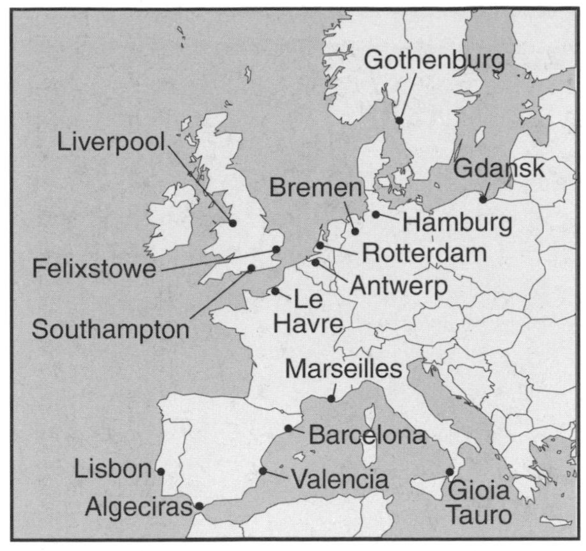

Europe

Alexa
Jeddah
Jebel Ali
Salalah
Abidjan
Durban

Africa and the Middle East

Dalian
Tianjin
Incheon
Chiba
Tokyo
Qingdao
Ulsan
Yokohama
Busan
Nagoya
Shanghai
Ningbo-
Zhoushan
Kobe
Osaka
Xiamen
Guangzhou
Keelung
Taichung
Kaohsiung
Karachi
Kolkata
Shenzhen
Honolulu
Mumbai
Nhava Sheva
Visakhapatnam
Hong
Kong
Manila
Bangkok
Laem
Chabang
Kochi
(Cochin)
Chennai
(Madras)
Colombo
Port Klang
Singapore
Tanjung
Pelepas
Tanjung Priok
Brisbane
Botany/
Sydney Harbour
Adelaide
Auckland
Melbourne

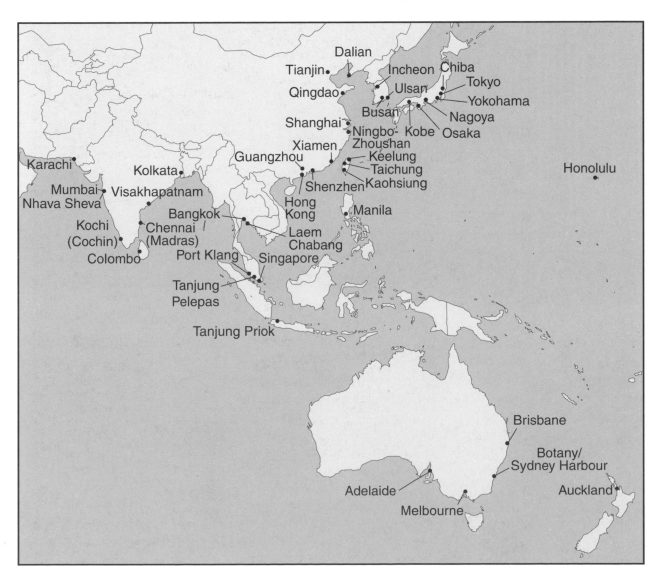

Asia, Australia and the South Pacific region

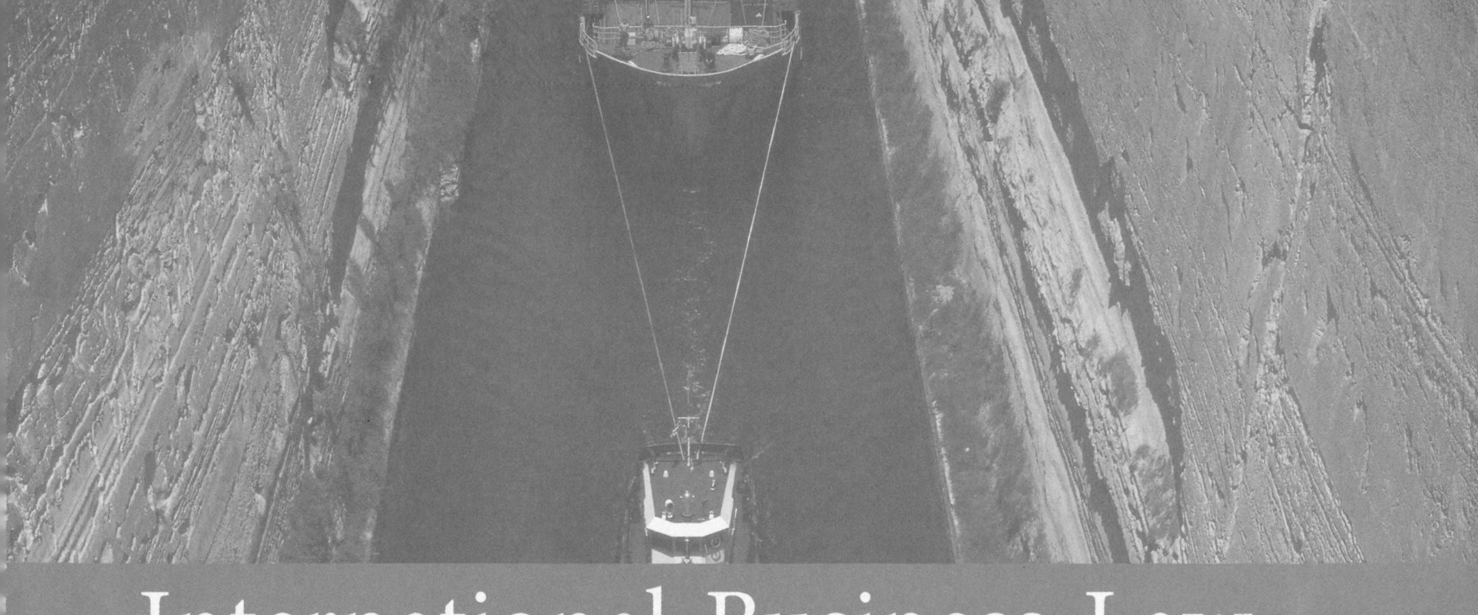

International Business Law and Its Environment

RICHARD SCHAFFER
Professor Emeritus (Ret.)
Walker College of Business
Appalachian State University

FILIBERTO AGUSTI
Senior Partner
Steptoe & Johnson LLP
Attorneys at Law
Washington, DC

LUCIEN J. DHOOGE
Sue and John Staton Professor of Law
College of Management
Georgia Institute of Technology

Australia • Brazil • Japan • Korea • Mexico • Singapore • Spain • United Kingdom • United States

International Business Law and Its Environment, 9e

Richard Schaffer, Filiberto Agusti, and Lucien J. Dhooge

Senior Vice President, LRS/Acquisitions & Solutions Planning: Jack W. Calhoun

Vice President, General Manager Social Science & Qualitative Business: Erin Joyner

Product Director: Mike Worls

Senior Product Manager: Vicky True-Baker

Managing Developer: Jennifer King

Product Assistant: Tristann Jones

Senior Brand Manager: Kristen Hurd

Associate Market Development Manager: Roy Rosa

Marketing Coordinator: Chris Walz

Production Management, and Composition: Integra Software Services Pvt. Ltd.

Senior Media Developer: Kristen Meere

Rights Acquisition Director: Audrey Pettengill

Rights Acquisition Specialist, Text and Image: Anne Sheroff

Manufacturing Planner: Kevin Kluck

Art Director, Art and Cover Direction: Emily Friel

Cover Designer: Rae Grant

Internal Designer: Integra Software Services Pvt. Ltd.

Cover Image(s): Steven Vidler/Eurasia Press/Corbis

Library of Congress Control Number: 2013952170

ISBN-13: 978-1-285-42704-1

ISBN-10: 1-285-42704-1

Cengage Learning
200 First Stamford Place, 4th Floor
Stamford, CT 06902
USA

Cengage Learning is a leading provider of customized learning solutions with office locations around the globe, including Singapore, the United Kingdom, Australia, Mexico, Brazil, and Japan. Locate your local office at: **www.cengage.com/global.**

Cengage Learning products are represented in Canada by Nelson Education, Ltd.

To learn more about Cengage Learning Solutions, visit **www.cengage.com.**

Purchase any of our products at your local college store or at our preferred online store **www.cengagebrain.com.**

1 2 3 4 5 6 7 17 16 15 14 13

R. S.

To Avery, for her love, patience, and encouragement.
And to Richard T. Fenton, formerly of West Publishing and Foundation Press, for having brought the first edition of this book to fruition.

F. A.

To my father, Filiberto, and my mother, Maria Luisa, who sacrificed so much that I might be free to write as I wish; and to my wife, Suki, and our daughters, Caroline, Olivia, and Jordan, for their abundant patience.

L. J. D.

To my wife, Julia, for her encouragement, support, and patience.

About the Authors

Richard Schaffer is Professor Emeritus of Business Law (retired) in the Department of Finance of the Walker College of Business at Appalachian State University. He has taught business law, international business law and transactions, and the law of international trade and investment since 1977. Professor Schaffer received his J.D. from the University of Mississippi and his LL.M. from New York University. From 1976 through 1982, he assisted United Nations agencies in New York, San Jose, and Vienna, with projects examining the relationship between corrupt practices, multinational corporations, and socioeconomic development, and served as rapporteur of UN working groups on international economic crime. Schaffer was director of international business studies at ASU and founder of its business study abroad programs. He has served as consultant to business schools on the internationalization of curriculum, and to industry trade groups. Professor Schaffer has extensive experience in business, including manufacturing and global sourcing, and he regularly consults on matters related to the international home textile industry.

Filiberto Agusti is a partner in the international law firm of Steptoe & Johnson LLP, where he has practiced law since 1978. He represents governments, multinational corporations, manufacturers, and investors in international arbitrations, lawsuits, and negotiations, including bankruptcy reorganizations. Mr. Agusti has authored articles for the *Harvard Law Review* and other legal publications. He is a frequent speaker at professional seminars around the world and is a regular on camera commentator for Univisión, Telemundo, and CNN en Español. Mr. Agusti was law clerk to Judge William H. Timbers at the U.S. Court of Appeals for the Second Circuit in 1977–78. He is a graduate of the Harvard Law School, where he was a senior editor of the *Harvard Law Review*. He graduated summa cum laude with a B.A. from the University of Illinois in 1974.

Lucien J. Dhooge is the Sue and John Staton Professor of Law at the Scheller College of Business at the Georgia Institute of Technology, where he teaches international business law and ethics and serves as the area coordinator in law and ethics. Prior to his tenure at the Georgia Institute of Technology, Professor Dhooge practiced law for eleven years and served on the faculty of the University of the Pacific in California for twelve years. He has authored more than fifty scholarly articles, co-authored and contributed to thirteen books, and is a past editor-in-chief of the *American Business Law Journal* and the *Journal of Legal Studies Education*. Professor Dhooge has presented courses and research throughout the United States, as well as in Asia, Europe, and Central and South America, and he has received numerous research and teaching awards, including six Ralph C. Hoeber Awards for excellence in published research. After completing an undergraduate degree in history at the University of Colorado, Professor Dhooge earned his J.D. from the University of Denver College of Law and his LL.M. from the Georgetown University Law Center.

Brief Contents

Contents

Table of Cases

Principal cases are in bold type.

Table of Treaties and International Agreements

Table of Statutes

Preface

It has been said that America's interest in international education has peaked and ebbed with the changing tide of the American political climate, rising in times of economic expansion and ebbing during periods of political isolation or economic protectionism. Perhaps, however, the cycle has finally been broken, and industry leaders, government policymakers, and educators alike have come to understand the importance of making a permanent commitment to international business education.

In the last half century America faced an increasingly competitive global marketplace and a mounting trade deficit. Rather than seek protection behind often-politicized trade laws, America's leaders committed the nation to policies of free trade and open investment. American managers realized that they had no choice but to compete aggressively with international competitors, in markets both at home and abroad. Witness not only America's great multinational corporations but also the successes of the many small and medium-sized companies that today do business internationally.

Among nations, the spirit of free trade has become contagious. Examples can be seen everywhere: The rush of nations to join the World Trade Organization, the growth of regional economic integration, privatization of national economies, the opening of once tightly controlled markets in developing countries and in formerly communist countries, and China's rise to prominence. The outcome has been the globalization of firms and of world markets for goods, services, and ideas, and the interdependence of national economies. It is in this climate that we have seen perhaps the greatest renewal of interest in international business education in America's history.

TRADE, INTELLECTUAL PROPERTY, AND FOREIGN DIRECT INVESTMENT: A THEMATIC APPROACH

International Business Law and Its Environment is intended for use in such courses as International Business Law, International Business Transactions, or The Law of International Trade and Investment. Our thematic approach tracks the basic market-entry strategies of many firms as they expand into international markets: Trade in goods and services, the protection and licensing of intellectual property rights, and foreign direct investment. Through the study of law, we examine each of these market-entry methods – and their variations and combinations – as they might fit into the overall strategy of a firm. We begin our discussion with trade, which involves the least penetration into the international market, and progress to the protection and licensing of intellectual property, and end with foreign direct investment, which immerses the firm completely in the social, cultural, and legal systems of its host country. Each step in the progression presents new and more complex risks, and following the old adage, we hope the sequence of this book teaches us to walk before we run. This progression patterns the life cycle of many firms, as well as the careers of many of our graduates, as they mature and then move more aggressively into new international markets.

PRIVATE AND PUBLIC INTERNATIONAL LAW

International Business Law and Its Environment emphasizes both private and public law. The private law applicable to international business transactions includes the law of international sales, trade finance and letters of credit, licensing and distribution agreements, agreements with foreign sales representatives, and other governing law.

Public international law includes conventions, treaties, and agreements among nations that make up the legal framework within which international business takes place. Customs and tariff laws are good examples, as are laws that open markets to international investors. The treaties of the European Union, the GATT agreements, the agreements of the World Trade Organization, and NAFTA are prime sources of public international law. Public international law provides the basis for government regulation of international business. It affects the environment within which a firm develops its international business strategies, and establishes the firm's responsibility under national laws and administrative regulations. We also treat general principles of the law of nations, the jurisdiction and work of international courts and tribunals, as well as the work of various intergovernmental organizations (such as UN agencies, the WTO, and the OECD), because these are fundamentals needed for study.

INTERNATIONAL AND COMPARATIVE APPROACH

No text can attempt to teach the law of every nation in which a firm might do business, and we have resisted the temptation to merely catalog foreign laws. Instead, we present foreign laws and foreign court decisions throughout the book for comparison purposes, to illustrate differences in legal or economic systems, and to show how business is done in other countries. Where applicable, we compare civil law, common law, socialist law, labor and employment law, Islamic law, and concepts from different legal systems. Examples include comparative sales law, labor and employment law, advertising law, agency law, and competition law. For instance, our discussion of Chinese law provides U.S. readers with many interesting comparisons, because the United States and China are in different stages of development, with very different political systems. We discuss European law throughout the book, and frequently use Japan for comparison purposes as well. Of course, we treat U.S. law in greater detail. However, the text focuses on relevant international agreements, uniform codes, and the decisions of international tribunals. Moreover, its focus on international law, the legal environment in developing countries, and a comparative view of national laws, makes the text perfect for use anywhere.

THE MECHANICS AND THEORY OF INTERNATIONAL BUSINESS TRANSACTIONS

International Business Law and Its Environment not only teaches the "hands on" mechanics of international business transactions but also provides the theory needed for businesspeople to understand the consequences of their actions.

Commercial transactions are thoroughly examined and explained. This includes negotiating contracts for the sale of goods and services, negotiating contractual terms of trade, handling shipping contracts and cargo insurance, making agency contracts, dealing with letters of credit and other banking arrangements, considering alternatives for dispute settlement, and much more. Many sample forms and documents are included. Methods for protecting one's intellectual property are closely considered, as are the handling of international investment arrangements, employing persons abroad, and other issues. Similarly, we take readers through many thorny problems of dealing with the government, such as learning how to use the harmonized tariff code when entering goods and "clearing customs," or when licensing exports.

A BUSINESS AND MANAGERIAL PERSPECTIVE

We begin with the premise that the world of international business is a dangerous place, and that the management of international business is the management of risk. Whether one is developing and implementing an international business strategy or managing an international business transaction, an understanding of the special risks involved will help ensure a project's success. In keeping with our thematic approach, we examine the risks of trade (for example, managing credit and marine risk); protecting and licensing intellectual property (for example, dealing with gray-market goods and registering foreign patents); handling foreign mergers and acquisitions (for example, coping with unexpected differences in foreign corporate or labor law); and evaluating political risk in less stable regions of the world. We then show how to avoid, reduce, or shift the risk to other parties or intermediaries. The case study approach is excellent for this purpose, as it shows readers the mistakes others have made, and how disputes have been resolved.

We also stress strategic business decision making. For example, our chapter on imports, customs, and tariff law does not view importing as an isolated transaction. Rather, it addresses the importance of customs and tariff law.

THE CULTURAL, POLITICAL, SOCIAL AND ECONOMIC ENVIRONMENT, AND HUMAN RIGHTS CONCERNS

As with each previous edition, we have made a special effort to discuss the cultural, economic, political, and social aspects of international business as they bear on differences in attitudes toward the law, their impact on trade relations, and how they affect the way we do business in another country.

In discussing trade issues, it is almost impossible to separate politics, foreign policy, and trade. This is evident in our coverage of export controls and trade sanctions imposed for reasons of foreign policy or national security. We have also devoted considerable attention to current events in many countries and their impact on international business there.

Many topics require a historical perspective, such as the *Smoot-Hawley* era of the 1930s, the development of GATT in the 1940s, export controls and the Cold War, the Iranian Revolution of 1979 or fifty years of U.S.-Cuba relations. We often try to draw on the lessons of history, such as the implications of President Carter's grain embargo of the Soviet Union in response to that nation's invasion of Afghanistan, or President Reagan's embargo of U.S. participation in the construction of the Siberian natural gas pipeline to Western Europe.

Throughout the book, readers are asked to consider the impact of world current events on their strategic business decisions, particularly in unstable regions or under hostile political and economic conditions.

We believe that it is impossible to cover the real world of international business without exploring the larger problems of human rights. Thus, we treat the areas of human rights law and international criminal law as global issues of concern to international business.

DEVELOPING COUNTRIES

The developing countries of Africa, Asia, Latin America, and the Caribbean present special problems for their richer trading partners. We have tried to paint a realistic picture of trade opportunities, colored by the realities of disease, poverty, and environmental degradation that threaten much of our planet.

Trade and investment issues in developing countries are incorporated in all parts of the book. Examples include the *Generalized System of Preferences*, the CARICOM *Single Market and Economy Treaty*, the *Doha Development Agenda*, labor and environmental issues in developing countries, and U.S. trade initiatives for Latin America, the Caribbean, and Africa. Many special issues related to doing business in the independent republics of the former Soviet Union are covered. The integration of China, Vietnam, and other countries into the world's economic system is stressed.

ETHICS AND SOCIAL RESPONSIBILITY

Because ethical questions can arise in varying contexts, we have chosen to integrate the subject throughout the book. However, we give a more focused treatment to ethics, social responsibility, and corporate codes of conduct in Chapter Two, the chapter on international law. All chapters conclude with a hypothetical case problem on ethics, called *Ethical Considerations.* Examples include, among others:

- *Codes of conduct*
- *Bribery and corruption*
- *Child labor*
- *Workers' rights*
- *Protection of the environment and of fish and wildlife*
- *Prison and forced labor*

- *Fair trade initiatives*
- *Human rights issues*
- *AIDS and other world health issues*
- *Discrimination issues in foreign countries*
- *Special issues related to U.S. investments*
- *Mexican* maquiladora *plants*
- *The ban on asbestos products*
- *Maritime fraud*

WHY STUDY INTERNATIONAL BUSINESS LAW?

As you begin your study of international business law using this text, realize that no book can tell you what the law "is." We can only introduce you the legal environment of international business, explain some basic principles of international law and international business law, and challenge you to consider the legal implications of any international business strategy or transaction. Thus, we study international business law because we want to understand:

1. How the legal and regulatory environment affects firms operating internationally;
2. The legal issues bearing on international business (IB) decision-making or strategies;
3. That the management of IB is the management of risk;
4. The sources of public and private international law, particularly international business law, as reflected in treaties and other international agreements, harmonized codes, national laws, and the decisions of national and international courts and tribunals.
5. The mechanics and legal implications of common IB transactions, particularly regarding trade in goods, the licensing of intellectual property, and foreign direct investment;
6. The influence of ethics and social responsibility in IB and when doing business in foreign countries, to encourage the development of an individual ethical value system for IB managers, and in particular to develop an appreciation for the rights of workers, consumers, and other stakeholders in civil society when doing business in foreign countries;
7. The importance of advance planning for dispute resolution in IB and the alternatives for dispute resolution;
8. The special legal and regulatory issues facing the multinational firm, and the relationship between the firm and host governments;
9. How to better communicate with attorneys on IB matters;
10. The role of agents, contractors, and intermediaries in IB, particularly those involved in international sales, transportation, banking, insurance, and customs brokerage.

TO OUR INTERNATIONAL READERS

We are pleased to know that our work is contributing to student learning at universities on virtually every continent and in every region of the world. Naturally, our audience is primarily an American one. We necessarily devote a major portion of the text to American law, U.S. trade relations, and the needs of the American firm. However, we have made every effort to maintain our international perspective and to draw important international comparisons. Cases from countries other than the United States appear throughout the book, as do decisions of international courts and tribunals, and discussions of foreign codes and practices. Moreover, the increased reliance on uniform rules, harmonized codes, and international standards makes the book suitable for any student interested in international business law.

KEY REVISIONS TO THE NINTH EDITION

Despite many changes in content in the ninth edition of *International Business Law and its Environment*, surely our greatest challenge was to make it more readable and manageable. To this end, we have tried to condense an ever-expanding body of legal material, clarify and simplify key terms and concepts, and refocus on the essentials of international business law. The writing style is tighter, boxed cases are shorter, coverage has been streamlined, and many details not necessary to an introductory course have been eliminated. Although dated material has been removed throughout, some historical perspectives are richer and more meaningful. Following are some of the major content changes to the ninth edition.

Part One: The Legal Environment of International Business

- *Chapter 1 has been largely rewritten to better prepare readers for the remainder of the book. The statistical data on international trade and investment has been eliminated and non-core areas condensed. The chapter now focuses on introducing the legal environment of international business and on key concepts and definitions needed in later reading. Chapter 1 contains four cases new to this edition.*
- *Chapter 2 on international law has been greatly revised, with two case replacements plus a significantly re-edited version of* Nottebohm. *The chapter is even more relevant to business readers: A new section looks at the nature and sources of international business law, and international criminal law and human rights issues now focus on international business issues. Any duplication of subjects in Chapter 2 (on international law) and Chapter 8 (national lawmaking powers) has been eliminated.*
- *Chapter 3 on dispute resolution now has a greater emphasis on key areas: Arbitration and alternative dispute resolution, jurisdiction in the Internet age, including the Ninth Circuit's* Pebble Beach *decision, personal jurisdiction and the recognition of judgments in China and India. It consolidates and includes new sections on sovereign immunity, abstention, act of state, comity, and political question doctrines.*

Part Two: International Sales, Credits, and the Commercial Transaction

- *Chapter 4 has been retitled as* The Formation and Performance of Contracts for the Sale of Goods, *and has a new focus on contract formation, performance, breach, and damages, as reflected in the new title.*
- *Chapter 5 on documentary sales has an updated discussion of international commercial terminology governing the use and interpretation of trade terms.*
- *Chapter 6 is now titled* Legal Issues in Transportation *to reflect its broader coverage. Aviation law has been fully updated post-Montreal. It includes all-new presentations of general maritime law (including a discussion of the historical development of maritime law) and admiralty jurisdiction. The carriage of goods by sea sections have been condensed and updated. A challenging but fun ethics case related to maritime fraud has been added to the chapter.*
- *Chapter 7 has been updated.*

Part Three: International and U.S. Trade Law

- *Chapter 8 on national lawmaking powers has been reorganized and focuses on core subjects, including U.S. trade agreements and key U.S. trade legislation. The role of the Department of Treasury in regulating international transactions has been added. The U.S. Supreme Court decision in* Arizona v. U.S. *is used to discuss federal preemption, while also introducing readers to immigration issues in the United States. The section on presidential powers in the war on terror has been eliminated.*
- *Chapter 9 on the WTO has also been completely reorganized to focus on basic WTO principles. New subjects include overview of trade preferences and free trade, which has been removed from Chapters 12 and 15 and consolidated here. Most other sections have been completely rewritten to simplify and condense. Materials on* Jackson-Vanik, *normalization of relations with China, Russia, and Vietnam were eliminated; historical materials on GATT reduced; materials on import licensing, custom procedures, quotas and other non-tariff barriers have been rewritten for clarity.*
- *Chapter 10 on market access updated throughout, and includes new WTO* U.S.-Clove Cigarettes *case on technical barriers to trade.*
- *Chapter 11 on import competition has been significantly rewritten for clarity, the WTO* Argentina-Footwear *decision has been re-edited for easier reading, the dumping section greatly simplified, subsidies and nonmarket economies updated, and the China safeguard materials eliminated reflecting end of that program.*
- *Chapter 12 on imports and customs has been condensed, simplified, and reorganized with a greater focus on the foundations of customs and tariff law. Sections on U.S. administration of customs law and enforcement issues has been moved to later in the chapter. The three major subject areas — classification, valuation, and rules of origin — are largely rewritten. Other changes include: Rules for using the harmonized tariff code are simplified, complex rules of origin for textiles eliminated, materials on electronic entry processing updated, trade preference material removed from this chapter. Other additions include the frequently cited* Carl Zeiss *customs classification case, and a new managerial case question provides a more realistic experience.*
- *Chapter 13 has been retitled,* Export Controls and Sanctions *to more accurately describe the material covered. It has been significantly rewritten,*

condensed, and updated, with non-essential material eliminated or reduced. New sections on today's export environment, policy issues related to balancing national security with competitiveness, on-going reform of export controls, and the automated export system. The sanctions material has been simplified but strengthened, with the elimination of narrower issues related to the war on terror. Chapter 13 also has a new case selection, with two cases removed and three shorter cases added.

- *Chapter 14 clarifies the distinctions between economic integration in federal models, free trade agreements, customs unions, and common markets; contains updated general and sectoral North American trade information.*
- *Chapter 15 now focuses entirely on the EU and includes key updates on the accession process, expansion, the financial crisis, and monetary issues, with new and updated cases on the supremacy doctrine and free movement of goods.*

Part Four: Regulation of the International Marketplace

- *Chapter 16 has been significantly revised to reflect changes in enforcement of the corrupt practices statute in the United States and by the EU of the OECD bribery convention. The chapter includes several new cases, including* World Duty Free *on bribery.*
- *Chapter 17 has been completely revised to emphasize intellectual property as a company asset. New material on IPR litigation, standard essential patents, strategic use of cross-licensing agreements, legal implications of IPR transfer, and U.S.-China relations. The chapter includes cases on software inventions, China IPR protection (WTO), and discusses international issues related to recent changes in U.S. patent legislation. The 2013* Apple v. Samsung *decision is included.*
- *Chapter 18 materials on foreign direct investment has been entirely revised, and includes litigation over recent expropriations in Latin America, revised material on U.S. taxation of international transactions (including new material on transfer pricing), and addresses both legal and illegal methods used by multinational companies to reduce global taxes. Also includes a new ICSID case involving remedies for expropriation.*
- *Chapter 19 expands its comparative legal view of different employment laws and practices, and now includes the "Chinese Approach" (as well as U.S., EU, and Japanese approaches) to the subject. Additions to the chapter include the new role of the WTO as a multilateral tool for dealing with labor conditions in developing countries, institutional discrimination in China, discrimination against women (particularly in emerging economies), and includes the Supreme Court decision in* Kiobel v. Royal Dutch Petroleum.
- *Chapter 20 new topics include: Environmental litigation at the International Court of Justice, international law implications of "swine flu," new rulings by the NAFTA environmental commission, the EU ban on GMOs, updates on global warming treaty issues and U.S. legislation.*
- *Chapter 21 now expands the discussion of competition law from the U.S. and EU to include a larger perspective of competition laws around the world, including those of Japan and China. Includes new Animal Science decision on extraterritoriality of U.S. antitrust laws.*

OUR GREATEST CHALLENGE

Perhaps the greatest challenge in preparing any edition is simply to keep up with the rapid pace of political, economic, and legal changes around the world. We had to make revisions almost daily to keep abreast of current developments. There are countless topics that had to be included or revised at the last moment. Other issues are still outstanding. Will the U.S. Congress renew the president's trade promotion authority? Will the *Doha Development* rounds conclude successfully? Will there be progress toward a free trade area of the Americas? How will the future U.S. response to international terrorism affect U.S. business interests? Will American consumers pressure U.S. clothing and apparel retailers and firms in their global supply chain to increase wages and provide safe working conditions in developing country factories? These and many other questions must await the next edition.

PEDAGOGICAL FEATURES OF THE NINTH EDITION

The *Key Terms* section at the end of each chapter gives the most important international business vocabulary and operative terminology expected of the successful student. The *Ethical Considerations* feature provides end-of-chapter case studies containing ethical or social responsibility issues. Examples include:

- *Bribery and corruption*
- *Environmental litigation in Ecuador and India*
- *Sales law and "ethically tainted" goods*
- *Insurance coverage in the wake of September 11*
- *The use of* maquiladoras *in Mexico*
- *The HIV epidemic in sub-Saharan Africa*
- *Gender discrimination in the global marketplace*
- *Sewing contractors in India*
- *Sales commissions on arms sales in the Middle East*
- *Exports of outdated pharmaceuticals to Africa*
- *Letter of credit fraud*
- *Free trade vs. cultural diversity*
- *Trade in genetically modified foods*
- *Chinese dumping: Is low cost selling unfair?*
- *Fair trade products—will paying a higher price for coffee eradicate poverty?*
- *Lobbying to decontrol exports of dual-use chemical*
- *Maritime fraud*

Other end-of-chapter features include *Managerial Implications*, which provides case problems suitable for extended discussions and end-of-chapter questions, many of which are based on actual cases (citations provided).

Primary source materials include landmark and cutting-edge cases from U.S. and foreign courts, and decisions of the WTO, NAFTA, ICSID, International Court of Justice, European Court of Justice, and other international judicial and arbitral tribunals.

In addition, we have incorporated

- *Business and industry examples, sample documents, and forms*
- *A transactions-oriented approach to those areas likely to be encountered by students, including international sales contracts, documentary sales and trade terms, handling letters of credit, procedures for import customs clearance and export licensing are examples.*
- *An expanded list of acronyms frequently used in international business*

COMPREHENSIVE LEARNING RESOURCES

Online Resources for Instructors and Students. The *International Business Law and Its Environment* instructor supplements are available exclusively on the textbook companion site, which is accessible through www.cengagebrain.com. You must log in using your Faculty SSO account.

- *The Instructor's Manual has been revised and enhanced by to align with all of the new book content. The Instructor's Manual provides answers to case questions and problems, end-of-chapter questions, Managerial Implications, and Ethical Considerations. It also offers teaching summaries, supplemental cases and exercises, teaching suggestions, and class activities.*
- *Chapter PowerPoint® slides are also available to instructors for use during lectures.*
- *NEW! The fully revised and updated Test Bank is now available in the Cognero online testing system. Cengage Learning Testing Powered by Cognero provides you with an easy interface that guides you through the creation and management of your tests. Choose from a variety of question types, and use the searchable metadata tags to ensure your tests are complete and compliant.*

Student Guide to the Sarbanes-Oxley Act. This brief overview for undergraduate business students explains the Sarbanes-Oxley Act, describes its requirements, and shows how it potentially affects students in their business life. The guide is available as an optional package with the text.

Business Law Digital Video Library. Featuring more than seventy-five video clips that spark class discussion and clarify core legal principles, the Business Law Digital Video Library is organized into five series: Legal Conflicts in Business (includes specific modern business and e-commerce scenarios); Ask the Instructor (presents straightforward explanations of concepts for student review); Drama of the Law (features classic business scenarios that spark classroom participation); Real World Legal (presents legal scenarios encountered in real businesses); and Business Ethics (presents ethical dilemmas in business scenarios). For more information about the Digital Video Library, visit **www.cengagebrain.com**.

Cengage Learning Custom Solutions. Whether you need print, digital, or hybrid course materials, Cengage Learning Custom Solutions can help you create your perfect learning solution. Draw from Cengage Learning's extensive library of texts and collections, add or create your own original work, and create customized media and technology to match your learning and course objectives. Our editorial team will work with you through each step, allowing you to concentrate on the most important thing—your students. Learn more about all our services at **www.cengage.com/custom**.

Cengage Learning's Global Economic Watch. Make the current global economic downturn a teachable moment with Cengage Learning's Global Economic Watch—a powerful online portal that brings these pivotal current events into the classroom. The watch includes:

- *A content-rich blog of breaking news, expert analysis, and commentary—updated multiple times daily—plus links to many other blogs*
- *A powerful real-time database of hundreds of relevant and vetted journal, newspaper, and periodical articles, videos, and podcasts—updated four times every day*
- *A thorough overview and timeline of events leading up to the global economic crisis*
- *Discussion and testing content, PowerPoint® slides on key topics, sample syllabi, and other teaching resources*
- *Social Networking tools: Instructor and student forums encourage students*

Visit **www.cengage.com/thewatch** for more information.

Acknowledgements

Cengage Learning and the authors would like to thank the following Business Law instructors for their insights and feedback in the preparation of this edition:

MICHAEL A. BAKER
University of California, Los Angeles

ANDREA BOGGIO
Bryant University

LINDA BRANDMILLER
University of the Incarnate Word

MARK P. CAZEM
University of California, Berkeley

JONATHAN J. DARROW
Bentley University

C. KERRY FIELDS
University of Southern California

WENDY D. GELMAN
Florida International University

F. WILLIAM MCCARTY
Western Michigan University

FAYE ROSENBERG
Northwood University

KURT M. SAUNDERS
California State University, Northridge

NORMAN GREGORY YOUNG
California Polytechnic Pomona

The authors wish to express their gratitude to the following reviewers for their help in preparing past editions:

THOMAS M. APKE
California State University—Fullerton

MARK B. BAKER
University of Texas—Austin

PATRICIA B. BARTSCHER
San Francisco State University

ANNE BERRE, J.D
Schreiner University

ROBERT BIRD
University of Connecticut

KAREN BORK
Northwood University

NIVEA CASTRO
Upper Iowa University—Fayette

PATRICK CIHON
Syracuse University Whitman School of Management

RAVEN DAVENPORT
Houston Community College

SANDRA J. DEFEBAUGH
Eastern Michigan University

LARRY A. DI MATTEO
University of Florida

RAFI EFRAT
California State University—Northridge

JOHN ELLIOTT
Pepperdine University

JOAN T. A. GABEL
University of Missouri

JOHN M. GARIC
University of Central Oklahoma

CHRISTOPHER GIBSON
Suffolk University

REX D. GLENSY
Drexel University

DAVID P. HANSON
Duquesne University

MICHAEL E. JONES
University of Massachusetts—Lowell

ROMAIN M. LORENTZ
University of St. Thomas—Minneapolis

SEAN P. MELVIN
Elizabethtown College

CAROL J. MILLER
Missouri State University

FRED NAFFZIGER
Indiana University—South Bend

GREGORY T. NAPLES
Marquette University

LYNDA J. OSWALD
University of Michigan

MARISA ANNE PAGNATTARO
University of Georgia—Athens

KIMBERLIANNE PODLAS
University of North Carolina—Greensboro

EMILIA JUSTYNA POWELL
Georgia Southern University

BRUCE L. ROCKWOOD
Bloomsburg University

JOHN C. RUHNKA
University of Colorado—Denver

MARTIN L. SARADJIAN
Boston University

LISA SPEROW
Cal Poly—San Luis Obispo

RICHARD STILL
Mississippi State University

CLYDE D. STOLTENBERG
Wichita State University

JAN TUCKER
Kaplan University

MICHAEL A. VALENZA
Temple University

SUSAN M. VANCE
St. Mary's College

MARTHA WEISEL, ESQ.
Hofstra University

JOHN WRIEDEN
Florida International University

Each of us would like to express our sincere gratitude to our editors at Cengage Learning, Vicky True-Baker and Jennifer King, who not only skillfully guided the development of one of the most important revisions of International Business Law, but whose candor, friendship, and invaluable advice gave us clarity and direction as we worked. We also want to thank Mike Worls, Michelle Kunkler, Tristann Jones, Kristen Hurd, and Robin LeFevre for their efforts in the development and promotion of this edition.

Richard Schaffer
Filiberto Agusti
Lucien J. Dhooge

PART 1

The Legal Environment of International Business

Part One of *International Business Law and Its Environment* provides a framework for understanding both international business and the legal environment in which it operates. This part covers several main areas: international business, the nature and sources of international business law, international public law, and the resolution of international business disputes. It also covers the economic, social, political, and historical forces that have influenced the development of the national and international law.

Chapter One introduces international business from a legal perspective. It explains the three major forms of international business: trade (importing and exporting); licensing agreements for the transfer and legal protection of patents, copyrights, trademarks, and other intellectual property; and direct investments in foreign firms. The reader is also introduced to the environment of doing business in the developing and newly industrialized countries. This chapter discusses how the risks of international business differ from those of doing business at home; how a firm deals with the added risks of doing business over great distances, including those associated with language and cultural barriers, country financial and political risk, the risks of trade controls or restrictions on investment, and the risks of foreign laws and foreign litigation. By illustrating some of the risks of international business, Chapter One sets the stage for the remainder of the book, which teaches that the law is an important tool for managing international business risk.

Chapter Two defines and explains international business law and the larger area of international law. It explains the sources of international law, including custom, treaties, and international conventions; its basic concepts; and the role of intergovernmental organizations in developing international standards and legal codes, which become binding on the nations that adopt them. Many of these directly affect business operations worldwide. Whether a problem is related to humanitarian issues such as the ethical treatment of labor in developing countries, laundering of drug money through the international banking system, setting standards for the protection of the world's oceans, or developing uniform rules for international sales contracts, international organizations can be useful in bringing individual nations to agreement on difficult issues. Many of the international codes address ethical issues facing businesses operating globally, such as corruption or child labor, and these, too, are examined. The chapter takes a comparative look at different legal systems, including the common law, civil law, and Islamic law systems, with a special emphasis on China and the Middle East. We examine several legal topics and see how culturally diverse countries in different regions of the world approach these subjects differently.

Chapter Three discusses how disputes are settled in an international business transaction, including both litigation and arbitration. It addresses issues of jurisdiction and procedural rules for litigating international cases. For instance, the chapter attempts to answer such questions as: If a company does business in a foreign country, can the company be sued there? If a buyer purchases goods from a foreign firm that does not regularly do business in the United States, under what circumstances can the buyer sue that firm in U.S. courts? If a product that is produced in one nation injures a consumer in another nation, where should the injured party's claim be heard? If a firm obtains a court judgment in one country, can the firm enforce it against the defendant's assets held in another country? Finally, because the costs and risks of foreign litigation are substantial, the chapter addresses what the parties can do in advance to provide an alternative to litigation should a dispute result.

CHAPTER 1

Introduction to International Business

INTRODUCTION

Today most people agree that no business is purely domestic and that global competition and world events affect even the smallest local firms. The realities of the modern world make all business international. No longer can an economic or political change in one country occur without reverberations throughout world markets. A tsunami in Asia interrupts global supply chains and brings distant assembly lines to a halt. War in the Middle East brings international shipping to a crawl. Contagious disease in Hong Kong or Toronto slows international business travel. The failure of China to safeguard American copyrights on films or software results in the United States imposing retaliatory tariffs and affects the price of Chinese-made clothing in American stores. Terrorist attacks not only affect business operations worldwide but also affect the ability of managers to travel and live safely in foreign lands.

As countries lower entry barriers to foreign goods and services, more and more foreign goods now appear in local stores around the world. Brand names once recognized only at home are now global brand images. And giant multinational corporations now move people, money, and technology across national borders in the blink of an eye. Clearly, no firm can remain isolated from international forces for long. As you will see in this chapter, just as national economies have become more interdependent, and businesses more globalized, so too has business law become more international. Our goal in this chapter is to explain the forms of international business, to explore the risks of international business transactions, and to set the stage to learn how international business law can be a tool to help manage these risks.

FORMS OF INTERNATIONAL BUSINESS

This text classifies international business into three categories: (1) trade, (2) licensing of intellectual property, and (3) foreign direct investment. To the marketer, these broad categories describe three ways a firm may enter a foreign market, or foreign market entry methods. To the international lawyer, they represent three forms of doing business in a foreign country and the legal relationship between parties to an international business transaction. Each form represents a different level of commitment to a foreign market, a different level of involvement in the life of a foreign country, and a different set of managerial challenges. Each form exposes firms to different sets of business and legal risks. Trade usually represents the least involvement, and thus the least political, economic, and legal risk; we buy or sell goods or services to others in foreign countries. A firm that wants to use its intellectual property worldwide must contract to let others distribute it, license it to users, and then protect it from infringement. However, the greatest risks come with owning and operating a foreign firm, perhaps a factory. This carries with it the obligations of corporate citizenship and means the complete involvement in all aspects of life in the foreign country—economic, political, social, cultural, and legal.

The three forms in international business are not mutually exclusive, and each can play a role in an international firm's strategy. One of the best examples is the vertically integrated firm that holds minority or majority ownership interest in other firms along the supply chain. One firm may be engaged in production of raw materials or component parts which are exported to an affiliated company in another country for final assembly. Still another company, owned by the same parent corporation may own the trademark for the product and have responsibility for global distribution. Here the production and marketing of a single product involves elements of trade, licensing, and investment. For firms just entering a new foreign market, the method of entry might depend on a host of considerations, including the sophistication of the firm, its overseas experience, the nature of its products or services, its commitment of capital resources, and the amount of risk it is willing to bear.

Trade

Trade is the import or export of goods and services across national borders, usually as part of an exchange. **Exporting** is the shipment of goods out of a country or the rendering of services to a foreign buyer located in a foreign country. **Importing** is the entering of goods into the customs territory of a country or the receipt of services from a foreign provider. **Trade in services** refers to the providing of services to a customer or the operation of service companies in a foreign country. Examples can be found in transportation, package delivery, banking, insurance, securities brokerage, law, accounting, architecture, waste management, environmental engineering, software development, and management consulting.

Exporting. Exporting is often a firm's first step into international business. Compared to the other forms of international business, exporting is relatively uncomplicated. It may provide the inexperienced or smaller firm with an opportunity to reach new customers and to tap new markets. It usually requires only a modest capital investment, and the risks are generally manageable by most firms. It also permits a firm to explore its foreign market potential before venturing further. For many larger firms, including multinational corporations, exporting may be an important portion of their business operations. The U.S. aircraft industry, for example, relies heavily on exports for significant revenues.

Direct exporting refers to a type of exporting in which the exporter, often a manufacturer, assumes responsibility for most of the export functions, including marketing, export licensing, shipping, and collecting payment. Many firms engaged in direct exporting on a regular basis reach the point at which they must hire their own full-time export managers and international sales specialists. These people participate in making export marketing decisions, including product development, pricing, packaging, and labeling for export. They should take primary responsibility for dealing with foreign buyers, attending foreign trade shows, complying with government export and import regulations, shipping, and handling the movement of goods and money in the transaction. Many direct exporters use the services of foreign sales representatives or foreign distributors.

Foreign sales representatives are independent sales agents who solicit orders on behalf of their principals and receive compensation on a commission basis. They have the advantage of knowing the foreign market, having established customer loyalty, and carrying a range of complementary products. For instance, one agent may represent several different manufacturers of U.S. sporting goods in Japan—one that makes baseball bats, another that makes gloves, and a third that makes baseballs.

Foreign distributors are independent firms, usually located in the country or region to which a firm is exporting, that purchase and take delivery of goods for resale to their customers. Exporters use foreign distributors when their products require service or a local supply of spare parts or if they are perishable or seasonal. Foreign distributors assume the risks of buying and warehousing goods in their markets and provide additional product support services. The distributor usually services the products they sell, thus relieving the exporter of that responsibility. They often train the end users of the products, extend credit to their customers, and bear responsibility for local advertising and promotion.

Companies that do not have the experience, personnel, or capital to tackle a foreign market alone use **indirect exporting**. They may be unable to locate foreign buyers or are not yet ready to handle the mechanics of a transaction on their own. By indirect exporting, the firm can use specialized intermediaries that can take on many of the export functions—marketing, sales, finance, and shipping. Two types of intermediaries include export trading companies and export management companies.

International Trading Companies. These are firms that specialize in all aspects of import/export transactions by either buying goods on their own accounts for resale or by acting as middlemen to bring other buyers and sellers together. Many trading companies handle particular types of goods, such as commodities, energy, minerals and metals, or general merchandise. They can be as small as one individual or a sprawling multinational corporation. They come from both developed and developing countries. They have extensive sales contacts overseas and experience in international finance, air and ocean shipping, preparing legal documents for import and export, and in dealing with customs authorities in many countries.

Japanese trading companies (called *sogo shosha*) are well known for their successes worldwide. Their early advantage over trading companies in the United States was their ability to bring together many competing producers in the Japanese market to take advantage of economies of scale in exporting. For example, a trading company might bring together several makers of competing large appliances and coordinate pricing and distribution in foreign countries. This proved to be very effective for the Japanese. In the United States, until 1982, any collusion by competitors to fix prices and market jointly would have been considered a violation of the U.S. antitrust laws. In that year the U.S. Congress passed the *Export Trading Company Act*, giving American exporters the same competitive advantage as the Japanese. U.S. **export trading companies**, or ETCs, can apply for and receive certificates from the U.S. Department of Justice that waive the application of U.S. antitrust laws to their export activities. For example, it is illegal for two competing firms that manufacture similar products to agree to fix prices in the U.S. market. However, if both companies are members of an approved ETC, they may jointly establish export prices, enter into joint export marketing arrangements, allocate export territories, and do business in ways that would be illegal if done with the U.S. market. The waiver is issued only if it is shown that the advantage will not lessen competition within the United States, or unreasonably affect domestic prices of the exported products.

There are many other advantages in selling through an ETC, such as teaming up to bid on large foreign projects, filling large and complex foreign orders, joint marketing of complementary or competing products, division of foreign territories by competing firms, sharing of marketing and distribution costs, and reducing rivalry between U.S. firms in dealing with foreign customers. The following case, *Tarbert Trading v. Cometals*, involves two trading companies that were apparently overly anxious to make the sale and a fraudulent **certificate of origin**—one of the most important legal documents used in import/export transactions.

Tarbert Trading, Ltd. v. Cometals, Inc.

663 F. Supp. 561 (1987) United States District Court (S.D.N.Y.)

BACKGROUND AND FACTS

Cometals, a New York commodities trading corporation, purchased 2000 tons of Kenyan red beans from Tarbert Trading, an English commodities trading company. The beans would be shipped from a warehouse in Rotterdam, the Netherlands. Cometals purchased the beans for "back to back" resale to a buyer in Colombia. However, the government of Colombia required a certificate of origin issued by a Chamber of Commerce showing that the beans were a product of the European Economic Community (EEC, now the European Union). Cometals requested that Tarbert supply such a certificate and Tarbert agreed. Employees of the two firms collaborated on the wording of the certificate even though they understood that Kenyan red beans originated in Africa. Later, Cometals refused the beans due to insect damage and Tarbert sued. Cometals maintained that the agreement should be declared void because Tarbert could not, except through fraud, have supplied an EEC certificate of origin for the beans. Tarbert later resold the beans to the original seller.

NEWMAN, SENIOR JUDGE

Concededly, both Tarbert and Cometals were cognizant of the fact that an EEC certificate of origin stating that the Kenyan beans were of the origin of an EEC member would be false and would be shown to third persons. * * * Simply put, [Cometals] intended to deceive the Colombian customs officials with a false certificate as to the beans' country-of-origin so that they would allow the importation of the beans by Cometals' customer.

Irrespective of the rather incredible explanations of [Tarbert's employees] as to what they understood to be the purport of the requested certificate of origin, they finally and grudgingly conceded that an EEC certificate stating that the goods were of the origin of an EEC member would be understood by anyone reading it to mean that the beans were grown in an EEC country and not simply shipped from such country. * * *

It is evident from the Kenyan origin of the beans that it would have been impossible for Tarbert to honestly obtain from a Chamber of Commerce and furnish Cometals with a bona fide EEC certificate of origin stating that the goods were of the origin of a member of the EEC since concededly Kenya is not an EEC member. Thus, the only way in which Tarbert could have complied with the agreement would have been to convince an official of a Chamber of Commerce to issue a fraudulent certificate or to obtain a forged certificate. Both acts are obviously illegal.

"No one shall be permitted to profit by his own fraud, or take advantage of his own wrong, or to found any claim upon his own iniquity, or to acquire property

continues

continued

by his own crime. These maxims are dictated by public policy, have their foundation in universal law administered in all civilized countries, and have nowhere been superseded by statutes." [citations omitted] * * * Plainly, enforcement of the agreement for either party would be contrary to public policy ...

Decision. The complaint and counterclaim were dismissed. Agreements that violate the law are void. In this case, an agreement calling for the delivery of a fraudulent certificate of origin is illegal and contrary to public policy.

Comment. Trading companies play an important role in world trade. While what happened here is obviously a rare case, it does give us an opportunity to introduce some of the documents required in international trade and to question the legal and ethical conduct of the parties. It also teaches us the importance of knowing more about the people we do business with.

Case Questions

1. Import/export transactions usually require much more documentation than domestic transactions. These include detailed invoices, packing lists, shipping and insurance documents, and specialized certificates. In this case, a "certificate of origin" was required by the government of Columbia before the goods could be imported. Does it refer to the country from which the goods were shipped or where they were grown or made? Why do you think Columbia required a certificate of origin? What is its purpose?
2. Suppose that the beans had arrived in Columbia and were then stopped by Columbian customs authorities because of a fraudulent certificate. What do you think might have happened to the beans? What would the risk have been to Cometals and Tarbert? What if the Columbian buyer had already paid for the beans?
3. Evaluate and discuss the conduct of Cometals and Tarbert. Fraudulent documentation is not uncommon in international trade, especially when parties do not have a history of business together. What are the lessons to be learned by all parties?

Export Management Companies. Independent firms that assume a range of export-related responsibilities for manufacturers, producers, or other exporters are called **export management companies**, or EMCs. They might do as little as render advice and training on how to export, or they might assume full responsibility for the entire export sales process. Many EMCs specialize in specific industries, products, or foreign markets. Firms that cannot justify their own in-house export departments use EMCs. Foreign market research, establishing foreign channels of distribution, exhibiting goods at foreign trade shows, working with foreign sales agents, preparing documenting for export, and handling language translations and shipping arrangements are also among the services EMCs provide.

Successful Small Business Exporting. When we think of international business, usually the largest multinational corporations come to mind. It is true that the largest companies, those with more than 500 employees, still dominate the total share of U.S. export volume. Nevertheless, many small- and medium-sized U.S. exporters (less than 500 employees) do extremely well in foreign markets. According to the U.S. Department of Commerce *Exporter Database,* for example, in 2010 there were more than 293,000 individual companies exporting goods from the United States. Ninety-eight percent of those were small- to medium-sized exporters, accounting for one-third of the total exports of goods. About one-quarter of those were manufacturers. The Department of Commerce points out that because the majority of companies ship only to one foreign country, this group as a whole could increase its export sales by entering additional foreign markets.

What does it take for a small business to be a successful exporter? First, most people agree that looking to foreign markets is not a panacea for a company's failures at home. Due to the time and resources necessary to enter a foreign market, a firm that is already failing at home will likely be unable to bear the cost of expansion and will probably repeat its same mistakes again. Second, experience shows that success or failure in entering a foreign market is often due to the commitment made to international business at a company's executive level. Many small companies that are new to exporting may lack the global view and commitment to foreign customers of a multinational corporation. In some cases they wrongly look for new customers abroad only when the economy declines at home. But this has proven shortsighted. During the time needed to gear up for the export process, which can take months or years, the domestic economy may heat up again, domestic customers return, and the new-to-export firm may lose interest in its new-found foreign customers. Without a long-term commitment, foreign buyers view these firms as unreliable suppliers. Many small companies soon learn that entering international markets requires time, patience, and commitment. Third, many small companies learn too late that international business is not merely a distant extension of domestic business. It requires the company to adapt to a new social, cultural, political, and economic environment and to be prepared to meet new challenges. For example, it may have to adapt its products and services to the expectations of the foreign market, develop new channels of distribution, visit foreign customers, and comply with new legal regulations, and so on. Finally, one of the greatest mistakes made by small business exporters, especially "new-to-export" firms, is the failure to have an **export plan** (see Exhibit 1.1).

Licensing and Protection of Intellectual Property Rights

The *Intellectual Property Handbook* of the World Intellectual Property Organization broadly defines **intellectual property (IP)**, also called **intellectual property rights**, as "legal rights which result from intellectual activity in the industrial, scientific, literary, and artistic fields." The most common forms are patents, trademarks, copyrights, and trade secrets. Patents have many different forms. In addition to the traditional patents on apparatus, they include methods for achieving a commercial objective, industrial designs, utility models, and geographical indications. The IP owner has the right to use, reproduce, distribute, and profit from its property, to license its use or distribution to others, and to protect it from unauthorized infringement. Firms with significant intellectual property assets must protect their legal rights in every country in which they plan to do business or even in which their patent, trademark, or copyright might be stolen, or infringed. Each country governs the recognition and protection of IP rights within its borders. In the

Exhibit 1.1

Components of an Export Plan

- Assessing the firm's readiness for export markets and its willingness to commit financial resources, human resources, and production output to foreign customers
- Making a long-term commitment to exporting and to foreign customers on the part of senior management and executives
- Identifying foreign-market potential of the firm's products, including economic, political, cultural, religious, and other factors
- Identifying the risks involved in exporting to that foreign market, including an evaluation of cost-effective shipping arrangements, banking arrangements for getting paid, and political risks
- Evaluating the legal aspects of the firm's export plan for compliance with government rules and customs regulations, including identifying legal controls on exporting its products out of the United States as well as legal barriers to importing and selling its products in the foreign country, and whether there are any patents, copyrights, or trademarks that must be protected abroad
- Determining the export readiness and suitability of the firm's products for the export market, including whether the products meet the quality standards, technical regulations, and foreign language requirements of foreign countries and whether any redesign, re-engineering, or relabeling of products is needed
- Identifying members of the "export team," comprising management, outside advisors, and trade specialists from banking, shipping, and government
- Identifying possible financing arrangements to assist foreign buyers
- Establishing foreign market channels of distribution, including deciding whether to export directly to customers or indirectly through intermediaries, deciding whether to use a sales representative or foreign distributor, identifying potential buyers, and participating in foreign trade shows
- Re-evaluating the firm's export performance over time, reconsidering its export plan, and determining whether the firm should increase its penetration of foreign markets beyond exporting

United States, IP law is almost entirely the province of federal law, although state law does apply in some areas not covered by federal law. A large body of state contract law and tort law also applies to many cases involving IP infringement. Most countries maintain a registration system for creating and protecting rights to patents, trademarks, and copyrights. Several important intellectual property treaties provide for streamlined procedures for mutually recognizing and enforcing IP rights. Many countries cooperate on IP policy and enforcement efforts.

International Licensing Agreements. IP is a valuable asset that can be transferred by the owner or holder to licensee through a grant of rights in that property, called a **license**. The license is usually part of a larger business arrangement represented in a licensing agreement. **Licensing agreements** are contracts by which the holder of intellectual property will grant certain rights (the "license") in that property to another party under specified conditions and for a specified time, in return for consideration, such as a fee or royalty or as a part of a larger business arrangement. Licenses can be either exclusive or nonexclusive, and frequently limit distribution to a certain geographical area, to certain uses, or to a certain period of time.

In the following case, *Russian Entertainment Wholesale, Inc. v. Close-Up International, Inc.*, the court was asked to resolve a conflict between two licensees of exclusive distribution rights to Russian films in the United States.

Russian Entertainment Wholesale, Inc. v. Close-Up International, Inc.

767 F. Supp. 2d 392 (2011) United States District Court (E.D.N.Y.)

BACKGROUND AND FACTS

Two Russian film studios [the studios] granted rights to produce and distribute DVD versions of their films to multiple licensees. Each licensee received different limited exclusive rights. Krupny Plan, which could distribute the films only in the original Russian language, sublicensed its rights to the films for home use in the United States and Canada to Close-Up, a New York corporation. Ruscico could distribute multilingual versions of the same films that were dubbed or subtitled and sublicensed its rights to its distributor in the United States, Image. At the time of licensing, none of the parties considered that a viewer of the subtitled films could simply turn off the subtitles and hear the film in any of several languages, including Russian. None of the agreements had a requirement that the films prevent the disabling of subtitles. Close-Up brought this action against Ruscico and Image for damages from copyright infringement, claiming that it is the "exclusive" U.S. licensee of the Russian-language-only versions of the films. The federal district court held for the defendants, and Close-Up appealed.

COGAN, DISTRICT JUDGE

The Copyright Act establishes that the "legal or beneficial owner of an exclusive right under a copyright" may bring suit for infringement under the act [citations omitted]. However, when this provision is invoked by an exclusive licensee, the licensee may seek relief from infringement only for the rights that the licensee has been exclusively licensed by the copyright holder. Plaintiff has shown that ... it was the legal and beneficial licensee of the narrow right to reproduce and distribute *Russian-language-only* versions of the subject works. Therefore, even if plaintiff had a valid sublicense, plaintiff would still only have standing to sue for infringement of the narrow right to reproduce and distribute Russian-language-only DVDs.... * * *

The evidence presented at trial proves that [the studios] elected to grant a "Russian language only" right to one licensee, and a separate "multilingual" right to another. The rights-holders did not consider sales of the multilingual DVDs manufactured by [the defendants] to violate the "Russian language only" license separately given to Krupny Plan. Instead, they considered the multilingual DVDs to be a distinct line of products, geared towards the separate non-Russian-speaking market. * * *

Plaintiff has failed to put forth any evidence that defendants ever produced or distributed works that infringed plaintiff's limited rights in Russian-language-only DVDs ... Instead, the evidence shows that all of the DVDs produced and distributed by defendants were multilingual DVDs, which [the studios] viewed as being distinct from the Russian-language-only DVDs that they had authorized Krupny Plan to reproduce and

continues

continued

distribute. Plaintiff thus has failed to make out a claim for copyright infringement against any of the defendants. * * *

Because there is no evidence that defendants reproduced or distributed DVD copies of the [films] that did not contain subtitles or dubbing in foreign languages, defendants' conduct was entirely within the scope of their rights ...

Plaintiff next argues that paragraph 1.2.1 [of defendants' license], which states that "[r]eproduction of the Films in the original language without the accompaniment of the picture by sound and/or subtitles in a foreign language is a violation of the present Agreement," should be interpreted to mean that production of DVDs that *could be watched* in Russian without subtitles or dubbing was a violation of the agreement. However, plaintiff reads too much into this provision, which explicitly states that its purpose was to ensure that the DVDs produced by [the defendants] would be "multilingual versions." In this context, it is clear that paragraph 1.2.1 simply forbade [the defendants] from producing DVD copies ... that did not include foreign subtitles or dubbing accompanying the films. Because all of the DVDs produced by defendants were multilingual versions that included subtitles in numerous foreign languages, defendants did not violate this provision of the agreement by producing DVDs that did not contain a disabling feature. * * *

Decision. Judgment affirmed for the defendant. A licensee of a limited exclusive license may seek relief from infringement only for the exclusive rights received from the copyright holder. Here, the plaintiff received only the rights to reproduce or distribute Russian-language-only DVDs. Defendants, pursuant to their license, distributed only multilingual (dubbed) versions and versions with subtitles.

Case Questions

1. What are the "limited exclusive" rights granted to the licensees in this case?
2. What is the difference between the rights granted to the plaintiff and those granted to the defendants?
3. Do you agree or disagree with the court's interpretation of the license agreements?
4. What does this case tell you about negotiating and drafting a licensing agreement?

Case Comment

The district court's opinion was affirmed in *Russian Entertainment Wholesale, Inc. v. Close-Up International, Inc.,* 482 Fed. Appx. 602 (2d Cir. 2012).

International Organizations and IP. The most important international IP organization is the **World Intellectual Property Organization**, or **WIPO**, a specialized agency of the United Nations, headquartered at Geneva. It was established in 1967 and currently has 185 member countries. WIPO fosters government cooperation in developing IP policies and coordinates registrations in some IP areas. It administers an arbitration center to resolve IP disputes between private parties, such as individual inventors, corporations, and universities (including patent, trademark, industrial design, and domain name dispute resolution). Another organization, the **World Trade Organization** (WTO), helps member countries assure a more uniform application and enforcement of their national IP laws. Its Dispute Settlement Body is a forum for resolving IP disputes between governments.

Infringement, Piracy, or Counterfeiting. The term **infringement** refers to the violation of the IP rights of another, and often occurs in the unauthorized use, distribution, or appropriation of those rights. IP infringement is often referred to as piracy or counterfeiting.

Intellectual property rights are the reward for innovation. Without laws to protect IP, and without the ability to enforce those laws, innovation in the arts, sciences, and industry would be destroyed. Thus enforcement of IP rights is a worldwide effort. However, many countries find it difficult to prevent IP piracy. Some developing countries have even encouraged it because of the perceived financial gains to their economies. For example, a few developing countries have not protected pharmaceutical and chemical patents, believing that some products are so indispensable to the public that low-cost generic versions should be encouraged regardless of the IP rights of the inventor. Ecommerce and mobile technologies have magnified the problem, not just in the sale of goods, but in many areas, such as the retransmission of performances, sports events, and films. Reports of the Office of the U.S. Trade Representative highlight the lack of enforcement of IP laws in China, India, Indonesia, Russia, Ukraine, and Venezuela, and many others.

Transfer of Technology. The sharing of scientific information, technology, and manufacturing know-how between firms, universities, or other institutions is known as the **transfer of technology**. It is important to building business alliances and is often accomplished through complex licensing agreements that include patent and other forms of intellectual property.

International Franchising. **Franchising** is a business arrangement that uses an agreement to license, control, and protect the use of the franchisor's patents, trademarks, copyrights, or business know-how, combined with a proven plan of business operation in return for royalties, fees, or commissions. The most common form of franchising is known as a business operations franchise and is usually used in retailing. Under a typical franchising agreement, the franchisee is allowed to use a trade name or trademark in offering goods or services to the public in return for a royalty based on a percentage of sales or other fee structure. The franchisee usually obtains the franchisor's rules for operating and managing the enterprise, along with the brand and other trademarks to attract customers. Franchising in the United States accounts for a large proportion of total retail sales. When American markets became saturated for franchise opportunities several decades ago, U.S. firms began looking for growth overseas. As in the United States, foreign franchising has been successful in fast-food retailing, hotels, car rental, automobile maintenance, educational courses, convenience stores, printing services, and real estate services, to name a few. U.S. firms have excelled in franchising overseas, making up the majority of new franchise operations worldwide. The prospects for future growth in foreign markets are enormous, especially in China and the developing countries of Asia, the Middle East, and Latin America.

Some Legal Aspects of Franchising. Franchising is a good vehicle for entering a foreign market because the local franchisee provides capital investment, entrepreneurial commitment, and on-site management to deal with local issues, such as labor and employment. However, franchisors face many legal requirements. Franchising in the United States is regulated primarily by the Federal Trade Commission at the federal level, which requires the filing of extensive disclosure statements to protect prospective investors. Other countries have also enacted franchise disclosure laws. Some developing countries have restrictions on the amount of money the franchisor can remove from the country and others might have restrictions on importing supplies (ketchup, paper products, etc.) for the operation of the business. While these restrictions protect local suppliers, more progressive developing countries are now abandoning them because they recognize that foreign franchises bring high-quality consumer products and managerial talent to their countries. Having eliminated many of its restrictions on franchising in recent years, franchises in China today are governed by a 2007 law, and are subject to approval by the China Ministry of Commerce.

The following case, *Dayan v. McDonald's,* illustrates the difficulty in supervising the operations of a franchisee in a foreign country. Consider how any U.S. franchiser will allow its franchisees to adapt to the cultural environment in a foreign country while still providing the same consistent quality and service that is expected whenever anyone patronizes one of its establishments anywhere in the world.

Dayan v. McDonald's Corp.

125 Ill. App.3d 972, 466 N.E.2d 958 (1984) Appellate Court of Illinois

BACKGROUND AND FACTS

Dayan received an exclusive franchise to operate McDonald's restaurants in Paris, France. The franchise agreement required that the franchise meet all quality, service, and cleanliness (QSC) standards set by McDonald's. The agreement stated that the rationale for maintaining QSC standards was that a "departure of restaurants anywhere in the world from these standards impedes the successful operation of restaurants throughout the world, and injures the value of [McDonald's] patents, trademarks, trade name, and property." Dayan agreed not to vary from QSC standards without prior written approval. After several years of quality and cleanliness violations, McDonald's sought to terminate the franchise. Dayan brought this action to enjoin the termination. The lower court found that good cause existed for the termination and Dayan appealed.

continues

continued

BUCKLEY, PRESIDING JUSTICE

Dayan also argues that McDonald's was obligated to provide him with the operational assistance necessary to enable him to meet the QSC standards.

... Dayan verbally asked Sollars (a McDonald's manager) for a French-speaking operations person to work in the market for six months. Sollars testified that he told Dayan it would be difficult to find someone with the appropriate background that spoke French but that McDonald's could immediately send him an English-speaking operations man. Sollars further testified that this idea was summarily rejected by Dayan as unworkable even though he had informed Dayan that sending operations personnel who did not speak the language to a foreign country was very common and very successful in McDonald's international system. Nonetheless, Sollars agreed to attempt to locate a qualified person with the requisite language skills for Dayan.

Through Sollars's efforts, Dayan was put in contact with Michael Maycock, a person with McDonald's managerial and operational experience who spoke French. Dayan testified that he hired Maycock sometime in October 1977 and placed him in charge of training, operations, quality control, and equipment.

As the trial court correctly realized: "It does not take a McDonald's-trained French-speaking operational man to know that grease dripping from the vents must be stopped and not merely collected in a cup hung from the ceiling, that dogs are not permitted to defecate where food is stored, that insecticide is not blended with chicken breading; that past-dated products should be discarded; that a potato peeler should be somewhat cleaner than a tire-vulcanizer; and that shortening should not look like crank case oil."

Clearly, Maycock satisfied Dayan's request for a French-speaking operations man to run his training program ... The finding that Dayan refused non-French-speaking operational assistance and that McDonald's fulfilled Dayan's limited request for a French-speaking operational employee is well supported by the record. To suggest, as plaintiff does, that an opposite conclusion is clearly evident is totally without merit. Accordingly, we find McDonald's fulfilled its contractual obligation to provide requested operational assistance to Dayan.

In view of the foregoing reasons, the judgment of the trial court denying plaintiff's request for a permanent injunction and finding that McDonald's properly terminated the franchise agreement is affirmed.

Decision. Judgment was affirmed for McDonald's. McDonald's had fulfilled all of its responsibility under the agreement to assist the plaintiff in complying with the provisions of the license. The plaintiff had violated the provisions of the agreement by not complying with the QSC standards. The plaintiff was permitted to continue operation of his restaurants, but without use of the McDonald's trademarks or name.

Comment. Today most international franchise agreements call for dispute resolution through arbitration.

Case Questions

1. What social or cultural factors might have affected McDonald's presence in Paris?
2. How could McDonald's have exercised greater control over its foreign franchisee?
3. What types of products or services are most suitable for foreign licensing?

Foreign Direct Investment

In this text, the term **foreign direct investment (FDI)** refers to the ownership and operation or effective control of the productive assets of an ongoing business by an individual or corporate investor who is a resident or national of another country. FDIs are "active investments," as distinguished from passive investments (such as the purchase of stock for dividends or appreciation). They are generally made for the long term and with the expectation of being involved in company management and producing a profit from operations. FDI may include investments in manufacturing, mining, farming, assembly operations, and other facilities of production, as well as in service industries.

Throughout this book, distinctions are made between the home and host countries of the firms involved. The **home country** refers to that country under whose laws the investing corporation was created or is headquartered. For example, the United States is home to multinational corporations such as Ford, Exxon, and Coca-Cola, but the companies operate in **host countries** in every region of the world. Of the three forms of international business, FDI provides the firm with the greatest opportunity for market penetration, the most involvement, and perhaps the greatest risk of doing business abroad. Investment in a foreign plant is often a result of having had successful experiences in exporting or licensing and of the search for ways to overcome the disadvantages of those other entry methods. For example, by producing its product in a foreign country, instead of exporting, a firm can become more competitive in the host market. It can avoid quotas and tariffs on imported goods, avoid currency fluctuations on the traded goods, provide better service and spare parts, and more quickly adapt products to local tastes and market trends. Manufacturing overseas can mean taking advantage of local natural resources, labor, and manufacturing economies of scale.

Forms of Investment. Firms entering a foreign market through direct investment can structure their business arrangements in many different ways. Their options and eventual course of action may depend on such factors as industry and market conditions, capitalization of the firm and financing, and legal considerations. Some of these options include the start-up of a new foreign subsidiary company, the formation of a joint venture with an existing foreign company, a merger with a foreign company, or the acquisition of a foreign company by stock purchase.

A **foreign branch** is a business presence by the investor in the host country. It might be a branch office or an entire network of operational facilities. The branch is a part of the home country entity, with operations in the host country. A **foreign subsidiary** is a "foreign" company organized under the laws of a foreign host country, but owned and controlled by the parent corporation in the home country. A parent company that controls a majority of the stock of a subsidiary can control management and financial decision making. A subsidiary can also be part of a joint venture with another investor. Several subsidiaries owned by one parent, are called **affiliates**.

The **joint venture** is a cooperative business arrangement between two or more companies for profit. A joint venture may take the form of a partnership or corporation. Typically, each party contributes a different type of expertise and each contributes different amounts of capital, each bringing its own special resources to the venture. A joint venture is often used where the laws of a host country require local some ownership or require that the investing foreign firm has a local partner. **Local participation** means that a share of the business is owned by nationals of the host country. Developing countries have a history of having local participation requirements, although these have been reduced to attract more investment. A disadvantage of the joint venture is that a company may have to share its technology, expertise, and profits with another company, or give up control over local operations.

Multinational Corporations. **Multinational corporations**, or multinationals, are firms that have significant foreign direct investment assets or that derive a significant portion of their revenues from more than one country. Typically a multinational is comprised of a parent company in the home country and foreign affiliates located in host countries. A multinational is usually not a single legal entity. It is a global enterprise that consists of any number of interrelated corporate entities, connected through complex chains of stock ownership. Some "multinationals" are not actually corporations, but can take other forms, and some are state-owned trading organizations. They are characterized by their abilities to derive and transfer capital resources worldwide, move management and technology across national borders, operate facilities of production, deliver services, and penetrate markets in more than one country—often on a global scale. They can be domiciled in both developed and developing countries. The term **transnational corporation** is often used in the United Nations system, reflecting that the corporation's operations and interests "transcend" national boundaries.

One significant trend in business during the last half of the twentieth century has been the "globalization" of multinational corporations. At one time, multinational corporations were simply large domestic companies with foreign operations. Today, they are global companies. They typically make decisions and enter strategic alliances with each other without regard to national boundaries. They move factories, technology, and capital to those countries with the most hospitable laws, the lowest tax rates, the most qualified workforce, or abundant natural resources. They see market share and company performance in global and regional terms.

CONDUCTING BUSINESS IN DEVELOPING AND NEWLY INDUSTRIALIZED COUNTRIES

While our introduction to the forms of international business applies generally to firms doing business anywhere in the world, companies do face special problems in developing countries, newly industrialized countries, and in emerging market economies. In this section we'll take a brief look at the legal and economic environment of doing business there.

It is often useful to group countries according to socioeconomic criteria, even though they may be otherwise very different and in different geographic regions. For example, the countries of Vietnam in Asia, Libya in North Africa, and Bolivia in South America each have different cultures, religions, geography, per capita income levels, and very different political and trade relationships with the United States and other Western countries. Yet they have many of the same traits as other developing countries. So too are the countries of India, Brazil, and Malaysia; they are vastly different in their locations, cultures, geographies, and even sizes. However, the socioeconomic data of these countries show that they have much in common with each other and with other newly industrialized countries. Grouping like this is helpful in discussion and aids in statistical analysis. However, there is no one universally accepted definition for the terms "developing" or "newly industrialized" because economists are grouping countries for different purposes, and because there are so many different indicators of socioeconomic development.

Developed Countries

The developed countries generally have a high per capita income, have a high standard of living, and are in the later stages of industrialization. They are characterized by advanced technology, modern production and management methods, and advanced research facilities. They have diversified economies not dependent on agriculture, oil, or mining alone. Although the oil-dependent countries of the Middle East are very wealthy with a high standard of living, for example, they are not considered developed countries. It can be said that many developed countries are entering a postindustrial economy, with declining manufacturing but a growing service sector. The best examples of developed countries are the United States and Canada, the Western European nations, Israel, Japan, Australia, and New Zealand. The countries of Eastern Europe, most of which were freed from communist domination at the end of the 1980s, are for the most part considered to be developed countries.

Developing Countries

Compared to developed countries, developing countries generally have a lower per capita income, a lower standard of living, higher foreign debt, more rapid population growth, and a history of greater state control over their economy. The "typical" developing country is impossible to describe. Some rely almost exclusively on petroleum exports as their source of income. Many have large agrarian populations, densely populated cities, and a plentiful supply of unskilled labor. Many support high-tech industries. Although some are rich in natural resources, such as Brazil, others have depleted theirs. The protection of the environment often takes a back seat to industrialization and economic "progress," and so pollution often chokes their air and water. Sanitation and water systems are often inadequate. In some areas, toxic waste dumps may threaten entire communities. Economic crimes such as smuggling, hijacking and ocean piracy, organized crime, government corruption, and illicit drug production are frequently major problems. Education levels are generally far below that of the developed countries. Poor communication and transportation systems make business difficult. Inadequate distribution systems make it costly to get goods to market. Floods and natural disasters, exacerbated by inappropriate agricultural, land management, and industrial policies have disrupted entire populations. Overpopulation, homelessness, malnutrition, and disease are still common in many areas. The epidemic of plague that struck India in 1994, for example, caused workers to flee industrial communities in fear and forced the closing of many factories. Despite this bleak picture, developing countries do present trade, franchising, and investment opportunities for U.S. companies.

A wide disparity in social and economic classes exists in many developing countries, with great inequality in income and education between the rich and poor. Also, political systems differ widely in developing countries. Some have stable, democratic governments; others do not. For instance, Costa Rica has the oldest continuing democracy in Central America, dating back to 1948. Other less-stable Central and South American countries experience varying degrees of political and economic freedom, from parliamentary rule to military dictatorship.

Trade and Investment Policies in Developing Countries. Firms that do business in developing countries can face a host of adverse government policies, including high tariffs, taxes, import licensing requirements, financial regulation, controls on technology transfer, and trade and investment barriers that protect local industries from competition. Consider these examples: Governments in developing countries might allow the import of goods and services needed for their own socioeconomic development plans, such as tractors, machine tools, or power plants. However, they might ban or discourage the import of goods and services considered nonessential, or those that are available from local producers. They may allow investment in a chemical or pharmaceutical plant, but not one making consumer goods for local sale. They may allow a foreign firm to produce there, but only if it does so in a joint venture with a local partner, to whom it must disclose or license its latest technology patents.

Another problem in doing business in developing countries is that the rules affecting international business often lack transparency; government regulations are often not published or made easily available to foreign firms. This makes regulations feel more like "red tape," and compliance almost impossible. In addition, in many developing countries bribery and corruption make it difficult to deal with local officials, even though such practices may be illegal and violators are prosecuted.

Each year the Office of the U.S. Trade Representative issues the *National Trade Estimate Report on Foreign Trade Barriers,* which reports on foreign barriers to trade and investment. The 2012 report on India illustrates some of the restrictions developing countries place on foreign business. Retailing, especially larger "multi-brand" stores, is largely closed to foreign companies. Many products may not be imported without a license, creating long delays and uncertainty, with many licenses simply being denied. Private package delivery services are regulated to protect the government-owned postal service. Foreign investment is prohibited or restricted in agriculture, railways, and real estate. Although it has become easier to invest in the banking, telecommunications, and insurance sectors in recent years, these areas are still not widely open to foreign firms. Government procurement contracts for goods and services rarely go to foreign firms, but are usually granted to Indian state-owned firms. Entrance to the accounting and legal professions is highly restricted.

Many of the hostile policies in developing countries, dating back to the first half of the last century, were based on socialist agricultural and economic policies that led to central planning and the government ownership of some farms, businesses, and industries. Some developing countries that had been subject to colonialization by European countries continued their resentment even long after gaining independence, and later directed it at the power and influence of Western multinational corporations. Some argued that multinationals were only present in their countries to exploit their natural resources and cheap labor, and to circumvent laws by bribing local officials. They felt that multinationals should be controlled for the good of society. Needless to say, these attitudes did not help attract foreign investment.

Today most developing countries recognize that foreign firms bring capital, technology, innovation, jobs, and tax revenues. In recent decades most developing countries have slowly loosened controls over trade and investment. As the developing countries joined the World Trade Organization they became committed to opening their markets to foreign goods and services, and to removing barriers to investment.

The following case, *In re Union Carbide Corporation Gas Plant Disaster at Bhopal,* involves a U.S. multinational company that faced problems in owning and operating a plant in India.

The Newly Industrialized Countries

The **newly industrialized countries** are developing countries that have made rapid progress toward becoming industrialized or technology-based economies. They are located in all regions of the world, including Latin America, the Middle East, and Southern and Southeast Asia. Much of their successes in recent years are due to highly motivated workforces and stable climates for foreign investment. Typically they are transitioning from agricultural economies to industrial ones, with burgeoning urban populations in the manufacturing centers. Their manufacturing is export oriented, producing a broad mix of high-quality products from computers to steel. Indeed, many newly industrialized countries are home to multinational corporations that operate in foreign countries. They are magnets for foreign investment and have reserves of foreign exchange. Their successes have led to dramatic rises in per capita gross domestic product and to improvements in jobs, wages, education, health care, living accommodations, and overall quality of life. Newly industrialized countries have also benefited from many social and political reforms that have led to democracy and fundamental freedoms. In Asia, the countries of Indonesia, Malaysia, the Philippines, Thailand, China, and India are considered

In re Union Carbide Corporation Gas Plant Disaster at Bhopal

809 F.2d 195 (1987) United States Court of Appeals (2d Cir.)

BACKGROUND AND FACTS

Union Carbide Corporation (UCC) had been one of the largest chemical and industrial companies in the world, operating in dozens of countries. UCC's subsidiary in India, UCIL, had grown to fourteen plants, employing more than 9,000 Indian citizens, manufacturing a variety of products, including chemicals, plastics, batteries, fertilizers, and pesticides. UCIL was incorporated under the laws of India. Fifty-one percent of UCIL stock was owned by UCC, 24 percent by the government of India, and the balance by approximately 23,500 Indian citizens. The stock was publicly traded in India. In the 1970s, India issued a license to UCIL to produce pesticides at a plant to be built in Bhopal. UCC provided the basic design for the plant, but India insisted that its own engineering firms and contractors build it. From 1972–1980, the construction was supervised by Indian engineers and many changes were made to the design. Labor and employment policies were set by the Indian government and the construction was managed and operated entirely by Indian citizens. The operations of the plant were regulated by more than two dozen Indian governmental agencies; however, enforcement of environmental, health, and safety standards by regulators was weak and ineffective. Maintenance procedures and record keeping at the plant were inadequate. In 1984, poisonous methyl isocyanate gas was released from the plant and blew into densely occupied parts of the city of Bhopal, resulting in the deaths of several thousand Indian citizens (estimates range from 2,000–10,000) and severe injuries to several hundred thousand others.

In April 1985, the Indian government filed a complaint in the federal courts in New York on behalf of the victims. UCC contended that the action should properly be heard in the courts of India. The district court agreed and dismissed the action.

MANSFIELD, CIRCUIT JUDGE

The vital parts of the Bhopal plant, including its storage tank, monitoring instrumentation, and vent gas scrubber, were manufactured by Indians in India. Although some 40 UCIL employees were given some safety training at UCC's plant in West Virginia, they represented a small fraction of the Bhopal plant's employees. The vast majority of plant employees were selected and trained by UCIL in Bhopal. The manual for start-up of the Bhopal plant was prepared by Indians employed by UCIL.

In short, the plant has been constructed and managed by Indians in India. No Americans were employed at the plant at the time of the accident. In the five years from 1980 to 1984, although more than 1,000 Indians were employed at the plant, only one American was employed there and he left in 1982. No Americans visited the plant for more than one year prior to the accident, and during the five-year period before the accident the communications between the plant and the United States were almost nonexistent.

The vast majority of material witnesses and documentary proof bearing on causation of and liability for the accident is located in India, not the United States, and would be more accessible to an Indian court than to a U.S. court. The records are almost entirely in Hindi or other Indian languages, understandable to an Indian court without translation. The witnesses for the most part do not speak English but Indian languages understood by an Indian court but not by an American court. These witnesses could be required to appear in an Indian court but not in a court of the United States. * * * The accident and all relevant events occurred in India. The victims, over 200,000 in number, are citizens of India and located there. The witnesses are almost entirely Indian citizens. The Union of India has a greater interest than does the United States in facilitating the trial and adjudication of the victims' claims.

India's interest is increased by the fact that it has for years treated UCIL as an Indian national, subjecting it to intensive regulations and governmental supervision of the construction, development, and operation of the Bhopal plant, its emissions, water and air pollution, and safety precautions. Numerous Indian government officials have regularly conducted on-site inspections of the plant and approved its machinery and equipment, including its facilities for storage of the lethal methyl isocyanate gas that escaped and caused the disaster giving rise to the claims. Thus India has considered the plant to be an Indian one and the disaster to be an Indian problem. It therefore has a deep interest in ensuring compliance with its safety standards. Moreover, plaintiffs have conceded that in view of India's strong interest and its greater contacts with the plant, its operations, its employees, and the victims of the

continues

continued

accident, the law of India, as the place where the tort occurred, will undoubtedly govern.

Decision. The district court's dismissal of the actions against UCC was upheld. The doctrine of *forum non conveniens* is a rule of law, stating that to further the administration of justice, where a case is properly heard in the courts of more than one country, it should be heard in the country with the greater interest in the outcome of the case, and where it is most convenient. In this case that is India.

Comment. In 1989, the Supreme Court of India approved a settlement fund of $470 million to compensate the victims of the disaster. The company has long maintained that the tragedy resulted from employee sabotage at the plant.

Case Questions

1. India gained its independence from Great Britain in 1947. Like many developing countries with agrarian economies, independent India embarked on a long period of socialist and protectionist policies. How do you think this affected the investment climate in India? How do you think this defined the relationship between UCC and the Indian government prior to 1984?
2. Why do you think UCC might have chosen to produce agricultural pesticides in India rather than export those products to India from plants in developed countries?
3. Why did India require local management and control? What are the advantages and disadvantages of local management, and what problem does it present to the multinational?
4. Had the legal requirements in India concerning the handling of hazardous chemicals been less than those required in the United States, should UCC have ethically followed the higher U.S. standard?
5. Do you think that a parent corporation, like UCC in this case, should be financially liable for torts committed by its foreign subsidiary? Should the parent be protected by the limited liability of its corporate veil, or should a multinational firm with a "global purpose" be responsible under some theory of "single-enterprise" liability? How would this affect the attitude toward investment worldwide?

newly industrialized. Other countries outside of Asia that may be described as transitioning to newly industrialized status are Mexico, Brazil, Turkey, and South Africa.

Although they are now widely considered to have highly developed economies, the best-known newly industrialized economies are the four "Asian Tigers": Hong Kong, Singapore, Taiwan, and South Korea.

Emerging Market Economies. The term **emerging market economy** is often used to describe countries or regions with the potential for rapid economic growth. Many of them are transitioning from heavily state controlled economies to market economies. The term can apply to countries or regions that are considered newly industrialized developing, or even developed. There is no precise definition, and the term is most frequently used in the investment field when referring to countries viewed as having growth opportunities for foreign investors. The largest emerging markets include China, India, Brazil, and Russia, but could also include smaller countries such as Saudi Arabia, Thailand, and Mexico. The term **countries in transition** refers to those countries that are transitioning from centrally planned economies (usually based on communist doctrine) to free markets. These include the countries of the former Soviet Union and its former Eastern European allies, China, and a few others.

The Least Developed Countries

The **least developed countries (LDCs)** are those defined by the United Nations on the basis of several socioeconomic criteria. Examples include low per capita income, poor nutrition and health, high adult literacy, unstable agricultural production, weak export economy, and large populations displaced by natural disasters. Examples of least-developed regions or countries include most of sub-Saharan Africa, such as Rwanda and Somalia, Haiti in the Caribbean, Bangladesh and Cambodia in Asia, and Afghanistan in Central Asia. They lack many of the basic resources needed for development and require vast amounts of foreign aid from the wealthier nations. Many of these countries have inadequate roads and bridges, inadequate public utilities and telephone systems, poor educational and health-care facilities, a lack of plentiful drinking water, unstable governments, little or no technological base, high infant mortality, AIDS and other diseases, rampant crime, ethnic and tribal warfare, public corruption, and weak or nonexistent financial institutions. According to the United Nations, most of the population is under the age of 25. Business opportunities for trade in consumer goods and for the products and services of most Western companies are limited. Least-developed countries are in need of investments and products that will help them deal with these basic problems.

SOME COMMON RISKS OF INTERNATIONAL BUSINESS

International business differs from business at home for many obvious reasons. Distance, culture, language, currency, and government control are a few examples. As you will see in this section, they can present new challenges and risks to international managers.

Distance and Logistics

Managing many international transactions means managing the risks of shipping goods, getting paid, and doing business over great distances. In an import/export transaction, the risk that the buyer will fail or refuse to pay, is called **payment or credit risk**. This may mean finding special ways of assuring payment for goods being shipped to far-off countries, including the use of international banking services. For many exporters it means attending international trade shows and visiting their customers to get to know them personally.

Similarly, importers and purchasing managers for international firms learn to manage **supplier risk**, such as the possibility of being victims of fraud or receiving defective goods. Most experienced managers visit their suppliers, tour their plants, and work as partners. Purchasers also frequently use foreign agents to inspect cargo before shipment to make sure it complies with the contract. Purchasers come to quickly appreciate the words of one experienced purchasing manager: "There is no substitute for personally knowing your supplier."

Distance also means that parties must consider **property or marine risk** to cargo. Goods can be damaged by salt water or air, ships wreck, planes crash, refrigeration breaks down, food spoils, "sealed" ocean containers are pilfered, grain becomes infested, and so on. As between buyer and seller, who bears the risk of loss to goods at sea or in the air? And when is and isn't the carrier responsible? Exporters also learn how to arrange transportation and manage their shipping costs. With rates often based on the greater of weight or volume, they learn to creatively compress and package for shipment. For instance, items can be vacuum packed to remove air, liquids can be dehydrated to remove water, and both can be added back in the country of destination. After all, why pay to ship air or water?

All international firms are subject to the risks of war, terrorism, or international hostilities. This includes the risks to international shipping. The following case, *Transatlantic Financing v. United States*, is one of many cases resulting from the closing of the Suez Canal during a war in the Middle East.

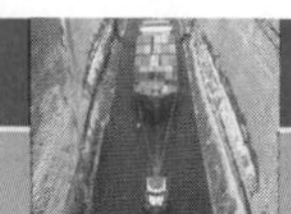

Transatlantic Financing Corporation v. United States

363 F.2d 312 (1966) United States Court of Appeals (D.C. Cir.)

BACKGROUND AND FACTS

The United States contracted with Transatlantic Financing, the operator of a cargo ship, to transport wheat from Texas to Iran in 1956. The parties never agreed on the route the ship would take. Six days after the ship left Texas, the government of Egypt was at war with Israel and blockaded the Suez Canal. As a result, the ship had to sail around the Cape of Good Hope on the southern tip of Africa, extending the voyage several thousand miles and adding an additional 14 percent to Transatlantic's costs. Transatlantic sued for the added expense, claiming that it had agreed only to travel the "usual and customary" route to Iran through Suez, and that its performance became legally impossible. The lower court ruled infavor of the United States, and Transatlantic appealed.

J. SKELLY WRIGHT, CIRCUIT JUDGE

* * * It is now recognized that "A thing is impossible in legal contemplation when it is not practicable; and a thing is impracticable when it can only be done at an excessive and unreasonable cost." [citations omitted]. * * *

continues

continued

It seems reasonable, where no route is mentioned in a contract, to assume the parties expected performance by the usual and customary route at the time of contract. Since the usual and customary route from Texas to Iran at the time of contract was through Suez, closure of the Canal made impossible the expected method of performance. But this unexpected development raises rather than resolves the impossibility issue, which turns additionally on whether the risk of the contingency's occurrence [closure of the canal] had been allocated and, if not, whether performance by alternative routes was rendered impracticable.

The contract in this case does not expressly condition performance upon availability of the Suez route. Nor does it specify 'via Suez' or, on the other hand, 'via Suez or Cape of Good Hope.' Nor are there provisions in the contract from which we may properly imply that the continued availability of Suez was a condition of performance. Nor is there anything in custom or trade usage, or in the surrounding circumstances generally, which would support our constructing a condition of performance. The numerous cases requiring performance around the Cape when Suez was closed, *see e.g., Ocean Tramp Tankers Corp. v. V/O Sovfracht* (*The Eugenia*), (1964) 2 Q.B. 226 ... indicate that the Cape route is generally regarded as an alternative means of performance. [Thus, the risk of canal closure was not allocated by contract or custom to either party.]* * *

We turn then to the question whether occurrence of the contingency rendered performance commercially impracticable under the circumstances of this case. The goods shipped were not subject to harm from the longer, less temperate Southern route. The vessel and crew were fit to proceed around the Cape. Transatlantic was no less able than the United States to purchase insurance to cover the contingency's occurrence. If anything, it is more reasonable to expect owner-operators of vessels to insure against the hazards of war. They are in the best position to calculate the cost of performance by alternative routes (and therefore to estimate the amount of insurance required), and are undoubtedly sensitive to international troubles which uniquely affect the demand for and cost of their services. The only factor operating here in Transatlantic's favor is the added expense, allegedly $43,972.00 above and beyond the contract price of $305,842.92, of extending a 10,000-mile voyage by approximately 3,000 miles. While it may be an overstatement to say that increased cost and difficulty of performance never constitute impracticability, to justify relief there must be more of a variation between expected cost and the cost of performing by an available alternative than is present in this case—where the promisor can legitimately be presumed to have accepted some degree of abnormal risk and where impracticability is urged on the basis of added expense alone.

Decision. Judgment affirmed for the United States. The closure of the canal and the resulting additional expenses of the alternate route did not make the contract commercially impracticable, (and therefore not legally impossible) to perform.

Case Questions

1. Did the parties agree on what would happen if the Suez Canal had closed? In other words, did they allocate the risk of closure? Would that have changed the result?
2. What is Transatlantic's argument? If admiralty law implies that a ship's journey will be by the "usual and customary" route, why did the court not hold that the contract had become impossible to perform? How does the court define "impossible?"
3. Did Transatlantic's performance become *impracticable*? How difficult was it for Transatlantic to take the alternate route around Africa?
4. Suppose it had been bad weather instead of a blocked canal? Would the case outcome have been different? How about a tsunami? What if a government order had prohibited the ship from departing Texas?

Language and Cultural Differences

International business people know the importance of language and culture in every business relationship and the ability to speak a foreign language is certainly an advantage. But the international business world is filled with successful people who are not fluent in a foreign language. They adapt by learning some basic courtesies in the language of a country they are visiting, and being especially sensitive to social conventions, cultural issues, and religious beliefs. There is some truth in the saying that if you're the buyer, the seller will find a way to speak your language; but if you're the seller, you must find a way to communicate with your customer. One corporate CEO argued that he could not possibly know all the languages of all the countries in which he does business. While true, that argument may not be

Gaskin v. Stumm Handel GMBH

390 F. Supp. 361 (1975) United States District Court (S.D.N.Y.)

BACKGROUND AND FACTS

The plaintiff, a U.S. citizen, entered into an employment contract with the German firm of Stumm Handel, the defendant. The contract was written entirely in German. Without being able to speak or read German, the plaintiff signed the contract. He never received an English language version. However the terms of the contract were explained to him in English. One of the terms of the contract, known as a "forum selection clause," provided that any disputes that might arise between the parties would be settled in the courts of Germany. Later, when the parties reached a disagreement, the plaintiff brought this action against the defendant in the United States, contending that his failure to understand German rendered the forum selection clause invalid.

CANELLA, DISTRICT JUDGE

With regard to such translation, Gaskin asserts that "I was never informed that by executing the (contract), I was consenting to the Republic of West Germany [now Germany] as the forum within which I must submit all controversies" and that "had I known this, I would not have agreed to the same, as such an obligation is onerous and unconscionable, and a deterrent to bringing any actions whatsoever."... We find that in making the foregoing assertions, Gaskin flies in the face of well-settled contract law principles and has failed to sustain his burden.

It is a settled proposition of contract law in this state and nation that "the signer of a deed or other instrument, expressive of a *jurai* act, is conclusively bound thereby. That his mind never gave assent to the terms expressed is not material. If the signer could read the instrument, not to have read it was gross negligence; if he could not read it, not to procure it to be read was equally negligent; in either case the writing binds him (citations omitted) ... "

While Mr. Gaskin's apparent "blissful ignorance" with regard to the contract under which he was to render his labors to the defendant strikes us as highly incredible as a matter of common sense, we take note of certain facts which are relevant to the disposition of this matter. It must be remembered that Mr. Gaskin is not an ignorant consumer, unlearned in the language of the contract, who has become entangled in the web of a contract of adhesion through the overreaching or other unconscionable practices of the defendant. The contract at bar does not involve the credit sale of a refrigerator or color television set, but rather compensation of some $36,000 per annum for Mr. Gaskin's services as the manager in charge of the defendant's New York operations which were to be conducted under the name Stumm Trading Company. His office (Park Avenue, New York City) is not located in an area which would have precluded his easy access to a competent translation of the involved document. There existed no emergency condition or other exceptional circumstances at the time plaintiff entered into this contract; conditions which might now serve to excuse his present plight. Mr. Gaskin has advanced no evidence to support a finding that the contract sued upon is other than one which was fairly negotiated at arm's length and in a businesslike fashion between the parties and voluntarily entered into by him in the hope of reaping a great economic benefit ...

Thus, we find that the instant transaction was a commercial arrangement of a nature which warranted the exercise of care by Mr. Gaskin before his entry into it and that his conduct with regard to this undertaking can only be characterized as negligent, the consequences of which he must now bear ...

Decision. The court dismissed the plaintiff's action, holding that the plaintiff's failure to speak or read German was not grounds for invalidating any of the provisions of the contract.

Case Questions

1. Why did Gaskin claim that he was not bound by the forum selection clause included in the contract to which he agreed?
2. In business, is a party to contract negotiations obligated to provide translation services to other parties?
3. If the parties to a contract execute two copies of a contract, one in each language, which is the operable and effective document?

so valid for an international sales manager who does business in one or two primary foreign markets. Some positions require an even greater level of foreign language competency. As a firm moves toward greater penetration of a foreign market, for instance, when negotiating a licensing or investment contract, it will become crucial to use native speakers or nationals of the host country. Contracts will often be written in the languages of both parties, and so the use of foreign lawyers may also be necessary. The case of *Gaskin v. Stumm Handel* illustrates what can happen when a party is not able to read and understand a foreign language contract.

Cross-Border Trade Controls

Whenever goods, services, money, or people cross an international border, they are regulated by government. The movement of goods is governed by the laws and regulations of the countries through which they pass. The most common regulations are controls on exports, tariffs, and non-tariff barriers to trade.

Export Controls and Sanctions. An **export control** is a restriction on exports of goods, services, or technology to a country or group of countries imposed for reasons of national security or foreign policy. All countries have export controls. Those in the United States are enforced through an export licensing system administered by the Bureau of Industry and Security of the U.S. Department of Commerce. Export licensing requirements can apply to exports of almost any type of goods or technology, although advanced technology items that can contribute to the military capability of a foreign nation are most strictly regulated. **Sanctions** are broader and more comprehensive restrictions on trade and financial transactions with countries, who sponsor international terrorism, engage in the proliferation of weapons of mass destruction, threaten international peace, or violate major principles of international law. Sanctions can include restrictions on travel to those countries, and are often based on resolutions of the United Nations Security Council. In the United States, they are primarily administered by the Department of Treasury.

Tariff and Non-tariff Barriers. The most common import barriers are tariffs and non-tariff barriers. A **tariff** is an import duty or tax imposed on goods entering the customs territory of a nation. Most tariff rates today are determined by trade negotiations between nations and are no longer the great barrier to trade that they were at one time. U.S. Customs and Border Protection of the Department of Homeland Security enforce tariff laws in the United States.

Non-tariff barriers are all barriers to the import of foreign goods or services other than tariffs. They usually are laws or administrative regulations that have the effect, directly or indirectly, of restricting access of foreign goods or services to a domestic market. A **quota** is a quantitative restriction on imports that limits the quantity of an item that may enter a country annually. International trade laws today prohibit countries from using quotas to keep out foreign goods, except in very limited circumstances. Examples of indirect non-tariff barriers include health and safety regulations, environmental regulations, and industrial and agricultural standards.

Currency Risk

A firm is exposed to currency risk whenever it transacts business in a foreign currency or makes an investment in a host country whose currency is different from that of the home country. Examples are pricing and selling goods for export in a currency other than your own, or operating a business in a foreign country where the profits are derived in that country's currency. Currency risk includes (1) exchange rate risk and (2) currency control risk. Currency risk exists when a firm must convert one currency to the currency of another country before it can be used.

Exchange rate risk. **Exchange rate risk** results from the fluctuations in the relative value of two currencies when one is exchanged for the other. In a simple export/import transaction, the party dealing in the foreign currency bears the exchange rate risk. If the contract calls for payment in the seller's currency at some future date, the buyer bears the exchange rate risk in the intervening period. By quoting prices in its own currency, the seller has shifted the exchange rate risk to the buyer. Of course, if the seller quoted prices in a buyer's currency, the seller would be assuming the exchange rate risk. The ability of a firm to manage its currency risk depends on the firm's size, sophistication, and global resources. Multinational corporations also have other, more complex and sophisticated options for managing exchange rate risk. For instance, a multinational corporation's subsidiary in a foreign country may have excess local currency derived from revenues there. These assets can be transferred to affiliated units owned by the parent company for use anywhere in the world. In the following case, *Bernina Distributors v. Bernina Sewing Machine Co.*, the parties failed to consider the impact of currency fluctuations on their contract.

Bernina Distributors v. Bernina Sewing Machine Co.

646 F.2d 434 (1981) United States Court of Appeals (10th Cir.)

BACKGROUND AND FACTS

The defendant purchased sewing machines from a Swiss manufacturer in Swiss francs. The machines were imported into the United States for sale to distributors. The contract with the distributor in this case allowed the importer to pass on cost increases to the distributor. When the Swiss franc rose "precipitously" in value against the dollar, the importer imposed a 10 percent surcharge to protect itself. Eventually the increased value of the Swiss franc doubled the importer's costs. The distributor did not feel that this additional "cost" fell under the terms in the contract and sued to have the contract enforced at its original price. The importer argued that increased costs due to currency fluctuations could be passed on to the distributor as any other "cost." It also argued that the exchange risk had rendered performance of the contract commercially impracticable. Just prior to the contract the dollar had fallen 7 percent on the franc. The district court interpreted the contract terms to find for the distributor, and the importer appealed.

LOGAN, CIRCUIT JUDGE

* * * [The contract] limits all price increases incurred by reason of invoice, duty, insurance, freight, handling, broker, port fees, and "other similar charges" to the extent of the increases. Thus, we believe the contract places the risk of a diminishing profit margin on Importer in case of increasing costs and find the trial court's holding that the Importer bears the risk of currency fluctuations, once a price is established for a model, is amply supported by the record. * * *

Importer asserts that the court's interpretation makes the contract impracticable under *Utah Code Ann. s 70A-2-615 (1980).* [The contract stated that it was to be governed by Utah law]. That U.C.C. section excuses performance under the contract "(e)xcept so far as a seller may have assumed a greater obligation" when performance "has been made impracticable by the occurrence of a contingency the nonoccurrence of which was a basic assumption on which the contract was made." In our view the instant contract is not one made "impracticable" by the contingency of the devalued dollar. The contract, as interpreted by the trial court, always allows a gross profit margin, although the return on capital investment has been reduced considerably because of the devaluation of the dollar. Moreover, there is considerable evidence that Importer assumed this particular risk. The contract lumps all the shipping and invoice costs in one provision which allows price increases only to the extent of the cost increases to Importer. Importer's letter to Distributor concerning a 7 percent devaluation of the dollar in relation to the franc, sent three weeks prior to the contract execution, shows clear foreknowledge of the possibility of currency fluctuations and, thus, supports the finding that section 2-615 is inapplicable. [citations omitted]

Finally, cost increases alone, though great in extent, do not render a contract impracticable. In *Gulf Oil Corp. v. F. P. C.,* 563 F.2d 588, 600 (3d Cir. 1977), the Third Circuit held that the doctrine of impracticability was not available unless the party seeking to excuse performance could show he could perform only at a loss, and that the loss would be especially severe and unreasonable. We hold the defense of impracticability is unavailable in the instant case. * * *

Decision. Judgment affirmed for the distributor. The importer had assumed the exchange rate risk. The language of the contract did not include currency fluctuations as one of the cost increases that could be passed on to the distributor, thus the exchange rate risk remained with the importer. Cost increases and currency fluctuations alone do not render a contract too "impracticable" to perform.

Case Questions

1. What were the importer's two arguments in this case? How did the court address each?
2. What is the effect of the fact that just prior to executing the contract, the dollar had fallen by 7 percent against the Swiss franc?
3. In any international business transaction which party assumes the exchange rate risk?

Currency Controls. **Currency controls** are restrictions on foreign currency transactions used by some developing countries that do not have large reserves of foreign currency. Controls can take many forms, such as prohibiting residents from making payments in a foreign currency; prohibiting any foreign payments unless on government approval or through authorized bank accounts; prohibiting the removal of foreign currency from the country by individuals traveling abroad, prohibiting the exchange of foreign currency for local currency at other than the official rate of exchange; and controls on foreign investors, prohibiting them from removing or **repatriating profits** earned by their subsidiary companies within the country. To preserve foreign currency, some governments in developing countries have prohibited the import of luxury or consumer goods or other products that the government deems nonessential. Currency controls can be enforced with criminal penalties. Most countries, such as Russia and India, have loosened or eliminated currency controls in recent years due to the requirements of the International Monetary Fund and the World Trade Organization.

Political Risk. **Political risk** is generally defined as the risk to a firm's business interests resulting from political instability or civil unrest, political change, war, or terrorism in a country in which the firm is doing business. Political risk is sometimes unpredictable, and is greatest in countries undergoing rapid economic or political change, such as in developing countries. Even though foreign business interests may have been welcomed by one government, its successor may take a different view. For many years, a nation may welcome foreign investment, consumer products, and Western culture, and then virtually overnight turn to resent any foreign influence at all. Cuba and Iran are two key examples. For much of U.S. history, U.S. firms had friendly relationships and extensive investments there. Yet after political upheaval, these countries became hostile to Americans and American investment. Exhibit 1.2, *Major Constraints on Foreign Investment in Emerging Markets,* illustrates that political risk is one of the biggest concerns for corporate investors in emerging markets.

Political Risk: Loss of the Investor's Property. The transfer of private-sector firms to government ownership and control, usually with payment to shareholders and pursuant to a larger plan to restructure a national economy, is known as **nationalization**. In developing countries, political reasons or socialist

Exhibit 1.2

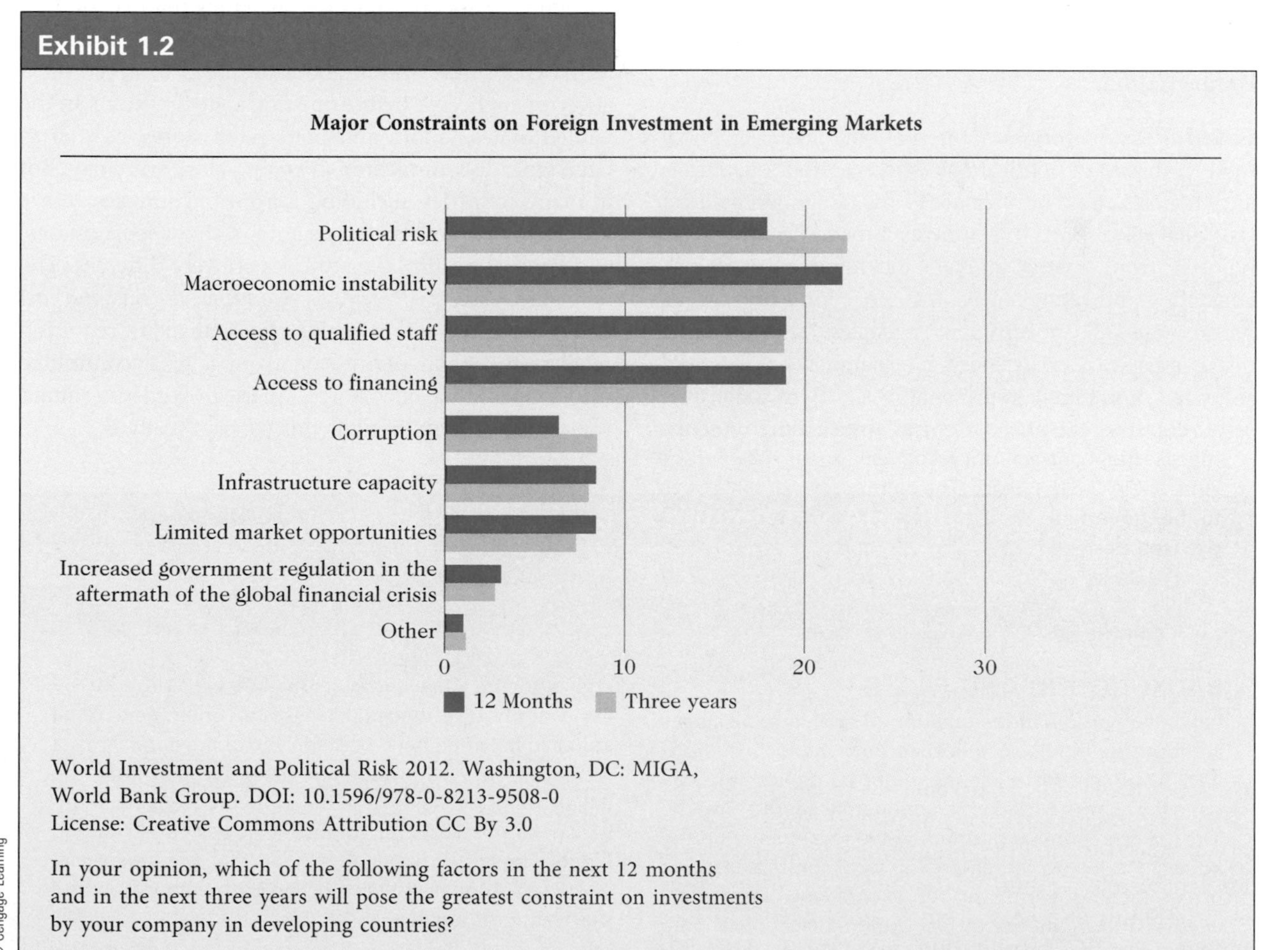

World Investment and Political Risk 2012. Washington, DC: MIGA, World Bank Group. DOI: 10.1596/978-0-8213-9508-0
License: Creative Commons Attribution CC By 3.0

In your opinion, which of the following factors in the next 12 months and in the next three years will pose the greatest constraint on investments by your company in developing countries?

inspired economics are often the motivation behind nationalization. A recent example is Venezuela's nationalization of its oil and gas industries by its socialist government, which asserted legal ownership over all oil and gas deposits and control over distribution. But nationalization also occurs in Western nations, including the UK, Canada, and even the United States, for reasons such as to save a dying but needed industry. For example, in 1971 the UK purchased Rolls Royce, the critical British maker of aircraft engines. Rolls Royce was returned to private ownership in 1987. There are many other policy reasons for nationalizing an industry. After the terrorist attacks in the United States in 2001, for example, the air transportation security industry was taken out of private hands, nationalized, and put under the Department of Homeland Security.

Expropriation is the taking by a government of privately owned assets, such as real estate, factories, farms, mines, or oil refineries, with the payment of some compensation. Although the compensation is supposed to be "just," in some countries it often is not. **Confiscation** is expropriation without payment of any compensation.

Political Risk Analysis. International managers know to keep abreast of political risk wherever their operations and interests could be affected. Firms can obtain political risk analysis reports (as well as broader country risk reports) from many sources, including country risk consulting and ratings firms, insurance industry reports, reports of U.S. government agencies, and informal discussions with experienced international bankers and shipping company representatives. Two published resources are the U.S. Central Intelligence Agency *World Fact Book*, and the U.S. Department of Commerce *Country Commercial Guides*. In some cases, political risk insurance is available to firms making investments in foreign countries where their exposure is great. A firm engaged in strategic corporate planning should consider this information when developing its global business strategy and when transacting business.

Exposure to Foreign Laws. We are all responsible for complying with the laws of the every country in which we do business. Foreign criminal laws apply to each of us as individuals and to corporate entities. Many acts that are perfectly legal in one country can be illegal in another. Moreover, in some countries, local laws may not be readily understandable to the average foreign guest, and the costs of not complying can be great. The same can be true for business laws. The greater the firm's penetration into the foreign market, the greater its risk. Thus foreign investors have great liability for failing to comply with local laws and regulations.

Many people are at first surprised at the laws they encounter in foreign countries. After all, many laws have social and cultural underpinnings. For example, Americans would never think about the need to apply for a government license before opening a grocery store. In the United States, "mom and pop" retail stores, as well as large-scale discount stores, open and close every day. But in many countries, including European countries with a long history of powerful trade unions, shopkeeper unions, and apprenticeships, the attitudes are very different. The following case, *DIP SpA v. Comune di Bassano del Grappa*, considered the legality of an Italian law requiring retailers to obtain permission from a local committee before opening a new store. American students should consider just how "foreign" this concept really is.

DIP SpA v. Comune di Bassano del Grappa

Case 140-142/94 joined, [1995] ECR I-03257
Court of Justice of the European Communities (2nd Chamber)

BACKGROUND AND FACTS

Italian law prohibits the opening of certain retail stores without first obtaining a license from the local authorities. A request for a license might be denied if it was believed that the market is adequately served already. The license could be granted by the local mayor on the advice of a ten- to fifteen-person local committee made up of local government representatives, local merchants, and members of local unions of shopkeepers and workers. This particular action was brought by three applicants whose licenses to open new retail stores in Italy had been denied. One of the applicants, a subsidiary of a German company, argued that the Italian retail licensing law discriminated against non-Italian companies and imported goods, and lead to higher consumer prices. It argued that the Italian law was invalid under the laws of the European Union and the Treaty of Rome.

continues

continued

HIRSCH P.C., PRESIDING

During the oral hearing the applicants submitted that, because the Act operated effectively to exclude new entrants, many of whom would be non-Italian operators desirous of establishing large-scale and sometimes discount outlets which might sell more non-Italian goods than existing traders, it was likely, either actually or at least potentially, to hinder intra-Community trade.

I believe that this argument must be rejected. [W] hile the limits the Act overall number of trading licenses, it does not necessarily produce an overall decrease in the number or value of goods sold on the Italian market nor does it necessarily render more difficult the sale of imports as opposed to domestic goods. I accept the Commission's observation that this type of provision is not capable of hindering intra-Community trade ...

The Italian Act provides that licenses are to be issued by the mayor of the municipality concerned, taking into account the criteria laid down in the municipal commercial development plan. The purpose of that plan is to provide the best possible service for consumers and the best possible balance between permanent trading establishments and foreseeable demand from the population.

National rules which require a license to be obtained before a new shop can be opened and limit the number of shops in the municipality in order to achieve a balance between supply and demand cannot be considered to put individual traders in dominant positions or all the traders established in a municipality in a collective dominant position, a salient feature of which would be that traders did not compete against one another.

On this point, it is sufficient to observe that rules such as those contained in the Italian Act make no distinction according to the origin of the goods distributed by the businesses concerned, that their purpose is not to regulate trade in goods with other Member States and that the restrictive effects which they might have on the free movement of goods are too uncertain and indirect for the obligation which they impose to be regarded as being capable of hindering trade between Member States.

Decision. The Italian law requiring the licensing of new retail stores by local committees is not invalid under the laws of the European Union and the Treaty of Rome.

Comment. Consider the dual effect of this law. It not only barred entry to multinational retailers from outside of Italy, but also to the large volume of imported products they would be likely to sell.

It was soon evident that supermarkets and mass retailers would change the face of Italy. Since this decision, the number of supermarkets in Italy has almost doubled, and traditional family-owned businesses, with all the character, richness, and history they represent, has sadly declined. But even a country like Italy, where for generations shoppers made daily stops at the meat, produce, or dairy store, they seemed to enjoy the new convenience and lower prices.

Case Questions

1. What was the ostensible purpose of the Italian law? What was its effect?
2. Do you think this law creates a climate ripe for corruption?
3. Why was the law not found to be discriminatory?
4. Assume that a municipality in a foreign country passes a law limiting the size of retail stores in the city. How might this affect U.S. firms wanting to open stores there?

Country Risk: Exposure to Foreign Courts. Settling disputes between companies can be much more difficult in international business than in domestic business. Litigating a case in a court in a foreign country is both costly and time consuming. A firm may need representation by attorneys in its own country *and* in the country of litigation. Frequent court appearances could require great travel expense. International cases also involve complex procedural problems: Which country's courts should hear the case? Which country's laws should apply? How does a court compel the testimony of witnesses or the production of business records not found in that country? Should the case be submitted to arbitration—perhaps in some "neutral" country? When a firm is negotiating an agreement with a foreign party, such as a contract to sell goods or to franchise a business, both parties will usually want to reach an agreement on these issues, and so the advice of an attorney at this stage in a transaction is extremely important.

Obtaining Professional Assistance

International managers must often rely on professional advice from attorneys, bankers, freight forwarders and customs brokers, insurance carriers and agents, government trade specialists, and others.

Attorneys who practice in international business can be either in private practice or employed as in-house counsel to larger or multinational firms. Their work might include export law, customs and tariff law, immigration and nationality law, the licensing of intellectual property, foreign investment contracts, international antitrust law, admiralty or maritime law, drafting and negotiating international contracts, and other legal issues. Private practice attorneys who specialize in these areas are usually located in larger cities and have associations with other lawyers in foreign countries. Attorneys who are employees of multinational corporations regularly advise management, develop internal corporate policies, work on external government relations at home and abroad, take responsibility for international tax matters, supervise litigation abroad, and coordinate the work of foreign counsel.

Freight forwarders and **customs brokers** act as the agent for the exporter or importer in arranging transportation and insurance for goods, preparing import or export documents, and moving goods through customs. A power of attorney is required when acting as customs broker for the importer. Many forwarding and brokerage companies operate with offices in several major port cities. Customs brokerage firms in the United States are licensed and bonded under the rules of the Federal Maritime Commission and the U.S. Bureau of Customs and Border Protection.

The international divisions of major banks not only provide important financing but also offer a range of specialized international banking and foreign exchange services necessary to international firms. Many international bankers possess a great wealth of expertise and foreign contacts and can play an advisory role in international business.

CONCLUSION

One primary objective of this chapter was to set the stage for the remainder of the book by surveying the legal environment of international business. Another broader objective is to illustrate how international business differs from domestic business, especially in developing countries, and how those differences affect the risks of an international business transaction. As your education progresses, you should see how the study of international business law can help you plan strategies and enter transactions with a greater awareness of these risks and if necessary how to communicate with your attorney on these issues.

Chapter Summary

1. The three forms of international business, or methods of entering a foreign market, are trade, the licensing of intellectual property, and foreign direct investment.
2. Trade consists of importing and exporting, including trade in goods and services.
3. Successful exporters make a long-term commitment to their foreign markets and customers and undertake an export plan. Success also requires building interpersonal relationships with foreign business associates and fostering an attitude of trust.
4. Cross-border trade in services includes business services such as passenger fares, shipping, package delivery, banking, insurance, securities brokerage, accounting, management and engineering consulting, and other professional services.
5. Importing should not be viewed as an isolated, one-time transaction. Most successful importers have a "global sourcing" strategy.
6. Intellectual property rights can be transferred through a licensing agreement in return for a royalty or other compensation arrangement. IPRs can be rendered worthless if they are not protected and infringement occurs.
7. Foreign direct investment refers to the long-term ownership and operation or active control of an ongoing business in a foreign "host" country with the expectation of producing a profit.
8. Multinational corporations are firms with significant foreign direct investment assets. They are increasingly "globalized," meaning that they have the ability to derive and transfer capital resources worldwide and to operate facilities of production and penetrate markets in more than one country, usually on a global scale.
9. While the developing countries attract hundreds of billions of dollars in investments each year, the economic and political climate in many developing countries still presents many obstacles to trade and investment.

10. International business differs from domestic business because of distance, currency, language, culture, national controls over trade and investment, country risk, and differences in national laws and legal systems.
11. In international business there is no substitute for knowing your suppliers, customers, and partners, visiting their facilities, and building relationships based on trust.
12. An important lesson of this chapter is that the management of international business is the management of risk. By understanding the legal environment of international business we are better prepared to evaluate, manage, and reduce these risks.

Key Terms

trade 2
exporting 3
importing 3
trade in services 3
direct exporting 3
indirect exporting 3
foreign sales representatives 3
foreign distributors 3
export trading companies 4
certificate of origin 4
export management companies 5
export plan 6
intellectual property (IP) 6
intellectual property rights 6
licensing agreements 7
license 7
infringement 8
franchising 9
transfer of technology 9
foreign direct investment (FDI) 10
home country 10
host countries 10
foreign branch 11
foreign subsidiary 11
foreign affiliate 11
joint venture 11
multinational or transnational corporation 11
local participation 11
newly industrialized countries 13
emerging market economy 15
least developed countries (LDCs) 15
countries in transition 15
payment or credit risk 16
supplier risk 16
property or marine risk 16
tariff 19
non-tariff barrier 19
quota 19
export controls 19
sanctions 19
exchange rate risk 19
currency controls 20
repatriating profits 21
expropriation 22
nationalization 21
political risk 21
confiscation 22
freight forwarders 24
customs brokers 24

Questions and Case Problems

1. Two cases in this chapter, *Transatlantic Financing* and *Bernina Distributors*, involved very different facts but similar issues of law. What legal issues do they have in common? In each case there is some unexpected "supervening event" that interfered with one party's ability to perform and with their expectations in the contract. In either case, did the nonperforming party have a legally recognized "excuse for nonperformance"? Why or why not? While you might have to wait until a later chapter for a full answer, how do you think parties to a contract might deal with these uncertainties in advance?
2. How does international business differ from domestic business? Explain how those differences affect the risk of doing business internationally. What factors influence that risk?
3. International business managers try to build trust with their foreign counterparts, whether it's a customer, supplier, or partner. How would you suggest they do this? Why is trust important to the long-term relationship, and what might it mean to managing the risks of international business?
4. Pro Golf, a U.S. company, manufactured and sold golf equipment under the brand name "First Flight," which had been registered in the United States and certain other foreign countries. Pro Golf negotiated with Wynn to act as its foreign sales representative in Japan. Wynn incorporated First Flight Associates, Inc. (FFA) under Japanese law for the purposes of selling Pro Golf's products there. The parties then entered into an informal trademark agreement, evidenced only by a letter from Pro Golf's president to FAA, permitting FAA to use Pro Golf's "First Flight" trademark

on "soft goods" such as golf bags and clothing, in return for a royalty. There were no restrictions on sub-licensing. FFA attempted to sub-license the trademark to another Japanese company, Teito, for a royalty much larger than that paid to Pro Golf. When Pro Golf objected, the company learned that its attempt to register the trademark in Japan had not been completely successful, but that third parties had obtained the right to use the "First Flight" trademark in Japan in marketing soft goods. Pro Golf terminated the agency agreement with Wynn and FFA, and FFA brought this action for breach of contract. What is the result? Do you agree with Pro Golf's strategy for entering the Japanese market? What advice would you have given Pro Golf on entering the Japanese market? *First Flight Associates v. Professional Golf Co., Inc.* 527 F.2d 931 (6th Cir. 1975)

5. Plaintiff, a Swiss corporation, entered into contracts to purchase chicken from B.N.S. International Sales Corporation. Defendant was a New York corporation. The English language contracts called for the delivery of "chicken" of various weights. When the birds were shipped to Switzerland, the 2-lb. sizes were not young broiling chickens as the plaintiff had expected, but mature stewing chickens or fowl. The plaintiff protested, claiming that in German the term *chicken* referred to young broiling chickens. The question for the court was: What kind of chicken did the plaintiff order? Was it "broiling chicken," as the plaintiff argued, or any chickens weighing 2 lbs., as the defendant argued? *Frigaliment Importing Co., Ltd. v. B.N.S. International Sales Corp.*, 190 F. Supp. 116 (S.D.N.Y. 1960). What could the parties have done to avoid this misunderstanding?
6. Successful international managers agree that success in entering a foreign market comes from planning and commitment. What does this mean? What kind of commitment do you think they are referring to? It is also often said that exporting is not an "elixir" for a company that is failing in its home market and is looking for new sales elsewhere. Evaluate this statement. Do you think it is true?
7. What industries in your state are the leading exporters? Who are the leading export firms? What do you think is the impact of exports on your state's economy? Where would you go for information? What role does your state government play in promoting exports?
8. U.S. firms have been successful in foreign franchising, particularly in fast food and other retail businesses and service companies. How do you account for this success? Where do you think the best opportunities and hottest markets are for foreign franchising?
9. There are many U.S. government programs to aid American firms in boosting exports. The International Trade Administration and its U.S. Commercial Service, as well as the Small Business Administration administer several of these programs. Undertake an Internet search of government resources for small- and medium-sized exporters. What services does the U.S. Commercial Service offer? What trade statistics are available? Country information? Foreign market information? Export counseling? Matchmaking and trade contact programs?

Managerial Implications

Your company, Quiet-Maid, manufactures home washers and dryers in the United States that use a patented technology to make them run virtually silent. Having been successful in the United States, Quite-Maid's CEO wants your opinion on exporting to the European market.

1. What are the advantages of Quite-Maid exporting appliances to Europe from the United States?
2. What problems do you foresee with exporting large appliances there? What barriers and or problems do you think the company might face?
3. What factors might influence success in Europe?

The CEO now decides that the best course of action is to enter the European market by forming a joint venture with a Spanish manufacturer of home appliances. Quiet-Maid would contribute its quiet technology and financial and technical assistance in return for a 40 percent share. The Spanish company would oversee manufacturing, sales, and service and receive a 60 percent share.

1. Why did Quiet-Maid choose a joint venture as its vehicle to enter Europe? In addition to manufacturing, sales, and service, what else might the local Spanish firm do for the joint venture?
2. What reasons do you think Quiet-Maid had for not starting a new subsidiary in Europe on its own?

During negotiations, Quiet-Maid's management went to Spain to review its prospective partner's finances. During their visit, they were asked "which set of books and numbers" they wanted to review—the real financial records of the Spanish company or those used to report to Spanish tax authorities. Quiet-Maid became uneasy about their potential exposure as a minority partner in a foreign investment with this company, and decided to withdraw.

1. What did Quiet-Maid discover on its trip to Spain?
2. What are the risks of making an investment in this foreign joint venture?
3. If Quiet-Maid decides that there is no other possible joint venture partner available in Europe, and if it does not have the resources to start a new subsidiary, what is its alternative? What other significant assets does Quiet-Maid have that it could leverage to still do business with the Spanish firm? Explain.

Ethical Considerations

All of us understand that the law is a floor for judging our behavior, an absolute minimum standard of conduct that one must follow. Anyone doing business in a foreign country understands that he or she must abide by the laws of the host country. But what about the unwritten or informal rules of doing business there—rules based on culture, religious codes, and societal constraints? Sometimes these laws can be very different from those in one's home country or in other countries in which one is working. Pollution may be a crime in one country and tolerated in another; bribery may be a crime in one country and customary in another. What is an accepted practice for employing children in industry in one country may be abhorrent in another, and so on. How does the multinational manager reconcile differences like these? What is the appropriate standard of ethical conduct for a multinational manager—that of his or her home country, the host country, or of some internal personal value system? How will the laws, unwritten rules, and cultural values of the host country influence the manager? How does one balance his or her social responsibility regarding the health, safety, and well being of the people of the host country with the company's overall objective of maximizing shareholder profit? What can a multinational corporation do to aid its managers in the development of a personal value system that is in keeping with the legal and cultural values of their host countries? Consider some of the legal and ethical issues in the following problems.

1. You have been negotiating with a representative of a government in Africa to sell products to them for a new state building project in his country. The negotiations are finalized during your trip to his offices in Africa. After easily negotiating a fixed price and delivery, he "suggests" that you prepare a price quotation on a "pro forma invoice"—at double the negotiated price. His government will pay the full amount shown on the invoice through a foreign bank, and your firm will pay him the difference as a "commission" in U.S. dollars deposited to his personal bank account in New York. He convincingly argues that this practice is customary in his country. The temptation for you is great; the deal would be a profitable one. Should you make the payment? Does it matter that it is customary in his country? Do you think it is lawful under American law? Does it matter that this is taking place in Africa, far from the United States? Is there a "victim" in this case?
2. Your company intends to locate a plant in Mexico to manufacture tires for sale in both Mexico and the United States. If the plant were in the United States, the laws would require expensive safeguards to protect the health and safety of U.S. workers, as well as the added cost of minimum wage rules, Social Security contributions, health insurance, retirement benefits, and other employee benefits. Assume that Mexican law is not so strict, wages and operating costs are less, and that benefit programs are either nonexistent or far less costly. To what extent should you conform to the legal standards applicable in the United States? Should you comply with American labor rules and environmental rules, even though they are not enforceable in Mexico? After all, should not all workers be safe from harm? Does not polluted air in Mexico travel to the United States? Do you think that any firm operating in a host country should carry with it the ethical codes of its home country? What about competition from firms in Japan or Germany that are operating their plants in Mexico? If they don't comply with American labor and environmental standards in Mexico, how will you compete with them? How does the international manager justify decisions in cross-cultural situations?
3. You are an international manager for a U.S. apparel designer that sells to major U.S. department stores and retailers. Several years ago, your firm decided to have clothing sewn in India and Pakistan, which resulted in tremendous cost savings over having the work done in the United States. In making the decision, the firm considered its impact on U.S. families who depend on the income from these jobs. It opted for the cost savings, seeing its responsibility to produce a profit for shareholders as more important than its responsibility

to provide jobs in the United States. Now, however, it finds that its contractor in India is overworking and abusing child labor in violation of internationally accepted standards for the treatment of children in the workplace. The Indian government shows little interest in policing its own labor practices. The sad story of the Indian children runs on national television and appears in the national press. What course of action should you take? If you decide to discontinue working with sewing contractors in India, do you do so to protect Indian children, because of the adverse publicity in the United States, or for both reasons? What do you expect the reaction would be from shareholders? From consumers?

4. While your answer to this question may have to wait until the next chapter, do you think that a written corporate code would aid a manager in resolving these conflicts and in making difficult choices? How would a corporation draft such a code, and what sources would it draw on?

CHAPTER 2

International Law and the World's Legal Systems

INTRODUCTION

This chapter examines the law of treaties, customary international law, principles of international jurisdiction, and the role of international organizations in fostering international laws and ideals. We will look not only at the historical development of international law, but how it addresses a range of current issues, particularly international business, commerce, and transnational crimes. Because much international law stems from international norms, we will also briefly look at developing norms for the social responsibility of multinational corporations. Finally, we will take a comparative look at three of the major legal systems in place around the world today, including the common law, civil law, and Islamic legal systems.

INTERNATIONAL LAW

The exact origins of international law, and whether it dates to antiquity or to the Middle Ages, is debatable. The ancient Greeks, Chinese, and Romans all recognized some rudimentary concepts of international law. However, the term *international law* is thought to be derived from the Latin term *jus gentium,* meaning "**the law of nations**." That term was used in reference to that part of **Roman law** that governed public and private relations with foreigners and with the rulers of foreign lands.

Many legal historians believe that it was the rise of the European nation-state, first ruled by monarchs and later by sovereign governments, that led to the development of modern international law. In the sixteenth and seventeenth centuries, legal scholars from Spain, Italy, and Holland developed the first modern European concepts of international law. In 1625, Hugo Grotius, a diplomat and lawyer for the Dutch East India Company, wrote *On the Law of War and Peace,* which brought together various schools of thought on the nature of law and international obligations. It was a time of colonialism, trade, and the rise of nations. Grotius wrote that the law of nations was not just divinely given, as was commonly believed in his day, but also that law arose by common agreement, by consensus, and by the accepted practice of nations. He premised these ideas on the idea of national sovereignty and on the recognition that all states are equal. To this day, it is accepted that international law arises not from the work of some supranational legislature, but because nations have agreed to follow customary and accepted rules or norms and to comply with treaties and conventions on which they agree.

Definition and Characteristics of International Law

International law is the body of rules applicable to the conduct of nations in their relationships with other nations, and with individuals and other private parties, rules for settling disputes between nations, as well as rules for intergovernmental organizations. It can also include crimes and criminal procedures applicable to genocide, war crimes, and offenses against humanity committed by individuals in an official capacity.

International law has several characteristics that distinguish it from a country's national or domestic law. First, instead of being dictated by a legislative body, international law consists of rules that countries agree to follow. It is lawmaking by choice and by consent. Indeed, international law exists because nations agree that it is in their best interests to cooperate and to conform to commonly accepted norms. Second, despite some commonly misunderstood beliefs about the United Nations and other international bodies, there is no global authority for enforcing international law. It is true that international courts and tribunals do issue judgments against nations. However, nations must agree to be a party to these cases. The judgments are "binding" only according the authority of the court or tribunal under international law, and "hard" enforcement mechanisms of the kind used in national law do not really exist. There are courts, but no international sheriffs or marshals. Enforcement of international law relies on remedies that countries have agreed to in advance, or on economic or political sanctions. International law relies greatly on "soft" enforcement mechanisms such as the force of public opinion, diplomacy, or the withholding of foreign aid or other assistance. Of course, the ultimate sanction against a country for violating international law is war, or at least the threat of it. But the use of force is also limited by international law. Later we will see that domestic and international courts do add to the enforcement capabilities of international law.

Public and Private International Law. There are many ways of classifying types of international law. Two broad categories are public international law and private international law. **Public international law** deals with those rules affecting the conduct of nations in their relationships with each other and with individuals as citizens or residents. For example, this might include rules for resolving territorial or boundary disputes, for conducting diplomacy or war, for determining nationality, and for how nations treat foreign citizens. It also includes the rules governing the status and operation of intergovernmental organizations, such as the United Nations (UN) or the International Court of Justice.

Private international law deals with the rights and responsibilities of individuals, corporations, or other private parties in their cross-border or international activities, as well as procedural rules for how courts resolve private international disputes. For example, private international law might include family law and rules for international adoptions, wills and decedents' estates who own property in more than one nation, and rules for international business transactions, such as sales contracts, international shipping, or the liability of commercial airlines to injured passengers.

Sources of International Law. The most frequently cited authority for the sources of international law is the *Statute of the International Court of Justice*, the judicial arm of the United Nations. It sets out both primary and secondary sources of international law. According to Article 38, the primary sources of international law are: (1) international treaties and conventions, (2) international custom, as evidence of a general practice accepted as law, and (3) the general principles of law recognized by civilized nations. Secondary sources provide evidence of what international law might be or how it should be interpreted. These include the decisions of international courts and tribunals, and to a lesser extent, the scholarly writings of respected jurists and legal scholars. For example, in the United States, the *Restatement of Foreign Relations Law*, published by the American Law Institute, is considered a secondary source of customary law. Resolutions of the UN General Assembly are also a nonbinding secondary source. Like scholarly writings, UN resolutions are of persuasive value only.

We begin our study with treaties.

The Law of Treaties

Sovereign governments have been entering into military and trade alliances with one another for thousands of years. While treaties have always played an important role in international life, today they have taken on a new meaning. As the world becomes "smaller" and more interdependent, new issues take on global proportions requiring global solutions. Scientific and technological advances are proceeding more rapidly than ever before. Air and water pollution know no national boundaries. Illegal drug trafficking, terrorism, computer crime, and other crimes have taken on transnational dimensions. The problems we all face have one thing in common: Resolving each of them requires cooperation and agreement. Treaties are the most important form of international agreement and a primary source of international law.

A **treaty** is a legally binding agreement between two or more nations that is recognized and given effect under international law. A treaty between two countries is said to be **bilateral**, and a treaty between three or more countries is **multilateral**. One of the most important principles of treaty law is *pacta sunt servanda* ("the pact must be respected"), meaning that treaties are binding on the parties by consent and must be performed by them in good faith.

A **convention** is a legally binding multilateral treaty on matters of common concern, usually negotiated on a regional or global basis and open to adoption by many nations. Many conventions are negotiated under the auspices of the United Nations, the European Union, or the Council of Europe.

Other Treaty Terminology. An agreement that modifies or adds to a treaty or convention, or that deals with matters less significant than those dealt within treaties, is known as a **protocol**. It usually addresses matters that are ancillary to a main treaty or convention. Nations adopt a treaty or convention when it is completed in its final form and is ready for nations to ratify. Nations that express their willingness to join a treaty are called **signatories. Ratification** is the formal agreement of a signatory nation to be bound by the treaty, usually by its own legislative approval. Countries that have ratified become **contracting parties**. A treaty becomes effective on the date set out in the treaty for it to "enter into force," which is usually after some minimum number of nations become parties. A **reservation** is an exception to a treaty set out by a signatory country at the time of ratification. **Abrogation** is an act of a legislature that renders a treaty null and void.

A word of caution when referring to treaties by name: Many people abbreviate the names of treaties by referring to the name of the city in which the treaties were completed. Examples of common names are "the Vienna Convention," and "the Montreal Convention." Many treaties discussed in this book were completed in Madrid, Vienna, Geneva, Budapest, Kyoto, Montreal, Paris, Warsaw, and other cities. Some cities have been the site of many treaties. For example, a reference to the "the Vienna Convention" can either mean the *Vienna Convention on Diplomatic Relations* or the *Vienna Convention on Protection of the Ozone Layer*—a big difference. Be careful when abbreviating treaty names.

The Legal Status and Domestic Law Effect of Treaties. To understand the legal effect of a treaty in a country that is a party to it, we must ask whether that treaty is self-executing or non-self-executing. A **self-executing treaty** (known in Europe as a treaty with "**direct effect**") is one that automatically creates rights that are enforceable in the courts of that country, without any further legislative action. The treaty is immediately binding on courts, government agencies, and individuals. An example of a self-executing treaty enforceable by courts in the United States is the *Montreal Convention for the Unification of Certain Rules for International Carriage by Air*, that sets out the rights of airlines and airline passengers for personal injuries or damage to baggage or cargo on international flights.

A **non-self-executing treaty**, or one without direct effect, is one that requires some additional legislative act before it becomes enforceable in national courts. In some countries, most notably the United Kingdom, Canada, and Australia, few if any treaties have direct effect. Treaties there require parliamentary action before they are enforceable by private parties. In a few other countries, such as the Netherlands and France, treaties are given greater legal effect. The status of treaties may be found in the written constitution of a country (if that country is one with a written constitution), in a legislative act, or by judicial interpretation. The legal status of treaties in the United States has been the subject of many federal appellate court decisions. Whether a treaty is self-executing or not depends on the wording and history of the treaty itself and the intent of Congress.

In *Medellin v. Texas*, 552 U.S. 491 (2008) the U.S. Supreme Court held that judgments of the International Court of Justice (ICJ) were not enforceable by U.S. courts because the *UN Charter*, which created the ICJ, was non-self-executing. The case involved Jose Medellin, an 18-year-old Mexican national who had been arrested in the United States for murder. While in prison the International Court of Justice, sitting in The Hague, Netherlands, issued a judgment that Medellin (and 50 other Mexicans in U.S. prisons) had been deprived of rights under international law because Medellin had never been told that he had the right to notify the Mexican embassy of his arrest. The Court stated,

> Article 94(1) [of the UN Charter] provides that "[e]ach Member of the United Nations undertakes to comply with the decision of the [ICJ] in any case to which it is a party." The Executive Branch contends that the phrase "undertakes to comply" is not "an acknowledgement that an ICJ decision will have immediate legal effect in the courts of U.N. members," but rather "a commitment on the part of U.N. Members to take future action through their political branches to comply with an ICJ decision."
>
> We agree with this construction of Article 94. The Article is not a directive to domestic courts. It does not provide that the United States "shall" or "must" comply with an ICJ decision, nor indicate that the Senate that ratified the *U.N. Charter* intended to vest ICJ decisions with immediate legal effect in domestic courts.... In other words, the *U.N. Charter* reads like "a compact between independent nations" that "depends for the enforcement of its provisions on the interest and the honor of the governments which are parties to it."

Treaties of Friendship, Commerce, and Navigation. **FCN treaties** are bilateral agreements that provide a broad range of protection to foreign nationals doing business in a host country. Most countries are party to many FCN treaties. In the United States, FCN treaties are self-executing. Although each treaty is different, they typically state that each country will allow the establishment of foreign branches or subsidiaries, the movement of capital and technology, the right of travel, and the right to own real estate. FCN treaties also assure the payment of just compensation for property taken by government action and the nondiscriminatory treatment of personnel.

The following case, *Ventress v. Japan Airlines*, involves an FCN treaty between the United States and Japan in a case for wrongful termination of employment. It illustrates the relationship between treaties and legislation, and that treaty interpretation is a matter for domestic courts.

Ventress v. Japan Airlines

486 F.3d 1111 (2007) United States Court of Appeals (9th Cir.)

BACKGROUND AND FACTS

Japan Airlines (JAL) is a Japanese air carrier based in Tokyo, with offices in California and Hawaii. The plaintiffs were employed by a Hawaiian company that contracted to perform services for JAL flights. They alleged that JAL had required a seriously ill pilot to fly, in violation of aviation laws. After expressing their concerns to a JAL official and to aviation regulators, they claimed they experienced harassment from superiors, including required psychiatric evaluations, unsatisfactory evaluations, and termination. They sued in federal court seeking recovery for violation of California's whistle blower protection statute and wrongful termination. The court dismissed the claims on the basis that the state statute had been preempted by the 1953 *Treaty of Friendship, Commerce, and Navigation* (FCN) between the United States and Japan. The plaintiffs appealed.

GOODWIN, CIRCUIT JUDGE

* * * A treaty preempts inconsistent state law. *United States v. Pink*, 315 U.S. 203 (1942). [other citations omitted] Federal law must also be strictly construed to avoid conflict with treaty obligations. The district court premised its judgment on article VIII(1) of the *Japan FCN Treaty*, which provides:

> Nationals and companies of either Party shall be permitted to engage, within the territories of the other Party, accountants and other technical experts, executive personnel, attorneys, agents and other specialists *of their choice* ... [emphasis added by court].

* * * "The purpose of the Treaties was not to give foreign corporations greater rights than domestic companies, but instead to assure them the right to conduct business on an equal basis without suffering discrimination based on their alienage." *Sumitomo Shoji Am., Inc. v. Avagliano,* 457 U.S. 176 (1982) ("Sumitomo II"). "The Treaties accomplished their purpose by granting foreign corporations 'national treatment' in most respects." Id. at 188. National treatment entitles a foreign national to "carry on his chosen business under conditions of non-discrimination, and to enjoy the same legal opportunity to succeed and prosper on his merits as is allowed citizens of the country." *MacNamara v. Korean Air Lines*, 863 F.2d 1135, 1143 (3d Cir. 1988). * * *

Given the purpose and history of the FCN treaties, our sister circuits have consistently held that foreign employers do not enjoy immunity from domestic employment laws that do not interfere with the employers' ability to hire their fellow citizens. In *MacNamara*, the Third Circuit considered a provision in the *Korea FCN* treaty that is identical in language to article VIII(1). The [U.S.] plaintiff, having been terminated by his Korean employer and replaced by a Korean citizen, sought recovery for race, national origin and age discrimination. The employer argued that it enjoyed treaty conferred immunity from federal anti-discrimination statutes. The court disagreed. The court explained that the treaty's negotiating history "[w]as barren of any suggestion that Article VIII(1) was intended to achieve anything other than the right to utilize one's own citizens in the capacities specified." * * * Although the Korean employer had a treaty right to discriminate in favor of Korean *citizens*, the treaty afforded no immunity from liability for race, age and *national origin discrimination*. [emphasis added]

We hold that the district court erred by construing article VIII(1) to confer on Japanese employers blanket immunity from state employment law. * * * California's whistle-blower protection laws merely prevent JAL from retaliating against employees for reporting and resisting the employer's domestic law violations; the laws in no way conflict with JAL's limited treaty right to discriminate in favor of Japanese citizens. In the absence of conflict, there can be no preemption.

Decision. Judgment reversed for plaintiffs. Although the FCN treaty does allow Japanese companies in the United States to give preference to hiring Japanese citizens as executives, professional staff, and technical

continues

continued

experts "of their choice," it does not give them blanket immunity from state and federal employment laws.

Case Questions

1. What was the purpose of article VIII(1) of the FCN treaty? In what way would this give them greater control of their U.S. operations?
2. What was the basis of the court's ruling? Does the California whistle blower protection statute "interfere with the employer's ability to hire their fellow citizens"?
3. In citing *MacNamara v. Korean Airlines*, the court refers to the difference between "citizenship" and "national origin." What is the difference, and why was that important here?

The Vienna Convention on the Law of Treaties. The interpretation of treaties is governed by customary international law rules. The *Vienna Convention on the Law of Treaties*, which became effective in 1980 in about half of the countries of the world, codified many of the customary rules. It covers such issues as when treaties enter into force, how they are interpreted or amended, and the rights and duties of contracting parties. Although the treaty has not been ratified by the United States, many U.S. courts apply its provisions as customary law.

Customary International Law

Custom has always been at the root of legal development, and that includes international law. **Customary international law** is a body of commonly accepted rules of conduct, or **international norms**, that have arisen out of consistent and long-standing practice, and that nations have followed out of a sense of binding obligation. Historically, examples of customary international law include rules for prosecuting the crimes of slavery, piracy, or genocide, rules for diplomatic immunity and the protection of ambassadors, rules for the inviolability of embassies, rules that protect civilians during war, or rules governing the seizure of private vessels during wartime. The legal effect of customary international law is different from country to country. Even within the common law countries of the United Kingdom, Canada, and Australia, there are differences. Some judges in the United Kingdom have held that customary norms are automatically a part of the common law. Other judges rely on customary norms for their persuasive value. On the other hand, in a landmark 1999 Australian case, the court held that crimes under customary law, like treaties, are not part of Australian domestic criminal law unless specifically enacted in legislation.

In recent years there has been increasing debate over whether customary international law is part of American law, and if so, which customs and norms are part of it and which are not. In the United States, however, it is generally accepted as a part of American law to be applied by courts where there is no contradictory statute or treaty and where there is no other way to resolve the case other than by applying customary norms. The following well-known decision of the U.S. Supreme Court, *The Paquette Habana*, reflects this view.

The Paquette Habana

175 U.S. 677 (1900) United States Supreme Court

BACKGROUND AND FACTS

During the Spanish-American War, the United States Navy seized two commercial fishing ships sailing from Havana. The unarmed ships were owned by a Spanish citizen living in Cuba and sailed under Spanish flags. The owners were unaware of the hostilities between the United States and Spain and of the U.S. blockade of Cuba. The fishing ships were sold by the Navy in Florida as "prizes of war." Their original owner sued for damages in U.S. District Court. The court upheld the seizure and the owner appealed.

JUSTICE GRAY

By an ancient usage among civilized nations, beginning centuries ago, and gradually ripening into a rule of international law, coast fishing vessels, pursuing their vocation of catching and bringing in fresh fish, have been recognized as exempt, with their cargoes and crews, from capture as prize of war * * *

The doctrine which exempts coast fishermen, with their vessels and cargoes, from capture as prize of war, has been familiar to the United States from the time of the War of Independence * * *

continues

continued

International law is part of our law, and must be ascertained and administered by the courts of justice of appropriate jurisdiction as often as questions of right depending upon it are duly presented for their determination. For this purpose, where there is no treaty and no controlling executive or legislative act or judicial decision, resort must be had to the customs and usages of civilized nations, and, as evidence of these, to the works of jurists and commentators who by years of labor, research, and experience have made themselves peculiarly well acquainted with the subjects of which they treat. Such works are resorted to by judicial tribunals, not for the speculations of their authors concerning what the law ought to be, but for trustworthy evidence of what the law really is * * *

This review of the precedents and authorities of the subject appears to us abundantly to demonstrate that at the present day, by the general consent of the civilized nations of the world, and independently of any express treaty or other public act, it is an established rule of international law, founded on consideration of humanity to a poor and industrious order of men, and of the mutual convenience of belligerent states, that coast fishing vessels, with their implements and supplies, cargoes and crews, unarmed and honestly pursuing their peaceful calling of catching and bringing in fresh fish, are exempt from capture as prize of war * * *

This rule of international law is one which prize courts administering the law of nations are bound to take judicial notice of, and to give effect to, in the absence of any treaty or other public act of their own government in relation to the matter * * *

Decision. The Supreme Court reversed and said that under an established rule of international law peaceful fishing vessels are exempt from capture as prizes of war. The Court acknowledged that it was bound to take judicial notice of international law.

Case Questions

1. Under what conditions is customary international law a part of U.S. domestic law?
2. Which international norm or custom applies to this dispute?

Limits on International Customary Law: The U.S. Alien Tort Statute. The *U.S. Alien Tort Statute* (ATS) was enacted in 1789. It gave the U.S. federal courts jurisdiction over civil actions for damages brought by non-U.S. citizens for torts committed against them by other non-citizens outside of the United States in violation of the norms of customary international law. For almost two hundred years the statute was seldom used. However, in the 1980s, a number of cases were brought under the statute to recover damages from U.S. companies accused of cooperating with foreign governments in abusing human rights. Many executives of U.S. multinational corporations were concerned that they could be sued in the United States by non-citizens who were accusing them of supporting, or participating in, human rights violations such as unfair or abusive labor practices, environmental damage, or worse (such as aiding and abetting foreign government-sponsored torture and killings). In the following case, *Sosa v. Alvarez-Machain*, the court discussed the limitations on the incorporation of customary international law into U.S. law through the ATS.

Sosa v. Alvarez-Machain

542 U.S. 692 (2004) United States Supreme Court

BACKGROUND AND FACTS

Alvarez, a Mexican physician, was wanted by the U.S. Drug Enforcement Agency for the torture and murder of one of its agents in Mexico in 1985. When Mexico would not extradite Alvarez, the agency employed Sosa to kidnap Alvarez from his home and fly him by private plane to Texas, where he was arrested by federal officers. Alvarez was tried and acquitted in a U.S. court. After the acquittal, Alvarez brought this civil suit in U.S. District Court against Sosa for damages under the U.S. Alien Tort Statute (ATS). The ATS reads: *"The district courts shall have original jurisdiction of any civil action by an alien for a tort only, committed in violation of the law of nations or a treaty of the United States." 28 U.S.C. §1350.* Alvarez sued on the theory that the abduction and arrest were a tort committed in violation of customary international law. Alvarez won a judgment against Sosa in District Court, and it was upheld by the U.S. Court of Appeals. Sosa appealed to the U.S. Supreme Court.

continues

continued

JUSTICE SOUTER

Alvarez says that the ATS was intended ... as authority for the creation of a new cause of action for torts in violation of international law. We think that reading is implausible. As enacted in 1789, the ATS ... bespoke a grant of jurisdiction, not power to mold substantive law. * * *

"When the United States declared their independence, they were bound to receive the law of nations, in its modern state of purity and refinement." *Ware v. Hylton*, 3 Dall. 199 (1796). [William Blackstone, in 4 *Commentaries on the Laws of England* 68 (1769)] ... mentioned three specific offenses against the law of nations addressed by the criminal law of England: violation of safe conducts, infringement of the rights of ambassadors, and piracy. An assault against an ambassador, for example, impinged upon the sovereignty of the foreign nation and if not adequately redressed could rise to an issue of war. It was this narrow set of violations of the law of nations, admitting of a judicial remedy and at the same time threatening serious consequences in international affairs, that was probably on minds of the men who drafted the ATS with its reference to tort. * * *

The second inference to be drawn from the history is that Congress intended the ATS to furnish jurisdiction for a relatively modest set of actions alleging violations of the law of nations ... As Blackstone had put it, "offences against this law [of nations] are principally incident to whole states or nations," and not individuals seeking relief in court. 4 *Commentaries* 68. * * *

[A]lthough the ATS is a jurisdictional statute creating no new causes of action, the reasonable inference from the historical materials is that the statute was intended to have practical effect the moment it became law. The jurisdictional grant is best read as having been enacted on the understanding that the common law would provide a cause of action for the modest number of international law violations with a potential for personal liability at the time.

We think it is correct, then, to assume that the First Congress understood that the district courts would recognize private causes of action for certain torts in violation of the law of nations, though we have found no basis to suspect Congress had any examples in mind beyond those torts corresponding to Blackstone's three primary offenses: violation of safe conducts, infringement of the rights of ambassadors, and piracy.

Accordingly, we think courts should require any claim based on the present-day law of nations to rest on a norm of international character accepted by the civilized world and defined with a specificity comparable to the features of the eighteenth-century paradigms we have recognized. This requirement is fatal to Alvarez's claim. * * * Since many attempts by federal courts to craft remedies for the violation of new norms of international law would raise risks of adverse foreign policy consequences, they should be undertaken, if at all, with great caution. * * *

[Alvarez] attempts to show that prohibition of arbitrary arrest has attained the status of binding customary international law. * * * It is this position that Alvarez takes now: that his arrest was arbitrary and as such forbidden by international law not because it infringed the prerogatives of Mexico, but because no applicable law authorized it. * * * Alvarez cites little authority that a rule so broad has the status of a binding customary norm today. He certainly cites nothing to justify the federal courts in taking his broad rule as the predicate for a federal lawsuit, for its implications would be breathtaking. His rule would support a cause of action in federal court for any arrest, anywhere in the world, unauthorized by the law of the jurisdiction in which it took place, and would create a cause of action for any seizure of an alien in violation of the Fourth Amendment. * * *

Whatever may be said for the broad principle Alvarez advances, in the present, imperfect world, it expresses an aspiration that exceeds any binding customary rule having the specificity we require. It is enough to hold that a single illegal detention of less than a day, followed by the transfer of custody to lawful authorities and a prompt arraignment, violates no norm of customary international law so well defined as to support the creation of a federal remedy.

Decision. Judgment reversed for Sosa. Alvarez's arrest did not violate any norm of customary international law that would permit an action for damages under the *Alien Tort Statute*. Recovery under the ATS should be limited to well-defined violations of norms of international law that are accepted by the civilized world, "principally incident to whole states or nations, and not individuals seeking relief in court." The abduction and arrest in this case did not meet that standard.

Comment. In *Kiobel v. Royal Dutch Petroleum Co.*, 133 S.Ct. 1659 (2013), the Supreme Court held that, perhaps with the exception of piracy on the high seas, the First Congress in 1789 did not intend that the ATS would apply extraterritorially (outside the United States). In Kiobel, Nigerian nationals residing in the United States sued Dutch, British, and Nigerian oil companies under the ATS for allegedly aiding and abetting the Nigerian government in the torture and execution of

continues

continued

Nigerian environmentalists who were protesting oil exploration in Nigeria. The Court referred to its warning in *Sosa* that lawsuits under the ATS should not be permitted where they would cause "unwarranted judicial interference in the conduct of foreign policy." The Court stated, "These concerns ... are all the more pressing when the question is whether a cause of action under the ATS reaches conduct within the territory of another sovereign." 133 S.Ct. at 1664, 1665. The Court stated that although the ATS could be applied to violations of safe conduct and assaults on ambassadors within the United States, it could not be applied outside the United States. With regard to whether piracy on the high seas could be a violation of international customary law, the Court noted, "Pirates were fair game wherever found, by any nation, because they generally did not operate within any jurisdiction. We do not think that the existence of a cause of action against them is a sufficient basis for concluding that other causes of action under the ATS reach conduct that does occur within the territory of another sovereign; pirates may well be a category unto themselves." *Id.* at 1667.

Case Questions

1. What were the three specific offenses mentioned by Blackstone that were recognized as violations of customary international law at the time the ATS was enacted?
2. Is the Court willing to expand the ATS beyond these original three offenses? According to Justice Souter, what types of torts would give rise to jurisdiction under the ATS?
3. Do you feel that this decision grants too much or too little power to the federal courts to hear tort claims occurring outside the country?
4. What foreign policy implications are involved in a U.S. court hearing a case under the ATS?
5. In what way did the Supreme Court's subsequent decision in Kiobel further limit the application of customary international law?

INTERNATIONAL BUSINESS LAW AND CRIMES

In this book, **international business law (IBL)** is the body of law and regulations, derived from national and international sources, that governs cross-border business transactions, the activities of those doing business in foreign countries or subject to the jurisdiction of foreign courts, and the resolution international business disputes. IBL includes both public and private international law, and overlaps with "international economic law," a term used by some international lawyers. Several main subject areas of IBL that we introduced in the last chapter are international trade and transportation (import and exports), the international aspects of licensing and protecting intellectual property, foreign direct investment, and the operations of firms in foreign host countries.

Sources of International Business Law

IBL today is found in modern treaties, multilateral conventions, statutes, the acts of government departments and agencies, court decisions, and the decisions of international courts and tribunals. However, many basic concepts of modern IBL developed over centuries from the ***law merchant*** and maritime law—the accepted customs and practices of ancient and medieval merchants, traders, bankers, mariners, and ship owners. The practices were local at first, but spread rapidly as people began sharing customs and learning that consistent rules were enhancing commerce. Soon private merchant courts and maritime courts in port cities were adopting these customs. Kings and princes were permitting this self-governance because it functioned well to enhance commerce, and that increased tax revenues. A few centuries later the same customs were influencing legislative codes in the new nation-states of continental Europe, and the common law and admiralty courts in England were relying on them as precedents in their written judgments. Many of the same rules, in modern form, are now found in negotiable instruments law, sales and contract law, maritime and shipping law, insurance law, and many other areas.

One important modern code—embodied in an international convention—is the *UN Convention on Contracts for the International Sale of Goods*. We will cover this is some detail later in the book. The code was written by legal scholars of commercial law from around the world, brought together over the course of many years by the *UN Commission on International Trade Law* (UNCITRAL), located in Vienna. The code covers subjects similar to those in Article 2 of the *Uniform Commercial Code*, the primary body of sales law in the United States. However, the UN code applies to international sales between a buyer and seller in countries that are party to the convention. This includes most trading nations of the world today.

Another source of IBL are the non-binding standards of conduct, or guidelines, published by respected international organizations and disseminated worldwide. Examples include standards for the fair treatment and protection of workers in a developing country, a set of voluntary standards for socially responsible corporations, or recommendations for the protection of the environment. Although these are not technically "law" and may not be enforceable in courts of law, there exists a "*soft enforcement*" mechanism by virtue of their moral authority and the willingness of companies to comply in the face of public opinion. In some cases these norms do find their way into binding legal codes. Universal norms and standards are therefore considered a source of IBL. We will discuss a few of these later in this chapter.

Uniformity in International Business Law. Business functions best when law is clear and predictable. This lets people know the legal ramifications of future business plans and tells them their rights and obligations in advance of entering into business arrangements. This is especially true for firms operating in different countries. Complying with the maze of laws and regulations is difficult enough at home; it might be far too dangerous to embark on a business venture in a foreign country, if the laws there are unpredictable, arbitrary, unfair to foreigners, or just unknown. Despite its many differences worldwide, IBL has become more uniform between countries and regions of the world for several reasons:

1. The forces of free trade, economic integration, and the globalization of business have accelerated the need for greater uniformity in the law for international business.
2. Nations have had to cooperate in their legal responses to global issues, common problems, and technologies. For example, as intellectual property, ecommerce, and other technologies have grown in economic importance, IBL has adapted to keep pace.
3. Intergovernmental organizations such as the UN and the World Trade Organization have played an important role by producing uniform codes on many business subjects, from food safety to contract law.
4. International tribunals for dispute resolution have caused the greatest change in IBL in the modern era. They issue written reports and render judgments affecting national laws that do not conform to international treaties or customary international law.
5. The roles of private industry organizations and trade associations have had an important role in encouraging the growth of uniform IBL. One prominent example is the International Chamber of Commerce in Paris, which has developed standard terms for international business contracts, arbitration, and international banking. While not "law," these customs and practices are regularly incorporated into business and banking contracts, and are relied on by business people and international lawyers and applied by courts in legal disputes.

Why International Business Law Retains Its National Character. Although IBL has become more uniform, there are important reasons why it remains diverse and "national" in character:

1. National courts interpret and apply IBL according to their own legal rules, case precedents, and histories.
2. Differences in national legal systems reflect different legal and regulatory approaches to business law. For example, legal systems may be based on the common law of English tradition, on the civil law of European, Scandinavian, or Latin American tradition, on state socialist law, on religious law, or on mix of these.
3. The level of socioeconomic development in a country influences its legal development. It depends, for example, if a country has an industrialized economy like the United States, if it is a developing country, or if it has an agrarian economy.
4. National attitudes toward economics affect attitudes toward law and regulation. For example, one country may have a strong tradition of private enterprise and a free market economy. Other countries may believe in greater government regulation, more government ownership of industry, and more control over business. Some countries may pursue free trade and investment policies, while others may take a protectionist approach.

Crimes Related to International Business

Another special issue in the field of international law is that of jurisdiction for crimes. While **jurisdiction** is the power of a court to act, criminal jurisdiction is the power of a court to hear a criminal case and to act over a defendant. Today jurisdiction has become an important international issue because just as business has become more international, so too has criminality. We all understand that nations have jurisdiction over crimes that occur within their territorial borders—"territorial jurisdiction." But what if a crime that affects citizens or their national interests within the country is committed outside of a country?

Transnational Organized Crime. Before we return to the question of jurisdiction, let's mention two major types of international crime. One type is transnational organized crime. Examples include the illegal drug and firearms trade, smuggling, human trafficking, prostitution and sex crimes, cybercrime, counterfeiting, ocean piracy, money laundering, and similar crimes. This might be the work of the Russian or Sicilian mafias, the Japanese yakuza, Colombian drug cartels, Chinese triad, or one of many gangs that engage in organized crime at the international level—a serious issue for law enforcement.

Transnational Business Crime. Another type of international crime is transnational business crime, including crimes that occur incident to or in the course of legitimate business, and that either take place across national borders or have an effect in more than one country. Sometimes referred to as "white collar crime" or "economic crime," these include bribery and corruption, tax evasion, customs fraud, criminal violations of export control laws, business fraud, financial crimes, criminal violations of environmental laws, securities laws, and antitrust laws. The perpetrator might be an individual business person or the corporate entity itself.

UN Convention Against Corruption. The *UN Convention Against Corruption* (2003) has 165 contracting parties, including the United States. It calls for nations to (1) criminalize the offering or giving of a bribe or undue advantage to a public official, including a foreign official, to influence his or her official acts or to obtain business; (2) criminalize money laundering (passing money through otherwise legitimate businesses or banks to disguise its illicit origins); (3) improve enforcement by changing national bank secrecy laws so that the illicit proceeds of crimes can be tracked, identified, and seized; and (4) establish corporate criminal liability for legal entities. Some of these concepts are already a part of the national laws of many countries, including the United States, but not of all countries. One positive effect of more uniform laws against bribery and corruption is that it would level the business "playing field," allowing government contracts to go to the most efficient companies worldwide or to those that produced the best product or service at the best price, instead of to the most corrupt companies located in countries with the most lax laws. American business and government leaders and others around the world recognize this positive benefit.

Criminal Jurisdiction and the Extraterritorial Reach of Domestic Law

In a world where national political and economic interests span the globe, it is more important than ever for countries to deal with transnational crime—to protect their interests and the interests of their citizens. To set the stage, consider these jurisdictional problems:

- Industry executives from competing firms in the United States meet on a golf course on a Caribbean Island to fix prices and divide up territories among them in the U.S. market. On what jurisdictional grounds can these executives be prosecuted in the United States?
- An American businessperson doing business in Kuwait pays a cash bribe to a Kuwaiti government or military official to obtain business. Can the U.S. government arrest and prosecute this American on his or her return home?
- An executive of a Canadian corporation knowingly causes the discharge of a toxic waste into a river that runs into the United States. It poisons most life in the river for miles downstream and renders the water unsuitable for use. Can the business executive be prosecuted for crimes in both countries?
- A citizen of Russia, living in London, attacks and disrupts a major computer network in the United States. Where can he or she be tried?

What would happen in these cases? There are several issues raised here: May a country pass laws affecting conduct outside its territory? May it exert jurisdiction over individuals or corporations outside its territory? And if so, does this include jurisdiction only over its own citizens who commit crimes abroad, or also over foreign individuals and foreign corporations? The answers to these questions are often "yes," although it does depend on the facts of each case and the laws of each country involved.

The principle that a nation can project its laws—its jurisdiction—beyond its territorial borders is known as **extraterritoriality** or **extraterritorial jurisdiction**. It applies to both civil and criminal statutes, although our discussion here applies to criminal law. All countries have different views toward the use of extraterritoriality. Some countries, such as the United States, are more willing to project their laws to individuals in foreign countries than, say, Canada or the countries of Europe. In the United States many criminal statutes affecting business apply extraterritorially. These include statutes on discrimination in employment, price-fixing and antitrust violations, securities laws, transportation of counterfeit films and other intellectual property, interference with a flight crew, trading with the enemy during time of war, country embargoes, banking and financial crimes, bribery, and more.

We are not speaking of any one country becoming the world's police force. Extraterritorial jurisdiction does not mean that one nation's law enforcement officials can enter another to make arrests. Normally, it requires a measure of compromise and mutual assistance in law enforcement. Any attempt by one country to enforce its laws against a citizen of another country might be very controversial and viewed as a violation of a country's sovereignty. It can even prompt diplomatic or trade retaliation. As a result, courts say there is a presumption that national laws do not have extraterritorial reach, particularly where they conflict with international law or the laws of another nation. This helps to avoid conflicts in foreign relations. Extraterritoriality is least controversial when it is done by international agreement. A U.S. criminal statute may be applied extraterritorially if the language and history of the statute shows that Congress had intended for it to apply outside the United States. Jurisdiction must also be based on one of the following five basic principles: territoriality, nationality, the protective principle, passive personality, and universality.

Territoriality. Territoriality or **territorial jurisdiction** refers to a nation's jurisdiction over all persons (citizens and noncitizens), places, and property within the territory, airspace, or territorial waters of a country and to crimes committed on vessels flying that nation's flag. In the case of jurisdiction for crimes, subjective territorial jurisdiction exists where a crime was actually committed within the territory. It is the least controversial form of exerting state power because it does not directly interfere with the sovereignty of other nations. Objective territorial jurisdiction, also called the "effects" principle, exists where an act was committed outside a country's territory, but had a substantial effect inside the country. An example of objective territorial jurisdiction in criminal law is the prosecution of foreign citizens in U.S. courts for attempting to smuggle illegal drugs into the United States aboard a foreign-flag ship in international waters.

Nationality. Under the principle of **nationality jurisdiction**, individuals and corporate citizens owe duties to comply with the laws of their countries of nationality no matter where they are in the world. It is considered one of the obligations of citizenship. For example, an American banker in Hong Kong must comply with both Hong Kong and U.S. banking laws. If an executive order of the president states that no funds may be transferred to an account of a party believed to support international terrorism, then the American in Hong Kong is bound just as though he or she were in the United States. In another example a country may tax the income of its citizens earned anywhere in the world, subject of course to certain rules set out in international treaties on income taxation.

Protective Jurisdiction. The protective principle allows jurisdiction over noncitizens for acts committed abroad on the basis of a country's need to protect its national security, vital economic interests, and governmental functions. **Protective jurisdiction** has been used as a basis of extraterritorial jurisdiction to prosecute terrorism, espionage, counterfeiting, making false statements to customs and immigration officers, and falsifying U.S. government documents (such as passports and visas). In one reported case, it was the basis for prosecuting a foreign citizen who conspired with an American to set up a sham marriage for the sole purpose of gaining entrance to the United States.

Passive Personality. **Passive personality** jurisdiction gives a country the right to hear cases stemming from crimes committed against their own citizens by noncitizens outside of their own territories. Passive personality is controversial because the only connection to the prosecuting nation may be the nationality of the victim. This raises the question of whether one nation should attempt to criminalize and prosecute acts committed by foreign citizens in foreign countries. Most countries, including the United States, have been reluctant to rely only on passive personality for jurisdiction and are willing to exercise it only in the case of heinous crimes, such as terrorism or other crimes with a significant nexus to the United States. One case, *United States v. Roberts,* 1 F. Supp. 2d 601

(E.D.La.1998), involved a sexual assault of an American minor aboard a cruise ship in international waters by a non-U.S. citizen working aboard. The ship was registered in Panama and was flying the flag of Liberia. On the perpetrator's prosecution in the United States, the court held that there was passive personality jurisdiction because the ship had departed on its cruise from Miami; the ship's corporate officers were located in Miami; the company's stock was traded on the New York Stock Exchange; and a trial in the United States would not infringe the sovereignty of any other nation.

Universal Jurisdiction. Finally, the **universality** principle of jurisdiction permits any country to prosecute perpetrators of the most heinous and universally condemned crimes regardless of where the crimes occurred or the nationality of the perpetrators or victims. The main offenses universally punishable are piracy, slavery, war crimes, torture, genocide, crimes against humanity, and extrajudicial killings. One famous case of universality is Israel's 1961 public trial of Nazi war criminal Adolf Eichmann for holocaust atrocities committed in Europe during World War II. However, in more recent years, universality jurisdiction has not been widely in use.

Interestingly, acts of terrorism have not been held to fall within universal jurisdiction. As a result, prosecution of a terrorist must be based on one of the other jurisdictional grounds. In *U.S. v. Ramzi Yousef*, 327 F.3d 56 (2d Cir. 2003), the defendant was convicted of conspiracy to bomb an American-flagged airline in Asia. On appeal he argued that the U.S. statute on destruction of aircraft could not be applied outside the United States. The court rejected the argument, stating that jurisdiction was consistent with a treaty and with three of the five principles of customary international law criminal jurisdiction—objective territorial, protective, and passive personality. The court stated

> First, jurisdiction... is consistent with the "passive personality principle" of customary international jurisdiction because [this] involved a plot to bomb United States-flag aircraft that would have been carrying United States citizens and crews and that were destined for cities in the United States. Moreover ... jurisdiction is appropriate under the "objective territorial principle" because the purpose of the attack was to influence United States foreign policy and the defendants intended their actions to have an effect—in this case, a devastating effect—on and within the United States. Finally, there is no doubt that jurisdiction is proper under the "protective principle" because the planned attacks were intended to affect the United States and to alter its foreign policy.

The court went on to say that terrorism, unlike genocide, had not yet risen to a crime under customary international law. Noting the cliché that "one man's terrorist is another man's freedom fighter," the court felt that there was yet no universal definition of "terrorism" and thus universal jurisdiction could not apply.

In the following case, *United States v. Campbell*, a federal court permitted the prosecution in the United States of an Australian citizen arrested in India for a business crime committed against the U.S. government in Afghanistan. The court discusses extraterritoriality both under United States and international law.

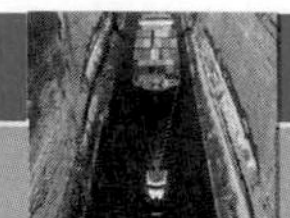

United States v. Campbell

798 F. Supp. 2d 293 (2011) United States District Court (D.D.C.)

BACKGROUND AND FACTS

Campbell, an Australian citizen, was employed in the construction of health care facilities and schools in Afghanistan. The projects were funded by a U.S. government agency that extends financial and technical assistance to foreign countries to support U.S. foreign policy objectives. Campbell was on a panel that selected subcontractors to work on projects. The U.S. government alleged that Campbell demanded and received a cash payment in return for granting $14 million worth of work to a subcontractor. The money had been paid by an undercover federal investigator in Kabul, Afghanistan, posing as an agent of the subcontractor. Campbell was indicted in the United States for bribery (18 *U.S.C.* Sec. 666), arrested in India several months later, and brought to the United States for prosecution. Campbell moved for dismissal claiming that his prosecution was barred because the events occurred outside the United States, he is not an American citizen, prosecution would violate his due

continues

continued

process rights, and his prosecution would violate international customary law.

ROSEMARY M. COLLYER, DISTRICT JUDGE

* * * Courts have long recognized a presumption against reading a statute to have extraterritorial effect. "It is a 'longstanding principle of American law that legislation of Congress, unless a contrary intent appears, is meant to apply only within the territorial jurisdiction of the United States.'" *Morrison v. Nat'l Australia Bank Ltd.*, 561 U.S. ——, 130 S.Ct. 2869 at 2877 (2010). [most citations omitted].

Despite this seemingly unequivocal pronouncement, the Supreme Court earlier cautioned that "the same rule of interpretation should not be applied to criminal statutes which are, as a class, not logically dependent on their locality for the Government's jurisdiction, but are enacted because of the right of the Government to defend itself against obstruction, or fraud wherever perpetrated, especially if committed by its own citizens, officers or agents." *United States v. Bowman,* 260 U.S. 94, 98, (1922). * * * *Bowman* concerned a ... "conspiracy to defraud ... the United States ... after defendants submitted a false claim for fuel oil for one of its steamships. [T]he Supreme Court reasoned:

> Crimes against private individuals or their property, like assaults, murder, burglary, larceny, robbery, arson, embezzlement, and frauds of all kinds, which affect the peace and good order of the community, must of course be committed within the territorial jurisdiction of the government where it may properly exercise it. If punishment of them is to be extended to include those committed outside of the strict territorial jurisdiction, it is natural for Congress to say so in the statute, and failure to do so will negative the purpose of Congress in this regard ...
>
> But the same rule of interpretation should not be applied to criminal statutes which are, as a class, not logically dependent on their locality for the Government's jurisdiction, but are enacted because of the right of the Government to defend itself against obstruction, or fraud wherever perpetrated, especially if committed by its own citizens, officers, or agents. Some such offenses can only be committed within the territorial jurisdiction of the government because of the local acts required to constitute them. Others are such that to limit their locus to the strictly territorial jurisdiction would be greatly to curtail the scope and usefulness of the statute and leave open a large immunity for frauds as easily committed by citizens on the high seas and in foreign countries as at home. In such cases, Congress has not thought it necessary to make specific provision in the law that the locus shall include the high seas and foreign countries, but allows it to be inferred from the nature of the offense. * * *

Mr. Campbell argues that his prosecution violates customary international law. "[I]nternational law itself imposes limits on the extraterritorial jurisdiction that a domestic court may exercise. It generally recognizes five theories of jurisdiction, the objective territorial, national, passive, protective and universal." *Tel-Oren v. Libyan Arab Republic,* 726 F.2d 774 (D.C.Cir. 1984). An act of Congress should not be construed in a manner that violates the laws of nations if a non-violative interpretation is possible. *Hartford Fire Ins. Co. v. California,* 509 U.S. 764, (1993).

Here, the protective principal—specifically articulated in *Bowman*—supports the prosecution of Mr. Campbell. "The protective principle permits a nation to assert jurisdiction over a person whose conduct outside the nation's territory threatens the nation's security or could potentially interfere with the operation of its governmental functions." *United States v. Romero-Galue,* 757 F.2d 1147 (11th Cir. 1985); Bribery in connection with contracts backed by U.S. financing is illegal precisely because it implicates and adversely affects the interests and purse of the United States. The United States has the right "to defend itself against obstruction, or fraud wherever perpetrated." [*Bowman*]. The protective principle amply supports prosecution of Mr. Campbell in this Court.

Decision. Motion to dismiss is denied. The defendant's prosecution under this statute for bribery occurring outside the United States does not violate the principle against extraterritorial application of U.S. law because, under *U.S. v. Bowman* (cited above), the government has an interest in protecting itself from fraud wherever it occurs. The statue does not violate international customary law because it falls within the protective jurisdiction.

Comment. The court also held that because of the real harm done to the United States, there was a sufficient "nexus" or connection to the United States such that prosecution was not unreasonable or fundamentally unfair in violation of the defendant's constitutional rights.

Case Questions

1. If Congress did not state in the statute that it applied outside the U.S., how did the court arrive at its conclusion?
2. What is meant by the "*Bowman* Exception?"

INTERNATIONAL COURT OF JUSTICE

The most important international judicial body is the International Court of Justice, or ICJ. Formed in 1945 as the primary judicial arm of the United Nations, the ICJ is the arbiter of international law disputes between nations—cases brought by nations, against nations. It sits at The Hague, Netherlands, and bases its work on the *Statute of the International Court of Justice.* The fifteen independent judges are selected from the leading jurists and scholars of international law on a worldwide basis. Individuals and private corporations are not parties to cases before the ICJ (although one nation may bring an action against another nation alleging a violation of the rights of one of their citizens under international law). In addition to dispute resolution the ICJ renders non-binding advisory opinions to the UN.

Specifically, the ICJ has jurisdiction over cases brought under the *UN Charter* or that involve a treaty, convention, international obligation, or question of international law. Jurisdiction over any nation is completely voluntary in that no nation must appear unless it consents to jurisdiction. Nations that agree in advance to submit certain types of cases to the ICJ are said to have submitted to **compulsory jurisdiction**, although this too is voluntary and may be withdrawn.

The ICJ's judgments are made public, and there is no appeal. The judgments are binding only on the parties to the case, and not to all nations of the world. They are enforced primarily on the basis of world public opinion, diplomatic pressure, and good faith of the countries involved. In a principle established in the *Case Concerning the Factory at Chorzów (Poland v. Germany,* P.C.I.J., 1927), decided by the Permanent Court of International Justice, the forerunner of the modern ICJ, any violation of an international obligation requires the payment of financial reparations or damages. Typical cases heard by the ICJ have included land and maritime boundary disputes and the use of waterways; unlawful detaining of diplomats (e.g., Iran holding U.S. diplomats hostage in 1979); violations of sovereignty by neighboring armies (e.g., Uganda's plundering of the Democratic Republic of the Congo and the killing and torture of civilians from 1996–2001); violations of humanitarian law (e.g., Bosnia and Serbia from 1992–1995); violations of human rights (e.g., the ICJ's 2003 decision holding that the United States had violated the rights of 51 Mexican citizens on death row in the United States by not permitting them to have the assistance of the Mexican embassy in their defense).

Many of these decisions are highly controversial and, as would be expected, subject to criticism from many quarters. Many decisions cannot be enforced. For instance, in the above examples, Iran did not comply with the ICJ's judgment, Uganda will probably never pay the ordered $10 billion in reparations, and the United States did not overturn the sentences of the Mexican nationals and, indeed, withdrew from the treaty on which the court's decision was based.

In the following case, Mr. Nottebohm was seeking diplomatic protection by Liechtenstein, of which he was a naturalized citizen, against the acts of Guatemala, where he resided. **Diplomatic protection** is the right of one nation to take diplomatic or judicial action to protect the rights of a person to whom it has granted nationality from a violation of international law by another nation. (Case on *Mavrommatis Palestine Concessions,* Judgment of Aug. 30, 1924 P.C.I.J.)

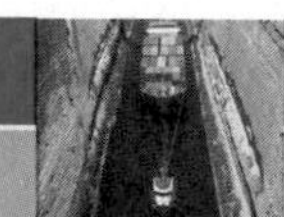

Nottebohm Case [Liechtenstein v. Guatemala]

Judgment of April 6th, 1955: I.C.J. Reports 4 International Court of Justice

BACKGROUND AND FACTS

Friedrich Nottebohm was born in Germany in 1881. He moved to Guatemala for business reasons in 1905 and lived there until 1943, except for business trips and visits to his brother in Liechtenstein. He remained a German citizen during that time. One month after Germany's invasion of Poland and the start of World War II in 1939, while visiting Liechtenstein, Nottebohm applied to become a naturalized citizen. Liechtenstein waived the three-year residency requirement. Nottebohm paid taxes and fees to Liechtenstein and filed the requisite forms, and Liechtenstein swore him in as a citizen and issued him a passport. Nottebohm returned to Guatemala in 1940. In 1943, Guatemala entered World War II, siding with the United States. Upon his return to Guatemala, Nottebohm was arrested as a German enemy and turned over to the United States for internment. His property was seized by Guatemala. Nottebohm was released in 1946, but his

continues

continued

property was not returned. Liechtenstein filed a "memorial" for diplomatic protection of its citizen, as the complaint is called, before the International Court of Justice, claiming that Guatemala had violated international law by refusing to recognize Liechtenstein as his country of nationality. Liechtenstein claims that it is entitled to damages.

JUDGMENT

... [I]nternational law leaves it to each State to lay down the rules governing the grant of its own nationality. * * * On the other hand, a State cannot claim that the rules it has thus laid down are entitled to recognition by another State unless it has acted in conformity with this general aim of making the legal bond of nationality accord with the individual's genuine connection with the State ...

According to the practice of States, to arbitral and judicial decisions and to the opinions of writers, nationality is a legal bond having as its basis a social fact of attachment, a genuine connection of existence, interests and sentiments, together with the existence of reciprocal rights and duties. It may be said to constitute the juridical expression of the fact that the individual upon whom it is conferred, either directly by the law or as the result of an act of the authorities, is in fact more closely connected with the population of the State conferring nationality than with that of any other State. * * *

Naturalization is not a matter to be taken lightly. To seek and to obtain it is not something that happens frequently in the life of a human being. It involves his breaking of a bond of allegiance and his establishment of a new bond of allegiance. It may have far-reaching consequences and involve profound changes in the destiny of the individual who obtains it. It concerns him personally, and to consider it only from the point of view of its repercussions with regard to his property would be to misunderstand its profound significance. In order to appraise its international effect, it is impossible to disregard the circumstances in which it was conferred, the serious character which attaches to it, the real and effective, and not merely the verbal preference of the individual seeking it for the country which grants it to him. * * *

At the time of his naturalization does Nottebohm appear to have been more closely attached by his tradition, his establishment, his interests, his activities, his family ties, his intentions for the near future to Liechtenstein than to any other State? * * *

At the date when he applied for naturalization Nottebohm had been a German national from the time of his birth. He had always retained his connections with members of his family who had remained in Germany and he had always had business connections with that country. His country had been at war for more than a month, and there is nothing to indicate that the application for naturalization then made by Nottebohm was motivated by any desire to dissociate himself from the Government of his county.

He had been settled in Guatemala for 34 years. He had carried on his activities there. It was the main seat of his interests. He returned there shortly after his naturalization, and it remained the centre of his interests and of his business activities. He stayed there until his removal as a result of war measures in 1943. * * *

In contrast, his actual connections with Liechtenstein were extremely tenuous. No settled abode, no prolonged residence in that country at the time of his application for naturalization: the application indicates that he was paying a visit there and confirms the transient character of this visit by its request that the naturalization proceedings should be initiated and concluded without delay. No intention of settling there was shown at that time or realized in the ensuing weeks, months or year-on the contrary, he returned to Guatemala very shortly after his naturalization and showed every intention of remaining there. * * * Furthermore, other members of his family have asserted Nottebohm's desire to spend his old age in Guatemala.

These facts clearly establish, on the one hand, the absence of any bond of attachment between Nottebohm and Liechtenstein and, on the other hand, the existence of a long-standing and close connection between him and Guatemala, a link which his naturalization in no way weakened. * * * It was granted without regard to the concept of nationality adopted in international relations.

Naturalization was asked for not so much for the purpose of obtaining a legal recognition of Nottebohm's membership in fact in the population of Liechtenstein, as it was to enable him to substitute for his status as a national of a belligerent State that of a national of a neutral State, with the sole aim of thus coming within the protection of Liechtenstein but not of becoming wedded to its traditions, its interests, its way of life or of assuming the obligations - other than fiscal obligations - and exercising the rights pertaining to the status thus acquired.

Guatemala is under no obligation to recognize a nationality granted in such circumstances. Liechtenstein consequently is not entitled to extend its protection to Nottebohm vis-à-vis Guatemala and its claim must, for this reason, be held to be inadmissible.

continues

continued

Decision. Guatemala was not required to recognize the citizenship granted by Liechtenstein in a way that did not follow well-established principles of international law.

Comment. Nottebohm was a naturalized citizen of Liechtenstein and citizenship is a domestic law concept. He was a citizen for purposes of the laws of Liechtenstein when in Liechtenstein. Nationality, however, is an international law concept, important in the international arena, and Guatemala's recognition of nationality was based on international law.

Case Questions

1. May individuals bring an action against a nation at the ICJ?
2. On what basis did Liechtenstein file this action?
3. Although a nation can determine its own criteria for citizenship, must that be recognized by other nations?
4. Do you feel that this judgment interfered with Liechtenstein's sovereignty? Why or why not?
5. Would this case be considered one of international public or private law?

International Criminal Court. The *Rome Statute of the International Criminal Court* (122 parties as of 2013), is a 2001 treaty that created the International Criminal Court, which sits at The Hague, Netherlands. It is independent, and not a part of the United Nations. The Court hears three types of crimes: genocide, crimes against humanity (attacks against civilians through murder, slavery, forced deportations, torture, rape and sexual violence, disappearances, apartheid and other persecutions on the grounds of religion, race, ethnicity, national origin, political beliefs, or gender), and war crimes. Terrorism and drug trafficking are not within the Court's jurisdiction. Jurisdiction applies to nationals of a country that has ratified the treaty, even if the nationals were acting in an official (government) capacity. There is no statute of limitations—perpetrators can be apprehended and tried any time during their lifetimes. The Court does not have exclusive jurisdiction over these crimes, as the right of any nation to prosecute genocide, crimes against humanity, and war crimes still exits under international customary law and domestic law.

The United States, Russia, China, India, and Iran are among the countries that have not joined the Rome Convention. Many critics believe that the Court impinges on national sovereignty, that it could subject government and military leaders to prosecutions solely on political grounds, and that it lacks fair procedures and appeal mechanisms.

ETHICS, SOCIAL RESPONSIBILITY, AND CODES OF CONDUCT

In international business, the law is a floor above which our ethical conduct should rise. Lawyers can tell us what the law is, or what conduct is lawful or unlawful. They can do a good job of telling us what a likely fine or prison sentence will be for commission of a crime, and they are fairly good at estimating future damages to injured consumers, or anyone else with a legal claim against us. But it would be difficult for anyone to tell us what is ethical, or socially responsible, or right or wrong. Compliance with the laws of all countries in which we work is difficult enough. Rising to a higher ethical standard is even harder. After all, ethics are based on one's own experience, knowledge, culture, beliefs, and personal value system. And in international business, what is ethical in one culture or in one country might not be ethical in another. However, it is easier to evaluate our own notions of right and wrong, and to conform to a higher international standard, when there is a growing international consensus on business ethics and social responsibility expressed in international norms. Norms and standards—the conscience of world public opinion—can be found in codes of conduct drafted by public and private international organizations, and by companies themselves. Although the codes are voluntary and non-binding, they do have the soft enforcement mechanisms that we spoke of earlier in the chapter. They are enforceable because each corporate stakeholder has an interest in them being enforced, as those stakeholders are not just the owners and directors, but also the subcontractors and business partners, customers, employees, managers of large investment funds and other investors, and the public. Indeed, taken together, these codes contain a framework for promoting ethical conduct and social responsibility in international business.

International Business and Human Rights

International human rights law protects individuals and groups from the acts of governments that violate their civil, political, or human rights. Sources of human rights law includes customary international law and many international conventions. Today human rights law issues are seen as a broader concept that have ramifications in international business, and especially to large, multinational firms. The *Guiding Principles for Business on Human Rights* (2011), published by the UN Office of the High Commissioner for Human Rights, addresses this. Although not a legally binding document, it does reflect the thinking about human rights and business: Article 23 states,

In all contexts, business enterprises should

(a) Comply with all applicable laws and respect internationally recognized human rights, wherever they operate
(b) Seek ways to honour the principles of internationally recognized human rights when faced with conflicting requirements
(c) Treat the risk of causing or contributing to gross human rights abuses as a legal compliance issue wherever they operate

We started this section with the idea that the law is a floor for our ethical conduct. This is reflected in a quote from the *Guiding Principles.*

> The responsibility to respect human rights is a global standard of expected conduct for all business enterprises wherever they operate. It exists independently of States' abilities and/or willingness to fulfill their own human rights obligations, and does not diminish those obligations. *And it exists over and above compliance with national laws and regulations protecting human rights.*

International Labour Organization

The International Labour Organization (ILO), located in Geneva, was founded in 1919 and became a part of the UN system in 1946. The objectives of the ILO are to bring together government, industry, and labor groups, with a focus on developing countries, to help promote the rights of workers, create decent and beneficial employment opportunities, eliminate child labor, and help foster ideas and the means for the economic and social protection of the poor, the elderly, the unemployable, women, and children. The governing body of the ILO is made up of individual representatives of government, industry, and labor.

Perhaps the most important undertaking of the ILO has been the creation of international labor standards, embodied in 188 conventions and almost 200 non-binding "recommendations" for minimum standards of basic workers' rights. These include the right of workers to freely associate, the right to organize and bargain with employers collectively, abolition of forced labor and child labor, creation of a safe working environment, protection of migrant workers and workers at sea, elimination of discrimination at work, equality of opportunity and treatment for men and women workers, and other standards addressing workplace health and safety. ILO conventions are legally binding on a member nation only when ratified by the member nation's government. Not all countries have ratified all conventions. For example, the United States has ratified only fourteen ILO conventions.

The OECD Codes of Conduct

The *Organisation for Economic Cooperation and Development* (OECD), located in Paris, is an intergovernmental organization whose members consist of national governments, with nongovernmental organizations joining as observers. The OECD comprises 34 industrialized countries, including the United States, Canada, Mexico, Israel, Japan, Korea, Turkey, and the European countries. Some of the formerly communist countries of Eastern Europe are also members.

The *OECD Guidelines for Multinational Enterprises* are a set of voluntary recommendations to multinationals encouraging responsible business conduct when they operate in host countries. They cover the entire range of business ethics and social responsibility issues. They are not legally enforceable, but are well known and reflect the consensus of many governments. They encourage self-enforcement through accountability, reporting, and internal controls, such as encouraging "whistle blowing" by employees who become aware of corporate violations. The guidelines were first issued in 1976 and revised in 2000. A few representative standards include those for employment, environmental protection, corruption, consumer privacy, and diffusion of technology in developing countries. One interesting environmental standard calls on countries to "not use the lack of full scientific certainty as a reason for postponing measures to prevent or minimize serious damage to the environment."

You can find other OECD recommendations in specific areas in the OECD *Convention on Combating Bribery of Foreign Public Officials in International Business Transactions* (1997), *Guidelines for Protecting*

Consumers from Fraudulent and Deceptive Commercial Practices Across Borders, and the *Guidelines for Consumer Protection in the Context of Electronic Commerce.*

United Nations Global Compact

The ***UN Global Compact*** is a partnership of international companies, public interest groups, and UN agencies who pledge to support a set of voluntary principles on human rights, labor standards, the environment, and corruption. The ten core principles are presented in very general terms. For instance, one states that, "Businesses should make sure that they are not complicit [with governments] in human rights abuses." Another states that, "Businesses should support a precautionary approach to environmental challenges." Of course, the *Global Compact* is not without criticism from those who are generally critical of all UN activities. However, the core principles are merely a statement of the most basic, universally recognized principles of corporate social responsibility. According to the UN, as of 2012 there were 7,000 corporate signatories from around the world, although reception of the compact has been greatest in Europe (56 percent of signatories), Latin America (18 percent), Asia (14 percent), and North America (5 percent).

CERES Principles

The **Coalition for Environmentally Responsible Economies**, or CERES, is a private, mostly American network of environmental groups, socially conscious investors, and companies committed to following the **CERES Principles** of environmental and social accountability. One provision of the CERES Principles requires that in selecting a board of directors the company will look for individuals with demonstrated environmental commitment, and the CEO and directors will take responsibility for the firm's environmental policy.

Corporate Codes of Conduct

In recent years, many companies have had an increased interest in enacting their own codes of conduct. There are surely many reasons for a company doing this. It might be seen as good business, in that it creates goodwill with customers and investors. Some might see it as an opportunity to foster an ethical and responsible attitude in their employees while others may view it as an opportunity for self-regulation that could forestall the enactment of more restrictive national laws and regulations. In the United States, the guidelines for sentencing corporate offenders allow for reduced fines and sentences if a defendant can show that it has had a **code of conduct** and compliance program to reduce the likelihood of criminal conduct.

A good example of a corporate ethics code is the *Levi Strauss & Co. Global Sourcing and Operating Guidelines.* It is generally recognized as the first code of conduct created by a multinational corporation and made applicable to its foreign suppliers. While these guidelines address issues important to an apparel company like Levi Strauss, their basic ideas can be applicable to any firm that does business through a global supply chain or with a supplier or contractor in a developing country in an industry that is highly labor intensive.

The guidelines include the *Business Partner Terms of Engagement,* representing an effort by Levi Strauss to control the activities of its more than 500 overseas contractors and suppliers. In the 1990s, the company discovered (as did many U.S. apparel and footwear makers) that a large number of its subcontractors were maintaining substandard working conditions or using child labor in some fashion. The company not only reacted quickly to stop these practices, it began developing guidelines to end them. The *Business Partner Terms of Engagement* sets out, in more than 70 pages, the minimum standards for the fair treatment of workers that must be met by any foreign firm wishing to supply or contract with Levi Strauss. It addresses specifics such as wages, working hours, the use of corporal punishment, and how to treat workers on the factory floor. Levi Strauss provides its suppliers with manuals and training programs to implement its standards. The company also makes public its list of all overseas factories producing Levi Strauss products.

Other apparel companies, with similar codes, include The Gap (*Code of Vendor Conduct*), The Limited (*What We Stand For*), Sara Lee (*Global Business Standards and Global Standards for Suppliers*), Wal-Mart (*Ethical Standards Program*), and many others. It is generally agreed that for any company's code of conduct to be effective it must be communicated to its employees, become a part of its corporate culture, include disciplinary measures and other methods for ensuring compliance, include a system for measuring its effectiveness, and provide a means of shareholder and public accountability.

COMPARATIVE LAW: DIFFERENCES IN NATIONAL LAWS AND LEGAL SYSTEMS

The study of "comparative law" refers to the study of differences in national laws and legal systems. These differences cover the entire range of law—marriage and family law, business law, liability for wrongful torts, crimes, and more. There are also differences in legal procedures, the role of legislation and case law, the function of judges, the conduct of trials, the use of legal remedies in civil cases, and punishments in criminal cases. These differences are rooted deep in national culture, politics, economics, and especially history, and often are the result of centuries of gradual evolution, combined with rapid change caused by wars, revolution, and political turmoil. Even the opening of world markets for commerce and trade—globalization—has influenced the development of law. There is no better example of how legal systems adapt to change than the case of modern Japan.

Modern Japan: An Example of Legal Change

Japan's earliest legal records date back to at least 500 A.D., and for most of its history it was a feudal system whose laws were based on early Confucian and Buddhist principles taken from China. Japan had been largely closed to Westerners and Western trade, except for some trade with the Dutch until the mid-nineteenth century. As the Japanese opened their doors to trade, they recognized that a modern legal system, one on an equal footing with those of the Americans and Europeans, was necessary and would enhance their bargaining position in negotiating trade agreements. In response, during the 1860s, the Japanese started a national effort to modernize their legal system. New law schools opened in Japan, and law professors were exchanged with foreign institutions. Japan sent out legal scholars around the world, primarily to Europe, to study foreign legal codes and to find ways to adapt these to Japan. By the end of the nineteenth century, Japan had remade its legal system largely in the image of the European countries, primarily of Germany. The result was the adaptation of European civil law principles to Japanese culture and society. These included written codes in commercial law, real property law, family law, criminal law, and others, as well as procedures for trials and deciding cases.

After World War II the United States became the major influence in Japan, resulting in a parliamentary democracy and bill of rights, while preserving the symbolic role of the Emperor. The United States also revised many of Japan's business laws. To this day, it is safe to say that Japan's laws are an amalgamation of European civil criminal law, American constitutional and administrative law, and Japanese cultural values.

We began this section by mentioning some of those forces that influence legal change—war and history, culture, religion, globalization, and international trade. In the case of Japan, we see all of these forces at play.

Modern Legal Systems of the World

While it is obvious that laws can differ from country to country, the differences in legal systems are largely differences in the role of legislatures in enacting statutes or codes, the role of judges and the courts in applying and interpreting the law, and in legal procedures. Here we briefly describe the most widespread modern legal systems found in the world today. These are the common law, civil law, Islamic law, and mixed systems that incorporate characteristics of more than one.

Origins of Civil Law Systems

Civil law includes most of Eastern and Western Europe, Scandinavia, Latin America, Japan, and Russia. **Mixed civil law** systems include much of Africa (including tribal law). China's system is largely civil, mixed with principles of socialist economic law and traditional Confucian values.

While the term "civil law" can have several different meanings, the most common meaning to Americans is in reference to the laws affecting private rights and remedies, such as contract law, family or inheritance law, or tort law. However, in this chapter, *civil law* refers to those modern legal systems that are derived from ancient Roman law.

Early Roman Law and Its Revival. The early Romans had a penchant for writing, or most likely carving, very simple laws into bronze or marble tablets and placing them in public places. These became the earliest written Roman codes. Rome's conquering armies carried Roman law far and wide. Eventually, Rome had amassed thousands of edicts, rules, and penalties created by generations of emperors. Over the centuries, they had become unwieldy and outdated. By 529 A.D., Rome had long ceased to be the capital of the Roman Empire, and the Emperor Justinian ruled the Eastern Roman Empire from his seat of government in Byzantium (modern Istanbul). In that year, Justinian presided over the rewriting of Roman law, which was condensed and compiled into one code, known as the ***Justinian Code***. It classified legal rules and organized them into a logical system that created a "body" of law, in a form that could be learned, understood, and applied. However, Rome had already been overrun by Germanic hordes in the West. The Roman Empire had been lost, and in time, Justinian's code was forgotten—some say lost—almost forever.

Hundreds of years later, around 1100 A.D., copies of Justinian's long-lost code were discovered. Legal scholars from Italy and around the world began to take great interest. They were impressed by how comprehensive it was and how it had arranged legal principles in an orderly and systematic manner. For centuries, Roman law was taught only as an academic discipline, primarily in Italian universities.

Centuries later, the Emperor Napoleon found the clarity and organization of the Roman system to be very appealing, and in 1804, he used Roman principles as the basis for consolidating all French law into one code. The ***Napoleonic Code*** was soon translated into almost every language, and adaptations of it spread throughout Europe and the world. It was the model for the new legal systems of Latin America on their independence. The legal systems in civil law countries still have their distant roots in Roman law.

In the nineteenth century Germany started work on a uniform code, also closely based on the organization of Roman law. In 1900, it enacted its *Bürgerliches Gesetzbuch,* the German civil code, as well as codes of commercial law and criminal law. The *Bürgerliches Gesetzbuch* is still the codified law of Germany to this day, having been amended through the twentieth century, and most recently in 2002. These two codes have been an important influence on the growth of civil law internationally. The German legal codes influenced the legal systems of Japan, China, Portugal, Brazil, and many other countries. Today, the civil law system is the predominant legal system in the world. Despite common legal heritage, there still are many national differences in the civil law systems. Scotland, South Africa, and the Scandinavian countries have variations of the traditional civil law system.

Origins of Common Law Systems

It amazes many American students to learn that English law originated in the Normandy region of France via the Norman Conquest of 1066. While many English and American legal terms come from French and Latin (after all, the Romans had conquered Gaul and Britain), the revival of Roman law in the eleventh and twelfth centuries that occurred on the European continent completely skipped Britain, which by then was branching off on its own legal track.

The job of describing one thousand years of English legal history in a few paragraphs is not easy. But it is an interesting tale. Anglo-Saxon law governed much of Britain from the fall of the Roman Empire until the Norman Conquest in 1066. Law came partly from the early kings and their councils and partly from local custom. By 1066, legal disputes were being heard by Anglo-Saxon courts. There were early forms of trial, but there was no evidence or factual proof offered. There were no witnesses as we know them today. Proof at trials was based on the ceremonious recitation of a formal oath by the parties and their "oath helpers." The higher one's social status, the fewer helpers he needed. One mistake in the recitation, one slip of the tongue, and the accused was deemed to have lied, and was thus guilty by divine intervention. There was also trial by ordeal—perhaps by placing a hand in fire. Again, by divine intervention, if the hand became infected over time, the accused had lied. If the hand healed, he had told the truth. It was primitive and archaic. Perhaps the most common method of proof was "trial by battle." Needless to say of course, justice was not kind to some.

Then, after 1066, William the Conqueror introduced a political and economic system commonly called *feudalism.* All land was parceled out to his closest followers, the lords, who in turn gave parcels to subtenants, who in turn did the same. Each took his land with certain rights and in return for certain duties owed to the tenant above, or to his lord. The duties might be farming, knight service, or castle guard, for example. Even the church received land in return for prayers. The very first laws developed by William were created to enforce feudal rights in land.

While European feudalism no longer exists, the legal system that William and the kings that followed introduced to England does. They decreed that all justice flowed from the king, and from the King's Court, or *Curia Regis* (the king's closest advisors, sitting at Westminster). Justice from the king was obtainable through one of many formal, written writs. Soon traveling judges were sent into the countryside to hold court. Eventually, the king's judges brought with them a new concept, trial by jury.

As one would expect, the popularity of trial by jury over trial by ordeal or battle led to the eventual demise of the old Anglo-Saxon courts. As these itinerant judges decided cases, they wrote down their decisions and shared them with other judges of the King's Court. Judges could now justify their decisions by citing the decisions of other judges in similar cases. A "common" body of law resulted. Thus began the **common law system** that we know today—where the reasoned decisions of judges become the law of the case, a legal precedent that binds judges in deciding similar cases in the future. This is expressed in the common law doctrine of *stare decisis,* meaning that courts should "let the decision stand" unless it is overruled by a higher authority.

The common law spread with the British Empire. Examples of common law countries today include Australia, Canada, Ghana, Great Britain, the United States, and many Caribbean island nations. India has a mixed system that is largely based on the common law. Even many civil law nations have adopted common law principles.

Differences between Modern Civil Law and Common Law Countries

Civil law and common law systems today have many differences and many similarities. Both systems rely on legislative codes, or statutes, as the primary source of law. However, in civil law countries the legal codes are more comprehensive, establishing general principles that are interpreted by judges and applied to the case before them. Where there are gaps in the code law, the judge will draw from the code's principles and doctrine to decide a case. The courts in both systems issue judicial decisions. While civil law judges often cite earlier court decisions that they consider representative of settled law, they are not bound to follow them. Civil law judges do not render opinions that make new law in the form of binding precedent, as do common law judges. It can be said that civil law lawyers are more trained in the interpretation of code law, while common law lawyers are more skilled in using case precedent to develop legal arguments for their clients. It is probably true that researching case law is far more difficult in common law systems, where lawyers must find and piece together common legal principles from unrelated cases and justify the application of those principles to their client's case. Of course, in common law countries, case decisions can always be overridden by statute, as long as the statute does not violate a constitutional doctrine.

The role of judges is also different in civil law countries. The professional judge is schooled for a career as a judge, not a lawyer. In criminal cases, judges take a more inquisitorial role, as do the lawyers for both sides, in an investigative search for the truth. The process is less adversarial than in common law countries. In other legal matters, such as contract or tort cases, judges do the work that both judge and jury would do in common law countries. Unlike common law judges, they can undertake their own investigations of the facts and decide what witnesses to call and what questions to put to them. Much of this is done in writing. In common law countries, the judge is an arbiter between opposing counsel, ruling on what evidence or testimony is admissible, and maintaining a fair trial.

Islamic Law

Over 20 percent of the world's population is Muslim. They are located in some of the very richest and very poorest countries on earth, in the Middle East, Northern Africa, and Central and Southeast Asia. The largest Muslim populations are in Indonesia, Pakistan, India, Bangladesh, Turkey, Iran, and Egypt. In less than 50 years, the Muslim countries of the Middle East have gone from the age of antiquity to the modern age of information, technology, and oil wealth.

The poorer Muslim countries are undergoing tremendous social and political change. Some have adopted Western practices in business, society, and to a lesser extent, family life. Others have returned to strict Islamic principles. Some Muslim countries give limited rights to women; others abide by strict fundamentalist principles. For example, in Saudi Arabia unmarried women are the wards of their fathers, and widowed women are the wards of their sons.

All Muslim countries seem caught in the political, social, and religious struggle between the Western nations and Islamic fundamentalism. Because of the importance of the Muslim countries today, business students should have some understanding of their basic laws.

Most Muslim countries today have modern legal systems, based on civil law or common law, mixed with principles of Islamic law. Islamic law is known as ***Sharia*** (or *Shari'ah*), meaning "divine law." It is derived from the Koran (*Qur'an*), and from the *sunna*. The Koran is the main religious book of the Islamic religion that expresses fundamental Islamic values. The *sunna* is the written record of the teachings and actions of the prophet Muhammad. In addition, Islamic jurists and scholars qualified to interpret the scriptural sources have produced opinions known as *fiqh*. An understanding of the *Sharia* requires reference to the *fiqh* for guidance. Islamic judges do not issue written opinions with the force of law, and they are not bound by the precedents of other courts. They are attempting to seek the truth, the divine word of God.

Saudi Arabian Legal System. An example of a strict Muslim country that is governed by *Sharia* is Saudi Arabia. It is a monarchy and all laws are decreed by the King, in consultation with his highest ministers, in accordance with *Sharia*. The basic law sets out very general legal principles. For example, Article 41 states, "Foreign residents in the Kingdom of Saudi Arabia shall abide by its regulations and shall show respect for Saudi social traditions, values, and feelings."

All Saudi citizens must be of the Muslim faith. Serious crimes are punishable by capital punishment, stoning, amputations, or floggings. Rape, theft, the possession or use of alcohol, fornication, and adultery are serious crimes. Drug smuggling can be punishable by death. The *Sharia* courts hear cases involving crimes, family matters, property, and torts. In the last few years, Saudi Arabia has enacted new business regulations on product labeling, insurance, foreign investment, corporate income tax, trademarks, and others. These are considered to supplement Islamic law and must never conflict with it. Commercial and business disputes are heard by special commissions for grievances appointed by the King.

Pakistani Legal System. Other Muslim countries that had been colonized by Western nations in past centuries, such as Pakistan, have closer historical ties to Western legal systems. Pakistan's legal system has been influenced by the British, but is governed in part by Islamic principles. Today, Pakistan has a modern, written constitution, with a bill of rights that has some language that is similar to the American Constitution. It does declare Islam as the state religion.

Pakistan has secular civil and criminal courts, as well as a *Federal Shariat Court,* which has the power to invalidate any public law if it violates Islamic law. Appeals go to the Supreme Court of Pakistan.

The case of *M. Aslam Khaki v. Syed Muhammad Hashim* (2000) illustrates the great differences between banking and finance in Western nations and Islamic law nations. The Muslim countries have both international banks and Islamic banks. Islamic banks abide by *Sharia* law that prohibits the payment of interest on loans and deposits (although they do have alternative forms of compensation that substitute for interest). In its decision, the Supreme Court of Pakistan struck down the use of interest on all loans and bank deposits (including personal loans, commercial and corporate loans, and interest paid by the government on foreign loans). In 2002, the same court reconsidered its opinion, citing errors, and ruled that invalidating the payment of interest to non-Muslims would "pose a high degree of risk to the economic stability and security of Pakistan." Given that there are now many purely Islamic banks in the Muslim world that follow Islamic law, cases like this one could have a tremendous effect on international business worldwide.

M. Aslam Khaki v. Syed Muhammad Hashim

Shariah Appellate Bench PLD 2000 SC 225 Supreme Court of Pakistan (2000)

BACKGROUND AND FACTS

This case illustrates a classic case of the conflict between Islamic law and modern business. In 1991, the Federal Shariah Court of Pakistan declared the payment of interest (*riba*) by banks on loans and deposits to be contrary to Islamic law. During the 1990s, Pakistani banks adopted many banking techniques to avoid the payment of interest, such as equity investments, profit sharing, and service charges. The government, together with several banks, brought this appeal to the Supreme Court of Pakistan. The court's entire opinion was 1,100 pages long. Below are excerpts from the individual opinion of Maulana Justice Taqi Usmani, an Islamic scholar trained in strict *Sharia* law. As you read, consider the political overtones of the opinion and the economic analysis of interest that would be considered contrary to Western, capitalist economic theory.

MAULANA JUSTICE TAQI USMANI

40. Imam Abubakr Al-Jassas (D.380 AH) in his famous work Ahkamul Qur'an has explained *riba* in the following words: "And the *riba* which was known to and practiced by the Arabs was that they used to advance loan in the form of *Dirham* (silver coin) or *Dinar* (gold coin) for a certain term with an agreed increase on the amount of the principal advanced."

continues

continued

138. Firstly, money (of the same denomination) is not held to be the subject-matter of trade, like other commodities. Its use has been restricted to its basic purpose, i.e., to act as a medium of exchange and a measure of value.

139. Secondly, if for exceptional reasons, money has to be exchanged for money or it is borrowed, the payment on both sides must be equal, so that it is not used for the purpose it is not meant for, i.e., trade in money itself.

140. Imam Al-Ghazzali (d. 505 A.H.) the renowned jurist and philosopher of the Islamic history has discussed the nature of money in an early period when the Western theories of money were non-existent. He says: "... And whoever effects the transactions of interest on money is, in fact, discarding the blessing of Allah and is committing injustice, because money is created for some other things, not for itself." * * *

151. This is exactly what Imam Al-Ghazzali had pointed out nine hundred years ago. The evil results of such an unnatural trade have been further explained by him at another place, in the following words: *"Riba* is prohibited because it prevents people from undertaking real economic activities. This is because when a person having money is allowed to earn more money on the basis of interest, either in spot or in deferred transactions, it becomes easy for him to earn without bothering himself to take pains in real economic activities. This leads to hampering the real interests of the humanity, because the interests of the humanity cannot be safeguarded without real trade skills, industry and construction."

153. Another major difference between the secular capitalist system and the Islamic principles is that under the former system, loans are purely commercial transactions meant to yield a fixed income to the lenders. Islam, on the other hand, does not recognize loans as income-generating transactions. They are meant only for those lenders who do not intend to earn a worldly return through them. They, instead, lend their money either on humanitarian grounds to achieve a reward in the Hereafter, or merely to save their money through a safer hand. So far as investment is concerned, there are several other modes of investment like partnership ... which may be used for that purpose. The transactions of loan are not meant for earning income.

159. Once the interest is banned, the role of "loans" in commercial activities becomes very limited, and the whole financing structure turns out to be equity-based and backed by real assets. In order to limit the use of loans, the *Shar'iah* has permitted to borrow money only in cases of dire need, and has discouraged the practice of incurring debts for living beyond one's means or to grow one's wealth. * * *

160. Conversely, once the interest is allowed, and advancing loans, in itself, becomes a form of profitable trade, the whole economy turns into a debt-oriented economy which not only dominates over the real economic activities and disturbs its natural functions by creating frequent shocks, but also puts the whole mankind under the slavery of debt.

* * *

164. Since in an interest-based system funds are provided on the basis of strong collateral and the end-use of the funds does not constitute the main criterion for financing, it encourages people to live beyond their means. The rich people do not borrow for productive projects only, but also for conspicuous consumption. Similarly, governments borrow money not only for genuine development programs, but also for their lavish expenditure and for projects motivated by their political ambitions rather than being based on sound economic assessment.

204. The basic and foremost characteristic of Islamic financing is that, instead of a fixed rate of interest, it is based on profit and loss sharing. We have already discussed the horrible results produced by the debt-based economy. Realizing the evils brought by this system, many economists, even of the Western world are now advocating in favor of an equity-based financial arrangement.

Decision. Interest on the use of money is unjustified and unearned income. A financial system based on the lending of money for interest is unjust and contrary to Islamic law. Equity investments are lawful where all parties share the risk of profit and loss.

Comment. The Islamic banking community in many countries has been innovative in developing lending and banking programs that they feel are both in keeping with Islamic principles and adaptive to modern banking.

Case Questions

1. What is *riba?* Why is *riba* not permitted pursuant to the *Sharia* law?
2. What would the effect be on Pakistan if the decision were implemented in Islamic banks?
3. In what other ways have culture and religion influenced modern legal systems?

CONCLUSION

Although international law is rooted in centuries of customary law and treaties, it affects modern international relations and international business every day. It affects the movement of people, goods, and money across national borders. Virtually every area of international trade, foreign investment, and intellectual property rights is governed by at least one international convention. International law offers solutions to some of humankind's greatest challenges: human rights abuses by rogue governments, pollution that knows no national boundaries, transnational crimes, international terrorism, and more. However, international solutions depend on the willingness of nations to cooperate, and that is not always politically possible. One can only hope that humankind is up to that challenge.

As we said at the beginning of the chapter, our discussion of international law was guided by our broader interest in understanding the legal environment of international business. For that reason, our approach and coverage is somewhat different from that applied in traditional courses in international law.

Finally, there are several topics traditional to the study of international law that must wait for the next chapter on the resolution of international commercial disputes.

Chapter Summary

1. International law includes public and private international law. Public international law governs the conduct of nations with other nations or the conduct of nations in their relationships with individuals. Private international law governs the rights and responsibilities of private individuals or corporations operating in an international environment, such as international sales contracts or shipping. International law relies primarily on "soft" enforcement mechanisms: the force of public opinion, trade and diplomatic sanctions, and the withholding of foreign aid. The ultimate sanction is war.
2. Customary international law is derived primarily from the widespread and long-standing practices of nations. International law also arises from agreement. A treaty is a legally binding agreement between two or more nations that is recognized and given effect under international law. A convention is a multilateral treaty on a topic of broad international concern.
3. International business law is any law or regulation, whether derived from national or international sources, that governs cross-border business transactions, the activities of those doing business in foreign countries or subject to the jurisdiction of foreign courts, or the resolution of international business disputes.
4. Uniformity and predictability in international business law are important to companies that do international business.
5. Transnational business crimes are major problems calling for global solutions. Typical crimes include bribery and corruption, tax evasion, customs fraud, criminal violations of export control laws, financial crimes, and criminal violations of environmental laws, securities laws, and antitrust laws.
6. Jurisdiction means the power of a nation to create laws that proscribe conduct and to act over individuals, corporations, or their property in the application or enforcement of those laws. When used in reference to a court, it is the power of a court to act or to hear a case—to adjudicate. There are five doctrines of international criminal jurisdiction: territoriality, nationality, the protective principle, passive personality, and universality.
7. Extraterritoriality refers to a nation's jurisdiction that extends beyond its territorial borders.
8. The International Court of Justice hears cases brought by nations against other nations. Individuals and private corporations are not parties to cases before the court. The court has jurisdiction over all cases brought by nations under the *UN Charter* or involving treaties, conventions, international obligations, or questions of international law. Jurisdiction is not compulsory; each nation must agree to submit to the court's jurisdiction.
9. Business ethics and social responsibility are important to the stakeholders of all companies. But these can be vague concepts for firms

operating in different parts of the world. One solution, in addition to legal penalties, are voluntary codes of conduct produced by international organizations and corporations. While some people can argue their effectiveness, they do provide a common framework for management, and they do focus the spotlight of world public opinion on the problem and its solutions.

10. Comparative law refers to the study of differences in national laws and legal systems. These differences cover the entire range of law—marriage and family law, business law, torts, crimes, and more. There are also differences in legal procedures, the role of legislation and case law, the function of judges, the conduct of trials, the use of legal remedies, and punishments in criminal cases.

Key Terms

the law of nations 29
Roman law 29
international law 29
public international law 30
private international law 30
treaty 30
bilateral treaty 30
multilateral treaty 30
convention 30
protocol 31
signatories 31
ratification 31
contracting parties 31
reservation 31
abrogation 31
FCN treaties 31
self-executing treaty 31
non-self-executing treaty 31
direct effect 31
customary international law 33
international "norms" 33
international business law (IBL) 36
law merchant 36
jurisdiction 37
extraterritorial jurisdiction 38
territorial jurisdiction 39
nationality jurisdiction 39
protective jurisdiction 39
passive personality 39
universality 40
compulsory jurisdiction 42
diplomatic protection 42
code of conduct 46
CERES Principles 46
civil law 47
Justinian Code 48
Napoleonic Code 48
common law system 49
Sharia or *Shari'ah* law 49

Questions and Case Problems

1. Kiobel and other environmental activists were arrested, tortured, and executed by the Nigerian military in 1995. They had been protesting Shell's oil exploration in the Ogoni region of Nigeria. A lawsuit was brought by Kobel's widow and others under the *Alien Tort Statute* (ATS) in the United States against three Royal Dutch Shell companies alleging that the companies had aided and abetted the Nigerian military in committing human rights abuses in violation of customary international law. The defendant corporations are incorporated or headquartered in the Netherlands, the United Kingdom, and Nigeria. None of the plaintiffs or defendants are citizens of, or incorporated in, the United States. May an individual may bring an action under the ATS against a corporation for violations of customary international law? If not, do you think that international law should permit damage suits against individuals but leave corporations free to violate the law without consequences? Should a corporation be able to shield its profits from human rights abuses by simply doing business as a corporate entity? *Kiobel v. Royal Dutch Petroleum Co.*, 621 F.3d 111 (2nd.Cir. 2010), cert.granted, 132 S.Ct. 472.
2. The defendants conspired to transport 191 Ecuadorian nationals into the United States illegally aboard a 54-foot fishing vessel. A U.S. Navy helicopter sighted the overcrowded vessel off the Guatemalan coast and saw that it had no lights and flew no flag. A Coast Guard detachment found the passengers with little food or water, and the defendants had left the vessel. The defendants were indicted in the United States for conspiracy to induce aliens to illegally enter the United States, and attempting to bring unauthorized aliens to the United States. (8 *U.S.C.* § 1324). The statute does not mention jurisdiction. The defendants argued that the statute did not apply extraterritorially. Does it? Why or why not? Do you think the "*Bowman* Exception" applies in this case as described in *U.S. v. Campbell*, earlier in the chapter? Why or why not? The terrorist attacks of

September 11, 2001 were planned overseas. Where are immigration offenses planned? How is that relevant to your legal analysis? Explain. *U.S. v. Delgado-Garcia*, 374 F.3d 1337 (D.C.Cir. 2004).

3. Assume that someone in a foreign country poisons a shipment of pharmaceuticals destined for the United States, resulting in death of an American consumer in violation of 18 *U.S.C.*1365 (tampering with a consumer product). Under what circumstances could they be prosecuted in the United States? Would any principle of international law justify bringing them to trial in the United States? Could you argue that the decision in *U.S. v. Campbell* (see chapter) would apply to this situation?
4. What types of issues lend themselves to international solutions through international law?
5. You overhear someone say, "International law does not exist." What do they mean? What evidence can you provide to persuade them that they are mistaken?
6. Internationalists often refer to the "unification" or "harmonization" of international law. What do you think these terms mean? What factors have influenced the harmonization of international business law? In what ways do you think IBL is more "national" than international?
7. Do you think corporate codes of conduct can have an effect on making firms more socially responsible? Are they a substitute for government regulation or do they complement it? Explain.
8. What ideas do you have for setting up an accountability system to ensure compliance with codes of conduct and other ethical and social responsibility standards for business?
9. Why must corporations be concerned about human rights issues when doing business internationally? Who are the "stakeholders" of a public corporation, and what is management's responsibility to them?
10. What are the different forms of criminality that are of concern to international businesses? Explain why international solutions are important. Give some examples.
11. Describe the five theories of international criminal jurisdiction. How have these been made applicable to international terrorism? What types of crimes are covered under the principle of universality? From an international law perspective, do you think that terrorism should be a universal crime? Why or why not?
12. Students often confuse the International Court of Justice with the International Criminal Court. What is the difference between them? Although not covered in this chapter, what is the European Court of Justice and what is its jurisdiction?

Managerial Implications

1. You are a vice president of a multinational corporation headquartered in North America. You are asked to visit Latin America to meet with government officials to consider a location for a new factory. On your arrival, you are met at the airport by one of your hosts, who spends some time that day taking you on a tour of the city and getting acquainted. That evening you are invited to his home for dinner with government representatives. After dinner, one of the guests who works for a key government ministry asks what you think of your company's role in his country as an employer, taxpayer, and corporate good citizen. He makes it clear that his country is no longer a "puppet" of the North Americans. He asks you to show him that you understand his concerns and to show him that your company will be respectful of his country's culture, environment, natural resources, and local laws. How do you respond?
2. Assume that a Korean company manufacturing critical tail assemblies for commercial aircraft ships several defective assemblies to manufacturers in the United States. The CEO, a Korean national, was not only aware of the defects at the time the assemblies were being made but was also responsible for knowingly using inferior parts. He even threatened an engineer with termination if he leaked the truth. One of the assemblies failed on the American-made plane, leading to the crash of a Canadian-flag passenger airline on takeoff from New York. When the investigation leads to him, he flees Korea for Saudi Arabia, where he lives for several years in luxury. Which countries have jurisdiction to prosecute the Korean citizen, and under what legal principles? You do not need to research any international treaties, but you should base your analysis on general principles from this chapter.
3. Your company owns and operates a factory in a foreign country when it is invaded by a neighboring army over a border dispute. The invading government claims that your factory is actually on land belonging to them. Their soldiers destroy your buildings, threaten your employees, and arrest your local manager. While a complete answer to resolving this question will have to wait until later in the book, what recourse do you think you might have under international law against the invading country, if any? How might you proceed? Do you think it would be of any help to contact the U.S. State Department? Why?

Ethical Considerations

We have considered many subjects in this chapter that raise ethical issues—human rights law, international criminal law, international labor standards, bribery and corruption, and others. Here are two cases to consider as food for thought.

Exports of "Unsafe" Pharmaceuticals

Some years ago, it was reported in the world's press that American pharmaceutical companies were selling in developing countries expired medicines that were no longer permitted to be sold in the United States. Assess the validity of the following arguments:

> "There are two sides to every debate. We are talking about antibiotics that are lifesaving and in short supply in some developing countries. True, they are expired under federal regulations in the United States, but they will still be effective for some time to come. It is not illegal overseas, and maybe not illegal to export them, so why should I do anything more than just obey the law? After all, we are selling them at reduced prices to the governments of developing countries. They probably have foreign aid money to buy these with. They will sell them, or give them away, to poor people that otherwise would not be able to afford any medicine at all. Why should I destroy them? After all, we are not talking about AIDS, are we? I wonder what the world and big pharmaceutical companies are doing about that problem?"

Bribery as a "Cost of Doing Business"

What are the economic, political, and social arguments for and against criminalizing the bribery of foreign government officials in developing countries by employees and representatives of Western companies? Assess the validity of each of the following arguments in this statement:

> "I've always thought that bribery is endemic in the developing countries, so 'When in Rome, do as the Romans do.' It's legal there, isn't it? Nothing would happen to me if I get caught there, would it? My government does not have the right to say whether what I do in a foreign country is a crime. They can't tell me what is legal or illegal over there. And I don't have a moral problem, either. I see it as a small price to pay—my company just considers this another 'cost of doing business.' We might even try to deduct it on our corporate income tax returns. If I don't offer cash payments or gifts to my customers in government offices overseas, then my competitors from other countries will. Foreign customers will just buy from my competitors. If I don't pay, I'd just be giving my competitors a 'corruption advantage.' And what difference does this make anyway? Why should my country care? I've heard about companies that gave cash payments to the Shah of Iran when he was in power in the 1970s, to his government ministers, even to members of his family. They got contracts worth tens and hundreds of millions of dollars to install everything—telecommunications systems, power plants, and refineries, and, most of all, armaments and weapons. I heard he was a brutal dictator, but so what? That's not my problem. I don't see what the problem is."

CHAPTER 3

Resolving International Commercial Disputes

AVOIDING BUSINESS DISPUTES

Long-term business relationships are generally the most profitable ones. Experienced executives and international managers know this, and they work very hard to foster them, at both the personal and organizational levels. Long-term relationships are based on trust. In a world where we do business with people who look, speak, and act differently from ourselves and who live and work oceans away, trust takes on a new and even more important significance. Indeed, it has been said that all of international business is based on trust. Any dispute that threatens the bonds of trust can threaten future business opportunities, do irreparable harm to individual and corporate reputations, and permanently damage long-term relationships. Moreover, when disputes become combative, it can be costly, time consuming, and physically and mentally exhausting for all parties. After all, there is the real possibility that one or both of the parties will have to litigate in a protracted and expensive trial in a foreign court, before a foreign judge, and in a foreign language, and have their rights determined under foreign procedural rules and possibly foreign law. Quite often the parties must retain attorneys in more than one country. So, when disagreements break out, amicable settlements are usually the best outcome and offer the best hope of salvaging a business relationship. It is always helpful if the parties have a reservoir of trust and goodwill that they can draw on to settle the dispute in a friendly way. But, of course, this is not always possible, and the prudent international businessperson, in any contract or any venture, will seek good legal advice and always "hope for the best and plan for the worst."

Nowhere is this more important than in negotiating and drafting business contracts. The contract is the basis of any bargain and its importance cannot be overstated. If and when a dispute arises, the terms of the contract provide the basis for dispute resolution.

Cultural Attitudes toward Disputes

Keep in mind that cultural factors will influence a party's attitude toward how disputes are settled. Americans are notorious litigators, quickly turning to the courts to redress grievances. Their combative stance can result in a "win or lose" mentality. On the other hand, Asians are notable for going to great lengths to seek an amicable settlement. After all, by tradition, it is a virtue to seek harmony and a vice to seek discord. These differences are evident in the way American and Japanese businesspeople approach contract or business negotiations. It is quite common for Americans to include their attorney or corporate counsel as a member of the negotiating team. Indeed, many Western managers and executives would never dream of it being any other way. But to the Japanese, this may seem a little confrontational, a little unnecessary, and a bad omen or a sign that disagreement is inevitable.

All too often, Americans view the negotiating process as something to be gotten out of the way so the deal can be closed, the contract signed, and all can go back home. People of many other cultures, from Asia to Latin America, might see the negotiating process as a time to build a relationship and new friendships. Of course, these attitudes differ throughout the world, and from country to country, and no generalizations should be made. But one thing is certain, and that is that the rest of the world views Americans as confrontational and quick to call in the lawyers. Perhaps the words of the English Lord Denning best sum up the foreign view:

> As the moth drawn to the light, so is a litigant drawn to the United States. If he can only get his case into their courts, he stands to win a fortune. At no cost to himself; and at no risk of having to pay anything to the other side ... The lawyers will charge the litigant nothing for their services but instead they will take forty percent of the damages ... If they lose, the litigant will have nothing to pay to the other side. The courts in the United States have no such cost deterrents as we have. There is also in the United States a

right to trial by jury. These are prone to award fabulous damages. They are notoriously sympathetic and know that the lawyers will take their forty percent before the plaintiff gets anything. All this means that the defendant can be readily forced into a settlement. Smith Kline and French Laboratories v. Bloch, [1983] 1 W.L.R. 730, 733-4 (Eng. C.A.).

The resolution of disputes between citizens of different countries, with business transactions that span continents and cultures, raises many complicated legal and tactical problems. Consider a dispute involving an American manufacturer that purchases thousands of meters of cloth from a Chinese supplier. The cloth is shipped to Vietnam where the manufacturer contracted to have it embroidered and sewn into pillow shams. When the finished goods arrive in the United States, it is discovered that they are damaged. Apparently the fabric was shipped from China in a defective condition, but the Vietnamese firm failed to inspect for damage as it normally did. The Chinese company claims that the time for bringing the defective fabric to its attention has long passed. The Vietnamese company says it was not its responsibility. Consider all the questions presented. To whom does the manufacturer look for remuneration? Is the relationship between the parties worth keeping, and is the case capable of being settled or should the manufacturer "take the gloves off?" Was there a contract with either party and did it specify the method of resolution, such as mediation, arbitration, or litigation, and, if so, where and under what law? If the contract does not specify, what legal rules apply to determine where the case should be heard and what law should govern? Finally, if a judgment is obtained through litigation, how will it be enforced across international borders? These are some of the questions we will discuss in this chapter.

Methods of Resolution

This chapter presents several alternatives for dispute resolution, including mediation, arbitration, and litigation. Consider a domestic dispute in which a New York supplier tries to sue a Texas distributor. This situation raises several questions: Should the parties settle, mediate, arbitrate, or litigate? Where should the dispute be heard—in New York or Texas? In federal or state court? Which law applies to the transaction—the law of New York, Texas, or some other jurisdiction? Finally, if a resolution is reached (be it a settlement, a verdict, or a judgment), how will it be enforced?

Changing the parties to an American supplier and a foreign distributor adds several dimensions to the problem. Many of the same questions that are relevant to a domestic dispute are equally relevant to an international dispute, but they become infinitely more complex. This chapter examines these questions as they apply to commercial disputes in international business.

ALTERNATIVE DISPUTE RESOLUTION

Alternative dispute resolution (ADR) usually offers a faster, cheaper, and more efficient alternative to resolving international commercial disputes than litigation. Unlike litigation, ADR requires that the parties voluntarily submit to the resolution process.

Mediation

Mediation is a voluntary, nonbinding, conciliation process. The parties agree on an impartial mediator who helps them reach a solution amicably. The final decision to settle rests with the parties themselves. It is private, and there are no public court records or glaring articles in the local press to influence local opinion about the firms. The parties reserve all legal rights to resort to binding arbitration or litigation.

Arbitration

Arbitration is a more formalized process resulting in a binding award that the courts of law in many countries will enforce. The parties must agree to arbitration, and once they do, they may not withdraw. Arbitration is frequently used in international business because it "levels the playing field" since the case may be heard in a more impartial tribunal. First, arbitration may permit the resolution of the case in a third "neutral" country, rather than in the country of one of the parties. The parties are generally free to choose a location for arbitration that is mutually convenient. For example, a dispute between an American company and a Russian company might be arbitrated in Paris or Stockholm. Disputes between American companies and Chinese companies are often arbitrated in Hong Kong. (Not only is Hong

Exhibit 3.1

Some Arbitration Treaties in Force Worldwide

Arab Convention on Commercial Arbitration (1987)

Convention on the Recognition and Enforcement of Foreign Arbitral Awards (New York Convention, 1959)

Convention on the Settlement of Investment Disputes Between States and Nationals of Other States (Washington Convention, 1966)

European Convention Providing a Uniform Law on Arbitration (Strasbourg Convention, 1966)

Geneva Protocol on Arbitration Clauses (1923)

Geneva Convention on the Execution of Foreign Arbitral Awards (1927)

Inter-American Convention on International Commercial Arbitration (Organization of American States, Panama Convention, 1975)

Kong still considered a neutral site, but its awards are enforceable by the courts of both the United States and China.) Secondly, the arbitrator may be chosen by the parties from a roster of impartial industry experts or distinguished lawyers, who may also be from a third country. Finally, the case may be resolved using the impartial and straightforward rules of the arbitrating organization, rather than the procedures buried in the statutes or rules of a court of the country of one of the parties. **Arbitration rules** are the rules of arbitral tribunals that address issues such as the qualification and appointment of arbitrators, the conduct of proceedings, procedures for finding the facts and applying the law, and the making of awards. These rules are often published in multiple languages.

There are other advantages to arbitration besides neutrality. Pretrial discovery is faster and more limited than that available in the United States, resulting in less expense and delay. The process is private and records of proceedings are not publicly available as are court records. Arbitration and attorney fees are far less than similar fees in a court of law. The rules for evidence admissibility are more flexible than in many national courts. And finally, a party's right to appeal is more limited.

Although parties can always agree to arbitration, a requirement to submit to arbitration is often set out in many international contracts. Contracts for the sale of goods, commodities, or raw materials might include arbitration clauses. International shipping contracts, employment contracts, international construction contracts, financing agreements, and cruise ship tickets, to name a few, as well as in multimillion- or billion-dollar contracts may also use them Today, arbitration helps to resolve disputes over intellectual property and licensing agreements.

Despite its reputation for being less costly than litigation, arbitration is not cheap. The International Chamber of Commerce (ICC) estimates that for a $1 million claim before its International Court of Arbitration in Paris, the average arbitrator's fee is $39,378, plus $21,715 in administrative expenses, for a total of $61,094 in costs—or about 6 percent. For a $100,000 claim, the average arbitrator's fee is $10,060, plus $5,365 in administrative expenses, for a total of $15,424 in costs—or about 15 percent.

There are other disadvantages to arbitration in addition to cost:

- The losing party in an arbitration has a limited right to appeal the decision, which is usually reserved for rare cases involving misconduct or fraud by the arbitrator or the arbitrator exceeding his or her authority or refusing to consider material evidence.
- Discovery is limited in arbitration proceedings, and parties may proceed to an arbitration hearing without full awareness of the other side's case or all of the facts.
- Relaxed procedural rules may permit the admission of evidence that would otherwise be excluded from consideration in a court of law.
- As previously mentioned, the widespread use of arbitration clauses in contracts may result in the limitation of the right to initiate litigation for an unwary party who has not carefully read the agreement.
- Less sophisticated parties may also be at a disadvantage in such circumstances due to limited experience in the selection of an arbitrator.
- Finally, there is no precedential value to an arbitrator's decision meaning that it cannot be relied upon in future proceedings to the same extent as judicial opinions.

National Arbitral Laws. Most commercial nations today have laws permitting arbitration and specifying the effect of an arbitral award (see Exhibit 3.1). The *British Arbitration Act* went into effect in 1996. The *Arbitration Law of the People's Republic of China,* which became effective in 1994, provides that arbitrators must have eight years' prior legal experience. The Russian arbitration law, which was enacted in 1993, provides that arbitration may be conducted in Russia in any language agreed upon by the parties. The laws of many countries, such as China, Russia, Mexico, and Canada, were patterned after the *1985 Model Law on International Commercial Arbitration* of the United Nations' Commission on International Trade Law (UNCITRAL). The U.S. *Federal Arbitration Act* dates back to 1925, but it has been modernized; it applies to both domestic and international arbitration and defers to the specific procedural rules of the arbitral body conducting the arbitration proceedings. Many U.S. states (e.g., California, Connecticut, Illinois, Oregon, and Texas) have enacted statutes on international commercial arbitration, some patterned after the UNCITRAL model.

Arbitration Bodies. Many organizations worldwide provide arbitral services. The choice is up to the parties, and this is often decided in advance and set out in the terms of the contract. Some leading private organizations for arbitration of commercial disputes include:

- American Arbitration Association
- Arbitration Institute of the Stockholm Chamber of Commerce
- Cairo Regional Center for International Commercial Arbitration
- China International Economic and Trade Arbitration Commission
- Dubai International Arbitration Center
- Hong Kong International Arbitration Centre
- International Court of Arbitration of the International Chamber of Commerce (ICC)
- Japan Commercial Arbitration Association
- London Court of Arbitration
- St. Petersburg International Commercial Arbitration Court
- Singapore International Arbitration Centre
- World Intellectual Property Organization (WIPO) Arbitration and Mediation Center

Two additional organizations provide dispute resolution between private parties and national governments:

- The *International Centre for the Settlement of Investment Disputes* (ICSID), a part of the World Bank group, provides arbitration for the settlement of disputes between member countries and investors who qualify as nationals of other member countries.
- The *Permanent Court of Arbitration at The Hague* provides arbitral services for commercial disputes to states, private parties, and intergovernmental organizations, including handling mass claims and environmental disputes where one of the parties is a national government.

Each of these organizations operates under a different set of procedural rules. The ICC uses its own, highly respected rules. Many other arbitral bodies use the widely accepted rules drafted by UNCITRAL, which take into account the various legal systems and countries in which they might be used. The Hong Kong Arbitration Center, WIPO, and other organizations throughout the world, for example, use the UNCITRAL rules.

Arbitration Clauses. Many contracts contain clauses requiring that disputes be submitted for arbitration because doing so removes much of the uncertainty in the event of a breach of contract or other dispute. Here is a typical example:

> All disputes or claims arising out of this contract, or breach thereof, shall be resolved by arbitration before [name of arbitral body], and according to the rules of that body. Any award rendered thereby may be entered in any court of competent jurisdiction.

While the validity of these clauses is now generally accepted, that was not always clear. In the following case, *Scherk v. Alberto-Culver,* the U.S. Supreme Court considered an arbitration clause in an international contract calling for arbitration in Paris.

Enforcement of Arbitration Awards. The courts of most nations recognize and enforce arbitral awards. In the United States, for example, an arbitral award will usually be enforced if the following conditions are met:

- The award is enforceable under the local law of the country where the award was made.
- The defendant was properly subject to the jurisdiction of the arbitral tribunal.
- The defendant was given notice of the arbitration proceeding and an opportunity to be heard.
- Enforcement of the award is not contrary to public policy.
- The subject matter of the contract at issue is not unlawful under applicable law.
- The contract at issue is not void for reasons of fraud or the incapacity of one of the parties.

Scherk v. Alberto-Culver

417 U.S. 506 (1974) United States Supreme Court

BACKGROUND AND FACTS

Alberto-Culver Co., a Delaware corporation with its principal office in Illinois, manufactured toiletries and hair products in the United States and abroad. In February 1969, Alberto-Culver signed a contract in Austria to purchase three businesses of Fritz Scherk (a German citizen) that were organized under German and Liechtenstein law, as well as the trademarks to related cosmetics. In the contract, Scherk warranted that he had the sole and unencumbered ownership of these trademarks. The contract also contained a clause that provided that "any controversy or claim [that] shall a rise out of this agreement or the breach thereof would be referred to arbitration before the International Chamber of Commerce in Paris, France, and that the laws of Illinois shall govern." One year after the closing, Alberto-Culver discovered that others had claims to Scherk's trademarks. Alberto-Culver tried to rescind the contract; Scherk refused, and Alberto-Culver filed suit in federal court in Illinois claiming that the misrepresentations violated the Securities and Exchange Act, Sec. 10(b), and SEC rule 10b-5. Scherk moved to dismiss or to stay the action pending arbitration. In the U.S. District Court, the motion to dismiss was denied and arbitration was enjoined. The U.S. Court of Appeals affirmed. The U.S. Supreme Court granted certiorari.

JUSTICE STEWART

The United States Arbitration Act, *now* 9 U.S.C. 1 et seq., reversing centuries of judicial hostility to arbitration agreements, was designed to allow parties to avoid "the costliness and delays of litigation," and to place arbitration agreements "upon the same footing as other contracts ... "

Alberto-Culver's contract to purchase the business entities belonging to Scherk was a truly international agreement. Alberto-Culver is an American corporation with its principal place of business and the vast bulk of its activity in this country, while Scherk is a citizen of Germany whose companies were organized under the laws of Germany and Liechtenstein. The negotiations leading to the signing of the contract in Austria and to the closing in Switzerland took place in the United States, England, and Germany, and involved consultations with legal and trademark experts from each of those countries and from Liechtenstein. Finally, and most significantly, the subject matter of the contract concerned the sale of business enterprises organized under the laws of and primarily situated in European countries, whose activities were largely, if not entirely, directed to European markets.

Such a contract involves considerations and policies significantly different from those found controlling in *Wilko v. Swan* [citation omitted]. In *Wilko,* quite apart from the arbitration provision, there was no question but that the laws of the United States generally, and the federal securities laws in particular, would govern disputes arising out of the stock-purchase agreement. The parties, the negotiations, and the subject matter of the contract were all situated in this country, and no credible claim could have been entertained that any international conflict-of-laws problems would arise. In this case, by contrast, in the absence of the arbitration provision considerable uncertainty existed at the time of the agreement, and still exists, concerning the law applicable to the resolutions of disputes arising out of the contract.

Such uncertainty will almost inevitably exist with respect to any contract touching two or more countries, each with its own substantive laws and conflict-of-laws rules. A contractual provision specifying in advance the forum in which disputes shall be litigated and the law to be applied is, therefore, an almost indispensable precondition to achievement of the orderliness and predictability essential to any international business transaction. Furthermore, such a provision obviates the danger that a dispute under the agreement might be submitted to a forum hostile to the interests of one of the parties or unfamiliar with the problem involved.

A parochial refusal by the courts of one country to enforce an international arbitration agreement would not only frustrate these purposes, but would invite unseemly and mutually destructive jockeying by the parties to secure tactical litigation advantages. In the present case, for example, it is not inconceivable that if Scherk had anticipated that Alberto-Culver would be able in this country to enjoin resort to arbitration he might have sought an order in France or some other country enjoining Alberto-Culver from proceeding with its litigation in the United States. Whatever recognition the courts of this country might ultimately have granted to the order of the foreign court, the dicey atmosphere of such a legal no-man's-land would surely damage the fabric of international commerce and trade, and imperil the willingness and ability of businessmen to enter into international commercial agreements ...

continues

continued

For all these reasons we hold that the agreement of the parties in this case to arbitrate any dispute arising out of their international commercial transaction is to be respected and enforced by the federal courts in accord with the explicit provisions of the Arbitration Act.

Decision. Reversed and remanded.

Comment. The Court understood that an arbitration agreement was the ultimate type of forum selection clause. The Court made reference to national legislation that indicated an acceptance of arbitration (the Arbitration Act, 9 U.S.C 1 et. seq.). Other countries have similar national legislation or are signatories to the New York Convention and/or the European Convention on International Arbitration.

Case Questions

1. What were the Court's reasons for upholding the arbitration provision?
2. What needs of international businesses were served by the Court's holding? How were these needs addressed?
3. What factors would Alberto-Culver need to have shown in order to have overturned the arbitration provision?

More than 140 nations have signed the *1958 United Nations Convention on the Recognition and Enforcement of Foreign Arbitral Awards,* known as the *New York Convention,* further strengthening the ability to enforce awards in those countries. The New York Convention requires that an arbitral award made in one country be honored and enforced by the courts of another country, where both countries are parties to the convention. The award will be enforced unless one of the defenses listed above exists or if the original award has been set aside or suspended by a court in the country in which it was made.

LITIGATION

Litigation in a court of law is the final alternative for resolving a dispute. It is used more frequently in the United States than in virtually any other country. Many countries have different procedural rules for litigating cases. First, many concepts familiar to American and English students, such as trial by jury and other traditions, may not be used in the civil law countries. While we take jury trials in criminal and civil cases almost for granted in the United States, the same is not true throughout the world. The role of the judge may be very different; in some countries, the judge is an impartial arbiter of fairness and procedure, while in other countries, he or she may examine witnesses and take an active role in the search for the truth. The discovery process, by which the parties attempt to uncover evidence in advance of trial, can also be different. For instance, oral depositions taken under oath outside of court may be routine in the United States, while China and some other countries prohibit their use. There are different rules for compensating lawyers; in the United States, for instance, contingent fees are widely used in tort cases, while in other countries, they are barred. The entire issue of damages is frequently handled differently. Finally, many countries handle appeals differently, with some, like the United States, limiting appeals to reconsidering issues of law applied by the trial courts. In other countries, appellate courts will consider new or additional evidence.

There can also be many differences in substantive law ("the law of the case"), although this topic is too broad for this chapter. Suffice it to say that almost every body of law—contracts, torts, crimes, property, business regulation, intellectual property, and so forth—can vary from legal system to legal system and country to country. This has a tremendous impact on the outcome of litigation. Certainly, parties to a contract can have some control over the choice of substantive law and procedural rules by incorporating a *choice of law clause* in the contracts. They may also have control over where the litigation takes place by using a forum selection clause in the contract. Keep these critical issues in mind as you read on.

Jurisdiction

Jurisdiction, one of the key concepts of jurisprudence, is the power of a court to hear and decide a case. A court that has jurisdiction is said to be a "competent" court. The term has different meanings depending on how it is used. For example, **territorial jurisdiction** refers to the power of criminal courts to hear cases involving crimes committed within their territory.

In rem jurisdiction refers to a court's power over property within its geographical boundaries. **Subject matter jurisdiction** refers to the court's authority to hear a certain type of legal matter, such as tort cases or breach of contract. In the United States, for example, federal courts have subject matter jurisdiction over cases involving federal statutes and federal government agencies, constitutional issues, and cases arising between citizens of different states or between citizens of the United States and citizens of foreign countries (where the amount in controversy exceeds $75,000). The latter is known as **diversity jurisdiction**. Thus, we see that there are many different uses for the term "jurisdiction." But one thing is certain, without it, courts are powerless to act.

In Personam Jurisdiction. **In personam jurisdiction** or "jurisdiction over the person" refers to the court's power over a certain individual or corporation. No party can be made to appear before a court unless that court has personal jurisdiction. If there is no personal jurisdiction, the case will be dismissed upon the defendant's motion. Typically, jurisdiction is obtained by having a summons served on an individual or on the legal agent of a corporation. In certain types of cases, service over those not present in the territory can be done by registered mail or even through publication in the "legal notices" section of approved newspapers. In the United States, the Due Process Clauses of the 5th and 14th Amendments to the U.S. Constitution require obtaining service of process on a defendant in a case, and of having jurisdiction over them. The method used must be authorized by statute and be fundamentally fair. The basic concept is that one should not be "hauled into court" in some distant state or country unless that person has some connection to that place.

Requirement for In Personam Jurisdiction: Minimum Contacts. At one time in U.S. legal history, the U.S. Supreme Court had interpreted the Due Process Clause to limit personal jurisdiction to people physically present in the court's territory. As the nation grew and as interstate commerce expanded, the concept was broadened to allow jurisdiction over persons who were not present within the court's geographical territory, but who, for reasons of justice and fairness, should be held to answer a complaint there. A modern example is a state "implied consent" statute, by which one operating a motor vehicle on the highways of a state "impliedly consents" to submitting to the jurisdiction of the courts of that state for all suits arising out of the operation of the vehicle there.

The due process requirements for *in personam* jurisdiction over persons absent from a state or territory have been carefully considered by the courts. In the now famous language of U.S. Supreme Court decisions dealing with both interstate and international commerce, "due process requires only that in order to subject a defendant to a judgment *in personam,* if he be not present within the territory of the forum, he have certain minimum contacts with it such that the maintenance of the suit does not offend traditional notions of fair play and substantial justice." *International Shoe Co. v. Washington,* 326 U.S. 310 (1945).

Just how much of a connection to a foreign state or country does it take for the courts to require one to defend a case there? The courts answer the question on a case-by-case basis, looking to see whether it would be fair to ask a nonresident to come to their jurisdiction to defend a case. The courts look at many factors, including the extent of the defendant's presence in the state, what business he or she may have conducted there, the burden on the defendant, fairness to the plaintiff, and the interest of the state in having the case resolved there. Did the defendant have an office, branch location, or salespeople in the territory of the forum? Did any of its employees or agents travel there on business? Did it advertise or otherwise solicit business there? Did it ship goods there? Did it enter into a contract there, or was the contract to be performed there? In *Worldwide Volkswagen Corp. v. Woodson,* 444 U.S. 286 (1980), the U.S. Supreme Court stated that a New York automobile distributor was not required to appear in Oklahoma to defend a products liability suit based on the sale of a vehicle that took place in New York and was later involved in a serious accident in Oklahoma.

> Petitioners carry on no activity whatsoever in Oklahoma. They close no sales and perform no services there. They avail themselves of none of the privileges and benefits of Oklahoma law. They solicit no business there either through salespersons or through advertising reasonably calculated to reach the State. Nor does the record show that they regularly sell cars at wholesale or retail to Oklahoma customers or residents or that they indirectly, through others, serve or seek to serve the Oklahoma market. In short, respondents seek to base jurisdiction on one, isolated occurrence and whatever inferences can be drawn therefrom: the fortuitous circumstance that a single Audi automobile, sold in New York to New York residents, happened to suffer an accident while passing through Oklahoma.

A similar concept exists in the international context. The following case, *Asahi Metal Ind. v. Superior Ct. of California,* questions whether a Japanese manufacturing company should be forced to defend a lawsuit in California for an accident that occurred there. As you read, keep in mind that these cases are resolved on a case-by-case basis after a consideration of all of the facts. A decision on jurisdiction may depend on one or more different factors not present in other cases. In other words, it is very difficult for lawyers to counsel whether your actions will or will not subject you to a foreign court's jurisdiction sometime in the future. In reading this case, think about what factors, if they had been present, might have forced Asahi to appear in court in California.

Asahi Metal Industry, Co. v. Superior Court of California, Solano County

480 U.S. 102 (1987) United States Supreme Court

BACKGROUND AND FACTS

Asahi Metal Industry, a Japanese corporation, manufactured valve assemblies in Japan and sold them to tire manufacturers including Cheng Shin (a Taiwanese corporation) from 1978–1982. Cheng Shin sold tires all over the world, including in California. On September 23, 1978, in Solano County, California, Gary Zurcher was injured riding his motorcycle. His wife was killed. He filed a products liability action against Cheng Shin, the manufacturer of his motorcycle's tires, alleging that the tires were defective. Cheng Shin filed a cross-complaint seeking indemnification from Asahi. Cheng Shin settled with Zurcher. However, Cheng Shin pressed its action against Asahi. The California Supreme Court held that California state courts possessed personal jurisdiction over Asahi, and Asahi sought review by the U.S. Supreme Court. The case presented the question of whether a dispute between a Taiwanese company and a Japanese company with the above-described relationship to California should be heard by the California courts. In other words, did the California courts have personal jurisdiction over Asahi?

JUSTICE O'CONNOR

The placement of a product into the stream of commerce, without more, is not an act of the defendant purposefully directed toward the forum State. Additional conduct of the defendant may indicate an intent or purpose to serve the market in the forum State, for example, designing the product for the market in the forum State, advertising in the forum State, establishing channels for providing regular advice to customers in the forum State, or marketing the product through a distributor who has agreed to serve as the sales agent in the forum State. But a defendant's awareness that the stream of commerce may or will sweep the product into the forum State does not convert the mere act of placing the product into the stream into an act purposefully directed toward the forum State.

Assuming, *arguendo,* that respondents have established Asahi's awareness that some of the valves sold to Cheng Shin would be incorporated into tire tubes sold in California, respondents have not demonstrated any action by Asahi to purposefully avail itself of the California market. It has no office, agents, employees, or property in California. It does not advertise or otherwise solicit business in California. It did not create, control, or employ the distribution system that brought its valves to California. There is no evidence that Asahi designed its product in anticipation of sales in California. On the basis of these facts, the exertion of personal jurisdiction over Asahi by the Superior Court of California exceeds the limits of due process.

The strictures of the Due Process Clause forbid a state court from exercising personal jurisdiction over Asahi under circumstances that would offend "traditional notions of fair play and substantial justice." *International Shoe Co. v. Washington,* 326 U.S. 310, 316 (1945), quoting *Milliken v. Meyer,* 311 457, 463 (1940).

We have previously explained that the determination of the reasonableness of the exercise of jurisdiction in each case will depend on an evaluation of several factors ...

Certainly the burden on the defendant in this case is severe. Asahi has been commanded by the Supreme Court of California not only to traverse the distance between Asahi's headquarters in Japan and the Superior Court of California in and for the County of Solano, but also to submit its dispute with Cheng Shin to a foreign nation's judicial system. The unique burdens placed upon one who must defend oneself in a foreign

continues

continued

legal system should have significant weight in assessing the reasonableness of stretching the long arm of personal jurisdiction over national borders.

When minimum contacts have been established, often the interests of the plaintiff and the forum in the exercise of jurisdiction will justify even the serious burdens placed on the alien defendant. In the present case, however, the interests of the plaintiff and the forum in California's assertion of jurisdiction over Asahi are slight. All that remains is a claim for indemnification asserted by Cheng Shin, a Taiwanese corporation, against Asahi. The transaction on which the indemnification claim is based took place in Taiwan; Asahi's components were shipped from Japan to Taiwan. Cheng Shin has not demonstrated that it is more convenient for it to litigate its indemnification claim against Asahi in California rather than in Taiwan or Japan.

Because the plaintiff is not a California resident, California's legitimate interests in the dispute have considerably diminished. The Supreme Court of California argued that the State had an interest in "protecting its consumers by ensuring that foreign manufacturers comply with the state's safety standards."...The State Supreme Court's definition of California's interest, however, was overly broad. The dispute between Cheng Shin and Asahi is primarily about indemnification rather than safety. Moreover, it is not at all clear at this point that California law should govern the question whether a Japanese corporation should indemnify a Taiwanese corporation on the basis of a sale made in Taiwan and a shipment of goods from Japan to Taiwan.

Considering the international context, the heavy burden on the alien defendant, and the slight interests of the plaintiff and the forum State, the exercise of personal jurisdiction by a California court over Asahi in this instance would be unreasonable and unfair.

Because the facts of this case do not establish minimum contacts such that the exercise of personal jurisdiction is consistent with fair play and substantial justice, the judgment of Supreme Court of California is reversed, and the case is remanded for further proceedings not inconsistent with this opinion.

It is so ordered.

Decision. The U.S. Supreme Court reversed the California Supreme Court and found that there was no jurisdiction. This Supreme Court case is significant because it lists several factors that will be taken into account in determining whether a court has personal jurisdiction.

Case Questions

1. Why did the Court refuse to hold that the California courts had personal jurisdiction over Asahi?
2. In what activities would Asahi need to have engaged in order for the Court to determine that it had purposefully availed itself of California law? Are some of these activities more important than others? If so, which ones?
3. Did the Court give adequate weight to California's interest in the safety of products distributed in the state? Why or why not?

Jurisdiction in the European Union. Jurisdiction in civil and commercial cases between parties domiciled in two or more European Union (EU) countries is determined by EU *Council Regulation No. 44/2001.* This law became effective in 2002 and replaced the 1968 *Brussels Convention on Jurisdiction and the Enforcement of Judgments in Civil and Commercial Matters.* The general rule is that jurisdiction is determined by the domicile of the defendant. The regulation states that "persons domiciled in a Member State shall, whatever their nationality, be sued in the courts of that Member State." Corporations are domiciled in the Member State (i.e., member country of the EU) where they are incorporated, where they have their primary administrative offices, or where they have their principal place of business.

There are several exceptions to this general rule:

1. Cases involving commercial contracts for the sale of goods within the EU will be heard in the country where the goods were or should have been delivered.
2. Cases involving a breach of contract for services (other than insurance or employment) within the EU will be heard where the services were or should have been provided.
3. Tort cases, such as an action arising out of an automobile accident, will be heard before the courts in the country where the wrong occurred.
4. In consumer contract cases, a consumer may bring an action against the other party to the contract either in the country in which that party is domiciled or in the country where the

consumer is domiciled. Lawsuits against a consumer to enforce the contract can only be brought in the courts of the consumer's home country.

5. An employer may sue its employee or former employee only in the employee's place of domicile. However, an employee may bring a lawsuit against an employer either in the country where the employee is domiciled; where the employer is domiciled, or, if not domiciled in the EU, where a branch or agent is located; or in the country where the employee regularly or last worked.
6. Where at least one of the parties is domiciled in the EU, by an agreement specifying the courts of a certain EU country, provided that the agreement is in written or electronic form, or in international cases, in a form that the parties should have known amounted to a forum selection.

Jurisdiction in China. Chinese courts may not exercise jurisdiction over non-resident defendants who are merely present in China. Rather, the non-resident defendant must have a meaningful connection to China which provides a "sufficient ground" warranting the exercise of the court's power. The *Civil Procedure Law of 1991* grants jurisdiction to Chinese courts based upon a non-resident defendant's conduct or property. For example, courts may exercise jurisdiction if a contract was concluded or performed in China. In such a circumstance, the Chinese court at the place of the contract or performance would possess jurisdiction over the parties. A non-resident defendant may be subject to personal jurisdiction if the subject matter of a claim is located in China, if the defendant has property in China or maintains a representative office in China. An additional "sufficient ground" for exercising personal jurisdiction is if the non-resident defendant committed a tort in China.

Jurisdiction in the Internet Age. As electronic commerce brings the world closer together, there will likely be more disputes between parties in distant countries. How will the courts fashion rules for deciding when a party must defend itself against litigation in foreign courts? Just as the meaning of "minimum contacts" adapted to the rise of interstate commerce in the United States over 60 years ago, it is now adapting to the rise of the Internet age. The following case, *Pebble Beach Company v. Caddy,* involves trademark infringement and dilution and demonstrates the challenges litigants and courts confront in determining whether and under what circumstances a presence on the Internet subjects a defendant to personal jurisdiction.

Pebble Beach Company v. Caddy

453 F.3d 1151 (2006) United States Court of Appeals (9th Cir.)

BACKGROUND AND FACTS

Plaintiff Pebble Beach Company (Pebble Beach) is a well-known golf course and resort located in Monterey County, California. The golf resort has used "Pebble Beach" as its trade name since 1956. Pebble Beach contended that the trade name has acquired secondary meaning in the United States and the United Kingdom. Pebble Beach operates a website located at www.pebblebeach.com. Defendant Caddy ran a three-room bed and breakfast, restaurant, and bar located in southern England. Caddy's business operation was located on a cliff overlooking the pebbly beaches of England's south shore, in a town called Barton-on-Sea. The name of Caddy's operation was "Pebble Beach." Caddy advertised his services, which did not include a golf course, at his website, www.pebblebeach-uk.com. Caddy's website included information about the accommodations he provided, including lodging rates in pounds sterling, a menu, and a wine list. The website was not interactive. It did not have a reservation system and did not allow potential guests to book rooms or pay for services online. Visitors to the website who had questions about Caddy's services were required to fill out an online inquiry form. Pebble Beach sued Caddy for infringement and dilution of its "Pebble Beach" trademark in the United States District Court for the Central District of California. Caddy moved to dismiss the complaint for lack of personal jurisdiction. The district court granted Caddy's motion, and Pebble Beach appealed to the United States Court of Appeals for the Ninth

TROTT, NINTH CIRCUIT JUDGE

The general rule is that personal jurisdiction over a defendant is proper if it is permitted by a long-arm statute and if the exercise of that jurisdiction does not

continues

continued

violate federal due process ... For due process to be satisfied, a defendant, if not present in the forum, must have "minimum contacts" with the forum state such that the assertion of jurisdiction "does not offend traditional notions of fair play and substantial justice." *Int'l Shoe Co. v. Washington*, 326 U.S. 310, 315, 66 S. Ct. 154, 90 L. Ed. 95 (1945).

In this circuit, we employ the following three-part test to analyze whether a party's "minimum contacts" meet the Supreme Court's directive. This "minimum contacts" test is satisfied when (1) the defendant has performed some act or consummated some transaction within the forum or otherwise purposefully availed himself of the privileges of conducting activities in the forum, (2) the claim arises out of or results from the defendant's forum-related activities, and (3) the exercise of jurisdiction is reasonable.

Bancroft & Masters, Inc. v. Augusta Nat'l Inc., 223 F.3d 1082, 1086 (9th Cir. 2000).

* * *

In order to satisfy the first prong of the "minimum contacts" test, Pebble Beach must establish either that Caddy (1) purposefully availed himself of the privilege of conducting activities in California, or the United States as a whole, or (2) that he purposefully directed its activities toward one of those two forums.

Pebble Beach fails to identify any conduct by Caddy that took place in California or in the United States that adequately supports the availment concept. Evidence of availment is typically action taking place in the forum that invokes the benefits and protections of the laws in the forum. Evidence of direction generally consists of action taking place outside the forum that is directed at the forum. All of Caddy's action identified by Pebble Beach is action taking place outside the forum. Thus, if anything, it is the type of evidence that supports a purposeful direction analysis. Accordingly, we reject Pebble Beach's assertion that Caddy has availed himself of the jurisdiction of the district court ... and proceed only to determine whether Caddy has purposefully directed his action toward one of two applicable forums.

In *Calder v. Jones*, the Supreme Court held that a foreign act that is both aimed at and has effect in the forum satisfies the first prong of the specific jurisdiction analysis 465 U.S. 783, 104 S. Ct. 1482, 79 L. Ed. 2d 804 (1984). We have commonly referred to this holding as the "*Calder* effects test." To satisfy this test the defendant must have (1) committed an intentional act, which was (2) expressly aimed at the forum state, and (3) caused harm, the brunt of which is suffered and which the defendant knows is likely to be suffered in the forum state. However ... we have warned courts not to focus too narrowly on the test's third prong-the effects prong-holding that "something more" is needed in addition to a mere foreseeable effect. *Bancroft*, 223 F.3d at 1087... . Thus, the determinative question here is whether Caddy's actions were "something more"—precisely, whether his conduct was expressly aimed at California or alternatively the United States.

* * *

In support of its contention that Caddy has expressly aimed conduct at California, Pebble Beach ... asserts that Caddy's website and domain name are sufficient to satisfy the express aiming standard that it is required to meet. We disagree.

* * *

In *Rio Properties, Inc. v. Rio Int'l Interlink*, 284 F.3d 1007, 1020 (9th Cir. 2000), we cited *Cybersell, Inc. v. Cybersell, Inc.*, 130 F.3d 414, 418-20 (9th Cir. 1997), for the proposition that when a "website advertiser [does] nothing other than register a domain name and post an essentially passive website" and nothing else is done "to encourage residents of the forum state," there is no personal jurisdiction.... These cases establish two salient points. First, there can be no doubt that we still require "something more" than just a foreseeable effect to conclude that personal jurisdiction is proper. Second, an Internet domain name and passive website alone are not "something more," and, therefore, alone are not enough to subject a party to jurisdiction.

* * *

Even if Pebble Beach is unable to show purposeful direction as to California, Pebble Beach can still establish jurisdiction if Caddy purposefully directed his action at the United States.

* * *

Pebble Beach claims that because Caddy selected a ".com" domain name it shows that the United States was his "primary" market and that he is directly advertising his services to the United States. Second, Pebble Beach asserts that his selection of the name "Pebble Beach" shows the United States is his primary target because "Pebble Beach" is a famous United States trademark. Third, Pebble Beach asserts that Caddy's intent to advertise to the United States is bolstered by the fact that Caddy's facilities are located in a resort town that caters to foreigners, particularly Americans. Finally, Pebble Beach asserts that a majority of Caddy's business in the past has been with Americans.

Pebble Beach's arguments focus too much on the effects prong and not enough on the "something more" requirement. We conclude that the selection of

continues

continued

a particular domain name is insufficient by itself to confer jurisdiction over a non-resident defendant where the forum is the United States. The fact that the name "Pebble Beach" is a famous mark known worldwide is of little practical consequence when deciding whether action is directed at a particular forum via the world wide web. Also of minimal importance is Caddy's selection of a ".com" domain name instead of a more specific United Kingdom or European Union domain. To suggest that ".com" is an indicator of express aiming at the United States is even weaker than the counter assertion that having "U.K." in the domain name, which is the case here, is indicative that Caddy was only targeting his services to the United Kingdom. Neither provides much more than a slight indication of where a website may be located and does not establish to whom the website is directed.

This leaves Pebble Beach's arguments that because Caddy's business is located in an area frequented by Americans, and because he occasionally services Americans, jurisdiction is proper. These arguments fail for the same reasons; they go to effects rather than express aiming. Pebble Beach's arguments do have intuitive appeal-they suggest a real effect on Americans. However, as reiterated throughout this opinion, showing "effect" satisfies only the third prong of the *Calder* test—it is not the "something more" that is required... . The "something more" additional requirement is important simply because the effects cited may not have been caused by the defendant's actions of which the plaintiff complains. Here, although Caddy may serve vacationing Americans, there is not a scintilla of evidence indicating that this patronage is related to either Caddy's choice of a domain name or the posting of a passive website.

Decision. Caddy did not purposefully avail himself of U.S. law nor expressly aim his conduct at California or the United States. Therefore, he is not subject to the personal jurisdiction of the district court. A passive website and domain name alone do not satisfy the effects test, and there was no other action expressly aimed at California or the United States that would justify personal jurisdiction. Pebble Beach's complaint was properly dismissed.

Case Questions

1. On what basis did the court hold that Caddy had insufficient minimum contacts with the United States such as to support the exercise of personal jurisdiction?
2. Is the court's focus on the passivity of Caddy's website valid? What factors determine whether a website is interactive or passive?
3. Is the Internet sufficiently different from non-electronically based businesses to merit different treatment for purposes of jurisdiction? Why or why not?

Obtaining Jurisdiction by Service of Process. As we have learned, a court must have personal jurisdiction over individuals or corporate entities before they can be made to appear and defend a civil case. Personal jurisdiction is obtained through lawful service of process. Without proper service, any judgment that might be taken will not be enforceable. This is especially problematic when attempting to enforce a judgment internationally. To illustrate, imagine that an American plaintiff files suit in a U.S. court against a resident of France on a contract that was performed in the United States. Assume that the plaintiff's attorney is able to obtain service of process upon the defendant in France. The French citizen does not appear in the United States and a default judgment is entered. When the American attempts to enforce the U.S. judgment in the courts of France, the defendant will claim that the method of service of process upon him was unsatisfactory under French law. If the French courts agree, the plaintiff's judgment may be worth nothing if the defendant's only assets are in France. Thus, international lawyers trying to obtain jurisdiction over a foreign defendant are advised to consult an attorney in the defendant's country and to follow the requirements of both U.S. and French law to the letter.

Service of process upon a foreign defendant is addressed in *The Hague Convention on the Service Abroad of Judicial and Extra-judicial Documents in Civil or Commercial Matters,* in force in more than 60 countries. Authorized methods of service are different even for countries that are members of the treaty. Some countries permit service through the use of registered or certified mail, with a return receipt signed by the defendant being served, although other countries (e.g., Germany, Norway, Egypt, China, and others) do not permit this method. Some countries permit personal service by an agent or attorney of the plaintiff located in the defendant's country who signs an "affidavit of service" at a nearby U.S. embassy affirming that he or she has served the defendant with notice and a copy of the complaint. Most countries require the complaint to be in the local language as well as in English. Perhaps the safest method, but one that can cause very long delays (up to a year, according to the U.S. State Department), is a formal request for service made through a **letter rogatory** (a "letter of request" sent through diplomatic channels) that results in personal service on the defendant by the courts of the country in which he or she is found. Defendants located in countries not parties to this convention can also be served with process with a letter rogatory.

Venue

Jurisdiction is often confused with the concept of venue. **Venue** refers to the geographical location of a court of competent jurisdiction where a case can be heard. While the courts of several different states or countries may have proper jurisdiction, the concept of venue helps decide which one of these should actually hear the case. For instance, in some civil lawsuits between citizens of different states, we know that the federal courts may have jurisdiction. But in which federal districts should the suits be tried?

Imagine an automobile accident in which the passengers of one car are residents of Pennsylvania, while the driver of the other vehicle is a resident of North Carolina, and the accident occurs while they are both on vacation in California. We know that jurisdiction is proper in the federal courts (and it may also be proper in some state courts). But we certainly would not expect that the case could be tried in a federal court located in Montana. Federal rules generally permit the case to be heard where all of the plaintiffs reside, where all of the defendants reside, or where the cause of action arose. (In complex transnational litigation, it is not unusual that courts in several countries might attempt to exercise jurisdiction over the matter.) While typically the plaintiff will initially choose where to file its suit, it is not unusual for a defendant to request a change of venue, asking that the case be removed to a location that is more convenient and that has a closer connection to the facts of the particular case.

Forum Non Conveniens

The legal doctrine of ***forum non conveniens*** (meaning "inconvenient forum") refers to the discretionary power of a court to refuse to hear a case, even though jurisdiction and venue are otherwise proper, because a court in another jurisdiction or location would be more convenient and justice would be better served. According to this doctrine, whenever a case is properly heard in the courts of more than one jurisdiction, it should be heard in the jurisdiction that is more convenient and has the closer connection to the cause of action that led to the case. In deciding on where to hear a case, the courts will examine both "private factors" (factors affecting the convenience of the parties and their ability to pursue their claims) and "public factors" (factors related to the public interest). For example, it may be more convenient to hear a case where the action arose, where witnesses and evidence are located, where the parties reside, or in the state or country whose law applies to the case.

Imagine an airline disaster in the United States, with many plaintiffs and one airline. Jurisdiction may be proper in any number of locations, including the airline's principal place of business. But would it not be more convenient to hold the trial where the crash occurred? After all, that is where the wreckage is located, and where the controllers and other witnesses live and work. *Forum non conveniens* is applied by courts in the United States, as well as in many other countries. In the United States, it is applied by the federal courts in determining where to hear lawsuits between citizens of different states. It is also used in determining whether an international case should be heard by U.S. courts or by the courts of some other country. It is not unusual for one of the parties to a case to ask a court to transfer the case to another judicial district or location for reasons of convenience. The factors generally considered are described by the U.S. Supreme Court in *Gulf Oil v. Gilbert,* 330 U.S. 501 (1947).

> Important considerations are the relative ease of access to sources of proof; availability of compulsory process for attendance of unwilling [witnesses] and the cost of obtaining attendance of willing witnesses; ... and all other practical problems that make trial of a case easy, expeditious and inexpensive. There may also be questions as to the enforceability of a judgment if one is obtained ... It is often said that the plaintiff may not, by choice of an inconvenient forum, "vex," "harass," or "oppress" the defendant by inflicting upon him expense or trouble not necessary to his own right to pursue his remedy. But unless

> the balance is strongly in favor of the defendant, the plaintiff's choice of forum should rarely be disturbed ... There is a local interest in having localized controversies decided at home. There is an appropriateness, too, in having the trial of a diversity case in a forum that is at home with the state law that must govern the case, rather than having a court in some other forum untangle problems in conflict of laws, and in law foreign to itself.

Forum non Conveniens* in Action: *In re Union Carbide Gas Plant Disaster at Bhopal. After a chemical leak at a plant in Bhopal, India, killed almost 2,000 people, Indian citizens filed suit in the United States against Union Carbide. At one point, almost 145 legal actions on behalf of some 200,000 plaintiffs had been consolidated for trial in federal court in New York. However, the case was subsequently dismissed on the basis of *forum non conveniens* in favor of the case being heard in India. The judge gave many reasons for the decision: the Indian legal system was better able to determine the cause of accident and assign liability; the overwhelming majority of witnesses and evidence were in India; the records of plant design, safety procedures, and training were located in India; most records were not in English and many witnesses did not speak English; the court would be unable to compel witnesses to appear and the cost to transport them to the United States would be prohibitive; visits to the plant might be necessary; there was the likelihood that the U.S. court would have to apply Indian law (the tort law of the jurisdiction where the accident occurred); and the undue burden of this immense litigation would unfairly tax an American tribunal. Also considered was India's substantial interest in the accident and the outcome of the litigation: The Indian government and Indian citizens owned 49 percent of the plant, with Union Carbide owning the rest. As the judge expressed in the opinion:

> To retain litigation in this forum would be another example of imperialism, another situation in which an established sovereign inflicted its rules, its standards and values on a developing nation. This Court declines to play such a role. The Union of India is a world power in 1986, and its courts have the proven capacity to mete out fair and equal justice. To deprive the Indian judiciary of this opportunity to stand tall before the world and to pass judgment on behalf of its own people would be to revive a history of subservience and subjugation from which India has emerged. India and its people can and must vindicate their claims before the independent and legitimate judiciary created there since the Independence of 1947. This Court defers to the adequacy and ability of the courts of India. Their interest in the sad events ... in the City of Bhopal, State of Madhya Pradesh, Union of India, is not subject to question or challenge. *In re Union Carbide Gas Plant Disaster at Bhopal*, 634 F. Supp. 842, 867 (S.D.N.Y. 1986).

The case was settled in India prior to trial in 1989 when Union Carbide agreed to pay $470 million in compensation. In 2010, an Indian court convicted several former Union Carbide officers of crimes arising from the accident.

Forum Shopping. It is not unusual that requests to transfer on the basis of *forum non conveniens* are in truth attempts by counsel to "shop around" for a better legal deal. They may be looking for laws that are more favorable to their cases or for juries that might be more sympathetic to their sides. After all, in federal lawsuits between residents of different states, such as in tort cases, the federal courts apply the laws of the states in which they sit.

Although there are procedural rules that discourage "forum shopping," it still weighs on the minds of most trial lawyers. The same is true, perhaps even more so, in international cases which may involve several considerations. For example, there may be procedural reasons for forum shopping, such as the availability of a jury trial, class action procedures, and liberal discovery rules. The availability of property that may be readily attached may lead some litigants to select specific forums. Forum shopping may occur in order to avoid resolution of a dispute in a country where the judicial system suffers from a perceived lack of integrity. Provisions affecting the compensation of attorneys, such as the availability of contingent fees and awards of attorney's fees, may also encourage forum shopping.

A significant motivation for forum shopping is the perception that U.S. courts will be more likely to award larger amounts of damages to injured parties than courts in other countries. This perception is very strong in the area of **punitive damages**, which are designed to punish a defendant for particularly offensive behavior (such as intentional torts, fraud, and bad faith) and deter future misconduct. Punitive damages are recognized in other common law countries such as Australia, Canada, England, India, and New Zealand, although with different restrictions and in lesser amounts than may be awarded in the United States. The majority of the rest of the world's legal systems reject punitive damages. For example, as a matter of public policy Japanese courts do not award punitive damages and Japanese law prohibits the recognition of foreign judgments containing punitive awards. Like most civil law countries, France and Germany have long adhered to the traditional rule that prohibits awards of punitive damages in civil actions. The French Civil Code limits damages in civil actions to placing the injured party in the position it would have occupied had the defendant's conduct not occurred. German courts traditionally consider the prohibition on punitive damages to be a matter of fundamental public policy.

However, there has been a gradual move away from wholesale rejection of punitive damages in states whose legal systems derive from traditions other than common law. For example, in 2010, the French Cour de Cassation (French Supreme Court) refused to recognize a U.S. court judgment that awarded the plaintiffs $1.46 million in punitive damages. However, the basis for the decision was that the amount was disproportionate to the $1.39 million compensatory damages award rather than that punitive damage awards are contrary to French public policy. Also, recent German court judgments contain elements that are not purely compensatory in nature such as for claims of invasion of personal privacy and employment discrimination and for pain and suffering. Although Spanish courts do not award punitive damages in private actions, in 2001, the Tribunal Supremo enforced a Texas judgment that included treble damages arising from misuse of a U.S. trademark by a Spanish company.

Other countries limit punitive damages through statutes. Perhaps most importantly is the enactment of the People's Republic of China's *Tort Liability Law* in December 2009. Effective in July 2010, the law unifies tort law in numerous fields including product liability, environmental pollution, medical malpractice, and motor vehicle accidents. Of particular importance is the section devoted to product liability. In response to several tainted product scandals in the country, the new law permits an award of punitive damages against a manufacturer or seller who knows that a product is defective but nevertheless continues to manufacture or sell the product if such product subsequently results in death or serious physical injury to consumers. The law represents the first time that the term "punitive damages" officially appears in Chinese law. However, the method by which such damages are to be calculated and any limits on their amounts are undefined.

In the following case, *Iragorri v. United Technologies,* the appellate court had to decide whether a case for wrongful death should be heard in Connecticut or in Cali, Colombia. The plaintiffs wanted the case heard in Connecticut because, as one would expect, the possibility of winning a large damage award was much greater than in Colombia.

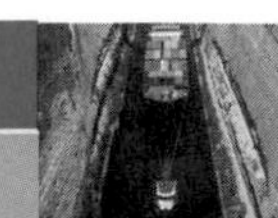

Iragorri v. United Technologies Corp. & Otis Elevator Co.

274 F. 3d 65 (2001) United States Court of Appeals (2d Cir.)

BACKGROUND AND FACTS

Iragorri and his family had been residents of Florida since 1981, and naturalized citizens of the United States since 1989. In 1993, while visiting his mother in Cali, Colombia, Iragorri fell to his death through an open elevator shaft. Iragorri's children had been attending school there as exchange students from their Florida high school. His surviving wife and children brought this action in U.S. District Court in Connecticut for damages against two American companies, Otis Elevator and its parent corporation, United Technologies. They alleged that employees of International Elevator had negligently wedged a door open with a screwdriver during repairs, leaving the shaft open. International Elevator was a Maine corporation doing business in South America. Both Otis and United had their principal place of business in Connecticut. The complaint alleged that Otis and United were liable because (1) International had acted as their agent in negligently repairing the elevator, and (2) Otis and United were liable under Connecticut's products liability statute for the defective design and manufacture of the elevator that had been sold and installed by their affiliate, Otis of Brazil. Otis and United moved to dismiss the case on the basis of

continues

continued

forum non conveniens, arguing that it should be heard in the Colombian courts. The U.S. District Court dismissed the case, and the plaintiffs brought this appeal.

OPINION BY PIERRE N. LEVAL AND JOSÉ A. CABRANES, CIRCUIT JUDGES FOR THE COURT SITTING EN BANC

We regard the Supreme Court's instructions that (1) a plaintiff's choice of her home forum should be given great deference, while (2) a foreign resident's choice of a U.S. forum should receive less consideration, as representing consistent applications of a broader principle under which the degree of deference to be given to a plaintiff's choice of forum moves on a sliding scale depending on several relevant considerations.

The Supreme Court explained in *Piper Aircraft Co. v. Reyno,* [citation omitted] that the reason we give deference to a plaintiff's choice of her home forum is because it is presumed to be convenient. ("When the home forum has been chosen, it is reasonable to assume that this choice is convenient.") In contrast, when a foreign plaintiff chooses a U.S. forum, it "is much less reasonable" to presume that the choice was made for convenience. In such circumstances, a plausible likelihood exists that the selection was made for forum-shopping reasons, such as the perception that United States courts award higher damages than are common in other countries. Even if the U.S. district was not chosen for such forum-shopping reasons, there is nonetheless little reason to assume that it is convenient for a foreign plaintiff.

Based on the Supreme Court's guidance, our understanding of how courts should address the degree of deference to be given to a plaintiff's choice of a U.S. forum is essentially as follows: The more it appears that a domestic or foreign plaintiff's choice of forum has been dictated by reasons that the law recognizes as valid, the greater the deference that will be given to the plaintiff's forum choice. Stated differently, the greater the plaintiff's or the lawsuit's bona fide connection to the United States and to the forum of choice and the more it appears that considerations of convenience favor the conduct of the lawsuit in the United States, the more difficult it will be for the defendant to gain dismissal for *forum non conveniens.* Thus, factors that argue against *forum non conveniens* dismissal include the convenience of the plaintiff's residence in relation to the chosen forum, the availability of witnesses or evidence to the forum district, the defendant's amenability to suit in the forum district, the availability of appropriate legal assistance, and other reasons relating to convenience or expense. On the other hand, the more it appears that the plaintiff's choice of a U.S. forum was motivated by forum-shopping reasons—such as attempts to win a tactical advantage resulting from local laws that favor the plaintiff's case, the habitual generosity of juries in the United States or in the forum district, the plaintiff's popularity or the defendant's unpopularity in the region, or the inconvenience and expense to the defendant resulting from litigation in that forum—the less deference the plaintiff's choice commands and, consequently, the easier it becomes for the defendant to succeed on a *forum non conveniens* motion by showing that convenience would be better served by litigating in another country's courts.

We believe that the District Court in the case before us, lacking the benefit of our most recent opinions concerning *forum non conveniens,* did not accord appropriate deference to the plaintiff's chosen forum. Although the plaintiffs had resided temporarily in Bogota at the time of Mauricio Iragorri's accident, it appears that they had returned to their permanent, long-time domicile in Florida by the time the suit was filed. The fact that the children and their mother had spent a few school terms in Colombia on a foreign exchange program seems to us to present little reason for discrediting the bona fides of their choice of the Connecticut forum. Heightened deference to the plaintiffs' chosen forum usually applies even where a plaintiff has temporarily or intermittently resided in the foreign jurisdiction. So far as the record reveals, there is little indication that the plaintiffs chose the defendants' principal place of business for forum-shopping reasons. Plaintiffs were apparently unable to obtain jurisdiction in Florida over the original third defendant, International, but could obtain jurisdiction overall three in Connecticut. It appears furthermore that witnesses and documentary evidence relevant to plaintiffs' defective design theory are to be found at the defendants' installations in Connecticut. As we have explained, "live testimony of key witnesses is necessary so that the trier of fact can assess the witnesses' demeanor." *Alfadda v. Fenn,* 159 F.3d 41, 48 (2d Cir. 1998). Also, in assessing where the greater convenience lies, the District Court must of course consider how great would be the inconvenience and difficulty imposed on the plaintiffs were they forced to litigate in Cali. Among other factors, plaintiffs claim that they fear for their safety in Cali and that various witnesses on both sides may be unwilling to travel to Cali; if these concerns are warranted, they appear highly relevant to the balancing inquiry that the District Court must conduct.

continues

continued

Decision. Remanded to the U.S. District Court for adetermination in accordance with this opinion. In deciding whether to hear the case, the district court should consider the degree of deference to which plaintiffs' choice is entitled, the hardships of litigating in Colombia versus the United States, and the public interest factors involved.

Case Questions

1. What were the court's reasons for refusing to apply *forum non conveniens* to this case and requiring refiling of the litigation in Colombia?
2. Does the court's opinion reward forum shopping to the extent the plaintiffs were likely to receive a larger damages award in the United States than in Colombia? Why or why not?
3. The court cited concern regarding the unstable political situation in Colombia as a reason for refusing to apply *forum non conveniens.* Given the changes that have occurred in the country in the past decade, would the court reach the same conclusion today?

Forum Selection Clauses

Businesspeople and lawyers negotiating international contracts can avoid much of the uncertainty over jurisdiction and venue by including a forum selection clause in their contracts. A **forum selection clause** is a provision in a contract that fixes in advance the jurisdiction in which any disputes will be arbitrated or litigated. It provides certainty because the parties know where and how a dispute will be resolved in the event of a breach. One of the major advantages of these clauses is that they eliminate the last-minute attempt by lawyers to go "forum shopping" by filing suits in jurisdictions that offer the best law for their cases. The last chance for forum shopping may very well be during contract negotiations. This allows both parties to agree on a forum, perhaps the courts of a certain country, which they find acceptable. Of course, the reality is that these clauses are often not open for negotiation at all—the party to the contract with the greatest bargaining power will simply include a fine print provision calling for disputes to be resolved in the courts of the country where it is located.

Historically, any attempt by private parties to control jurisdiction was viewed with hostility by the courts as an effort to usurp their authority. However, the realities of the international marketplace and the need to reduce uncertainty in a dispute have persuaded many courts to accept forum selection clauses. Today, they are generally accepted as valid provided that the forum chosen has some reasonable connection to the transaction. In the following case, *M/S Bremen v. Zapata,* the U.S. Supreme Court upheld a clause calling for disputes to be resolved before the English courts, noting that U.S. courts can no longer remain geocentric in light of modern-day international trade.

CONFLICT OF LAWS

As a general rule, courts apply the law in force in their jurisdictions to the cases before them. In the United States, state courts usually apply their own states' laws. Federal courts hearing **diversity of citizenship** cases, such as breach of contract or tort actions between residents of different states, generally apply the laws of the states in which they sit (unless a federal statute or treaty controls). But these are general rules only, and there are many cases where courts apply the laws of other states, or even of foreign countries. The term **conflict of laws** refers to the rules by which courts determine which jurisdiction's laws apply to a case and how to reconcile differences between laws. In turn, the choice of law ultimately determines whether a court has jurisdiction, the rights and liabilities of the parties, and how to enforce a judgment or monetary award.

The Restatement (Second) of the Conflict of Laws

Conflict of laws rules are some of the most complex in procedural law, with different jurisdictions following different rules. However, the concepts found in the *Restatement (Second) of the Conflict of Laws,* drafted under the auspices of the American Law Institute in 1971, provide a clear and widely accepted explanation of these rules. As a general rule, courts apply the law of the state, country, or jurisdiction that has the closest relationship to the action before them. The *Restatement (Second)* addresses different types of actions, including actions for breach of contract and for tort.

Contracts. It has been said that deciding which law governs a contract is like finding its "center of

M/S Bremen v. Zapata Off-Shore Co.

407 U.S. 1(1972) United States Supreme Court

BACKGROUND AND FACTS

In 1967, Zapata, a Houston-based corporation, entered into a contract with Unterweser, a German corporation, to tow Zapata's drilling rig from Louisiana to Ravenna, Italy. The contract the parties signed contained the clause "Any dispute arising must be heard before the London Court of Justice." During a storm, the rig was damaged, and Zapata instructed Unterweser's tug, the *Bremen,* to tow instead to Tampa, Florida, the nearest port. Immediately thereafter, Zapata filed suit in federal district court in Tampa, Florida, on the basis of admiralty jurisdiction, seeking $3,500,000 damages *in personam* against Unterweser and *in rem* against the *Bremen.* Unterweser moved to dismiss for lack of personal jurisdiction on the basis of the forum selection clause and *forum non conveniens.* Unterweser sought a stay of action pending resolution in the London Court of Justice.

The U.S. District Court and Court of Appeals denied the motion to stay, thus allowing the case to proceed in U.S. court despite the forum selection clause. Unterweser filed a petition of certiorari to the U.S. Supreme Court.

CHIEF JUSTICE BURGER

We hold, with the six dissenting members of the Court of Appeals, that far too little weight and effect were given to the forum clause in resolving this controversy. For at least two decades we have witnessed an expansion of overseas commercial activities by business enterprises based in the United States. The barrier of distance that once tended to confine a business concern to a modest territory no longer does so. Here we see an American company with special expertise contracting with a foreign company to tow a complex machine thousands of miles across seas and oceans. The expansion of American business and industry will hardly be encouraged if, notwithstanding solemn contracts, we insist on a parochial concept that all disputes must be resolved under our laws and in our courts. Absent a contract forum, the considerations relied on by the Court of Appeals would be persuasive reasons for holding an American forum convenient in the traditional sense, but in an era of expanding world trade and commerce, [prior cases that have decided otherwise] have little place and would be a heavy hand indeed on the future development of international commercial dealings by Americans. We cannot have trade and commerce in world markets and international waters exclusively on our terms, governed by our laws, and resolved in our courts.

Forum-selection clauses have historically not been favored by American courts. Many courts, federal and state, have declined to enforce such clauses on the ground that they were "contrary to public policy," or that their effect was to "oust the jurisdiction" of the court. Although this view apparently still has considerable acceptance, other courts are tending to adopt a more hospitable attitude toward forum-selection clauses. This view, advanced in the well-reasoned dissenting opinion in the instant case, is that such clauses are prima facie valid and should be enforced unless enforcement is shown by the resisting party to be "unreasonable" under the circumstances. We believe this is the correct doctrine to be followed by federal district courts sitting in admiralty ...

This approach is substantially what is followed in other common-law countries including England. It is the view advanced by noted scholars and that adopted by the Restatement of the Conflict of Laws. It accords with ancient concepts of freedom of contract and reflects an appreciation of the expanding horizons of American contractors who seek business in all parts of the world ... The choice of that forum was made in an arm's length negotiation by experienced and sophisticated businessmen, and absent some compelling and countervailing reason it should be honored by the parties and enforced by the courts.

The elimination of all such uncertainties by agreeing in advance on a forum acceptable to both parties is an indispensable element in international trade, commerce, and contracting. There is strong evidence that the forum clause was a vital part of the agreement, and it would be unrealistic to think that the parties did not conduct their negotiations, including fixing the monetary terms, with the consequences of the forum clause figuring prominently in their calculations.

Thus, in the light of present-day commercial realities and expanding international trade we conclude that the forum clause should control absent a strong showing that it should be set aside. Although their opinions are not altogether explicit, it seems reasonably clear that the District Court and the Court of Appeals placed the burden on Unterweser to show that London would be a more convenient forum than Tampa, although the contract expressly resolved that issue. The correct approach would have been to enforce the forum clause specifically unless Zapata

continues

continued

could clearly show that enforcement would be unreasonable and unjust, or that the clause was invalid for such reasons as fraud or overreaching. Accordingly, the case must be remanded for reconsideration.

Decision. Vacated and remanded for proceedings consistent with the opinion.

Comment. The Supreme Court noted the possible reasons that a forum selection clause could be unenforceable, including: (1) if it contravenes strong public policy and (2) if the forum is seriously inconvenient. These reasons still hold true today. Other reasons forum selection clauses may be ignored by the courts are because parties are of unequal bargaining power; counsel was not consulted; the clause was written in a foreign language; the clause violates federal law; or circumstances have changed (where the forum is the site of a revolution hostile to one party's country—for example, a forum selection clause choosing Iran after the Islamic Revolution). Many other countries also support the validity of forum selection clauses, including Austria, the United Kingdom, France, Germany, Italy, and many Latin American and Scandinavian countries.

Case Questions

1. What was the Court's holding with respect to the general enforceability of forum selection clauses?
2. How would you define "public policy reasons" or "serious inconvenience" for purposes of refusing to uphold a forum selection clause? What factors would you take into account in making this determination?

gravity." In other words, in the absence of an agreement by the parties, contracts should be governed by the law of the jurisdiction that has the most significant relationship to the transaction and the parties. The *Restatement (Second)* sets out five factors to be considered: (1) the place of contracting (i.e., where the acceptance took place); (2) the place where the contract was negotiated (particularly if the parties met and negotiated at length); (3) the place where the contract will be performed; (4) the location of the subject matter of the contract; and (5) the domicile, residence, nationality, place of incorporation, and place of business of the parties. If the contract was both negotiated and performed in the same jurisdiction, then the law of that jurisdiction will apply (except for contracts involving real estate or life insurance, which have special rules). Of these, the place of negotiation and performance is often the most important factor, especially if both parties are performing within the same jurisdiction. The place of contracting and the domicile of the parties, while not critical by themselves, are important when supporting other factors.

Torts. Traditionally, the law in the United States and in most countries has been that **tort actions,** including personal injuries, product liability, wrongful death, fraud, and business torts, should be governed by the law of the place where the injury or damage occurred (known as *lex loci delicti*). In the United States, many courts are adopting the broader view taken by the *Restatement (Second)* that tort liability should be governed by the law of the jurisdiction that has the most significant relationship to the tort and to the parties. The *Restatement (Second)* lists the following factors to be considered: (1) the place where the injury occurred; (2) the place where the conduct causing the injury occurred; (3) the domicile, residence, nationality, place of incorporation, and place of business of the parties; and (4) the place where the relationship between the parties is centered.

Choice of Law Clauses

Choice of law clauses are contract provisions that stipulate the country or jurisdiction whose law will apply in interpreting the contract or enforcing its terms. Lawyers are quite aware that laws can be very different from state to state or country to country and will consider this in contract negotiations. Indeed, the choice of law may well become a bargaining point in international contract negotiations. As a general rule, the choice of law selection will be upheld as long as there is a reasonable relationship between the transaction and the jurisdiction chosen. As one court put it, parties today have several choices of law that could apply to their dealings, but they could not choose to have their disputes decided under the ancient *Code of Hammurabi.* For example, imagine a Japanese manufacturer who enters into a contract with a buyer in New York for the shipment of goods to New York. Both parties have offices in California and sign the contract there. A clause making California law applicable to the contract would be valid, because there is a sufficient nexus, or connection, between the contract and the state of California.

Choice of law clauses are often used in conjunction with a forum selection agreement. Such concurrent use ensures that the selected forum is consistent with the selected law. A selected court thus would not be required to speculate on what law may be applicable to the case and the requirements of such law. A recent example includes the passenger tickets of guests upon the *Costa Concordia* cruise ship, which capsized off the Italian coast in January 2012. The accident resulted in 32 fatalities and 64 injured passengers. Despite the fact that the victims haled from eight different countries, they were all bound by Section 2 of their tickets which provided as follows:

> All claims, controversies, disputes, suits and matters of any kind whatsoever arising out of, concerned with or incident to any voyage that does not depart from, return to, or visit a U.S. port ... shall be instituted only in the courts of Genoa, Italy, to the exclusion of the courts of any other country, state or nation. Italian law shall apply to any such proceedings.

This language will most likely serve to prevent successful lawsuits in the United States and other locations where recoveries may be larger than available in Italian courts.

The Application of Foreign Law in American Courts

If an American court determines that it should apply foreign law to the case, how does it know what that law is? At one time, foreign law was required to be proven in court as fact. Today, in the federal courts, that has changed. Courts are free to determine as a matter of law what the foreign law is. The federal courts will follow the *Federal Rules of Civil Procedure.* Rule 44.1 states:

> A party who intends to raise an issue about a foreign country's law must give notice by a pleading or other writing. In determining foreign law, the court may consider any relevant material or source, including testimony, whether or not submitted by a party or admissible under the Federal Rules of Evidence. The court's determination must be treated as a ruling on a question of law.

Accordingly, judges may conduct their own research on foreign law, they may request briefs provided by the parties' lawyers, or they may rely on the testimony of foreign lawyers in or out of court. The following case, *Finnish Fur Sales Co., Ltd. v. Juliette Shulof Furs, Inc.*, involves a U.S. court in New York that had to decide a case under the laws of Finland. It offers an explanation of how a choice of law clause works and shows how a U.S. court applies the law of a foreign country to resolve a contract dispute. Notice the interplay of federal and state law and the application of Rule 44.1.

Finnish Fur Sales Co., Ltd. v. Juliette Shulof Furs, Inc.

770 F. Supp. 139 (1991) United States District Court (S.D.N.Y.)

BACKGROUND AND FACTS

Juliette Shulof Furs (JSF) is a New York corporation that has been in the fur-dealing business for fifteen years. George Shulof, an officer of JSF, attended two auctions conducted by Finnish Fur Sales (FFS) in Finland in 1987. He purchased more than $1.2 million worth of skins at the auctions. Shulof attended each auction and was the actual bidder. The conditions of sale were listed in the auction catalog in English. JSF paid for the majority of the skins purchased, leaving an unpaid balance of $202,416.85. FFS brought this action to recover the contract price of the skins from Shulof, claiming he was personally liable for payment under Finnish law. Shulof responded that he was acting only as the agent for JSF and that under New York law he was not personally responsible for the contracts of the corporation he represented at the auction.

LEISURE, DISTRICT JUDGE

Section 4 of the *Conditions of Sale* provides:

Any person bidding at the auction shall stand surety as for his own debt until full payment is made for purchased merchandise. If he has made the bid on behalf of another person, he is jointly and severally liable with the person for the purchase.

continues

continued

George Shulof denies any personal liability on the grounds that the provision is unenforceable under both New York and Finnish law.

Section 15 of the *Conditions of Sale* provides that "[t] hese conditions are governed by Finnish law." Choice of law clauses are routinely enforced by the courts of this Circuit, "if there is a reasonable basis for the choice." *Morgan Guaranty Trust Co. v. Republic of Palau, 693* F. Supp. 1479, 1494 (S.D.N.Y. 1988). New York courts also generally defer to choice of law clauses if the state or country whose law is thus selected has sufficient contacts with the transaction. Under those circumstances, "New York law requires the court to honor the parties' choice insofar as matters of substance are concerned, so long as fundamental policies of New York law are not thereby violated." *Woodling v. Garrett Corp.,* 813 F.2d 543,551 (2d Cir. 1987). Finland's contacts with the transactions at issue are substantial, rendering the choice of law clause enforceable unless a strong public policy of New York is impaired by the application of Finnish law. Plaintiff FFS is a Finnish resident, which held auctions of Finnish-bred furs in Finland. All bids were made in Finnish marks, with payment and delivery to take place in Finland. Mr. Shulof voluntarily traveled to Finland in order to partake in FFS's auctions. Thus, virtually all of the significant events related to these transactions took place in Finland. Finland also has an obvious interest in applying its law to events taking place within its borders relating to an important local industry, and in applying uniform law to numerous transactions with bidders from foreign countries.

Mr. Shulof argues that the choice of Finnish law provision should be held invalid ... According to Mr. Shulof, New York has the following interests in this action: it is the place of business and of incorporation of JSF; FFS has a representative with a New York office who communicated with Mr. Shulof about the fur auctions; and that New York is, allegedly, "the economic and design center for the world's fur industry." Mr. Shulof also argues that, under New York law. Section 4 of the *Conditions of Sale* would be invalid as contravening New York's policy against imposing personal liability on corporate officers ...

Under Federal Rule of Civil Procedure 44.1, a court, "in determining foreign law, may consider any relevant material or source, including testimony." Both parties have submitted affidavits of Finnish attorneys on the issue of Mr. Shulof's liability under Finnish law. FFS's expert, Vesa Majamaa, a Doctor of Law and Professor of the Faculty of Law at the University of Helsinki, gives as his opinion that the provision of Section 4 of the *Conditions of Sale* imposing personal liability upon the bidder, regardless of whether he bids on behalf of another, is valid both as a term of the particular auctions at issue and as a general principle of Finnish and Scandinavian auction law. According to Majamaa, it is "commonly accepted in Scandinavia that a bidder, by making a bid, accepts those conditions which have been announced at the auction." Further, he states: According to the Finnish judicial system, no one may use ignorance of the law as a defense ... This same principle is also ... applicable when the matter in question concerns ... terms of trade ... If the buyer is not familiar with the terms observed in an auction, he is obliged to familiarize himself with them. In this respect, failure to inquire will result in a loss for the buyer ... If a businessman who has been and is still active in the fields falls back on his ignorance in a case in which he has been offered an actual opportunity to find out about the terms of the auction, his conduct could be considered to be contrary to equitable business practices [and] the "Principle of Good Faith." ...

Majamaa also notes that under Danish law, which he maintains would be applied by a Finnish court in the absence of Finnish decisional or legislative law on point, "It is taken for granted that someone who has bid on merchandise on someone else's account is responsible for the transaction, as he would be for his own obligation, together with his superior ... Hence the auction buyer's responsibility is not secondary, as is, for example, the responsibility of a guarantor." ...

Majamaa also opines that the terms of Section 4 are neither unexpected nor harsh because "the liability has been clearly presented in the terms of the auction,' and because the same rule of liability would apply under Finnish law in the absence of any provision.

...[T]he Court concludes that a Finnish court would enforce the provisions of Section 4 and impose personal responsibility upon George Shulof for his auction bids on behalf of JSF.

Moreover, even if a New York court would not enforce such a provision in a transaction to which New York law clearly applied, this Court does not find New York's interest in protecting one of its residents against personal liability as a corporate officer to constitute so fundamental a policy that New York courts would refuse to enforce a contrary rule of foreign law. Indeed, the New York Court of Appeals has held that "foreign-based rights should be enforced unless the judicial enforcement of such a contract would be the approval of a transaction which is

continues

continued

inherently vicious, wicked or immoral, and shocking to the prevailing moral sense." *Intercontinental Hotels Corp. v. Golden,* 15 N.Y.2d. 9, 13, 254 N.Y.S.2d 527, 529, 203 N.E.2d 210 (1964). Given the lack of a clear conflict with either New York law or policy, this Court concludes that a New York court would apply Finnish law to the issue before the Court. The Court also notes that a similar result has often been reached under New York conflict rules even in the absence of a contractual choice of law clause. Thus, Mr. Shulof must be held jointly and severally liable with JSF for any damages owed to FFS for the furs purchased.

Decision. Under conflict of law rules, the U.S. court applied Finnish law to hold Shulof personally liable for the contract debt.

Case Questions

1. What was the court's holding with respect to the enforceability of the choice of law clause?
2. What factors did the court use in its decision to uphold the choice of law provision?
3. How would you define a "fundamental" public policy that would cause a court to refuse to enforce a choice of law provision?

ENFORCEMENT OF FOREIGN JUDGMENTS

At the close of a judicial proceeding, a winning party might obtain a judgment for damages or some other award. Once a judgment is taken against a defendant, it must be enforced. If necessary, it can be done through a legal process, including the seizure of the losing party's property. But what if a judgment is won in a state or country where that party has no money or property? This is where some good detective work comes in handy. In the United States, judgments taken against a party by a court of competent jurisdiction in one state will be enforced by all other states under the ***Full Faith and Credit Clause*** of the U.S. Constitution. This provision, however, does not apply to the recognition of judgments from foreign countries. Rather, the issue of whether to recognize a foreign judgment is governed by state law.

Many states have statutes specifically permitting the enforcement of foreign judgments. More than 30 states have adopted either the *Uniform Foreign Money Judgments Recognition Act of 1962* or its successor the *Uniform Foreign-Country Money Judgments Recognition Act of 2005.* The remaining states rely on the requirements of comity in determining whether to recognize a foreign judgment. Regardless of the source of recognition, U.S. courts will usually recognize a final and conclusive foreign money judgment based on a full and fair trial on the merits of the case by an impartial tribunal. The foreign court must have had jurisdiction over the subject matter and over the parties or property involved, and the defendant must have been given notice of the action and an opportunity to appear. Judgments may not be enforced where they violate due process or public policy, where they were procured by fraud, where the original proceeding contravened a forum selection clause in the contract, where the foreign court was a seriously inconvenient forum, or where there is serious doubt about the integrity of the foreign court.

Foreign courts often enforce judgments of U.S. court on the basis of reciprocity and comity in countries where the losing party or its property can be found. Foreign courts, including several in Europe, have been known to refuse to honor the judgments of U.S. courts where in the view of the foreign court the amount of money awarded was excessive, or represented punitive damages, or where in the opinion of the foreign judge the U.S. court extended its net of jurisdiction too widely. To ensure that U.S. judgments will be enforceable in foreign courts, or foreign judgments enforceable in the United States, it is a good idea for the plaintiff's counsel here to coordinate with counsel in the foreign country. That way they can develop some reasonable assurance that the procedures used to obtain the judgment will satisfy the courts of the country in which property is located or it will otherwise be enforced.

Rules regarding recognition of foreign judgments are similar in other jurisdictions. For example, effective March 1, 2003, a European Union regulation required mutual recognition of court judgments among EU member countries, without requiring any special procedures. Exceptions to recognition and enforcement include judgments in violation of public policies of the state in which enforcement is sought and lack of adequate service of process and notice.

Foreign judgments are subject to review by the intermediate people's court in China to determine their consistency with treaties to which China is a party and applicable case law. This review is limited to formalities and does not question the foreign court's findings of fact or application of the law. The court may issue an order of recognition and writ of enforcement unless it determines that the judgment contravenes Chinese law, sovereignty, public security, or social interests. Additional grounds upon which China refuses to recognize foreign judgments include lack of subject matter or personal jurisdiction, lack of notice of the foreign proceeding, and concurrent litigation regarding the same subject matter and issues in China.

The *Code of Civil Procedure*, adopted in 1908 when India was a British colony, governs recognition of foreign judgments in India. Under Section 44-A of the Code, a party seeking to enforce a foreign judgment must present an Indian district court with a certified copy of the judgment within three years of its entry. The judgment must meet several prerequisites under Section 13 of the Code, including subject matter and personal jurisdiction of the foreign court, a final decision on the merits, the absence of fraud in the procurement of the judgment, and the consistency of the judgment with international law, Indian law, and principles of natural justice. Foreign judgments meeting these conditions are deemed conclusive and binding.

Uniform Foreign Money Claims Act. As a general rule, courts award money judgments in their own currencies. For many years, U.S. courts were only able to award judgments in dollars. This rule was rooted in English law dating back several hundred years. However, it created some problems. If an international contract called for payment in the year 2009 in Japanese yen, and a judgment for a breach of the contract is awarded in 2012 in dollars, fluctuations in currency exchange rates may have distorted the value of the judgment relative to the contract terms. One of the parties may be greatly disadvantaged, while the other may receive a windfall profit. The question of whether or not a foreign money judgment can be awarded is, in the United States, a matter of state law, not federal law. In recent years, about half of the states have enacted the *Uniform Foreign Money Claims Act.* This statute gives state courts the authority to issue a judgment in a foreign currency. Some state courts have permitted foreign money awards by judicial decision, acknowledging the need to make the parties whole. Foreign money awards have been available in Great Britain since 1975.

COMMERCIAL DISPUTES WITH NATIONS

This chapter deals with commercial disputes between private parties. Of course, governments, too, are players in commercial transactions because they are the largest purchasers of goods and services in the world. Resolving disputes with nations is quite a different matter. When governments act in their capacity as a sovereign, it is very difficult to bring them to answer in court. When they act in a commercial capacity, it is easier.

Sovereign Immunity

Sovereignty is defined as the supreme and absolute power that governs an independent state or nation. Of course, in reality, sovereignty can have a range of meanings. For example, in the United States, sovereignty can be shared between the federal government, the states, and even Native American tribes. In Europe, some national sovereignty had to be sacrificed by countries that joined the European Union. For our purposes, we should recognize that all independent countries are equal with one another and that each has the exclusive right over its citizens, its territory, all property within that territory, and its internal affairs.

It follows that the doctrine of **sovereign immunity** states that the courts of one country cannot hear cases brought against the government of another country and that courts cannot involve themselves in the internal affairs of a foreign country. In English law this is derived from the feudal notion that the "king can do no wrong." This principle was firmly established in the United States in *Schooner Exchange v. McFaddon,* 11 U.S. 116 (1812), in which an American merchant ship was seized by Emperor Napoleon and pressed into service with the French navy. When the ship docked at Philadelphia, its original owners filed suit to have it returned. The U.S. Supreme Court ruled that under sovereign immunity, a warship of a foreign nation was not subject to seizure by U.S. courts. Today, sovereign immunity is recognized by most nations of the world and defined by statute in many.

In the United States, the *Foreign Sovereign Immunities Act of 1976* defines jurisdiction of U.S. courts over foreign nations. This takes a somewhat restrictive view of immunity by creating exceptions courts must consider. These exceptions generally are waiver (by statute or by agreement in a contract); commercial activity; certain violations of international law such as torture, terrorism, and unlawful expropriation of private property without payment of compensation; and lawsuits for money damages for torts committed within the United States. Examples might include a lawsuit by the victim of state-sponsored terrorism or a lawsuit against a foreign government for negligence in the operation of a motor vehicle within the United States.

Commercial Activity Exception. Sovereign immunity protects foreign governments from suit when they are acting as political entities. When foreign governments or their agencies enter the commercial field, engaging in business for profit, as would a private company, or engaging in essentially private functions, they can be sued in the courts of a foreign country. When agencies of government buy and sell goods or services, they become liable for damages for breach of contract. An example is a contract between a private company in the United States and a government-owned company in China for the supply of raw materials. If the Chinese government is acting as a private company in mining, marketing, and selling raw materials, it is liable to suit in the United States (assuming other jurisdictional requirements are met) for delivering materials that do not conform to the contract specifications.

Abstention Doctrines

There are three abstention doctrines worthy of mention which may impact litigation with a foreign sovereign or relating to an action taken by a foreign sovereign. In each of these circumstances, a U.S. court may refuse to exercise jurisdiction.

Comity. **Comity** refers to the willingness of one court or department of government to respect the rules or decisions of another or to grant it some privilege or favor. International comity is a judicial doctrine, not an international law, based on the desire for courtesy and reciprocity between countries. It also serves to prevent courts from embroiling themselves in matters of foreign affairs and thereby helps to avoid diplomatic conflicts. Comity allows the courts of one country to recognize the laws and court decrees of another country or to defer hearing a case that is more appropriate for hearing in the courts of another country. Under comity, for example, a court that otherwise might be entitled to hear a case may allow it to be transferred to a court in a foreign country with a greater interest in the case.

Assume, for example, there is a breach of contract for the sale of goods between two parties, the buyer residing in the United States and the seller in Japan. Assume that the contract does not mention where disputes should be resolved and that jurisdiction in the case would be appropriate in the courts of either country. If the seller files suit for payment in the courts of Japan, and subsequently the buyer (not wanting to defend the case in a foreign country) files suit in a U.S. court alleging damages for defective goods, the U.S. court will likely dismiss the case on the basis of comity to avoid a conflict with the courts of Japan. Now assume that the seller wins a money judgment in Japanese courts, but the buyer has no assets there to satisfy the judgment. The seller can take the judgment to U.S. courts for enforcement. (Keep in mind that U.S. courts will only enforce civil judgments from countries that guarantee fair trials and due process. U.S. courts will not enforce foreign tax liens or verdicts in foreign criminal cases.)

Act of State. The **act of state doctrine** is a principle of domestic law (not international law) that prohibits the courts of one country from inquiring into the validity of the legislative or executive acts of another country. It was first announced in the United States in the case of *Underhill v. Hernandez,* 168 U.S. 250 (1897) where it was held that " … [T]he courts of one country will not sit in judgment on the acts of the government of another done within its own territory. Redress of grievances by reason of such acts must be obtained through the means open to be availed of by sovereign powers as between themselves."

Many of the U.S. cases discussing the Act of State doctrine involve the confiscation of American-owned property by foreign governments without the payment of compensation, such as occurred with Fidel Castro's communist takeover of Cuba in 1959 and with the Islamic revolution in Iran in 1979. As a general rule, the Act of State doctrine prohibits courts from embroiling themselves in such politically charged issues. The doctrine is based on the idea that courts should not intervene in matters of foreign affairs. These matters are best left to the executive branch, which has the benefit of a diplomatic corps, foreign embassies, and the ability to talk directly to foreign governments. There is also the practical reason that it may very well be impossible for domestic courts to enforce their decisions against foreign governments, as it certainly would have been in the case of both Cuba and Iran. In the latter case, a treaty between the United States and Iran led to the creation of an impartial tribunal in the Netherlands to resolve outstanding claims between U.S. citizens and the Iranian government. Courts in the United States, the United Kingdom, Germany, France, Italy, Japan, and many other countries recognize the Act of State doctrine.

Political Question Doctrine. The **political question doctrine** traces its origin to the U.S. Supreme Court's 1803 opinion in *Marbury v. Madison* in which Chief Justice Marshall stated "[q]uestions, in their nature political, or which are, by the constitution or laws submitted to the executive, can never be made in this court." The modern version of this doctrine requires courts to consider six different factors before dismissing a lawsuit on political question grounds. These factors are: (1) constitutional commitment of the question to the executive or legislative branch, (2) a lack of judicially manageable and discoverable standards for resolving the question, (3) the impossibility of resolving the question without making a policy determination of a kind clearly for nonjudicial determination. (4) the determination of the question will result in the expression of lack of judicial respect for the executive or legislative branches, (5) the need for adherence to a previously-made political decision, and (6) the potential for embarrassment of the U.S. government by differing pronouncements of policy by multiple branches of government.

CONCLUSION

When negotiating international transactions, the prudent businessperson or lawyer will hope for the best but always plan for the worst. Planning for disputes in advance is a proper method of minimizing risk in a transaction. This planning includes obtaining expert legal advice in negotiating and drafting business contracts. The importance of the contract cannot be overstated because if and when a dispute arises, the terms of the contract provide the basis for dispute resolution.

Chapter Summary

1. Alternate dispute resolution usually offers a faster, cheaper, and more efficient alternative to litigation. Mediation is a voluntary, non-binding conciliation process. Arbitration is a more formalized process, resulting in a binding award that courts in many countries will enforce. The parties must agree to arbitration, but once they do, they cannot withdraw. Most commercial nations today have laws permitting arbitration and recognizing arbitral awards.
2. Litigation is the final step in attempting to resolve a dispute. It is in use more frequently in the United States than in virtually any other country. Many litigants from foreign countries seek ways for American courts to hear their cases. American juries are known for giving larger verdicts, and punitive damage awards are possible.
3. Jurisdiction is the power of a court to hear and decide a case. *In personam* jurisdiction, or "jurisdiction over the person," refers to the court's power over a certain individual or corporation. No court can enter a judgment against an individual or corporate defendant unless they have such jurisdiction. When a defendant is not physically present in the state, a court can obtain jurisdiction only if the party has had sufficient minimum contacts with the territory of the forum such that it is fair for the defendant. The Internet is leading to new jurisdictional issues.
4. Jurisdiction is often confused with the concept of venue. Venue refers to the geographical location of a court of competent jurisdiction where a case can be heard.
5. According to the legal doctrine of *forum non conveniens,* whenever a case can be properly heard in the courts of more than one jurisdiction, it should be heard in the jurisdiction that is most convenient.
6. The term *conflict of laws* refers to the rules by which courts determine which state or country's laws will apply to a case and how to reconcile differences between laws. In breach of contract cases, in the absence of an agreement by the parties, the law of the jurisdiction that has the

most significant relationship to the transaction and the parties usually governs the contracts. The law of the place where the injury or damage occurred usually governs tort cases, although today many courts are adopting the broader view that the law of the jurisdiction that has the most significant relationship to the tort and to the parties should govern liability.

7. A forum selection clause is a provision in a contract that fixes in advance the jurisdiction in which any disputes will be litigated. A choice of law clause is a contract provision that stipulates which country or jurisdiction's law will apply in interpreting the contract or enforcing its terms.
8. As a general rule, U.S. courts honor the judgments of foreign countries when the requirements of comity are satisfied and when the foreign judgment was rendered by an impartial tribunal in a fashion that would not offend American notions of fundamental fairness and due process of law.
9. Foreign courts often enforce judgments of U.S. courts on the basis of reciprocity and comity in countries where the defendant or its property can be found. Some foreign courts have been known to refuse to honor the judgments of U.S. courts where, in the view of the foreign court, the amount of money awarded was excessive.
10. Commercial disputes with foreign sovereigns present many difficulties including barriers to the initiation of litigation. These barriers include sovereign immunity, comity, the act of state doctrine, and the political question doctrine.

Key Terms

alternative dispute resolution (ADR) 57
mediation 57
arbitration 57
arbitration rules 58
litigation 61
jurisdiction 61
territorial jurisdiction 61
in rem jurisdiction 62
subject matter jurisdiction 62
diversity jurisdiction 62
in personam jurisdiction 62
letter rogatory 68
venue 68
forum non conveniens 68
punitive damages 69
forum selection clause 72
diversity of citizenship 72
conflict of laws 72
torts 74
choice of law clauses 74
Full Faith and Credit Clause 77
sovereign immunity 78
act of state doctrine 79
comity 79
political question doctrine 80

Questions and Case Problems

1. Explain the concepts of jurisdiction and minimum contacts. What application do they have in international disputes?
2. Sarl Louis Feraud International is a French corporation that designs high-fashion clothing and other items for women. Viewfinder, Inc., a Delaware corporation, operated a Website called "firstView. com," on which it posted photographs of fashion shows held by designers around the world, including photographs of Feraud's fashion shows. The firstView Website contained both photographs of the current season"s fashions, which could be viewed only upon subscription and payment of a fee, and photographs of past collections, which were available for free. In January 2001, Feraud, along with several other design houses, filed suit against Viewfinder in the Tribunal de grande instance de Paris seeking money damages for alleged unauthorized use of their intellectual property and unfair competition. Viewfinder failed to respond, and the French court entered a default judgment in which it ordered Viewfinder to remove the offending photographs, and awarded damages of 500,000 francs for each plaintiff and a fine of 50,000 francs for each day Viewfinder failed to comply. In December 2004, Feraud sought recognition of the judgment in U.S. district court in New York. The district court found that enforcing the French judgment would be repugnant to New York public policy because it would violate Viewfinder's First Amendment rights. The district court concluded that the "First Amendment simply does not permit plaintiffs

to stage public events in which the general public has a considerable interest, and then control the way in which information about those events is disseminated in the mass media." Feraud filed an appeal in the U.S. Court of Appeals for the Second Circuit. What should be the outcome on appeal? *Sarl Louis Feraud International v. Viewfinder, Inc.*, 489 F.3d 474 (2d Cir. 2007).

3. Two teenagers residing in North Carolina were fatally injured when the bus upon which they were riding overturned on a roadway outside of Paris, France. The parents of the decedents brought a lawsuit in North Carolina state court against Goodyear Tire and Rubber Company and its subsidiaries based in Luxembourg, Turkey and France alleging that the accident was caused by negligent design and production of the bus tires. The subsidiaries moved to dismiss for lack of personal jurisdiction. The plaintiffs alleged that North Carolina courts had personal jurisdiction due to the fact that the subsidiaries placed their tires into the stream of commerce and some of these tires ended up in North Carolina. The subsidiaries alleged that there was no personal jurisdiction as the mere placement of a product in the stream of commerce is an insufficient basis for the assertion of personal jurisdiction especially when the accident had no connection with the forum other than the residence of the decedents. Additionally, the mere placement of tires into the stream of commerce did not constitute a continuous and systematic presence in North Carolina as to subject the subsidiaries to personal jurisdiction. The North Carolina state courts disagreed and exercised personal jurisdiction over the subsidiaries. The subsidiaries appealed to the U.S. Supreme Court. Do the North Carolina courts have personal jurisdiction over Goodyear's foreign subsidiaries arising from the accident in France? *Goodyear Dunlop Tires Operations, S.A. v. Brown*, 131 S. Ct. 2846 (2011).
4. Nicastro was severely injured at his workplace in New Jersey by an industrial metal shearing machine manufactured by J. McIntyre Machinery, Ltd., an English company. Nicastro filed a product liability claim against McIntyre in New Jersey state court. McIntyre denied that the New Jersey state courts had personal jurisdiction. The machinery in question was manufactured in England and was not directly sold to Nicastro's employer in New Jersey. McIntyre had no office, did not pay taxes, own property, advertise, or maintain employees in New Jersey. Although McIntyre had a U.S. distributor for its products and sent its employees to the United States to attend trade shows, its only contact with New Jersey was the presence of the metal shearing machine at Nicastro's workplace. The New Jersey Supreme Court disagreed with McIntyre's contentions and held that state courts could exercise personal jurisdiction with respect to Nicastro's claim. McIntyre appealed this decision to the U.S. Supreme Court. Do the New Jersey courts have personal jurisdiction over McIntyre arising from Nicastro's injuries? *J. McIntyre Machinery, Ltd. v. Nicastro*, 131 S. Ct. 2780 (2011).
5. Why do so many litigants, "like moths to a flame," want to litigate in the United States?
6. Seung was a passenger on the *M/S Paul Gauguin* cruise ship owned by Regent Seven Seas Cruises. The cruise ship operated exclusively in French Polynesia. Seung's ticket contained a forum selection clause that designated Paris, France as the sole location for any lawsuit that might be filed arising from passenger injuries on cruises that did not include a U.S. port. Seung was injured on her cruise and filed a lawsuit in the U.S. District Court for the Southern District of Florida. Regent Seven Seas Cruises moved to dismiss the lawsuit on the basis of the forum selection clause. Seung claimed that the clause violated U.S. public policy, was unfair and unreasonable as she was financially and medically unable to bring a lawsuit in Paris, and that Paris was a "remote alien forum" designated for the sole purpose of discouraging passengers from bringing legitimate claims. The district court disagreed with Seung and dismissed her lawsuit. Seung appealed to the U.S. Court of Appeals for the Eleventh Circuit. Is the forum selection clause as drafted enforceable against Seung such as to bar her lawsuit in the United States? Why or why not? *Seung v. Regent Seven Seas Cruises, Inc.*, 2010 U.S. App. LEXIS 17449 (11th Cir. 2010).
7. The Uniform Foreign Money Judgments Recognition Act of 1962 and the Uniform Foreign-Country Money Judgments Recognition Act of 2005 do not mention any requirement of reciprocity. However, several states will not recognize foreign judgments without assurance that judgments entered in their courts will be enforced overseas. Criticism of such a requirement has focused on the absence of reciprocity in English common law and U.S. statutes and common law, the holding of the interests of private litigants hostage to the government's interest in promoting reciprocity, and the gridlock that results as the United States and foreign states refuse to recognize one another's judgments due to failure to reciprocate. Should recognition of foreign judgments in U.S. state courts be subject to a reciprocity requirement? Why or why not?
8. In 1995, Jorge Luis Machuca Gonzalez purchased a Chrysler LHS in Mexico. In May 1996, Gonzalez's wife was involved in a collision with another moving vehicle

while driving the Chrysler LHS in Mexico. The accident triggered the passenger-side air bag. The force of the air bag's deployment instantaneously killed Gonzalez's three-year-old son, Pablo. Gonzalez brought suit in Texas district court against Chrysler, TRW, Inc., and TRW Vehicle Safety Systems, Inc. (the designers of the front sensor for the air bag), and Morton International, Inc. (the designer of the air bag module). Gonzalez asserted claims based on products liability, negligence, gross negligence, and breach of warranty. The district court dismissed the case on the basis *of forum non conveniens* as the car was manufactured, purchased, and operated in Mexico, and the accident involved Mexican citizens. On appeal, Gonzalez claimed that Mexico was an inadequate forum because Mexican law capped the maximum award for the loss of a child's life at approximately $2,500. Does the enormous disparity between what Gonzales could recover for the death of his son in the United States and Mexico render Mexico an inadequate forum? What did the court of appeals decide? *Gonzales v. Chrysler Corp.,* 301 F.3d 377 (5th Cir. 2002).

9. Badbusinessbureau.com was a limited liability company organized and existing under the laws of St. Kitts/Nevis, West Indies. Badbusinessbureau owned and operated "The Rip-Off Report," a Website displaying consumer complaints about various businesses, including 30 or 40 complaints about Hy Cite Corporation, a Wisconsin-based marketer of dinnerware, glassware, and cookware. Badbusinessbureau did not have any assets, offices, or employees in Wisconsin. No Wisconsin company had purchased a rebuttal to a consumer complaint or ad space on the site or had enrolled in the company's "Corporate Consumer Advocacy Program." However, the Website was viewable in Wisconsin, and one Wisconsin resident purchased a copy of "The Rip Off Revenge Guide" through a link on the site. Hy Cite filed suit and contended that by operating the Website, Badbusinessbureau had engaged in unfair competition, false advertising, disparagement, and trademark infringement. Badbusinessbureau filed a motion to dismiss for lack of personal jurisdiction. How should the district court resolve this motion? What challenges does the Internet present in the area of personal jurisdiction? Should the rules regarding personal jurisdiction be different for Web-based businesses and transactions? Why or why not? *Hy Cite Corp. v. Badbusinessbureau.com L.L.C.,* 297 F. Supp.2d 1154 (W.D. Wisc. 2004).

Managerial Implications

1. You are CEO of a large publicly traded company. You are negotiating several contracts with foreign governments in Vietnam, India, and Brazil to provide hardware and software to government agencies. Are you interested in including an arbitration clause in the contract? What are the pluses and minuses of such a clause? What alternatives do you have? How does your plan change, if at all, if you are dealing with multiple corporations in the same countries? What if you are dealing with one corporation in the United Kingdom and one in New York? Discuss how these variables may affect your decision.
2. You have started a small high-tech company in New York.
   a. You are running an informational Website. Customers must call your 800 number to place an order. A customer in Alaska is very unhappy with your product. Can he or she successfully sue you in Alaska?
   b. You decide you want to be clear in all your future dealings, so you insert a forum selection clause in all of your contracts with your customers that stipulates arbitration in New York under the rules of the American Arbitration Association. Would this be enforceable?
   c. What if the forum selection clause stated that all disputes would be heard in Tibet?
   d. What ramifications are there to changing your Website and making it more interactive so that people can place orders there?
   e. What if your competitor is using your trade secrets and your patents without your permission or payment? Would you be interested in arbitrating this dispute? Explain.
   f. What difference would it make if your competitor were a Dutch company?
   g. The CEO has asked you to outline a comprehensive strategy to deal with customers, suppliers, and citizen groups complaining about a myriad of issues as well as employee complaints (both domestic and foreign). Prepare a short memo addressing key principles, major concerns, and suggested actions.

Ethical Considerations

The Bhopal disaster litigation presented the anomaly of Indian plaintiffs seeking to maintain their lawsuit in the United States on the basis of the inadequacy of the Indian legal system while, at the same time, a U.S. company sought to have the case heard in India. Union Carbide was ultimately successful in having the U.S. case dismissed in favor of litigation in India. Although the subsequent $470 million settlement sounds very large, the ultimate breakdown was approximately $600 for each injured person and $3,000 for each fatality. Union Carbide's legal strategy of forcing the litigation to proceed in India where it could be settled for much less than a U.S. jury may have awarded was very successful.

But was it ethical? The answer may depend on the ethical theory one applies to the question. For example, teleological frameworks focusing on the consequences of one's actions lead to mixed results. One such framework, ethical egoism, recognizes that people act in their own self-interest and thus a person should act in a manner that best promotes his or her interests unless the net result will generate negative rather than positive results. Union Carbide clearly acted in its own self-interest in forcing the litigation to India, but the net result was a significant financial undervaluation of the victims' lives. Another theory within the teleological framework is moral relativism, which focuses on determining what is right behavior based on the time and place of the circumstances. Were the terms of the settlement proper given the location of the catastrophe and the financial circumstances of the largely poor and undereducated victims of the gas leak? Finally, utilitarianism focuses on whether an individual's action adds to the overall utility of the community. Ethical conduct is that which is likely to produce the greatest overall good not just for the decider but for all persons who will be affected by the decision. The financial well-being of the victims may have been enhanced had the litigation been permitted to proceed in the United States, although it is equally possible that this wellbeing would have been diminished by procedural delays and appeals. However, if one determines that the greater good resides with those interested in the continued financial well-being of Union Carbide, then the outcome was ethically defensible.

By contrast, deontological frameworks focus on duties rather than outcomes. For example, Immanuel Kant's *Categorical Imperative* provides that "[o]ne ought to act such that the principle of one's act could become a universal law of human action in a world in which one would hope to live" and that "[o]ne ought to treat others as having intrinsic value in themselves, and not merely as a means to achieve an end." Would anyone want Union Carbide's conduct in the Bhopal disaster litigation to become an example for companies confronted with similar catastrophes in the future? Was the settlement simply a means of preserving the company's assets and shareholder value at the victims' expense?

The theory of *contractarianism* holds that membership in society is imbued with certain duties and responsibilities and that rational people will always select the course of action that is the fairest and most equitable resolution of a dilemma without regard for personal consequences. Did Union Carbide abide by its duties and responsibilities to the community in Bhopal, especially given the lethal nature of the products it was producing and the large information gap between itself and the people living close to the plant? Did Union Carbide choose the fairest and most equitable resolution of the litigation without regard for consequences? As a profit-driven entity, should it have made such a choice? Is contractarianism unrealistic given that inequality is a fact of life?

What conclusions do you reach and why?

PART 2
International Sales, Credits, and the Commercial Transaction

Early in this book we said that the management of international business is the management of risk. Nowhere is this adage more relevant than in Part Two, *International Sales, Credits, and the Commercial Transaction.* International business lore is filled with stories about sellers who shipped goods to buyers on the other side of the world, on the basis of a written contract, only to find that the buyer has refused to take delivery or has vanished. The risk is equally as great to the unsuspecting buyer who pays in advance, only to find that the seller has delivered an ocean container filled with worthless merchandise. The risks do not end there. Almost daily, there are reports of cargo being damaged by weather, spoilage, contamination with salt water or chemicals, infestation, inadequate packing, and more. It is not uncommon for cargo vessels to go down in storms or to run aground as a result of errors in navigation. Modern day pirates still plow the high seas and dangerous inland waterways, kidnapping crews, plundering cargo, and seizing entire ships for ransom. These are only a few examples of the transaction risks inherent in an international sale. In this part of the book, we hope to expose readers to the risks of the international sale, and to suggest methods for dealing with such risks. In doing so, we explore traditional business law topics: contracts, sales, commercial law, bank collections, letters of credit, aviation and maritime law, and marine insurance.

In this area, the law is derived from both national and international law. This includes many international conventions, national statutes, and the decisions of national courts. The court decisions appearing in this section are composed of both "landmark" cases that explain longstanding and widely accepted legal principles, and those that illustrate common problems faced in international business. Some of the landmark decisions are rooted in the English *Law Merchant* of hundreds of years ago, or early maritime law, although none in this text is so old.

In Chapter Four, *Sales Contracts and Excuses for Nonperformance,* we will study basic principles of international sales law under *The Formation and Performance of Contracts for the Sale of Goods.* This is the first widely accepted body of international sales law, in force in over 70 nations, governing two-thirds of world trade in goods. The chapter discusses the validity and formation of contracts, their interpretation and performance, remedies for breach, and whether or not events beyond control of the parties (e.g., a fire, storm, or terrorist act) will excuse performance.

In Chapter Five, *The Documentary Sale and Terms of Trade,* we cover two important transaction risks facing the buyer and seller in an international sale—the seller's credit risk and the buyer's delivery risk. We examine the use of the documentary sale as a secure payment method and the role of the bill of lading and other negotiable transport documents in facilitating the exchange of goods and money across international borders. We will also look at the importance of trade terms in the contract as a means of allocating, as between buyer and seller, the responsibility for arranging the international transportation of goods, as well as for allocating the risk of loss or damage to the goods while in transit. We will also see the crucial role that ocean carriers and international banks play in facilitating the international sale.

Chapter Six, *Legal Issues in International Transportation,* deals with important areas of aviation and maritime law. The first portion of the chapter covers the liability of air carriers for damage or loss to cargo, and for baggage claims and bodily injuries to passengers. Next, the chapter covers the liability of ocean carriers for damage or loss to cargo at sea, as well as important legal issues affecting marine insurance policies. No area of international business engenders as much litigation in the courts as the carriage of goods. This is a fascinating and important area of study.

In Chapter Seven, *Bank Collections, Trade Finance, and Letters of Credit,* we build on the material presented in Chapter Five. The chapter gives an overview of the law of negotiable instruments in the context of international trade and discusses issues related to trade finance. Although the bank letter of credit is in wide use in international trade, it is not well understood by most businesspeople. Therefore, we devote considerable time to following a typical letter of credit transaction and to understanding both the law and practice of documentary letters of credit.

CHAPTER 4

The Formation and Performance of Contracts for the Sale of Goods

INTRODUCTION TO CONTRACTS FOR THE INTERNATIONAL SALE OF GOODS

The sales contract is universally recognized as the legal mechanism for conducting trade in goods. The contract for purchase and sale embodies the agreement of the parties, the buyer and seller. It expresses their intention to be bound by the contract's terms, commits them to perform their part of the bargain, and makes them responsible for breach of contract if they do not. The sales contract is essential because it sets out rights and liabilities that may extend well into the future. Any agreement to buy and sell goods, especially an international one, usually takes some time to perform. If buyer and seller could do all that was required at the moment the agreement was reached, or if every seller handed over the goods at the moment the purchase price was paid, there would be far less need for a detailed sales contract. In the real world, however, the risks are usually too great to begin performance without first reaching an agreement on all essential terms, especially when the contract extends well into the future.

The contract allows buyer and seller to agree on all essential terms of the contract in advance, and to begin performance, knowing there is an understanding of their rights and obligations. The contract might call for shipment at a future date, or for several shipments to be made over many years. The seller might need time to secure raw materials, or to gear up for the engineering and design phase, and for manufacturing. The buyer may want to arrange advance financing for the purchase, to plan future deliveries to meet production schedules, do advance marketing, or plan the introduction of new products. Whatever the case, both buyer and seller can proceed with some confidence, knowing their contract is sealed.

During the negotiating process the parties can tend to the details of the contract, air their concerns, and negotiate an agreement on all the terms important to them. After all, there are more details to consider besides quantity and price. There are payment terms, shipping and insurance arrangements, specifications and warranties, remedies on default, and more. There is the question of who will bear the risk of loss if the goods are destroyed in transit. Hopefully, everything will go well and neither party will ever have to pull out the document and read its fine print. Yet if performance breaks down, and a dispute arises, that is the first thing the parties and their attorneys will do. If the case proceeds to litigation and a court or arbitrator must resolve their dispute, they will look to the governing law of sales to interpret and enforce the contract.

CULTURAL INFLUENCES ON CONTRACT NEGOTIATIONS

An important factor to keep in mind throughout this chapter is the influence of culture upon contract negotiations. Americans tend to approach contract negotiations in an aggressive, adversarial manner and often view negotiations as a win-lose proposition. Similarly, U.S. lawyers, who are accustomed to practicing in a highly litigious society, press for every legal advantage. They draft their contracts in calculated, technical, and detailed language, setting forth exactly how the parties are to perform and what their legal rights are if the deal falls apart.

Negotiating Contracts in Japan

By contrast, contract negotiations in many countries take a much different form. Japan presents perhaps the best example. Three aspects of Japanese culture and ancient Confucian thinking tremendously influence the role of a contract in Japanese society. First, every person must strive to maintain harmony and accord in society. Second, the maintenance of harmony and the importance placed on personal dignity stress the importance of not causing others to "lose face" or become embarrassed. Third, the Japanese attach the utmost importance to the social group to which one belongs, particularly to one's school or company. Thus, group loyalty and the desire for group harmony and consensus may characterize Japanese businesspeople.

These attributes affect the way the Japanese view contractual relationships. A contract is a relationship, and as much a social one as a business one. Instead of the combative approach of U.S. lawyers, Japanese negotiators view the contract as an expression of a common goal and of a desire for a long-lasting business relationship.

These cultural and societal influences affect the manner in which contracts are negotiated and drafted. Japanese firms normally prefer that lawyers not be involved in negotiating, because they feel that lawyers interfere with the parties' concentration on their mutual business interests. Western negotiators also must remember that they must never put the other parties in a situation in which losing face is the only out such as making demands without offering something in exchange.

In addition, a Western company must be prepared to carry out negotiations for an extended period. In many cases, the Japanese firm will require a long time to reach a group consensus before a decision can be made. The U.S. managers may not realize that, while they have the authority to bind their firm to the agreement, the foreign negotiator may require approval from superiors or from a working group. When doing business in Asia, the watchwords are not only "trust" and "respect" but "patience" as well.

When the contract is finally put into writing, it is typically short and written in little detail. The Japanese consider this necessary because a long-term relationship requires a flexible agreement, and one that the parties can easily modify in the future.

These attitudes also affect the manner in which contract disputes are resolved. Japanese contracts might state that, in the event of a dispute, "the parties will resolve their disagreement harmoniously and in mutual consultation with each other." If a dispute arises, it is more likely to be settled through private conciliation. Litigation is to be avoided if at all possible.

THE LAW OF SALES

The Origin of Modern Sales Law

Sales law, or the **law of sales**, is generally that body of law which governs contracts for the present or future sale of goods. In most countries, the term **sale** means a transfer of the ownership and possession of tangible goods (sometimes referred to simply as "things which are movable" or "tangible personal property") from seller to buyer in return for a price or monetary payment. The "law of sales" does not apply to contracts for the sale of real estate or intangibles, such as stocks, bonds, patents, copyrights, and trademarks. It does not apply to contracts of employment, of insurance, or to the provision of services. The reason for the distinction, as we will see, is that sales law developed out of the practices of merchants and traders who dealt in goods. Generally speaking, courts look to the governing sales law to determine whether a valid and enforceable agreement exists, how to interpret contractual provisions, what remedies are available in the event of a breach, and what damages can be awarded. Sales law is a sub-category of both contract law and commercial law. Today, the sales law of most nations can be found in modern statutes, or codes, supplemented by extensive case decisions. Surprisingly, many countries, particularly developing countries, have newly enacted sales codes that have only recently replaced outdated codes from the nineteenth and early twentieth centuries. Several Latin American countries have only recently modernized their codes, which dated to the mid-1800s. China's modern sales law is a little more than ten years old.

The Law Merchant and English Sales Law. In the twelfth century, medieval Europe experienced a renaissance of trade and commerce. Merchants met at trade fairs and city markets to exchange goods such as wool, salted fish, cotton cloth, wine, fruit, and oils. Trade routes to the East were opening, with access to silk and spices. Rudimentary banking systems were founded so that money could be used as payment in long-distance transactions. Over time, the merchants developed a set of customs for exchanging goods for money—an unwritten code that protected their words, gave them the benefit of their bargains, and helped foster commerce and trade. These customs became known as the ***lex mercatoria*** or ***law merchant****, and they were "enforced" by the merchants themselves.*

In the centuries to follow, the local courts in both England and continental Europe recognized the *law merchant* and used juries made up of other merchants to decide cases. As trade spanned greater distances, merchants took on greater risks, and transactions required more complex legal rules. In England, by the eighteenth century, the *law merchant* became a part of the common law when noted English jurist Lord Mansfield ruled that it was up to the English courts to say what the *law merchant* was and not merely what merchants thought it to be. In continental Europe, the *law merchant* gave way early on to more formal legal codes enacted by legislatures in the nineteenth century, based on legal concepts dating to the Roman period.

More than a hundred years after the merger of the *law merchant* with the common law, England enacted the *English Sale of Goods Act of 1894,* which codified many customary rules and adapted the common law to business needs of the time. The 1894 act and subsequent legislation were consolidated into the *United Kingdom Sale of Goods Act of 1979.* English sales law was transplanted to most of England's colonies and remains a strong influence around the world to this day. Virtually all common law nations today have modern commercial codes and extensive case law governing the sale of goods. Canadian sales law, for example, borrows principles from both the English common law and from the American *Uniform Commercial Code* (UCC).

The U.S. Uniform Commercial Code. In the United States, the law of sales was originally drawn from the English common law of contracts and the *law merchant.* In 1906, the *Uniform Sales Act,* codifying the law of sales, was passed in many U.S. states. (It is no longer in effect.) As the business world became more complex, and with the dawn of air travel and worldwide communications, there was a need for a clearer set of modern rules. This led to the creation in 1951 of the UCC, which has become the primary body of commercial law for domestic transactions in the United States. The UCC has been adopted (with some minor differences) in each of the fifty states plus the District of Columbia. Louisiana has not adopted UCC Article 2 on the Sale of Goods, preferring to follow the rules in its French-influenced Civil Code. The UCC covers many areas of commercial law, including bank deposits and negotiable instruments as well as the sale of goods, and makes the law uniform throughout the United States. Common law controls contracts not governed by the UCC, such as contracts for employment, insurance, and services, the transfer of intellectual property rights, and sales of real property.

National Differences in Sales Law. In an international contract for the sale of goods, at least one party is likely to have its rights decided under the law of a foreign country. In the last chapter, we learned that "conflict of laws" rules determine the country in which a breach of contract case will be heard, and under which country's law will the case be decided. In the absence of a "choice of law" provision in a contract, a court must determine which law will govern—and that could be the law of the country where the contract was made, where it was to be performed, where the goods were to be delivered, where the subject matter is located, where either party resides or has its principal place of business, or in some other country with a close connection to the contract. This could lead to some surprising results. Different countries, even with modern codes, often have different rules for interpreting contracts, for remedies and awarding damages, or even for determining if a contract exists at all. This is especially true when buyer and seller come from countries with different legal systems—common law, civil law, or Islamic law. No international businessperson or attorney can possibly know all the laws of every country in which they do business. Attorneys may feel uncertain about negotiating and drafting contracts for their clients that would be governed by foreign codes that are unfamiliar or that are available only in a foreign language. If they do not have foreign legal experience, have not read the foreign case law, and do not have the advice of foreign counsel, then it becomes very difficult for them to advise their clients on the legal ramifications of a contract. Of course, the parties are free to negotiate and agree on their choice of national law. However, while it may seem like a freely bargained agreement, the choice is usually that of the party with the greatest bargaining power. It is this unpredictability of foreign law that is the unknown factor in contracting, and that can lead to a tremendous uncertainty in buying and selling goods across national borders.

The ability to predict what will happen in the event of a breach of contract is essential to commerce. For centuries, legal scholars and lawmakers everywhere have realized that no nation can be open for business with the rest of the world without a stable and predictable body of sales law. No nation can expect to attract foreign traders and firms without a modern body of governing law to protect the contract rights of both its own citizens and foreigners alike.

The Unification of Sales Law. The history of legal development in many nations has often coincided with its history of opening to the world through foreign trade. As trade expanded, and as foreigner merchants came to trade, so did nations require a more universally accepted set of laws. English common law spread through the early British Empire, including the American colonies. Civil law and Napoleonic codes spread through Europe, Latin America, Japan, and even China. This gradual process certainly unified laws, one country at a time. However, as the twentieth century brought the world closer together, there were calls for more organized efforts at unifying the sales laws of diverse countries around the world.

The process of making national laws more uniform is known as the **unification of law**. The unification of modern sales law has been ongoing since the early part of the last century. Early efforts were made by the League of Nations, and by private organizations and law societies, although those largely turned out to be unsuccessful. In 1966, the United Nations created a new organization responsible for unifying trade law, the *United Nations Commission on International Trade Law,* or UNCITRAL (Vienna). UNCITRAL's work led to a very successful effort in unifying the law applicable to the international sale of goods and the adoption in 1980 of the *United Nations Convention on Contracts for the International Sale of Goods,* or CISG. The CISG now forms the basis for a widely accepted body of international sales law, now implemented into the national codes and statutes of more than 70 nations, including the United States and its largest trading partners—Canada, Mexico, China, and most of Europe. The great feat of the United Nations in creating the CISG was that it was able to bring together legal scholars from all regions of the world, representing diverse legal systems. It was able to develop a code acceptable to the common law countries and civil law countries, including both developed and developing countries as well as the socialist countries of the time. The CISG is the primary subject of this chapter. We will look at contract formation, interpretation, warranties, rights and remedies on default, excuses for nonperformance, and more. We begin, however, by briefly tracing the historical development of sales law at the national level in England, the United States, and in modern China.

THE CONVENTION ON CONTRACTS FOR THE INTERNATIONAL SALE OF GOODS (CISG)

Throughout most of the twentieth century, international legal scholars envisioned a near-universally accepted, uniform law of sales. In 1980, that work came to fruition in the form of the CISG. It was drafted by representatives from many different countries at meetings that took place over many years around the world.

The CISG is now in effect in over 70 countries that account for more than two-thirds of all world trade. It was ratified by the U.S. Senate and became effective in the United States in 1988. The CISG is effective for trade within North America, as it has also been ratified by Canada and Mexico. It has also displaced the Chinese law of contracts for international sales. Interestingly, the United Kingdom, which is so firmly rooted in common law traditions, has not adopted the CISG. As of 2012, it has been adopted by the countries shown in Exhibit 4.1. Translations are available in the official languages of the United Nations (Arabic, Chinese, English, French, Russian, and Spanish) and in many others. An edited copy of the CISG appears in the appendix of this book, and you are encouraged to refer to it often while reading this chapter.

This chapter examines the following aspects of the CISG: (1) its applicability to international sales, (2) rules of contract formation, validity and interpretation; (3) performance and nonperformance by the parties (4) remedies and damages for breach of contract; and (5) excuses for nonperformance of a contract.

Applicability of the CISG to International Sales

The CISG applies if the following conditions are met:

1. The contract is for the commercial sale of goods (the CISG does not define the term "goods.").
2. It is between parties whose places of business are in different countries (nationality or citizenship of individuals is not a determining factor).
3. The parties' places of business are located in countries that have ratified the convention.

Exhibit 4.1

Countries that Have Ratified or Acceded to the CISG

Argentina	Latvia
Albania	Lebanon
Armenia	Lesotho
Australia	Liberia
Austria	Lithuania
Belarus	Luxembourg
Belgium	Macedonia (Republic of)
Benin	Mauritania
Bosnia and Herzegovina	Mexico
Bulgaria	Moldova
Burundi	Mongolia
Canada	Montenegro
Chile	Netherlands
China	New Zealand
Colombia	Norway
Croatia	Paraguay
Cuba	Peru
Cyprus	Poland
Czech Republic	Romania
Denmark	Russian Federation
Dominican Republic	San Marino
Ecuador	St. Vincent-Grenadines
Egypt	Serbia
El Salvador	Singapore
Estonia	Slovakia
Finland	Slovenia
France	Spain
Gabon	Sweden
Georgia	Switzerland
Germany	Syrian Arab Republic
Greece	Turkey
Guinea	Uganda
Honduras	Ukraine
Hungary	United States
Iceland	Uruguay
Iraq	Uzbekistan
Israel	Zambia
Italy	
Japan	
Korea (Republic of South)	
Kyrgyzstan	

Assume that a dispute arises over a contract between a buyer whose business is located in the United States and a seller whose business is located in France. Regardless of who initiates the lawsuit or whether it is brought in the United States or France, if no choice of law provision specifies otherwise, their rights will be determined by the CISG—not by the UCC or the French Civil Code. Similarly, if the same dispute arises between a U.S. buyer and an English seller whose business is located in the United Kingdom, and there is no choice of law provision in the contract, the applicable law is likely to be that of the country with the closest connection to the contract. Here, one of the parties is not located in a country that has ratified the convention—the United Kingdom. Now take another, perhaps more important, example. Assume that American and Chinese firms are in the process of negotiating a contract, but that neither will agree to have a dispute heard under the other's law (assume they disagree on the forum as well). There is no arbitration provision. The CISG provides a solution: The contract can be drafted to call for any dispute to be brought before the courts of Hong Kong and to be decided according to the CISG, thus providing a neutral forum and a neutral law.

In the United States, the UCC will continue to apply to purely domestic sales and to sales between firms located in the United States and countries that have not ratified the CISG.

Place of Business Requirement. In the case of buyers or sellers with places of business in more than one country, such as multinational corporations, "place of business" would be considered to be the country that has the closest relation to the contract and where it will be performed. This could mean, at least theoretically, that if two American companies negotiated a contract entirely within the United States, but one of them had a place of business outside of the United States and the contract was to be performed outside the United States (e.g., the contract called for delivery of the goods to a point outside the United States), then the CISG might govern the transaction.

Choice of Law Provisions. Despite the widespread acceptance of the CISG, many attorneys recommend that their clients negotiate a choice of law provision calling for the resolution of disputes according to their own national laws. Many U.S. lawyers prefer to have the more familiar UCC govern their clients' contracts. Article 6 of the CISG allows parties to "exclude the application of this Convention… or vary from any of its provisions." This is often called the "opting out" provisions of the CISG. Any attempt to "opt out" must be stated in clear and unequivocal language and should only be done by attorneys experienced with the CISG.

The following case, *Asante Technologies, Inc. v. PMC-Sierra, Inc.*, discusses three important provisions of the CISG: the place of business requirement, the ability of the parties to "opt out" of the CISG by using a choice of law clause, and the concept that in international transactions the CISG preempts the contract laws of U.S. states.

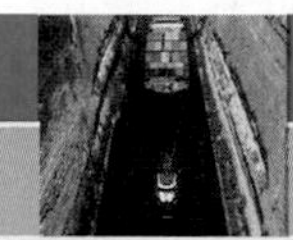

Asante Technologies, Inc. v. PMC-Sierra, Inc.

164 F. Supp. 2d 1142 (2001) United States District Court (N.D. Cal.)

BACKGROUND AND FACTS

The plaintiff, Asante, purchased electronic parts from the defendant, PMC, whose offices and factory were in Canada. Asante placed its orders through defendant's authorized distributor, Unique Technologies, located in California. Asante's order stated that the contract "shall be governed by the laws of the state shown on buyer's address on this order." PMC's confirmation stated that the contract "shall be construed according to the laws of Canada." Invoices were sent from Unique, and payment remitted to Unique, either in California or Nevada. Asante claimed that the goods did not meet its specifications and filed suit in California state court to have its claim decided under California law. When the case was transferred to a U.S. federal court, Asante requested that the case be remanded back to state court.

WARE, DISTRICT JUDGE PLACE OF BUSINESS REQUIREMENT

The *Convention on Contracts for the International Sale of Goods* ("CISG") is an international treaty which has been signed and ratified by the United States and Canada, among other countries ... The CISG applies "to contracts of sale of goods between parties whose places of business are in different States ... when the States are Contracting States." CISG Art. 1 (1) (a). Article 10 of the CISG provides that "if a party has more than one place of business, the place of business is that which has the closest relationship to the contract and its performance." CISG Art. 10 ...

It is undisputed that plaintiff's place of business is Santa Clara County, California. It is further undisputed that...defendant's corporate headquarters, inside sales and marketing office, public relations department, principal warehouse, and most of its design and engineering functions were located in Canada. However, plaintiff contends that, pursuant to Article 10 of the CISG, defendant's "place of business" having the closest relationship to the contract at issue is the United States ...

Plaintiff asserts that Unique acted in the United States as an agent of defendant, and that plaintiff's contacts with Unique establish defendant's place of business in the United States for the purposes of this contract. Plaintiff has failed to persuade the Court that Unique acted as the agent of defendant ... To the contrary, a distributor of goods for resale is normally not treated as an agent of the manufacturer ... Furthermore, while Unique may distribute defendant's products, plaintiff does not allege that Unique made any representations regarding technical specifications on behalf of defendant ... Plaintiff's dealings with Unique do not establish defendant's place of business in the United States.

Plaintiff's claims concern breaches of representations made by defendant from Canada. Moreover, the products in question are manufactured in Canada, and plaintiff knew that defendant was Canadian, having sent one purchase order directly to defendant in Canada by fax ... Moreover, plaintiff directly corresponded with defendant at defendant's Canadian address ... In contrast, plaintiff has not identified any specific representation or correspondence emanating from defendant's Oregon branch. For these reasons, the Court finds that defendant's place of business that has the closest relationship to the contract and its performance is British Columbia, Canada. Consequently, the contract at issue in this litigation is between parties from two different Contracting States, Canada and the United States. This contract therefore implicates the CISG.

CHOICE OF LAW CLAUSE

Plaintiff next argues that, even if the Parties are from two nations that have adopted the CISG, the choice of law provisions in the [buyer's purchase order and seller's confirmation] reflect the Parties' intent to "opt out" of application of the treaty. The Court finds that the particular choice of law provisions in the "Terms and Conditions" of both parties are inadequate to effectuate an "opt out" of the CISG.

continues

continued

Although selection of a particular choice of law, such as "the California Commercial Code" or the "Uniform Commercial Code" could amount to implied exclusion of the CISG, the choice of law clauses at issue here do not evince a clear intent to opt out of the CISG. For example, defendant's choice of applicable law adopts the law of British Columbia, and it is undisputed that the CISG is the law of British Columbia. Furthermore, even plaintiff's choice of applicable law generally adopts the "laws of" the State of California, and California is bound by the Supremacy Clause to the treaties of the United States. Thus, under general California law, the CISG is applicable to contracts where the contracting parties are from different countries that have adopted the CISG ...

FEDERAL PREEMPTION

It appears that the issue of whether or not the CISG preempts state law is a matter of first impression. In the case of federal statutes, "the question of whether a certain action is preempted by federal law is one of congressional intent ... The Court concludes that the expressly stated goal of developing uniform international contract law to promote international trade indicates the intent of the parties to the treaty to have the treaty preempt state law causes of action. The availability of independent state contract law causes of action would frustrate the goals of uniformity and certainty embraced by the CISG. Allowing such avenues for potential liability would subject contracting parties to different states' laws and the very same ambiguities regarding international contracts that the CISG was designed to avoid. As a consequence, parties to international contracts would be unable to predict the applicable law, and the fundamental purpose of the CISG would be undermined.

Finally, plaintiff appears to confuse the matter of exclusive federal jurisdiction with preemption ... Even where federal law completely preempts state law, state courts may have concurrent jurisdiction over the federal claim if the defendant does not remove the case to federal court [citation omitted]. This Court does not hold that it has exclusive jurisdiction over CISG claims.

Decision. The federal court had concurrent jurisdiction over this case (even though the case could also have been heard in state court) because the applicable law was the CISG, an international convention ratified by the United States.

Case Questions

1. What were the court's holdings with respect to place of business, choice of applicable law and preemption of state contract law?
2. On what basis did the court conclude that the parties had not sufficiently evidenced an intent to opt out of the CISG? What language would you have included in the purchase and confirmation orders to clearly evidence such an intent?
3. What reasons did the court give for preempting state contract law in favor of the CISG?

Sales Excluded from the CISG. The following types of sales have been specifically excluded from the convention:

1. Consumer goods sold for personal, family, or household use
2. Goods bought at auction
3. Stocks, securities, negotiable instruments, or money
4. Ships, vessels, or aircraft
5. Electricity
6. Assembly contracts for the supply of goods to be manufactured or produced wherein the buyer provides a "substantial part of the materials necessary for such manufacture or production"
7. Contracts that are in "preponderant part" for the supply of labor or other services
8. Contracts imposing liability on the seller for death or personal injury caused by the goods
9. Contracts where the parties specifically agree to "opt out" of the convention or where they choose to be bound by some other law

In the United States, Article 2 of the UCC applies to both consumer and domestic commercial transactions. Consumer sales were excluded from the CISG because consumer protection laws are so specific to every country that it would have been very difficult to harmonize them. Further, consumer sales are usually domestic in nature.

VALIDITY AND FORMATION OF INTERNATIONAL SALES CONTRACTS

Although readers who have studied contract law may be acquainted with the general concepts of contract validity and formation, they may find that many of the specific rules applicable to international contracts are different from what they learned. The following sections discuss the requirements for a valid contract, including the intention of the parties to be bound, mutual assent (offer and acceptance), and other rules.

General Requirements for a Valid Contract

Under the common law, a **valid contract** is an agreement that contains all of the essential elements and meets all the requirements of a binding contract, including:

1. It is an agreement between parties entered into by mutual assent and resulting from their words or from conduct that indicates their intention to be bound.
2. It must be supported by consideration (the bargained-for exchange of a legal benefit or incurring of a legal detriment).
3. The parties must have legal capacity (they may not be minors, legally incompetent, or under the influence of drugs or alcohol).
4. The contract must not be for illegal purposes or contrary to public policy.

If an agreement is missing any one of these essential elements, the courts will not enforce it under the common law.

The CISG only governs the formation of a contract and the rights and obligations of the seller and buyer. The Convention does not provide rules for determining whether a contract is valid, for determining whether a party to a contract is legally competent, or for determining whether a party is guilty of fraud or misrepresentation. These rules are left to individual state or national laws. Consideration is not mentioned, and Article 29 seems to state that consideration is not required in order to modify or terminate a contract under the CISG, although in *Geneva Pharmaceuticals Technology Corp. v. Barr Laboratories Inc.*, 201 F. Supp. 2d 236 (S.D. N.Y. 2002), a U.S. federal court stated that issues of validity, including consideration, were a matter of state law and not governed by the CISG. Two additional federal courts in *Barbara Berry, S.A. v. Ken M. Spooner Farms, Inc.*, 2006 U.S. Dist. LEXIS 31262 (W.D. Mich. 2006) and *Norfolk Southern Railway Co. v. Power Source Supply, Inc.*, 2008 U.S. Dist. LEXIS 56942 (W.D. Pa. 2008) have reached similar conclusions.

The Effect of Illegality

A generally recognized principle of contract law is that, in all legal systems, agreements that violate the laws of a state or nation are void. A void agreement is of no legal effect and will not be enforced by a court.

The Writing Requirement

The laws of many nations differ as to whether contracts for the sale of goods must be in writing. Under the UCC, American law requires that contracts for the sale of goods of $500 or more be in writing. (Under proposed amendments to the UCC, the requirement would be increased to $5,000 and the requirement of a signed "writing" would be changed to signed "record.") Writing requirements in common law countries date back to an act of the English Parliament in 1677. In 1954, however, the United Kingdom repealed its law.

Under CISG Article 11, a contract for the international sale of goods "need not be concluded in or evidenced by writing and is not subject to any other requirement as to form. It may be proved by any means, including witnesses." This is in keeping with a basic concept found in the CISG: that the parties should have flexibility in contracting and as much freedom of contract as possible.

Several countries, including Argentina, Chile, Hungary, Russia, and a few others, have elected to omit Article 11 from their version of the CISG. In those countries, foreign sales contracts governed by the CISG must still be in writing. In China, one provision of the 1999 *Contract Law for the People's Republic of China* prevails over CISG Article 11, even for international sales otherwise governed by the CISG. This permits foreign sales contracts to be either written or oral, unless some other statute or administrative regulation requires that they be in writing. That requires knowledge of many different administrative regulations. By practice, almost all foreign trade contracts involving Chinese firms are in writing.

Digital Signatures in Electronic Commerce. The United States, Japan, China, and members of the European Union have enacted laws recognizing the validity of electronic or digital signatures on contracts and legal documents. The U.S. law, the *Electronic Signatures in Global and National Commerce Act*, makes an electronic signature on a contract as legally binding as a handwritten one on a paper document.

Problems of Contract Interpretation

Due to the great distances involved in international business, negotiations are often conducted through a series of conversations, meetings, and communications by mail, package delivery, telephone, fax, e-mail, and sharing of digital files. The parties may make reference to ancillary materials, such as spec sheets and price lists. Samples, models, and prototypes may be exchanged. The negotiations may take place in more than one country and more than one language. The buyer may visit the seller's factory to see the seller's capabilities firsthand. Discussions might take place through "delegations" or negotiating teams of salespeople, technical specialists, agents, and attorneys. Technical discussions are often left to engineers or others experts. Negotiations may be heavily influenced by language barriers and cultural differences, and terminology peculiar to the industry will be used. The parties may have thought that they were close to agreement many times, only to reach an impasse, resuming negotiations at a later time. In the end, the final agreement may be recorded in one written document.

On the other hand, it is not unusual for the parties to fail to put their agreement into a complete and final written document. This can happen out of ignorance, a history of past dealings with one another, time constraints, or other reasons. And as we saw, in most countries, a contract for the international sale of goods does not have to be in writing to be enforceable under the CISG. In the event that a dispute ends in court, it might be possible for the court to look at the chain of negotiations and to piece together the intentions of the parties on the basis of the testimony and other evidence. But this can be expensive and lead to an uncertain result. More experienced firms, at the close of negotiations, would be careful to put their complete agreement in writing. If the complete and final agreement has been put into writing, we say that the contract has become "integrated." An **integrated contract** is a written document or documents that evidence the final and complete agreement of the parties. Mere informal notes of one of the parties, or an unsigned document marked "draft," would not be a fully integrated contract.

The Parol Evidence Rule and the Common Law. The common law **parol evidence rule** states that a court may not consider in evidence any written or oral statements that were made by the parties prior to or at the time of concluding a fully integrated written contract if the statements are offered to contradict, vary, or add to the terms of the written contract. The court may not look to prior negotiations, correspondence, or verbal statements offered by one of the parties at trial for the purpose of denying or contradicting the written contract. Parol evidence may be introduced to clarify an ambiguity (but not to contradict the "plain meaning" of a term); to prove fraud, undue influence, or lack of capacity; or to prove the existence of a later agreement that modified or terminated an earlier contract. The parol evidence rule is a common law rule, applicable to all contracts, not just sales contracts. It prevents extrinsic evidence from reaching the ears of a jury and lessens the chance of perjury and unreliable testimony. The civil law systems, which generally do not use jury trials in these cases, do not have the same strict rule against the admissibility of parol evidence in most breach of contract cases.

Parol Evidence and the CISG. The parol evidence rule has not been incorporated into the CISG. Article 8 of the CISG allows a court, when considering the intent of the parties to a contract, to consider "all relevant circumstances of the case, including the negotiations, any practices which the parties have established between themselves, usages, and any subsequent conduct of the parties."

In *MCC-Marble Ceramic Center, Inc. v. Ceramica Nuova D'Agostino, S.P.A.*, 144 F.3d 1384 (11th Cir. 1998), a U.S. citizen signed a contract for the purchase of Italian ceramic tile while at a trade fair in Bologna. The document consisted of the seller's order form and included preprinted terms on the front and reverse sides. The terms stated that if the goods did not conform to the contract, notice had to be given to the seller within ten days. When the tile arrived, the buyer believed it was inferior, but never gave notice of this fact to the seller. There was uncontradicted evidence that, at the time of signing the contract, all parties had a verbal understanding that the preprinted terms would not be applicable. Applying the CISG, the court ruled that parol evidence could be considered to contradict the written terms of the contract. In other words, the trial court could consider the subjective intent of the parties, as well as their verbal understanding at the time of signing the contract, in order to invalidate the preprinted terms. With no preprinted terms, the buyer would be permitted to withhold payment because the goods did not conform to the contract specifications.

The Role of Customs, Practices, and Trade Usages. It is usually not possible, in an international transaction, for the parties to expressly state or write every single detail into their contract. There are bound to be gaps in most contracts. Firms that have done business in a certain way for many years often expect, and are justified in expecting, that they will continue the same practice. A buyer who has always ordered products and materials of specified quality may not recite that in every order placed with his or her supplier. They may assume that their past dealings will become a part of their future dealings, unless specified. Another issue is that in many industries, it is common to use language and terminology specific to that industry. For example, in purchasing silk from China, a silk buyer in the United States may order "hand-pulled mulberry silk" or "habotai" or "tussah" or "10-momme weight." These are terms that may have very special meanings to merchants but mean nothing to the rest of us.

To fill in these gaps, or to interpret specific contract provisions, the courts of the United States and most other common law countries will look to **trade usages** for guidance. Trade usages are rules derived from the widespread customs of an industry, the practices of merchants in their past dealings, and the usages of trade terminology and language. Examples include use of specific descriptive terms, guarantees that the goods "will be of average and acceptable quality for the kind and type of goods sold in the trade," and inclusion of trade terms to refer to which party is responsible for shipping expenses and the risk of damage or loss of goods during shipment.

Trade Usages and the CISG. The CISG provisions of Article 9 resemble how U.S. law handles trade usages. The only trade usages that can be used to interpret or fill in the gaps in a contract are (1) those to which the parties have agreed or that they have established between themselves and (2) those usages of which the parties knew or ought to have known, and that are widely known in international trade (or at least in those countries in which both buyer and seller are located) and regularly observed in the industry or trade involved.

Mutual Assent: The Offer

The contract laws of all countries require that the parties reach a mutual agreement and understanding about the essential terms of a contract. This is known as **mutual assent**. The agreement is reached through the bargaining process between offeror and offeree. The offeror, by making the offer, creates in the offeree the power of acceptance, or the power to form a contract. A contract arises upon acceptance by the offeree.

The Intention to Be Bound. Under Article 14 of the CISG, a communication between the parties is considered an offer when (1) it is a proposal for concluding a contract and (2) it is "sufficiently definite and indicates the intention of the offeror to be bound." An offer is considered sufficiently definite if it (1) indicates or describes the goods, (2) expressly or implicitly specifies the quantity, and (3) expressly or implicitly specifies the price for the goods. However, one should not think that just because an item of communication includes a description of the goods, the quantity, and the price, that it always indicates an offer to conclude a contract. In many international contracts involving a great deal of money, no firm would make a commitment without reaching an agreement on many other terms, such as methods of payment, delivery dates, allocation of shipping costs, quality standards, installation and training, warranties, and responsibility for duties or taxes. In cases where the court does find that the parties had the intention to be bound, it can supply many of the missing terms by looking to their past dealings and to the customs in the trade or industry, or by referring to the applicable provisions of the CISG.

Public Offers. If an offer must express the offeror's intention to be bound, how does the law treat advertisements, brochures, catalogs, and Websites? Are they offers, inviting acceptance, or are they mere **invitations to deal**—invitations to the public to make an offer? The laws of some nations hold that an offer must be addressed to one or more specific persons. In those countries, an advertisement will not create the power of acceptance in a member of the public who reads the ad. Other countries, while treating most advertisements as mere invitations to deal, do recognize that specific advertisements that describe the goods, their quantity, and price may be considered an offer.

The CISG takes a middle position by creating a presumption that an advertisement, catalog, price list, or Website is not an offer. Article 14 states, "A proposal other than one addressed to one or more specific persons is to be considered merely as an invitation to make offers, unless the contrary is clearly indicated by the person making the proposal." Consequently, to be on the safe side, many attorneys recommend that a seller include in all of its price sheets and literature, and on its Website, a notice that the content does not constitute an offer.

Open Price Terms. In international transactions between companies familiar with their industry or market, it is not unusual that a contract can be concluded without any mention of price. It is not that it was overlooked; it may just have been that they were relying on some external market factor or prior course of dealings to determine price. A contract may even refer to a market price on a date that is months or even years away. If the price is left "open," is the parties' understanding sufficiently definite to constitute a valid contract? In the United States, most state UCC laws provide that if price is not specified, a "reasonable price" will be presumed. Other countries take different approaches which may not favor open price terms.

Although some conflict stems from the language of the CISG regarding open price terms (see Articles 14 and 55), the CISG provisions seem similar to those of U.S. state law. Article 55 states that where price is not fixed, the price will be that charged "for such goods sold under comparable circumstances in the trade concerned." Accordingly, if the buyer and seller fail to specify the price of the goods, a court might look to the trade or to the market price of comparable goods to make its own determination of price, and the contract and all its other provisions will remain in effect.

Firm Offers. As a general rule, an offer may be revoked at any time prior to acceptance. Under the UCC, as between merchants, an offer may not be revoked if it is made in a signed writing that gives assurance that it will remain open for a stated period of time, not to exceed three months. Under the CISG, firm offers are valid even if they are not in writing. Moreover, an offer may not be revoked if the offeree reasonably relies on the offer as being irrevocable and the offeree has acted in reliance on the offer. Some civil law countries, such as Germany, France, Italy, and Japan, prohibit revocation during the period of time normally needed for the offeree's acceptance to arrive.

The Pro Forma Invoice. One very common method of offering goods for sale to a foreign buyer is through the pro forma invoice (Exhibit 4.2). The ***pro forma* invoice** is a formal document addressed to a specified buyer to sell the products described according to certain terms and conditions. Most pro forma invoices are specific and definite enough to meet the requirements of an offer. The pro forma invoice sets out the price for the goods in the currency stated, plus any additional charges payable by the buyer's account, including the cost of packing and crating; the cost of inland freight; the cost of ocean or air freight, freight forwarder's fees, and pier delivery charges; wharfage and warehouse charges; and insurance. The *pro forma* invoice specifies the mode of shipment, the method of payment, the length of time for which the quoted terms will be valid, and any and all other terms required by the seller as a condition of sale. Sellers usually require the buyer to accept the offer by signing it and returning it to them before shipment. In other cases, a buyer might accept an offer by sending its own purchase order form. *The pro forma* invoice should not be confused with the commercial invoice, which is the final bill for the goods that accompanies the request for payment.

Mutual Assent: The Acceptance

A contract is not formed until the offer is accepted by the offeree. The acceptance is the offeree's manifestation of the intention to be bound to the terms of the offer. Modern legal rules applicable to the sale of goods give great flexibility to the offeree as to the manner and method of accepting—certainly greater flexibility than under the common law. Under the CISG, an acceptance may take the form of a statement or conduct by the offeree that indicates the offeree's intention to be bound to the contract. CISG Article 18 states that "a statement made by or other conduct of the offeree indicating assent to an offer is an acceptance." (UCC 2-206 states that "an offer to make a contract shall be construed as inviting acceptance in any manner and by any medium reasonable in the circumstances.") This rule has day-to-day applicability. It is very common for a prospective buyer to place an order to purchase goods, with the seller responding not with a verbal or written confirmation, or not by initialing the order and returning it to the buyer, but simply by shipping the goods called for. For instance, the seller may be shipping urgently needed replacement parts for a stopped assembly line. Similarly, it is not uncommon for a buyer to accept the delivery of goods by simply remitting payment (as in the case where the seller

Exhibit 4.2

Pro Forma Invoice

DownPillow International, Inc.
Pro Forma Invoice
Boone, North Carolina, U.S.A.

Invoice to:	Japanese Retailer Osaka, Japan	Date of pro forma invoice: Oct. 12, 2009
Ship/Consign to:	as per buyer's instructions	This pro forma no. 000044372
Shipment via:	U.S. port to destination Kobe	Terms of Payment
Notify Party:	Buyer to advise	Cash against documents,
Country-of-Origin:	U.S.A	irrevocable LC payable in U.S. dollars
Total weight (est.):	9405 lbs/4266 kg.	Shipment Date
Shipping volume (est.):	3000 cu.ft./85 cu.m.	45 days after receipt of LC

Quantity	Item Code	Description	Price	Amount
5,000	5WGD-1	Bed pillows of white goose down total fill weight 26 oz./0.74 kg, contents sterilized shell: 100% cotton, with piping size 26" × 26", 66 cm × 66 cm	$32.00	$160,000
		PRICE Ex Works, Domestic packing		$160,000
		Export packing/vacuum pack charges		850
		Cartage/Inland freight charge		1,250
		Pier delivery charge		150
		Freight forwarder's fees		200
		PRICE F.A.S. NC PORT		$162,450
		Ocean freight charges port to port		$3,355
		Container rental charge		450
		Marine insurance charges		640
		PRICE C.I.F. Port of KOBE, Japan		$166,895

DownPillow International, Inc.

____________________ ____________________

by, Export Sales Manager Authorized buyer's signature

All terms of sale interpreted by *Incoterms* 2000. This quotation is valid for a period of sixty days from above date. Any changes in the actual cost of shipping, handling, packaging, insurance, or other charges not a part of the actual cost of the goods are buyer's responsibility.

SEE OTHER SIDE FOR ADDITIONAL TERMS AND CONDITIONS

ships blue widgets instead of the red ones ordered; if the buyer pays for the nonconforming red ones, there is a contract). Both the UCC and the CISG cover these situations. CISG Article 18 states that an offeree may accept by "dispatching the goods or payment of the price, without notice to the offeror" provided that the parties have established this as a practice or it is routinely accepted in the trade, and if the act is performed within the time for acceptance fixed by the offeror or within a reasonable time.

Silence Not an Acceptance. The general rule in most countries is that the offeree's silence or inactivity alone should not be interpreted as an acceptance. If you unexpectedly receive goods that you did not order, you should not have to pay for them (although in most legal systems, you might have to safeguard them until the sender retrieves them). Moreover, it would be unfair if a seller could force you to take goods simply by stating, "If I don't hear from you, I assume you will keep them and pay for them." On the other hand, there are situations where the parties can agree that silence is an acceptance. If seller makes an offer to you, and you reply, "If you do not hear from me by 5:00 p.m., ship the goods," then you have made your silence an acceptance.

Another exception occurs when the parties' previous dealings oblige them to speak up and not remain silent. Consider this case: For the past five years, DownPillow, Inc., has regularly ordered quantities of white goose down from Federhaus GmbH for shipment within three months. At first, Federhaus confirmed all orders. Soon, Federhaus stopped sending written confirmations of orders and just shipped.

This time, DownPillow placed the order and Federhaus never shipped. DownPillow suffered damages when it unexpectedly ran out of feathers. It can sue Federhaus for breach of contract on the basis that the established practice of the parties presumed Federhaus's acceptance of DownPillow's order.

When an Acceptance is Effective. Under the common law, and in virtually all legal systems, the offeree may accept at any time until the offer is revoked by the offeror, until the offer expires due to the passage of time, until the original offer is rejected by the offeree, until the offeree makes a counteroffer in return, or until the offer terminates (such as through the death of one of the parties or destruction of the subject matter). Thus, it is often important to know when an acceptance becomes effective because it cuts off the offeror's ability to revoke the offer, and it is at that point in time when contractual rights and obligations arise. Time constraints can be even more critical in international transactions between buyers and sellers located in different time zones and using several different means of communications—next-day letters, e-mail, telephone, and facsimile transmissions.

Under the common law, a contract is formed when the acceptance is dispatched by the offeree In the case of an acceptance by letter or written document, the time of dispatch is the time the letter is put into the hands of the postal authorities, courier service, or other carrier. This is commonly called the **mailbox rule**. The rule assumes that the correct mode of transmission is used (i.e., one that the offeror specifies or, if none, one that is reasonable under the circumstances) and that it is properly addressed. This assumption makes commercial sense, for if a fax arrives offering to sell fresh roses sitting on the hot tarmac in Colombia, one does not accept by letter and expect a contract to be formed on dispatch. Hence, if a buyer submits an order to a seller, a contract is formed upon the dispatch of the seller's acceptance. The buyer's power to withdraw the offer to purchase ended at the time the contract was formed. While the mailbox rule was developed long before the existence of electronic communications, and while it has lost some of its significance in the age of fax machines and e-mail, it is still relevant and applicable.

The CISG follows a somewhat different approach. Under Article 18, an acceptance is not effective upon dispatch, but is effective when it reaches the offeror (or in the case of electronic transmission, appears on the offeror's fax machine or in his or her e-mail inbox). Article 16 protects the offeree by stating that the dispatch of an acceptance cuts off the offeror's right to revoke the offer. Thus, an acceptance may possibly be withdrawn if the withdrawal reaches the offeror before or at the same time as the acceptance does (Article 22). Recall that under the common law, the offeree would not have had the same right because the contract would have been formed at the moment of dispatch. This CISG rule follows the basic rules in effect in China and civil law countries. The following case, *Solae, LLC v. Hershey Canada, Inc.*, discusses the formation of a contract and one party's futile attempt to modify it.

The Mirror Image Rule. Students of the common law of contracts are very familiar with the **mirror image rule**. The rule requires that an offeree respond to an offer with an acceptance that is definite and

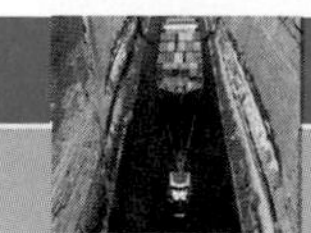

Solae, LLC v. Hershey Canada, Inc.

557 F. Supp. 2d 452 (2008) United States District Court (D. Del.)

BACKGROUND AND FACTS

Solae, a U.S. limited liability company with its principal place of business in St. Louis, Missouri, had sold soy lecithin to Hershey Canada, Inc., a Canadian corporation with its primary place of business in Mississauga, Ontario (Canada) since 2003. The soy lecithin was incorporated into Hershey's products sold throughout Canada. Solae and Hershey negotiated contracts at the end of each calendar year for Hershey's orders of soy lecithin in the upcoming year. In January 2006, the parties reached an agreement whereby Hershey would order up to 250,000 pounds of soy lecithin from Solae in 2006 at a price of U.S. $1.2565 per pound.

In June 2006, Hershey faxed a purchase order to Solae for 40,000 pounds of soy lecithin to be delivered to Hershey's manufacturing plant in Smith Falls, Ontario, in September 2006. Solae sent an order confirmation to Hershey in June 2006. The order confirmation did not contain Solae's standard conditions of sale nor did it contain a forum selection clause. In September 2006, Solae shipped 40,000 pounds of soy lecithin to Hershey. An invoice sent to Hershey concurrent with the shipment contained the conditions of sale, including a forum selection clause providing that "the courts of Delaware shall have exclusive jurisdiction over any disputes or issues arising under this Agreement."

In October 2006, Hershey discovered that the soy lecithin was contaminated with salmonella. The contamination was discovered after Hershey had incorporated the contaminated soy lecithin into over two million units of product shipped throughout Canada. The contamination resulted in a large-scale recall of Hershey's chocolate products, the temporary closure of the Smith Falls plant, and an extensive investigation by the Canadian government. Hershey notified Solae of the contaminated soy lecithin, informed Solae that it would hold Solae responsible for damages incurred as a result of the incident, and refused to accept delivery or pay for any additional lots of soy lecithin, including a lot for which an order had been placed in October 2006.

Solae filed a lawsuit in March 2007 seeking a determination of the parties' rights with respect to the June and October 2006 orders. Hershey moved to dismiss Solae's complaint for lack of personal jurisdiction. The issue before the court was whether the forum selection clause contained within Solae's conditions of sale were part of the parties' contract such that the court could exercise personal jurisdiction over Hershey.

FARNAN, DISTRICT JUDGE

The parties dispute the relevant contract governing this dispute. If the relevant contract contains a forum-selection clause, Hershey Canada's contentions regarding personal jurisdiction are largely irrelevant. Accordingly, the Court must determine whether Hershey Canada is bound by a forum selection clause.

The parties agree that the *United Nations Convention of Contracts for the International Sale of Goods* ("CISG ") governs contract formation here. Under the terms of the *CISG, "a* contract is concluded at the moment when an acceptance of an offer becomes effective in accordance with the provisions of this Convention." *CISG,* Art. 23. An offer must be "sufficiently definite," and "demonstrate an intention by the offerer to be bound if the proposal is accepted." *Id.* Art. 14. An offer is accepted, and a contract is formed when the offeree makes a statement or other conduct, "indicating assent to an offer." *Id.* Art. 18. The CISG does not contain a statute of frauds, stating that "a contract of sale need not be concluded in or evidenced by writing and is not subject to any other requirement as to form." *Id.* Art. 11. Courts have held that a binding contract exists when the parties sufficiently agree to the goods, the quantity and the price. See, *e.g., Chateau Des Charmes Wines, Ltd. v. Sabate U.S.A., Ltd.* [citation omitted].

Having reviewed the record in light of the applicable legal standard, the Court is not persuaded by Solae's contention that its Conditions of Sale control the disputed transaction.... The record is clear that [the parties] reached agreement as to the amount of soy lecithin Solae was obligated to sell Hershey Canada during the calendar year 2006, and the price at which Solae was obligated to sell. Under this agreement, Hershey Canada was obligated to purchase a substantial quantity of soy lecithin from Solae at the price agreed upon. The Court concludes that this is sufficient to create a complete and binding contract under the CISG (the "2006 Contract").

Because the 2006 Contract did not include a forum-selection clause, the Court must now determine if the forum-selection clause contained in the Conditions of Sale subsequently became part of the 2006 Contract under the CISG. As Hershey Canada points out, this issue was addressed by the Ninth Circuit in *Chateau Des Charmes Wines Ltd.,* 328 F.3d 528:

> Under the Convention, a "contract may be modified or terminated by the mere agreement of the

continues

continued

> parties." [CISG], art. 29(1). However, the Convention clearly states that "[a]dditional or different terms relating, among other things, to ... the settlement of disputes are considered to alter the terms of the offer materially." *Id.* art 19(3). There is no indication that [the buyer] conducted itself in a manner that evidenced any affirmative assent to the forum selection clauses in the invoices. Rather, [the buyer] merely performed its obligations under the oral contracts. Nothing in the Convention suggests that the failure to object to a party's unilateral attempt to alter materially the terms of an otherwise valid agreement is an "agreement" within the terms of Article 29.

Id. at 531. Here, as in *Chateau,* Solae has set forth no substantive evidence indicating that Hershey Canada agreed to a modification of the terms of the 2006 Contract, beyond Hershey Canada's receipt of the Conditions of Sale. Solae has not set forth evidence refuting statements that Hershey Canada's material analyst at the Smith Falls plant was not authorized to negotiate contractual terms or to commit Hershey Canada to Solae's Conditions of Sale, and the Court does not agree with Solae's contention that because multiple invoices and pre-shipment confirmations containing these Conditions of Sale were sent to Hershey Canada over "years of sales and dozens of transactions," these terms necessarily became part of the 2006 Contract. "[A] parties' multiple attempts to alter an agreement unilaterally do not so effect." *Chateau,* 328 F.3d at 531. In sum, the Court concludes that Hershey Canada's continued performance of its duties under the 2006 Contract did not demonstrate its acceptance of the terms contained in the Condition of Sales, and the Court further concludes that Solae's Conditions of Sale did not modify the 2006 Contract to add a forum-selection clause.

Decision. The parties' January 2006 contract for the sale and purchase of soy lecithin in 2006 was valid and binding. The forum selection clause contained in Solae's conditions of sale and incorporated in later sales documents was not a part of this contract. The buyer did not assent to the forum selection agreement simply by receiving and paying for the goods. The seller's complaint was thus dismissed for lack of personal jurisdiction.

Comment. In addition to its holding on new and additional terms, this case is instructive in its determination of the minimum requirements to form a contract pursuant to the CISG and its disregard of terms apparently incorporated into the sales documents between the parties for three years prior to this lawsuit.

Case Questions

1. What was the court's holding with respect to the inclusion of the forum selection clause in the parties' contract?
2. What are the requirements for the formation of a contract pursuant to the CISG?
3. Did the court improperly excuse Hershey's failure to object to the forum selection clause given the parties' extended dealings (which included conditions of sale containing a forum selection clause)? Why or why not?

unconditional and that matches the terms of the offer exactly and unequivocally. Under the mirror image rule, a purported acceptance that contains different or additional terms, no matter how minor, is considered a counteroffer and, thus, a rejection of the original offer. The principle that an acceptance must be definite and unconditional is found in the civil law countries and in the CISG. Article 19(1) states, "A reply to an offer which purports to be an acceptance but contains additions, limitations or other modifications is a rejection of the offer and constitutes a counteroffer." Thus, if the buyer places an order for a quantity of goods of a certain description, for shipment by air no later than "next Tuesday," and the seller replies by promising shipment no later than "next Wednesday morning," there is no contract. For many contracts this rule works fine, because it prevents contracts from arising when there was actually no mutual assent. It lessens the possibility of contract disputes. However, there are a few situations where strict adherence to the mirror image rule is not commercially practical. One of these situations is where the offeror and offeree, the buyer and seller, are communicating through an exchange of standard business forms, each of which contains extensive "fine print" provisions.

Standard Business Forms and Contract Modifications

Buyers and sellers often use standard business forms for quoting prices, placing orders, and acknowledging receipt of those orders. Two of the most common that we will discuss are the purchase order and the order confirmation. Business buyers commonly use a **purchase order** for placing orders for goods from their vendors. Typically, it includes the description and quantity of the goods ordered, a delivery address, and authorized buyer's signature. It may also recite the prices that the buyer believes to be accurate and current for the goods, a desired shipping date, and any other contractual requirements the buyer may have. The **order confirmation** (also called a "sales acknowledgment") is the seller's formal confirmation of the buyer's order, either accepting the order, rejecting it, or modifying its terms. Typically, these forms leave room on the front so the parties may insert important contract terms—those that they "bargained for," such as price, quality, or ship date. The reverse side often contains detailed "fine print" provisions or standard clauses, often called terms and conditions or general conditions of sale (Exhibit 4.3).

An attorney often drafts these **terms and conditions** to limit his or her client's liability by placing greater responsibility on the other party. The parties may not even be aware of the legal significance of these seldom-read fine print provisions. For the most part, a seller would only read the most crucial

Exhibit 4.3

Seller's Terms and Conditions of Sale

(Seller's Order Confirmation—Reverse Side)

Pro Forma Invoice or

TERMS AND CONDITIONS OF SALE

1. *Acceptance*

This constitutes acceptance by Seller of Buyer's purchase order. This acceptance is expressly made conditional upon Buyer's assent, express or implied, to the terms and conditions set forth herein without modification or addition. Buyer's acceptance of these terms and conditions shall be indicated by any part of the following, whichever first occurs: (a) Buyer's written acknowledgment hereof; (b) Buyer's acceptance of shipment of the goods herein described; (c) Buyer's failure to acknowledge or reject these terms and conditions in writing within five business days after delivery; or (d) any other act or expression of acceptance by the Buyer. Seller's silence or failure to respond to any such subsequent term, condition, or proposal shall not be deemed to be Seller's acceptance or approval thereof.

2. *Price and Delivery*

The quoted price for the goods may be varied by additions upwards by the Seller according to market conditions at the date of shipment and the Buyer shall pay such additions in addition to the quoted price, including but not limited to increases in the cost of labor, material, operations, and/or transport. Delivery and payment terms shall be made according to this order confirmation. Trade formulas used herein (e.g., CIF, CPT, FAS, or FOB) shall be interpreted according to *Incoterms* 2010. Payment in the currency and at the conditions of this confirmation.

3. *Force Majeure*

Seller shall not be liable for loss or damage due to delay in manufacture, shipment, or delivery resulting from any cause beyond Seller's direct control or due to compliance with any regulations, orders, acts, instructions, or priority requests of any government authority, acts of God, acts or omissions of the purchaser, fires, floods, epidemics, weather, strikes, factory shutdowns, embargoes, wars, riots, delays in transportation, delay in receiving materials from Seller's usual sources, and any delay resulting from any such cause shall extend shipment or delivery date to the extent caused thereby, and Seller shall be reimbursed its additional expenses resulting from such delay. In the case of delay lasting more than eight weeks, Seller has the right to cancel the contract. Receipt of merchandise by the Buyer shall constitute a waiver of any claims for delay.

4. *Warranties*

The Seller makes no representations or warranties with respect to the goods herein. Seller hereby disclaims warranties, express or implied, as to the products, including but not limited to, any implied warranty of quality or merchantability or fitness for any particular purpose, and the Buyer takes the goods on the Buyer's own judgment. Seller is not liable for any damage or loss for a breach of warranty.

5. *Limitation of Liability*

Seller is not liable for any special, consequential, or incidental damages arising out of this agreement or the goods sold hereunder, including but not limited to damages for lost profits, loss of use, or any damages or sums paid by Buyer to third parties, even if Seller has been advised of the possibility of such damages.

6. *Governing Law*

In respect of any standard, test, mode of inspection, measurement, or weight, the practice governing the same adopted for use in United States shall prevail. This agreement shall be governed by the Laws of North Carolina and in the event of any dispute arising, whether touching on the interpretation hereof or otherwise, the same shall be resolved before the General Court of Justice of the State of North Carolina.

provisions on the front page of a buyer's purchase order to see what was ordered. A buyer may only glance at the key provisions of the seller's confirmation to see when the goods will be shipped. The preprinted terms on these forms may differ, sometimes in significant ways.

Here are several examples of how they might differ:

- Buyer's purchase order allows the buyer to bring suit for consequential damages if the seller breaches the contract. Seller's confirmation specifically excludes consequential damages.
- Buyer's purchase order calls for disputes to be resolved in the buyer's country. Seller's confirmation calls for disputes to be heard in the courts of the seller's country.
- Buyer's purchase order requires shipment by a certain date named in the order. Seller's confirmation allows a grace period for late shipping or provides for excuses for late shipment.
- Buyer's purchase order is silent about whether the buyer has to notify the seller in the event of problems with the merchandise. Seller's confirmation requires buyer to notify the seller of any problems in the order within seven days.

The potential for conflict is almost endless. When this occurs, lawyers call it a **battle of the forms**.

The "Battle of the Forms" under the Common Law and Civil Law. If a seller sends a confirmation in response to a buyer's purchase order and the seller's form contains differing or additional terms, no matter how minor, then no contract exists. The mirror image rule has been violated. Each form or correspondence between them is considered a counteroffer, canceling the previous one. If the parties do not perform, then no contract is formed. If the parties do perform—the seller ships the goods—then that action is an acceptance of the terms on the other party's last form. The result usually is that the form sent last in time will prevail as the contract. The rule is, however, different in the United States.

The "Battle of the Forms" under the UCC. In the United States, the mirror image rule has been modified by statute to deal with modern business practices and to avoid the problems in the preceding examples. Under subsections 1 and 2 of the original UCC 2-207:

1. A written confirmation that is sent within a reasonable time operates as an acceptance even though it states terms additional to or different from those in the purchase order, unless the confirmation "is expressly made conditional on assent to the additional or different terms."
2. If both parties are merchants, any additional terms contained in the seller's confirmation automatically become a part of the contract *unless:*
   a. The buyer's purchase order "expressly limits acceptance" to the terms in that order;
   b. The additional terms in the confirmation *materially alter* the terms of the order; or
   c. The buyer notifies the seller of an objection to the additional terms within a reasonable time after receiving the confirmation containing the new terms.

A careful reading of UCC 2-207 shows that the UCC attempts to uphold the intentions of the parties by keeping the contract in existence where there are only *minor differences* between the forms used by the parties. The UCC states that, between merchants, an acceptance by a confirmation that contains additional terms that reflect only minor changes from the buyer's order will be effective to produce a contract, and the minor terms become a part of it (unless the buyer notifies the seller of an objection to the new term). A minor term might be one that is in usual and customary usage in the trade. Adding a provision that calls for an interest penalty for late payment is an example of a minor term (only because such penalties are common in sales contracts).

The situation is different in the case of new terms in the acceptance that attempt to *materially alter* the offer. A material term is generally considered to be one that is not commonly accepted in the trade and that would result in surprise hardship to one party if unilaterally included in the contract by the party. Such new terms do not become a part of the contract unless accepted by the other party. Sellers who wish for assurance that their order confirmation will comprise the entire agreement should request that the buyer show its acceptance of the new terms by signing the confirmation and returning the completed contract to them.

Proposed amendments to UCC 2-206 and 2-207, if adopted, would simplify the "battle of the forms" problem (Exhibit 4.4).

The Battle of the Forms under the CISG. The CISG rules fall somewhere between the rules set out by the common and civil law and the UCC. In an international sales transaction governed by the CISG, an acceptance containing new terms that do

Exhibit 4.4

Proposed Amendments to UCC 2-206 and 2-207*

§2-206. Offer and Acceptance in Formation of Contract.

(3) A definite and seasonable expression of acceptance in a record operates as an acceptance even if it contains terms additional to or different from the offer.

§2-207. Terms of Contract; Effect of Confirmation.

If (i) conduct by both parties recognizes the existence of a contract although their records do not otherwise establish a contract, (ii) a contract is formed by an offer and acceptance, or (iii) a contract formed in any manner is confirmed by a record that contains terms additional to or different from those in the contract being confirmed, the terms of the contract, subject to Section 2-202, are:

(a) terms that appear in the records of both parties;
(b) terms, whether in a record or not, to which both parties agree; and
(c) terms supplied or incorporated under any provision of this Act.

Preliminary Official Comment

1. This section applies to all contracts for the sale of goods, and it is not limited only to those contracts where there has been a "battle of the forms."

* Subject to enactment by state legislatures.

not materially alter the terms of the offer becomes a part of the contract, unless the offeror promptly objects to the change. However, a purported acceptance that contains additional or different terms that materially alter the terms of the offer would constitute a rejection of the offer and a counteroffer. No contract would arise at all unless the offeror in return accepted all of the terms of the counteroffer. Under the CISG, an acceptance of the counteroffer may arise by assent or *by performance.* In other words, if the original offeror takes some steps toward performing the contract after having received a counteroffer, the offeror will be deemed to have accepted the counteroffer and a contract will be created on the new terms.

Unlike the UCC, the CISG states those key elements of a contract that will materially alter a contract: price, payment, quality and quantity of goods, place and time of delivery, extent of one party's liability to the other, and settlement of disputes. This list is so broad that almost any term could conceivably be interpreted as "material." Thus, under the CISG, almost any new or different term in the acceptance could constitute a counteroffer. The effect is that many businesspeople may believe that they are "under contract" when they really are not.

The Validity of Standard Contract Terms: A Comparison. Today, there is wide use of so-called fine print or standard terms in contracts. They offer many advantages to businesses by eliminating the need to negotiate all the details of a contract every time goods are sold. In the United States, standard terms are generally permitted in business-to-business contracts unless in violation of a statute or struck down by the courts for other reasons. However, in some civil law countries, such as China or Germany, to take two examples, the statutes are quite specific about the kinds of standard contract terms that are permissible.

China takes a clear legal approach to the validity of standardized terms. Chinese law requires standardized terms to be fair in limiting the rights and liabilities of the parties. The terms must be brought to the attention of the other party, and they must be explained if requested. Caution should be used when using standardized terms in China because, if they are not fairly negotiated between both parties, they might be declared invalid. Grounds for invalidation include fraud, duress, illegality, harm to the public interest or the interest of the state, and exclusion of one party's liability for personal injury or property loss caused by intentional misconduct or gross negligence.

The German Civil Code has more detailed provisions dealing with standard contract terms. Standard business terms are defined as "contract terms preformulated for more than two contracts which one party to the contract presents to the other party upon the entering into of the contract." The form of the contract, typeface, font, or physical separation of terms in different documents is irrelevant to this determination. Individually negotiated terms take precedence over standard business terms. Parties may agree in advance to the application of particular standard business terms. In the absence of such advance agreement, standard business terms are incorporated into a contract only if the user expressly draws the other party's attention to them, gives the other party a reasonable opportunity to gain knowledge of their content, and the other party is agreeable to their application. Standard terms that unreasonably disadvantage a party are ineffective. Examples include terms providing for unreasonably long periods of time for acceptance or performance and unilateral reservation of the rights to revoke or modify the contract. If all or some standard business terms do not become part of the contract or are invalidated, the remainder of the contract continues to be valid unless its performance would be an unreasonable hardship for one party. In the event of doubt, standard business terms are to be interpreted against the user.

PERFORMANCE OF CONTRACTS

The primary responsibility of the buyer (Articles 53-60) is to pay the price for the goods and take delivery at the time and in the manner promised. The primary responsibility of the seller (Articles 30-35) in performing a contract for the sale of goods is to deliver conforming goods in the manner specified and within the time called for in the contract.

Performance of Seller

One of the primary responsibilities of the seller is to deliver conforming goods. CISG Article 35 states, "The seller must deliver goods which are of the quantity, quality and description required by the contract and which are contained or packaged in the manner required by the contract." Goods that do not conform to the requirements of the contract are said to be nonconforming. This includes all express descriptions, specifications, representations, and warranties set out in the contract. They must also comply with representations implied in the contract by law.

Implied Warranties. In the United States, the UCC creates certain implied warranties on goods that become a part of the contract by law (Exhibit 4.5). This includes the warranty of merchantability (drawn from the English common law), the warranty of fitness for a particular purpose in which the buyer relies on the skill and expertise of the seller, and the warranty of title. The CISG has similar provisions. Under CISG Article 35, unless otherwise agreed by the parties, the seller must deliver goods that are of the quantity, quality, and description required by the contract and that

1. Are fit for the purposes for which goods of the same description would ordinarily be used (unless at the time of contracting, the buyer knew or could not have been unaware that the goods were unfit; the seller's knowledge in this case is not relevant). This corresponds to the warranty of

Exhibit 4.5

UCC Implied Warranties, Merchantability, and Usage of Trade

§2-314(2)	Goods to be merchantable must be at least such as
	(a) pass without objection in the trade under the contract description; and
	(b) in the case of fungible goods, are of fair average quality within the description; and
	(c) are fit for the ordinary purposes for which such goods are used; and
	(d) run, within the variations permitted by the agreement, of even kind, quality, and quantity within eachunit and among all units involved; and
	(e) are adequately contained, packaged, and labeled as the agreement may require; and
	(f) conform to the promises or affirmations of fact made on the container or label if any.
§2-314(3)	(a) Unless excluded or modified other implied warranties may arise from course of dealing or usage of trade.

merchantability under the common law and the UCC and to the implied representation that goods be of "average quality" under European civil law.
2. Are fit for any particular purpose expressly or impliedly made known to the seller at the time of the conclusion of the contract, except where the circumstances show that the buyer did not rely, or that it was unreasonable for him to rely, on the seller's skill and judgment.
3. Possess the qualities of goods that the seller has held out to the buyer as a sample or model.
4. Are contained or packaged in the manner usual for such goods or, where there is no such manner, in a manner adequate to preserve and protect the goods (unless at the time of contracting, the buyer knew or could not have been unaware that the goods were not properly packaged).

The CISG does not prevent parties from waiving these representations. The drafters of the CISG wanted to give the parties as much freedom of contract as possible, in part because the Convention does not apply to consumer sales.

Conformance to Laws and Regulation in Buyer's Country. Technical regulations setting standards for product design and performance can vary widely from country to country. This might include safety standards for foods, pharmaceuticals, automobiles, toys, and consumer goods; flammability standards for children's clothing; fire and electrical codes; health codes; environmental standards; and rules for packaging or labeling products. Obviously, these issues are more important in international trade, where the standards are far less uniform, than in domestic commerce. Does Article 35 require the seller to supply goods that conform to the national laws of the buyer's country? The cases seem to depend on the factual situations. The issue often turns on whether the seller knew the uses to which the goods would be put, whether it knew of the regulations in the buyer's country affecting that use, and whether the buyer had relied on the seller's knowledge and expertise. It is usually only then that a court would hold that goods are nonconforming if they do not meet the regulations for sale in the buyer's country.

This issue was addressed by the Federal Supreme Court of Germany in 1995, in the *Case of New Zealand Mussels.* (Translations available online from the Pace Law School Institute of International Commercial Law or from UNCITRAL.) This case dealt with a shipment of mussels from New Zealand to Germany that contained concentrations of cadmium exceeding those recommended by German health authorities. Generally, foodstuffs must be sold in a condition "fit for human consumption." However, the court held that since the mussels were still edible (they are generally not dangerous unless eaten in large quantities) they had conformed to the contract. The court held that the seller was not responsible for complying with the German standards unless it had known of the standards and was aware that this was essential to the buyer, or if similar standards had existed in the exporting country. It did not seem to matter to the German court whether the food safety standards were binding rules or simply "recommended" limits. This should send a warning to international buyers. If it is important that foreign goods meet local standards or regulations, this requirement should be clearly set out in the contract.

Performance of Buyer

We said that the buyer's main responsibility is to pay the price for the goods and take delivery of them as required (Article 53). In addition, the buyer has an obligation to inspect the goods and notify the seller of any nonconformity.

Inspection and Notice of Nonconformity. The buyer must inspect the goods within "as short a period as is practicable in the circumstances" after they have arrived at their destination (Article 38). Obviously, foodstuffs and perishables require inspection more quickly than durable goods like machinery. The buyer must then give notice of any defect or nonconformity in the goods within a reasonable time after it is discovered or ought to have been discovered. If the defect can be discovered only upon use, the buyer has a reasonable period from that time to notify the seller. Some defects or other nonconformities may be latent, or hidden, and may take longer to detect. There is no set time limit on discovering these, although the time within which notice must be given to the seller of the nonconformity begins to run at the time that the seller "ought to have discovered" the hidden defect (Article 39). In any event, notice must be given within two years from the date on which the goods were "handed over" to the buyer. If the buyer fails to give timely and proper notice, the buyer loses the right to assert the breach against the seller. The parties are free to agree on other inspection and notice requirements and frequently do so in international business.

The notice of nonconformity should specifically, and in necessary detail, state how the goods are nonconforming. This is necessary so a breaching party can send substitute goods or otherwise correct the problem. In one German case, a German fashion retailer purchased clothing from an Italian manufacturer. The buyer refused to pay and notified the seller that the clothes were of "poor workmanship and improper fitting." The German court, applying the CISG, ruled that the buyer had lost his breach of warranty claim because the notice did not precisely say why the goods were defective or nonconforming. Another German case refused to excuse a German purchaser of chrysanthemums and hydrangeas from payment in full to an Italian seller on that the plants were of "poor quality" and were "miserable." An American example of the buyer's inspection and notification obligations pursuant to the CISG is set forth in the court's opinion in *Chicago Prime Packers, Inc. v. Northam Food Trading Co.*

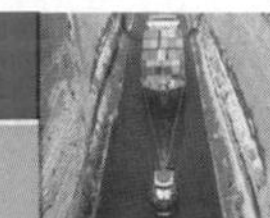

Chicago Prime Packers, Inc. v. Northam Food Trading Co.

320 F. Supp. 2d 702 (2004) United States District Court (N.D. Ill.)

BACKGROUND AND FACTS

Chicago Prime Packers, Inc., was a Colorado corporation with its principal place of business in Avon, Colorado. Northam Food Trading Company was a Canadian corporation with its principal place of business in Montreal, Quebec, Canada. Chicago Prime and Northam were wholesalers of meat products. In March 2001, Chicago Prime contracted with Northam to sell 1,350 boxes of government inspected fresh, blast frozen pork back ribs, which Chicago Prime purchased from Brookfield Farms, a meat processor. The agreed on price for the ribs was $178,200.00, and payment was required within seven days from the date of shipment. The ribs were stored at three different locations en route to Northam's customer Beacon Premium Meats but at all times were stored at or below acceptable temperatures. However, the ribs ultimately proved to be spoiled and were condemned by the U.S. Department of Agriculture. Nevertheless, Chicago Prime continued to demand payment from Northam. Chicago Prime sued Northam for breach of contract because it refused to pay for the ribs.

MEMORANDUM OPINION AND ORDER

In this case, it is undisputed that the parties entered into a valid and enforceable contract for the sale and purchase of pork loin ribs, Chicago Prime transferred a shipment of pork loin ribs to a trucking company hired by Northam, Northam has not paid Chicago Prime for the ribs pursuant to the contract, and Chicago Prime has suffered damages in the amount of the contract price. Therefore, Chicago Prime has established the essential elements for a breach of contract claim. Northam asserts, however, that the ribs were spoiled at the time of transfer and, as a result, it is relieved of its duty to pay under the contract. The burden is on Northam to establish non-conformity. The evidence is evaluated in light of that burden.

1. Northam has failed to prove that the ribs were non-conforming at the time of transfer ...

Chicago Prime produced evidence ... that the ribs delivered by Brookfield were processed and stored in acceptable conditions and temperatures from the time they were processed until they were transferred to Northam on April 24, 2001 ... The ribs were appropriately processed and maintained in acceptable temperatures while at Brookfield; and no other meat products that were processed and stored at the same time and under the same conditions as the ribs were found to be spoiled or objectionable ...

Northam argues that Chicago Prime has "utterly failed to establish that the ribs were damaged while at Beacon." That argument ignores the fact that Northam carries the burden of proving that the ribs were non-conforming at the time of receipt.

2. Northam failed to prove that it examined the ribs, or caused them to be examined, within as short a period as is practicable under the circumstances.

Northam is correct that "there were no contractual [terms] requiring inspection upon delivery." ... When an issue is not addressed by the contract, the provisions of the CISG govern. Because the contract at issue did not contain an inspection provision, the requirement under the CISG that the buyer examine the goods, or cause them to be examined, "within as short a period as is practicable in the circumstances" is controlling. *CISG,* Art. 38(1). Decisions under the CISG indicate that the buyer bears the burden of proving that the goods were inspected within a reasonable time. See, *e.g., Fallini Stefano & Co. s.n.c. v. Foodic BV,* [citation omitted] ...The determination of what period of time is "practicable" is a factual one and depends on the circumstances of the case ...

continues

continued

Section 3 of Article 38 of the CISG provides that "if the goods are redirected in transit or redispatched by the buyer without a reasonable opportunity for examination by him and at the time of the conclusion of the contract the seller knew or ought to have known of the possibility of such redirection or redispatch, examination may be deferred until after the goods have arrived at the new destination." *CISG,* Art. 38(3). In this case, Chicago Prime knew, or ought to have known, that the ribs would be redirected or redispatched after receipt because Chicago Prime knew that Northam was only a "trading company," which is defined as a company that buys and sells meat, but does not own any facilities, brick and mortar, or trucks. Thus, under the CISG, examination of the ribs could have been deferred until after they arrived at Beacon.

It is notable, however, that Northam did not present any testimony or evidence as to why the ribs or a portion of the ribs were not and could not have been examined by Northam, Beacon, or someone acting on their behalf when the shipment was delivered to Beacon or within a few days thereafter ... Northam points out that the ribs were wrapped and shipped in sealed non-transparent cartons or packages that are either white or brown. However ... nothing would have precluded a Beacon representative from opening and inspecting the boxes of ribs ... Northam simply did not present any evidence indicating why the boxes or at least enough of the boxes to constitute a reasonable inspection could not have been opened and examined when they arrived at Beacon or shortly after arrival ... Accordingly, Northam has failed to demonstrate that it examined the ribs, or caused them to be examined within as short a period as is practicable under the circumstances.

3. Northam also failed to prove that it gave notice to Chicago Prime of the alleged lack of conformity within a reasonable time after it ought to have discovered the alleged lack of conformity.

Article 39 of the CISG states that "[a] buyer loses the right to rely on a lack of conformity of the goods if he does not give notice to the seller specifying the nature of the lack of conformity within a reasonable time after he has discovered it or ought to have discovered it." *CISG,* Art. 39. A buyer bears the burden of showing that notice of nonconformity has been given within a reasonable time. The evidence shows that, shortly after Beacon discovered the ribs were "off condition" and did not "look good," both Northam and Chicago Prime were notified of a potential problem. Chicago Prime therefore received notice within a reasonable time after Northam discovered the problem; however, the question here is whether Chicago Prime was notified within a reasonable time after Northam should have discovered the problem.

A court in Italy found that the reasonableness of the time for a notice of non-conformity provided in Article 39 is strictly related to the duty to examine the goods within as short a period as is practicable in the circumstances set forth in Article 38. See *Sport D'Hiver di Genevieve Culet v. Ets Louys et Fils,* [citation omitted]. The court further noted that when defects are easy to discover by a prompt examination of the goods, the time of notice must be reduced. The putrid condition of the meat was apparent even in its frozen state ...

Because this court has found that Northam failed to examine the shipment of ribs in as short a period of time as is practicable, it follows that Northam also failed to give notice within a reasonable time after it should have discovered the alleged non-conformity.

In summary, the object of the CISG in requiring inspection in as short a period of time as is practicable, and notice promptly thereafter, is to avoid controversies such as this—where, because of the passage of time, the condition of the goods at the time of transfer cannot be reliably established. When that happens, the burden falls on the buyer, who had the opportunity to inspect the goods, but failed to do so.

Decision. The district court concluded that the buyer failed to satisfy its obligations with respect to the inspection of the goods and notification of the seller of non-conformities within a reasonable time. As a result, the court entered judgment in favor of the seller in the amount of $178,200.00 plus $27,242.63 in interest for a total payment of $205,442.63.

Comment. This case is interesting not only with respect to ascertaining the buyer's duties of inspection and notification but also for its discussion of sources for interpretation of the CISG. The court cited Dutch and Italian case law in reaching its conclusion and additionally noted that the CISG must be interpreted in a manner consistent with its international character and the need to promote uniformity and good faith in international trade.

Case Questions

1. What was the court's decision with respect to Chicago Prime Packer's claim for breach of contract?
2. What should Northam have done in order to avoid the result in this case?
3. Is the court's opinion overly harsh given that Northam was only a trading company and not the end user of the product? Why or why not?

REMEDIES FOR BREACH OF CONTRACT

In the event of a breach of contract, the remedies available to a buyer or seller are set out in the CISG. In principle, these remedies are drawn from both the common law and civil law systems. They are intended to give the parties the benefit of their bargain and to put the parties into the economic position they would have been in had the breach not occurred. The remedies outlined in the CISG include (1) avoidance (cancellation) of the contract; (2) the right to remedy or cure; (3) the setting of an additional time, or extension, for performance; (4) price reduction; (5) money damages; and (6) specific performance. The right to a remedy depends on whether or not the failure of performance amounted to a fundamental breach.

The Requirement of Fundamental Breach

The CISG distinguishes between a serious or fundamental breach of the contract and one that is minor or less than fundamental. Article 25 defines a **fundamental breach** as a breach of contract committed by one of the parties that "results in such detriment to the other party as substantially to deprive him of what he is entitled to expect under the contract, unless the party in breach did not foresee and a reasonable person of the same kind in the same circumstances would not have foreseen such a result." Examples of fundamental breaches include shipment of less than the full quantity of goods ordered by the buyer, the seller's shipment of seriously defective goods that cannot be repaired or replaced on time, or that have no value to the buyer under the contract and, of course, the seller's failure or refusal to ship at all. Late shipments are more problematic, because this is so common in international shipping. Most late shipments are not a fundamental breach, and under the CISG sellers are usually given additional time to perform even when they are late. A partial shipment may also amount to a fundamental breach if it presents a serious problem for the buyer and one that cannot quickly be remedied. A buyer may also be in fundamental breach of a contract. This usually results from the buyer's refusal or inability to live up to its two primary responsibilities—to take delivery and to pay for the goods.

Seller's Right to Cure

The CISG attempts to encourage the parties to stay in their contract rather than to repudiate it in the event of a dispute. It does this by giving the seller (and the buyer) additional time to perform.

Both the UCC and the CISG allow the seller to remedy, or cure, a nonconforming shipment if it can be done within the time for performance called for in the contract. So, if the contract calls for the seller to deliver goods to the buyer by October 1, but defective goods arrive on September 15, then the seller may "cure" by delivering a second shipment of conforming goods by October 1.

Nachfrist Period. Unlike the UCC, civil law systems traditionally grant an extension of time, beyond the date called for in the contract, within which the parties may perform. French civil law often refers to this grace period as *mise en demeue*, while German law calls it **nachfrist**, meaning "the period after." The CISG adopts this civil law rule in Articles 47-49. In the event that the seller has failed to deliver the goods, or has already delivered nonconforming goods, and the time for their shipment or delivery has passed, the seller may request the buyer to grant a reasonable extension of time to perform (or to "cure" the problem), at the seller's own expense, if it can be done without causing the buyer unreasonable inconvenience or the uncertainty of reimbursement of expenses incurred during the extension. If the breach is fundamental and, a "cure" seems impossible, the buyer need not grant the extension. In the case of the delivery of nonconforming goods resulting in a breach that is not fundamental, or in the case of a nondelivery that can be cured by the seller within a reasonable time, the buyer may not unreasonably refuse the extension. If the buyer does not respond to the seller's request within a reasonable time, the seller is entitled to the requested extension. If the seller still does not perform within the extension of time, the buyer is then released from the contract whether or not the breach was fundamental.

Buyer's Right to Avoidance. When one party fails to perform, the contract does not automatically end. The contract, or certain provisions of it, must be declared to be at an end, or "avoided" by one of the parties. A buyer may declare a contract avoided where the seller's failure to perform any obligation amounts to a fundamental breach (Article 49). If the seller requests additional time to cure a fundamental breach, the buyer need not grant it. If the buyer takes delivery of goods and learns they are so seriously defective as to amount to a fundamental breach, the buyer must declare avoidance within a reasonable time after he or she became aware, or should have become aware, of the breach. The buyer need not pay for the goods or find a substitute buyer to take them. After notifying the seller of the avoidance, the buyer may simply return them for a full refund of money paid or institute an action for breach of contract. When the goods can rapidly deteriorate or decay, such as with certain foods, the buyer may notify the seller and then take steps to sell them. These rights are especially important to a buyer in an international transaction because of the hardships associated with having to accept delivery and then reselling or disposing of imported goods in a foreign (i.e., the buyer's) market.

In the case of nondelivery, the buyer may avoid the contract only at the end of the *nachfrist* period—at the end of additional time that the seller was given to perform. The buyer may bring an action for damages against the seller at that time.

Seller's Right to Avoidance. The seller also may avoid a contract. A seller may avoid a contract if a buyer fails to either take delivery or pay the purchase price or otherwise commits a fundamental breach (Article 64). The effect of avoidance is that the seller is released from the contract, need not deliver the goods still in the seller's possession, and may claim their return if they have already been delivered. The seller also may bring a legal action for damages.

Price Reduction

One solution for the buyer in the event that the seller ships defective or nonconforming goods is that of **price reduction** (CISG Article 50). A buyer who would like to retain the goods, even though they are perhaps not the quality or specifications called for, may adjust the amount paid by withholding a part of the purchase price in order to offset the reduced value of the nonconforming goods. If the buyer can repair the goods or bring them up to contract specifications, the buyer may adjust the price paid accordingly. If the goods have already been paid for, the buyer may ask that the seller return a portion of the amount paid. The buyer may use the remedy of price reduction whether or not the seller's breach has been fundamental.

Money Damages

In breach of contract cases, the usual remedy granted by common law courts is the awarding of money damages. Damages for breach of contract are addressed in Articles 74-77. The CISG provides that a breaching party, whether buyer or seller, shall be liable for damages in an amount sufficient to make the injured party whole in the event of a breach. Article 74 states that damages to an injured party shall consist of a "sum equal to the loss."

Compensatory Damages. In the event of a breach of contract by either buyer or seller, and the nonbreaching party has exercised their right to avoidance of the contract, the method of measuring money damages depends on whether the nonbreaching party has been able to enter into a substitute transaction. For example, if the seller fails to deliver or delivers nonconforming or worthless goods, and the buyer has been able to purchase substitute goods, the buyer may claim damages if the substitute goods cost more than the contract price. If the buyer has not purchased substitute goods, damages are measured by the difference between the contract price and the current market price or the price of a reasonable substitute. Similarly, if the buyer refuses delivery or fails to pay and the seller has avoided the contract and resold the goods, the seller may recover damages in the amount by which the contract price exceeded the price received in the substitute transaction.

Consequential Damages. The CISG also permits recovery of **consequential damages**. Consequential damages are those special or indirect damages arising as a "reasonably foreseeable" consequence of the breach. They normally result from some special circumstances involving one of the parties to the contract, where those special circumstances were made known, or should have been known, by the other party. For example, assume that the buyer is purchasing the goods in order to resell them at a higher price under a separate contract to a third party. That fact is made known to the seller. If the seller breaches, it may be liable for the buyer's **lost profits** as well as other consequential damages resulting from the buyer's breach to the third party. Consequential damages are limited under Article 74 to those that the parties "foresaw or ought to have foreseen at the time of the conclusion of the contract." To compare the provisions for consequential damages in the CISG and the UCC, see Exhibit 4.6.

Exhibit 4.6

Comparison of Consequential Damage Provisions of the CISG and the UCC

CISG Article 74

Damages for breach of contract by one party consist of a sum equal to the loss, including loss of profit, suffered by the other party as a consequence of the breach. Such damages may not exceed the loss which the party in breach foresaw or ought to have foreseen at the time of the conclusion of the contract, in the light of the facts and matters of which he then knew or ought to have known, as a possible consequence of the breach of contract.

UCC 2-715
Buyer's Incidental and Consequential Damages

1. Incidental damages resulting from the seller's breach include expenses reasonably incurred in inspection, receipt, transportation, and care and custody of goods rightfully rejected, and commercially reasonable charges, expenses, or commissions in connection with effecting cover and any other reasonable expense incident to the delay or other breach.
2. Consequential damages resulting from the seller's breach include
   a. any loss resulting from general or particular requirements and needs of which the seller at the time of contracting had reason to know and which could not reasonably be prevented by cover or otherwise; and
   b. injury to person or property proximately resulting from any breach of warranty.

Liquidated Damages. **Liquidated damages** are monetary awards set forth and agreed to by the parties within the express terms of a breached agreement. The CISG does not expressly address liquidated damages as a measure of damages. Rather, it indirectly addresses liquidated damages in several provisions. CISG Article 6 allows for the incorporation of agreed sums into a contract for the sale of goods through its recognition of the principle of freedom of contract. Articles 46 and 62 recognize the principle of *pacta sunt servanda*, specifically, that contractual obligations must be kept. Finally, Article 74 recognizes the necessity of providing full compensation for injured parties in the event of breach of contract. In *American Mint LLC v. GOSoftware, Inc.*, a U.S. district court held that these provisions would not preclude enforcement of a liquidated damages clause pursuant to the CISG.

Specific Performance

The usual legal remedy in contract cases in common law countries is an award for money damages. The usual remedy in civil law countries, on the other hand, is that of **specific performance**. Specific performance is used when a court requires a party to the contract to perform, or carry out its part of the bargain. To be sure, courts in the United States and other common law countries hesitate to require parties to specifically perform. It is considered a harsh remedy for use only where money damages cannot be calculated or are inadequate, which may occur when the subject matter of the contract is unique.

Specific Performance Under the CISG. The CISG draws strongly on the civil law's acceptance of specific performance as a remedy in contract cases. Under Article 46, a court may grant specific performance only if all of the following conditions are met: (1) the buyer has not resorted to another remedy; (2) the seller failed to deliver or, in the case of nonconforming goods, the nonconformity was so serious that it constituted a fundamental breach; (3) the buyer gave timely notice to the seller that the goods were non-conforming; and (4) the buyer made a timely request that the seller provide substitute goods. The court may grant specific performance without regard to whether money damages are inadequate.

The provisions of the CISG probably will not have much effect on the law in common law countries. Article 28 places a limit on the buyer's right to specific performance by providing that a court need not grant specific performance unless "it would do so under its own law." Thus, the CISG will have little effect on the use of specific performance in the United States.

Anticipatory Breach

Anticipatory breach occurs when one party clearly sees that the other party to the contract either will not perform a substantial part of its obligations or will commit a fundamental breach. The breach may occur as a result of one party repudiating the contract and notifying the other that it will not perform, or it may be determined from the conduct of the breaching party.

Right to Suspend Performance. Either party may **suspend performance** under a contract if one party realizes that the other party will not perform a "substantial part" of its obligations. A buyer may suspend payment when aware of evidence that the seller cannot or will not ship. A seller may suspend shipment when the buyer obviously cannot pay or take delivery of the goods. A seller who has already shipped may stop the goods in transit. The right to suspend performance ends when the other party provides adequate assurance that it will perform. If adequate assurance becomes impossible, the other party may then avoid the contract entirely.

Right to Avoid Performance for Anticipatory Breach. If prior to the date of performance it becomes clear that one of the parties is likely to commit a fundamental breach in the future, the other party may avoid the contract. This is similar to the common law concept of "anticipatory breach." In contrast to the right to suspend, avoidance for anticipatory breach is allowed where one party will *never* be able to perform. For instance, if the seller's plant burns down, or if an embargo in the seller's country makes it legally impossible to ship the contracted goods, then the buyer may avoid the contract.

Avoidance of Installment Contracts. When a contract calls for the delivery of goods by installments, the rules of avoidance apply to each individual delivery. Therefore, a buyer may refuse a single nonconforming shipment if the seller has committed a fundamental breach. Where the breach of one installment indicates strong grounds that a party will breach future installments, the nonbreaching party may declare the contract avoided if done within a reasonable time. So, if a buyer refuses to pay for one or two installments, the seller may avoid the remainder of the contract.

EXCUSES FOR NONPERFORMANCE

Occasionally, a party will find that circumstances make carrying out its part of the contract difficult, unprofitable, or even impossible. As a defense to an action for breach of contract, it may claim that it has been excused because intervening events beyond its control have made performance impossible or financially impracticable. Whether an intervening event will cause a party to be excused and discharged from its contractual promise depends on the reasoning the court uses. Some courts reason that a party's performance is excused (1) if performance of the contract has been rendered physically or legally impossible, (2) if the underlying purposes of the contract no longer exist, or (3) if a change in circumstances has rendered the contract commercially or financially impracticable.

Impossibility of Performance

Under English law, a court may excuse a party's nonperformance where it becomes objectively impossible for it to perform. **Objective impossibility** means that it must be impossible for anyone to perform, not just this particular party, and that the parties did not expressly assume such risk. Examples of objective impossibility include death of one of the parties, the destruction of the specific subject matter of the contract, or when performance of the contract has been rendered illegal or made impossible due to the fault of the other party. The inability to pay money is not usually an acceptable excuse.

Supervening Illegality. A contract becomes impossible to perform and the parties excused when performance becomes illegal or prohibited by supervening government regulation. For instance, suppose that a U.S. company is under contract to ship computers to Syria. As a result of the ongoing Syrian civil war, the U.S. government declared that such sales were illegal. Because the contract has been rendered illegal, nonperformance is excused.

Frustration of Purpose

Under the English common law, a party's performance could be excused if some unforeseen event occurred that frustrated the purposes of the contract. This event, called **frustration of purpose**, would have to totally destroy the value of the contract to the party relying on the excuse. Moreover, both parties must have known the purposes of the contract. To understand, one might ask the question, "Had this event existed at the time of the contract, would the parties have gone through with it?" Today, the United States does not widely recognize frustration of purpose.

Commercial Impracticability

A party to a contract that is prevented from performing may attempt to be excused under the doctrine of **commercial impracticability**. The United States uses this modern doctrine today. It dates back to 1916 when the California Supreme Court stated in *Mineral Park Land Co. v. Howard,* 156 P. 458 that "[a] thing is impossible in legal contemplation when it is not practicable; and a thing is impracticable when it can be done only at an excessive and unreasonable cost." Today, impracticability in the United States has been codified in the UCC (Exhibit 4.7) and in Article 79 of the CISG. Remember, courts hesitate to excuse parties from contracts. Accordingly, the breaching party will be excused only if performance would result in extreme hardship, difficulty, or unreasonable expense as a result of an unforeseen event.

Extreme Hardship, Difficulty, or an Unreasonable Expense. The courts have experienced some difficulty in determining what is a "hardship" and how much additional cost is "unreasonable." If the cost of performing the contract becomes so excessive that performance is rendered unrealistic and senseless and threatens the viability of the business itself, performance may be excused. Of course, what is a lot of money to one company may be a drop in the bucket to another. Thus, if a large multinational corporation contracts to deliver goods at a contract price and discovers that wage increases or an increase in the price of raw materials will cause it to lose millions of dollars on the deal, the courts still may not release the company from its obligation.

Unforeseen Events. Courts also look to see whether the party claiming the excuse should have foreseen the likelihood of its occurrence. If the event was foreseeable, the nonperforming party will not be released from its obligations. This does not mean that the parties had to foresee the specific event that actually occurred. Rather, the parties *should have* foreseen that an event *of this kind* could occur. Thus, if a party is a sophisticated business, experienced and familiar with the risks of entering into this kind of contract, they might have difficulty in proving that they should not have foreseen a particular risk. The courts generally feel that if a particular risk was foreseeable, then the parties would have provided in their contract that performance would be excused if it occurred. If they did not provide for the excuse in the contract, then they must have intended to bear this risk.

Exhibit 4.7

Excuse by Failure of Presupposed Conditions

Uniform Commercial Code

2-615. Except so far as a seller may have assumed a greater obligation and subject to the preceding section on substituted performance:

a. Delay in delivery or nondelivery (performance or nonperformance, 2003 amendments) in whole or in part by a seller who complies with paragraphs (b) and (c) is not a breach of his duty under a contract for sale if performance as agreed has been made impracticable by the occurrence of a contingency the nonoccurrence of which was a basic assumption on which the contract was made or by compliance in good faith with any applicable foreign or domestic governmental regulation or order whether or not it later proves to be invalid.
b. Where the causes mentioned in paragraph (a) affect only a part of the seller's capacity to perform, the seller must allocate production and deliveries among its customers but may at its option include regular customers not then under contract as well as its own requirements for further manufacture. The seller may so allocate in any manner which is fair and reasonable.
c. The seller must notify the buyer reasonably that there will be delay or nondelivery and, when allocation is required under paragraph (b), of the estimated quota thus made available for the buyer.

For the most part, parties to a contract can anticipate shortages, inflation, and even dramatic fluctuations in market prices.

The CISG Exemption for Impediments Beyond Control

CISG Article 79 provides that a party is not liable for a failure to perform any obligations if (1) it was due to an *impediment beyond control,* (2) the impediment was not reasonably foreseeable at the time the contract was concluded, (3) the impediment was unavoidable and could not be overcome, and (4) notice was given to the other party of the impediment and of its effect on the contract. Unless an impediment renders performance permanently impossible, it does not entirely excuse performance, but merely suspends it during the time that the impediment exists.

Avoiding Performance Disputes: Force Majeure Clauses

Courts do not like to release parties from a contract on the basis of an excuse. As a result, lawyers frequently advise their clients to incorporate a *force majeure* clause into their contracts.

The term **force majeure** means "superior force." It is a clause in a contract that excuses a party from failing to perform on the occurrence of one or more specified events. These clauses usually list with specificity those events that will excuse nonperformance. These events might include war, blockades, fire, acts of governments, inability to obtain export licenses, acts of God, acts of public enemies, failure of transportation, quarantine restrictions, and strikes. Of course, such a clause assumes the party claiming the *force majeure* did not cause the event and could not control it. In practice, most *force majeure* clauses do not excuse a party's nonperformance entirely, but only suspend it for the duration of the *force majeure.* For an example of a *force majeure* clause, see the *Terms and Conditions of Sale,* Exhibit 4.3.

Another special type of *force majeure* clause is the *government approval* clause. Because government permission is often needed to transact business across national borders, many companies include a provision in their contracts stating that they are subject to obtaining government approvals or licenses. The *Harriscom Svenska, AB v. Harris Corp.* case illustrates the operation of a *force majeure* clause.

Harriscom Svenska, AB v. Harris Corp.

3 F. 3d 576 (1993) United States Court of Appeals (2d Cir.)

BACKGROUND AND FACTS

RF Systems, a division of Harris Corporation, manufactures radio communications products in New York. It appointed Harriscom, a Swedish firm, as its exclusive distributor to the Islamic Republic of Iran. The contract contained a *force majeure clause.* In 1985, the U.S. Customs Service detained a shipment of radios ordered by Harriscom and bound for Iran. The government prohibited all sales to Iran of goods it categorized as military equipment. In 1986, RF Systems negotiated a compromise under which it agreed to "voluntarily withdraw from all further sales to the Iranian market." Harriscom brought this action for a breach of contract against RF Systems. The District Court granted judgment for the defendants on the basis of commercial impracticability and *force majeure,* and the plaintiff appealed.

CARDAMONE, CIRCUIT JUDGE

One of the issues before us is whether the manufacturer's refusal to ship the spare parts was a voluntary act on its part, subjecting it to liability to its distributor for damages for breach of contract. We think it a foregone conclusion that a government bureaucracy determined to prevent what it considers military goods from leaving this country and with the will to compel compliance with its directives is an irresistible force, one that cannot reasonably be controlled. The government in these circumstances may be likened to the wife of "Rumpole of the Bailey," John Mortimer's fictional barrister, who describes his wife as "she who must be obeyed." ...

What appellant ignores is the overwhelming and uncontradicted evidence that the government would not allow RF Systems to continue sales to Iran. RF Systems established the affirmative defense of commercial impracticability because it complied in good faith with the government's informal requirements. Further, for RF Systems to have failed to comply would have been unusually foolhardy and recalcitrant, for the government had undoubted power to compel compliance. Like commercial impracticability, a

continues

continued

force majeure clause in a contract excuses nonperformance when circumstances beyond the control of the parties prevent performance. The contracts between these parties specifically contained force majeure clauses to excuse RF Systems' performance under the present circumstances, namely, "governmental interference."

Decision. Summary judgment for the defendant, RF Systems, was affirmed. The *force majeure* clause in the distributorship agreement excused the manufacturer from performance on the grounds of "government interference."

Case Questions

1. On what basis did the court deny Harriscom's claim of breach of contract against RF Systems?
2. How much "government interference" should be required to invoke a *force majeure* clause?
3. Who should bear the risk in transactions with customers in risky locations such as Iran, the seller or the buyer?

CONCLUSION

All commerce and trade require a stable and predictable legal environment in which to prosper. In recent years, the international community has agreed on a common body of international sales law, the *U.N. Convention on Contracts for the International Sale of Goods* (CISG). The CISG is important not only because it governs transactions for the trade in goods between parties in those nations that have adopted it but also because it represents internationally accepted legal principles of sales law. One of its key doctrines is that business parties should have the greatest freedom to contract possible.

The CISG was drafted under the aegis of the United Nations by representatives from countries with diverse political, economic, and legal systems. Thus it draws on common law, civil law, and even socialist law principles. It has already been adopted by countries whose trade volume represents two-thirds of world trade.

This chapter does not purport to cover all aspects of international sales law. For example, later we will discuss the actual mechanics of the transaction—how parties carry out contracts.

The next two chapters look at how companies ship goods and exchange money and what happens if the goods are lost at sea. These chapters also examine the responsibility of carriers for transporting the goods and carriers' relationships to buyers and sellers.

Chapter Summary

1. The *U.N. Convention on Contracts for the International Sale of Goods* (CISG) was ratified by the United States in 1988 and applies to commercial contracts for the sale of goods between buyers and sellers located in different countries, both of which have ratified the CISG. The CISG is not applicable to consumer contracts, liability for injury or death caused by defective products, or the sale of services.
2. Under the CISG, contracts for the sale of goods need not be in writing, although most international business transactions are.
3. Evidence as to trade usages is admissible to interpret or fill in the gaps in a contract. It may include those usages derived from past dealings or those that the parties knew of, should have known of, or are regularly observed in their countries in their type of business.
4. An acceptance may take the form of a statement or conduct by the offeree that indicates the offeree's intention to be bound to the contract. An offeree may accept by "dispatching the goods or payment of the price, without notice to the offeror," provided that the parties have established this as a practice or it is routinely accepted in the trade.
5. In an international sales transaction governed by the CISG, a confirmation or other acceptance containing new terms that do not materially alter the terms of the offer becomes a part of the contract, unless the offeror

promptly objects to the change. However, a purported acceptance that contains additional or different terms that do materially alter the terms of the offer would constitute a rejection of the offer and a counteroffer.

6. Unless otherwise agreed by the parties, the seller must deliver goods that are fit for the purposes for which goods of the same description would ordinarily be used and fit for any particular purpose expressly or impliedly made known to the seller.
7. Generally, a seller is not responsible for delivering goods that fail to conform to technical regulations and standards in the buyer's country. However, the seller would be responsible if it knew the uses to which the goods would be put, if it knew of regulations in the buyer's country affecting that use and if the buyer had relied on the seller's knowledge and expertise.
8. Unless otherwise agreed in the contract, a buyer must inspect the goods within as short a period as is practicable under the circumstances after the goods have arrived at their destination and notify the seller of any nonconformity within a reasonable time after it is discovered. In no case may the notice be made more than two years from the date the goods were handed over.
9. The remedies outlined in the CISG include (1) avoidance (cancellation) of the contract; (2) the right to remedy or cure; (3) the setting of an additional time, or extension, for performance; (4) price reduction; (5) money damages; and (6) specific performance. The right to a remedy depends on whether or not the failure of performance amounted to a fundamental breach.
10. A *fundamental breach* is one that the seller knew or should have known would result in such detriment to the buyer as substantially deprive him of what he is entitled to under the contract.
11. Performance may be suspended or excused for an impediment beyond the control of the parties that was unavoidable and not reasonably foreseeable at the time the contract was concluded, provided notice was given to the other party. A *force majeure* clause excuses a party from failing to perform on the occurrence of a specified event, such as plant closings or natural disasters.

Key Terms

sales law (law of sales) 87
sale 87
lex mercatoria 87
unification of law 89
United Nations Commission on International Trade Law (UNCITRAL) 89
valid contract 93
integrated contract 94
parol evidence rule 94
trade usages 95
mutual assent 95
invitations to deal 95
pro forma invoice 96
mailbox rule 98
mirror image rule 98
purchase order 101
order confirmation 101
terms and conditions 101
battle of the forms 102
fundamental breach 108
nachfrist 108
price reduction 109
compensatory damages 109
consequential damages 109
lost profits 109
liquidated damages 110
specific performance 110
anticipatory breach 111
suspend performance 111
objective impossibility 111
frustration of purpose 112
commercial impracticability 112
force majeure 113

Questions and Case Problems

1. Lucent Technologies International, Inc., subcontracted with a Saudi Arabian company, National Group, for work that Lucent was doing as part of a $4 billion telecommunications project for the Saudi government. National Group sued Lucent for damages for terminating the contract. The damages included an amount for lost profits. The contract contained no choice of law provision and Saudi law applied. The U.S. court had to decide if recovery of lost profits was prohibited as *gharar*. After all, *gharar* prohibits gambling, or the sale

of the "calf while still in the womb" or of "fish in the sea." What is *gharar,* and how does this Islamic law principle affect calculation of damages for breach of contract under Islamic law? Would this decision have been different under the CISG? *National Group for Communications and Computers, Ltd. v. Lucent Technologies International, Inc.,* 331 F. Supp. 2d 290 (D.N.J. 2004).

2. Bende had a contract to sell boots to the government of Ghana for $158,500. Bende promised to deliver the boots "as soon as possible." Bende then contracted with Kiffe, who agreed to make the boots in Korea and to deliver them in Ghana within sixty to ninety days at a price of $95,000. The contract contained no *force majeure* clause. Kiffe knew that Bende was going to resell the boots. Kiffe failed to deliver the boots on the agreed date because a train carrying the boots had derailed in Nebraska. Bende brought this action against Kiffe for breach of contract. *Bende and Sons, Inc. v. Crown Recreation and Kiffe Products,* 548 F. Supp. 1018 (E.D.N.Y. 1982).
   a. Kiffe claimed that the contract had been rendered commercially impracticable and that performance was excused. Do you agree? Why or why not? Was the train wreck foreseeable or unforeseeable?
   b. What could Kiffe have done in negotiating the contract to protect itself from this contingency?
   c. If Bende would have incurred an additional $18,815 in freight charges and miscellaneous costs had the breach not occurred, what would be its measure of damages? Is Bende entitled to lost profits? How are damages measured in a case such as this?
   d. In this case, the risk of damage or loss to the boots while in transit remained with the seller, Kiffe. How would the case differ if the parties had agreed that Kiffe would merely ship (not deliver) the goods by a certain date and that Kiffe would bear the risk of loss during transit? (You may have to wait until the next chapter to answer this question.)
3. Rotorex, a New York corporation, agreed to sell air compressors to Delchi, an Italian company. The compressors were for use in producing Ariele air conditioners. The first shipment reached Delchi, and Delchi paid $188,000. In preparation, Delchi had spent 39 million lire for special tooling, and 27 million lire for special insulation and tubing for use in making Arieles. Delchi expended 18 million lire in shipping and customs duties. Delchi then paid $130,000 to Rotorex for a second shipment. While the second shipment was en route, Delchi discovered that the first lot was nonconforming. It rejected the compressors and canceled the contract. Delchi spent several million lire to replace problem grommets, inspect, repair, and retest the compressors in an effort to make them usable. During this time, Delchi's assembly line shut down, incurring unproductive assembly worker wages. Delchi was able to obtain some substitute compressors from other sources in time for the selling season, which it had to adapt for Ariele units at additional expense. It arranged to have a shipment of Sanyo compressors, which it has previously ordered, sent to it by air freight so that it could fill some orders. Delchi was also unable to fill some orders, amounting to millions of lire in lost profit. Delchi brought this action for damages. What expenses should Delchi be allowed to recover from Rotorex as a result of its delivery of nonconforming and why? How should the court measure each element of damages? *Delchi Carrier, SpA v. Rotorex Corp.,* 1994 WL 495787 (N.D.N.Y. 1994).
4. Your company, Acme Widgets, sells its widgets worldwide. Acme has a contract for 250,000 widgets to be shipped to the Czech Republic. The price stated in the offer and acceptance is $1 per widget, C.I.F. Prague. During the production of the widgets, the price of one component increases 250 percent due to a shortage. In addition, these widgets are due for shipment on June 15 and arrival in Prague no later than July 1. On June 15, a stevedores' strike begins, which lasts for 60 days. Are either or both of these factors—the material price increase and the stevedores' strike—an excuse for Acme's nonperformance? What legal theory might Acme use under U.S. common law as an excuse? Under the CISG?
5. A German seller sued a Russian buyer because the buyer failed to pay for the equipment supplied to the buyer pursuant to their contract. The buyer acknowledged it had received the goods but said its nonpayment should be excused because it was due to the failure of the bank responsible for the buyer's foreign currency transactions to make payment to the seller. The buyer claimed the bank's lack of the available currency resources should be regarded as a *force majeure,* discharging it from liability for nonpayment to the buyer. The contract did include a *force majeure* clause, but it did not refer to the buyer's lack of foreign currency. Do you agree with the buyer? *Tribunal of International Commercial Arbitration at the Russian Federation Chamber of Commerce and Industry 17 October 1995.* (See case law on UNICTRAL texts Abstract No. 142; reproduced with permission on Pace University's CISG Website.)
6. A U.S. software manufacturer sold software for processing credit card charges to a U.S. limited liability company that

was a wholly-owned subsidiary of a German corporation. The software did not function properly and generated erroneous reports of charges. The U.S. buyer and its German parent sued the software manufacturer for breach of contract. The plaintiffs asserted that the CISG was applicable to the transaction as the head of the German parent company signed the purchase and sales contract. The software manufacturer alleged that the CISG was inapplicable as the contract was addressed to the U.S. limited liability company, and the purchase price was paid with a check tendered by the U.S. purchaser. Is the CISG applicable to this transaction? Why or why not? *American Mint LLC v. GOSoftware, Inc.*, 2006 U.S. Dist. LEXIS 1569 (M.D. Pa. 2006).

7. A Canadian seller sued a U.S. purchaser for the purchaser's refusal to pay for concrete light poles utilized in a construction project in Florida. The purchaser counterclaimed that it had sustained damages because the poles had not been delivered on time. The seller admitted that it had problems with production and was unable to ship a truck load of poles every two weeks as it had done in the past. Nevertheless, the purchaser accepted the poles that had been shipped. Applying the CISG, the court interpreted Article 39 to encompass not only nonconforming goods but also goods that were not shipped in a timely manner pursuant to the contract. Thus, the light poles could be deemed nonconforming based not on their performance but rather on their untimely delivery. As the purchaser had given notice of the untimely delivery of the light poles within two years from their delivery, it was free to pursue its counterclaim. Do you agree with this result? Is the court's interpretation of Article 39 too expansive? Was Article 39 intended to include untimely delivery as well as nonconforming goods? *Sky Cast, Inc. v. Global Direct Distribution, LLC*, 2008 U.S. Dist. LEXIS 21121 (E.D. Ky. 2008).

8. A U.S. purchaser sued a German limited partnership alleging that the partnership breached a contract to deliver 15,000-18,000 metric tons of used Russian railroad rail to the U.S. company for recycling into other products. The rail was to be shipped from the port in St. Petersburg, Russia, travel by sea for four weeks, and be delivered to the purchaser at its factory in Illinois by December 31, 2002. The seller failed to meet this deadline allegedly due to the unexpected early freezing of the St. Petersburg port on approximately December 1, 2002. The seller thus alleged that its performance was subject to *force majeure.* In denying the purchaser's motion for summary judgment, the court acknowledged that the contract was governed by the CISG and, specifically, Article 79 relating to *force majeure.* It also noted the absence of U.S. case law interpreting Article 79. However, instead of applying foreign case law or scholarly commentary to the interpretation of Article 79, the court simply applied similar provisions contained within § 2-615 of the UCC. Applying the UCC, the court concluded that the freezing of the port rendered the seller's performance impracticable, and the premature freezing was unforeseeable. The court's opinion has been condemned as "the worst CISG decision in twenty-five years" due to its disregard of the international character of the CISG and the need for uniformity in international trade. It has also been cited as an example of the "homeward trend" in improperly utilizing analogous domestic law to interpret the CISG. What is meant by "homeward trend"? Do you agree with the application of this trend and result in this case? Compare the opinion with that in *Chicago Prime Packers Inc.* issued by the same court in the same year. What are the possible explanations for the divergence in sources utilized to interpret the CISG? *Raw Materials, Inc. v. Manfred Forberich GMBH & Co.*, 2004 U.S. Dist. LEXIS 12510 (N.D. Ill. 2004).

Managerial Implications

You are the vice president of sales for DownPillow International, Inc., a U.S. manufacturer of bed pillows. The raw materials needed for making pillows are all sourced from suppliers overseas. Your firm purchases feathers from exporters in China who maintain large flocks of geese and ducks for breeding and cotton ticking and other textiles from mills in Germany. Every year you show your products at the International Bed Show in New York. This year, a delegation of Japanese buyers, representing several well-known Tokyo stores, showed interest in your best quality pillows. The president of your firm expressed interest in these contacts because although Americans use the same pillow for long periods of time, the Japanese are fastidious about their bedding. You followed up with samples, product, and pricing information. After several discussions and months of correspondence, you now expect to receive your first overseas orders.

You are to meet with legal counsel next week to discuss this opportunity. What questions might you want to ask about entering a sales contract with a Japanese buyer? If a buyer shows interest in purchasing large quantities, should you consider a visit to the buyer's Tokyo office? What would you accomplish? Should your attorney conduct negotiations there for you? If you and your buyer agree to put your agreement in writing, what terms might the document contain? Your customers want assurances that their pillows will be made of the finest white goose down, with less than 10 percent feathers. What assurance will you be able to give them regarding product quality and specifications? What factors might influence the selection of a choice of law clause? Do you think your lawyer will insist on a *force majeure* clause? Can you suggest some of the things DownPillow might want in its clause?

If you anticipate having several accounts in Japan, and each of them will be sending in purchase orders for each order, will you need a confirmation form? Will your attorney recommend that you develop a standard form to use for confirming all export orders? How will this form differ from the form you use for domestic shipments? What kind of provisions should it have?

How might negotiating your supply contracts with the Chinese differ from dealing with German textile mills? You have some concern about making sure that the quality of the down from China remains consistent. What will assure you that you will receive goose down and not duck down? What other precautions should you take? The German mill wants you to mail in or fax your orders. Your lawyer recommends that certain terms be put into your purchase order form. What might they be? Your purchase order states that the seller is liable for consequential damages for late shipment. The mill's confirmation states that "the liability of the seller is limited to the replacement of returned goods." In the event of a dispute, which will prevail under U.S. law? Under German law? Under the CISG?

Your contract with the Japanese buyer specifies that the CISG is to govern the transaction. Your pillows arrive in Japan and the buyer discovers that they contain only 13 ounces of down instead of the full 16 ounces of down as promised. You admit the error and want to resolve the problem. However, the buyer has just been offered the same quality pillow at considerably lower prices from a firm in Taiwan and wants to cancel the contract. Discuss the rights of each of the parties under the CISG.

Ethical Considerations

Most commentators agree that nonpecuniary injuries resulting from breach of a sales contract (such as reputational harm, injury to goodwill, pain and suffering, and emotional distress) cannot be compensated under the damages provision of the CISG. However, other efforts to unify or harmonize contract law on an international or regional level have considered allowing monetary compensation for nonpecuniary injuries. This has caused a minority of commentators to advocate a similar interpretation of the CISG on the basis that some breaches of contract cannot be adequately addressed if only economic losses can be awarded as damages. Such a circumstance may arise in cases involving "ethically tainted" goods, such as those which are the product of child or forced labor or are produced under circumstances that pose grave health hazards to workers.

In an article published in the *Pace International Law Review* in 2007, noted scholar Peter Schlechtriem denounces any such interpretation of the CISG on several grounds. Schlechtriem contends that the CISG was not the proper instrument to promote moral convictions. Rather, adequate remedies addressing such convictions may exist in other areas of international law as well as in domestic law (such as causes of action for fraud and misrepresentation and mandatory production and manufacturing standards). Parties could also establish standards with respect to the goods for which they have contracted in their agreements, the violation of which gives rise to a cause of action for breach of contract. Second, there are few if any shared ethical values across and within populations. Similar problems exist with respect to product lines. For example, one may object to the animal testing in the development of cosmetics but not in the development of life-saving pharmaceuticals. Third, any ethics-based damages award pursuant to the CISG would circumvent the burden of proof for pecuniary losses "by reverting to the 'penal' sanction of non-pecuniary damages, which could result in extremely diverging awards around the globe and, in some instances, in 'hometown justice.'" Finally, any such interpretation could impose one party's social, religious, and ideological beliefs on other parties. The consequence of such interpretation would be irreparable harm to the CISG's neutrality, objectivity, and uniformity on which its worldwide acceptance rests.

Do you agree with Schlechtriem? Is the CISG "ethically challenged"? Is the CISG the proper tool by which to address trade in "ethically tainted" goods? Why or why not?

CHAPTER 5

The Documentary Sale and Terms of Trade

Imagine that your firm is a manufacturer of specialty cotton yarn, which it sells to domestic knitting and weaving mills. You receive an inquiry from a potential foreign customer expressing an interest in your yarn and requesting a price quote or *pro forma* invoice showing the price for the goods and two different shipping and cargo insurance options: one if the customer takes delivery of the yarn at a named seaport in your country and arranges ocean transport and insurance himself, and another if you arrange for all insurance on the goods and their transportation to a seaport near the buyer. This will let the customer determine if it is more cost-effective for you to arrange and pay the cost of ocean shipping or for the customer to do it.

The customer also requests your "most favorable payment terms" and supplies you with banking and credit information and trade references. Typically, your shipments to established domestic customers are on "open account" terms, and you offer a 30-day credit period for payment. However, you are uncertain about granting the same terms to a new foreign customer because there it is possible that you may never see your money. If the customer fails to pay, it may be difficult for you to find a substitute buyer in that part of the world. Moreover, you would like your money as quickly as possible. On the other hand, if you demand cash in advance the customer may take his business elsewhere. After all, you realize that the customer probably has no more reason to trust you to ship as promised than you have reason to trust the customer to pay. Being new to exporting, you begin to do some research and consult several international trade specialists from government, freight forwarding, and banking. You would like to know if there are payment options other than open account or cash in advance.

Evaluating your customer's creditworthiness and deciding on payment terms is not your only concern. The customer wants you to quote a price for the yarn using two shipping alternatives. The first requires you to make the goods available to the buyer at a seaport in your country. This means that you must determine the costs of packing, crating, and ground transportation to the port named by your customer. The second alternative requires you to calculate the costs of ocean transport and marine cargo insurance to a foreign port in your customer's country. You calculate the weight and number of pallets of yarn to be shipped and estimate that it will fill one ocean container. On that basis, you request your freight forwarder to provide land and ocean transportation costs, container fees, dock fees, forwarder's fees, insurance coverage, and other costs.

You need the answer to one remaining question before you can produce your *pro forma* invoice: What is your liability for damage to the yarn during shipment? You know the perils of the sea are great. What if the ship goes down in a storm or the yarn is stolen or damaged by saltwater condensation? Which party, buyer or seller, will bear the risk of loss? Even if the insurance covers the loss, and even if the law permits a claim against the carrier (the topics of the next chapter), as between buyer and seller, which party must try to recover it? At what moment or at what place, does the risk of loss shift from the seller to the buyer? Are you free from responsibility when the goods leave your hands, when the goods reach the buyer's mill, or at some point in between? Does it matter which party, buyer or seller, owns the goods at the time they are lost or damaged? You want to know if you can "negotiate away" the responsibility for damage to the goods as quickly as possible after they leave your hands. Is there any way to put language in the contract that assigns the risks of the ocean voyage to the buyer? We will try to answer these questions in this chapter in our coverage of several basic subjects:

1. A brief description of the transaction risks facing the buyer and seller
2. The legal nature of documents of title, such as ocean bills of lading, and the significance of their negotiability to international commerce
3. The documentary sale and collection process used in exchanging goods for money
4. The role of ocean carriers and international banks in facilitating the documentary sale
5. An explanation of the difference between "shipment contracts" and "destination contracts"
6. The use of shipping terms and trade terms in sales contracts to assign the shipping responsibilities and the risk of loss between buyer and seller

TRANSACTION RISK

For purposes of this book, the term **transaction risk** refers to the risks facing the buyer and seller when they move money and goods in an international sales transaction. Transaction risks arise from barriers that separate buyer and seller, including distance, oceans, the time that the cargo is out of possession of the parties, communication and language difficulties, cultural differences, national boundaries, interference by local customs authorities, and legal systems.

Delivery Risk

Two of the most obvious forms of transaction risk are delivery risk and payment risk. **Delivery risk** is the risk to the buyer that the seller will fail to ship the goods as called for in the contract. For instance, the seller might fail to ship the goods at all, or on time, properly packaged, adequately insured, and using the agreed mode of transportation. There is much greater delivery risk in an international sale than in a domestic sale because the buyer may not know the seller very well. The seller may fail to ship due to any number of business reasons. In addition, the seller may not have the same commitment to its foreign customers as it does to its domestic customers. The seller may even be a cheat and fill the containers with worthless rubbish or ship less than the quantity billed. Indeed, international business can be fraught with peril.

Distance and the use of ocean transport also increase delivery risk. Despite the importance of air transport today, most cargo is still carried by sea. Although all forms of transportation put cargo at risk, ocean cargo can be imperiled by time, moisture, storms, shipwreck, pilferage of ocean containers, and, even today, piracy. In addition, *multimodal transport* (the use of more than one mode of transportation, such as truck plus ocean vessel) places the goods at risk during transfers and at times when they are temporarily warehoused.

Payment Risk

Payment risk (also called credit risk) is the risk to the seller that the buyer will fail to pay as promised. Payment risk is compounded by the difficulty the seller may have getting a credit history on a foreign customer or obtaining banking and trade information. The buyer's distance, and location in a foreign country with an unfamiliar legal system, means that any attempt to collect payment can be costly and time consuming. If the buyer fails or refuses to pay, the seller might have to resort to litigation in the buyer's country to recover the money owed. Even then, recovery might become impossible, if the buyer becomes insolvent or bankrupt. If a foreign buyer refuses delivery, it may not be cost-effective to ship the goods home, and the seller may have difficulty locating a substitute buyer that far away.

Ideally, if sellers could have their way, they would have *cash in advance* from new foreign buyers before the goods leave their hands. That is certainly the most secure form of payment. On the other hand, few buyers would part with their money merely in the hope that the goods they order will ever arrive. An unscrupulous seller who already has the cash, may be tempted to walk away without shipping or to ship goods other than those that were ordered. The seller may have no long-term interest in exporting to a foreign market or may just be dishonest. Cultural and language barriers might make it especially hard to gauge a seller's honesty or intentions. So, cash in advance as a payment option usually will not serve to bring buyer and seller together.

On the other hand, all buyers would like to buy on open credit terms, or on **open account**. With open account terms, the seller grants an extended credit period for the buyer to pay, typically 30 days. In domestic sales, for the seller who has had an opportunity to learn the creditworthiness of the buyer, sales are often made on open account terms. However, few sellers would risk shipping their goods, perhaps halfway around the world, giving up possession, control, and even ownership of the goods to a foreign buyer, without some adequate assurance of payment. Perhaps after a long relationship has developed between them, they may agree to do business this way, but an open account sale is usually not secure enough for most large international transactions. In addition, a seller who agrees to sell on open account in a foreign currency bears the risk that the currency will fall in value during the open credit period. Thus, if cash in advance or open account terms were the only payment options, buyer and seller would be at an impasse. Bringing them together requires some other form of payment. One method that provides assurances to both parties is the documentary sale.

THE DOCUMENTARY SALE

The **documentary sale** is a type of contract for the sale of goods in which possession and ownership of the goods are transferred from seller to buyer through negotiation and delivery of a negotiable document of title issued by an ocean carrier. The seller's obligation is to place the goods in the hands of an ocean carrier within the time called for in the contract, in exchange for a negotiable document of title and to negotiate the document of title to the buyer in return for either immediate payment or, if an extension of credit is anticipated by the contract, for the buyer's promise to pay at a future date. The buyer's obligation is to "purchase" the document in a timely fashion and to take delivery of the goods. Correspondent banks in the buyer's and seller's countries handle the process of exchanging a document of title in return for money. It reduces the transaction risks between a buyer and a seller who are great distances apart by ensuring that if one releases the title to the goods, the other will release the money. The documentary sale is a unique method of exchange devised by early traders when their sailing vessels traveled medieval trade routes. The method spread by custom and practice and eventually became recognized in early English law, in the modern common law countries, and in the civil law countries of Europe. Today, the documentary sale is a common type of contract for the sale of goods.

The Document of Title

The first step to understanding the documentary sale is to understand the nature of a negotiable document of title. A negotiable **document of title** is a document that evidences the ownership of goods it represents. It entitles the person who possesses the document to possess the goods. Documents of title are created out of a special "bailment" relationship between the owner of personal property, the **bailor**, and one to whom its possession is entrusted, the **bailee**. A **bailment** is a relationship involving the separation of ownership and possession of personal property. The bailee receives the property on the condition that it will care for and return the property in the condition in which it was given or will transfer or dispose of it in accordance with the terms of the bailee's agreement with the bailor. Bailments are common in everyday life and are treated in more depth in other law classes. One example of a commercial bailment occurs when a bailor places goods in a warehouse for storage. The warehouse operator (the bailee) issues a document of title known as a *warehouse receipt*. The document serves as a receipt for goods taken into its possession, and also as a document of title. For example, a farmer may place leaf tobacco in a warehouse, receive a warehouse receipt, and either reclaim the tobacco or sell it at auction by delivering the warehouse receipt to the buyer. In international trade, the most commonly used documents of title are bills of lading and multimodal transport documents.

Negotiability of Documents of Title. Documents of title may either be negotiable or nonnegotiable. A negotiable document of title is one stating that the goods will be delivered "to the order of a named person or assigns" or "to the bearer." Negotiable documents can be transferred by negotiation from one party to another in return for value or payment. **Negotiation** is the transfer of a document of title by its owner to another in a manner that passes title to the document, title to the goods, and the right to claim the goods from the issuer of the document. Order documents are negotiated by delivery. Bearer documents are negotiated by a signed indorsement and delivery. Documents of title are used to transfer ownership of goods from one party to another without the necessity of transferring physical possession of the goods themselves. When a negotiable document of title is sold in the ordinary course of trade, the seller is said to have made a **constructive delivery** of the goods to the seller. The property can stay in the possession of the bailee while the owner or subsequent owners sell or resell it or pledge it as collateral for a loan. In this chapter, we will discuss just one type of document of title used for moving goods by ocean—the ocean or maritime bill of lading. In a later chapter, we will cover air cargo and the use of air waybills in some detail.

The Bill of Lading

A negotiable ocean **bill of lading** is a document of title that an ocean carrier issues to a shipper upon receiving goods for transport (see Exhibit 5.1). Having first been used in the sixteenth century, the bill of lading plays a vital role in international trade. It has three roles.

1. It is a receipt for the goods from the carrier, indicating any damage to the goods that was visible or apparent at the time of loading.
2. It is the contract of carriage between the shipper and the carrier (i.e., a *transport document*).
3. It is the document of title to the goods described in it.

For the purposes of this chapter, unless otherwise noted, we refer only to negotiable ocean bills of lading. Later in this chapter, we describe different types of

Exhibit 5.1

Ocean Bill of Lading

OCEAN BILL OF LADING

Shipper/Exporter	Export References
Shipper's name Address	Invoice or order number (Not negotiable unless consigned to order)
Consignee: (Complete Name and Address) To the order of: Shipper	Forwarding Agent – References Shippers Freight Forwarder Forwarding Agent – References: U.S.A. Forwarding Agent – References
Notify Party (Complete Name and Address) Buyer or buyer's import agent	Domestic Routing/Export Instructions Pre-carriage These commodities licensed by U.S. for ultimate destination Japan and for resale to any destination except North Korea, Iraq, Cambodia, or Cuba.
Pier	Onward Inland Routing / Place of delivery
Ocean Vessel / Flag / Port of Loading	
Port of Discharge / For Transshipment To	

Carrier's Receipt — Particulars Furnished By Shipper

Marks and Numbers	No. of Cont. or Other Pkgs.	Description of Goods	Gross Weight	Measurement
Container No. UP 362459 Seal # 2398112	95	1 x 40' container said to contain down pillows on invoices to be as per proforma invoices nos. 2368714, 2368715 dated April 15, 2008.		
Shipping Marks: Down Bedding		"Shipper Load, Stuff & Count"	1,550 Kg (Net)	
ON BOARD		Clean Shipped on board 5/10/2008 "Freight Prepaid" House to port basis Signed ______ Title of Company Official		

Received in apparent good order and condition except as otherwise noted hereon the goods, containers, or other packages, or units mentioned above for transportation from the place of receipt if named above or (if not named) the port of loading to the port of discharge or place of delivery (as the case may be) subject to exceptions, limitations, conditions and liberties hereof and there to be delivered to the consignee or his or their assigns.

(TERMS OF THIS BILL OF LADING CONTINUED ON REVERSE SIDE HEREOF)

Freight Charges	Prepaid	Collect
Land Charges		
Port Charges		
Ocean Charges		
Container Rental		
Total	4850.00	

B/L No.

IN WITNESS WHEREOF, The Master or Agent of said vessel has affirmed to THREE (3) ______ Bills of Lading, all of this tenor and date, one of which being accomplished, the others stand void.

Carrier TAMPA BAY STEAMSHIP
JACKSONVILLE, FLA.

By ______
Agent (for the Master) TBS

Dated at Port of Shipment	Mo.	Day	Yr.
	5	10	08

ocean bills, including nonnegotiable bills, as well negotiable multimodal transport documents. In the United States, the laws governing the negotiability of bills of lading are the *Federal Bills of Lading Act* (for bills originating in the United States for export shipments) and the *Uniform Commercial Code.*

Rights of Purchasers of Documents of Title

Although some readers may be familiar with the rights of parties that purchase **negotiable instruments**, such as checks and promissory notes, the law regarding the transfer and sale of **negotiable documents** is somewhat different because the functions of the two are different. Negotiable instruments serve as a substitute for money, whereas negotiable documents are used to move goods and to transfer their ownership and possession.

Good-Faith Purchasers of Documents of Title. The legal rights of the purchaser of a document of title in the United States depend on whether the case is governed by Article 7 of the *Uniform Commercial Code* or by the *Federal Bills of Lading Act*. The *Federal Bills of Lading Act* (enacted in 1916) is probably the more important of these, because it applies to all bills of lading issued by any common carrier for the shipment of goods in interstate or international commerce. This discussion generally applies to both laws. In order for negotiable documents of title to be freely accepted in commerce and trade, the law gives special protection to those who purchase negotiable documents under such circumstances as to become holders by due negotiation.

A holder by due negotiation (otherwise referred to as a good-faith purchaser) is one who purchases a negotiable document (1) for value (and not in settlement of a past debt), (2) in good faith and without any notice of any adverse claim against it, and (3) in the ordinary course of business or financing. If it is an order instrument, then the good-faith purchaser must take it by indorsement.

When a buyer, bank, or other party takes a document as a good-faith purchaser, it not only takes title to the document and to the goods it represents, but it acquires even greater rights in the document and to the goods than were had by the party who negotiated it to the purchaser. The rule states as follows: A good-faith purchaser takes a negotiable document of title free from the adverse claims that third parties might have against the goods represented in the document (excluding claims of the carrier for unpaid shipping charges or the claims of government customs authorities). Thus, a good-faith purchaser of a negotiable document of title, as a general rule, will get clear title to the goods described therein, and must not be concerned that someone else may have a greater right to claim the goods. For example, assume that a firm is having financial difficulties. It delivers goods to a carrier for shipment to a foreign buyer, obtains a bill of lading, and negotiates the document to the buyer. In the meantime, a creditor of the seller attempts to put a lien on the goods to satisfy its debt. If the buyer is a good-faith purchaser, then his or her rights to the goods will prevail over the creditor's lien.

Now consider a slightly different case: A entrusts goods to B for storage. B delivers the goods to a carrier, obtains a bill of lading, negotiates the document to C, and absconds with the money. C, who is a good-faith purchaser, takes title to both the document and the goods. A may not reclaim them because C takes **paramount title**. This means that C's rights are superior, even against the original owner, because B was entrusted with the goods and then wrongfully sold them.

There are many cases where the good-faith purchaser takes greater rights than the transferor of the document had. But in certain other instances, a good-faith purchaser might not enjoy greater rights. For instance, if a thief steals goods and obtains a bill of lading, a purchaser of the document does not obtain paramount title over the original owner. In the following case, *Banque de Depots v. Ferroligas*, the court addresses the rights of a party who takes a bill of lading by "due negotiation." Notice how the court attempts to protect the rights of these purchasers of negotiable documents.

Different rules apply to transferees of nonnegotiable bills of lading and to transferees of negotiable bills of lading who did not take them by due negotiation or in good faith. In these cases, the holder receives only those rights that the transferor had or that the transferor had the actual authority to convey. Recall the example in which A entrusted goods to B for storage. Now assume that B transfers a nonnegotiable bill of lading to C and absconds with the money. A can reclaim the goods from C.

Carrier's Liability for Misdelivery. The carrier may deliver the goods only to the holder of an original bill of lading. Assume that A entrusts a shipment of goods to an ocean carrier and obtains a bill of lading. The carrier delivers the goods to B without asking B to produce the document. Without knowledge of what has occurred, A sells the bill to C, who takes it for value and in good faith. C is the good-faith purchaser

Banque de Depots v. Ferroligas

569 So. 2d 40 (1990) Court of Appeals of Louisiana

BACKGROUND AND FACTS

Banque de Depots, a Swiss bank, brought an action against Bozel, a Brazilian exporter, seeking a money judgment because Bozel had allegedly misapplied the bank's funds. The bank obtained an order seizing 1,300 metric tons of calcium silicon located in a Louisiana port. The calcium silicon was shipped under ocean bills of lading by Bozel from Rio de Janeiro to New Orleans for transit to three purchasers, none of whom were domiciled in Louisiana. The documents were still in the hands of the collecting banks and had not yet been negotiated to the buyers. Bozel asked the court to free the goods because he was not the owner of the bills of lading.

LOBRANO, JUDGE

Bozel asserts that ... title to the cargo follows the bills of lading, and once those were transferred to the collecting banks, they [Bozel] were no longer the owner of the cargo.

The Bank asserts that ... only bills of lading which are "duly negotiated" transfer ownership of goods ... They contend that the bills of lading may have been transferred to the collecting banks, but they were not "duly negotiated" ... since there was no value given prior to the attachment ...

We agree that Louisiana law governs the ownership of the cargo when it reached Chalmette, La. Article 2 of the UCC has not been adopted in Louisiana, hence the courts must look to the Louisiana Civil Code in determining the ownership of movables ...

The holder of a duly negotiated bill of lading acquires title to the document and title to the goods described therein. It is clear that once a carrier has issued a negotiable bill of lading for goods being placed in commerce, the intent of the law is to protect those who subsequently become holders through "due negotiation." Part and parcel of that intent is the protection afforded the [carrier] in relinquishing possession of the goods to the holder of the document. Thus, although goods in the possession of a [carrier] may have been seized, if the document's negotiation has not been enjoined or the document is not in its possession, [Louisiana law] permits the [carrier] to surrender the goods to the duly negotiated holder. The law protects that holder from acquiring goods that are subject to a seizure. Any other conclusion would lead to the absurd result of requiring the holder, prior to his purchase of the bill of lading, to check every jurisdiction through which the goods passed to determine if it has been seized by judicial process. This would defeat the purpose of our commercial laws.

The record is clear that on May 14, 1990, the date of the seizure, the negotiable bills of lading were outstanding. They were not in the hands of the carrier and their negotiation had not been enjoined. As discussed, the validity of the attachment must be determined as of the date it was issued. The Bank cannot cure this defect by seeking to impound the bills of lading after it obtained the seizure. To hold otherwise would create an impossible contradiction in our commercial laws since the "seized" goods would still be subject to the legal effects of the unimpaired "due negotiation" of the corresponding bills of lading. The legal "capture" of the bills of lading is a prerequisite to the seizure of the goods.

We order that the writ of attachment be dissolved.

Decision. A court-ordered seizure of goods in transit cannot stand when the title to the goods is represented by a bill of lading and the bill of lading itself was not seized by the court order.

Comment. The Swiss bank was attempting to assert jurisdiction over Bozel by seizing its cargo in the United States. Although this attempt failed, the court stated that the bank was free to continue to find other ways to get jurisdiction over Bozel.

Case Questions

1. Why did the court not permit Banque de Depots to seize the cargo Bozel shipped?
2. What are the policy reasons for not allowing a creditor, such as Banque do Depots, to seize cargo that is being shipped to a buyer under a bill of lading?
3. What are the expectations of a good faith purchaser of a bill of lading?

and the owner of the goods and may bring an action to reclaim the goods from B. C also has a cause of action against the carrier for misdelivery of the goods because the carrier violated the terms of the contract of carriage. A further example of a carrier's liability for misdelivery may be found in the following case of *Lite-On Peripherals, Inc. v. Burlington Air Express, Inc.*

Lite-On Peripherals, Inc. v. Burlington Air Express, Inc.

1999 U.S. Dist. LEXIS 23701 (1999) United States District Court (C.D. CA)

BACKGROUND AND FACTS

Lite-On Peripherals, Inc. was a California-based corporation engaged in the computer hardware business. Lite-On's parent company was Silitek Corporation, a Taiwan-based corporation. On January 22, 1996, Burlington Air Express, Inc. ("Burlington") received 1,000 cartons comprised of 5,000 computer keyboards from Silitek in Keelung, Taiwan for transportation to Los Angeles, California. Burlington issued a bill of lading in the form of its own negotiable combined transport bill of lading. The bill provided that the goods were "consigned to order of" Reveal Computer Products, Inc. ("Reveal") in California and were to be delivered to Reveal only upon surrender of a duly endorsed copy of said bill. The price of all 5,000 keyboards contained in the 1,000 cartons was $202,800.

Despite the presence of such provision on the face of its bill, Burlington delivered the computer keyboards to Reveal without obtaining a copy of the bill. In fact, the bill was in the hands of Lite-On, Silitek's assignee, at the time the goods were delivered to Reveal. Furthermore, type-written portions of the bill of lading provided that Lite-On was to be notified before delivery to Reveal was attempted. Burlington made no efforts to notify Lite-On. Finally, Lite-On, prior to delivery, notified Burlington by telephone and faxed letter that no delivery was to be made to Reveal as its creditworthiness was in question and the original bill of lading was in Lite-On's possession.

Notwithstanding such warning from Lite-On or the terms of the bill of lading, Burlington delivered the entire shipment to Reveal on or about February 6, 1996. Lite-On was eventually able to recover 2,495 of the 5,000 keyboards from Reveal. However, 2,505 of the items were never recovered. Reveal failed to pay Silitek or Lite-On for the computer keyboards and subsequently filed bankruptcy. The value of the 2,505 keyboards improperly delivered to Reveal and unrecoverable by Lite-On was $101,602.80. Lite-On sued Burlington for misdelivery, conversion, negligence, and breach of contract.

LETTS, DISTRICT COURT JUDGE

Where a carrier is obligated by its bill of lading terms, as Burlington was in this case, to obtain the bill before delivering the goods, failure to do so constitutes actionable misconduct. See, for example, *Pere Marquette Railway Co. v.* J.F. French *& Co., 254* U.S. 538 (1921) (conversion); *C-ART, Ltd. v. Hong Kong Islands Line America*, S.A., 940 F.2d 530 (9th Cir. 1991) (misdelivery); *Allied Chemical International Corp. v. Companhia*, 775 F.2d 476 (2d Cir. 1985) (breach of contract and conversion); and *Iowa Beef Processors, Inc. v. Grand Trunk Western Railroad Company*, 493 F.2d 665 (6th Cir. 1974) (misdelivery and conversion).

Furthermore, where bills of lading contain language requiring surrender of the bill prior to delivery of the goods, "[a]ny interpretation of the bill of lading, other than one requiring the surrender of a duly endorsed original bill of lading in exchange for the goods, would require this Court to contradict the language of the contract and render this language of the bill of no affect. Such an interpretation strains credulity." *International Knitwear Company Limited v. M/V Zim Canada*, 1994 U.S. Dist. LEXIS 14180, 1994 WL 924203 (S.D.N.Y. 1994).

The language in Burlington's own bill requiring surrender of the endorsed bill before delivery is clear. There exists no reason for this Court to disregard such language or to look beyond the bill to determine the rights and liabilities of the parties.

Burlington's argument that, because the goods were shipped F.O.B. point of origin, the consignee named in the bill was the owner of the goods and therefore was entitled to delivery without surrender of the bills of lading, is unfounded. Such an assertion has been rejected by the Ninth Circuit in *C-Art v. Hong Kong*, supra, 940 F.2d 530. There the Court stated that "this argument is inimical to the express provisions of the bill of lading, as well as contradictory to the applicable authorities."

Based upon the weight of authority, Burlington's delivery of the goods to Reveal without obtaining the endorsed bill of lading constitutes actionable breach of contract, misdelivery and/or conversion.

The basic recovery under any of the theories propounded by Lite-On is the value of the property with interest ... Lite-On is therefore entitled to recover from Burlington the sum of $101,602.80 plus interest and costs of suit.

Decision. The carrier disregard of the limitations contained within the bill of lading and instructions received from the shipper subjected the carrier to liability for misdelivery in an amount equal to the value of the property which could not be recoverable from the purchaser.

Case Questions

1. Why did the court not permit Burlington to diverge from the terms of the bill of lading?
2. What are the policy reasons for not allowing a carrier, such as Burlington, to disregard the terms of a bill of lading?
3. When combined with the opinion in *Banque de Depots v. Ferroligas*, what does this case tell you about the legal nature and effect of the bill of lading to trade?

Importance of Negotiability to Trade. The negotiability of the bill of lading is what makes it so important to trade. As the document is bought and sold, so too are the goods it represents. Negotiability permits merchants to trade in cargo while it is still afloat. With a bill of lading, goods can be bought and sold, time and again, while they are still on the high seas, with the bill of lading circling the globe from one buyer to the next. This practice is, in fact, quite common. Persian Gulf oil can change hands twenty or thirty times in the six weeks that it takes a tanker to reach U.S. waters.

The negotiability of bills of lading was recognized in most European trading centers at least as early as the sixteenth century. Early records of them have been found in many languages. In 1883, Lord Justice Bowen described the bill of lading in this time-honored description from *Sanders Brothers v. Maclean* & Co., (1883) 11 Q.B.D. 327 at 341.

> The law as to the indorsement of bills of lading is as clear as in my opinion the practice of all European merchants is thoroughly understood. A cargo at sea while in the hands of the carrier is necessarily incapable of physical delivery. During this period of transit and voyage, the bill of lading by the law merchant is universally recognized as its symbol, and the indorsement and delivery of the bill of lading operates as a symbolical delivery of the cargo. Property in the goods passes by such indorsement and delivery of the bill of lading, whenever it is the intention of the parties that the property should pass, just as under similar circumstances the property would pass by an actual delivery of the goods. And for the purpose of passing such property in the goods and completing the title of the indorsee to full possession thereof, the bill of lading, until complete delivery of the cargo has been made on shore to someone rightfully claiming under it, remains in force as a symbol, and carries with it not only the full ownership of the goods, but also all rights created by the contract of carriage between the shipper and the shipowner. It is a key which in the hands of a rightful owner is intended to unlock the door of the warehouse, floating or fixed, in which the goods may chance to be.

As the vessel bearing the goods proceeds out of the harbor and onto the open ocean, the seller safely retains the title to the merchandise, literally held in hand. The seller can sell the goods as planned by sending the bill of lading ahead to the buyer, divert the shipment to another buyer around the globe, pledge it for a loan, or bring it home. This unique flexibility has made the documentary sale essential to world trade and the international economy.

Documentary Collection. **The documentary collection** is the process by which banking institutions serve as intermediaries between seller and buyer to handle the exchange of the bill of lading for payment (see Exhibit 5.2). The documentary collection is an integral part of the documentary sale. It provides a safer alternative for payment than either cash in advance or sale on open account. The parties might indicate their desire for a documentary collection by specifying in the contract that payment terms are "cash against documents" or "documents against payment" (sometimes abbreviated CAD or D/P). Such an indication is not always essential because the collection process is implied in most documentary sales contracts.

Here is a simplified description of how the documentary collection process works: Seller places the goods in the hands of a carrier and in return receives a negotiable bill of lading or multimodal **transport document** made to its order or assigns. Seller indorses the bill of lading and presents it to the bank for collection. Along with the bill of lading, the seller includes other essential documents that the contract requires it to submit, such as a **marine insurance** policy on the goods covering the risks of the ocean voyage. The customs regulations in the buyer's country may require a **certificate of origin**. The seller's **commercial invoice** describing the goods and showing the price to be paid is always required. Finally, a **documentary draft** is necessary to expedite the exchange of money. The draft is a negotiable instrument for making payment for the invoice and for the bill of lading. In a later chapter we describe the draft as a negotiable "order to pay" made out by the seller, drawn on the buyer for collection, and payable to the order of the seller. Its purpose is to tell the parties how much to pay when purchasing the bill of lading. The bank also needs the draft if financing is to be provided for the sale. Other documents may be required, as well, depending on the needs of the parties or the export-import regulations of their countries.

The seller's bank forwards the draft and documents to a **collecting bank** in the buyer's country, with instructions to release the documents to the buyer only on payment of the draft. A collecting bank is any bank authorized to collect on an instrument. When the buyer pays the draft, the collecting bank remits the money back to the seller's bank.

If the documents are presented in good order, the collection process should work smoothly, with buyer and seller each getting what they bargained for in

Exhibit 5.2

The Documentary Sale

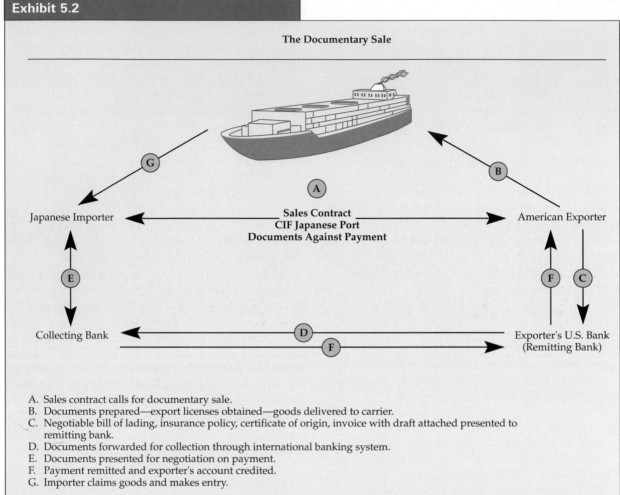

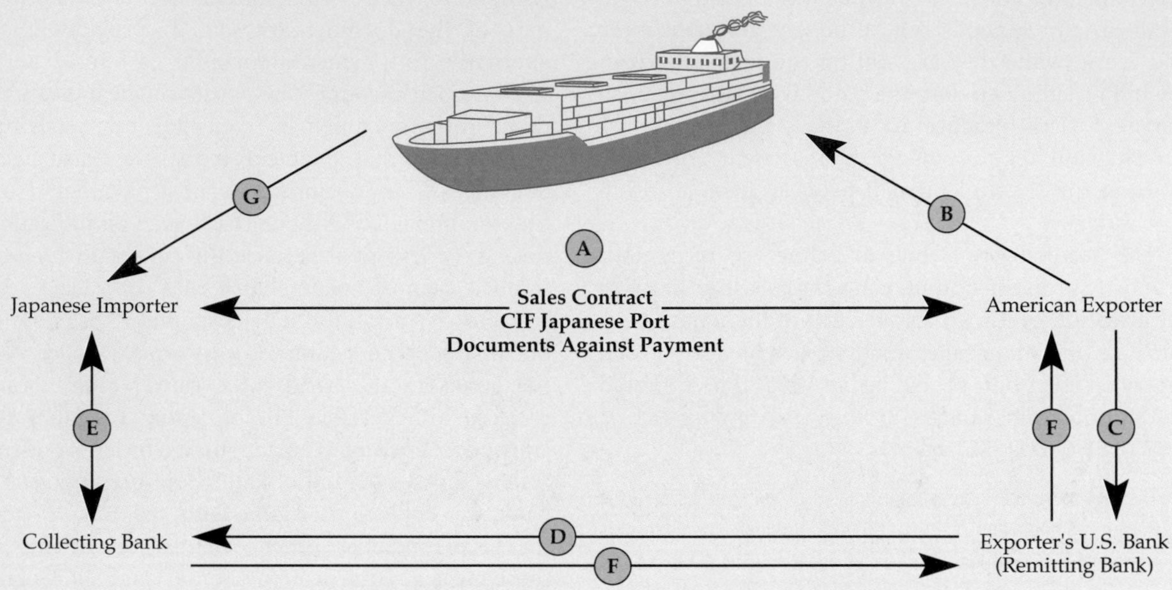

A. Sales contract calls for documentary sale.
B. Documents prepared—export licenses obtained—goods delivered to carrier.
C. Negotiable bill of lading, insurance policy, certificate of origin, invoice with draft attached presented to remitting bank.
D. Documents forwarded for collection through international banking system.
E. Documents presented for negotiation on payment.
F. Payment remitted and exporter's account credited.
G. Importer claims goods and makes entry.

the contract. The process may not be so smooth, however, if the documents tendered contain one or more obvious defects. If they appear forged, or if they show that the goods were shipped later than the date called for in the contract, or on an improper vessel, or if the goods are inadequately insured, or if the documents on their face appear fraudulent (e.g., a nonexistent shipping line), the buyer may refuse them. The buyer's refusal could come as quite a surprise to the seller, who in good faith shipped and tendered documents to the buyer only to find that they have been rejected and the draft unpaid due to some "technicality." Of course, the point of contention may be more than just a technicality to the buyer, who may feel the rejection was based on good cause. Either way, the seller is left with a good deal of exposure while the goods remain in a distant foreign port.

CIF Contracts and the English Common Law. There are many variations on the documentary sale. However, under one of the oldest and most typical variations, the seller must not only tender a bill of lading to the buyer for payment but also provide marine insurance on the goods and prepay the freight charges to the foreign port. These contracts are called **CIF contracts**. The acronym CIF is a trade term which stands for "cost, insurance, and freight." Trade terms are shorthand abbreviations drafted into a contract that assign the risk of loss, freight charges, and other responsibilities to either buyer or seller. Later in the chapter we discuss CIF and other trade terms, including some not used in documentary sales, are discussed later in the chapter.

In the following English case, the seller in San Francisco tendered documents covering a shipment of hops to the buyer in London. The buyer wanted to inspect the merchandise first and refused to pay until delivery was made. The seller claimed that payment was due immediately upon presentation of the documents, even though the hops were still somewhere aboard ship on the ocean. The Kennedy dissent in *Biddell Brothers* represents a virtually universal view of CIF and other documentary sales contracts today. This rule has been adopted by the UCC, is incorporated into statutes in other countries, and has long been recognized by courts in the United States and throughout the world.

Certificates of Inspection or Analysis

The documentary sales transaction serves to protect the buyer as well as the seller. The bill of lading ensures that the goods have been loaded aboard ship for transport on the date shown, and the insurance policy protects against covered marine losses. However, the buyer must take the description of the goods in the bill of lading, and in the invoice that usually accompanies it, at face value. If the goods are nonconforming or defective, or if a lesser quantity was shipped, the buyer's only remedy may be an action for breach of contract. In many industries, buyers will require that an inspection report of a reputable, independent testing laboratory or inspection service, usually located in the seller's country, accompany a bill of lading. These might certify the quantity, quality, or other characteristic of the goods being purchased. Examples include **certificates of inspection**, **certificates of weight**, or **certificates of analysis**. Inspections are common in the chemical, extraction, and commodities businesses, as well as throughout other types of international trade. For instance, major apparel retailers in the United States typically arrange for pre-shipment inspection of garments for defects in the country of assembly.

Biddell Brothers v. E. Clemens Horst Co.

1 King's Bench 934 (1911) Court of Appeal

BACKGROUND AND FACTS

The defendant entered into a contract to sell hops to the plaintiff in London, as follows:

> ... one hundred bales, equal to or better than choice brewing Pacific Coast hops of each of the crops of the years 1905 to 1912 Inclusive. The said hops to be shipped to Sunderland. The [buyer] shall pay for the said hops at the rate of ninety shillings sterling per 112 lbs. CIF to London, Liverpool, or Hull. Terms net cash.

The seller wrote to the buyer stating that they were ready to ship and that they expected payment upon presentation of a negotiable bill of lading. The buyer replied that it was prepared to take delivery but insisted that the seller either submit samples for prior inspection or that it be permitted to inspect each bale prior to payment. The buyer was unwilling to accept a certificate of inspection from the San Francisco Merchant's Exchange as assurance of quality. The seller refused to ship, and the buyer brought this action. The seller counterclaimed for the buyer's refusal to pay on the documents. The lower court ruled in for the defendant buyer. The Court of Appeals affirmed, with Kennedy, L.J., dissenting. On appeal to the House of Lords, the judgment was reversed.

LORD JUSTICE KENNEDY, DISSENTING

The plaintiffs' case is that the price was not to be paid until they had been given an opportunity of inspecting the shipment, which could not be given until after its arrival in this country. The defendants contend that the plaintiffs' obligation was to pay for the hops, whether they arrived or not, against tender of the shipping documents. The Court, therefore, has in the present case to decide what are the true conditions of the right of the seller to payment under a CIF contract, if that commercial contract is to be performed strictly according to its tenor.

Let us see, step by step, how according to those principles and rules the transactions as in such a CIF contract as that before us is and, I think, must be carried out in order to fulfill its terms.

At the port of shipment—in this case San Francisco—the vendor ships the goods intended for the purchaser under the contract. Under the Sale of Goods Act, 1893, [section] 18, by such shipment the goods are appropriated by the vendor to the fulfillment of the contract, and by virtue of [section] 32 the delivery of the goods to the carrier—whether named by the purchaser or not—for the purpose of transmission to the purchaser is prima facie to be deemed to be a delivery of the goods to the purchaser. Two further legal results arise out of the shipment. The goods are at risk of the purchaser, against which he has protected himself by the stipulation in his CIF contract that the vendor shall, at his own cost, provide him with a proper policy of marine insurance intended to protect the buyer's interest, and available for his use, if the goods should be lost in transit. How is such a tender to be made of goods afloat under a CIF contract? By tender of the bill of lading, accompanied in case the goods have been lost in transit by the policy of insurance. The bill of lading

continues

continued

in law and in fact represents the goods. Possession of the bill of lading places the goods at the disposal of the purchaser.... But then I understand it to be objected on behalf of the plaintiffs: "Granted that the purchaser might, if he pleased, take this constructive delivery and pay against it the price of the goods; what is there in the 'cost freight and insurance' contract which compels him to do so? Why may he not insist on an option of waiting for a tender of delivery of the goods themselves after having had an opportunity of examining them after their arrival?"

There are, I think, several sufficient answers to such a proposition. In the first place, an option of a time of payment is not a term which can be inferred, where the contract itself is silent. So far as I am aware, there is no authority for the inference of an option as to times of payment to be found either in the law books or in the Sale of Goods Act. Secondly, if there is a duty on the vendor to tender the bill of lading, there must, it seems to me, be a corresponding duty on the part of the purchaser to pay when such tender is made. For thereunder, as the bill of lading with its accompanying documents comes forward by mail, the purchaser obtains the privilege and absolute power of profitably dealing with the goods days or weeks, or, perhaps, in the case of shipments from a distant port, months, before the arrival of the goods themselves. This is, indeed, the essential and peculiar advantage which the buyer of imported goods intends to gain under the CIF contract according to the construction which I put upon it.

Finally, let me test the soundness of the plaintiffs' contention that according to the true meaning of this contract their obligation to pay arises only when delivery of the goods has been tendered to them after they have an opportunity of examination, in this way. Suppose the goods to have been shipped, the bill of lading taken, and the insurance for the benefit of the buyer duly effected by the seller, as expressly stipulated in the contract. Suppose the goods then during the ocean transit to have been lost by the perils of the sea. The vendor tenders the bill of lading, with the insurance policy and the other shipping documents (if any) to the purchaser, to whom from the moment of shipment the property has passed, and at whose risk, covered by the insurance, the goods were at the time of loss. Is it, I ask myself, arguable that the purchaser could be heard to say, "I will not pay because I cannot have delivery of and an examination of the goods?" But it is just this which is necessarily involved in the contention of these plaintiffs. The seller's answer, and I think conclusive answer, is, "You have the bill of lading and the policy of insurance."

In my judgment, the judgment of Hamilton, J., was right, and this appeal, so far as relates to the plaintiffs' claim, should be dismissed.

Decision. Under a CIF sales contract, the buyer has no right to inspect the goods but is obligated to pay upon the presentation of the proper documents.

Case Questions

1. Why did the court rule that the buyer was not entitled to inspect the goods prior to paying for them?
2. What assurance did the buyer have that conforming goods were actually shipped?
3. What terms could the buyer have negotiated in the contract to assure that the goods shipped would be as ordered?
4. Assume that the documents arrive well ahead of the ocean cargo and that they are purchased by the buyer. A day later, the ship and cargo go down at sea. Assuming that the carrier was not at fault, what is the buyer's recourse?
5. In a CIF contract, which party assumes the risk of changes in the cost of ocean freight after the signing of the contract but before shipment?

In the *Basse and Selve v. Bank of Australasia* case, the buyer claimed that its bank should have been more diligent in accepting an inspection certificate that the seller had obtained from a chemist by fraud and trickery.

How Secure Are Documentary Payment Terms?

No reader should be left with the impression that documentary payment terms are appropriate for all parties or for all transactions. They are appropriate for shipments that are of low to moderate value, shipments to repeat customers, and shipments of goods that may cost-effectively be returned home or resold to a substitute buyer if the original buyer rejects the documents. Traders that buy and sell commodities, natural resource materials, or other goods while they are still in transit also use documentary sales.

By establishing a regular course of business on documentary terms, the seller may become more comfortable in advancing to open credit account terms later. However, a documentary sale is not the most secure method of doing business because it offers no guarantee that the buyer will actually purchase the documents when presented. There is always the possibility that the buyer may become insolvent, find the goods more cheaply from another source, or change his or her mind.

Even though the seller can maintain possession, ownership, and control of the goods through the bill of lading and can attempt to resell them to a substitute customer, that may not be so easy when the goods are in a foreign country or if they have a custom design and are not readily saleable. Therefore, the seller may want to require some additional security where the goods are of a very high value, specially manufactured, for first-time orders to new customers, or where a seller is uncertain as to the creditworthiness or integrity of a prospective foreign customer. In this case it may be wise to require full or partial payment in advance of shipment. The seller may also want to consider another advance payment alternative that we will study in a later chapter: the use of a "letter of credit" from the buyer's bank wherein the bank irrevocably promises to become primarily responsible for purchasing the documents in lieu of the buyer. This added layer of security substitutes the creditworthiness and integrity of a bank for that of the buyer.

Measuring Damages for Breach of the Documentary Sale

In the previous chapter we discussed the remedies available to a buyer and seller for breach of contract. In the case of the documentary sale, if the buyer sues the seller for nondelivery or other breach of contract,

Basse and Selve v. Bank of Australasia

90 Law Times 618 (1904) King's Bench

BACKGROUND AND FACTS

The plaintiff had purchased ore from Oppenheimer. The plaintiff requested that the defendant bank negotiate documents on its behalf from Oppenheimer covering a shipment of "cobalt ore analysis not less than 5 per cent peroxide." The plaintiff specified that the bill of lading must be accompanied by a policy of insurance and a certificate of analysis from Dr. Helms, a Sydney chemist. Oppenheimer submitted for analysis phony samples of ore to the chemist, who, on the basis of this small sample, issued his certificate indicating the quality to be as described in the bill of lading. In fact, the ore contained in the actual shipment was worthless. The plaintiff brought this action in order to recover amounts paid by the bank against the documents.

JUSTICE BIGHAM

It was no part of their duty to verify the genuineness of the documents; the duty was not cast upon them of making inquiries at the office of the ship's agent as to whether the goods had, in truth, been received on board; nor were they to examine the contents of the packages to see whether they were right; nor were they to communicate with Dr. Helms in order to ascertain whether he had properly made the analysis mentioned in the certificate. The plaintiffs' mandate amounted in business to a representation to the defendants that upon all such matters they might rely on Oppenheimer, and the legal effect of such a representation is now to preclude the plaintiffs from questioning the validity of any apparently regular documents which Oppenheimer might tender. If this is so, then the only question left on this part of the case is whether the documents were apparently regular. It is admitted by the plaintiffs that the bill of lading and the policy of insurance were apparently regular, but an objection is made on this score to Helms's certificate. It is said that it professes to show merely the test of the contents of a sample packet with a mark upon it, and does not purport to show a test of the bill of lading of 100 tons of ore. This, I think, is a fanciful objection. Large quantities of produce are necessarily tested by means of samples. Such samples are drawn either by the servants of the owner of the goods or (as it seems) by the servants of the analyst, and if the samples are carefully and skillfully drawn they generally fairly represent the bulk. But in this case it would be no part of the bank's duty to see to the sampling or to ascertain that it was fairly done. The bank was entitled to assume that it was so just as they were entitled to assume that the analyst had acted skillfully in making the analysis. The certificate is, in my opinion, regular on its face, and comes within the meaning of the mandate under which the bank was acting, and the bank in taking it acted carefully and properly.

Judgment for defendants.

Decision. The court ruled that because the certificate on its face was regular, the bank had acted properly in paying the seller. The bank had no duty to inspect the ore itself.

Case Questions

1. Why do buyers in international transactions often use inspection firms?
2. If the seller fails to provide an inspection certificate as required in the contract, can the buyer refuse to accept the documents?
3. Give examples of industries or products that would benefit from the following: health certificate, ingredients certificate, fumigation certificate, inspection certificate, certificate of chemical analysis, certificate of quantity or weight, social compliance audit certificate.

you can measure the buyer's damages by the difference between the contract price for the goods and the cost or fair market value of replacement goods. How do you determine the market value in a documentary sale? Is it the market value at the time that the goods ship, the time of delivery of the goods, or the time of payment?

Under the English view, damages are based on the market value as of the date when the buyer would have paid for the goods had the seller not breached. In *Sharpe & Co., Ltd. v. Nosawa* & Co., (1917) 2 K.B. 814, a Japanese seller entered into a contract to ship peas to an English buyer under a documentary sale, CIF London. Neither the goods nor the documents were ever sent, and the buyer sued for damages. The question was whether the buyer's damages should have been calculated on the basis of the difference between the contract price (£10.15 sterling per ton) and the market price of peas at the time of the anticipated August delivery (£17.10 sterling per ton), or the difference between the contract price and the market price of peas on July 21, when the documents would have been tendered in London (£12.00 sterling per ton). The court held that the seller's responsibility under this contract would have been incomplete until he delivered the shipping documents to the buyer in London, at which time he would have been paid, and that the damages should therefore be measured by the price of peas on that date, July 21.

In a market with rapidly fluctuating prices, this question becomes especially important. *Seaver v. Lindsay Light* Co., 135 N.E. 329 (N.Y. 1922) illustrates how American courts have diverged from the English rule. The seller and buyer entered a CIF contract for the shipment of thorium from Chicago to London. After the seller refused to ship, the buyer brought an action for breach of contract. Contrary to the English rule, the New York court looked at the nature of a shipment contract and stated:

Where was the delivery of the thorium in the present case to be made? Was it at Chicago or at the London dock? When the correspondence and cablegrams are all construed together, as they must be, then it seems to me they clearly indicate an intention on the part of both parties that the delivery was to be made at Chicago, and when the defendant delivered to a carrier at that point, paid the freight to point of destination, and forwarded the other necessary documents, he had fully completed his part of the contract.

The court then concluded that damages for breach of a shipment contract should be measured by the market price of the goods *at the port of shipment on that date.*

Types of Ocean Bills of Lading

Bills of lading can take a variety of forms with different functions and usages in trade. The legal significance of each is important to all parties to the document.

Clean Bills of Lading. In addition to being a document of title, the bill of lading is also a receipt for the goods. A **clean bill of lading** is one that contains no notations by the carrier that indicate any visible damage to the goods, packages, drums, or other containers being loaded. Buyers should insist that all contracts call for the seller to provide a clean bill.

A bill of lading that is not clean is *foul.* Normally, this description applies only to the external appearance of the goods. For instance, the bill of lading must note leaking containers, rust on metal products, and external evidence of infestation by insects. As a generally accepted practice, the bill of lading must state the condition of the goods themselves, even if they are not externally observable, if the carrier knows or should have known that the goods are damaged. This type of inspection serves to protect the carrier from responsibility for pre-shipment damage.

A buyer who receives a clean bill still has no assurance that the goods will arrive in good condition. A clean bill of lading means only that the carrier noted no obvious or visible damage to the goods when they were loaded aboard ship. A clean bill of lading is no guarantee as to the quality of the goods or their conformance to the description in the sales contract. Moreover, it is no guarantee that the goods will not be damaged during the voyage.

On-Board Bills of Lading. An **on-board bill of lading**, signed by the ship's master or other agent of the carrier, states that the goods have actually been loaded aboard a certain vessel. In most documentary sales, the buyer would want to specify that payment is conditioned upon receipt of a negotiable, clean onboard bill of lading. This document gives some assurance that the goods described in the bill of lading have actually been loaded on board and are under way to the buyer. It also insulates the exporter from loss of the goods before loading. An importer who buys an on-board bill also has an approximate idea of when the goods will arrive.

Received-for-Shipment Bills of Lading. A **received-for-shipment bill of lading**, on the other hand, is issued by a carrier only upon having received goods for transport. It has limited use in cases of a delay between the delivery of the goods to the carrier and their being loaded aboard ship. Imagine a buyer who is asked to pay for a received-for-shipment bill of lading for bananas being shipped from Honduras to the United States. The buyer has no guarantee that they will not spoil on the sun-parched dock weeks before they are loaded. Most documentary sales contracts will require that sellers tender on-board (and clean) bills of lading. A received-for-shipment bill of lading can be converted into an on-board bill of lading if the carrier notes the vessel name and date of loading on the face of the bill.

Straight Bills of Lading. The bill of lading used in a documentary sale is negotiable. In nondocumentary sales, a nonnegotiable or **straight bill of lading** will suffice. A straight bill of lading should not be confused with a sea waybill which is used in some countries and is a nonnegotiable receipt for goods received by the carrier containing the contract of carriage and identifying the party to whom the goods may be released. Sea waybills are used less frequently than bills of lading.

Ocean carriers use a straight bill of lading only if the seller intends that the goods be delivered directly to a **consignee**, a specific person, named in the bill. The consignee may be the foreign buyer, as in the case of a sale on open account terms. It also may be the buyer's bank or customs agent. There is no requirement for the consignee to produce the actual straight bill of lading to the carrier in order to take delivery in the United States; generally the only requirement is proof of identification. However, courts in Canada, the United Kingdom, and some other countries require consignees to produce a straight bill of lading when claiming their goods from the carrier.

Straight bills of lading are also used when the exporter is shipping to its own agent (or subsidiary company) in the foreign country, with the expectation that the agent will make direct arrangements with the buyer for payment before turning over the goods. As in the case of negotiable documents, the carrier may deliver only to the party named in the bill. If the carrier delivers the goods to anyone else, it will be liable for misdelivery. Straight bills do not represent transferable title to the goods and cannot be used as the sole collateral for a loan. Thus, the typical use of straight bills of lading is when there is no financing involved.

Other Types of Transport Documents

Many specialized types of transport documents are in use today. The ocean bills of lading just described are only a few of the most common types. Transport documents have specific uses, depending on the type of carrier and the function the document is to perform. Many new types of transport documents have been developed because of modern shipping techniques. The following summary describes the different types of transport documents.

Air Waybills. Most air transport is handled through nonnegotiable **air waybills** issued by air cargo carriers. The carrier will make delivery only to the consignee named in the bill. The importance of negotiability in air transport is not as important as in ocean freight because the goods are not out of the control of the parties for long periods. The air waybill contains a mechanism by which the seller can guarantee payment, even though the sale is not a documentary sale. The air waybill can name a foreign bank as consignee and specify that the goods be held at the point of destination until the bank guarantees payment or until the bank approves release to the buyer. COD services are also available.

Forwarder's Bills of Lading. **Freight forwarders** (who usually also act as customs brokers for importers) are federally licensed individuals who act as agents for sellers. They handle their foreign shipments, book transportation, prepare documents and customs forms, and perform other functions. They are excellent sources of information on packing and transporting cargo, evaluating alternative shipping options, and obtaining freight rates. Freight forwarders can issue either straight or order bills of lading. Only certain forms of forwarder's bills are acceptable in a documentary sale. Forwarder's bills allow claims only against the forwarder itself, not the carrier. The carrier is liable only to the forwarder who holds the carrier's bill of lading.

Forwarder's bills must be distinguished from forwarder's receipts, which are mere acknowledgments that the forwarder has received goods for shipment. Such receipts are nonnegotiable and usually will not be accepted for payment under a draft unless specifically allowed.

Multimodal Transport Documents. When goods are transported by only one mode of transportation, the transport is referred to as *unimodal*. If the transport is executed using more than one mode of transportation, the transport is **multimodal**. **Multimodal transport operators**, sometimes called **combined transport operators**, are firms that arrange for cargo to be sent via several different carriers in one journey—truck, rail, barge, and/or ship. Multimodal transport was made possible by new methods of containerizing freight that replaced "break bulk" cargo for all but the smallest shipments. The **multimodal transport document**, or **combined transport document**, is a single contract between the shipper and the operator, who, in turn, contracts with each of the carriers involved. They are sometimes referred to as "through bills of lading." The operators become responsible for the shipment of goods throughout the time of their transport.

Electronic Data Interchange

Paper transport documents are rapidly being replaced by **electronic data interchange** (EDI), whereby shipping data is transmitted over the Internet using one of several standards. Under this practice, trade documents such as bills of lading, letters of credit, and certificates of origin may be filed electronically at a central database.

The electronic transfer of documents has several advantages over paper-based transfers. First, it lets buyers and sellers track goods that are in transit and lets the parties make necessary adjustments when the goods are delayed. Second, the faster transmission of bills of lading and other documents lets the seller get faster payment for goods, which in turn translates into an improved cash flow for the seller. Third, it eliminates the need to prepare multiple copies of documents manually, which reduces redundant paperwork and improves efficiency and accuracy.

The use of EDI raises several issues. A principal concern is security. Traditionally, the buyer has had to present an original signed bill of lading to receive the goods. Although a "digital signature" may replace the written signature requirement, such documents may not be protected against unauthorized access. Infrastructure is another issue. Not all geographic regions have reliable telecommunication networks.

Another obstacle to the global paperless system of trade is the lack of standardization. A particular trade document, such as a bill of lading, may have several different formats depending on the country and practices it uses. For a global system to work, there must be a standard format of trade documents.

ALLOCATING SHIPPING RESPONSIBILITIES AND THE RISK OF LOSS

Earlier in this chapter, and in the *Biddell Brothers case*, we saw that in certain documentary sales the seller is responsible for arranging and paying for ocean transportation and that risk of loss shifts to the buyer when the goods are properly delivered to the carrier at the port of shipment.

In the following sections, we look at how shipping responsibilities and risk of loss are allocated in general. The material in the following sections applies to all contracts for the sale of goods, not just those with documentary payment terms.

Freight and Transportation Charges

Shipping terms are integral to the price term itself. Because of the high cost of air and ocean freight, a buyer and seller must do more than merely agree on a price for the goods; they must also agree on who is going to pay the transportation and cargo insurance charges. For the price quoted, will the seller deliver the goods to the buyer, put them aboard a ship, or just make them available to a common carrier at the factory door? For instance, a seller might say, "This is the price if you come to my factory and pick up the goods. If you want me to pay to get them to the seaport in my country, or even across the ocean to your country, I will, but this is what the price of the goods will be then."

A seller will frequently present a proposal to a buyer offering a choice of shipping terms. For instance, one proposal may show a price with ocean freight, another without. These choices provide the buyer with a breakdown of the costs and responsibility for those costs within the transaction. Buyers who have an itemized breakdown of the various transportation, handling, and insurance charges from the seller can compare those with the costs of making the shipping arrangements themselves. Furthermore, transportation costs are needed if the buyer is comparing prices from two different foreign suppliers located in different parts of the world.

A buyer who requests all suppliers to quote prices with the same shipping terms can compare "apples to apples." A buyer might also request certain shipping terms because of the nature of their business. A buyer who imports regularly may have buying agents in the seller's country who can handle the details of moving the goods. Similarly, a buyer may take full responsibility for chartering its own ships, as in the case of a developing country making a large purchase of grain. They may want the grain made available to them alongside their ship, and they will pay all expenses and bear all risks from that point. In many cases, a seller who maintains a warehouse in the buyer's country will price the goods for pickup there.

Unless a seller is in such a dominant position in the market that it can dictate terms, it may want to offer more flexible shipping terms to make the sale. Even if a competitor offers a lower price, a firm with better shipping terms may get the order. The buyer may lack experience in moving cargo or may just not want to deal with arranging transportation in the seller's country.

For instance, imagine a Japanese buyer who attends a trade fair in New York and concludes a contract with a company from Boone, North Carolina. The buyer may not want to bother with getting the goods from "the Boonedocks" to a U.S. seaport and then on to Japan. Rather, the buyer just wants the best price for the goods delivered and unloaded from a ship at a Japanese seaport nearest the buyer's factory.

Allocating the Risk of Loss

The parties to a contract must know when they are responsible for damage or loss to goods and when they are not. Clearly, the seller is responsible if fire destroys the goods during production at the seller's plant. Likewise, if the goods are destroyed after they have been moved into the buyer's warehouse, then the buyer is responsible. But when does the risk pass from one party to the other? In some countries, in the absence of a provision in the contract, the risk of loss is on the party who has "title" to the goods—the party who owns them, or the bill of lading, at that moment. However, because the bill of lading does not move physically with the goods, a determination of who owned the goods at the time of their destruction is often difficult. For example, the bill of lading may have been negotiated to the buyer at 2:12 in the afternoon, but we have no evidence as to what time the ship actually sank. Here, there is no way of determining who actually "owned" the goods at the exact moment of loss. This "title" method has not been employed in the United States for many decades.

Ideally, the seller wants to be free of the risk of loss as soon as the goods leave the back door. The buyer would like to delay it for as long as possible. The ability to negotiate, of course, stems from the relative bargaining position of the parties. If the seller's products contain superior technology or if they are commodities in short supply or patented products that the buyer needs, then the seller may be in a stronger position to shift the risk to the buyer. Similarly, if the buyer is in a dominant economic position, such as by being able to order in large quantities, the buyer may be able to dictate the terms of the contract. For example, the owner of a rare 1927 Rolls-Royce in London may say to a U.S. buyer, "You may purchase my Rolls in London and drive it away, but if you want it shipped to you, you must bear all the risks of the journey from the moment it leaves my door."

Buyer and seller are always free to decide in their contract when the risk of loss will pass from one to the other. However, if the parties fail to do so and a dispute arises, the courts will be forced to decide on the basis of whether the contract is of the shipment type or of the destination type.

Destination Contracts. How the responsibilities of the parties are defined determines whether a contract is a shipment or a destination contract: Who has responsibility for shipping or transporting the goods? Who is paying the freight charges? By what means will the buyer remit payment? If the contract calls for the seller to deliver the goods to a particular destination, such as the buyer's city or place of business, the contract is a **destination contract** (also known as an "arrival" contract). Under UCC §2-509 (see Exhibit 5.3), the risk of loss in a destination contract passes to the buyer when the goods are tendered to the buyer at the point of destination.

Shipment Contracts. If the contract calls for the seller to ship the goods by carrier but does not require the seller to deliver the goods to a named place, then it is a shipment contract (also known as a "departure" contract). In a **shipment contract**, the risk of loss or damage to the goods passes to the buyer when the goods are given to the first carrier—be it truck, airline, or ocean carrier. Shipment contracts are more common in international trade because sellers usually prefer not to be responsible for the goods at sea.

Exhibit 5.3

2003 Amendments to UCC 2-513*

§2-513 Buyer's Right to Inspection of Goods

1) Unless otherwise agreed and subject to subsection (3), where goods are tendered or delivered or identified to the contract for sale, the buyer has a right before payment or acceptance to inspect them at any reasonable place and time and in any reasonable manner. When the seller is required or authorized to send the goods to the buyer, the inspection may be after their arrival.
2) Expenses of inspection must be borne by the buyer but may be recovered from the seller if the goods do not conform and are rejected.
3) Unless otherwise agreed, the buyer is not entitled to inspect the goods before payment of the price when the contract provides
   a) for delivery on terms that under applicable course of performance, course of dealing, or usage of trade are interpreted to preclude inspection before payment; or
   b) for payment against documents of title, except where such payment is due only after the goods are to become available for inspection.

* Subject to enactment by state legislatures.

The Risk of Loss in International Sales under the CISG

The **Convention on Contracts for the International Sale of Goods** contains provisions that assign the risk of loss in Articles 66–70, reproduced in Appendix A of this book. The basic rule of Article 66 is that, unless the parties agree otherwise, any loss or damage to the goods occurring after the risk of loss has passed from seller to buyer does not relieve the buyer of his or her obligation to pay for the goods, unless the loss or damage is the fault of the seller. According to Article 67, if the contract calls for the goods to be handed over to a carrier at a particular place, then the risk passes to the buyer at that place. However, if the seller is simply expected to ship and no particular place is mentioned, the risk passes to the buyer when the goods are handed over to the first carrier for shipment to the buyer. For instance, assume that a company located in Boone, North Carolina, confirms an order for the export of its product to a foreign customer. The contract reads simply "Seller will handle all transportation charges and arrangements." The seller arranges for a trucking company to pick up the goods and deliver them to the air carrier's terminal at the airport in Charlotte, 100 miles away. The risk of loss will pass from seller to buyer when the goods are first handed over to the trucking company at the seller's factory or warehouse in Boone. If the goods are damaged from that point forth, on land or in the air (or at sea, in the case of ocean shipment), the loss falls on the buyer. Of course, the seller is responsible for properly packaging and preparing the merchandise for shipment. The buyer would be relieved from any obligation to pay for the goods if the loss was due to an act or omission of the seller (Article 66).

Trade Terms

While it is possible to draft a detailed agreement for allocating shipping and transportation charges between buyer and seller and to specify when the risk of loss shall pass, in most routine cases this is done by using **trade terms**, sometimes called *shipping terms*. Trade terms are usually expressed in the form of abbreviated symbols, such as FOB or CIF. They are a shorthand method that permits the parties to express their agreement quickly, with little confusion, and with few language problems. If the parties use a trade term in their contract, they must define it. If it is not defined in the contract, a court would have to look to the applicable law for its interpretation. The most common method of defining trade terms, however, is to incorporate them into the contract by reference to some independent source or publication.

International Rules for the Interpretation of Trade Terms

The most important set of trade term definitions are the *International Rules for the Interpretation of Trade Terms*, or ***Incoterms 2010***, published by the Paris-based *International Chamber of Commerce*. These definitions have the support of important business groups, including manufacturing, shipping, and banking industries worldwide. Courts and legal scholars in many countries cite them as having the effect of customary law. First published in 1936, the current revision was released in January 2011.

Incoterms include eleven trade terms classified into four groups—E, F, C, and D—according to the relative responsibilities of each party and to the point at which the risk of loss passes from seller to buyer. Exhibit 5.4 arranges the terms with the minimum responsibility of the seller and the maximum responsibility of the buyer appearing at the top; the minimum responsibility of the buyer and maximum responsibility of the seller appear at the bottom. International salespeople, export managers, and world traders benefit from a working knowledge of these terms. Because *Incoterms* are not automatically part of a contract for the sale of goods, parties should include a clause, such as "This contract is to be interpreted in accordance with *Incoterms*."

The following case, *St. Paul Guardian Ins. Co. v. Neuromed Medical Systems & Support, GmbH*, illustrates the wide acceptance of *Incoterms*. Here, an American court was called on to decide who was responsible for goods damaged at sea, the German seller or the U.S. buyer. The contract used a common trade term, CIF (cost, insurance, and freight; see Exhibit 5.4), but did not define CIF. The contract also specified that it was governed by the laws of Germany. The court stated that under German law the CIF term, and thus the rights of the parties, would be defined by *Incoterms*. The court reasoned that *Incoterms* were so commonly used that they had become a trade usage to which the parties were bound in the absence of their agreement to the contrary.

The following section looks at some hypothetical illustrations to see how these terms are used. Keep in mind that the terms were drafted by their authors to reflect how companies actually do business. Selecting a term for incorporation in a contract is more than just bargaining over who will pay freight costs or bear the risk of loss. Certain terms may fit better with the needs of the parties. Some are suited for ocean carriage, some for air transport, and others for **multimodal transport**. Some terms are suited for a documentary form of payment while others are suited to open account payment terms. Also, keep in mind that the terms are for maritime and inland waterway transport only: FAS, FOB, CFR, and CIF. Others are for any mode of transport.

E Terms

E terms place the lowest amount of responsibility on the seller. In the following hypothetical situation, assume a buyer in the Netherlands is placing an order with a supplier in Albany, New York. The buyer states that its U.S. subsidiary will pick up the goods at the Albany plant and arrange export. Therefore, the seller will probably quote its price in terms *EXW Albany factory*. Under this term, the seller need only make the goods available at its factory (or mill, farm, warehouse, or other place of business) and present the buyer with an invoice for payment. The buyer must arrange all transportation and bear all risks and expenses of the journey from that point. The buyer must also clear the goods for export by obtaining export licenses from the U.S. government.

This term is most often used when the buyer will pick up the goods by truck or rail. Therefore, for international shipments, EXW terms are common in Europe where goods frequently move across national boundaries by ground transportation. This term is likely to become more popular in trade between Canada, the United States, and Mexico in the future. But unless the buyer requests this term, use of it may show that the seller is not really interested in exporting and is unwilling to accommodate a foreign buyer.

F Terms

The **F terms** are shipment contracts similar to those studied earlier. Under F terms, the seller must deliver the goods to the designated point of departure "free" of expense or risk to the buyer. At that point, the risk of loss passes from seller to buyer. The buyer arranges the transportation and pays all freight costs. However, if it is convenient and the parties agree, the seller may pay the freight and add that amount to the invoice price already quoted. F terms are often used when the buyer contracts for a complete shipload of materials or commodities and thus has reason to assume the responsibility for arranging carriage. F terms may also be used because the buyer feels that it can obtain better freight rates than the seller. Some F terms are for ocean shipment only. Others can be used for all modes of transport.

Assume that the buyer in the Netherlands wants to arrange its own ocean transportation. The seller in Albany wants to deliver the goods to a carrier near it, for transportation to the Port of New York, making it necessary for different forms of transportation. For instance, the seller might deliver the goods to a barge hauler for a trip down the Hudson, or to a railroad or trucking company. The seller may want to hand over the goods to a multimodal terminal operator nearby and let it handle the goods from there. This inland

Exhibit 5.4

Explanation of *Incoterms 2010:* ICC Official Rules for the Interpretation of Trade Terms

Group and Type	Term Abbreviation/ In Full	Mode of Transportation	Seller's Responsibilities	Buyer's Responsibilities	Passage of Risk
E Group	EXW Ex Works	All modes	Have the goods ready for pickup at the location specified in the contract, usually seller's place of business.	Provide vehicle or rail car and load goods. Obtain export licenses. Enter goods through customs.	When the goods are made available by seller at named location.
F Group	FCA Free Carrier	All modes	Place the goods in the hands of a carrier named by the buyer at the place specified. Provide export license.	Choose carrier, arrange transport, and pay freight charges. On arrival, enter goods through customs.	When the goods are delivered to the carrier or terminal operator at the named place of shipment.
	FAS Free Alongside Ship	Sea and inland waterway only	Place the goods alongside the ship specified by the buyer (on the dock or barge) within the time required by the contract, ready for loading. Obtain export license.	Choose ocean carrier, arrange transport, and pay freight. Enter goods through customs.	When the goods are delivered alongside the ship specified by buyer.
	FOB Free on Board	Sea and inland waterway only	Load the goods on board the ship specified by the buyer within the time required by the contract. Pay costs of loading. Obtain export license.	Choose ocean carrier and pay freight charges. Enter goods through customs.	When the goods are on board at port of shipment.
C Group	CFR Cost and Freight	Sea and inland waterway only	Contract for transport and pay freight charges to the named port of destination. Arrange for loading of goods on board ship, usually of seller's choice, and pay costs of loading. Obtain export license. Notify buyer of shipment. Documentary sale is assumed. Tender documents to buyer.	Purchase document of title and take delivery from ocean carrier. No date of delivery at buyer's port is implied. Pay import duties. Enter goods through customs.	When the goods are on board at port of shipment. Buyer must procure own insurance or else use CIF term.

continued

Group and Type	Term Abbreviation/ In Full	Mode of Transportation	Seller's Responsibilities	Buyer's Responsibilities	Passage of Risk
	CIF Cost, Insurance, and Freight	Sea and inland waterway only	Same as CFR, with added requirement that seller purchase marine insurance. Insurance policy is assigned to buyer. Documentary sale is assumed.	Same as CFR, except seller supplies insurance. Buyer may request additional insurance coverage at own expense.	When the goods are on board at port of shipment. If damage or loss, buyer files a claim with insurer.
	CPTCarriage Paid To	All modes	Similar to CFR, but for all modes of transport. Deliver goods to truck, rail, or multimodal carrier, or to ship, and arrange for transport to destination. Freight charges prepaid. Obtain export license. Notify buyer of shipment. Seller need not insure goods. Documentary sale is assumed.	Similar to CFR. Purchase document of title and take delivery of goods from carrier. Enter goods through customs. Pay import duties.	When the goods are delivered by the seller to the first carrier. Buyer must procure own insurance or use CIP term.
	CIP Carriage and Insurance Paid To	All modes	Same as CPT, with added requirement that seller purchase insurance. Insurance policy assigned to buyer.	Same as CPT. Purchase document of title and take delivery of goods from carrier. Enter goods through customs. Pay import duties.	When the goods are delivered by the seller to the first carrier. If damage or loss, buyer files a claim with insurer.
D Group	DAT Delivered at Terminal	All modes	Seller clears the goods for export and bears all costs associated with delivering the goods and unloading them at the terminal at the named port or destination.	Take delivery of goods at specified location. Buyer is responsible for all costs after delivery and unloading of the goods including clearing the goods for import in the named country of destination.	When the goods are unloaded and delivered to buyer at specified location.

continued

Group and Type	Term Abbreviation/ In Full	Mode of Transportation	Seller's Responsibilities	Buyer's Responsibilities	Passage of Risk
	DAP Delivered at Place	All modes	Seller clears the goods for export and bears all costs associated with delivering the goods at the named place of destination not unloaded.	Take delivery of goods at specified location. Buyer is responsible for all costs after delivery including unloading of the goods and clearing the goods for import in the named country of destination.	When the goods are delivered to buyer at specified destination.
	DDP Delivered Duty Paid	All modes	Same as DAT, except that seller obtains import licenses, pays import duties, and clears goods through customs. Place of destination specified is usually buyer's place of business.	Take delivery of goods at specified location.	When the goods are unloaded and deliv-ered to buyer at specified location. Seller should insure for own protection.

SOURCE: export.gov, *Incoterms* 2010, located at http://export.gov/faq/eg_main_043740.asp.

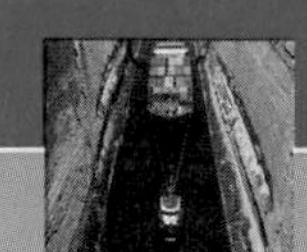

St. Paul Guardian Ins. Co. v. Neuromed Medical Systems & Support, Gmbh

2002 U.S. Dist. LEXIS 5096 United States District Court (S.D.N.Y.)

BACKGROUND AND FACTS

Shared Imaging, an American company, agreed to purchase an MRI machine from Neuromed, a German seller. The one-page contract of sale stated that the delivery terms were "CIF New York Seaport, the buyer will arrange and pay for customs clearance as well as transport to Calumet City." In addition, under "Disclaimer" it stated, "system including all accessories and options remain the property of Neuromed till complete payment has been received." Payment was to be made when the machine was received in Calumet City. The contract also stated that it was to be governed by the laws of Germany. The MRI was loaded aboard the vessel *Atlantic Carrier* undamaged and in good working order. When it reached its destination of Calumet City, Illinois, it had been damaged and was in need of extensive repair, which led plaintiff to conclude that the MRI had been damaged in transit. Shared Imaging filed its claim for insurance with St. Paul Guardian, who brought this action against Neuromed for damages. Neuromed argues that the case should be dismissed because it is not liable under German law.

STEIN, DISTRICT J.

Neuromed contends that because the delivery terms were "CIF New York Seaport," its contractual obligation, with regard to risk of loss or damage, ended when it delivered the MRI to the vessel at the port of shipment and therefore the action must be dismissed because plaintiff has failed to state a claim for which relief can be granted. Plaintiff responds that the generally accepted definition of the "CIF" term, as defined in *Incoterms* 1990, is inapplicable. Moreover, the plaintiff suggests that other provisions of the contract are inconsistent with the "CIF" term because Neuromed, pursuant to the contract, retained title subsequent to delivery to the vessel at the port of shipment and thus Shared Imaging manifestly retained the risk of loss.

APPLICABLE GERMAN LAW

The parties concede that pursuant to German law, the *U.N. Convention on Contracts for the International Sale of Goods* ("CISG") governs this transaction because (1) both the U.S. and Germany are Contracting States to that Convention, and (2) neither party chose, by express provision in the contract, to opt out of the application of the CISG ... [citations hereinafter omitted]. Germany has been a Contracting State since 1991, and the CISG is an integral part of German law. To hold otherwise would undermine the objectives of the Convention which Germany has agreed to uphold.

CISG, INCOTERMS, AND "CIF"

"CIF," which stands for "cost, insurance, and freight," is a commercial trade term that is defined in *Incoterms* 1990, published by the International Chamber of Commerce ("ICC"). The aim of INCOTERMS, which stands for international commercial terms, is "to provide a set of international rules for the interpretation of the most commonly used trade terms in foreign trade...." INCOTERMS are incorporated into the CISG through Article 9(2) which provides that, "The parties are considered, unless otherwise agreed, to have impliedly made applicable to their contract or its formation a usage of which the parties knew or ought to have known and which in international trade is widely known to, and regularly observed by, parties to contracts of the type involved in the particular trade concerned." CISG, art. 9(2).... INCOTERMS defines "CIF" (named port of destination) to mean the seller delivers when the goods pass "the ship's rail at the port of shipment." The seller is responsible for paying the cost, freight and insurance coverage necessary to bring the goods to the named port of destination, but the risk of loss or damage to the goods passes from seller to buyer upon delivery to the port of shipment ...

Plaintiff's legal expert contends that INCOTERMS are inapplicable here because the contract fails to specifically incorporate them. Nonetheless, he cites and acknowledges that the German Supreme Court (Bundesgerichtshof)—the court of last resort in the Federal Republic of Germany for civil matters—concluded that a clause "FOB" without specific reference to INCOTERMS was to be interpreted according to INCOTERMS "simply because the INCOTERMS include a clause 'FOB.'"

Conceding that commercial practice attains the force of law under section 346 of the German Commercial Code (citing the German Court), plaintiff's expert concludes that the opinion of the German Court "amounts to saying that the INCOTERMS definitions in Germany have the force of law as trade custom." As encapsulated by defendant's legal expert, "It is accepted under German law that in case a contract refers to CIF-delivery, the parties refer to the INCOTERMS rules ... " Thus, pursuant to CISG art. 9 (2), INCOTERMS definitions should be applied to the

continues

continued

contract despite the lack of an explicit INCOTERMS reference in the contract.

EFFECT OF TRANSFER OF TITLE CONTRACT PROVISIONS

Plaintiff argues that Neuromed's explicit retention of title in the contract to the MRI machine modified the "CIF" term, such that Neuromed retained title and assumed the risk of loss. INCOTERMS, however, only address passage of risk, not transfer of title. Under the CISG, the passage of risk is ... independent of the transfer of title. Moreover, according to Article 67(1), the passage of risk and transfer of title need not occur at the same time, as the seller's retention of "documents controlling the disposition of the goods does not affect the passage of risk." CISG, art. 67(1).

EFFECT OF OTHER DELIVERY TERMS

Plaintiff next contends that ... the other terms in the contract are evidence that the parties' intention to supersede and replace the "CIF" term such that Neuromed retained title and the risk of loss. That is incorrect. Citing the "Delivery Terms" clause in the contract, plaintiff posits that had the parties intended to abide by the strictures of INCOTERMS there would have been no need to define the buyer's obligations to pay customs and arrange further transport. Plaintiff's argument, however, is undermined by *Incoterms* 1990, which provides that "[i]t is normally desirable that customs clearance is arranged by the party domiciled in the country where such clearance should take place." The "CIF" term as defined by INCOTERMS only requires the seller to "clear the goods for export" and is silent as to which party bears the obligation to arrange for customs clearance. The parties are therefore left to negotiate these obligations. As such, a clause defining the terms of customs clearance neither alters nor affects the "CIF" clause in the contract.

Plaintiff also cites to the "Payment Terms" clause of the contract, which specified that final payment was not to be made upon seller's delivery of the machine to the port of shipment, but rather, upon buyer's acceptance of the machine in Calumet City. These terms speak to the final disposition of the property, not to the risk for loss or damage. INCOTERMS do not mandate a payment structure, but rather simply establish that the buyer bears an obligation to "[p]ay the price as provided in the contract of sale." Inclusion of the terms of payment in the contract does not modify the "CIF" clause.

The terms of the contract do not modify the "CIF" clause in the contract such that the risk of loss remained with Neuromed. The fact remains that the CISG, INCOTERMS, and German law all distinguish between the passage of the risk of loss and the transfer of title. Thus, because (1) Neuromed's risk of loss of, or damage to, the MRI machine under the contract passed to plaintiff upon delivery of the machine to the carrier at the port of shipment and (2) it is undisputed that the MRI machine was delivered to the carrier undamaged and in good working order, Neuromed's motion to dismiss for failure to state a claim is hereby granted.

Decision. The U.S. court, interpreting German law, held that a delivery term in a sales contract (here CIF) should be defined according to *Incoterms*, in the absence of contractual provisions specifying otherwise. The court reasoned that under the CISG, merchants impliedly agree to trade usages of which they should have known. *Incoterms* are so widely used that they have become a trade usage, or international custom, applicable to this contract. The risk of loss passed to the buyer at the port of shipment.

Comment. *Incoterms* 2010 eliminates the rule regarding passage of risk in C terms when goods pass over the ship's rail in favor of passage of risk when the goods are on board the vessel. According to the International Chamber of Commerce, the new rule on passage of risk "more closely reflects modern commercial reality and avoids the rather dated image of the risk swinging to and fro across an imaginary perpendicular line."

Case Questions

1. If the contract stated that it was governed by the laws of Germany, why did the court apply the law of the CISG?

carrier will then transport the goods to the Port of New York for shipment to the foreign destination. If this inland carrier is in Albany, then the seller should quote prices *FCA Albany*. Here, for the contract price, the seller bears the costs and assumes all risks of getting the goods from its factory to the carrier or terminal in Albany. The seller then has the responsibility to obtain any necessary government export licenses. This term can also be used for air transport. A term *FCA JFK Airport* means that the seller has agreed, for the contract price, to deliver the goods from Albany to the airline in New York for shipment.

Assume now that the Dutch buyer is purchasing a bulk cargo, such as agricultural commodities, and will charter a full ship for the overseas voyage—*a voyage charter*—departing from New York to Rotterdam. The buyer may find the voyage charter more convenient and cheaper to arrange than leaving the shipping up to the seller. The buyer wants the seller to place the goods on barges or on the pier alongside the ship, *Queen Anna E*, docked at the Port of New York. The appropriate contract terms are *FAS Queen Anna E*. (If the name of the vessel is not yet known, the parties can contract on terms *FAS New York*.) The risk of loss passes from seller to buyer once the goods are alongside the ship. The buyer, having arranged the ocean transport, will pay the separate costs of loading the vessel. The seller must obtain an export license and clear the goods for export. An FAS buyer should also provide the seller with notice of the ship's departure date and loading times. The seller's obligation is to place the goods alongside the vessel within the time called for in the contract.

Under FOB (free on board) contracts, the seller bears slightly more responsibility. In addition to obtaining export clearance, the seller must place the goods aboard the ship. Risk of loss passes to the buyer once the goods are on board. Therefore, if the contract is on terms *FOB New York* or *FOB Queen Anna E*, the seller must secure export licenses, pay all costs of loading, and deliver the goods over the ship's rail. Notice that under *Incoterms*, the seller's responsibility does not end until the goods are actually on board the vessel. Exporters should always use the FOB term as a shipment contract as it was intended. Using it in conjunction with a destination location (e.g., *FOB foreign port*) contradicts the *Incoterms* definition and shifts the risk of the voyage to the exporter.

C Terms

C terms are also shipment contracts. The letter C indicates that the seller is responsible for certain costs after the delivery of goods to the carrier. Like the FOB term, however, risk of loss passes to the buyer when the goods are on board the vessel or carrier. Assume that our Dutch buyer requests pricing information from Albany. As an experienced exporter, the seller might understand that the buyer has little interest in arranging transportation, let alone coming to pick up the goods. The buyer simply wants the goods delivered to the port of entry in its country closest to its company. If this requires ocean shipment, the seller will prepare a price quotation *CFR Port of Rotterdam* (formerly called *C & F*) or *CIF Port of Rotterdam*. For the price quoted, the seller will deliver the goods to an ocean carrier, arrange shipment, prepay the freight charges to the agreed-on port of destination, obtain a clean on-board bill of lading marked *freight prepaid*, and forward it along with the invoice to the buyer for payment.

The only difference between CFR and CIF terms is that under CIF terms the seller must also procure and forward to the buyer a policy of marine insurance to cover the risk of loss once it passes to the buyer. (This amount is the minimum coverage; the buyer may want to request the purchase of additional insurance for its own protection.) By providing both carriage and insurance coverage, the seller is able to earn additional profit yet retain its rights in the goods until payment is made against documents. Upon presentation of the bill of lading, the Dutch buyer must make payment, but once it receives the bill of lading, it can resell the goods, or if the goods are lost, it is entitled to collect the insurance money. However, both *Incoterms* and maritime practice seem to indicate that, if the seller desires, it may forgo its right to collect on the documents, negotiate the bill of lading directly to the buyer, and make other arrangements for payment or credit.

If the seller intends to arrange ocean transportation but will deliver the goods to a road or rail carrier, inland waterway, or to a multimodal terminal operator for transit to the seaport, the seller may wish to quote *CPT, Port of Rotterdam*. Here, the risk of loss shifts to the buyer when the goods are delivered to the first carrier. CIP terms are the same as under CPT, with the added requirement that the seller procure insurance to cover the buyer's risk of loss.

D Terms

Contracts with **D terms** of sale are destination (or "arrival") contracts. If the seller in Albany is willing to enter into a destination contract, then it must be willing to accept far greater responsibility than under any other terms. For the price stated in the contract, the seller must deliver the goods at the port of destination and bear the risk of loss throughout the journey. Thus, if the goods are lost in transit, the Dutch buyer would not be entitled to claim the insurance money, although the buyer may have lost profits it was hoping to make on the goods.

The *D terms* may be used for any mode or modes of transport. If the contract terms are *DAT Rotterdam*, the seller must clear the goods for export and bears all costs and risks associated with their delivery and unloading at the terminal in Rotterdam. The Dutch buyer is responsible for all costs and risks going forward including clearing the goods for import in the Netherlands. The parties' responsibilities are identical if the contract terms are *DAP Rotterdam* with the exception that the seller is responsible for delivery to the named destination not unloaded, and the buyer is responsible for the costs and risks associated with unloading in addition to clearing the goods through customs. Finally, the seller's responsibilities are at their maximum if the contract terms are *DDP Rotterdam* in which the seller bears all risks and costs associated with delivery of the goods ready for unloading and cleared for import. Clearly, the seller will not want to take on the responsibility and risks of a DDP shipment unless it is experienced in importing into the Netherlands and familiar with customs regulations and tariff laws there.

Today, destination contracts are actually becoming more popular due to an increasingly competitive and globalized marketplace. Many manufacturers and other shippers find they must do more and more to win and keep customers. In other words, shippers often have to provide credit terms to their customers by shipping on open account and giving the customer time to pay. Shippers are also being forced to take greater responsibility for getting the goods into the customer's hands. For these reasons, more and more shippers are quoting prices on D terms than ever before. Still others are quoting prices on C terms to shift the risk of the voyage but voluntarily forgoing the documentary collection and sending the bill of lading directly to the customer for payment on open account.

Modification of Trade Terms

On occasion, the parties may be tempted to alter the meaning of a trade term in their contract to meet their own business requirements. The International Chamber of Commerce and many experienced lawyers usually recommend that buyer and seller do not attempt to add to, explain, or change the meaning of any trade term without legal advice. This "customizing" only causes needless confusion. The problem usually arises in CIF contract cases. The general rule is that if the additional shipping terms added by the parties to a CIF contract do not

On the other hand, by inserting additional terms that are contrary to the usual meaning of CIF, they can destroy the CIF terms. For instance, assume that the parties enter into a contract labeled "CIF." They then add that "payment is not due until the goods are sold by the buyer." A court must then decide, looking at all the evidence, whether the contract was on CIF terms. The court in *Kumar Corp. v. Nopal Lines, Ltd.* discusses this issue. As you read, notice that the court decides the case on the basis of the seller's failure to obtain insurance on the cargo as required under CIF terms.

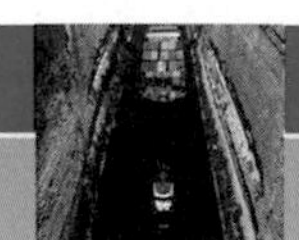

Kumar Corp. v. Nopal Lines, Ltd.

462 So. 2d 1178 (1985) District Court of Appeals of Florida, Third District

BACKGROUND AND FACTS

Kumar sold 700 television sets to one of its largest customers, Nava, in Venezuela. The contract was on CIF terms, Maracaibo. However, they agreed that Nava would not pay Kumar until Nava actually sold the merchandise. Kumar obtained the televisions from its supplier, received them in its Miami warehouse, loaded them on a trailer, delivered the trailer to its freight forwarder, Maduro, in Florida, and obtained the shipping documents. The trailer was stolen from the Maduro lot and found abandoned and empty. Kumar had failed to obtain marine insurance on the cargo. Kumar sued Maduro and the carrier. The defendants argued that, because the risk of loss had passed from Kumar to Nava, Kumar did not have standing to sue. The trial court agreed with the defendants and dismissed Kumar's case. Kumar appealed.

DANIEL S. PEARSON, JUDGE

Kumar's argument that it is the real party in interest proceeds ... from the premise that its agreement to postpone Nava's obligation to pay for the goods modified the ordinary consequence of the CIF contract that the risk of loss shifts to the buyer. A CIF contract is a recognized and established form of contract, the incidents of which are well known. Thus, if a buyer and seller adopt such a contract, "they will be presumed, in the absence of any express term to the contrary, to have adopted all the normal incidents of that type of contract," D. M. Day, *The Law of International Trade*, 4

continues

continued

(1981), one of which is that the buyer, not the seller, bears the risk of loss when the goods are delivered to the carrier and the seller's other contractual obligations are fulfilled. A CIF contract is not a contract "that goods shall arrive, but a contract to ship goods complying with the contract of sale, to obtain, unless the contract otherwise provides, the ordinary contract of carriage to the place of destination, and the ordinary contract of insurance of the goods on that voyage, and to tender these documents against payment of the contract price." C. Schmitthoff, *The Law and Practice of International Trade*, 26-27 (7th ed. 1980).

It is clear, however, that parties may vary the terms of a CIF contract to meet their own requirements. But where the agreed-upon variation is such that it removes a vital ingredient of a CIF contract, then the contract ceases to be a CIF contract. Thus, "if according to the intention of the parties the actual delivery of the goods [to the buyer] is an essential condition of performance, the contract is not a CIF contract." C. Schmitthoff, *supra.*

In the present case, Kumar and Nava agreed to payment upon Nava's sale of the goods in Venezuela... [thereby negating an essential ingredient of the CIF contract].... [T]he use of the term CIF does not ipso facto make the contract a CIF contract if the contract has been altered in a manner that is repugnant to the very nature of a CIF contract. Therefore, because the record before us does not ... conclusively show that the contract remained a true CIF contract despite the agreement between Kumar and Nava concerning the payment for the goods, it was improper for the trial court to conclude as a matter of law that the risk of loss passed to Nava when Kumar delivered the goods to the shipper.

But even assuming, *arguendo*, that we were to conclude, as did the trial court, that the risk of loss passed to Nava merely by virtue of the label CIF on the contract, Kumar must still prevail. Under the CIF contract, Kumar was obliged to procure insurance, and by not doing so, acted, intentionally or unintentionally, as the insurer of the shipment. As the insurer of the shipment, Kumar was obliged to pay Nava, the risk bearer, for the loss when the goods were stolen. Being legally obliged to pay Nava's loss, Kumar would thus be subrogated to Nava's claims against the appellees. Since a subrogee is the real party in interest and may sue in its own name, Kumar would have standing to sue under this theory.

Reversed and remanded for further proceedings.

Decision. The court held that where, under a CIF contract, the seller fails to obtain marine cargo insurance on behalf of the buyer, the risk of loss remains with the seller, who becomes a self-insurer of the property. As such, the seller has standing to sue the carrier for the cargo loss.

Case Questions

1. In what way did the wording of the contract contradict the CIF term?
2. If the court said that the parties may vary the terms of their contract to meet their own requirements, why did the court not recognize the contradictory wording?
3. Assume that a seller fails to procure insurance on a shipment as required by contract and that the shipment is lost at sea. As between buyer and seller, which party will bear the loss?

CONCLUSION

Transaction risks can threaten significant costs to doing international business. Contract negotiations represent a good opportunity to address transaction risks in advance. In an international contract for the sale of goods, the terms of sale are as essential to the contract as the quality of the goods themselves. Moving goods around the world is expensive and risky. If a contract does not specify the terms of sale and who bears the risk of loss, the parties may be in for a tremendous surprise. Moreover, because of the risks of nonpayment and nondelivery, the parties may not wish to do business on cash or open account terms until a business relationship is established. Thus, an understanding of the documentary sale, as well as of the most common trade terms, is necessary for any international sales specialist or export manager.

Despite the continued and widespread use of the documentary sale, its use has declined somewhat in the past 30 years due to a number of factors. First, the greater reliability of international credit reporting makes open account transactions between foreign parties much safer than in previous years. Second, increasing globalization means closer, long-term relationships between vendors in a global supply chain. Third, it is possible to purchase many of the same products on other terms from domestic sources, such as domestic subsidiaries of foreign manufacturers or through local distributors. Nevertheless, the documentary sale is often used when the credit risk is significant. It is also used when the goods will be resold while in transit. Common examples are agricultural commodities, oil, and fungible goods. The bill of lading, which serves as a document of title, permits the goods to be bought and sold, time and again, even though they remain aboard ship on the high seas or are sitting in a foreign port.

No reader should be left with the impression that the documentary sale eliminates the risk of foreign shipments. The buyer might refuse the documents when they are presented by its bank or it may be unable to pay. Similarly, the buyer might purchase documents that appear to be in order only to find defective merchandise in the containers—or no merchandise at all. The solution to some of these problems is the subject of the next chapter.

Chapter Summary

1. *Transaction risks* are those risks to buyer and seller resulting from moving money and goods under an international sales contract. Transaction risks arise from barriers that separate buyer and seller, including distance, oceans, the time that the cargo is out of possession of the parties, communication and language difficulties, cultural differences, national boundaries, interference by local customs authorities, and differences in legal systems.
2. The *documentary sale* is one type of contract for the international sale of goods, using ocean transport, in which the buyer must pay upon the presentation of a negotiable document of title by the seller. The parties might indicate their desire for a documentary sale by specifying in the contract that payment terms are "cash against documents" or "documents against payment."
3. A *bill of lading* is a document of title that an *ocean carrier* issues to a shipper upon receiving goods for transport. Bills of lading can be negotiable or nonnegotiable. Nonnegotiable bills are contracts of carriage and receipts for depositing goods with a carrier for shipment. Additionally, negotiable bills of lading serve as a document of title. Only negotiable bills of lading can be used in the documentary sale.
4. The documentary sale is critical to world trade because it allows the holder of the document of title to trade in the goods while they are still at sea. The documents may be bought and sold many times before they reach a final destination.
5. The *documentary collection* is the process by which international banks serve as intermediaries between seller and buyer to handle the exchange of the bill of lading in return for payment.
6. In a documentary sale, the buyer is given no opportunity to inspect the goods. In essence, the buyer is not buying goods, but is buying documents that represent ownership of the goods. The seller's basic obligation is to ship the good in accordance with the contract and to tender a clean bill of lading to the buyer. The buyer's obligation is to purchase the bill of lading when presented by a bank in the buyer's country. A "clean" bill is one with no notations from the carrier or carrier's agent indicating that damage to the goods was observable at the time of loading. Cargo insurance is a key component of most documentary sales.
7. Due to the expense of ocean shipment, and the perils of the sea, it is important for the parties to know that they have the freedom to negotiate which of them, buyer or seller, will pay for transportation expenses and insurance, and which of them will bear the risk of loss or damage during transit. This is often done using shorthand *trade term* in the contract. The most commonly used definitions for trade terms are *Incoterms*, published by the International Chamber of Commerce, a private group. If used in a contract, they will be recognized and enforced by courts.
8. *Incoterms* include eleven trade terms, classified into four groups—E, F, C, and D—according to the relative responsibilities of each party and to the point at which the risk of loss passes from seller to buyer. As Exhibit 5.4 shows, *Incoterms* are arranged in order ranking the responsibility of buyer and seller. The *E term* EXW, or *Ex Works*, represents the maximum responsibility of the buyer and minimum responsibility of the seller. The *D term* DDP, or *Delivery Duty Paid*, represents the maximum responsibility of the seller and the minimum responsibility of the buyer. The C *terms* are shipment contracts. The *D terms* are destination contracts.

9. Some trade terms are appropriate for documentary sales; others can be used for contracts that call for open account or other payment terms.
10. While the documentary sale is still widely used as a safe payment mechanism, experienced parties attempt to forge long-term business relationships with flexible payment terms.

Key Terms

transaction risk 121
delivery risk 121
payment risk (credit risk) 121
open account 121
documentary sale 121
document of title 122
bailor 122
bailee 122
bailment 122
negotiation 122
constructive delivery 122
bill of lading 122
negotiable instrument 124
negotiable document 124
holder by due negotiation (good-faith purchaser) 124
paramount title 124
documentary collection 127
transport document 127
marine insurance 127
certificate of origin 127
commercial invoice 127
documentary draft 127
collecting bank 127
CIF contracts 128
certificates of inspection 129
certificates of weight 129
certificates of analysis 129
clean bill of lading 132
on-board bill of lading 132
received-for-shipment bill of lading 133
straight bill of lading 133
consignee 133
air waybills 133
freight forwarder 133
multimodal 134
multimodal transport operators 134
combined transport operators 134
multimodal transport document 134
combined transport document 134
electronic data interchange (EDI) 134
destination contract 135
shipment contract 135
trade terms 136
Incoterms 2010 136
multimodal transport 137
E terms 137
F terms 137
C terms 143
D terms 143

Questions and Case Problems

1. Bruitrix held a bill of lading covering a shipment of washing machines that it had purchased. The washing machines were placed into a bonded warehouse operated by the British Transport Commission. Bruitrix pledged the bill of lading to its creditor, Barclay's Bank, as security for an outstanding debt. Two months later, the defendant, the Commissioners of Customs, obtained a judgment against Bruitrix for a delinquent tax. The bank attempted to take possession of the goods in order to satisfy Bruitrix's outstanding debt. On the same day, the Commissioners attempted to take possession of the goods to satisfy their judgment. The bank brought this action claiming that the pledge had transferred title to the goods to it and that as the holder of the bill of lading it was entitled to the goods. Who has a greater right in the property, Barclays Bank or the Commissioners? Why? How does the bill of lading serve as a financing device? The bill of lading is a contract of carriage. When does the carrier discharge its performance under the contract? *Barclay's Bank, Ltd. v. Commissioners of Customs and Excise*, (1963) 1 Lloyd's 81, Queen's Bench.
2. Colorado Fuel sold caustic soda to a buyer in Bombay under a CIF contract. The soda was fully loaded aboard a ship when a labor strike made it impossible for the vessel to sail. As a result, the soda arrived in Bombay six months late. The buyer sued for the late shipment. Was Colorado Fuel liable for damages? Does it matter that Colorado Fuel may have known that a strike was imminent? *Badbwar v. Colorado Fuel and Iron Corp.*, 138 F. Supp. 595 (S.D.N.Y. 1955).
3. Buyer and seller entered into a contract for the sale of sugar from the Philippines to New York on CIF terms. They added language to the contract that delivery was to be "at a customary safe wharf or refinery at New York, Philadelphia, or Baltimore to be designated by the buyer." Before the sugar arrived, the United States placed a quota on sugar imports. The sugar was not

allowed to be imported and was placed in a customs warehouse. The buyer refused the documents and the seller sued, claiming that the import restriction was no excuse for the buyer's nonpayment. The buyer argued that the language calling for delivery to a U.S. port converted a shipment contract into a destination contract. Was this a CIF contract or a destination contract? What was the effect of the additional shipping language the parties used? Why should the parties not attempt to modify a trade term or add other delivery language? *Warner Bros. & Co. v. A.C. Israel*, 101 F.2d 59 (2d Cir. 1939).

4. Phillips contracted to buy naphtha from Tradax for shipment from Algeria to Puerto Rico on C&F terms. Shipment was to be made between September 20–28, 1981. The agreement incorporated the ICC *Incoterms*. It also contained *a force majeure* clause that stated, "In the event of any delay in shipment or delivery of the goods by the seller, the unaffected party may cancel the unfulfilled balance of the contract." On September 16, Tradax shipped on the *Oxy Trader*. While en route, the *Oxy Trader* was detained by maritime authorities at Gibraltar, deemed unsafe, and not allowed to proceed. Tradax informed Phillips, which telexed back on October 1 that October 15 was the last acceptable delivery date. On October 7, its cargo had to be offloaded in Portugal for shipment on another vessel. On October 13, Phillips refused payment of the documents due to the delay. In November, Tradax sold the cargo to a third party at a loss. Phillips brought this action in the United States. Tradax claimed that it had ceased to bear responsibility for the goods when it transferred the goods to the carrier for shipment. Phillips maintained that it was excused from performance because the ship's delay constituted *force majeure*. Judgment for whom, and why? *Phillips Puerto Rico Core, Inc. v. Tradax Petroleum Ltd.*, 782 F.2d 314 (2d Cir. 1985).

5. Design, Inc., in Newport, Rhode Island, entered into a contract with Buenavista, S.A. in Barcelona, Spain, to buy 1,000 sheets of stained glass. The contract contained a delivery clause that read "FOB Hasta Luego." The contract also stated that it was to be interpreted in accordance with *Incoterms*. While the glass was being loaded onto the ship *(Hasta Luego)*, one of the crates slipped from the loading mechanism and landed in the water before it crossed the ship's rail. Who bears the risk of loss of the glass? Would the answer change if the contract was governed by the UCC?

6. The defendant agreed to sell watches to the buyer in Mexico. A notation was printed at the bottom of the contract that, translated into English, reads as follows: "Please send the merchandise in cardboard boxes duly strapped with metal bands via air parcel post to Chetumal. Documents to Banco de Commercio De Quintana Roo S.A." There were no provisions in the contract that specifically allocated the risk of loss on the goods sold while in the possession of the carrier. When the goods were lost in transit, the buyer sued for a refund of his purchase price. Judgment was entered for the defendant, and the buyer appealed. Judgment for whom, and why? Was this a shipment or destination contract? When or where did the risk of loss pass? *Pestana v. Karinol Corp.*, 367 So. 2d 1096 (Fla. Dist. Ct. App. 1979).

7. Allied Chemical, a U.S. exporter, shipped chemicals to Banylsa in Brazil under bills of lading showing that the goods were consigned to the order of Banylsa. Allied sent the bill of lading, draft, and invoice to a Brazilian bank for collection, together with a letter of instruction to deliver the documents only on payment of the sight drafts. In the meantime, the goods had arrived in Brazil and were put into a warehouse under the supervision of the port authority. However, in Brazil and in some other Latin American countries, it is customary for goods to be released from a state warehouse to anyone holding either a bill of lading or a *carta declaratoria*. The latter is not a bill of lading, but only a document indicating that Brazilian import fees have been paid. Banylsa obtained a *carta declaratoria* from Lloyd and used it to obtain possession of the goods from the warehouse. Banylsa never purchased the bill of lading and never paid for the goods. Banylsa then became insolvent and filed for receivership in Brazilian civil court. Allied sued Lloyd for misdelivery in New York. Judgment for whom, and why? Explain a bailment. *Allied Chemical International Corp.* v. Companhia De Navegacao Lloyd Brasileiro, 775 F.2d 476 (2nd Cir. 1985).

8. Empresa Estatal Petroleos de Ecuador (PetroEcuador) contracted with BP Oil International, Ltd. for the purchase of 140,000 barrels of gasoline to be delivered CFR from Texas to Ecuador. The contract separately provided that the terms were governed by Ecuadorian law. The contract also required that the gasoline have a gum content of less than three milligrams per one hundred milliliters to be determined at the port of departure in Texas. The gasoline was tested for gum content upon departure and was deemed satisfactory. However, the gum content exceeded the contractual limit upon retesting in Ecuador, and PetroEcuador refused to accept delivery. BP resold the gasoline at a loss of $2 million and sued PetroEcuador for breach of contract. BP claimed that the

Convention on Contracts for the International Sale of Goods was applicable to the transaction. As such, BP contended that the risk of loss passed to PetroEcuador upon the loading of the goods in Texas. However, PetroEcuador claimed that local law required the delivery of conforming goods to the agreed destination despite the ratification of the CISG by Ecuador. Which party is correct? When did the risk of loss pass in this case? *BP Oil International, Ltd. v. Empresa Estatal Petroleos de Ecuador*, 332 F.3d 333 (5th Cir. 2003).

Managerial Implications

You receive a fax transmittal from Japanese buyers you met in New York. They indicate that they want to order 5,000 down bed pillows. The pillows must contain no less than 85 percent cluster prime white goose down. To make the transportation as cost-effective as possible, they want pricing for a full ocean container. Before placing the order, they want to discuss the details of the sale.

Their fax indicates that although the buyers prefer to pay for the pillows on open account terms, they will consider your suggestions for payment options. Also they are unwilling to purchase against the documents unless they can first inspect the pillows on their arrival in Japan. They want this right of inspection to find out if the quality is what they ordered and to look for possible freight damage. They feel strongly about this issue and insist on these conditions, unless you can provide them with adequate protection. In addition, they want to consider the cost of alternative shipping arrangements before deciding whether to handle these themselves.

1. Prepare a *pro forma* invoice giving your buyer several options for shipping the pillows. Consider how to pack and transport them to the closest or best seaport. What facilities are available for handling containerized cargo or for multimodal transport in your region? Using *Incoterms*, present a breakdown of the shipping alternatives and costs involved in the transaction. Contact a freight forwarder and inquire as to what services it can provide. Can the freight forwarder assist you in obtaining the information you need to prepare your *pro forma* invoice?
2. In determining your export price, what other factors must you consider in addition to freight costs? Do you consider additional communication expenses, port fees, trade show expense, forwarder fees, sales agents, and clerical expenses? Discuss your export pricing with your marketing team and decide on your pricing strategy.
3. Prepare a letter to accompany the *pro forma* invoice explaining why payment by "cash against documents" is fair to both parties. What can you propose to address the buyers' concerns that the goods shipped will conform to their quality specifications? How will the goods be protected from marine risks?

Ethical Considerations

Your company is expecting a shipment of 10,000 T-shirts from a company in Pakistan. You recently received a call from a nearby bank that it was in possession of a negotiable bill of lading aboard the ship *Jhelum* and documents from Pakistan covering a shipment of T-shirts, and that they were awaiting your payment. However, you are concerned.

The Pakistani company made the initial contact with your firm via the Internet, locating you through one of several trade directories in which you are listed. The prices quoted for shirts are considerably less than what you currently pay or are able to pay for a comparable quality. You begin to do some research. You find the company's site on the Internet, with pictures of its mill and textile products. Several days after you make enquiries through the U.S. Commercial Service, you receive an e-mail from its office in Karachi indicating that one of its staff officers was unable to locate the mill, but thought that the company "was currently exporting from Pakistan."

Recently you have been hearing of many international business scams. You are worried about what might really be in the ocean container and wonder if you should purchase the documents from the bank or refuse them just in case. You look at the documents and see that the bill of lading is dated one day later than the date for shipment called for in the contract. You are getting cold feet, and think you might want out. (1) Do you think, under the circumstances, that it is ethical to refuse the documents based on a minor technicality? Why or why not? Do you believe you have enough information to make a fair decision? What are your options? (2) Now assume that you contacted the ocean carrier and they said that they do not have a ship named *Jhelum* currently in the fleet. Does this change your decision? (3) If this is a fraudulent scheme, how could it be perpetrated on an unsuspecting buyer?

CHAPTER 6

Legal Issues in International Transportation

This chapter is about international aviation and maritime law. Our discussion is limited to a few crucial areas of international business law that concern almost everyone doing business internationally: the legal aspects of moving goods and people by air and sea. We will not cover domestic transportation or those narrow regulatory issues that directly concern only firms operating in the transportation industry. Our focus is on the liability of air carriers for death or bodily injury to passengers traveling internationally and for loss or damage to baggage or air cargo; the liability of marine carriers for damage or loss to cargo; the liability of freight forwarders and other transport intermediaries; and selected issues in maritime and marine cargo insurance law.

You will see many common solutions to common problems, because there is probably more uniformity in aviation and maritime law around the world than there is with other laws. There are likely two reasons. First, both modern aviation and maritime law rely heavily on international conventions. This has had a harmonizing effect on national legislation. This does not mean that all national aviation or maritime laws are completely alike, or that courts in all countries render the same decisions. Of course they do not. But they each have common objectives and take similar approaches to handling legal issues. We will see this throughout the chapter. Secondly, in the maritime area, the law grew out of customary law, based on the traditions of ancient and medieval mariners, ship owners, and merchants. The customs were enforced by early maritime courts in port cities whose judgments were put into medieval maritime codes that spread westward from the eastern Mediterranean around the coastline of Europe to the Baltic. After all, those who go to sea share similar problems and common dangers. It is no wonder then, that so much of our modern maritime law concepts are so similar around the world.

THE LIABILITY OF INTERNATIONAL AIR CARRIERS

Commercial air transportation developed rapidly in the first few years after the Wright Brothers' famous flight at Kitty Hawk in 1903. In 1911 the first airmail service began in the United States, and the first scheduled passenger service, albeit very rudimentary, was only a few years after that. By the 1920s the race was on to develop regular commercial air service, and by the 1930s newly started companies were vying for the first transatlantic cargo and passenger services. The pace was accelerated by innovations in engineering, the bravery of young pilots, the backing of the military and government, savvy business investors, and by the demand for faster, safer air transportation. The pace of aviation development was indeed rapid, almost too rapid for legal change to keep up. But soon after World War I governments around the world recognized the need for international cooperation in regulating air transportation, including uniformity in the laws relating to the use of airspace, the nationality of aircraft, and rules for navigation. Of importance to this chapter, governments realized that one of their most important goals was to protect the fledgling air industry from financial disaster by placing limits on the liability of air carriers for damages. After all, investors feared that their fortunes could be wiped out in one air disaster, and insurance companies feared insuring air carriers. Out of the early work of the League of Nations and several international air conferences came several air treaties, including the *Warsaw Convention of 1929*.

For more than 70 years, the *Warsaw Convention of 1929* was the most important law governing the liability of air carriers for loss or damage to cargo or baggage during international shipping, and for death or bodily injury to passengers engaging in international travel. The Convention limited what damages were recoverable by a plaintiff, and under what circumstances, and it placed caps on the amount that could be recovered. By the late 1990s, a passenger could recover no more than $75,000 in proven damages for death or bodily injury and only more than that if the plaintiff could prove the airline's "willful misconduct" (which was often difficult to prove). Liability for loss or damage to baggage or cargo was also limited. As the air industry grew out of its infancy, these limits became unreasonably low. After all, damages awarded in a wrongful death action in an automobile crash might amount to many, many times that, and are based on economic and other measures of the value of a human life. Another problem with the *Warsaw Convention* was that it was never modernized or adapted to electronic commerce and modern air transportation methods. By the end of the twentieth century it was clear that a new treaty was needed.

The Montreal Convention of 1999

The most important change to air transportation law in 70 years occurred with the adoption of the *Montreal Convention for the Unification of Certain Rules for International Carriage by Air* (1999), referred to in this chapter as the *Montreal Convention.* It now replaces the outdated *Warsaw Convention* in those countries where ratified (the *Warsaw Convention* remains in effect in about 50 others). As of 2013, the *Montreal Convention* had been ratified in 130 countries, including the United States, Canada, Mexico, Japan, China, and the European Union, to name a few. The *Montreal Convention* eases restrictions and raises the limits on recovery from air carriers above those of the *Warsaw Convention*, and accommodates the use of electronic tickets and other documents. It also requires that airlines maintain adequate insurance for losses or damages and include provisions for compensating passengers for flight or baggage delays.

The language of the *Montreal Convention* is patterned after the older *Warsaw Convention.* This was intended by the drafters, so that there could be continuity in its interpretation by courts. The legislative history of the U.S. Senate in considering the ratification of the *Montreal Convention* makes it clear that Congress had intended that much of the case law decided by U.S. courts under the earlier convention was to apply to the new convention.

International Carriage. The *Montreal Convention* applies "to all international carriage of persons, baggage and cargo by aircraft" in which the *place of departure* and the *place of destination* are in two countries that are party to the Convention. The place of departure and place of destination is that destination listed in the ticket and not where the passenger intended to fly. If the aircraft is diverted to some other country due to weather or accident, or even returns to the departing airport, the place of destination is still that listed in the ticket for purposes of determining if the flight is an international one. The Convention does not apply to a passenger who is ticketed for travel between two countries that are not party to the Convention or for domestic travel solely within one country.

The Convention also applies where the place of departure and place of destination are within a single country that is party to the Convention if there is an *agreed stopping place* in another country, even if that other country is not party to the Convention. This includes round trip tickets. Assume a passenger has a round trip ticket from the United States for travel to a foreign country and returning to the United States. The flight is covered by the Convention regardless of whether or not that foreign country is party to the Convention.

Next, consider a passenger who is traveling internationally, but whose journey includes a domestic leg. Assume that a U.S. passenger is ticketed for round-trip travel from Chicago to Los Angeles, connecting on another flight with a different airline from Los Angeles to Tokyo. Is the flight from Chicago to Los Angeles considered part of the "international carriage" and governed by the Convention? Here, the determining factor is how the passenger was ticketed and whether he or she was engaged in a *continuous international journey.* The answer for that passenger is "yes" if the flight from Chicago to Los Angeles is deemed to be *one undivided carriage* that is part of a *single operation.* If all legs of a journey, international and domestic, are booked on the same ticket, then they are presumed to be one undivided carriage. Even where the separate flights are purchased and booked on different tickets, or even on different airlines, they may still be considered one undivided journey if the domestic and international legs may be considered a "single operation."

The *Montreal Convention* provides the exclusive remedy to a plaintiff to the extent that the Convention covers the plaintiff's claim. If a passenger files suit in state court against an airline, alleging damage to checked baggage (or a shipper for damage to cargo), the airline may "remove" the case to federal court because the Convention specifically addresses damage to baggage (and cargo) and provides a remedy. In other words, if both a state law and the Convention address the same issue, and there is a conflict between them, the Convention will prevail. In the following case, *El Al Israel Airlines, Ltd. v. Tseng*, the U.S. Supreme Court ruled that the *Warsaw Convention* provided the exclusive cause of action against an air carrier for injuries incurred during international travel.

El Al Israel Airlines, Ltd. v. Tseng

525 U.S. 155 (1999) United States Supreme Court

BACKGROUND AND FACTS

Tseng purchased a ticket on an El Al flight from New York to Tel Aviv. Prior to boarding, an El Al security guard questioned her about her travel plans. The guard considered her response "illogical" and ranked her as a security risk. Tseng was taken to a private security room and told to remove her shoes and to lower her blue jeans to mid-hip. A female guard then searched her body outside her clothing by hand. Nothing was found, and she was allowed to board. She did not suffer any bodily injury. Tseng sued El Al in New York state court for assault and false imprisonment under New York law. El Al removed the case to a federal district court. The district court dismissed, concluding that Tseng's only remedy was under the Warsaw Convention, and that the Convention precluded recovery unless there was bodily injury. On appeal, the U.S. Court of Appeals held that a plaintiff who did not qualify for relief under the Convention could seek relief under local law for an injury sustained in the course of international air travel. El Al then appealed to the U.S. Supreme Court.

JUSTICE GINSBURG

[Tseng's] case presents a question of the Convention's exclusivity: When the Convention allows no recovery for the episode-in-suit, does it correspondingly preclude the passenger from maintaining an action for damages under another source of law, in this case, New York tort law? * * * We ... hold that recovery for a personal injury suffered "on board [an] aircraft or in the course of any of the operations of embarking or disembarking," if not allowed under the Convention, is not available at all. Recourse to local law, we are persuaded, would undermine the uniform regulation of international air carrier liability that the Warsaw Convention was designed to foster, [citations omitted] * * *

The Warsaw Convention ... declares ... that the "[C]onvention shall apply to all international transportation of persons, baggage, or goods performed by aircraft for hire." * * * Article 17 establishes the conditions of liability for personal injury to passengers: "The carrier shall be liable for damage sustained in the event of the death or ... bodily injury suffered by a passenger, if the accident which caused the damage so sustained took place on board the aircraft or in the course of any of the operations of embarking or disembarking." * * *

We accept it as given that El Al's search of Tseng was not an "accident" within the meaning of Article 17, for the parties do not place that Court of Appeals conclusion at issue ... The parties do not dispute that the episode-in-suit occurred in international transportation in the course of embarking. * * *

The cardinal purpose of the Warsaw Convention, we have observed, is to "achiev[e] uniformity of rules governing claims arising from international air transportation." *Eastern Airlines, Inc. v. Floyd*, 499 U.S. 530, 111 S.Ct. 1489 (1991). The Convention signatories, in the treaty's preamble, specifically "recognized the advantage of regulating in a uniform manner the conditions of ... the liability of the carrier." To provide the desired uniformity, the Convention sets out an array of liability rules which, the treaty declares, "apply to all international transportation of persons, baggage, or goods performed by aircraft." * * * Given the Convention's comprehensive scheme of liability rules and its textual emphasis on uniformity, we would be hard put to conclude that the delegates at Warsaw meant to subject air carriers to the distinct, nonuniform liability rules of the individual signatory nations. * * *

Construing the Convention, as did the Court of Appeals, to allow passengers to pursue claims under local law when the Convention does not permit recovery could produce several anomalies. Carriers might be exposed to unlimited liability under diverse legal regimes, but would be prevented, under the treaty, from contracting out of such liability. Passengers injured physically in an emergency landing might be subject to the liability caps of the Convention, while those merely traumatized in the same mishap would be free to sue outside of the Convention for potentially unlimited damages. The Court of Appeals' construction of the Convention would encourage artful pleading by plaintiffs seeking to opt out of the Convention's liability

continues

continued

scheme when local law promised recovery in excess of that prescribed by the treaty. Such a reading would scarcely advance the predictability that adherence to the treaty has achieved worldwide. * * *

Decision. The decision of the Court of Appeals was reversed. Under the Warsaw Convention a passenger may not bring an action for personal injury damages under state law when his or her claim does not satisfy the conditions for liability under the Convention.

Case Questions

1. Why was Tseng not able to pursue a remedy under New York state law?
2. What policy reasons does the Court give for holding that the air liability convention should preclude remedies under local or state law?
3. Why would Tseng not be successful in an action against the airline in federal court under the Convention?

Jurisdiction. In summary, lawsuits governed by the *Montreal Convention*, whether for death, bodily injury, cargo damage, or baggage claims, can be brought only in a country that is party to the Convention and, at the option of the plaintiff, in one of the following locations: (1) the country where the passenger's tickets were purchased or the air waybill for cargo issued, (2) the country of final destination, (3) the country where the carrier is incorporated or domiciled, (4) the country where the carrier has its principal place of business, or (5) in addition to the first four locations, in the case of claims for bodily injury or death, in the country of the passenger's "principal and permanent residence," if the carrier provides air service there. This "fifth jurisdiction" prevents many passengers or their families from having to litigate cases in far-off countries.

Air Carrier's Liability for Death or Bodily Injury

The plaintiff in an air accident is usually the injured passenger or the estate or heirs of a deceased passenger. Article 17 of the Convention states,

> The carrier is liable for damage sustained in case of *death or bodily injury* of a passenger upon condition only that the *accident* which caused the death or injury took place *on board the aircraft or in the course of any of the operations of embarking or disembarking.* [emphasis added]

The sections in italics show the three basic requirements for liability: (1) death or bodily injury of a passenger, (2) resulting from an accident, (3) on board the aircraft or while embarking or disembarking. Thousands of litigated cases exist on these issues.

Accident. There are many court decisions discussing the meaning of "accident." It generally requires that the cause of injury be an event that presents a risk peculiar to air travel and "external" to the passenger. This might include injuries resulting from a fall while boarding, the spilling of hot coffee on a passenger, air turbulence, or a crash landing. In *Air France v. Saks*, 470 U.S. 392 (1985), the Supreme Court attempts to explain the meaning of the term "accident." The plaintiff was on a 12-hour flight from Paris to Los Angeles when she felt a severe pressure and pain in her ear during descent. The flight was routine and the plane landed normally. She disembarked without informing the airline of her ailment. Five days later, she consulted a doctor who concluded that she had become permanently deaf in her left ear. The trial court said it was not an accident. The U.S. Court of Appeals reversed, believing that the *Warsaw Convention* imposed absolute liability on airlines for injuries caused by the risks inherent in air travel. The U.S. Supreme Court disagreed and reversed, stating that,

> Liability under Article 17 of the *Warsaw Convention* arises only if a passenger's injury is caused by an *unexpected or unusual event or happening that is external to the passenger.* This definition should be flexibly applied after assessment of all the circumstances surrounding a passenger's injuries ... But when the injury indisputably results from *the passenger's own internal reaction to the usual, normal, and expected operation of the aircraft,* it has not been caused by an accident, and Article 17 of the *Warsaw Convention* cannot apply." [emphasis added]

The court went on to give some examples of accidents from prior cases. These included torts committed by terrorists, a drunken passenger who fell and injured a fellow passenger, and a "sudden dive" that led to pressure change, which caused hearing loss. The general rule of *Air France v. Saks* was accepted by the British House of Lords in 2005 in litigation involving cases of deep vein thrombosis (formation of blood clots in the legs from sitting for long periods during flight). American and British cases have held that blood clots result from a passenger's internal reaction to the usual, normal, and expected operation of an aircraft and thus are not accidents. However, in the following case, *Olympic Airways v. Husain,* 540 U.S. 644 (2004) the U.S. Supreme Court arrived at a different conclusion in the case of an asthmatic passenger aboard a passenger aircraft who died from an allergic reaction to secondhand smoke resulting from the flight attendant's refusal to move his seat further from the smoking section.

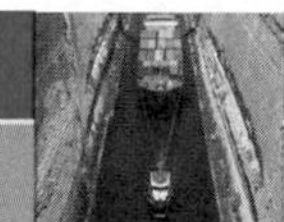

Olympic Airways v. Husain

540 U.S. 644 (2004) United States Supreme Court

BACKGROUND AND FACTS

Dr. Abid Hanson was traveling with his wife and family aboard an Olympic Airways flight from Athens to New York. He suffered from asthma and was affected by second-hand smoke. They were seated in a non-smoking section, three rows from the smoking section. As Dr. Hanson was struggling to breathe, his wife, Rubina Husain, made three urgent requests that he be moved away from the smoke. Her requests were refused. The flight attendant claimed that the flight was "totally full" (which was not correct) and that she was "too busy." Dr. Hanson walked to the front of the plane for air. He died shortly later, despite attempts to revive him. At trial, the court awarded Mrs. Husain a $1.4 million judgment due to the willful conduct of the flight attendant. The U.S. Court of Appeals affirmed. Olympic Airways appealed to the Supreme Court, arguing that Dr. Hanson's death was the result of his internal reaction to the usual and expected operation of the airplane and thus not the result of an accident.

JUSTICE THOMAS

* * * Petitioner [Olympic] argues that the "accident" inquiry should focus on the "injury producing event," which, according to petitioner, was the presence of ambient cigarette smoke in the aircraft's cabin. Because the petitioner's policies permitted smoking on international flights, the petitioner contends that Dr. Hanson's death resulted from his own internal reaction—namely, an asthma attack—to the normal operation of the aircraft. The petitioner also argues that the flight attendant's failure to move Dr. Hanson was inaction, whereas Article 17 requires an action that causes the injury. We disagree. * * *

The petitioner's focus on the ambient cigarette smoke as the injury producing event is misplaced. We do not doubt that the presence of ambient cigarette smoke in the aircraft's cabin during an international flight might have been "normal" at the time of the flight in question. But the petitioner's "injury producing event" inquiry—which looks to "the precise factual 'event' that caused the injury"—neglects the reality that there are often multiple interrelated factual events that combine to cause any given injury. In [*Air France v. Saks,* 470 U.S. 392 (1985)], the Court recognized that any one of these factual events or happenings may be a link in the chain of causes and—so long as it is unusual or unexpected—could constitute an "accident" under Article 17. Indeed, the very fact that multiple events will necessarily combine and interrelate to cause any particular injury makes it difficult to define, in any coherent or non-question-begging way, any single event as the "injury producing event."

The petitioner's only claim to the contrary here is to say: "Looking to the purely factual description of relevant events, the aggravating event was Dr. Hanson remaining in his assigned non-smoking seat and being exposed to ambient smoke, which allegedly aggravated his pre-existing asthmatic condition leading to his death," and that the "injury producing event" was "not the flight attendant's failure to act or violation of industry standards." [Brief for Petitioner] The petitioner ignores the fact that the flight attendant's refusal on three separate occasions to move Dr. Hanson was also a "factual 'event,'" that the District Court correctly found to be a "'link in the chain'" of causes that led to Dr. Hanson's death. The petitioner's statement that the flight attendant's failure to reseat Dr. Hanson was not the "injury producing event" is nothing more than a bald assertion, unsupported by any law or argument. * * * The exposure to the smoke and the refusal to assist the passenger are happenings that both contributed to the passenger's death.

And the petitioner's argument that the flight attendant's failure to act cannot constitute an "accident" because only affirmative acts are "events or happenings" under *Saks* is unavailing ... The relevant "accident" inquiry under *Saks* is whether there is

continues

continued

"an unexpected or unusual event or happening." The rejection of an explicit request for assistance would be an "event" or "happening" under the ordinary and usual definitions of these terms. See *American Heritage Dictionary* 635 (3rd ed. 1992) ("event": "something that takes place; an occurrence"); *Black's Law Dictionary* 554-555 (6th ed. 1990) ("event": "Something that happens").

Decision. The flight attendant's "unexpected or unusual" refusal to move the passenger to another seat, contrary to airline policy and industry standards, was an "accident" that was "external to the passenger" within the meaning of Article 17 of the *Montreal Convention.* It was a link in a chain of causation that resulted in the aggravation of a passenger's pre-existing medical condition by exposure to a normal condition (smoking, which was permitted at the time) in the aircraft cabin.

Case Questions

1. Why were the events in this case deemed "unexpected or unusual"?
2. Why did the Court reject Olympic's argument that the term "accident" refers only to affirmative acts?
3. What is the significance of the attendant's failure to move the asthmatic passenger away from the smoke when that was contrary to airline industry procedures?
4. How does this case differ from *Air France v. Saks* and the British "deep vein thrombosis" cases, cited in the text?

Embarking or Disembarking. A carrier is only liable for damages occurring "on board the aircraft or in the course of any of the operations of embarking or disembarking." Whether a passenger is embarking or disembarking often turns on their proximity to the security or boarding gate, the *imminence of boarding,* whether their movements were under the control of the airline or security officials, and the activity of the passenger at the time. If they were actually in the process of boarding or exiting the aircraft, then the airline is responsible. However, the airline would generally not be responsible where the passenger is outside of the control of airline employees and moving about the terminal. In one case, an airline was held not responsible where the passenger was injured approximately one-half hour before the flight and several hundred feet from the departure gate, and the passengers had not yet been called to board the flight. Other cases have held the airlines not liable for injuries in corridors and on moving stairs or sidewalks that are under the control of the terminal, not the airline.

In most cases, there is no liability for injuries sustained while a passenger is dining or shopping, or at the baggage claim. However, many cases are more complicated. In *Singh v. North American Airlines,* 426 F.Supp.2d 38 (E.D.N.Y. 2006) the passenger was arrested and imprisoned for several months when illegal drugs were discovered in his baggage on arrival in New York on a flight from Guyana. It was later discovered that airline employees had placed Singh's name and identification tags on the bags to illegally transport drugs. Singh sued the airline. The District Court ruled that this was "an accident" covered by the Convention because the process of checking baggage in Guyana and obtaining baggage claim tags was a necessary part of the embarkation process there. The court added that it did not matter in this case that the damage arose later, when Singh was imprisoned. It was sufficient, the court believed, that the "accident itself took place on board the aircraft or in the course of any of the operations of embarking or disembarking."

Limitations on Liability for Death or Bodily Injuries. The monetary limit of an air carrier's liability is set not in the currency of any one country, but in **special drawing rights** (SDRs). SDRs represent an amount equal to a mix of currency values (the euro, Japanese yen, British pound sterling, and U.S. dollar) developed by the International Monetary Fund (IMF). This facilitates an easy conversion from the limits expressed in the Convention into any currency. SDR values are listed daily on the IMF Web site. For example, on January 2, 2013, one SDR was worth approximately $1.54 (rounded). The *Convention* calls for the review of the limits every five years (they were raised in 2009) so they can be adjusted for inflation. The review is done by the International Civil Aviation Organization, a specialized agency of the United Nations, charged with assisting nations in developing international policies and standards for air safety, security, and operations.

The *Montreal Convention* sets up a two-tiered liability system. First, the carrier is strictly, or absolutely, liable for all damages from death or bodily injury that can be proven by the passenger or the representative of their estate, in an amount not exceeding 113,100 SDRs per passenger (about $174,000 in early 2013), arising out of an accident. Strict or absolute liability means that the carrier is liable without regard to fault. In addition, the carrier is presumed to be liable for all proven damages above 113,100 SDRs, with no limit on the amount, unless the carrier can show that the damages were not due to its negligence, willfulness, or other wrongful act or omission or to that of its employees or agents.

Compensable Damages. The Convention does not specify the types of compensatory damages (medical, loss of earnings, etc.) that a plaintiff can recover. Local law determines that an air carrier is exonerated to the extent that the passenger's own negligence contributed to his or her injuries or death. Thus, if a passenger is scalded by hot coffee on the seat-back table in front of him because he was not careful while removing his coat, he is most likely unable to recover anything from the carrier. Punitive damages are never allowed under the *Montreal Convention.* Where damages for mental anguish or emotional distress are permitted by state or federal law, or by national law in another country, they may only be awarded to a plaintiff under the *Montreal Convention* if they are actually caused by bodily injury. In *Ehrlich v. American Airlines, Inc.*, 360 F.3d 366 (2004), the U.S. Court of Appeals sitting in New York considered a claim by passengers for mental anguish resulting from an emergency evacuation of the aircraft. The passengers testified that they suffered from nightmares and anxiety from the evacuation. In the course of the evacuation, they also sustained knee injuries. The court did not allow recovery for the mental anguish because it was not "caused by" the bodily injury to the knee, but merely accompanied it.

In a case with a nearly tragic ending, *Eastern Airlines, Inc. v. Floyd,* 499 U.S. 530 (1991), the U.S. Supreme Court considered a passenger's suit for emotional distress resulting from the pilot's announcement that three engines had failed, and that the aircraft was losing altitude and would ditch in the Atlantic Ocean. After a period of descending flight without power, the crew was able to restart an engine and land the plane safely in Miami. The court concluded that "an air carrier cannot be held liable under Article 17 when an accident has not caused a passenger to suffer death, physical injury, or physical manifestation of injury." In other cases, it has been held that passengers could not recover damages for emotional distress merely because of stolen baggage or because their seat had been downgraded from first class to economy.

Third-Party Suits. The *Montreal Convention* applies only to claims against air carriers. It does not prohibit or govern claims brought against third parties, such as the manufacturer of a defectively designed or built airplane, the company that serviced or maintained it, the owners or operators of the airport, private security firms, retailers or vendors operating within airport facilities, or other passengers. These cases are primarily governed by ordinary tort law of the state or jurisdiction in which the case is heard.

Air Waybills and Air Cargo Losses

Unlike passengers who are "ticketed" for travel, cargo moves pursuant to a transport document called an air waybill. It serves as a contract between the **consignor** (shipper) and carrier that states the freight charges and other conditions of transport. It is also a receipt from the carrier for having received the goods in good condition, and instructions for delivery to a named **consignee**. Unlike typical marine bills of lading, air waybills are nonnegotiable, and are not documents of title. An example appears in Exhibit 6.1. A **master air waybill** is one issued directly to a shipper by an air carrier. A **house air waybill** is one issued by a freight forwarder to the shipper (thus representing a contract between them), and is also used where the shipments of several shippers are being consolidated by the forwarder to one destination. There is a movement toward the use of electronic air waybills, just as there has been with passenger tickets. In 2012 the United States began accepting electronic air waybills for shipments crossing U.S. borders. The **International Air Transport Association** (IATA), a trade association of airlines, expects that most air waybills will be electronic by 2016.

An air carrier is only liable for loss or damage to cargo under its control up to 19 SDRs per kilogram (2009), unless the shipper has declared a higher actual value on the air waybill and paid an additional fee if required. The carrier is not responsible for damages resulting from an inherent defect or quality of the cargo, defective packing by the shipper, an act of war or armed conflict, or an act of public authority, such as customs authorities.

Exhibit 6.1

International Air Waybill

AIRPORT OF DEPARTURE

037– 0226 0123 INTERNATIONAL AIR WAYBILL 037– 0226 0123

SHIPPER'S NAME AND ADDRESS | SHIPPER'S ACCOUNT NUMBER

ABC Company
123 Elm St.
Anytown, NC 12345

NOT NEGOTIABLE
AIR WAYBILL
(AIR CONSIGNMENT NOTE)

USAIR
USAir, Inc.
NATIONAL AIRPORT, WASHINGTON, D.C. 20001

Copies 1, 2 and 3 of this Air Waybill are originals and have the same validity.

It is agreed that the goods described herein are accepted in apparent good order and condition (except as noted) for carriage SUBJECT TO THE CONDITIONS OF CONTRACT ON THE REVERSE HEREOF. THE SHIPPER'S ATTENTION IS DRAWN TO THE NOTICE CONCERNING CARRIERS' LIMITATION OF LIABILITY. Shipper may increase such limitation of liability by declaring a higher value for carriage and paying a supplemental charge if required.

TO EXPEDITE MOVEMENT, SHIPMENT MAY BE DIVERTED TO MOTOR OR OTHER CARRIER AS PER TARIFF RULE UNLESS SHIPPER GIVES OTHER INSTRUCTIONS HEREON.

CONSIGNEE'S NAME AND ADDRESS | CONSIGNEE'S ACCOUNT NUMBER

XYZ Corporation
456 Wind St.
Anycity, France

ISSUING CARRIER'S AGENT NAME AND CITY

ALSO NOTIFY NAME AND ADDRESS *(OPTIONAL ACCOUNTING INFORMATION)*

Foreign Custom Broker
1001 Maple St.
Anycity, France

AGENT'S IATA CODE: 1-5678 | ACCOUNT NUMBER

ACCOUNTING INFORMATION (SHIPPER CHECK ONE): XX AIR FREIGHT | AIR EXPRESS | COMAT

AIRPORT OF DEPARTURE (ADDR OF FIRST CARRIER) AND REQUESTED ROUTING: Charlotte

ROUTING AND DESTINATION

TO	BY FIRST CARRIER	TO	BY	TO	BY
CDG	US				

CURRENCY	CHGS CODE	WT/VAL PPD	WT/VAL COLL	OTHER PPD	OTHER COLL	DECLARED VALUE FOR CARRIAGE	DECLARED VALUE FOR CUSTOMS
USD			X		X	NVD	5000

AIRPORT OF DESTINATION | FOR CARRIER USE ONLY: FLIGHT/DATE US 8/15/08 | FLIGHT/DATE

AMOUNT OF INSURANCE: NIL

INSURANCE– If shipper requests insurance in accordance with conditions on reverse hereof, indicate amount to be insured in figures in box marked amount of insurance. | TC

HANDLING INFORMATION These commodities licensed by US for ultimate destination. Diversion contrary to US law is prohibited.

MKD: AS Addr. PO# 0001

NOTIFICATION (PERSON NOTIFIED) | BY | DATE/TIME | DISPOSITION

NO. OF PIECES RCP	GROSS WEIGHT	Kg/lb	RATE CLASS / COMMODITY ITEM NO.	CHARGEABLE WEIGHT	RATE / CHARGE	TOTAL	NATURE AND QUANTITY OF GOODS (INCL. DIMENSIONS OR VOLUME)
10	109	K		109	2.10	228.90	Leather aprons

	PREPAID	COLLECT
A. WEIGHT CHARGE		228.90
D. VALUATION CHARGE		
I. TAX		
TOTAL OTHER CHARGES DUE AGENT		58.00
TOTAL OTHER CHARGES DUE CARRIER		10.00
TOTAL PREPAID / TOTAL COLLECT		296.00
CURRENCY CONVERSION RATES / TOTAL COLLECT IN DEST. CURRENCY		

P–UP ZONE | B. PICK–UP CHARGES 25.00 | ORIGIN ADVANCE CHARGES K. | DESCRIPTION OF ORIGIN ADVANCE | ITEMS PREPAID

DEL. ZONE | C. | DEST. ADVANCE CHARGES L. | DESCRIPTION OF DESTINATION ADVANCE | ITEMS COLLECT

SHIPPER'S R.F.C. (AMOUNT TO BE ENTERED BY SHIPPER) J. | OTHER CHARGES AND DESCRIPTION F.

SHIPPER CERTIFIES THAT THE PARTICULARS ON THE FACE HEREOF ARE CORRECT AND THAT INSOFAR AS ANY PART OF THE CONSIGNMENT CONTAINS RESTRICTED ARTICLES, SUCH PART IS PROPERLY DESCRIBED BY NAME AND IS IN PROPER CONDITION FOR CARRIAGE BY AIR ACCORDING TO APPLICABLE NATIONAL GOVERNMENT REGULATIONS, AND FOR INTERNATIONAL SHIPMENTS THE CURRENT INTERNATIONAL AIR TRANSPORT ASSOCIATION'S RESTRICTED ARTICLES REGULATIONS.

SIGNATURE OF SHIPPER OR HIS AGENT

I. COD → | CURRENCY

EXECUTED ON (Date) (Time) at (Place) SIGNATURE OF ISSUING CARRIER OR ITS AGENT

CARRIER CERTIFIES GOODS DESCRIBED ABOVE WERE RECEIVED FOR CARRIAGE SUBJECT TO THE CONDITIONS ON THE REVERSE HEREOF, THE GOODS THEN BEING IN APPARENT GOOD ORDER AND CONDITION EXCEPT AS NOTED HEREON.

FOR CARRIERS USE ONLY AT DESTINATION | CHARGES AT DESTINATION | TOTAL COLLECT CHARGES

(ALL COLLECT CHARGES IN DESTINATION CURRENCY)

037– 0226 0123

Baggage Losses. The liability of the carrier in the case of loss, damage, or delay to baggage on board an aircraft or under their control is limited to 1,131 SDRs (2009) per passenger, unless the passenger has declared a higher actual value and paid any additional fees required.

Delay. Travelers will appreciate the new provisions of the *Montreal Convention,* which make airlines liable for delays in transporting passengers, baggage, or cargo. However, the carrier is not liable if it proves that it and its servants and agents took reasonable measures to avoid the damage or that it was impossible for it or them to take such measures. Liability for delays is limited to 4,694 SDRs per passenger (2009).

Time Limitations. All legal actions against air carriers for damages must be brought within two years of the date of arrival at the destination, or from the date on which the aircraft ought to have arrived, or from the date on which the carriage stopped. Where baggage or cargo are damaged, the carrier must be notified immediately and no later than seven days from the date of receipt in the case of checked baggage and 14 days from the date of receipt in the case of cargo. Claims for damages for delayed baggage or cargo must be made in writing and at the latest within 21 days from the date on which the baggage or cargo was actually delivered.

MARITIME LAW AND THE CARRIAGE OF GOODS BY SEA

An understanding of maritime law and the jurisdiction of admiralty courts is crucial to anyone shipping goods by ocean carrier. The overwhelming volume of goods shipped overseas moves by water, as compared to air, road, or rail. Estimates are that between 80–90 percent of overseas shipments, measured by weight or volume, moves by water, and about 35 percent by volume moves by air (IATA).

Maritime law, as it is used in this book, refers to that body of law within the admiralty jurisdiction of a court that governs private rights and obligations arising out of the operation of vessels on navigable waters or in maritime commerce. It covers activities on the water and can also cover certain related activities on land. Examples include maritime torts and contracts, bills of lading, ship owner's liability for cargo, the law of collision, maritime liens, **salvage** (the rescue or recovery of a ship or cargo that is lost or damaged in navigable waters), **jettison** (throwing cargo or property overboard to save the ship), marine insurance, and the relationship between a ship's crew, master, and ship owner, and other areas. Maritime law also applies to claims for death or injury to mariners or **seamen** (persons employed on vessels regardless of their jobs), or to **longshoremen** (those employed to load and unload ships), and to harbor workers. In the United States these claims are governed by both federal and state statutes. Maritime law is also referred to as admiralty law, although the latter term is often used when referring to a court's **admiralty jurisdiction**.

There are three main sources of modern maritime law. These are international conventions, national legislation, and the **general maritime law**. The general maritime law in the United States is made up of the decisions of U.S. courts of "admiralty" jurisdiction, as it was handed down from the English admiralty courts when the United States was founded. That precedent was based on customary maritime law—the customs and practices of early mariners and merchants and the early codes of marine courts dating to ancient and medieval times.

History of the General Maritime Law. Maritime law has its roots in the antiquity of the eastern Mediterranean. Although the Phoenicians were great sea traders, the earliest maritime law of which we have much understanding comes from (the Greek island of) Rhodes, dating from 800 BC to 1000 BC. **Rhodian law** came from the customs and practices of the sea trade. Although there is no known written record of Rhodian law, it has been referred to in the written writings of other maritime codes that it influenced. It was so important in its time that some of its concepts were incorporated into Roman code law.

Rhodian law greatly influenced the westward expansion of maritime law. Principles of Rhodian law were found inscribed on tablets in the (now Italian) port city of Amalfi, and influenced maritime laws to Barcelona, and northward to the Baltic. Local **maritime courts**—private courts—developed in the port cities, far from the dictates of distant kings and rulers. These courts dealt with problems unknown on land—"jettison," "salvage," "perils of the sea," and so on. They rendered judgments based on the custom and practice of mariners, ship owners, and merchants who often traveled on the very ships that carried their cargos. Those judgments soon became the basis for

maritime "codes" that dealt with uniquely marine problems, including shared responsibility for the ship and cargo at sea, ship owners' responsibility for caring for mariners who fell ill in foreign ports, hiring local pilots to steer through unknown harbors, diversions to save life and property at sea, and enforcing liens on ships for supplies or repairs made in a foreign port.

It was during the twelfth century that perhaps the most influential and detailed medieval maritime code appeared—the **Rolls of Oleron** (*Rôles d'Oléron*) or "Judgments of the Sea." They were judgments in actual cases heard in local maritime courts in the seaport towns of Normandy and Britain. They were originally in French, but translated later to English, Dutch and other languages. Here are three actual judgments (that you will be asked about later):

> 3. If a ship is lost in any land or in any place whatever, the mariners are bound to save the most that they can; and if they assist, the master is bound, if he have not money, to pledge some of the goods which they have saved, and to convey them back to their country. And if they do not assist, he is not bound to furnish them with anything or to provide them with anything, on the contrary, they shall lose their wages, when the ship is lost. And this is the judgment in this case.
>
> 8. A ship loads at Bordeaux, or elsewhere, and it happens that a storm overtakes her at sea, and that they cannot escape without casting over some of the goods on board, the master is bound to say to the merchants: "Sirs, we cannot escape without casting overboard some of these wines or goods" ... Those goods which are cast overboard, ought to be appraised at the market price of those which have arrived in safety, and shall be sold and shared pound by pound amongst the merchants; and the master ought to share [in the loss] reckoning his ship or his freight at his choice, to reimburse the losses. And this is the judgment in this case.
>
> 9. It happens that the master of a ship cuts his mast from stress of weather [or cables or anchors]; he ought to call the merchants, and show them that it is expedient to cut the mast, to save the ship and the goods; they ought to be reckoned pound by pound as jettison; and the merchants shall share and pay without any delay, before their goods are landed from the ship. And this is the judgment in this case. [Studer, ed., *The Oak Book of Southampton*, Vol. 2. (1911). Available at *OpenLibrary.org*]

During the first few hundred years of its development, maritime law (as with the law merchant on land) applied only to the commercial classes, and not to the "common" people. The maritime law of England was separate and distinct from the "common law," and continued to be heard by local merchant and maritime courts. By at least the seventeenth century the demands of international commerce, diplomacy, and even war caused English monarchs to demand greater control over foreign trade and maritime issues. Maritime law became more national in character, no longer just the law of a local port.

In England, the king's courts began to subsume jurisdiction of maritime and commercial cases. It was **Lord Mansfield**, one of the England's most renowned common law judges and commonly called the "founder of English commercial law," who said from the King's Bench court, "The maritime law is not the law of a particular country, but the general law of nations," *Luke v. Lyde* [1759] 2 Burr. 882, 887. The days of local courts deciding maritime cases on the basis of custom were over; they had become the province of formal English common law and special admiralty courts. By the mid-eighteenth century, maritime law was received into the common law of England, and common law courts became willing to hear maritime and commercial law cases. Yet the customs and traditions lived on. Lord Mansfield and other judges of the king's realm continued to cite and rely on the *Rolls of Oleron*, and even the older Rhodian law, to guide their decisions from that day forward.

By the seventeenth century, maritime law in continental Europe also began to take on a national character in the form of new maritime codes. The most important of these was the *Marine Ordinance of France of 1681*, the creation of **Jean Baptiste Colbert**, who is considered by some historians as the greatest lawmaker in French history. The ordinance turned the customary maritime law of local courts into national law enforced by royal courts. It was a model for a new generation of national maritime law in Europe.

The first maritime law in the American colonies came from the English vice-admiralty courts that sat in American port cities. Those courts did not survive. After 1789, U.S. courts with admiralty jurisdiction cited English cases, as well as the medieval maritime codes, although American judges were not hesitant to break from English precedent when justified.

Admiralty Jurisdiction in the United States

When any case arises out of events on or near the water, the most immediate question is whether or not there is admiralty jurisdiction. Cases heard in admiralty are subject to different procedural and substantive rules than would apply in an ordinary law court. Admiralty cases are heard without a jury, and the judge serves as the trier of fact. In addition, admiralty courts apply different laws and defenses, and the time limitations for bringing lawsuits are different. One example is a U.S. maritime statute that limits a ship owner's liability, under certain circumstances, for damages caused by its ship to little more than the value of the ship itself. 46 U.S.C. Sec. 30505. Admiralty law is a specialized area and the province of admiralty lawyers.

Admiralty jurisdiction in the United States stems from Article III, Section 2, of the *U.S. Constitution,* that states, "The judicial power shall extend … to all cases of admiralty and maritime jurisdiction." U.S. statutes grant jurisdiction to the federal district courts "of any civil case of admiralty or maritime jurisdiction." 28 U.S.C. 1333. Admiralty jurisdiction is primarily federal, although state courts have concurrent jurisdiction in some areas. To maintain uniformity, federal admiralty law preempts state law whenever there is a conflict.

Navigable Waters. Admiralty jurisdiction applies to cases occurring on navigable waters. The term **navigable waters** includes not only the oceans and seas, but also large lakes (such as the Great Lakes), rivers, and waterways, regardless of size, that are *used or capable of being used for commercial activity.* For example, in one case salvors were attempting to recover and obtain ownership of cut logs that had been lost and submerged for over a hundred years in a Georgia river. It's likely that no commerce had been done on that river since that time. The court held that admiralty jurisdiction applied because the waterways were *capable* of commercial activity.

Vessels in Navigation. Admiralty jurisdiction applies to the operation and management of vessels during navigation on navigable waters. U.S. statutes define **vessel** as "every description of watercraft or other artificial contrivance used, or *capable of being used,* as a means of transportation on water." 1 U.S.C. §3. A vessel does not have to be a ship or boat. A dredge, used to scoop up silt and deepen harbors and channels, has been considered a vessel despite its very limited means of self propulsion. Even an oil-drilling rig is a vessel if it is mobile and not permanently affixed to the ocean floor. Anything permanently moored to the shore or permanently anchored is not a vessel.

Maritime Torts. When is a tort case heard in admiralty court? According to U.S. court decisions, admiralty jurisdiction applies to a tort that: (1) occurs on navigable water, or if the injury or damage is suffered on land then it was caused by a vessel in navigable water; (2) has a substantial relationship to traditional maritime activity; and (3) the incident has the potential to disrupt maritime commerce.

Historically, jurisdiction over **maritime torts** applied only if the tort occurred *and the injury was sustained* on navigable waters. If the injury was sustained on land it was not a maritime tort. That changed in 1948 when Congress passed the *Extension of Admiralty Jurisdiction Act* (46 U.S.C. 30101). It extends admiralty jurisdiction of the United States to injuries or property damage "caused by a vessel on navigable waters, even though the injury or damage is done or consummated on land." Thus jurisdiction in admiralty now includes damage to a bridge that has been struck by a vessel in navigable waters, to buildings burned as a result of sparks thrown from a vessel, or to environmental damage done to the coastline resulting from a discharge of oil, chemicals, or other pollutants by a vessel in navigable waters. Maritime law regulates recreational activity as well as commercial activity, such as the collision of pleasure boats on navigable waters.

Maritime torts must have a connection to a traditional maritime activity. In *Executive Jet Aviation, Inc. v. Cleveland,* 409 U.S. 249 (1972), the Supreme Court held that the crash of a commercial airliner into Lake Erie was not an admiralty case because it did not have a connection to a "traditional maritime activity," even though it went down in a navigable water.

Maritime Contracts. Admiralty jurisdiction applies to maritime contracts, such as those that relate to a vessel, to commerce or navigation on navigable waters, or to maritime employment. It does not matter if a contract is made on land or at sea. Marine insurance contracts fall within admiralty jurisdiction even though they are made on land, because they "relate to the navigation, business or commerce of the sea." Joseph Story in *Delovio v. Boit,* 2 Gall. 398 (1815). **Maritime contracts** include ocean bills of lading, marine insurance contracts, contracts for towing or

wharfage (a charge for the use of a wharf or dock), contracts for fuel, supplies for or repairs to vessels, contracts to pilot or guide vessels through harbors or canals, and contracts with longshoremen or **stevedores** (companies that employ longshoremen).

Cargo Losses and the Carriage of Goods by Sea

In this section we switch to a specialized area of maritime law; the liability of ocean carriers for the "carriage of goods by sea." Before we begin, some definitions will be helpful. **Cargo** is the term for goods carried aboard ships. **Freight** is the price charged to transport cargo. **Ships** are large vessels intended to carry cargo or passengers.

The different types of vessels used in the ocean or seaborne trade are **break-bulk** or general cargo ships (where goods are stowed in individual containers or on pallets in the ship's hold), **dry bulk ships** (for carrying coal, ore, and other minerals, grains and cereals, steel, forest products, fertilizers, etc.), **tankers** (for oils, chemicals and other liquids), roll-on-roll-off or "Ro-Ro" ships (for carrying vehicles, aircraft, boats, and heavy equipment), specialized vessels such as refrigerated units (called **reefer ships**), and others. Container ships are often used to transport merchandise inside sealed ocean containers. **Containerized ocean cargo** is the fastest-growing mode of ocean transport. Today's modern containers were developed in the 1950s to eliminate excessive handling of bulk cargo and to reduce pilferage and damage. They are packed and sealed by the shipper at its place of business, and opened only for customs inspection until they reach their destination. The containers revolutionized ocean shipping by allowing above-deck storage on container vessels, and by permitting efficient intermodal transportation. According to U.S. Customs and Border Protection, some seven million ocean containers enter U.S. ports annually.

Ocean-going cargo is constantly at risk, from the time it leaves the shipper's door until it reaches its destination. Typical examples of cargo damage from reported legal cases include the wrecks, storm damage from rain and seawater, the jettison of cargo, containers washing overboard, infestation from insects or molds, flooding of tankers, contamination from chemicals carried in previous shipments, rust and other moisture damage from saltwater condensation inside the hold, damage from broken refrigeration units and other equipment, losses from fire, damage done to cargo while rescuing the ship from peril, damage resulting from cargo being improperly stowed above deck, losses from theft and modern-day piracy on the seas, damage from acts of war, and many others.

Historically, carriers attempted to limit their liability for cargo damage through exculpatory clauses in bills of lading. With the growth of trade and the advent of large steamship companies in the nineteenth century, ocean carriers became more economically powerful and were able to do this. The exculpatory clauses attempted to free the carrier from all responsibility, including negligence or even for providing an unfit vessel. The small shippers were at the mercy of the steamship companies. The result was a period of great uncertainty over the liability of ocean carriers.

The Hague Rules. At the end of the First World War, there was a worldwide effort to develop uniform rules governing ocean bills of lading. The result was the 1924 *International Convention for the Unification of Certain Rules of Law relating to Bills of Lading*, known as the *Hague Rules.* You could say that the *Hague Rules* were a trade-off. Although carriers could no longer use "fine print" provisions in bills of lading to limit their liability, COGSA defined their responsibilities to the cargo and cargo owners, and limited the carrier's liability for loss or damage to cargo by law. The *Hague Rules* were essentially adopted in the national legislation of many countries, including the U.S. After 1968 some countries adopted the *Visby Amendments* to the *Hague Rules* which made some changes to the *Hague Rules.* The *Visby Amendments* have been adopted in Canada, the UK and most of Europe, Japan, Hong Kong, India, and Singapore. They have not been adopted in the United States.

The Carriage of Goods by Sea Act. The *Hague Rules* were codified in the U.S. *Carriage of Goods by Sea Act* or COGSA *(1936).* COGSA applies to every bill of lading for the carriage of goods by sea between a U.S. port and a foreign port. It does not apply to shipments between two U.S. ports. COGSA governs the liability of a carrier from the time goods are loaded onto the ship until the time the cargo is unloaded. COGSA does not apply to losses that occur prior to loading or after discharge from the vessel. Thus, it is commonly said that COGSA applies from "tackle to tackle." Another federal law, the *Harter Act* (1893), applies to goods damaged during all ocean shipments not covered by

COGSA, including shipments between two U.S. ports and while goods are warehoused prior to loading aboard ship or after discharge.

The protections in COGSA that limit a carrier's liability for damage to goods usually apply to stevedoring companies and to subcontractors that transport or handle goods—not just to the ocean carrier. This is because many bills of lading issued by ocean carriers contain written provisions extending these protections "downstream" to other parties involved in the transport. Such a provision is known as a "**Himalaya" clause** (for a ship of that name). In *Norfolk Southern Railway Co. v. James N. Kirby, Ltd.,* 543 U.S. 14 (2004), a multimodal shipment of machinery going from Australia to Savannah by sea, and then to Alabama by rail under a through bill of lading, was damaged when the train derailed in Georgia. The railroad claimed the protections of COGSA. The Supreme Court considered whether COGSA, a maritime statute, should apply to the inland portion of a multimodal shipment. Writing for the Court, Justice Sandra Day O'Connor's opening sentence foretold how the case would be decided, "This is a maritime case about a train wreck." She explained,

> Conceptually, so long as a bill of lading requires substantial carriage of goods by sea, its purpose is to effectuate maritime commerce - and thus it is a maritime contract. Its character as a maritime contract is not defeated simply because it also provides for some land carriage. Geography, then, is useful in a conceptual inquiry only in a limited sense: If a bill's sea components are insubstantial, then the bill is not a maritime contract, 543 U.S. at 27.

In a similar case several years later, *Kisen Kaisha Ltd. v. Regal-Beloit Corp.*, 130 S.Ct. 2433 (2010), the Court held that COGSA (and not *Carmack*, a federal railroad statute) applied to the rail portion of a multimodal ocean shipment. Justice Kennedy explained the practical problems that would result if two different laws applied to one multimodal shipment.

> Applying two different bill of lading regimes to the same through shipment would undermine COGSA and international, container-based multimodal transport. As *Kirby* explained,"[t]he international transportation industry `clearly has moved into a new era—the age of multimodalism, door-to-door transport based on efficient use of all available modes of transportation by air, water, and land.'" 543 U.S. at 25. If *Carmack* applied to an inland segment of a shipment from overseas under a through bill, then one set of liability and venue rules would apply when cargo is damaged at sea (COGSA) and another almost always would apply when the damage occurs on land (*Carmack*). Rather than making claims by cargo owners easier to resolve, a court would have to decide where the damage occurred to determine which law applied. As a practical matter, this requirement often could not be met; for damage to the content of containers can occur when the contents are damaged by rough handling, seepage, or theft, at some unknown point. Indeed, adopting the Court of Appeals' approach would seem to require rail carriers to open containers at the port to check if damage has been done during the sea voyage. This disruption would undermine international container-based transport. 130 S.Ct. at 2447.

Liability of the Carrier

When cargo damage is visible at the time of delivery, written notice must be given by the consignee to the carrier before the goods are taken from the carrier's custody. If the loss is not visible or apparent, written notice must be given to the carrier within three days of delivery. Failure to do so does not prevent the plaintiff's claim, but does make it procedurally more difficult. The statute of limitations for filing claims under COGSA is one year.

In the event of a cargo dispute, the claims are generally brought by the "cargo interest," typically the holder of the bill of lading, such as a shipper, consignee, or the insurer. If unresolved, and the case proceeds to court, the plaintiff must show that the goods were lost or damaged while in the carrier's custody. One way of doing this is to prove that the damage was of the type that could only have occurred while the goods were at sea, such as having been soaked with sea water. The burden then shifts to the carrier to prove that it cared for the goods appropriately or that the loss occurred in a manner for which the carrier is not legally responsible under COGSA.

To determine if the loss or damage occurred while the carrier had custody of the goods, we begin by looking at the bill of lading. If goods are not sealed and locked in an ocean container but are visible and open to inspection by the carrier, then the issuance of a **"clean" bill of lading** to the shipper is proof that the goods were shipped in good condition and not damaged. (Recall a clean bill is one with no notations by the carrier or its agent showing visible or apparent damage to the goods on loading). However, if the goods are enclosed and sealed in a package or container of any type and the carrier is unable to inspect them, then a clean bill is not evidence of the condition or even the quantity of the goods inside. Carriers do not open sealed containers to routinely count packages as that would only open them to liability. *Asoma Corp. v. M/V Land*, 46 Fed. Appx. 34 (2d Cir.2002) involved coils of water-sensitive steel that had rusted. The coils had been oiled, covered in laminated paper, and enclosed in galvanized steel cans sealed with strapping bands. The court held that a clean bill of lading does not prove that the cargo was in good condition when received from the shipper because the carrier could not inspect the cargo. Moreover, the shipper did not produce any other evidence that the goods were in good condition when handing them over to the carrier.

Carrier's Responsibilities for Cargo Shortages. A dispute over whether goods were stolen or lost overboard at sea may depend on whether there is a difference in the weight of the goods on loading and on unloading. A statement of the weight of the cargo in a bill of lading issued by a carrier is binding on the carrier, even where it is the shipper that provides the weight. This is true even where the shipper provides the weight of cargo that had been sealed in an ocean container at their inland factory. The carrier can simply weigh the full container at the port and subtract the weight of the metal box. In the case of cargo missing from sealed containers, it is easier to prove a discrepancy in weight than in the number of cartons.

Carrier's Responsibilities for Stowing Cargo. COGSA strictly defines the liability of a carrier for damage to oceangoing cargo. To understand the carrier's liability under COGSA we must distinguish between damages resulting from improperly loading and caring *for the cargo itself*, and damage to cargo resulting from improperly navigating, handling, or caring for *the ship*. With regard to the cargo, it is the responsibility of the carrier and its crew to "properly and carefully load, handle, stow, carry, keep, care for, and discharge the goods carried" throughout the voyage. For example, the carrier may not stow cargo above deck (other than in a sealed ocean container) because of exposure to the rain and seas, unless the bill of lading specifically allows it, or unless the shipper knows that it is the common practice with that type of cargo. A carrier should not stow cargo in a manner that causes it to shift and be crushed. Cargo should not be exposed on deck to rain and seas.

Carrier's Responsibilities for a Seaworthy Ship. The rules are different if the cargo is lost or damaged due to a problem with the ship itself. Here the carrier must use *due diligence before and at the beginning of the voyage* to (1) provide a seaworthy ship; (2) properly man, equip, and supply the ship; and (3) make the refrigerated units and all areas where cargo is carried "fit and safe" for the cargo. For example, the cargo holds must not become contaminated by oil or fuel, and tankers must not be contaminated by chemicals carried on a previous shipment. A ship is **seaworthy** if it is the proper type of ship to carry the type of cargo at issue, is reasonably fit for the intended journey, is prepared for the weather and seas expected, and complies with Coast Guard regulations and relevant shipping industry standards. The requirement that the ship be made seaworthy only "before and at the beginning of the voyage" is due to the fact that a ship could be rendered unseaworthy by events that are unavoidable and beyond the control of the carrier while on the ocean.

Specific Exceptions to Liability. COGSA not only sets out what the carrier must do in preparing the ship for voyage and in handling cargo, but it also lists 16 specific exceptions, or events, for which the carrier is not liable. (See Exhibit 6.2). The most striking of these exceptions is that the carrier is not liable for **errors in navigation** or in managing the ship, even if the crew's negligence causes the ship to collide or run aground. However, distinguish that from the carrier's corporate management that fails to use due diligence in hiring an unseaworthy or incompetent crew; here, the ship owner is liable. Similarly, the carrier is not liable if the crew's negligence starts a fire aboard ship, but the carrier is liable if it's corporate management fails to use due diligence in providing appropriate firefighting equipment and training prior to the voyage. The last exception for discussion here are the "perils of the sea," our next subject.

Perils of the Sea. Ships encounter tremendous forces of water and weather on the high seas. COGSA exempts carriers from liability for damage resulting from these "perils, dangers, and accidents of the sea." A **peril of the sea** is a fortuitous action of the sea or weather of sufficient force to overcome the strength of a seaworthy ship or the diligence and skill of a seaworthy crew. If the

Exhibit 6.2

Carriage of Goods by Sea Act Specific Exceptions to Liability

Carriers are not liable for losses resulting from a number of specific causes listed in the statute. These exceptions include the following:

1. Errors in the navigation or in the management of the ship
2. Fire, unless caused by the actual fault of the carrier (the ship owner)
3. Perils, dangers, and accidents of the sea
4. An act of God (an unpreventable loss from natural causes or disaster)
5. An act of war
6. An act of public enemies
7. Legal seizure of the ship
8. Quarantine restrictions
9. An act or omission of the shipper or owner of the goods
10. Labor strikes or lockouts
11. Riots and civil commotions
12. Saving life or property at sea
13. An inherent defect, quality, or vice of the goods that causes wastage in bulk or weight or other damage or loss
14. Insufficiency of packing (by shipper)
15. Inadequate marking of goods or containers (by shipper)
16. Latent defects in ship or equipment (that might render the ship unseaworthy) that were not discoverable by due diligence

ship is seaworthy when it leaves port and is prepared for expected weather and conditions, the carrier is not liable for cargo damage from a storm so strong that it represents a peril of the sea. The following case, *J. Gerber & Co. v. S.S. Sabine Howaldt,* illustrates damage resulting from a peril of the sea.

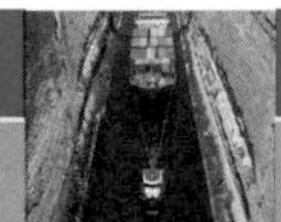

J. Gerber & Co. v. S.S. Sabine Howaldt

437 F.2d 580 (1971) United States Court of Appeals (2d Cir.)

BACKGROUND AND FACTS

The S.S. Sabine Howaldt, a small cargo vessel, was chartered for a voyage from Antwerp, Belgium, to Wilmington, Delaware. The ship was carrying steel products consigned to the plaintiff. The cargo was in good condition when loaded at Antwerp. On arrival at the port of destination in the United States, however, the steel showed extensive saltwater damage from rust and pitting. The Sabine Howaldt encountered extremely heavy weather on the Atlantic. Water penetrated the ventilators and damaged the cargo. The carrier argued that the damage was caused solely by a peril of the sea and that the ship was seaworthy. The trial court found that the ship was unseaworthy due to the negligence of the defendant and that the winds and seas that the vessel encountered did not constitute a peril of the sea. The carrier appealed.

ANDERSON, CIRCUIT JUDGE

* * * The ship's log records that ... the ship was badly strained in her seams and sea water was breaking over forecastle deck, hatches, and upper works. It was necessary for the vessel to heave to and she so remained for 12 hours. [Winds reached 63 knots]. The hull of the Sabine Howaldt was twisted and strained in the turbulent cross seas; she rolled from 25 degrees–30 degrees; waves constantly broke over her; and she shuddered and vibrated as she was pounded and wrenched by the heavy seas ... Subsequently it was discovered that during this period of hurricane ... a port hole in the galley was smashed; the catwalk or gangway from the amidships housing aft over the hatches and the well-deck to the poop was destroyed when it was torn loose and landed against a ventilator, which it dented. * * *

On arrival at Wilmington, Delaware ... the chief officer examined the hatches and found no damage to the hatches, the hatch covers, or their rubber gaskets—all were in good condition. There was no evidence in the case that at any relevant time anything was wrong with the hatches or their MacGregor covers, or that they were at any time damaged or defective. No alterations, changes or repairs were made to the

continues

continued

hatches or covers after arrival and before the ship's next voyage from Santo Domingo to Norway in which she encountered heavy seas and shipped green water over decks and hatches but no leaks occurred. All the evidence showed they were in good condition both before and after the voyage. * * *

The standard of seaworthiness must remain uncertain because of the imponderables of the forces exerted upon a ship by the winds and seas. Ship design and construction over many centuries of experience have evolved to meet the dangers inherent in violent winds and tempestuous seas. But for the purpose of deciding whether or not they constitute perils of the sea for a particular vessel for the purpose of the statutory exception there is the question of how violent and how tempestuous. These are matters of degree and not amenable to precise definition ... Other indicia are, assuming a seaworthy ship, the nature and extent of the damage to the ship itself, whether or not the ship was buffeted by cross-seas which wrenched and wracked the hull and set up unusual stresses in it and like factors. While the seaworthiness of a ship presupposes that she is designed, built, and equipped to stand up under reasonable expectable conditions, this means no more than the usual bad weather, which is normal for a particular sea area at a particular time. It does not, however, include an unusual combination of the destructive forces of wind and sea which a skilled and experienced ship's master would not expect and which the ship encountered as a stroke of bad luck. Hurricane-force winds and turbulent cross-seas generating unpredictable strains and pressures on a ship's hull are an example.

We are satisfied that the Sabine Howaldt was a seaworthy vessel when she left Antwerp ... Throughout the voyage she was operated in a good and seamanlike manner. There was no negligence on the part of the carrier. The damage to the cargo was caused by violence of the wind and sea and particularly by the resulting cross-seas which, through wrenching and twisting the vessel, set up torsions within the hull which forced up the hatch covers and admitted sea water to the holds.

Decision. The decision of the trial court is reversed. The defendant carrier met its burden of proof that the vessel was seaworthy when it left port and that the damage to the cargo resulted solely from a peril of the sea.

Case Questions

1. What is a "peril of the sea?" Why do you think maritime law relieves a carrier from liability for damages resulting from a peril of the sea?
2. Describe the sea and weather conditions here and explain whether they amounted to an exculpatory peril of the sea.
3. If an insurance company pays a claimant for goods damaged during ocean transit, may the insurance company bring the action against the carrier under COGSA?

The Per-Package Limitation

Imagine that you travel to England in search of antiques for sale in your antique store in the United States. You find many pieces from the late eighteenth century. You purchase regency tables, writing desks, chairs, settees, decorative objects, and other smaller pieces from the George II period. You arrange with a reputable freight forwarder to package everything and ship it to you in the United States. The forwarder packages everything individually in cardboard and then places them with other items on wooden pallets for wrapping with heavier cardboard and fastening with steel bands. There are 200 pieces of furniture and decorative objects on 26 pallets. The forwarder arranges for an ocean carrier to deliver a steel container to your warehousing agent for loading. On delivering the container to the carrier, the forwarder receives an ocean bill of lading showing the receipt of "2 x 40 ft. container STC [said to contain] 26 pallets antique furniture." The bill of lading contains no value for the goods, and the forwarder does not object, because the value appears on other customs documentation. You return to the United States and await delivery. Unfortunately, as your container was being unloaded, it was dropped from the crane and the contents were completely destroyed. You request reimbursement from the carrier in the amount of $250,000, based on the actual value of the antiques. The carrier says that it is only responsible for $13,000 and no more. What do you think?

COGSA's Per-Package Liability Limitation. All countries have some limitation on the carrier's liability for loss or damage to goods, expressed either as a monetary limit per package (or shipping unit) or per unit of weight. The limits can be found in the domestic law of each country. In the United States, the limit of a carrier's liability under COGSA is $500 per package or customary freight unit, provided the shipper gets a "fair opportunity" to declare the "nature and value" of the goods and to state the quantity and description on the bill of lading. The shipper is free to declare any value up to the actual value of the goods, but a higher value may mean a higher freight rate. If no value is stated, the limit applies. A package can be a box of merchandise, a bale of cotton, a coil of wire, a barrel of oil, or something much larger, as in the following case, *Z.K. Marine, Inc. v. M/V Archigetis.*

Z.K. Marine, Inc. v. Archigetis

776 F. Supp. 1549 (1991) United States District Court (S.D.Fla.)

BACKGROUND AND FACTS

The plaintiff, Z.K. Marine, is an importer of yachts for sale in the United States. In 1987, five yachts were shipped from Taiwan to the United States aboard the MV Archigetis. Each yacht was shipped under a clean negotiable bill of lading. Each of the five bills of lading provided on its face that one unit only was being shipped, that the yacht was being shipped on deck at the shipper's risk, and that the value of the goods could be declared with prior notice. On the back of each bill of lading, the liability for danger or loss was limited to $500 per package or customary freight unit. During transit, one yacht was lost and the other four were damaged. The bills of lading were purchased by the plaintiffs while the yachts were in transit. The defendant claims that it is liable only in the amount of $500 per yacht.

HOEVELER, DISTRICT JUDGE

Defendants argue that pursuant to the *Carriage of Goods by Sea Act*, and the explicit provisions of the bills of lading, damages are limited to $500 per package. Because the bills of lading are clearly stamped "one unit," defendants contend that their liability is limited to $500 per yacht. Alternatively, defendants argue that if the yachts are not one package, they are each a customary freight unit—since the freight charges were based upon a customary freight unit and yacht was used as the basis of a single freight charge— and consequently subject to the $500 limitation.

First, [plaintiffs] argue that there is no opportunity to declare a higher value because the bills of lading themselves provide no space to do so.. Although there is no specific slot for the shipper to write in its higher value, there appears plenty of space on the face of the bills for it to do so, if desired. The bills plainly afford space and, by their terms, opportunity for the shipper to declare a higher value.

Plaintiffs argue in the alternative that even if the bills of lading offer the shipper opportunity to declare a higher value, the plaintiffs, as purchasers of the negotiable bills, had no such opportunity. Therefore, they argue that the limitation provisions should not be enforced. Purchasers of a negotiable bill of lading, however, purchase only those rights which the shipper had. The right to declare a higher value and pay higher freight ended when the goods were delivered on board the ship. Therefore, the purchasers of the bills cannot now complain if a higher value was not declared.

Plaintiffs' next contention is that each yacht is not a package so that the limitation to $500 per package does not apply. Plaintiffs contend that the cradles attached to the yachts for ease in transporting them do not suffice as packaging because the cradles do not enclose the yachts. Plaintiffs are mistaken in this regard. A package is some class of cargo, irrespective of size or weight, which has been prepared for transportation by the addition of some packaging that facilitates handling, but which does not necessarily enclose the goods ... In the instant case, the yachts were all transported on cradles, analogous, for purposes of the package analysis, to skids. Accordingly, this court finds that each yacht constituted a package within the purview of COGSA's liability limitation provisions. Therefore the limitation of $500 per package on the bills of lading applies to limit liability of the carrier to $500 per yacht ...

Decision. court held that each yacht constituted one customary freight unit or "package," that the shipper had been given a fair opportunity to declare a higher value, and that the carrier's liability was limited to $500 per package. The purchasers of the bills of lading were bound by the terms of the bills of lading, including the limitation provisions.

Comment. COGSA generally does not apply to goods carried above deck unless specifically permitted in the bill of lading., or unless the bill of lading states that COGSA govern, as was the case here. This is known as a clause paramount. Thus, the court

continues

continued

held that the COGSA package limitation applied to these yachts.

Case Questions

1. Why might an unknowing or unadvised shipper fail to value marine cargo properly?
2. What is the proper role of the shipper's freight forwarder in giving advice and in arranging transport for ocean cargo?
3. How could the shipper have avoided the result in this case?

The meaning of the term "package" became more complicated after the introduction of containerized freight in the 1960s. Carriers have occasionally argued that the ocean shipping container is itself the "package," which makes them liable for only $500 for the entire shipment. Steel containers are 8' wide by 20' or 40' long and are usually stowed one on top of the other, above deck. Carriers usually provide the containers and shippers pack and transport them by road or rail to the ports for loading. Sometimes they are used to consolidate goods from several different shippers, perhaps containing thousands of different items valued at up to millions of dollars. The question of whether or not a container is a "package" under COGSA has resulted in many conflicting court opinions over the past 30 years. Courts have held that a container is not a "package," unless the bill of lading (accidentally?) describes the quantity as "one container."

The purpose of disclosing the number of packages in the bill of lading is to give the carrier a better idea of its total liability if a container is damaged. If the number of packages are not given, but only the total number of items or pieces within a container, then the carrier's liability may be limited to only $500 per container. *Binladen BSB Landscaping v. The Nedlloyd Rotterdam*, 759 F.2d 1006 (2d Cir. 1985) involved a shipment of potted plants to Saudi Arabia that were stuffed into a container individually, without any prior packing. The bill of lading stated, "1 x *40 ft. reefer container, said to contain 7,790 live plants.*" The court noted that stating the number of plants was not the same thing as stating the number of packages (or customary freight units) and the carrier was liable for only $500 in the destruction of the cargo.

Another common problem in defining the term "package" involves shipments of cartons strapped to wooden pallets or skids by steel bands, cardboard, or shrink-wrapping. Different courts have resolved this differently, even in the United States. Many courts hold that the number of "packages" is the number of pallets. *Tokio Marine & Fire Ins. Co., Ltd. v. Nippon Express U.S.A.* 155 F. Supp. 2d 1167 (C.D. Cal. 2000) involved a shipment of car radio components shipped in 177 cardboard cartons on 33 wooden pallets. Each pallet was wrapped in heavy cardboard and strapped with plastic bands, so that the cartons inside were not visible. The bill of lading showed the quantity as "1 *container STC 33 skids.*" The goods were then described as "177 *pieces, car radio components.*" The court held that each of the 33 skids, and not each of the 177 cartons, was a $500 "package." There seemed to be two reasons: The quantity section of the bill of lading clearly specified "33 skids" and the smaller cartons could not be seen through the heavy outer cardboard wrapping. The court distinguished this from other cases where the pallets were shrink-wrapped in transparent polyethylene, noting that with shrink-wrapping the carrier could plainly see the number of smaller cartons on each skid and read the markings on each.

These cases give due warning that an export sales manager or freight forwarder should follow good shipping practices and get expert advice when needed. Goods should always be prepared and packaged for shipment in a customary and safe manner. The shipper should always be certain that the goods are correctly described, weighed, and counted and that their value is correctly stated on the bill of lading. The number of COGSA packages being shipped, based on the smallest *unit of packaging,* should be declared in the quantity section of the bill of lading (e.g., "1 x *40 ft. container STC 1,000 cases red table wine*"). A shipper should also use caution when declaring a quantity of goods based on individual unpacked units or pieces. Of course, a shipper must never knowingly or fraudulently misstate the identity of cargo or its value on the bill of lading, or the carrier cannot be held liable for any damage to the goods.

The Proposed Rotterdam Rules. In 2009 a new treaty, *United Nations Convention on Contracts for the International Carriage of Goods Wholly or Partly by Sea,* was adopted, and will go into effect if, and when, ratified by 20 countries. Known as the *Rotterdam Rules,* the Convention would replace the *Hague-Visby Rules* in those countries that ratify it, and it would be the most

Exhibit 6.3

The Proposed Rotterdam Rules* (2008)
A Few Key Differences with the *Hague Rules* of 1924

1. **When Carrier Responsible.** The carrier's responsibility for the goods extends to cover the entire multimodal carriage, "door to door," from initial receipt to delivery at the destination, not just from loading to unloading.
2. **Electronic Documents.** An electronic "transport record" has the same legal effect as a paper transport document or bill of lading. The term "bill of lading" is not used in the Convention.
3. **Carrier Obligation Before and During Voyage.** The carrier's obligation to use due diligence to make and keep the ship seaworthy, to properly crew and equip the ship, and to keep the holds and all other parts of the ship in which the goods are carried (including containers) fit and safe for the carriage, applies to the entire voyage (not just at the beginning of the voyage as under the Hague Rules).
4. **Errors in Navigation.** Carriers are liable for errors in navigation and mismanagement of the ship.
5. **Apportioning Fault.** When damage or loss is attributable both to a cause for which the carrier is not liable (e.g. a peril of the sea) and one for which it is liable (e.g. unseaworthy crew or vessel), then a court may apportion the loss accordingly.
6. **Limits on Liability.** The limit on the carrier's liability is increased to 875 SDRs "per package or other shipping unit" or three SDRs per kilogram of gross weight of the goods lost or damaged, whichever is the higher (unless actual value is declared). The benefit of this limit would not apply if the corporate owner of the ship acted recklessly and with knowledge that loss would probably result.
7. **Package.** When goods are carried in or on a container or pallet, the number of packages is that number listed on the transport record. If the number of packages or shipping units is not listed, then the container or pallet is considered one package or shipping unit.
8. **Negligence of Shipper.** If the negligence of the shipper (e.g. improperly marking or shipping dangerous cargo) causes damage or loss to the vessel or to other cargo, there is no monetary limit placed on the shipper's liability under the Convention.
9. **Delay.** Economic loss due to delay in delivery is limited to 2.5 times the freight payable for the carriage.
10. **Notice.** Notice of damage that is not apparent must be given to the carrier at the port of delivery within seven days. Notice of loss due to delay must be given within 21 days.
11. **Time Limit for Suits.** The time limit for lawsuits has been extended to two years from the date the goods were delivered, or should have been delivered.

**United Nations Convention on Contracts for the International Carriage of Goods Wholly or Partly by Sea* (2008). Adopted by the UN General Assembly, 2009. Will go into force when ratified by 20 nations.

important change in ocean cargo law in over 85 years. As of 2013 the Convention had only ratified by two countries. Anyone with an understanding of maritime law and the Hague Rules would understand the *Rotterdam Rules*. Exhibit 6.3 shows some of the important changes.

THE LIABILITY OF OCEAN TRANSPORTATION INTERMEDIARIES

Many companies that ship or receive goods internationally often use the services of intermediaries—service companies that handle the cargo, arrange transportation with air or ocean carriers, assist shippers in clearing legal hurdles in moving freight internationally, and provide many other services. The ocean transportation intermediaries discussed here include *freight forwarders* and *non-vessel operating common carriers.*

Freight Forwarders

Transporting goods over great distances and across national borders is often costly, complex, and highly susceptible to error and unexpected delays. Most exporters (as well as importers) rely on the services of professional **freight forwarders** for assistance. Forwarders act as agents for shippers in contracting with air, land, or sea carriers for the transportation of goods to a place of destination. These are some of the functions that forwarders provide to shippers:

- advice on shipping alternatives and cost information
- contracting with carriers for transportation of cargo by air, land, and sea
- obtaining cargo insurance
- assisting in packing, crating, and containerizing cargo
- advice on marking of packages, cartons, and pallets
- assisting in consolidating smaller shipments of several different shippers into one container
- arranging warehousing of goods pending shipment or delivery
- preparing shipping and customs documents
- assisting in moving goods through customs and across national borders

Many forwarders specialize in moving complex or dangerous cargo, such as explosives. Some have foreign offices and are familiar with foreign import regulations. When forwarders receive cargo for shipment, they issue **forwarder's receipts** or house bills of lading (called consignment notes in some countries). These do not have the same legal effects as ocean bills of lading and are not negotiable.

Non-Vessel Operating Common Carriers

Shippers who can fill an entire ocean container with goods can receive more favorable shipping rates than those shippers who must move small amounts of break-bulk cargo without a container. **Non-vessel operating common carriers** (commonly referred to as NVOCCs) act as freight consolidators for small shipments, permitting them to take advantage of lower freight rates. A **NVOCC** is a common carrier that functions like an ocean carrier but does not operate the vessels by which transportation is provided. It issues bills of lading and assumes liability for goods due to loss or damage during transport. It also performs many of the same services as a freight forwarder. The *Federal Maritime Commission* licenses and regulates ocean transportation intermediaries that operate in the United States. Ocean carriers, freight forwarders, and NVOCCs in the United States are governed by the *Shipping Act of 1984* and the *Ocean Shipping Reform Act of 1998.* The latter represents an attempt by the U.S. Congress to reform ocean shipping regulation by allowing carriers greater flexibility in contracting with shippers and establishing shipping rates. Because these agreements are considered private contracts (with no bill of lading) they are not subject to COGSA. States and municipalities in the United States are prohibited from regulating freight forwarders.

The following case, *Prima U.S. Inc. v. Panalpina, Inc.*, compares the liability of a freight forwarder with that of an NVOCC.

Prima U.S. Inc. v. Panalpina, Inc.

223 F.3d 126 (2000) United States Court of Appeals (2d Cir.)

BACKGROUND AND FACTS

Westinghouse contracted with Panalpina, a freight forwarder, to arrange for the transportation of an electric transformer from Italy to Iowa. Panalpina stated to Westinghouse, "[R]est assured your shipment will receive door to door our close care and supervision…." Westinghouse paid Panalpina over $20,000 for its services. As was the industry custom, Panalpina did not issue a bill of lading for the shipment.

Panalpina hired an Italian company to coordinate the movement of the transformer through Italy, who then hired a local stevedoring company, to load the transformer aboard the ship for the voyage to the United States. Panalpina never inquired of the stevedore how the transformer was lashed for the ocean voyage, nor did it supervise the endeavor. During the ocean voyage, the ship encountered heavy seas and the transformer broke loose, crushing a laser-cutting machine owned by Prima. Prima sued the owner of the ship, Westinghouse, and Panalpina for damages to the laser. The district court held Panalpina liable, and Panalpina appealed.

MCLAUGHLIN, CIRCUIT JUDGE

The job of a non-vessel operating common carrier ("NVOCC") is to consolidate cargo from numerous shippers into larger groups for shipment by an ocean carrier. An NVOCC—as opposed to the actual ocean carrier transporting the cargo—issues a bill of lading to each shipper. If anything happens to the goods during the voyage the NVOCC is liable to the shipper because of the bill of lading that it issued.

A freight forwarder like Panalpina, on the other hand, simply facilitates the movement of cargo to the ocean vessel. The freight forwarder secures cargo space with a steamship company, gives advice on governmental licensing requirements, proper port of exit and letter of credit intricacies, and arranges to

continues

continued

have the cargo reach the seaboard in time to meet the designated vessel. Freight forwarders generally make arrangements for the movement of cargo at the request of clients and are vitally different from carriers, such as vessels, truckers, stevedores or warehouses, which are directly involved in transporting the cargo ... As long as the freight forwarder limits its role to arranging for transportation, it will not be held liable to the shipper. Panalpina did not issue a bill of lading and it did not consolidate cargo. It was hired by Westinghouse simply as a freight forwarder to arrange for the transportation of a transformer from Italy to Iowa. By analogy, Panalpina was hired to act as a "travel agent" for the transformer: it set things up and made reservations, but did not engage in any hands-on heavy lifting. Admittedly, Panalpina did state that Westinghouse's "shipment [would] receive door to door our close care and supervision...." However, because of the well settled legal distinction between forwarders and carriers, that statement—mere puffing—cannot transform Panalpina into a carrier, and bestow liability upon it.

Decision. Judgment reversed for Panalpina. Panalpina was a freight forwarder hired by Westinghouse to arrange for transportation and other services. It was not a carrier and was not liable for the cargo during shipment. Freight forwarders must use due diligence and reasonable care in performing their functions. Panalpina was reasonable in its selection of its stevedore to load the ship.

Case Questions

1. Explain the difference between a carrier, a freight forwarder, and a NVOCC.
2. How does the liability of each of the above differ for damage or loss to goods?
3. Why did Panalpina's assurance that the shipment would "receive door to door our close care and supervision" not subject the freight forwarder to liability?

MARINE CARGO INSURANCE

Cargo insurance is an essential element of international trade. The potential for damage and loss to goods, particularly during ocean shipments, which are lengthier and more hazardous than air shipments, is tremendous. Sellers, buyers, and even banks that finance international sales want to be certain that their interest in the goods is fully insured. If not, the property risks will be unacceptably high.

Marine Insurance Policies

Although policies of insurance cover individual shipments, many shippers who do large volumes of business overseas maintain **open cargo policies**. An open policy offers the convenience and protection of covering all shipments by the shipper of certain types of goods to certain destinations and over specified routes. With an open policy in effect, insurance company authorizes the exporter to issue a certificate of insurance on a form the company provides. Exporters shipping on CIF terms often use open cargo policies. These certificates are negotiable and are transferred along with the bill of lading to the party who purchases and takes title to the goods. The type or form of the certificate is determined by the contract between the parties or by the requirements of the bank that is providing financing for the sale. The insurance company must be notified as soon as possible after shipment under an open policy.

Marine insurance policies cover several different types of losses, including: (1) total losses of all or part of a shipment, (2) general averages or general average losses, and (3) partial or particular average losses.

General Average

The concept of general average is derived from ancient mariners, ship owners, and merchants who understood that ocean voyages were a shared venture. After all, lives and commercial interests of all three groups depended on one another while at sea. So early maritime principles developed to assure that each could rely on the other, by seeing that they all shared in the gain and loss of the voyage. By now you should have realized that the three judgments of the *Rolls of Oleron* that appeared earlier in this chapter illustrate this important principle of shared responsibility.

The word "average" in marine insurance law means loss. A **general average** is a loss that results when extraordinary expenses or losses are incurred in saving the vessel or its cargo from danger at sea. It spreads the risk of a disaster at sea by making all parties to the voyage contribute to any loss incurred. Under this rule, if A's cargo is damaged or "sacrificed" in the process of saving the ship, and B's cargo is saved as a result, B or its insurer must contribute to A for the loss. A's claim is a general average. In other words, the owner of the cargo that was sacrificed would have a general average claim for contribution against the owner of the cargo that was saved. For example, when fire threatens an entire ship and certain cargo is damaged by water in putting the fire out, the owners of all of the cargo must contribute to the loss of the cargo that was damaged by the water. The owners of cargo that is thrown overboard to save a sinking ship may have a claim against those whose cargo was thereby saved. General average claims are typically covered by marine insurance.

Modern cases hold that, to prove a general average claim, the claimant must show that (1) the ship, cargo, and crew were threatened by a *common danger*; (2) the danger was *real and substantial* (the older cases required that the danger be imminent); and (3) either the cargo or ship was voluntarily sacrificed for the benefit of both or extraordinary expenses were incurred to avert a common danger.

General Average Claims by the Carrier. Under general average, ship owners can also bring general average claims against the owners of cargo. The principles of general average apply when a carrier incurs extraordinary expenses in rescuing, saving, or repairing an endangered ship that is in a real and substantial danger. In *Eagle Terminal Tankers, Inc. v. Insurance* Co. *of USSR*, 637 F.2d 890 (2d Cir. 1981), the ship had traveled for more than a day with a damaged propeller. It dry-docked, unloaded the cargo, had the damage repaired at a cost of $127,000 (which included the crew's expenses during that time), reloaded, and completed its voyage to Leningrad. The court awarded the carrier the general average claim. It noted that "a ship's master should not be discouraged from taking timely action to avert a disaster," and need not wait until the peril is imminent to claim general average.

The results of general average law must have been quite surprising to the plaintiff in *Amerada Hess Corp. v. S/T Mobil Apex*, 602 F.2d 1095 (2d Cir. 1979). Plaintiff shipped gasoline and naphtha. When the cargo was destroyed by an explosion and fire that had been started by sparks from machinery in the engine room, the plaintiff sued the carrier for damages. The carrier counter-claimed for general average losses. The court denied recovery to the cargo owner under COGSA, holding that the carrier was not liable for the fuel because the ship was not unseaworthy. The court then held, much to the chagrin of the plaintiff, that it was actually liable to the carrier for towing and salvage expenses incurred in arresting the fire and saving the ship.

The York-Antwerp Rules. The *York-Antwerp Rules* are a set of standardized rules on general average. An effort to develop commonly accepted principles of general average began in England as early as 1860, with work on the rules being completed in 1890. Following World War II, an international effort to achieve universally accepted general average rules resulted in the revised *York-Antwerp Rules* of 1950. The rules have achieved widespread acceptance by the maritime industry; the latest version was agreed to in 1994. The rules are not the subject of treaty or convention and have not been enacted into national laws. They traditionally have become a part of the contract of carriage because their provisions are generally incorporated into all modern bills of lading.

Particular Average Claims

Although total and general average losses are ordinarily covered up to the policy amount, special problems result from partial or particular average losses. A **particular average** is a partial loss to the insured's cargo. Many insurance policies limit the insurer's liability for particular average losses. Because many losses only partially damage the cargo, a shipper must understand the particular average terms of the policy. A policy that is *free of particular average* (or said to be on "FPA terms") will not cover any partial losses. A policy FPA, followed by certain specified losses, will not pay for any partial or particular average losses of that nature. As such, an "FPA fire" policy will not pay for partial losses to the cargo due to fire.

Types of Coverage

Marine cargo insurance is available for virtually any type of risk, for any cargo, destined for almost any port (see Exhibit 6.4). The only limitations are the willingness of the insurer to undertake the risk and the price. The perils clause of the policy describes the types of risk it covers.

The Perils Clause. The **perils clause** covers the basic risks of an ocean voyage. It generally covers extraordinary and unusual perils that are not expected during a voyage. Examples of perils that are included are bad weather sufficient to overcome a seaworthy

Exhibit 6.4

Marine Cargo Insurance Policy

CHUBB GROUP
of Insurance Companies
100 William Street, New York, N.Y. 10038

CARGO POLICY OF INSURANCE

$ Number

Issued by the stock insurance company shown below

Open Policy No.

FEDERAL INSURANCE COMPANY
Incorporated under the Laws of New Jersey

In consideration of a premium as agreed, the Company
Does insure (lost or not lost)
to the amount of Dollars,
on
valued at to be shipped on board of the B/L Date
at and from
to
and it is hereby understood and agreed, that in case of loss, such loss is payable to the order of
on surrender of this Policy.

(continued)

Touching the Adventures and Perils which said Assurers are contented to bear, and take upon themselves, in this Voyage, they are of the Seas, Fires, Assailing Thieves, Jettisons, Barratry of the Master and Mariners, and all other like Perils, Losses and Misfortunes that have or shall come to the Hurt, Detriment or Damage of the said Goods and Merchandise, or any part thereof except as may be otherwise provided for herein or endorsed hereon. AND in case of any Loss or Misfortune, it shall be lawful and necessary to and for the Assured, his or their Factors, Servants and Assigns, to sue, labor and travel for, in and about the Defense, Safeguard and Recovery of the said Goods and Merchandise, or any part thereof, without Prejudice to this insurance; nor shall the acts of the Assured or Assurers, in recovering, saving and preserving the property insured, in case of disaster, be considered a waiver or an acceptance of an abandonment; to the charges whereof, the said Assurers will contribute according to the rate and quantity of the sum hereby insured.

In case of loss, such loss to be paid in thirty days after proof of loss and proof of interest in the property hereby insured.

In case the interest hereby insured is covered by other insurance (except as hereinafter provided) the loss shall be collectedfrom the several policies in the order of the date of their attachment, insurance attaching on the same date to be deemed simultaneous and to contribute pro rata; provided, however, that where any fire insurance, or any insurance (including fire) taken out by any carrier or bailee is available to the beneficiary of this policy, or would be so available if this insurance did not exist, then this insurance shall be void to the extent that such other insurance is or would have been available. It is agreed, nevertheless, that where these Assurers are thus relieved of liability because of the existence of other insurance, these Assurers shall receive and retain the premium payable under this policy and, in consideration thereof, shall guarantee the solvency of the companies and/or underwriters this clause, but not exceeding, in any case, the amount which would have been collectible under this policy if such other insurance did not exist.

In all cases of damage caused by perils insured against, the loss shall, as far as practicable, be ascertained by a separation and a sale or appraisement of a damaged portion only of the contents if the packages so damaged and not otherwise.

Losses arising from breakage and/or leakage and/or loss of weight and/or loss of contents are excluded from this insurance unless caused by stranding or collision with another vessel, or unless this insurance has been expressly extended to include such losses.

Warranted free from Particular Average unless the vessel or craft be stranded, sunk or burnt, but notwithstanding this warranty these Assurers are to pay any loss of or damage to the interest insured which may reasonably be attributed to fire, collision or contact of the vessel and/or conveyance with any external substance (ice included) other than water, or to discharge of cargo at port of distress. The foregoing warranty, however, shall not apply where broader terms of average are provided for herein or by endorsement hereon.

If the voyage aforesaid shall have been terminated before the date of this policy, then there shall be no return of premium on account of such termination of the voyage.

Wherever the words "ship", "vessel", "seaworthiness", "ship or vessel owner" appear in this Policy, they are deemed to include also the words "aircraft", "airworthiness", "aircraft owner".

THIS INSURANCE IS SUBJECT TO THE AMERICAN INSTITUTE CARGO CLAUSES (FEB. 1949) (INCLUDING THE WAREHOUSE TO WAREHOUSE CLAUSE), SOUTH AMERICAN 60 DAY CLAUSE WHEN APPLICABLE. ALSO SUBJECT TO THE AMENDED F. C. & S. AND S. R. & C. C. WARRANTIES (OCT. 1959) (*SEE REVERSE*)

continues

continued

Original and Duplicative issued, one of which being accomplished the other to stand null and void

SPECIAL CONDITIONS	**Marks and Numbers**
ON DECK—Merchandise and/or goods shipped on deck to an On Deck Bill of Lading *which must be so specified in this policy* are insured.—Free of particular average unless caused by the vessel being stranded, sunk, burnt, on fire, or in collision, but including jettison and/or washing overboard, irrespective of percentage.	

Where the words "including M. E. C." are typed in the space below at the time the policy is issued, this insurance is subject to the American Institute Marine Extension Clauses.

Where the words "including Strike Risks" are typed in the space below at the time the policy is issued, this insurance is subject to the Current American Institute S. R. & C. C. Clauses.

Where the words "including War Risk" are typed in the space below at the time the policy is issued, this insurance is subject to the Current War Risk Clauses.

In Witness Whereof, the Company issuing this policy has caused this policy to be signed by its authorized officers, but this policy shall not be valid unless signed by a duly authorized representative of the Company.

FEDERAL INSURANCE COMPANY

Date: *Henry G Gubel* Secretary *Henry L. Harlon* President __________ Authorized Representative

The following Warranties shall be paramount and shall not be modified or superseded by any other provision included herein or stamped or endorsed hereon unless such other provision refers specifically to the risks excluded by these warranties and expressly assumes the said risks.

(A) "Notwithstanding anything herein contained to the contrary, this insurance is warranted free from capture, seizure, arrest, restraint, detainment, confiscation, preemption, requisition or nationalization, and the consequences thereof or any attempt thereat, whether in time of peace or war and whether lawful or otherwise; also warranted free, whether in time of peace or war, from all loss, damage or expense caused by any weapon of war employing atomic or nuclear fission and/or fusion or other reaction or radioactive force or matter or by any mine or torpedo, also warranted free from all consequences of hostilities or warlike operations (whether there be a declaration of war or not), but this warranty shall not exclude collision or contact with aircraft, rockets or similar missiles or with any fixed or floating object (other than a mine or torpedo), stranding heavy weather, fire or explosion unless caused directly (and independently of the nature of the voyage or service which the vessel concerned or, in the case of a collision, any other vessel involved therein, is performing) by a hostile act by or against a belligerent power; and for the purposes of this warranty 'power' includes any authority maintaining naval, military or air forces in association with a power.

Further warranted free from the consequences of civil war, revolution, rebellion, insurrection, or civil strife arising therefrom, or piracy."

(B) Warranted free of loss or damage caused by or resulting from strikes, lockouts, labor disturbances, riots, civil commotions or the acts of any person or persons taking part in any such occurrence or disorder.

NOTE: It is necessary for the assured to give prompt notice to these Assurers when they become aware of an event for which they are "held covered" under this policy and the right to such cover is dependent on compliance with this obligation.

Source: Sample policy provided courtesy of Chubb Group of Insurance Companies.

vessel, shipwreck, stranding, collision, and hitting rocks or floating objects. (An example of a perils clause follows in the next case.) However, this clause does not cover every event that can damage goods. The perils clause does not include damage due to the unseaworthiness of the vessel or loss from explosion or pilferage. The clause only covers losses while at sea. Moreover, it only covers **fortuitous losses**. "Fortuitous" is a concept that runs throughout insurance law. It means that the loss occurred by chance or accident and could not have reasonably have been predicted. For example, damage due to predictable winds or waves are generally not considered fortuitous. Courts have held that damage from seawater due to improper stowage of goods is not fortuitous. Losses due to the "inherent vice" or nature of the goods are not fortuitous, such as steel that rusts or materials that absorb water from humidity in the air. A loss from improper packaging is not fortuitous.

A shipper who desires additional coverage can purchase it from the insurer at an added charge. This is called a **specially to cover clause**. For instance, a standard perils clause does not generally cover damage resulting from explosion, but a shipper can obtain insurance to cover it in the form of an explosion clause. Similarly, a shipper can purchase additional coverage to protect against the risks of freshwater damage, moisture damage, and rust or contamination of the cargo from chemicals, oil, or fuel. Many insurers offer specially designed import-export insurance packages for shippers of perishable foodstuffs, tobacco, steel, and other products and commodities.

The *Shaver* case discusses a standard perils clause and several additional types of coverage purchased by the insured. Unfortunately, none of them covered the loss that the plaintiffs had incurred.

Shaver Transportation Co. v. The Travelers Indemnity Co.

481 F.Supp. 892 (1979) United States District Court (D. Or.)

BACKGROUND AND FACTS

Shaver, a barge company, contracted with Weyerhauser, the shipper, to transport caustic soda to a buyer. Shaver arranged for marine cargo insurance with Travelers. Several different types of coverage were discussed. Shaver decided on "free from particular average" and "standard perils" provisions, supplemented with "specially to cover" clauses. Shaver loaded the first shipment of caustic soda on one of its barges and transported it to the buyer. The buyer refused delivery because it had been contaminated with tallow. The contamination occurred as Shaver was loading the caustic soda aboard the barge. The barge had previously carried a load of tallow, and Shaver had not thoroughly cleaned the barge input lines. The barge was returned to Shaver's dock. Shaver and Weyerhauser filed a claim with Travelers. Travelers argued that the contamination did not represent a recoverable loss under the policy. Shaver and Weyerhauser brought this action against Travelers.

SKOPIL, CIRCUIT JUDGE, SITTING BY DESIGNATION

Although the plaintiffs request recovery under several theories, there is only one major issue in the case: Are the losses incurred by the plaintiffs the consequences of an insured event under the marine cargo insurance policy? If the losses are not insured against, no recovery is possible.

[RECOVERY UNDER THE PERILS CLAUSE AND FREE FROM PARTICULAR AVERAGE CLAUSE]

The perils clause, almost identical to ancient perils provisions dating back several hundred years, defines the risks protected by the policy. In addition to a long list of "perils of the sea," the clause concludes with "and all other perils, losses, and misfortunes, that have, or shall, come to the hurt, detriment, or damage to the said goods and merchandise." Plaintiff argues that the "forced" disposition of the caustic soda was like jettison (an enumerated peril) and is covered by the concluding language of the clause. That language has been interpreted to include only perils that are similar to the enumerated perils.

Whether or not I conclude the forced disposition was a type of jettison, plaintiffs are unable to show an insurable loss due to jettison. The loss contamination of the cargo occurred at the time of loading ... [P]laintiffs cannot recover under the perils clause of the policy. The term "jettison" also appears in the Free from Particular Average clause. If jettison did occur, this clause affords coverage regardless of the amount of cargo damage. However, I find that a jettison did not occur in this instance. Jettison is the act of throwing overboard from a vessel a part of the cargo, in case of extreme danger, to lighten the ship. The orderly unloading and sale of the cargo to a chemical salvage company is not "jettison." Plaintiff cannot recover under the Free from Particular Average clause.

continues

continued

[RECOVERY UNDER THE ... SHORE COVERAGE CLAUSE]

The shore coverage clause provides coverage for enumerated risks occurring on shore. Plaintiffs argue that contamination while loading is a shore accident. However, since the contamination occurred within the barge's intake lines, the incident arose "on board." Therefore shore coverage does not apply. Even if it were to apply, contamination of cargo is not within the enumerated risks covered by the shore coverage clause....

[RECOVERY UNDER THE INCHMAREE CLAUSE]

The purpose of the Inchmaree clause is to expand the coverage of the policy beyond the perils provision. Federal law allows a vessel owner to become exempt from liability for fault or error in navigation or management of the ship. In contrast, the ship owner must retain liability for negligence in the care and custody of the cargo. The Inchmaree clause is intended to provide coverage to a cargo owner when a loss is due to error in navigation or management of the vessel since the carrier is exempt from liability. Plaintiffs argue the contamination was the result of an error in management and therefore covered under the Inchmaree clause. Defendant naturally urges the court to find the loss caused by fault in the care and custody of the cargo.

The United States Supreme Court has addressed the distinction between error in management and error in care of cargo but has not articulated a clear test. The Ninth Circuit, noting that no precise definitions exist, advocates a case-by-case determination using the following test: "If the act in question has the primary purpose of affecting the ship, it is 'in navigation or in management'; but if the primary purpose is to affect the cargo, it is not 'in navigation or in management.'" *Grace Line, Inc. v. Todd Shipyards Corporation*, 500 F.2d 361, 374 (9th Cir. 1974).

Using this test, I find that the contamination of the cargo in this case was caused by fault in the care, custody, and control of the cargo. The Inchmaree clause will not provide coverage for plaintiffs' losses under the facts of this case.

[RECOVERY UNDER NEGLIGENCE CLAUSE]

The Negligence clause provides coverage against losses due to enumerated perils caused by the unseaworthiness of the vessel ... This unseaworthiness must then cause a loss through one of the enumerated perils: "sinking, stranding, fire, explosion, contact with seawater, or by any other cause of the nature of any of the risks assumed in the policy." ...

Since contamination is not an enumerated peril, plaintiff urges coverage .... by suggesting the barge was in imminent danger of sinking. Although there is evidence that the caustic soda would have eventually corroded through the barge and caused it to sink, the process would have taken three to five years. This possibility is too far removed to find coverage under a provision providing for loss due to sinking. No recovery is possible under the Negligence clause of this policy ...

Plaintiffs suggest a number of theories of recovery under the marine cargo insurance policy. None is suited to this case. I am aided in my construction of this policy by one additional fact. Shaver rejected insurance coverage costing more but did not believe contamination was covered under the policy. Plaintiffs' present attempt to include this type of loss within the coverage of the policy is an afterthought.

Judgment shall be entered for the defendant.

Decision. The plaintiffs' loss due to contamination was not covered under any of the clauses of the insurance policy.

Comment. The following clauses were at issue in this case.

[THE PERILS CLAUSE]

"Touching the adventures and perils which the said Assurers are contended to bear, and take upon themselves, they are of the seas and inland waters, man of war, fires, enemies, pirates, rovers, assailing thieves, jettisons, letters of mart and countermart, reprisals, taking at sea, arrests, restraints and detainments of all kings, princes of people of what nation, condition or quality soever, barratry of the master and mariners, and all other perils, losses, and misfortunes, that have or shall come to the hurt, detriment, or damage to the said goods and merchandise, or any part thereof."

[THE SHORE CLAUSE]

"Including while on docks, wharves, or elsewhere on shore and/or during land transportation, risks of collision, derailment, fire, lightning, sprinkler leakage, cyclones, hurricanes, earthquakes, floods, the rising of navigable waters, or any accident to the conveyance and/or collapse and/or subsidence of docks and/or structures, and to pay loss or damage caused thereby, even though the insurance be otherwise FPA."

[THE INCHMAREE CLAUSE (NAMED AFTER A FAMOUS BRITISH CASE)]

"This insurance is also specially to cover any loss of or damage to the interest insured hereunder, through the bursting of boilers, breakage of shafts, or through any latent defect in the machinery, hull, or appurtenances, or from faults or errors in the navigation and/ or

continues

continued

management of the vessel by the Master, Mariners, Mates, Engineers, or Pilots; provided, however, that this clause shall not be construed as covering loss arising out of delay, deterioration, or loss of market, unless otherwise provided elsewhere herein."

[THE NEGLIGENCE CLAUSE]

"... [T]he Assurers agree that in the event unseaworthiness or a wrongful act or misconduct of shipowner, character, their agents or servants, shall, directly or indirectly, cause loss or damage to the cargo insured by sinking, stranding, fire, explosion, contact with seawater, or by any other cause of the nature of any of the risks assumed in the policy, the Assurers will [subject to the terms of average and other conditions of the policy] pay to an innocent Assured the resulting loss."

Case Questions

1. Tell whether coverage was awarded or denied under each of the following insurance provisions, and why or why not: the perils clause, the shore clause, the "Inchmaree" clause, the negligence clause.
2. How could the shipper have avoided this problem?

All Risks Coverage. An all risks policy covers all risks except those specifically excluded in the policy. Today, virtually all marine policies are issued with all risks coverage (although as we have already learned, that does not mean that all "losses" are covered, but only fortuitous losses). These policies usually exclude damage from certain specific causes, such as acts of war, damage or loss from delay in reaching the destination, and damage resulting from strikes and civil commotion. Coverage for strikes is available, but usually at additional cost.

War Risk. Typically, marine insurance policies do not cover the risks of war. War risk insurance is available for ocean shipments. If the shipper desires war risk insurance, it must purchase it separately from the insurer. If the buyer wants war risk coverage, it must agree on the price separately from the marine insurance provisions. The rates for war risk insurance are relatively stable in peacetime, but fluctuate almost daily in times of war.

CONCLUSION

This chapter began by discussing the liability of air carriers for the death or injury of passengers, for damage to baggage or cargo, and for flight delays affecting international travel and shipments. Airline-related litigation is very common. Some cases involve individual claims for single incidents. Others involve highly publicized major air disasters. Critics of the American legal system are quick to point out that airline litigation is a big business with American law firms and that much of it is frivolous and unnecessary. On the other hand, it would be nearly impossible for victims of air disasters to seek recovery without the benefit of experienced aviation lawyers because of the complexity of aviation law and the technical and engineering knowledge required to handle these cases. To put this in perspective, according to the IATA, some three billion passengers were carried by air in 2012, on 37.5 million flights worldwide. Yet there were only 414 fatalities in 15 fatal accidents; the safest year on record for air travel.

Air freight, both domestic and international, is the fastest growing method of cargo transportation. Although only a small fraction of goods by weight moves by air, it accounts for much higher percentage when measured by value. This is due to shipments of higher-value goods and perishables and increased package delivery services.

It has been over 50 years since the beginning of the modern era of containerized ocean cargo. In 1956 the first containers were loaded atop a converted tanker, the *Ideal X,* at the Port of Newark, bound for Houston. They were no more than truck trailer bodies, with the wheels and running gear removed. There were 56 trailers on the *Ideal X.* In 2013, the shipping firm Maersk announced a new container ship capable of carrying 16,000 containers. There are several million ocean containers in transit at any given time. No one knows for sure the number of containers lost at sea each year, or their value. Although it is a relatively small percentage of total ocean freight, by all estimates, it runs into the tens of thousands of containers and billions of dollars annually. There is perhaps no other single area of international business that has engendered as much litigation as ocean cargo losses. It is incumbent on anyone shipping goods to understand the risks involved and what can be done in advance to protect against them.

Finally, anyone working in the field of international transportation should follow the progress of the *Rotterdam Rules,* which may someday replace the Hague/COGSA rules.

Chapter Summary

1. The *Montreal Convention* (MC) makes the carrier strictly liable for the death or injury of a passenger ticketed for international travel, or for damages to baggage or cargo, up to an amount equal to 113,100 Special Drawing Rights. In addition, the carrier is liable for all proven damages above that unless the carrier can show that it or its employees were not at fault.
2. The MC applies only to passengers ticketed for "international carriage." Travel on a domestic flight is included, if it is a part of one continuous international journey.
3. If the MC applies, then it provides the exclusive cause of action against air carriers, preempting state or local law. Lawsuits may be brought against third-party defendants, other than the carrier, who were at fault in causing an injury or damage.
4. An air carrier is liable for damage sustained in case of death or bodily injury of a passenger only if the accident that caused the death or injury took place on board the aircraft or in the course of any of the operations of embarking or disembarking. An "accident" is an unexpected or unusual event or happening that is external to the passenger. It is not an accident if death or injury is caused by the passenger's own internal reaction to the usual, normal, and expected operation of the aircraft.
5. The carrier is not liable to the extent that the passenger's own negligence contributed to the accident or to his or her loss. Injuries for mental harm or emotional distress are only permitted if they were caused by a bodily injury. Punitive damages are not permitted under the MC.
6. Our maritime law developed out of the customs of ancient medieval ship owners, mariners, and merchants of the Mediterranean, and was adopted into maritime codes used in local courts in port cities. The most famous code is the *Rolls of Oleron*. Important principles of jettison, general average, salvage, maritime liens, the treatment of the ship's crew, all came from these early codes.
7. In the United States, maritime cases are heard in the admiralty jurisdiction of the federal district courts. Some admiralty cases are also heard in the state courts.
8. In most nations of the world, the *Hague Rules,* adopted in the United States as the *Carriage of Goods by Sea Act* (COGSA), govern the liability of a carrier for damage or loss to oceangoing goods.
9. COGSA provides many limitations on the liability of ship owners. The carrier's primary obligation is to use due diligence to provide a seaworthy ship at the beginning of the voyage. A vessel is seaworthy if it is reasonably fit to carry the cargo it has undertaken to carry on the intended journey. Carriers are generally not liable for damage to cargo resulting from errors in navigation, mismanagement of the ship, acts of god, acts of war or public enemies, labor strikes, damage resulting from saving lives at sea, inherent defects in the goods, or perils of the sea. Liability for damage due to fire aboard the ship is limited to fires caused by the actual fault of the ship's owner.
10. In the United States, COGSA also provides that carriers are not liable for amounts in excess of $500 "per package" or "customary freight unit" unless the shipper has indicates a higher amount on the bill of lading.
11. The *Rotterdam Rules,* a convention adopted in 2009, will change the rules of ocean carrier liability if it becomes law. An understanding of the current *Hague Rules* will be a good foundation for learning the *Rotterdam Rules.*
12. Maritime and marine insurance law is a complicated and specialized area of the law, with concepts dating back to the days of the ancient mariners. Under the law of general average, a carrier can assert a general average claim against the owners of cargo demanding that they (or their insurers) contribute to expenses incurred in saving a vessel from a common peril on the seas.

Key Terms

international carriage 152
special drawing rights 156
consignee 157
consignor 157
master air waybill 157
house air waybill 157
maritime law 159
salvage 159
jettison 159
seamen 159
longshoremen 159
admiralty jurisdiction 159
general maritime law 159
Rhodian law 159
maritime courts 159
maritime codes 160
Rolls of Oleron (*"Judgments of the Sea"*) 160
navigable waters 161
vessel 161
maritime tort 161
maritime contract 161
wharfage 162
stevedore 162
cargo 162
freight 162
ship 162
break-bulk 162
dry bulk ships 162
tanker 162
reefer ship 162
Himalaya clause 163
clean bill 163
seaworthy 164
containerized cargo 164
errors in navigation 164
peril of the sea 164
freight forwarder 169
forwarder's receipt 170
non-vessel operating common carrier (NVOCC) 170
open cargo policy 170
general average 171
particular average 172
perils clause 172
fortuitous losses 175

Questions and Case Problems

1. The plaintiff was traveling by air from Rome to Philadelphia. Being highly allergic to gluten, she had requested a gluten-free meal at the time she booked the flight. She again informed the flight attendant that she required a gluten-free meal. She was served a vegetarian meal, but it was not gluten-free. After taking a few bites she suffered an allergic reaction, developed hives, and had difficulty breathing. Was this a compensable accident under the *Montreal Convention*? The plaintiff contends she suffered post-traumatic stress disorder. May she recover damages for mental injury? *Schaefer-Condulmari v. U.S. Airways Group, LLC,* WL 4729882 (E.D.P.A. 2009).
2. The Plaintiff purchased a round-trip ticket on British Airways between London and Denver. Three days later she purchased a round-trip ticket on American Airlines between Denver and Washington, DC. During the flight between Denver and Washington, she was burned by dry ice accidentally given to her by a flight attendant. When booking her flights, the plaintiff had scheduled her connection in Denver so that her flight to Washington would depart within about three hours of her arrival from London, with as short a layover as possible. She had no reason to be in Denver on that day other than to make the plane connection. Plaintiff brought this action for damages more than two years after the flight. Should her case be dismissed? Does the *Montreal Convention's* two-year statute of limitations apply? *Robertson v. American Airlines, Inc.,* 401 F.3d 499 (D.C. Cir. 2005).
3. In 2004, Ellen Kruger was boarding a flight from San Francisco to Seattle, on her way home from Australia, when she was struck on the head with a backpack swung by another passenger. During the flight she became ill, vomited, and remained unconscious for much of the flight. She sued the airline for pain and suffering, emotional distress, and punitive damages. Her husband also sued for loss of consortium and companionship of his wife. United Airlines argued that these were not compensable damages under the *Montreal Convention.* Does the *Montreal Convention* specify what types of damages are recoverable or whether the husband may bring an action? How is this decided? *Kruger v. United Airlines, Inc.* 481 F. Supp. 2d 1005 (N.D. Cal. 2007.) How would this case be decided if the injuries were the result of the aircraft plunging into the middle of the Pacific Ocean?
4. Fishman shipped a container of boys' pants on a ship owned by Tropical. The container was lost at sea due to improper storage. The pants were packed into bundles

of 12 each and placed into what is known in the industry as a "big pack." A "big pack" is similar to a 4' × 4' pallet, partially enclosed in corrugated cardboard, with a base and cover made of plastic. The bill of lading stated, "1 × *40 ft. [container] STC [said to contain] 39 Big Pack Containing 27,908 units boy's pants."* Fishman maintains that Tropical is liable for an amount up to $500 for each of the 2,325 bundles. If the carrier is liable for up to $500 per "package," what is the limit of the carrier's liability? *Fishman & Tobin, Inc. v. Tropical Shipping & Const. Co., Ltd.*, 240 F.3d 956 (11th Cir. 2001).

5. Assume a passenger dies aboard an international flight, and that there was no defibrillator aboard the aircraft that might have been used to revive him. Do you think the failure to have a defibrillator is an event "external to the passenger?" Do you think it is an "unexpected or unusual" event? Would it make a difference if there was a legal requirement to have a defibrillator aboard, or that it was or was not industry practice to do so?
6. Sony Corp. packed a shipment of videocassette tapes into a 40-foot ocean container for transport to England. Sony put the tapes into 1,320 cardboard cartons, then strapped the cartons onto 52 wooden pallets. The pallets were put into one shipment container. The bill of lading stated "1 × 40 ft. container: 1,320 ctns. magnetic tape." The value of the tapes shown on the export certificate was $400,000. On loading, the ship's deck crane dropped the container 60 feet to a concrete deck. Sony claims it can recover the value of the tapes. The ship maintains that under COGSA its liability is limited to 52 pallets. How many "packages" were involved here and what do you think should be the outcome? *Sony Magnetic Products Inc. of America v. Merivienti O/Y*, 863 F.2d 1537 (11th Cir. 1989).
7. A shipper of fruits and vegetables delivered a refrigerated van of produce to the S.S. *Bayomon* at the port of Elizabeth, New Jersey, on September 22 for shipment to San Juan, Puerto Rico. The ship was supposed to sail that day but was unable to do so because of repairs needed to correct a boiler problem. The ship sailed on September 25 and arrived in Puerto Rico on September 27. A clause paramount incorporated COGSA into the bill of lading. Upon arrival in Puerto Rico, part of the produce was found to be rotten. The shipper claims that the carrier is liable because the ship was not "seaworthy." COGSA states that the carrier shall not be liable unless it shows a failure to make the ship seaworthy before and at the beginning of the voyage. Does COGSA apply here, considering that the port is domestic rather than foreign? Is the carrier liable for an unseaworthy vessel? What is the outcome? *Squillante & Zimmerman Sales, Inc. v. Puerto Rico Marine Management, Inc.*, 516 F. Supp. 1049 (D.Puerto Rico 1981).
8. Three judgments of the *Rolls of Oleron* appear in this chapter. Early ship owners, mariners, and merchants found it necessary for all parties aboard ship to share in the risks of the voyage. Explain how these judgments accomplished that.

Managerial Implications

1. Reconsider the hypothetical case presented earlier in this chapter involving the shipment of English antiques to the United States. Do you think that the $500 per package limitation applies to the container, to each wooden skid, or to each of the individually wrapped pieces of furniture or objects fastened onto the skid? What could have been done differently, if anything, to avoid the confusion and problems in this case? Discuss the ramifications of this case.
2. You are CEO of a firm that regularly imports consumer electronic devices from plants in Thailand, Malaysia, Indonesia, and the Philippines. The devices are shipped to you by ocean carrier through the South China Sea and then are sold in the United States and exported to ports in Europe and the Middle East. What kind of information do you need to assess the potential risk to your cargo passing through the dangerous waters of the South China Sea? From what sources will you receive your information? What sources are available in your library? Which are commercially available? If part of your job is to keep abreast of developments on a daily basis, where will you obtain that information? What types of information might be available from freight forwarders, steamship companies, local port authorities, and insurers?

Ethical Considerations

O. L. Salt had a long career in the merchant trade of the western hemisphere, running voyage charters in old tramp freighters and hauling whatever cargo came his way. He had since retired, living on a houseboat south of Miami when he decided to return to the sea. He acquired an old rust-bucket tanker, the *Q. Anne's Revenge II*, from an acquaintance in Panama who found the old ship no longer worth the upkeep. But she would do for hauling small cargos of crude oil. O. L. Salt contracted with an oil trader in Venezuela to haul 40,000 tons of crude oil, worth $28 million, to a buyer in Houston. All went well, until a few days out from port when the ship's engines apparently gave in under the strain. Sailors on a passing container ship reported seeing fire on the *Q. Anne Revenge II*, as they watched her disappear into thousands of feet of water near the Cayman Trench in the Caribbean Sea. Those observing reported that the ship had been setting low in the water, appropriate for a tanker with a full load of cargo. Fortunately, Salt and his Jamaican crew were found dry and safe, suitcases in hand, in a Jamaican hotel. They had lost all else, even the ship's log. Luckily for the environment, hardly a trace of an oil spill could be found. The owner of the cargo filed a cargo insurance claim. Salt filed a hull and machinery claim with his insurer for the loss of the *Q. Anne's Revenge II*, a loss that would surely end his long career. O. L. Salt had had enough of old ships and the sea, so he left Miami, and retired to a Greek island.

A few days later a marine publication reported that an old tramp vessel, sailing under the name *Corfu Sunset*, and flying a Liberian flag of convenience, had been seen entering a Cuban harbor near a refinery there. The reporter who covers maritime news noted that the owner of the cargo surely received a sum well in excess of the market price of oil from Cuba's communist government. After all, Cuba is under a U.S. embargo, its attempts at deep sea oil drilling have failed, and the Russians no longer send them oil.

What happened? Can you speculate on some of the details? Bonus points: What hidden clues are given in the case? While this is not a true story, it is based on many true stories that are not all that uncommon in the maritime trade. If you are still not clear as to what happened, consider the case of the supertanker, *Salem*, lost at sea in 1980. Conduct some research on the issues presented here. Find out what sources of information are available. Identify the extent of the problems as they exist in the maritime trade, and find out what is being done to deal with them. Consider beginning your research with the *International Maritime Bureau* of the International Chamber of Commerce.

CHAPTER 7

Bank Collections, Trade Finance, and Letters of Credit

The previous chapters include discussions of contracts for the sale of goods, documentary sales, the risk of loss, and the liability of air and sea carriers. This chapter now turns the use of the international banking system to move money in an international trade transaction. We will see how sellers collect for their shipments and how buyers remit payments for their purchases. We will also learn how sellers are assured of payment for their goods or services through the use of bank letters of credit and will briefly discuss some issues related to financing the sale. Keep in mind that most of the concepts covered here do not just apply to collecting money for the sale of goods but are equally applicable to many different types of international transactions involving the movement of money internationally and the use of banks to provide an assurance of contractual commitments.

THE BILL OF EXCHANGE

An understanding of how international payments or movements of money are made to fulfill contract obligations requires some basic understanding of the law of negotiable instruments. In general, courses on business law cover the law of negotiable instruments. For our purposes, we assume you have some limited understanding of this field. Our concern here is not with their technical requirements, but with their use in international trade. A **negotiable instrument** is a signed writing, containing an unconditional promise or order to pay a fixed sum of money, to order or to bearer, on demand or at a definite time. Common negotiable instruments include promissory notes, which are two-party instruments containing a promise to pay, and drafts, which are three-party instruments containing orders to pay. In this chapter, our concern is only with drafts. A **draft** is the signed order of the drawer, given to a drawee who is in possession of money to which the drawer is entitled, to pay a sum of money to a third party, the payee, on demand or at a definite time. A common *check* is a special form of draft, which is drawn on a bank and payable on demand. The three parties to a check include the drawer, who gave the order to pay, the drawee bank to whom the order to pay is given, and the payee. The **bill of exchange** is a specialized type of international draft commonly used to expedite foreign money payments in many types of international transactions. A **documentary draft** is used to expedite payment in a documentary sale. The word *draft* is more frequently in use in U.S. law and banking practice, while the term *bill of exchange* is more frequently in use outside the United States, particularly in England. Generally, we use the term *draft* in this text except when referring specifically to an English bill of exchange. These negotiable instruments can serve two purposes: (1) they act as a substitute for money and (2) they act as a financing or credit device.

Although it is beyond the scope of this text to offer a thorough treatment of the law of negotiable instruments, an understanding of the importance of the draft is essential to anyone engaging in international trade.

The Origin of Bills of Exchange

The origin of the bill of exchange lies in the history of the merchants and traders of fourteenth- and fifteenth-century Europe. Merchants visiting the markets of distant cities to buy and sell their wares sought a safer means of transferring their gold or money than carrying it in their caravans. It might have worked like this: Assume Merchant A delivers goods in a distant city to Merchant B, who becomes indebted to A for the amount of the purchase. Later Merchant A desires to purchase goods from Merchant C. Merchant A can pay Merchant C for the goods with a written piece of paper—an order-addressed by A to B to pay that money to C. Assume further that Merchant B is wealthy and respected in the trade—one whose credit is highly regarded. Merchant C can present the written order to B for payment immediately, or should he wish, he can simply ask B to sign (or "accept") the order for future payment. Thus, the written order to pay becomes an *acceptance.* With the acceptance in hand, Merchant C can purchase new wares from yet another merchant and use the acceptance in payment. Eventually, merchants turned to wealthy families, Italian banking societies, or medieval bankers spread throughout Europe to transfer money over great distances by issuing payment orders to their correspondents living in distant cities. As merchants recognized that these orders could be bought and sold, the concept of negotiability evolved and negotiable instruments were born. At first, English law did not recognize the validity of negotiable instruments. But merchants accepted them as substitutes for money, and they were enforceable in the merchant's private courts under the Law Merchant. As their importance and use evolved, so did their validity and treatment under the law. They became formally recognized by statute in England in 1822 in the *English Bills of Exchange Act* and in the United States in 1866 in the *Uniform Negotiable Instruments Law.*

In the United States today, the *Uniform Commercial Code* (UCC) governs bills of exchange or drafts, while the *Bills of Exchange Act* governs in England, and the 1930 *Convention Providing for a Uniform Law for Bills of Exchange and Promissory Notes* governs in more than 25 other countries. Despite their common history, these laws differ in their treatment of the creation and transfer of negotiable instruments, as well as in the rights of the parties should an instrument be dishonored or refused.

Brief Requirements of a Bill of Exchange

The English *Bills of Exchange Act* requires that a bill of exchange be: (1) an unconditional order in writing, (2) addressed by one person to another, (3) signed by the person giving it, (4) with a requirement that the person to whom it is addressed pay on demand or at a fixed or determinable future time, (5) a sum certain in money, and (6) to or *to the order of* a specified person, or to bearer. These characteristics are similar to the requirements for a draft set out in the UCC. (The *Convention on Bills of Exchange* requires that the words "bill of exchange" appear on the instrument, but English and U.S. laws do not.)

Basically, a bill of exchange or international draft is similar to a check, in that it is an unconditional order to pay a sum of money. (Drafts can be made payable in any currency.) In the case of a check, the **drawer** orders its bank, the **drawee,** to pay the amount of the check to the **payee.** However, instead of being drawn against funds held on deposit in a bank (as with a check), an international draft is an order from the seller to the buyer or buyer's bank to pay the seller upon the delivery of goods or the presentation of shipping documents (e.g., an ocean bill of lading or air waybill). Thus, the seller is both the drawer (the one giving the order to pay) and the payee (the one entitled to payment under the instrument). The drawee is either the buyer or its bank, depending on the arrangements made for payment.

Negotiation and Transfer of Negotiable Instruments. The commercial use of a draft or other negotiable instrument is derived from its negotiability, the quality that allows it to act as a substitute for money. **Negotiation** is the transfer of an instrument from one party to another so that the transferee (called a *holder*) takes legal rights in the instrument. The correct manner of negotiation depends on whether the instrument is a bearer or order instrument. Most drafts used in international trade are order instruments because they are payable to a named payee. To negotiate an order instrument, **indorsement** (by signature) **and delivery** of the instrument to the holder must take place. References to the negotiation of international drafts appear throughout this chapter.

The Documentary Draft and the Bank Collection Process

Drafts come in several different types. A draft that is to be paid upon presentation or demand is known as a **sight draft** because it is payable "on sight." The seller prepares the sight draft and sends it to the buyer along with the shipping documents (e.g., the bill of lading) through banking channels, moving from the seller's bank in the country of export to a foreign correspondent bank in the buyer's country and city. The draft is sent "for collection," known as a **documentary collection.** The banks act as agents of the seller for collection purposes. A *collection letter* that provides instructions from the seller on such matters as who is responsible for bank collection charges, what to do in the event the buyer dishonors the draft, and how the proceeds are to be remitted to the seller, accompany the draft and documents. Thus, the collection letter may specify that in the event of the buyer's dishonor of the draft, the seller's agent in the buyer's country is to be notified, and that the goods are to be properly warehoused and insured pending resolution of the problem or sale of the goods to another party.

Essentially, documentary collections function like a cash-on-delivery (COD) transaction. When the buyer receives the sight draft at its bank or place of business, the draft is paid, and the payment is remitted to the seller. Only then does the bank turn over the shipping documents with which the buyer can claim its cargo from the carrier. The transaction is somewhat risky, however, because when presented with documents, there is no guarantee that the buyer will actually pay. Assuming the buyer does pay, the average cycle for completing a documentary collection is approximately three weeks (although most banks offer accelerated schedules). If a sales contract between buyer and seller calls for payment upon presentation of a sight draft, the contract terms commonly call for *cash against documents.* (See Chapter Five for a discussion of sales contracts with documentary payment terms.)

The Swift System. The **Society for Worldwide Interbank Financial Telecommunication**, an industry-owned cooperative commonly known as the SWIFT network, is a high-speed communications network between banks, set up to transfer funds worldwide. It originated through the cooperative efforts of major banks in Europe, the United States, and Canada in the mid-1970s, and it is used by 9,000 institutions throughout the world. It has largely replaced the use of telex and mail-in fund transfers. In fact, the SWIFT network transmits most international letters of credit. It is cost-effective and has greatly expedited the remission of payments in a documentary collection.

In 1998, SWIFT and the TT Club (the international transport and logistics industry's leading provider of insurance and risk management services) created a joint venture to market and support the *Bolero Project.* Bolero seeks to replace the paper-based transfer of trade documents with electronic transmissions on a global scale.

Documentary Drafts Used in Trade Finance

Banks and other financial institutions involved in commercial lending provide a wide range of financing packages for international trade, commonly called **trade finance.** Trade finance not only assists the buyer in financing its purchase but also provides immediate cash to the seller for the sale and is profitable for the lending institution.

The documentary draft can serve as an important financing or credit device, providing the seller and buyer with a mechanism for financing the international sale. In a competitive marketplace, an exporter must be able to offer its customers credit or other financing for their purchases. Many firms consider their ability to arrange credit a crucial component of their marketing strategies. If an exporter can prearrange financing for the buyer, it has an advantage over a competitor who cannot.

The Use of Time Drafts and Acceptances. The use of the draft in trade finance works like this: Seller agrees to issue a draft that is due, say, 60 days after shipment of the goods. The draft states that it is due in 60 days or on a future date specified on the instrument. A draft due at a future date or after a specified period is known as a **time draft**, as shown in Exhibit 7.1. The time draft is sent to the buyer for its **acceptance.** Typically, acceptance is done by stamping the date and the word "accepted" across the face of the draft, together with the name and signature of the drawee, because no party is obligated on a draft unless its signature appears on it. Under the UCC, the acceptance "may consist of the drawee's signature alone." The buyer has thus created a *trade acceptance.* The buyer's acceptance indicates the buyer's unconditional obligation to pay the draft on the date due. A draft payable at "60 days after date" is payable by the drawee 60 days after the original date of the instrument. A draft payable at "60 days sight" means that it is due to be paid 60 days after the date of the acceptance.

As with a sight draft, a seller usually sends the time draft together with the shipping documents to the buyer through banking channels with instructions to the banks that the shipping documents should be handed over to the buyer only upon acceptance of the draft. The sales contract would have indicated the parties' agreement to this arrangement by calling for "documents against acceptance," or other clear language of similar meaning. After acceptance, the draft is returned through banking channels to the seller. The seller can then hold the draft to maturity or sell it at a discount to a local bank or commercial lending institution for immediate cash. The commercial lender takes the acceptance by negotiation. The greater the creditworthiness of the buyer, the greater the marketability of the trade acceptance. Where the foreign buyer is unquestionably creditworthy, such as a major multinational corporation, the trade acceptance carries little risk and is easily saleable.

Exhibit 7.1

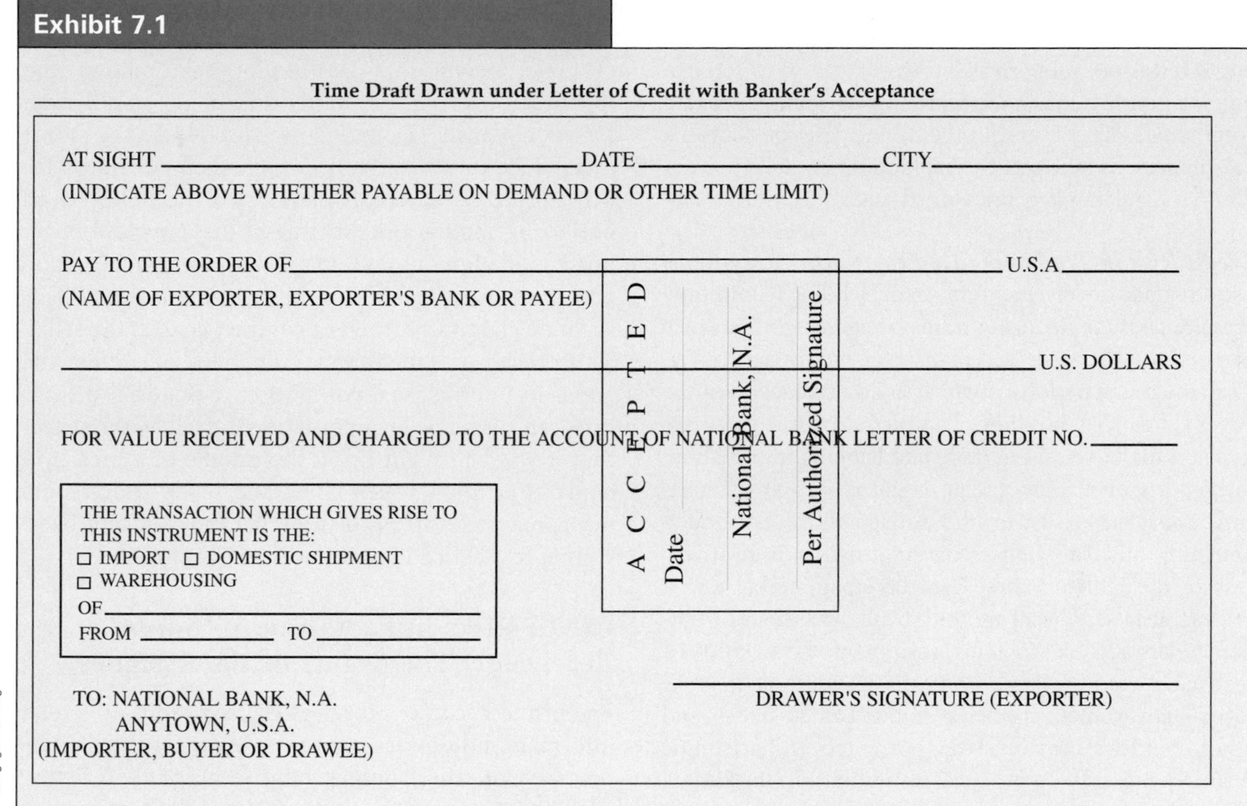

Time Draft Drawn under Letter of Credit with Banker's Acceptance

AT SIGHT ______ DATE ______ CITY ______
(INDICATE ABOVE WHETHER PAYABLE ON DEMAND OR OTHER TIME LIMIT)

PAY TO THE ORDER OF ______ U.S.A ______
(NAME OF EXPORTER, EXPORTER'S BANK OR PAYEE)

______ U.S. DOLLARS

FOR VALUE RECEIVED AND CHARGED TO THE ACCOUNT OF NATIONAL BANK LETTER OF CREDIT NO. ______

THE TRANSACTION WHICH GIVES RISE TO
THIS INSTRUMENT IS THE:
☐ IMPORT ☐ DOMESTIC SHIPMENT
☐ WAREHOUSING
OF ______
FROM ______ TO ______

ACCEPTED
Date
National Bank, N.A.
Per Authorized Signature

TO: NATIONAL BANK, N.A.
ANYTOWN, U.S.A.
(IMPORTER, BUYER OR DRAWEE)

______
DRAWER'S SIGNATURE (EXPORTER)

Banker's Acceptances and Acceptance Financing. A **banker's acceptance** is a negotiable instrument and short-term financing device in wide use to finance international (as well as domestic) sales. The purpose of an acceptance is to substitute a bank's credit for that of the buyer to finance the sale. A banker's acceptance is a time draft drawn on and accepted by a commercial bank. The bank stamps its name, date, and signature on the face of the draft to create the acceptance and thereby becomes obligated to pay the amount stated to the holder of the instrument on the date specified. The holder of the acceptance can convert it to cash immediately at a discounted rate or hold it until it matures.

Banker's acceptances are flexible instruments, with many creative uses. Either a buyer's or a seller's bank can handle the acceptance. Importing buyers can use a banker's acceptance for short-term borrowing until they can resell and liquidate the goods being purchased. Sellers to export markets can use a banker's acceptance for short-term, pre-export financing of raw materials and production costs until the goods are sold to the foreign customer and payment is received. Exporters can also use acceptances to grant credit terms to foreign customers. For instance, in a sale on open account, an exporter might draw a time draft on its own bank for the amount of its overseas sale. The exporter's bank accepts the draft, the discounted amount is paid to the exporter, and the acceptance is negotiated and discounted in the credit markets. When the importer pays the invoice amount to the exporter, the proceeds are used to satisfy the acceptance at maturity. In another arrangement, the exporter's draft may be accepted by the importer's bank, and then discounted in the credit markets. In any case, the acceptance is satisfied at maturity through the proceeds of the sale.

In essence, the acceptance financing is self-liquidating because repayment is made from the underlying sales transaction, using credit market monies to finance business. The bank charges the borrower a commission and the discount rate for acceptance financing, which is usually deducted from the face amount of the acceptance when paid to the borrower. Depending on market conditions, acceptance financing is often cheaper for companies than regular credit borrowing.

Banker's acceptances are generally short-term instruments because they must be for a period of six months or less. An eligible banker's acceptance is one that qualifies for discount at the U.S. Federal Reserve Bank, which will buy it if it is not sold privately. Acceptances thus serve to finance international trade with outside capital. Because commercial banks create them, the use of banker's acceptances is subject to banking laws and Federal Reserve regulations in the United States.

Credit Risk in Trade Finance Programs. Institutions with regular involvement in trade lending commonly prearrange these financing terms by agreeing in advance to purchase the trade acceptances of the foreign buyer. They must first perform an analysis and evaluation of the buyer's financial position. Thorough credit checks are done on the buyer, using trade and banking information, the reports of U.S. or foreign credit reporting agencies, and even site visits to the foreign firm. (Although obtaining and verifying credit information is relatively easy in the United States, Canada, Japan, and Western Europe, it is somewhat more difficult, and the information is less reliable, in other regions of the world.) To reduce the credit risk and lower the cost of trade finance, several government agencies in the United States and other countries provide credit guarantees to back trade finance lending by commercial institutions. In the United States, these agencies include Eximbank, the Commodity Credit Corporation, and the Agency for International Development (discussed later in this chapter).

Credit Risk in Acceptance Financing: Rights of the Holder in Due Course. One of the primary reasons for the popularity of the acceptance as a financing device is the protection it provides to the financial institution or other party who purchases it, provided that party is a holder in due course. The UCC spells out the detailed requirements to become a holder in due course. A **holder in due course** is a holder in possession of a negotiable instrument (such as a draft or acceptance) that has been taken: (1) for value, (2) in good faith, (3) without notice that it is overdue or has been dishonored, and (4) without notice that the instrument contains an unauthorized signature or has been altered (UCC 3-302). If all of the requirements for transferring a negotiable instrument are met and the transferee qualifies as a holder in due course, the transferee can take greater rights in the instrument than the transferor had.

According to the *holder in due course rule,* the purchaser of an acceptance, or any negotiable instrument, takes it free from most disputes that might arise between the drawer and drawee—the original parties to the underlying transaction. The most common type of dispute that might arise is breach of contract. For example, assume that DownPillow sells pillows to a Japanese buyer and forwards documents and a draft for acceptance. DownPillow discounts the trade acceptance to a U.S. bank, which then discounts the instrument in the credit markets. If the pillows turn out to be moldy and worthless, the Japanese buyer must still honor and pay the acceptance upon presentation in Japan. The buyer may then assert its separate claim for breach of contract against the seller. This rule ensures the free transferability of commercial paper in international commerce. A financial institution can discount an international draft without fear that it will be caught up in the middle of a breach of contract action between buyer and seller. If drafts did not come with this protection, banks might not be so willing to finance international sales.

Credit Risks in Factoring Accounts Receivable: The Rights of the Assignee

As firms become more globalized and as credit information becomes more widely available, many firms are offering open account terms to their better, long-term foreign customers. These sellers are giving their customers an open credit period, typically from 30 days to several months, to pay for goods received. However, companies engaged in exporting products are not in business to loan money. Thus, banks are providing open account trade finance services, including the factoring of foreign accounts receivable.

An account receivable is no more than a representation of a *contract right* belonging to the seller—the right to collect money owed by the buyer under the contract for goods shipped. Contract rights can be assigned to another party. In a typical financing arrangement, the seller (assignor) assigns its right to collect the account to the financial institution (assignee). This is also called *factoring,* and the assignee is sometimes called the *factor*. Under basic contract law, the assignee "steps into the shoes" of the assignor and acquires only those rights under the contract that the assignor had against the other party to the contract (e.g., the buyer of the goods).

Take the following example: Assume that DownPillow ships an ocean container of pillows to Japan and factors the account receivable with a U.S. bank (the assignee). DownPillow now has its money and the bank is awaiting payment directly from Japan. (Of course, it is important for the Japanese buyer to be notified of the assignment and instructed to pay only the assignee bank.) If a dispute later breaks out over the quality of the pillows, the Japanese buyer may legally assert any claims and defenses against collection by the bank that it otherwise would have had against DownPillow. Thus, for example, the buyer can successfully argue that it does not have to pay the bank because of the breach of warranty by DownPillow. DownPillow must repay the bank for money it receives and resolve the breach of contract suit with the buyer. For this reason, banker's acceptance financing offers some advantages over accounts receivable financing. Unlike a factor, the rule protects a holder in due course of a banker's acceptance. Thus, the fact that the products are defective does not provide a defense against payment to one liable on the negotiable instrument. Some insurance companies today offer commercial *credit insurance* to protect against accounts receivable that become uncollectible bad debts.

THE LETTER OF CREDIT

We will devote considerable attention to letters of credit issued by commercial banks. These flexible banking instruments are in wide use around the world. As much as $1 trillion in goods is purchased worldwide by letter of credit every year, according to most banking and government sources. In broad terms, we can say that a **letter of credit** is an obligation of a bank, usually irrevocable, issued on behalf of one of its customers and promising to pay a sum of money to a beneficiary upon the happening of a certain event or events. In a sense, it is the substitution of the credit and good name of a bank for that of its customer, permitting the customer to do business with other individuals or firms on terms that otherwise might not be available to them. Letters of credit can be either domestic or international. They can be used in transactions for the sale of goods or services or to guarantee performance of other business obligations. Evidence exists that early forms of letters of credit were in use in Renaissance Europe and in ancient Greece and Egypt. Today, almost all large banks can issue a letter of credit, although in practice a small fraction of the world's largest banks located in major banking centers of the world issue most of them. In this chapter we discuss two types of letters of credit: the international documentary letter of credit for use in the sale of goods and the standby letter of credit for guaranteeing performance or payment obligations of a bank's customer.

The Documentary Letter of Credit

Suppose that you are an American manufacturer and a buyer in a foreign country approaches you. The buyer makes initial inquiries about your products, engineering and manufacturing capabilities, and installation and service after the sale. You do some informal background checking within the industry and determine that this is a serious customer. You receive its credit statement, containing banking and trade references. You may even obtain a credit report on the buyer. You learn that the buyer has been in business for relatively few years, so you are not willing to enter the sale without some security. After all, you would be manufacturing these goods to conform to their specifications and shipping them halfway around the world on the basis of their promise to take delivery and remit payment. In earlier chapters we studied some of your options. The risk is too great to ship the goods on 30-day open account terms and hope for your money, and if you demand cash in advance the customer is not likely to agree. After all, the buyer may not trust you any more than you trust the buyer.

You could use a documentary sale, quoting prices to the customer as "cash against documents," but even then you may never see payment. If you send the documents to the buyer's bank for collection, it is still possible for the buyer to avoid the transaction. The buyer might not be able to pay, may have changed his or her mind, or may even have gone out of business. It is often possible for the buyer to find the same goods for less from another supplier. While probably not an issue in our hypothetical instance, in cases where substitute goods are freely available (and that might include everything from agricultural commodities to computer chips), a buyer might look for a way out of a contract where there has been a sharp decline in market prices. In any event, your customer could simply disappear, leaving the bank with documents to be returned to you and leaving you with specially manufactured goods in a customs warehouse halfway around the world. Unless you can find another foreign customer, which may be unlikely, you must pay the freight costs of returning the goods to your plant. To add a level of security to the documentary sale, you might propose contract terms calling for the buyer to provide an irrevocable, documentary letter of credit issued by a bank and addressed to you. This substitutes the credit and good name of a bank for that of the buyer and is a fairly good assurance (although nothing is absolute) that if you do your part that will be paid, and paid quickly.

A letter of credit would have another advantage to you in this example. If you ship goods to your customer on open account, you may have to wait several weeks or months to receive your money. By using a letter of credit, you will probably receive payment within a few days. Moreover, because the letter of credit is so secure, it can serve as security, or collateral, for you to obtain a short-term loan to help finance the purchase of materials for manufacturing or other start-up costs.

The Parties to the Transaction. A buyer that has committed in the sales contract to obtain a letter of credit begins by applying to its bank for a letter of credit issued "in favor of" or "for the benefit of" the seller. In this arrangement, the buyer is known as the **account party**, the buyer's bank is the **issuing bank**, or **issuer**, and the seller is the **beneficiary.** Exhibit 7.2 illustrates a typical documentary sale with a letter of credit.

Documentary Letter of Credit Defined. The **documentary letter of credit** is defined as:

1. The definite undertaking of a bank,
2. issued in accordance with the instructions of their customer,
3. addressed to, or in favor of, the beneficiary,
4. wherein the bank promises to pay a certain sum of money (or to accept or negotiate the beneficiary's drafts up to that sum) in the stated currency,
5. within the prescribed time limits,
6. upon the complying presentation,
7. of the required and conforming documents.

The requirement that the bank will pay the seller only on the presentation of documents is what gives the documentary credit its name. The documents might differ greatly depending on whether the transaction is a domestic or an international one, the needs of the parties, or the method for shipping the goods. Letters of credit can be used for many different types of shipments, including ocean, air, rail, and road shipments, and with multimodal freight. In reality, they can be used with almost any type of document, from simple invoices to postal receipts. However, we are limiting our discussion to letter of credit transactions involving ocean transport, where the most common documents required by the letter of credit are the ocean bill of lading, the commercial invoice, and the marine insurance policy.

Throughout this chapter, we use the terms "letter of credit," "credit," or "documentary credit" interchangeably, although the latter refers only to credits payable on the presentation of documents.

The Legal Status of the Letter of Credit. There has long been an academic argument over whether or not the letter of credit is a contract between the issuing bank and the beneficiary. The letter of credit does act like a promise from an issuing bank to a beneficiary, and it seems to be treated at times like a contract and discussed in terms of the principles of contract law. However, the general consensus is that it is not a contract. If you recall the requirements for a contact, a letter of credit does not come about through offer and acceptance or mutual assent, nor is there any requirement for consideration. The basic requirements of a contract are missing. The bank and the beneficiary do not negotiate about anything; in fact, they usually have no contact whatsoever. The letter of credit is not a negotiable instrument, like a check or a promissory note. Nor is it a third-party beneficiary contract because the beneficiary's rights do not derive from the contract between the buyer/account party and its bank. The letter of credit is a legal animal all of its own species; it is created by statute. It gives the beneficiary a statutory right to enforce the letter of credit against the bank that issues it, rather a contract right. Moreover, both the UCC and banking customs refer to the letter of credit not as a contract, but as a "definite undertaking."

Law Applicable to Letters of Credit

All legal systems of the world recognize letters of credit. In the United States, Article 5 (2003 revision) of the *Uniform Commercial Code* codifies the law governing letters of credit. In addition, in some states, notably New York, letters of credit are responsible for a great body of case law. Perhaps the most important rules affecting letters of credit are not laws at all, but a privately developed set of guidelines based on the customs and commonly accepted practices of merchants and bankers, known as the **Uniform Customs and Practice for Documentary Credits**.

The Uniform Customs and Practice for Documentary Credits. The *Uniform Customs and Practice for Documentary Credits* (UCP) is a document that international bankers know well. It is a set of standardized rules for issuing and handling letters of credit that the International Chamber of Commerce (which publishes *Incoterms,* covered in Chapter Five) drafts and

Exhibit 7.2

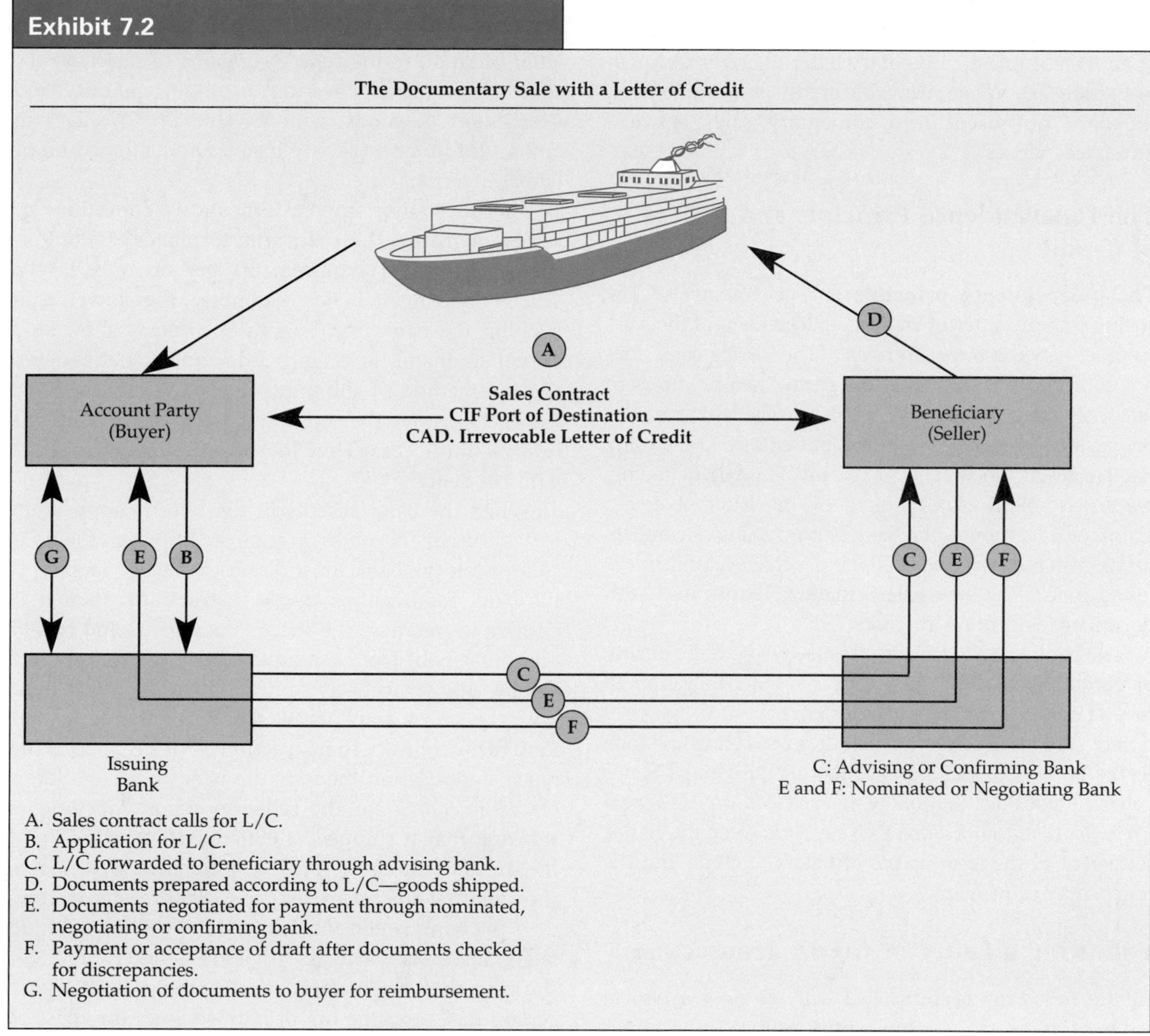
The Documentary Sale with a Letter of Credit
A
D
Account Party
(Buyer)
Sales Contract
CIF Port of Destination
CAD. Irrevocable Letter of Credit
Beneficiary
(Seller)
G
E
B
C
E
F
C
E
F
Issuing
Bank
C: Advising or Confirming Bank
E and F: Nominated or Negotiating Bank
A. Sales contract calls for L/C.
B. Application for L/C.
C. L/C forwarded to beneficiary through advising bank.
D. Documents prepared according to L/C—goods shipped.
E. Documents negotiated for payment through nominated, negotiating or confirming bank.
F. Payment or acceptance of draft after documents checked for discrepancies.
G. Negotiation of documents to buyer for reimbursement.

publishes with the assistance of the international banking community. The UCP establishes the format for letters of credit, sets out rules by which banks process letter of credit transactions, and defines the rights and responsibilities of all parties to the credit. Because banks were the main drafters of the UCP, its provisions tend to protect their rights in any transaction. The UCP was first introduced in the early 1930s, with the latest revision (UCP 600) becoming effective in 2007. The UCP is in use in virtually every nation of the world and applies to most letters of credit issued worldwide.

The International Chamber of Commerce is not a government or lawmaking body, and the UCP is not law. The UCP "governs" a letter of credit only to the extent that it states that the letter of credit is to be "interpreted" according to the UCP (which almost all do). Judges use the UCP in deciding letter of credit cases, and references to the UCP appear in virtually every reported decision on international letters of credit. The *Uniform Commercial Code,* Article 5 (2003 revision), now defers to the UCP and specifically states that the UCC is *not* applicable to any letter of credit to the extent that it is in conflict with the UCP. As a result, the UCP has a far greater impact on the law of international letters of credit than does the *Uniform Commercial Code.*

Irrevocability of Letters of Credit. Letters of credit issued under UCP 600 are presumed irrevocable unless clear language is used to make them revocable.

Nevertheless, most sales contracts recite that the buyer's letter of credit is to be irrevocable. An example of an irrevocable documentary letter of credit is shown in Exhibit 7.3. While revocable credits have some uses, they are not used in documentary sales between unrelated parties.

The Independence Principle and Letters of Credit

The **independence principle** is a general rule of law stating that the letter of credit is independent of the sales contract between buyer and seller. The issuing bank does not concern itself with what the parties had promised to do, or should do, under their contract. The issuing bank's only concern is that the buyer presents to the issuing bank certain "documents" (i.e., invoice, bill of lading, insurance policy, etc.) required by the letter of credit. Think of it as though the bank is purchasing documents for its customer, not goods. The independence principle is found in UCP 600, Article 5, stating, "Banks deal with documents and not with goods … "

The banks do not concern themselves with the quality or condition of the goods. They have no obligation to inspect goods or to investigate rumors about them. They do not care if the ship on which they are sailing has gone to the bottom of the sea. Scholars in the United States generally consider the following case, *Maurice O'Meara Co. v. National Park Bank of New York*, to be the classic statement of the legal nature of letters of credit and the independence principle.

Following a Letter of Credit Transaction

In the following sections, we will see how a typical letter of credit transaction works. Some of the topics include the contract between the buyer and the buyer's bank to issue a letter of credit, what the seller should do when the letter of credit arrives, rules for the seller to follow in presenting documents for payment, and the process by which the bank inspects documents and honors or dishonors the seller's request for payment.

The Buyer's Application and Contract with the Issuing Bank. Once the buyer has finalized a sales contract calling for payment to the seller under a letter of credit, it is up to the buyer to apply for that letter of credit at a bank. The application for the credit, usually done on the bank's form and accompanied by an initial fee, contains the buyer's instructions and conditions upon which the issuing bank may honor the seller's documents. These instructions are based on the details of the original sales contract between buyer and seller. The application requests the bank to issue a letter of credit to the seller promising to purchase the seller's documents covering a certain quantity and description of goods, with a value up to a certain amount of money, that are insured and shipped on or before a certain date.

The buyer may impose almost any conditions or requirements on the seller's performance, as long as the conditions or requirements pertain only to the seller's documents. For example, the buyer can prohibit the bank from taking documents showing a partial shipment, or require a document that shows a specific method of shipping, or even name a specific vessel. However, the buyer must remember that this information is based on the buyer's final agreement with the seller.

When the bank accepts it, the buyer's application for the credit becomes a contract between them. It states what the bank must do on the buyer's behalf. If the bank follows the buyer's instructions, then it is entitled to purchase the seller's documents and obtain reimbursement from the buyer. If it does not, or if it violates any terms of its contract, then the buyer need not take the documents or reimburse the bank that took them contrary to instructions. For instance, if the buyer's application requests the bank to issue a letter of credit calling for the seller to submit documents showing that it shipped "1,000 electric toasters," and the bank, without approval, purchases documents showing that the seller shipped "1,000 toaster ovens," then the bank is not entitled to reimbursement. If the buyer instructs the bank to issue a letter of credit showing that the toasters must ship on or before a certain date, and the bill of lading shows the toasters were shipped after that date, the bank is not entitled to reimbursement. Indeed, banking lore is filled with stories of banks getting "stuck" with cargo like this. So (we say only half-jokingly), the next time you are in your bank and you see a sign offering a free toaster oven to anyone opening a new account, you might think of this example and wonder whether it was a marketing decision or a way to unload unwanted cargo. If you choose a career in banking, you might want to remember that banks deal with money and documents. They do not like to deal in goods or to be stuck with them.

The buyer may not make any demands on the issuing bank that are not related to the seller's documents. For example, the application may not attempt to require the bank to inspect goods or to

Exhibit 7.3

Irrevocable Documentary Letter of Credit

IMPORTER'S BANK
CONFIRMATION OF BRIEF CABLE

Irrevocable
Documentary Letter of Credit

Importer's Bank	Date of Issue	
Charlotte, NC	February 1, 2013	
	Issuing Bank Letter of Credit No.	Advising Bank Letter of Credit No.
	78346	

Advising Bank	Applicant
German Bank F.R.G.	Downpillow, Inc. North Carolina

Beneficiary	Expiratory Date (For Negotiation)		
	Day	Month	Year
Federhaus, GIN F.R.G.	30	April	2013

Currency	Amount	
U.S.A.	35,00000	Thirty-Five Thousand Dollars

Gentlemen:
We hereby issue this documentary Letter of Credit in your favor which is available against your draft at sight drawn on Importer's Bank, Charlotte, North Carolina for 100% of the invoice value bearing the clause "Drawn under documentary letter of Credit Number 78346" Accompanied by the following documents:

1. Commercial invoice in triplicate
2. U.S. special customs form #1111 in triplicate
3. Insurance policy/certificate in duplicate covering all risks
4. Certificate of origin "form A" in duplicate
5. Full set 3/3 clean on-board bills of lading issued to the order of Importer's bank, marked "Freight prepaid," notify applicant.

Purporting to cover: 3000 lbs washed white goose down in machine compressed bales, CIF Norfolk, Va.

Shipment from	Partial Shipments	Transshipments
F.R.G. To Norfolk, Va	Prohibited	Prohibited

Special conditions

Documents must be presented to negotiating bank within 10 days of issuance of shipping documents but within the validity of the credit.
Latest ship date March 15, 2013.

Negotiating bank is authorized to forward all documents to us via airmail. All banking charges outside the United States are for account of the beneficiary.

We hereby engage with the bona fide holders of all drafts under and in compliance with the terms of this letter of credit that such drafts will be duly honored upon presentation to us. The amount of each drawing must be indorsed on the reverse side of this letter of credit by the negotiating bank.

B. G. DeWoolfson
Authorized Signature

Indications of the Advising Bank

Place, Date, Name, and Signature of the Advising Bank

Except so far as otherwise expressly stated this documentary letter of credit is subject to the Uniform Customs and Practices for Documentary Credits (1993 Revision) the International Chamber of Commerce Document No. 500.

Maurice O'Meara Co. v. National Park Bank of New York

146 N.E. 636 (1925) Court of Appeals of New York

BACKGROUND AND FACTS

National Park Bank issued a letter of credit addressed to Ronconi & Millar, beneficiary, at the request of its account party, Sun Herald, "covering the shipment of 1,322 tons of newsprint paper in 72½-inch and 36½-inch rolls to test 11-12, 32 lbs. at 8½ cents per pound net weight—delivery to be made in December 1920 and January 1921." The letter of credit did not require that a testing certificate from an independent laboratory accompany the documents. When Ronconi & Millar's invoice and draft were presented to the bank, the documents described the paper as was required in the letter of credit. However, the bank refused payment because it had no opportunity to test the tensile strength of the paper. (Interestingly, the market price of newsprint paper had fallen sharply in the time period between the contract of sale and the presentation of documents, amounting to over $20,000 in this case.) Ronconi & Millar transferred their rights to collect payment to Maurice O'Meara, a financial institution, who brought this action to collect the full amount of the drafts. Maurice O'Meara claims that the issuing bank had no right to test or inspect the paper.

MCLAUGHLIN, JUDGE

[The letter of credit] ... was in no way involved in or connected with, other than the presentation of the documents, the contract for the purchase and sale of the paper mentioned. That was a contract between buyer and seller, which in no way concerned the bank. The bank's obligation was to pay sight drafts when presented if accompanied by genuine documents specified in the letter of credit. If the paper when delivered did not correspond to what had been purchased, either in weight, kind or quality, then the purchaser had his remedy against the seller for damages. Whether the paper was what the purchaser contracted to purchase did not concern the bank and in no way affected its liability. It was under no obligation to ascertain, either by a personal examination or otherwise, whether the paper conformed to the contract between the buyer and seller. The bank was concerned only in the drafts and the documents accompanying them. This was the extent of its interest. If the drafts, when presented, were accompanied by the proper documents, then it was absolutely bound to make the payment under the letter of credit, irrespective of whether it knew, or had reason to believe, that the paper was not of the tensile strength contracted for. This view, I think, is the one generally entertained with reference to a bank's liability under an irrevocable letter of credit of the character of the one here under consideration.

The defendant had no right to insist that a test of the tensile strength of the paper be made before paying the drafts; nor did it even have a right to inspect the paper before payment, to determine whether it in fact corresponded to the description contained in the documents. The letter of credit did not so provide. All that the letter of credit provided was that documents be presented which described the paper shipped as of a certain size, weight, and tensile strength. To hold otherwise is to read into the letter of credit something which is not there, and this the court ought not to do, since it would impose upon a bank a duty which in many cases would defeat the primary purpose of such letters of credit. This primary purpose is an assurance to the seller of merchandise of prompt payment against documents.

It has never been held, so far as I am able to discover, that a bank has the right or is under an obligation to see that the description of the merchandise contained in the documents presented is correct. A provision giving it such right, or imposing such obligation, might, of course, be provided for in the letter of credit. The letter under consideration contains no such provision. If the bank had the right to determine whether the paper was of the tensile strength stated, then it might be pertinent to inquire how much of the paper must it subject to the test. If it had to make a test as to tensile strength, then it was equally obligated to measure and weigh the paper. No such thing was intended by the parties and there was no such obligation upon the bank. The documents presented were sufficient. The only reason stated by defendant in its letter of December 18, 1920, for refusing to pay the draft, was that—"There has arisen a reasonable doubt regarding the quality of the newsprint paper ... Until such time as we can have a test made by an impartial and unprejudiced expert we shall be obliged to defer payment."

This being the sole objection, the only inference to be drawn there from is that otherwise the documents presented conformed to the requirements of the letter of credit. All other objections were thereby waived.

Judgment should be directed in favor of the plaintiff.

Decision. National Park Bank's obligation to pay the beneficiary's drafts submitted under its letter of credit

continues

continued

was separate and distinct from the contract of sale between the buyer and seller. Banks deal in documents only. Therefore the defendant, National Park Bank, could not withhold payment of the drafts even if it believed that the paper was not of the weight, kind, or quality ordered by Sun Herald. Defendant also had no right to demand testing of the paper or to inspect it prior to payment.

Case Questions

1. Had the bank been aware that the newsprint shipment did not conform to the requirements of the underlying sales contract, would it have still been required to pay under the letter of credit?
2. If the bank pays for documents that conform to the letter of credit, but the goods themselves turn out to be nonconforming, is the buyer legally justified in refusing to reimburse its bank?
3. Do you think, under current law and banking practice, that bankers should physically inspect the goods when they arrive before honoring their customer's letter of credit?

make the letter of credit conditional on an investigative report of the seller, on a criminal background check, on the buyer's receipt of financing, or on a contract to resell the goods.

The buyer's international banker and customs broker are two good sources of information and advice on what documents a buyer should require from a seller. Buyers would be well warned to heed their advice or consult an attorney experienced in handling international letters of credit.

The willingness of the bank to issue the letter of credit for the buyer—its customer—depends on the buyer's creditworthiness and the banking relationship between them. More than likely, the buyer and its bank have an established history of banking and commercial lending. The buyer will be responsible to the bank for fees and a percentage of the value of the letter of credit, so the buyer should have already considered these additional costs when agreeing to original sales contract.

Advising the Letter of Credit to the Beneficiary. The issuing bank will send the letter of credit to the seller via a foreign *correspondent bank* (a bank with whom the issuing bank has a reciprocal banking relationship) located in the seller's country. This bank is called the *advising bank.* An advising bank merely informs or "advises" the seller that the letter of credit is available for pick up. An advising bank has no responsibility to honor a draft or purchase the seller's documents. It is not liable on the credit. It provides the service of forwarding the letter of credit to the seller, but it has no obligation to advise the credit and may refuse if it wishes. The bank's only responsibility is to satisfy itself that the credit is authentic and accurate as received (e.g., that there were no errors in transmission). For example, it might compare the signature on the credit as advised to them with the authorized signature of the banking officer at the issuing bank. Letters of credit are commonly transmitted between banks using the SWIFT network.

Seller's Compliance with the Letter of Credit. Until the seller receives the letter of credit and reads it carefully, he or she might not want to begin manufacturing, packaging, arranging transportation, or preparing the documents. The letter of credit tells the seller what it must do to be paid. It tells the seller what to ship, how to ship, when to ship, and more. It contains specific terms and conditions drawn from the original sales contract and included in the letter of credit, such as the quantity and description of the goods, shipping dates, the type or amount of insurance, markings on packages, and so on. The letter of credit also tells the seller what documents are needed in addition to the usual ones. For instance, assume a buyer in California wants to import foreign-made beanbag chairs that must meet California's strict flammability standards for upholstered furniture. The letter of credit might call for an inspection certificate showing that the chairs "were tested pursuant to and are compliant with California Technical Bulletin 117." This tells the seller that this test must be performed, probably by an independent laboratory, and the inspection certificate obtained before the shipping date.

The seller will want to decide if the letter of credit is in keeping with his or her agreement with the buyer in the underlying contract of sale. If the letter of credit shows any significant differences from the sales contract, the seller will want to contact the buyer to inquire why. For instance, assume that a sales contract calls for shipment of "4,000 lbs. washed white goose down in machine-compressed bales," and the letter of credit reads "3,000 lbs. washed white goose down in machine-compressed bales." The seller must stop and inquire why a difference appears in the quantities expressed. Did the buyer decide to purchase only 3,000 pounds instead of the 4,000 pounds agreed to? If so, why didn't the buyer contact the seller to confirm the new order? Perhaps the bank erred in transmitting the letter of credit. Whatever the reason, the seller should do nothing until the problem is resolved or until an amended letter of credit is received. If the seller ships 4,000 pounds, its drafts may be refused and it may only get paid for 3,000 pounds; if it ships 3,000 pounds, it may be losing a sale for the 1,000 pounds difference.

The seller should examine other conditions of the credit to be certain they can be met. Can the seller acquire materials and manufacture on time for the shipment deadline in the letter of credit or before the expiry date of the credit? Does the credit call for a particular shipping method or route or specify a particular carrier or ship that cannot be used? If a license is necessary to export the products from the seller's country, is it possible to process and receive it on time from the government agency?

The seller should also review the credit for accuracy. Is the total amount of the letter of credit sufficient to cover the drafts? Is it in the currency called for in the sales contract? Do the provisions for insurance and the payment of freight charges meet the terms of the contract of sale, and are they agreeable to the seller? Does the letter of credit allow partial shipments?

If the seller is unable to comply with the letter of credit for any reason, the buyer must be contacted immediately, before shipment, so that an amended credit can be issued. In one case, a U.S. furniture manufacturer received a letter of credit from Kuwait calling for the shipment of furniture in "one 40' ocean container." Only after packaging and loading did the manufacturer realize that some of the furniture would not fit into one container. If the manufacturer's documents had shown two containers, or had it shown less furniture than was called for in the letter of credit, the bank would have rejected the documents. An amended credit had to be issued before it was safe to crate and ship the furniture.

Complying Presentation. A *presentation* is the delivery of the seller's documents and draft to the nominated bank or directly to the issuing bank. A **complying presentation** is one in which

1. the seller delivers all of the required documents,
2. within the time allowed for presentation and prior to the expiry date of the credit,
3. containing no discrepancies, and
4. which complies with all other terms of the letter of credit, the provisions of the UCP, and standard banking practices.

The **nominated bank,** usually in the seller's country has been appointed or "nominated" by the issuing bank to honor the documents. The nominated bank is often the advising bank that originally transmits the documents to the seller. If no bank is nominated, then the letter of credit is said to be "freely available" and can be negotiated through any bank of the seller's choice.

Article 14(c) of the UCP requires, in most cases, that presentation of the documents be within 21 days of the date of shipment (determined by the date of the bill of lading) and before the expiry date stated in the credit. Documents will be refused for late presentment unless waived by the buyer.

Examination of Documents for Discrepancies. If the seller's presentation complies, the nominating bank will purchase the seller's documents and honor the draft. If the credit calls for payment on sight, the nominated bank will honor and pay the seller's draft on sight. If the credit calls for payment of the draft at some other time, the nominated bank will honor the draft by acceptance. However, if the seller's documents do not comply with the terms of the letter of credit or if they contain irregularities or discrepancies, the documents will be held pending instructions from the buyer or rejected by the banks. If the bank purchases noncomplying documents, it cannot seek reimbursement from the buyer.

Article 14(b) of UCP 600 gives banks up to five banking days to examine the seller's documents to determine if they conform to the requirements of the letter of credit, or if they contain any discrepancies or irregularities. A **discrepancy** is any difference, no matter how minor, between the terms of a required document and the terms required by the letter of credit. The discrepancy may be caused by some wording or data in a document that is not exactly what was required in the credit. The seller's documents and letter of credit are literally put side by side and compared by a bank's professional document checker. Each term in the documents is matched to the requirement of the letter of credit. For instance, a discrepancy exists if the quantity or description of the goods in the invoice does not match that in the credit, if the bill of lading is dated later than required, if any documents are missing, or if they show signs of fraud, forgery, tampering, or missing signatures.

A bank may not try to interpret the wording of a document. The UCP permits banks only to examine the documents "on their face" to see if they comply with the letter of credit or if there is a discrepancy. Banks may not look to any outside sources or conduct any independent investigation to see if the seller's shipment to the buyer is in good order. It is the documents alone that must be in good order and compliant with the letter of credit. For example, assume a letter of credit calls for the shipment of "1,000 blood pressure monitoring kits." The shipper's invoice shows the sale and shipment of "1,000 sphygmomanometers and cuffs." The document checker may or may not know if items are the same, nor does it matter. The document checker may not consult dictionary definitions, encyclopedias, medical textbooks, or other outside references. The bank is not responsible for interpreting technical or foreign language. The bank may not telephone the seller and ask what was meant in the invoice. In this case there is a discrepancy, and the documents will be rejected, unless the buyer waives the discrepancy. Neither the buyer nor his or her bank is obligated to take the documents.

In the following sections, we will look at the most important documents required under a letter of credit, and some common discrepancies. These derive from the UCP, standard international banking practices, and common requirements on letters of credit. The most common discrepancies found in documents are related to descriptions, time, amounts, missing documents, missing signatures, and contradictions among documents. (See Exhibit 7.4.) Other documents frequently required in a letter of credit include a packing list, certificate of origin, consular invoice, and many others. The seller should not submit documents that the letter of credit does not require; under the UCP, the banks will disregard them and may return them to the seller.

Exhibit 7.4

Common Discrepancies Found in Documentation

Bill of Lading/Air Waybill

- Incomplete set of bills (originals missing)
- Onboard notations not dated and signed or initialed
- Time for shipment has expired
- Unclean bill of lading shows damage
- Indorsement missing
- Evidence of forgery or alteration
- Does not show freight prepared if required under the letter of credit
- Description of goods differs substantially from letter of credit
- Name of vessel differs from one required
- Shows partial shipment or transshipment where prohibited by the letter of credit

Commercial Invoice

- Description of goods does not conform to description in letter of credit
- Does not show terms of shipment
- Amount differs from that shown on draft
- Amount exceeds limits of letter of credit
- Weights, measurements, or quantities differ

Draft

- Draft and invoice amounts do not agree
- Draft does not bear reference to letter of credit
- Evidence of forgery or alteration
- Draft not signed
- Maturity dates differ from letter of credit
- Currency differs from letter of credit

Insurance Policy

- Description of goods differs from invoice
- Risks not covered as required by the letter of credit
- Policy dated after date of bill of lading
- Amount of policy insufficient
- Certificate or policy not indorsed
- Certificate presented instead of policy, if required in letter of credit

General Discrepancies

- Letter of credit has expired
- Letter of credit is overdrawn
- Draft and documents presented after time called for in letter of credit
- Incomplete documentation
- Changes in documents not initialed
- Merchandise description and marks not consistent between documents

The Commercial Invoice. Buyers, banks, and customs authorities require the commercial invoice in every international sale. It must be made out by the seller and addressed to the buyer and be in the same currency as the letter of credit. It need not be signed, notarized, or verified, unless the credit requires. Where a commercial invoice is required, a preliminary "pro forma" invoice will not be accepted.

Perhaps the most important requirement is that the description of the goods in a commercial invoice must correspond to that in the credit. Most courts hold that the description must be exactly the same. As we will see in the next section, sellers are encouraged to use the same description in the invoice as the issuing bank used in the letter of credit, misspellings and all. Where bulk items are involved, the invoice should be for the quantity of goods ordered, or within 5 percent of the amount specified in the credit. However, the 5 percent rule does not apply to letters of credit covering a specific number of items or packages. In such a case, the amount of the invoice cannot exceed the amount of the letter of credit. For example, a seller may ship and bill for 5 percent more grain than was ordered, but not for more cases of soft drinks, or tractors.

The Ocean Bill of Lading. For transactions in which the letter of credit calls for presentment of an "on-board" bill of lading, the seller must present to the issuing bank a bill of lading showing the actual name of the ship and containing the notation "on board," to indicate that the goods have been actually loaded. Where the buyer and seller have agreed, and where it is approved in the letter of credit, it is acceptable for the bill of lading to show that the carrier has received the goods for shipment (but are not yet loaded on board). The dates of receipt or loading must be shown. The seller must present the *original* bill of lading, and if it was issued in a set of more than one original, then all originals must be presented. When all originals are present, this is known as a *full set*. The bill of lading must be dated within the time set in the credit for shipping. It must show the name of the carrier and be signed by the carrier's agent or ship's master. It must state either that the goods have been taken in charge for shipment, or that they were shipped "on board." It must be a "clean" bill—one that has no wording or notations indicating that damage to the goods or packaging was apparent or visible at the time of loading. In transactions where the seller has agreed to arrange and pay for the cost of international freight, the bills of lading must be marked "freight prepaid." Similar requirements exist for road, rail, inland waterway, or air transportation.

The Insurance Policy. The insurance policy should be of the type and coverage required by the letter of credit, and in the same currency and in the amount specified in the credit or, if none is specified, in the amount of the invoice, plus 10 percent. It should be effective on or before the date of the bill of lading to show that the goods were insured during loading. The policy itself should be used; alternatively, a certificate of insurance may be used unless a certificate is not permitted by the letter of credit. Companies that have open policies that "float" over many shipments use declarations. They must be signed by an agent for the company. Cover letters from agents are not acceptable.

Certificates of Analysis or Inspection. Although certificates of analysis or inspection are not required for letter of credit transactions, they are common and deserve to be mentioned. Frequently, a buyer requires the seller to submit documentary proof of inspection from an independent inspection firm. A seller may require submission of a certificate of inspection for merchandise, a certificate of laboratory analysis, or a certificate of compliance with health, safety, or technical standards from an approved testing lab. Analysis or inspection certificates can be required for almost any product, such as an inspection of the sewing quality of blue jeans, an analysis of the mold content of grain, or a laboratory analysis of the lead content of the paint on children's toys. Sellers should ensure that certificates they include with their documents meet all the terms the letter of credit requires.

The Rule of Strict Compliance

The prevailing standard established by the courts for examining documents is found in the **rule of strict compliance**. According to this view, the terms of the documents presented to the issuing bank must strictly conform to the requirements of the letter of credit and the UCP. This rule is almost as old as letter of credit law itself. It is stated in the famous words of Lord Sumner in *Equitable Trust* Co. *of New York v. Dawson Partners Ltd.* [1927] 2 Lloyd's Rep 49: "There is no room for documents which are almost the same, or which will do just as well." This does not mean that every "i" must be dotted and every "t" crossed. As one court states, it is not a discrepancy if Smith is spelled "Smithh." Some typographical errors are excusable, of course. But the thrust of the rule is that every provision of the bill of lading, invoice, insurance policy, and any other required shipping document must match the letter of credit. Even a small discrepancy can cause the bank to reject the documents. The reason for such a harsh rule is simple: it relieves bankers from the duty of interpreting the meaning of the discrepancy or its possible impact on their customers, and it relieves them of the liability of interpreting it incorrectly.

In the following case, *Courtaulds North America, Inc. v. North Carolina National Bank,* the court considers a discrepancy between the description of the goods on the letter of credit and on the invoice.

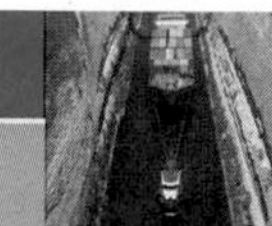

Courtaulds North America, Inc. v. North Carolina National Bank

528 F.2d 802 (1975) United States Court of Appeals (4th Cir.)

BACKGROUND AND FACTS

The defendant bank issued an irrevocable letter of credit on behalf of its customer, Adastra Knitting Mills. It promised to honor sixty-day time drafts of Courtaulds for up to $135,000 covering shipments of "100% Acrylic Yarn." Courtaulds presented its draft together with a commercial invoice describing the merchandise as "Imported Acrylic Yarns." The packing lists that were stapled to the invoice contained the following description: "Cartons marked: 100% Acrylic." The bank refused to accept the draft because of the discrepancy between the letter of credit and the commercial invoice. (The buyer had gone into bankruptcy, and the court-appointed trustee would not waive the discrepancy.) The documents were returned and the plaintiff brought this action. The lower court held that the bank was liable to the plaintiff for the amount of the draft because the packing lists attached to each carton stated that the cartons contained "100% Acrylic," and the bank appealed.

BRYAN, SENIOR CIRCUIT JUDGE

The defendant denied liability chiefly on the assertion that the draft did not agree with the letter's conditions, viz., that the draft be accompanied by a "Commercial invoice in triplicate stating (inter alia) that it covers ... 100% acrylic yarn"; instead, the accompanying invoices stated that the goods were "Imported Acrylic Yarn."

... [T]he District Court held defendant Bank liable to Courtaulds for the amount of the draft, interest, and costs. It concluded that the draft complied with the letter of credit when each invoice is read together with the packing lists stapled to it, for the lists stated on their faces: "Cartons marked: 100% Acrylic." After considering the insistent rigidity of the law and usage of bank credits and acceptances, we must differ with the District Judge and uphold Bank's position.

In utilizing the rules of construction embodied in the letter of credit—the *Uniform Customs* and state statute—one must constantly recall that the drawee bank is not to be embroiled in disputes between the buyer and the seller, the beneficiary of the credit. The drawee is involved only with documents, not with merchandise. Its involvement is altogether separate and apart from the transaction between the buyer and seller; its duties and liability are governed exclusively by the terms of the letter, not the terms of the parties' contract with each other. Moreover, as the predominant authorities unequivocally declare, the beneficiary must meet the terms of the credit—and precisely—if it is to exact performance of the issuer. Failing such compliance there can be no recovery from the drawee. That is the specific failure of Courtaulds here.

... [T]he letter of credit dictated that each invoice express on its face that it covered 100% acrylic yarn. Nothing less is shown to be tolerated in the trade. No substitution and no equivalent, through interpretation or logic, will serve. Harfield, *Bank Credits and Acceptances* (5th ed. 1974), commends and quotes aptly from an English case: "There is no room for documents which are almost the same, or which will do just as well." Although no pertinent North Carolina decision has been laid before us, in many cases elsewhere, especially in New York, we find the tenet of Harfield to be unshaken.

At trial Courtaulds prevailed on the contention that the invoices in actuality met the specifications of the letter of credit in that the packing lists attached to the invoices disclosed on their faces that the packages contained "cartons marked: 100% acrylic." ... But this argument cannot be accepted.

The district judge's pat statement adeptly puts an end to this contention of Courtaulds: "In dealing with letters of credit, it is a custom and practice of the banking trade for a bank to only treat a document as an invoice which clearly is marked on its face as 'invoice.'" This is not a pharisaical or doctrinaire persistence in the principle, but is altogether realistic in the environs of this case; it is plainly the fair and equitable measure. (The defect in description was not superficial but occurred in the statement of the quality of the yarn, not a frivolous concern.) Bank was not expected to

continues

continued

scrutinize the collateral papers, such as the packing lists. Nor was it permitted to read into the instrument the contemplation or intention of the seller and buyer ...

Had the Bank deviated from the stipulation of the letter and honored the draft, then at once it might have been confronted with the not improbable risk of the bankruptcy trustee's charge of liability for unwarrantably paying the draft monies to the seller, Courtaulds, and refusal to reimburse Bank for the outlay. Contrarily, it might face a Courtaulds claim that since it had depended upon Bank's assurance of credit in shipping yarn to Adastra, Bank was responsible for the loss. In this situation Bank cannot be condemned for sticking to the letter of the letter.

Nor is this conclusion affected by the amended or substituted invoices which Courtaulds sent to Bank after the refusal of the draft. No precedent is cited to justify retroactive amendment of the invoices or extension of the credit beyond the August 15 expiry of the letter.

For these reasons, we must vacate the decision of the trial court, despite the evident close reasoning and research of the district judge ...

Reversed and remanded for final judgment.

Decision. The judgment is reversed for the defendant bank. The description of the goods in the invoice did not match the description of the goods in the credit, and the defect was not cured by a correct description in the packing list.

Case Questions

1. Why did the bank refuse to accept the draft upon presentation of the documents?
2. Had the bank known that the yarns described in the invoice as "imported acrylic yarns" were actually 100% acrylic, as called for in the letter of credit, would the outcome of the case have been different?
3. What is the liability of a bank for paying or accepting a draft when the documents contain a discrepancy?

Apply the strict compliance rule of the *Courtaulds* case to the following situation: Suppose that a seller receives a letter of credit from a foreign buyer covering "1,000 standard-size bed pillows." Seller's export manager completes an invoice for "1,000 bed pillows, size 20 × 26 in." A discrepancy exists. Bankers are not expected to know that a "standard" bed pillow is 20 × 26 inches, and even if the banker did know, he or she would still have to refuse the document because of the discrepancy. Assume now that the invoice matches the letter of credit, but that the bill of lading shows shipment of "1,000 pillows." On this point the UCP is clear: the description in a document other than an invoice may be "in general terms not conflicting with their description in the credit." Here the documents show no discrepancy.

The Functional Standard of Compliance. While the strict compliance rule remains the prevailing view in most jurisdictions, some courts in the United States and in some European countries have used a more practical "functional standard" of compliance. These courts do not require a bank to reject documents with obviously minor typographical errors. *Voest-Alpine Trading Co. v. Bank of China,* 167 F. Supp. 2d 940 (S.D. Tex. 2000), aff'd 288 F.2d 262 (5th Cir. 2002), involved a shipment of styrene from Voest-Alpine to a customer in China under a $1.2 million letter of credit issued by the Bank of China. Apparently the market value of the styrene at the time the documents were presented for payment had fallen well below the contract price. Voest-Alpine refused a price concession requested by the buyer, and the bank started looking for discrepancies. There was no question that the two documents contained discrepancies. The question was whether they were sufficient to justify the bank's refusal to pay for the documents. The beneficiary's name in the letter of credit, Voest-Alpine *Trading USA,* was transposed in the documents to "*USA Trading.*" The letter of credit required three "original" bills of lading, but none were stamped "original," one was stamped "duplicate" and another "triplicate." All three, however, contained original hand signatures in blue ink. The survey report for damage was dated a day after the bill of lading, even though the report stated that the goods had been inspected upon loading. Although the reference number of the letter of credit was incorrect on the cover letter prepared by Voest-Alpine, it was correct elsewhere. Finally, the name of the port city, Zhangjiagang, was spelled several different ways in various documents. The Bank of China argued that under a strict compliance standard it was justified in rejecting the documents. Voest-Alpine argued for a "functional standard" of compliance, contending that the bank should have looked at documents as a whole. In agreeing with Voest-Alpine, the court rejected the notion that the documents should be a "mirror image" of those called for in the letter of credit, and adopted a more moderate approach. The district court stated:

> A common sense, case-by-case approach would permit minor deviations of a typographical nature because such a letter-for-letter correspondence between the letter of credit and the presentation documents is virtually impossible. While the end result of such an analysis may bear a strong resemblance to the relaxed strict compliance standard, the actual calculus used by the issuing bank is not the risk it or the applicant faces but rather, whether the documents bear a rational link to one another. In this way, the issuing bank is required to examine a particular document in light of all documents presented and use common sense but is not required to evaluate risks or go beyond the face of the documents. The Court finds that in this case the Bank of China's listed discrepancies should be analyzed under this standard by determining whether the whole of the documents obviously relate to the transaction on their face.

The UCP 600 Rule. The general principles of letter of credit law that we have discussed up to this point have been developed by courts in countries around the world. Often, these decisions are based on the courts' interpretation of the UCP because the UCP contains its own standards for gauging when documents comply with the letter of credit. Article 14(d) of UCP 600 takes a modified strict compliance approach by stating that, while "data in a document" (here "data" means such things as the description of the goods, names of the parties, quantities and weights, addresses, and similar relevant terms) does not have to be "identical" to other data in the same document, or to data in any other required document, or data in the credit itself, it may not conflict with it. The UCP has specific provisions regarding the description of the goods—one of the key terms in any letter of credit. The UCP states that a document (other than an invoice) may describe the goods "in general terms not conflicting with their description in the credit." However, the rule of strict compliance is retained in Article 18(c) with regard to the invoice, which states, "The description of the goods ... in a commercial invoice must correspond with that appearing in the credit." The UCP also requires that the name, address, and contact details for the consignee or notify party on the transport documents must appear exactly as in the letter of credit. Thus a warning to export managers and to bankers who advise them: Be certain that you describe your goods in your invoice in the exact wording and form that is used in the letter of credit. Be consistent in your data throughout all documents, and conform your data and wording to that used in the credit itself.

Every export manager, freight forwarder, carrier's agent, and international banker should have his or her own reference copy of the UCP readily at hand when drafting documents or dealing in transactions governed by the UCP.

An Ethical Issue in Handling Letters of Credit. In most cases, buyers will waive a minor discrepancy. However, sellers and bankers must beware: If a buyer is looking for a reason to reject the documents (e.g., if the ship has gone down at sea, the market price of similar goods has fallen dramatically, etc.), a discrepancy will give the savvy (or unscrupulous?) buyer a way out. If the buyer is looking for a way to chisel a better price out of the deal, then a discrepancy will give him or her leverage. The buyer can reject the documents, and only later reluctantly agree to waive the discrepancy—but only for a huge discount off the contract price! Issuing banks may on occasion want to find discrepancies. If they discover that their customers—the buyers—are going to back out of the deal, they can use the discrepancy to reject the documents. (An old adage states that any banker who cannot find a discrepancy is not worth his or her salt.) Of course, almost all discrepancies are honest accidents or commercial mistakes and are easily resolved.

Procedures for Dishonor. A bank must follow the UCP guidelines for rejecting or dishonoring a presentation. The first step is to ask the buyer for a waiver. If the buyer decides to refuse the documents, the bank must give notice of its refusal to the presenting bank by telecommunication within five banking days. The notice must inform the presenter whether the documents are being held pending further instructions or are being returned. If the issuing bank fails to do this, it is precluded from claiming that the documents were properly presented.

Enjoining Banks from Purchasing Documents in Cases of Fraud

Earlier in this chapter you read the case of *Maurice O'Meara,* which illustrates the important principle that letters of credit are independent of the underlying sales contract. An issuing bank is responsible only for the seller's documents and is not concerned with the quality of the goods or whether the seller shipped the correct goods. If the goods are defective or non-conforming, the buyer's remedy is against the seller for breach of contract.

What if the buyer's problem is not that the quality or condition of the goods is defective, but that he or she has fallen victim to a fraud or a scam? What good would a breach of contract suit be against the perpetrator of a fraud who disappears with the cash? To address these situations, a partial exception to the independence principle exists where documents presented by the seller (the beneficiary of the credit) are fraudulent, or forged, or if *fraud in the transaction* exists in the underlying sales contract. For instance, suppose that the buyer in a letter of credit transaction learns, almost too late, that the purported bill of lading is actually a fake, that no ship or carrier by that name exists, and that the goods the buyer was awaiting do not exist. Here the issuing bank would be justified in refusing to pay for fraudulent documents. Similarly, consider the case where an unscrupulous seller places worthless junk into a sealed ocean container and delivers it to an ocean carrier, obtains a bill of lading, and presents it to the issuing bank for payment under a letter of credit. Here too, the issuing bank would be justified in dishonoring the letter of credit because of fraud in the transaction. Of course, banks do not want to refuse documents without cause (especially where they have already been purchased by a nominated bank that is looking for reimbursement). After all, their international reputation is at stake, and no bank wants to be known for refusing to honor its letters of credit. One solution that will preserve the reputation of the bank is for the buyer to obtain a court injunction stopping the bank from honoring its letter of credit.

The UCP is silent on the question of when a court may enjoin a letter of credit for fraud. This is left to the law of individual jurisdictions. In the United States, the authority of a court to enjoin payment under a letter of credit is found in the case law and in Article 5 of the *Uniform Commercial Code.* According to UCC Section 5-109 (2003 revision), the standard for enjoining payment under a letter of credit is whether or not "a required document is forged or materially fraudulent or that honor of the presentation would facilitate a material fraud by the beneficiary on the issuer or applicant." Courts may not enjoin payment if the documents are presented by a holder in due course or by a nominating bank that "has given value in good faith and without notice of the forgery or material fraud." Although the line between what is fraud and what is not fraud is unclear, the fraud must be material and significant to the parties. Such would be the case where worthless rubbish is shipped in lieu of genuine goods. On the other hand, if the seller intentionally ships only 998 pounds of goose feathers but presents a draft and documents for 1,000 pounds, it is probably neither material nor significant. Some of the cases have said that the fraud must be "egregious," or that the seller's demand for payment has "no basis in fact," or to allow him to collect payment would be "unjust."

The following pre-UCC case, *Sztejn v. J. Henry Schroder Banking Corp.*, presents a clear distinction between a mere breach of warranty and fraud. Recall that the last case, *O'Meara*, involves a breach of warranty—the seller shipped newsprint paper of inferior quality. *Sztejn* involves **fraud in the transaction**—*the* presentation of documents covering goods and the shipment of bales of worthless rubbish. The *Sztejn* case is one of the most widely cited cases in U.S. letter of credit law. Today, the UCC provisions largely follow the rule first set out by the *Sztejn* case.

Fraud in the transaction can take many forms. In *Regent Corp., U.S.A. v. Azmat Bangladesh, Ltd.*, 686 N.Y.S.2d 24 (1999), a textile company located in Bangladesh represented to a U.S. buyer that bedsheets and pillowcases were to be manufactured in Bangladesh. In fact, the seller knew that the goods were a product of Pakistan but provided a fake certificate of origin because they were trying to circumvent U.S. import quotas on Bangladeshi linens. The New York court ruled that there was sufficient fraud in the transaction to justify the bank's refusal to honor the draft under the letter of credit. Another example may be found in the following case of *Semetex v. UBAF Arab American Bank*.

Confirmed Letters of Credit

In most cases, a letter of credit is adequate assurance for payment. In certain instances, however, a seller may want an additional layer of security. Where a seller is uncertain about the soundness of an issuing bank in a foreign country, or of the integrity of the banking system there generally, or the stability of the government, the seller may want to request that a bank in its own country confirm the letter of credit. A

Sztejn v. J. Henry Schroder Banking Corp.

31 N.Y.S.2d 631 (1941) Supreme Court, Special Term, New York County

BACKGROUND AND FACTS

The plaintiff contracted to purchase hog bristles from Transea Traders in India. The defendant bank issued an irrevocable letter of credit to Transea covering a shipment of hog bristles and payable upon presentation of the proper documents. Transea filled fifty cases with cow hair and other worthless rubbish in order to obtain an ocean bill of lading from the steamship company showing the shipment of fifty cases of hog bristles. The documents and draft were presented to the defendant bank by The Chartered Bank of India, acting as agent for Transea. The plaintiff brought this action against the issuing bank to restrain it from paying on the letter of credit.

SHIENTAG, JUSTICE

One of the chief purposes of the letter of credit is to furnish the seller with a ready means of obtaining prompt payment for his merchandise. It would be a most unfortunate interference with business transactions if a bank before honoring drafts drawn upon it was obliged or even allowed to go behind the documents, at the request of the buyer and enter into controversies between the buyer and the seller regarding the quality of the merchandise shipped ... Of course, the application of this doctrine presupposes that the documents accompanying the draft are genuine and conform in terms to the requirements of the letter of credit.

However, I believe that a different situation is presented in the instant action. This is not a controversy between the buyer and seller concerning a mere breach of warranty regarding the quality of the merchandise; on the present motion, it must be assumed that the seller has intentionally failed to ship any goods ordered by the buyer. In such a situation, where the seller's fraud has been called to the bank's attention before the drafts and documents have been presented for payment, the principle of the independence of the bank's obligation under the letter of credit should not be extended to protect the unscrupulous seller. It is true that even though the documents are forged or fraudulent, if the issuing bank has already paid the draft before receiving notice of the seller's fraud, it will be protected if it exercised reasonable diligence before making such payment. However, in the instant action Schroder has received notice of Transea's active fraud before it accepted or paid the draft ...

Although our courts have used broad language to the effect that a letter of credit is independent of the primary contract between the buyer and seller, that language was used in cases concerning alleged breaches of warranty; no case has been brought to my attention on this point involving an intentional fraud on the part of the seller which was brought to the bank's notice with the request that it withhold payment of the draft on this account. The distinction between a breach of warranty and active fraud on the part of the seller is supported by authority and reason. As one court has stated: "Obviously, when the issuer of a letter of credit knows that a document, although correct in form, is, in point of fact, false or illegal, he cannot be called upon to recognize such a document as complying with the terms of a letter of credit." *Old Colony Trust Co. v. Lawyers' Title & Trust Co.,* 297 F. 152 at page 158 (2nd Cir. 1924).

No hardship will be caused by permitting the bank to refuse payment where fraud is claimed, where the merchandise is not merely inferior in quality but consists of worthless rubbish, where the draft and the accompanying documents are in the hands of one who stands in the same position as the fraudulent seller, where the bank has been given notice of the fraud before being presented with the drafts and documents for payment, and where the bank itself does not wish to pay pending an adjudication of the rights and obligations of the other parties. While the primary factor in the issuance of the letter of credit is the credit standing of the buyer, the security afforded by the merchandise is also taken into account. In fact, the letter of credit requires a bill of lading made out to the order of the bank and not the buyer. Although the bank is not interested in the exact detailed performance of the sales contract, it is vitally interested in assuring itself that there are some goods represented by the documents. * * * Accordingly, the defendant's motion to dismiss the supplemental complaint is denied.

Decision. The court held in favor of the plaintiff and enjoined the bank's payment. A court can enjoin an issuing bank from honoring a draft if the bank learns that its customer will suffer irreparable harm as a result of fraud in the transaction.

Case Questions

1. What basic principle of letter of credit law does this decision challenge?

continues

continued

2. How would the result be different if the draft and documents had been sold and negotiated to a holder in due course who took with no knowledge of the fraud, and who then presented the documents to the issuing bank for payment?
3. Explain the misrepresentation that took place in this case. How was this "fraud in the transaction"? Can you think of other examples of how fraud could occur in a documentary letter of credit transaction between foreign parties?
4. What steps could a buyer and seller take to avoid falling victim to an international fraud? How could they learn more about each other, and what sources could they consult?

Semetex Corp. v. UBAF Arab American Bank

853 F. Supp. 759 (1994) United States District Court (S.D.N.Y.)

BACKGROUND AND FACTS

In 1988, Semetex entered into an agreement with the Al-Mansour Factory in Baghdad, Iraq, an enterprise owned and operated by the government of Iraq, in which Semetex agreed to provide Al-Mansour with an "ion implanter" used to mark circuitry pathways on microchips. Payment to Semetex was to be made through an irrevocable documentary letter of credit in the amount of $7,462,500. The letter of credit was issued by the Central Bank of Iraq in February 1990 and confirmed by a bank in the United States, specifically, UBAF.

The letter of credit conditioned payment solely on presentation of commercial invoices; a certificate of origin; an air waybill evidencing air shipment, freight prepaid, from the United States to Baghdad via Iraqi Airways or carriers authorized by Iraqi Airways; and a cable to Al-Mansour advising Al-Mansour of the flight number and date of arrival in Baghdad. It did not require evidence that control of the ion implanter had passed to a designated carrier before payment could be made.

Semetex engaged Eaton Corporation to manufacture the ion implanter to Al-Mansour's specifications. Semetex engaged Alison Transport, Inc., a freight-forwarding company, to ship the equipment from Eaton's factory in Austin, Texas, to Baghdad. The shipment was scheduled in several stages by van from Austin to John F. Kennedy International Airport in New York, followed by a Lufthansa flight to Frankfurt and a connecting Iraqi Airways flight to Baghdad. While the truck carrying the ion implanter was in transit to New York, Iraq invaded Kuwait, which caused President George H. W. Bush to issue an executive order blocking Iraqi assets in the United States. The ion implanter was subsequently diverted to a warehouse in Massachusetts in order to comply with the assets freeze.

Semetex made demand for payment upon UBAF, which demand was rejected. UBAF claimed that the documents evidencing transport of the ion implanter as prepared by Alison contained inconsistent information and fraudulent representations regarding the dates of shipment and the identities of carriers. Semetex applied for a license from the U.S. Office of Foreign Assets Control to sue UBAF for payment on the letter of credit, which application was granted.

SAND, JUDGE

UBAF invokes the fraud exception to the letter-of-credit independence principle. UBAF admits that the documents presented to it on August 1, 1990, complied on their face with the requirements of the Letter of Credit. It contends, however, that the documents were in compliance only because Plaintiffs misrepresented the flight information on the air waybill and forged the signature of an Iraqi Airways representative. Alison noted flight dates of July 26 and 29 on the air waybill when it made its second drawing attempt on August 1, UBAF contends, even though Alison and Plaintiffs knew that the ion implanter had only been picked up by truck in Austin on July 31 and that it was not scheduled to reach JFK Airport until August 2. UBAF contends that these discrepancies rise to the level of "outright fraudulent practice" that is required under New York law to supersede the independence principle ....

Fraud provides a well-established exception to the rule that banks must pay a beneficiary under a letter of credit when documents conforming on their face to the terms of the letter of credit are presented.... The fraud defense, however, is a narrow one. The defense is available only where intentional fraud is shown, not where the party alleges improper performance or breach of warranty.... As the Second Circuit stated in Rockwell:

> The "fraud in the transaction" defense marks the limit of the generally accepted principle that a letter of credit is independent of whatever obligation it secures. No bright line separates the rule from the exception, to be

continues

continued

> sure, but ... "fraud" embraces more than mere forgery of documents supporting a call. The logic of the fraud exception necessarily entails looking beyond supporting documents .... We must look to the circumstances surrounding the transaction and the call to determine whether [the] call amounted to an "outright fraudulent practice." *Rockwell Int'l Systems, Inc. v. Citibank, N.A.*, 719 F.2d 583, 588–89 (2d Cir. 1983).

UBAF argues that ... Semetex presented a false air waybill to the confirming bank UBAF purporting to evidence shipment and export days earlier than in fact the shipment was scheduled. The air waybill was dated July 24 and signed by Iraqi Airways at Robert Mueller Airport in Austin, Texas, purporting to evidence consignment to that carrier on that date and a flight on July 26. In reality, by August 1, the ion implanter had not been delivered to the designated air carrier, Lufthansa.... Although UBAF raises evidence of substantial discrepancies between the actual facts of the ion implanter's transport and the information on Semetex's transport documents, we conclude that UBAF has not presented evidence that rises to the level of "outright fraudulent practice." In particular, evidence of Plaintiffs' fraudulent intent is lacking.

UBAF has presented no evidence that Plaintiffs "first caused the default and then attempted to reap the benefit of the guarantee." Semetex and Eaton, defaulted on their obligations on the underlying contract because of an event over which they had absolutely no control—the Iraqi assets freeze.

UBAF likewise has presented no evidence that Plaintiffs either (1) failed to comply with an explicit term of the letter of credit or (2) did so with intent to defraud.... UBAF has presented no evidence that Plaintiffs' alleged "forgery" of dates and a signature on the air waybill was material to the requirements of the Letter of Credit or was committed with intent to defraud. There is no dispute that Eaton in fact manufactured an ion implanter to Al-Mansour's specifications, and there is likewise no dispute that, had it not been for the invasion of Kuwait and the subsequent Iraqi sanctions orders, the equipment would have reached its destination in Baghdad.... UBAF has presented no evidence of ... fraudulent intent behind the seven-day discrepancy between the July 26 departure date represented on the air waybill and the actual planned flight date of August 2, and have presented no evidence that that discrepancy would have been material in any way in the absence of the unannounced invasion of Kuwait. Similarly, they have presented no evidence of fraudulent intent behind Plaintiffs' signing the air waybill as agents of Iraqi Airways and designating Robert Mueller Airport as the point of departure.

In this regard, it is significant that the Letter of Credit did not specify that shipment in the United States must begin at Robert Mueller Airport, or otherwise specify how the equipment was to be moved within the United States.... [T]he UCP ... does not assign significance to the date of delivery to a designated air carrier unless the parties expressly incorporate such a term into their letter of credit....

In sum, none of the discrepancies on which UBAF focuses would have been material to Plaintiffs' ability to draw on the Letter of Credit if the parties' plans had not been unexpectedly dashed by the invasion of Kuwait and the subsequent freezing of Iraqi assets. [UBAF's cited authorities] would be analogous to this case only if Semetex had had foreknowledge of the invasion of Kuwait and the resulting freeze of Iraqi assets, and so had conspired with Alison to falsify the dates on the air waybill in order to draw on the letter of credit funds before actually shipping the ion implanter. Of course, no such evidence was presented....

The parties are thus left with the rights and obligations they bargained for: Semetex bargained for the right to be paid from UBAF's non-Iraqi assets, and UBAF attempted to protect itself against the risk of nonpayment by the Iraqi bank by fully collateralizing its obligation to Semetex. The parties having thus entered into the Letter of Credit arrangement, the material question regarding UBAF's liability is not whether control of the ion implanter had passed to Al-Mansour at the time that Plaintiffs attempted to draw on the Letter of Credit; rather, the question is whether UBAF has demonstrated either that the documents presented by Semetex failed to satisfy the Letter of Credit's terms, or that they were forged or fraudulent or there was fraud in the transaction. As set out above, UBAF admits that the documents satisfy the Letter of Credit's terms on their face, and it has failed to present evidence from which a reasonable factfinder could conclude that the fraud exception applies.

Conclusion. For the reasons set forth above, we conclude that Plaintiffs have demonstrated that they are entitled to judgment as a matter of law.

Case Questions

1. What basic principle of letter of credit law does this decision uphold?
2. Is the court's decision correct given the many problems with the documentation as prepared by the freight forwarder and the additional complication of the Iraqi government asset freeze? Why or why not?
3. Is the court's definition of "outright fraudulent practice" too restrictive? What would be the consequences for letter of credit law if the court adopted a more liberal interpretation of fraud?
4. What could UBAF have done in the negotiation and drafting process to prevent the ultimate outcome in this case?

confirmed letter of credit is one in which a second bank, usually in the seller's country, agrees to purchase documents and honor drafts on the same terms as the original issuing bank. Suppose a seller is shipping to a country that has a shortage of foreign currency, large foreign debts, and a poor balance of payments record. It is always possible that foreign government currency restrictions, imposed between the time the contract is agreed to and the time the drafts are tendered for payment, could prevent the issuing bank from honoring its letter of credit in dollars. A letter of credit confirmed by a bank in the seller's country will ensure prompt payment regardless of financial or political instability in the country where the issuing bank is located. Additionally, should legal action ever be necessary to collect on a letter of credit, a seller can much more easily sue a U.S. confirming bank in the United States than a foreign bank in foreign courts. Of course, a confirmed credit is far more expensive than one that is unconfirmed because two banks are exposed to the risk of the transaction. The parties must weigh these costs in determining the level of acceptable risk in the transaction.

Banks in the United States that confirm foreign letters of credit continuously monitor the economic and political conditions in those foreign countries. If a foreign buyer is unable to have its bank's letter of credit confirmed by a U.S. bank, then that may be a signal that the political and credit risks are too high. After all, if no U.S. bank will confirm a foreign letter of credit, why would the seller want to accept it? In this case, the seller might want to reconsider requesting some amount of cash in advance or other secure arrangement.

Standby Letters of Credit

A **standby letter of credit** (also called a standby credit, or simply a standby) is one in which the issuer is obligated to pay a beneficiary upon the presentation of documents indicating a default by the account party in the payment of a debt or the performance of an obligation. The documents might be as simple as a notice of default by the account party, signed by the beneficiary, and accompanied by a demand for payment. A standby letter of credit is a backup payment mechanism that the parties hope they will never have to use. It can be used to guarantee performance under a service or construction contract, to guarantee repayment of a loan, or as security for almost any other type of contract. The standby works much like the "performance guarantee" used by banks in other countries (or the "performance bond" in the UK) but is legally different. A standby is subject to the *International Standby Practices* (ISP 98), a set of rules and standards published by the International Chamber of Commerce. A standby letter of credit is flexible and can be tailored for almost any use. Most are used in large, complex transactions. Assume that a construction firm enters into a contract with a foreign government to construct a public works project. The government wants assurances that the firm will complete the work as promised by being named as beneficiary of a standby credit. The credit could be payable upon the government's presentation of a written demand for payment and a notice of default to the issuing bank stating that the construction firm has failed to complete the required work in the manner and within the time called for in the contract. Like the documentary requirements we have already studied, the language of default must strictly comply with the language used in the standby letter of credit. Documentary requirements depend on the transaction and the needs of the parties, but could include independent testing reports, architect's reports, court judgments, certified public accounting statements, or a signed statement by the beneficiary or an authorized corporate officer.

In the sale of goods, a standby can be used in lieu of a conventional letter of credit. Assume that a seller agrees to grant 30-day open account terms to a buyer. In a standby credit, the bank is "standing by" as a backup, ready to purchase the documents if the buyer does not remit payment within 30 days. A standby can also guarantee the *seller*'s performance, that is, that the seller will ship conforming goods within the time called for.

Standby letters of credit can ensure the repayment of a loan. Suppose, for example, that a subsidiary of a U.S. company operating in Latin America borrows money from a local bank. The bank can require a standby letter of credit from a U.S. bank that would allow it to draw against the credit should the subsidiary default on its obligation.

A standby can ensure compliance with almost any obligation. In the Exxon Valdez oil spill that occurred in Alaska in 1989, the court required that Exxon provide a $6 billion standby letter of credit to ensure that Exxon would meet its obligations of environmental cleanup and payment of damages.

Not surprisingly, standby letters of credit have led to a great deal of litigation in the courts. To protect an account party under a standby credit from an "unfair" demand by the beneficiary, many international business lawyers structure the standby credit to require that the beneficiary's request for payment be accompanied by a written, independent confirmation of the account party's default by a third party.

Other Specialized Uses for Letters of Credit

Many specialized types of letters of credit provide a mechanism for financing a sale or other business transaction. We discuss some of these types here.

Transferable Credits. International traders usually use **transferable credits**. Traders buy and sell goods in international trade quickly and with no view to actually using the goods themselves. They bear considerable risk every day. Traders operate on little capital, buying merchandise or commodities in one country, taking title through the documents, and then, through their business contacts built up over years of experience, selling at a profit. Some traders specialize in trade with the developing world, often trading commodities for raw materials or merchandise when dollars or hard currency is not available. For instance, assume a Swiss bank issues a letter of credit for the account of an African country in favor of the trader, with a part of the credit transferred to the trader's supplier in the Philippines for the cost of the goods it is supplying to the African country. This letter of credit can be split up among many suppliers around the world, each presenting documents for payment, with the trader taking its profit out of the balance of the credit. Shipments of crude oil are often bought and sold in this fashion.

Red Clauses in Credits. The **red clause** is a financing tool for smaller sellers who need capital to produce the products to be shipped under a letter of credit. A red clause in a letter of credit is a promise (usually written or underlined in red ink) by the issuing bank to reimburse the seller's bank for loans made to the seller. The loan, then, is really an advance on the credit. Loans can be used only for purchasing raw materials or for covering the costs of manufacturing or shipping of the goods described in the credit. Ultimately, the liability will fall on the buyer if the seller defaults on shipment or repayment of the amounts taken under the credit. This form of financing is risky for the buyer and its bank.

Revolving Credits and Evergreen Clauses. When a buyer is planning on purchasing from a foreign seller on a regular basis, the buyer may use a **revolving letter of credit**. Instead of having to use several different credits, one may be used with a maximum amount available during a certain period. As the draws against the credit are paid, the full amount becomes available again and continues until the expiration of the credit. An **evergreen clause** provides for automatic renewal of the letter of credit until the bank gives "clear and unequivocal" notice of its intent not to renew.

Back-to-Back Letter of Credit Financing. A **back-to-back letter of credit** is a special type of financing arrangement in which the proceeds of one credit serve as security to obtain a second credit. It might be used where a manufacturer or other exporter has a contract to sell finished goods to a buyer but needs financing to purchase needed component parts or raw materials from a supplier. The exporter, as beneficiary of a letter of credit from its buyer's bank, can assign the proceeds of that credit to its bank as security for a separate letter of credit being issued to the exporter's supplier. Thus, a back-to-back credit is really two credits, one issued in favor of the exporter that serves as security for a second issued in favor of the exporter's supplier. Many banks will issue the second credit only if they had issued the first one (known as a *countercredit*). Back-to-back credits are also used as a financing arrangement by traders with minimal capital resources.

Electronic Data Interchange and the eUCP

Like funds transfers, letters of credit have been issued and transmitted to advising banks electronically for many years (and from advising bank to beneficiary usually by mail). The use of electronic documentation has increased over time, and beneficiaries are presenting documents electronically to banks for payment.

In 2002, the International Chamber of Commerce published the *eUCP*, a set of rules that extends the UCP to electronic documents. When documents are submitted electronically, eUCP rules apply by agreement of the parties. The eUCP addresses the format for electronic documents (the rules are flexible and include signed e-mail attachments or secured transfer), authentication and digital signatures, transmission errors, the manner of presentation, and other issues.

Bolero is a technical infrastructure created by the world's banking and logistics firms for exchanging electronic documents in a common format, including bills of lading, letters of credit, and other bank documents. *Identrus* is a private company founded by a small consortium of the world's largest banks to provide secure "digital identities" or signatures for confidentiality and authentication of financial and legal documents. Both *Identrus* and *Bolero* represent technological innovations necessary to move the centuries-old banking and shipping industries to the paperless age.

Letters of Credit in Trade Finance Programs

Letter of credit financing plays an important role in export financing by government and intergovernmental agencies. U.S. exports are financed by such agencies as the Agency for International Development (AID), the World Bank (which provides financial and technical assistance to developing countries to stimulate economic growth), the Commodity Credit Corporation (which assists with commerce in surplus agricultural products), and the Export-Import Bank of the United States (Eximbank). These agencies often insure payments made to U.S. sellers under letters of credit that are confirmed by U.S. banks using a letter of commitment from the agency to the issuing bank.

AID Financing. A typical AID financing situation might include a letter of credit. A country wishing to import U.S. products, usually for use in developmental projects such as building roads, power-generating facilities, and the like, applies to AID for financing. AID then issues its commitment to a U.S. bank that issues its letter of credit for the benefit of the U.S. supplier of eligible goods for use in the project. The issuing bank receives reimbursement for payments under its letter of credit from AID.

Eximbank Financing. **Eximbank** is the largest U.S. export financing agency. It can provide guarantees on loans made by commercial banks and insurance on credit extended by U.S. exporters to their foreign customers. It also makes loans directly from Eximbank funds, including fixed-rate loans to creditworthy foreign buyers of American-made exports. Under another Eximbank loan program, a U.S. bank designated by the foreign buyer opens a letter of credit on behalf of the buyer for the benefit of a U.S. supplier. Eximbank guarantees the issuing bank repayment of sums that it pays out under the credit. Eximbank then receives its payments under the loan agreement worked out in advance between it and the foreign buyer. Eximbank programs cover both the risk of nonpayment and political risk (such as the outbreak of war or government controls that prohibit currency exchange). Despite the importance of the U.S. Eximbank, it only finances a small percentage of U.S. exports. Industries receiving substantial Eximbank support include aircraft manufacturing, oil and gas, mining, construction equipment manufacturing, energy production and agribusiness. In fiscal year 2012, Eximbank authorized almost 3,800 export sales for over $35.7 billion in export loans, guarantees, and export-credit insurance. In the past, Eximbank had been subject to criticism for not assisting small business U.S. exporters. In fiscal year 2012, however, more than 3,300 transactions (87 percent of total transactions), representing $6.1 billion (17 percent of Eximbank total financial support) went to aid small businesses. Eximbank has increased its lending guarantees for U.S. goods going to developing countries. Other countries have export-import banks of their own to assist in financing their exports.

Commodity Credit Corporation. The U.S. Department of Agriculture's Commodity Credit Corporation provides payment assurances to U.S. sellers of surplus agricultural products to approved foreign buyers. Standby letters of credit are often in use, whereby the seller can draw under the credit for invoices that remain unpaid by the overseas buyer.

CONCLUSION

The letter of credit is a flexible banking arrangement that can be structured according to the needs of the parties. It is a security device and a tool for financing. It provides enough security for companies to do business safely over great distances. One indirect result of using the letter of credit is that it gives the parties an opportunity to experiment with doing business with each other. It allows them to build trust, which is essential to generating repeat business. If the buyer and seller are both pleased with each other's performance, they may eventually decide to omit the letter of credit from future transactions. The seller may be satisfied by selling on documentary terms alone, and eventually, on open account terms. Each step becomes easier and less expensive for the buyer, and that in turn may translate into additional business for the seller.

Chapter Summary

1. The *bill of exchange* or *international draft* is a specialized type of *negotiable instrument* commonly used to expedite foreign money payments in many types of international transactions.
2. The commercial and financing use of a draft or other negotiable instrument is derived from its *negotiability*, which is the quality that allows it to act as a substitute for money. When a draft is negotiated to a *holder in due course*, that party takes it free from most disputes that might arise between the drawer and drawee (the original parties to the underlying transaction). This protection for the holder in due course allows banks and other parties to purchase or accept drafts without fear of becoming embroiled in litigation over the original contract for which the draft was drawn.
3. A draft that may be paid upon presentation or demand is known as a *sight draft* because it is payable "on sight." The seller prepares the sight draft and presents it with the shipping documents through banking channels, moving from the seller's bank in the country of export to a foreign correspondent bank in the buyer's country and city. The draft is thereby sent "for collection," a process known as a *documentary collection.*
4. Banks and other financial institutions involved in commercial lending provide a wide range of financing packages for international trade, commonly called *trade finance.* A draft due at a future date or after a specified period of time is known as a *time draft.* The buyer's acceptance indicates the buyer's unconditional obligation to pay the draft on the date due.
5. A *banker's acceptance* is a negotiable instrument and short-term financing device widely used to finance international (as well as domestic) sales.
6. The documentary *letter of credit* is the definite undertaking of a bank, issued in accordance with the instructions of their customer, addressed to, or in favor of, the beneficiary, wherein the bank promises to pay a certain sum of money (or to accept or negotiate the beneficiary's drafts up to that sum), in the stated currency, within the prescribed time limits, upon the complying presentation of the required and conforming documents.
7. The *Uniform Custom and Practice for Documentary Credits* (UCP No. 600, 2007) is a set of standardized rules for issuing and handling letters of credit, drafted and published by the *International Chamber of Commerce.*
8. The letter of credit is a separate transaction and independent from the underlying sales contract on which it was based. Bankers deal in documents and not in goods, so they are not concerned with the quality or condition of goods represented in the credit.
9. The buyer's application for a credit forms a contract between the buyer and the issuing bank.
10. Credits are transmitted to the beneficiary through an *advising bank* (or through a *confirming bank,* in the case of a confirmed letter of credit).
11. The seller must make a *complying presentation* to the *nominated bank* within the time limits of the credit and according to the terms of the credit, the provisions of the UCP, and standard banking practices.
12. Documents containing discrepancies will be rejected and held for the buyer's instructions or returned to the seller. A discrepancy exists if the seller's documents, *on their face,* do not conform to the terms of the letter of credit. The description of the goods in the commercial invoice must correspond exactly to that in the credit. Documents are usually interpreted according to the *strict compliance rule.*
13. Courts have the power in certain cases to enjoin banks from honoring documents that are fraudulent or where there was fraud in the transaction.
14. *Confirmed letters of credit* contain the additional obligation of a second bank, usually in the seller's country, to honor a complying presentation. They are the next best alternative to receiving cash in advance for an international sale.
15. A *standby letter of credit* is one in which the issuer is obligated to pay a beneficiary upon the presentation of documents indicating a default by the account party in the payment of a debt or the performance of an obligation.

Key Terms

negotiable instrument 182
draft 182
documentary draft 182
bill of exchange 182
drawer 183
drawee 183
payee 183
negotiation 183
indorsement and delivery 183
sight draft 183
documentary collection 183
trade finance 184
time draft 184
banker's acceptance 185
holder in due course 186
letter of credit 187
issuer or issuing bank 188
account party 188
beneficiary 188
documentary letter of credit 188
Uniform Customs and Practice for Documentary Credits 188
independence principle 190
complying presentation 194
nominated bank 194
discrepancy 194
rule of strict compliance 196
fraud in the transaction 200
confirmed letter of credit 204
standby letter of credit 204
transferable credits 205
red clause 205
revolving letter of credit 205
evergreen clause 205
back-to-back letter of credit 205

Questions and Case Problems

1. Wade entered into a contract to sell irrigation equipment to Ribadalgo, its Ecuadorian distributor. Ribadalgo obtained an irrevocable letter of credit in the amount of $400,000 from Banco General Runinahui, S.A. (Banco), a bank in Quito, Ecuador. The letter of credit provided that Wade was to ship by July 30, 1992. Wade was to present documents for payment "no later than 15 days after shipment, but within the validity of the credit." The expiry date of the letter of credit was August 21, 1992. Partial shipments were acceptable. The letter of credit stated that it was governed by the UCP. Citibank confirmed the letter of credit. Wade shipped a portion of the goods on July 7. On July 21, just before the document presentment deadline, Wade presented the requisite documents to Citibank for payment. Two days later, on July 23, Citibank informed Wade that the documents contained discrepancies and that it therefore would not honor Wade's request for payment. In response, Wade forwarded amended documents to Citibank on July 24 and July 27. Although Citibank conceded the documents as amended contained no discrepancies, it nevertheless rejected them as untimely because they were not received within fifteen days of the July 7 shipment date as required by the credit. On July 17, the Ecuadorian government issued an order freezing all Ribadalgo's assets and precluding payment on any lines of credit made available to Ribadalgo due to alleged drug trafficking. Four days later, Ecuadorian banking authorities entered an order barring Banco from making payment under the letter of credit. In turn, Banco advised Citibank not to honor any request for payment made by Wade thereunder. Is Wade entitled to payment under the letter of credit from Citibank? Wade argues that the documents did not have to be conforming before the presentment deadline, but only before the expiry date of the credit. Is Wade correct? Why do you think Citibank rejected the documents on July 21? *Banco General Runinahui, S.A. v. Citibank*, 97 F.3d 480 (11th Cir. 1996).
2. The rule of strict compliance in New York is best illustrated by *Beyene v. Irving Trust Co.*, 762 F.2d 4 (2d Cir. 1985). The letter of credit specified that payment be made on presentation of a bill of lading naming "Mohammed Sofan" as the party to be notified when the goods arrive. However, the bill of lading submitted to the bank with the demand for payment misspelled the name as "Mohammed Soran." The confirming bank refused payment because of this discrepancy, and the beneficiary sued. Was this a "material" discrepancy, or was it "so insignificant as not to relieve the issuing and confirming bank of its obligation to pay"? The court compared and contrasted the misspelling of "Sofan" as "Soran" to the misspelling of "Smith" as "Smithh." The court stated that the misspelling of "Smith" is not a discrepancy because the meaning is "unmistakably clear despite what is obviously a typographical error." How did the court decide? Is there a difference between the misspellings of "Smith" and "Sofan"? For a more recent

example, see *Hanil Bank v. Pt. Bank Negara Indonesia (Persero),* 2000 U.S. Dist. LEXIS 2444 (S.D.N.Y.). The case involves an Indonesian bank that refused payment on a letter of credit it issued which had been subsequently negotiated to a Korean bank on the basis that the beneficiary was identified as Sung Jin Electronics Company rather than by its correct name Sung Jun Electronics Company.

3. Hambro Bank, Ltd., an English bank, received a cable from a Danish company, A.O., requesting that an irrevocable letter of credit be opened in favor of J. H. Rayner and Company. A.O. instructed Hambro Bank that the letter of credit be for "... about \P16,975 [pounds] against invoice full straight clean bills of lading ... covering about 1,400 tons Coromandel groundnuts." The bill of lading presented to Hambro by J. H. Rayner stated "... bags machine-shelled groundnut kernels," with the abbreviation "C.R.S." in the margin. Hambro refused to pay on the letter of credit. J. H. Rayner sued Hambro. The custom of trade holds that C.R.S. is short for Coromandel groundnuts. Why did the bank not want to pay on this letter of credit? Was the bank correct in denying payment on this letter of credit? *J. H. Rayner and Co., Ltd. v. Hambro's Bank, Ltd.* [1943] 1 K.B. 36.
4. The buyer, a Peruvian company, entered into a contract to purchase glass fibers from an English seller. Payment was to be made under an irrevocable letter of credit confirmed by Royal Bank of Canada. The letter of credit called for a bill of lading dated no later than December 15, 1976. The goods were in fact loaded onto the vessel on December 16, but the loading brokers wrongfully issued a bill of lading dated December 15, 1976. Unaware of the false statement, the sellers submitted documents to Royal Bank, who refused to pay because it suspected fraud in the documents. How does this situation differ from that in the *Sztejn v. J. Henry Schroder Banking Corporation* case? Does this case involve "fraud in the transaction"? Why or why not? Should the bank be permitted to refuse payment on the documents for apparently conforming documents where it has reason to believe a third party, here the loading broker, committed an act of fraud? See, *United City Merchants (Investments), Ltd. v. Royal Bank of Canada* [1982] 2 W.L.R.1039 (HL).
5. The seller of goods has a right to proceed judicially against an issuing bank that dishonors its obligation under an irrevocable letter of credit, just as the seller has the right to proceed directly against the buyer. Should the issuing bank also be liable for consequential damages that are reasonably foreseeable? See *Hadley v. Baxendale* [1854] 9 Ex. 341.
6. A South African firm applied for a revolving letter of credit in favor of a German exporter at a branch of Barclays Bank in Johannesburg. The letter of credit was issued covering shipments of pharmaceuticals and was confirmed by Deutsche Bank in Germany. Shipments proceeded with no problem, growing larger and more frequent. Barclays increased the amount of the letter of credit on several occasions to accommodate the growing business. To Barclays' knowledge, their account party had always taken possession of the goods and sold them quickly for a profit. Barclays was pleased with their customer's history and increased their financing. In the last shipment, the largest of all, Deutsche Bank honored the seller's sight draft for the full amount of the letter of credit and presented the documents to Barclays. While Barclays was inspecting the documents, it learned that the South African buyer had ceased business. In the meantime, Deutsche Bank discovered that the seller has ceased business also. On inspection by Barclays, the cargo containers were found to contain only worthless junk. Investigative reports placed both buyer and seller in Brazil. What happened? What are the rights and liabilities of the advising and confirming bank? How do banks handle problems like this?

Managerial Implications

1. Your firm regularly sells to customers in Germany, Poland, Japan, Canada, and Venezuela. How would you evaluate the creditworthiness of firms in each of these countries? How would the credit risk differ in each of these countries? What sources of information would you use? Under what circumstances would you consider selling to firms in these countries without a letter of credit? In which of these countries would you want an American bank to confirm the buyer's letter of credit? Why? What additional protection does confirming the credit provide?
2. An advising bank presents documents to you for payment. How would you respond to each of the following discrepancies? Explain your answers.
   a. The letter of credit calls for an ocean bill of lading. The seller presents a trucker's bill of lading showing shipment to an ocean port.
   b. The sales contract and the letter of credit call for shipment of "Soda Ash Light." The invoice shows shipment of "Soda Ash Light," but the bill of lading describes the shipment as "Soda Ash."

c. The letter of credit calls for shipment of 1,000 kilograms. The invoice shows shipment of an equal amount in pounds.

d. The CIF contract with the letter of credit calls for onboard bill of lading to be dated by December 20. The bill of lading is dated December 20, but the insurance policy is dated December 21.

Ethical Considerations

1. Corby, an experienced tire broker in Wales, offered to sell tires to Chappell, a tire broker in California. Chappell contacted two U.S. tire distributors, Jenkins in Tennessee and Hein in Ohio, and agreed to act as their agent in negotiations with Corby. Corby claimed that he had a large client who had negotiated an arrangement directly with Michelin to handle all of its overstock blemished tires from France and who could offer 50,000 to 70,000 Michelin tires per quarter at 40–60 percent below the U.S. market price on an exclusive and ongoing basis. Corby faxed a list of tires, showing that the tires bore the designation "DA/2C." Chappell faxed the list to Jenkins and Hein. They knew that the "DA" meant "defective appearance." When Chappell asked Corby about the "/2C" he was told that it meant the tires were located at a different warehouse. Chappell told Corby on several occasions that since it was October 1998, the season for selling winter tires was almost over and that he required summer tires as well, to bundle with the winter tires. A second list showed no summer tires and nowhere near the 50,000 tires promised. In November and December, Corby pressured Chappell and Jenkins to open the letter of credit, asserting that if they did not do so the deal would be ended, thus preventing the buyers from being able to procure the requested summer tires. In late December, Jenkins began having reservations regarding the deal because Corby's representations were becoming suspicious. Jenkins requested to speak to Corby's source. Corby put him in touch with Evans, a tire distributor in England. In January, Evans sent the following fax to Jenkins:

> There are large stocks of Michelin summer pattern tyres being made available within the next 7/10 days and we will be pleased to offer these to you when an acceptable Letter of Credit is received for the winter pattern tyres. We will be very happy to work with you on Michelin tyres on a long term basis and give you first option on offers. May we once again stress the urgency of letting us have the Letter of Credit for the Michelin winter tyres so that we can commence business on a long term basis?

Evans faxed a *pro forma* invoice requesting a letter of credit in favor of PTZ Trading Company in Guernsey as the beneficiary. Evans said that the letter of credit had to be sent immediately. The buyers felt that they had to comply as a show of good faith. An irrevocable credit was issued by an Ohio bank according to the terms of the *pro forma* invoice and stated:

> Covering shipment of: "14,851 Michelin tyres at usd 34.83 per tire in accordance with seller's *pro forma* invoice 927-98 dated 11-19-98. Shipping terms: EXWORKS any European location. The credit is subject to UCP Publication 500. Expiry date April 2, 1999. The credit was advised to the sellers through Barclays Bank.

Shortly later, the negotiations broke down over the issue of summer tires, and the parties became hostile. In February, Corby sent a list of summer tires that had fewer units than promised, contained sizes not used in the United States, included various tires not manufactured by Michelin, and specified prices that were often higher than the cost of purchasing the tires one at a time from most dealers in the United States. In March, the buyers discovered that the "DA/2C" designation, attached to many of the tires, actually meant that the U.S. Department of Transportation serial numbers had been buffed off those units, rendering them illegal for import to or sale in the United States. Just before the letter of credit expired, Jenkins was informed by Sievers, a German tire distributor who was shipping the tires for PTZ Trading Co., that the tires were about to ship. Jenkins protested that he had not given permission to ship the tires because there was no agreement on summer tires. He threatened legal action. Sievers responded that he did not need permission and proceeded to ship. Sievers obtained a bill of lading and presented all documents to Barclays Bank for payment. The documents strictly complied with the credit. Jenkins petitioned an Ohio court for a restraining order preventing the issuing bank from honoring the credit. Barclays Bank learned of the order and refused Sievers' presentment. The carrier billed Jenkins for the ocean freight, and the tires remained in a warehouse in Savannah, Georgia. After a hearing in July, the court denied the buyer's petition for the restraining order. The Ohio Court of Appeals reversed, and the buyer appealed to the Ohio Supreme Court. See *Mid-America Tire, Inc. v. PTZ Trading Ltd.*, 768 N.E.2d 619 (2002).

a. What are the buyer's legal arguments supporting its petition for a restraining order? How do the facts support that argument? What precedent can it cite?
b. What are the seller's arguments opposing the petition for a restraining order?
c. What do you think about the way the buyer handled this from the beginning? What does this say about its level of expertise in international business? Explain.
d. If you had been in the buyer's position, what would you have done differently?
e. If the documents had not strictly complied with the credit, would this case have turned out differently?
f. This court's decision only addressed the petition for a restraining order. How will the parties finally resolve the dispute on the underlying sales contract? What do you think will happen to the tires? Who is responsible for their warehousing fees?

2. Your firm has contracted to purchase silk from overseas suppliers on letter of credit terms. After contracting but before presentment of the seller's documents, China expands its production and floods the market with raw silk. The price of silk plummets on world markets. Comment on whether you should try to find a minor discrepancy in the documents to justify rejecting the documents. Is it ethical for a buyer to reject documents presented under a letter of credit that contains only a minor discrepancy between the documents and the credit? Do the reasons matter? Does it matter that the buyer may know that the shipment actually conforms to the requirements of the contract and of the letter of credit? What does the following statement mean? "Buyers and their banks have on occasion been known to 'invent' discrepancies; to make a 'mountain out of a molehill.'"

PART 3
International and U.S. Trade Law

In Part Three we examine the legal relationship between countries as they set the "rules of the game" for world trade in goods and services. We will study various international agreements intended to promote world trade, by removing trade barriers and lowering tariffs for example, and how nations implement those agreements into their national legislation. We will also see how the countries resolve trade disputes and avoid "trade wars."

Chapter Eight discusses the various branches of the U.S. government that share responsibility for regulating foreign commerce and trade, important U.S. trade legislation and U.S. trade agreements, and restrictions on U.S. state involvement in international trade. Chapters Nine, Ten, and Eleven cover the basics of international trade law. Chapter Nine examines important terminology and basic principles of international trade and tariff law, the role of the World Trade Organization, and processes for resolving trade disputes between countries. Chapter Ten examines laws that help keep markets open to foreign firms, and thus to foreign competition. It is about the process called "trade liberalization," through which countries negotiate freer and fairer methods of trade regulation to open markets and further world trade. This chapter focuses on non-tariff barriers that have blocked the import of U.S. goods and services in foreign countries. Chapter Eleven addresses the issues of free trade versus protectionism and the regulation of import competition. Many of these topics, such as dumping and subsidies, may be familiar to the reader from courses in economics. In this chapter, we will examine the very interesting legal aspects and political ramifications of these issues.

Chapter Twelve examines customs and tariff laws that govern the importing of goods into the United States and the relationship between a U.S. importer and the U.S. government. This chapter is important not only to American importers, but to any foreign firm that exports to the United States. We will learn how to determine the dutiable status of foreign goods and how to move them into the United States through the "entry process." We will look closely at the role of U.S. Customs and Border Protection, the U.S. agency charged with administering U.S. customs laws. This chapter focuses on importing as an integral part of the global strategy of the firm, in the context of global sourcing and the location of factories and assembly plants in different regions of the world.

Chapter Thirteen discusses legal restrictions on the export of goods and technology out of the United States. It addresses the national security and foreign policy implications of exports, such as the use of trade sanctions and other controls to stop the spread of weapons of mass destruction and missile technology, to fight international terrorism, and to further human rights.

Chapter Fourteen covers the *North American Free Trade Agreement* (NAFTA) and trade issues affecting the Western Hemisphere. This subject is near the end of this part because it builds on the principles of global trade covered in the earlier chapters.

Finally, Chapter Fifteen covers the European Union which has a level of economic integration far greater than that of NAFTA. Although NAFTA is a "free trade area," the European Union takes the process of economic integration several steps further and is both a "customs union" with common tariff laws and a "monetary union" with a common currency.

CHAPTER 8

National Lawmaking Powers and the Regulation of U.S. Trade

The U.S. Constitution provides for a separation of powers between the executive and legislative branches of government. In the field of international economic affairs, however, the roles of Congress and the president are not clearly defined. We know that Congress has the authority to impose duties, to regulate commerce with foreign nations, to punish offenses against the law of nations, and to declare war. But what of the president? The Constitution tells us that the president appoints ambassadors, negotiates with foreign nations, and is the commander-in-chief of the armed forces. The president also makes treaties, although only with the advice and consent of the Senate.

Even this cursory reading of the Constitution suggests that most of the authority to regulate U.S. commerce and trade with foreign countries rests with Congress and not with the president. Most scholars would agree. After all, the Constitution tells us that Congress "regulates" commerce with foreign nations, while the president merely "negotiates." In practice, it is not so simple. The system of checks and balances between the two branches has taken well over 200 years to develop. One established principle of American government is that Congress, within limits set out by decisions of the Supreme Court interpreting the Constitution, has the authority to delegate aspects of its legislative authority to the executive branch. Congress can enact a statute setting forth the goals to be accomplished and the means by which to achieve them and then authorize the president to carry them out. It can authorize the creation of a regulatory agency and provide funding for its work. As long as the president and the executive branch agencies are complying with the will of Congress, they are acting with the full force of law and usually with a large measure of congressional backing. This applies to the regulation of commerce with foreign nations and the establishment of U.S. trade policies.

In this chapter, we begin by exploring the basic concepts of the separation of powers in a modern business context. We will examine the balance of power over foreign commerce and foreign relations, the "inherent" authority of the president as chief executive and commander in chief, and the delegations of power from Congress to the president. We will see the difference between "treaties" and "executive agreements," both of which are used to implement the trade policies of the nation. We will also see how Congress has enacted statutes giving the president the authority to negotiate foreign trade agreements, including "fast track" trade promotion authority.

The chapter then briefly traces the history of American trade and tariff laws from the protectionist days of the *Smoot-Hawley Tariff Act of 1930*, which raised tariffs on imported goods to historic highs just at the start of the Great Depression, to the free trade programs that gave birth to modern free trade areas. Finally, we will look at the issue of federal-state relations and see the limits placed on state power when it comes to international affairs. This material provides an important background for later chapters.

THE SEPARATION OF POWERS

At the time the Constitution was drafted, people were greatly concerned with how to regulate foreign commerce. During this period of U.S. history, each state's primary interest was in its own economic well being. States imposed regulations on commerce to protect their own local industries, their ports, and their agricultural interests.

To ensure that states would not erect barriers to commerce between them and to guarantee a source of revenue to the federal government in the form of import duties, the drafters of the Constitution placed the power to regulate international commerce in the hands of the federal government. The drafters believed, for example, that economic disintegration could result if states were free to tax exports or if states located along the seacoast could tax imports passing through to states located inland. Moreover, they wanted the United States to be able to deal with foreign nations from a position of political strength and unity. The framers of the Constitution understood that trade relations with foreign nations could not be handled successfully by each state on its own, but only by a strong federal government that could speak for the economic and political interests of the nation as a whole.

Legislative Power of Congress

Today, the concept that the power over both foreign affairs and foreign trade rests with the federal government arouses little controversy. Considerable debate has arisen, however, over how the Constitution divides that power between Congress and the president. Article I of the Constitution confers "all legislative powers" on Congress, including the power "to regulate commerce with foreign nations, and among the several states" (Section 8, clause 3). In addition, Congress has broad power to pass domestic laws, raise and support armies, provide and maintain a navy, declare war, appropriate monies, and levy and collect taxes. The Senate has the authority to give advice and consent to the president in making treaties with foreign nations and to approve treaties by a two-thirds vote.

Considering these powers as a whole, the U.S. Supreme Court has consistently held that Congress has wide-ranging constitutional power to establish overall economic and trade policy for the United States and to put it into effect through legislation. Congress has recognized, however, that the day-to-day conduct of trade relations with foreign nations is often best accomplished through a strong executive branch. As a result, Congress has delegated authority to the president to carry out the trade policies set by statute.

Presidential Power

Article II of the Constitution confers executive power on the president. The executive power is not clearly specified, and many court decisions interpret what the Constitution meant to confer. However, both courts and legal scholars have said that the president has greater and wider-reaching power over foreign affairs than over domestic policy. An important argument in favor of a strong executive branch is that the nation must "speak with one voice" in international affairs. If each senator or representative, perhaps motivated by the local interests of his or her own constituents, attempts to negotiate agreements with foreign nations on matters such as tariff reductions, trade in agriculture or semiconductors, provisions for military assistance, or even nuclear disarmament, the process would be encumbered by local interests and would be ineffective and potentially disastrous. One of the most famous statements about the power of the president over foreign affairs is found in *United States v. Curtiss-Wright Export Co.,* 299 U.S. 304 (1936).

> Not only, as we have shown, is the federal power over external affairs in origin and essential character different from that over internal affairs, but participation in the exercise of the power is significantly limited. In this vast external realm, with its important, complicated, delicate and manifold problems, the President alone has the power to speak or listen as a representative of the nation. He makes treaties with the advice and consent of the Senate; but he alone negotiates. Into the field of negotiation the Senate cannot intrude; and Congress itself is powerless to invade it. As Marshall said in his great argument of March 7, 1800, in the House of Representatives, "The President is the sole organ of the nation in its external relations, and its sole representative with foreign nations." ... It is quite apparent that if, in the maintenance of our international relations, embarrassment—perhaps serious embarrassment—is to be avoided and success for our aims achieved, congressional legislation which is to be made effective through negotiation and inquiry within the international field must often accord to the President a degree of discretion and freedom from statutory restriction which would not be admissible were domestic affairs alone involved. Moreover, he, not Congress, has the better opportunity of knowing the conditions which prevail in foreign countries, and especially is this true in time of war. He has his confidential sources of information. He has his agents in the form of diplomatic, consular and other officials. Secrecy in respect of information gathered by them may be highly necessary, and the premature disclosure of it productive of harmful results.

The president's powers over foreign affairs are derived from (1) inherent power, including the power to conduct foreign affairs, appoint ambassadors, receive foreign ambassadors, and to act as commander-in-chief of the armed forces; (2) the treaty power; and (3) powers delegated by Congress in a statute. Each of these is addressed here in turn, to provide a better understanding of the interplay between the president and Congress in setting trade policies and carrying out trade relations with foreign countries.

President's Inherent Powers

The president's **inherent powers** are those that are either expressly granted to the president in the Constitution or found to be there by judicial interpretation. These may be powers necessary to conduct foreign affairs, to appoint ambassadors, to receive foreign ambassadors, or to act as commander-in-chief of the armed forces. The president may only rely on these inherent powers when Congress has not passed a law directing otherwise. In limited situations, the president can use the inherent power to justify entering into a sole executive agreement.

Sole Executive Agreements. A **sole executive agreement** is one negotiated and put into legal effect on the basis of the inherent authority of the president, and does not require congressional approval. The president's authority to enter a sole executive agreement is based on powers inherent in being the chief executive of the nation and commander-in-chief of the armed forces. Sole executive agreements are used to execute and carry out existing laws, or to enter into agreements with foreign countries that do not create broad new national policies. They are not treaties or substitutes for treaties. Examples include an agreement with a foreign country to lease property for the site of an American embassy, or an agreement for scientific cooperation or the exchange of technical information. Most sole executive agreements, such as the one in the following case, *Dole v. Carter*, relate to specific matters.

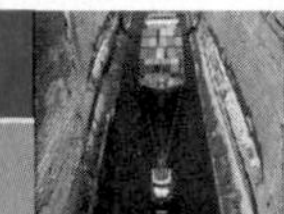

Dole v. Carter

444 F. Supp. 1065 (1977) United States District Court (D. Kan.)

BACKGROUND AND FACTS

This action was brought by a U.S. senator against the president to enjoin him from returning the Hungarian coronation regalia to the People's Republic of Hungary. The Holy Crown of St. Stephen had been held by the Hungarian people as a treasured symbol of their statehood and nationality for nearly 1,000 years. At the close of World War II, it was entrusted to the United States for safekeeping by Hungarian soldiers. In 1977, the governments of the United States and Hungary entered into an agreement returning the crown to Hungary. Many Hungarians living in the United States were opposed to the return of the crown. The plaintiff filed this action seeking an injunction against delivery of the crown to Hungary on the ground that such action was tantamount to a treaty undertaken by the president without the prior advice and consent of the Senate.

DISTRICT JUDGE O'CONNOR

We turn now to the plaintiff's argument that the agreement to return the coronation regalia to Hungary in and of itself constitutes a treaty which must be ratified by the Senate. It is well established, and even plaintiff admits, that the United States frequently enters into international agreements other than treaties. Indeed, as of January 1, 1972, the United States was a party to 5,306 international agreements, only 947 of which were treaties and 4,359 of which were international agreements other than treaties. These "other agreements" appear to fall into three categories: (1) so-called congressional-executive agreements, executed by the President upon specific authorizing legislation from the Congress; (2) executive agreements pursuant to treaty, executed by the President in accord with specific instructions found in a prior, formal treaty; and (3) executive agreements executed pursuant to the President's own constitutional authority (hereinafter referred to as "executive agreements"). Defendant contends that his agreement to return the coronation regalia to Hungary falls into the latter category, and the court agrees. * * *

The United States enters into approximately 200 executive agreements each year, and it has been observed that the constitutional system "could not last a month" if the President sought Senate or congressional consent for every one of them. L. Henkin, *Foreign Affairs and the Constitution* ... Congress itself recognized this fact in passing P.L 92-403, 1 U.S.C. §112b, requiring the secretary of state to transmit for merely informational purposes the text of all international agreements other than treaties to which the United States becomes a party. The House Committee on Foreign Affairs stated in recommending passage of that statute that while it wished to be apprised of "all agreements of any significance," "[c]learly the Congress does not want to be inundated with trivia." 1972 U.S. Code Cong, and Admin. News, p. 3069. While the President's understanding to return the Hungarian coronation regalia is hardly a "trivial" matter to either the United States or the people of Hungary, the court is yet convinced that the President's agreement in this regard lacks the magnitude of agreements customarily concluded in treaty form. The President's agreement

continues

continued

here involves no substantial ongoing commitment on the part of the United States, exposes the United States to no appreciable discernible risks, and contemplates American action of an extremely limited duration in time. The plaintiff presented no evidence that agreements of the kind in question here are traditionally concluded only by treaty, either as a matter of American custom or as a matter of international law. Indeed, while the court has not exhaustively examined all possibly pertinent treaties, the court can hardly imagine that any such examination would lend support to the plaintiff's position. Finally, the agreement here encompasses no substantial reciprocal commitments by the Hungarian government. As a matter of law, the court is therefore persuaded that the President's agreement to return the Hungarian coronation regalia is not a commitment requiring the advice and consent of the Senate under Article II, Section 2, of the Constitution.

Decision. The plaintiff's motion for a preliminary injunction was denied. The agreement to return the coronation regalia was found to be not a treaty requiring ratification by the Senate, but a valid executive agreement based on the president's inherent power.

Case Questions

1. Why did the president use a sole executive agreement resolving this issue with Hungary instead of relying on the treaty power?
2. Was the president's action required to be authorized by the Congress?
3. What kinds of agreements are usually reserved for treaties, and what kinds are handled through executive agreements?

If Congress has passed a statute on a subject, the president's inherent power does not grant "license" to violate that law. There are also limitations on the president's power as commander in chief, especially during peacetime and at home. Many controversies arise when Congress fails to address an issue through legislation, and the president acts to "fill the void" by dealing with the issue alone, without the consent of Congress. For example, the president cannot "stretch" his title as commander-in-chief to achieve an objective not normally within the purview of the armed forces. To this day, one of the most frequently cited cases on the president's inherent power is *Youngstown Sheet & Tube v. Sawyer.* In this case, President Truman had relied on his inherent power as chief executive and as commander-in-chief of the armed forces to force the continued operation of the nation's steel mills during the Korean War in the face of a threatened labor strike. Notice the differences with the last case. Pay particular attention to Justice Jackson's concurring opinion.

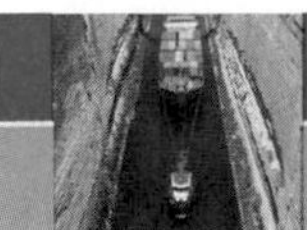

Youngstown Sheet & Tube v. Sawyer

343 U.S. 579 (1952) United States Supreme Court

BACKGROUND AND FACTS

In the early 1950s, the United States was at war in Korea as part of a United Nations "police action." American steelworkers were threatening to strike over wages and collective bargaining disagreements with steel companies. The president made every attempt to intervene and to help the parties negotiate an agreement. A strike would have disrupted the supply of steel, leading to a possible shortage of steel during the war effort and an increase in prices in all products made of steel. Despite all efforts, the parties were unable to reach agreement. Just before the steelworkers were to go on strike, President Truman ordered Secretary of Commerce Charles Sawyer to seize the steel mills and keep them in operation. The president based his authority for doing so on Article II of the Constitution and on his power as commander in chief of the armed forces. A district court granted the request of the steel companies for a temporary injunction against the president's order, the Court of Appeals agreed, and the secretary of commerce appealed to the Supreme Court.

DECISION MR. JUSTICE BLACK DELIVERED THE OPINION OF THE COURT

* * *

The President's power, if any, to issue the order must stem either from an act of Congress or from the Constitution itself. There is no statute that expressly authorizes the President to take possession of property as he did here. Nor is there any act of Congress to which our attention has been directed from which such

continues

continued

a power can fairly be implied. Indeed, we do not understand the Government to rely on statutory authorization for this seizure

Moreover, the use of the seizure technique to solve labor disputes in order to prevent work stoppages was not only unauthorized by any congressional enactment; prior to this controversy, Congress had refused to adopt that method of settling labor disputes. When the *Taft-Hartley Act* was under consideration in 1947, Congress rejected an amendment which would have authorized such governmental seizures in cases of emergency. Apparently it was thought that the technique of seizure, like that of compulsory arbitration, would interfere with the process of collective bargaining. * * *

The order cannot properly be sustained as an exercise of the President's military power as Commander in Chief of the Armed Forces. The Government attempts to do so by citing a number of cases upholding broad powers in military commanders engaged in day-to-day fighting in a theater of war. Such cases need not concern us here. Even though "theater of war" be an expanding concept, we cannot with faithfulness to our constitutional system hold that the Commander in Chief of the Armed Forces has the ultimate power as such to take possession of private property in order to keep labor disputes from stopping production. This is a job for the Nation's lawmakers, not for its military authorities.

Nor can the seizure order be sustained because of the several constitutional provisions that grant executive power to the President. In the framework of our Constitution, the President's power to see that the laws are faithfully executed refutes the idea that he is to be a lawmaker. The Constitution limits his functions in the lawmaking process to the recommending of laws he thinks wise and the vetoing of laws he thinks bad. And the Constitution is neither silent nor equivocal about who shall make laws which the President is to execute. The first section of the first article says that "All legislative Powers herein granted shall be vested in a Congress of the United States. * * * The power of Congress to adopt such public policies as those proclaimed by the order is beyond question. It can authorize the taking of private property for public use. It can make laws regulating the relationships between employers and employees, prescribing rules designed to settle labor disputes, and fixing wages and working conditions in certain fields of our economy. The Constitution did not subject this law-making power of Congress to presidential or military supervision or control. * * *

The judgment of the District Court is affirmed.

MR. JUSTICE JACKSON, CONCURRING IN THE JUDGMENT AND OPINION OF THE COURT

* * *

When the President acts pursuant to an express or implied authorization of Congress, his authority is at its maximum, for it includes all that he possesses in his own right plus all that Congress can delegate. In these circumstances, and in these only, may he be said (for what it may be worth), to personify the federal sovereignty. If his act is held unconstitutional under these circumstances, it usually means that the Federal Government as an undivided whole lacks power. A seizure executed by the President pursuant to an Act of Congress would be supported by the strongest of presumptions and the widest latitude of judicial interpretation, and the burden of persuasion would rest heavily upon any who might attack it.

When the President acts in absence of either a congressional grant or denial of authority, he can only rely upon his own independent powers, but there is a zone of twilight in which he and Congress may have concurrent authority, or in which its distribution is uncertain. Therefore, congressional inertia, indifference or quiescence may sometimes, at least as a practical matter, enable, if not invite, measures on independent presidential responsibility. In this area, any actual test of power is likely to depend on the imperatives of events and contemporary imponderables rather than on abstract theories of law.

When the President takes measures incompatible with the expressed or implied will of Congress, his power is at its lowest ebb, for then he can rely only upon his own constitutional powers minus any constitutional powers of Congress over the matter. Courts can sustain exclusive Presidential control in such a case only by disabling the Congress from acting upon the subject. Presidential claim to a power at once so conclusive and preclusive must be scrutinized with caution, for what is at stake is the equilibrium established by our constitutional system. * * *

In view of the ease, expedition and safely with which Congress can grant and has granted large emergency powers, certainly ample to embrace this crisis, I am quite unimpressed with the argument that we should affirm possession of them without statute. Such power

continues

continued

either has no beginning or it has no end. If it exists, it need submit to no legal restraint. I am not alarmed that it would plunge us straightway into dictatorship, but it is at least a step in that wrong direction.

Decision. The lower court's injunction against the President's action was upheld. The President was not acting pursuant to an act of Congress, nor could the seizure of private property during wartime be justified on the basis of his inherent power as President or as Commander in Chief.

Comment. The concurring opinion by Justice Jackson is one of the most frequently cited opinions in American constitutional history regarding presidential powers. Justice Robert Jackson was America's chief prosecutor of Nazi war criminals at the Nuremberg Trials. Where, as in this case, the President's action is in contradiction to acts of Congress, the President's power is at its "lowest ebb."

Case Questions

1. On what grounds did Justice Black reject President Truman's seizure order?
2. Explain Justice Jackson's tripartite classification of presidential power. How did he classify President Truman's action in seizing the steel mills, and why?
3. Considering that the United States was engaged in a brutal war in Korea, and that steel was needed for the war effort, do you agree with this decision (three justices dissented)? If the Court had permitted the seizure of a private business in this case, could that have led to a "slippery slope" and ultimately future seizures on somewhat lesser grounds?

The Treaty Power

In Chapter Two we discuss the legal status of self-executing and non-self-executing treaties under international and national law. The term **treaty power** refers to the authority of the United States to enter treaties pursuant to Article II of the Constitution. U.S. treaties are negotiated by the executive branch with the "advice and consent" of the Senate and approved by a two-thirds vote of the Senate. The House does not vote on treaties. Treaties are binding on both the federal and state governments with the same force as an act of Congress. This is known as the **equal dignity rule**; both statutes and treaties are of equal importance. In the event of a conflict between a treaty and statute, the last in time prevails. A treaty will override an inconsistent prior act of Congress. Similarly, an act of Congress can override an inconsistent prior treaty, provided that Congress had expressed its intention to do so. Treaties of the United States can be found in the U.S. State Department document, *Treaties in Force.* For a discussion of treaties under international law, and an explanation of the different types of treaties, see Chapter Two.

Congressional-Executive Agreements. Treaties are not the only type of international agreement. **Congressional-executive agreements** are international agreements between the president, representing the United States, and a foreign country, negotiated and concluded by the president and voted into law by a simple majority vote of both the Senate and the House of Representatives. Congressional-executive agreements serve much the same purpose as treaties, but they are entered into without resort to the treaty process. Their legal nature, however, is different. Unlike treaties, congressional-executive agreements are not described in the Constitution. They are a creature of compromise between the president and Congress. Congressional-executive agreements date to the Roosevelt era of the 1930s and 1940s, when the president was seeking new and more flexible ways of dealing with the nation's economic problems during the Great Depression and World War II. By the close of World War II, the House and Senate had informally agreed with the president to provide a substitute process for approving international agreements—one that would not require a two-thirds vote of approval of the Senate, as do treaties. Instead, they agreed on a substitute process permitting international agreements to be approved either by statute or by joint resolutions of both houses of Congress. Statutes and joint resolutions can pass on a *simple majority vote* of both houses. Presidents usually prefer the congressional-executive agreement process to the treaty process because it is often easier for them to obtain congressional approval by simple majority vote of both the House and Senate than it is to obtain a two-thirds vote of the Senate. Since World War II, most international agreements of the United States have been executive agreements, not treaties. Congressional-executive agreements, as a delegated power, clearly meet the standard for presidential power set out in Justice Jackson's concurring opinion in *Youngstown Steel.*

Presidential Power and U.S. Trade Relations

From the time of America's first tariff act in 1790 through the early 1900s, the concern of Congress was more with setting tariffs than setting trade policy. Tariff setting was a unilateral process—rates were not set by negotiations with foreign governments so much as by negotiation in the halls of Congress, no doubt under some political influence. U.S. law gave little authority to the president other than to collect the tariffs on imported goods according to the rates set by Congress. Congress saw tariffs as a way to collect revenue and protect American industry and workers. Shortly after World War I, partially as a result of isolationist sentiments at home, the United States began to increase tariffs on imported goods. Under the *Smoot-Hawley Tariff Act of 1930,* signed into law by President Herbert Hoover, the U.S. Congress imposed the highest tariff levels in the nation's history. The levels were so high that other nations raised their tariffs in retaliation. Some tariff rates reached nearly 100 percent of the cost of the goods. It was disastrous. Economic activity declined precipitously. When the U.S. slowed imports of foreign goods, buyers in those countries no longer had the U.S. dollars to purchase U.S. goods. Foreign nations retaliated and imposed burdensome tariffs on their imports. It became a worldwide problem, and it is generally accepted today that it exacerbated the Great Depression of the 1930s.

While President Franklin Roosevelt recognized the immediate need to reduce tariffs, he simply did not have the legal authority to take any significant action without congressional approval, and the treaty process was too cumbersome. Roosevelt therefore worked with Congress to pass the *Reciprocal Trade Agreements Act of 1934,* which provided the president with the authority needed to lower tariffs.

The Reciprocal Trade Agreements Act of 1934

The *Reciprocal Trade Agreements Act of 1934* created a partnership between the executive and congressional branches of government in setting tariff and trade policy. It not only provided the president with a mechanism for lowering "the *Smoot-Hawley* tariff rates" but for encouraging other countries to lower their rates on our products in return. This act granted the president far more flexible powers to adjust tariffs than under any prior legislation. The president was granted the authority to negotiate tariff reductions on a product-by-product basis with other countries on the basis of **reciprocal trade**. The United States would reduce a tariff on a foreign product if the foreign country would reciprocate by lowering its tariffs. An agreement to reduce a tariff to a specified level is known as a **tariff concession**. If the United States lowers an existing tariff on an imported product from France, for example, then France must make similar concessions on the same or other products coming from the United States.

Unconditional Most-Favored-Nation Trade. The 1934 *Reciprocal Trade Agreements Act* also introduced most-favored-nation or *MFN trade.* MFN trade can be conditional or unconditional. **Conditional MFN trade** means that any trading advantage (such as a reduced tariff rate) applied to an item imported into a country will also be applied to the same or like items coming from any other country that has MFN status with the importing country, *provided that country reciprocates and lowers its tariff rates in an equivalent amount in return.* Prior to the 1930s the United States relied on conditional MFN trade. The concept of unconditional MFN trade, however, came into U.S. law in 1934. In **unconditional MFN trade** any new lower tariff that applies to an item imported from one MFN trading partner *automatically applies to the same or like items imported from all other nations that are in MFN status with the importing country, without any concession being required from those nations in return.* Thus, if the United States negotiates a lower tariff rate on raw shrimp coming from one MFN trading nation, then that rate *automatically applies* to raw shrimp coming from all other MFN trading nations without them having to do anything in return. Unconditional MFN trade is one of the foundations of the modern trading system today.

One country grants MFN legal status to another by international treaty or congressional-executive agreement, and the executive branch negotiates MFN tariff rates. While the logic of unconditional MFN trade may not be clear, it makes economic and political sense. It helps to lower global tariff rates much faster than would otherwise occur, and it is fairer. It allows for equal treatment, without discrimination, of all countries designated as MFN partners. In the United States, unconditional MFN trade has been renamed by Congress as **normal trade relations**. Countries with whom the United States has normal trade relations receive a favorable, negotiated rate well below the original 1930 *Smoot-Hawley* rate.

In the following case, *Star-Kist Foods, Inc. v. United States*, the constitutionality of the tariff-setting process of the *Reciprocal Trade Agreements* the president. In doing so, the court upheld the foundations of U.S. customs and tariff laws in use today.

Star-Kist Foods, Inc. v. United States

275 F.2d 472 (1959) United States Court of Customs and Patent Appeals

BACKGROUND AND FACTS

Star-Kist Foods, a U.S. producer of canned tuna, instituted a lawsuit to protest the assessment of duties made by the collector of customs on imported canned tuna. Duty was assessed on the canned tuna at the rate of 12.5 percent pursuant to a trade agreement with Iceland. Prior to the agreement, the tariff rate had been set by Congress in the *Tariff Act of 1930* at 25 percent *ad valorem.* The trade agreement with Iceland, which resulted in lowering the rate of duty, was executed pursuant to the *Reciprocal Trade Agreements Act of 1934.* That act authorized the president to enter into foreign trade agreements for the purpose of expanding foreign markets for the products of the United States by affording corresponding market opportunities for foreign products in the United States. To implement an agreement, the president was then authorized to raise or lower any duty previously set by Congress, but not by more than 50 percent. Star-Kist brought this action, contending that the delegation of authority under the 1934 act, and the agreement with Iceland, were unconstitutional.

JUDGE MARTIN

A constitutional delegation of powers requires that Congress enunciate a policy or objective or give reasons for seeking the aid of the President. In addition the act must specify when the powers conferred may be utilized by establishing a standard or "intelligible principle" which is sufficient to make it clear when action is proper. And because Congress cannot abdicate its legislative function and confer carte blanche authority on the President, it must circumscribe that power in some manner. This means that Congress must tell the President what he can do by prescribing a standard which confines his discretion and which will guarantee that any authorized action he takes will tend to promote rather than flout the legislative purpose. It is not necessary that the guides be precise or mathematical formulae to be satisfactory in a constitutional sense.

In the act before us the congressional policy is pronounced very clearly. The stated objectives are to expand foreign markets for the products of the United States "by regulating the admission of foreign goods into the United States in accordance with the characteristics and needs of various branches of American production so that foreign markets will be made available to those branches of American production which require and are capable of developing such outlets by affording corresponding market opportunities for foreign products in the United States. ..."

Pursuant to the 1934 act the presidential power can be invoked "whenever he [the President] finds as a fact that any existing duties or other import restrictions of the United States or any foreign country are unduly burdening or restricting the foreign trade of the United States and that the [purpose of the act] will be promoted." ...

Under the provisions of the 1934 act the President by proclamation can modify existing duties and other import restrictions but not by more than 50 percent of the specified duties nor can he place articles upon or take them off the free list. Furthermore, he must accomplish the purposes of the act through the medium of foreign trade agreements with other countries. However, he can suspend the operation of such agreements if he discovers discriminatory treatment of American commerce, and he can terminate, in whole or in part, any proclamation at any time ...

In view of the Supreme Court's recognition of the necessity of flexibility in the laws affecting foreign relations ... we are of the opinion that the 1934 act does not grant an unconstitutional delegation of authority to the President.

Decision. The court held for the United States. The congressional delegation of authority under the 1934 statute was constitutional because Congress had provided the president with a sufficiently discernible standard to guide any decisions in carrying out the purposes of the act.

Case Questions

1. What was the constitutional authority for the agreement with Iceland?
2. What was the policy objective of Congress in enacting the *Reciprocal Trade Agreements Act* noted by the court? How was the president to implement this policy?
3. Why was the congressional delegation of authority constitutional?

Trade Agreements and Trade Promotion Authority

A **trade agreement** is an international agreement between nations on matters related to trade and tariffs. In addition to reducing tariffs or other barriers to trade in goods or services, trade agreements can achieve far broader objectives. For example, some agreements manage or control trade in endangered wildlife, forestry products, or antiquities, while others might also address "side-issues," such as the protection of intellectual property, the rights of workers in developing countries, the rights of investors, or cross-border transportation. Some trade agreements have a mechanism for resolving disputes between countries over trade issues. Trade agreements can be either bilateral or multilateral. Many trade agreements are completed between neighboring countries or those with regional concerns. America's first trade agreement was a bilateral agreement with France in 1778.

A **free trade agreement** usually refers to a trade agreement with broader coverage that establishes a "free trade area" in which special tariff and customs provisions govern the flow of trade between the participating countries. Goods moving between these countries usually have no tariffs and few restrictions.

Although trade agreements can be concluded by treaty, the United States usually uses the congressional-executive process instead. Of course, there is always the risk that a politicized Congress might later reject any agreement that the executive branch and a foreign country reach. Imagine the executive branch taking years to negotiate trade agreements with dozens of countries, covering thousands of products affecting hundreds of industries, only to have a senator or representative vote against it because it would reduce import duties on foreign products that compete with those made by his or her special interests back home. A potential rejection by Congress or delay of many years might also make a foreign nation less willing to enter trade negotiations.

To avoid this, the *Trade Reform Act of 1974* set up a "fast-track" process for approving trade agreements, known as the president's **trade promotion authority**. The statute gave the president authority to negotiate trade agreements pursuant to the objectives set out by Congress. During trade negotiations, the president must consult with Congress and notify it of proposed changes to U.S. trade laws. Congress can then comment on the negotiations before there is a final agreement and while there is still time for the president to modify it. At the conclusion of negotiations, both houses of Congress must vote on a bill submitted by the president. The agreement must pass a simple majority vote in its entirety without amendment. This process helps ensure the passage of trade agreements into U.S. law because it eliminates the possibility of Congress trying to rewrite agreements under pressure from special interests. Trade promotion authority has been used successfully to negotiate many trade agreements since the end of World War II. The president's trade promotion authority expired in 2007, however, and Congress has yet to renew it as of 2013.

Survey of U.S. Trade Legislation since 1962

In 1962 Congress authorized the president to negotiate across-the-board tariff reductions instead of using the tedious product-by-product system set up in 1934. This allowed for an even faster reduction of tariffs worldwide. By the mid-1970s tariff rates had been reduced significantly, and it was the non-tariff barriers that were seen as interfering with the worldwide free flow of goods and services. Recall that a **non-tariff barrier** is any barrier to trade other than tariffs intended to prohibit or discourage imports, including quotas on imported products, special licenses for importing, and hidden "red tape" in the customs laws. In the 1970s, and continuing to this day, Congress has given additional authority to the president to use the economic leverage of U.S. trade, and the threat of trade sanctions, to force foreign governments to remove unfair non-tariff barriers to the entry of U.S. goods and services.

Also in the 1970s, the trade concerns of developing countries were taken more seriously—concerns that are of importance today in all global trade negotiations. For example, during this period the United States initiated a program giving trade preferences to goods imported from developing countries. A **trade preference** is a law that grants favorable trade and tariff treatment to products coming from developing countries, and is intended to aid in their economic development. Various U.S. programs dating to the mid-1970s grant trade preferences and lowered rates of duty on goods from Africa, the Caribbean, and developing countries throughout the world. Most developed countries have similar programs. Trade preference rates of duty are generally lower than even the MFN rate.

By the 1980s and 1990s the focus of U.S. trade objectives changed, geographically and in scope.

There were several new areas of concern: (1) removing barriers to trade in high technology industries, (2) removing barriers to trade in services, (3) incorporating the protection of intellectual property and investment concerns into trade laws, (4) negotiating free trade areas, and perhaps most importantly, (5) a commitment to formalize multilateral trade negotiations and dispute settlement procedures in one permanent international organization. The *Omnibus Trade and Competitiveness Act of 1988* extended the president's authority to negotiate trade agreements, which led to the *North American Free Trade Agreement* (1994), the *Central American Free Trade Agreement* (2004), and the *Agreement Establishing World Trade Organization* (1994). In addition, the president and Congress have also passed a number of trade agreements dealing with specific issues, or affecting U.S. trade with specific world regions. This led to the eventual passage of the *Caribbean Basin Economic Recovery Act of 1983,* the *Andean Trade Program and Drug Eradication Act of 2002,* and the *African Growth and Opportunity Act of 2000,* as well as other important trade laws.

As a result of the process started in the 1980s, as of 2013 the U.S. had bilateral or regional free trade agreements with Australia, Bahrain, Canada, Chile, Colombia, Costa Rica, Dominican Republic, El Salvador, Guatemala, Honduras, Israel, Jordan, Korea, Mexico, Morocco, Nicaragua, Oman, Panama, Peru, and Singapore.

Enhanced and Emergency Powers of the President

Today, the president is authorized not just to reduce duties on products but also to take a wide range of executive actions to deal with the complexities of the modern business world. This authority is in keeping with the modern notion that the president needs increased flexibility in handling matters related to international trade and foreign affairs. For example, the president has authority to negotiate special trade relations with developing countries; negotiate rules for dealing with agricultural trade problems; coordinate international monetary policies; negotiate better mechanisms for protecting copyrights, patents, and trademarks in foreign countries; negotiate a reduction of barriers to trade in high technology; and ensure equal access to foreign high technology by U.S. firms.

In addition, the president has broader powers to deal with a range of complex economic problems. For example, the president may take certain specific measures approved by Congress to protect U.S. industries from foreign competition. These powers can be used under well-defined circumstances defined by Congress, such as when U.S. industry is being injured by increased imports of particular foreign products.

Congress also grants the president **emergency powers** for responding to international emergencies. International emergencies are generally unexpected international events that threaten American national security. The *International Emergency Economic Powers Act* enables the president to block financial transactions or restrict the flow of trade with foreign countries, or seize the assets of governments, individuals, or organizations responsible. These issues are discussed in Chapter Thirteen.

FEDERAL-STATE RELATIONS

Thus far our discussion focuses on the relation between the executive and legislative branches of the federal government. But the notion of "federalism" also implies that the United States has two levels of government—state and federal. The Constitution has several provisions that touch on the relations between the state and federal governments and that determine a state's authority to regulate international (as well as interstate) trade.

The Supremacy Clause

When a law or regulation of the federal government directly conflicts with those of the state (or local) government, the federal law will generally prevail when Congress expresses the intention that the federal law shall prevail or when that intention may be inferred from the legislation or from the circumstances. This is known as **federal preemption**. Where Congress enacts a comprehensive scheme of legislation, such as statutes and federal regulations governing commercial aviation, the federal rule will prevail over an inconsistent state rule. The inconsistent state law is void to the extent it conflicts with the federal scheme.

In the following case, *Arizona v. United States*, the U.S. Supreme Court considered an attempt by the State of Arizona to deal with illegal immigration there. Arizona, like other border states, does indeed have many problems stemming from illegal immigration. The Court was aware of the "epidemic of crime, safety risks, serious property damage and environmental problems associated with the influx of illegal migration" from Mexico. It also noted that hundreds of thousands of deportable aliens are apprehended in Arizona each year. However, the issue confronting the Court was not what Arizona should do about the immigration problem, but about what the Constitution permitted it to do considering the limits of federal preemption.

Arizona v. United States

132 S.Ct. 2492 (2012) United States Supreme Court

BACKGROUND AND FACTS

During a time of political controversy in the United States over immigration policy and enforcement, the State of Arizona enacted a statute to deal with the large number of unlawful aliens in the state. Section 3 made it a misdemeanor under Arizona law for any person to violate federal alien-registration laws. Section 5(c) made it a misdemeanor for an unauthorized alien to seek or engage in work in the state. Section 6 authorized state and local officers to arrest without a warrant any person they believed could lawfully be removed from the United States. Section 2(B) required state and local officials to contact federal officials for the purpose of verifying the immigration status of any person who had been lawfully stopped or detained. The United States brought this action against Arizona challenging the constitutionality of the statute. A federal district court enjoined enforcement of the statute, and Arizona appealed. The Supreme Court granted certiorari.

JUSTICE KENNEDY DELIVERED THE OPINION OF THE COURT

The Government of the United States has broad, undoubted power over the subject of immigration and the status of aliens. See *Toll v. Moreno,* 458 U.S. 1, 10, 102 S.Ct. 2977 (1982) [citations omitted]. This authority rests, in part, on the National Government's constitutional power to "establish an uniform Rule of Naturalization," *U.S. Const.*, Art. I, §8, cl. 4, and its inherent power as sovereign to control and conduct relations with foreign nations.

The federal power to determine immigration policy is well settled. Immigration policy can affect trade, investment, tourism, and diplomatic relations for the entire Nation, as well as the perceptions and expectations of aliens in this country who seek the full protection of its laws. Perceived mistreatment of aliens in the United States may lead to harmful reciprocal treatment of American citizens abroad.

It is fundamental that foreign countries concerned about the status, safety, and security of their nationals in the United States must be able to confer and communicate on this subject with one national sovereign, not the 50 separate States. This Court has reaffirmed that "[o]ne of the most important and delicate of all international relationships ... has to do with the protection of the just rights of a country's own nationals when those nationals are in another country." *Hines v. Davidowitz,* 312 U.S. 52, 64, 61 S.Ct. 399 (1941).

Federal governance of immigration and alien status is extensive and complex. Congress has specified categories of aliens who may not be admitted to the United States. Unlawful entry and unlawful reentry into the country are federal offenses. Once here, aliens are required to register with the Federal Government and to carry proof of status on their person. Failure to do so is a federal misdemeanor. Federal law also authorizes States to deny noncitizens a range of public benefits, and it imposes sanctions on employers who hire unauthorized workers.

Congress has specified which aliens may be removed from the United States and the procedures for doing so. Aliens may be removed if they were inadmissible at the time of entry, have been convicted of certain crimes, or meet other criteria set by federal law. Removal is a civil, not criminal, matter. A principal feature of the removal system is the broad discretion exercised by immigration officials. Federal officials, as an initial matter, must decide whether it makes sense to pursue removal at all. If remo-val proceedings commence, aliens may seek asylum and other discretionary relief allowing them to remain in the country or at least to leave without formal removal.

Discretion in the enforcement of immigration law embraces immediate human concerns. * * * Some discretionary decisions involve policy choices that bear on this Nation's international relations. Returning an alien to his own country may be deemed inappropriate even where he has committed a removable offense or fails to meet the criteria for admission. The foreign state may be mired in civil war, complicit in political persecution, or enduring conditions that create a real risk that the alien or his family will be harmed upon return. The dynamic nature of relations with other countries requires the Executive Branch to

continues

continued

ensure that enforcement policies are consistent with this Nation's foreign policy with respect to these and other realities. * * *

Federalism, central to the constitutional design, adopts the principle that both the National and State Governments have elements of sovereignty the other is bound to respect. From the existence of two sovereigns follows the possibility that laws can be in conflict or at cross-purposes. The Supremacy Clause provides a clear rule that federal law "shall be the supreme Law of the Land; and the Judges in every State shall be bound thereby, any Thing in the Constitution or Laws of any State to the Contrary notwithstanding." Art. VI, cl. 2. Under this principle, Congress has the power to preempt state law. See *Crosby v. National Foreign Trade Council*, 530 U.S. 363, 372, 120 S.Ct. 2288 (2000); *Gibbons v. Ogden*, 9 Wheat. 1, 210–211 (1824).

State law must also give way to federal law in at least two other circumstances. First, the States are precluded from regulating conduct in a field that Congress, acting within its proper authority, has determined must be regulated by its exclusive governance. * * * Second, state laws are preempted when they conflict with federal law. * * *

The four challenged provisions of the state law each must be examined under these preemption principles.

Section 3 of the Arizona Statute Section 3 creates a new state misdemeanor. It forbids the "willful failure to complete or carry an alien registration document ... in violation of [federal law]. * * *

Federal law makes a single sovereign responsible for maintaining a comprehensive and unified system to keep track of aliens within the Nation's borders. If §3 of the Arizona statute were valid, every State could give itself independent authority to prosecute federal registration violations, "diminish[ing] the [Federal Government]'s control over enforcement" and "detract[ing] from the 'integrated scheme of regulation' created by Congress." *Wisconsin Dept. of Industry v. Gould Inc.*, 475 U.S. 282, 288–289, 106 S.Ct. 1057 (1986). Even if a State may make violation of federal law a crime in some instances, it cannot do so in a field (like the field of alien registration) that has been occupied by federal law. * * *

Section 5(C) Unlike §3, which replicates federal statutory requirements, §5(c) enacts a state criminal prohibition where no federal counterpart exists. The provision makes it a state misdemeanor for "an unauthorized alien to knowingly apply for work, solicit work in a public place or perform work as an employee or independent contractor" in Arizona. The United States contends that the provision upsets the balance struck by the *Immigration Reform and Control Act of 1986* (IRCA) and must be preempted as an obstacle to the federal plan of regulation and control. * * * Congress enacted IRCA as a comprehensive framework for "combating the employment of illegal aliens." *Hoffman Plastic Compounds, Inc. v. NLRB*, 535 U.S. 137, 147, 122 S.Ct. 1275 (2002). The law makes it illegal for employers to knowingly hire, recruit, refer, or continue to employ unauthorized workers. It also requires every employer to verify the employment authorization status of prospective employees. These requirements are enforced through criminal penalties and an escalating series of civil penalties tied to the number of times an employer has violated the provisions. * * *

The legislative background of IRCA underscores the fact that Congress made a deliberate choice not to impose criminal penalties on aliens who seek, or engage in, unauthorized employment. * * * In the end, IRCA's framework reflects a considered judgment that making criminals out of aliens engaged in unauthorized work—aliens who already face the possibility of employer exploitation because of their removable status—would be inconsistent with federal policy and objectives. * * *

Although §5(c)attempts to achieve one of the same goals as federal law—the deterrence of unlawful employment—it involves a conflict in the method of enforcement. * * *

Section 6 [Section 6 allows a state officer to arrest without a warrant anyone that they believe is removable from the United States for a violation of the law.] The United States argues that arrests authorized by this statute would be an obstacle to the removal system Congress created.

As a general rule, it is not a crime for a removable alien to remain present in the United States. See *INS v. Lopez-Mendoza,* 468 U.S. 1032, 1038, 104 S.Ct. 3479 (1984). If the police stop someone based on nothing more than possible removability, the usual predicate for an arrest is absent. When an alien is suspected of being removable, a federal official issues an administrative document called a Notice to Appear. The form does not authorize an arrest. Instead, it gives the alien information about the proceedings, including the time and date of the removal hearing. If an alien fails to appear, an *in absentia* order may direct removal. * * *

Section 6 attempts to provide state officers even greater authority to arrest aliens on the basis of possible removability than Congress has given to trained federal immigration officers. * * * This would allow the State to achieve its own immigration policy. The result could be unnecessary harassment of some aliens (for instance, a veteran, college student, or someone assisting with a criminal investigation) whom federal officials determine should not be removed. * * *

continues

continued

By authorizing state officers to decide whether an alien should be detained for being removable, §6 violates the principle that the removal process is entrusted to the discretion of the Federal Government. * * *

Section 2(B) [Section 2(B) requires state officers contact the federal government to determine the immigration status of any person they detain or arrest on some other legitimate grounds if they have a "reasonable suspicion that the person is an alien unlawfully present in the United States.] Congress has done nothing to suggest it is inappropriate to communicate with [federal officials] in these situations, however. Indeed, it has encouraged the sharing of information about possible immigration violations. See 8 U.S.C. §1357(g)(10)(A). A federal statute regulating the public benefits provided to qualified aliens in fact instructs that "no State or local government entity may be prohibited, or in any way restricted, from sending to or receiving from [federal officials] information regarding the immigration status, lawful or unlawful, of an alien in the United States." §1644. The federal scheme thus leaves room for a policy requiring state officials to contact [federal officials] as a routine matter.

The National Government has significant power to regulate immigration. With power comes responsibility, and the sound exercise of national power over immigration depends on the Nation's meeting its responsibility to base its laws on a political will informed by searching, thoughtful, rational civic discourse. Arizona may have understandable frustrations with the problems caused by illegal immigration while that process continues, but the State may not pursue policies that undermine federal law. * * *

Decision. Affirmed in part and reversed in part. Those sections of the Arizona statute [Sections 3, 5(c), and 6] are preempted by federal law and invalid. Section 2(B) which encourages consultation between state and federal officials does not conflict with federal immigration law and is valid.

Case Questions

1. Where does the federal government derive its authority to regulate immigration?
2. What policy arguments does the court give for the federal government's regulation of immigration?
3. On what grounds did the Court strike down three parts of the Arizona statute?
4. Why did the court uphold the fourth part of the Arizona statute (2B)?

Federal Preemption of Trade Policy. The doctrine of federal preemption has also been applied to attempts by state governments to regulate imports of foreign goods into the state or to conduct their own trade relations with foreign countries. In 1996, the Commonwealth of Massachusetts passed a law prohibiting all commonwealth and municipal government agencies from buying goods or services from any person or firm that did business in Burma. Congress took a different strategy with a federal statute to ban all economic aid to the Burmese government except for humanitarian assistance, deny U.S. entry visas to Burmese citizens, and authorize the president to prohibit "new investment" in Burma if the Burmese government continued its violent suppression of democracy. The powers delegated to the president were specific and directed him to work with other Asian countries to promote democracy in Burma through diplomatic means.

In *Crosby v. National Foreign Trade Council*, 530 U.S. 363 (2000), the U.S. Supreme Court struck down the Massachusetts law on the basis of federal preemption. The Court noted the difference between the federal and state sanctions. The Massachusetts sanctions were immediate and direct in prohibiting business in Burma. The federal sanctions were more flexible, gradually allowing the president to increase pressure on Burma as needed and to do so through both specific legal and diplomatic means. The court reasoned, "If the Massachusetts law is enforceable the president has less to offer and less economic and diplomatic leverage as a consequence." Thus, the state law undermined the intended purpose and "natural effect" of the federal act. In deciding that federal law preempted the state statute, the Court repeated that the federal government must "speak with one voice" in foreign policy matters and that Congress had left little or no role for states or municipalities.

The Import-Export Clause

The **Import-Export Clause** prohibits the federal government from taxing exports and prohibits the states from taxing either imports or exports. Historically, three reasons prompted such a provision. First, the federal government needed to be able to "speak with one voice" on matters related to foreign affairs. Second, import duties provided an important source of revenue for the federal government. And third, seaboard states were prevented from imposing burdensome regulations and taxes on "in transit" goods that were destined for inland states.

In *Michelin Tire Corp. v. Wages*, 423 U.S. 276 (1976), the U.S. Supreme Court addressed the issue of the state's power to tax imports. Michelin Tire Corporation imported tires manufactured in France and Nova Scotia, Canada, by Michelin Tires, Ltd. The company maintained a distribution warehouse in Georgia. The state assessed an *ad valorem* property tax against the tires that were held in inventory. The tax was nondiscriminatory in nature in that the same tax was imposed on all property similarly being held for resale in Georgia. The petitioner filed suit to have the collection of the tax enjoined as unconstitutional under the Import-Export Clause. The Supreme Court ruled that the tax was permitted under the Import-Export Clause because the tax was imposed on all products for the purpose of supporting the cost of public services, the tax was nondiscriminatory, and it did not interfere with the federal government's regulation of international commerce.

In 1978, the Supreme Court considered the constitutionality of a Washington state tax on stevedoring (the process of loading and unloading cargo on ships). Relying on the *Michelin* decision, the Court in *Department of Revenue of the State of Washington v. Association of Washington Stevedoring Cos.*, 435 U.S. 734 (1978) held that,

> the tax does not restrain the ability of the federal government to conduct foreign policy. As a general business tax that applies to virtually all businesses in the state, it has not created any special tariff. The assessments in this case are only upon that business conducted entirely within Washington. No foreign business or vessel is taxed... The tax merely compensates the state for services and protection extended by Washington to the stevedoring business.

In discussing interstate rivalries, the Court concluded that if it were to strike down the tax, then the state of Washington would be forced to subsidize the commerce of inland consumers. The tax was upheld under the Import-Export Clause.

The Commerce Clause

As discussed earlier in the chapter, the broadest power of the federal government to regulate business activity is derived from Article I, Section 8 of the Constitution. The **Commerce Clause** vests the federal government with exclusive control over foreign commerce. Conversely, in the negative implication doctrine, state governments may not enact laws that impose a substantial burden on foreign commerce. Where there is an existing federal law governing some aspect of foreign commerce, a conflicting state statute may be invalid (preempted) under the **Supremacy Clause**.

The Commerce Clause and Multiple Taxation

A state's authority to tax a business engaged in foreign commerce is also determined by whether or not the tax imposed results in **multiple taxation**. Multiple taxation occurs when the same service or property is subjected to the same or a similar tax by the governmental authorities of more than one nation. The following case, *Japan Line, Ltd. v. County of Los Angeles*, discusses the problems of multiple taxation. The purpose of restricting multiple taxation is to strengthen the government's ability to foster domestic participation in the international marketplace. By not prejudicing foreign companies operating in the United States, this country does not risk retaliation by foreign governments against U.S. firms operating abroad

The issue of multiple taxation was considered in *Barclays Bank PLC v. Franchise Tax Board of California,* 512 U.S. 298 (1994). The Court upheld the constitutionality of California's "unitary" method of assessing income tax on companies in California that are subsidiaries of foreign multinational corporations.

Barclays Bank of California (Barcal), a California banking institution, was a subsidiary of the Barclays Group, a multinational banking enterprise based in the United Kingdom. The Barclays Group included more than 220 corporations doing business in 60 nations. In 1977, Barcal reported taxable income only from its own operations within California. California claimed that Barcal was a part of a multinational **unitary business** (an affiliated or related group of companies under common control) and that the entire worldwide income of the unitary business (the income of all of the subsidiaries within the Barclays Group operating anywhere in the world) was taxable in California. Under the unitary method, taxes were assessed on the percentage of worldwide income equal to the average of the proportions of worldwide payroll, property, and sales located in

Japan Line, Ltd. v. County of Los Angeles

441 U.S. 434 (1979) United States Supreme Court

BACKGROUND AND FACTS

The state of California imposed an *ad valorem* property tax on cargo containers owned by Japanese companies and temporarily located in California ports. The containers were used exclusively for transporting goods in international commerce. They were based, registered, and subjected to property taxes in Japan. The containers spent, on average, only three weeks a year in California. Japan Lines contended that the tax was invalid because it subjected the containers to multiple taxation in Japan and the United States. The California Supreme Court upheld the statute and the ship owners appealed.

JUSTICE BLACKMUN

This case presents the question whether a state, consistently with the Commerce Clause of the Constitution, may impose a nondiscriminatory *ad valorem* property tax on foreign-owned instrumentalities (cargo containers) of international commerce ...

In order to prevent multiple taxation of commerce, this Court has required that taxes be apportioned among taxing jurisdictions, so that no instrumentality of commerce is subjected to more than one tax on its full value. The corollary of the apportionment principle, of course, is that no jurisdiction may tax the instrumentality in full. "The rule which permits taxation by two or more states on an apportionment basis precludes taxation of all of the property by the state of the domicile ... Otherwise there would be multiple taxation of interstate operations." The basis for this Court's approval of apportioned property taxation, in other words, has been its ability to enforce full apportionment by all potential taxing bodies.

Yet neither this Court nor this Nation can ensure full apportionment when one of the taxing entities is a foreign sovereign. If an instrumentality of commerce is domiciled abroad, the country of domicile may have the right, consistently with the custom of nations, to impose a tax on its full value. If a state should seek to tax the same instrumentality on an apportioned basis, multiple taxation inevitably results. Hence, whereas the fact of apportionment in interstate commerce means that "multiple burdens" logically cannot occur, the same conclusion, as to foreign commerce, logically cannot be drawn. Due to the absence of an authoritative tribunal capable of ensuring that the aggregation of taxes is computed on no more than one full value, a state tax, even though "fairly apportioned" to reflect an instrumentality's presence within the state, may subject foreign commerce "to the risk of a double tax burden to which [domestic] commerce is not exposed, and which the commerce clause forbids."

Second, a state tax on the instrumentalities of foreign commerce may impair federal uniformity in an area where federal uniformity is essential. Foreign commerce is preeminently a matter of national concern. "In international relations and with respect to foreign intercourse and trade the people of the United States act through a single government with unified and adequate national power." *Board of Trustees v. United States*, 289 U.S. 48 (1933). Although the Constitution, Art. I, §8, cl. 3, grants Congress power to regulate commerce "with foreign Nations" and "among the several States" in parallel phrases, there is evidence that the Founders intended the scope of the foreign commerce power to be the greater. Cases of this Court, stressing the need for uniformity in treating with other nations, echo this distinction. * * *

A state tax on instrumentalities of foreign commerce may frustrate the achievement of federal uniformity in several ways. If the State imposes an apportioned tax, international disputes over reconciling apportionment formulae may arise. If a novel state tax creates an asymmetry in the international tax structure, foreign nations disadvantaged by the levy may retaliate against American-owned instrumentalities present in their jurisdictions. Such retaliation of necessity would be directed at American transportation equipment in general, not just that of the taxing state, so that the Nation as a whole would suffer ...

It is stipulated that American-owned containers are not taxed in Japan. California's tax thus creates an asymmetry in international maritime taxation operating to Japan's disadvantage. The risk of retaliation by Japan, under these circumstances, is acute, and such retaliation of necessity would be felt by the Nation as a whole ...

We hold the tax, as applied, unconstitutional under the Commerce Clause.

Decision. The Supreme Court reversed, holding that the tax was unconstitutional. The Court ruled that an *ad valorem* property tax applied to cargo containers used exclusively in foreign commerce violates the Commerce Clause because it resulted in multiple taxation of instrumentalities of foreign commerce.

Case Questions

1. What rule does the Court espouse for the state taxation of cargo containers and other instrumentalities of foreign commerce?
2. How does this case affect taxation by foreign countries?
3. What effect would multiple taxation have on international commerce?

California. Thus, if a multinational corporation had 8 percent of its payroll, 3 percent of its inventory and other property, and 4 percent of its sales in California, the state imposed its tax on 5 percent of the multinational's total income. (The weight given to each category can vary under different formulas.) California used the unitary method because it believed that under traditional methods of tax accounting, conglomerates had the ability to manipulate transactions between affiliated companies so as to shift income to low-tax jurisdictions (although to guard against such manipulation, transactions between affiliated corporations are generally scrutinized to ensure that they are reported on an "arm's-length" basis). Barclays claimed that California's tax resulted in multiple taxation, in violation of the Commerce Clause.

Citing its previous decisions, the U.S. Supreme Court upheld the California tax because seven requirements were met:

1. The tax applied to an activity with a substantial connection to California.
2. The tax was "fairly apportioned."
3. The tax did not discriminate against interstate commerce.
4. The tax was fairly related to the services provided by the state.
5. The tax did not result in multiple taxation.
6. The tax did not impair the federal government's ability to "speak with one voice when regulating commercial relations with foreign governments."
7. Compliance with the formula was not so impossible as to deprive the corporation of due process of law.

Even before this case went to court, foreign corporations doing business in California had objected strongly to the unitary tax. Foreign governments also objected, claiming it violated international law.

In response to this outcry, the state of California in 1986 instituted a **water's edge election** allowing "multinational" corporate taxpayers the option of excluding the income of related entities that are incorporated in a foreign country or that earn a majority of their income in a foreign country. The result is that today, in California and several other states, the taxpayer has the option of being taxed as a unitary business according to the Supreme Court's decision in *Barclays*, or only on its California (or taxing state) income—up to the "water's edge." Most states, however, require reporting on the "water's edge" basis. Income tax regulations are complicated for any firm engaged in a multistate business, and even more so for related multinational parent-subsidiary corporations. Professional tax advice is crucial.

State Restrictions on Exports. The Commerce Clause prohibits state governments from restricting, taxing, or otherwise imposing undue burdens on exports. In *South-Central Timber Development, Inc. v. Wunnicke*, 467 U.S. 82 (1984), the Supreme Court considered a challenge to an Alaska regulation that required that all timber taken from state lands be processed within the state prior to being exported. South-Central was an Alaskan company engaged in purchasing timber and shipping logs overseas. It filed suit claiming that the regulation violated the negative implications of the Commerce Clause. Alaska argued that the Commerce Clause did not apply because the state was acting as a "market-participant" (a vendor of lumber), not as a regulator. The Court agreed with South-Central:

> The limit of the market-participant doctrine must be that it allows a State to impose burdens on commerce within the market in which it is a participant, but allows it to go no further. The State may not impose conditions, whether by statute, regulation, or contract, that have a substantial regulatory effect outside of that particular market ... [A] lthough the state may be a participant in the timber market, it is using its leverage in that market to exert a regulatory effect in the processing market, in which it is not a participant.... In light of the substantial attention given by Congress to the subject of export restrictions on unprocessed timber, it would be peculiarly inappropriate to permit state regulation of the subject.

State Restrictions on Imports. State government restrictions on imports are severely limited. User fees for the use of port facilities are generally permitted. Also, states may impose restrictions directly related to the protection of the public health and safety. For example, Florida could limit, restrict, or ban the import of fruits or vegetables suspected of carrying a disease that could contaminate the local crop. In one case, however, a labeling and licensing statute was invalidated by the courts even though its alleged purpose was the protection of the public health and safety. Tennessee had enacted a statute calling for the licensing of all persons who deal in foreign meat products in the state and the labeling of all foreign meats sold in the state as being of foreign origin. The court, in *Tupman Thurlow Co. v. Moss*, 252 F. Supp.

641 (M.D. Tenn. 1961), concluded that "The regulation here involved cannot fairly be construed as a consumer protection measure, and if it should be, it would be interdicted by the Commerce Clause because it unreasonably discriminates against foreign products in favor of products of domestic origin."

FEDERAL AGENCIES AFFECTING TRADE

Many U.S. government agencies provide technical and financial assistance for international firms. These include the Small Business Administration, the Export-Import Bank, the Overseas Private Investment Corporation, the Commodity Credit Corporation, the Agency for International Development, the Trade and Development Program, the U.S. Department of Agriculture, and any others. We mention a few here and will discuss those that are highlighted in bold in more detail in later chapters.

United States Department of Commerce

The U.S. Department of Commerce has broad authority over many international trade issues. The department's functions include fostering trade and promoting exports of U.S. goods and services (trade promotion), investigating and resolving complaints by U.S. firms that foreign governments are unfairly blocking access to foreign markets (market access), administering U.S. unfair import laws (import administration), issuing export licenses for certain products, developing U.S. international trade statistical information, and many other functions. The **International Trade Administration** (ITA), housed within the department, performs many of the trade promotion, market access, and import administration functions. Within the ITA, the **U.S. Commercial Service** maintains a network of offices at home and abroad to assist U.S. firms in developing export opportunities. The **U.S. Bureau of Industry and Security** regulates the export of sensitive goods and technologies for national security and foreign policy and administers U.S. export control laws.

United States Department of Homeland Security

The Department of Homeland Security was created as an executive department of the federal government in 2003. Its creation was part of the largest reorganization of the American government in over a half-century. The new department brought together many existing government agencies with a common responsibility for protecting the American "homeland." The department is organized into four directorates: Border and Transportation Security, Emergency Preparedness and Response, Science and Technology, and Information Analysis and Infrastructure Protection. Its primary mission is to prevent terrorist attacks within the United States.

The **Border and Transportation Security Directorate** brings together the major border security and transportation security functions of Homeland Security. This includes the following agencies: **U.S. Customs and Border Protection (CBP), U.S. Immigration and Customs Enforcement (ICE), U.S. Citizenship and Immigration Services, the Transportation Security Administration**, the Secret Service, the Federal Emergency Management Agency, and the U.S. Coast Guard.

The agency with the greatest impact on our reading is the **Bureau of Customs and Border Protection** (CBP). This agency brings together many functions of the former U.S. Customs Service, the Border Patrol, and the Immigration and Naturalization Service. Its functions include preventing suspected terrorists from entering the United States; apprehending individuals attempting to enter the United States illegally; stemming the flow of illegal drugs and other contraband; protecting American agricultural and economic interests from imported pests and diseases; preventing the illegal import of goods in violation of U.S. copyright, patent, and trademark laws; enforcing U.S. import and export laws; and collecting import duties.

United States Trade Representative

The **United States Trade Representative** (USTR) is a cabinet-level post reporting directly to the president. The USTR carries on all bilateral and multilateral trade negotiations on behalf of the United States, is the principal adviser on trade matters to the president, represents the United States at all WTO meetings, coordinates the trade agreements program, and coordinates all U.S. trade policies, including those related to commodity trade and unfair trade practices. The USTR now handles much of the responsibility for trade matters once held by the Department of State. Each year the USTR prepares the president's report to Congress on U.S. trade activities. These reports are in the president's annual *Trade Policy Agenda*, the *Annual Report of the United States on the Trade Agreements Program*, and the annual *National Trade Estimate Report on Foreign Trade Barriers.*

United States Department of the Treasury

The Treasury Department has a tremendous impact on all international business transactions because of its near total control of U.S. currency moving in and out of the United States and control over U.S. banks worldwide. Since 2001 the role of Treasury has grown considerably as it took on a major role in fighting the financial war on terror by denying terrorist groups access to financing. The **Bureau of Financial Crimes Enforcement Network** (known as "FinCEN") fosters domestic and international cooperation among law enforcement agencies in dealing with financial crimes. The **Office of Foreign Assets Control** administers U.S. trade sanctions enacted by Congress on the basis of U.S. foreign policy and national security objectives it is targeted against foreign terrorists, international drug traffickers, and individuals or groups that illegally proliferate weapons of mass destruction.

International Trade Commission

The **International Trade Commission** (ITC), formerly the U.S. Tariff Commission, is an independent agency of government created by Congress in 1916. The ITC maintains a highly trained cadre of professional economists and researchers who conduct investigations and prepare extensive reports on matters related to international economics and trade for Congress and the president. Because of the highly political nature of many of the investigations related to the impact of imported goods on U.S. domestic industry, the ITC is a bipartisan agency. The members of the commission are appointed by the president from both political parties and are subject to Senate confirmation. We will thoroughly discuss the role of the ITC (along with that of the International Trade Administration) in investigating unfair trade practices in future chapters.

The U.S. Court of International Trade

The **Court of International Trade** (CIT) consists of nine judges who hear cases arising from the trade or tariff laws of the United States. Appeals from U.S. Customs and Border Protection regarding duties assessed on imported goods and appeals from decisions of the ITC in unfair import cases are heard by the CIT. Appeals from the CIT go to the Court of Appeals for the Federal Circuit and, where appropriate, to the U.S. Supreme Court.

The court has exclusive jurisdiction over all civil actions commenced against the United States involving (1) revenue from imports or tonnage; (2) tariffs, duties, fees, or other taxes on importation of merchandise for reasons other than the raising of revenue; (3) embargoes or other quantitative restriction of the importation of merchandise for reasons other than the protection of the public health or safety; and (4) administration or enforcement of the customs laws. The court is located in New York City.

CONCLUSION

Many students are surprised at the limited powers granted to the president in the Constitution. The president's power is not unlimited and is derived from the treaty power (with the advice and consent of the Senate), the power to conduct foreign affairs, the inherent power under Article II as chief executive and as commander-in-chief of the armed forces, and the power delegated to the president to enforce and carry out acts of Congress. As Justice Jackson said in his famous concurring opinion in the *Youngstown* case, "When the president takes measures incompatible with the expressed or implied will of Congress, his power is at its lowest ebb, for then he can rely only upon his own constitutional powers minus any constitutional powers of Congress over the matter."

Presidents have wide latitude in the exercise of their powers in foreign affairs, especially during times of war. Virtually every U.S. president in the twentieth century had disputes with Congress over the extent of presidential power. While this chapter can do no more than describe the separation of powers, we hope you now have a better understanding of the limits on presidential power.

For additional information on the topics in this chapter, consider looking at an annual publication of the United States International Trade Commission, *The Year In Trade: Operation of the Trade Agreements Program*. It is an annual survey of U.S. trade statistics, trade laws and regulations, trade agreements, and recent developments between the United States and its major trading partners. This publication also provides an excellent way to stay current on this material in the years ahead.

Chapter Summary

1. U.S. trade law is that body of public law that governs America's trade relations with foreign countries, including the import and export of goods and services. Trade law is used to implement American trade policies as well as American foreign policy and thus can be used to encourage trade with a political ally or to discourage trade with a potential foe. Using trade policy as a tool of foreign policy can lead to many conflicts.
2. Article I of the Constitution confers "all legislative powers" on Congress, including the power "to regulate commerce with foreign nations, and among the several states." In addition, Congress has broad power to pass domestic laws, raise and support armies, provide and maintain a navy, declare war, appropriate monies, and levy and collect taxes. The Senate has the authority to give advice and consent to the president in making treaties with foreign nations and to approve treaties by a two-thirds vote.
3. Treaties are binding on both the federal and state governments and have the same force as an act of Congress.
4. The president's powers are derived from two sources: those powers delegated to the president by Congress, and those "inherent" powers set out in Article II of the Constitution. Inherent powers include the treaty power, the power to appoint ambassadors, the power to receive foreign ambassadors, and the power inherent in being commander-in-chief of the armed forces.
5. The primary instrument for implementing foreign political and economic affairs is the *international agreement.* International agreements include treaties and executive agreements.
6. An *executive agreement* is an international agreement between the president and a foreign country, entered into without resort to the treaty process. The two types of executive agreements are *sole executive agreements* (based on the president's inherent powers) and *congressional-executive agreements* (based on authority delegated by Congress). Sole executive agreements are usually reserved for agreements with foreign countries that do not affect the broad interests of the nation as a whole. Congressional-executive agreements, based on the majority vote of both houses of Congress, are recognized as having the same binding legal effect as treaties.
7. A *trade agreement* is an agreement between nations on matters involving trade, tariffs, and related issues. A *free trade agreement* seeks to eliminate or substantially reduce tariffs and non-tariff barriers and often sets up a mechanism for resolving trade disputes between the countries. Trade agreements can be bilateral, multilateral, or regional.
8. *Trade promotion authority* allows the president to negotiate trade congressional-executive trade agreements. The *North American Free Trade Agreement* and many other trade pacts were successfully negotiated under trade promotion authority.
9. The *Smoot-Hawley Tariff Act of 1930* placed the highest tariffs on goods in U.S. history. It was one of the causes of the Great Depression.
10. Beginning with the *Reciprocal Tariff Act of 1934* and continuing to this day, tariff reductions have been negotiated on a reciprocal basis. As a result, tariffs today are not a major barrier to trade.
11. In the United States, the role of state or local governments in regulating or interfering with trade relations with foreign countries is very limited. States have no authority to regulate imports or exports of foreign goods or services. In case after case, legislation enacted by state or local governments that restricts trade with foreign countries has been ruled unconstitutional under either the Supremacy Clause or the Commerce Clause of the Constitution.

Key Terms

inherent powers 216
sole executive agreement 216
treaty power 219
equal dignity rule 219
congressional-executive agreement 219
reciprocal trade 220
tariff concession 220
conditional most-favored-nation (MFN) trade 220
unconditional most-favored-nation (MFN) trade 220
normal trade relations 220
trade agreement 222
free trade agreement 222
trade promotion authority 222
non-tariff barrier 222
trade preference 222
emergency powers 223
federal preemption 223
Import-Export Clause 226
Commerce Clause 227
Supremacy Clause 227
multiple taxation 227
unitary business 227
water's edge election 229

Questions and Case Problems

1. In 2013, President Obama's *Trade Policy Agenda* reported that the United States was in its third year of negotiating a new trade agreement, the *Trans-Pacific Partnership Trade Agreement,* between 11 pacific countries. Included are Australia, Brunei Darussalam, Canada, Chile, Malaysia, Mexico, New Zealand, Peru, Singapore, Vietnam, and the United States. The president maintained that in terms of both trade policy and foreign policy, the United States would refocus itself on "engaging" Asia in the coming years. At the same time, the president announced that he would negotiate a new *Transatlantic Trade and Investment Partnership* with the European Union intended to reduce non-tariff barriers to trade in technology products. Because the president's trade promotion authority to negotiate trade agreements expired in 2007, these face real scrutiny from Congress. What is the status of these negotiations? What are their objectives and what industry sectors are they primarily intended to benefit? What are their chances of passing either as a treaty or a congressional-executive agreement
2. Together, North Carolina, South Carolina, and Georgia produce a large amount of cotton each year. In an effort to protect their farmers from overseas competition, the governors of these three states met and agreed on a uniform "inspection fee" to be imposed on all foreign cotton coming into their states through their ports. They vowed to do their best to get their state legislatures to adopt this fee as law. Would any legal problem arise with such a fee?
3. Due to threats by the president to set import quotas, the U.S. State Department negotiated directly with European and Japanese steel producers to limit their companies' exports to the United States. No foreign government was party to the agreement. Although the president has express authority to limit imports by an act of Congress, this act required that he either hold public hearings through the Tariff Commission about setting import quotas or deal directly with foreign governments about limiting imports. The Consumers Union of U.S., Inc., felt that when Congress gave the president this express power, it preempted any other action by the president. They brought an action against the secretary of state to have the president's agreement with private steel producers in Europe and Japan declared illegal. What should be the result of such an action? See *Consumers Union of U.S., Inc. v. Kissinger,* 506 F.2d 136 (D.C. Cir. 1974).
4. The *Trade Expansion Act of 1962* as amended by the *Trade Act of 1974* states that if the secretary of the treasury finds that an "article is being imported into the United States in such quantities or under such circumstances as to threaten to impair the national security," the president is authorized to "take such action ... as he deems necessary to adjust the imports of the article ... so that [it] will not threaten to impair the national security." Does this grant of power by Congress allow the president to establish quotas? If importation of foreign oil is deemed "a threat to national security," can the president implement a \$3–\$4-per-barrel license fee? See *Federal Energy Administration v. Algonquin SNG, Inc.,* 426 U.S. 548 (1976).
5. Future U.S. trade negotiations will focus both on the U.S. trade relationships with the world through the World Trade Organization and on special trade

relationships with countries in Latin America. Some leaders of Congress want to use trade negotiations to push Latin American countries to protect worker's rights, conserve tropical forests, and protect the environment. Such issues may dominate U.S. trade relations for most of this decade. As of today, what is the status of the president's fast-track authority? What has Congress required of the president in leading current or future U.S. trade negotiations? To what extent has Congress included side issues such as labor rights or the environment? Research the topic and discuss the pros and cons of linking trade relations to these and other social and political side issues.

6. During the 1940s, the U.S. government instituted a price support system for domestic potatoes. To protect the potato market from imported Canadian potatoes, the U.S. secretary of state entered into an executive agreement with the Canadian ambassador in which they agreed that Canada would permit the export of potatoes to the United States for use only for seed and not for food. The agreement was not submitted to or approved by Congress. The *Agricultural Act of 1948* permitted the president to restrict potato imports by requesting an investigation by the Tariff Commission and considering its recommendations. Guy W. Capps, Inc., the importer, assured the Canadian exporter that the potatoes were destined for planting, but while they were in transit, they were sold to the A&P grocery store chain for resale. The United States brought suit against Guy Capps for damages. The court entered judgment for Guy Capps and the government appealed. Was the U.S.-Canadian agreement valid under the U.S. Constitution? Was the president acting under his inherent constitutional authority, under power delegated from Congress, or neither? What did Congress say the president could do to restrict agricultural imports? See *United States v. Guy W. Capps, Inc.*, 204 F.2d 655 (4th Cir. 1953).
7. Xerox manufactured parts for copy machines in the United States that were shipped to Mexico for assembly. The copiers were designed for sale exclusively in Latin America. All printing on the machines was in Spanish or Portuguese. The copiers operated on a 50-cycle electric current unavailable in the United States. The copiers had been transported by a customs bonded warehouse in Houston, Texas, where they were stored pending their sale to Xerox affiliates in Latin America. The copiers had previously been stored in Panama. Under federal law, goods stored in a customs bonded warehouse are under the supervision of the U.S. Customs Service. Goods may be brought into a warehouse without the payment of import duties and stored for up to five years. At any time they may be re-exported duty-free or withdrawn for domestic sale upon the payment of the duty. Harris County and the city of Houston assessed a nondiscriminatory *ad valorem* personal property tax on the copiers. Xerox claimed that the local tax is preempted by the federal legislation. What did the Court decide? Would it have made any difference whether the goods were needed for domestic use or intended for re-export? See *Xerox Corporation v. County of Harris, Texas*, 459 U.S. 145 (1982).
8. The state of Tennessee passed legislation requiring that any person selling or offering for sale in the state of Tennessee any meats that are the products of any foreign country must so identify any such product by labeling it "This meat is of foreign origin." The state law did not require a higher standard of purity and sanitation than that required by the U.S. Department of Agriculture. A New York corporation selling imported meats to customers in Tennessee challenged this state statute in U.S. District Court. The corporation's sales of imported meat to customers in Tennessee were one-half of its volume prior to enactment of the statute. What do you think was the legal basis for this challenge to the Tennessee law? What do you think was Tennessee's argument for passing the law? What do you think the court decided? See *Tupman Thurlow Co. v. Moss*, 252 F. Supp. 641 (M.D. Tenn. 1966).

Managerial Implications

Your firm, Day-O Shoes, Inc., manufactures deck shoes in the Caribbean island country of Haiti, the poorest nation in the Western Hemisphere. Your plant there employs more than 400 workers and has always considered itself a good citizen of both Haiti and the United States. Most of the shoes are imported for sale into the United States, where you maintain a 30 percent share of a competitive market. In 1991, the freely elected President of Haiti is removed from office by military officers who install a dictator of their choice. In response, the President of the United States exercises authority under the *International Economic Emergency Powers Act* and issues an executive order imposing a complete embargo on trade with Haiti. The Treasury Department's Office of Foreign Assets Control is charged with enforcing the embargo. Facing the impending embargo, your firm shut down its production operations there one week prior to the date set for the embargo. Feeling some obligation to the unemployed workers, your company's chief executive ships over ten tons of food and clothing to the people who have lost their jobs.

Believing that the United States is serious about the embargo and that it will remain in effect until the rightful president is returned to Haiti, your firm ships its U.S.-made raw materials, such as rubber soles and leather uppers, from Haiti to your other factory in Costa Rica. However, you soon discover, much to your surprise, that your competitors are continuing to produce and stockpile their shoes in Haiti in the belief that the embargo will soon be lifted. Three months after you cease operations, the U.S. government decides to lift the embargo because it has resulted in the loss of 50,000 Haitian jobs. With no inventory of finished shoes and your raw materials en route to Costa Rica, your firm is unable to fill existing orders. Your competitors are ready to ship their shoes from Haiti immediately.

1. Evaluate the course of action taken by Day-O Shoes. How did Day-O Shoes balance its responsibility under U.S. law to comply with the embargo with its need to remain competitive in the industry? What could it have done differently? Evaluate the ethics of Day-O's actions.
2. Was Day-O Shoes required to stop producing in Haiti? Were its competitors violating U.S. law by continuing to produce and stockpile their inventories? Were they violating any moral code or even the "spirit of the law" by continuing to produce there? Evaluate the risks taken by the competitors in continuing their operations in Haiti during the embargo.
3. The embargo was intended to put economic pressure on Haiti to encourage political reform. Is the U.S. government saying that the embargo worked too well? Do you think that the embargo was lifted because of its impact on the Haitian workers or on U.S. firms doing business there? Critics argue that the U.S. government's attempts to use trade policy as a means of conducting foreign policy lead to confusion and uncertainty and are counterproductive. Evaluate this argument.

Ethical Considerations

It is clear that Congress has the authority to require that any trade agreement negotiated by the president take into account environmental and labor issues. At least since 1974, U.S. trade laws have instructed the president to consider foreign worker rights and workplace conditions in negotiating trade agreements. One U.S. statute, which fosters U.S. trade with developing countries, contains provisions for labor standards. The 1994 *North American Free Trade Agreement* contained specific provisions for protecting worker rights and the environment. More recently, the *Trade Act of 2002* called for countries entering trade agreements with the United States to abide by the "core labor standards" of the International Labour Organization, including the freedom of association, the right to form unions and to bargain collectively, minimum age requirements and limitations on child labor, maintenance of safe working conditions, and a ban on forced labor.

Some U.S. trade agreements also reflect environmental concerns. They do not set environmental standards, but they call for each nation to enforce its own standards and to ensure that environmental protections are not weakened in order to promote foreign trade.

Do you think that the United States should require foreign countries to address worker rights, worker safety, and environmental harm in return for trade privileges with the United States? Find out how U.S. trade agreements incorporate concerns over the environment and worker's rights. What has been the policy of presidential administrations in this regard? What are the competing economic and political issues in domestic politics? Should trade be used to accomplish these political and social objectives? How much focus should be placed on human rights? Why or why not?

CHAPTER 9

The World Trade Organization: Basic Legal Principles

In the last chapter we saw the impact of the high tariffs and protectionism of the early 1930s. Our story left off with the worldwide Great Depression, and the ever-lasting reminder that protectionist attitudes in one country, with unbridled tariff increases and quotas on imports, will only be met by retaliation by other countries. The result was disastrous to national economies. Realizing this, the United States and other nations began the process of negotiating a reduction of tariff rates. It was a slow bilateral process, with countries bargaining with each other over the reciprocal reduction of tariffs on thousands of items. By the end of the decade there had been some success in lowering tariff rates overall, but it was a process that could not be completed before the world entered World War II.

This chapter picks up the story after the war, as nations sought a faster and better means of reducing tariff rates and other protectionist barriers to international trade. The postwar period saw the growth of multilateralism: multilateral trade agreements concluded on a wide range of trade topics, multilateral negotiations to reduce tariff and non-tariff barriers to trade, and the rise of multilateral organizations—first the GATT and later the World Trade Organization, to coordinate the process. This chapter covers the major trade agreements that govern most of the world's trade in goods and services.

You may ask why we are studying "trade agreements?" Is that not the stuff of foreign relations, diplomats and international lawyers? It is, but it also affects everyone involved in international business. A trade agreement is a nation's commitment to other nations to conform its national laws and regulations to the terms of that agreement. A trade agreement is a legal framework for national laws. It may be a commitment to lower the tariff rate on certain goods imported from specific countries, or it may be a change in the rules for delivering services to consumers or customers in foreign countries. The trade agreement is the mold from which national laws are cast. In turn, these laws govern the day-to-day international business transactions of companies doing business in those countries. And it does not matter if they are small exporters or importers, larger service-oriented companies such as those in telecommunications or insurance, technology companies managing their intellectual property rights, or multinational industrial giants with goods moving through global supply chains. In other words, this chapter explains how the rules are made that govern individual firms that move goods and services from one country to another.

INTRODUCTION TO TRADE REGULATION

Every country establishes its own trade policies according to its own national interests. Domestic politics heavily influences trade policies. Left to its own devices, any nation would want to protect its industries from foreign competitors by erecting a maze of import trade barriers. These might include high tariffs, quotas, or complex regulations designed to keep out foreign goods and services. A **trade barrier** is any impediment to trade in goods or services. An import trade barrier is any impediment, direct or indirect, to the entrance or sale of imported goods or services existing in the country of importation. Typically, trade barriers are tariffs or taxes on imported goods or laws, government regulations, or national industrial standards that make importing or selling foreign-made goods or services more difficult or that make imported goods or services more costly to produce, market, or sell.

Reasons for Regulating Imports

Nations regulate imports for economic, political, and public policy reasons. These include the following:

- Collection of revenue
- Protection or safeguarding of domestic industry and employment
- Prohibition of unfair trade (trade distorting subsidies, dumping, and others)

- Retaliation against foreign government trade barriers
- Implementation of foreign policy (to aid friends and punish enemies—prohibition on import of goods from a country that violates international norms or is a military adversary)
- Implementation of national economic policies (preservation of foreign exchange; implementation of industrial policy)
- Protection of the national defense (erection of barriers to foreign firms selling defense-related equipment or essential products such as machine tools; protection of strategic national industries such as aerospace or telecommunications)
- Protection of natural resources or of the environment (ban on export of scarce minerals; requirement that imported cars be equipped with antipollution devices; ban on import of tuna caught in fishing nets that trap dolphins)
- Protection of public health, safety, and morals (to stop the spread of human disease; to ensure safety in consumer goods, pharmaceuticals, construction equipment, etc., or to prevent the import of banned obscene materials)
- Protection of plant and animal life (ban on import of disease-carrying fruit or foreign species of wildlife)
- To ensure uniform compliance with common standards and standard-setting codes (compliance with electrical codes, fire codes, standards for automotive transportation or aviation; and other technical codes)
- Protection of local cultural, religious, or ethnic values (limitations on foreign television programming; prohibition of import of religiously offensive materials in Islamic countries; ban on export of artifacts or antiques)
- To aid in the economic development of poorer, developing countries by encouraging imports of their products through tariff preferences

Import trade barriers can take many different forms and are usually classified as either tariff or non-tariff barriers.

Tariffs

The most common device for regulating imports is the tariff or import duty, terms that we use interchangeably in this text. A **tariff** is a tax levied on goods by the country of importation. It is usually computed either as a percentage of value (***ad valorem* tariffs**) or on the basis of physical units (**specific or flat tariffs**). Goods that are fungible (e.g., crude oil, wheat, or standard-size graded lumber) are usually subject to a specific or flat-rate tariff, while non-fungible goods (e.g., chairs, machinery, or specialized steel) are usually subject to an *ad valorem* tariff. **Global tariffs** are imposed on a particular classification of goods without regard to the country of origin of the goods. Tariffs are generally considered to be one of the least restrictive types of trade barriers (assuming the tariff rate is reasonable and not prohibitive) because tariff rates are published, easily calculated, and capable of being passed on in the price of goods.

Non-tariff Barriers to Trade

Non-tariff barriers are any impediment to trade other than tariffs. Non-tariff barriers can be direct or indirect. Some non-tariff barriers serve socially beneficial purposes and are permitted by international law. Others, which violate international agreements and are not permitted, can lead to trade disputes unless removed.

Direct non-tariff barriers specifically limit imports of goods or services or deny access of foreign firms to local markets. Examples are embargoes, quotas, complex and discriminatory import licensing schemes, and other prohibitions on trade. Most direct non-tariff barriers are not permitted unless, as we will see later in the chapter, they fit into certain exceptions.

While **indirect non-tariff barriers** may seem perfectly neutral and nondiscriminatory on their face, their effect is to discriminate against foreign-made products or firms. They may take the form of laws, regulations, or rules of administrative agencies that make it difficult or costly to import foreign made goods or services. For example, a government may enact a regulation to achieve a perfectly valid policy objective, such as the protection of human or animal health, public safety, or the environment. But the mechanism to achieve that objective may have the unintended (or intended!) effect of discriminating against foreign-made products, by making their importation more difficult or costly. Examples might include national standards for electrical appliances, health standards for food or cosmetics, and safety standards for industrial and consumer goods. The refusal to allow imports of foreign beef containing growth hormones would effectively shut down imports of beef from countries in which virtually all cattle are fed growth hormones. Government restrictions on the use of food preservatives are another excellent example of a trade barrier in disguise, because it is more difficult and expensive to transport and warehouse food products in distant foreign countries.

Many non-tariff barriers are permitted under international agreements. For instance, we are all familiar with laws requiring foreign goods to be labeled with the country of origin, requirements that instruction manuals for consumer goods be written in the language of the importing nation, or that metric sizes appear on the product or packaging. Manufacturers and exporters with a global marketing vision must learn to adapt to the regulatory hurdles of nontariff barriers in foreign markets.

Consider this overly simplistic story: Assume that all passenger cars sold in the United States have wheel assemblies with either four or five lug nuts. U.S. tests show that this number is adequate for safety. But the Bureau for the Protection of Wheel Assemblies of the Government of Zimbabwe passes a rule requiring that all wheels be assembled with at least six lug nuts. It just so happens that all Zimbabwean automobile manufacturers already use six nuts. Zimbabwean tests show that six nuts are safer than five. The cost of redesigning, retooling, and testing U.S.-made cars for shipment to Zimbabwe may be tens of millions of dollars. Do you think that the U.S. firms can justify the expenditures? Probably not, and Zimbabwean drivers will have to be content with driving Zimbabwean cars. While this may appear to be a perfectly legitimate safety regulation on its face, it also has the effect of being a non-tariff barrier to trade.

Case Example: Large-Scale Retail Stores in Japan. A well-known example of an indirect non-tariff barrier is the 1974 *Japanese Large-Scale Retail Stores Law*. Japan has always had many small, neighborhood retail shops and grocers, many of which are "mom and pop" owned. Small local shops existed in an atmosphere that fit into the Japanese consumer's cultural expectations of quality, freshness, and personal attention. The law limited the number, location, and operations of large retail stores and supermarkets in Japan with over 500 square meters in floor space, and gave a voice to existing small shops in the approval process. The process often took seven or eight years to complete and usually required the large store operator to make many concessions to the small store owners to obtain their approval. If the government found that the proposed store posed a risk of adversely affecting nearby shops, it could require the large store to reduce its floor space or limits days and hours of operation. Of course, large retailers in the United States and Europe were not very happy about the law. After all, for a foreign retail chain to justify its investment in Japan it would have to be a "big-box" store. Small stores are not economically feasible. In addition to protecting politically powerful small business owners, the law also perpetuated the vertically integrated distribution system in Japan by giving large Japanese manufacturers greater control over the distribution of their products being sold through many small retail stores. Large foreign retail chains, on the other hand, might favor purchasing from U.S. exporters accustomed to selling to high-volume purchasers.

The law was an excellent example of a non-tariff barrier that on its face was completely neutral. It was enacted for many economic, political, and cultural reasons, and it did not discriminate against products because they were of foreign origin. However, it did have the effect of limiting access to the Japanese retail market by American and other foreign big-box and discount chains. As a result of negotiations in the 1980s and 1990s, the law was eventually repealed and replaced with laws focused more on environmental and city-planning policies. After the law's repeal large-scale American and European volume discounters entered the Japanese market and almost immediately began to transform retailing in Japan.

HISTORY OF GATT 1947

Even while World War II was being fought, the United States and its allies were charting a course to rebuild and revitalize the world's economy and to ensure that the economic mistakes of the 1930s would not be repeated. In 1944, the Allied nations met at the Bretton Woods Conference in New Hampshire to create several important international economic and political institutions, including the **International Monetary Fund**, and the International Bank for Reconstruction and Development, also called the **World Bank**. The **United Nations** was created at about the same time. In addition to these economic and political institutions, world leaders had a vision of another international organization dedicated to preventing the kinds of protectionism and rising tariffs seen in the 1930s. So a third specialized organization, the **International Trade Organization**, was planned to promote and stabilize world trade by reducing tariffs.

At international meetings held in 1947, a multilateral trade agreement was reached between 23 nations. Called the *General Agreement on Tariffs and Trade* (GATT 1947), it reflected a more international view of the world's economic and trading system than had existed, and would become the most important trade agreement of the twentieth century. However, the International Trade Organization never materialized, due in part to the lack of support in the U.S.

Congress for yet another international organization. But eventually a professional staff was needed to administer the GATT agreement, and a headquarters was established in Geneva. Thus, ironically, a GATT organization arose by default in the place of the aborted International Trade Organization and functioned successfully for nearly 50 years. Interestingly, although GATT 1947 was never ratified by the U.S. Congress as a treaty, it was consistently accepted as a binding legal obligation of the United States under international law.

Trade negotiations were conducted on the basis of agreed-upon international rules, with common objectives and greater transparency, or openness, than ever before. Disagreements and trade disputes were handled through consultations at the GATT headquarters in Geneva, and a non-binding dispute settlement process was put in place to prevent trade wars before they occurred.

GATT Multilateral Trade Negotiations

One of the cornerstones of the GATT system was a commitment by member countries to conduct **multilateral trade negotiations**, and on a regular basis, under the auspices of the GATT organization. Negotiating sessions are called "rounds." The following is an overview of the most important **negotiating rounds** from 1947–present. Although the focus of each round was different, they all had the same goal of **trade liberalization**—the process of reducing tariffs and removing artificial barriers and restrictions on trade.

- Geneva, Switzerland, 1947
- Annecy, France, 1949
- Torquay, England, 1951
- Geneva, Switzerland, 1956
- Geneva, (Dillon Round) 1960–1961
- Geneva, (Kennedy Round) 1964–1967
- Tokyo Round, 1973–1979
- Uruguay Round, 1986–1994
- Doha Development Round, 2001–present (as of 2013)

In the early rounds, from 1947–1961, countries negotiated on a product-by-product basis by presenting lists of tariff reductions they desired from other countries. These rounds resulted in a lowering of *ad valorem* tariffs from roughly 40 percent in 1945 to approximately 20 percent in 1961. The Kennedy Round, which took place from 1964–1967, resulted in even larger across-the-board tariff cuts, particularly in manufactured goods, averaging nearly $40 billion in trade. Sixty-two nations participated in the Kennedy Round. During this period, many developing countries joined the GATT organization.

By the 1970s, GATT's efforts had proven so successful that tariffs ceased to be the world's greatest barrier to trade in goods. Indeed, without GATT, decades of bilateral negotiations may have been necessary to achieve the reductions that multilateral negotiations reached within a few years. In the Tokyo Round, more than 100 participating nations agreed to tariff cuts averaging 34 percent and covering $300 billion in trade, which effectively lowered the average level of tariffs to about 5 percent. In addition, the parties established a number of GATT codes that called for the removal of non-tariff barriers and forms of protectionism that are considered to be "unfair."

The Uruguay Round negotiations lasted from 1986–1994, with 123 countries participating. Its tariff and market access negotiations resulted in worldwide tariff cuts averaging 35–40 percent on merchandise, agricultural products, and industrial goods. Tariffs were eliminated in several industry sectors: agricultural equipment, medical equipment, construction equipment, beer, distilled spirits, chemicals, furniture, paper and printed matter, pharmaceuticals, and toys. Tariffs on information technology products were eliminated by 2005. In addition to tariff cuts, tariffs were bound, or capped, on most products at the rate effective at the time of the agreement. The round also eliminated many non-tariff barriers to trade.

The newest negotiating round, known as the Doha Development Agenda, has been ongoing since 2001. As of 2013 the negotiations had not been completed. The focus of the negotiations is to reach an agreement to reduce agriculture subsidies (domestic price supports and export incentives) by developed countries. This is an area of great disagreement between the rich and poor countries because subsidies by rich countries to agricultural producers makes it more difficult for developing countries to compete in world markets. Although this is the most polarizing of topics, other issues include liberalizing trade in environmental technology products, such as wind turbines, and ecommerce issues related to trade.

Transition from GATT to the WTO

The most important work of the Uruguay Round was in devising solutions to the deficiencies of GATT 1947. The first dealt with coverage: GATT 1947 applied only to trade in goods. Even though the service sector had become the fastest growing sector of the world's economy, it was not subject to GATT rules. Trade in services, such as banking, insurance, telecommunications, or professional services, was specifically excluded. In addition, GATT 1947 failed to regulate agricultural trade, an area of constant dispute among nations, especially between developed and developing countries. Until 2005, trade in textiles and apparel was also outside the scope of GATT because of the politically sensitive nature of these industries. GATT 1947 did little or nothing to address trade-related aspects of intellectual property or the use of restrictions on foreign investment that interfered with the free movement of goods. Finally, the process used to resolve trade disputes between countries was non-binding, filled with loopholes, and often ineffective.

The Uruguay Round ushered in a new era of international trade regulation. It replaced the original GATT organization with the World Trade Organization (WTO). It modernized and expanded the scope of the world trade agreements and instituted a binding dispute settlement process. The Uruguay Round resulted in the conclusion of over 60 major trade agreements that make up a large part of "WTO law."

THE WORLD TRADE ORGANIZATION AND WTO LAW

The year 1995 was one of the most important in the modern history of international trade law. It saw the birth of the World Trade Organization and the conclusion of more than 60 multilateral trade agreements that provide the framework by which we regulate world trade today. The five most important of these agreements that are covered in this chapter are the original 1947 *General Agreement on Tariffs and Trade,* the 1994 *General Agreement on Tariffs and Trade* (covering trade in goods), the *General Agreement on Trade in Services* (to open domestic markets to foreign service providers), the *Agreement Establishing the World Trade Organization*, and the *WTO Dispute Settlement Understanding.* There are also more than a dozen other agreements that apply to specific industry sectors that we will study in later chapters. As a group, we will refer to these as either the "Uruguay Round agreements" or the "GATT/WTO agreements." Some of the most important of agreements include:

- *Agreement on Agriculture*
- *Agreement on Sanitary and Phytosanitary Measures* (animal and plant safety)
- *Agreement on Textiles and Clothing* (terminated as of 2005)
- *Agreement on Technical Barriers to Trade*
- *Agreement on Trade-Related Investment Measures*
- *Agreement on Implementation of Article VI* (dumping as an unfair trade practice)
- *Agreement on Implementation of Article VII* (Customs Valuation)
- *Agreement on Preshipment Inspection*
- *Agreement on Rules of Origin*
- *Agreement on Import Licensing Procedures*
- *Agreement on Subsidies and Countervailing Measures* (unfair trade)
- *Agreement on Safeguards (Import Relief)*
- *Agreement on Trade-Related Aspects of Intellectual Property Rights*
- *Dispute Settlement Understanding*
- *Trade Policy Review Mechanism*
- *Financial Services Understanding*
- *Agreement on Government Procurement*
- *Balance-of-Payments Understanding*

Organization of the WTO

The WTO is today the most important intergovernmental organization for world trade, with 159 member nations as of 2013. Two of the more controversial admissions to WTO membership were China (2001) and Russia (2012). It is headquartered in Geneva. The WTO is not a United Nations agency, but cooperates with the UN as well as the IMF and World Bank. The functions of the WTO are (1) to facilitate international cooperation on trade issues, (2) to administer the GATT/WTO agreements, (3) to provide a forum for future trade negotiations, (4) to monitor national trade policies, (5) to assist developing countries in complying with GATT/WTO agreements by giving technical assistance, and (6) to provide a forum for the settlement of trade disputes..

The organization of the WTO is shown in Exhibit 9.1. The WTO is overseen by the **Ministerial Conference**, made up of high-ranking representatives from all WTO member countries. They meet at least once every two years to direct the policies, activities, and future direction of the WTO by consensus. The Ministerial Conference appoints the *Director-General* and specifies his duties. The WTO Secretariat staff supports the work of the Director-General. Beneath the Ministerial Conference is the *General Council,* which is made up of representatives of each nation and is responsible for overall supervision of the WTO's activities. The General Council also oversees the work of the lower councils, which carry out the work of the WTO in specialized areas. The **Dispute**

Exhibit 9.1

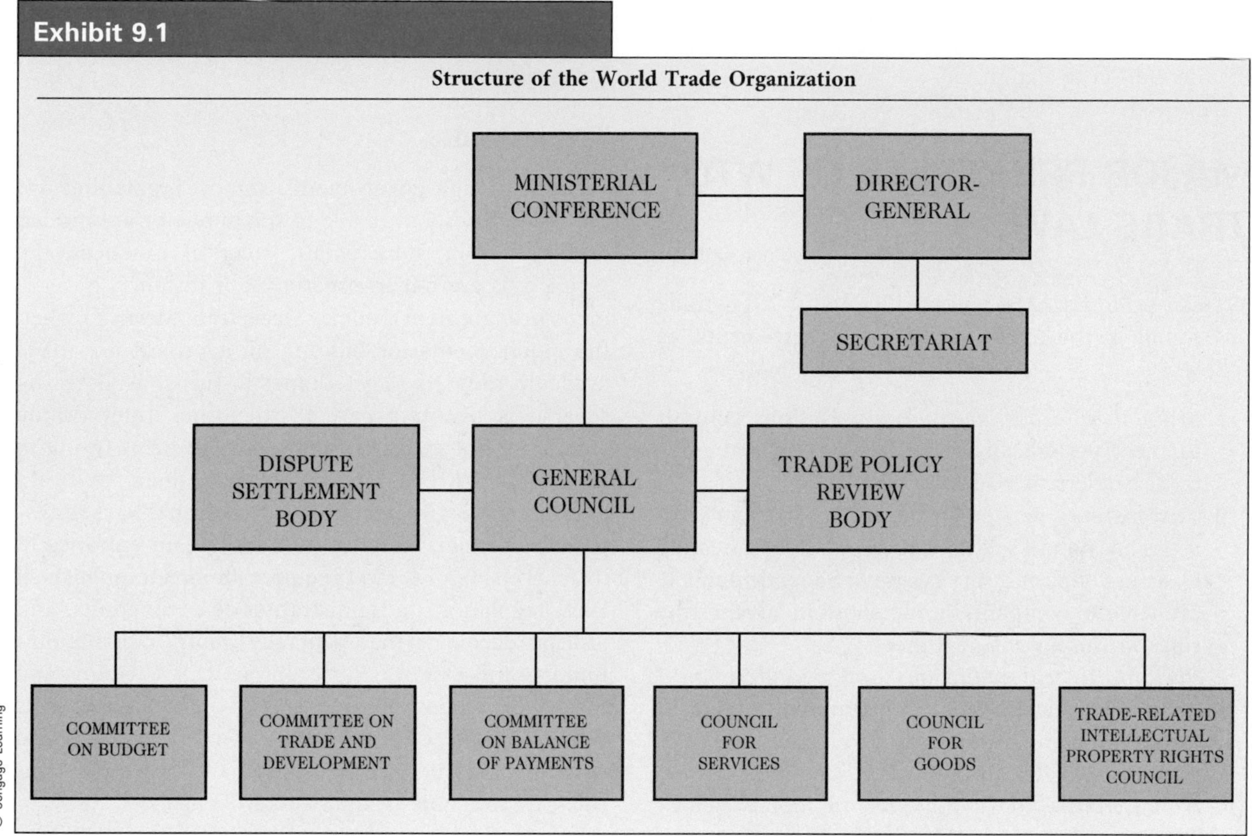

Settlement Body is made up of member governments through the General Council.

The WTO Trade Policy Review Body periodically reviews the trade policies and practices of member countries for transparency and to ensure that member nations adhere to the rules and commitments of the agreements. It is a policy body only and has no enforcement powers. The WTO Council for Trade in Goods oversees the functioning and implementation of the multilateral trade agreements. The WTO Committee on Trade and Development reviews the treatment received by least-developed countries, considers their special trade problems, and makes recommendations to the General Council.

The WTO and U.S. Law

The United States negotiated the Uruguay Rounds and adopted the GATT/WTO agreements under "fast-track" trade promotion authority. The agreements are not treaties, but were enacted into U.S. law through the "congressional-executive" process discussed in Chapter Eight. The agreements were submitted to Congress by President Clinton in the U.S. *Uruguay Round Agreements Act*, and became effective in 1995.

The GATT/WTO agreements do not provide individual rights and remedies to private parties. Private litigants cannot use them to assert rights or claims for compensation in lawsuits against the U.S. government or to challenge the legality of a tariff or federal statute. The *Uruguay Round Agreements Act* states: "No provision of the Uruguay Round agreement … that is inconsistent with any law of the United States shall have effect. Nothing in this Act shall be construed to amend or modify any law of the United States relating to the protection of human … life, the protection of the environment, or worker safety."

If a private firm or industry in the United States believes that its rights under the GATT/WTO agreements are being violated by a foreign company or foreign government, it may seek redress either with the appropriate federal administrative agency or before the courts on the basis of a U.S. statute, but not at the WTO. Of course, it can also communicate its grievance to the U.S. government, which can, at its discretion, negotiate with the foreign government under WTO rules in an attempt to resolve the trade dispute nation to nation.

MAJOR PRINCIPLES OF WTO TRADE LAW

We can summarize the basic principles of WTO trade law found in the major GATT/WTO agreements, as follows:

1. *Multilateral trade negotiations:* Nations commit to meet periodically to reduce tariffs and non-tariff barriers to trade.
2. *Transparency and predictability of trade opportunities:* A nation's laws and regulations affecting trade in goods and services must be made publicly available so companies understand in advance the rules for doing business there.
3. *Reciprocal tariff reductions and bound commitments.* Nations commit to maximum bound tariff rates on specific products and to make those rates publicly available in their tariff schedules.
4. *Nondiscrimination and unconditional most-favored-nation trade:* Members will not give any import advantage or favor to products coming from one member over the goods of another member.
5. *National treatment:* Members will not discriminate in favor of domestically produced goods and against imported goods or treat the two differently under their internal tax laws, regulations, and other national laws.
6. *Elimination of quotas and tarrification and other non-tariff barriers:* Nations must first "convert" their non-tariff barriers to tariffs (through a process called tariffication) and then engage in negotiations to reduce the tariff rates.
7. *Consultations and dispute resolution*: An agreement to resort to the WTO consultation and dispute settlement process and to not engage in unilateral retaliation against countries that violate WTO rules.

In addition, GATT contains provisions to promote trade with developing nations and special rules allowing the establishment of free trade areas and customs unions. Other special rules allow restrictions on imports when necessary to protect the public health and safety or to protect domestic firms from unfair trade practices or increased levels of imports that might cause serious economic injury to domestic industries.

Transparency

When a foreign government's import regulations are not made readily available to the public or are hidden or disguised in bureaucratic rules or practices, the regulations are not transparent. For instance, government procurement policies "lack transparency" when the requirements for bidding on a project are made available only to select domestic firms. A licensing scheme is not transparent when the "rules of the game" are not made known to foreign firms trying to apply for a license to do business there. When a nation's import regulations or procedures lack transparency, foreign firms cannot easily gain entrance to its markets. GATT 1994 requires nations to publish all laws, regulations, administrative determinations, and judicial decisions that generally apply to a nation's imports and exports. For example, U.S. Customs and Border Protection provides public online access to its ruling requests, customs rulings, weekly bulletins and decisions, and its directives and handbooks. Customs rules are available in the Federal Register.

Tariff Concessions, Bound Rates, and Tariff Schedules

GATT calls for member nations to cooperate in lowering tariffs through tariff concessions. A **tariff concession** is each country's promise to reduce tariffs on imports of a given item in return for tariff concessions from other countries. Most concessions are made during the major negotiating rounds. In negotiating tariff concessions, each country takes into account the total economic effect of a concession on its national economy. For example, if Honduras wants the United States to lower the tariff rate on U.S. imports of Honduran coffee beans, then the United States could request that Honduras reciprocate by lowering duties on, say, U.S.-made medical devices in an amount equivalent to the value of the tariff reduction granted to Honduran coffee. Concessions can be on a single product, by entire product categories, or across the board. The agreed tariff rates are known as **tariff bindings** because the rates become *bound,* or capped, at that rate. The **bound rate** is the maximum tariff rate a country may charge on an item, although tariff rates may be reduced below the bound rate.

A country's tariff bindings are recorded in that country's **schedule of concessions** at the WTO. The schedules are legal commitments considered part of the GATT agreement itself. Bound rates are published in each country's **tariff schedules**, which are the detailed product-by-product listings of all tariffs for that country. Tariff schedules for the United States are found in the *Harmonized Tariff Schedule of the United States*, available online from the United States International Trade Commission. If a country later wishes to **modify or withdraw a concession** and raise its bound rate on an item it must negotiate directly with the countries most affected (those countries which are the major suppliers of that item) and by agreement reduce or offset tariffs on other items equal to an equivalent amount in trade.

The case *GATT Report on European Economic Community—Import Regime for Bananas* (1995) illustrates the importance of countries honoring their tariff rates granted by concession to foreign countries. The GATT Panel (pre-WTO) ruled that the change in European Economic Community (now EU) tariff schedules had "nullified and impaired" the rights of foreign banana exporters who should have been able to rely on the existing tariff structure.

European Economic Community—Import Regime for Bananas

Report of the Dispute Settlement Panel, 34 I.L.M. 177 (1995)
General Agreement on Tariffs and Trade, Geneva

BACKGROUND AND FACTS

Since 1963 the European Economic Community (EEC), had negotiated tariff rates with the developing countries that export bananas, and these concessions were bound in the tariff schedules at 20 percent *ad valorem.* In 1993 the EEC took over banana import regulation from the individual countries. The EEC set up uniform rules on quality, marketing standards, and tariffs. Under the EEC regime, the tariff rates on bananas from the Latin American countries were increased between 20 and 180 percent. A complex licensing scheme was also set up to limit the access of foreign banana traders (e.g., Chiquita, Dole, and Del Monte) to sell in the EEC. The Latin American countries claimed that the regulations impaired their Article II tariff concessions and violated Article I, MFN principles, and other GATT provisions. Notice that prior to the WTO's founding in 1995, countries that were party to the GATT agreement were called "contracting parties."

REPORT OF THE PANEL

Article II—Schedules of Concessions: [Central and South American] banana producers had assessed their competitive position on the basis of the bound tariff level. They had made strategic decisions and investments on that basis; they had cultivated substantially more land specifically for this export trade; and they had pursued marketing ties with European importers. The new tariff quota undermined the legitimate expectations upon which these actions were based and severely disrupted the trade conditions upon which these producers had relied, regardless of the actual protective effect of the new regime.

The Panel noted that Article II required that each contracting party "accord to the commerce of the other contracting parties treatment no less favourable than that provided for in the ... *Schedule of Concessions.*" The Panel then considered whether the introduction of a specific tariff for bananas in place of the *ad valorem* tariff provided for in its *Schedule* constituted "treatment no less favourable" in terms of Article II ... The Panel consequently found that the new specific tariffs led to the levying of a duty on imports of bananas whose *ad valorem* equivalent was, either actually or potentially, higher than 20 percent *ad valorem* ...

The Contracting Parties had consistently found that a change from a bound specific to an *ad valorem* rate was a modification of the concession. A working party examining a proposal by Turkey to modify its tariff structure from specific to *ad valorem* had stated: "The obligations of contracting parties are established by the rates of duty appearing in the schedules and any change in the rate such as a change from a specific to an *ad valorem* duty could in some circumstances adversely affect the value of the concessions to other contracting parties. Consequently, any conversion of specific into *ad valorem* rates of duty can be made only under some procedure for the modification of concessions."

Decision. The panel held that the EEC had deprived the complaining Latin American countries of the benefits to which they were entitled under the schedule of concessions. The

Case Questions

1. What action did the EEC take that violated its tariff concessions?
2. Why is it important that countries maintain their tariff commitments?
3. What is the GATT basis for its objections?

Nondiscrimination, Most-Favored-Nation Trade, and National Treatment

The principle of nondiscrimination has long been a guiding concept of international economic relations and of trade liberalization. **Nondiscrimination** is one of the basic rights of membership in the WTO. It means that every WTO member country must treat the goods and services from all other WTO member countries equally and without discrimination. Simply put, nations should not "play favorites" with each other's goods or services. The principle of nondiscrimination is embodied in two important principles of international trade law: the principle of unconditional most-favored-nation trade and the concept of national treatment.

Most-Favored-Nation Trade. When one country grants **most-favored-nation trading status** to another country, it is agreeing to accord items imported from that country the most favorable treatment or the lowest tariff rates that it gives to like products imported from other MFN trading nations. In the United States, an act of Congress grants MFN trading status to a foreign country. According to the WTO/GATT agreements, all countries that are members of the WTO should automatically be entitled to MFN trading status with other WTO countries (although in reality this may not be the case—Cuba is a WTO member but as of 2010 had not received MFN trading status from the United States). Although MFN trade has been in use for at least 300 years, it is now a basic principle of GATT law and is found in Article I of the GATT, which says,

> With respect to customs duties and charges of any kind imposed on or in connection with importation or exportation ... and with respect to the method of levying such duties and charges, and with respect to all rules and formalities in connection with importation and exportation.... Any advantage, favour, privilege, or immunity granted by any other member to any product originating in or destined for any other country shall be accorded immediately and unconditionally to the like product originating in or destined for the territories of all other contracting parties [countries].

MFN principles also apply to trade in services under Article II of the *General Agreement on Trade in Services.*

> With respect to any measure covered by this Agreement, each Member [country] shall accord immediately and unconditionally to services and service suppliers of any other Member treatment no less favourable than that it accords to like services and service suppliers of any other country.

Unconditional MFN Trade. **Unconditional MFN trade** requires that if a nation negotiates a reduced tariff rate on a certain product imported from one WTO member, that rate of duty automatically becomes applicable to like products imported from any and all other WTO members. This means that if country A agrees to reduce its tariff rate to 5 percent on a particular product imported from WTO country B, that new rate becomes applicable to like products imported from all other WTO member countries. Moreover, if country A later agrees to reduce the same tariff to a rate of 3 percent on like products coming from nation C, then like products originating in country B will automatically be entitled to the lower 3 percent rate.

Many people erroneously think that MFN trade is some "special treatment" applied as a favor to products coming from a foreign country. That is not the case. Actually, under WTO rules, most-favored-nation treatment is the norm. All WTO member countries must, under normal trading circumstances, apply MFN tariff rates to products being imported from any and all other WTO member countries. WTO member countries normally give MFN status (and thus MFN tariff rates) to all countries except those that abuse human rights, support terrorism, engage in acts of aggression toward their neighbors, attempt to spread weapons of mass destruction, or are otherwise in violation of international law. Moreover, as we will see later in the chapter, many countries grant better-than-MFN tariff rates to developing countries or to countries within a free trade area.

In the United States, the term "most favored nation" is now referred to as **normal trade relations** or NTR because Congress considers it to more accurately describe the "normal" tariff treatment for most countries. The term "most favored nation" is still in use in international documents and in other countries, however.

National Treatment

Under Article III, once goods enter a nation's stream of commerce, they must not be subjected to different taxes or regulations than domestic goods. For example, goods may not be subject to internal taxes or charges in excess of those applied to like domestic products. Article III provides,

1. [Internal taxes, laws, and regulations] should not be applied to imported or domestic products so as to afford protection to domestic production.
2. [Imports] shall not be subject, directly or indirectly, to internal taxes or other internal charges of any kind in excess of those applied, directly or indirectly, to like domestic products. * * *
3. [Imports] shall be accorded treatment no less favourable than that accorded to like products of national origin in respect of all laws, regulations and requirements affecting their internal sale, offering for sale, purchase, transportation, distribution, or use.

Article III prohibits discrimination against imports resulting from a wide range of non-tariff barriers to trade, including discriminatory customs procedures, government procurement policies, and product standards. In the following case, *WTO Report on Japan—Taxes on Alcoholic Beverages (1996),* the WTO Appellate Body undertook a thorough analysis of the *Japan Liquor Tax Law* and found that the Japanese tax was in violation of GATT Article III. As you read, look not only for its interpretation of national treatment but also look at the Appellate Body's reflections on GATT as international law.

Japan—Taxes on Alcoholic Beverages

Report of the Appellate Body, WT/DS11/AB/R (1996) World Trade Organization

BACKGROUND AND FACTS

The *Japan Liquor Tax Law,* or *Shuzeiho,* taxes liquors sold in Japan based on the type of beverage. There are ten categories of beverage (the categories are *sake, sake* compound, *shochu, mirin,* beer, wine, whiskey/brandy, spirits, liqueurs, and miscellaneous). *Shochu* is distilled from potatoes, buckwheat, or other grains. *Shochu* and vodka share many characteristics. However, vodka and other imported liquors fall in categories with a tax rate that is seven or eight times higher than the category for *shochu.* Foreign spirits account for only 8 percent of the Japanese market, whereas they account for almost 50 percent of the market in other industrialized countries. The United States, the European Union, and Canada called for consultations and brought this complaint at the WTO. The panel held that the Japanese tax law violated GATT, and Japan appealed to the Appellate Body.

REPORT OF THE APPELLATE BODY

The WTO Agreement is a treaty—the international equivalent of a contract. It is self-evident that in an exercise of their sovereignty, and in pursuit of their own respective national interests, the Members of the WTO have made a bargain. In exchange for the benefits they expect to derive as Members of the WTO, they have agreed to exercise their sovereignty according to the commitments they have made in the WTO Agreement. One of those commitments is Article III of the GATT 1994, which is entitled *National Treatment on Internal Taxation and Regulation.*

The broad and fundamental purpose of Article III is to avoid protectionism in the application of internal tax and regulatory measures. More specifically, the purpose of Article III is to ensure that internal measures not be applied to imported or domestic products so as to afford protection to domestic production. Toward this end, Article III obliges Members of the WTO to provide equality of competitive conditions for imported products in relation to domestic products. "[T]he intention of the drafters of the Agreement was clearly to treat the imported products in the same way as the like domestic products once they had been cleared through customs. Otherwise indirect protection could be given." *Italian Discrimination Against Imported Agricultural Machinery,* BISD 7S/60, para.11. Moreover, it is irrelevant that "the trade effects" of the tax differential between imported and domestic products, as reflected in the volumes of imports, are insignificant or even nonexistent. Article III protects expectations not of any particular trade volume but rather of the equal competitive relationship between imported and domestic products. Members of the WTO are free to pursue their own domestic goals through internal taxation or regulation so long as they do not do so in a way that violates Article III or any of the other commitments they have made in the WTO Agreement. * * *

[I]f imported products are taxed in excess of like domestic products, then that tax measure is inconsistent with Article III ...[We must determine first] whether the taxed imported and domestic products are "like" and, second, whether the taxes applied to the imported products are "in excess of" those applied to the like domestic products. If the imported and domestic products are "like products," and if the taxes applied to the imported products are "in excess of" those applied to the like domestic products, then the measure is inconsistent with Article III:2.

We agree with the Panel also that the definition of "like products" in Article III:2 should be construed narrowly. How narrowly is a matter that should be determined separately for each tax measure in each

continues

continued

case. [A 1970 GATT Report] set out the basic approach for interpreting "like or similar products":

> [T]he interpretation of the term should be examined on a case-by-case basis. This would allow a fair assessment in each case of the different elements that constitute a "similar" product. Some criteria were suggested for determining, on a case-by-case basis, whether a product is "similar": the product's end-users in a given market; consumers' tastes and habits, which change from country to country; the product's properties, nature and quality. *Report of the Working Party on Border Tax Adjustments* 18S/97, para. 18. * * *

The concept of "likeness" is a relative one that evokes the image of an accordion. The accordion of "likeness" stretches and squeezes in different places as different provisions of the WTO Agreement are applied. [The definition of "likeness" must be narrowly interpreted.] The Panel determined in this case that *shochu* and vodka are "like products."

A uniform tariff classification of products can be relevant in determining what are "like products." Tariff classification has been used as a criterion for determining "like products" in several previous adopted panel reports ... There are risks in using tariff bindings that are too broad as a measure of product "likeness. "... It is true that there are numerous tariff bindings which are in fact extremely precise with regard to product description and which, therefore, can provide significant guidance as to the identification of "like products." Clearly enough, these determinations need to be made on a case-by-case basis. However, tariff bindings that include a wide range of products are not a reliable criterion for determining or confirming product "likeness" under Article III:2.

The only remaining issue under the first sentence of Article III:2 is whether the taxes on imported products are "in excess of" those on like domestic products. If so, then the Member that has imposed the tax is not in compliance with Article III. Even the smallest amount of "excess" is too much. The prohibition of discriminatory taxes in Article III is not conditional on a "trade effects test" nor is it qualified by a *de minimis* standard.

If imported and domestic products are not "like products" ... those same products may well be among the broader category of "directly competitive or substitutable products" that fall within the domain of the second sentence of Article III:2. How much broader that category of "directly competitive or substitutable products" may be in any given case is a matter for the Panel to determine based on all the relevant facts in that case. In this case, the Panel emphasized the need to look not only at such matters as physical characteristics, common end-uses, and tariff classifications, but also at the "market place." This seems appropriate. The GATT 1994 is a commercial agreement, and the WTO is concerned, after all, with markets. It does not seem inappropriate to look at competition in the relevant markets as one among a number of means of identifying the broader category of products that might be described as "directly competitive or substitutable." Nor does it seem inappropriate to examine elasticity of substitution as one means of examining those relevant markets. In the Panel's view, the decisive criterion in order to determine whether two products are directly competitive or substitutable is whether they have common end-uses, *inter alia,* as shown by elasticity of substitution. We agree.

Our interpretation of Article III is faithful to the "customary rules of interpretation of public international law." WTO rules are reliable, comprehensible and enforceable. WTO rules are not so rigid or so inflexible as not to leave room for reasoned judgements in confronting the endless and ever changing ebb and flow of real facts in real cases in the real world. They will serve the multilateral trading system best if they are interpreted with that in mind. In that way, we will achieve the "security and predictability" sought for the multilateral trading system by the Members of the WTO through the establishment of the dispute settlement system.

Decision. The *Japan Liquor Tax Law* was found to violate the national treatment provisions of GATT Article III. *Shochu* is a "like product" and is "directly competitive and substitutable" with other imported spirits. The imported spirits were taxed higher than the *shochu.* The decision of the panel was upheld and Japan was requested to bring its tax law into compliance with GATT.

Comment. In 1997, the United States was forced to seek binding arbitration when it became apparent that Japan did not intend to bring its liquor tax into WTO compliance within a "reasonable period" as required by WTO rules. The arbitration ruling supported the U.S. position. Japan agreed to revise its tariff system in stages and to eliminate tariffs on most spirits. The U.S. distilled spirits industry reported that, as expected, the change in taxation has increased exports of U.S. distilled spirits to Japan.

Case Questions

1. What is the purpose of GATT's Article III and how is that purpose served?
2. Is it necessary that the complaining party show that a discriminatory tax has a negative effect on trade? Is a remedy possible even where the discrimination has no adverse impact on the sales volume of the imported products?
3. How does a WTO panel determine whether two products are "like products" for purposes of the first sentence of Article III(2) or "directly competitive or substitutable products" that fall within the domain of the second sentence of Article III(2)?

Licenses, Quotas, and Prohibitions on Imports

GATT favors the use of tariffs over any other method of regulating imports, while specifically prohibiting all other restrictions on trade. Article XI reads as follows:

> No prohibitions or restrictions other than duties, taxes, or other charges, whether made effective through *quotas, import or export licenses, or other measures,* shall be instituted or maintained . . . on the importation of any product . . . or on the exportation or sale for export of any product . . .

Import Licensing and Customs Procedures as Trade Barriers. Article XI prohibits a country from using an import license as a protectionist measure. In the years after World War II many governments, particularly in developing countries, required importers to apply for permission to import products, subjecting them to many complex and often discriminatory requirements. The licensing was often an expensive, time consuming, regulatory maze. Rather than being "rules-based" they often gave the ultimate discretion to government bureaucrats to decide which license applications to accept and which to deny. In many cases license applications were lost in government red tape and endless delay. Paperwork and inspection requirements caused delays and expense.

To illustrate, in 1995 the United States accused South Korea of using delaying tactics in the form of "inspections" that held shipments of U.S.-grown fresh produce on the docks until it had rotted. According to the annual *National Trade Estimate Report on Foreign Trade Barriers*, prepared by the U.S. Trade Representative, unfair licensing requirements and similar restrictions exist to this day. Article XI was used against the United States in the Report of the Appellate Body in *United States—Import Prohibition of Certain Shrimp and Shrimp Products*, WT/DS58/AB/R (1998). The United States banned imports of shrimp harvested by vessels of foreign nations that had not been certified by the United States as using methods that would not kill sea turtles. Although it was an import ban for good reason, conservation, it was not implemented in a fair, open, and transparent manner. The U.S. approval process was so informal, arbitrary, and discretionary, that foreign shrimpers found it very difficult to obtain approval. The U.S. restrictions were held to violate Article XI, much to the chagrin of environmental groups. When faced with foreign licensing schemes, exporters around the world use local agents and attorneys to advise them on import regulations and customs procedures in the foreign market. Chapter Ten discusses a WTO side agreement on import licensing.

Quotas and Quantitative Restrictions on Imports. Article XI reflects a general policy in the GATT agreement against the use of quotas to protect domestic companies. A **quota** is a quantitative restriction on imports. **Absolute quotas** are those that strictly prohibit imports of an item above a pre-determined limit, based either on the value or quantity of specific goods (weight, number of pieces, etc.), or as a percentage of the domestic market for that item.

There are different types of absolute quotas. **Global quotas** are imposed by an importing nation on a particular product regardless of its country of origin. An **allocated quota** is one in which the total limit is "allocated" among several specific countries. The term **zero quota** is sometimes used when referring to a complete ban on the import of a product in that it permits *zero* quantities to be imported. An **auctioned quota** is one in which the quota rights are sold to the highest bidder.

Historically, countries that wanted to protect domestic industries used absolute quotas because they worked quickly to block imports. Their impact was immediate, while tariffs took time to take effect. But GATT prohibits absolute quotas because of the many economic arguments against them, including the following:

- Quotas distort the free market through government restrictions on supply, causing price increases.
- Domestic producers become "dependent" on quotas to protect them from foreign competition, and it often becomes politically difficult to remove them.
- Unlike tariffs, quotas can deprive importers and consumers of the ability to make a choice of products in the marketplace and are therefore politically unpopular with consumers.
- Unlike tariffs, quotas provide no tariff revenue to the importing nation.
- The limited number of firms that are able to import an item within the quota limit can earn a "monopoly profit."
- Without foreign competition, domestic producers are free to raise prices, to the detriment of consumers.
- Quotas require a complex and costly government licensing scheme and record-keeping system to enforce them.
- The licensing schemes used to enforce quotas were often viewed as inherently unfair, and were difficult for many foreign exporters to comply.

Despite the provisions in GATT 1947 prohibiting quotas, many countries continued to use them for decades. Quotas were used to regulate trade in textiles and apparel worldwide for many years prior to 2005, when the quota system on textiles was abolished. There were so many quotas in place protecting farmers from foreign competition, that removing quotas on the import of agricultural items was a main focus of the Uruguay Round negotiations. The WTO was instrumental in removing quotas through tarrification. **Tariffication** is the process by which a country agrees to "convert" its quotas, import licenses, and other non-tariff barriers on specific items to tariffs. Reciprocal tariff concessions can then gradually reduce tariffs, while giving domestic producers time to adapt to new foreign competition.

Tariff-Rate Quotas. A **tariff-rate quota** (also called a "tariff quota") is not really a quota at all, but a tariff rate that increases according to the quantity of goods imported. It is a limitation or ceiling on the quantity of goods that may be imported into a country at a given tariff rate. Unlike absolute quotas, tariff-rate quotas leave the price mechanism in effect in regulating imports. They are also allocated to specific supplying countries without discrimination. Consider bedspreads as an example. A country that wants to protect its domestic textile industry might impose a tariff rate of, say, 7 percent on the first 500,000 bedspreads to be imported into the country in a given year; 14 percent on the next 500,000; and an even higher rate, perhaps 25 percent, on all bedspreads imported above 1,000,000 pieces. The use of tariff-rate quotas is quite common worldwide. After 1994 and the Uruguay Rounds, many absolute quotas were converted to a system of tariff-rate quotas. In the United States, for example, tariff-rate quotas are used to limit imports of raw cane sugar, tuna, dairy products, peanuts, brooms, olives, and some cotton and wool products. A similar system exists in Canada. Some tariff-rate quotas are determined by obligations under free trade agreements. Quotas on agricultural products are administered by the U.S. Department of Agriculture, and like other tariff-rate quotas, are enforced by U.S. Customs and Border Protection.

Quantitative Restrictions: The Balance-of-Payments Exception and Developing Countries. GATT permits quotas under limited circumstances, such as those related to national policies affecting agriculture or fisheries. Quotas may also be used during certain national financial emergencies. When a nation's payments of foreign exchange exceed receipts, a **balance-of-payments** (BOP) deficit can arise. The fastest way to halt the outflow of foreign exchange by local companies is to place quantitative restrictions on imports of goods and services through quotas or licensing schemes. (Tariffs would take much longer to have the same effect.)

Although both developed and developing countries can face a BOP deficit, the problem is exacerbated in developing countries because their international transactions are usually done with one of the major currencies, not with their own. Historically, many developing countries were agrarian economies, some with only a few "cash crops" that could be sold for export. Others were able to develop basic industries in steel or textiles that provided export revenues. Often this was their only source of scarce foreign exchange, which was needed to purchase essential foreign goods, such as medicine, fertilizer, or farm equipment or to repay international debts. After all, dollars, pounds, or yen could be used for trade anywhere on the globe, but usually their local currency could not. Despite GATT's prohibition of quotas, any nation (including developed nations) may resort to quantitative restrictions in a BOP crisis. Article XII applies to a developed country "with very low monetary reserves" and allows the use of quantitative restrictions to "safeguard its external financial position and its balance-of-payment … necessary to forestall the imminent threat of, or to stop, a serious decline in its monetary reserves." Article XVIII applies to a developing country that "can only support low standards of living and is in the early stages of development." For these countries the rule is more liberal, allowing the use of quantitative restrictions "in order to safeguard its external financial position and to ensure a level of [foreign exchange] reserves adequate for the implementation of its program of economic development." In any case, the restrictions must be temporary and phased out as economic conditions improve and they are no longer required.

GATT 1994 instituted a new requirement that a WTO member must use the least restrictive means possible for correcting a BOP emergency, preferably a price-based measure, such as a surcharge or tariff increase, rather than a pure quantitative limit on imports. Restrictions should not be targeted at individual products, but should affect the "general level" of all imports to the country. The restrictions must be transparent and the government must publicly announce its timetable for removing them. Members must provide justification for the measure to the WTO **Balance-of-Payments Committee**, and the action is subject to WTO surveillance and periodic review. Exporters who do business in developing countries should pay particular attention to this issue. In the following *WTO Panel Report on India—Quantitative Restrictions on Imports of Agricultural Textile, & Industrial Products,* the United States sought to have India remove a complex scheme of import restrictions that had existed for almost 50 years. The panel addressed the Indian licensing scheme as a prohibition on imports under Article XI and the BOP exception.

India—Quantitative Restrictions on Imports of Agricultural, Textile, & Industrial Products

Report of the Dispute Settlement Panel, WT/DS90/R (1999)
World Trade Organization

BACKGROUND AND FACTS

For 50 years prior to this case, India had placed complex restrictions on the import of agricultural, industrial and consumer goods from other countries. Goods placed on the "negative list" could only be imported by special license, which was generally only granted to the "actual user," rather than to firms in the normal chain of distribution. Many goods could only be imported by state agencies. The restrictions were, in many cases, applied arbitrarily and in the discretion of Indian government officials on a case-by-case basis. As a result, it was often impossible to know at any given time what goods might be allowed into the country. Goods imported with a license were subject to confiscation or a fine of five times the value of the goods. In 1997, the United States brought this complaint at the WTO against India requesting that restrictions on thousands of products be removed. India claimed that without restrictions its foreign exchange would leave the country, upsetting its balance of payments and inhibiting its economic development.

REPORT OF THE PANEL

The United States contended that ... persons wishing to import an item on the Negative List had to apply for a license and explain their "justification for import": the authorities provided no explanation of the criteria for judging applications, and no advance notice of the volume or value of imports to be allowed. In fact, licenses were routinely refused on the basis that the import would compete with a domestic producer. The leading item on the Negative List was consumer goods (including many food items), and for many consumer goods inclusion on the Negative List had amounted to an import ban or close to it.

The United States considered that the restrictiveness of India's licensing of consumer goods imports was demonstrated by the trade statistics ... *zero imports for 1995/96,* including meat; fish; cereals; malt and starches; preparations of meat or fish; cocoa, chocolate and cocoa preparations; nuts, canned and pickled vegetables and fruits, and fruit juices; wine, beer, spirits and vinegar; leather articles; matting and baskets; carpets; knitted fabrics; clothing; headgear; umbrellas; and furniture. [Imports of hundreds of other products were allowed in only minute quantities for a population of 1 billion.] Thus, in many cases import licensing amounts to an import ban, or close to it.

The United States noted that ... the "Actual User condition" ruled out any imports by wholesalers or other intermediaries, and itself was a further quantitative restriction on imports. * * *

Thus, according to the United States, the generally applicable import licensing process was a complete black box for the importer and for the foreign exporter. No information was provided on the Government's sectoral priorities with respect to products or on what its views of "merit" might be. All that the United States knew was that the Indian licensing authority generally refused to grant import licences for "restricted" items when it was considered prejudicial to the state's interest to do so.

The United States added that the broad definition of "consumer goods," and the fact that some goods were *only* restricted if they were consumer goods, created considerable confusion, commercial uncertainty and distortion of trade. * * * The 1996 study on *Liberalisation of Indian Imports of Consumer Durables* by the Export-Import Bank of India had noted that the only two commonly-used consumer durable goods that were freely importable were cameras and nail cutters. * * *

India said that it needed to use discretionary licensing on a case-by-case basis for the following reasons. India's economy had been almost totally closed to imports barely 15 years ago. Because of the size and structure of the economy, it was impossible for India to estimate precisely the level of demand for imports, the import elasticity of demand for a huge number of products, as well as the elasticity of substitution of domestic products by consumers, and the effective rate of protection for all these products.

continues

continued

Accordingly, India considered recourse to discretionary licensing to be unavoidable. Further, India was progressively phasing out its import restrictions. As part of its autonomously initiated programme of economic liberalization, India had already reduced the number of items on which there were import restrictions to just 2,296 as of 1998, from about 11,000 HS-lines in I991. * * *

The United States stated that India's quantitative restrictions and licensing regimes had damaged and continued to damage U.S. trade interests ... In 1996, the United States exported $1.3 billion to India in goods subject to quantitative restrictions. However, while the ASEAN area had a population half the size of India's, U.S. exports to ASEAN were eight times the value of U.S. exports to India. As the panel on *"Japanese Measures on Imports of Leather"* noted, "the fact that the United States was able to export large quantities of leather to other markets [than Japan] ... tended to confirm the assumption that the existence of the restrictions [on leather imports] had adversely affected [the] United States' exports."

The nature and operation of India's import licensing regimes also damaged and continued to damage U.S. trade interests. The uncertainty and limitations imposed by India's licensing regime deterred or prevented exporters from undertaking the investments in planning, promotion and market development necessary to develop and expand markets in India for their products. No exporter would put resources into developing a product's market in India without some assurance that it would be able to export some minimum amount per year, and the Indian system provided no such assurance—only a guarantee of continuing uncertainty—if the product in question was on the Negative List of Imports. * * *

In light of the foregoing, we note that it is agreed that India's licensing system for goods in the Negative List of Imports is a discretionary import licensing system, in that licences are not granted in all cases, but rather on unspecified "merits." We note also that India concedes this measure is an import restriction under Article XI: 1. * * *

Having determined that the measures at issue are quantitative restrictions within the meaning of Article XI:1 and therefore prohibited, we must examine ... India's defence under the balance-of-payments provisions of GATT 1994. * * *

In this connection, we recall that the IMF reported that India's reserves as of 21 November 1997 were $25.1 billion and that an adequate level of reserves at that date would have been $16 billion. While the Reserve Bank of India did not specify a precise level of what would constitute adequacy, it concluded only three months earlier in August 1997 that India's reserves were "well above the thumb rule of reserve adequacy" and although the Bank did not accept that thumb rule as the only measure of adequacy, it also found that "[b]y any criteria, the level of foreign exchange reserves appears comfortable." It also stated that "the reserves would be adequate to withstand both cyclical and unanticipated shocks." * * *

For the reasons outlined ... we find that ... India's monetary reserves of $25.1 billion were not inadequate as that term is used in Article XVIII:9(b) and that India was therefore not entitled to implement balance-of-payments measures to achieve a reasonable rate of growth in its reserves. * * *

The institution and maintenance of balance-of-payments measures is only justified at the level necessary to address the concern, and cannot be more encompassing. Paragraph 11, in this context, confirms this requirement that the measures be limited to what is necessary and addresses more specifically the conditions of evolution of the measures as balance-of-payments conditions improve: at any given time, the restrictions should not exceed those necessary. This implies that as conditions improve, measures must be relaxed in proportion to the improvements. The logical conclusion of the process is that the measures will be eliminated when conditions no longer justify them. * * *

In conclusion ... we have found that India's balance-of-payments situation was not such as to allow the maintenance of measures for balance-of-payments purposes under the terms of Article XVIII9, that India was not justified in maintaining its existing measures under the terms of Article XVIII: 11, and that it does not have a right to maintain or phase-out these measures on the basis of other provisions of Article XVIII:B which it invoked in its defence. We therefore conclude that India's measures are not justified under the terms of Article XVIII:B. * * *

This panel suggests that a reasonable period of time be granted to India in order to remove the import restrictions which are not justified under Article XVIII:B. Normally, the reasonable period of time to implement a panel recommendation, when determined through arbitration, should not exceed fifteen months from the date of adoption of a panel or Appellate Body report. However, this 15-month period is "a 'guideline for the arbitrator,' not a rule," and ..."that time may be shorter or longer, depending upon the particular circumstances."

Decision. India's quantitative restrictions and the licensing scheme violated Article XI because they were discriminatory and not "rules based," and were no longer justified to preserve its balance of payments. The panel's decision was upheld by the WTO Appellate

continues

continued

Body in its report of August 1999 and later adopted by the Dispute Settlement Body.

Comment. Complex licensing restrictions like the one used by India for decades following World War II were not uncommon in developing countries. While it protected domestic producers, many of which were state-owned enterprises, it also kept their markets closed to foreign technology, innovation, capital, and the many benefits of competition. But consider how life in many developing countries has changed since the 1980s and 1990s. Most developing countries, including India, have dramatically opened their markets to foreign competition and foreign investment (although certainly not in all industry sectors). Many are no longer totally dependent on an agricultural economy. And many that once feared imports because they did not have the foreign currency to pay for them, now have vibrant export- based manufacturing industries.

Case Questions

1. Compare the system of import licensing in effect in India during that time to what you know in the United States today. Are there any industries you can think of in the United States that are subjected to import licensing? What industries are so highly regulated?
2. Why did the licensing scheme violate Article XI?
3. What causes a balance-of-payments problem, and why can this be a critical problem for many developing countries?
4. Why did the panel not accept India's balance-of-payments argument?

Exceptions Permitting Import Restrictions

GATT Article XX provides that countries may restrict imports when necessary to meet the following public policy goals:

- When necessary to protect public morals
- When necessary to protect human, animal or plant life or health
- Relating to imports of gold or silver
- Prohibitions on trade in products made by prison labor
- Protection of national artistic, historic, or archaeological treasures
- Conservation of exhaustible natural resources if done in conjunction with domestic controls
- When necessary to stop infringement of intellectual property rights
- Relating to traffic in nuclear materials, arms, or ammunition
- During time of war

WTO DISPUTE-SETTLEMENT PROCEDURES

The GATT/WTO agreements can only work when national legislatures and governments choose to comply with WTO principles when setting tariff rates and regulating imports. When one WTO member nation acts contrary to its commitments in a GATT/WTO agreement, such as raising a tariff above the bound rate or imposing an unjustified quota on imports, that country is said to have "nullified or impaired" the rights of other WTO member countries that are affected by that country's action. Consider this example: Assume that under domestic pressure from local chair makers, Australia raises the tariff rate on imported beach chairs above the bound rate. WTO countries whose companies ship beach chairs to Australia may file a complaint with the WTO for **nullification or impairment** of their national rights under a trade agreement. These governments must first engage in **trade consultations** with Australia at the WTO, and if no resolution is possible they may request binding dispute resolution before the WTO **Dispute Settlement Body** (WTO-DSB).

The GATT/WTO agreements envision that nations will not take unilateral retaliatory action against any other nation in a trade dispute, but will instead rely on WTO dispute-settlement procedures to avert a trade war. These procedures are a quasi-judicial process for resolving trade disputes when attempts by the countries involved to reach a settlement become deadlocked. Dispute resolution is intended to resolve a conflict before a "trade war" erupts. For instance, if nation A imposes a quota on nation B's products, then nation B may file a complaint with the WTO-DSB. In the meantime, nation B may not unilaterally retaliate with quotas or tariffs on A's products and, in fact, it needs approval of the WTO-DSB to do so. Only a government can bring a complaint for nullification and impairment against another government. Complaints are not filed by or against firms or individuals (although, as a practical matter, WTO cases are often brought by nations upon the instigation of private industry). Unlike GATT panel decisions prior to 1995, WTO-DSB decisions are released to the public and available online. WTO-DSB decisions are binding, and unlike the previous GATT panels, the parties cannot "block" or veto a panel's decision. Countries generally want to support and abide by the decisions because they might want to rely on the process in the future. Furthermore, WTO decisions carry the voice of world opinion and serve as an international conscience for determining which trade practices are acceptable and which are not.

The following provisions are from the *WTO Understanding on Rules and Procedures Governing the Settlement of Disputes,* also known as the *WTO Dispute-Settlement Understanding* (DSU):

- The WTO's General Council has responsibility for the dispute resolution process, and oversees the work of the WTO-DSB. The WTO-DSB appoints panels, adopts panel decisions, and authorizes the withdrawal or suspension of concessions.
- A complaining party can request consultations to seek a solution. If no solution is found within 60 days, the complaining party may request that a panel hear the case. (Historically, most disputes are resolved in the consultation stage, which in some cases can last for years.) There is a process for handling urgent cases. The panel consists of three to five individuals nominated by the WTO Secretariat.
- Other member nations with a "substantial interest" in the case may join in a complaint, make written submissions, and appear at the oral argument before the panel.
- A panel determines the facts of the case and whether there have been violations of the terms of a GATT/WTO agreement. It may call on experts for advice on scientific and technical matters. All panel deliberations are confidential. The panel must submit a written report to the parties and to other members within six months (three months in urgent cases).
- Unless the parties file for an appeal to the Appellate Body, the panel's report goes to the WTO-DSB where it will automatically be upheld unless there is a consensus of all member countries to reject the decision. A WTO-DSB vote to reject must be by consensus. Thus the "losing" nation in a dispute settlement case cannot block the decision of a panel without a unanimous vote of all members (including getting the "winning" party in the dispute to agree to block a decision it just won). The process takes about one year, from the beginning of consultations to adoption of a report by the WTO-DSB.
- Panel decisions may be appealed to the WTO **Appellate Body** on issues of law related to interpretation of the relevant provisions of the GATT/WTO agreement in question. Each case is heard by three judges (out of a permanent body of seven judges). They may uphold, modify, or reverse a panel decision. Judges serving on the Appellate Body will be chosen by the WTO-DSB on the basis of their expertise in international trade law to serve for four-year terms. They usually come from government, universities, or international law practices. Other member nations with a substantial interest in the case may file written submissions and appear before the Appellate Body. Appeals are limited to issues of law covered in the panel report and legal interpretations considered by the panel. The appellate report is final unless the WTO-DSB rejects it by consensus vote within 30 days.
- If the panel report finds that the offending party has violated a GATT/WTO agreement, the WTO-DSB can recommend ways for the offending party to come into compliance. The offending party has thirty days in which to state how it plans to comply with the panel's ruling. Compliance must be within a reasonable time. If no immediate solution is available, the offending party can voluntarily make compensatory adjustments to the complaining party as a temporary measure.
- If no settlement is reached or if the trade violation is not removed, the panel may recommend that the General Council authorize the **withdrawal or suspension of a concession** by the complaining party. This is the equivalent of a trade sanction. The sanction should be imposed on the same type of goods imported from the offending nation or on goods from the same type of industry or economic sector. Sanctions should be in an amount equal to the impact that the breach of agreement had on the complaining party. Sanctions are to be temporary and remain in force only until the offending party's violation is removed.

The following case, *WTO Report of the Appellate Body on European Communities—Regime for the Importation, Sale and Distribution of Bananas (1997)* involves a long-running trade dispute among the European Community, Latin America, and the United States. It addresses the issue of who may request a WTO panel in a trade dispute.

WTO Reports as Legal Precedent

Do WTO reports carry precedential value for future panels, as judicial decisions do in common-law courts? According to Appellate Body decisions, the answer seems to be no. The *WTO Report of the Appellate Body on Japan—Taxes on Alcoholic Beverages* (1996) addressed the status of a report that had been adopted by the WTO-DSB:

European Communities—Regime for the Importation, Sale & Distribution of Bananas

Report of the Appellate Body, WT/DS27/AB/R (1997) World Trade Organization

BACKGROUND AND FACTS

The European Community (EC) had been the world's largest importer of bananas, two-thirds of which was grown in Latin America. A large percentage came from developing countries that were once colonies of Britain, Spain, and France, located in Africa, the Caribbean, and the Pacific (known as ACP countries). Growers in the ACP countries could not compete with the highly efficient non-ACP producers, most of which are in Latin America. In order to encourage the import of ACP-grown bananas and to aid in the development of ACP economies, the EC devised a host of tariff and non-tariff barriers aimed at non-ACP bananas. For example, a complex quota scheme was used permitting only a limited quantity of non-ACP bananas to be imported each year. While licenses to import ACP bananas were granted routinely, only importers who met strict requirements could receive licenses to import Latin American and other non-ACP bananas. Whereas most ACP bananas entered duty free, other bananas had a very substantial tariff rate. Several Latin American countries requested consultations, claiming that the EC regulations violated GATT by discriminating against bananas grown in their countries. The United States joined with them in bringing this complaint, arguing that the United States also had a substantial interest in the issue. While the United States was not an exporter of bananas, the U.S. government noted that U.S. companies, such as Chiquita Brands and others, conducted a wholesale trade in bananas amounting to hundreds of millions of dollars a year and would lose market share because of the EC's actions. The EC maintained that the United States had no grounds for complaining about the EC regulations because it was not a producer and grower. A WTO panel was convened, and its decision was appealed to the WTO Appellate Body.

REPORT OF THE APPELLATE BODY

The EC argues that the Panel infringed Article 3.2 of the Dispute Settlement Understanding (DSU) by finding that the United States has a right to advance claims under the GATT 1994. The EC asserts that, as a general principle, in any system of law, including international law, a claimant must normally have a legal right or interest in the claim it is pursuing... . The EC asserts that the United States has no actual or potential trade interest justifying its claim, since its banana production is minimal, it has never exported bananas, and this situation is unlikely to change due to the climatic and economic conditions in the United States. In the view of the EC, the panel fails to explain how the United States has a potential trade interest in bananas, and production alone does not suffice for a potential trade interest. The EC also contends that the United States has no right protected by WTO law to shield its own internal market from the indirect effects of the EC banana regime....

We agree with the Panel that no provision of the DSU contains any explicit requirement that a member must have a "legal interest" as a prerequisite for requesting a panel. We do not accept that the need for a "legal interest" is implied in the DSU or in any other provision of the WTO Agreement ... [We believe] that a member nation has broad discretion in deciding whether to bring a case against another member nation under the DSU...

The participants in this appeal have referred to certain judgments of the International Court of Justice and the Permanent Court of International Justice relating to whether there is a requirement, in international law, of a legal interest to bring a case. We do not read any of these judgments as establishing a general rule that in all international litigation, a complaining party must have a "legal interest" in order to bring a case. Nor do these judgments deny the need to consider the question of standing under the dispute settlement provisions of any multilateral treaty, by referring to the terms of that treaty.

We are satisfied that the United States was justified in bringing its claims under the GATT 1994 in this case. The United States is a producer of bananas, and a potential export interest by the United States cannot be excluded. The internal market of the United States of bananas could be affected by the EC banana regime, in particular, by the effects of that regime on world supplies and world prices of bananas. We also agree with the Panel's statement that: "... with the increased interdependence of the global economy ... member nations have a greater stake in enforcing WTO rules than in the past since any deviation from the negotiated balance of rights and obligations is more likely than ever to affect them, directly or indirectly."

Accordingly, we believe that a member nation has broad discretion in deciding whether to bring a case against another member under the DSU. The language of Article XXIII: 1 of the GATT 1994 and of the DSU

continues

continued

suggests, furthermore, that a member is expected to be largely self-regulating in deciding whether any such action would be "fruitful."

Decision. The Appellate Body held that the United States could call for the convening of a WTO panel to question EC import barriers even though its exports were not directly affected.

Comment. The United States sought WTO authorization to "suspend concessions" (i.e., impose retaliatory tariffs) on a wide range of EU products, the value of which was equivalent to the nullification or impairment sustained by the United States. Consider the impact of a trade war over bananas: In 1999 the Dispute Settlement Body authorized the United States to impose 100 percent *ad valorem* duties on a list of EU products with an annual trade value of $191.4 million. The range of European products included bath preparations, handbags of plastic, paperboard, lithographs not over twenty years old, cotton bed linens that are printed and do not contain any embroidery or trimming, lead-acid batteries, "articles of a kind normally carried in the pocket or handbag, with outer surface of reinforced or laminated plastics," electric coffeemakers, and other products. In 2001, an agreement was reached to end the trade dispute. The EU restrictions were dismantled, and U.S. tariffs were lifted. The "Banana Wars" were the largest trade war to date with tremendous economic and political ramifications.

Case Questions

1. When may a member bring a complaint against another member of the WTO?
2. What was the basis for the EC's argument in this case?
3. The EU-Latin America banana dispute did not end until 2012. What was the ultimate conclusion to this WTO issue?

> We do not believe that [WTO member nations], in deciding to adopt a panel report, intended that their decision would constitute a definitive interpretation of the provisions of GATT 1947. Nor do we believe that this is contemplated under GATT 1994 . . . Adopted panel reports can play an important part of the GATT *acquis.* They are often considered by subsequent panels. They create legitimate expectations among WTO members, and, therefore should be taken into account where they are relevant to any dispute. However, they are not binding . . .

This statement is reaffirmed in the actual language of GATT 1994, which states that interpretations of the agreement may only be made by the Ministerial Conference and the General Council. Nevertheless, WTO Appellate Body reports continue to cite prior reports for their persuasive value.

In the United States, WTO Panel and Appellate Body decisions are not binding on the courts. However, there are several cases in which the federal courts have cited WTO decisions for their persuasive authority. For example, in *Hyundai Electronics Co., Ltd. v. United States,* 53 F. Supp. 2d 1334 (1999), the Court of International Trade stated, "Thus, the WTO panel report does not constitute binding precedential authority for the court. Of course, this is not to imply that a panel report serves no purpose in litigation before the court. To the contrary, a panel's reasoning, if sound, may be used to inform the court's decision." This means that a U.S. court cannot strike down a U.S. law or regulation merely because a WTO decision has ruled that it is in violation of an international agreement. For instance, if a WTO panel rules that a U.S. Department of Energy regulation regarding the sale of imported oil is held to be in violation of GATT's nondiscrimination provisions, a U.S. court cannot rely on that decision in striking down the regulation. It would be a matter for the U.S. Congress or the executive branch of government, and not the judiciary, to bring that regulation into compliance with a WTO decision.

EXCEPTIONS TO NORMAL WTO TRADE RULES

Earlier we said that most-favored-nation tariff rates, which must be granted to goods coming from all WTO member countries, were not the lowest rates, nor a type of special treatment for "favored" nations. Since 1947 the GATT/WTO agreements have provided for two categories of trading arrangements that provide better-than-MFN tariff treatment. These are (1) trade preferences for developing countries and (2) free trade areas, customs unions, and common markets.

Trade Preferences for Developing Countries

The GATT/WTO agreements permit the granting of **trade preferences**, or preferential tariff treatment, to developing countries to help further their social and economic developments. Most developed nations, including the United States, Canada, Japan, the European Union, and the Scandinavian countries grant trade preferences to developing countries, not only in their own hemispheres but also around the world. Three important U.S. programs for developing countries are the *Generalized System of Preferences,* the *Caribbean Basin Initiative,* and the *African Growth and Opportunity Act.*

The Generalized System of Preferences. The most well-known trade preference is the *Generalized System of Preferences* (GSP), under which the United States aids in the economic development of certain developing countries by allowing their products to enter the United States at reduced rates of duty, or duty-free. Developing countries eligible for preferential treatment under U.S. GSP legislation are known as **beneficiary developing countries**. The GSP programs of most developed countries are very similar to those of the United States. The program was begun in the United States in 1974 and Congress renews it regularly. In 2013 there were 129 countries eligible for GSP status under U.S. law. Beneficiary developing countries remain eligible for tariff preferences until such time as their own companies become competitive. More liberal rules apply to certain products from *least developed beneficiary countries.*

Eligibility for GSP Status. Every developed country has its own criteria for designating a beneficiary developing country. In the United States a GSP country must cooperate with the enforcement of narcotics laws, not aid international terrorists, not have unlawfully expropriated the property of U.S. citizens, and not be controlled by a communist government. The beneficiary country must also recognize internationally accepted standards for worker rights and safety and prohibit the worst forms of child labor. In addition, the president has wide authority under the GSP statute to deny duty-free treatment on political and economic grounds. For instance, the president can deny GSP status to any country that does not protect the patents, trademarks, and copyrights of U.S. citizens, maintains unreasonable restrictions on U.S. investment, does not grant internationally recognized worker rights to its workers, or that exports goods to the United States in such large quantities that it injures a competing U.S. industry.

Another requirement for GSP eligibility is that a product must be approved under U.S. law for duty-free treatment. About 5,000 types of products are eligible and many of them are agricultural. A few examples include sugar, jewelry, leather shoe uppers, wooden furniture, Christmas tree lighting, and telephones. Certain import-sensitive products, such as footwear, steel, watches, and some electronic items, are not eligible. The Office of the U.S. Trade Representative conducts an annual review of product eligibility, with opportunities for public filing of petitions. A developing country may lose GSP benefits for specific products when the benefits are economically no longer needed. Once a developing country reaches a higher level of per capita gross national product it "graduates" out of the GSP program. The list of countries eligible for GSP preferences and the rates of duty are available from the Office of the U.S. Trade Representative and can be found in the *Harmonized Tariff Schedules of the United States.*

The U.S. Caribbean Basin Initiative. America's imports from the Caribbean include petroleum products, chemicals, natural gas, textiles and apparel, agricultural products, such as coffee and tropical fruits, electrical parts, and many others. The *Caribbean Basin Initiative* (CBI) is the name collectively given to several laws that grant trade preferences to goods imported from the Caribbean. These include several special programs allowing duty-free imports of textiles and other products from impoverished Haiti. These statutes give the president the authority to grant tariff reductions or duty-free status to imports from eligible countries in order to encourage trade and investment in the Caribbean. A few of the products benefiting from the preferences are cane sugar, communications equipment, electrical and non-electrical machinery, medical appliances, orange juice, bananas, ethyl alcohol, baseballs, and rum. Countries must meet the same mandatory criteria as under the GSP. Many CBI countries, but not all, also qualify for benefits under the GSP. However, the CBI covers a wider range of products, there is no annual review, and countries do not "graduate" out of the programs. In 2013 there were 17 countries benefiting from the CBI programs.

U.S. Preferences for Africa. The *Africa Growth and Opportunity Act* (AGOA) aids in the economic growth and the establishment of political freedom in 48 poor countries in sub-Saharan Africa where the per capita annual income averages about $500 per year. The law encourages U.S. trade and investment there and improves access for African products to U.S. markets. To qualify for the benefits of the act, the African countries must try to improve their own conditions through progressive economic and social policies. The country must abide by human rights standards, eliminate abuses of child labor, not support terrorism, enforce laws against corruption, and move toward a free-market economy. Forty-seven countries are now eligible for AGOA. AGOA preferences are even more favorable than the GSP. Almost all of the 6,500 eligible products enter the U.S. duty free. The largest AGOA sectors are petroleum, minerals (including platinum and diamonds), motor vehicle parts, steel, textiles, jewelry, fruit and nuts, leather, and cocoa.

Free Trade Areas and Customs Unions

Another exception to normal MFN rules applies to goods traded within free trade areas and customs unions. A **free trade area** consists of two or more countries that are party to a free trade agreement that reduces or eliminates tariffs on goods, removes trade barriers, and usually addresses other common concerns affecting trade between them. For example, goods traded between Canada, Mexico, and the United States, qualify for better-than-MFN tariff rates, or may pass duty free, under the *North American Free Trade Agreement.* In Chapter Eight we discuss other countries with which the United States has bilateral free trade agreements. In 2012 the United States and South Korea signed the *U.S.-Korea Free Trade Agreement* (KORUS FTA), and is expected to be the most economically important bilateral free trade agreement that the United States has entered in recent decades.

In 2005, the United States entered into the *United States-Central America-Dominican Republic Free Trade Agreement* (CAFTA-DR) with Costa Rica, El Salvador, Guatemala, Honduras, Nicaragua, and the Dominican Republic. Unlike the GSP, CAFTA-DR is not a trade preference program, but a free trade agreement based on reciprocity and mutual agreement. The agreement phased out all tariffs on goods over a five to ten year period (15 years for agricultural products). The agreement also addresses many collateral issues, such as corruption, labor standards, environmental protection, and the protection of intellectual property.

A **customs union** is a free trade area with a common external tariff. A **common market** takes the integration one step further: it is a customs union that also removes restrictions on the free movement of money, labor, and factors of production. The European Union is a common market and monetary union that functions at a high level of economic, legal, and political integration. Because both the North American and European trading blocs are so highly integrated and economically important, each has its own chapter later in this book. Here we discuss some of the smaller trade blocs in Latin America, Africa, and Asia.

Importantly, some leading international economists and supporters of the role of the WTO view regional trading blocs as a threat to further trade liberalization on a global scale. They are concerned that the world will divide into geographic or regional trading blocs and fear that this could become a method of regional protectionism rather than a means of fostering free trade. They encourage the focus of trade liberalization to be through the WTO system.

- **Caribbean Community**. Caribbean Community (CARICOM) members include Antigua and Barbuda, the Bahamas, Barbados, Belize, Dominica, Grenada, Guyana, Haiti, Jamaica, Montserrat, Saint Lucia, St. Kitts and Nevis, St. Vincent and the Grenadines, Suriname, and Trinidad and Tobago. CARICOM associate members are Anguilla, Bermuda, British Virgin Islands, Cayman Islands, Turks, and Caicos Islands. CARICOM is a highly integrated political and economic common market with executive and legislative bodies and specialized institutions. It has its own *Caribbean Court of Justice* that resolves disputes over the treaty and hears civil and criminal appeals from national courts in member nations. CARICOM is transitioning into a fully integrated "single market" economy similar to what Europe has done.
- **Common Market of the South**. The Common Market of the South (*Mercado Común del Sur* or MERCOSUR) includes Argentina, Brazil, Paraguay, Uruguay, and Venezuela. Its associate members are Bolivia, Chile, Columbia, Ecuador, and Peru.
- **Andean Community of Nations.**The Andean Community of Nations (*Comunidad Andina or* CAN) includes Bolivia, Colombia, Ecuador, and Peru. Its associate members are the MERCOSUR nations (see above). Both organizations have discussed merging. There has been some significant progress in permitting the free movement of people among the CAN member nations. Beginning in 2005, citizens from one member country could enter the other member countries without a visa and only a national identity card.
- **African Regional Economic Communities.** Africa consists of many small trading blocs in Africa, including the world's oldest customs union, the *South Africa Customs Union* (South Africa, Botswana, Lesotho, Swaziland, and Namibia), founded in 1910. The *Common Market for Eastern and Southern Africa* (COMESA) is the largest free trade area in Africa, with 20 member nations and a population of 390 million. Civil war, violence, and internal corruption affect several COMESA countries. There are also sub-regional customs unions in both East Africa *(East African Community)* and West Africa (*West*

African Economic and Monetary Union). The *African Economic Community* is an ambitious, long-term plan to unite the various regional economic communities into a larger pan-African union. The *African Union* is the most important intergovernmental organization in Africa, not a free trade area, comprised of over 50 member countries. Its role is to unify Africa through economic, social, and political development.

- **Asian Free Trade Initiatives.** Free trade initiatives have not progressed as quickly with respect to countries located in the Asia-Pacific region as they have in other parts of the world. Economic integration in the Asia-Pacific region has more often taken the form of enhanced cooperation rather than free trade initiatives. The *Association of South East Asian Nations* (ASEAN) is comprised of Brunei, Myanmar, Cambodia, Indonesia, Laos, Malaysia, the Philippines, Singapore, Thailand, and Vietnam. There is an inter-ASEAN common preferential tariff on goods; however, unlike the treaties underlying the EU and CARICOM, ASEAN does not have a legal mechanism to harmonize laws or enforce the rules of a common market. ASEAN does negotiate as a whole with major economic players for common tariff agreements and has free trade agreements with China and Japan on goods and services.
- **Middle East Economic Integration**. The *Gulf Cooperation Council* (GCC) is comprised of the Persian Gulf states of Bahrain, Kuwait, Oman, Qatar, Saudi Arabia, and the United Arab Emirates. All of the countries are oil-wealthy monarchies, sharing a similar language, culture, religion, and political interests. It is a broad political and security organization, a customs union, and it is progressing to a common market. Some members have hopes of it becoming a monetary union with a single currency. The *Greater Arab Free Trade Area* (GAFTA) is an agreement developed out of the broader intergovernmental organization of Arab countries called the *Arab League*. GAFTA has 17 member countries and spans the Middle East and North African regions. All internal tariffs have been eliminated, and other barriers to trade reduced.

CONCLUSION

The GATT has provided a framework for the international trading system since the close of World War II. It established the principles of international trade law on which national trade laws are based. The GATT agreement and its principles of trade liberalization prevented reactionary forces from drawing the world back into the isolationism and protectionism of the 1930s. Multilateral trade negotiations have resulted in tariff concessions and a worldwide lowering of duties. Today, tariffs are at reasonable levels compared to the 1930s, and rates no longer act as a barrier to world trade.

Although non-tariff barriers are still obstacles to free trade, they have been slowly reduced by a number of important GATT/WTO agreements and through dispute resolution. Some of the most difficult issues facing global trading nations today are the government subsidies for agricultural trade, tariff barriers to trade in services, and finding ways to use trade to promote the economies of the poorest developing countries. Readers are encouraged to follow the work of the WTO and the meetings of the WTO Ministerial Conference as they address these issues.

It seems that all countries, perhaps the United States more than others, use their trade policies as tools of foreign policy. The United States has linked its trade policies with China and Russia to its foreign policy goals. For example, the United States has used the granting of MFN/NTR tariff rates on imports from many countries as an enticement to encourage these and other countries to move toward democracy, respect for human rights, freedom of emigration, and the development of free-market economies. China and Russia are now both members of the WTO and are in normal trade status with the United States.

Some issues not covered here will have to wait for later chapters. How is trade regulated within a customs and monetary union like the European Union? How do the rules governing trade within the North American free trade area differ from the global rules? What specific tariff and customs regulations are necessary to import goods into the United States? What types of "unfair trade" are regulated by the GATT/WTO agreements? As you complete this chapter, remember that the "global rules" presented here are the basis for understanding more specific rules later.

Chapter Summary

1. Nations regulate trade for several important reasons, including collection of revenue, regulation of import competition, retaliation against foreign trade barriers, implementation of foreign policy or national economic policy, national defense, protection of natural resources and the environment, protection of public health and safety, and protection of cultural values or artifacts.
2. The terms *tariff* and *import duty* are used interchangeably. Tariffs are a tax levied on goods by the country of importation. A non-tariff barrier is broadly defined as any impediment to trade other than a tariff. The most severe form of import restriction is the embargo. Countries usually use it as a drastic measure for reasons of foreign policy or national security.
3. An import licensing scheme is a form of non-tariff barrier to trade that is often hidden in administrative regulations and bureaucratic red tape. Exporters faced with foreign licensing schemes often have to retain local agents and attorneys to advise them on import measures in the foreign market. Import regulations that are not made readily available to foreign exporters are said to lack *transparency.*
4. The *General Agreement on Tariffs and Trade,* or GATT, includes the original 1947 agreement, the 1994 agreement that founded the WTO, and many side agreements on specific trade issues. The original agreement only covered trade in goods. In 1994, a *General Agreement on Trade in Services* was added.
5. GATT's major principles include a commitment to multilateral trade negotiations, tariff bindings, transparency, non-discrimination, unconditional MFN trade, national treatment, and the elimination of quotas and other non-tariff barriers.
6. Through multilateral trade negotiations at the WTO, countries make reciprocal tariff concessions that bind tariff rates. The bound rate is the maximum rate that can be charged on an item and is in the schedule of concessions which is kept on record at the WTO. This rate then appears in that country's tariff schedules. The schedules are made available to all exporting and importing countries.
7. WTO dispute-settlement procedures provide a legal forum for nations to resolve trade disputes. No single country can veto the decisions of a WTO panel. If a settlement is not reached, the WTO Dispute Settlement Body may authorize countries whose rights have been nullified and impaired to impose retaliatory tariffs against another that has violated a GATT/WTO agreement.
8. The principles of most-favored-nation (MFN) trade mean that a nation must accord products imported from any country with which it has MFN trading status the most favorable treatment or the lowest tariff rates that it gives to similar products imported from other MFN countries. Unconditional MFN treatment means that if a country negotiates a lower tariff rate with one MFN country, that rate is automatically applicable to all MFN countries. The United States applies MFN tariff rates to those countries that qualify for "normal trade relations." The MFN/NTR rate is considered the normal tariff rate for goods coming from most developed countries. Goods imported from developing countries or within free trade areas often qualify for better-than-MFN rates.
9. Under the national treatment provisions of GATT Article III, imported products must not be regulated, taxed, or otherwise treated differently from domestic goods once they enter a nation's stream of commerce.
10. GATT outlaws most quantitative restrictions on imports, such as quotas. Quotas on imported products are permitted only in certain situations, such as when a nation has insufficient foreign exchange to meet its foreign payments obligations.
11. Many developed countries grant trade preferences to beneficiary developing countries around the world.
12. The GATT/WTO agreements permit countries to form free trade areas, customs unions, and common markets. Although the largest are in Europe and North America, important free trade areas and customs unions exist in Africa, Asia, and Latin America. Some economics criticize the concept of regional economic integration as distracting from the benefits of a globalized world trading system.

Key Terms

trade barrier 240
tariff 241
ad valorem tariffs 241
specific or flat tariffs 241
global tariffs 241
non-tariff barriers (direct and indirect) 241
multilateral trade negotiations 243
trade liberalization 243
negotiating rounds 243
transparency 243
tariff concession 246
tariff binding 246
bound rate 246
schedule of concessions 247
tariff schedules 247
modify or withdraw a concession 247
nondiscrimination 248
most-favored-nation (MFN) trading status 248
unconditional MFN trade 248
normal trade relations (NTR) 248
quota 251
absolute quota 251
global quota 251
allocated quota 251
zero quota 251
auctioned quota 251
tarrification 251
tariff-rate quota 252
balance-of-payments (BOP) 252
nullification or impairment 255
trade consultations 255
withdrawal or suspension of a concession 256
trade preferences 258
beneficiary developing country 259
free trade area 260
customs union 260
common market 260

Questions and Case Problems

1. Visit the Website of the World Trade Organization (www.wto.org). It is a practical, user-friendly guide that offers complete information on the WTO's role and organizational structure as well as access to the GATT/WTO legal texts and dispute settlement cases.
   a. As a beginning point, from the home page click on *Documents and Resources.* From there you will have access to *WTO Distance Learning, WTO Videos, audio podcasting,* the *WTO Library,* and a helpful *WTO Glossary.* The *Distance Learning* page offers training modules and excellent multimedia presentations on the basics of world trade and on many of the more technical WTO issues. You can also link to the international trade *statistics* page. From the *WTO Videos* page, you can view programs or link to the *WTO Channel on YouTube.*
   b. For links to all GATT/WTO agreements from 1947 to the present, navigate from the home page to *Documents and Resources* and choose *Legal Texts of the WTO Agreements.* Accessing WTO materials through the *Legal Texts* page is quick and easy. You can find Web documents either by browsing or searching.
   c. For access to major WTO trade issues, from the home page click on *Trade Topics* and navigate to the *Trade Topics Gateway* and choose a subject, trade in goods, services, intellectual property, dispute settlement, or "Other topics," including electronic commerce, investment, government procurement, or trade and the environment.
   d. The highest decision-making body of the WTO is the Ministerial Conference, which brings together all members of the WTO for meetings every two years. The Ministerial Conference can make decisions on all matters under any of the multilateral trade agreements. Ministerial Conferences have been held in Bali (2013), Geneva (2009, 2011), Hong Kong (2005), Cancún (2003), Doha (2001), Seattle (1999), Geneva (1998), and Singapore (1996). From the *Trade Topics* menu, navigate to *Ministerial Conferences.* What topics were on the most recent Ministerial agenda?
   e. For access to the reports of WTO dispute settlement panels and the Appellate Body, from the home page navigate to *Trade Topics* > *Dispute Settlement,* and look for *The Disputes.* From here you may search either chronologically, by country involved in the dispute, by the GATT/WTO agreement at issue, or by subject. Notice that disputes are cited as *DS* followed by a number. The numbers are sequential; for example, DS1 designates the first dispute filed in 1995, and so forth. Citations for panel reports will generally appear as WT/DS#/R, and reports of the Appellate Body will appear as WT/DS#/AB/R.
   f. From the Dispute Settlement page, find *The Disputes,* and click on *Disputes by Subject.* Assume you are researching a Japanese restriction on the import of apples

from the United States. Click on *Apples*. This is a search function, with results listed for you at the bottom of the page. Enter the case and find the link to the *one page summary*. What actions did Japan take against U.S. apples? Why? What was the result of the dispute resolution?

2. One of the most controversial areas for the WTO and its member governments has been the relationship between trade and the environment. What are the overlapping issues? What is the impact of trade or trade negotiations on environmental issues? How do these issues affect the developing countries, and what position have various developing countries taken? Explain the relationship between protection of the environment and economic development.
    a. Consider the following major trade-related environmental disputes at the WTO: *U.S.—Standards for Reformulated and Conventional Gasoline* (provisions of the U.S. *Clean Air Act,* DS52)
        - *U.S.—Import Prohibition of Certain Shrimp and Shrimp Products* (selling of shrimp caught in nets without turtle extractors, DS58)
        - *European Communities—Measures Affecting Asbestos and Asbestos-Containing Products* (DS135)
        - *European Communities—Measures Concerning Meat and Meat Products* (containing growth hormones, DS26, DS48, DS39)
        - *European Communities—Measures Affecting the Approval and Marketing of Biotech Products* (genetically engineered foods, DS291)

       Using one of these cases, write a case study on the relationship between trade and environmental issues. Be sure to explore both sides of the debate.
    b. For alternative views on trade and the environment, see the Websites of Public Citizen and the Sierra Club and a highly educational site presented by the Levin Institute at the State University of New York, aptly called *Globalization101.org*. To learn more about the important Shrimp/Turtle case at the WTO, see the Website of the National Wildlife Federation.
3. Every year, the U.S. Trade Representative issues a report on foreign government trade barriers to U.S. goods and services. Locate these reports and describe the nature of these trade barriers. Which countries are the greatest offenders? What industries are most affected?
4. In 1990, a Korean law established two distinct retail distribution systems for beef: one system for the retail sale of domestic beef and another system for the retail sale of imported beef. A small retailer (not a supermarket or a department store) designated as a "Specialized Imported Beef Store" may sell any beef except domestic beef. Any other small retailer may sell any beef except imported beef. A large retailer (a supermarket or department store) may sell both imported and domestic beef, as long as imported and domestic beef are sold in separate sales areas. A retailer selling imported beef must display a sign reading "Specialized Imported Beef Store." The dual retail system resulted in a reduction of beef imports. By 1998, there were approximately 5,000 imported beef shops as compared with approximately 45,000 shops selling domestic beef. Korea claims that stores may choose to sell either domestic or imported beef and that they have total freedom to switch from one to another. Moreover, Korea argues that the dual system is necessary to protect consumers from deception by allowing them to clearly distinguish the origin of the beef purchased. Is the Korean regulation a valid consumer protection law? Do you think this system is necessary to protect consumers from fraudulent misrepresentation of the country of origin of the beef? Does it matter that scientific methods are available to determine the country of origin of beef? How do you think the dual system might affect the prices of imported beef versus domestic beef? Assuming that countries have the right to protect consumers from deception, what other methods might be available to accomplish this goal? WTO *Report on Korea—Measures Affecting Imports of Fresh, Chilled and Frozen Beef,* World Trade Organization Report of the Appellate Body, WT/DS161/AB/R, WT/DS169/ AB/R (11 December 2000).
5. One of the central obligations of WTO membership is a limit on tariffs on particular goods according to a nation's tariff commitments. If a member does not abide by its agreement, can another WTO member unilaterally raise its agreed-upon tariff? Explain.
6. The U.S. auto industry has had its problems in the past from foreign competition. If the auto industry lobbied the president and Congress for implementation of a quota on the total number of imported automobiles and trucks, would such a quota be in violation of GATT 1994? Under what circumstances may a country impose a quota?
7. The WTO comprises many nations from all regions of the world. As such, the GATT/WTO system takes a global view of trade liberalization based on nondiscrimination, unconditional MFN, national treatment, tariffication, and multilateral trade negotiations. The GATT agreements recognize that nations may form bilateral or regional free trade areas and customs unions. Yet a free trade area only has free trade between the countries that belong to it. How does the concept of a free trade area, such as the *North American Free Trade Agreement* (NAFTA), fit into the GATT/WTO global framework? Do bilateral or regional free trade areas violate the principles of nondiscrimination and MFN trade? Evaluate these arguments.

Managerial Implications

Your firm designs, manufactures, and markets children's toys for sale in the United States. Almost 90 percent of your production is done in the People's Republic of China. During the 1990s, U.S. relations with China improved. Even though there were many disagreements between the two countries, the United States granted normal trade status to China and supported China's membership in the WTO in 2001. Your firm invested heavily in China during that time. You have developed close ties to Chinese suppliers and have come to depend greatly on inexpensive Chinese labor and the lower costs of doing business there.

You are now concerned about increasing political tension between China and the United States over a variety of issues: China's s treatment of the Tibetan people, reports about the use of prison labor to manufacture goods for export, China's population policies, and differences over relations with communist North Korea. The United States has also accused China of corporate and industrial espionage in the United States to obtain scientific, industrial, and trade secrets, and of hacking into corporate and government computer networks. There are also disagreements over China's censorship of Internet search providers, and over the protection of U.S. intellectual property rights in China. The United States is also concerned with China's tax policies, which are said to discriminate against imported goods, and also with China's state subsidies to domestic industry. The U.S. accuses China of currency manipulations of the yuan, making Chinese goods unfairly cheap in foreign markets and imports into China artificially expensive. Most worrisome is the potential for conflict over Taiwan, with which the United States has had a mutual defense pact for 60 years. China claims Taiwan under its "One China" reunification policy, while accusing the United States of fostering "independence" there. Despite the issues, both countries recognize their deep economic reliance on each other. With that background, consider the following:

1. Describe the impact that a trade dispute between the U.S. and China would have on your firm.
2. Describe the impact on your firm if China were to lose its MFN trading status.
3. What strategic actions might you consider to reduce your firm's exposure to political risk?
4. What are the current areas of agreement or disagreement between the United States and China, and how do you think they will affect future trade relations between the two countries?
5. The United States often links trade policy with a nation's foreign policy. Do you agree with this? What do you think of U.S. trade policies toward China being linked to foreign policy issues?
6. Although both mainland China and Taiwan are "Chinese," doing business in Taiwan differs greatly from doing business in China. Investigate and describe that difference. How do business opportunities differ on the mainland versus the island?
7. Explain the importance of sound country risk analysis in doing business abroad. What sources of information do you think you would use to evaluate your international business strategies in China?
8. Do you think it would be advantageous to visit China, and to visit your suppliers there? If so, what would you hope to accomplish in your visits?

Ethical Considerations

How do you reconcile free trade with the protection of cultural diversity? Free trade in goods and services means that a country will necessarily open itself to foreign influences. Just look at the impact of American fast-food restaurants, hotels, and large retail outlets on the American landscape and particularly on small-town America. Now imagine the influence of American companies and American culture in foreign countries. Consider the long-term impact of American music and film on the indigenous culture of a foreign country. Despite these impacts, free trade agreements mandate the opening of local markets to foreign goods, services, and advertising, including music and film. The French, as well as French-Canadians, are notorious for trying to manipulate trade rules to preserve their French language and French culture. Examples might include limits on foreign advertising, television programming, or films. Consider the *Convention on the Protection and Promotion of the Diversity of Cultural Expressions,* which has been ratified or approved by 69 nations and entered into force in 2007. The Convention states:

> Nations may adopt measures aimed at protecting and promoting the diversity of cultural expressions within its territory. Such measures may include (a) regulatory measures aimed at protecting and promoting diversity of cultural expressions; (b) measures that, in an appropriate manner, provide opportunities for domestic cultural activities, goods and services among all those available within the national territory for the creation, production, dissemination, distribution and enjoyment of such domestic cultural activities, goods and services, including provisions relating to the language used for such activities, goods and services.

In addition, a country may take "all appropriate measures to protect and preserve cultural expressions" that are "at risk of extinction, under serious threat, or otherwise in need of urgent safeguarding."

The United States is not a party to the Convention. In response to the Convention, the U.S. State Department stated, "The United States is a multicultural society that values diversity… Governments deciding what citizens can read, hear, or see denies individuals the opportunity to make independent choices about what they value."

1. Do you feel that countries should limit the influence of foreign cultures in their communities? How should they do that? Do you think that a country should restrict the foreign content of advertising, television, music, or film?
2. Do you think that this Convention might be used as a means of restricting trade in the guise of protecting cultural expressions and national identity?
3. Reconcile the terms of this convention with principles of free trade. What will be the effect on trade in audiovisual products? How would American industry respond?

CHAPTER 10

Laws Governing Access to Foreign Markets

Few would disagree that governments have a critically important role in protecting public health, safety, and welfare, and in the economic well-being of their people and industries. We accept government's role in preventing the spread of human disease; in setting standards for occupational health and safety; in protecting plant, animal, and marine life; in protecting air, water, and natural resources; in assuring viable farms and an agricultural base that feeds a nation; and in regulating economic activity. But, consider what happens when national regulations, designed for the public good, conflict with the rules of international trade.

In the last chapter, you learned that one of the pillars of world trade law is that companies should have nondiscriminatory access to foreign markets and customers, unimpeded by artificial import barriers or local regulations that discriminate against foreign goods or services without justification. In this chapter we look at specific WTO **market access agreements**—agreements that provide exporters of goods and services with market access to foreign countries in the following areas: (1) technical barriers to trade, including product standards; (2) government procurement of goods and services; (3) trade in services, including consulting, engineering, banking and financial services, insurance, telecommunications, and the professions; (4) trade in agricultural products; (5) trade-related investment measures; and (6) trade-related aspects of intellectual property rights. As you read, consider how a nation balances its sovereign right to protect the public welfare through government regulation while abiding by world trade rules that cede some of its authority to international dispute resolution panels. The chapter concludes with a look at the U.S. response to foreign trade barriers that deny access to U.S. products and services or that treat U.S. firms unfairly. This includes U.S. laws that permit retaliation against illegal foreign trade barriers.

THE GENERAL PRINCIPLE OF LEAST RESTRICTIVE TRADE

We begin with one of the broadest and most important legal concepts in the body of international trade law: the principle of **least restrictive trade**. The principle states that WTO member countries, in setting otherwise valid restrictions on trade, shall make them no more onerous than necessary to achieve the goals for which they were imposed. For example, if a country requires inspections of foreign fruit arriving from countries affected by a plant disease, the inspection procedures must be no more arduous, rigorous, or expensive than is needed to achieve those ends. They may not be a trade barrier in disguise.

A corollary is that national laws and regulations passed for purely internal purposes, such as the protection of the general health, welfare, and safety, must also pose the fewest barriers to trade as possible. This principle is relevant to all types of regulations: health codes, environmental regulations, worker safety laws, and uniform technical specifications for a wide range of industrial or consumer products. Examples might include laws regulating the sale of alcohol or tobacco or banning the sale of beef containing growth hormones, genetically modified foods, or toxic lead paint. It might include testing requirements for the fire resistance of fabrics or the safety of children's toys or set mandatory standards for the practice of law or medicine. The list is endless; the concept is the same. Countries may protect their citizens to the extent they deem necessary but must choose those methods that do not unduly burden international trade and/or single out foreign goods or service providers for unfair or discriminatory treatment.

The WTO Appellate Body has stated that this is a balancing test: nations must weigh the necessity of protecting the public against restrictions on free trade. The principle of least restrictive trade appears throughout the *General Agreement on Tariffs and Trade* (GATT) and other WTO agreements, and applies to most of the discussions in this chapter.

The following case, *Thailand—Restrictions on Importation of Cigarettes (1990)*, is an early GATT panel decision that the WTO Appellate Body still cites. It considers Thailand's options for reducing tobacco use. As you read, consider reviewing the GATT/WTO national treatment provisions in the previous chapter.

Thailand—Restrictions on Importation of Cigarettes

Report of the Dispute Settlement Panel, DS10/R, BISD, 37th Supp. 200 (1990)
General Agreement on Tariffs and Trade, Geneva

BACKGROUND AND FACTS

The Royal Thai government maintains restrictions on imports of cigarettes. The *Tobacco Act of 1966* prohibited the import of all forms of tobacco except by license of the Director-General of the Excise Department. Licenses have only been granted to the government-owned Thai Tobacco Monopoly, which has imported cigarettes only three times since 1966. None had been imported in the ten years prior to this case. The United States requested the panel to find that the licensing of imported cigarettes by Thailand was inconsistent with GATT Article XI and could not be justified under Article XX(b) since, as applied by Thailand, the licensing requirements were more restrictive than necessary to protect human health. Thailand argued that cigarette imports were prohibited to control smoking and because chemicals and other additives contained in American cigarettes might make them more harmful than Thai cigarettes.

REPORT OF THE PANEL ADOPTED ON 7 NOVEMBER 1990

The Panel, noting that Thailand had not granted licences for the importation of cigarettes during the past ten years, found that Thailand had acted inconsistently with Article XI:1, the relevant part of which reads: "No prohibitions or restrictions ... made effective through ... import licenses ... shall be instituted or maintained by any [country] on the importation of any product of the territory of any other [country] ...

The Panel proceeded to examine whether Thai import measures affecting cigarettes, while contrary to Article XI:1, were justified by Article XX(b), which states in part:

> [N]othing in this Agreement shall be construed to prevent the adoption or enforcement by any [country] of measures: ... (b) necessary to protect human, animal or plant life or health.

The Panel then defined the issues which arose under this provision ... [The] Panel accepted that smoking constituted a serious risk to human health and that consequently measures designed to reduce the consumption of cigarettes fell within the scope of Article XX(b). The Panel noted that this provision clearly allowed [countries] to give priority to human health over trade liberalization; however, for a measure to be covered by Article XX(b) it had to be "necessary ...

The Panel concluded from the above that the import restrictions imposed by Thailand could be considered to be "necessary" in terms of Article XX(b) only if there were no alternative measure consistent with the GATT Agreement, or less inconsistent with it, which Thailand could reasonably be expected to employ to achieve its health policy objectives. The Panel noted that [countries] may, in accordance with Article III:4 of the GATT Agreement, impose laws, regulations and requirements affecting the internal sale, offering for sale, purchase, transportation, distribution or use of imported products provided they do not thereby accord treatment to imported products less favourable than that accorded to "like" products of national origin. The United States argued that Thailand could achieve its public health objectives through internal measures consistent with Article III:4 and that the inconsistency with Article XI:1 could therefore not be considered to be "necessary" within the meaning of Article XX(b). The Panel proceeded to examine this issue in detail. * * *

The Panel then examined whether the Thai concerns about the quality of cigarettes consumed in Thailand could be met with measures consistent, or less inconsistent, with the GATT Agreement. It noted that other countries had introduced strict, non-discriminatory labeling and ingredient disclosure regulations which allowed governments to control, and the public to be informed of, the content of cigarettes. A non-discriminatory regulation implemented on a national treatment basis in accordance with Article III:4 requiring complete disclosure of ingredients, coupled with a ban on unhealthy substances, would be an alternative consistent with the GATT Agreement. The Panel considered that Thailand could reasonably be expected to take such measures to address the quality-related policy objectives it now pursues

continues

continued

through an import ban on all cigarettes whatever their ingredients.

The Panel then considered whether Thai concerns about the quantity of cigarettes consumed in Thailand could be met by measures reasonably available to it and consistent, or less inconsistent, with the GATT Agreement. The Panel first examined how Thailand might reduce the demand for cigarettes in a manner consistent with the GATT Agreement. The Panel noted the view expressed by the World Health Organization (WHO) that the demand for cigarettes, in particular the initial demand for cigarettes by the young, was influenced by cigarette advertisements and that bans on advertisement could therefore curb such demand. At the Forty-third World Health Assembly a resolution was approved stating that the WHO is: "Encouraged by ... recent information demonstrating the effectiveness of tobacco control strategies, and in particular ... comprehensive legislative bans and other restrictive measures to effectively control the direct and the indirect advertising, promotion and sponsorship of tobacco."

A ban on the advertisement of cigarettes of both domestic and foreign origin would normally meet the requirements of Article III:4 ... The Panel noted that Thailand had already implemented some non-discriminatory controls on demand, including information programmes, bans on direct and indirect advertising, warnings on cigarette packs, and bans on smoking in certain public places.

The Panel then examined how Thailand might restrict the supply of cigarettes in a manner consistent with the GATT Agreement. The Panel noted that [countries] may maintain governmental monopolies, such as the Thai Tobacco Monopoly, on the importation and domestic sale of products. The Thai Government may use this monopoly to regulate the overall supply of cigarettes, their prices and their retail availability provided it thereby does not accord imported cigarettes less favourable treatment than domestic cigarettes or act inconsistently with any commitments assumed under its Schedule of Concessions. * * *

For these reasons the Panel could not accept the argument of Thailand that competition between imported and domestic cigarettes would necessarily lead to an increase in the total sales of cigarettes and that Thailand therefore had no option but to prohibit cigarette imports.

In sum, the Panel considered that there were various measures consistent with the GATT Agreement which were reasonably available to Thailand to control the quality and quantity of cigarettes smoked and which, taken together, could achieve the health policy goals that the Thai government pursues by restricting the importation of cigarettes inconsistently with Article XI:1. The Panel found therefore that Thailand's practice of permitting the sale of domestic cigarettes while not permitting the importation of foreign cigarettes was an inconsistency with the GATT not "necessary" within the meaning of Article XX(b).

Decision. The licensing system for cigarettes was contrary to Article XI:1 and is not justified by Article XX(b). The panel recommended that Thailand bring its laws into conformity with its obligations under the GATT.

Comment. GATT Article XVII permits a country to create state agencies and "marketing boards" that have the authority to import and export goods. The Thai Tobacco Monopoly is an example. Developing countries often use state trading enterprises that often have the exclusive right to import or export certain classifications of goods. Products traded by state enterprises might include foodstuffs, medicines, liquor, or, as in this case, tobacco. Article XVII requires that state enterprises not discriminate against the purchase of foreign goods or treat them differently than domestic goods.

Case Questions

1. What reasons did Thailand give for restricting imports of cigarettes? What GATT provision did Thailand rely on to restrict cigarette imports?
2. The panel states that GATT permits countries to give priority to human health over trade liberalization only under certain conditions. What are those conditions?
3. How was the doctrine of "least restrictive trade" used in this case?
4. What alternative means could Thailand have used to achieve its objectives that would have not singled out imported cigarettes for discriminatory treatment?

TECHNICAL BARRIERS TO TRADE

A **technical regulation** is a law or regulation affecting a product's characteristics—such as its performance, design, construction, chemical composition, materials, packaging, or labeling—that must be met before a product can be imported or sold in a country. A **product standard,** also called a "standard" in this chapter, is usually used when referring to a voluntary guideline for product characteristics established by a recognized private or industry organization or association. However, even when a standard is voluntary, many consumers may look for the seal of compliance in making a purchasing decision. We caution against over reliance on the differences betweem the terms "technical regulation" and "standard" as they are sometimes used interchangeably. In some countries "standards" can also be mandatory. Technical regulations and standards that apply to imported foreign products, even if they also apply equally to domestic products, are called **technical barriers to trade**.

The Protection of Public Health, Safety, or Welfare

Almost all products are subject to technical regulations or standards set by either government regulators or private standard-setting groups. They are generally imposed for the protection of public health, safety, or welfare to promote uniform design, engineering, and performance standards or to ensure product quality or purity. Examples include standards for the safe design of consumer goods, for automotive safety, vehicle emissions, or fuel economy, for safe foods and pharmaceuticals, standards of weights and measures, or worker safety standards for machinery and industrial equipment. Other standards protect consumers from fraud or deception (such as labels that disclose the product's content or warn of safe uses); impose environmental criteria on appliances and other products, such as restrictions on ozone-damaging refrigerants or eliminating dangerous formaldehyde or heavy metals from bed linens, carpeting, or construction materials; set packaging requirements for products such as plastic bottles that aid in recycling or for energy efficiency; require technical specifications standardizing electrical power and telecommunications, building and construction standards, such as common sizes for lumber and building materials, standards for barcodes and barcode readers, and many others. Imagine multinational companies such as Ford, General Electric, Electrolux, or Bosch-Siemens and the incredibly diverse product standards they must meet in each country in which their products are sold.

Product Testing, Inspections, and Certifications. Most countries require some type of testing, inspection, or certification of regulated products. There are two major regulatory approaches: **prior approval** and **prior certification**. In "prior approval" countries, regulated products must undergo testing and inspection by an approved laboratory, receive a certification of compliance with technical standards, and then receive prior regulatory approval before sale. In other countries, regulated products need only undergo testing or inspection and certification. The testing lab's certification remains on file with the manufacturer or importer, and no regulatory approval is needed prior to import or domestic sale.

Different countries have different philosophies and thus take different approaches. For instance, in the United States, the *U.S. Flammable Fabrics Act* places technical restrictions on the sale of all bed mattresses. The law is administered through regulations of the Consumer Products Safety Commission. Six prototypes of a given mattress are subjected to a controlled cigarette burn test under laboratory conditions to determine whether they meet federal safety requirements. If the length of the char is longer than allowed or if the mattress ignites, then it does not pass. Manufacturers usually arrange to have independent laboratories perform the tests. They are required to keep photographs and records of the results at their places of business and to make them available to retailers, customers, or agency regulators who request them. Importers are also subject to these regulations; any of their products entering into the United States must meet these standards. If they cannot produce the certification, their goods will be denied entry or removed from stores. Thus, certification and compliance are required, but advance regulatory approval is not. Foreign manufacturers and importers alike must be familiar with the regulatory systems of the countries where their products will be sold.

Foreign inspection and testing requirements can prove to be a tremendous barrier to trade. This is especially true if the product has a short shelf life, as with produce or other food products, or a short technological life (semiconductors or computer parts). In 1989, the European Communities complained that the United States was delaying the inspection of perishable products by making them wait in turn behind nonperishable goods such as steel products, causing the perishables to spoil in the process. It was necessary to dump entire shipments of citrus fruit from Spain without any compensation to the importer.

In the United States, technical regulations and product standards are set by many federal agencies, including the Department of Agriculture, the Consumer Product Safety Commission, the Food and Drug Administration, the Federal Communications Commission, the Department of Energy, and the Department of Transportation. To illustrate, law requires the U.S. Department of Agriculture to review meat inspection standards in foreign countries to ensure that imported meat products comply with

USDA standards. The Federal Communications Commission promulgates uniform standards for telecommunications equipment that apply to foreign products. The Consumer Product Safety Commission's rules apply to all consumer products, regardless of where they are made. In 1994, Chinese crayons were removed from sale because they were found to contain dangerous levels of lead, a known carcinogen. In 2007, Chinese-made toys were also found to contain lead, as well as other chemicals that could cause seizures, coma, and death. Millions upon millions of these toys were found in countries around the world. The event caused an outcry of public opinion, a reawakening of consumer safety sentiment, a review of consumer legislation in the United States and elsewhere, and a vast change in concern and oversight by the Chinese government.

Transparency. Many technical regulations and standards are not transparent. **Transparency** refers to ability of the public, particularly foreign firms, to have open access to government rules or private standards that are published and made readily available to foreign firms. If a technical regulation is made known only to domestic firms, then it indirectly becomes a technical barrier to foreign firms who are unable to comply. Indeed, many foreign firms never learn of foreign technical barriers until it is too late—only after their shipments to customers are turned away by foreign customs agencies. Moreover, foreign companies are generally not a part of the standard-setting process. Domestic firms are typically invited to participate in developing and writing regulations or standards; foreign firms are not. Thus, they often experience delays in adapting their products for sale in the foreign market, causing them to lose competitive advantage to local firms. The U.S. Department of Commerce maintains a collection of international standards so that U.S. exporters will have access to foreign technical regulations and standards applicable to their industries. Some countries also require inspections of the factories where products are made (e.g. food or drugs), including foreign factories, or advance approval of certifying laboratories. This makes it extremely difficult and expensive to import these products.

European Union Standards and Technical Regulations

The problem of technical barriers is critical to firms operating in the European Union (EU), where national standards vary tremendously. Consider the impact of national standards on a firm such as Phillips, a Dutch multinational electronics company, which has had to manufacture products to conform to dozens of different standards. Thus, the standards policy of the EU is designed to balance the health and safety interests of member countries with the need for the free flow of goods. Despite decades of work by the EU Commission to reduce technical barriers to trade, thousands of new national standards have arisen. Even after years of debating detailed standards for thousands of products, companies wishing to sell their products in Europe still face a maze of complex regulations, applicable to a wide range of products from beer to hair dryers and automobiles to plywood. However, EU countries understand that uniform standards are essential to achieving a unified market.

It is interesting that technical regulations imposed in a large, important market and considered popular by consumers, can have global consequences. For example, in 2013 the EU instituted a ban on the import or sale of all cosmetics that were tested on animals (for cruelty reasons). That move seems to have spurred a change in practices by many global cosmetic's firms.

Many opinions of the European Court of Justice reflect the EU's effort to reduce technical barriers. In one case, arising over the sale of liquor made in France and sold in Germany, the Court ruled that an EU member country could not prohibit the sale of a product produced in another EU member country when that product had already met the technical specifications of the producing country.

In decisions handed down in the 1980s, the Court rejected attempts by two EU countries to protect centuries-old industries. Disregarding consumer-protection arguments, the Court of Justice struck down Germany's beer purity law, which had kept out foreign beers containing preservatives and required that beer only be made from wheat, barley, hops, and yeast (beer made in other European countries often contains rice and other grains). The Court also struck down Italy's pasta content regulations. In one long-standing dispute with the United States, the EU prohibited the import of beef containing growth hormones. Because these hormones are widely used in the United States, U.S. beef was kept out of European markets.

Standard setting in the EU for nonelectrical products is a focus of the **European Committee for Standardization.** This intergovernmental agency works with manufacturers, including some European subsidiaries of U.S. firms, and with scientists to develop workable product standards. When adopted by directive of the European Council, the standards become legally binding for products sold in Europe (see Exhibit 10.1).

The EU has attempted to increase its standardization through the **CE Mark**. (CE means *Conformité Européene.)* The CE Mark is an internationally recognized symbol for quality and product safety for many different types of products, such as children's toys, gas appliances, machinery, and medical and electrical equipment. European manufacturers seeking the mark are inspected and audited by an EU-authorized body and an independent laboratory must test their products. Once a European manufacturer receives the mark, it may sell its products throughout the EU without undergoing inspections in each individual country. Manufacturers outside the EU may submit their products to independent laboratories for testing before attaching the CE Mark. The U.S. government estimates that soon half of the U.S. products shipped to Europe will require CE Mark compliance.

Japanese Standards and Technical Regulations

U.S. and other non-Japanese firms have lodged many complaints against Japan's technical barriers to trade, most of which involve unreasonable and burdensome inspection procedures or import licensing requirements and the arbitrary enforcement of overly strict standards. Japan maintains complex technical regulations on thousands of important products, including electrical appliances, telecommunications and medical equipment, lumber, electronic components, pharmaceuticals, and food. The prolific use of technical requirements in Japan is rooted in Japan's protective attitude toward consumers, the historical role of the Japanese government in economic life, and the Japanese people's acceptance of governmental regulation of business. Product standards in Japan have generally taken the form of **design standards**—characteristics that govern how a product should be designed. U.S. standards, by contrast, are usually based on **performance standards** that describe how products should function. It is usually more cost-effective for a manufacturer to meet foreign performance standards than design standards. Thus, it is easier for Japanese manufacturers to meet U.S. performance standards than for U.S. manufacturers to meet Japanese design standards. In Japan, products capable of inflicting injury on consumers or products that affect public health are more highly regulated than other products. For example, for many years Japan banned the import of cosmetics containing colorants and preservatives for health reasons, despite the approved use of the ingredients in the United States.

Japanese agencies that enforce technical regulations include the **Japanese Ministry of Economy, Trade, and Industry**, which has the widest authority, and the ministries that oversee the health, agriculture, and transportation sectors. Many products require testing and prior approval before they can be sold in Japan. For instance, prior to the mid-1980s, foreign products could not be inspected for pre-clearance at the foreign factory, but could only be inspected, shipment by shipment, as they arrived in Japan. Items had to be individually inspected and tested for compliance with the applicable technical regulations or standards. Legal changes have now made it possible for a foreign firm to register with the appropriate regulatory ministry and to obtain advance product approval without going through a Japanese importer or intermediary.

Another problem occurs when Japanese technical regulations and standards lack transparency. Their agencies still generally do not permit foreign input into the drafting of the regulations, although on occasion U.S. industry groups, under pressure, have succeeded in being heard by Japanese standard-setting groups. The **Japan External Trade Organization** (JETRO) maintains an online database of standards and technical regulations in the areas of food and plant safety, electronic products and electrical appliances, household goods, consumer and industrial products, chemicals, food imports, and others. The **Japanese Standards Association** works to develop and disseminate standards in many areas.

The symbol of an approved product in Japan is the government-authorized **Japan Industrial Standards Mark** (JIS Mark). Its appearance on a product, although voluntary, indicates that the manufacturer has submitted to on-site inspections by the appropriate Japanese ministry and has met accepted standards for quality control, production techniques, and research methods. Because of this mark's wide recognition, foreign products without it are often not competitive in the Japanese market.

Chinese Standards and Technical Regulations

China has a complex regulatory system governing product quality, safety, and other standards and technical regulations. As a socialist country, the

Exhibit 10.1

EU Council Directive Concerning the Safety of Toys*

Article 1.1. This Directive shall apply to toys. A "toy" shall mean any product or material designed or clearly intended for use in play by children of less than 14 years of age.

2. Taking account of the period of foreseeable and normal use, a toy must meet the safety and health conditions laid down in this Directive.

Article 5.1. Member states shall presume compliance with the essential requirements referred to in Article 3 in respect of toys bearing the EC mark provided for in Article 11, hereinafter referred to as "EC mark," denoting conformity with the relevant national standards which transpose the harmonized standards the reference numbers of which have been published in the Official Journal of the European Communities.

Article 7.1. Where toys bearing the EC mark are likely to jeopardize the safety and/or health of consumers, it shall withdraw the products from the market.

Article 8.1. Before being placed on the market, toys must have affixed to them the EC mark by which the manufacturer or his authorized representative established within the Community confirms that the toys comply with those standards; ...

3. The approved [inspection firm] shall carry out the EC type-examination in the manner described below:
-it shall check that the toy would not jeopardize safety and/or health, as provided for in Article 2.
-it shall carry out the appropriate examinations and tests—using as far as possible the harmonized standards referred to in Article 5 (1).

Article 11.1. The EC mark shall as a rule be affixed either to the toy or on the packaging in a visible, easily legible and indelible form.

2. The EC mark shall consist of the symbol "CE."

3. The affixing to toys of marks or inscriptions that are likely to be confused with the EC mark shall be prohibited.

Article 12.1. Member States shall take the necessary measures to ensure that sample checks are carried out on toys which are on their market and may select a sample and take it away for examination and testing.

ANNEX II ESSENTIAL SAFETY REQUIREMENTS FOR TOYS
II. PARTICULAR RISKS

1. Physical and mechanical properties:
   (a) Toys must have the mechanical strength to withstand the stresses during use without breaking at the risk of causing physical injury.
   (b) Edges, protrusions, cords, cables, and fastenings on toys must be so designed and constructed that the risks of physical injury from contact with them are reduced as far as possible....
   (d) Toys, and their component parts, and any detachable parts of toys which are clearly intended for use by children under thirty-six months must be of such dimensions as to prevent their being swallowed or inhaled....
   (e) Toys, and their parts and the packaging in which they are contained for retail sale must not present a risk of strangulation or suffocation.
   (h) Toys conferring mobility on their users must, as far as possible, incorporate a braking system which is suited to the type of toy and is commensurate with the kinetic energy developed by it.
2. Flammability: (a) Toys must not constitute a dangerous flammable element in the child's environment. They must therefore be composed of materials which... irrespective of the toy's chemical composition, are treated so as to delay the combustion process.

ANNEX IV WARNINGS AND INDICATIONS OF PRECAUTIONS TO BE TAKEN WHEN USING TOYS

1. Toys which might be dangerous for children under thirty-six months of age shall bear a warning, for example: "Not suitable for children under thirty-six months."

5. Skates and skateboards for children. If these products are offered for sale as toys, they shall bear the marking: "Warning: protective equipment should be worn."

*Exhibit text was edited for student use by the authors.
Council Directive 88/378/EEC of 3 May 1998 concerning the safety of toys. *Official Journal I.* 187, 16/07/1988, p. 0001–0013;
Document 388L0378.
SOURCE: EU Website.

enormous bureaucracy dwarfs any similar agencies in Western countries. The laws are administered by China's **General Administration of Quality Supervision, Inspection, and Quarantine** (AQSIQ). In 2008, AQSIQ had 19 major departments, 15 national institutes and research centers, 35 inspection and quarantine bureaus in 31 provinces, 500 branches and local offices across the country, and over 30,000 employees at Chinese seaports, airports, and other ports of entry. Over 180,000 employees work for provincial or municipal bureaus in developing and enforcing quality and standards laws. These bureaus are also responsible for enforcing Chinese laws against counterfeit products. Ten industry trade associations are allied with AQSIQ in setting standards and technical regulations.

China enforces its product quality standards through compulsory product testing, factory inspections and certifications, and by the accreditation of testing laboratories. The country's compulsory certification and inspection system covers thousands of consumer and industrial products. Chinese rules require that covered products receive certification prior to import. Companies must ship product samples to approved laboratories in China for inspection and testing for compliance with Chinese quality, safety, and environmental standards. Chinese inspectors must then visit the foreign plants, whether they are in the United States, Canada, or Europe, that produce goods destined for China. Products that meet the quality and safety requirements for certification may receive the **China Compulsory Certification** Mark (CCC). China will not accept imports of covered products without the mark. Under the regulations, fines may be imposed for falsification of marks. Anyone who plans to export goods to China should check the AQSIQ and CCC Mark Websites to determine whether Chinese regulations cover their products. The Chinese certification process can be expensive and time consuming. Follow-up supervision and reviews are conducted annually. Many companies wishing to ship to China find that they must employ a consulting firm to manage the certification process. Many of the regulations, such as those related to human health, apply to all travelers to China.

The **American National Standards Institute** (ANSI) maintains an online "standards portal" that gives firms access to English translations of standards and technical regulations in China, India, and Korea, as well as various U.S. standards in English, Mandarin Chinese, and Korean.

The WTO Agreement on Technical Barriers to Trade

The *WTO Agreement on Technical Barriers to Trade (TBT Agreement)* is one of the 1994 Uruguay Round agreements. It governs the use of technical regulations, product standards, testing, and certifications by WTO member countries. The *TBT Agreement* is binding on all WTO member countries. Remember that this agreement does not contain standards of its own. It makes no attempt to say how a product should perform or be designed or when a product is safe or unsafe. These are matters for nations and governments to decide. But the *TBT Agreement* does prohibit countries from using their regulations or standards to discriminate against the import of foreign goods.

Harmonization, Equivalence, and Mutual Recognition. The primary goal of the *TBT Agreement* is to minimize technical barriers to trade. It sets out three methods of achieving this goal. The first is *harmonization*, by which nations attempt to bring their standards and technical regulations into harmony with internationally accepted standards. The second is *equivalence,* by which nations agree to accept foreign standards that are functionally equivalent to their own. The third is *mutual recognition*. Nations are encouraged to enter into mutual recognition agreements, whereby they recognize the certifications, or **conformity assessments**, of foreign inspection firms and laboratories approved in the country where the article is manufactured. For example, if a manufacturer ships telephones to several different markets, it would be far cheaper if all countries accepted the certification of an inspection firm in the manufacturer's country that the device conforms to the telecommunications standards in the importing country. This avoids the expense of having to perform multiple tests.

Main Provisions of the TBT Agreement. The WTO *Agreement on Technical Barriers to Trade* applies to all products, including agricultural, industrial, and consumer goods. An outline of the agreement's main provisions follows:

1. All technical regulations shall be applied on a nondiscriminatory basis, without regard to the national origin of the products.
2. Technical regulations must not be made or applied to create an unnecessary obstacle to trade, and they must not be more trade restrictive

than necessary to fulfill a legitimate objective such as national security, preventing fraud or deception of consumers, protecting public health or safety, or protecting the environment.

3. Countries should take into account available scientific and technical information in writing their standards. This provision is intended to ensure that standards are not just made to keep out foreign goods, but have some scientific foundation.
4. Wherever possible, performance abilities of the product rather than on design or descriptive characteristics should be the basis for product requirements. For example, there are several different mechanisms in use to hold automobile doors securely closed. Government regulations that require industry to use a mechanism of a certain type or design are creating a barrier to trade. Instead, the agreement encourages governments to set a performance standard requiring that the door remain securely closed during certain collisions, leaving the design up to the manufacturer.
5. Countries should develop and use internationally accepted standards where they exist. International standards will be presumed to be in compliance with the *TBT Agreement.*
6. Countries should work toward the goals of harmonization of standards and equivalence.
7. Proposed standards must be published and made available to foreign countries, and those countries must be given an opportunity to make written comments prior to adoption.
8. Final regulations must be published a reasonable time before they become effective so that foreign producers have time to adapt their products.
9. Testing and inspection procedures should restrict trade as little as possible and should not discriminate. The agreement encourages on-site factory inspections instead of port-of-entry inspections for foreign goods.
10. Nations should accept the testing reports and certifications from approved foreign inspection firms and laboratories (mutual recognition of conformity assessments).
11. Countries should try to ensure that state and local governments, as well as private standard-setting groups, comply with the agreement.
12. Disputes between countries may be referred to the WTO for negotiation and settlement.

The following case, *WTO Report of the Appellate Body on Measures Affecting the Production and Sale of Clove Cigarettes* discusses the nondiscrimination provisions of the *TBT Agreement*, and pits one nation's effort to protect public health with its commitments to follow international trade rules.

United States—Measures Affecting the Production and Sale of Clove Cigarettes

Report of the Appellate Body WT/DS406/AB/R (2012) World Trade Organization

BACKGROUND AND FACTS

The United States has long sought ways to reduce smoking by children. In 2009 the United States enacted the *Family Smoking Prevention and Tobacco Control Act* [the Act] that prohibited the import or sale of cigarettes with any flavor, herb, or spice, including fruit, chocolate, cinnamon, and clove. Of course, menthol cigarettes are produced primarily in the United States, whereas clove cigarettes are produced primarily in Indonesia. This is a complaint by the government of Indonesia that the ban on clove-flavored cigarettes unlawfully discriminated against flavored tobacco products made in other countries. The United States claimed that it had excluded menthol from the regulations, despite the fact that menthol is also known to make cigarettes more appealing to adolescents, because it feared withdrawal by menthol smokers, and by the likely creation of a black market in menthol cigarettes. After consultations at the WTO, Indonesia requested dispute panel resolution. The panel held that the United States had acted in violation of Article 2.1 of the *Agreement on Technical Barriers to Trade* (TBT Agreement), and the United States appealed to the Appellate Body.

REPORT OF THE APPELLATE BODY

Article 2.1 of the *TBT Agreement* provides that, with respect to their central government bodies:

> Members shall ensure that in respect of technical regulations, products imported from the territory of any Member shall be accorded treatment no less favourable than that accorded to like products of national origin and to like products originating in any other country.

continues

continued

Article 2.1 of the *TBT Agreement* contains a national treatment and a most favoured nation treatment obligation. In this dispute, we are called upon to clarify the meaning of the national treatment obligation. For a violation of the national treatment obligation in Article 2.1 to be established, three elements must be satisfied: (i) the measure at issue must be a technical regulation; (ii) the imported and domestic products at issue must be like products; and (iii) the treatment accorded to imported products must be less favourable than that accorded to like domestic products. The United States' appeal concerns only the second and the third elements of this test ...

[T]he determination of likeness under Article 2.1 of the *TBT Agreement* is a determination about the nature and the extent of a competitive relationship between and among products, and that the regulatory concerns that underlie a measure may be considered to the extent that they have an impact on the competitive relationship. * * *

[W]here the technical regulation at issue does not *de jure* discriminate against imports, the existence of a detrimental impact on competitive opportunities for the group of imported vis-à-vis the group of domestic like products is not dispositive of less favourable treatment under Article 2.1. Instead, a panel must further analyze whether the detrimental impact on imports stems exclusively from a legitimate regulatory distinction rather than reflecting discrimination against the group of imported products. In making this determination, a panel must carefully scrutinize the particular circumstances of the case, that is, the design, architecture, revealing structure, operation, and application of the technical regulation at issue, and, in particular, whether that technical regulation is even-handed, in order to determine whether it discriminates against the group of imported products.

Given the above, the design ... and application of [the Act] strongly suggest that the detrimental impact on competitive opportunities for clove cigarettes reflects discrimination against the group of like products imported from Indonesia. The products that are prohibited under [the Act] consist primarily of clove cigarettes imported from Indonesia, while the like products that are actually permitted under this measure consist primarily of domestically produced menthol cigarettes.

Moreover, we are not persuaded that the detrimental impact of [the Act] on competitive opportunities for imported clove cigarettes does stem from a legitimate regulatory distinction. We recall that the stated objective of [the Act] is to reduce youth smoking. One of the particular characteristics of flavoured cigarettes that makes them appealing to young people is the flavouring that masks the harshness of the tobacco, thus making them more pleasant to start smoking than regular cigarettes. To the extent that this particular characteristic is present in both clove and menthol cigarettes, menthol cigarettes have the same product characteristic that, from the perspective of the stated objective of [the Act], justified the prohibition of clove cigarettes. Furthermore, the reasons presented by the United States for the exemption of menthol cigarettes from the ban on flavoured cigarettes do not, in our view, demonstrate that the detrimental impact on competitive opportunities for imported clove cigarettes does stem from a legitimate regulatory distinction. The United States argues that the exemption of menthol cigarettes from the ban on flavoured cigarettes aims at minimizing: (i) the impact on the U.S. health care system associated with treating "millions" of menthol cigarette smokers affected by withdrawal symptoms; and (ii) the risk of development of a black market and smuggling of menthol cigarettes to supply the needs of menthol cigarette smokers. Thus, according to the United States, the exemption of menthol cigarettes from the ban on flavoured cigarettes is justified in order to avoid risks arising from withdrawal symptoms that would afflict menthol cigarette smokers in case those cigarettes were banned. We note, however, that the addictive ingredient in menthol cigarettes is nicotine, not peppermint or any other ingredient that is exclusively present in menthol cigarettes, and that this ingredient is also present in a group of products that is likewise permitted under [the Act], namely, regular cigarettes. Therefore, it is not clear that the risks that the United States claims to minimize by allowing menthol cigarettes to remain in the market would materialize if menthol cigarettes were to be banned, insofar as regular cigarettes would remain in the market.

Therefore, even though [the Act] does not expressly distinguish between treatment accorded to the imported and domestic like products, it operates in a manner that reflects discrimination against the group of like products imported from Indonesia. Accordingly, despite our reservations on the brevity of the Panel's analysis, we agree with the Panel that, by exempting menthol cigarettes from the ban on flavoured cigarettes [the Act] accords to clove cigarettes imported from Indonesia less favourable treatment than that accorded to domestic like products, within the meaning of Article 2.1 of the *TBT Agreement*. * * *

While we have upheld the Panel's finding that the specific measure at issue in this dispute is inconsistent with Article 2.1 of the *TBT Agreement*, we are not saying that a Member cannot adopt measures to pursue legitimate health objectives such as curbing and preventing youth smoking. In particular, we are not saying that the United States cannot ban clove

continues

continued

cigarettes; however, if it chooses to do so, this has to be done consistently with the *TBT Agreement.* Although [the Act] pursues the legitimate objective of reducing youth smoking by banning cigarettes containing flavours and ingredients that increase the attractiveness of tobacco to youth, it does so in a manner that is inconsistent with the national treatment obligation in Article 2.1 of the *TBT Agreement* as a result of the exemption of menthol cigarettes, which similarly contain flavours and ingredients that increase the attractiveness of tobacco to youth, from the ban on flavoured cigarettes.

Decision. The U.S. regulation is not justified. The *TBT Agreement* prohibits technical regulations that treat imported products less favorably than "like products" of domestic origin. Clove-flavored cigarettes and menthol-flavored cigarettes are "like products" due to their competitive relationship in the marketplace. The less favorable treatment accorded flavored cigarettes from Indonesia was not justified by a *"legitimate regulatory distinction."*

Comment. The Dispute Settlement Body requested the United States to remove the ban on clove cigarettes, and if it did not, Indonesia was authorized to impose $15 million in trade sanctions on U.S. exports to Indonesia.

Case Questions

1. Did the U.S. prohibition on clove cigarettes prohibit the import of Indonesian cigarettes on its face, or did it merely prohibit a flavor of cigarette that happens to be produced primarily in Indonesia? Was this *de facto* or *de jure* discrimination in this case? How did this affect the Appellate Body's decision?
2. The report (not reproduced here) noted the similarities between Article 2.1 of the *TBT Agreement,* under which this dispute was decided, and Article III.4 of GATT 1994. Review Article III.4 of GATT 1994 in the last chapter and explain the differences between the two articles. The *TBT Agreement* applies to "technical regulations" but GATT 1994 applies to a broader range of discriminatory measures. Explain.
3. What were the options left to the United States after this report? What action did the United States take in response to the report?
4. How well do you think the report balances trade liberalization with a country's need to protect public health? How well suited do you think a WTO panel is to determining matters of public health?

International Organization for Standardization

The **International Organization for Standardization** (ISO), based in Geneva, is a non-governmental organization comprising the national standards institutes of 163 countries. It has developed over 19,500 standards for goods, services, manufacturing and technology in many industries. ISO standards are voluntary and not legally binding, and the organization has no legal authority to enforce them. However, the standards have been accepted by businesses and entire industries worldwide and are legally enforceable in countries where they have been incorporated into a treaty or into national law. In general, the standards are intended to ensure product quality, safety, efficiency, and interchangeability, although some standards have been adopted to minimize the impact of manufacturing or the use of products on the environment. Generally speaking, standards foster international business and trade, because they make it easier and cheaper to design and build products that comply with one international standard than to design products that comply with dozens of local standards. Consider the impact of ISO standards that set the dimensions of screw threads and other fasteners, the size and dimensions of international freight containers, methods of storing data on credit cards, warning and information symbols for signs and labels, ergonomics, computer protocols, food safety management, life vests, and inflatable boats.

One of the most commonly known ISO standards is ISO 9000. Since 1987, ISO 9000 has become the standard for ensuring product quality through the product design and manufacturing process. Companies become ISO 9000-certified through a costly and rigorous inspection of their facilities and documentation of their quality control systems. They are audited on a regular basis for compliance. To sell in Europe, many U.S. firms have obtained ISO certification. By meeting ISO requirements, firms no longer have to certify each product individually in every European country.

EU law requires ISO certification for certain regulated products, such as medical devices and construction equipment. Market demands make compliance for other products equally essential. In the United States, a number of firms offer assistance to U.S. companies seeking ISO certification.

Another standard, known as ISO 14000, provides guidelines for environmental management. It does not set criteria for pollution or environmental impact. Rather, it requires that a firm establish a management system for setting its own environmental objectives, complying with national or local environmental laws, and continuing to improve its environmental performance.

GOVERNMENT PROCUREMENT

Government procurement is the purchase of goods and services by government agencies at all levels. Governments are among the largest business customers in the world. GATT contains an exception to its national treatment provision that permits government agencies to favor domestic suppliers when making purchases.

Most nations require their government agencies to give a preference to domestically made products. The laws often apply to goods purchased by defense-related agencies or by the military. Other laws might require that the purchased product contain a certain proportion of domestically made component parts or raw materials.

In the United States, the *U.S. Buy American Act* (enacted in 1933 during the Great Depression) requires federal agencies to purchase goods of U.S. origin rather than foreign-made goods. There are several exceptions. The restrictions do not apply if U.S.-made goods are not available in sufficient quantities or quality, if the U.S.-made goods are unreasonably more expensive (generally 6–12 percent higher), to purchases under $2,500, to goods purchased for use outside the United States, where purchasing domestic goods would not be in the public's best interest, or where the terms of a trade agreement provide for nondiscrimination in procurement. There are also specific buy-American provisions in the other statutes applicable to procurement for mass transit projects and to procurement by the U.S. Department of Defense that must purchase domestic products unless those products are more than 50 percent more expensive than competing foreign goods. Most food, textiles, and apparel purchased by the Defense Department and the Department of Homeland Security must be grown or produced in the United States of entirely U.S. components.

The *WTO Agreement on Government Procurement*

As a general rule, large-scale procurement by governments or government agencies is exempt from the normal WTO rules for trade in goods and services. Instead, the *WTO Agreement on Government Procurement* (1994), known as AGP, governs most large-scale government procurement.

The AGP brought about many changes in procurement practices in the United States and other countries. The agreement requires fair, open, and nondiscriminatory procurement practices and sets up uniform procurement procedures to protect suppliers from different countries. It applies to the purchase of goods or services by national governments worth more than 130,000 IMF Special Drawing Rights (approximately $200,000 on January 2, 2013) and to construction contracts (buildings, dams, power plants, etc.) worth more than 5 million SDRs (approximately $7.7 million as of 2013). Unlike other WTO agreements, the AGP applies only to those countries that have signed it. Approximately 40 nations participate in the AGP, including the United States, Canada, Japan, and the EU.

The AGP applies to almost 90 U.S. federal agencies, large and small—from the Department of Labor to the American Battle Monuments Commission, for example—and to the executive branch departments. There are several exclusions from the procurement rules, including purchases to be sent to foreign countries as foreign aid; purchases by the Department of Agriculture for food distribution or for farm support programs; and some purchases made by the Federal Aviation Administration, the Department of Energy, and the Department of Defense related to national security. In the United States, many states are also bound by the AGP.

Procurement Rules. The AGP reverses the general WTO rules that allow government agencies to favor domestic products. It brings the principles of MFN trade, nondiscrimination, and transparency to government procurement. A procuring agency must treat foreign suppliers equally with domestic suppliers. Moreover, a government agency may not discriminate against local suppliers just because they are foreign-owned. The agreement also prohibits a procuring agency from awarding a contract to a foreign firm on the basis of certain conditions, called **procurement offsets**. For example, an offset might be a condition that the foreign firm awarded the contract must use local subcontractors, domestically made materials, or local labor; that the firm agree to license its technology to local firms; that the firm make local investments; or that the firm engage in countertrade. Offsets can be complex. For instance, assume that Aeroflop, a U.S. firm, wants to sell several million dollars' worth of airplanes to a government-owned airline in a European country famous for cheese. To get the contract, the firm agrees to pay a 5 percent kickback to another U.S. company, Cheezy, if Cheezy agrees to buy all of its cheese from a seller in that European country. If the cheese-producing country requires Aeroflop to make the offset, it violates the AGP.

To ensure that the procurement rules are applied fairly, the AGP sets up procedures for governments to follow. Agencies must give adequate notice to potential bidders when a procurement contract is announced and must disclose all the information necessary for foreign bidders to participate. In the event of a disagreement between a supplier and a procuring agency, a country must allow the supplier to challenge the contract before either an independent administrative review board or the courts.

Procurement Rules in the United States. According to Congress, the responsibility for implementing the AGP lies with the president. The president may waive the requirements of the *Buy American Act* for suppliers from any country that is party to the AGP and complies with the AGP's terms in its own procurement practices. Suppliers from least-developed countries also receive the waiver, which entitles them to nondiscrimination and equal treatment with U.S. domestic suppliers.

The president must compile an annual report of those countries that have adopted the AGP but do not abide by it. The U.S. Trade Representative (USTR) negotiates with violating countries to get them to end their unfair practices and give equal access to U.S. firms. If no agreement is reached, then the USTR must present the case to the WTO for dispute settlement. If an agreement or resolution is still not reached, the president must revoke the waiver of the *Buy American Act,* and preferences for domestic suppliers will be allowed.

TRADE IN SERVICES

Trade in services includes areas such as professional services (law, accounting, architecture, engineering, and others); travel, recreation, and tourism; health care; transportation and distribution; finance, banking, and insurance; computer and data processing services; research and development; business services such as advertising, market research, and consulting; education; environmental engineering and waste management; and telecommunications. According to the WTO, exports of commercial services (non-governmental) exceeded $4 trillion in 2012. That represents about 20 percent of total world trade in goods and services. The United States was the leading exporter of commercial services, followed by Germany and the United Kingdom. Services account for the majority of the gross domestic product in the United States and most developed countries. Although the GATT agreement regulated trade in goods for more than 45 years, it did not regulate trade in services until the Uruguay Round agreements. The *North American Free Trade Agreement* governs the free flow of services among Canada, Mexico, and the United States.

The *WTO General Agreement on Trade in Services*

The *WTO General Agreement on Trade in Services (1994),* or GATS, establishes rules for international trade in services. It is a part of the WTO system and is overseen by the **Council for Trade in Services**. The agreement is largely patterned after the concepts that GATT applies to trade in goods. It covers trade in most services, including health services, architecture, engineering and construction, travel and tourism, legal and other professional services, rental and leasing, distribution and courier services, education, management and environmental consulting, market research and advertising consulting, computer services, repair and maintenance, sanitation and disposal, franchising, entertainment, and others. Trade in services could be as large as a billion-dollar contract to install a telecommunications system in a country, or as small as a model's appearance at a foreign fashion show. Two areas, telecommunications and financial services, are treated in separate GATS agreements. GATS applies to the federal government as well as to state and local governments.

GATS defines four different ways of providing an international service:

1. Services supplied from one country to another (e.g., international telephone calls), officially known as cross-border supply.
2. Consumers or firms making use of a service in another country (e.g., tourism), officially known as **consumption abroad**.
3. A foreign company setting up subsidiaries or branches to provide services in another country

(e.g., foreign banks setting up operations in a country), officially known as **commercial presence**.

4. Individuals traveling from their own country to supply services in another (e.g., teachers or consultants), officially known as **presence of natural persons**.

GATS principles are similar to the GATT principles studied in the last chapter. Rules affecting service providers must be transparent and made readily available. Signatory countries to the agreement can place no limit on the number of foreign service providers or on the number of people they may employ. The agreement also prohibits countries from imposing a requirement that local investors own any percentage of the service company (leaving that up to the parties). These are known as the GATS "market access" provisions. Like GATT, the GATS agreement also contains MFN trade and national treatment (nondiscrimination) provisions. Countries may not treat foreign service providers less favorably than they treat domestic providers. Laws and regulations must be reasonable, objective, and impartial. Also, countries may not unreasonably restrict the international transfer of money by service industries or the movement of people across borders for the purpose of providing a service.

GATS contains a set of schedules, or commitments, that lists each country's specific provisions related to each type of service. For instance, if you want to find out if Japan has separate requirements for foreign lawyers, or perhaps package delivery services, as opposed to the requirements for Japanese lawyers or Japanese couriers, you can consult the schedules. Of course, for the specific regulations you must research the issue with the appropriate Japanese authority. The schedules are available online from the WTO in its searchable **WTO Services Database**. A country may not treat foreign services or service providers any less favorably than promised in the schedules. As a result, no new or additional restrictions may be imposed in the future. Countries also are bound to negotiate an eventual elimination of the exceptions made in the schedules.

Licensing and Professional Qualifications. GATS also has special provisions governing the qualifications of service providers set by national or local governments. Most governments license certain service providers at some level; in the United States, licensing generally occurs at the state level. Of course, areas such as law, medicine, nursing, engineering, architecture, surveying, and accounting will continue to have more strict professional licensing requirements than, say, management consulting. Countries can continue to license professionals and other service providers as necessary to ensure the quality of the service, provided that licensing is not made overly burdensome just to restrict trade. Licensing must be based on objective criteria, such as education, experience, or ability. It must not discriminate on the basis of the person's citizenship. Countries may recognize licenses granted by other countries, but only if they choose to do so.

The WTO Agreement on Trade in Financial Services. Over 100 nations, including the EU and the United States, have joined the *WTO Agreement on Trade in Financial Services,* a part of the GATS agreement. The purpose of the agreement is to open commercial banking, securities, and insurance industries to foreign competition. The agreement is intended to promote efficiency, reduce costs, and provide consumers with a greater choice of service providers, while still permitting countries to regulate these industries for the protection of investors, depositors, and consumers.

The WTO Agreement on Basic Telecommunications. The *WTO Agreement on Basic Telecommunications* is also part of the larger GATS agreement. Its services include voice and facsimile telephone systems, data transmission, fixed and mobile satellite systems and services, cellular telephone systems, mobile data services, paging, personal communications systems, and others. The agreement binds 108 countries, including the United States, Canada, the EU, and Japan, to MFN trade and to honor their specific commitments to open their telecommunications markets to foreign competitors. It includes local, long distance, and international communications.

TRADE IN AGRICULTURE

Trade in agriculture has always been a contentious issue between nations because no nation wants to be totally dependent on other nations for its food supply. In addition, both large scale farming conglomerates and family farmers represent politically powerful and important constituencies in most countries. So to protect farmers, many governments control the domestic pricing structure to provide market stability. These agricultural price supports set prices at higher-than-world-market prices and contribute to the buildup of food surpluses. To avoid disrupting their price support systems, some countries impose import restrictions on both raw and processed food products. There are many programs that provide guaranteed incomes to farmers. Other programs provide disaster aid for weather-related and other natural disasters, rural development, conservation, wildlife preservation, and more. GATT Article XI, which prohibits quantitative restrictions, contains a loophole allowing quotas on agricultural imports when necessary to protect government price support programs.

Some Agricultural Trade Issues in the EU and Japan

The United States, Japan, and the EU provide subsidies to farmers and controls on agricultural prices through a morass of complex legislation and government programs. In the United States, federal legislation (commonly called the *Farm Bill)* is enacted every five years. It establishes U.S. agricultural and food policies, programs, and funding for that period. Congress was debating the U.S. farm bill in 2013, and will likely include several hundred billion dollars in funding with billions of dollars in farm aid, price supports, and subsidies for farm exports. Several agricultural issues in the European Union and Japan are of special interest to students of world trade law.

The EU Common Agricultural Policy. Agricultural policies in the EU are governed by its Common Agricultural Policy. The policies are rooted in the period following World War II, when a war-devastated continent needed government policies that assured adequate food supplies by promoting food production and aiding farmers. Today, expenditures for agricultural subsidies and price supports cost billions of euros each year, constituting over one-third of the annual total budget of the EU. The system has long been very controversial, and has become unpopular with consumers, taxpayers, and free-market economists. Of course, farmers are a powerful political force in Europe, as they are in all countries. In more recent years, the Common Agricultural Policy has undergone many changes. While expensive subsidies, cash payments to farmers, and some quotas still exist, there is a new focus on helping farmers deal with natural disasters, controlling plant and animal disease, promoting ecological standards, assuring food quality and safety, improving land and water management, and support for renewable energy sources in rural areas. Subsidies are no longer dependent on crop production. The United States has generally demanded that EU farm subsidies, including direct payments to European farmers, be reduced.

Japanese Rice: A Trade Dilemma. An excellent example of how nations feel about their agricultural trade is the Japanese treatment of rice imports. Rice has long been considered the staple food of Japan, and rice farming lies at the center of its agricultural community. Rice is a food that is symbolic of Japanese culture. The Japanese government's objective is to maintain self-sufficiency in rice production by ensuring the economic health of rice farmers. Since World War II, Japanese laws have been placing strict limitations on rice imports and imposed governmental controls on rice pricing and distribution. As a result, the domestic price of rice in Japan has often been many times higher than the price of rice in international markets. One small but vivid example of protectionism occurred in 1991, when U.S. rice exhibitors at a Japanese trade fair were threatened with arrest for merely exhibiting American-grown rice products there. The American rice had to be removed from the show.

Today, Japan permits rice imports, although they are still subject to tariff and non-tariff barriers. Rice illustrates the dilemma facing protectionist nations. The Japanese are self-sufficient in rice production; they produce enough for their own needs. There is also some reduced demand because the Japanese diet is becoming more Westernized and is incorporating more grains other than rice. But for decades other rice-producing nations, including the United States, have been pressuring Japan to reduce tariffs and to accept more rice imports. Of course, any economist will tell you that these forces should combine to reduce the price of rice in Japan. But the Japanese government had feared that this would lead to a loss of self-sufficiency in rice, and an end to family rice farming. In the 1990s, other governments put pressure on Japan to purchase a minimum quantity of foreign rice annually. According to Japanese government and industry sources, and to reports of the U.S. Trade Representative, the government now purchases about three-quarters of a million tons of foreign rice each year. Most of it is unneeded, warehoused, and sold for food processing, animal feed, or re-exported as foreign aid to poorer countries (leaving the government with regular annual surpluses). Only a tiny portion of American rice is consumed at the dining table. In addition, private farmers have stockpiled millions of tons more of surplus rice. As prices fall, the government then is forced to artificially maintain them, through import barriers, cash subsidies to farmers, market controls, and a system of incentives and disincentives for rice farmers. In all, it is a "perfect storm" of market disruption from excessive government intervention.

The WTO Agreement on Agriculture

The 1994 Uruguay Round called for many significant changes in government control of agricultural trade. The *WTO Agreement on Agriculture* began the process of removing government intervention in the farming sector and ending government programs that distort normal market conditions. The agreement has three main objectives:

1. Cutting domestic subsidies and other direct payments to farmers. **Domestic subsidies** distort markets by causing overproduction and suppressing prices while protecting the incomes of farmers. The agreement prohibits domestic subsidies, except for research, disease control, environmental protection, and rural development. It also permits cash payments to farmers during emergencies.
2. Cutting programs that subsidize exports of farm products. **Agricultural export subsidies** are payments or other benefits given to farmers that directly encourage, or are conditional upon, the export of food or agricultural products. Government subsidized food exports that are part of a foreign aid program to needy countries are not considered illegal subsidies under the agreement.
3. Assuring greater market access for imported farm products by converting quotas and other non-tariff barriers into tariffs.

SANITARY AND PHYTOSANITARY MEASURES: FOOD, ANIMAL, AND PLANT SAFETY

Trade in agricultural goods has been impeded because some countries use food safety as an excuse for blocking agriculture imports. No one doubts the right of a government to take extraordinary measures to protect its citizens from contagious disease or to protect food or agricultural products from infestation. If a blight, fungus, or insect were found in orange groves in Mexico, no one would argue against the right of the United States to keep out Mexican oranges to protect the U.S. crop. A **sanitary and phytosanitary measure** is a government rule or regulation that protects or enhances food, animal, or plant safety or quality, including preventing the spread of pathogens and disease. The *WTO Agreement on the Application of Sanitary and Phytosanitary Measures* (the *SPS Agreement)* is specifically designed to allow governments to protect human, animal, and plant life from infestations, contaminants, pesticides, toxins, harmful chemicals, or disease-carrying organisms. However, governments may not use restrictions as excuses to keep out foreign goods.

The *SPS Agreement* opens markets for agricultural exports by requiring that the protective measures taken by nations (1) may not be more trade-restrictive than required and may be applied only to the extent necessary for the protection of human, animal, or plant life; (2) may not be a disguised restriction on trade; (3) must be based on a risk assessment made according to scientific principles and scientific evidence; (4) may not unjustifiably discriminate between countries where similar threats prevail; and (5) countries must ensure that inspections of imported products are fair and reasonable and are completed without delay. Consider an example: A country that sets an unreasonably short shelf-life for dairy products may actually be discriminating against foreign-produced dairy products whose shelf-life expires during the time it takes for shipment. Under the *SPS Agreement,* the shelf-life restriction cannot stand unless based on scientific evidence. A novel example is the strict Japanese law prohibiting thoroughbred racehorses from entering Japan. This prohibition might violate the agreement if the restriction is unnecessary, discriminatory toward the United States, or not based on scientific evidence. Citing the *SPS Agreement,* the U.S. Department of Agriculture in 1995 repealed an 81-year-old prohibition against the import of Mexican avocados.

Codex Alimentarius

Whenever possible, countries must rely on internationally accepted standards or recommendations for the protection of their plants, animals, and foodstuffs. The most notable are found in the ***Codex Alimentarius.*** This "food code" for the protection of the world's food supply developed slowly over most of the last century. Today, the *Codex Alimentarius* Commission develops these important standards on the basis of worldwide scientific studies and disseminates them to government agencies and lawmakers. The commission is based in Rome and is made up of countries that belong to the UN World Health Organization and the UN Food and Agricultural Organization. If a country's national standards are based on the *Codex Alimentarius,* they are deemed to be in compliance with the *SPS Agreement.*

In the following 1997 WTO panel decision, *WTO Report on EC Measures Concerning Meat & Meat Products (Hormones),* the panel held that the European ban on the sale of beef containing residues of growth hormones violated the *SPS Agreement.*

European Communities—Measures Concerning Meat and Meat Products (Hormones)

Report of the Dispute Settlement Panel, WT/DS26/R/USA (1997) World Trade Organization

BACKGROUND AND FACTS

Throughout the 1970s, European consumers became more concerned over the use of hormones to speed the growth of livestock. Their fears were in part based on the fact that some people had been injured by the illegal use of certain banned hormones. Some consumer organizations boycotted meats. By 1986, the EC had banned the sale of beef from cattle given growth hormones. The EC maintained that such measures were necessary to protect public health (primarily from hormone-related illnesses and cancer) and necessary to restore confidence in the meat industry. The United States began contesting the hormone ban in 1987 at GATT. In January 1989, the United States introduced retaliatory measures in the form of 100 percent *ad valorem* duties on a list of products imported from the European Communities. The United States, together with Australia, Canada, New Zealand, and Norway maintained that the ban was unlawful under the 1994 *Agreement on the Application of Sanitary and Phytosanitary Measures* (*SPS Agreement*) and brought this complaint. The United States argued that the ban was not based on an assessment of risk, not based on scientific principles, more trade-restrictive than necessary, and a disguised restriction on trade. In June 1996, the European Communities requested the establishment of a panel to examine this matter, and the United States terminated its retaliatory action entirely. Prior to the ban, U.S. firms had exported hundreds of millions of dollars of goods annually to Europe. After the ban, exports plummeted to nearly zero. The European Communities argued that its measures offered equal opportunities of access to the EC market for all third-country animals and meat from animals to which no hormones had been administered for growth promotion purposes.

REPORT OF THE PANEL

Article 3.1 requires Members to base their sanitary measures on international standards, guidelines or recommendations [where they exist]. We note, therefore, that even if international standards may not, in their own right, be binding on Members, Article 3.1 requires Members to base their sanitary measures on these standards ... We shall therefore, as a first step, examine whether there are international standards, guidelines or recommendations with respect to the EC measures in dispute and, if so, whether the EC measures are based on these standards, guidelines or recommendations in accordance with Article 3.1[of the *SPS Agreement*]:

> To harmonize sanitary and phytosanitary measures on as wide a basis as possible, Members shall base their sanitary and phytosanitary measures on international standards, guidelines or recommendations, where they exist, except as otherwise provided for in this Agreement ...

For food safety ... the *SPS Agreement* defines "international standards, guidelines or recommendations" as "the standards, guidelines and recommendations established by the *Codex Alimentarius* Commission relating to food additives, veterinary drug and pesticide residues, contaminants, methods of analysis and sampling, and codes and guidelines of hygienic practice." We note that [there are] five Codex standards ... relating to veterinary drug residues ... with respect to five of the six hormones in dispute when these hormones are used for growth promotion purposes ... We find, therefore, that international standards exist with respect to the EC measures in dispute. * * *

The amount of residues of these hormones administered for growth promotion purposes allowed by these Codex standards is ... higher than zero (a maximum level of such residues has not even been prescribed). The EC measures in dispute, on the other hand, do not allow the presence of any residues of these three hormones administered for growth

continues

continued

promotion purposes. The level of protection reflected in the EC measures is, therefore, significantly different from the level of protection reflected in the Codex standards. The EC measures in dispute are … therefore, not based on existing international standards as specified in Article 3.1. * * *

[For those sanitary measures for which no international standards exist] … a Member needs to ensure that its sanitary measures are based on an assessment of risks. The obligation to base a sanitary measure on a risk assessment may be viewed as a specific application of the basic obligations contained in Article 2.2 of the *SPS Agreement* which provides that "Members shall ensure that any sanitary … measure is *applied only to the extent necessary to protect* human, animal or plant life or health, is *based on scientific principles* and is *not maintained without sufficient scientific evidence …*" (emphasis added). Articles 5.1 to 5.3 sum up factors a Member needs to take into account in making this assessment of risks … [A]n assessment of risks is, at least for risks to human life or health, a scientific examination of data and factual studies; it is not a policy exercise involving social value judgments made by political bodies. * * *

We recall that under the *SPS Agreement* a risk assessment should, for the purposes of this dispute, identify the adverse effects on human health arising from the presence of the specific hormones at issue when used as growth promoters in meat or meat products and, if any such adverse effects exist, evaluate the potential or probability of occurrence of these effects. We further recall that a risk assessment should be a scientific examination of data and studies and that *the SPS Agreement* sets out factors which need to be taken into account in a risk assessment.

[The panel conducted a review of the scientific studies.] All of the scientific studies outlined above came to the conclusion that the use of the hormones at issue for growth promotion purposes is safe; most of these studies adding that this conclusion assumes that good practice is followed. We note that this conclusion has also been confirmed by the scientific experts advising the Panel. Accordingly, the European Communities has not established the existence of any identifiable risk against which the EC measures at issue … can protect human life or health.

Decision. The EC's ban on the sale of beef containing residues of growth hormones was found to violate the *Agreement on the Application of Sanitary and Phytosanitary Measures.* Where an existing internationally accepted standard permits beef to contain a residue of a certain growth hormone, an EC regulation permitting zero residue is in violation of the agreement. Where no internationally accepted standard exists on the residue of a certain hormone, the EC ban on that hormone is not permitted because it is not based on a risk assessment made using scientifically accepted principles.

Comment. The panel's decision was upheld by the WTO Appellate Body in 1998 and accepted by the WTO Dispute Settlement Body. The United States and Canada were authorized to impose retaliatory tariffs on EU imports. The United States imposed 100 percent duties on a range of European products valued at $116 million per year (Canada at CDN$11.3 million). In 2009, an agreement was finally reached in which the EU would allow increased duty free imports of U.S. beef produced without hormones in return for the United States eliminating the retaliatory tariffs over a period of several years.

Case Questions

1. What was the role of the panel in settling this dispute under the *SPS Agreement?* Did it make its own determination and draw its own scientific conclusions about the effect of beef hormones on human health, or did it give total deference to the conclusions of the EU scientists?
2. What factors were taken into account to determine whether a sanitary measure violates the *SPS Agreement?*
3. It is an interesting irony in this case, that today many scientists, environmentalists, and consumer groups in the United States are calling for a similar domestic ban on beef growth hormones. How do you feel about the use of hormones in beef cattle?

OTHER WTO "TRADE-RELATED" AGREEMENTS

Two other agreements that will have an effect on world trade are the *WTO Agreement on Trade-Related Investment Measures* and the *WTO Agreement on Trade-Related Aspects of Intellectual Property Rights.* While we only mention them briefly here, we discuss these issues more fully in Part Four of this book.

Trade-Related Investment Measures

There is no question today that trade and foreign direct investment are interrelated. To be competitive in a global market, firms must do more than just produce in one country and sell in another. They must be able to supply services or conduct procurement, manufacturing, assembly, and distribution operations on a global scale. This requires the freedom to build foreign factories, open new foreign subsidiaries, or merge with foreign firms. The link between investment and trade becomes even more obvious when looking at the volume of trade between related companies. According to UNCTAD, trade between foreign affiliated companies or between subsidiaries and their parent companies—accounts for over one-third of world trade. Government controls that hamper the freedom of firms to acquire or merge with foreign firms or to make critical investment decisions will have an adverse effect on trade in goods and services, especially between these multinational affiliates.

The 1994 Uruguay Round agreements resulted in the *WTO Agreement on Trade-Related Investment Measures* (commonly called *TRIMS*). A **trade-related investment measure** is a national rule or regulation on foreign investment that has a direct or indirect effect on trade in goods. The agreement does not set broad rules for local investing, such as rules affecting domestic stock exchanges. It does attempt to reduce restrictions on foreign investment that might restrict cross-border trade in goods and services. It also eliminates discrimination against foreign firms and their goods and services to the extent that those restrictions distort or restrict trade. For example, TRIMS prohibits **trade balancing requirements**—laws that condition a company's right to import foreign goods on the basis of the volume of goods that company exports. TRIMS also prohibits **local content requirements**—regulations dictating that a foreign company or other producer must use a certain minimum percentage of locally made parts or components in the manufacture of a product. For instance, Argentina may not say to a U.S. multinational corporation, "We will finance the construction of a new automobile factory for you, but only if you guarantee us that 25 percent of the component parts used in assembling cars are made in this country," or "You may only import foreign raw materials on the condition that you export an equal volume of finished goods from our country." These requirements would violate the prohibition of quantitative restrictions of GATT Article XI. Also prohibited are laws that condition the receipt of foreign exchange on the company's foreign exchange revenues. Thus, Argentina may not demand, "Our central bank will only permit you to transfer U.S. dollars out of the country if you have brought into the country an equivalent amount this year in dollars, yen, or other hard currency."

Trade-Related Aspects of Intellectual Property Rights

Because intellectual property rights (IPRs) are not "goods," they did not fall within the bounds of the 1947 GATT agreement. However, IPRs are often attached to goods and used to sell them. Thus, if IPRs are not protected from unauthorized use, then trade in goods and services will suffer. For this reason, the Uruguay Round negotiations focused on IPRs and resulted in the *WTO Agreement on Trade-Related Aspects of Intellectual Property Rights,* or TRIPS. **Trade-related aspects of intellectual property rights** refers to government rules or regulations on IPRs that have a direct or indirect effect on trade in goods.

TRIPS sets new, comprehensive standards for the protection of IPRs in all member countries of the WTO. It requires every WTO country to abide by the most important international intellectual property conventions and then calls on countries to grant even greater protection to inventors, authors, and trademark owners. The agreement requires that all domestic and foreign IPR owners, regardless of their citizenship, be treated the same under a country's IPR laws. It prohibits countries from imposing requirements on foreign firms in exchange for being granted trademarks, patents, or copyrights. For instance, a WTO country may not condition the award of a patent on the inventor's promise to manufacture the item in that country. Countries must publish all laws, regulations, and administrative rulings that pertain to the availability, application, protection, or enforcement of IPRs. Enforcement efforts will be strengthened worldwide to reduce the billions of dollars' worth of losses every year due to counterfeit and pirated goods (e.g., fake Rolex watches or unauthorized copies of Microsoft software). WTO member countries will bring their IPR laws into compliance with TRIPS, as the United States has already done. For example, in 1995 the United States increased the patent period from 17–20 years to comply with TRIPS' longer period. The TRIPS Council of the WTO monitors compliance with TRIPS. TRIPS disputes are settled by the WTO Dispute Settlement Body.

TRADE SANCTIONS AND *U.S. SECTION 301*: THE THREAT OF RETALIATION

One of the most important legal weapons in the U.S. arsenal against foreign trade barriers and unfair trade practices is commonly known to businesspeople and lawyers alike as "Section 301." *Section 301 of the U.S. Trade Act of 1974* has been amended by Congress several times and is still in effect today. The law permits the United States Trade Representative (USTR) to take retaliatory trade action against other countries whose trade policies toward the United States are unreasonable or discriminatory.

The purpose of the law is to discourage foreign countries from violating their trade agreements with the United States. If they do, or if they unreasonably restrict access of U.S. goods or services to their markets, they face losing access to the U.S. market. Retaliation would subject their products to punitive tariffs or other trade restrictions upon entering the United States. Even prior to the GATT agreements of the mid-1990s and the founding of the WTO, *Section 301* had already proven to be a significant threat to foreign countries for discriminating against U.S. goods and services.

The manner in which the United States, or any country, takes retaliatory action in a trade war has long been a subject of argument. Some commentators and politicians argue for **unilateralism**: the policy that a nation should retaliate unilaterally against another country that discriminates against its products or firms rather than relying on an established international or multilateral framework for resolving trade disputes. Those who favor unilateralism usually do so because they believe it furthers a nation's self-interest. Those opposed to unilateralism believe that a nation's self-interest is best furthered by gaining support from other nations. Unilateralism is in direct conflict with the principles of the WTO system. After the creation of the WTO in 1995, the United States, like other member countries, became obligated to seek consultations at the WTO and approval from the WTO Dispute Settlement Body before imposing retaliatory measures. For instance, if the European Union imposes a licensing scheme on imports that unfairly discriminates against products from the United States, the United States must first attempt to resolve the matter by negotiations. If this fails, the United States must invoke WTO dispute settlement procedures, seek WTO authorization for retaliation, and gain approval of the amount of punitive tariffs and the types of European goods to which they will apply.

In the 1990s, the EU argued that *Section 301* violated WTO dispute settlement procedures. In the following case, *WTO Report on United States—Sections 301-310 of the Trade Act of 1974* (1999), a dispute settlement panel held that *Section 301* does not violate U.S. obligations under GATT if it is applied in accordance with WTO dispute settlement provisions.

United States—Sections 301-310 of the Trade Act of 1974

Report of the Panel, WT/DS152/R (1999) World Trade Organization

BACKGROUND AND FACTS

The European Communities requested a WTO panel to decide whether U.S. Sections 301-310 [the Act] violated GATT dispute settlement procedures. The Act permits the USTR to investigate possible violations of GATT or other international trade agreements, to negotiate a settlement of the dispute, and to request a WTO dispute settlement panel if necessary. The Act also permits the USTR to impose retaliatory tariffs or other trade sanctions either unilaterally or if authorized by the WTO Dispute Settlement Body. The EC argued that the Act violated WTO rules.

REPORT OF THE PANEL

The European Communities argues that [WTO rules] prohibit unilateralism in the ... dispute settlement procedures. Members must await the adoption of a panel or Appellate Body report by the Dispute Settlement Body, or the rendering of an arbitration decision ... before determining whether rights or benefits accruing to them under a WTO agreement are being denied. * * *

The European Communities ... took the position in the Uruguay Round that a strengthened dispute settlement system must include an explicit ban on any government taking unilateral action to redress what that government judges to be the trade wrongs of others.

The United States argues that nothing in Sections 301-310 requires the U.S. government to act in violation

continues

continued

of its WTO obligations. To the contrary, the Act requires the USTR to undertake WTO dispute settlement proceedings when a WTO agreement is involved, and provides that the USTR will rely on the results of those proceedings when determining whether U.S. agreement rights have been denied. Likewise, [the Act] explicitly indicates that the USTR need not take action when the DSB has adopted a report finding no denial of U.S. WTO rights.

Under well-established GATT and WTO jurisprudence and practice which the European Communities appears to accept, a law may be found inconsistent with a Member's WTO obligations only if it precludes a Member from acting consistently with those obligations. The European Communities must therefore demonstrate that Sections 301-310 do not permit the United States government to take action consistent with U.S. WTO obligations—that this legislation in fact mandates WTO-inconsistent action. The European Communities has failed to meet this burden. Its analysis of the language of Sections 301-310 ignores pertinent statutory language and relies on constructions not permitted under U.S. law. Sections 301-310 of the Trade Act of 1974 are fully consistent with U.S. WTO rights and obligations. * * *

If a law does not make it compulsory for authorities to act so as to violate their international obligations, that law may not be said to command such action. This can be illustrated through a simple example. A law which provides, "the Trade Representative shall take a walk in the park on Tuesdays, unless she chooses not to" does not oblige the USTR to walk in the park on Tuesdays. She has complete discretion not to take a walk in the park on Tuesdays; the law in no way obliges or commands her to do so. This remains true despite the use of the word "shall" in that law.

Decision. Sections 301-310 of the U.S. *Trade Act of 1974* were found to be valid under the GATT 1994 agreements. The panel clarified that the United States may impose retaliatory trade sanctions against other WTO members only where the United States strictly followed WTO dispute settlement rules and when authorized by the Dispute Settlement Body.

Comment. Upon entering the WTO, the United States had filed a binding "Statement of Administrative Action," in which it committed to abide by all WTO dispute settlement procedures and to not act unilaterally. That was noted by the panel in its report and was a factor in the panel's decision.

Case Questions

1. What does the panel mean by "unilateralism"?
2. If a trade dispute arises, what is the proper procedure under WTO rules for settling that dispute?

Basic *Section 301*

Basic **Section 301** sets two different standards for retaliation against different types of foreign trade barriers: The first defines when retaliatory action by the USTR is discretionary, and the second defines when it is mandatory. Discretionary retaliatory action may be taken at the option of the USTR, under the direction of the president, against any foreign country whose policies or actions are found by the USTR to be *unreasonable or discriminatory and burden or restrict U.S. commerce.* A foreign country acts unreasonably if its policies toward U.S. firms are unfair and inequitable, even if they are not in violation of any international agreement. This includes the unfair restriction of foreign investment, denial of equal access to their markets, failure to protect U.S. intellectual property rights, or the subsidization of a domestic industry. In this case, the USTR determines whether any action is necessary, and if so, what action to take. The USTR also has the discretion to take retaliatory action when a foreign government (1) fails to allow workers the right to organize and bargain collectively; (2) permits forced labor; (3) does not provide a minimum age for the employment of children; or (4) fails to provide standards for minimum wage, hours of work, and the health and safety of workers. This gives the USTR sufficient discretionary authority and flexibility to attack a wide variety of foreign unfair trade practices.

Mandatory trade retaliation is required if the USTR determines that (1) a foreign country has denied the United States its rights under any trade agreement or (2) a foreign country's actions or policies are *unjustifiable and burden or restrict* U.S. commerce. An act, policy, or practice is unjustifiable if it is in violation of the international legal rights of the United States. Examples of unjustifiable acts or policies include tariffs above the agreed rate, quotas, denial of MFN treatment, illegal import procedures, overly burdensome restrictions on U.S. foreign investment, and IPR violations. In a case of a violation of GATT, the "burden" to U.S. commerce is presumed. Mandatory action is waived if a WTO panel has upheld the foreign government action, if the foreign country has agreed to eliminate the illegal policy, if the USTR believes that a negotiated solution is imminent, or, in extraordinary cases, if the USTR believes that the adverse effects of retaliation on the U.S. economy would exceed the benefits. A Section 301 action begins with the filing of a petition by an interested party, such as a U.S. company, or on the initiative of the USTR.

Sanctions and Retaliatory Measures. Trade sanctions can only be imposed after the USTR conducts an investigation into the foreign trade practices and an attempt at dispute resolution has failed. The imposition of trade sanctions are for the purpose of ending an illegal foreign practice, not to compensate the petitioning U.S. firm. No benefits accrue directly to the petitioning firm other than those that affect all U.S. companies or industries in a similar position.

The most common form of retaliation is the assessment of additional import duties on products from the offending nation in an amount that is equivalent in value to the burden on U.S. firms that country imposes. The products affected are said to be placed on the USTR's "retaliation list" or "hit list." The USTR may impose sanctions against any type of goods or any industry. If a country puts quotas on U.S. food products, the United States can retaliate against imports of any type, such as electronic parts. For instance, when the United States threatened trade sanctions against Japan for unfairly keeping out U.S. auto parts, the USTR proposed 100 percent import duties on imports of Japanese luxury automobiles. When China refused to protect U.S. copyrights, the United States threatened to impose over $1 billion a year in trade sanctions on all Chinese imports. When the EU refused to comply with a WTO panel decision and lift its ban on U.S. beef containing growth hormones in 1999, the United States imposed 100 percent duties on $117 million in European imports. Tariffs of this magnitude are calculated to temporarily raise prices on imported goods and to discourage their purchase, until such time as foreign trade barriers are lifted and the trade dispute is resolved.

Special 301. The United States uses so-called *"Special 301"* to assure that American-owned intellectual property rights (IPRs) are adequately protected in foreign countries. Each year, the USTR must identify those foreign countries that deny adequate protection to American IPRs. An offending country can be designated either as a **priority foreign country** (the worst offenders), or be placed on the **watch list** or the **priority watch list.** If a country is designated as a priority foreign country, the USTR must conduct an investigation to decide whether to invoke sanctions. In 2013, the USTR placed ten countries on the priority watch list: Algeria, Argentina, Chile, China, India, Indonesia, Pakistan, Russia, Thailand, and Venezuela. Thirty countries were on the watch list. From 2001–2005, Ukraine was subjected to $75 million per year in U.S. trade sanctions, and as of 2013 it remained a priority foreign country.

CONCLUSION

This chapter discusses the "market access" provisions of WTO law. This represents a worldwide effort to move from economic protectionism to freer and fairer trade. While it does seem that modern economists generally support free trade attitudes, protectionist habits are difficult to break. Nevertheless, it is safe to say that the general trend internationally has been away from protectionism and toward greater open market access for foreign firms.

The United States has generally taken a pro-free-trade stance ever since the 1930s. This is despite quite a bit of protectionist talk from lawmakers representing old-industry and organized labor states and from some candidates for public office, a few news commentators, and some think tanks and economists. Every U.S. president has had to balance free trade with domestic political pressure to protect industries at home. However, as U.S. firms became more dependent on export sales, they also became more vulnerable to foreign trade barriers that denied them access to export markets. For this reason, almost all Americans agree with the need to remove foreign trade barriers to the sale of U.S. goods and services abroad. This requires reciprocity—a give and take—with America's trading partners so that all will follow the rules of international trade law for the improvement of the business environment around the world.

Chapter Summary

1. The Uruguay Round trade negotiations resulted in many important trade agreements designed to remove trade barriers and improve access to foreign markets, including agreements on technical barriers, import licensing, government procurement, trade in services, agriculture, and textiles.
2. The *WTO Agreement on Technical Barriers to Trade* does not set standards of its own for product performance, design, safety, or efficiency, but it guides nations in the application of their own regulations and standards through legal principles of nondiscrimination, transparency, and MFN trade. The agreement applies broadly to regulations imposed to protect the public health, safety, and welfare, including consumer and environmental protection. Health and safety regulations may not be used unless they are "trade neutral" and restrict trade no more than necessary, according to the principle of least restrictive trade.
3. Governments are some of the largest consumers of goods and services in the world. *The WTO Agreement on Government Procurement* requires that countries "free up" their procurement policies and practices by giving foreign firms equal access to bidding on government contracts and by providing transparent and easily obtained rules for submitting bids.
4. About 20 percent of world trade is in services. The *General Agreement on Trade in Services* (1995) applies basic GATT principles to service industries for the first time since 1947. This agreement has already opened access to foreign markets in construction, engineering, health care, banking, insurance, securities, transportation, and the professions.
5. Trade in agriculture has been distorted by billions of dollars' worth of government subsidies granted to farming interests worldwide that artificially lower the cost of agricultural exports. In turn, importing nations artificially raise the price of agricultural imports with trade restrictions and tariffs. Attempts to limit government support of agriculture have been met by attacks from politically powerful farm groups, particularly in France and other European countries. Negotiations during the Doha Rounds of trade negotiations focus on making agricultural trade freer and fairer.
6. Exports of farm products have suffered because of discriminatory trade barriers imposed under the guise of health standards. Under the *WTO Agreement on Sanitary and Phytosanitary Measures,* countries cannot impose restrictions to protect animal and plant life from pests or contagious diseases unless those restrictions are applied fairly and equally to goods from all countries that present a risk of infection. Restrictions must be supported by scientific evidence and be as unrestrictive of trade as possible. These issues are critical to all humankind, as we face potential scourges like "mad cow" disease and hoof-and-mouth disease.
7. The *U.S. Trade Act of 1974* (Sections 301-310) provides the United States Trade Representative, under the direction of the president, with the tools needed to retaliate against foreign government trade barriers that breach trade agreements with the United States or that deny fair and equal access of U.S. goods and services to foreign markets. The United States is committed to only using *Section 301* retaliation after it has unsuccessfully resorted to the dispute settlement process at the WTO.

Key Terms

market access agreements 267
least restrictive trade 267
technical regulations 269
product standards 269
technical barriers to trade 270
prior approval 270
prior certification 270
transparency 271
CE Mark 272
design standard 272
performance standard 272
Japan Industrial Standards Mark 272
China Compulsory Certification Mark 274
conformity assessments 274

procurement offsets 278
trade in services 279
consumption abroad 279
commercial presence 280
presence of natural persons 280
domestic subsidies 282
agricultural export subsidies 282
sanitary and phytosanitary measures 282
Codex Alimentarius 283
trade-related investment measure 285
trade balancing requirements 285
trade-related aspects of intellectual property rights 285
local content requirements 285
unilateralism (in trade relations) 286
Section 301 288
priority foreign country 288
watch list 288
priority watch list 288

Questions and Case Problems

1. In 2002, the U.S. Congress passed a law requiring the Department of Agriculture to develop country of origin label ("COOL") requirements for fresh meats, fish, fruits, and vegetables sold to American consumers. It was a time of public concern over "mad cow" disease that had been found in some foreign cattle, and there were calls from consumer groups and many in government demanding that consumers be told the source of their food. After several years of public hearings, deliberations, and amendments to the rules, the COOL requirements went into effect in early 2009. Only meat from animals that were born, raised, and slaughtered in the United States could be labeled as products of the United States. Complex rules governed the labeling of meats sold from non-U.S. animals. Because of the need to segregate animals throughout the feeding and packing process, the record keeping requirements, and a mandatory animal identification system, U.S. importers found it too expensive, time consuming, and difficult to purchase imported animals. Potential fines were $1,000 per violation. Mexico and Canada filed a complaint at the WTO claiming that the rules caused price suppression in livestock of foreign origin. The United States argued that all health and safety regulation comes at some cost, and that the added costs here were not a result of discrimination. In 2012, a dispute panel ruled that the COOL requirements treated foreign livestock "less favorably" than domestic livestock, and thus violated Article 2.1 of the *Agreement on Technical Barriers to Trade.* On appeal, how did the Appellate Body rule? *United States—Certain Country of Origin Labeling (COOL) Requirements*, WT/DS384/AB/R; WT/DS386/AB/R (2012). Is this a technical regulation under the *TBT Agreement*? Was the discrimination against foreign livestock "arbitrary and burdensome," or was it a "legitimate regulatory distinction?"
2. In 2001, an outbreak of hoof-and-mouth disease threatened the meat supply of Europe. This virus is spread through the air or by contact. To control its spread, millions of cattle, sheep, and pigs were slaughtered and burned; export and transportation of British livestock, meat, and dairy products were halted; and many areas of Great Britain were placed off limits to travelers. Certain areas of the country were quarantined, with "Keep Out" notices posted on the roads. Officials sprayed chemicals to kill the virus on the soles of shoes and automobile tires. The virus quickly spread to continental Europe, and even the United States banned the import of meat from Europe. Explain the application of the WTO *Agreement on Sanitary and Phytosanitary Measures* to this issue. Does the agreement tell countries specifically what actions to take? What action does the agreement permit nations to take to fight a disease like this? Do you think that the agreement gave sufficient latitude to countries to fight the disease? For additional information, see the Website for the World Organization for Animal Health, a Paris-based government organization comprising 178 nations.
3. Businesses and consumers in China process more than $1 trillion (U.S. equivalent) in electronic payments every year. The United States claimed that the Chinese government used several regulatory requirements that had the effect of only allowing one company, the government-owned China Union Pay, to process all electronic payment services (EPS) in the country denominated in Chinese currency, the *renminbi* or yuan. The world's leaders in EPS, however, are U.S. firms, and they were virtually locked out of the China market. The United States brought a complaint before a WTO panel claiming that the Chinese government violated its obligations under Article XVI of GATS by granting one company a monopoly on clearing credit card transactions denominated in Chinese currency. Did China violate GATS Article XVI:2 (a) that prohibits a country from limiting the number of service suppliers in service sectors where it has made commitments? Did

this violate the principle of nondiscrimination? How was the dispute resolved? *China—Certain Measures Affecting Electronic Payment Services, Report of the Panel,* WT/DS413/R (2012).

4. Assume the United States and Japan are unable to resolve a trade war over trade in automobiles and auto parts. Acting unilaterally, the United States imposes punishingly high tariffs of 100 percent on Japanese cars. What are the real economic impacts and long-term effects of trade sanctions? Immediate costs might be borne by the Japanese manufacturers, U.S. dealerships, or consumers, but what does such a measure do to the long-term health and competitiveness of the U.S. car industry? Could you see any impact on the United States lead in innovation, design, and quality? Discuss.
5. At the request of the Canadian owner of a country music channel, Canada removed a Nashville-based country music channel from the air. This was only one in a series of attempts by Canada to restrict U.S. programming. Canadians argued that their country was dominated by U.S. culture on television and wanted it restricted. The U.S. firm petitioned the USTR to impose trade sanctions unless the Canadian policy was changed. After an investigation, the USTR threatened the Canadian government with $500 million in punitive tariffs. Discuss whether the USTR should have threatened sanctions before the case is heard by the WTO. See *Initiation of Section 302 Investigation Concerning Certain Discriminatory Communications Practices,* 60 FR 8101 (February 10, 1995).
6. The marketing and sale of beer and alcoholic beverages in Canada are governed by Canadian provincial marketing agencies or "liquor boards." In most of the ten Canadian provinces, these liquor boards not only regulate the marketing of domestic beer in the province but serve as import monopolies as well. They also warehouse, distribute, and retail imported beer. Canada imposed restrictions on the number of locations at which imported beer could be sold; authorization from the liquor board was needed to sell a brand of beer in the province; and higher markups were required on the price of foreign beer than on domestic beer sold by the liquor boards. Do the regulations violate the nondiscrimination provisions of GATT? May Canada use state trading monopolies to regulate imports of this kind? Are Canada's provisions valid public health regulations or illegal discrimination? If trade statistics showed that foreign beer sales have actually increased, could an exporting country's rights under GATT still be subject to "nullification and impairment"? Would *Section 301* apply to this case? See 56 FR 60128 (1991). See also *GATT Dispute Settlement Panel Report: Canada Import, Distribution and Sale of Alcoholic Drinks By Canadian Provincial MarketingAgencies* (1988).
7. Each year the USTR publishes an annual report to Congress entitled the *National Trade Estimate Report on Foreign Trade Barriers.* The report details trade barriers, by country and industry sector, U.S. firms face in exporting goods and services to foreign markets. The *Special 301 Report* is an annual assessment of the effectiveness of foreign intellectual property rights laws and enforcement efforts in foreign countries. Starting in 2010, the USTR introduced two new reports: *The Report on Technical Barriers to Trade* and the *Report on Sanitary and Phytosanitary Measures.* Find these reports, and select several countries of interest. What is the USTR's position with regard to trade barriers in those countries?

Managerial Implications

1. Your company is a U.S. multinational corporation with a 40 percent share of the world market for its product. Over the past decade, management has invested more than $100 million trying to get its products into Japanese stores. Despite all of its efforts, the company still has less than a 10 percent share of the Japanese market, and only 15 percent of Japanese stores carry its products. Company investigations show that its major Japanese competitor has a virtual monopoly there and has violated Japanese antitrust laws by fixing prices and refusing to sell to any store that carries your firm's products. Most distributors and retailers are linked to your competitor through *keiretsu* relationships. Management believes that by having the Japanese market all to itself, the competitor is able to maintain sufficiently high prices in Japan to permit them to undersell your company in the United States. Apparently, the Japanese government simply "looks the other way." Moreover, your firm has been effectively restrained by the bureaucracy that administers government procurement contracts in Japan. As a result, management estimates that it has lost several billion dollars in exports since the company first entered the Japanese market. Your competitor responds that it is not the only producer

in Japan, that the market there is very competitive, and besides, it also outsells your firm's products in several other Asian countries.

a. If you petition for a *Section 301* action, do you think the USTR will begin an investigation? What political factors in the United States might affect the USTR's decision to investigate? What is the attitude of the current U.S. administration toward the use of *Section 301?*

b. Management thinks that the Japanese government should require distributors to agree to import a given quantity of U.S.-made products in a year's period. How would the Japanese government mandate this? Do you think the Japanese distribution system or its *keiretsu* practices can be reformed? What other remedies or sanctions might be appropriate in this case? What is the likelihood that the threat of sanctions by the United States will affect the Japanese position? Given the history of U.S.-Japanese trade relations and the authority of the WTO, what do you think is the likely outcome of this case? Based on your study of the last two chapters, what provisions of the GATT agreement, if any, might apply to this case?

c. Are the market share statistics relevant to your case? What other data or information will be important?

2. The Asian country of Tamoa imports large quantities of down pillows each year. DownPillow, a U.S. company, wants to do more business there; however, Tamoa has a number of regulations affecting the importation and sale of down bedding. Consider the following five regulations:

a. Pillows made from down harvested from Tamoan flocks may be labeled as "goose down," even though they may contain up to 25 percent duck down. If the pillow is made from foreign down, then a pillow labeled "goose down" may contain no more than 5 percent duck down. Duck down is a cheaper alternative to goose down. Virtually all U.S. state regulations permit goose down to contain up to 10 percent duck down.. Tamoa believes that the stricter standard for imported pillows is justified to protect Tamoan consumers from fraud.

b. Tamoa also requires that the cotton coverings of all pillows be certified to meet certain ecology and human health standards for textiles: they may not contain any harmful chemicals, such as formaldehyde or chlorine, and they must be tested according to minimum standards set by the International Organization for Standardization. Certifications are accepted from qualified testing laboratories in any country. U.S. regulations do not require certification.

c. All pillow imports must be inspected on arrival in Tamoa. No inspections are permitted at the foreign factory. Tamoa has only one full-time inspector, who must remove down from at least three pillows from every shipment and subject it to laboratory analysis. Given the current backlog, inspections and analysis are taking up to four weeks, during which time the pillows are often damaged by Tamoa's high humidity.

d. Tamoan regulations also require that DownPillow's plant be inspected and that the sterilization process be approved by Tamoan officials. In the United States, the down is washed, sanitized, and subjected to hot air heat several hundred degrees in temperature, all under health department supervision. The Tamoan ministry of agriculture refuses to accept the sterilization permits, inspections, and approvals from state health departments in the United States. Tamoa does not pay the overseas travel expenses of its inspectors.

e. Tamoan regulations prohibit pillows and comforters from being compressed or vacuum packed for shipment to ensure the down will not be damaged in shipment.

DownPillow ships smaller orders by air freight and larger orders by ocean container. DownPillow and other U.S. firms are not pleased with these requirements. Evaluate the legality of the regulations and their impact on DownPillow. What course of action should DownPillow take?

Ethical Considerations

The concern of many proponents of environmental safety and public health includes creation, spread, and potential impact of genetically modified foods. The United States, along with Canada and Argentina, is one of the leading producers of genetically modified foods made from bioengineered organisms (GMOs). The U.S. government believes that GMOs are important for the world's food supply because they can boost food production and nutrition and lead to both disease-resistant crops and better-tasting foods. Many respected scientific studies vouch for the safety of GMOs for human and animal consumption and on the Earth's environment. GMOs are important to U.S. agriculture economically. According to the U.S. Department of Agriculture, approximately three-quarters of U.S. soybean and cotton production and over one-third of corn production are genetically modified. However, many consumer groups and countries argue that the dangers to humans, wildlife, and the environment are unknown. Genetically modified corn and soy were approved for sale in the EU prior to 1998, but the European countries ceased new approvals after that time. In addition, the EU and several other countries have adopted regulations requiring the tracing of biotech crops through the chain of distribution, and they imposed strict labeling requirements on all foods and animal feed containing more than 1 percent GMO. European consumers who fear GMO foods will not purchase products with these labels. The United States claims that the requirements are expensive and unnecessary and have cost U.S. farm exporters hundreds of millions of dollars in lost revenues. In 2003, the United States requested a WTO panel to decide whether the moratorium and labeling requirements violate the *WTO Sanitary and Phytosanitary Agreement.* Research the history of the WTO's deliberations. What was the outcome? Can you find any decisions of the European Court of Justice on GMOs? What is the current state of EU legislation on GMOs? What is your opinion? Do you think that GMOs should be permitted, or do you think they present some possible harm to the environment or to public health?

CHAPTER 11

Regulating Import Competition and Unfair Trade

The last two chapters examined the basic principles of world trade law found in the *General Agreement on Tariffs and Trade* (GATT), the other WTO agreements, and in the dispute resolution cases of the World Trade Organization (WTO). We studied the key principles of nondiscrimination and national treatment, MFN trade, the elimination of quotas and non-tariff barriers, and specific agreements affecting trade in services, agriculture, and other sectoral areas. This chapter covers two main areas The first is the protecting or "safeguarding" of domestic industries from foreign competition. These laws protect industries that say, "We're doing the best we can to compete, but the same products we make are coming in from overseas with few tariffs. Our foreign competitors have lower wage rates, lower employee benefit costs, fewer government rules, and they are becoming more efficient and more productive. They are shipping ever-greater quantities here, and we need time to adjust—to retool our plants and retrain our workers to become more competitive again. Just give us some time!"

The second part of this chapter covers the regulation of unfair trade, and the two most common unfair trade practices in international business: dumping and government subsidies. You might hear a business manager say, "Foreign firms compete unfairly. They dump their goods in our market at ridiculously low prices. They absorb the losses until they drive us all out of business so they will have the whole U.S. market to themselves!" Or you might hear: "How can we expect to sell our products here at home when we cannot match the price of imports? We may be more efficient than our overseas competitors, but they are subsidized; they are paid by their own governments, with their taxpayers' money, to build products and ship them here."

We will learn how **import competition** affects the private firm, and what remedies it might have against a barrage of competing imports or unfair trade practices. We will learn what the firm can do at home by petitioning the responsible government agency for a legal remedy, and see what remedies its government can pursue through the World Trade Organization (WTO). Although we will focus on the United States, what you will study is not that different from what is done in Canada, the EU, or in many other countries. In part, this is due to the internationalization of trade law through the WTO agreements, which require that national laws meet basic guidelines.

Remember, you can view the regulation of import competition from two directions. Not only can it be seen as a means of protecting industries at home, perhaps your firm or firms in your country, but it can also be seen as limiting the attempts of foreign governments to protect their industries by denying foreign firms, perhaps yours, access to their markets. Thus international rules for safeguarding domestic industries are also an important part of trade liberalization and market access efforts.

In this chapter, we frequently mention two U.S. government agencies: the **International Trade Commission (ITC)**, an "independent" agency, and the **International Trade Administration (ITA)**, a "dependent" agency and part of the U.S. Department of Commerce. Readers who are unfamiliar with these, or the differences between independent and dependent agencies, should review the material in Chapter Eight or consult the agencies for information.

SAFEGUARDS AGAINST INJURY

Governments of WTO nations normally may not raise tariff rates on imported goods simply because of political pressure to protect a domestic industry or jobs. However, under limited conditions a government may use temporary safeguards to protect a domestic industry from injury caused by increased imports. **Safeguards against injury** are *emergency remedies* provided by law, usually tariffs, used to protect a domestic industry from injury resulting from increased imports of a like or competing products. The legal authority and requirements for a WTO member nation to use a safeguard are set out in two important WTO agreements: Article XIX of GATT (1947), known as the "escape clause," and in the *WTO Agreement on Safeguards* (1994).

The GATT Escape Clause

Nations enter into trade agreements and make tariff concessions to boost two-way trade. If one country agrees to a reduced duty on semiconductors in return for another country granting a reduced duty on auto parts, one of the countries should be prepared to see an increase in imports of semiconductors and the other will see an increase in imports of auto parts. However, the resulting increases in imports can disrupt domestic markets and injure competing domestic producers far more than had been expected. **Market disruption** from increased imports of foreign goods might include decreased sales volume, price suppression, lower profitability, lower wages, and other economic consequences to domestic firms.

The original drafters of GATT in 1947 were aware of the economic and possible political ramifications of tariff concessions and built in a mechanism, commonly called the **escape clause**, that permits a country to temporarily "escape" or be relieved from its tariff concessions under certain conditions. Article XIX permits a country to take temporary corrective action (also called "emergency action") to safeguard its domestic industry where (1) as a result of *unforeseen developments*, (2) and due to the effect of a tariff concession or obligation under a trade agreement, (3) *increased quantities* of an imported product, (4) are causing or threaten to cause *serious injury to domestic producers of like or directly competitive products.* The escape clause is not meant to be used as an excuse for raising tariffs just because there are increased imports of foreign goods. It may only be used when the increase is a result of "unexpected developments," such as a sudden surge of imports resulting from an unexpected economic event. The most famous example of an unforeseen development occurred around 1950. The United States had agreed to lower tariff rates on fur hats at a time when fur hats were at the peak of fashion. When sales of women's fur felt hats later "dropped off the charts," due to an unexpected change in fashion, the United States invoked the escape clause. This was known as the GATT *Hatters' Fur* case.

The *WTO Agreement on Safeguards*

The *WTO Agreement on Safeguards* (1994) provides details lacking in the 1947 GATT Article XIX escape clause and sets out the procedural steps for countries imposing a safeguard.

Safeguards may only be used after an independent administrative agency in the importing country has conducted an investigation of the industry and determines that the legal requirements to impose safeguards have been met. Article 4.2 of the *Agreement on Safeguards* requires that the investigating agency "evaluate all relevant factors of an objective and quantifiable nature having a bearing on the situation of that industry, in particular, the *rate and amount* of the increase in imports of the product concerned in absolute and relative terms ..." The investigation must show that the increases in imports are the actual cause of the domestic industry's decline. An overall decline in the economy due to a recession, or new technology breakthroughs by domestic competitors, are not reasons to impose safeguards.

The following report of the WTO Appellate Body, *Argentina—Safeguard Measures on Imports of Footwear*, discusses Article 4.2 and the requirements of a safeguard investigation.

Global Safeguards. Safeguards applicable to WTO member countries must be in the form of **global safeguards**—safeguard measures placed on imports of specific products without discrimination as to their countries of origin. Safeguards must be applied "globally" to all imports of like products. For example, in the last case Argentina had applied the safeguards to footwear imported from all countries except the MERCOSUR countries, a regional customs union of South American nations to which Argentina belongs. The Appellate Body ruled that Argentina's safeguards must be applied without discrimination and could not be applied only to non-MERCOSUR countries.

WTO Limits on the Use of Safeguards. Safeguards may be used for no longer than four years (with an extension to eight years). Appellate Body reports have

Argentina—Safeguard Measures on Imports of Footwear

Report of the Appellate Body, WT/DS121/AB/R (1999)
World Trade Organization

BACKGROUND AND FACTS

Argentina conducted a safeguard investigation into imports of footwear during the period from 1991–1996 and found the following data related to absolute levels of imports:

TOTAL IMPORTS OF FOOTWEAR INTO ARGENTINA, 1991–1996		
	QUANTITY (MILLION PAIRS)	VALUE (US$ MILLIONS)
1991	8.86	44.41
1992	16.63	110.87
1993	21.78	128.76
1994	19.84	141.48
1995	15.07	114.22
1996	13.47	116.61

Argentina then imposed safeguard measures that increased import duties on footwear from the bound rate of 35 percent to 200 percent. The European Community (now EU) and the United States brought an action at the WTO claiming that the data do not show an increase in absolute levels of imports as required by GATT Article XIX and the *WTO Agreement on Safeguards*. Argentina compared the 1991 figures to 1996 to show an increase. The EU and U.S. argued that using end points only was improper because it ignored intervening, declining trends over the period. A WTO panel held that Argentina's safeguard investigation was inadequate, and Argentina appealed to the WTO Appellate Body.

REPORT OF THE APPELLATE BODY

* * * We note once again, that Article XIX:1(a) requires that a product be imported "in such increased quantities and under such conditions as to cause or threaten serious injury to domestic producers." [emphasis in Report] Clearly, this is not the language of ordinary events in routine commerce. In our view, the text of Article XIX:1(a) of the GATT 1994, read in its ordinary meaning and in its context, demonstrates that safeguard measures were intended by the drafters of the GATT to be matters out of the ordinary, to be matters of urgency, to be, in short, "emergency actions." And, such "emergency actions" are to be invoked only in situations when, as a result of obligations incurred under the GATT 1994, a Member finds itself confronted with developments it had not "foreseen" or "expected" when it incurred that obligation. The remedy that Article XIX:1(a) allows in this situation is temporarily to "suspend the obligation in whole or in part or to withdraw or modify the concession". Thus, Article XIX is clearly, and in every way, an extraordinary remedy. * * *

We agree with the Panel that Articles 2.1 and 4.2(a) of the *Agreement on Safeguards* require[s] a demonstration not merely of any increase in imports, but, instead, of imports "in such increased quantities ... and under such conditions as to cause or threaten to cause serious injury." In addition, we agree with the Panel that the specific provisions of Article 4.2(a) require that "the rate and amount of the increase in import ... in absolute and relative terms" [emphasis in Report] must be evaluated. Thus, we do not dispute the Panel's view and ultimate conclusion that the competent authorities are required to consider the trends in imports over the period of investigation (rather than just comparing the end points) under Article 4.2(a). As a result, we agree with the Panel's conclusion that "Argentina did not adequately consider the intervening trends in imports, in particular the steady and significant declines in imports beginning in 1994, as well as the sensitivity of the analysis to the particular end points of the investigation period used." * * *

Although we agree with the Panel that the "increased quantities" of imports cannot be just any increase, we do not agree with the Panel that it is reasonable to examine the trend in imports over a five-year historical period. In our view, the use of the present tense of the verb phrase "is being imported" in both Article 2.1 of the *Agreement on Safeguards* and Article XIX:1(a) of the GATT 1994 indicates that it is necessary for the competent authorities to examine recent imports, and not simply trends in imports during the past five years – or, for that matter, during any other period of several years. In our view, the phrase "is being imported" implies that the increase in imports must have been sudden and recent.

We recall here our reasoning and conclusions above on the meaning of the phrase "as a result of unforeseen developments" in Article XIX:1(a) of the GATT 1994. We concluded there that the increased quantities of imports should have been "unforeseen" or "unexpected." We also believe that the phrase "in such increased quantities" in Article 2.1 of the *Agreement on Safeguards* and Article XIX:1(a) of the

continues

continued

GATT 1994 is meaningful to this determination. In our view, the determination of whether the requirement of imports "in such increased quantities" is met is not a merely mathematical or technical determination. In other words, it is not enough for an investigation to show simply that imports of the product this year were more than last year—or five years ago. Again, and it bears repeating, not just any increased quantities of imports will suffice. There must be "such increased quantities" as to cause or threaten to cause serious injury to the domestic industry in order to fulfill this requirement for applying a safeguard measure. And this language in both Article 2.1 of the *Agreement on Safeguards* and Article XIX:1(a) of the GATT 1994, we believe, requires that the increase in imports must have been recent enough, sudden enough, sharp enough, and significant enough, both quantitatively and qualitatively, to cause or threaten to cause "serious injury." * * * We ... uphold the Panel's ultimate conclusion that "Argentina's investigation provides no legal basis for the application of the definitive safeguard measure at issue, or any safeguard measure."

Decision. The Appellate Body agreed with the conclusion (but not completely with the reasoning) of the Panel that Argentina's investigation was inadequate under the standards of the WTO safeguard provisions.

Case Questions

1. What is the role of a WTO panel in reviewing the safeguard investigations conducted by a national administrative agency?
2. What kind of "increased quantities" of imports must be found by the investigating authority to impose safeguard measures?
3. Locate the *Agreement on Safeguards* and read Article 2. Why did Argentina's exemption for footwear imported from MERCOSUR countries violate the WTO Agreements?

held that they not be greater or more restrictive than necessary to prevent injury, and must be gradually lifted when conditions warrant. Tariffs are the preferred safeguard. A quota, if used, may not reduce the quantity of imports below the average level of imports of the prior three years. Quotas should be allocated among supplying nations based on their proportion of the total quantity of imports during the preceding years. Safeguards can only apply to imports from developing countries if a particular developing country is supplying more than 3 percent of the total imports of that product. Where critical circumstances exist that could cause irreparable harm to a domestic industry, **provisional safeguards**, consisting of tariffs only, can be used if clear evidence justifies the safeguards, but they must be lifted within 200 days.

Trade Compensation. WTO agreements encourage a country imposing a safeguard to compensate a supplying nation for the burden the safeguard measure has imposed on it. For example, if the United States imposes safeguard tariffs on imported bicycles and Taiwan supplies large numbers of bicycles to the United States, then the United States should make trade compensation to Taiwan by reducing tariffs on other Taiwanese imports in an equivalent amount. Thus, **trade compensation** is the act of lowering import duties on certain products coming from a foreign country for the purpose of offsetting increased duties imposed on other products from that country. The countries are expected to negotiate trade compensation; if they fail to reach agreement, then the supplying nation may "suspend ... substantially equivalent concessions" or raise tariffs in retaliation.

Safeguards against Injury under U.S. Law

The U.S. safeguards law is found in *Section 201* of the *Trade Act of 1974* as amended by later statutes and are codified in Title 19 of the U.S. Code on "Customs Duties." The law does not follow the specific language and guidelines of GATT Article XIX and the *WTO Agreement on Safeguards* completely, but is similar. The law does not refer to the term "safeguards," but rather to a "positive adjustment to import competition" or **import relief**. The two greatest differences between the WTO safeguards provisions and U.S. law is that U.S. law lacks the requirement that safeguards only be imposed where the injury to industry results from "unforeseen developments," and the requirements for determining "serious injury" are different. These differences have caused the WTO Dispute Settlement Body to rule against the United States in a number of safeguard actions reviewed at the WTO since 1994.

Under the U.S. statute, the president can grant import relief when the International Trade Commission (ITC) determines that "an article is being imported into the United States in such increased quantities as to be a *substantial cause of serious injury*, or threat thereof, to the domestic industry producing an article like or directly competitive with the imported article." A "substantial cause" is that cause of the industry's decline that is the most important cause, and "not less than any other cause." Thus, the ITC may look to see what factors other than the increase in imports contributed to the industry's decline, although it may not consider overall economic trends, such as the impact of a recession on the industry. In determining "serious injury" the ITC may look at all relevant factors including:

1. A significant idling of productive facilities in the industry
2. The inability of firms to operate at a reasonable profit
3. Unemployment or underemployment in the industry Where serious injury to a domestic industry is threatened, or *clearly imminent*, the commission may consider all relevant factors including:
4. A decline in sales or market share
5. A downward trend in production, profits, wages, productivity, or employment
6. Growing inventories
7. A firm's inability to generate capital for plant and equipment modernization or for research and development
8. An actual increase in imports or in market share held by imports
9. Other factors that may account for the serious injury to the domestic industry (e.g., incompetent management or lack of technological innovation)

A petition for import relief may be filed with the ITC by any firm, trade association, union, or group of workers, or by Congress or the president, or the commission may initiate an investigation itself. The ITC gives public notice in the *Federal Register* of its investigations and hearings. The commission conducts public hearings at which interested parties may present evidence and make suggestions as to the form of import relief. The ITC prepares a detailed economic analysis of the affected market and then makes either an affirmative or negative determination as to injury. If the ITC finds that the requirements of the law are met, it can recommend a remedy or course of action to the president.

Remedies under U.S. Law. The president may make an **adjustment to imports** if, in the president's discretion, it will help the domestic industry make a positive adjustment to import competition and if it will provide *greater economic and social benefits than costs*. Because of this discretionary power, a president who adopts free trade or free-market concepts might be reluctant to apply a safeguard remedy at all. Although largely political in nature, a president's decision is usually based on the national interest. Although U.S. safeguard actions were common in the 1970s, their use has declined in recent decades, and their use to protect U.S. industry from foreign competitions is now rare. The same has been true in Canada, where safeguards are now seldom imposed.

Any relief that the president grants must be temporary (limited to four years, with an extension to eight years if the firms in the industry are making needed changes) and designed to allow those firms sufficient time to regain their competitive positions in the market. Relief should only provide time to retool, modernize, streamline, recapitalize, improve quality, or take other actions to better meet new competitive conditions in the market. The president's options for adjusting imports include (1) tariff increases, (2) tariff-rate quotas, (3) absolute quotas, (4) auctioned quotas, or (5) grant trade adjustment (financial) assistance to workers or to the domestic industry.

In the following *ITC Report on Heavyweight Motorcycles*, the commission found that increased imports of motorcycles threatened serious injury to the petitioner, Harley-Davidson, despite the severe impact of a long recession on total sales in the industry.

Heavyweight Motorcycles & Engines & Power-Train Subassemblies

Report to the President on Investigation No. TA-201-47 (1983) United States International Trade Commission

BACKGROUND AND FACTS

In 1982, the ITC instituted an investigation to determine if motorcycles having engines with displacement more than 700 cubic centimeters were being imported into the United States in such increased quantities as to be a substantial cause of serious injury, or threat thereof, to domestic industry producing like or directly competitive articles. The investigation was in response to a petition for relief filed by Harley-Davidson Motor Co., a U.S. firm. The investigation showed that from 1977 to 1981, U.S. shipments of motorcycles grew by 17 percent, with domestic production capacity increasing by nearly 82 percent (largely as a result of American Honda's increased production in the United States). During that

continues

continued

same period, the number of U.S. jobs increased by 30 percent. In 1982, however, consumption fell, domestic shipments declined, and employment dropped. In the first nine months of 1982, domestic shipments fell by 13 percent and inventories rose, leaving large numbers of unsold motorcycles. Production during that period showed a decline of 36 percent, profits were down by 20 percent, and employment was down by 12 percent. Inventories of imported motorcycles doubled in that period, representing a tremendous threat to Harley-Davidson. The country as a whole was in the midst of a recession, and demand for heavyweight motorcycles was depressed.

VIEWS OF CHAIRMAN ALFRED ECKES

* * *

It is evident that inventories of imported motorcycles have increased significantly during the most recent period. These increases exceed growth in consumption and surpass historical shipment trends for importers. The mere presence of such a huge inventory has had and will continue to have a depressing effect on the domestic industry. Also, given the natural desire of consumers for current design and up-to-date performance capabilities, motorcycles cannot be withheld from the market indefinitely. They must be sold. And given the realities of the market place, there is a strong incentive to liquidate these inventories as quickly as possible. The impact of such a massive inventory build-up on the domestic industry is imminent, not remote and conjectural.

I have seen no persuasive evidence that would suggest imports of Japanese heavyweight motorcycles will decline in the near future. Instead, the Japanese motorcycle industry is export oriented ... exporting in 1982 some 91 percent of the heavyweight motorcycles produced in Japan. Because motorcycles of more than 750cc, which include the merchandise under investigation here, cannot be sold in Japan under current law, Japanese producers cannot consider domestic sales as a replacement for exports. The other option, which they apparently pursued in 1982, is to push export sales in the face of declining demand in the U.S. market. This tactic helps to maintain output and employment in the producing country but it shifts some of the burden of adjustment to competitors in the importing country. Evidence that the Japanese producers will seek to maintain a high level of export sales to the U.S. is found in an estimate of the Japanese Automobile Manufacturer's Association. This organization estimated that exports of 700cc or over motorcycles to the United States for 1982 and 1983 would average 450,000 units or less for both years combined. That figure results in import levels higher than recent levels.

Finally, imports of finished heavyweight motorcycles pose a "substantial cause" of threat of serious injury. Under section 201(b)(4), a "substantial cause" is a "cause which is important and not less than any other cause." In my view, there is no cause more important than imports threatening injury to the domestic motorcycle industry.

In reaching this conclusion I have considered the significance of the present recession in my analysis. Without a doubt the unusual length and severity of the present recession has created unique problems for the domestic motorcycle industry. Without a doubt the rise in joblessness, particularly among blue-collar workers, who constitute the prime market for heavyweight motorcycles, has had a severe impact on the domestic industry. Nonetheless, if the Commission were to analyze the causation question in this way, it would be impossible in many cases for a cyclical industry experiencing serious injury to obtain relief under section 201 during a recession. In my opinion Congress could not have intended for the Commission to interpret the law this way.

There are other reasons for doubting the domestic recession is a substantial cause of injury or threat to the U.S. industry. During the current recession, imports from Japan have increased their market share from domestic producers, gaining nearly six percentage points. Imports have taken market share from the domestic facilities of Honda and Kawasaki as well as Harley-Davidson.

Moreover, while the current recession has undoubtedly depressed demand for heavyweight motorcycles, economic conditions are beginning to improve in this country ... As demand responds to this improvement, the domestic industry will be pre-empted from participating in any growth because of the presence of a one-year supply of motorcycles poised and ready to capture market share. Consequently, not the recession, but the inventory of motorcycles coupled with anticipated future imports constitute the greatest threat of injury in the months ahead.

Decision. The commission recommended that incremental duties be imposed for five years at the declining rates of 45, 35, 20, 15, and 10 percent, in addition to the existing rate of 4.4 percent *ad valorem*.

Comment. President Reagan followed the commission's recommendations, but added tariff-rate quotas of 5,000 units to keep the U.S. market open to European firms that exported to the United States in smaller quantities. The remedy has been considered one of the most successful uses of safeguards. Under protection, Harley-Davidson recapitalized, introduced quality control

continues

continued

processes and just-in-time inventory control, and regained its competitiveness. The safeguards were discontinued in 1987. Within a few years, Harley was one of the most demanded motorcycles in the world, including in Japan. In 2012, 35 percent of Harley's sales were outside the U.S.

Case Questions

1. In the early 1960s, Honda entered the U.S. motorcycle market with the slogan, "You meet the nicest people on a Honda." During the next two decades, the Japanese company not only made motorcycling acceptable and fun but it also introduced motorcycles known for quality, dependability, and easy starting. By 1982, Japanese motorcycles had reached their peak sales in the United States. In the meantime, Harley-Davidson was plagued with quality and image problems. Do you think this should have been considered in the ITC's recommendations or considered by President Reagan?
2. Assume that a domestic firm is not competitive in price and quality with foreign firms, but that competition by high tariffs protects it. What are the effects of the protection on the firm in the short term? How might it affect the firm's competitiveness in the long term?
3. President Reagan later rejected recommendations to place quotas on footwear because of estimates it would have cost American consumers $3 billion in increased tariffs, and because there was no indication it would have helped American manufacturers return to competitiveness. How important do you think cost is to a president's decision?
4. Although the administrative process is handled through a bipartisan, independent commission (the ITC), in what way might the process still be very political?
5. What do you think the role would be of the president's economic advisors in an unfair imports case?

Trade Adjustment Assistance

Workers who become unemployed as a result of increased imports of foreign goods may be entitled to federal financial assistance, known as **trade adjustment assistance (TAA)**. The Trade Adjustment Assistance Program was originally created by President Kennedy in 1962, and modified by the *Trade Act of 1974*. It is administered by the U.S. Department of Labor. A group of three or more workers, an employer, a state workforce or jobs agency, or a labor union representing affected workers may file petitions for TAA with the department.

For workers to be eligible to apply for TAA, the Secretary of Labor must determine (1) that a significant number or group of workers in a firm have become, or are threatened to become, partially or totally separated from their employment; (2) that the firm's sales or production have decreased absolutely; and (3) that increased imports of like or directly competitive products contributed importantly to the separation and to a decline in the firm's sales or production. Once a group of workers is certified as eligible, the workers in that group apply individually for benefits with their local state job agency office. Assistance to workers, in the form of cash benefits, tax credits, or vouchers, is available to cover the expenses of job search, retraining and relocation, and health insurance coverage. Under certain conditions, and in lieu of other benefits, workers age 50 or older who find reemployment at lower wage rates have the option to receive wage subsidies (a portion of the difference between what they were earning and what they can earn now).

The industries with the largest concentration of certified workers during the last several decades have been automotive equipment, textiles and apparel, furniture, leather and leather products, industrial machinery, and electrical and electronic equipment. A special TAA program exists for farmers, and it is administered by the U.S. Department of Agriculture. TAA programs are amended frequently and every few years Congress renews their authority.

Trade Assistance to Firms. Trade adjustment assistance is not just available for U.S. workers but also for U.S. companies. The U.S. Department of Commerce administers it. It is intended to help U.S. companies become more competitive. Companies are eligible if increased imports contributed importantly to a decline in sales and to the unemployment of a significant number of its workers. Twelve assistance centers nationwide help certified companies develop business recovery plans over a two-year period. The plans include such things as improving production capabilities, marketing, computer systems and Website development, and standards certification. To receive financial assistance, the certified firm must contribute its own matching funds.

UNFAIR IMPORT LAWS: DUMPING

Dumping is the selling of goods in a foreign country for less than the price charged for "like" or comparable products in the exporter's or producer's home market. Dumping is an **unfair trade practice** in the form of export price discrimination. It causes injury to domestic producers through artificially low prices against which they cannot compete at a profitable level. Dumping has been a fairly persistent problem in international trade and it is not uncommon. The original GATT agreement has prohibited dumping since 1947.

Reasons for Price Cutting in a Foreign Market

The theories that explain the economics of dumping, its causes and effects, fill entire volumes, and any detailed discussion is certainly beyond the scope of this book. Exporting goods to a foreign market at an unfairly low price might be done by a firm wanting to sell its excess production capacity at bargain prices to cover fixed costs and to avoid cyclical worker layoffs. As long as dumped products are not sold in the exporter's own country, causing price suppression in its home market, then it has everything to gain and little to lose. In some cases, an exporter may simply not be able to command the same prices for their goods in a foreign market as at home, such as where they do not have the same market power, brand recognition, or brand loyalty. So there may be some perfectly valid business reasons for dumping. Nevertheless, dumping is recognized as a predatory practice.

At first glance, one might wonder what is wrong with consumers in one country being able to buy the products of another nation cheaply. As long as the products remain available at reasonable market prices there may be little harm to consumers at first. But selling at an unfairly low price in a foreign market is often intended to drive local firms out of business so that the foreign dumping firms will ultimately be free to raise their prices to monopoly levels.

Of course, while the explanations for dumping are of interest to economists, the reasons why an individual firm sells its products at an unfairly low price in a foreign country are irrelevant in determining whether the dumping was unlawful. Thus we leave that part of the discussion to our economist friends.

Remedies for Dumping. The usual remedy for dumping is for the importing country to place **antidumping duties** on the dumped products. Antidumping duties are special import tariffs assessed in addition to normal tariffs imposed for the purpose of offsetting the unfairly low price of dumped goods. They are not criminal fines, and they are not "damages" that are awarded to an injured firm.

Virtually all developed nations have antidumping statutes that define dumping and that set out the administrative procedures and remedies available in dumping cases. The United States has had antidumping laws since 1916. Current U.S. antidumping laws are found in Title 19 of the U.S. Code. China enacted its antidumping law in 1997. In the EU, the antidumping laws are imposed only on trade between a member country and a nonmember country. Japan has similar laws, although they are not widely enforced. Developing countries, such as Mexico, Brazil, Argentina, India, and Korea, also have antidumping codes. It is important to point out that many economists disagree with the use of antidumping duties. Some claim that the laws injure consumers by "fixing prices" at high levels. Once the prices rise for imported products, domestic manufacturers follow suit by raising their prices as well.

The WTO Antidumping Agreement

The laws of WTO member countries must meet the requirements of GATT 1994 Article VI and the 1994 *WTO Antidumping Agreement.* The agreement permits the imposition of antidumping duties only when dumping threatens or causes "material injury" to a domestic industry producing "like products," and only after an investigation determines the amount of the dumping and the extent of material injury.

U.S. Antidumping Investigations

In the United States, antidumping investigations involve two different federal agencies: the United States International Trade Administration (ITA), which determines whether dumping occurred and the extent of it; and the International Trade Commission (ITC), which determines whether the dumping has caused, or threatens to cause, a material injury to U.S. producers of like products. Petitions for an investigation may be filed by producers of like or competing domestic products, including manufacturers, sellers, or labor groups. By law, U.S. producers or workers who account for at least 25 percent of the total production of the domestic like products must support the petition. The ITA can poll industry and labor to see if that support exists. Most WTO member countries have a similar administrative process, patterned after the WTO requirements. For example, in Canada, Canada Border Services Agency and the Canadian International Trade Tribunal handle unfair trade law investigations.

Calculating the Dumping Margin. The U.S. statute provides that antidumping duties may be imposed on imported merchandise if that merchandise is sold or is likely to be sold in the United States at *less than its fair value.* Contrary to popular belief, dumping does not require that the foreign products be sold for less than the cost to produce them, although a sale at below cost is certainly "less than its fair value." A sale at "less than fair value" is one in which the "export price" of merchandise sold in the United States is less than the "normal value" of like or similar merchandise sold for consumption in the exporter's or producer's country home market. This is also known as the **dumping margin**. Antidumping duties may be assessed on the merchandise in an amount equal to the dumping margin. If the dumping margin is less than 2 percent of the value of the products no duties are imposed.

Calculating the Export Price in the United States. Let's examine some of the terminology a little closer. The **export price** is the price at which a product is sold to an unaffiliated or unrelated buyer in the importing country, exclusive of shipping and insurance charges. When a price charged for a product does not reflect an "arm's-length" (freely negotiated) transaction, a **constructed export price** must be used. A constructed export price is also necessary when the exporter and importer are "affiliated," or related companies, or when the product's price is "hidden" in some other type of compensatory arrangement (such as barter). In these cases, the constructed export price is deemed to be the price at which the imported product is first resold in its original condition to an independent buyer. For this purpose, an "affiliated buyer" is a U.S. company or corporation in which the foreign seller owns a 5 percent equity ownership or more, or one over which the foreign seller is in a position to control, manage, or direct. This may also include companies where the seller has a degree of control as a result of having an exclusive supplier arrangement or where the same individuals sit on the boards of directors of both companies.

Calculating the Normal Value of Like Products in the Exporting or Producing Country. **Normal value** is the price at which foreign like products are sold for consumption in the exporting or producing country in usual commercial quantities and in the ordinary course of business, and at the same level of trade—in other words, comparing wholesale sale to wholesale sale, or retail to retail—as the dumped product. If there are insufficient quantities of like products sold in the exporting country (if sales of the product in the exporting country are less than 5 percent of the total sales volume of the dumped product in the U.S. market) the dumping margin is calculated by comparing the dumped product to the price of a like product exported to a third country. If there are insufficient third country sales, then a constructed value is used instead. **Constructed value** is the price of the dumped product compared to the cost of producing the product in the exporting country plus a reasonable amount for selling, packaging, administration, and other costs and for a reasonable profit. The amount of profit to be added into constructed value is based on either (1) actual profits in the transaction, (2) average profits on sales of the same product made by other producers, or (3) profits made on different products sold by the same producer.

The ITA, like agencies in other countries, sends questionnaires to foreign exporters requesting cost and pricing data based on generally accepted accounting principles. The agencies rely on the responses in determining the dumping margin.

What Is a "Like Product"? One common problem in comparing the price of the dumped product to "like products" sold for normal value in the exporting country is defining the term **like product**. First, many antidumping actions are taken against an entire category, kind, or classification of merchandise, not just on a single item or product. The ITA must determine which products to include in its price analysis and which to exclude. Also keep in mind that in many cases the products sold by a manufacturer or producer in one country are not like those sold in foreign countries. For example, the range of qualities, specifications, or dimensions may differ. The products may be packaged differently or in different quantities and bulk packs. For example, in the home market bed sheets may be packaged separately, with customers purchasing the flat sheet, fitted sheet, and pillowcases individually. However, in the export market they may be packaged and sold as "sheet sets." Adjustments must be made to make "like" comparisons.

During an investigation, the ITA looks at many factors, including whether the products are identical in physical characteristics, whether the same or different firms produce them, whether they are made of the same or similar component materials, whether they are of equal commercial value, and whether their use is for the same purpose. The following case, *Pesquera Mares Australes Ltda. v. United States*, illustrates a typical problem that might face the ITA in determining a "like product." It is actually one of the more readable opinions in this area of the law, as most cases deal with far more complex industrial product classifications than salmon. As you read, consider how the agency made its decision and the deference given to that decision by the Court of Appeals for the Federal Circuit.

Pesquera Mares Australes Ltda. v. United States

266 F.3d 1372 (2001) United States Court of Appeals (Fed. Cir.)

BACKGROUND AND FACTS

Pesquera Mares Australes, a Chilean salmon exporter, was accused of dumping salmon in the U.S. market at less than fair value. An antidumping petition was filed in 1997 by the Coalition for Fair Atlantic Salmon Trade. The U.S. Department of Commerce (ITA) conducted an investigation to compare the price of the salmon sold in the United States with its "normal value" in the home market. Finding no sales of Mares Australes' salmon in Chile during that time, ITA based normal value on the price of the salmon sold in Japan. However, while the salmon sold in the United States was of the "premium" grade, the salmon sold in Japan was of both "premium" and "super-premium" grades. ITA nevertheless found that the salmon sold in Japan and in the United States had "identical physical characteristics" and thus were "like products" as defined by the U.S. statute. ITA then included the price of the super-premium Japanese grade in its determination of normal value. This resulted in the ITA finding a larger dumping margin and imposing higher antidumping duties. The duties were affirmed by the Court of International Trade, and Mares Australes appealed to the Court of Appeals for the Federal Circuit.

DYK, CIRCUIT JUDGE * * *

[T]he antidumping statute specifically defines "foreign like product," as ... merchandise *which is identical in physical characteristics* ... . In this case ITA ... sought to identify salmon sold by Mares Australes to Japan that was "identical in physical characteristics" to salmon exported by that company to the United States. It is ITA's interpretation of the phrase "identical in physical characteristics" that is at issue. * * *

Mares Australes argued that the super-premium salmon it sold to Japan could not be considered "identical in physical characteristics" to the premium grade salmon it sold to the United States. As evidence of this distinction, the company stressed ... that certain physical defects (such as external lacerations to the salmon) were present in premium but not super-premium salmon; that super-premium salmon enjoyed a darker, redder color than premium salmon; and that its customers in Japan, recognizing these physical and color distinctions, paid higher prices for premium-grade salmon ... . But ITA noted that "the record also contains evidence that the distinctions between the two grades were, in practice, nominal ... ."

As support for its conclusion that super-premium was not a commercially recognized separate grade, ITA also pointed to commercial practice in countries (other than Chile) exporting to Japan, whose salmon industries did "not recognize any grade higher than 'superior.'" [In its final determination] ITA stated: "... The Norwegian, Scottish, Canadian, and U.S. salmon industries do not recognize any grade higher than "superior." The "superior" grade is consistent with the premium grade and permits minor defects ... . Nonetheless, all salmon in this range are graded equally, and are comparable products in the market place. *[Notice of Final Determination of Sales at Less Than Fair Value: Fresh Atlantic Salmon From Chile,* 63 Fed. Reg. 31411 (June 9, 1998)]. ITA thus determined that "salmon reported as super-premium are in fact of premium grade," and accordingly compared the sales of both super-premium and premium salmon to Japan to corresponding sales of premium salmon only in the United States. The practical consequences of ITA's decision to classify the two grades of salmon as "identical in physical characteristics" was to increase Mares Australes' dumping margin from the *de minimis* level (1.21%) to a final dumping margin of 2.23%. * * *

This case requires us to interpret the phrase "identical in physical characteristics" as that phrase appears in the definition of "foreign like product" [U.S. Code]. In order to ascertain the established meaning of a term such as the word "identical," it is appropriate to

continues

continued

consult dictionaries. There are a variety of dictionary definitions of "identical." Some require exact identity. See, *e.g., American Heritage Dictionary, 896* (3d ed. 1996) (defining "identical" as "being the same" and "exactly equal and alike")... . Others allow "minor differences" so long as the items are "essentially the same." See, *e.g., The American Heritage Dictionary,* 639 (2d ed. 1991)... . We find nothing in the statute to suggest that Congress intended to depart from the ordinary definition of the term "identical." But that leaves the question of which of the two common usages was intended by Congress: *exactly the same* or *the same with minor differences?*

We conclude that Congress intended the latter usage... . As Coalition for Fair Atlantic Salmon Trade points out, Congress could hardly have intended to require ITA in each and every instance to compare *all* the physical characteristics of the goods. It might not be possible, for example, with certain types of merchandise to "account for every conceivable physical characteristic" of that merchandise.

Despite our conclusion that Congress intended to allow identical merchandise to have minor differences, the phrase "identical in physical characteristics" [as used in the U.S. statute] remains ambiguous, and, as we learn from *Chevron U.S.A., Inc. v. Natural Resources Defense Council, Inc.,* 467 U.S. 837, 104 S.Ct. 2778 (1984), ITA has discretion to define the term.

The ITA has concluded that merchandise should be considered to be identical despite the existence of minor differences in physical characteristics, if those minor differences are not commercially significant. We conclude that this standard adopted by ITA constitutes "a permissible construction of the statute." We conclude that this finding is supported by substantial evidence, and that it has been adequately explained. * * *

Decision. The Chilean salmon exporter violated the antidumping laws of the United States by selling foreign salmon in the U.S. at less than fair value. The super-premium salmon sold by Mares Australes in Japan was similar enough to the premium grade sold in the United States to be considered a "foreign like product," the price of which should be included in determining the normal value for purposes of calculating the dumping margin.

Case Questions

1. What is the purpose of comparing the price of salmon sold in the United States to that sold in Japan?
2. Why did Mares Australes not want the ITA to compare the price of salmon sold in the United States to the price of the "super-premium" salmon it sold in Japan?
3. Explain the problem confronting the ITA in determining "foreign like product." How did the court define that term?

Adjustments to Normal Value and Export Price. A fair comparison often requires adjustments to either the export price or to normal value to compensate for differences in the sale—comparing "apples to apples." For example, if the German manufacturer of ball bearings must pay a sales commission to sales representatives for ball bearings sold in Germany but does not pay commissions on sales to the United States, then the difference must be accounted for in the calculation. Adjustments can be made for differences in the terms and conditions of sale, the cost of ocean containers and packaging, freight and warehouse expenses, customs brokerage fees, insurance on the goods in transit, and other expenses. Adjustments should also be made for differences in taxes, advertising and sales commission expenses, quantity discounts, and other factors that might legitimately cause the export price to be lower than normal value. The federal law spells out the rules for making adjustments in U.S. dumping cases.

The Material Injury Requirement

Antidumping duties only apply where the ITC finds that an industry in the United States is materially injured, or threatened with material injury, by reason of dumped imports. **Material injury** is injury that is "not inconsequential, immaterial, or unimportant." In determining material injury, the ITC must consider all relevant economic factors, including (1) the volume of the dumped imports (Have dumped imports increased significantly?); (2) the effect of the imports on prices in the domestic market for like products (Have prices been undercut significantly? Have prices been depressed? Are domestic firms unable to raise prices to cover increased costs?); and (3) the impact on domestic industry, including data on sales, profits, market share, productivity, wages, unemployment, growing inventories, and other measures of economic health. A finding of material injury must be reviewed every five years if the antidumping order is still in effect at that time. The "material injury" standard under the antidumping law is less than the "serious injury" standard in safeguard actions (studied earlier). Later in the chapter, we will see that another U.S. unfair trade law (on countervailing duties) will also rely on the same definition of material injury.

WTO Dispute Settlement in Dumping Cases

Prior to the WTO agreement in 1994, the original GATT 1947 had been criticized for its inability to control dumping or resolve dumping disputes. The 1994 agreement created the WTO Committee on Antidumping Practices, which is responsible for assisting countries in implementing the agreement.

Dumping disputes may be taken to the WTO Dispute Settlement Body for negotiation or resolution. (See Chapter Nine for a discussion of the procedures for WTO dispute settlement.) The parties to dispute settlement are the nations involved and not the sellers and buyers of the dumped products—although individual companies often have considerable influence in initiating dumping investigations.

The WTO panel may review a final antidumping order of an administrative agency in the importing country to determine if it is consistent with the *WTO Antidumping Agreement*. The panel can look to see if the agency misinterpreted the provisions of the agreement or whether it properly followed all administrative procedures in an unbiased and objective manner. If the panel finds that an antidumping order violates WTO rules, the panel can recommend measures to be taken against the importing country.

The scope of review of an agency's investigation and antidumping order is limited. A dispute panel cannot reconsider issues of fact determined during a dumping investigation or overturn an interpretation of the agreement made by the investigating agency. Thus, in reviewing U.S. dumping cases, a panel must accept the facts as found by the ITA and ITC in their investigations. This standard of review is similar to the process found in the United States in which courts of law review decisions of administrative agencies. Of course, as discussed in earlier chapters, an adverse ruling by the WTO Dispute Settlement Body does not have legal effect on U.S. agencies or courts, but does permit other WTO countries to impose retaliatory sanctions.

Dumping and Nonmarket Economy Countries

The United States has long had special rules for antidumping investigations involving goods it imports from **nonmarket economy countries** (NMEs). These are countries whose political and economic systems are rooted in the socialist principles of a state-controlled economy. The number of NME countries has declined greatly since the late 1980s due to the fall of communist governments and the integration of others into the world economy. Some are still in a stage of transition. By agreement, the United States will presume that China is an NME country until 2016, and Vietnam until 2018. In determining if goods are being imported from an NME country, U.S. statutes give the ITA considerable discretion, but require the agency to look at the following factors: (1) the extent to which the currency of the foreign country is convertible into the currency of other countries, (2) the extent to which wage rates in the foreign country are determined by free bargaining between labor and management, (3) the extent to which joint ventures or other investments by firms of other foreign countries are permitted in the foreign country, (4) the extent of government ownership or control of the means of production, and (5) the extent of government control over the allocation of resources and over the price and output decisions of enterprises.

In antidumping cases involving NMEs, it is difficult or even impossible to determine the "normal value" of merchandise sold in a NME because of likely government manipulation of costs and prices. Instead, the ITA looks at the value of the **factors of production** that would be incurred if the subject merchandise had been produced in a **surrogate market economy country** that is at a level of economic development comparable to that of the NME country and that is a significant producer of comparable merchandise. The factors of production include raw materials used, hours of labor required, energy and utilities consumed, capital costs and depreciation, packaging, other general expenses, plus a reasonable amount for profit. The ITA presumes that the normal value established by the factors of production method is applicable to all firms in that industry, unless in an antidumping duty action a firm can prove that it is a "market-oriented exporter."

Market-Oriented Exporters. In countries with a history of socialist or communist control, the transition to a market economy does not occur overnight. Rather, it might take place in steps, with the government freeing certain market sectors to competition or by selling state-owned companies through privatization. So, even if the exporting country has an NME, the ITA may look to see if the particular firm producing the dumped products in that country is a market-oriented exporter. A **market-oriented exporter** is an exporting firm in an NME country that is not under government control and that does business on competitive terms. Generally, management negotiates export contracts and prices autonomously, and the government does not share in the profits of the firm. Some industries in an NME country can also be considered market-oriented industries. A **market-oriented industry** is one in which resources (materials, energy, etc.) and labor costs are procured at free-market prices, where there is little government involvement in controlling production and capacity decisions, where prices are set by markets, and where the producers are mostly privately owned. Very few industries in NME countries have ever been given market-oriented industry status in U.S. antidumping actions.

In the following case, *Bulk Aspirin from the People's Republic of China*, a French-owned chemical giant with a plant in the United States petitioned the government for antidumping duties against its Chinese competitors. As you read the case, and especially the comment that follows, consider the ironies in the case, the impact of the antidumping laws on workers and consumers, and the place of dumping laws in the future of the global economy.

Bulk Aspirin from the People's Republic of China

Notice of Preliminary Determination of Sales at Less Than Fair Value
65 Fed. Reg. 116 (2000) International Trade Administration

BACKGROUND AND FACTS

Rhodia Pharma Solutions is one of the world's leading manufacturers of specialty chemicals, including acetylsalicylic acid (bulk aspirin). With corporate headquarters in France, it has about 25,000 employees in offices and manufacturing plants in the United States and throughout the world. In 1999, Rhodia filed a petition with the Department of Commerce (ITA) alleging that imports from the People's Republic of China (PRC) were being dumped in the United States for less than fair value. Based on industry information, Rhodia believed that their customers were paying less than half of Rhodia's price for the same product. No other firms joined the petition, and Rhodia was apparently the only producer of aspirin in the United States at the time. Rhodia's petition identified several potential Chinese exporters of bulk aspirin. Only two Chinese firms, Jilin and Shandong, responded to the petition. The ITA sent questionnaires to Jilin and Shandong and to the Chinese government, asking that it be forwarded to other Chinese producers. Jilin and Shandong responded with the price and market information requested by the ITA. No other Chinese firms responded. After an investigation, the agency issued this preliminary determination.

PRELIMINARY DETERMINATION

The ITA has treated the PRC as a nonmarket economy ("NME") country in all past antidumping investigations. A designation as an NME remains in effect until it is revoked by the ITA.

Separate Rates: Both Jilin and Shandong have requested separate company-specific rates. These companies have stated that they are privately owned companies with no element of government ownership or control. To establish whether a firm is sufficiently independent from government control to be entitled to a separate rate, the ITA analyzes each exporting entity. Under the separate rates criteria, the ITA assigns separate rates in NME cases only if the respondents can demonstrate the absence of both *de jure* and *de facto* governmental control over export activities.

Absence of *De Jure* Control: The respondents have placed on the record a number of documents to demonstrate absence of *de jure* government control, including the *Foreign Trade Law of the People's Republic of China* and the *Company Law of the People's Republic of China.* The ITA has analyzed these laws in prior cases and found that they establish an absence of *de jure* control ... over export pricing and marketing decisions of firms.

Absence of *De Facto* Control: Shandong and Jilin have each asserted the following: (1) they establish their own export prices; (2) they negotiate contracts without guidance from any governmental entities or organizations; (3) they make their own personnel decisions; and

continues

continued

(4) they retain the proceeds of their export sales and use profits according to their business needs without any restrictions. Additionally, these two respondents have stated that they do not coordinate or consult with other exporters regarding their pricing. This information supports a preliminary finding that there is no *de facto* governmental control of the export functions of these companies. Consequently, we preliminarily determine that both responding exporters have met the criteria for the application of separate rates.

Use of Facts Available: The PRC-Wide Rate: U.S. import statistics indicate that the total quantity of U.S. imports of aspirin from the PRC is greater than that reported by Jilin and Shandong ... . Accordingly, we are applying a single antidumping deposit rate—the PRC-wide rate-to all exporters [other than Jilin and Shandong] based on our presumption that the export activities of the companies that failed to respond to the ITA's questionnaire are controlled by the PRC government. The PRC-wide antidumping rate is based on adverse facts available. The exporters that decided not to respond in any form to the ITA's questionnaire failed to act to the best of their ability in this investigation. Thus—we are assigning the highest margin in the petition, 144.02 percent, which is higher than any of the calculated margins. * * *

Normal Value in the Surrogate Country: [The Act] requires the ITA to value the NME producer's factors of production, to the extent possible, in one or more market economy countries that: (1) Are at a level of economic development comparable to that of the NME, and (2) are significant producers of comparable merchandise. The ITA has determined that India, Pakistan, Sri Lanka, Egypt, Indonesia, and the Philippines are countries comparable to the PRC in terms of overall economic development. We have further determined that India is a significant producer of comparable merchandise. Accordingly, we have calculated NV using mainly Indian values, and in some cases U.S. export values, for the PRC producers' factors of production. * * *

Factors of Production: [W]e calculated NV based on factors of production reported by the companies in the PRC which produced aspirin and sold aspirin to the United States. Our NV calculation included amounts for materials, labor, energy, overhead, SG&A, and profit. To calculate NV, the reported unit factor quantities were multiplied by publicly available Indian and U.S. export price values.

Decision. Based on the calculations of normal value, two producers, Jilin and Shandong, were able to show that their export pricing was not under government control and received separate antidumping duty rates based on their individual dumping margins (which ranged from 4 to 42 percent). Bulk aspirin imports from all other Chinese exporters received the PRC-wide rate of 144 percent.

Comment. Shortly thereafter, the Court of International Trade reversed parts of the ITA's methodology of obtaining surrogate values for certain factors of production because it was not based on substantial evidence. *Rhodia v. U.S.* 240 F. Supp. 2d 1247 (CIT 2002). The ITA then changed its methods of calculating overhead and labor, with the result that Jilin and Shandong's antidumping duties were cut to zero, although the PRC-wide rate was not affected. In 2003, a Rhodia representative stated in testimony before the U.S. House of Representatives that at first the new duties had helped it regain customers and become profitable again, but when ITA changed its methodology and the antidumping duties disappeared, so did its customers. Rhodia's business in the United States had been devastated. And with that, Rhodia closed the last remaining aspirin plant in America and moved it to—you guessed it—China. A few years later another Chinese importer of bulk aspirin, Bimeda, petitioned for a review of the antidumping duty order, asking that the antidumping duties be removed. Its logic was that since Rhodia had closed its U.S. plant, and there was no longer any aspirin produced in the U.S., that there was no longer any "like domestic product"—and therefore antidumping duties were now inapplicable. The ITA agreed. (69 FR 35286; 69 FR 77726).

Case Questions

1. What are the special problems of determining the dumping margin of goods exported from an NME country?
2. What is the difference between *de jure* and *de facto* control by the government over Jilin and Shandong? Did either exist?
3. Why is the ITA using a surrogate country, India, to determine normal value?
4. What are the functions of U.S. antidumping duty laws? Explain.
5. While many U.S. jobs were unfortunately at stake in the proceedings, do you not see irony in the fact that U.S. laws were used to protect a French multinational (Rhodia) from low-cost dumping by a Chinese company, all while maintaining higher aspirin prices for American consumers?

UNFAIR IMPORT LAWS: SUBSIDIES

There are government programs in all countries that grant benefits to local industries and firms to achieve some specific social or economic objective or for the greater social good. They might be tax credits to encourage alternative energy technologies or conservation, grants to the defense industry to aid in the development of new technologies or weapons, or incentives to rebuild old factories. Some subsidies are used to protect critical domestic industries, such as steel, aircraft, or agriculture. For instance, a government that enacts a tax credit for homeowners who install insulation, or energy efficient windows, is subsidizing the purchase and installation of those products to achieve environmental and economic objectives, whether those objectives are conservation or just a boost for makers of insulation and windows.

All nations grant subsidies to virtually all segments of their economies, including to manufacturing and agriculture (recall our discussion of agricultural subsidies in Chapter Ten). The EU, the United States, and Japan each spend tens of billions of dollars annually on agricultural subsidies alone, including direct payments to farmers. These programs create a problem in international trade relations when they are in the form of subsidies that give an unfair cost/price advantage in foreign export markets.

Subsidies have long been recognized as damaging to the international economy. Subsidized industries can sell their products in foreign markets at prices lower than would otherwise be possible, which distorts trade patterns based on comparative advantage and gives an unfair competitive advantage to subsidized industries. Subsidies might also encourage firms to embark on commercial ventures that, once the subsidy ends, may prove unprofitable or commercially disastrous. A good example is the Concorde supersonic aircraft, which could fly from Europe to the United States in less than half the time of a regular jet. The aircraft's development by a consortium of European companies was spurred not by demand, but by a host of EU subsidies. In commercial use, the plane turned out to be highly unprofitable. The last Concorde was taken out of service in 2003. Without the subsidy, the plane would likely have proved too costly to have merited production in the first place.

Government subsidies for a program as large and well known as the Concorde, of course, are a matter of public information; however, most subsidies involve industries and products that are smaller, less known, and less glamorous. Just a quick glance at recent subsidy cases shows products such as crepe paper, electric blankets, narrow woven ribbons, furniture, or endless varieties of food, chemicals, or steel products. The fact that a subsidy might exist on an imported product is usually discovered by a competing firm that is affected by the unreasonable or unexplainable low prices foreign competitors offer to customers. Not surprisingly, knowledge of pricing, as well as rumors about government aid programs that affect pricing, fly quickly through most industries. If a subsidy (or dumping, for that matter) is expected, it is usually the affected industry that brings this to the attention of the appropriate government agency in its country.

WTO Agreement on Subsidies and Countervailing Measures

Subsidies have been regulated by the GATT agreement since 1947. Today, subsidies are governed by the original 1947 GATT agreement, by the 1994 WTO *Agreement on Subsidies and Countervailing Measures* (*SCM Agreement*), and by national laws and regulations. The *SCM Agreement* defines subsidies, clarifies those subsidies that are permissible and those that are not, and sets out the procedures for resolving subsidy disputes.

Definition of a Subsidy. A **subsidy** is defined in the *SCM Agreement* as a financial contribution, including any form of income or price support, made by a government that confers a benefit on a specific domestic enterprise or industry. Examples of financial contributions include:

1. Directly transferring money or grants, making loans at less than prevailing commercial interest rates, or providing loan guarantees that allow the company to receive loans at rates more favorable than non-guaranteed commercial loan rates.
2. Not collecting revenue or taxes otherwise due or providing tax credits.
3. Providing investment capital in a private company if the investment decision is inconsistent with the usual practices of private investors.

4. Furnishing goods or services (including the supply of energy or natural resources) other than general infrastructure.
5. Purchasing goods from firms at a higher price than would be paid in the marketplace.

Two key concepts to remember: there must be a *financial contribution* from government that *confers a benefit.* Many WTO panels have addressed the meaning of these terms. Generally, the financial contribution must be made by government on terms that are more favorable than would otherwise be available in the marketplace, and the benefit must make the recipient better off than it otherwise would have been.

WTO Rules Apply to "Specific Subsidies." The *SCM Agreement* only applies to subsidies considered to be "specific." Nonspecific subsidies are not prohibited. A **specific subsidy** is one given to a select company or limited number of companies, to a select industry or group of industries, or to firms in a select geographical region of a country. A subsidy is usually specific *unless* eligibility is automatic upon the meeting of certain neutral, objective criteria. For instance, suppose that tax authorities allow all corporate taxpayers to deduct $50,000 of the cost of new machinery as an ordinary operating expense in the year of purchase instead of the $25,000 that had been allowed. Because the criteria for qualifying for the tax reduction is objective and neutral, made generally available to all taxpayers, and does not favor one company or one industry over another, it is not specific and does not fall under WTO rules. Of course, government programs that benefit industry are common. So, clearly, not all specific subsidies are impermissible. For a specific subsidy to violate WTO rules, it must either be a prohibited subsidy or an actionable subsidy.

Prohibited Subsidies. The *SCM Agreement* provides for two types of subsidies: prohibited subsidies and actionable subsidies. **Prohibited subsidies** are impermissible per se and banned under all conditions. Their harmful effects are presumed; no proof is necessary to show that they cause any adverse effects to a foreign country or foreign competitor because they so clearly distort international competition between firms. The two types of prohibited subsidies are export subsidies and import substitution subsidies. An **export subsidy** is made available to domestic firms upon the export of their products or made *contingent on export performance.* Examples of export subsidies might include a grant or tax credit to cover the cost of transportation of goods from a manufacturing site to an ocean port for shipment to foreign customers, a tax credit for energy consumption for use in manufacturing goods for export, or the special tax treatment of income earned on export sales. Another prohibited export subsidy is a loan from a government agency on terms not available from commercial banks, and which is either conditional on the export of goods to a foreign customer or repayable only out of the proceeds of a contract of sale with a foreign customer. All export subsidies are deemed to be specific, as discussed in the last section, because they target a specific group of recipients—exporters. An **import substitution subsidy** is a government subsidy whose payment is contingent on its recipient using or purchasing domestically made goods over imported goods.

U.S.-Brazil Dispute over Cotton Subsidies. Both export subsidies and import substitution subsidies were at issue in a dispute over U.S. subsidies to the U.S. producers and exporters of upland cotton. The United States is the world's second largest producer of cotton (after China) and the largest exporter (China is a net importer), with almost 60 percent of production exported. The United States spends billions of dollars on cash payments, loans, and guarantees to boost U.S. cotton exports, lower the price of U.S. cotton on world markets, and raise farmer income. U.S. cotton subsidies have been the subject of a long-running trade dispute.

At issue was a U.S. program that provided loan ("export credit") guarantees to private lenders that financed shipments of cotton to countries where credit and financing were not available. In a "special competitiveness program," the United States actually paid American textile mills and exporters to purchase U.S. cotton instead of lower priced foreign cotton. Brazil (joined by the EU and 14 other cotton exporting countries) requested dispute resolution at the WTO claiming that the U.S. programs constituted prohibited subsidies under the *SCM Agreement.* (Brazil also claimed violations of the *WTO Agreement on Agriculture,* discussed in the last chapter.) In *WTO Report on the United States—Subsidies on Upland Cotton,* WT/DS267/AB/R (2005) it was held that the export credit guarantees were a prohibited export subsidy, and that the payments to mills and exporters constituted a prohibited import substitution subsidy, both in violation of the *SCM Agreement.* Brazil was then authorized to take retaliatory measures. Brazil announced that it would impose a tariff of 100 percent on 102 American-made products valued at $830 million and impose restrictions on U.S. pharmaceuticals, biotech products, films, and other intellectual property entering Brazil. Negotiations in 2010, just days before Brazil's tariffs were set to begin, temporarily ended the dispute much to the relief of U.S. exporters. The payments to U.S. mills were ended, discussions were still ongoing about modifications to the loan guarantee program, and the United States agreed to pay Brazil $147 million per year until a permanent solution to the cotton subsidy problem could be reached.

Actionable Subsidies. **Actionable subsidies**, also known as **adverse effects subsidies**, are subsidies that are not automatically prohibited, but may still be "actionable" because of their harmful effect. An actionable subsidy is one that: (1) causes material injury to the domestic producers of a like product in the complaining country, (2) violates a trade agreement, or (3) causes "serious prejudice" to the interests of the complaining country. An actionable subsidy exists if the subsidy exceeds 5 percent of a product's value, if the subsidy covers a firm's operating losses, or if the government forgives a debt owed to it. Actionable subsidies must also have been the cause of significant price undercutting, price suppression, or lost sales in the same market.

Upstream Subsidies. An **upstream subsidy** is a subsidy bestowed on raw materials or component parts ("inputs") for use in an exported product. For instance, a subsidy on coal might also be considered a subsidy on steel made in furnaces that burn that coal. A subsidy on European wheat might be considered a subsidy on Italian pasta made from that wheat. Similarly, a subsidy on live swine might be considered an upstream subsidy of processed pork exports. Upstream subsidies are subject to countervailing duties if the input product is made available at a below-market price and has a significant effect on lowering the cost of manufacturing the final product.

WTO Subsidy Dispute Settlement

Subsidy disputes can be resolved either nation to nation, through the dispute settlement procedures of the WTO, or, as we will see in the next section, through administrative remedies available to injured domestic industries in the country where the subsidized products were imported.

Nations wanting to challenge another nation's subsidization of a domestic industry may seek dispute settlement at the WTO. Dispute settlement procedures in subsidy cases are similar to those used generally at the WTO, as discussed in Chapter Nine. WTO dispute settlement begins with the complaining country's formal request for "consultations," and if unresolved can proceed to an investigation by a panel, a possible appeal to the Appellate Body, and consideration of their recommendations by the Dispute Settlement Body (DSB). If a subsidy is found, the DSB must recommend its removal or it may authorize the complaining country to take **countermeasures**, such as tariff increases in an amount needed to offset the subsidy. A WTO arbitration panel determines the amount of the countermeasures.

Countervailing Duty Actions

The second method for dealing with a subsidy is through an administrative proceeding in the country to which the subsidized goods are imported. All trading nations have some administrative process for addressing subsidized imports. These are commonly called countervailing duty actions. A **countervailing duty** (CVD) is a special tariff, levied in addition to the normal tariff, imposed on imports of subsidized goods for the purpose of offsetting the subsidy. The result is that the cost of imported goods is brought back to where it would have been had the goods not been subsidized. The use of a CVD discourages subsidization, eliminates market distortions and the harmful effects of the subsidy, and protects domestic industry in the importing country from injury. A CVD action may be brought at the same time as the WTO dispute settlement action. However, only one form of relief is available: either the CVD or a countermeasure approved by the WTO. All CVD laws must comply with the *SCM Agreement.*

Countervailing Duty Actions in the United States. U.S. CVD laws date as far back as the late 1800s. The laws changed little over the years until recent decades, when they were revised to comply with the requirements of the *SCM Agreement.* CVD actions are administrative, similar to that used in antidumping duty cases, described earlier. In the United States, an action is begun by the filing of a petition with both the ITA and the ITC. The ITA may initiate an action on its own, but that does not occur frequently. If the ITA finds that a subsidy exists, and the ITC finds that it caused *material injury* to domestic producers, then a countervailing order may be awarded. (The standard for material injury is the same as for antidumping duty actions, described earlier.) It generally takes from 12 to 18 months for an order to be issued.

Subsidies and Nonmarket Economy Countries

For many years, the CVD law did not apply to imports from nonmarket economy countries, including China and Vietnam. The Department of Commerce, which manages the ITA, did not believe that Congress had intended to apply the CVD law to government-controlled, centrally planned economy countries, where many producers and export firms are little more than government agencies acting as private firms. After all, it could be argued that "everything and anything" might be subsidized, so a real determination of a subsidy was impossible. The U.S. courts agreed. Only the antidumping law was used against imports from nonmarket countries where the legal requirements under that statute were met. However, by the mid-2000s, China's economy had undergone many structural changes. There was increasing private ownership of Chinese firms (including American foreign investment) and a loosening of state control over many industries. In addition, there was a growing U.S. trade imbalance with China, and increased demands from members of Congress to stop Chinese subsidies. In 2007 the ITA applied the CVD law to China for the first time, in a case involving imports of Chinese coated paper used in quality, full-color publications. From 2007 to 2009, almost two dozen CVD actions were brought against China.

In 2012, the U.S. Congress and the Obama administration enacted new legislation specifically applying the CVD law to subsidized imports from nonmarket economy countries, including China and Vietnam. However, CVDs will not be used if the ITA is unable to identify and measure government subsidies because the economy of that country is essentially comprised of a "single entity." If the CVD law is not applicable, then antidumping duties become the only unfair trade remedy. The law also contains a special provision to avoid "double counting" in cases where both antidumping and countervailing duties might both be imposed on the same goods. The law was made retroactive to 2006, and upheld in *GPX International Tire Corp. v. U.S.*, 893 F. Supp. 2d 1296 (2013).

Exports from Newly Privatized Enterprises. What happens when a state-owned enterprise transitions into private ownership? Do the subsidies once provided when the enterprise was government owned continue to benefit the now privately owned firm? Understand that state-owned enterprises exist not just in nonmarket economies or socialist countries but also in many countries that we think of as being "free market" or "capitalist." These include Western nations like the UK, Sweden, and France, as well as developing countries such as Mexico, Chile, and Brazil. For example, government ownership of communications or energy industries is not unusual.

Since the late 1980s, there has been a worldwide trend away from government ownership of industry and toward private investment. Known as **privatization**, the term refers to the process by which a government sells or transfers government-owned industries or other assets to the private sector.

The next case, *United States—Countervailing Measures Concerning Certain Products from the European Communities* ("*European Steel*"), sees the largest European steel mills go from their days of near-financial collapse in the late 1960s, through a government bailout and the privatization of ownership, decades later. The United States believed that the financial contributions made to the firms while they were government owned were benefits that passed through to the newly privatized companies. This, in turn, continued to permit low-cost steel exports to the United States. The issue ultimately reached the WTO Appellate Body in Geneva.

United States—Countervailing Measures Concerning Certain Products from the European Communities ("European Steel")

Report of the Appellate Body, World Trade Organization, WT/DS212/AB/R (2002)

BACKGROUND AND FACTS

During the 1960s and 1970s, the European steel industry was near financial collapse. With the support of labor groups, the largest firms were kept alive with government money, low-interest loans, and equity investments from European governments. Many mills became government owned. In the early 1980s, the equivalent of tens of billions of dollars of public money was used to keep the mills running. The money financed operations, revitalized equipment, lowered the firms' debt, trained steelworkers, and permitted the export of low-priced steel. The United States responded

continues

continued

with a host of trade remedies, including countervailing duties. When the political climate changed in Europe, governments decided to sell off their interests to private investors in free-market stock sales. Since 1988, many large steel mills have been privatized, including British Steel (today Corus), Germany's Saarstahl, France's Usinor, and others. The new privately owned companies continued to sell steel in America.

The International Trade Administration imposed countervailing duties on European steel imports despite the fact that the European mills had been privatized. The agency believed that the benefits granted while the companies were government owned continued to "pass through" to the same steel companies (arguing that the companies were still the "same legal person") even after the change in ownership. After all, it was assumed, the new shareholders received the modern equipment, trained workers, and other assets paid for by the government. The European Communities maintained that the privatizations took place at arm's length and for fair market value, that the government no longer had any ownership interest or control, and thus that public monies were no longer subsidizing steel production. The EC argued that the U.S. "same person" rule violates the *WTO Agreement on Subsidies and Countervailing Measures [SCM Agreement].* Consultations between the governments failed, and in 2001, the EC requested that the WTO Dispute Settlement Body convene a dispute panel. After the decision of the panel, the United States appealed to the Appellate Body.

REPORT OF THE APPELLATE BODY * * *

[W]e find that the Panel erred in concluding that "[p]rivatizations at arm's length and for fair market value *must* lead to the conclusion that the privatized producer paid for what he got and thus did not get any benefit or advantage from the prior financial contribution bestowed upon the state-owned producer." [emphasis Panel's] Privatization at arm's length and for fair market value *may* result in extinguishing the benefit. Indeed, we find that there is a rebuttable presumption that a benefit ceases to exist after such a privatization. Nevertheless, it does not *necessarily* do so. There is no inflexible rule *requiring that* investigating authorities, in future cases, *automatically* determine that a "benefit" derived from pre-privatization financial contributions expires following privatization at arm's length and for fair market value. It depends on the facts of each case. * * *

With all this in mind, we now turn to the administrative practice of the [ITA] that is the source and subject of this dispute ... . Generally, the ITA applies the "same person" method to countervailing duty determinations following a change in ownership. * * *

The Panel stated, and the United States agreed before the Panel and on appeal, that the "same person" method requires the ITA to "consider that the benefit attributed to the state-owned producer can be automatically attributed to the privatized producer without any examination of the condition of the transaction" when the agency determines the post-privatization entity is not a new legal person. It is only if the ITA finds that a new legal person has been created that the agency will make a determination of whether a benefit exists, and, in such cases, the inquiry will be limited to the subject of whether a new subsidy has been provided to the new owners. Thus, under the "same person" method, when the ITA determines that no new legal person is created as a result of privatization, the ITA will conclude from this determination, without any further analysis, and irrespective of the price paid by the new owners for the newly-privatized enterprise, that the newly-privatized enterprise continues to receive the benefit of a previous financial contribution. This approach is contrary to the *SCM Agreement* that the investigating authority must take into account in an administrative review "positive information substantiating the need for a review." Such information could relate to developments with respect to the subsidy, privatization at arm's length and for fair market value, or some other information. The "same person" method impedes the ITA from complying with its obligation to examine whether a countervailable "benefit" continues to exist in a firm subsequent to that firm's change in ownership. Therefore, we find that the "same person" method, as such, is inconsistent with ... the *SCM Agreement.*

Decision. The Appellate Body found that in CVD actions, national administrative agencies must consider a broad range of criteria on a case-by-case basis in determining whether prior subsidies to a former government-owned company have "passed through" to the newly privatized company. The "same person" test used by the U.S. Department of Commerce violated the *SCM Agreement.*

Comment. In 2003, the ITA announced a new rule based on the presumption that a government subsidy can benefit a company over a period of time, corresponding to the useful life of the assets. However, the presumption is rebuttable if it can be shown that the government sold its ownership of all or substantially all of a company or its assets, retaining no control, and that the sale was an arm's-length transaction for fair market value.

Case Questions

1. What is "privatization" and how might it affect a subsidies case?
2. Why did the ITA conclude that the EC steel mills were the "same legal person"?
3. What factors should be considered in determining whether the European mills were still benefiting from earlier subsidies?

JUDICIAL REVIEW IN UNFAIR TRADE CASES

Decisions of the ITA or ITC in both CVD cases and antidumping duty cases are reviewable in the U.S. Court of International Trade if they are final decisions or if they are negative determinations. **A negative determination** is a decision by the agency either to not initiate an investigation or that a material injury does not exist. If an antidumping determination involves Canadian or Mexican goods, appeals may be made to a binational arbitration panel established under the North American Free Trade Agreement.

CONCLUSION

Most readers are accustomed to hearing arguments in the news, television, and popular press about free trade versus protectionism. The debates seem to be especially vociferous as national elections approach, whether in the United States or elsewhere in the world. Other readers have had the opportunity to study the issues more academically, perhaps in courses in economics. This chapter, however, looks at the issues of free trade and protectionism from a purely legal perspective. We examine the tools, administrative procedures, and remedies available at the international level, through the WTO, and under American law, for dealing with (1) increased imports that threaten to injure a domestic industry and (2) unfair trade.

Anyone interested in additional reading on the law or economics of international trade from a U.S. perspective should consider using the reports and publications of the U.S. International Trade Commission (ITC). It produces authoritative reports that examine trends in international trade and analyze the impact of trade and trade agreements on American industries. Readers who want to know more about bringing and handling unfair trade actions in the United States should consult the *Antidumping and Countervailing Duty Handbook,* published by the ITC (latest edition). The text is an excellent summary and informal resource for business. Another excellent source of information from the ITC is *The Year in Trade: Operation of the Trade Agreements Program* (latest edition). For statistical data on unfair import cases, see *Import Injury Investigations Case Statistics* (latest edition). All three publications are available from the ITC Website.

A 2011 report of the ITC examines the economic impact of U.S. import restrictions on the most protected U.S. industries (sugar, ethanol, canned tuna, dairy products, tobacco, textiles and apparel, footwear and leather products; glass and glass products; ball and roller bearings; ceramic tile; china tableware; costume jewelry; hand tools; tires; and agricultural chemicals, and other high-tariff manufacturing sectors). The ITC used an economic model to estimate what would happen if all significant U.S. trade barriers were removed in those industries. It gave us food for thought when it concluded.

> [P]ublic and private consumption would increase by about $2.6 billion annually by 2015 if the United States unilaterally ended ("liberalized") all significant restraints quantified in this report. Exports would expand by $9.0 billion and imports by $11.5 billion. [*The Economic Effects of Significant U.S. Import Restraints, Seventh Update,* USITC Pub. 4253, August 2011.]

Chapter Summary

1. The terms "safeguard," "import relief," and "adjustments to imports" all refer to the WTO-recognized rights of a nation to protect a domestic industry from increasing foreign imports.
2. The *WTO Agreement on Safeguards* provides that a member may apply a temporary safeguard measure (e.g., increase tariffs) to a product only if that product "is being imported in such increased quantities and under such conditions as to cause or threaten to cause serious injury to the domestic industry that produces like or directly competitive products." WTO safeguards are global safeguards, meaning that they must be applied to imports of specific products without regard to the country of origin.
3. In the United States, the International Trade Commission (ITC), an independent agency of government, investigates safeguard actions and

conveys its recommendations to the president. The willingness of the president to protect an industry depends on national interests and the president's own economic and trade philosophies. Special safeguard actions apply to imports from China.

4. Trade adjustment assistance is available to workers, firms, and farmers whose jobs are lost to foreign imports or by the relocation of factories to foreign countries.
5. Dumping is the unfair trade practice of selling goods in a foreign country for less than the normal value of like products in the home market. It is a form of international price discrimination by exporters. National laws and practices on antidumping must follow the basic framework of the *WTO Agreement on Antidumping.* Antidumping duties can only be imposed on dumped products by the country of import where the dumping causes or threatens material injury to a domestic industry producing like products. Much of the litigation in this area involves determining normal value and the calculation of the dumping margin. In the United States, the International Trade Administration determines the dumping margin, and the International Trade Commission determines if the dumping caused material injury to a domestic firm.
6. A subsidy is a financial contribution or benefit conferred by a government to a domestic firm or firms, directly or indirectly, to achieve some industrial, economic, or social objective. Subsidies that are prohibited include export subsidies, import substitution subsidies, and adverse effects subsidies. The *WTO Agreement on Subsidies and Countervailing Measures* permits the country of import to impose countervailing duties on illegally subsidized imports to offset the value of the benefit. In the United States, the ITA determines the amount of a subsidy, if any, and the ITC determines material injury.
7. In 2007, for the first time since 1984, the United States began applying the U.S. countervailing duty law to nonmarket economy countries, including China. This change in policy was due to the growing influx of Chinese imports into the United States, the increasing privatization of Chinese firms, and the demands from members of Congress to stop Chinese subsidies.
8. Throughout the area of unfair trade law, the decisions of the WTO Appellate Body in Geneva, Switzerland, are becoming increasingly important. In several cases, the United States has had to reform or repeal its laws and administrative practices to comply with WTO rules.
9. Books and articles on the economics of dumping and subsidies could fill entire libraries. Readers interested in this area should consider furthering their theoretical study of international economics or the economics of international trade.
10. Websites for both the ITA (Import Administration unit) and the ITC are excellent starting points for additional information and industry research.

Key Terms

import competition 290
safeguards against injury 290
escape clause 291
global safeguards 291
market disruption 291
provisional safeguards 293
trade compensation 293
import relief 293
adjustment to imports 294
trade adjustment assistance (TAA) 296
unfair trade practice 297
dumping 297
antidumping duties 297
normal value 298
constructed value 298
export price 298
dumping margin 298
constructed export price 298
like product 298
material injury 300
nonmarket economy country 301
factors of production 301
surrogate market economy 301
market-oriented exporter 302
market-oriented industry 302
subsidy 304
specific subsidy 305
prohibited subsidy 305
export subsidies 305
import substitution subsidy 305
actionable subsidy 306
adverse effects subsidy 306
upstream subsidy 306
countermeasures 306
countervailing duty 306
privatization 307
negative determination 309

Questions and Case Problems

1. In an antidumping investigation the ITA finds that the dumping firm was experiencing a downturn in its domestic economic cycle, and that there had been no intent to harm a U.S. industry. Can antidumping duties still be applied?
2. A foreign shoe manufacturer sells shoes to a wholly-owned subsidiary company in a foreign market at $20. The subsidiary sells to an independent distributor at $40, who sells to a retailer at $80.00. The retailer sells the shoes to a consumer for a price of $160. In comparing the export price to the normal value, which price should the ITA use, and why? Which allowances or adjustments to the export price, if any, can the ITA make? Give several examples.
3. A country enacts a law that denies import privileges for five years to any firm that "dumps" products for sale in its markets at less than normal value. Do the WTO antidumping agreements permit such a remedy?
4. Why does the U.S. Congress subsidize agriculture? What is the economic impact of subsidies on worldwide agricultural prices? Why are subsidies a subject of dispute between the United States, Europe, and the developing countries?
5. What do you think of the results of the USITC report, *The Economic Effects of Significant U.S. Import Restraints, Seventh Update*, cited in the chapter conclusion? Considering the net effect of import restraints on the volume of imports and exports, and considering the costs incurred in administering all import restraint laws, do you have an opinion of their effectiveness?
6. In this chapter we discuss U.S. safeguards on Chinese products in existence from 2001 to 2013. These safeguards protected American industries from injury due to increased Chinese imports after China was admitted to the WTO in 2001. Research the subject to determine how the records of President Bush and President Obama may have differed on this issue of safeguards. Did either president invoke safeguards against Chinese products, and under what conditions? What does your outside reading tell you were the arguments for and against imposing duties on Chinese imports? Describe the economic, political, and foreign policy implications of the safeguard laws. See, USITC Investigation of *Pedestal Actuator Imports from the People's Republic of China*, Inv. No. TA-421-1 (2002), USITC Publication No. 3557 and the USITC Investigation of *Certain Passenger Vehicle and Light Truck Tires from China*, Inv. No. TA-421-7, USITC Publication 4085. Also see, *United States—Measures Affecting Imports of Certain Passenger Vehicle and Light Truck Tyres from China*, Report of the WTO Appellate Body, WT/DS399/AB/R (2011).
7. What makes an import practice "unfair"? What remedies are available under U.S. law to protect domestic industries from unfair import competition?
8. Describe the different functions of the ITA and the ITC in regulating import competition.
9. The plaintiff, Smith Corona, was the last remaining manufacturer of portable electric typewriters in the United States. An action was brought to challenge the method used by the International Trade Administration to determine whether the Japanese typewriter companies, Brother and Silver Seiko, had engaged in dumping in the United States. The typewriters in question were sold in Japan (the home market) under different circumstances of sale than in the United States. In Japan, Silver Seiko provided volume rebates to its customers based on total sales of all merchandise sold. Brother incurred advertising expenses in Japan, as well as expenditures for accessories that accompany typewriters sold in Japan but not in the United States. The ITA subtracted these amounts from foreign market value in calculating the dumping margin. Was the ITA correct? See *Smith-Corona Group v. United States*, 713 F.2d 1568 (Fed. Cir. 1983).
10. The American Grape Growers alleged that imports of wine from France and Italy were being subsidized and sold in the United States at less than fair value. The ITC's preliminary review found that no U.S. industry was threatened with material injury. The American growers said the ITC decision did not include the imports from both France and Italy as it should have done. Instead it considered the two products different because the French wines were primarily white wines and the Italian wines were primarily red and effervescent. The growers also said the ITC was wrong to base its decision on whether an injury had been proved, as opposed to whether there was a possibility of injury. Do you agree with the grape growers that the ITC's preliminary decision was wrong?

Managerial Implications

Your firm is a U.S. manufacturer of optic transistors (OTs) for use in robotic applications. A few years ago the United States entered into an OT trade agreement with Asian countries reducing tariffs on most OTs made worldwide. Over the past two years foreign imports of OTs have risen by over $100 million per year, and now account for 60 percent of the U.S. market. During this time you noticed a drop in your firm's share of the U.S. market for OTs from more than 25 percent to less than 20 percent. In addition, your firm's total sales are in decline, its inventories are at their highest levels, and you have had to postpone hiring new employees. One of your better customers informs you that it can purchase comparable OTs for 25 percent less than yours from a supplier in Taiwan. Furthermore, you learn that the government of Taiwan assists OT manufacturers by rebating taxes on the value of OTs they export. To complicate your problems, you have been experiencing difficulty cracking export markets, and countries where robots are assembled, such as Korea, Singapore, and Taiwan, have been restricting your firm's imports through a maze of complex regulations. Also, to receive import licenses, these regulations require you to disclose important manufacturing and design techniques. You are also concerned that your design patents will not be protected there, because there is no enforcement of Korean patent protection laws. Korea has imposed quotas on OTs that make it virtually impossible to export to that market.

Considering your work in the last three chapters, what remedies are available to your firm under U.S. law that would help protect its U.S. market? What are the available remedies that the U.S. government has to help improve market access to your customers who manufacture robots in Asia? What factors (economic, political, or other) will affect the outcome of the case? How might these legal implications affect your global business strategy? Discuss.

Ethical Considerations

Your firm is a paper converter. It converts paperboard into various articles for use in homes and restaurants for food preparation, sale, and storage. Its products include pizza boxes, ice cream boxes, bakery and deli boxes, and paper plates as well as boxes and trays for use in fast food operations. You purchase paperboard from both domestic and foreign sources. Recently, a Chinese supplier has begun offering paperboard at extremely low prices—far lower than what you have been paying domestically. One of your colleagues at your firm calls the offer "too good to be true." You have always had reliable sources of supply, but the offer is very tempting. Why might the foreign exporter be cutting prices to U.S. customers? What information do you think you need before committing to a purchase? Specifically, what pricing information do you need? If it turns out that the products are being "dumped" in the U.S. market, what would be the result and how might it affect your firm and your purchasing decision? Do you think it is fair or unfair for an exporter to dump its goods in a foreign market? Evaluate the statement, "Selling at a low price can't be unfair."

CHAPTER 12

Imports, Customs, and Tariff Law

Importing is the entering of goods into the customs territory of a country. All commercial shipments must go through an administrative **entry process** supervised by national customs authorities and informally referred to as "clearing customs." The purpose of the entry process is for customs authorities to determine whether any import prohibitions or restrictions apply to the goods, whether the goods are subject to any other laws or regulations affecting their entry (e.g., such as product labeling, etc.), and whether any tariffs or import duties are due. This requires that the importer and the customs authorities know the tariff classification, customs value, and country of origin of the goods. This information determines what tariffs and regulations apply to the goods being entered. This chapter begins by explaining these concepts. Later in the chapter we discuss the use of several tariff-saving devices, such as customs drawbacks and foreign trade zones. The chapter concludes with a review of customs enforcement issues, including civil and criminal penalties for customs violations.

Many of the broad concepts discussed here are applicable to importing in almost any country because many rules are uniform or "harmonized" internationally. However, because customs and tariff law is based on national law and regulation, we focus on specific rules and case law from the United States, particularly in the country-specific area of enforcement and penalties. This area should be particularly helpful to importers in the United States as well as to exporters in other countries who are shipping goods to the United States. In discussing U.S. imports, we will frequently mention the role of the **U.S. Bureau of Customs and Border Protection,** the customs regulatory authority in the United States. We will refer to this bureau as "U.S. Customs" or simply "Customs."

As you study this chapter, remember that importing is too often viewed from the perspective of a single, isolated transaction. You might be tempted to think in terms of an individual or small firm that imports only occasionally. However, importing is often a part of a global company's larger operation and international business strategy. Imagine a leading apparel designer that ships garments to the United States that were assembled in Honduras, from parts of clothing that were cut and sewn at plants in Hong Kong, from fabric that had been woven in China. Imagine an automobile company ships car to the United States from assembly plants in Mexico that used component parts sourced from Japan or Europe. Outside the manufacturing context, consider an importer of Swiss watches, Danish cheese, or French wine that might import foreign brands for national distribution. These are simple examples of how import operations can be an integral part of a firm's global or international business strategy, linking all entities and processes along a global supply chain. Customs and tariff laws will have a great influence on strategic and operational decisions. They can determine the countries where raw materials are purchased and factories are built and even influence the engineering, packaging, labeling, and pricing of the final product. Naturally, due to the complexity of customs and tariff laws and the range of civil and criminal penalties, we caution readers to seek the assistance of a licensed customs broker or customs attorney in more complex commercial transactions.

There is a fine line between the term "customs law" and "tariff law," and many lawyers might be pressed to find a practical difference. However, for purposes of this chapter, we could say that **tariff law** is the body of laws and regulations that determines the tariff or "dutiable" status of goods and the rate of duty. As used here, the term **customs law** is somewhat broader, and while including tariff law, it extends to other areas of regulatory control over goods and people as they cross international borders.

DUTIABLE STATUS OF GOODS

The **dutiable status** of goods (in this section "goods" may also called "articles" or "items") refers to the legal status of imported goods at the time of entry for purposes of compliance with the tariff and customs laws. Dutiable status is determined by three factors:

(1) the *classification and coding* of the article, (2) the *customs value* of the article, and (3) the *country of origin* of the article. In other words, importers must know what it is that they are importing, what it's worth, and where it came from according to law. It is the importer's responsibility to use reasonable care to determine the dutiable status of an import, to accurately report it to their customs authorities, and to provide the necessary documentation to verify the information. The time to begin thinking about an article's dutiable status is not when the goods arrive at the port of entry—which is far too late. Dutiable status—which ultimately determines the tariff rate, possible quotas, country of origin marking and labeling, and more—should be considered in the earliest planning stages. It gives the importer and product manager essential information for determining product costs, pricing, marking and labeling, and it may even affect a product's design characteristics and choice of suppliers.

Classification of Goods

The first step in determining the dutiable status of an item is to determine its tariff classification. A **tariff classification** is a method of categorizing different types or kinds of goods based on a uniform descriptive nomenclature or terminology, according to their tariff name, use, or physical characteristics. Classifications are found in a nation's official **tariff schedule**, together with the tariff rate for each item according to the country from which it originated. Tariff schedules are found in national codes or legislation.

The Harmonized Commodity Description and Coding System. The tariff schedules of virtually all nations are based on the *Harmonized Commodity Description and Coding System*, an international convention that uses uniform rules and a standardized tariff nomenclature to describe and code—or classify—goods. The harmonized system was developed by the World Customs Organization, an international organization located in Brussels with 179 member nations. The harmonized system is used by virtually every trading nation of the world. Goods that fall into a certain classification in one country should be similarly classified in all countries. Of course, customs authorities and even courts in different countries may arrive at different classifications for the same goods, but the uniformity of descriptions and coding at least provides a common nomenclature and understanding. Thus, a company that knows the classification of its product in the United States, for example, will have a general idea of the classification of its product in a foreign country (even though the importer-of-record in the country of import will be entering the goods there). Although the schedule does show the tariff rates for every item, the rates are not set by the harmonized system. Tariff rates for each country can be very different and are determined by each country's tariff binding as a result of trade negotiations.

The harmonized system was adopted by the United States in 1989 and forms the basis of the *Harmonized Tariff Schedule of the United States* (HTSUS or "tariff schedule"). U.S. importers must have a working knowledge of the tariff schedule, an example of which is shown in Exhibit 12.1. In the United States, the tariff schedule is maintained by the **International Trade Commission**. It is not published in the *U.S. Code* but is available online directly from the ITC or through a link on the U.S. Customs and Border Protection's Website. The harmonized schedule of the European Union is called the *Combined Nomenclature (CN) of the European Union* and is published in the *Official Journal of the European Union*. Although the European Union utilizes the harmonized tariff code and has a common external tariff rate and trade policies, each of the EU countries maintains its own customs enforcement agency. The Canadian version of the harmonized schedule is called the *Customs Tariff* and is administered by the **Canada Border Services Agency**. Although the discussion that follows does focus on tariff classification in the United States, it explains broad, internationally accepted principles applicable to almost all countries that have adopted the harmonized system.

An Outline of the U.S. Harmonized Tariff Schedule

The *Harmonized Tariff Schedule of the United States* divides products into several thousand tariff classifications, ranging from basic commodities and agricultural products to manufactured goods. It is organized into sections and chapters, each covering different kinds of commodities, materials, and products. The chapters are arranged in a progression from crude materials, livestock, and agricultural products through manufactured goods such as vehicles, aircraft, and even spacecraft and their component parts.

Chapters are broken down into headings and then into subheadings, and tariff items. Tariff classifications are standardized internationally through the subheading (six-digit) level. Tariff items are further broken down to

Exhibit 12.1

Harmonized Tariff Schedule of the United States (2013)

Annotated for Statistical Reporting Purposes

XI
63–18

Heading/ Subheading	Stat. Suf-fix	Article Description	Unit of Quantity	Rates of Duty 1 General	Rates of Duty 1 Special	2
6306		Tarpaulins, awnings and sunblinds; tents; sails for boats, sailboards or landcraft; camping goods:				
		Tarpaulins, awnings and sunblinds:				
6306.12.00	00	Of synthetic fibers (669).	kg.	8.8%	Free (BH,CA,CL, CO,IL,JO,KR,MA, MX,OM,P,PA,PE, SG) 3% (AU)	90%
6306.19		Of other textile materials:				
6309.19.11	00	Of cotton (369).	kg.	8%	Free (BH,CA,CL, CO,IL,JO,KR,MA, MX,OM,P,PA,PE, SG) 3% (AU)	90%
6306.19.21	00	Other.	. . . .	5.1%	Free (BH,CA,CL, CO,E*,IL,JO,KR, MA,MX,OM,P,PA, PE,SG) 3% (AU)	40%
	10	Of artificial fibers (669).	kg			
	20	Other (899).	kg			
		Tents:				
6306.22		Of synthetic fibers:				
6306.22.10	00	Backpacking tents.	No. . . . . . kg	Free		90%
6306.22.90		Other.	. . . .	8.8%	Free (BH,CA,CL, CO,IL,JO,KR,MA, MX,OM,P,PA,PE, SG) 3% (AU)	90%
	10	Screen houses.	kg			
	30	Other (669).	kg			
6306.29		Of other textile materials:				
6306.29.11	00	Of cotton.	kg.	8%	Free (BH,CA,CL, CO,IL,JO,KR,MA, MX,OM,P,PA,PE, SG) 3% (AU)	90%
6306.29.21	00	Other.	kg.	2.9%	Free (AU,BH,CA CL,CO,E*,IL,J*, JO,KR,MA,MX, OM,P,PA,PE,SG)	40%
6306.30.00		Sails.	. . . .	Free		30%
	10	Of synthetic fibers.	kg			
	20	Of other textile materials.	kg			
6306.40		Pneumatic mattresses:				
6306.40.41	00	Of cotton.	kg.	3.7%	Free (BH,CA,CL, CO,IL,JO,KR,MA, MX,OM,P,PA,PE, SG) 3% (AU)	25%
6306.40.49	00	Of other textile materials:.	kg.	3.7%	Free (A,BH,CA,CL, CO,E,IL,J,JO,KR, MA,MX,OM,P,PA, PE,SG) 3% (AU)	25%
6306 (con.)		Tarpaulins, awnings and sunblinds; tents; sails for boats, sailboards or landcraft; camping goods (con.):				
6306.90		Other:				
6306.90.10	00	Of cotton.	kg.	3.5%	Free (BH,CA,CL, CO,IL,JO,KR,MA, MX,OM,P,PA,PE, SG) 3% (AU)	40%
6306.90.50	00	Of other textile materials.	kg.	4.5%	Free (BH,CA,CL, CO,E*,IL,J*,JO, KR,MA,MX,OM,P, PA,PE,SG) 3% (AU)	78.5%

continues

continued

Harmonized Tariff Schedule of the United States (2013)

General Notes to the Harmonized Tariff Schedule of the United States (2013) [edited for student use].

3. *Rates of Duty.* The rates of duty in the "Rates of Duty" columns designated 1 ("General" and "Special") and 2 of the tariff schedule apply to goods imported into the customs territory of the United States as hereinafter provided in this note
   a) Rate of Duty Column 1.
      i) Except as provided in subparagraph (iv) of this paragraph, the rates of duty in column 1 are rates which are applicable to all products other than those of countries enumerated in paragraph (b) of this note. Column 1 is divided into two subcolumns, "General" and "Special," which are applicable as provided below.
      ii) The "General" subcolumn sets forth the general or normal trade relations (NTR) rates which are applicable to products of those countries described in subparagraph (i) above which are not entitled to special tariff treatment as set forth below.
      iii) The "Special" subcolumn reflects rates of duty under one or more special tariff treatment programs described in paragraph (c) of this note and identified in parentheses immediately following the duty rate specified in such subcolumn. These rates apply to those products which are properly classified under a provision for which a special rate is indicated and for which all of the legal requirements for eligibility for such program or programs have been met. Where a product is eligible for special treatment under more than one program, the lowest rate of duty provided for any applicable program shall be imposed. Where no special rate of duty is provided for a provision or where the country from which a product otherwise eligible for special treatment was imported is not designated as a beneficiary country under a program appearing with the appropriate provision, the rates of duty in the "General" subcolumn of column 1 shall apply.
      vi) Products of Insular Possessions (omitted)
      v) Products of the West Bank or Gaza Strip (omitted)
   b) Rate of Duty Column 2. Notwithstanding any of the foregoing provisions of this note, the rates of duty shown in Column 2 shall apply to products, whether imported directed or indirectly, of the following countries and areas:

      Cuba North Korea
   c) Products Eligible for Special Tariff Treatment.
      i) Programs under which special tariff treatment may be provided, and the corresponding symbols for such programs as they are indicated in the "Special" subcolumn, are as follows:

Program	Symbol
Generalized System of Preferences	A, A* or A+
United States–Australia Free Trade Agreement	AU
Automotive Products Trade Act	B
United States–Bahrain Free Trade Agreement Implementation Act	BH
Agreement on Trade in Civil Aircraft	C
North American Free Trade Agreement:	
Goods of Canada, under the terms of general note 12 to this schedule	CA
Goods of Mexico, under the terms of general note 12 to this schedule	MX
United States–Chile Free Trade Agreement	CL
African Growth and Opportunity Act	D
Caribbean Basin Economic Recovery Act	E or E*
United States–Israel Free Trade Area	IL
Andean Trade Preference Act or Andean Trade Promotion and Drug Eradication Act	J, J* or J+
United States–Jordan Free Trade Area Implementation Act	JO
Agreement on Trade in Pharmaceutical Products	K
Dominican Republic–Central America–United States Free Trade Agreement Implementation Act	P or P+

continues

continued

Uruguay Round Concessions on Intermediate Chemicals for Dyes	L
United States–Caribbean Basin Trade Partnership Act	R
United States–Morocco Free Trade Agreement Implementation Act	MA
United States–Singapore Free Trade Agreement	SG
United States–Oman Free Trade Agreement Implementation Act	OM
United States–Peru Trade Promotion Agreement Implementation Act	PE
United States–Korea Free Trade Agreement Implementaton Act	KR
United States–Colombia Free Trade Promotion Agreement Implementation Act	CO
United States–Panama Trade Promotion Agreement Implementation Act	PA

Source: U.S. International Trade Commission, Washington, D.C. USITC Publication 4368. Always be sure to consult the latest version of the code.

eight-digit codes. In some countries such as the United States, the schedule breaks out to ten digits to allow for compiling of statistical data on imports.

Chapter:	first two digits
Heading:	first four digits
Subheading:	first six digits
Tariff item:	first eight digits
Statistical break:	ten digits

Look at Exhibit 12.1. What is the classification shown for lightweight tents made of synthetic fibers, such as nylon, used for backpacking?

Chapter 63:	"Other textile articles"
Heading 6306:	"Tarpaulins, awnings and sunblinds, tents, sails for boats"
Subheading 6306.22:	"Tents: Of synthetic fibers"
Tariff item 6306.22.10:	"Backpacking tents"

The rate of duty is listed next to each tariff item. As shown in Exhibit 12.1, the schedule is divided into two columns. Column 1 contains the general rate of duty. The general rate is the tariff rate applicable to imports from countries with whom the United States has "normal trade relations" (formerly called the "most-favored-nation" rate). The special rate of duty is the tariff rate applicable to one or more tariff preference programs. This column indicates whether the item qualifies for special tariff treatment because it originated in a developing country under the *Generalized System of Preferences*, or from within a free trade area. So-called Column 2 rates are the original rates from the *Smoot-Hawley Tariff Act of 1930* that today are applicable only to countries not granted normal trade relations. Prior to the 1990s, the Column 2 rates had applied to goods from all communist countries. As of 2013, only goods from Cuba and North Korea fell into this category (trade with those countries is subject to other controls as well). Column 2 tariff rates are so high that trade becomes cost-prohibitive.

Tariffs are based on *ad valorem*, specific, or compound rates. The most common is the ***ad valorem tariff* rate**, based on a percentage of the value of the articles imported. A **specific tariff rate** is a specified amount per unit of weight or measure. A **compound tariff rate** is a combination of both *ad valorem* and specific rates.

Classification by Common and Commercial Meaning. To locate an article in the schedule, begin with its description. Articles are described in the tariff schedule in several ways: by common name (or *eo nomine* description), by a description of the article's physical characteristics, by a description of its component parts, or by its use.

If a term used to describe an article in the schedule is not specifically defined, then the *common meaning* of the term is used unless it can be proven that there is a different *commercial* or *scientific meaning* that is definite, uniform, and in general use throughout the industry or trade. Courts will often examine the legislative history of the tariff act to determine the intent of Congress and will consult dictionaries, encyclopedias, and other reliable sources to determine the common and commercial meaning of a term. The courts also rely on scientific authorities and expert witnesses during a trial.

The meaning of a term can change over time, or with technological developments. In *Texas Instruments v. United States*, 518 F. Supp. 1341 (C.I.T. 1981), *aff'd.* 673 F.2d 1375 (C.C.P.A. 1982), the court was faced with determining the common meaning of the term "watch movement." The plaintiff, Texas Instruments, Inc., had entered solid-state electronic watch modules consisting of an integrated circuit chip, a capacitor, a liquid crystal display for digital readouts, and plastic cases. Because digital watches had not yet been invented at the time this tariff schedule (prior to the harmonized schedule) was enacted by Congress, the court upheld Customs' determination that the common meaning of "watch movement" in the industry did not include these electronic modules. The court believed that Congress could not have intended the term "movement" to include the "essentially molecular vibration" in a digital watch. In addressing the impact of technological development on customs law, the Court of International Trade stated that

> The courts cannot be asked to restructure the tariff schedules by judicial fiat in order to accommodate scientific and engineering innovations which far transcend the vision and intent of the Congress at the time of the enactment of the tariff schedules. It is true ... that it is an established principle of customs law that tariff schedules are written for the future as well as for present application and may embrace merchandise unknown at the time of their enactment. It must be borne in mind, however, that ... in applying a tariff provision to an article, unknown at the time of the enactment thereof, such an article must possess an essential resemblance to the characteristics so described by the applicable tariff provision.

The court ruled that the solid-state electronic module was not a "watch movement."

Dictionary definitions are often used to interpret the tariff schedule. In *C. J. Van Houten & Zoon v. United States*, 664 F. Supp. 514 (Ct. Int'l. Trade 1987), the court ruled that tariff schedule items for "bars or blocks" of chocolate weighing 10 pounds or more did not apply to imports of molten, liquid chocolate imported into the United States in tank cars. Rather, the molten chocolate was to be classified as "sweetened chocolate in any other form." After consulting several dictionaries for the common meaning of the terms "bars and blocks," the court concluded that this meant only solid materials.

Classification by Use. Some articles are described in the schedule by their use. For example, a detergent additive for gasoline is described as a "preparation used to keep the carburetor ... clean." When an article has several different uses, the principal use controls. Principal use is that use to which articles of the class and kind being imported are usually put and which is greater than any other single use of the article. An article may be classified according to the actual use intended for that article. To classify by actual use, the article must be used for the purposes listed in the schedule. The actual use must be noted in customs documentation at the time of entry, the imported article must actually be used in that manner, and the use must be verifiable for three years after entry.

The following case, *Carl Zeiss, Inc. v. United States*, is one of the most frequently cited cases in this area of the law.

Carl Zeiss, Inc. v. United States

195 F.3d 1375 (1999) United States Court of Appeals (Fed. Cir.)

BACKGROUND AND FACTS

Zeiss imported ZMS 319 microscopes, stands, and accessories, including a camera—all specially tailored for neurosurgical use. Customs classified the ZMS 319 as a "stereoscopic compound microscope with a means for photographing the image." Zeiss argued that the article should be classified under heading 9018 for "Instruments and appliances used in medical, surgical, dental or veterinary sciences, including scintigraphic apparatus, other electro-medical apparatus and sight-testing instruments." Zeiss disagreed and filed a protest. Zeiss then brought this action in the Court of International Trade. The court held for the government, and Zeiss appealed.

LOURIE, CIRCUIT JUDGE

Zeiss challenges Customs' classification of the subject merchandise under heading 9011, which includes "compound optical microscopes." Zeiss argues that this term commonly refers to compound optical microscopes used for laboratory, industry, and research use, not for medical or surgical use. Zeiss concedes that the ZMS 319's OPMI ® microscope falls within the dictionary definition of a compound optical microscope in that it has multiple stages of magnification (an objective and two eyepieces), but maintains that it is not a compound optical microscope for tariff purposes because it only has surgical uses and has a different "commercial identity." The government responds that

continues

continued

the common meaning of the term is the same as its dictionary meaning, which is simply any light microscope with multiple levels of magnification, and that the ZMS 319's use is irrelevant.

Absent contrary legislative intent, HTSUS terms are to be construed according to their common and commercial meanings, which are presumed to be the same. A court may rely upon its own understanding of the terms used and may consult lexicographic and scientific authorities, dictionaries, and other reliable information sources. One who argues that a tariff term should not be given its common or dictionary meaning must prove that it has a different commercial meaning that is definite, uniform, and general throughout the trade.

We agree with the government that the merchandise is *prima facie* classifiable under the 9011 heading "compound optical microscopes." *Webster's International Dictionary* defines an "optical microscope" as "a microscope in which light rays are seen directly by the observer as distinguishable from one ([such] as an electron microscope) in which some transformation or system of indirect viewing is used." *Webster's Third International Dictionary* 1584 (1976). It further defines a "compound microscope" as "a microscope consisting of an objective and an eyepiece mounted in a drawtube and focused by means of screw arrangements." *Id.* at 467. *See also The Random House Unabridged Dictionary* 420 (2d ed. 1987).... There is no dispute that the ZMS 319 OPMI ® microscope conforms to these definitions.

Furthermore, heading 9011 is an *eo nomine* classification provision, not a use provision, as it describes the merchandise by name, not by use. It would be improper to narrow this provision to include those microscopes used in industry and research, but to exclude those microscopes used in medicine and surgery; a use limitation should not be read into an *eo nomine* provision unless the name itself inherently suggests a type of use. "[A]n *eo nomine* designation, with no terms of limitation, will ordinarily include all forms of the named article." *Hayes–Sammons Chemical Co. v. United States,* 55 C.C.P.A. 69, 75, (1968). Therefore, the fact that the ZMS 319's exclusive use is surgical is irrelevant to the question whether it falls under the *eo nomine* provision "compound optical microscope."

Lastly, the [lower] court found that Zeiss had not proved that the term "compound optical microscope" has a well-known signification in trade and commerce that is different from its common meaning. On appeal, Zeiss only argues that its own product has a separate "commercial identity." However, the fact that the ZMS 319 is designed, marketed, and used as a surgical instrument does not establish a separate commercial meaning for the HTSUS heading term. Thus, the court properly construed the term "compound optical microscope" in accordance with its common meaning and properly determined that the ZMS 319 fell within heading 9011.

Although we agree with the government that the ZMS 319 is classifiable under heading 9011, we agree with Zeiss that the ZMS 319 is also *prima facie* classifiable under the 9018 heading for instruments used in medical and surgical sciences, for there is no dispute that the ZMS 319 is such an instrument. Having determined that the ZMS 319 is *prima facie* classifiable under both headings 9011 and 9018, we must now determine which is the preferred heading for classification.

When a product is *prima facie* classifiable under two or more headings, "[t]he heading which provides the most specific description shall be preferred to headings providing a more general description." GRI 3(a). Under this rule of "relative specificity," "we look to the provision with requirements that are more difficult to satisfy and that describe the article with the greatest degree of accuracy and certainty." [citations omitted]

The government responds that ... the description "compound optical microscopes" is narrower and more specific than "instruments used in medical or surgical sciences...."

We agree with the government that the ZMS 319 should be classified under heading 9011 because the description "compound optical microscopes" more specifically describes the merchandise than "instruments used in medical or surgical sciences." The term "compound optical microscopes," even while encompassing microscopes with different specifications and uses, suggests specific structural requirements, *viz,* that it be "compound" and "optical." That provision, therefore, is narrower than "instruments and appliances used in medical or surgical sciences," which encompasses a wide variety of non-microscopic merchandise and does not suggest any structural features at all.

Decision. Affirmed for the government. Customs properly classified the ZMS 319 under heading 9011 as a "compound optical microscope." Items are to be construed according to their common and commercial meaning. The ZMS 319 meets the common dictionary meaning of compound microscope, and an *eo nomine* classification includes all forms of the named article, including this one adapted for surgery. Because the ZMS is also classifiable under 9018 as a "medical appliance," the court must then decide into which category the article fits. Heading 9011 for compound microscopes is narrower, more specific, and describes the article with more accuracy and certainty.

Case Questions

1. Describe the two-step process for classifying an article.
2. Why is "compound microscope" an *eo nomine* term, and what does the court mean when it says, "that includes all forms of the named article?"
3. Which of the two headings is more specific, and why?

The General Rules of Interpretation. To classify goods you must follow the **General Rules of Interpretation (GRI)** found at the front of the tariff schedules. The GRI contains both the procedural and substantive rules for arriving at the correct classification. Some of the substantive rules follow in the next sections. You must begin by classifying your goods at the four-digit heading level, looking for the heading that most specifically and completely describes your goods.

The Rule of Relative Specificity. The **rule of relative specificity**, found in the GRI, states that where an article could be classified under more than one heading, it must be classified under the one that most specifically—most narrowly—describes the article with the greatest degree of accuracy and certainty. The *Carl Zeiss* case is a good example of the application of this rule.

If an article can be classified under more than one heading, a description by name is more specific than a description of a class of merchandise. For example, tools used by a hair stylist would be classified as "shavers and hair clippers with self-contained electric motor" under heading 8510 because this description is more specific than "electromechanical tools for working in the hand with self-contained electric motor" under 8508.

Classification by Essential Character. Suppose an article is made of two or more different materials or components, each of which could be classified individually in the schedule under different headings. If two or more headings each describe only certain materials or components of the article, the GRI requires that the article be classified under the heading that describes those materials or components that give the article its **essential character**. This method is helpful to determine the classification of mixtures of chemicals, foodstuffs, and other substances or materials blended together, assuming that there is no classification that fits the mixture. The rule also applies to composite goods. *Composite goods* are goods made up of more than one component or material. For instance, imagine a somewhat dated notebook computer that also contains a standard AM/FM radio receiver. Should it be classified as "Reception apparatus for radio telephony" under heading 8527 or as an "Automatic data processing machine" under section 8471? If the notebook computer imparts the essential character to this odd contraption, it would probably be classified under 8471.

In *Pillowtex Corp. v. United States*, 111 F.3d 1370 (Fed. Cir. 1999), the court considered the tariff classification of comforters made from a 100 percent cotton shell and filled with white duck down. The court held that the down fill should control the classification because the essential character of the comforters was derived from the insulating ability of the filling, not from the shell. Cases involving the essential character test are very fact intensive; they turn on a detailed analysis of the facts of the case.

In the following case, *Better Home Plastics Corp. v. United States*, 916 F. Supp. 1265 (Ct. Int'l. Trade 1996), the court had to determine whether a shower curtain set was classified under the heading for "Curtains" or under the heading for "Tableware, kitchenware, other household articles and toilet articles, of plastics." Notice how the court applies the General Rules of Interpretation and the essential character test.

Better Home Plastics Corp. v. United States

916 F.Supp.1265 (1996) Court of International Trade

BACKGROUND AND FACTS

Plaintiff, Better Home Plastics Corp., imported shower curtain sets consisting of an outer textile curtain, an inner plastic liner, and plastic hooks. The liner prevented water from escaping and was color coordinated to match the curtain. The curtain was decorative and semi-transparent, permitting the color of the plastic liner to show when in use. Customs classified the merchandise under the provision for the set's outer curtain at a duty of 12.8 percent, under heading 6303 for *"Curtains and interior blinds; curtain or bed valances"* and Subheading 6303.92 as *"Other ... Of synthetic fibers."* Better Home argues that classification of the set should be based on the set's inner plastic liner under heading 3924 for *"Tableware, kitchenware, other household articles and toilet articles, of plastics,"* and item 3924.90.10 for *"Curtains and drapes"* at a duty of 3.36 percent *ad valorem.*

DICARLO, CHIEF JUDGE

Goods put up in sets for retail sale, which cannot be classified according to the most specific heading, are classified by the "component which gives them their essential character." GRI 3(b). Better Home Plastics

continues

continued

contends the court must apply the essential character test, in classifying the applicable merchandise. Application of the test, Better Home Plastics asserts, would mandate classification of the set on the basis of its inner plastic liner pursuant to Subheading 3924.90.10 ... .

Defendant contends the essential character of the curtains is embodied in the textile curtain. Defendant raises numerous arguments to support its position, particularly that (1) the plastic liner is replaceable at 1/3 to 1/4 the price of the set; (2) the consumer purchases the set because of the decorative function of the outer curtain, and not for the protection afford by the liner; and (3) the liner is only employed for the limited period that someone is utilizing the shower, whereas the decorative outer curtain is employed, at a minimum, when the bathroom is in use, and as much as 24 hours a day. Defendant also contends Better Home Plastics' invoice description supports Customs' classification. Pursuant to the invoice description, the set is sold as "Fabric Shower Curtain and Liner." Therefore, defendant argues, this description serves as an admission that the curtain provides the essential character of the set. * * *

Although the court agrees that the curtain in the imported set imparts a desirable decorative characteristic, nonetheless ... it is the plastic liner that provides the indispensable property of preventing water from escaping the shower enclosure. The liner (1) prevents water from escaping when the shower is in use; (2) protects the fabric curtain from mildew and soap scum; and (3) conceals the shower and provides privacy when the shower is in use. Further, the plastic liner can serve its intended function without the outer curtain and contributes to the overall appearance of the set. The outer curtain, in contrast, merely furthers the set's decorative aspect. The court therefore concludes the essential character of the set is derived from the plastic liner.

Defendant's other contentions are also unpersuasive. The manner in which the set is invoiced does not definitively determine which component provides the essential character of the set. The invoice description is intended to characterize the shipped item; it is not a declaration of the relative importance of its component parts. Finally, while the court takes into consideration the relative cost of the component parts, this point alone is not dispositive, nor very persuasive against the competing arguments.

It is the essential character of the set—derived in part from the plastic's ability to repel water—that denotes the set's utility, purpose, and accordingly, character. Inclusion of the textile curtain within the classification for the plastic liner does little to change the qualities or the basic nature of the set in meeting this purpose.

The court finds Better Home Plastics has overcome the presumption of correctness accorded to Customs, and the shower curtain sets were improperly classified under subheading 6303.92.00, HTSUS. In addition, the court agrees with Better Home Plastics' proposed classification of the sets under subheading 3924.90.10.

This decision is limited to its facts, i.e., that the set at issue is at the low end of the shower curtain market. The court does not offer an opinion on the proper classification of sets targeted to a different market segment.

Decision. When articles are made up of component parts, or are in sets, and their parts are referred to in two equally specific headings, then the rule of relative specificity does not apply, and their classification must be determined by which part gives the article its essential character. In this case, the shower liner imparted the essential character to the set.

Comment. Judge DiCarlo's opinion was affirmed by the U.S. Court of Appeals in *Better Home Plastics Corp. v. U.S.*, 119 F.3d 969 (Fed. Cir. 1997).

Case Questions

1. What are the two main components of this "set"? If they had been sold separately, how would each have been classified?
2. What is the "essential character" test, and how was it applied here?
3. At the end of the opinion the court clarifies that the opinion is limited to shower curtains at the "low end of the market." Why might that have made a difference?

Tariff Engineering. **Tariff engineering** is the process of modifying or engineering a product prior to importation for the purposes of obtaining a lower rate of duty. The general rule established by the U.S. Supreme Court long ago is that an article is to be classified according to its condition at the time it is imported. An 1881 case involved duties on imported sugar that were determined on the basis of its color and grade. In approving of tariff engineering, the Supreme Court stated that "if the manufacturer uses ... bleaching processes in order to make his sugars more saleable, why may he not omit to do so in order to render them less dutiable; nay, why may he not employ an extra quantity of molasses for that purpose?" *Merrit v. Welsh*, 104 U.S. 694 (1881). Tariff engineering also permits importers to enter their goods at any step in the manufacturing or assembly process in order to obtain a lower rate of duty.

Of course, there are some limits on tariff engineering. There must be no fraud or deception, the goods must be correctly described on the entry documents, and they must be honestly presented to Customs for inspection if requested. In *Heartland By-Products, Inc. v. United States*, 264 F.3d 1126 (Fed. Cir. 2001), the importer added molasses to sugar syrup in Canada and removed it after the syrup was imported into the United States. The syrup with molasses entered free from U.S. tariff-rate quotas on sugar syrup imports. Customs maintained that there had been no other purpose for adding molasses except to avoid the quota, that the molasses was a "foreign substance," and that adding it was not a genuine step in the manufacturing process. Because the molasses was later returned to Canada to be reused for the same purpose, Customs maintained that the process was done for "disguise or artifice" to circumvent the customs laws. There was no evidence that Heartland ever falsified or concealed the identity of its sugar syrup, its method of manufacture, or its use. The Court of Appeals agreed with Customs' argument and upheld its reclassification of the syrup.

Customs Valuation

The customs value, often called **dutiable value**, of goods entered into any country must be reported by the importer-of-record to national customs authorities at the time of entry. Customs value is the transaction value of the goods. In the United States, **transaction value** is the *price actually paid or payable* for the merchandise when sold for export to the United States, plus the following amounts if not included in the purchase price: (1) packing and container, (2) selling commission paid by the buyer, (3) the value of any "assist" as defined below, (4) any royalty or license fee that the buyer is required to pay as a condition of sale, and (5) the proceeds of any subsequent resale of the merchandise that accrues to the *seller*.

Transaction value *does not* include international freight charges, insurance or customs brokerage fees, inland freight after importation, charges for assembling or maintaining the goods after importation, or import duties.

If an importer is required, as a condition of the purchase, to make certain payments to foreign parties other than the seller, those payments may be included in transaction value. Examples include separate payments (i.e., license fees) made to the holders of copyrights, trademarks, or patents for the privilege of importing merchandise subject to those rights, and design and engineering fees paid to foreign firms separately from payments to the actual producer of the product. For instance, if a firm imports blue jeans manufactured in Hong Kong and as a condition of sale makes royalty payments to the designer of the jeans in Paris, the royalty would be included in the transaction value of the merchandise.

Agency Commissions. A buying agent is frequently used to locate foreign goods or foreign suppliers or to handle the details of import transactions. Transaction value can be affected by the terms of the relationship between the importer and the agent. Although commissions paid to an agent of the buyer/ importer are not included in transaction value, payments made to or for the benefit of the seller or seller's agent are included. Customs carefully scrutinizes the relationship between U.S. importers and their buying agents to be sure that dutiable value is accurately reported.

In *Monarch Luggage Co. v. United States*, 715 F. Supp. 1115 (C.I.T. 1989), the importer successfully structured a business transaction so that the buying commissions were excluded from transaction value. Although representatives of Monarch traveled to the Far East several times a year to meet with their suppliers, inspect their facilities, and place orders for luggage, they nevertheless maintained a local agent there. Under a written agreement, the agent was to locate the best sources for luggage and visit the suppliers to determine the quality of the luggage but could place orders only at Monarch's direction. The agent coordinated payment for the luggage and arranged transportation according to Monarch's explicit instructions. The supplier and not the agent absorbed the loss associated with defective merchandise. The agent bore no risk of loss to the goods and never took title to them. The agreement further stated that "the agent shall never act as a seller in any transaction involving the principal." Most importantly, Monarch made the payments to its agent directly and separately and not as a part of the invoice price paid to the supplier of the luggage. In other words, the agent was in fact a representative of thc buyer and not an agent of the seller. The fees paid to the agent were not included in dutiable value.

Production Assists. **Production assists**, also called *dutiable assists*, are goods, services, or intellectual property furnished by the importer to a foreign producer, free or at a reduced price, for use in producing merchandise for import and sale in the United States. The value of an assist must be included in transaction value when the goods are imported into the United States. For example, if a U.S. apparel importer provides sewing machines (i.e., the "assist") free to a foreign sewing contractor, then the value of the their use in sewing the apparel must be included in transaction value when the apparel enters the United States. Other production assists include the value of component parts supplied, tools, engineering and design services, or the value of artwork and sketches performed outside the United States and that are necessary for production. Production assists might be provided when a foreign firm needs special equipment or machinery to manufacture custom or specially designed goods. It might reduce costs by putting to use underutilized equipment belonging to the importer, while taking advantage of the foreign producer's low-cost labor or economies of scale. Assists might also allow the importer some greater control over the quality of the finished product.

Assists are often used in **contract manufacturing**—a business arrangement in which the production of goods is contracted or "outsourced" by one firm to a manufacturing firm, often overseas. They also result from multinational companies with operations in many countries. A multinational may have research and development facilities in one country, derive parts from other countries, and conduct final assembly in yet another country. These companies should maintain accurate accounting and documentation of all assists.

RULES OF ORIGIN

Imagine that it is 1989 and your trading company has firm commitments from buyers in the United States to take all of the ostrich chicks that you can provide during the next year. After considerable searching and time spent traveling the world, you find an ostrich hatchery in England. You enter into a sales contract with the hatchery, with payment to be made under a confirmed letter of credit. Your bank pays the seller cash on the documents, and the chicks arrive peeping and squawking at a U.S. port of entry. The chicks are entered with their country of origin listed as England. An astute customs inspector realizes that the chicks could not possibly have "originated" there and corrects the country of origin to South Africa where the eggs obviously originated. You agree that the fertilized eggs originated in South Africa but argue that their incubation and hatching in England amounts to a "substantial transformation" and that England therefore became the country of origin. U.S. Customs rules that the processing of the eggs in England is a natural biological consequence of the initial fertilization of the eggs in South Africa, that the chicks continue to be a product of South Africa, and that they are therefore prohibited from entering the United States under a U.S. law banning the import of products from South Africa. (The ban was lifted in the early 1990s following the end of apartheid racial discrimination and political changes in South Africa.) This not-so-hypothetical case illustrates how critical it is to know the proper rules of origin needed to determine the country of origin of imported goods—and to know them in advance of executing the transaction.

All goods have a type of "nationality," known as the country of origin. The **country of origin** is that country from which an imported article is said to have originated according to specific legal rules, known as *rules of origin*. The country of origin is used to determine the following:

- The normal tariff rate on an import
- Whether an import is subject to a preferential tariff rate or an increased rate
- Whether an import is subject to antidumping or countervailing duties
- Whether an import is subject to a quota, embargo, or other trade restriction
- The applicability of government procurement rules
- The proper country of origin marking or labeling of the product
- Statistical information

Determining the country of origin seems like it would be pretty simple to do. If all production processes for a product are conducted entirely in one country using raw materials and components originating there, the country of origin is not difficult to determine. For example, bananas grown in Honduras and shipped directly to supermarkets in the United States are products of Honduras. Plywood sheets glued and pressed in Brazil, from trees grown in Brazil, are products of Brazil. Men's shirts that were cut and sewn in China, from fabric dyed and woven there, from yarn spun there, from cotton grown there, are products of China. But as with our ostrich chicks, country of origin is not always so easy to determine. The country of origin is not merely the country from which the goods were purchased, or from where they were shipped, or from where they were subjected to some superficial processing. If that were the case, Chinese-made furniture could be routed through Mexico, subjected to some very minor "finishing," and then be relabeled and transshipped to the United States at the lower Mexican tariff rate. In today's global economy, raw materials and component parts circle the earth, finding their way into assembly lines and manufacturing plants stretched around the world. Thus, for most manufactured, processed, or assembled articles, the country of origin can only be determined by resorting to the rules of origin in effect in the importing country. Without rules of origin, the tariff system worldwide would quickly fall apart.

Definition and Types of Rules of Origin

Rules of origin are the legal rules used to determine the country of origin of imported products. They are found in national statutes, the regulations of customs authorities, and international agreements and can differ greatly from country to country. In the United States, many of the rules have been fashioned in court decisions and are administered and enforced by U.S. Customs. Penalties for willfully misstating a country of origin or procuring a false country of origin certificate are severe. Rules of origin can be complex and arcane, with different rules often applying to different products. Application of the rules often requires firms to seek expert professional advice or to obtain an advance ruling from customs authorities.

In the United States and most developed countries, there are two general types of rules of origin, non-preferential and preferential. **Non-preferential rules of origin** are those applicable to imports from developed countries that receive normal tariff treatment. Trade between the United States and Europe or between the United States and China is non-preferential trade. **Preferential rules of origin** are those applicable to goods traded within a free trade area or customs union, or that receive preferential tariff treatment under trade preference programs for developing countries. All free trade agreements, such as the *North American Free Trade Agreement* (NAFTA), have preferential rules of origin. (NAFTA rules of origin are discussed in more detail in Chapter fourteen.) Preference programs covering imports from developing countries, such as the *Generalized System of Preferences* (discussed in Chapter nine), also contain their own rules of origin. (See Exhibit 12.1 for a list of U.S. tariff preferences in effect at the time of this writing.)

Non-Preferential Rules of Origin

The general rule applicable to most non-preferential trade is that the country of origin of an article imported into the United States is the country in which the article was wholly obtained. *Wholly obtained* means that it was wholly the growth, product, or manufacture of one country. In other words, the country of origin is that single country where an article was wholly and completely produced or manufactured entirely from raw materials originating in that country. Of course, few products today are wholly made in one country entirely from materials derived there. More and more products are subjected to manufacturing, processing, and assembly operations on a global scale. Nevertheless, there can be only one country of origin for customs purposes.

If an article is *not* wholly the growth, product, or manufacture of one country, then the country of origin is that country where the article last underwent a substantial transformation into a new and different article of commerce. Importers are expected to track the movement of materials and understand the complex manufacturing or assembly processes, which in turn allows them to accurately determine an article's country of origin.

The Substantial Transformation Test. For more than a century, U.S. courts have held that a **substantial transformation** occurs when the original article loses its identity as such and is transformed into a new and different article of commerce having "a new name, character, or use" different from that of the original item. In 1908, the U.S. Supreme Court ruled that imported cork had not been substantially transformed when it was dried, treated, and cut into smaller sections for use in bottling beer. The Court stated, "Something more is necessary .... There must be a transformation; a new and different article must emerge, having a distinctive name, character or use. This cannot be said of the corks in question. A cork put through the claimant's process is still a cork." *Anheuser-Busch Brewing Association v. United States*, 207 U.S. 556 (1908). This is known as the **name, character, or use test**. Since then, many courts have tried to interpret this phrase and to apply it to many different types of products and manufacturing operations.

Suppose, for example, that stainless steel bars are made in Korea and shipped to Germany where they are turned into fine cutlery. The cutlery will then enter the United States under the tariff rate for German cutlery and be labeled "Made in Germany" if the processing in Germany amounted to a substantial transformation that created a new and different article of commerce with a new name, character, or use. Similarly, if foreign raw materials are imported into the United States and put through a manufacturing process that substantially transforms them into a product with a new name, character, or use, the new product need not be marked as of foreign origin when sold to the ultimate purchaser. In other words, the foreign raw materials were transformed into a product of the United States because that is where the last substantial transformation occurred.

The landmark case *Gibson-Thomsen Co. v. United States*, 27 C.C.P.A. 267 (1940), involved the application of the name, character, or use test under the marking and labeling laws of the United States. The court ruled that when wooden handles and blocks were imported into the United States from Japan, then drilled with holes into which American bristles were inserted, and with the final product being sold in the United States as toothbrushes and hairbrushes, the imported wooden components had "lost their identity in a tariff sense" and had been transformed into products of the United States. The court took account of the fact that the bristles, which had been of U.S. origin, were a key component of the new product. Because the transformation took place in the United States, the wooden handles did not have to be marked as having originated in Japan. *Gibson-Thomsen* is often cited by courts today.

Since 1940, the courts have looked to see if a "new article of commerce" emerges from the transformation. For instance, wooden sticks imported into the United States and then set into liquid ice cream and frozen have been held to be substantially transformed into a new article of commerce having a new name, character, and use. Although many cases look to see if the name commonly given the transformed article has changed, a product's name is generally considered to be only one of several factors to take into account. Greater emphasis is usually placed on whether the character—sometimes said to be the "essential nature"—of the product or its use has changed.

As a general rule, a simple assembly of component parts is not a substantial transformation, unless the assembly is meaningful and significant (in terms of time, skill, level of quality control, etc.) and if it results in the creation of an article with a new name, character, or use.

Value-Added. Many of the cases also look to see whether the substantial transformation has resulted in an increase in value, called the **value-added test**. In *National Juice Products Association v. United States*, 628 F. Supp. 978 (Ct. Int'l. Trade 1986), a U.S. company had imported evaporated orange concentrate and, at its U.S. plant, blended it with water, orange oils, and fresh juice to make frozen orange concentrate. The blending and processing in the United States had added only a 7 percent value to the orange juice. The court held that the blending in the United States was not a substantial transformation and that the orange juice sold to consumers could not be labeled as a product of the United States. Complying with a value-added test can be difficult and expensive in large-scale industrial applications because it requires firms to calculate, trace, and record all of the costs of processing, and many of these costs constantly fluctuate.

The following case, *Ferrostaal Metals Corp. v. United States*, illustrates the difficulty of determining whether a substantial transformation has occurred. It also illustrates how the courts have developed rules on a case-by-case basis.

Ferrostaal Metals Corp. v. United States

664 F. Supp. 535 (1987) Court of International Trade

BACKGROUND AND FACTS

Plaintiff attempted to enter steel products at the Port of Seattle. These products consisted of unpainted steel sheets that had originated in Japan but had been hot-dip galvanized in New Zealand. Plaintiff's entry documents identified New Zealand as the country of origin. Customs ruled that the country of origin was Japan and that the steel could not be entered due to an agreement between the United States and Japan. Customs contended that hot-dip galvanizing of Japanese steel sheets in New Zealand was merely a "finishing process" carried out to improve certain performance characteristics of the steel sheets and not a process that results in a substantial transformation so as to change the country of origin. The plaintiff disagreed and brought this action for review.

JUDGE DICARLO

Substantial transformation is a concept of major importance in administering the customs and trade laws. In addition to its role in identifying the country of origin of imported merchandise for purposes of determining dutiable status, or, as in this case, the applicability of a bilateral trade agreement, substantial transformation is the focus of many cases involving country of origin markings....

The essence of these cases is that a product cannot be said to originate in the country of exportation if it is not manufactured there. The question, therefore, is whether operations performed on products in the country of exportation are of such a substantial nature to justify the conclusion that the resulting product is a manufacture of that country. "Manufacture implies a change, but every change is not manufacture...."

continues

continued

There must be transformation; a new and different article must emerge, 'having a distinctive name, character, or use.'" *Anheuser-Busch Brewing Assn. v. United States,* 207 U.S. 556 (1908). The criteria of name, character, and use continue to determine when substantial transformation has occurred, and the prior cases of this court and our predecessor and appellate courts provide guidance in the application of this test.

* * *

Whether galvanizing and annealing change the character of the merchandise depends on the nature of these operations and their effect on the properties of the materials To produce one of the types of imported sheet the sheet must be heated to 1,350 degrees F, at which point recrystallization of the grains of steel occurs. The sheet is then brought down to 880 degrees F, before galvanizing begins. At 880 degrees F, the sheet enters a pot of molten zinc and is dipped. The molten zinc reacts immediately with the solid steel, and begins a process known as "alloying." Alloying constitutes a chemical change in the product, characterized by the formation of iron-zinc alloys at the interface between the steel and the zinc. The galvanized steel sheet emerging from the bath has a mixed zinc-steel surface with an identifiable atomic pattern. The formation of a galvanized surface is an irreversible process which provides electrochemical protection to the sheet. As a result of the galvanic protection, the steel will last up to twenty years, or ten times as long as ungalvanized steel ... .

The alloy-bonded zinc coating affects the character of the sheet by changing its chemical composition and by providing corrosion resistance. The court also finds that the hot-dip galvanizing process is substantial in terms of the value it adds to full hard cold-rolled steel sheet. The evidence showed that the Japanese product is sold for approximately $350 per ton, while the hot-dipped galvanized product is sold for an average price of $550 to $630.

Taken as a whole, the continuous hot-dip galvanizing process transforms a strong, brittle product which cannot be formed into a durable, corrosion-resistant product which is less hard, but formable for a range of commercial applications. Defendant's witness stated that the imported sheet has a "different character from the standpoint of durability." The court finds that the annealing and galvanizing processes result in a change in character by significantly altering the mechanical properties and chemical composition of the steel sheet.

The name criterion is generally considered the least compelling of the factors which will support a finding of substantial transformation. Nonetheless, the satisfaction of the name criterion in this case lends support to plaintiffs' claim. The witnesses for both parties testified that the processing of full hard cold-rolled steel sheet results in a product which has a different name, continuous hot-dip galvanized steel sheet.

The court also considers relevant whether the operations underlying the asserted transformation have effected a change in the classification of the merchandise under the Tariff Schedules of the United States. Change in tariff classification may be considered as a factor in the substantial transformation analysis. Here this factor supports a substantial transformation. Full hard cold-rolled steel sheet is classified under item 607.83, TSUS, while continuous hot-dip galvanized steel sheet is classifiable under item 608.13, TSUS. [The TSUS was the forerunner to the *Harmonized Tariff Schedule.*]

Based on the totality of the evidence, showing that the continuous hot-dip galvanizing process effects changes in the name, character, and use of the processed steel sheet, the court holds that the changes constitute a substantial transformation and that hot-dipped galvanized steel sheet is a new and different article of commerce from full hard cold-rolled steel sheet.

Decision. Japanese steel that had been galvanized in New Zealand prior to its importation into the United States was substantially transformed so that it had become a product of New Zealand and thus was not subject to voluntary restraint agreements between the United States and Japan.

Comment. "Voluntary restraint agreements," such as those described in this case to restrict steel imports from Japan, are no longer used as a method of limiting imports of foreign goods into the United States, as they do not fall under the permissible rules of the WTO. Nevertheless, this case serves well to illustrate the use of the substantial transformation test in tariff cases. The case has since been cited by U.S. Customs in determining the country of origin in other cases.

Case Questions

1. Why is the process of galvanizing steel important to the court's decision?
2. Consider the process of hot-dip galvanizing described here. Would you agree that the operations performed on the steel in New Zealand created a product with a new name, character, or use? Why or why not?
3. Of the three factors generally referred to—name, character, use—which seem to be the most or least important?
4. What other factors does the court consider in addition to a change in the name, character, and use of the product?

Preferential Rules of Origin

The tariff-shift rule and the local or regional value content rule of origin are two rules used to determine if an article qualifies for a tariff preference under a free trade agreement or preference program for developing countries, as well as in some non-preferential trade. These rules of origin are important for all North American trade between Canada, Mexico, and the United States.

The **tariff-shift rule** states that the country of origin is the last country in which all "inputs" (raw materials, component parts, etc.) into the finished article underwent a *defined* change in tariff classification. For example, under NAFTA, if raw materials or component parts from Europe are combined, altered, or subjected to a process in Canada, and that process results in a certain change in tariff classification, then the finished article is considered to have originated in Canada if the initial materials or components (called "inputs") underwent a change from one tariff classification to a new classification as defined in the NAFTA agreement. The finished article can then qualify for tariff-free treatment when sold in Mexico or the United States. A variation of the tariff-shift rule is also used to determine the country of origin of apparel and textiles.

The tariff-shift rule has the advantage over the name, character, and use test because it is more objective, concise, and easier to apply. It can also be the basis of an internationally accepted rule because most countries use the harmonized tariff classifications on which the rule is based. As a result, the rule is favored by WTO experts working on international rules of origin. U.S. Customs has actually considered adopting it in lieu of the more subjective substantial transformation test discussed earlier.

The other common preferential rule of origin is the **regional value content test**, a type of value-added test described earlier. This requires that some minimum percentage of the value of a finished article be added in a country in order for it to have "originated" there. For example, the U.S. preference program for Caribbean countries requires that at least 35 percent of the value of materials and/or labor be added there in order for the article to enter the United States at the lower Caribbean rate. The regional value content test is used to determine whether a vehicle originates in North American under NAFTA. Compliance requires automotive manufactures to trace the value of each component as it moves through the production and assembly process in North America.

WTO Agreement on Rules of Origin

Exporters and importers worldwide would benefit greatly from standardized rules of origin, which would let them more accurately determine the country of origin of their shipments in advance. This would help in product labeling as well as in determining the rate of duty and other laws applicable to their products. The WTO *Agreement on Rules of Origin* (1995) is a long-term project to achieve this goal. As of this writing, the WTO was in the process of developing new, uniform rules. Under a proposed rule, the country of origin for goods originating in all WTO countries would be determined by a tariff-shift rule, similar to that discussed.

Marking and Labeling of Imports

All countries require that imported goods be marked or labeled with the country of origin The United States has two key laws that require imports to be labeled with the country of origin: the marking rules of U.S. Customs and the Federal Trade Commission (FTC) rules. The rules of U.S. Customs apply to country of origin markings of all imported products sold in the United States. The FTC rules apply primarily to the use of "Made in U.S.A." or similar terms. To be labeled "Made in U.S.A.," a label must meet the requirements of both agencies.

Customs Marking Rules. Every article of foreign origin imported into the United States must be indelibly and permanently marked in English in a conspicuous place and in such a manner as to indicate the name of the country of origin of the article to the **ultimate purchaser** in the United States. The ultimate purchaser is the last person in the United States who receives an article in the form in which it was imported. If an imported article is to be sold at retail in the same form as it was imported, then the retail customer is the "ultimate purchaser."

If the imported article is converted, processed, or combined with other articles or ingredients in the United States so that it undergoes a substantial transformation resulting in a new article of commerce with a new name, character, or use, as defined by the *Gibson-Thomsen* case, then the U.S. firm that transformed the article is considered the ultimate purchaser. As a result, the new product need not be labeled with a foreign country of origin.

Items Not Requiring Marks. Customs regulations specify many articles by name that are exempt from marking requirements. These generally are objects that are incapable of being marked because of their size or special characteristics. Examples include works of art, unstrung beads, nuts, bolts, cigarettes, eggs, feathers, livestock, and vegetables. The following categories of products do not require marking: (1) products incapable of being marked; (2) products that cannot be marked without injury; (3) crude substances; (4) articles produced more than twenty years prior to importation; (5) products of possessions of the United States; (6) articles imported solely for the use of the importer and not intended for resale (e.g., personal articles purchased abroad by a tourist); (7) products of American fisheries that are entered duty-free; and (8) certain products of the United States that are exported (e.g., for repairs) and returned. In addition, articles used by an importer as samples in soliciting orders and that are not for sale are exempted from the marking requirements.

When an item is exempt from marking requirements, the container in which it is sold to the consumer must be marked. To illustrate, imported carpentry nails need not be marked, but the box in which they are sold to the consumer must be.

Federal Trade Commission "Made in U.S.A." Rules. In the United States, the FTC and U.S. Customs have overlapping jurisdiction with regard to country of origin claims. While Customs oversees foreign country of origin marking ("Made in China"), the FTC regulates the use of the term "Made in U.S.A." Customs rules apply only to product marking, whereas the FTC rules apply to all claims, including those on product labels, catalogs, packaging, and all forms of advertising. Customs rules are more complex and detailed, whereas the "Made in U.S.A." rules of the FTC are more flexible and are based on whether or not the claims would mislead or cause deception in the minds of the average consumer. The FTC bases its rules on its authority under the *Federal Trade Commission Act* to prevent unfair or deceptive trade practices.

There is no rule that requires a U.S.-made product to be labeled as such. Except for special rules applicable to automobiles and textile and fur products, U.S. content need not be disclosed. However, a seller may not claim that a product is "Made in U.S.A." unless *all or virtually all* of the materials, processing, or component parts are made in the United States and their final assembly or processing took place there. All significant parts and processing that go into the product must be of U.S. origin. That is, the product should contain only negligible foreign content. For instance, the FTC has held that a gas barbecue grill assembled entirely from U.S. parts could be labeled as "Made in U.S.A." despite the fact that the knobs were of foreign origin. The knobs were said to make up a small portion of the product's total cost and an insignificant part of the final product.

The FTC origin rules apply also to other more indirect forms of marketing and promotion that may be deceptive. In one case, a company packaged its Chinese-made product in a package covered with an American flag and eagle. Despite the statement "Made in China," which appeared in small print on the bottom and side panels of the package, the FTC held that the labeling was deceptive.

Partly Made in the U.S.A. Products that cannot be labeled as "Made in U.S.A." may still bear qualified claims. A qualified claim is one that indicates that the product was partially made or processed in the United States. An example would be a down comforter labeled "Shell constructed in Germany with filling and further processing in the U.S.A." To use a qualified claim, there must still be a significant amount of U.S. content. A product that is invented in the United States and made in India could *not* claim "Created in U.S.A.," as this would be deceptive. The term "Assembled in U.S.A." may be used only where the product has undergone a substantial transformation in the United States and where the use of the term would not be deceptive. For example, according to the FTC, component parts for computers made in Singapore and assembled in Texas with only a screwdriver and screws may *not* be labeled as "Assembled in U.S.A." Here there was no substantial transformation in the United States and the statement is deceptive.

OTHER CUSTOMS LAWS AFFECTING U.S. IMPORTS

This section examines two other programs affecting the import/export operations of international companies: drawback provisions allowing a refund of duties paid, and foreign trade zones. These are tariff-saving programs created by law to encourage the import/export trade. Most developing countries have similar programs for their importers and exporters.

Drawbacks

A **drawback** is a refund of duties already paid on imported goods when the goods (or other goods manufactured from the original goods) are re-exported or destroyed. Drawbacks are recognized by many countries around the world. The most common type in the United States is the **manufacturing drawback**, designed to encourage U.S. manufacturers to export. A manufacturing drawback is a 99 percent refund of duties and taxes paid on merchandise that is imported, subjected to manufacture or production, and then exported within five years. U.S. firms are becoming increasingly sophisticated in using manufacturing drawbacks. For instance, duties paid on imported yarn will be refunded to the importer who exports a finished fabric made from that yarn. Similarly, a poultry farm that imports chicken feed can receive a drawback on duties paid on the imported feed when the chickens are slaughtered and exported. Drawbacks allow the exporter to purchase materials from low-cost foreign suppliers without having to pay prohibitively high duties. There are no drawbacks allowed in trade between Canada, Mexico, and the United States.

A same-condition drawback is a drawback of duties paid on imported goods that are re-exported in the "same condition" as they were imported, provided they were not significantly altered. For example, nuts and bolts can be entered in bulk, cleaned, sorted, and repackaged with foreign-language labeling. On export, the drawback applies. Many trading companies utilize same-condition drawbacks.

A **substitution drawback** of duties paid on imported goods may be received by a U.S. firm that imports goods and then exports other goods of the "same kind and quality." Substitution drawbacks usually deal with fungible goods or agricultural commodities. Assume a U.S. manufacturer imports soda ash, pays import duties, and then sells it to a U.S. customer. Later, it exports the same quantity of U.S.-made soda ash to a foreign buyer. The importer can receive a drawback on duties paid on the imported soda ash.

A **rejected merchandise drawback** is allowed for imported merchandise that was shipped without consent, is defective, or does not conform to specifications or to samples (e.g., zippers that do not zip). The merchandise is returned to U.S. Customs within three years and either destroyed or re-exported.

Obtaining a drawback requires close cooperation between the firm and U.S. Customs. The procedures, time limits, documentation, and accounting requirements for drawbacks are complex and exact, and many companies use drawback consultants for advice or help in structuring drawback transactions. Some firms utilize specially developed software to help track and document a drawback transaction. Civil penalties are imposed for violating the provisions of the law. Many firms do not file for drawbacks for fear of being assessed a penalty for clerical errors.

Foreign Trade Zones

Foreign trade zones (FTZs) are legally defined sites within a country that are subject to special customs procedures. They are used widely around the world, and are monitored by, and under the control of, the customs authorities of that country. Foreign trade zones exist under the laws of most nations, including the United States. In the United States, FTZs operate under a license from the Foreign Trade Zone Board and according to regulations of the board and of U.S. Customs and Border Protection. Foreign trade zones must be within a 60-mile radius of a U.S. port of entry. Imported goods may be brought into an FTZ without being subjected to tariffs until such time as the goods are released into the stream of commerce in the United States.

FTZs are operated by state or local governments, airports or seaports, or specially chartered corporations who charge private firms for their use. Originally, FTZs were intended to encourage U.S. firms to participate in international trade by providing a "free port" into which foreign-made goods could be transported, stored, packaged, and then re-exported without the payment of import duties. Today, FTZs are used for many different purposes, ranging from warehousing to manufacturing. Goods may be assembled, exhibited, cleaned, manipulated, manufactured, mixed, processed, relabeled, repackaged, repaired, salvaged, sampled, stored, tested, displayed, and destroyed. Manufacturing may result in a change to the tariff classification of the goods only with permission of U.S. Customs. Retail sales are prohibited. The length of time that these goods can be held in a zone is not limited.

The flexibility offered to an importer through the use of FTZs provides many opportunities for creative importing strategies. For example, firms can ship goods to their zone duty-free and hold them for later entry and sale in the United States pending buyer's orders or more favorable market conditions. Foreign goods can also be held for exhibition and display in the zone for unlimited periods without the payment of duties. Foreign goods that arrive damaged or defective may be destroyed without the payment of duties. Goods in an FTZ are not subject to quotas and may remain in the FTZ until the quota opens and their entry is permitted. Title to goods held in an FTZ may be transferred to another party without the payment of duties (although not to a retail customer for consumption outside of the FTZ).

Opportunities for creative business planning are almost endless. For instance, in certain cases it is possible that foreign component parts can be assembled in an FTZ, making the duties payable when the finished product is sold less than what the duties would have been on the individual components. As another example, if a commodity is dutied by weight, it may be brought into an FTZ for drying; subsequently it may be entered without the excess weight caused by the moisture. But perhaps the most unusual use of an FTZ is the Cape Canaveral Zone in Florida. There, foreign payloads can be imported into the United States, processed, and made ready for a space launch, and then "exported" to space without the payment of U.S. import duties! More than 200 general-purpose foreign trade zones and more than 250 subzones exist in the United States.

In addition to general-purpose zones, firms are able to establish their own special-purpose subzones. Subzones can be placed anywhere in the United States with U.S. Customs approval. Most automotive manufacturers and oil refineries use subzones. They are also widely used in chemicals, pharmaceuticals, computer assembly, electronics, and shipbuilding and as retail distribution centers. The following case, *Nissan Motor Mfg. Corp. U.S.A. v. United States*, arose out of Nissan's importation of equipment into an automotive manufacturing subzone in Tennessee.

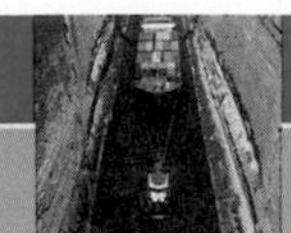

Nissan Motor Mfg. Corp., U.S.A. v. United States

884 F.2d 1375 (1989) United States Court of Appeals (Fed. Cir.)

BACKGROUND AND FACTS

Nissan operated a foreign trade zone subzone at its automotive manufacturing and assembly plant located in Smyrna, Tennessee. Nissan imported production machinery for use in the subzone consisting of industrial robots, automated conveyor systems, and a computerized interface. The machinery was to be assembled and tested in the zone, and if it proved unsatisfactory it was to be replaced, redesigned, or scrapped. Customs ruled that production equipment was not "merchandise" as defined under the FTZ act and was therefore dutiable. Duties were assessed at $3 million, and Nissan filed a protest. On denial, the Court of International Trade ruled that the equipment was dutiable, and this appeal was filed.

CIRCUIT JUDGE ARCHER

The activities performed by Nissan in the foreign trade zone subzone with the imported equipment are not among those permitted by a plain reading of the statute. Section 81c provides that merchandise brought into a foreign trade zone may be "stored, sold, exhibited, broken up, repacked, assembled, distributed, sorted, graded, cleaned, mixed with foreign or domestic merchandise, or otherwise manipulated, or be manufactured... ."

The act does not say that imported equipment may be "installed," "used," "operated" or "consumed" in the zone, which are the kinds of operations Nissan performs in the zone with the subject equipment. Alternative operations of a different character should not be implied when Congress has made so exhaustive a list.

Nissan relies upon the case of *Hawaiian Independent Refinery v. United States,* 460 F. Supp. 1249 (Cust. Ct.1978) in support of its position. The merchandise there involved was crude oil which was entered into a foreign trade zone for manufacture into fuel oil products. This, of course, is an activity delineated by the act and entry into the zone was exempted from Customs duties. Thereafter, a portion of the crude oil was consumed in the manufacturing process and Customs assessed duty on the theory that there had been a "constructive" entry into the Customs territory of the United States. In holding that the assessment was improper, the Court of International Trade did not have to deal with the question at issue here of whether the initial entry into the zone was exempt. Clearly, in that case the crude oil was exempt at the time of entry. Thus, the Court of International Trade properly concluded that the *Hawaiian Independent Refinery* case was not dispositive of this case.

We are convinced that the Court of International Trade correctly determined that the importation by Nissan of the machinery and capital equipment at issue into the foreign trade zone subzone was not for the purpose of being manipulated in one of the ways prescribed by the statute. Instead it was to be used (consumed) in the subzone for the production of motor vehicles. Under the plain language of the 1950 amendment to the act and the legislative history of that amendment, and Customs' published decision interpreting the act as amended, such a use does not entitle the equipment to exemption from Customs duties. Accordingly, the judgment of the Court of International Trade is affirmed.

Decision. The decision of the lower court was affirmed. Machinery entered into a foreign trade zone for use in the manufacture and assembly of automobiles is not "merchandise" under the act and may not be entered duty-free.

Case Questions

1. What purposes do FTZs serve? Why did Congress establish them?
2. What were the advantages to Nissan by assembling automobiles in an FTZ? How many can you list?
3. Why could Nissan not bring manufacturing equipment into its zone duty-free? Do you think this case applies to office chairs or personal computers? Explain.
4. Assume that you import merchandise subject to annual quotas. You have a shipment arriving, but the quota has filled. How might an FTZ help you?
5. What FTZs are located in your state or region?

THE ADMINISTRATION OF U.S. CUSTOMS AND TARIFF LAWS

The customs and tariff laws of the United States are administered and enforced by the U.S. Bureau of Customs and Border Protection, an agency within the Department of Homeland Security. The creation of the Department of Homeland Security in 2003 was a part of the largest reorganization of the American government in more than fifty years. The reorganization eliminated the U.S. Customs Service (which had been in the Department of the Treasury) and the Immigration and Nationality Service, and transferred those functions to the newly created Department of Homeland Security. Customs' responsibilities are to stop terrorists and terrorist weapons, as well as illegal drugs and drug traffickers, from entering the United States; to assess and collect the tariff revenue of the United States; and to enforce the customs and immigration laws at the border. The latter includes regulating the entry of products under quota or embargo, enforcing the country of origin labeling statutes, administering foreign trade zones, and performing other functions. As a law enforcement agency, U.S. Customs combats smuggling and investigates tariff fraud cases. Customs has the authority to bar the entry of goods that violate patent, trademark, or copyright laws, or that violate the food and drug laws.

The U.S. Border Patrol today is part of U.S. Customs. Customs has overlapping authority in the enforcement of customs and immigration laws with U.S. Immigration and Customs Enforcement (ICE), also within Homeland Security. While Customs' responsibilities are primarily at borders and points of entry to the United States, ICE has immigration responsibility elsewhere in the country. Customs also shares some responsibilities with other agencies in enforcing U.S. export laws. Some U.S. Customs officers are assigned to U.S. embassies or offices in foreign countries to assist in the administration of U.S. customs laws.

Customs is divided into seven geographic regions; the regions are divided into districts, each headed by a district director. Customs offices are located at the **ports of entry**, including major seaports, airports, inland ports, and border crossings. Within each district are *field import specialists*, who make initial determinations as to the entry of goods. They can seek advice from *national import specialists*. Some officers are specialists in particular types of products, such as textiles. The district director supervises all imports within the district and makes sure that imported goods are entered in accordance with the rules of the agency and decisions of the courts.

The Formal Entry

The **formal entry** refers to the administrative process required to import goods into the customs territory of a country. Goods have officially "entered" the United States only when the following requirements have been met.

1. The goods have arrived at a U.S. "port of entry."
2. The goods are not of a type that is not permitted entry or from an embargoed country.
3. Delivery is authorized by Customs after inspection and release.
4. Estimated duties have been paid or a customs bond posted.

The process begins upon the arrival of the merchandise at a U.S. port of entry. Goods not processed for entry within fifteen days are sent to a warehouse as "unclaimed freight." The goods may be entered by the owner, purchaser, consignee (the party to whom the goods are shipped or to be delivered), or licensed customs broker. A **customs broker** is an authorized agent, licensed by federal law, to act for and on behalf of importers in making entry of goods. (A broker is not needed to import goods for personal use.) More than 90 percent of all entries are made by customs brokers. A customs broker must possess a written power of attorney from the party making entry. Nonresident individuals and foreign corporations may make entry, but they are bound by much stricter rules. The entry process is not merely transporting the goods into the United States; it includes the filing of customs documents and the payment of duties.

Required Documentation. When goods are entered, the entry documents must be filed within five days. The documents necessary to enter goods generally include the following items:

1. An entry manifest or merchandise release form (see the *Entry/Immediate Delivery Form* in Exhibit 12.2)
2. U.S. Customs *Entry Summary Form* (Exhibit 12.3)
3. Proof of the right to make entry (a bill of lading, air waybill, or carrier's certificate)
4. The commercial invoice obtained from the seller (or a pro forma invoice, if the commercial invoice is temporarily delayed by the seller)

Exhibit 12.2

Entry/Immediate Delivery Form

U.S. DEPARTMENT OF HOMELAND SECURITY
Bureau of Customs and Border Protection

Form Approved
OMB No. 1651-0024
Exp. 01/31/2012

ENTRY/IMMEDIATE DELIVERY

19 CFR 142.3, 142.16, 142.22, 142.24

ABI CERTIFIED

1. ARRIVAL DATE	2. ELECTED ENTRY DATE	3. ENTRY TYPE CODE/NAME	4. ENTRY NUMBER
060908		01 ABI/S	669-2242260-6
5. PORT	6. SINGLE TRANS. BOND	7. BROKER/IMPORTER FILE NUMBER	
1512	X 891	61779SE	
	8. CONSIGNEE NUMBER		9. IMPORTER NUMBER
			12-34567
10. ULTIMATE CONSIGNEE NAME		11. IMPORTER OF RECORD NAME	
Importer's Company Anytown, NC 20000		SAME	
12. CARRIER CODE	13. VOYAGE/FLIGHT/TRIP	14. LOCATION OF GOODS-CODE(S)/NAME(S)	
111	444	L362	
15. VESSEL CODE/NAME			
LUFTHANSA			
16. U.S. PORT OF UNLADING	17. MANIFEST NUMBER	18. G. O. NUMBER	19. TOTAL VALUE
1704			$3331
20. DESCRIPTION OF MERCHANDISE			
Bedding			

21. IT/BL/ AWB CODE	22. IT/BL/AWB NO.	23. MANIFEST QUANTITY	24. H.S. NUMBER	25. COUNTRY OF ORIGIN	26. MANUFACTURER NO.
I	22069456995		6304.HS.60107	DE	DEBRILRHE4044KRA
M H	22069456995 48502287	5			

27. CERTIFICATION

I hereby make application for entry/immediate delivery. I certify that the above information is accurate, the bond is sufficient, valid, and current, and that all requirements of 19 CFR Part 142 have been met.

SIGNATURE OF APPLICANT
X Importer's Custom Broker

PHONE NO. | DATE

29. BROKER OR OTHER GOVT. AGENCY USE

28. CBP USE ONLY

☐ OTHER AGENCY ACTION REQUIRED, NAMELY:

☐ CBP EXAMINATION REQUIRED.

☐ ENTRY REJECTED, BECAUSE:

JUN 12 8.23 AM '08

DELIVERY AUTHORIZED: SIGNATURE | DATE

PAPERWORK REDUCTION ACT STATEMENT: An agency may not conduct or sponsor an information collection and a person is not required to respond to this information unless it displays a current valid OMB control number and an expiration date. The control number for this collection is 1651-0024. The estimated average time to complete this application is 15 minutes. If you have any comments regarding the burden estimate you can write to U.S. Customs and Border Protection, Office of Regulations and Rulings, 799 9th Street, NW., Washington DC 20229.

CBP Form 3461 (10/09)

5. Packing slips to identify the contents of cartons
6. Other documents required by special regulations (e.g., certificate of origin, quota visa, certificate of quality or inspection, etc.)

Within ten working days, the importer must file these completed documents with Customs at the port of entry. The information on the form is used to determine the amount of duties owed, to gather

Exhibit 12.3

Entry Summary Form

Form Approved OMB No. 1651-0022

DEPARTMENT OF HOMELAND SECURITY
U.S. Customs and Border Protection
ENTRY SUMMARY

1. Filer Code/entry No.	2. Entry Type	3. Summary Date
2242260-6		6/26/08

4. Surety No.	5. Bond Type	6. Port Code	7. Entry Date
891	SEB-9	1512	

8. Importing Carrier	9. Mode of Transport	10. Country of Origin	11. Import Date
LUFTHANSA	40	DE	06/06/08

12. B/L or AWB No.	13. Manufacturer ID	14. Exporting Country	15. Export Date
22069456995	DEBILRHE4044KRO	DE GERMANY	06/06/08

16. I.T. No.	17. I.T. Date	18. Missing Docs	19. Foreign Port of Lading	20. U.S. Port of Unlading
22069456995	06/06/08		Frankfurt	1704 ATLANTA

21. Location of Goods/G.O.No.	22. Consignee No.	23. Importer No.	24. Reference No.
L362		12-34567	

25. Ultimate Consignee Name and Address	26. Importer of Record Name and Address
Importer's Company	Same
City Anytown State NC Zip 20000	City State Zip

27. Line No.	28. Description of Merchandise: 29. A. HTSUS No. B. ADA/CVD No.	30. A. Grossweight B. Manifest Qty.	31. Net Quantity in HTSUS Units	32. A. Entered Value B. CHGS C. Relationship	33. A. HTSUS Rate B. ADA/CVD Rate C. IRC Rate D. Visa No.	34. Duty and I.R. Tax (Dollars / Cents)
	48502287					
	INV. No. 9999/99/8951					
001	FURN ARTICLES:N/KNIT:WOOL/HAIR					
	6304.9960107	193	193 KG	3331	6.4%	213.60
				709		
	MERCHANDISE PROCESSING FEE				.17%	5.66
INV	VAL 4039.98					
LESS	NDC 709.00					
	3330.98 US DOLLAR AT 1.00000000					
ENT.	VAL 3330.98 AS 3331		TOTAL			
	5 PCS TOTAL			3331		234.18
	BLOCK 39 SUMMARY:					
MPF	499 21.00					
TOTAL:	21.00		TEV:	3331		

Other Fee Summary for Block 39	35. Total Entered Value	**CBP USE ONLY**		TOTALS
	$	A. LIQ CODE	B. Ascertained Duty	37. Duty 213.18
	Total Other Fees $	REASON CODE	C. Ascertained Tax	38. Tax .00
			D. Ascertained Other	39. Other 21.00
			E. Ascertained Total	40. Total 234.18

36. DECLARATION OF IMPORTER OF RECORD (OWNER OR PURCHASER) OR AUTHORIZED AGENT

I declare that I am the [ ] Importer of record and that the actual owner, purchaser, or consignee for CBP purposes is as shown above, **OR** [X] owner or purchaser or agent thereof. I further declare that the merchandise [X] was obtained pursuant to a purchase or agreement to purchase and that the prices set forth in the invoices are true, **OR** [ ] was not obtained pursuant to a purchase or agreement to purchase and the statements in the invoices as to value or price are true to the best of my knowledge and belief. I also declare that the statements in the documents herein filed fully disclose to the best of my knowledge and belief the true prices, values, quantities, rebates, drawbacks, fees, commissions, and royalties and are true and correct, and that all goods or services provided to the seller of the merchandise either free or at reduced cost are fully disclosed.
I will immediately furnish to the appropriate CBP officer any information showing a different statement of facts.

41. DECLARANT NAME	TITLE	SIGNATURE	DATE
Importer's Broker			6/11/08

42. Broker/Filer Information (Name, address, phone number)	43. Broker/Importer File No.
Importer's Broker P.O. Box 123 Charlotle, N.C. 28219	123456ab-6

PaperWork Reduction Act Notice CBP Form 7501 (04/05)

import statistics, and to determine if the goods conform to other U.S. regulations.

The Commercial Invoice. A seller must provide a separate invoice for each commercial shipment entering the United States. The **commercial invoice** is required for all shipments intended for sale or commercial use in the United States. The invoice must provide all pertinent information about the shipment, in English, and be signed by the seller. One invoice can be used for installment shipments to the same consignee if the shipments arrive within ten days of each other. The invoice must include the following information:

- Names of the port of shipment and the destined port of entry
- Name of buyer and seller or consignee
- Common or trade name for the goods and their detailed description
- Country of origin
- Currency of payment
- Quantity and weight of the goods shipped
- Value of the goods accurately and correctly stated, including a breakdown of all itemized charges such as freight, insurance, packing costs, the costs of containers, any rebates and commissions paid or payable, and the value of any production assist
- A packing list stating in detail what merchandise is in each individual package
- Special information for certain classes of merchandise (e.g., bedspreads must indicate whether they contain any embroidery, lace, braid, or other trimming)

Payment of Duties. If import duties are assessed on the goods, the importer must deposit estimated duties with Customs at the time of filing the entry documents or the entry summary form. The duties must be in an amount determined by Customs, pending a final calculation of the amount actually owed. Payment to a customs broker does not relieve the importer of liability to pay the duties. The liability for duties constitutes a personal debt of the importer, and a lien attaches to the merchandise. In lieu of paying duties immediately, an importer may post a customs bond. This is more convenient for companies needing immediate delivery of their goods. A customs bond can be purchased for a single shipment or for all shipments over the course of a year and up to the amount stated in the bond. The purpose of the bond is to ensure the payment of duties on final calculation. In some cases, goods can be released for transportation or storage *in-bond*, meaning that the payments of duties are suspended until the goods are released for sale or use in the United States.

Informal Entries. Personal and some "low-value" commercial shipments valued at $2,500 or less may be cleared through an **informal entry** process. A surety bond is not required for informal entries, and import duties are payable immediately at the time of entry. Mail entries less than $2,500 may be processed through the U.S. Postal Service, in which case the goods are forwarded to a U.S. Customs mail branch for clearance.

Electronic Entry Processing. The Automated Broker Interface, created by U.S. Customs in the 1990s, allows qualified importers, brokers, and carriers to enter customs documents electronically. It has reduced the costs and time to process entries. Customs claims that 96 percent of entries are now done automatically. Brokers using the interface may also pay customs duties and received duty refunds electronically.

Remote Location Filing. Until recently, entry processing had to take place at the port where the goods were located. Thus, importers had to rely on the services of a broker at the port of entry, even if the goods were being entered in a distant location. Large importers who move goods through different ports asked Congress to permit entry processing from remote locations. The Remote Location Filing system, which did not officially operate nationwide until 2009, allows licensed customs brokers in all parts of the country to make remote entries at distant ports.

Liquidation and Protest

In a normal import transaction, assuming no errors or penalties are at issue, the entry will be liquidated. **Liquidation** is the final computation and assessment of the applicable duty on entered goods by Customs. This "closes the book," making the entry complete. If Customs accepts the entry as submitted on the importer's documents, liquidation occurs immediately. However, when Customs at the port of entry determines that additional duties are owed, a **notice of adjustment** is sent to the importer. The importer must respond to the notice, or the duty will be assessed as corrected. If a question or dispute arises concerning the goods themselves, as in the case of technical or unusual products, or in complex cases, the case may be referred to an import specialist familiar with that type of product. Either the importer or Customs officials may seek internal advice from the agency's headquarters. Officially, the liquidation becomes effective, and the entry closed, when it is posted at the "customs house" at the port of entry. A courtesy notice is sent to importers advising them of the liquidation, although this notice is not legally effective. If actual duties owed exceed the estimated duties paid at the time of entry, the importer must pay them within fifteen days of the posting of the noticc of liquidation.

Time Limits on Liquidation. Liquidation must occur within one year of entry. The time can be extended for good cause. An entry not liquidated within one year is deemed liquidated by operation of law. Under a **deemed liquidation**, the goods are dutied at the rate accepted on the entry summary form. A liquidation can be reopened within two years if there is evidence to suspect that the importer committed fraud.

Protesting Liquidations. An importer that wants to dispute a liquidation made by Customs may file a protest with Customs within ninety days at the port where the goods were entered. An importer may not file a protest where no change was made by Customs to the entry as filed by the importer. Customs has thirty days to respond in cases where the goods have been denied entry; otherwise it has two years to act. Appeals can be made to Customs headquarters in Washington, D.C.

Enforcement and Penalties

The Bureau of Customs and Border Protection has broad powers to establish regulations, carry out investigations, and impose penalties. All care must be used in complying with customs requirements, and many experienced importers will tell you that they make every effort to ensure the customs documents they submit are truthful and error-free.

The basic enforcement and civil penalty provisions of the customs laws are found in Title 19, Section 1592. The offenses set out here are civil violations calling for civil penalties imposed administratively by Customs. Criminal violations are addressed elsewhere in the U.S. criminal code. Section 1592 begins by setting out an importer's basic responsibility: "No person may enter or attempt to enter any merchandise into the United States by means of any written document, electronic transmission of information, oral statement, or other act that is both material and false or which omits any material information affecting the entry."

Making Materially False Statements to Customs. An act or statement is "material" if it refers to the identity, quality, value, source, or country of origin of the merchandise, or if it affects the rate of duty charged or the item's right to be imported into the United States. The most common, and often most serious, false statements involve undervaluation, incorrect descriptions, and misstatements as to country of origin. For instance, a statement to a Customs officer that cigars carried on your return flight from Honduras are of Honduran origin, when they are actually of Cuban origin, is materially false. Similarly, submitting a commercial invoice for a shipment of imported goods showing their value at less than that actually paid is materially false. Incorrect country of origin labeling on merchandise is a common false statement, usually resulting from a failure to properly understand customs law. An omission of material fact qualifies as a materially false statement.

A false statement can be material even if it does not actually cause a change in the rate of duty. Identifying an imported fabric as "100 percent cotton" when in fact it is made of a blend of cotton and silk would be material (and false) even though it may or may not actually result in a change in the rate of duty collected. The violation occurs whether the false statement was made intentionally or negligently. There is no violation if the falsity resulted from simple clerical errors or reasonable mistakes of fact outside the control of the importer (such as where a foreign supplier unexpectedly includes merchandise in a sealed container that you were not aware was being shipped to you, and you had no way to find out), as long as the errors are not part of a *pattern of negligent conduct*. The penalty, however, does depend on whether the offense resulted from negligence, gross negligence, or fraud.

Negligent Violations. A negligent violation is one in which the importer fails to use *reasonable care, skill, and competence* to ensure that all customs documents and statements are materially correct and all laws are complied with. It might result because the importer failed to accurately ascertain the facts or information required by Customs when making an entry. It could also result from a misinterpretation of customs regulations or a mistake in completing the customs documents. Negligence penalties can seem pretty severe: If duty has been lost, the penalty can be *the lesser of* the value of the goods or two times the loss of duty. If no duty is lost, then the penalty can be as high as 20 percent of the value of the goods, depending on whether there were mitigating or aggravating circumstances.

In the following case, *United States v. Golden Ship Trading Co.*, the importer was found negligent in misstating the country of origin of T-shirts, even though she based her information on assurances made by her supplier.

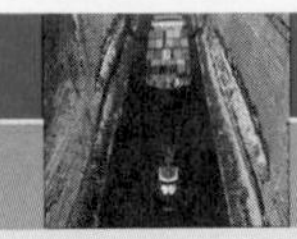

United States v. Golden Ship Trading Co.

2001 WL 65751 (2001) Court of International Trade

BACKGROUND AND FACTS

J. Wu entered three shipments of T-shirts purchased from Hui, who claimed that he operated a factory in the Dominican Republic. Hui furnished information necessary for the importer's broker to prepare the import documents and to obtain a permit for entry of wearing apparel into the United States (which was required at the time). Wu declared the country of origin of the T-shirts as the Dominican Republic. Customs discovered that Hui produced the body of the T-shirts in China and shipped them to the Dominican Republic, where sleeves were attached and "Made in Dominican Republic" labels inserted. The finished shirts were then transshipped to the United States. According to law, merely attaching the sleeves did not make the shirts a product of the Dominican Republic. Chinese-made shirts could not have been imported without a textile visa, which Hui may not have been able to obtain. The government alleged that Wu acted without due care in determining the country of origin and sought penalties of $44,000. Wu did not dispute that the country of origin was China but denied that she was negligent and claimed that Hui had duped her.

BARZILAY, J.

Section 1592(e) describes the burden of proof that each side bears in a penalty action based on negligence. The United States bears the burden of establishing that the material false act or omission occurred; the burden then shifts to the defendant to demonstrate that the act did not occur as a result of negligence. See 19 U.S.C. §1592(e)(4). In this action, Customs has adequately demonstrated that the material false act occurred.

Since the court holds that the statements on the entry papers were both material and false, the only remaining issue is whether Ms. Wu has carried her burden that "the act or omission did not occur as a result of negligence." To decide if the mismarking was the result of Ms. Wu's negligence the court must examine the facts and circumstances to determine if Ms. Wu exercised reasonable care under the circumstances.

Ms. Wu admits she relied on the information provided by the exporter and accepted his representations that the Dominican Republic was the country of origin of the tee-shirts because "all the documents that the exporter provided prior to entry stated the country of origin was the Dominican Republic." Further, she claims that she was the victim of the exporter's fraudulent scheme which was so elaborate that even Customs had difficulty discovering it. Ms. Wu points out that the exporter did have a T-shirt factory in the Dominican Republic and that the factory did perform some manufacturing operations on the imported T-shirts. Ms. Wu also claims "figuring out which (T-shirts) qualified as country of origin Dominican Republic and which did not required an entire team of Customs investigators, special agents and import specialists. Obviously, the exporter's fraud in this case was well-concealed." Furthermore, she contends, if Customs had difficulty investigating and uncovering the exporter's falsifications, how could Ms. Wu, with far fewer resources and less expertise, be expected to know that the entry papers falsely reflected the country of origin of the imported T-shirts. Therefore, Ms. Wu claims, she was justified in relying on the exporter's entry information.

The court finds that Ms. Wu failed to exercise reasonable care because she failed to verify the information contained in the entry documents. Under the regulation's definition of reasonable care, Ms. Wu had the responsibility to at least undertake an effort to verify the information on the entry documents. There is a distinct difference between legitimately attempting to verify the entry information and blindly relying on the exporter's assertions. Had Ms. Wu inquired as to the origin of the imported T-shirts or, at minimum, attempted to check the credentials and business operations of the exporter, she could make an argument that she attempted to exercise reasonable care and competence to ensure that the statements on the entry documents were accurate. Instead, Ms. Wu applies circular reasoning to prove she was not negligent. She assumes she would not have been able to discover that the exporter was misrepresenting the county of origin and therefore was not negligent even though she made no attempt to verify. The critical defect with Ms. Wu's argument is that it removes the reasonable care element from the negligence standard. The exercise of reasonable care may not have guaranteed success, but the failure to attempt any verification undercuts the argument that she would have been unable to determine the truth.

Ms. Wu failed to "exercise" reasonable care because she utterly failed to attempt to verify the exporter's information. Indeed, Ms. Wu admits, and the evidence is uncontroverted, that she relied solely on the word of the exporter.

continues

continued

Q. What information did you rely on when you signed this document that indicates that the single country of origin of the imported items was the Dominican Republic?
A. I believe [sic] Pedro. He said he sent me all the documents and the documents said it's made in the Dominican Republic so I just signed them.

Furthermore, Ms. Wu openly admits she did not inquire at all about the origin of the imported merchandise.

Q. Did you discuss with Mr. Hui (the exporter) where the fabrics from the T-shirts were made?
A. I never asked. I don't [sic] know how to ask. I never asked it.

Although it is apparent Ms. Wu did not directly research the authenticity of the exporter's claims, she argues that she employed the services of a licensed customs house broker and relied on the broker's expertise to properly prepare the import documents. However, Ms. Wu did not attempt to verify or ascertain the correctness of the information prepared by the broker.

Q. Did you discuss with the broker where he got the information from?
A. I did not discuss it with him.

Even though Ms. Wu did not attempt to verify the country of origin, she still signed and certified the accuracy of the information contained in the entry documents. Ms. Wu's reliance on the exporter and the broker does not remove the obligation to exercise reasonable care and competence to ensure that the statements made on the entry documents were correct.

The court finds that Ms. Wu's failure to attempt to verify the entry document information shows she did not act with reasonable care and did, therefore, attempt to negligently introduce merchandise into the commerce of the United States in violation of 19 U.S.C. §1592(a)(l)(A) and, therefore, must pay a civil penalty for her negligence pursuant to 19 U.S.C. §1592(c)(3)(B).

With regard to the amount of the penalty, the court directs the parties to attempt to settle the matter by consultation guided by the court's opinions in *United States v. Complex Machines Works Co.*, 83 F. Supp. 2d 1307 (1999) and *United States v. Modes, Inc.*, 826 F. Supp. 504 (1990) regarding mitigation.

Decision. Wu did not exercise reasonable care because she failed to verify the information contained in the entry documents. Customs could assess a penalty that took into account the mitigating circumstances of the case. Once the government proved the false act occurred, the burden shifted to Ms. Wu to prove that she was not negligent.

Case Questions

1. What was Wu's motivation in stating that the shirts were made in the Dominican Republic?
2. What is the burden of proof? Must the United States prove that Wu was negligent, or must Wu prove that she was not?
3. Can the importer (Wu) rely on the statements of the third party (here, the shirt exporter) to avoid responsibility?

Gross Negligence. An importer commits gross negligence if there is *clear and convincing evidence* that the act or omission was done with actual knowledge or reckless disregard for the relevant facts and with disregard for the importer's obligations under the law. The penalty is approximately twice that for negligent violations, up to the value of the goods.

Civil Fraud. **Customs fraud** is far more serious than negligence. A fraudulent violation exists where there is clear and convincing evidence that the importer *knowingly* made a materially false statement or omission while entering or attempting to enter goods into the United States. Examples are intentionally giving a phony description of the goods, understating their value by submitting a fake seller's invoice, concealing money paid to the seller, or altering the country of origin listed on a document. Although the act must have been done knowingly, it does not matter whether the importer intended to evade paying import duties. The maximum civil penalty is equal to 100 percent of the value of the goods, reduced for mitigating circumstances or where the fraud did not result in a loss of duty to the government. In many cases, Customs may seize the merchandise and either have it destroyed or sold at auction.

Crimes. Criminal penalties for customs fraud and smuggling are set out in Title 18, Chapter 27, of the *U.S. Code of Federal Regulations*, which specifies a range of criminal activities, including the use of false or fraudulent customs documents, destroying invoices on imported goods to cover up a fraud, making false statements to a Customs officer, smuggling, conspiracy, money laundering, and many other acts. The law provides a maximum sentence of two years' imprisonment, a fine, or both, for each violation and forfeiture of the goods that were the subject of the fraud. Anyone who knowingly and willfully, and with the intent to defraud the United States, clandestinely or secretly smuggles or attempts to smuggle goods into the country without customs clearance can receive up to a twenty-year prison sentence. Special criminal offenses apply to drug smuggling and to travelers entering the United States with merchandise in their baggage or on their person.

Aggravating and Mitigating Circumstances. Customs will consider aggravating and mitigating factors in determining the amount of a penalty. Aggravating factors include withholding evidence, providing misleading information, prior improper shipments, and illegal transshipments to hide the actual country of origin. Mitigating factors include erroneous advice from a Customs official, cooperating with the investigation, bringing the error to Customs' attention and voluntarily paying the duty, or a prior good shipment record.

Enforced and Informed Compliance. U.S. Customs takes a two-pronged approach to enforcement of the customs laws: enforced compliance and informed compliance. **Enforced compliance** refers to the active investigation of customs violations and the prosecution of violators. **Informed compliance** refers to "softer" mechanisms designed to place the burden of voluntary compliance on importers. Compliance with the customs laws is much like compliance with the income tax laws. Enforcement depends on the willingness of the majority of U.S. importers, like taxpayers, to voluntarily comply. Congress recognized this when it passed the *Customs Modernization and Informed Compliance Act of 1993* (called the *Mod Act*). It introduced the doctrine of informed compliance, which shifted to the importer a major responsibility to comply with all customs laws and regulations. It requires that importers, customs brokers, and carriers use reasonable care in complying with the law, in handling all import transactions, and in preparing all documentation for entered goods. "Reasonable care" means more than simply being careful. It means that those handling import transactions must be properly trained and that companies must establish internal controls over import operations to ensure compliance. When requirements are not understood, the importer should consult a licensed broker, customs law attorney, or U.S. Customs itself. Importers are expected to have enough information and knowledge to comply with the law. This includes having accurate information about the type of merchandise being imported, its value and origin, the identity of the seller, and so forth. It also requires importers to have a working knowledge of customs statutes, regulations, and rulings and U.S. Customs procedures.

The Reasonable Care Checklist. Customs understands that a "black-and-white" definition of reasonable care is impossible because interpretation of the concept depends on individual circumstances. As an aid to importers, Customs publishes a "checklist" to give less experienced importers a better understanding of their obligation to use reasonable care. The checklist is not a law or regulation; it merely helps importers to understand what is expected of them. Importers who fail to meet the reasonable care requirements on the checklist may be subjected to penalties for negligence. Exhibit 12.4 contains 20 edited provisions from more than 50 in the original document entitled, *What Every Member of the Trade Community Should Know About: Reasonable Care (A Checklist for Compliance)*, 2004.

Reporting Errors to Customs before an Investigation. Congress has enacted a statute to encourage importers to voluntarily report their own possible violations of the customs laws. This is called a **prior disclosure**. If an importer admits its mistake and informs Customs of a possible violation *before* learning that it is being investigated, the penalties are limited. The importer must completely disclose the materially false statements or omissions and the circumstances of the violation. Any unpaid duties must be remitted within thirty days. However, an attorney should be consulted before doing so. Some prior disclosures have reportedly saved companies many millions of dollars in potential fines.

The Statute of Limitations. The government is barred from bringing any action to collect an import duty after five years from the date of the violation involving negligence or gross negligence or five years from the date of discovery of a violation involving fraud.

Record-Keeping Requirements. Importers are required to keep records of all import transactions for five years from the date of entry and to give Customs access to those documents on demand. The records include all documents "normally kept in the ordinary course of business," including sales contracts, purchase orders, government certificates, letters of credit, internal corporate memoranda, shipping documents, correspondence with suppliers, and any other documents bearing on the entry of the merchandise. It is highly

Exhibit 12.4

Reasonable Care Checklist

1. If you have not retained an expert to assist you in complying with U.S. Customs requirements, do you have access to the Customs Regulations (Title 19 of the Code of Federal Regulations), the Harmonized Tariff Schedule of the United States, and the GPO publication Customs Bulletin and Decisions? Do you have access to the Customs Internet Web site, Customs Electronic Bulletin Board, or other research service to permit you to establish reliable procedures and facilitate compliance with customs laws and regulations?
2. Have you consulted with a customs "expert" (e.g., lawyer, broker, accountant, or customs consultant) to assist in preparation of documents and the entry of the merchandise?
3. If you use an expert to assist you in complying with U.S. Customs requirements, have you discussed your importations in advance with that person and have you provided that person with full, complete, and accurate information about the import transactions?
4. Has a responsible and knowledgeable individual within your organization reviewed the customs documentation prepared by you or your expert to ensure that it is full, complete, and accurate?
5. Are identical transactions or merchandise handled differently at different ports or customs offices within the same port? If so, have you brought this to the attention of the appropriate customs officials?
6. Have you established reliable procedures within your organization to ensure that you provide complete and accurate documentation to U.S. Customs?
7. Have you obtained a customs ruling regarding the importation of the merchandise?
8. Do you know the merchandise that you are importing and have you provided a detailed and accurate product description and tariff classification of your merchandise to U.S. Customs? Is a laboratory analysis or special procedure necessary for the classification?
9. Have you consulted the tariff schedules, U.S. Customs' informed compliance publications, court cases, or U.S. Customs rulings to assist you in describing and classifying the merchandise?
10. If you are claiming a free or special tariff treatment for your merchandise (e.g., GSP, HTS Item 9802, NAFTA, etc.), have you established a reliable program to ensure that you reported the required value information and obtained any required or necessary documentation to support the claim?
11. Do you know the customs value of the imported products? Do you know the "price actually paid or payable" for your merchandise?
12. Do you know the terms of sale; whether there will be rebates, tie-ins, indirect costs, additional payments; whether "assists" were provided, commissions or royalties paid? Have all costs or payments been reported to U.S. Customs? Are amounts actual or estimated? Are you and the supplier "related parties," and have you disclosed this to U.S. Customs?
13. Have you taken reliable measures to ascertain the correct country of origin for the imported merchandise? Have you consulted with a customs expert regarding the country of origin of the merchandise?
14. Have you accurately communicated the proper country of origin marking requirements to your foreign supplier prior to importation and verified that the merchandise is properly marked upon entry with the correct country of origin?
15. If you are importing textiles or apparel, have you developed reliable procedures to ensure that you have ascertained the correct country of origin and assured yourself that no illegal transshipment (rerouting through a third country for illegal purposes) or false or fraudulent documents or practices were involved? Have you checked the U.S. Treasury's published list of manufacturers, sellers, and other foreign persons who have been found to have illegally imported textiles and apparel products? If you have obtained your textiles from one of these parties, have you adequately verified the country of origin of the shipment through independent means?
16. Is your merchandise subject to quota/visa requirements and, if so, have you provided or developed a reliable procedure to provide a correct visa for the goods upon entry?
17. Have you determined or established a reliable procedure to permit you to determine whether your merchandise or its packaging bear or use any trademarks or copyrighted matter or are patented and, if so, that you have a legal right to import those items into, and/or use those items in, the United States?
18. If you are importing goods or packaging materials that contain registered copyrighted material, have you checked to ensure that it is authorized and genuine? If you are importing sound recordings of live performances, were the recordings authorized?

continues

continued

19. Have you checked to see that your merchandise complies with other government agency requirements (e.g., FDA, EPA/DOT, CPSC, FTC, Department of Agriculture, etc.) prior to or upon entry and procured any necessary licenses or permits?
20. Have you checked to see if your goods are subject to a Commerce Department dumping or countervailing duty determination and reported that to U.S. Customs?

Source: "What Every Member of the Trade Community Should Know About: Reasonable Care (A Checklist for Compliance)," U.S. Customs and Border Protection, 2004.

recommended that any corporate importer establish a customs records compliance program to avoid penalties. The willful failure to keep records about the entry is punishable by the lesser of a $100,000 fine or 75 percent of the value of the merchandise. Even negligent record keeping is punishable by fines up to $10,000 or 40 percent of the value of the goods, whichever is less. There is an exception if the records were destroyed by an act of God. Concealment or destruction of records carries an additional $5,000 fine or up to two years' imprisonment or both. U.S. Customs conducts audits to verify business records. Inspections can take place on reasonable notice to the importer. Documents can be seized by court order.

Enforcement of Penalty Actions. In any action to collect a penalty, U.S. Customs acts as plaintiff in bringing suit in the Court of International Trade. Quite often, Customs will ask the court to consider all theories of culpability—negligence, gross negligence, and fraud—hoping to win on one or the other theory. The burden of proof in court depends on the violation. Fraud and gross negligence must be proved by "clear and convincing evidence." In negligence cases, the government must prove only that the act or omission occurred; the burden then shifts to the defendant-importer to show that it did not occur as a result of negligence. (Note that this rule does not apply to importers seeking review of a protest to recover duties paid. In that case the importer brings the action and U.S. Customs is the defendant).

Binding Rulings

Imagine you work for a trading company in the United States and have an opportunity to sell imported women's "boxer shorts" to a leading U.S. department store chain. They would like you to quote "your best price," delivered with duties paid. If you underestimate your costs, you will end up eating your shorts on the deal. You learn that some women will wear the boxers as short pants, while others will wear the shorts as underwear. The question is whether Customs will consider the boxers to be "outerwear," which is dutied at 18 percent, or "women's slips and briefs," which are dutied at less than 12 percent. Importers faced with a situation like this may make a written request for a **binding ruling**, also called a *ruling letter*, from Customs in advance of an entry. A binding ruling represents the official position of Customs with respect to the *specific transaction for which it was issued.* It is binding on Customs personnel until revoked. Customs does not publish public notice in advance of a ruling, and there is no opportunity for the public to comment on the issue.

Rulings are important to importers, especially those dealing in new or unusual merchandise that they have not imported before. They relieve the recipient of a ruling of the uncertainty over the tariff rate and how the product will be treated by Customs. Importers can research the Customs Rulings Online Search System (CROSS) for rulings on articles similar to theirs. Although a ruling is only binding to the party to whom it is addressed, rulings found in CROSS do provide guidance. However, no one should rely on a ruling issued to someone else because rulings on similar products can seem inconsistent and unpredictable. A request for a ruling letter should be submitted in writing. It should contain all relevant information, and in some cases—like the boxer shorts case—the importer should send a sample of the article. Some ruling requests may be made online. The ruling letter is issued only on the basis of the exact facts given and ensures that the products described will be entered according to the terms set out in the letter. Customs' goal of a 90-day response period is often exceeded, and some can take up to nine months. Rulings are published in an official agency publication, *Customs Bulletin and Decisions* (commonly called the *Customs Bulletin*).

JUDICIAL REVIEW OF U.S. CUSTOMS

Judicial review of the rules and decisions of U.S. Customs is in the **Court of International Trade**. This is a specialized federal court located in New York City. Appeals from the court are to the **U.S. Court of Appeals for the Federal Circuit** in Washington, D.C. The use of a single, specialized court for customs and trade issues, with appeal to a single appellate court, provides uniformity of the law. If the many federal district courts and federal appellate courts around the country were deciding these cases, then the same goods might receive different tariff treatment at each U.S. port of entry according to the case law of that district or circuit.

The role of the courts in reviewing the decisions and actions of U.S. Customs and Border Protection depends on whether Customs was involved in formal rulemaking applicable to the public at large or whether it was an informal action, such as the issuance of a binding ruling or an action affecting a single shipment of goods belonging to a single importer, such as the classification of goods.

If U.S. Customs issues a final rule interpreting a statute enacted by Congress, and the rule is promulgated through formal rulemaking (called "notice and comment" rulemaking), applicable to all importers, and is published in the *Code of Federal Regulations,* then it has the "force of law." The U.S. Supreme Court held in *United States v. Haggar Apparel Co.*, 526 U.S. 380 (1999), that formal regulations of U.S. Customs are entitled to "judicial deference" where those regulations are a "reasonable interpretation" of a statute enacted by Congress. This is known as "Chevron deference," taken from the important case of *Chevron U.S.A. Inc. v. Natural Resources Defense Council, Inc.*, 467 U.S. 837 (1984).

Judicial Review of Customs Rulings

Not all rules of U.S. Customs, however, are a result of formal notice and comment rulemaking. Many rulings and routine decisions are made on an informal case-by-case basis involving entries and liquidations made every day—thousands every year—by Customs officials around the country. An importer is normally entitled to judicial review of Customs rules only after a shipment has been entered, liquidated, and a protest denied, and after all duties are paid. Unlike formal rulemaking, here Customs' decision affects only the importer and entry involved. If an importer seeks review of an informal Customs decision in the courts, to what extent will the court give deference to it? Should the court consider that the agency is an expert on customs matters and simply defer to its original decision? Or should the court undertake its own analysis and reach its own decision independent of the agency's determination? The following U.S. Supreme Court case, *United States v. Mead Corp.*, defines the scope of judicial review over Customs' rulings on liquidations, binding rulings, and other "informal" day-to-day decisions of Customs.

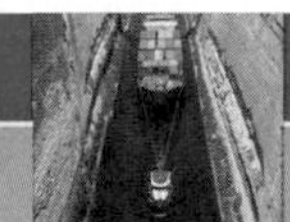

United States v. Mead Corp.

533 U.S. 218 (2001) United States Supreme Court

BACKGROUND AND FACTS

Mead had been importing "day planners" held together by a loose-leaf ringed binder. They were duty free. U.S. Customs later changed the classification to "bound diaries" with a 4 percent tariff. Mead argued that the day planners were not diaries and were not bound. Mead paid the duties and filed a protest. The protest was denied and Mead appealed. The Court of International Trade held for the government. The Court of Appeals reversed for Mead, holding that the planners were not "bound diaries" on the basis of the dictionary meaning of those words. The court held that it owed no deference to Customs' classification, but was free to decide the classification issue anew as a matter of law. The U.S. Supreme Court agreed to hear the case.

JUSTICE SOUTER DELIVERED THE OPINION OF THE COURT

We agree that a tariff classification has no claim to judicial deference under *Chevron U.S.A. Inc. v. Natural Resources Defense Council, Inc.*, 467 U.S. 837, (1984) there being no indication that Congress intended such a ruling to carry the force of law, but we hold that under *Skidmore v. Swift & Co.*, 323 U.S. 134 (1944), the ruling is eligible to claim respect according to its persuasiveness [most citations omitted].

"[T]he well-reasoned views of the agencies implementing a statute 'constitute a body of experience and informed judgment to which courts and litigants may properly resort for guidance,' *Skidmore,* and [w]e have long recognized that considerable weight should be accorded to an executive department's construction of

continues

continued

a statutory scheme it is entrusted to administer…" *Chevron.* The fair measure of deference to an agency administering its own statute has been understood to vary with circumstances, and courts have looked to the degree of the agency's care, its consistency, formality, and relative expertness, and to the persuasiveness of the agency's position…. Justice Jackson summed things up in *Skidmore:*

> The weight [accorded to an administrative] judgment in a particular case will depend upon the thoroughness evident in its consideration, the validity of its reasoning, its consistency with earlier and later pronouncements, and all those factors which give it power to persuade, if lacking power to control. * * *

There is room at least to raise a *Skidmore* claim here, where the regulatory scheme is highly detailed, and Customs can bring the benefit of specialized experience to bear on the subtle questions in this case: whether the daily planner with room for brief daily entries falls under "diaries," … and whether a planner with a ring binding should qualify as "bound… ." A classification ruling in this situation may therefore at least seek a respect proportional to its "power to persuade…." Such a ruling may surely claim the merit of its writer's thoroughness, logic, and expertness, its fit with prior interpretations, and any other sources of weight. * * *

Since the *Skidmore* assessment called for here ought to be made in the first instance by the [lower courts], we go no further than to vacate the judgment and remand the case for further proceedings consistent with this opinion. It is so ordered.

Decision. Judgment of the Court of Appeals was vacated and remanded. Courts should defer to Customs' ruling on a tariff classification or other matter related to the liquidation of an entry "according to the ruling's persuasiveness." The degree of deference depends on the agency's thoroughness in explaining the ruling, the validity of its reasoning, its expertise, and its "power to persuade."

Case Questions

1. When a court reviews a classification ruling, is the court free to disregard the position of Customs and consider all the evidence anew? Must the court give complete deference to Customs' rulings? What does the court say is the correct standard of review?
2. What was the rationale the Supreme Court used in holding for Mead?
3. What about the product, consisting of day planners in a loose-leaf binder? Do you think that a loose-leaf "day planner" is a "bound diary"? Could you locate these in the tariff schedule and determine the current rate of duty?

CONCLUSION

Most Americans recognize the enforcement predicament the U.S. Bureau of Customs and Border Protection faces: The agency must protect the borders of the United States from a range of dangers while considering the needs of American importers and exporters for expedited customs entry and delivery and the impact of cargo delays on the U.S. economy. The agency has shared responsibility with other federal agencies for protecting the borders from terrorist threats, including the potential smuggling of weapons of mass destruction; for interdicting illegal immigration; and for detecting the smuggling of drugs and other contraband. Given the numbers of ocean containers and international flights arriving at U.S. ports every day, most Americans recognize the immense job the agency has been given. The agency understands the need to balance security with the economic needs of U.S. importers and foreign exporters to enter their shipments with as little delay as possible. Americans also recognize that the effective and efficient enforcement of the customs laws and the movement of cargo are largely dependent on their cooperation and partnership with customs officials.

All businesspeople must be concerned about complying with the customs and tariff laws of the countries in which they import or export. Enforcement actions and penalties for violations can be severe. Individuals and firms must adhere to the concept of informed compliance. This means that importers and exporters must use reasonable care in handling entries and must either be adequately trained or rely on trained professionals.

Finally, customs compliance does not mean that importers should not plan their business strategies to take advantage of opportunities in the customs and tariff laws. To the contrary, tariff laws, like many other types of tax laws, are intended to encourage and reward certain business decisions. Multinational companies that structure their global operations to take advantage of incentives in the customs or tariff laws or that source materials and products made in certain countries that have tariff preferences under U.S. law, for example, are simply taking advantage of business opportunities legally provided by Congress. Customs laws will affect where multinationals build their plants, where they source their materials or component parts, how they move goods from country to country, and how they structure their overall global operations. Careful customs planning is essential to the success of any international business plan.

Chapter Summary

1. A formal entry is the administrative process required to import goods into the customs territory of a country. The goods may be entered by the owner, purchaser, consignee (the party to whom the goods are shipped or to be delivered), or a licensed customs broker.
2. The *Customs Modernization and Informed Compliance Act* introduced the doctrine of informed compliance, which shifted a major responsibility to comply with all customs laws and regulations to the importer. It requires that importers use reasonable care in complying with the law, in handling all import transactions, and in preparing all documentation for entered goods. Reasonable care means more than simply being careful. It means that those handling import transactions must be properly trained, that companies must establish internal controls over import operations to ensure compliance, and that professional advice must be sought when needed.
3. Binding rulings from the Customs Service are an important tool in properly and safely planning import transactions in advance.
4. Most trading nations of the world utilize the schedule of the *Harmonized Commodity Description and Coding System* for classifying products. In the United States, the *Harmonized Tariff Schedule* is a federal statute that includes virtually all goods sold in commerce and lists the tariff rate for each according to the country of origin. The U.S. schedule is maintained by the International Trade Commission.
5. Tariffs, restraints on imports, and other import controls are applied to goods according to their dutiable status. The dutiable status of goods is determined by the classification of the article, the transaction value of the article, and the country of origin of the article.
6. Goods are classified in the *Harmonized Tariff Schedule* either by name, by description of the article's physical characteristics, by a description of their component parts, or by a description of the article's use. Goods classified by name are defined by the common meaning of the name, unless it is clear that Congress had intended the commercial or scientific name to apply. Anyone attempting to research the classification of an article in the HTSUS must follow the rules set out in the General Rules of Interpretation. Where an article may be classified under more than one heading, it must be classified under the one that most specifically describes the item. If two or more headings each describe only certain materials or components of the article, the article must be classified under the heading that describes those materials or components that give the article its essential character.
7. The dutiable value of the goods is the transaction value. This is the cost of the goods adjusted for certain elements of cost set out in the statutes and regulations such as packing costs, assists, or royalty fees.
8. Rules of origin are the national laws and regulations of administrative agencies, usually customs authorities, which are used to determine the country of origin of imported products. There are few areas of customs law that are so complex and difficult for importers to understand. One of the reasons for the complexity is that there are so many different rules applicable to imports from different countries. The general rule is that the country of origin of an imported article is that country where it was wholly and completely produced, manufactured, or obtained entirely from raw materials originating in that country. Where goods are not wholly the product of one country, such as goods assembled in more than one country, importers must rely on the substantial transformation test or tariff-shift rules set out in the customs statutes and regulations.
9. Foreign trade zones are legally defined sites within a country that are subject to special customs procedures and under the supervision of U.S. Customs. Imported goods may be brought into an

FTZ without being subjected to tariffs until such time as the goods are released into the stream of commerce in the United States. They offer importers and exporters the opportunity for creative business planning to reduce tariff liability.

Key Terms

importing 313
entry process 313
tariff law 313
customs law 313
dutiable status 313
tariff classification 314
tariff schedule 314
ad valorem tariff rate 317
specific tariff rate 317
compound tariff rate 317
General Rules of Interpretation (GRI) 320
rule of relative specificity 320
essential character 320
tariff engineering 321
dutiable value 322
transaction value 322
production assists 322
contract manufacturing 323
country of origin 323
rules of origin 324
nonpreferential rules of origin 324
preferential rules of origin 324
substantial transformation 324
name, character, or use test 324
value-added test 325
tariff-shift rule 327
regional value content test 327
ultimate purchaser 328
drawback 328
manufacturing drawback 328
same-condition drawback 329
substitution drawback 329
rejected merchandise drawback 329
foreign trade zone (FTZ) 329
port of entry 331
formal entry 331
customs broker 331
commercial invoice 333
informal entry 334
liquidation 334
notice of adjustment 334
deemed liquidation 335
customs fraud 337
enforced compliance 338
informed compliance 338
prior disclosure 338
binding ruling 340

Questions and Case Problems

1. CamelBak imported back-mounted packs used for outdoor activities and designed to deliver "hands-free" water on-the-go. Each of the subject articles is a textile bag with padded shoulder straps and an insulated polyurethane reservoir, flexible tubing, a bite valve and a cargo compartment designed to hold food, clothing, and supplies. Each reservoir would hold 35 to 100 ounces of liquid, and each cargo compartment would hold 300 to 1,680 cubic inches, depending on the style of pack. U.S. Customs entered the articles under heading 4202 covering "backpacks" and subheading and item 4202.92.30 for "travel, sports and similar bags" at a rate of duty of 17.8 percent. CamelBak argued that the articles were "insulated food or beverage bags" under subheading 4202.92 dutiable at a rate of 7 percent. The Court of International Trade ruled in favor of Customs, holding that under GRI 1 the articles were specifically and completely encompassed under the heading for backpacks. CamelBak appealed to the Court of Appeals. What was the result? Are the articles "backpacks" or "insulated beverage bags"? Does GRI 1 apply, or are the articles "composite goods," requiring analysis under GRI 3? If so, what component makes up the "essential character" of the article? What is the effect of adding a feature to an article (i.e., insulated reservoir) that is *substantially in excess* of those within the common meaning of that article (i.e., backpacks)? In other words, does the addition of the insulated reservoir just make it an "improved" backpack or does it become something else for tariff purposes? Outdoor enthusiasts might be surprised at the result! *CamelBak Products, LLC v. U.S.*, 649 F.3d 1361 (Fed. Cir. 2011).
2. Inner Secrets entered 2,000 dozen boxer-style shorts from Hong Kong. The boxer shorts were made of cotton flannel in a plaid pattern, with a waistband, a side length of 17 inches, and two small nonfunctional buttons on the waistband above the fly. Two seams were sewn horizontally across the fly, dividing the fly opening into thirds. The boxers did not have belt loops, inner or outer pockets, or fly closures. They were marketed under the label "No Excuses." Customs

classified the garments as outerwear shorts under HTSUS 6204.62.4055: "Women's or girls' suits, ensembles, suit-type jackets and blazers, dresses, skirts, divided skirts, trousers, bib and brace overalls, breeches and shorts .... Trousers, bib and brace overalls, breeches and shorts ... of cotton ... 17.7%." The Customs Service based its decision on its determination that the boxers will be worn by women as outer clothing. Inner Secrets maintains that the items are not outerwear, as Customs claims, but are actually underwear properly classified under HTSUS 6208.91.3010: "Women's or girls' singlets and other undershirts, slips, petticoats, briefs, panties, nightdresses, pajamas, negligees, bathrobes, dressing gowns and similar articles ... of cotton ... 11.9%." Inner Secrets filed a protest with the agency, which was denied. Inner Secrets brought this action with the Court of International Trade. What is the proper classification of the boxers? How would a camisole worn under a sport jacket or a slip worn as a dress be classified? *Inner Secrets v. United States*, 885 F. Supp. 248 (C.I.T. 1995). See *also St. Eve International v. United States*, 267 F. Supp. 1371 (C.I.T. 2003).

3. Sports Graphics imported soft-sided "Chill" coolers from Taiwan, consisting of an outer shell of nylon, an insulating core of foam, a top secured by a zippered flap, an inner liner of vinyl, and a handle or shoulder strap. Customs classified the merchandise as "Travel goods, such as trunks... suitcases, overnight bags, traveling bags, ... and like articles designed to contain ... personal effects during travel ... and brief cases, golf bags, and like containers and cases designed to be carried with the person ... . Luggage and handbags, whether or not fitted with bottle, dining, drinking ... or similar sets ... and flat goods ... of laminated plastics ... " at a 20 percent rate of duty. Sports Graphics contended that the imported soft-sided coolers were properly classifiable as "Articles chiefly used for preparing, serving, or storing food or beverages" and were dutiable at a rate of 4 or 3.4 percent *ad valorem*. How do you determine the proper classification? Does the use of this product have a bearing on its classification? What result? *Sports Graphics, Inc. v. United States*, 24 F.3d 1390 (Fed. Cir. 1994).
4. You intend to import raw, frozen calamari (squid) from China, Vietnam, and Peru into the United States, where it will be defrosted and tenderized. The tenderization process entails placing the imported squid into a solution consisting of ice water mixed with salt, citric acid, sodium citrate, active oxygen, and potassium carbonate. The squid is kept cold as it sits in the solution within a large tank for a period of 15 to 18 hours. The process does not change the size or shape of the calamari, but makes it whiter and plumper. Then it is washed with clean water before being refrozen and repacked for sale. Can your calamari be labeled "Product of U.S.A."? Why or why not? Can you locate any cases like this in the *Customs Rulings Online Search System*?
5. You intend to import vodka that is produced in Denmark. The strength of the vodka when imported will be at least 80 percent by volume. In the United States, the vodka will be diluted with water, sugar, and flavor to produce flavored vodka with 35 percent alcohol by volume. What is the correct country of origin for labeling purposes? Why?
6. You intend to obtain a saw blade produced in England and then ship it to China to be assembled with a handle that is manufactured in China. The finished saw is then packaged in China for export. What is the country of origin of the saw? Why?
7. Visit the Website of the Bureau of Customs and Border Protection. What resources does it contain for the trade community? Go to the "Trade" page and link to "Legal Decisions/Publications." What legal resources appear here that you have studied or used in this chapter?
   a. The *Customs Rulings Online Search System* (CROSS) is a searchable database of about 100,000 ruling letters. Access the database and try locating rulings on some of the issues discussed in this chapter. For example, enter "country of origin" together with the name of a product or class of products and see what you can find. Remember, these letters are binding only for the individual to whom they are written and only for that transaction. Nevertheless, they are a helpful guide to importers.
   b. The *Customs Bulletins and Decisions* is a weekly diary of all official acts of the agency. What type of information does it contain, and who might want to follow this on a regular basis?
   c. Go to the "Trade" page and link to "Cargo Security." Look at the Container Security Initiative. More than eleven million ocean containers enter U.S. ports every year. Only a tiny fraction of the containers can be inspected by hand. Any one of them could be used to hide a weapon of mass destruction. Look at the Customs-Trade Partnership Against Terrorism (C-TPAT), a process for enhancing security between U.S. importers and their foreign supply chains based on utilizing intelligence, pre-screening, detection technology, and tamper-evident containers. How do you think the threat of terrorism and Customs' security programs will affect global transportation in the years to come? What is Customs' "24-hour rule" for loading cargo aboard ships destined for the United States?

8. Acquaint yourself with the *Harmonized Tariff Schedule of the United States.*
   a. Which countries receive GSP tariff preference treatment?
   b. Which countries qualify for duty-free treatment as "least developed beneficiary developing countries?"
   c. Which countries qualify for the *African Growth and Opportunity Act* preferences?
   d. A good portion of the HTSUS is devoted to the dutiable status of goods moving in North America. NAFTA is the subject of the next chapter. Can you locate the NAFTA rules of origin, known as the "tariff-shift rules," in the schedules?
   e. Choose several products with which you are familiar, and attempt to classify them using the schedule.
9. The primary body of U.S. customs law is found in Title 19 of the *U.S. Code*. The regulations are found in the *Code of Federal Regulations.* You can access the CFR either through the Website of the U.S. Customs and Border Protection ("Legal" section) or through the Government Printing Office site. Can you find Customs' record-keeping rules? What are the rules for filing a protest with U.S. Customs?

Managerial Implications

You are attending a product development meeting at your company, a U.S. manufacturer of outdoor equipment. Your firm designs and manufacturers tents, bivy sacks, backpacks, and other outdoor equipment and accessories. Your tents include expedition-quality, three- and four-season tents, lighter tents for backpacking, and larger tents used for camping and recreation. Most tents sleep from one to six people. While some sewing and construction is done at your U.S. plant, much of your work is contract manufactured for you in China. The Chinese firm maintains an inventory of the fabrics and hardware you use and supplies of your trademarked labels to sew in. The quality, reliability, and delivery of the Chinese firm has always been good, and you have no other foreign suppliers.

Today's meeting was called to discuss the opportunity to quote a tent design and prices to Z-Mart Sporting Goods, potentially your largest customer. They want only one tent of your quality and brand name, and they are leaving most of the tent design up to you. However, it must sleep three or four people and leave enough head-room to dress. It can be either a heavier three-season or lighter four-season tent, so you have some flexibility there. Most importantly, it cannot retail for more than $400 or they're not interested. Their retail price is double their total wholesale cost. That means you cannot price the tent for one penny more than $200, including the cost of the tent, import duties, overhead, and all transportation and insurance to Z-Mart's warehouse. To do business with Z-Mart, and still make a profit, your CEO demands that every penny of costs be shaved. He estimates that if the tariff rate is any more than 5 or 6 percent, then Z-Mart's target price will be difficult to meet. He schedules the next meeting for tomorrow and asks you to make a presentation on how U.S. tariff and customs law will affect costs. He wants to know the following (Hint: As you proceed, you may want to review the above facts):

1. Generally speaking, what factors will determine the U.S. tariff rate on your tents?
2. To import the tent at the lowest rate, what class and kind of tent should it be? What should be its "principal use"?
3. What textile material should the tent be made from to achieve the lowest tariff?
4. Access the Customs Rulings Online Search System and search for your tent. Are you able to locate any actual classification rulings that might give you some guidance? Would you advise the CEO to obtain a ruling?
5. Based on your research what are the key design characteristics necessary to import the tents at the lowest tariff rate possible? Specifically, what are the requirements for square-foot floor space, height, weight, and carry size?
6. Although a search for new suppliers is impossible at this time, your CEO wants to know if the U.S. gives any tariff preferences for tents originating in certain countries. Are your tents eligible for a tariff preference under the GSP for developing countries? The Caribbean Basin Initiative? Israel? Singapore? What is the rate from Australia?
7. At the last minute, Z-Mart calls your CEO to ask if you can produce "pickup truck tents"—tents that fit into the bed of a pickup truck. He asks if you think they will be classified as "tents" or as "parts and accessories of motor vehicles" in heading 8708. Can you find a previous customs ruling that you can cite to him?

Ethical Considerations

Fair trade is a worldwide movement based broadly based on the theory that trade between rich and poor should be based on notions of social and economic justice. It also advocates that small farms and farm workers in developing countries receive a fair price in return for their agricultural and handicraft products. Although the fair trade movement dates to the 1940s, it became popular in parts of Europe in the 1960s and more recently has taken hold in the United States. Fair trade is supported by consumers willing to pay a small additional price for goods knowing that the indigenous producers of the goods, living and working under the poorest conditions, receive a fair price for their product. Some fair trade farms consist of small cooperatives, with individual families farming only a couple of acres. Typical fair trade products include coffee, tea, bananas, wine, herbs and spices, honey, rice, and cocoa. Standards, minimum prices, inspections, and certifications of producers and traders are the responsibility of private, nonprofit organizations. Fair trade standards also require that certified farms practice sustainable farming techniques, follow rules on the use of pesticides and recycling, refrain from using child labor, and encourage farm children to attend school. These advances are made possible by the higher prices participants receive for their products.

By the early 2000s, labeling standards for fair trade-certified products became standardized, so that consumers could recognize fair trade products in stores. Participants in fair trade include the workers and producers themselves, the brokers and traders who deal in the products, the retailers and vendors in richer countries, and consumers. Some of the most important fair trade organizations are the Fairtrade Labelling Organizations International, the European Fair Trade Association, the International Fair Trade Association, and TransFair USA.

1. Would you be willing to pay a slightly higher price for sugar, coffee, fruits, and basic commodities, knowing that their producers, farmers in Central America or Africa, were paid an internationally established "fair price" for their labors? Do you believe that consumers will make ethical choices in the marketplace, or strictly economic ones?
2. Fair trade is based on the guarantee of a fair price. How is a "fair price" determined? What is the role of independent fair trade organizations in establishing price?
3. Critics suggest that fair trade does not address the root causes of poverty. Some economists argue that low prices for basic commodities, like coffee, result from oversupply. Moreover, fair trade also does not guarantee access to investment or technology. Do you think the fair trade movement can be successful in rooting out poverty in developing countries?
4. Although fair trade products account for a tiny volume of world trade relative to the total volume, they do focus concern on the plight of poor farmers, farm workers, and producers in agrarian regions. Some of America's largest and best-known retailers are selling fair trade products, including Sam's Club, McDonald's, Dunkin' Donuts, Starbucks, and many grocery chains. Based on your research and outside reading, what do you think the impact of fair trade programs can be?

CHAPTER 13

Export Controls and Sanctions

Throughout history, every civilization has had to decide whether it will trade with outsiders, and if so, on what terms. After all, there were economic, political, and military interests to protect. There were outlaw tribes and evil princes to punish. What better way than to deprive them of goods and treasures, be they coveted spices, colorful dyes, or prized horses. There were state-of-the-art technological secrets to guard. From the secrets of steelmaking and the fashioning of swords and armor, to the addition of the lowly stirrup to a horseman's saddle, to the invention of the bow and arrow and gunpowder, technology has helped to turned the tide of many battles and the course of history. Empires have been won or lost because of the technological advantage of one warrior, or one army, over another. The warlords and kings of ancient Europe and Asia knew this well and meted out punishments of torture and death to those who disclosed such closely guarded secrets or traded with the enemy. Imagine the diplomatic couriers of the ancient world, or medieval statesmen of later periods, who went out on foot or on horseback to distant kingdoms. They arranged alliances and orchestrated embargoes of common enemies. These were times of secret treaties, encrypted messages, intrigue, and danger.

This could just as well be the story of the modern world. All nations use trade to protect national military, industrial, and other technological secrets, and to reward allies and punish outlaw nations. Civilized people still war with barbarians and warlords, and deny aid and comfort to those who harbor them. There are, perhaps, a few differences today. The ancient warlords have been replaced by terrorists and outlaw nations, the horseman and archer have been replaced by computer hackers, and ancient secret societies have been replaced by international conventions and widely publicized United Nations resolutions. But unlike the past, one person with a weapon of mass destruction can destroy an entire city.

This chapter begins by examining international efforts to protect and "control" technology that began during World War II and that continue to this day. Although there is a good deal of international cooperation and coordination at the policy level, the protection of national technological secrets is still largely a matter of national law and law enforcement. For this reason the remainder of the chapter focuses on U.S. law and regulation.

The first and most important topic in this chapter is the system of U.S. **export controls**—laws and regulations that govern the licensing of certain goods and technology exported from the United States or "transferred" to non-U.S. citizens. These export controls apply to a wide range of commercial products that may be controlled for national security or foreign policy reasons, even though they are not in the category of guns, ammunition, or nuclear weapons. Keep in mind that although this chapter does briefly mention the control of arms and weapons systems, export controls apply to many commercial products and technologies that may also have common, civilian use. Thus this chapter is of broad interest to any firm involved in exporting any type of product. In addition, this chapter discusses export reporting requirements for all shipments leaving the United States as well as criminal penalties for violation of the export administration laws.

The second part of this chapter covers the use of **sanctions**, which are regulations that prohibit U.S. citizens or companies from doing business with certain foreign governments, organizations, or individuals who support international terrorism, violate treaties on the spread of nuclear weapons, or traffic in illegal drugs. Sanctions can be used to prohibit trade or financial transactions, to block bank accounts and freeze assets, or to prohibit travel to a foreign country. U.S. sanctions on Iran or Syria are an example. Some "international sanctions" result from international cooperation and agreement at the United Nations. Sanctions are primarily enforced by the U.S. Department of Treasury, Office of Foreign Assets Control, although the cooperation of many government agencies across many countries is often involved.

No person in any country has a guaranteed legal right to export, or to travel across international borders. In the United States, there is no unfettered constitutional right to export or to be permitted to travel to foreign countries. Exporting and travel are considered privileges that, while recognized in the law, can be granted or revoked according to law. Export controls and sanctions are enforced with civil and criminal penalties, and the reader should finish this chapter with an appreciation of the seriousness of violations.

MULTILATERAL COOPERATION IN CONTROLLING TECHNOLOGY

In 1949, the United States, Canada, Japan, Western Europe, and a few of their major cold war allies formed a multilateral "coordinating committee" within NATO—the North Atlantic Treaty Organization—to coordinate polices to keep military-critical technology from the Soviet Union and its then Eastern European allies. It was known by its acronym, COCOM. It now seems that it was much like a basketball game, where one side tried to keep the ball away from the other. Each "player" could hand the ball—products with possible military applications—off to someone on their own team, but they all worked to keep it from the other side. COCOM maintained lists of products and technologies that were subject to control and that could not be transferred to countries not part of COCOM. Exceptions could be reviewed and vetoed by any one COCOM member. COCOM facilitated trade between member countries because each country was assured that the other would be equally aggressive in keeping military-critical technology from the Soviet Union. COCOM was important in coordinating the export laws of individual countries and their enforcement. COCOM disbanded in 1994 with the collapse of the Soviet Union and communist governments in Eastern Europe.

The Wassenaar Arrangement

In 1995 COCOM was replaced by the **Wassenaar Arrangement on Export Controls for Conventional Arms and Dual-Use Goods and Technologies.** This is a voluntary arrangement, not a treaty, between more than 40 governments, including the United States, Canada, the eastern and western European countries, Japan, and Russia. Representatives meet periodically at permanent offices in Vienna to coordinate national export control strategies and to develop lists of items and technologies that should be controlled. The arrangement includes not only weapons, but also "dual-use items." Dual-use items are goods or technologies that have both commercial and military applications, or that might become a weapon in the hands of terrorists. We will discuss the concept of dual-use later in this chapter.

Unlike COCOM, no single Wassenaar-country has veto power over items that are controlled and subject to export licensing. The Wassenaar Arrangement is based on recommendations and statements of "best practices" about export controls. Its voluntary and nonbinding nature reflects the fact that there is no longer one, single "enemy" (the communist bloc) as well as a lack of consensus about the level of control necessary in today's world. The lack of an effective international control system over arms and technology is worrisome to many policymakers who realize that export controls by one nation are ineffective if the same technologies or weapons can be purchased freely on the open market in other countries.

Other Multilateral Export Control Groups. The **Australia Group** is a group of 41 countries that work together to combat the spread of biological and chemical weapons. They have set up a common list of controlled substances, equipment, and technologies that have weapons applications for nations to use in their licensing programs. The **Missile Technology Control Regime** is a voluntary association of 34 countries committed to keeping missile technology from rogue regimes and terrorist groups that could use it to deliver weapons of mass destruction. The **Nuclear Suppliers Group** is a group of 45 nuclear supplier nations that includes the United States, Russia, and China. Its purpose is to share information and to set voluntary guidelines for countries that want to control the export and proliferation of nuclear material, equipment, and technology, especially that used in the enrichment and conversion of nuclear material. The problem with these multilateral efforts is that they are voluntary and without enforcement powers. Nevertheless, they are an important way for nations to work together to address common terrorist threats.

Countries have common interests and shared concerns over the release of technology with potential military applications or that can be used by terrorists. Indeed, export controls in the industrialized countries are based on common security and foreign policy concerns. However, there is no single international treaty or law that governs what goods or technologies can be exported across national borders. That is a matter of national control. Thus, we turn to U.S. export controls and to their impact on U.S. firms doing business in world markets.

HISTORY OF U.S. EXPORT CONTROL LAWS

The Continental Congress passed the very first U.S. export law in 1775, restricting trade with Britain. Later in America's history, Congress enacted laws that restricted exports to enemies of the United States during time of war. Modern export control laws, however, can be traced to 1949 legislation enacted during the early days of the cold war and the communist threat. During the decades of the cold war, the United States cooperated with its allies in restricting goods or technologies that could give any economic or military advantage to China, the Soviet Union, or the Eastern European communist countries under Soviet control. In the 1950s and 1960s the export laws imposed an almost complete embargo on doing business with communist countries, most notably the Soviet Union and its then-communist allies in Eastern Europe, China, and Cuba.

In the late 1970s, American export control policy became more pragmatic and began to consider American competitiveness and the need of American companies to use their technological advantage to boost American export sales. Following the Soviet invasion of Afghanistan in 1979 and the election of President Reagan in 1980, the United States embarked on a military buildup to counter what was viewed as Soviet aggression and expansionism. President Reagan strengthened international cooperation to keep critical goods, technology, and money away from the Soviet Union, which he famously referred to as the "evil empire." But the 1990s saw the collapse of the Soviet Union, U.S. recognition of Russia and the newly independent central-Asian republics of the former Soviet Union, the rise of democracy in Eastern Europe, and the increasing importance of China as a global manufacturing base and trading partner.

Changes in the Export Environment since 2001

After 2001, three forces quickly reshaped U.S. export control policy. First, the rise of international terrorism and the "war on terror" created a get-tough political environment. This led to new laws that gave the president and U.S. law enforcement agencies far-reaching, but controversial, powers to investigate, track down, and prosecute anyone aiding terrorists, and to stop the flow of money to terrorist groups.

Second, renewed concerns and tensions arose over nuclear proliferation, especially in North Korea and Iran. There were also documented reports that Pakistani nuclear technology had spread to other countries and groups around the world, sold by unscrupulous scientists and businesspeople.

The third major change is that China has become a global economic powerhouse and is no longer satisfied to just be the source of cheap labor for the world. It is now a major purchaser of U.S. commercial technology and technology products. In 2009, nearly 10 percent of all export licenses issued by the United States were for exports to China. In recent years there have been widespread reports of foreign cyber-attacks on U.S. industry, many said to have originated in China in its attempt to acquire U.S. technology. China is obviously eager to acquire more than just commercial technology. Various U.S. government reports show that China is trying to obtain the latest military and strategic technology for its nuclear forces, missile guidance systems, avionics systems, submarines, and space program.

Despite conflict and competitiveness between the two countries, U.S. export policy with regard to technology exports to China balances the needs of business for open access to Chinese markets with the needs of national security. In recent years, the United States has loosened some controls on export of commercial technology to China, while significantly tightening controls and focusing enforcement efforts on those specific items that China could use to modernize its military.

Balancing National Security with Economic Competitiveness

The use of export controls presents a policy dilemma. How does a nation control exports for reasons of national security or foreign policy without harming business, jobs, or economic interests? If a nation restricts exports of goods that are widely available in world markets, then that nation's exporters will simply lose the business to foreign competitors. It does not matter whether the goods are semiconductors, agricultural commodities, or something else. Placing unnecessary restrictions on exports of technology products, beyond those that are necessary for national security, could unduly burden a key economic sector. Nations must consider this when trying to keep weapons or other sophisticated technology out of the hands of potential foreign enemies, outlaw nations, or terrorists. U.S. manufacturers have long complained that overly restrictive and unnecessary export controls have cost them billions of dollars in lost sales, especially in information technology, satellites and the aerospace industry, and dual-use products and technologies.

Keep in mind the immensity of the problem. We are not just speaking of controlling the export of, say, one ready-to-use nuclear bomb. That is a big enough problem. We are talking about trying to control the thousands of bits of technology, knowledge, critical components, and radioactive fuel that rogue scientists could use to build a bomb. The same issue arises when we think about the fundamental components of outlawed chemical weapons or missile guidance systems. Imagine the thousands of parts that go into advanced military aircraft and other weapons systems, and the thousands of pieces of information one needs to build and run these systems. Having just one more critical component, or one more piece of information, can give a huge advantage to a rogue nation, terrorist, or foreign military.

The problem is that many components of complicated weapons and defense systems may also have commercial applications and be widely available for commercial sale from suppliers in more than one country. Nations cannot control everything. The answer to the dilemma lies in knowing what to control, what not to control, who to keep it from, and how to control it effectively. This point was clearly expressed in an article, "Policing High Tech Exports," which appeared in *The New York Times* on November 27, 1983.

> The export-control process breeds ironies. Senator Paul E. Tsongas, Democrat of Massachusetts, used to tell the story of how the Ethiopian national airline, seeking to buy the latest model Boeing 767, was thwarted by the United States Government. If Ethiopia were allowed to purchase the plane, with its sophisticated laser gyroscope, the Government's reasoning went, that gyroscope could fall into the hands of the Soviet Union, currently Ethiopia's great friend. So the Ethiopians turned to the French for a new Airbus. The punch line: The American company that manufactures the gyroscope had already sold it to France, an ally, for incorporation into the Air-Bus. "We lose the technology, we lose the foreign business and we become known as an unreliable supplier," Senator Tsongas argued. Ultimately, in this instance, such arguments prevailed: The Commerce Department granted Boeing its license in December 1982.

The fact that the Department of Commerce administers most U.S. export laws covering commercial and dual-use goods and technologies is a recognition that economic and business interests are in play. The United States does not prohibit the foreign sale of all technology, because that would not be practical or commercially possible. Rather, U.S. policy balances security interests with commercial necessity. A good example is the decision made by the U.S. Department of Commerce in 1999 to loosen restrictions on the sale of certain high-speed computer components to China, India, and Russia. High-speed computers can design nuclear weapons and run simulated tests on detonations, design advanced military aircraft and torpedo guidance systems, do three-dimensional modeling, calculate fluid dynamics, and perform other complex functions. In 1999, the *The New York Times* reported that at a press briefing in the White House, then-Secretary of Commerce William H. Daley held a Sony Playstation in his hand and said that unless trade controls were eased, the new, more powerful Playstation 2, which was set to be released the following Christmas, would be classified as restricted due to its (at that time) high-speed computer technology. The event dramatizes how the Department of Commerce must balance national security and commercial interests.

EXPORT CONTROLS ON COMMERCIAL AND DUAL-USE GOODS AND TECHNOLOGY

In this section, we are concerned with U.S. export controls and government licensing procedures for commercial and dual-use goods and technology, and with compliance and enforcement mechanisms.

Export Administration Act of 1979 and EAR Regulations

The *Export Administration Regulations* (EAR or "regulations") were originally promulgated under the authority of the *Export Administration Act of 1979* by the **Bureau of Industry and Security** (BIS) of the U.S. Department of Commerce. In 2001, the act expired and was not renewed by Congress due to political disagreement. However, the regulations remain in effect pursuant to executive orders of the president issued under the authority of another statute, the *International Emergency Economic Powers Act of 1977*. As of this writing, the *Export Administration Act* has not been renewed, despite numerous proposals to do so. The *Export Administration Regulations* are available in the *Code of Federal Regulations* through the Internet from the BIS or the U.S. Government Printing Office.

Commercial and Dual-Use Goods and Technology. Items controlled by the EAR include the following: (1) All U.S.-origin goods and technology, wherever located, whether inside the United States or in a foreign country (2) Certain foreign-made items containing (usually more than 25 percent) U.S.-origin controlled content or technology; (3) Certain items made in a foreign country with U.S. technology; and (4) Items made at a plant located outside the United States if that plant was designed and built with U.S. technology.

Controlled items includes both commercial and "dual-use" items. **Commercial items** are intended primarily for civilian use. **Dual-use items** are commercial items that may also have military or "proliferation" uses (relating to the proliferation of nuclear, chemical, or biological weapons). For example, a set of brake pads made for a fire engine may also be used in heavy military equipment. Thermal imaging night vision has many civilian uses, including search and rescue, and hunting. But it clearly has military uses as well. Dual-use items do not include weapons, munitions, and defense systems that are controlled under a separate system administered by the U.S. State Department.

The EAR includes both goods and technology. The regulations define **controlled technology** as the specific information and know-how necessary for the development, production, or use of a product, including the results of proprietary research done by corporations, universities, or research labs. The information can take the form of technical data (blueprints, models, specifications, etc.) or technical assistance (training, imparting working knowledge, and providing consulting services). The EAR applies to exports of software, encryption technology, and source code.

The following examples of dual-use items are taken from actual cases that resulted in convictions and sentencing for violations of the export control regulations: semiconductors, scopes for sporting rifles, electric cattle prods, oil drilling equipment, pipe-cutting equipment, high-strength aluminum rods, fingerprinting powder, common chemicals that used in chemical weapons, advanced machine tools, medical and laboratory testing equipment (that could be used to develop and test toxins used in biological weapons), and parts for diesel engines that could become part of military vehicles or tanks.

Most dual-use goods and technology have commercial, civilian, or industrial applications that would not appear to have military or (nuclear) proliferation consequences. Indeed, in many cases, the engineers that designed them and the people that sold them would never have anticipated possible military uses. Consider this example: An American firm formulates a new super-hard alloy for use in its advanced drill bits, intended for deep-earth oil drilling. The drill bits are sold to an oil-exploration company in a foreign country so that it can tap its deep oil reserves and sell them to the United States. Then, a few years later, to the surprise of the American military, the foreign country rolls out a new tank with advanced armor that is almost impenetrable by ordinary antitank weapons. The armor, it turns out, was designed using the same technology that went into the manufacture of the drill bits, and the hardened alloy bits themselves were used to test the penetrability of the new armor. The clear message is that American companies cannot rely on their own intuition as to whether their goods or technology are controlled and require government approval for shipment. They must know the licensing requirements and follow all procedures for licensing their exports.

Reasons for Control

Under the *Export Administration Regulations*, there are three broad reasons for controlling exports. They are (1) To protect national security, (2) To promote U.S. foreign policy, or (3) To prevent the short supply of essential domestic materials. The Department of Commerce determines which items to control by consulting with other executive departments (such as Defense, State, and Agriculture), the intelligence community, and multilateral control or coordinating agencies, and then places those items on the **Commerce Control List** (CCL). The president establishes the list of controlled countries.

National Security Controls. **National security controls** are used to "prohibit or curtail" the export of goods or technology that would make "a significant contribution to the military potential of any other country or combination of countries which would prove detrimental to the national security of the United States."

Foreign Policy Controls. **Foreign policy controls** must not be merely idealistic, but also realistic. They must be able to achieve their purpose and be capable of being enforced. On balance, the benefit to U.S. foreign policy must be greater than the detrimental effects on U.S. companies. Export controls for foreign policy reasons are limited to a period of one year, after which they must be renewed by the president. The president is required to consult with Congress and report on the effectiveness of foreign policy controls.

An example of the use of foreign policy controls are U.S. controls on exports of crime control equipment to repressive governments and areas of civil disorder. These items can range from handcuffs, polygraphs, and tear gas to mobile crime labs and shotguns. At first glance, one would wonder why the United States would do this. But imagine what would happen if certain products used by law enforcement agencies got into the hands of repressive governments, such as Syria or North Korea. They could also be used to disrupt public demonstrations, arrest protesters, eavesdrop and investigate political opponents, conduct interrogations, and commit other human rights violations. They also may have military applications. In addition to blocking exports to the most egregiously dictatorial governments, in recent years the United States has scrutinized exports of crime control equipment to Saudi Arabia, Russia, and Venezuela. Foreign policy controls are an important tool of American foreign policy.

Trade Controls for Reasons of Short Supply. Another reason why nations control exports is that certain critical goods or strategic raw materials may be in short supply. **Short supply controls** might apply to certain foodstuffs, medicines, basic metals, or natural resources. For instance, during wartime, a country might limit exports of copper, brass, or steel because it may need these metals for making arms or ammunition. Even during peacetime, short-supply controls are sometimes used to limit inflationary effects on the domestic economy caused by strong foreign demand for scarce resources or materials. U.S. law permits use of short supply controls to protect the U.S. economy from excessive foreign demand for scarce materials. As of 2013, the United States had short supply controls on crude oil, some petroleum products, unprocessed Western red cedar from state and national forest lands, and shipments of horses by sea. In 2005, one American company paid a fine of nearly $500,000 for having exported cedar lumber to Canada for treatment with preservatives and processing.

Trade Controls for the Protection of Wildlife, the Environment, Public Safety, or of Antiquities. There are many other reasons why nations may restrict exports. Many countries prohibit the export of certain wildlife or endangered species, usually pursuant to international conventions. Some countries prohibit the export of artifacts and antiquities. A good example is Egypt, which prohibits the unlicensed export of antiquities found at archaeological sites. Many countries, including the United States, regulate the export of chemicals, hazardous waste, materials for recycling, unsafe products, controlled substances and medicines, medical devices, nuclear material, and other items. Governments often regulate agricultural exports, as well as pesticides, herbicides, and certain fertilizers. Many of these regulations result from international treaty obligations.

One important hallmark of the export regulatory system is that the decisions of the president and of the Department of Commerce, including decisions as to which items to put on the Commerce Control List and which countries to sanction, are largely exempt from the usual administrative procedures of public comment and virtually immune from judicial review. In the following case, *United States v. Mandel*, the court had to consider whether the defendants should be given access to the records and information that the Secretary of Commerce used in deciding to place the subject items on the control list.

Foreign Availability

At the start of the chapter we acknowledged that export controls are all about balancing the needs of national security and foreign policy with the needs of American firms to compete in world markets. The EAR states that controls shall not be imposed for foreign policy or national security purposes on the export of goods or technology if there is **foreign availability**. This means that controls may not be placed on the export of goods and technology that "are available without restriction from sources outside the United States in sufficient quantities and comparable in quality to those produced in the United States so as to render the controls ineffective in achieving their purposes." The government does not have to consider foreign availability if the president determines that the absence of such controls would be detrimental to foreign policy or national security.

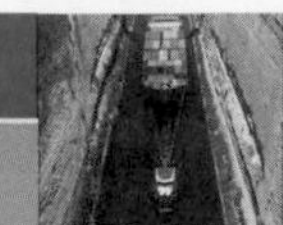

United States v. Mandel

914 F.2d 1215 (1990) United States Court of Appeals (9th Cir.)

BACKGROUND AND FACTS

Defendants were charged with illegally exporting high technology equipment without a license. The indictment alleged that their application for a license had been assigned an application number but was then returned as inadequate. Instead of resubmitting the application, the defendants are alleged to have shipped the equipment to a Hong Kong company placing the application number on the shipping documents in place of an actual license number. The equipment had been controlled for national security reasons. During discovery, they requested to see the records relied on by the Secretary of Commerce in deciding whether to place the subject items on the control list and the factual basis for national security controls related to each item. The government argues that the records are not material to the defense because a criminal defendant cannot challenge the Secretary's decision to place a commodity on the control list, and that the Secretary's decision to require export controls is a political question not reviewable in the courts. The District Court required the government to produce the records and the government appealed.

RYMER, CIRCUIT JUDGE

The [export administration laws] provide the executive branch with power to impose export controls for reasons of national security, foreign policy, or domestic short supply. These controls are implemented through licensing requirements for commodities which meet the criteria set forth in the Act. * * *

The Act contains an elaborate set of criteria which governs the Secretary's imposition of export controls. [The law] directs the Secretary to make a finding regarding the foreign availability of items before he may restrict their exportation. The Secretary must consider whether the commodities to be controlled are available without restriction from sources outside the United States, whether the export of those commodities is restricted pursuant to a multilateral agreement to which the United States is a party, and whether other nations possess capabilities with respect to such commodities comparable to those of the United States.

The items the defendants are charged with exporting were controlled for national security reasons. The Secretary may impose national security controls on a commodity "only to the extent ... necessary (A) to restrict the export of goods and technology which would make a significant contribution to the military potential of any other country or combination of countries which would prove detrimental to the national security of the United States." [citations omitted] * * *

The government contends that in any event the Secretary's decision to require export controls is an unreviewable political question. "Political questions" are controversies which revolve around policy choices and value determinations constitutionally committed to the Congress or the Executive Branch, and are not subject to judicial review. *Japan Whaling Ass'n v. American Cetacean Soc'y,* 478 U.S. 221, 230 (1986).... *Baker v. Carr,* 369 U.S. 186 (1962)....

The district court declined to decide if the political question doctrine applies. The Mandels argue that it correctly determined that judicial review limited to whether there was any basis in fact for the Secretary's decision raises no political question concerns.

Although the basis in fact inquiry is the narrowest form of judicial review, it is nevertheless a review of the merits of the Secretary's decision. A "basis in fact consists of 'some proof'—something which may be less than substantial evidence." *Petrie v. United States,* 407 F.2d 267 (9th Cir. 1969). Even that level of review carries with it the possibility that the court might reverse the Secretary's determination in a particular case.

The [law] requires the Secretary to consider such things as whether the imposition of export controls would be detrimental to the foreign policy or national security interests of the United States, whether restrictions on a given commodity would fulfill declared international obligations of this country, and whether the export of a given commodity would make a significant contribution to the military potential of other countries. These are quintessentially matters of policy entrusted by the Constitution to the Congress and the President, for which there are no meaningful standards of judicial review.

If a court were to review and reverse the Secretary's determination, it would call into question input from other agencies as well as Commerce. The [law] directs the Secretary of Defense to develop a list of militarily critical technologies for inclusion on the CCL, and provides for his concurrence in the Secretary of Commerce's decision. The Secretary of State must also be consulted. Finally, the [law] requires the Secretary to negotiate with allies of the United States to arrive at a mutually acceptable list of articles subject to export controls.

For these reasons the Secretary's decision to place an item on the Commodity Control List is a political question not subject to review to determine whether he

continues

continued

had a basis in fact. Accordingly it was error to allow discovery on that issue.

Decision. Reversed and remanded. The information and factual basis relied on by the Secretary of Commerce in deciding to place an item on the control list are not subject to discovery by the defendants and are not material to the defense. The Secretary's decision to place an item on the list is a political question; courts will not inquire into the national security or foreign policy reasons for controls.

Case Questions

1. What were the reasons for control in this case?
2. What might have been the broader implications, beyond this case, if the court had allowed the defendant access to the Secretary's records? Could it have an impact on national security?
3. If different judges had different opinions as to what goods may or may not be exported without a license, what would be the result?

Exports and Re-exports

U.S. export regulations prohibit the export *or re-export* of controlled items. The term **export** means the act of shipping controlled items out of the United States or the transfer of controlled items or technology to a foreign national whether they are located inside or outside the United States, including technology transferred electronically. The term **re-export** has similar breadth, but it refers to the shipment or transfer of American-controlled items or technology from one foreign country to another foreign country. For example, imagine that you have a license to ship a controlled item to a buyer in the United Arab Emirates. Now assume that the buyer in the UAE wants to sell or transfer the items to a buyer or subsidiary company in Iran. A new license is now required before the items can be transferred to Iran. The rules on re-exports can become complicated, because licensing depends on the items, the countries, and the identity of the parties involved.

Illegal Diversions of Controlled Items

In export control terminology, a **diversion** is the unlawful transfer, transshipment, rerouting, or re-exporting of controlled goods or technology from one destination, to which the goods or technology could legally be shipped, to another destination that has not been lawfully authorized to receive the items. In many cases, an American exporter may be an innocent victim of a scam to get around the export laws. For example, an agent of a foreign entity posing as a legitimate customer in a country not subject to controls may convince an American exporter that they are a legitimate business user with a real business need for the goods ordered. In other cases, the exporter may have been a willing participant in violating the law, having been tempted to skirt the export laws in return for receiving high price for the goods or a cash bribe.

During the cold war, operatives from the Soviet Union or its Eastern European allies would set up "dummy" companies in Western Europe, the Caribbean, or elsewhere, to place orders for U.S. products containing controlled technology. The goods would then be "diverted" to Soviet authorities or laboratories, where they could be analyzed and reverse engineered. The American exporter might have been tempted by offering to pay more than the asking price for the goods if the exporter would rush the shipment and forgo the often time-consuming license application process. Illegal diversions are still one of the most common, although criminal, methods used by rogue countries and terrorist groups to circumvent the export laws of all technology-based countries.

Deemed Exports

Export controls for national security reasons apply to more than just shipments of goods. They also apply to deemed exports. A **deemed export** is the communication or other transfer by an American citizen of technology, technical data, software and source code, encryption technology, or any other controlled information to a foreign national. A **foreign national** is an individual who is neither a U.S. citizen nor a permanent legal resident of the United States. A **deemed re-export**, or communication of information from someone who was licensed to receive it to a third person, must also be licensed.

A deemed export may occur when an American researcher communicates controlled technology or information to employees of a foreign subsidiary or parent company, to joint venture partners, or even to foreign customers. This can be a problem whenever U.S. plants, factories, research facilities, or offices are opened to visiting foreign customers and guests.

A deemed export can occur whenever American and foreign nationals work side-by-side. The communication can be in any form, including a verbal conversation, a visual inspection during site visits, or even casual observation of the controlled goods or technology. Sales of software via the Internet to overseas customers are deemed exports. It also applies to universities and research institutions that host foreign scholars and foreign students.

Licensing of deemed exports by the Department of Commerce depends on the type of research. Proprietary research, including industrial designs the results of which ordinarily are restricted for corporate or national security reasons, is controlled. However, fundamental research in science, engineering, or mathematics (i.e., basic or applied research in which the resulting information is ordinarily published and shared broadly with the scientific community), is not controlled or subject to licensing. Most technology companies and research universities have an internal management control program to ensure compliance with the law.

According to BIS reports, the agency has received the most deemed export license applications in the area of electronics (e.g., semiconductor manufacturing), telecommunications, computers, and aerospace. In recent years, almost 40 percent involved Chinese nationals working in U.S. companies, followed by foreign nationals from India, Iran, Russia, Germany, and the United Kingdom.

Export Licensing

U.S. exporters are responsible for determining if an **export license** is required for each export or re-export of a controlled item. The licensing requirement applies to each shipment and not to each customer "order." Thus if a customer places one order for several controlled items, and they are shipped separately, the exporter must apply for and receive a separate license for each shipment. Any firm or export manager must be familiar with the licensing process. As we will see, violations of the licensing regulations carry severe individual and corporate fines and criminal penalties.

Licenses are determined according to whether the item is controlled and the country of destination. This information is found in the Commerce Control List, which is a part of the *Export Administration Regulations*. Licenses are also determined according to the identity of the end-user.

End User Controls

Export controls are based not only on the article, technology, and country of destination, but also on the individual person or entity receiving it—known as the **end user**. It is unlawful to release any controlled item to anyone on the following lists

Entity List: A list originally set up to bar exports or diversions to organizations engaged in activities related to the proliferation of weapons of mass destruction. Today it has been expanded for other reasons. Most end users on this list are in China, Russia, Pakistan, or India.

Specially Designated Nationals and Blocked Persons List: A list maintained by the Department of Treasury, Office of Foreign Assets Control, comprising individuals and organizations deemed to represent restricted countries or known to be involved in terrorism and narcotics trafficking.

Unverified List: Firms for which an end use check could not be done in prior transactions. These firms present a "red flag" that exporters have a duty to investigate further. (For other **red flag indicators** warn of a possible illegal attempt to violate U.S. export controls, see Exhibit 13.1.)

Denied Persons List: A list of persons whose export privileges have been denied or revoked. They may be located abroad or within the United States. If an American firm believes that a "denied person" wants to buy its goods or acquire its technology, the firm must not make the sale and must report it to the BIS.

Debarred List: A list of parties barred from exporting defense articles, administered by the U.S. State Department.

Although there is a convenient **consolidated screening list**—an online compilation of prohibited end users—the individual lists shown above are the official sources on end users and are updated regularly in the *Federal Register*.

Licensing Review Process

According to the BIS's 2012 annual report, using data collected by the Bureau of the Census, in that year the agency processed more than 23,000 export license applications worth approximately $204 billion. The largest single approval was for a shipment of crude oil worth $113 billion. Overall, of course, this still represents a very small fraction of total U.S. trade.

Exhibit 13.1

Red Flag Indicators

Things to Look for in Export Transactions

These are possible indicators that an unlawful diversion might be planned by your customer:

1. The customer or its address is similar to one of the parties found on the BIS list of denied persons.
2. The customer or purchasing agent is reluctant to offer information about the end-use of the item.
3. The product's capabilities do not fit the buyer's line of business, such as an order for sophisticated computers for a small bakery.
4. The product ordered is incompatible with the technical level of the country to which the product is being shipped, such as semiconductor manufacturing equipment being shipped to a country that has no electronics industry.
5. The customer has little or no business background.
6. The customer is willing to pay cash for a very expensive item when the terms of the sale call for financing.
7. The customer is unfamiliar with the product's performance characteristics but still wants the product.
8. Routine installation, training, or maintenance services are declined by the customer.
9. Delivery dates are vague, or deliveries are planned for out-of-the-way destinations.
10. A freight forwarding firm is listed as the product's final destination.
11. The shipping route is abnormal for the product and destination.
12. Packaging is inconsistent with the stated method of shipment or destination.
13. When questioned, the buyer is evasive or unclear about whether the purchased product is for domestic use, for export, or for reexport.

Reprinted from the U.S. Bureau of Industry and Security.

Source: U.S. Bureau of Industry and Security.

The People's Republic of China was the destination for the largest number of approved licenses, with almost 3,100 individual licenses approved. License applications must be reviewed within 90 days, although in 2009 the average time for approval of license applications was only 26 days (a time frame critical to U.S. firms waiting to ship to foreign customers). Many applications go to the Department of Defense for technical review. The BIS also coordinates with the Department of Energy (nuclear issues), the Department of State (weapons issues), the Department of the Treasury, the U.S. Treasury's Office of Foreign Assets Control (terrorist groups and state sponsors of terrorism), the Department of Interior (fish and wildlife, endangered species), the Food and Drug Administration, the Arms Control and Disarmament Agency, and in some cases with intelligence agencies. Interagency disputes lead to a high-level review process, and eventually to the president.

Special Comprehensive Licenses. A **special comprehensive license** allows companies to make multiple shipments to the same consignee over an extended time. This might include shipments of spare or replacement parts, shipments for use in an ongoing construction project; routine shipments to subsidiary companies or recurring shipments to foreign distributors who regularly do business in the exporter's products. A special license requires advance registration with the BIS, approval of the consignee, and approval of a system of internal controls and record keeping to ensure compliance with the export regulations.

Validated End User Program. The **validated end user program** of BIS allows qualified exporters to preapprove foreign "trusted customers" and subsidiaries of American companies for shipments of certain high-technology, commercial, or dual-use items, without the need for individual export licenses. It is available to companies and end users that have a record of export compliance. It does not apply to any items that might have military or strategic value. Currently, the program is only used for exports to China and India. Critics claim that the program makes it too easy for controlled technologies to be illegally diverted.

Automated Export System

The **Automated Export System** is the online system of the U.S. Census Bureau used to collect information about export shipments. Exporters in the United

States use the automated system to file an **Electronic Export Information** (EEI), an electronic filing of information required for each export shipment leaving the United States. The Census Bureau is an agency of the U.S. Department of Commerce that compiles international trade statistics for the United States. It shares that information with the Bureau of Industry and Security, U.S. Customs, and other government agencies for export control purposes.

An EEI is required for each shipment for which an export license has been issued, and for most other shipments valued over $2,500 going to a foreign country, except those to Canada if the items are for use by a Canadian end user and will not be re-exported. The $2,500 limit applies not to the total value of an entire shipment, but to each commodity classification being shipped. The EEI may be filed by the exporter or by a freight forwarder acting as an authorized agent of the exporter. For most shipments, including those for which a license has been granted by BIS, the EEI must be filed prior to shipment. Only certain pre-approved exporters may file the EEI after shipment.

The EEI requires the item description, weight, and selling price, the U.S. state of origin, foreign consignee, port and transport information, the tariff classification number from the harmonized schedules, licensing information from BIS, and other data. Data entered on the automated system is a legal record, and submitting false statements is a violation of the export regulations. By using the automated system an exporter is certifying that the export has been authorized or licensed by the BIS, that the shipment conforms to the license, and that all statements are true. In the following case, *United States v. Chmielewski*, involved a prosecution for recording false information on export documents submitted to the government.

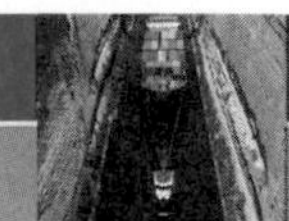

United States v. Chmielewski

218 F.3d 840 (2000) United States Court of Appeals (8th Cir.)

BACKGROUND AND FACTS

Chmielewski sold $2.7 million in slot machines to customers in South Africa. South Africa's import duty at the time was 69 percent *ad valorem*. In a scheme to help his customers avoid the duty, Chmielewski sent them false sales invoices grossly understating the value of the machines. The South African government lost $1.4 million in duties as a result. Chmielewski sent the false invoices to his U.S. freight forwarders who used that information for his export documentation with U.S. Customs. Chmielewski was paid by cash and travelers' checks. On his conviction for the crime of making and conspiring to make false statements to the United States (under Title 18 U.S.C 371 and 1001), Chmielewski appealed. He argued that there was insufficient evidence to convict. He also argued that the loss of tariff revenue—and thus the harm—occurred outside the United States (i.e. to South Africa) and therefore should not be considered as a factor in sentencing.

RICHARD S. ARNOLD, CIRCUIT JUDGE

Mr. Chmielewski also sent the false invoices to his U.S. freight forwarders. Freight forwarders arrange the shipment of goods overseas; their duties include filling out the required documentation for U.S. customs. Freight forwarders do not inspect the cargo themselves but rely on information provided by the exporter in completing the necessary customs declarations. Accordingly, the freight forwarders reported to the United States the false values contained in the defendant's invoices as part of the "Shipper's Export Declaration" [now the Electronic Export Information] required for such exports. If the freight forwarders had been given the true values, the scheme to defraud the South African government would have failed, because the values declared on the Shipper's Export Declaration are reported by the U.S. to the country receiving the exports.

The government presented sufficient evidence at trial that Mr. Chmielewski was aware of the Shipper's Export Declaration form and knew that the false values he supplied to his freight forwarders would be submitted in turn to the United States. First, Mr. Chmielewski received copies of the customs documentation prepared by the freight forwarders. These documents included completed copies of the Shipper's Export Declaration form with the false values that he had provided. The Shipper's Export Declaration form declares prominently on its face that it is used for official purposes by the Secretary of Commerce and that a criminal penalty may be imposed for falsified forms. * * *

From this evidence, the jury could have reasonably inferred that Mr. Chmielewski knew about the customs forms and intended the false statements of value to be made to the government. Based on his knowledge of the

continues

continued

forms, the jury could also infer that Mr. Chmielewski conspired to make false statements to the United States. Mr. Chmielewski admits that he and his business associates agreed to falsify the sales invoices to help his customers avoid South African duties. False U.S. customs forms were necessary to complete this scheme, and his co-conspirators' testimony shows that they understood this.

Likewise, the jury could have reasonably decided that the understatement of value on a Shipper's Export Declaration form was a material misrepresentation for the purpose of 18 U.S.C. §1001. A false statement is material if it has a natural tendency to influence or was capable of influencing the government agency or official to which it was addressed. *United States v. Gaudin,* 515 U.S. 506 (1995). At trial, the government presented evidence that the values submitted in the Shipper's Export Declaration are used by customs officials in determining which outbound cargo to inspect; higher-valued cargo suggests high-technology goods whose export may be restricted. Additionally, the values are used for statistical purposes which, *inter alia,* affect trade negotiations with other countries. The jury was supplied with sufficient evidence to decide that Mr. Chmielewski's misrepresentations were capable of influencing official action. * * *

Mr. Chmielewski argues that the sentencing enhancement was incorrect because the loss to South Africa occurred outside the United States ... . In this case, however, Mr. Chmielewski's false statements were domestic acts, and the crime charged is one against the United States. It is no intrusion to gauge the severity of Mr. Chmielewski's domestic crime by measuring the damage done to his extraterritorial victims. In doing so, we consider a foreign loss not to uphold a foreign law, but to uphold our own law, which directs us to consider the loss caused by fraud as a measure of a just punishment.

Decision. Judgment affirmed. There was sufficient evidence at trial to support the conviction. Making a materially false statement on official U.S. export documentation is a crime against the United States and the court may consider the harm done outside the United States (i.e. to South Africa) in increasing the sentence.

Case Questions

1. Imagine that you have a foreign customer who balks at your price, but then suggests that you send two invoices—one for them to submit to their customs authorities for far less than the agreed price of the goods, and a second for them to actually pay. How should you reply?
2. You apply for, and receive, an export license for a shipment to a foreign customer. After shipment, the customer places a new order for the same merchandise. May you use the license number and information from the first shipment and enter it on EEI for the second shipment? Why or why not?

Extraterritorial Jurisdiction of Export Control Laws

We begin this section with one of the most contentious questions in all of export control law: Should a nation, as a matter of law, be able to extend the power of its export control laws—its jurisdiction—over its goods and technology once they have left its territory? Most nations are not willing to say that goods and technology have "nationality" in the same sense that its citizens do. So the legal basis for extending jurisdiction over goods and technology once they leave the nation in which they originated is subject to debate. Most international lawyers reject the idea that one nation, in the absence of a treaty or convention, can control goods and technology within the borders of another nation. Consider a comparison to intellectual property law and the protection of patents, trademarks, and copyrights. We would not expect, for example, the United Kingdom to use its police and courts to take action in the United States to enforce a British patent that belongs to a British citizen. Such matters are usually covered by international treaty or convention, handled by local authorities under local law, or negotiated between governments.

However, for at least a half century, the United States has attempted to assert the extraterritorial jurisdiction of its export control laws over its goods and technology anywhere in the world. The *Export Administration Regulations* state that they are applicable to all "U.S. origin items wherever located," including "U.S. origin parts ... or other commodities integrated abroad into foreign-made products." In addition, the re-export provisions attempt to control U.S.-origin items long after they have left the United States. We have also seen this in the "deemed export" rules, under which the United States attempts to control and license the communication or transfer of technology by foreign subsidiaries of U.S. firms to foreign employees in foreign countries. In the example given in the following section, the American attempt to use extraterritorial export controls led to a serious international business crisis.

The Crisis over the Soviet Natural Gas Pipeline to Europe. In the early 1980s, the Soviet Union and European countries agreed to construct a 3,000-mile natural gas pipeline from Siberia, across Russia and communist Eastern Europe, to Western Europe. It was the height of the cold war: The Berlin Wall divided Germany, and U.S. and Soviet tanks faced each other along the border between East and West. President Reagan and the United States stood firmly against construction of the pipeline. The U.S. fear was that it would make America's allies in Western Europe too dependent on the Soviets, which could lead to disastrous consequences if war were to break out in Europe. It also would provide the Soviets with Western "hard currency" from the sale of gas, which would help take economic pressure off the Soviet Union's failing communist economy.

American companies in the United States, as well as their subsidiaries in Europe, produced advanced technology that could be used in drilling and in construction of the pipeline. General Electric produced the most advanced turbines for moving the gas, although less-effective alternatives were made by companies in the Soviet Union and elsewhere. Dresser France, S.A., a subsidiary of Dresser Industries of Dallas, Texas, produced gas compressors needed for the project. However, in an attempt to stop the project, President Reagan used the U.S. export control laws to order all American-owned companies and subsidiaries worldwide to refrain from exporting goods or technology for use in the pipeline project. The ban included goods and technology of U.S. origin, as well as those based on U.S. patents and technology licensed to foreign firms by American firms. France, Great Britain, (the former) West Germany, Italy, and other countries resented the order and considered it a "slap in the face" to their sovereignty. Their governments responded by making it unlawful for their companies to comply with the U.S. order.

Dresser was in a difficult position. The U.S. government threatened Dresser France, S.A., with sanctions, and possible criminal penalties, if it did not stop its shipment of compressors. The French government threatened to nationalize Dresser France, S.A., if it did. There was a diplomatic impasse. An article published in *Time* magazine in 1982 quoted John James, Dresser's chairman, as saying, "The laws of the United States are not the laws of the whole world." President Reagan had no support, either at home or abroad. In the end, the Reagan administration's attempt to assert the extraterritorial jurisdiction of U.S. export controls failed, and they were eventually rescinded.

Antiboycott Provisions

For our purposes, a **boycott** is an organized refusal of one or more nations, often backed by economic sanctions, to trade with one or more other nations. Boycotts are often used for political reasons. **Antiboycott** laws are legal responses by governments that make it unlawful for their citizens or companies to participate in a boycott. U.S. export control laws contain antiboycott provisions that make it illegal to "comply [with or] support any boycott fostered or imposed by a foreign country against a country which is friendly to the United States." Although the laws apply to any boycott not sponsored by the U.S. government, they primarily target some Middle Eastern countries that have been boycotting Israel for many decades. This boycott goes well beyond the Arab refusal to trade directly with Israel. Boycotting countries will not permit the import of any goods or services that have any Israeli components, and they will not do business with firms from anywhere in the world that also do business with Israel or that have ties to Israel. Firms that do business with Israel are "blacklisted."

U.S. antiboycott laws apply to any U.S. person or company located in the United States. They also apply to foreign affiliates of such persons and companies. The laws prohibit participation in the Arab boycott of Israel, refusal to do business with blacklisted companies, or agreements to do so. They also prohibit the furnishing of information relating to the boycott, relationships with or in Israel, or relationships with blacklisted companies. In addition, the laws prohibit discrimination based on, or the furnishing of any information about, the race, religion, sex, national origin, or nationality of another person.

Any request for information related to a boycott, or request to participate in a boycott, must not be answered, but must instead be reported to the Office of Antiboycott Compliance within the Bureau of Industry and Security. Some of these requests are cleverly disguised. For example, a bank letter of credit issued on behalf of a Lebanese buyer for goods being shipped to Lebanon required a "[c]ertificate issued by the shipping company or its agent testifying that the carrying vessel is allowed to enter the Lebanese port. . . . " This was a veiled attempt at enforcing the boycott on Israel, because ships that have carried Israeli goods, or that are Israeli owned, are not permitted to enter Lebanese ports. Violations of the antiboycott regulations by Americans are punishable under the export control laws. In the following case, *Briggs & Stratton Corp. v. Baldridge,* the court addresses a challenge to the U.S. antiboycott regulations.

Briggs & Stratton Corp. v. Baldridge

539 F. Supp. 1307 (1982) United States District Court (E.D. Wis.)

BACKGROUND AND FACTS

* * * In December 1954, the League of Arab States called for an economic boycott of Israel. Under the "General Principles" worked out by the Arab states, a firm could be blacklisted if it traded with Israel.

The plaintiff manufactures internal combustion engines. Its products are often used as component parts. Briggs had been blacklisted because of dealings with Israel.

In May of 1977, Briggs received a letter from its Syrian distributor telling it that it had been blacklisted and refused an import license. He also received a questionnaire, which was translated as follows:

1. Has the company now or in the past had main or branch factories in Israel?
2. Has the company now or in the past had general offices in Israel for its regional or international works?
3. Has it granted now or in the past the right of utilizing its name or trademarks or patents to persons or establishments or Israeli works inside or outside Israel?
4. Does it share in or own now or in the past share in Israeli works or establishments inside or outside Israel?
5. Does it now or did it offer in the past any technical assistance to any Israeli work or establishment?
6. Does it represent now or did it represent in the past any Israeli establishment or work inside or outside Israel?
7. What are the companies that it shares in or with, their nationalities, and the size or rate of these shares?

Briggs answered "no" to the questions, but did not have the questionnaire authenticated because of the new antiboycott regulations. The blacklisting continued, but subsequently the company was removed from the blacklist. Briggs was unquestionably injured economically by the blacklisting. Briggs brought an action against the officials charged with enforcing the act and regulations, claiming that they violated the First, Fifth, and Ninth Amendments to the U.S. Constitution.

DISTRICT JUDGE GORDON

The Commerce Department regulations are consistent with this express policy to require persons to refuse to furnish information which would have the effect of furthering a boycott against a nation friendly to the United States. Thus the regulations are not inconsistent with the policies of the act.

I also reject Briggs' argument that the regulations permit a firm to supply information in the absence of a questionnaire that it cannot supply if it gets one. Example (ix) following the intent regulation reads:

> U.S. company A is on boycotting country Y's blacklist. In an attempt to secure its removal from the blacklist, A wishes to supply to Y information which demonstrates that A does at least as much business in Y and other countries engaged in a boycott of X as it does in X. A intends to continue its business in X undiminished and in fact is exploring and intends to continue exploring an expansion of its activities in X without regard to Y's boycott.
>
> A may furnish the information, because in doing so it has no intent to comply with, further, or support Y's boycott. 15 C.F.R. 369.1(e).

Briggs' interpretation of this example goes too far. The example merely permits a company on its own initiative to demonstrate non-discriminatory conduct. . . . Example (ix) cannot be read to condone a company unilaterally providing a variety of information to a boycott agency. For example, I believe that the regulations quite reasonably prohibit a company from currying favor with boycott officials by unilaterally telling them that it will not trade with the boycotted country.

Briggs argues that because the regulations cause Briggs to be blacklisted, and thus affect its worldwide sales, the government has totally destroyed Briggs' rights to its foreign trade. Briggs likens the effect to a restriction on private property which "forces some people alone to bear public burdens which, in all fairness and justice, should be borne by the public as a whole."

continues

continued

* * * The regulations apply to all Americans equally. It is possible that they have a somewhat greater impact on Briggs than they do on others, but that does not constitute a taking. Briggs has lost some profits because it has lost some sales, but its property has not been seized or restrained by the government. There is no restriction by the challenged regulation on Briggs' efforts to export its products. In prohibiting Briggs from answering certain questions, the government has not taken Briggs' property in violation of the Fifth Amendment.

Decision. The antiboycott regulations were upheld by the court despite the difficulties of compliance or the economic consequences that may result. The district court's decision was affirmed by the U.S. Court of Appeals for the 7th Circuit at 728 F.2d 915 (1984).

Case Questions

1. What is the purpose of the antiboycott regulations?
2. On what basis did the company challenge the act and regulations?
3. Should a company respond to a questionnaire like the one Briggs received here? What action should it take?

Compliance and Enforcement

Compliance and enforcement are two sides of the same coin. No government agency, whether it collects taxes or fights water and air pollution, can rely solely on law enforcement to make the system work. Voluntary compliance by regulated companies is essential. Compliance with export controls is critical to national security. The exporter has the burden of using due diligence to comply with the law. Penalties for noncompliance are onerous.

Export Management and Compliance Programs. One of the best ways to ensure compliance is for a company to establish an internal **export management and compliance program**. Such programs are virtually mandatory today. An effective program should be in writing and state company compliance policies, involve senior management as well as personnel at all levels, use trained personnel or outside specialists to implement the policy, provide for a system of internal audits to prevent and detect violations, provide for compliance throughout a supply chain, and have provisions for notification of the Bureau of Industry and Security in case of a question, violation, or other irregularity. The policies should cover procedures for internal security; licensing; use of "red flag" indicators and blocked persons lists; screening of foreign customers; investigating end use destinations, foreign travel, Internet, and local area network use; shipping; security at trade shows; and more. The system should also include controls over record keeping and reporting. Technology companies, research and development facilities, and research universities are a few examples of institutions that should—or must—have deemed export compliance programs.

Record-Keeping Requirements. Exporters are required to keep records related to all licensed exports for a period of five years. These include all licenses, license applications and supporting documents, bills of lading or transport documents issued by carriers, memoranda, notes, correspondence, contracts, invitations to bid, books of account, financial records, and other records of the transaction. In particular, exporters should keep all formal and informal records related to their investigation into their end users and the end uses of their exports.

Investigations and Enforcement. Although the Bureau of Industry and Security (BIS) is the primary regulatory and licensing authority for the export laws, the responsibility for investigating and enforcing the U.S. export laws is spread across several departments and agencies of government. The **Office of Export Enforcement** (within BIS at the Department of Commerce) has authority for administrative (civil) and criminal investigations and enforcement. The BIS may detain shipments, issue "temporary denial orders" to prevent imminent illegal shipments, issue warning letters, and monitor compliance with the conditions of individual licenses. It may bring a civil action before an administrative law judge to impose civil fines or other administrative sanctions. Criminal cases are based on willful conduct or for **conscious avoidance**, meaning that the exporter purposely avoided learning information (e.g., not asking if the goods will be resold and diverted) that might have had a bearing on his or her license application. Criminal investigations are handled by the BIS, the Bureau of Customs and Border Protection, the Immigration and Customs Enforcement Agency, the FBI, the U.S. Postal Inspection Service, and often by the Internal Revenue

Service, and are prosecuted by the Department of Justice. In 2010, the president created the **Export Enforcement Coordination Center** within **U.S. Immigration and Customs Enforcement** (Department of Homeland Security) to coordinate the flow of information and activities between the 15 regulatory agencies, intelligence agencies, and law enforcement agencies involved in export administration.

Penalties for Export Violations. It is unlawful to export in violation of the terms of a license, to evade licensing controls, or to buy, use, sell, conceal, or transport any item exported or to be exported from the United States with knowledge that a violation of the export laws has occurred, is about to occur, or is intended to occur in connection with the item. Other violations include soliciting the export of a controlled item; possessing a controlled item with intent to export or re-export it in violation of the law; altering a license; making false statements in a license application or on government-required export documents, failing to comply with a lawful order of the BIS; failing to comply with reporting and record-keeping requirements; and conspiracy. Many investigations also uncover crimes of money laundering.

The penalties for violating the *Export Administration Regulations* are those found in the *International Emergency Economic Powers Enhancement Act of 2007*. A civil penalty may be imposed for each unlawful violation of the export regulations in an amount not to exceed the greater of $250,000 or twice amount of the transaction that is the basis of the violation. A willful violation (or a willful attempt or conspiracy to violate) is punishable by a criminal fine of not more than $1 million and imprisonment for not more than 20 years, or both. (50 U.S.C. §1705). In the following case, *United States v. Zhi Yong Guo*, the defendant attempted to argue that compliance with the export control laws was impossible because they were too vague and unclear.

Sentencing factors include the extent of the threat to national security, the number of shipments and their value, the degree of willfulness and planning, and the experience and sophistication of the exporter. Anyone who makes an "accurate and thorough" voluntary self-disclosure of an export violation is likely to receive a reduced penalty as a result.

Denial of Export Privileges. In addition to fines and imprisonment, individual violators and related parties (including freight forwarders or carriers) can be subject to a "denial order" that bars them from exporting for a specified number of years. It is also unlawful for any other person to participate in an export transaction with a "denied person."

United States v. Zhi Yong Guo

634 F.3d 1119 (2011) United States Court of Appeals (9th Cir.)

BACKGROUND AND FACTS

Defendant is a Chinese citizen who worked as an engineer in Beijing developing photoelectric technologies. Defendant's friend and accomplice, Chao, was a U.S. citizen who owned a printing business in California. On defendant's instructions Chao purchased three export-controlled thermal imaging cameras, called FLIR systems, and had them shipped to China. Defendant paid Chao a $900 commission. The export compliance staff at FLIR thought it strange that a printing company was purchasing such highly developed equipment and they notified the Department of Commerce. The defendant then came to Los Angeles, purchased ten additional cameras, hid them in his baggage, and was arrested by federal agents while attempting to board a return flight to China. Both were charged with knowingly and willfully conspiring to export, and attempting to export, controlled items without a license. Chao pled guilty, and the defendant was convicted at trial of violating the criminal provisions of the *International Emergency Economic Powers Act* (50 U.S.C. §1705) applicable to violations of the *Export Administration Regulations*. The defendant appealed, arguing that compliance was impossible because the regulations were too vague and unclear.

GRABER, CIRCUIT JUDGE

The *Export Administration Regulations* contain two provisions that are relevant to our discussion here. First, Supplement No. 1 to Part 774, entitled the *Commerce Control List*, contains the list of commodities, software, and technology subject to control. Each entry on the *Commerce Control List* has a particular export control classification number, describes the technical characteristics of the items classified with that number, and identifies the particular reasons for controlling the export of those items. Second,

continues

continued

Supplement No. 1 to Part 738 contains the *Commerce Country Chart*, which lists the restrictions relevant to each foreign country by setting out the reasons for control applicable to each country. A person can determine whether the regulations control the export of a particular item by (1) connecting the item to the relevant description in the *Commerce Control List*; (2) identifying the reasons for control applicable to that item; and (3) looking to see whether any of the reasons for control of that item are checked off next to the relevant country on the *Commerce Country Chart*.

Here, for example, export control classification number 6A003.b.4.b pertains to thermal imaging cameras incorporating certain focal plane arrays, of the kind that Defendant attempted to export. That classification has three reasons for its control: national security, regional stability, and anti-terrorism. The entry for China on the *Commerce Country Chart* shows restrictions for both national security and regional stability. Accordingly, the regulations required Defendant to obtain an export license before taking his thermal imaging cameras to China, and 50 U.S.C. §1705(a) [the statute] made it a crime for him *knowingly* to attempt to export the cameras without such a license.

We recognize that putting together the pieces of this regulatory puzzle is not easy. To understand the crime with which Defendant was charged, one must look at four sources and read them together: the statute and two implementing regulations, the *Commerce Control List* in 15 C.F.R. Part 774 and the *Commerce Country Chart* in 15 C.F.R. Part 738. But a statute does not fail the vagueness test simply because it involves a complex regulatory scheme, or requires that several sources be read together, and Defendant has not directed us to a single case in which we have held otherwise. *See United States v. Kennecott Copper Corp.,* 523 F.2d 821 (9th Cir. 1975) (rejecting a vagueness challenge premised on the complexity of a similar regulatory scheme and observing that the scheme was "simple as compared with some other statutory schemes carrying criminal penalties, such as the federal income tax statutes and regulations").

Rather, the test is whether the text of the statute and its implementing regulations, read together, give ordinary citizens fair notice with respect to what the statute and regulations forbid, and whether the statute and regulations read together adequately provide for principled enforcement by making clear what conduct of the defendant violates the statutory scheme. Although complicated, the *Export Administration Regulations* describe in detail the technologies subject to export control. That detailed description gave Defendant clear warning that the cameras he sought to export fell within the licensing requirement of the export regulations. Those regulations also provide law enforcement with clear guidance as to what technologies they may police. Because the regulations apprise those who take the time and effort to consult them as to what may and may not be taken to other countries without a license and do not allow for arbitrary enforcement, the regulations satisfy due process.

Moreover, the scienter requirement in [the statute] further alleviates any concern over the complexity of the regulatory scheme. To convict Defendant of willfully violating [the statute] the government was required to prove beyond a reasonable doubt that Defendant *knew* that a license was required for the export of the particular thermal imaging camera he was dealing with, and that Defendant intended to violate the law by exporting or attempting to export such a thermal imaging camera to China without such a license. The requirement that [the statute] places on the government to prove Defendant's knowledge of the law "'mitigate[s] a law's vagueness, especially with respect to the adequacy of notice to the complainant that his conduct is proscribed.'" *United States v. Jae Gab Kim,* 449 F.3d 933, 943 (9th Cir. 2006). (quoting *Village of Hoffman Estates v. Flipside, Hoffman Estates, Inc.*, 455 U.S. 489, 499 (1982)).

Statutes and regulations are often complex, and necessarily so. But complexity is not the same as vagueness. The export administration regulations describe in great detail the technologies for which the government requires a license for export. And, to convict anyone under [the statute] the government must prove beyond a reasonable doubt that the person *knew* that he needed a license but did not get one. We therefore see no danger that a person could violate [the statute] unwittingly, and we reject Defendant's vagueness challenge.

Decision. Affirmed. The *Export Administration Regulations* are neither vague nor so complex that compliance is impossible. Conviction only requires that the defendant knew that a license was required for shipment and that he had failed to get one, not that he was able to understand all of the intricacies and details of the regulations or the statute which gave them legal effect

Case Questions

1. From the limited facts presented here, do you think a reasonable juror could conclude that the defendant knew his conduct was illegal? Why or why not?
2. In addition to penalties faced during the sentencing in this case, what administrative or civil penalties did the defendant face?

ECONOMIC AND FINANCIAL SANCTIONS

An economic or **financial sanction** is a regulation that restricts or prohibits relationships with "targeted" foreign countries, foreign entities, or named foreign individuals because of their support for international terrorism, the proliferation of weapons of mass destruction, for international drug and narcotics trafficking, or other threats to national security. The restrictions can include a partial or total ban on trade and financial transactions, freezing of bank accounts and other physical assets, a ban on travel, and more. Many sanctions are coordinated between countries to assure they are effective and not circumvented. In 2013, the United States had comprehensive sanctions only on Iran, Sudan, Syria, and Cuba, as well as specific sanctions against North Korea. In decades past, well-known sanctions were used against South Africa (to end racial *apartheid*), Burma, Yugoslavia, Zimbabwe, and Iraq (under Saddam Hussein). A list of U.S. sanctions programs administered by the U.S. Treasury Department appears in Exhibit 13.2.

Exhibit 13.2

Sanctions Programs
U.S. Department of the Treasury Office of Foreign Assets Control as of August 2013
Balkans-related sanctions
Belarus sanctions
Burma sanctions
Cote d'Ivoire (Ivory Coast)-related sanctions
Counter Narcotics Trafficking sanctions
Counter Terrorism sanctions
Cuba sanctions
Democratic Republic of the Congo–related sanctions
Iran sanctions
Iraq-related sanctions
Lebanon-related sanctions
Former Liberian Regime of Charles Taylor sanctions
Libya sanctions
Magnitsky sanctions (Russia)
Non-Proliferation sanctions
North Korea sanctions
Rough Diamond trade controls
Somalia sanctions
Sudan sanctions
Syria sanctions
Transnational criminal organizations
Yemen-related sanctions
Zimbabwe sanctions

Effectiveness of Economic and Financial Sanctions

The use of trade controls to accomplish foreign policy objectives has been a subject of political and economic debate for many years. Proponents of the use of trade sanctions argue that they bring international attention to important world issues, and that they assert a moral stance. As examples, proponents point out that sanctions helped to end the civil war in the former Yugoslavia, and sanctions on Libya for harboring terrorists that shot down a commercial airliner over Lockerbie, Scotland, in 1988 eventually led to Libya handing over the terrorists for trial. Sanctions are also a very flexible foreign policy tool. They can be implemented gradually, increasing in severity to correspond with the seriousness of the violation and the willingness of the target country to comply with international law or UN resolutions.

Those who argue against the use of trade sanctions say that they are ineffective. They point out that imposing economic sanctions on an already poor country often affects innocent people more than it does those in power. Economic sanctions alone are rarely enough to cause a repressed people to rise up against a brutal military government. Most people would agree that almost 50 years of U.S. restrictions on trade with and travel to communist Cuba have done nothing to remove the Castro government or change its policies. Others argue that the Cuban sanctions did not work because they were not tough enough. Another argument against sanctions is that they are often easy for the targeted country to circumvent. Without universal cooperation, which there seldom is, sanctions by only one or a few countries quickly lose their effectiveness.

United Nations-Approved Sanctions. Sanctions that have broad international participation are easier to enforce and usually more effective. Sanctions authorized by the **United Nations Security Council** can be far more effective than unilateral controls by one country. They are harder to circumvent, and more importantly, they carry the backing of international law and the force of international moral opinion. United Nations sanctions are intended to force a government to comply with international law and are seen as a means of avoiding military intervention.

U.S. Agricultural Exports and the Soviet Invasion of Afghanistan. One of the most famous examples of a failed unilateral use of trade sanctions by the United States for foreign policy reasons occurred in 1979. The cold war was ongoing, and the Soviet Union had invaded Afghanistan. In retaliation, President Carter ordered an embargo of U.S. grain sales to the Soviet Union. This policy blocked the sale of millions of tons of American wheat. (In another bold move, he blocked U.S. participation in the 1980 Olympics.) President Carter had not garnered international support for the sanctions, and other countries did not back the United States. Major grain-producing nations, including Canada, Argentina, and Australia, continued to let their farmers sell to the Soviets. They did so and largely neutralized the embargo's impact. The only result of the United States having unilaterally used food exports as a weapon of trade, other than the making of a moral statement, was the devastating economic impact on American farmers who lost a key market. Although President Reagan revoked the embargo, the damage continued for years. American farmers had lost their position as the principal suppliers of grain to the Soviet Union. Subsequent American presidents have been, and should be, far more aware of the importance of getting international support before imposing trade sanctions.

Authority for U.S. Sanctions

Congress has passed a number of statutes granting the president exceptional powers during times of peace and war. Since the American Civil War era, Congress has granted extraordinary powers to the president to deal with national emergencies, such as an international economic, diplomatic, or military crisis. Although originally conceived to allow the president to deal with economic problems that arise during wartime, the concept of national emergency has gradually expanded to include a broad range of situations affecting foreign affairs and international trade during peace or war. The two most important are the *Trading with the Enemy Act* and the *International Emergency Economic Powers Act.*

Trading with the Enemy Act. Congress passed the *Trading with the Enemy Act* in 1917 to restrict trade with hostile countries during times of war or during a time of emergency declared by the president. In 1933, however, President Roosevelt used this statute during the Great Depression to declare a national banking emergency, close the nation's banks, and prevent the hoarding of cash and gold. In the 1970s Congress restricted the application of the TWEA to wartime (the TWEA still applies to U.S. relations with Cuba), and passed a new statute to deal with peacetime emergencies, the *International Emergency Economic Powers Act* (IEEPA).

International Emergency Economic Powers Act

This statute provides the current grant of authority to the president to regulate economic and financial transactions and to place restrictions on importing or exporting during a peacetime international emergency. The statute states that the president may declare a national emergency in the event of "any unusual and extraordinary threat, which has its source in whole or substantial part outside the United States, to the national security, foreign policy, or economy of the United States." IEEPA allows the president wide discretion in controlling international financial transactions, including the transfer of monies, goods, and securities to and from the United States. It allows the president to seize foreign assets, including money held in U.S. banks or foreign branches of U.S. banks, or other physical assets. The statute also allows the president to impose a trade embargo with a foreign country and to take a wide range of other economic sanctions. IEEPA is primarily enforced by the **Office of Foreign Assets Control** of the U.S. Department of Treasury.

USA Patriot Act. One of the major U.S. legal responses to the terrorist attacks of September 11, 2001, was the enactment of a statute with a rather cumbersome title, *Uniting and Strengthening America by Providing Appropriate Tools Required to Intercept and Obstruct Terrorism (2001),* commonly called the *USA Patriot Act.* The act made significant changes to IEEPA and other U.S. criminal statutes and gave far-reaching powers to law enforcement to deal with the threat of terrorism in America.

The act created new federal crimes and penalties for terrorism. These include new crimes (or increased penalties for existing crimes) for attacks on mass transportation, for harboring terrorists, for possession of biological toxins or weapons, for fraudulent charitable solicitation, and for providing material support to terrorists. The act also modified the immigration laws by giving the government greater freedom to detain and deport non-citizens where the U.S. Attorney General had reasonable grounds to believe that an individual belonged to a terrorist group or jeopardized U.S. national security. The act amended IEEPA to give the government greater flexibility to seize property of those who commit terrorist acts or who provide material support to terrorists. It permitted the president to order the confiscation of foreign property belonging to any individual, group, or country that planned, authorized, aided, or engaged in any attack against the United States. It also allowed assets belonging to individuals or organizations to be frozen pending (rather than following) an IEEPA investigation into its links to terrorists.

The *Patriot Act* amended U.S. laws on financial transactions and bank secrecy, so U.S. government agencies could better follow the trail of money supporting terrorists. The act expanded the record-keeping requirements for financial institutions and called for greater government scrutiny over international business transactions. Financial institutions were placed in the position of "knowing their customer." By consulting the government's list of specially designated nationals and blocked persons, banks could determine if any transaction included persons or organizations whose assets had been blocked or "frozen" under the law. Financial transactions, both inside and outside the United States, were to be tracked and reported to the government whenever there was suspicion of money laundering for terrorist groups. Cash transactions over $10,000 also had to be reported. The act also expanded the extraterritorial application of federal criminal law to terrorist acts committed against Americans or American property overseas. The law gave enforcement powers to the Department of Treasury, Office of Foreign Assets Control and the **Financial Crimes Enforcement Network** (often called "FinCen"), and other government agencies.

Court Challenges to IEEPA. When Libya was implicated in international terrorism in the late 1980s, President Reagan prohibited U.S. citizens from performing any contract in support of commercial, industrial, or governmental projects there. In *Herman Chang v. United States*, 859 F.2d 893 (Fed. Cir. 1988), a group of petroleum engineers brought suit against the United States alleging that the termination of their employment with a Libyan oil company by an executive order under IEEPA violated their constitutional protection against the taking of private property without the payment of just compensation. In upholding the president's order, the court dismissed the argument that the U.S. government may not act in an emergency in a way that causes economic harm to individuals or companies. The court stated,

> A new tariff, an embargo, a [military] draft, or a war may inevitably bring upon individuals great losses; may, indeed, render valuable property almost valueless. They may destroy the worth of a contract. But whoever supposed that, because of this, a tariff could not be changed ... or an embargo be enacted, or a war be declared?

IEEPA and the 1979 Iranian Revolution. In the late 1970s, the government of Iran was overthrown during an Islamic revolution. Islamic militants, angry at the United States for its support of the prior government, seized the U.S. embassy in Tehran and held the Americans there hostage for 444 days. At the time, American firms had considerable business interests and property in Iran. That property was also seized by the new government. In response, President Carter declared a national emergency under IEEPA and froze all Iranian property (worth a total of about $12 billion) held by U.S. banks and corporations, both in the United States and abroad. All trade was halted and travel was restricted between the two countries. In order to free the hostages, the United States and Iran signed the *Algiers Agreement* in 1981, by which the United States agreed to place the blocked Iranian money in trust accounts in British banks pending the settlement of claims by the newly created U.S.-Iranian Claims Tribunal (which sat at The Hague, Netherlands). Chas. T. Main International, Inc., a U.S. engineering firm that had been doing work on an Iranian hydroelectric power plant, brought a legal action of its own in a U.S. court against Iran seeking compensation for its lost property, and a declaration that the *Algiers Agreement* exceeded the president's powers under the Constitution. In *Chas. T. Main International, Inc. v. Khuzestan Water & Power Authority*, 651 F.2d 800 (1st Cir. 1981), the Court of Appeals ruled that the president had the authority to enter an agreement for the settlement of all claims between U.S. firms and Iran. The court further ruled that the agreement prevailed over all other attempts by Americans to regain their property in courts of law. In ruling that the president had the constitutional power to create a tribunal to settle international claims, the court stated: "This case well illustrates the imperative need to preserve a presidential flexibility sufficient to diffuse an international crisis, in order to prevent the crisis from escalating or even leading to war." Chas. T. Main had to proceed with its claim at The Hague, and it ultimately won an award against Iran there.

U.S. Sanctions on Trade with Cuba

Prior to 1959, the United States had strong ties to Cuba, an island nation just 90 miles off the coast of Florida. Many Americans had business investments there, and the country was a mecca for tourists from around the world. In 1952, an army general seized power in a military *coup d'état.* Political unrest fermented, culminating in the 1959 overthrow of the government by Fidel Castro's Marxist guerrilla army. Castro set up a communist government, with strong ties to the Soviet Union. Cuba nationalized the assets of American citizens and U.S. firms (including farms, factories, hotels, bank accounts, real estate, etc.) without compensation. Castro began an effort to "export communism" to other countries in Latin America and was a key player in the cold war between the United States and the Soviet Union. So began decades of anger between the United States and Cuba, beginning with the failed Bay of Pigs invasion in 1961 and the Cuban missile crisis in 1962.

In 1963, the United States began its efforts to isolate Cuba economically and politically. It banned all trade and financial transactions between Cuba and the United States and froze all U.S.-held assets of the Cuban government and of private Cuban citizens. It also prohibited almost all travel to Cuba by U.S. citizens. In the following case, *Freedom to Travel Campaign v. Newcomb*, a U.S. court ruled on the constitutionality of the Cuban travel restrictions. As you read, remember that although the case is about the Cuban regulations, the message to be learned is that as an American citizen, or national of any country, you have no constitution right to international travel in the absence of your government's approval.

Freedom to Travel Campaign v. Newcomb

83 F.3d 1431 (1995) United States Court of Appeals (9th Cir.)

BACKGROUND AND FACTS

Pursuant to the authority of the *Trading with the Enemy Act* (TWEA), in 1962 President Kennedy announced the *Cuban Asset Control Regulations*, which prohibited U.S. citizens from engaging in almost any economic activity with communist Cuba without a license. The regulations also restricted travel to Cuba, directly or through third countries. The embargo has remained in effect since then. At the time of this case, the regulations permitted some travel by journalists and government officials, those visiting "close relatives," and those engaging in professional research, in religious and humanitarian work, and some "educational activities." Traveling to Cuba without a license was a criminal offense, and violators were subject to imprisonment, fine, and property forfeiture. The Freedom to Travel Campaign (FTC) is an organization that organizes educational and other trips to Cuba. It brought this action challenging the regulations. The FTC claimed that (1) the government restrictions on travel violate the Constitution; and (2) the failure to define "educational activities" for which travel is permitted renders the regulations excessively vague, and therefore void.

HALL, CIRCUIT JUDGE

FTC argues ... that the Regulations' travel ban is unconstitutional because the Government lacks a sufficient foreign policy rationale to inhibit FTC's liberty interest in travel. In substance, this appears to be a substantive due process claim and we will treat it as such. A substantive due process claim involves the balancing of a person's liberty interest against the relevant government interests [most citations omitted]. FTC claims that its freedom to travel is trampled by the Regulations' travel ban. Although the freedom to travel internationally is a liberty interest recognized by the Fifth Amendment, *Kent v. Dulles,* 357 U.S. 116, 127 (1958) ("Freedom to travel abroad is, indeed, an important aspect of the citizen's 'liberty.'"), it is clearly not accorded the same stature as the freedom to travel among the states. Restrictions on international travel are usually granted much greater deference. Given the lesser importance of this freedom to travel

continues

continued

abroad, the Government need only advance a rational, or at most an important, reason for imposing the ban. This the Government can do. The purpose of the travel ban is the same now as it has been since the ban was imposed almost 35 years ago—to restrict the flow of hard currency into Cuba. That goal has been found [by other courts] "important," "substantial," and even "vital." Thus, the Government seems to have satisfied its obligation.

FTC, however, would have us evaluate the foreign policy underlying the embargo. It contends that the President's current reason for the embargo—to pressure the Cuban government into making democratic reforms—is not as compelling a policy for an embargo as were previous justifications that relied on national security concerns. FTC thus invites us to invalidate the ban. This is an invitation we must decline. It is well-settled that "[m]atters relating to the conduct of foreign relations ... are so exclusively entrusted to the political branches of government as to be largely immune from judicial inquiry or interference." See *Regan v. Wald,* 468 U.S. 222 (1984). This immunity manifests itself in a history of judicial deference.

Even were we to second guess the President, this is not a case where the Government has set forth no justifications at all. It has detailed numerous reasons for the embargo. We will look no further. The *Cuban Asset Control Regulations'* travel ban is constitutional.

FTC claims that two provisions [on travel] are void for vagueness and therefore infringe upon its freedom to travel ... . FTC correctly states that due process will not tolerate a law restricting the freedom of movement if its enforcement is left to the whim of government officials ... . The Treasury Department's recent amendment to the Regulations further cures any vagueness defects. Newly created Regulation 419 now defines "clearly defined educational activities" as (1) those conducted at an international meeting or conference; and (2) those related to undergraduate or graduate studies. Thus, this aspect of Regulation 560(b) is constitutional.

Decision. The ban on travel to Cuba imposed by the *Cuban Asset Control Regulations* are valid. The U.S. government need only have a "rational basis" for prohibiting travel by Americans to foreign countries, such as in this case, where the ban was intended to deprive the communist government of American or foreign currency.

Comment. During the Clinton administration the United States legalized sales of some food and medicines to Cuba, permitted travel to the island by religious groups and the media, and authorized direct charter flights. In 2009, President Obama lifted travel and spending restrictions for Americans with family in Cuba and on money that they can send to their families, as well as on telecommunications companies (in the hopes of getting more news and information to Cubans). Many people believe it will only be a short time until there is a thaw in U.S.-Cuba relations.

Case Questions

1. What was the purpose underlying the ban on travel to Cuba?
2. What is the legal standard for determining whether the U.S. government can restrict international travel?
3. Why was the prohibition on travel not "void for vagueness"?
4. Considering the cases presented in this chapter, what can you conclude about the relationship between the individual and government with respect to the regulation of imports, exports, international travel, and even international commerce?

The Effectiveness of Cuban Sanctions. Many people have condemned the Cuban sanctions for their harshness. Even the Vatican protested, claiming that trade sanctions increased the economic suffering of the Cuban people and travel sanctions separated families. Many business groups and internationalists argue that economic engagement promotes freedom in totalitarian countries. Indeed, every year since 1992 virtually every member nation of the UN, except the United States and a few supporters, has passed resolutions calling on the United States to end the sanctions. Ironically, surveys of American public opinion show that the vast majority of Americans also favor ending sanctions and recognizing the communist government. More than a half-century of communism has left the island nation in economic ruin.

However, a lack of necessities, modern transportation, and consumer goods has not spurred a democratic uprising, and many economists believe sanctions have had only a minimal impact on Cuba. They note that the government tends to make trade and investment decisions based on ideology and political factors, not on economic considerations. Perhaps the argument against modern-day Cuban sanctions was expressed best by Arthur Schlesinger, Jr., a noted U.S. historian and close advisor to President Kennedy, when he stated in a letter to the editor of the *The New York Times* that "A better policy ... would be to repeal [Cuban sanctions], lift the embargo and drown the [Castro] regime in American tourists, investments, and consumer goods." *The New York Times,* February 21, 1997, cited in *Havana Club Holding v. Galleon,* 961 F. Supp. 498 (S.D.N.Y. 1997).

CONCLUSION

For the United States, the pursuit of both export promotion and control will always be a deliberate balance between economic competitiveness and the needs of national security or foreign policy. It might be possible to have a country whose borders are impenetrable, whose technology products never reach the hands of an enemy, and who can stand by moral principles under all circumstances and refuse to do business with military dictators, communist regimes, or other despots. But the economic consequences for American exporters would be disastrous. The need to strike a balance between "controlling" exports and "administering" exports is reflected in the name of the export regulations—the *Export Administration Regulations.* This issue will continue to be debated in Congress and pondered by the president. How can government best maintain America's security in a dangerous world while fostering an environment for trade?

As of this writing in 2013, the Obama administration has embarked on significant export control reform. First, the administration wants to better balance the needs of national security with competitiveness, or, as it says, build "higher fences around fewer items." For example, it has begun the process of removing less-critical military items and technology from the strict controls of the State Department and placing them on the Commerce Control List where they are administered under the more flexible controls of the Commerce Department. A long-range objective is to consolidate the controls of both departments into one single export control list. The administration is also focusing on protecting technologies that give the United States a military or intelligence advantage, on stopping the proliferation of weapons of mass destruction, and on protecting technologies that no other country can easily duplicate (such as "stealth" technology or technology that render submarines virtually "silent").

The administration also proposes to better clarify which items are subject to control (such as specially designed items), and to use more objective criteria in describing items on the control list. The licensing process will be streamlined so that exporters clearly know what items are controlled, how they are controlled, and which government agency is responsible for licensing particular items. The administration is proposing a single information technology system to improve the sharing of licensing and enforcement of information between agencies, and, as we mentioned earlier, it has already created the Export Enforcement Coordination Center to coordinate interagency enforcement of the export laws. The administration has also proposed a long-range objective of combining all export control licensing within one agency, although this change would require new legislation. Many in Congress are not convinced that all controls should be put into the hands of one agency, especially given the fear of terrorism and nuclear proliferation.

Clearly economic and financial sanctions against rogue governments and terrorist groups work best when nations work together. The United Nations provides an important forum for building consensus. Although there are occasional calls for America to "go it alone," history tells us that international cooperation is the least dangerous solution.

Chapter Summary

1. The strategic environment affecting U.S. export controls changed greatly after 2001, as concerns shifted from keeping controlled items from the communist Soviet Union to concerns over terrorism, the proliferation of nuclear, biological, and chemical weapons (and missile delivery systems) in Iran and North Korea, and in securing U.S.-controlled technology from China.
2. The three primary reasons for control over exports of U.S. goods and technology are national security, foreign policy, and short supply controls to prevent excessive foreign demand on scarce materials.
3. The United States controls the export and re-export of all goods and technology (including software and source code) whether they have commercial (civilian) applications, military applications, or dual-use applications. Dual-use goods and technology are

those that have commercial uses, as well as military, intelligence-gathering, or other strategic applications. Nonproliferation controls apply to any goods or technology that can further the spread of weapons of mass destruction or missile technology. Diversion is the illegal transshipment, rerouting, or re-export of controlled goods or technology from a licensed destination to an unlicensed destination.

4. The U.S. Department of Commerce's Bureau of Industry and Security (BIS) is the lead agency for administering the export controls over commercial and dual-use goods.
5. Export licenses are issued according to the item, destination, end user, and end use. All goods and technology on the Commerce Control List require a license for export or re-export, unless it is classified as EAR99 or there is a specific exception.
6. A deemed export is the communication or release, by any means, of any technology, technical data, or software to a foreign national, whether done in the United States or in a foreign country.
7. The antiboycott laws prohibit Americans from participating in, or responding to requests for information about, the Arab boycott of Israel.
8. Violations of the export control laws and the antiboycott laws are punishable by civil penalties, denial orders, criminal fines, and imprisonment. Criminal charges can be brought for both willful violations and conscious avoidance, which is purposely avoiding learning information about an end user, end use, or destination, in order to evade the export laws. Technology exporters should have a solid corporate compliance plan.
9. Perhaps the most important and effective way to comply with the export laws is for every organization with exports or deemed exports to establish an effective Export Management and Compliance Program. This is true for every company exporting goods or technology, and institutions or universities with foreign researchers, foreign faculty, or foreign students that are involved in research.
10. Trade sanctions to achieve foreign policy objectives are generally more effective when done in coordination with other governments or in support of a United Nations resolution.
11. The *International Emergency Economic Powers Act* (IEEPA) gives the president authority to impose economic, trade, or financial controls during a declared international emergency. The president may seize assets, cancel contracts, impose export controls, and take a range of extraordinary actions. IEEPA was amended by the *USA Patriot Act* to grant exceptional powers against terrorist groups. This is administered by the Department of Treasury, Office of Foreign Assets Control.
12. The U.S. government is considering significant export control reform. The system will toughen controls and enforcement on items critical to U.S. military and intelligence gathering, while reducing confusion and delays in exporting non-critical items. There will be changes in the licensing process, and in the enforcement role of some of the government agencies that you studied in this chapter. Staying current on export control law is essential for anyone in international business.

Key Terms

export controls 348
sanctions 348
commercial items 352
dual-use items 352
controlled technology 352
Commerce Control List 352
national security controls 352
foreign policy controls 353
short supply controls 353
foreign availability 353
export 355
re-export 355
diversion 355
deemed export 355
foreign national 355
deemed re-export 355
export license 356
end user 356
entity list 356
specially designated nationals and blocked persons list 356
unverified list 356
red flag indicators 356
denied persons list 356
debarred list 356
consolidated screening list 356
special comprehensive license 357
validated end user program 357
Automated Export System 358
Electronic Export Information 358
extraterritorial jurisdiction 359
boycott 360
antiboycott 360
export management and compliance program 362
conscious avoidance 362
financial sanction 365

Questions and Case Problems

1. Beginning in 1995, both Presidents Clinton and Bush issued several executive orders under IEEPA declaring a national emergency in dealing with terrorism. The Department of the Treasury issued regulations prohibiting transactions with terrorist groups or providing services to them. Al Qaeda was named as a terrorist organization, along with the Taliban government of Afghanistan that supported them. During the U.S. war in Afghanistan, John Walker Lindh, an American citizen, was captured while fighting for the Taliban. He had undergone terrorist training in Pakistan and had allegedly met Osama bin Laden. He was charged in the United States under criminal statutes with conspiracy to murder Americans and with providing material support to foreign terrorist organizations in violation of the president's IEEPA orders. Lindh argued that IEEPA applied only to commercial transactions with terrorist groups and not to his conduct. Did IEEPA apply to Lindh's case? What was the result? *United States v. Lindh*, 212 F. Supp. 2d 541 (E.D. Va. 2002).
2. Do goods and technology have "nationality"? What is meant by this statement? Do you think that a nation's laws should apply to its goods and technology after they have left the territory of that nation? What principles of international law permit a nation to extend its jurisdiction over goods and technology that originated there? Can you make arguments for or against the extra territorial application of export control laws? Does this differ from the extraterritorial application of antitrust law or laws against bribery of foreign government officials?
3. Most readers are familiar with the debate over the use of trade sanctions as a means of carrying out foreign policy. President Carter's ban of grain sales to the Soviet Union in response to the Soviet invasion of Afghanistan failed when the Soviets simply started purchasing grain from other countries. Shortly after that, President Reagan angered American allies in Europe, as well as American businesses, by unilaterally imposing controls on the sale of equipment for use by the Soviets in constructing the Trans-Siberian natural gas pipeline. Can you cite any examples where trade sanctions have worked? Under what circumstances do you think that trade sanctions are likely to work?
4. What is a "deemed export"? How can this impact technology companies and research institutions in the United States?
5. Daniel Bernstein, while a graduate student, developed a software encryption program called "Snuffle" and wanted to post it on the Internet. The U.S. government said he needed a license. What was the result? How have the export regulations changed since Bernstein's case?
6. Is it ethical to hold a businessperson legally responsible if he or she sells controlled technology to a second party that is then diverted to a prohibited end user? What factors will influence your answer? How does "conscious avoidance" affect one's liability for an export violation?
7. Does the export of electric cattle prods require a license? Why? On what legal grounds?
8. Determine if and how U.S. export regulations apply to personal shipments made through the U.S. Postal Service or by air couriers such as FedEx or United Parcel Service.
9. What is the status of the *Export Administration Act of 1979* and the *Export Administration Regulations*? Has the statute been renewed or replaced since its lapse in 2001? Are the regulations still in force?

Managerial Implications

You are in charge of an American subsidiary company in France that manufactures advanced robotics equipment used in the automobile industry. You have engineering and research facilities in both countries. You receive an inquiry about your robotics from someone claiming to represent an upstart Chinese automobile manufacturer. He requests immediate information and explains that the plant is already well beyond the planning and financing stages and that things will soon begin to "move very quickly." Answer the following questions.

1. Do the U.S. export regulations apply to your firm in France? Why or why not?
2. Because this involves a potential sale to a customer, you question whether the U.S. regulations require an export license just to disclose some technical information. Does it? Explain.
3. How do you respond to his request for information? How much information may you give to him without a license? At what point do you have to stop? Explain.

4. You know that if you have to apply for a license, you will need more information about this individual, his company, and its location, the end use of the product, and the ultimate destination. How would you obtain that information? What sources would you use? Are there any industry, government, or banking sources that could help you? What special precautions would you want to take to ensure that his inquiry is legitimate and honest? Explain.
5. You and your prospective customer decide to meet and go over engineering and technical specifications. What steps must you take before the meeting to ensure compliance with the law? Does it matter whether you are meeting in the United States, France, or China?
6. It is some time later, and having worked out all necessary arrangements, you are ready to ship and arrange installation of your first pieces of equipment. In the interim, with no apparent provocation, China refuses to allow a U.S. naval ship to make a prearranged stop in Hong Kong. There are 1,000 sailors aboard who hope to spend Christmas with their family members, who have traveled all the way to Hong Kong for the holidays. You apply for a U.S. license with the BIS, and it is turned down based on a new ban on the sale of certain items to China, including robotics. You exhaust the administrative appeal process. Do you have any rights against the BIS? Are you protected by the U.S. Constitution, because the rule was changed just prior to your shipment date?
7. The French government is very interested in your company making the sale. The President of France considers it a technological *coup d'état*. On learning that the United States blocked your sale, he threatens to fine your company up to five times the value of the shipment and to throw you in a French prison. What do you do? Do you comply with the laws of the United States or the laws of France? What are the alternatives?

Ethical Considerations

1. Your company, Ajax Pharmaceutical, based in New Jersey, is approached by an agent for a company that has offices in Egypt and Jordan about participating in several joint ventures in the Middle East and Asia. The agent inquires about the status of your investment in Israel. You currently have an offer from a newly formed Israeli investment group to purchase your 30 percent share of Drugisco, an Israel-based company. How do you respond? What is your legal obligation? What other information do you need to answer the agent's question? He also asks about your ability to ship certain chemicals that are controlled. Do you have any obligation to report this inquiry? You initially ship the requested items to Japan. You discover during a late-night meeting in a karaoke bar that these items went to an intermediary and are now headed to Sudan. Do you have any legal responsibility? Ethical responsibility? What managerial controls can you implement to reduce the likelihood of this happening in the future?
2. Your company, Enzyme, Inc., manufactures biological and chemical agents that have potential military uses. You understand that Congress is considering the contentious issue of how to revamp the entire export control regimen. Prepare a letter to your state senators articulating your company's position about decontrol. Do you think your company should take an active role in lobbying for a new law? What are the risks associated with such a position? Will you discuss these issues with your board of directors? Would you make this public in a press release? How would you respond to reporters' questions?

CHAPTER 14

North American Free Trade Law

In previous chapters, we discussed principles of international trade law, including the General Agreement on Tariffs and Trade (GATT) agreements, the role of the World Trade Organization (WTO), laws regulating import competition and unfair trade, and laws governing access to foreign markets. We examined how the growth of free trade principles, or *trade liberalization,* has led to increased trade in goods and services and fostered an environment for economic development and globalization. That discussion focused on trade liberalization at the global level. For example, we saw how the principles of normal trade relations (NTR) are applied globally: If a nation reduces the tariff rate on a product imported from one NTR country, then it must automatically and unconditionally apply that rate to similar products imported from all NTR countries. Safeguards are another example of trade regulation at the global level. Increased tariffs temporarily imposed on a product to protect or safeguard a domestic industry from injury due to a flood of competing imports must be applied globally to imports of similar products coming from all WTO member countries and not just from a select few.

Although the focus of our discussions, up to this point in the book, has been on global trade, many regional trade issues are equally as important. Countries often enter trade agreements with each other that grant lower tariffs and other trade privileges that are more favorable than those granted to the rest of the world. These agreements may create regional free trade areas where goods and services can be bought and sold with few or no tariffs or other trade restrictions. Some free trade areas also have special rules for the cross-border movement of people, for protecting the environment of the region, or for cooperation on workplace health and safety issues. Regional trade areas might be created for economic, political, foreign policy, or security reasons in the region. For example, the United States may enter into a free trade agreement with a Latin American country partially for economic reasons, but also with the hope that it will slow the production of illegal narcotics and drugs.

However, the creation of free trade areas seems inconsistent with the philosophy and objectives of global free trade. After all, is it not protectionist if two or more countries single themselves out for even lower tariffs on goods traded between themselves than on goods imported from countries outside the trading area? Some supporters of global free trade would argue that, indeed, it is protectionist. Others argue that any effort to reduce trade barriers is a positive step, and those efforts eventually will spread to other countries. Moreover, regional agreements can address specific social, economic, and political issues that are incapable of being addressed globally.

This chapter examines the North American Free Trade Agreement (NAFTA) among Canada, Mexico, and the United States. These countries have agreed to rules that give the goods and services of each country even more favorable treatment than that given to most other WTO member countries. In addition to customs and tariff regulations, the agreement also addresses many broader issues of common concern, such as cooperation on labor and environmental issues, cross-border trucking, and more.

THE PHILOSOPHY OF ECONOMIC INTEGRATION

Of the numerous paradigms of economic integration, some involve comprehensive economic integration, while others are more limited in scope. The economic union created in the United States upon ratification of the Constitution in 1789 offers a good starting point for analysis.

Federal Model

The U.S. Constitution is so justly celebrated for its political attributes that its deeply economic character is often overlooked. During the first years of American independence, the states had different currencies and erected barriers against "imports" from other states. The resulting economic calamity inspired the economic provisions of the Constitution, a revolutionary compact among the states through which the states agreed to have their economies managed as a single unit by a strengthened federal government. Under the Constitution's Commerce Clause (Article I, Section 8, Clause 3), the states gave the federal Congress the exclusive power to manage trade among the states and with foreign nations. The federal court system—established by the Constitution's Article III—has interpreted this Clause as striking down any state law that would impede the free interstate movement of goods or people or any state law that would discriminate against businesses based in other states. This effectively created a highly integrated common market: the federal union.

Congress has used the Commerce Clause to grant the federal government primacy in the regulation of competition law issues. Article I, Section 8, Clause 5 gives the sole power of issuing currency to the federal government. Congress used that power to create the Federal Reserve System, which centrally controls the nation's monetary policy. Article II of the Constitution gives treaty-making power to the president, with Senate consent, and Article I, Section 10 absolutely forbade the states from entering into treaties. This concentrated all control over commercial policy toward other nations, expressed in international trade and customs treaties, in the hands of the federal government. In short, the loosely confederated American states united into a tight customs union and gave the federal government sweeping powers to create and regulate a vast common market encompassing the continent. In the economic arena, states retained control of legal areas in which the fundamental rules came from the states' Anglo-Saxon common-law tradition, such as contract and corporate law and the regulation of insurance. Even in those areas, the federal judiciary could review and strike down any state law that impinged on the federal common market.

The American experiment is now more than 220 years old and has convincingly proved the economic principle that completely eliminating commercial barriers among political entities, by permitting businesses in each to specialize in areas of competitive advantage and create a larger market for the best products, economically benefits the citizens of all states that join the union. Yet because such change necessarily brings short-term harm to those who cannot compete in the larger market, and those likely to be harmed inevitably have political power, it has proved quite difficult for other nations to forge economic agreements on the scale of the U.S. Constitution. We will now review the attributes of other, less comprehensive types of economic unions.

Free Trade Area

A **free trade area (FTA)** and a federal system represent the two extreme ends on the continuum of integration. An FTA develops when two or more countries agree to eliminate or phase out customs duties and other barriers to trade among the member countries. Because only products originating in the FTA countries may be shipped duty free, there is no need for the countries to have common commercial policies toward countries outside the FTA. For example, because Japanese steel imported into Mexico cannot be re-imported duty-free from Mexico to the United States, there is no need for Mexico and the United States to place the same customs duties on Japanese steel or have a common commercial policy toward Japan. Free trade agreements vary greatly in the degree to which FTA members have common policies for regulating business in their countries. Nevertheless, as with any system with common norms, an FTA needs a good dispute settlement mechanism.

The United States is a party to many FTAs. Table 14.1 lists some of these FTAs.

Customs Union

A **customs union** is more ambitious in scope than an FTA. In an FTA, there is free trade only in goods produced within the FTA. In a customs union, there is free trade in all goods that come through any of the union members, even imports from outside the customs union. Thus, Brazilian sugar imported into France should move from France into fellow European Union (EU) member state Germany just as freely as French wine would. By contrast, Brazilian sugar imported into Mexico may not freely move into the United States under NAFTA, whose free trade area applies only to products created in free trade area countries.

Because of this distinction, a customs union can only function if all of its members agree to a common tariff on imports from outside the union. Thus, the EU has a common customs tariff and, under its operating treaties, has the power to negotiate with other countries on behalf of all member states. The United States cannot negotiate with France over tariffs; it can only negotiate with the EU as a whole. This structure ensures that no outsider can gain an advantage by routing its imports through one member state.

Table 14.1 U.S. FREE TRADE AGREEMENTS (2013)

COUNTRY	EFFECTIVE DATE
Israel	1985
Jordan	2002
Chile	2004
Singapore	2004
Australia	2005
Bahrain	2006
Costa Rica	Part of CAFTA-DR 2006
Dominican Republic	Part of CAFTA-DR 2006
El Salvador	Part of CAFTA-DR 2006
Guatemala	Part of CAFTA-DR 2006
Honduras	Part of CAFTA-DR 2006
Morocco	2006
Nicaragua	Part of CAFTA-DR 2006
Oman	2009
Peru	2009
Colombia	2011
Panama	2011
South Korea	2012

In turn, the need of a customs union to have a single tariff policy for products from outside the union means that the members of the union must arrive at other common policies. If they are to impose common tariffs on a specific product, the member states must develop a consistent policy toward that product. For example, European nations have widely divergent interests in free entry of agricultural products, yet they must establish a common policy toward imported beef products from the United States and Australia. Similarly, the need to agree on a common tariff on products from a specific nation requires a common commercial policy toward that nation, even though the union members may have widely divergent views toward the nation's military or political policies.

Common Market

A **common market**, also called an *economic community,* goes further than a customs union. While a customs union ensures the free movement of goods within the union, a common market seeks to further facilitate free competition within a group of nations. To do so, it protects the right of all enterprises and persons within the area to do business, invest capital, and sell their services anywhere within the area without discrimination on the basis of national origin.

If they are to achieve free economic competition in a common market, the members of the market must establish certain common rules. If companies can compete everywhere within a market, the member nations must develop common policies and laws on what anticompetitive behavior is and how to curb it. To prevent national governments from unfairly favoring local firms over those from other member states, the members must develop rules on using tax dollars to subsidize industries. So that manufacturing concerns will not have a cost advantage in a particular nation, minimum market-wide environmental and consumer protection standards are appropriate.

For policy to be meaningful, it must be transformed into law. Its enforcement needs to be entrusted to a court with jurisdiction and power to enforce its rulings if the member states are to comply effectively with the standards and laws. Without effective enforcement, each member state can continue to operate its own protectionist barriers.

One way to substantially enhance commerce within a multinational market is to eliminate currency risk for businesses within that market. This can only be achieved by adoption of a common currency by all actors within the market. Adopting a common currency necessarily implies developing and maintaining a common monetary policy on things like how much of that currency to release into the market and what short-term interest rates to charge financial institutions. In addition, the member states need to agree on an institution that will protect and enforce that policy. The most significant customs union and common market, the EU, will be discussed in the next chapter.

Compatibility of Trade Areas with the WTO and GATT

At first glance, the principles underlying the formation of trade areas seem to contradict the basic principles of the WTO and GATT, which require nondiscrimination and reciprocity among all members. How can members of an FTA or customs union treat those members more favorably than other GATT members? Article XXIV of the GATT agreement states:

> [T]he provisions of this Agreement shall not prevent, as between the territories of contracting parties, the formation of a customs union or of a free-trade area . . . , Provided that: (a) with respect to a customs union, . . . the duties and other regulations of commerce imposed at the institution of any such union . . . in respect of trade with contracting parties not parties to such union . . . shall not on the whole be higher or more restrictive than the general incidence of the duties and regulations of commerce applicable in the constituent territories prior to the formation of such union. . . .

This section has been used to lower the rates of external tariffs within a trade area for the benefit of non-FTA WTO members. This achieves the goals of GATT for the benefit of WTO members.

THE NORTH AMERICAN FREE TRADE AREA

The North American Free Trade Area is comprised of Canada, Mexico, and the United States. These countries have different economic and political systems as well as different cultures, languages, geographies, and climates. Nevertheless, they have a long history of close economic ties. Together they encompass the largest free trade area in the world, with a market of about 461 million people and a combined gross domestic product of more than $17 trillion. (References to dollars in this chapter are to U.S. dollars or their equivalent unless otherwise noted.) The North American Free Trade Area was created in 1994 after a heated political debate. Its purpose was to spur trade and investment in North America and to improve the standard of living throughout the continent. Proponents in the United States viewed the creation of a free trade area in North America as a means of increasing U.S. exports of goods and services to Mexico, while promoting investment in Mexico, job creation, and economic growth. It was also seen as a means of reinforcing political ties with Mexico, fostering broader participation in democracy there, building a stronger Mexican middle class, stabilizing swings in the Mexican peso and Mexican economy, and stemming illegal immigration. It was also hoped that Asian manufacturers would invest in Mexican plants to gain favorable access to markets in the United States and Canada.

Critics claimed that NAFTA would cause a tremendous loss of manufacturing jobs in the United States, as well as hurt American agriculture. Perhaps the best-known critic was former independent presidential candidate Ross Perot, who claimed that on the creation of a free trade area with Mexico, the people of the United States would hear a "giant sucking sound"—the sound of jobs leaving America for Mexico, where wages were lower. It was also feared that American firms would relocate to Mexico to take advantage of reduced operating costs resulting from Mexico's lax labor and environmental laws. Proponents countered that NAFTA included "side agreements" calling for cooperation on labor and environmental issues.

In the United States, there was far greater concern about entering into a free trade area with Mexico than with Canada. While the U.S. and Canadian economies were similar, and had already been linked by a U.S.–Canadian free trade agreement since 1989, there were vast differences between the United States and Mexico. The United States and Canada are in advanced stages of economic development, with comparable levels of productivity and per capita gross domestic product. Canada and the United States are far more similar to each other than to their southern neighbor.

Mexico, on the other hand, is a developing country with a per capita GDP that is approximately 30 percent that of the United States, a poverty rate estimated as high as 50 percent, and the second-largest income disparity among Organization for Economic Co-operation and Development (OECD) member states. Also, Mexico has had a history of greater government control over industry, government ownership of key industrial sectors, higher tariffs, and greater barriers to foreign investment than has either the United States or Canada. Despite the controversy, the North American Free Trade Area was created on January 1, 1994, by the *North American Free Trade Agreement* (NAFTA).

CANADA–U.S. TRADE

Canada and the United States are each other's largest trading partners, with two-way trade in goods totaling more than $616 billion in 2012. Many people are surprised to learn that in 2012 the United States exported more than $292 billion in goods to Canada, an amount that was more than two and one-half times U.S. exports to China and more than four times the amount of exports to Japan. The United States purchased $323.9 billion in goods from Canada in 2012. Of Canada's total imports, about 51 percent come from the United States, while 74 percent of Canada's exports are destined for the United States. From the end of 1993, just prior to the creation of the North American Free Trade Area, to 2012, the annual volume of trade between the two countries increased from $211.6 billion to more than $616.4 billion. During that same period, America's trade deficit with Canada increased from $10.7 billion to more than $31 billion. The largest categories of products traded between the countries are automotive products, lumber, agricultural and fishing products, oil and gas products, machinery and industrial goods. Canada is also the leading export market for 36 of the 50 U.S. states. Canada has a population of 34.5 million (compared to 315 million in the United States).

Mexico–U.S. Trade

Mexico is the United States' number-three trading partner, with total two-way trade of more than $493 billion in 2012, which is more than a sixfold increase from $81.4 billion in 1993. In 2012, the United States purchased more than 78 percent of Mexico's exports and provided 50 percent of Mexico's imports. In 2012, U.S. sales of goods to Mexico totaled $215.9 billion while imports totaled $277.5 billion, leaving a trade deficit of $61.6 billion. The last year that the United States had a trade surplus with Mexico was in 1994, the year the North American Free Trade Area was created. Today, most Mexican products enter the United States duty-free or at a very low tariff rate. Most U.S. goods enter Mexico duty-free. Mexico offers U.S. firms low production costs, plentiful labor, easy transportation to the U.S. market, employees who respect and want to work for U.S. firms, and consumers that respect U.S. product brand names. Mexico's population is more than 116 million people, with almost three-quarters living in urban areas.

Until the mid-1980s, Mexico had a tightly controlled and protected economy. Its policies restricted imports and discouraged foreign investment. Many key industries were (and some remain) in the hands of government-owned monopolies. Foreign companies that wanted to do business there had to break through a mass of government bureaucracy, red tape, trade barriers, corruption, and outdated highway, transportation, and telecommunications infrastructures. Hampered by inefficient industries, Mexico during the 1970s and early 1980s suffered low productivity, staggering rates of inflation (as high as several hundred percent a year), and overwhelming foreign debt. Its foreign income was almost totally dependent on exports of oil and petroleum products.

New government policies in the late 1980s and 1990s opened the Mexican economy to trade and private investment. In 2000, Mexico announced that it had signed a trade agreement with the EU allowing European products to enter Mexico at reduced tariff rates. Privatization and deregulation also continued into this decade. Railroads, airports, natural gas transportation, telephone companies, banks, and power generation have all benefited from privatization. As a result of an influx of foreign capital, technology, and management skills, Mexican companies have become far more efficient. Mexican-made products have improved in quality and are now competitive in world markets. By 2000, inflation was down to the single-digit range and unemployment was at an all-time low, and these trends have largely continued. As a result, Mexico has become less dependent on oil exports and now has a more broadly based economy. It is safe to say that much of Mexico's economic success since 1993 has been attributable to political and economic reform and to factors other than just NAFTA.

The United States has considerable cross-border investment in both Canada and Mexico. Fifty-four percent of all foreign direct investment in Canada, $319 billion, originates in the United States. The United States also has $91.4 billion in foreign direct investment in Mexico.

The North American Free Trade Agreement

The *North American Free Trade Agreement* (NAFTA) created a free trade area between Canada, Mexico, and the United States on January 1, 1994. NAFTA is not a customs union or common market like the European Union. On trade issues, the EU deals with other countries as outsiders and represents its members in trade negotiations at the WTO. NAFTA does not. NAFTA instead fosters trade and investment among Canada, Mexico, and the United States by reducing tariffs and non-tariff barriers. It also facilitates transportation of goods, provision of services, and financial transactions among the three countries. Each country will generally continue to maintain its own tariff rates applicable to imports from outside the area. (Actually, NAFTA countries adopted a common external tariff on certain computer parts in 2004, but NAFTA is still not considered a customs union.) Each country will continue to establish its own economic policies, and each country will represent itself in the WTO system.

Long before NAFTA existed, many Mexican goods shipped to the United States were already receiving special tariff preferences under the **Generalized System of Preferences (GSP)**, which were available to selected products imported from any qualified developing country. Under the GSP, many Mexican products already qualified for either a low tariff or no tariff at all. Canada offered similar preferences for Mexican goods. The purpose of these programs was to encourage trade with developing countries to aid in their economic growth. However, the impact of NAFTA is much broader and much more important than GSP preferences.

Survey of NAFTA's Coverage. Historically, trade agreements focused on the lowering of tariffs, but NAFTA is a trade agreement that does more than just eliminate duties between Canada, Mexico, and the United States. It liberalizes trade in goods and services, contains specific provisions for protecting intellectual property rights, makes cross-border investment easier, and protects the interests of foreign investors from arbitrary government action. It allows easier access for commercial trucks and for business travel between the countries. NAFTA encourages cooperation between governments on antitrust policy dealing with monopolies and unfair methods of competition, worker safety, child labor, and environmental protection. Thus, NAFTA is far broader in scope than most typical trade or investment agreements. Only the EU treaties and perhaps GATT are as broad in scope as NAFTA.

NAFTA Trade and Tariff Provisions. NAFTA's basic trade and tariff provisions are patterned after the GATT agreements. Many principles are similar, including national treatment, nondiscrimination, tariff reduction, and elimination of non-tariff barriers. NAFTA tariff preferences only apply if the goods are of North American origin, and as we will see in the next section, this requires that you learn how to use the complex rules of origin. NAFTA set a limit of 15 years for the gradual phasing out of tariffs on goods that originated in North America. On January 1, 2008, all normal tariffs on goods originating and traded between Canada, Mexico, and the United States were eliminated.

National Treatment

NAFTA's **national treatment** principle is similar to that found in GATT. It states that once goods arrive from another NAFTA country, they must be treated without discrimination and no differently than domestically made goods. For example, the United States cannot require that only Mexican-made beer contain a certain alcohol content without setting the same standard for U.S.-brewed beer. Of course, the rule has wide application to all U.S. laws, regulations, and taxes and to a wide range of goods. This provision also applies to regulations of individual U.S. states and Canadian provinces.

Elimination of Non-tariff Barriers. Most quotas, import licenses, and other barriers have been eliminated. Of course, each country may impose import restrictions to protect human, animal, or plant life or the environment. Other special rules permit greater restrictions in key economic sectors, including automobiles, agriculture, energy, and textiles.

NAFTA prohibits new **export taxes** on goods, unless the taxes are also applied to similar goods sold for domestic consumption. **Customs user fees**—fees imposed on importers to help fund the cost of customs enforcement and port services—were eliminated by 1999. NAFTA also addresses issues related to customs administration, the public disclosure of customs regulations, fairness-in-labeling requirements for products, and other barriers to trade.

Continuing Non-tariff Barriers. Despite NAFTA, Mexico, Canada, and the United States have all been accused of maintaining non-tariff barriers. Following are some examples of trade problems that continue.

The United States argues that Mexico has found other ways to block or slow down U.S. imports. Mexico has imposed antidumping duties and safeguards on agriculture and chemical products.

It employs burdensome customs procedures that make it difficult for U.S. firms to export to Mexico. U.S. firms complain that regulations change without notice and are applied unfairly toward Americans. Some types of goods can only be entered through certain ports. Goods with counterfeit U.S. trademarks easily pass into Mexico without inspection at the border. Mexico has used sanitary and phytosanitary provisions to keep out U.S. farm products, even when health and safety were not at stake. For instance, it imposed agricultural inspections at the border, instead of in the United States at the time of packing, resulting in long delays. Some shipments were turned back at the border for mere typographical errors.

Similarly, in the *2012 National Trade Estimate Report,* prepared by the USTR, the United States alleges that Canada continues to maintain compositional standards for raw milk used in cheesemaking that severely limits U.S. access to the Canadian market. The importation of fresh or processed fruits and vegetables in packages exceeding standard package sizes, varietal controls on grains, warehousing policies applicable to alcoholic beverages, and limitations on the sale of foods fortified with minerals and vitamins remain as non-tariff barriers to U.S. products.

The Canadian government continues to restrict U.S. content in broadcasting media. Conventional over-the-air broadcasters must ensure that 60 percent of their overall broadcast time and 50 percent during evening hours consists of Canadian programs (this requirement is more than 50 percent of the channels received for cable television and direct television broadcast services). Thirty-five percent of popular musical selections broadcast on radio must qualify as Canadian. Even Canadian residents traveling to the United States are restricted in their access to U.S. goods. Residents visiting the United States for fewer than 24 hours are only permitted to return with C$50 in goods duty-free. Residents visiting for more than 48 hours and seven days are allowed C$400 and C$750 in duty-free goods respectively.

RULES OF ORIGIN

NAFTA tariff rates apply only to articles that originate in Canada, Mexico, or the United States. A foreign product cannot simply be channeled through one North American country for sale in another North American country to avoid the payment of duties. For example, European or Asian products cannot be brought into Canada and then imported duty-free into the United States as a product of Canada. In order to know which products qualify for NAFTA's duty-free treatment, one must consult the applicable rule of origin.

Rules of origin are a critical issue to importers and exporters. They offer the sole way to determine the rate of duty or even quotas that might apply to the product being bought or sold.

Only goods that qualify under NAFTA's rules of origin can obtain NAFTA tariff rates. The most important general rules are (1) the goods must be *wholly produced or obtained* in Canada, Mexico, or the United States and (2) the goods may contain non-originating inputs (components or raw materials), but must meet the regional value content requirements or the tariff shift rules of origin found in Annex 401 of the NAFTA agreement.

Goods Wholly Produced or Obtained in North America

NAFTA applies to goods wholly produced or obtained in North America. These goods may not contain any non-North American parts or materials. NAFTA Article 415 states that the qualifications apply only to minerals mined in North America, vegetables grown in North America, live animals born and raised in North America, fish and fish products, waste, and scrap derived from production in North America. "Produced or obtained" does not mean "purchased." The definition also includes goods produced in North America *exclusively* from the raw materials just mentioned. Thus, NAFTA applies to coal mined in Tennessee, lead mined in Canada, cotton grown in Mississippi, and cattle born in Mexico and raised in Mexico or Texas. It also includes silver jewelry made in Arizona from silver mined in Mexico and taco shells made in Mexico entirely from corn grown in Iowa. The producer, however, must be able to trace *all inputs to raw materials mined, grown, or born in North America.*

Annex 401 Tariff Shift Rule of Origin

The **substantial transformation test** is used to determine the country of origin of goods imported into the United States when the goods are produced or assembled in more than one country. This test is difficult to apply, and different courts often come up with different results. The variation in court decisions leads to great uncertainty in applying the test to any given case and complicates importers' sourcing decisions. NAFTA avoids this problem by setting out a simpler rule for when a foreign or non-North American product is "transformed" into a product of North America. NAFTA substitutes a tariff classification change for the vague substantial transformation test. When non-North American goods or materials are brought into a NAFTA country, they can be transformed into a product of North America as long as each non-North American input undergoes a tariff classification change as specified in NAFTA Annex 401. The Annex 401 rules of origin may be based on a *change in tariff classification,* a *regional value-content requirement,* or both, depending on the requirements for that particular product. This is known as the **tariff shift rule**. Annex 401 rules can be found in the *General Notes* of the *Harmonized Tariff Schedules.*

Changes in Tariff Classification. To know if a product imported into the United States has undergone a change in tariff classification, you must refer to the *General Notes* found at the beginning of the *Harmonized Tariff Schedules (HTS)* of the United States. The following example demonstrates how a product's tariff classification can change.

The harmonized system breaks down product classifications into ten digits. Countries that have adopted the HTS system have "harmonized" their classification of products internationally at the subheading level. After the first six digits, each country assigns its own numbers. For example, a down-filled comforter (HTS 9404.90.85) is classified in Chapter 94 (which covers a conglomerate of unrelated manufactured articles, including furniture), heading 9404 (covering bedding and similar furnishings, stuffed), subheading 9404.90 (other than sleeping bags), and tariff item 9404.90.85 (down-filled comforters).

To determine the import duty on a North American product, you must know the product's tariff classification at the subheading level. Imagine that you are in the business of making goose down comforters in the United States and Canada. You import unfilled cotton comforter shells from China and goose down fill from Europe. You want to know the U.S. rate of duty on the finished down comforters made at your Canadian plant. You also want to know the correct country-of-origin label to put on the comforter. So, you consult the HTSUS. Your main "non-originating inputs" are the European down (subheading 0505.10) and the cotton shell (subheading 6307.90). You also know that the finished comforter is classified under subheading 9404.90. You find the *General Notes* that contain the NAFTA tariff shift rules and read the following:

> A change to subheading 9404.90 from any other chapter, except from headings 5007, 5111 through 5113, 5208 through 5212, 5309 through 5311, 5407 through 5408 or 5512 through 5516.

Because the non-originating components, the down fill and the unfilled shell, are not in Chapter 94 and are not within any of the exceptions specified, they qualify as having undergone a tariff shift when they are changed to subheading 9404.90. Thus, we have learned that the finished down comforter may be assembled in Canada and shipped to the United States under the rate for Canadian-made comforters and are not subject to any quotas on comforters of Chinese origin (and if we do a little more research we would learn that the comforter can be labeled "Made in Canada"). But suppose we had instead imported Chinese-made cotton fabric and sewed it into an unfilled shell in Canada, filled it with down, and shipped it to the United States. Ironically, the fabric itself falls within subheading 5208 through 5212, and, according to the exceptions to the above rule, would *not* amount to a qualified tariff shift.

Now, consider pastries that are made in Canada for shipment to the United States. Pastries, breads, cakes, and biscuits fall under subheading 1905.90. Assume their only non-North American input is flour imported from Europe. The rule of origin for pastries in heading 1905 states that the item will be treated as a North American product if it undergoes "A change to heading 1905 from any other chapter." The pastries would qualify for NAFTA tariff treatment because the European-made flour was classified outside of HTS Chapter 19. However, the baker must be careful. If the pastries had been made from a prepared mix (containing flour, shortening, sugar, baking powder, etc.), they would not qualify as a North American product because mixes are classified under Chapter 19, the same chapter as the pastries themselves.

Regional Value Content Requirement. For most products undergoing a transformation in North America, the rule of origin will be based on its tariff classification. In limited cases, NAFTA requires a specified amount of **regional value content** (a similar rule is used for trade in automobiles and parts). For example, a rule might require that at least 50 percent of the value of a finished product be North American. Regional value may be calculated either by *transaction value* or *net cost* methods. Transaction value is the price actually paid for a good. The net cost method removes sales and marketing costs, shipping costs, and certain other expenses from the calculation. The value of non-North American materials is then subtracted from the total cost of the product. Usually the regional value content must be at least 60 percent for transaction value method and at least 50 percent for the net cost method. The value of packaging materials and containers in which a product is packaged for retail sale must be taken into account as either North American or non-North American materials, as the case may be.

Transaction Value Formula

$$RVC = \frac{TV-VNM}{TV} \times 100$$

Net Cost Formula

$$RVC = \frac{NC-VNM}{NC} \times 100$$

RVC = Percent regional value content
TV = Transaction value of good, FOB basis
VNM = Value of non-originating material
NC = Net cost of good

The importer may generally choose which method it wants to use. (For an example of the calculations, see Exhibit 14.1). For automobiles and auto parts, however, only the net cost method may be used.

Goods with Minimal Amounts of Non-North American Materials. If the amount of non-North American materials in a finished product is minimal (defined as less than 7 percent of the total cost of the product), the product will still be eligible for NAFTA tariff rates. Thus, if Japanese thread is used to sew together the sleeves on an otherwise 100 percent Mexican-made jacket, and the thread is less than 7 percent of the total cost of the jacket, the finished jacket can be exported to Canada or the United States under NAFTA tariff rates.

The NAFTA Certificate of Origin

A NAFTA **certificate of origin**, or CO (see Exhibit 14.2), is required for all shipments moving among the United States, Canada, and Mexico. It certifies that the goods qualify as having originated in North America for purposes of preferential tariff treatment under NAFTA. COs are required for all *commercial* shipments entering the United States where the total line item value for a good (*not* the total shipment value) is more than $2,500. For goods below these values, the invoice must state that the goods qualify as an originating good for purposes of preferential tariff treatment under NAFTA. A CO may cover a single shipment or it may be a *blanket certificate* that covers multiple shipments of identical goods. A CO is not required for temporary imports, such as those sent for repair or servicing. COs are not required for noncommercial shipments.

It is the responsibility of the exporter to provide a CO to the importer. The CO may be prepared by the exporter or by the exporter's customs agent with a written power of attorney. Frequently, the exporter is not the actual producer of the goods (as in cases where the exporter is a distributor or other intermediary). In this case, the exporter may complete and sign the certificate only with knowledge that the goods in fact originated in North America or if the producer has provided a written statement to that effect. An exporter that does not want to disclose the producer's identity to the importer may state that the producer's name is "available to Customs on request" (see field 3, Exhibit 14.2). It is unlawful to prepare or present a CO that is known to be false, inaccurate, or incorrect. If the preparer discovers an error in the certificate, it must be corrected within 30 days, with written notice of the corrections sent to all parties. COs may be completed in the language of either the exporting or importing country.

When completing the CO, follow the rules carefully. U.S. Customs and Border Protection Form 434 contains instructions on the reverse side (not reproduced here). Field 7 *(Preference Criterion)* requires a letter code indicating the reason why the goods are entitled to NAFTA treatment (i.e., that "wholly they may meet one of the rules of origin"). The form looks simple, but it is not intuitive, so caution must be used in preparing it.

U.S. importers must actually be in possession of an original CO before making entry or claiming the NAFTA tariff rate. If the importer does not have the certificate, the claim will be denied and penalties can be assessed. Faxed copies are accepted as originals. An importer who discovers errors in a certificate must notify Customs in writing within 30 days and pay any additional duties owed as a result. The importer must keep the certificate on file for five years.

Exhibit 14.1

Rules of Origin Example

Product: Wooden Furniture (HS # 9403.50)
Non–North American Inputs: Parts of furniture classified in 9403.90
Rule of Origin:

"A change to subheading 9403.10 through 9403.80 from any other chapter; or
A change to subheading 9403.10 through 9403.80 from subheading 9403.90, provided there is a regional value content of not less than:
a) 60 percent where the transaction value is used, or
b) 50 percent where the net cost method is used."

Explanation: Wooden furniture can qualify for NAFTA tariff preference under two scenarios—a tariff shift, or a combination of a tariff shift and regional value content requirement.

The first option—the tariff shift rule—requires that all non-originating inputs be classified outside of HS Chapter 94 (furniture and bedding). Since the non-originating inputs (furniture parts) are classified in Chapter 94 (subheading 9403.90), then the product cannot qualify based on tariff shift. However, it may still qualify based on the second part of the rule.

The second option has two components—a tariff shift requirement and a regional value content requirement. The tariff shift requirement is satisfied since the non-originating input (furniture parts) is classified in subheading 9403.90 as specified by the rule. The product must meet its regional value content requirement using the transaction value or the net cost methodology.

Given the following values, furniture qualifies for NAFTA tariff preference using the net cost methodology. The calculation is found below, with the following example.

Producer's Net Cost	$182.00 each (not including shipping, packing royalties, etc.)
Transaction Value	$200.00 each piece
Value of Non-Originating Parts	$90.00

Transaction Value Method

$$\frac{(200-90)}{200} \times 100 = 55$$

Good does not qualify under transaction value method because it does not have at least 60 percent regional value content.

Net Cost Method

$$\frac{(182-90)}{182} \times 100 = 50.5$$

Good qualifies under net cost regional value requirement because it has at least a 50 percent regional value content.

Source: U.S. Department of Commerce, 1995.

Standards and Technical Barriers to Trade

All countries can maintain product regulations to protect public health, consumer safety, the environment, and areas of public welfare. However, NAFTA encourages that standards and technical regulations not be used as a non-tariff barrier. For instance, Mexico cannot set unnecessary technical regulations and long, drawn-out approval processes for the sale of telecommunications equipment only to discourage entry to the Mexican market by U.S. or Canadian firms. Technical requirements for telecommunications equipment such as telephones may only require that the equipment not harm the telephone network in order to be approved for use or sale. Standards can be set for energy efficiency in appliances, safety in automobiles, or chemical additives in food. NAFTA requires that each country notify the others

Exhibit 14.2

NAFTA Certificate of Orgin

U.S. DEPARTMENT OF HOMELAND SECURITY
Bureau of Customs and Border Protection

OMB No. 1651-0096
See back of form for Paperwork Reduction Act Notice.

NORTH AMERICAN FREE TRADE AGREEMENT CERTIFICATE OF ORGIN

Please print or type

19 CFR 181.11, 181.22

Bill of Lading / Air Waybill No. :

1. EXPORTER NAME AND ADDRESS	2. BLANKET PERIOD
	FROM
TAX IDENTIFICATION NUMBER:	TO
3. PRODUCER NAME AND ADDRESS	4. IMPORTER NAME AND ADDRESS
TAX IDENTIFICATION NUMBER:	TAX IDENTIFICATION NUMBER:

5. DESCRIPTION OF GOOD(S)	6. HS TARIFF CLASSIFICATION NUMBER	7. PREFERENCE CRITERION	8. PRODUCER	9. NET COST	10. COUNTRY OF ORIGIN

I CERTIFY THAT:

- THE INFORMATION ON THIS DOCUMENT IS TRUE AND ACCURATE AND I ASSUME THE RESPONSIBILITY FOR PROVING SUCH REPRESENTATIONS. I UNDERSTAND THAT I AM LIABLE FOR ANY FALSE STATEMENTS OR MATERIAL OMISSIONS MADE ON OR IN CONNECTION WITH THIS DOCUMENT;
- I AGREE TO MAINTAIN AND PRESENT UPON REQUEST, DOCUMENTATION NECESSARY TO SUPPORT THIS CERTIFICATE, AND TO INFORM, IN WRITING, ALL PERSONS TO WHOM THE CERTIFICATE WAS GIVEN OF ANY CHANGES THAT COULD AFFECT THE ACCURACY OR VALIDITY OF THIS CERTIFICATE;
- THE GOODS ORIGINATED IN THE TERRITORY OF ONE OR MORE OF THE ARTIES, AND COMPLY WITH THE ORIGIN REQUIREMENTS SPECIFIED FOR THOSE GOODS IN THE NORTH AMERICAN FREE TRADE AGREEMENT AND UNLESS SPECIFICALLY EXEMPTED IN ARTICLE 411 OR ANNEX 401, THERE HAS BEEN NO FURTHER PRODUCTION OR ANY OTHER OPERATION OUTSIDE THE TERRITORIES OF THEPARTIES; AND
- THIS CERTIFICATE CONSISTS OF ______ PAGES, INCLUDING ALL ATTACHMENTS.

11a. AUTHORIZED SIGNATURE		11b. COMPANY	
11c. NAME (*Print or Type*)		11d. TITLE	
11e. DATE (*MM/DD/YYYY*)	11f. TELEPHONE NUMBER ▶	(*Voice*)	(*Facsimile*)

CBP Form 434 (04/97)

when the development of a technical regulation or standard begins, give public notice of the proposed regulations, and provide a 60-day comment period for interested firms or individuals to submit their arguments and concerns.

Standards and technical regulations in Mexico are called *normas. Normas* are either mandatory—the *Normas Oficiales Mexicanas,* or "official norms"—or voluntary, known simply as *Normas Mexicanas.* They are drafted by dozens of committees operating under the aegis of the Mexican Ministry of the Economy, the *Secretaría de Economía* (formerly the *Secretaría de Comercio y Fomento Industrial*). *Normas* are published in the *Diario Oficial de la Federación,* which is similar to the *Federal Register* in the United States. Mexico has hundreds of mandatory standards and more than 6,000 voluntary ones. Many U.S. exporters argue that these are really used to discourage the sale of their goods in Mexico. Other examples include lack of notification to U.S. parties before changing regulations and inconsistency with which customs agents apply the law.

Marking and Labeling Rules

The country-of-origin marking and labeling rules are set out in Annex 311 to NAFTA and enacted in the national customs regulations of the United States, Canada, and Mexico. The rules are not uniform among the three countries. The country of origin rules for marking and labeling goods are not the same rules that determine the country of origin for tariff purposes. It is actually possible for an item to be deemed a product of a NAFTA country for marking purposes without being eligible for lowered NAFTA tariff rates.

In an important case, the U.S. Court of Appeals held in *Bestfoods v. United States,* 165 F.3d 1371 (Fed. Cir. 1999), that only Annex 311 principles apply to NAFTA imports. The case was strongly argued by the maker of "Skippy" brand peanut butter, who wanted to be sure that its well-known "all-American" product obtained a "Made in U.S.A." label. The peanut butter was made in the United States from "peanut slurry"—a gritty, peanut-based paste—imported from Canada. Bestfoods argued that they should be allowed to label "Skippy" as "Made in U.S.A." because the U.S. process substantially transformed the peanut slurry into a product with a "new name, character, or use." However, the court held that NAFTA Annex 311 replaced the old "name, character, or use" test for North American trade. A reading of Annex 311 shows that the processing of Canadian (or Mexican) peanut slurry into peanut butter in the United States does not result in the type of tariff change that would transform the slurry into a U.S. product.

Mexico's marking and labeling requirements have been controversial. The *Normas Oficiales Mexicanas* contains specific labeling requirements for certain products (e.g., appliances, electronics, textiles, and food products). All others fall into the more general requirements for general merchandise. Mexico's labeling requirements are strict and often burdensome to U.S. and Canadian exporters. The cost of compliance is often so difficult that many small exporters cannot afford to sell their products in Mexico. Mexico has dictated the content, form, size, and even the appearance of product labels. The Spanish-language labels must include the generic name of the product, the name and address of the importer and exporter, the contents, and the country of origin. Instructions and warnings as to use and care of the product may be enclosed separately, but an invitation to read them must appear on the label. Product warranties must be clearly stated. However, in March 2011, the Mexican government announced a simplified labeling procedure for certain food and beverage products in border areas. These procedures exempted specified products from the Spanish-language requirement within designated "special zones" within the border regions. However, there are several required disclosures that must be included on such labels as well as required filings with the Mexican government.

Items Not Requiring Marks. Annex 311 exempts certain items from marking requirements: items incapable of being marked, items that would be injured by marking, items that cannot be marked except at a cost disproportional to the cost of the goods, items in containers that indicate the country of origin to the ultimate purchaser, crude or bulk materials, personal items for use by the importer and not intended for sale, items produced more than 20 years prior to importation, original works of art, and a few others.

TRADE IN GOODS: SECTORAL ISSUES

Sectoral issues are issues of concern to a particular industrial, agricultural, or service sector of the economy. Examples might be automobile manufacturing and assembly, telecommunications, agriculture, or financial services. NAFTA has specific provisions that reduce tariffs and liberalize trade and investment in these and other sectors. The most important and most controversial industry in North American trade relations is motor vehicles and parts.

Trade in Motor Vehicles and Parts

Perhaps no other sector has been affected by NAFTA as much as the automobile industry. Mexico had long tried to manage its automobile industry through strict trade and investment restrictions. For instance, prior to NAFTA, automobiles sold in Mexico had to contain a minimum of 36 percent Mexican-made parts. Tariffs were 20 percent on cars imported into Mexico and 13.2 percent on automobile parts (as compared to a 2.5 percent tariff on the import of Mexican-made cars into the United States). The result was a Mexican auto parts industry that was largely inefficient and noncompetitive in world markets. Of course, many modern automotive parts and assembly plants in Mexico are owned and operated by U.S., European, and Japanese firms. As discussed later in this chapter, cars assembled there cannot be released for sale into Mexico without meeting Mexican customs regulations and without the payment of duties. Cars assembled there from U.S. parts can only be returned to the United States at lowered tariff rates if they meet the strict requirements of U.S. customs law.

Canada and the United States eliminated duties on each other's automobiles even prior to NAFTA. By 2004, all three countries had eliminated tariffs and restrictions on automobiles, trucks, buses, and automotive parts originating in North America. However, restrictions on the cross-border trade in used cars will continue for many years to come.

Special Rules of Origin for Automobiles. To qualify for duty-free treatment, a motor vehicle that is made or assembled in North America must contain a specified percentage of North American content. For motor vehicles, these rules supersede the regional value content rules for other products, discussed earlier in the chapter.

Beginning in 2002, the content requirement for passenger cars rose to 62.5 percent. The same content requirements apply to engines and transmissions for these vehicles. Compliance with the rules requires complex calculations and the tracing of component parts throughout the supply chain. One of the major purposes of local content rules has been to encourage investment in North America. For example, Japanese manufacturers found it more efficient to build vehicles in North America than in Japan, in order to meet the North American content requirements.

Trade in Textiles and Apparel

The NAFTA textile provisions are of major significance because of the U.S. position as a major textile importer (with a large domestic industry arguing for protection from low-cost imports) and the role of Mexican plants in assembling apparel for sale in the United States. Prior to NAFTA, imports of Mexican textiles and apparel were limited by quotas in the United States and Canada. Mexico also had 20 percent tariffs on U.S. textile products. By 2004, Canada, Mexico, and the United States had phased out all quotas and tariffs on textile and apparel goods that meet the North American rules of origin. Now, textile quotas can only be used as a temporary safeguard in "emergency" situations.

There are specific rules of origin covering trade in textiles. They are complex and arcane, based largely on political considerations. Even the most experienced textile manufacturers and importers require an expert customs attorney and customs broker to move textiles and apparel across borders in North America.

With the expiration of the WTO *Agreement on Textiles and Clothing* in 2005 and the end of textile quotas and most trade restrictions at the global level (other than temporary safeguards), Chinese plants have rapidly begun to take the textile and apparel business away from plants in Mexico, the Caribbean, and Central America. China has quickly become the world's leader in low-cost textile production and is the largest supplier of textiles and apparel to the United States, Europe, and Japan. The international textile industry will surely undergo many more changes in the coming years.

Trade in Agriculture

Trade in agricultural products between the United States and Canada totaled more than $40 billion in 2012 according to the Office of the U.S. Trade Representative. The United States bought $20.2 billion of agricultural goods from Canada, which amount was more than 50 percent of Canada's agricultural exports. U.S. agricultural exports to Canada in 2012 were $20.6 billion, which made Canada the United States' second largest agricultural market. Agricultural trade between the United States and Mexico is equally impressive. The United States exported $18.9 billion in agricultural products to Mexico and imported $16.4 billion worth of such products from Mexico in 2012.

Prior to NAFTA, Mexico only permitted the import of U.S. agricultural products under a strict licensing scheme. Agricultural products were also protected by high tariff rates. The most sensitive products were corn, beans, sugar, powdered milk, and corn syrup, among many others. The United States also maintained protection on a variety of Mexican fruits and vegetable products intended to protect American farmers. NAFTA required an end to Mexico's licensing of agricultural imports and a phased-out end to tariffs. All tariffs on agricultural products originating in North America were completely eliminated by January 1, 2008. The 2008 deadline caused widespread protests throughout Mexico and remains controversial. Although large-scale American producers are pleased with open access to Mexican markets, many Mexicans argue that their system of small farms is threatened. Most Mexicans do not want to entertain the possibility that their country would one day be unable to produce its own corn, beans, and customary foods.

Agricultural Rules of Origin. NAFTA tariff preferences apply only to agricultural products that originate in North America. There are special rules of origin covering North American agricultural products. For example, for fresh or frozen juice (all single fruit juices, such as orange juice) to have "originated" in North America, the juice must be made of 100 percent North American fruit. Other bulk commodities, excluding juice, can have up to 7 percent non-North American content. There are other special rules of origin for sugar refining, peanuts, vegetable oils, and dairy products. For example, only North American milk can be used to make butter, cheese, yogurt, or ice cream, traded under NAFTA preferential rates.

Government Procurement

NAFTA allows North American companies to compete for contracts for the supply of goods and services to agencies of the three governments. NAFTA's government procurement rules apply to contracts for goods and services greater than $56,190 and construction contracts greater than $7.3 million for federal departments and agencies. For government-controlled enterprises, these amounts are $280,951 and $8.9 million respectively. The agreement does not cover weapons, equipment, and systems needed for national defense.

When a government agency announces its request for submission of bids, it must publish the technical specifications, qualifications for suppliers, and time limits for submission. Bids from suppliers in all NAFTA countries must be treated without discrimination. Each country has established a bid protest system that allows firms to challenge procurement procedures and awards. Countries will exchange information on bidding procedures to encourage cross-border bidding, particularly from small- and medium-sized firms.

Emergency Action to Protect Domestic Industry (NAFTA Safeguards)

When NAFTA was negotiated, it was clear that increased competition from foreign firms would cause some economic disruption and job loss, particularly to inefficient, uncompetitive, and outdated companies. NAFTA permits the United States, Canada, or Mexico to take very limited emergency action to safeguard a domestic industry. Emergency action may be taken only where increased quantities of a particular good are a *substantial cause of serious injury, or threat thereof to a domestic industry producing a like or directly competitive good* and only with the *consent* of the country from which the goods were exported. Generally, the right to invoke emergency safeguards under NAFTA is more limited than under GATT/WTO rules. For example, the country imposing the safeguard must agree with the exporting NAFTA country on trade compensation. The compensation must be equivalent in monetary terms to the safeguard action taken. For instance, if the United States seeks to impose safeguards on imports of light bulbs from Mexico, in order to save the U.S. lightbulb industry, then it will have to agree to concessions having substantially equivalent trade effects.

If a NAFTA country imposes emergency safeguards on certain imported goods arriving from all WTO member countries worldwide, then these *global safeguards* may be applied to the products entering from another NAFTA country only if they comprise a *significant share of the total imports* of that type of good and contribute importantly to the serious injury.

TRADE IN SERVICES

NAFTA provisions on cross-border services are aimed at facilitating trade in services in North America. The provisions affect a wide range of service providers, including transportation and package delivery, consulting, banking, insurance, and others. The principles of national treatment and NTR trade apply. No NAFTA country may require a North American service provider to have a residence or office within its borders. Each country will be able to continue to certify and license professionals, such as doctors, lawyers, and accountants; however, the countries are working to recognize the foreign credentials of a professional, especially foreign lawyers and engineers. For instance, many professional organizations from NAFTA countries are negotiating *mutual recognition agreements.* Once ratified by state and federal governments, they will permit recognition of professional licenses in all three countries. Citizenship requirements to obtain a professional license have been eliminated.

Financial Services

U.S.-Canadian cross-border investment in financial services was largely opened in 1989. Thus, the most important impact of NAFTA's financial services provisions is that they open Mexican financial service industries to investment by U.S. and Canadian companies. Banks, insurance companies, securities firms, and other financial service providers will now be able to open branches and offices throughout North America. Most restrictions were phased out by 2000, permitting 100 percent foreign ownership of Mexican financial institutions. Similar provisions apply to insurance companies (100 percent U.S. ownership of some Mexican insurance companies was permitted as early as 1996) and other finance companies (commercial credit, real estate lending, leasing, and credit card services).

Transportation

Nearly 90 percent of goods sold across the 2,000-mile U.S.-Mexican border—some five million truckloads a year—move by rail or truck transportation. In the past, both U.S. and Mexican truck regulations have severely limited truck access. On the American side, Mexican truckers have been limited to a 25-mile incursion across the border. Typically, carriers on one side of the border have had to hand over their cargo to transfer companies that specialize in moving goods through customs. The trucks and cargo are thoroughly inspected for customs compliance, illegal stowaways, drug smuggling, plants, and invasive insects. After inspection and a short trip across the border, the shipments are then handed over to truckers on the other side, perhaps in San Diego or Laredo for transport to their destination, or held in a warehouse for pickup. The long lines of trucks waiting to cross the borders have caused traffic congestion, idling engines, fuel consumption, pollution, and delays costing millions of dollars every year. Concerns over terrorism have worsened the situation.

NAFTA addresses the issue of cross-border road transportation. The agreement frees up cross-border road transportation by eliminating the intermediate transfer of cargo and eliminating the increased fees, costs, and delays that result. NAFTA does not affect regulations applied to purely domestic truck or bus transportation, and drivers will always be bound by the "rules of the road" in any foreign country in which they operate a vehicle. NAFTA does, however, permit U.S. and Canadian trucking companies to make deliveries and pickups in Mexico and permit Mexican trucking companies to have similar access to their customers north of the border. The three countries are developing common safety standards for vehicles—tires, brakes, truck and cargo weight, etc.—and driver's license certifications, including testing. NAFTA also permits the cross-border ownership of trucking companies. As of 2001, U.S. and Canadian companies were able to own a 51 percent interest in Mexican trucking companies and a 100 percent ownership interest after 2004. Despite the lifting of restrictions, U.S. and Canadian companies are still subject to long waits and other legal barriers to obtaining necessary permits.

No NAFTA provision has been more controversial or more difficult to implement than the open roads provisions. It has pitted the truckers' union, environmentalists, and Americans concerned about the safety of Mexican trucks against the Mexican trucking industry, farmers, importers and exporters, and other shippers. During the 1990s, the Clinton administration refused to admit Mexican trucks beyond the border zone until Mexican safety standards were on par with those in the United States and Canada. In the following 2001 decision, a NAFTA **arbitral panel**, which consists of five members who are experts in trade or law, ruled that the United States was in violation of NAFTA. As you read, consider the regulatory nightmare of enforcing U.S. safety standards on millions of Mexican trucks arriving in the United States every year.

In the Matter of Cross Border Trucking

No. USA-MEX-98-2008-01 (2001) (North American Free Trade Agreement Arbitral Panel Established Pursuant to Article 20)

BACKGROUND AND FACTS

To move goods between the United States and Mexico, shippers must typically deal with three trucking firms. Goods are shipped to a storage facility in a border town. The trailer is then detached from the tractor and picked up by a drayage company that moves it across the border, where a truck in that country picks it up to haul it to its final destination. The process is inefficient, and the border delays are a trucker's nightmare.

This handing off of cargo is necessary because the United States has prohibited Mexican trucks from carrying goods through to their U.S. destination for safety reasons. According to U.S. government studies, as many as 40 percent of the five million Mexican trucks that entered the United States in 1999 failed to meet U.S. safety requirements. Mexico does not have the same rigorous standards for driver regulation and truck inspections as does the United States, nor does it register or track safety statistics on its carriers. U.S. trucks must undergo periodic safety inspections by qualified personnel employed by the trucking company. Canadian regulations are similar to those in the United States, and Canadian drivers have been permitted on U.S. highways for decades. The United States maintains that because it can inspect less than 1 percent of the Mexican trucks arriving in the United States, it cannot open its border to Mexican trucking companies until Mexico also adopts comprehensive regulatory standards as tough as those in the United States and Canada. Mexico acknowledges that when its trucks operate in the United States they must comply with U.S. standards, but that the United States cannot dictate Mexican regulatory standards.

The United States also restricts Mexican investment in U.S. trucking firms. Mexico argues that the United States does not treat Mexican trucks as favorably as it does trucks from the United States and Canada and that the United States has violated NAFTA open investment rules by prohibiting Mexican ownership of U.S. trucking firms. The United States counters that under NAFTA Mexican trucks must be treated the same as U.S. and Canadian trucks only where there are "like circumstances" and that Mexican regulations are so unlike those in the United States and Canada that more restrictive treatment of Mexican trucks is warranted. An arbitral panel was convened to hear the dispute in 2000.

FINAL REPORT OF THE PANEL

Mexico asserts that no NAFTA provision entitles a party to impose its own laws and regulations on the other. This would be an unacceptable interference in the sovereignty of another state, and certainly not something to which any party to NAFTA has committed. Therefore, Mexico [argues that it] is under no obligation under NAFTA to enforce U.S. standards, despite cooperation between the United States and Mexico to make the regulatory systems compatible [since 1995]. However, according to Mexico, the United States has made adoption of an identical system of motor carrier regulation a condition of NAFTA implementation, even though NAFTA contemplates that harmonization would not be a condition.

According to the United States ... Mexico cannot identify its carriers and drivers so that unsafe conduct can be properly assigned and reviewed. Without such carrier safety performance history, the United States cannot conduct a meaningful safety fitness review of Mexican carriers at the application stage. The United States also contends that it would be futile to try to perform inspections of Mexican carriers in Mexico because "Mexican carriers are not required to keep the types of records that are typically reviewed in these inspections." In contrast to Mexico's system, the United States notes that "Canada's truck safety rules and regulations are highly compatible with those of the United States." Thus, "when Canadian-based commercial trucks cross into the United States, federal and state transportation authorities can have a high level of confidence that those trucks comply with U.S. standards and requirements at least to the same degree as U.S.-based trucks. That confidence level is bolstered by a fully functioning, computerized bilateral data exchange program." Given all of these considerations, the "United States has ... concluded that the 'circumstances' relevant to the treatment of Mexican-based trucking firms for safety purposes are not like those applicable to the treatment of Canadian and U.S. carriers." Accordingly, "the United States maintains that it may apply more favorable treatment to U.S. and Canadian trucking firms than to their Mexican counterparts without running afoul of Chapter 12's national treatment or most-favored-nation rules."

continues

continued

Article 1202 [national treatment] provides: Each Party shall accord to service providers of another Party treatment no less favorable than it accords, in like circumstances, to its own service providers. Similarly, Article 1203 [NTR] states: Each Party shall accord to service providers of another Party treatment no less favorable than it accords, in like circumstances, to service providers of any other Party or of a non-Party. In its most succinct terms, the disagreement between the United States on the one hand, and Mexico and Canada on the other, is over whether the "in like circumstances" language permits the United States to deny access to all Mexican trucking firms on a blanket basis, regardless of the individual qualifications of particular members of the Mexican industry, unless and until Mexico's own domestic regulatory system meets U.S. approval.

[T]he Panel is of the view that the proper interpretation of Article 1202 [and 1203] requires that differential treatment should be no greater than necessary for legitimate regulatory reasons such as safety... . Similarly, the Panel is mindful that a broad interpretation of the "in like circumstances" language could render Articles 1202 and 1203 meaningless. If, for example, the regulatory systems in two NAFTA countries must be substantially identical before national treatment is granted, relatively few service industry providers could ultimately qualify. Accordingly, the Panel concludes that the U.S. position that the "in like circumstances" language permits continuation of the moratorium on accepting applications for operating authority in the United States from Mexican-owned and domiciled carriers is an overly broad reading of that clause.

The United States claims that Mexico does not even allege that there is any interest on behalf of Mexican nationals to invest in U.S. trucking firms ... . [T]he prohibition on allowing Mexican investors to acquire U.S. companies that already have operating authority, on its face, violates ... NAFTA Articles 1102 and 1103 ... even if Mexico cannot identify a particular Mexican national or nationals that have been rejected.

Decision. The panel unanimously held that the U.S. restrictions on the Mexican trucking industry violated NAFTA. The inadequacies of the Mexican safety regulations were not sufficient reason for the United States to refuse applications from Mexican-owned trucking companies to operate on U.S. highways. The ruling preserved the right of the United States to hold Mexican trucks to the same regulations, safety standards, and inspections as any other vehicle on U.S. roads. Mexican drivers can be required to meet the same licensing and performance standards as U.S. drivers and observe all "rules of the road." Under special situations, the United States may establish different procedures to ensure that Mexican trucks and drivers comply with U.S. law, so long as the procedures are in good faith and not more restrictive to trade than necessary. The U.S. restrictions on investment are not valid because investment does not raise a safety issue.

Comment. Was the U.S. position strictly motivated by safety concerns? American truckers and organized labor have generally been opposed to opening the border. Mexican drivers make less than their American counterparts, and the border opening places them in competition with American drivers. Do you think this affected the U.S. government's position in the 1990s?

Case Questions

1. What were the panel's holdings with respect to the various restrictions on the free operation of the Mexican trucking industry in the United States?
2. As noted in the comment to this case, was the opposition to the operation of Mexican trucking companies in the United States based primarily on safety or economic considerations?
3. Does the example of the trucking dispute prove that despite NAFTA's free trade provisions, there are some areas where trade will never be free or without restrictions? Why or why not?

In response to the arbitral panel decision, the George W. Bush administration made efforts to give Mexican trucks full access to American highways. The Department of Transportation passed regulations to ensure that Mexican trucks complied with the same regulations that apply to American trucks. For example, the regulations require that all trucks comply with safety, environmental, and fuel efficiency standards. Mexican trucks are required to undergo registrations, safety inspections, and equipment checks. Drivers must have a federal license from Mexico and comply with all U.S. safety regulations, including those limiting the number of hours of continuous driving. Mexican trucking companies must implement drug and alcohol testing, maintain insurance, and keep safety-related records. U.S. law enforcement officers can run license checks on Mexican drivers. Mexican trucks may enter only at authorized points of entry when inspectors are present.

In the early 2000s, the truckers' union and environmentalists sought to block implementation of the NAFTA trucking provisions. A lawsuit was brought against the Bush administration, arguing that the administration had failed to comply with U.S. environmental laws. A federal appeals court agreed, but the U.S. Supreme Court unanimously reversed the decision in favor of the government. In *Department of Transportation v. Public Citizen,* 541 U.S. 752 (2004), the Court held that the government could implement the NAFTA transportation rules without an environmental impact statement addressing issues such as the effect on increased traffic, fuel consumption, and air pollution. Despite Court approval and the efforts of the Bush administration to ensure truck and driver safety, the U.S. Congress failed to implement the NAFTA cross-border transportation rules. Furthermore, the Obama administration canceled the cross-border trucking pilot program. Mexico responded to the failure to implement the cross-border transportation rules by imposing $1.5 billion in retaliatory tariffs on manufactured goods and $1 billion on U.S. agricultural products.

In July 2011, the United States and Mexico signed an agreement permitting unlimited access to the United States for Mexican trucks for a trial period of three years. The agreement required that all drivers qualify for necessary approvals and permits and agree to electronic monitoring to track hours of service, periodic drug and alcohol testing, and assessment of English language skills. All trucks must meet U.S. safety standards. Mexico agreed to reduce its retaliatory tariffs by 50 percent as a sign of good faith and eliminate such tariffs as soon as the first Mexican truck was allowed to enter the United States. This occurred in October 2011 when a truck operated by Transportes Olympic crossed the border at Laredo, Texas carrying a steel drilling structure to Garland, Texas. The cross-border trucking dispute is a prime example of the difficulties and delays encountered by more controversial provisions of free trade agreements.

Telecommunications

NAFTA eliminated all tariffs on telephones, cellular phones, and trade in telecommunications equipment by 2004. Given that the number of telephones per capita in Mexico is only a fraction of the per capita number of phones in the United States, Mexico is considered a giant untapped market for all forms of communications equipment and services. NAFTA provides that Canadian, Mexican, and U.S. telecommunications companies have nondiscriminatory access to all North American public telecommunications networks. They must be granted access to public and private (leased) lines and networks, and only conditions that are reasonable and necessary may be imposed on this access. Access to public telecommunications networks must be at rates related to the cost of operations. Technical standards may be imposed only for safety or to prevent damage to the equipment. Mexico's telephone system had been operated as a government-owned monopoly from 1972 to 1990, as *Telefonos de Mexico.* Today the company is privately owned and is even traded on the New York Stock Exchange. In the 1990s, Mexico developed a law that ended the monopoly on telecommunications and opened the Mexican market to foreign investment. Since then, many U.S. and Canadian telecommunications companies have teamed up with Mexican companies to take advantage of growing opportunities in the telecommunications market. More recently, the United States and Mexico disagreed over Mexican rules making it more difficult and costly for U.S. firms to connect international calls into Mexico. The United States complained to the World Trade Organization and requested a dispute settlement panel. In 2004, the panel ruled in favor of the United States and held that Mexican regulations discriminated against U.S. firms in violation of the WTO *General Agreement on Trade in Services.*

CROSS-BORDER INVESTMENT

Prior to the late 1980s, Mexico had a history of strictly regulating or even prohibiting foreign investment. For instance, Mexico required that foreign investors include local participants—Mexican stockholders or partners—in any new factory or investment venture. If a foreign firm wanted to purchase an interest in a local company, Mexico usually limited them to a minority, non-controlling interest. Mexico, as with many developing countries, required foreign manufacturing firms located there to export finished goods to other countries for foreign currency. Investors in manufacturing companies were required to use a certain portion of domestic content in the finished goods, thus discouraging imports. Limits were placed on how much money could be transferred out of the country. A common requirement was that foreign investors had to introduce their most advanced technology to the host country.

In the 1980s, Mexico turned away from the philosophy that government control is in the best interest of the country and recognized that the threat of expropriation and nationalization of industries would drive away foreign investors. Mexico became more hospitable toward foreign investment. It still exercises some control over foreign investment, particularly in the energy and petroleum industries, telecommunications, and a few other industries, but to a lesser extent than it did in the past.

NAFTA's Investment Provisions

NAFTA's investment provisions can be summarized as follows:

- NAFTA investors must be treated fairly, equitably, and in full accordance with basic principles of international law.
- NAFTA investors must be granted the basic protections of NTR (to be treated at least as favorably as investors from outside North America), *nondiscrimination,* and *national treatment* (to be treated no less favorably than a country's own investors or domestically owned firms are treated).
- NAFTA governments must adopt *open investment policies* and eliminate most restrictions on private investment from firms based in other NAFTA countries.
- Private property of a NAFTA investor may not be expropriated by the government without due process of law and the payment of fair compensation.
- Private investors may request an arbitral tribunal to hear an *investor claim* for money damages against a NAFTA country for violating the NAFTA investment provisions. NAFTA countries may invoke other procedures for settling investment disputes between themselves.

NAFTA's Investment Policies. Investors from all three countries can now establish new companies and purchase existing ones across North American borders. In addition, NAFTA sets limits on the government regulation of North American-owned companies. (These provisions were largely intended to break down the investment barriers in Mexico.) No NAFTA country can require a minimum level of local participation or ownership by nationals (other than in certain industries in which exceptions to this rule have been reserved). No NAFTA country may place restrictions on the conversion of foreign exchange and transfer of money between accounts in another NAFTA country. Similarly, no country may either require or prohibit a firm from transferring profits earned by a subsidiary in one NAFTA country to another NAFTA country. There can be no performance requirements on a NAFTA investor, such as minimum export requirements (where the host government requires foreign-owned firms to export a certain percentage of goods or services produced by the local subsidiary) or domestic content or purchasing requirements (where the host government requires that a minimum percentage of raw materials used in local operations be purchased from local companies). Governments may not require that parent companies in one NAFTA country transfer advanced technology (via patents, licensing, or "know-how" agreements) to a subsidiary in another NAFTA country, and they may not require that senior managers and corporate directors be of any particular nationality.

Environmental Measures Applicable to Investments. Mexico does not have the strict environmental laws that the United States has. For many U.S. firms, compliance with U.S. laws can be costly. When NAFTA was negotiated, heated debate surrounded the issue of whether U.S. companies, especially polluting ones, would flock to open plants in Mexico to avoid U.S. law. As a compromise in the negotiations, NAFTA provides that "it is inappropriate to encourage investment by relaxing domestic health, safety, or environmental measures. Accordingly, a [NAFTA country] should not waive … such measures as an encouragement for the establishment, acquisition, expansion or retention in its territory of an investment."

Exceptions to the Investment Agreement. Canada reserved the right to review acquisitions of local companies exceeding a set threshold. In 2012, the review threshold was C$330 million or more under the *Investment Canada Act.* This amount is scheduled to increase to C$1 billion by 2016. Canada also restricts foreign investment in cultural industries (such as publication and distribution of written materials, film, video and music recordings, and television, cable television, and satellite broadcasting), commercial aviation, energy and mining, telecommunications, and fishing. Real estate ownership may be restricted as primary responsibility for property law rests with the provinces. In Mexico, several sectors of the economy are reserved exclusively for the state. These sectors include petroleum exploration and exploitation, telegraphic services, electric power generation, transmission, and distribution, nuclear energy, and airports. Other sectors are reserved exclusively for Mexican nationals. These sectors include retail sales of gasoline, non-cable radio and television services, development banks, and domestic transportation for passengers, tourism, and freight (except messenger and package delivery services). The United States excluded investments in nuclear power, broadcasting, mining, customs brokerages, and air transportation and may block the takeover of U.S. firms on the basis of national security.

Protecting Investors from Expropriation. The legal requirement that governments must compensate owners of private property whose property is taken for public use is a virtually universal concept. It is based on the notion that at times governments must take private property for public purposes, or for uses such as conservation or environmental protection, and that the property owners should not have to shoulder the cost of the public welfare. NAFTA Article 1110 states that no NAFTA country may expropriate property of a NAFTA investor, unless it is done pursuant to internationally accepted rules, that is, that private property may only be taken for a public purpose or for public use on a nondiscriminatory basis, using procedures that are open, fair, and in accordance with due process of law, and fair compensation must be paid according to the market value of the property taken.

The *Metalclad Corp. v. United Mexican States* case is one of the most interesting and controversial cases to come out of NAFTA. This is a case involving a U.S. firm that attempted to build a hazardous waste landfill in Mexico. It was told that all permits necessary to build the facility had been obtained. After making significant progress to complete the project, the municipality where the landfill was claimed one additional permit was missing, and the state issued a decree turning the property into a wildlife refuge. Work was ordered stopped, and Metalclad requested that an arbitral tribunal award damages.

Investor Claims and Dispute Settlement Procedures. Investor claims are actions for damages brought by a NAFTA investor before an arbitral tribunal against a host NAFTA government for having violated NAFTA investment rules. Investor suits maybe brought either under the arbitration rules of the U.N. Commission on International Trade Law (UNCITRAL) or, as in the *Metalclad* award, the International Centre for the Settlement of Investment Disputes (ICSID). ICSID is an organization closely allied with the World Bank and is headquartered in Washington, DC. Investor suits may be brought by either citizens or corporations of another NAFTA country or by investors from other countries that have substantial business activities in a NAFTA country. For example, if a parent company in Sweden owns an incorporated subsidiary company in the United States, then the U.S. subsidiary may make investments in Canada or Mexico according to the open investment policies of NAFTA. Investors may bring suits for monetary damages (no punitive damages are allowed) or restitution of property, but not to force a government to change its laws or policies (as can a WTO panel wherein the cases are brought by complaining governments). There are usually three arbiters, selected by the parties, and their awards are binding on the parties. The awards are effective only for that case and do not establish binding rules that countries must follow in future disputes. NAFTA governments may also bring dispute actions against each other, not for damages, but to compel compliance with NAFTA rules.

There were 59 notices of intent to submit a claim filed pursuant to Chapter 11 of NAFTA between 1994 and 2009. Only 41 of such claims were ever filed seeking damages of $5 billion. Although these numbers appear large, it is important to place them in the context of the size of the free trade zone created by NAFTA and amount of foreign investment within its three member states. A study published in 2011 concluded that cases such as *Metalclad Corporation v. United Mexican States* were rare. In fact, of the 41 filed claims, only seven resulted in findings of a violation of Chapter 11. This includes five such cases against Mexico (including *Metalclad*) and two against Canada with total compensation of less than $200 million. The vast majority of cases filed against national governments were dismissed without any award of damages. In this regard, the result in *Metalclad* has proven to be the exception rather than the rule.

OTHER NAFTA PROVISIONS

In negotiating NAFTA, the United States was able to see the broader implications of free trade and investment in North America. For instance, what if an unscrupulous company in Mexico produces counterfeit software and smuggles it across the border in violation of the copyrights of a U.S. company? Or suppose that a firm emits poisonous gas or pollutants from a smokestack at its Mexican plant, and they are carried by air currents to the United States? What if the top managements of

Metalclad Corporation v. United Mexican States

International Centre for the Settlement of Investment Disputes
No. ARB(AF)/97/1 Award of the Arbitral Tribunal (August 30, 2000)

BACKGROUND AND FACTS

In 1993, a Mexican firm, Coterin, received a permit from the Mexican government to build a hazardous waste treatment plant in the La Pedrera valley in the state of San Luis Potosi, near the city of Guadalcazar. Metalclad, a U.S. company, was interested in acquiring Coterin. Several Mexican government authorities assured Metalclad that Coterin had obtained all required construction permits for the facility. One month later, Metalclad purchased Coterin. In 1994, amid much opposition to the plant from local residents and environmental protestors, the city of Guadalcazar ordered a halt to construction, claiming that no municipal permit had been obtained. Metalclad responded that the Mexican federal government had told it that no further state or municipal permits were needed. Metalclad even promised to create a reserve for native species and a local scientific advisory council, give discounts for local waste, contribute to local charities, and provide some free medical services to local residents. But, without reason, the city informed Metalclad that it could not begin operations. In 1997, the state governor issued a decree designating the landfill as a protected ecological and wildlife area, putting an end to Metalclad's business there. Having expended \$16.5 million on the project, Metalclad requested that a NAFTA arbitral tribunal be convened to resolve the dispute. The company maintained that it had not been given fair and equitable treatment, that the Mexican regulations lacked transparency, and that Mexico had in fact expropriated their property without payment of fair compensation.

AWARD OF THE ARBITRAL TRIBUNAL

For the reasons set out below, the Tribunal finds that Metalclad's investment was not accorded fair and equitable treatment in accordance with international law, and that Mexico has violated NAFTA Article 1105(1).

Prominent in the statement of principles and rules that introduces NAFTA is the reference to "transparency." The Tribunal understands this to include the idea that all relevant legal requirements for the purpose of initiating, completing and successfully operating investments made, or intended to be made, under NAFTA should be capable of being readily known to all affected investors. There should be no room for doubt or uncertainty on such matters.... The absence of a clear rule as to the requirement or not of a municipal construction permit, as well as the absence of any established practice or procedure as to the manner of handling applications for a municipal construction permit, amounts to a failure on the part of Mexico to ensure the transparency required by NAFTA. Metalclad was entitled to rely on the representations of federal officials and to believe that it was entitled to continue its construction of the landfill. Moreover, the permit was denied at a meeting of the Municipal Town Council of which Metalclad received no notice, to which it received no invitation, and at which it was given no opportunity to appear. The Town Council denied the permit for reasons which included, but may not have been limited to, the opposition of the local population, the fact that construction had already begun when the application was submitted ... and the ecological concerns regarding the environmental effect and impact on the site and surrounding communities. None of the reasons included a reference to any problems associated with the physical construction of the landfill or to any physical defects therein. The Tribunal therefore finds that the construction permit was denied without any consideration of, or specific reference to, construction aspects or flaws of the physical facility.

Mexico failed to ensure a transparent and predictable framework for Metalclad's business planning and investment. The totality of these circumstances demonstrates a lack of orderly process and timely disposition in relation to an investor of a Party acting in the expectation that it would be treated fairly and justly in accordance with the NAFTA. The Tribunal therefore holds that Metalclad was not treated fairly or equitably under the NAFTA and succeeds on its claim under Article 1105.

NAFTA provides that "no party shall directly or indirectly ... expropriate an investment ... or take a measure tantamount to ... expropriation ... except: (a) for a public purpose; (b) on a nondiscriminatory basis; (c) in accordance with due process of law and Article 1105(1); and (d) on payment of compensation. Thus, expropriation under NAFTA includes not only open, deliberate and acknowledged takings of property, such as outright seizure or formal or obligatory transfer of title in favor of the host State, but also covert or incidental interference with the use of property which has the effect of depriving the owner, in whole or in significant part, of the use or reasonably to be expected economic benefit of property even if not necessarily to the obvious benefit of the host

continues

continued

State. By permitting or tolerating the conduct of Guadalcazar ... Mexico must be held to have taken a measure tantamount to expropriation in violation of NAFTA.

NAFTA provides for the award of monetary damages and applicable interest where a Party is found to have violated a Chapter 11 provision. With respect to expropriation, NAFTA specifically requires compensation to be equivalent to the fair market value of the expropriated investment immediately before the expropriation took place. However, where the enterprise has not operated for a sufficiently long time to establish a performance record or where it has failed to make a profit, future profits cannot be used to determine going concern or fair market value. Rather, the Tribunal agrees with the parties that fair market value is best arrived at in this case by reference to Metalclad's actual investment in the project. For the reasons stated above, the Tribunal hereby decides that the Respondent shall pay to Metalclad the amount of $16,685,000.

Decision. Through the actions of city, state, and federal officials, Mexico had violated Metalclad's investor rights. The Mexican regulations were not transparent, the procedures were unfair, and Mexico's actions were an indirect expropriation of Metalclad's property. As a U.S. investor in Mexico, Metalclad was not granted fair and equitable treatment.

Case Questions

1. What was the panel's decision with respect to the restrictions placed on Metalclad's operations by Guadalcazar?
2. The *Metalclad* decision and similar cases have been criticized as placing the rights of foreign investors ahead of the rights of local communities with respect to fundamental concerns such as environmental protection. Is this criticism valid? How would you resolve the fundamental conflict between protection of local community interests and investor's rights? Should the community pay for actions that interfere with the expectations of foreign investors? Why or why not?

several competing companies meet in Denver or Mexico City and fix consumer prices for a product that they all make? Although these problems undoubtedly occurred prior to NAFTA and are tremendous issues that no one trade agreement is likely to change, the U.S. negotiators of the agreement used the opportunity to address them openly.

Intellectual Property Rights

Intellectual property rights (IPRs) are generally protected by national law but are also the subject of several international conventions (e.g., the *Berne Convention)* and agreements (e.g., GATT/TRIPS). Intellectual property is covered in greater detail in Part Four of this book. NAFTA adopts the basic tenets of these international agreements and builds on them. NAFTA's provisions protect the IPRs of North American firms. No country can make citizenship a requirement for IPR protection. Applicants for trademarks, copyrights, and patents must be treated equally and without discrimination. NAFTA guarantees that any IPR is freely transferable by the owner to another party.

Trademarks. Trademarks and service marks are protected under NAFTA for 10 years and can be renewed indefinitely. The owner of a registered trademark has the right to prevent others from using identical or similar signs for goods or services if it would result in a *likelihood of confusion* (which is presumed unless the offender can prove otherwise). Specific provisions prohibit the use of the names of geographical regions (e.g., Tennessee Whiskey), unless the products are actually derived from that area. Actual use of a trademark cannot be a condition for filing an application for registration. NAFTA requires fair procedures for obtaining a trademark, including notice and an opportunity to be heard. Registration may be canceled if the trademark is not used for an uninterrupted period of at least two years.

Copyrights. Copyrights are protected equally in all three countries. Computer programs are protected as literary works, and motion pictures and sound recordings are protected for at least 50 years. (Canada has made some exceptions for "cultural industries.") NAFTA prohibits the importation of copies of a sound recording made without the producers' authorization.

Patents. Patents must be made available for any invention "in all fields of technology" (including pharmaceuticals), whether it is a product or process. It must be new, result from an inventive step (be "nonobvious"), and be capable of industrial application (be "useful"). They are effective for a period of 20 years from the date of application or 17 years from the date when the patent was granted.

Enforcement and Penalties. NAFTA requires that each country enforce its IPR laws, both internally and at the border to prevent smuggling of counterfeit items. IPR owners will be able to protect their rights through administrative action and judicial relief. Courts will have the authority to order seizure and destruction of infringing items, to issue injunctions against their sale, and to permit lawsuits for damages against infringers. The NAFTA countries must provide criminal penalties for cases in which willful trademark counterfeiting or copyright piracy occurs on a commercial scale. Penalties may include imprisonment or monetary fines or both.

Environmental Cooperation and Enforcement

The *North American Agreement on Environmental Cooperation* (NAAEC) does not set environmental or ecological standards, but it does call for the three countries to cooperate in protecting the environment. The countries have promised to enforce their laws more effectively. They also promise to develop environmental emergency procedures and to share information on protecting the environment. They are also working to develop common environmental standards. All countries must notify the others before banning a pesticide or chemical, and afterward, all are urged to prohibit the export of such products to other countries.

The NAAEC created the *North American Commission for Environmental Cooperation* (CEC) to oversee this portion of the agreement. The commission is headed by a council made up of three cabinet-level officers of the three governments. The commission may convene panels to resolve disputes between countries. The arbitral panels can authorize tariff increases against a country that fails to enforce its environmental laws or is otherwise found in violation of the environmental provisions of the agreement, or can impose a monetary penalty.

One of NAFTA's first environmental cases was reported in *The Journal of Commerce* in 1995. The CEC was called on to investigate the death of 40,000 wild birds in Mexico. The commission acted quickly to determine the cause—apparently the birds died from the industrial dumping of either chromium or red dye—and made recommendations in order to protect other migratory birds that were due to return to the area. Mexico took quick action as a result of the commission's investigation. It was the first time in North America that authorities from other countries investigated an environmental disaster solely within another country. As of 2012, there have been a total of 91 requests for investigation submitted to the CEC. Forty of these requests concern environmental injuries alleged in Mexico. Environmental practices in Canada and the United States are the subject matter of 31 and 10 requests respectively. However, the effectiveness of the CEC investigative process in changing environmental practices among the member states remains an open question.

Labor Cooperation and Worker Rights

Many people worried that NAFTA would cause U.S. companies to move to Mexico to take advantage of cheap labor and weakly enforced labor laws. With this in mind, the United States insisted on a side agreement called the *North American Agreement on Labor Cooperation* (NAALC), intended to make labor policies more uniform by promoting the following basic labor principles in the region:

- Freedom of association and right to organize
- Right to bargain collectively
- Right to strike
- Prohibition of forced labor
- Protection for children and young persons
- Minimum working conditions
- Elimination of employment discrimination
- Equal pay for women and men
- Prevention of accidents and occupational disease and injuries, and compensation to workers
- Protection of migrant workers

NAFTA does not set specific rules or domestic labor standards but requires countries to enforce those standards that they already have. Indeed, Mexico's labor laws meet all international standards. The problems lie in the enforcement of Mexican laws, notably in the *maquiladoras* and factories along the border region. A **North American Commission for Labor Cooperation** was created to oversee the agreement and to promote cooperation in labor issues. The commission is headed by a council consisting of the U.S. Secretary of Labor and labor ministers from the other countries. An arbitral panel may be convened to investigate issues involving worker health or safety, child labor, or the failure to enforce minimum wage laws, and it may make recommendations for solutions and impose fines.

There is some criticism of the efficacy of this agreement. One attorney quoted in *The Wall Street Journal* who litigated five cases before the NAO (National Administrative Office) noted:

> Technically speaking in all cases we won. But in all cases workers are left with a piece of paper that says "you were right." Not a single worker was ever reinstated, not a single employer was sanctioned, no union was ever recognized.

At best, the agreement provides a forum to discuss disputes.

Rights to Temporary Entry

Unlike the EU, NAFTA does not create a common market in labor. Each country may still determine its own qualifications for employment and its own immigration policies. NAFTA countries, however, have agreed to give businesspeople easy access to their customers, clients, factories, and offices across the borders. NAFTA permits temporary entry in the following cases:

1. Business visitors engaged in international business activities related to research, manufacturing, marketing, sales, and distribution; those who are service providers; and those servicing products after the sale (repair or maintenance of products after the sale must be done pursuant to a warranty or other service contract on the products).
2. Traders employed by a company in a NAFTA country and those who are buying and selling substantial amounts of goods and services
3. Potential investors
4. Management or executive employees transferred to subsidiary companies in another NAFTA country
5. Qualified professionals entering to do business (in professions ranging from teaching and law to hotel management); separate licensing qualifications must also be met if they intend to practice a profession

Mexico requires these travelers to obtain an FMN card (*Formulario Migratorio* NAFTA), which is valid for 30 days. Special visas are available for periods of stay longer than 30 days. Normal tourist cards are still available.

ADMINISTRATION AND DISPUTE SETTLEMENT

NAFTA does not have the type of lawmaking institutions that the EU has. However, an administrative body oversees implementation of the agreement, and a dispute resolution process is available to NAFTA countries. The dispute resolution process is similar to that of the WTO.

NAFTA Fair Trade Commission

The NAFTA **Fair Trade Commission** supervises the implementation of the agreement and attempts to resolve disputes that may arise regarding its interpretation or application. One cabinet-level official from each of the three governments, supported by an administrative staff and committees, form the commission.

Arbitral Panels. When one NAFTA country accuses another of violating NAFTA's principles, it must first attempt to negotiate a settlement. If a settlement is not reached, then the countries can seek dispute resolution. When the issue falls under both NAFTA and GATT, the countries must agree on whether it will be heard by the NAFTA Fair Trade Commission or the WTO. If they cannot agree on which forum, the case will normally be heard before the Fair Trade Commission. If a settlement is not reached, the commission may convene an *arbitral panel*, which consists of five members who are experts in trade or law. They decide whether one country has violated NAFTA and recommend a solution. If the recommendations of the arbitral panel are not followed and no agreement is reached within 30 days, the complaining country may retaliate by raising tariffs. No arbitral panel has the authority to tell a country to actually change its laws or policies. For example, if a panel rules that a regulation of the U.S. Consumer Product Safety Commission, the National Park Service, or other agency is violating NAFTA, an individual cannot obtain a court order compelling the agency to alter its decision solely on the basis of the panel report.

Antidumping and Countervailing Duty Cases. The Fair Trade Commission also hears cases involving countervailing and antidumping duties. These cases are treated differently from other disputes. Recall that countervailing duties are imposed on imported goods that received an unfair price advantage because a part of their cost of production was subsidized by the exporting country. Antidumping duties are imposed on "dumped" products. Dumping, another unfair trade practice, is the selling of goods in a foreign market for less than the price charged in the country in which they were produced. Antidumping and countervailing duties are only imposed pursuant to an order of an administrative agency in the importing country.

This practice continues under NAFTA; however, the appellate process has been changed greatly. In the United States, an appeal of an agency decision in an international trade case normally goes to the U.S. Court of International Trade, but appeals from administrative orders in NAFTA cases now go to NAFTA **binational panels**, not to courts of law. The role of these panels and their standard of review in reviewing agency decisions are limited. Binational panels apply the same standard of review as would a court of law convened in the country where the case originated. Because it is not an appellate court, a panel does not make law in the traditional sense, but it applies the existing law of the country from which the case was appealed. This legal process is quite unusual and controversial, because private businesses will be bound by the decision of an intergovernmental panel with no recourse to judicial review.

Extraordinary Challenge Committees. Appeals of a binational panel decision may be taken only to a NAFTA **Extraordinary Challenge Committee**, and not to courts of law. A challenge committee examines a case only to see if a panelist was biased or guilty of misconduct, or whether the panel departed from a fundamental rule of procedure, or exceeded its powers, authority, or jurisdiction. A binational panel must apply the correct standard of review. Under NAFTA, a binational panel that fails to apply the correct standard of review would be considered to have exceeded its powers, authority, or jurisdiction. Panelists for binational panels and extraordinary challenge committees are chosen from a roster of impartial judges or former judges whenever possible.

PRODUCTION SHARING: ASSEMBLY PLANTS AND THE MEXICAN MAQUILADORAS

The process of spreading manufacturing and assembly operations across international borders is often called **production sharing**, a term coined by business theorist Peter Drucker. One type of production sharing involves the manufacture or fabrication of articles or component parts in one country and their assembly into finished goods in another. While this is not a part of NAFTA, production sharing is discussed in this chapter because of its importance to industry and trade in North America and the entire Western Hemisphere. Historically, global manufacturing firms have invested in manufacturing operations in developed countries that offered higher-skilled workers, technology, capital investment, research and development, quality control, and state-of-the-art production and management methods, as well as political and economic stability. The manufactured articles were then shipped to "assembly plants" in lower-wage countries for assembly into the final product.

To economists and management theorists, production sharing makes perfect economic sense. It allows countries to specialize in what they do best, be it research and development, highly skilled manufacturing, or low-wage labor. Production sharing also has been a major force for investment, employment, and the transfer of technology and know-how to developing countries. Today, modern production sharing techniques are integral to efficient global manufacturing operations and supply chain management.

Since the mid-1960s, U.S. legislation has encouraged the manufacture of articles in the United States and their assembly in foreign plants. Section 9802 of the *Harmonized Tariff Schedules of the United States* contains a special provision allowing U.S.-made articles or component parts to be shipped to factories in a foreign country where the articles are assembled or joined to other articles and then returned to the United States with duties assessed only on the value of the newly assembled product less the value of the U.S.-made component parts. In essence, import duties are placed only on the low-wage labor and the relatively inexpensive overhead of the foreign plants. For example, a cellular telephone manufacturer can assemble a telephone in a Mexican assembly plant, using parts sourced from North America and from other countries, and then re-export the finished telephone to the United States. Tariffs on the telephone are based on the value of the phone, less the value of the U.S. component parts.

Foreign assembly operations are common in industries that produce electronic goods, home furnishings and appliances, automobiles and automotive parts, textiles and apparel, and many others. Assembly plants can be locally owned or owned by companies from the United States or other countries. They can be located in countries all over the world, although most are located in low-wage countries.

Many are located in Mexico. Some of the largest users of assembly plants are Honeywell, General Electric, Ford, General Motors, Siemens, Sony, Whirlpool, Sanyo, Samsung, Motorola, Hyundai, Bose, Mattel, Fisher Price, Toshiba, and Nokia, to name just a few common brand names among hundreds.

During the 1990s, automobile firms from all over the world invested heavily in assembly plants in Japan, Canada, Sweden, Germany, and Mexico, while the electronics and apparel industries invested heavily in Asia, Mexico, and the Caribbean. Production-sharing plants are also called *offshore assembly plants,* or in the case of Mexico, *border plants,* because of their location along the U.S. border. The Spanish term for these plants is ***maquiladora***, derived from the word *maquilar,* meaning "to process." Production-sharing plants are common not only in Mexico but also throughout the Caribbean and Central America. Plants in Mexico have the advantage of being located close to the U.S. border, accessible by road and rail transportation. Proximity to the United States means faster shipping, lower inventory requirements, and lower transportation costs. This is particularly important for industries assembling products with short shelf lives, for products that can quickly become obsolete, or for managing just-in-time inventory in global manufacturing.

Many Asian firms have taken advantage of assembly operations in Mexico, giving them a platform for shipping throughout North America, as well as to Central and South America.

Assembly Plant Tariff Rules

Under Section 9802, the tariff assessed on an assembled article upon re-importation to the United States is calculated on the value of the newly assembled article less the value of the U.S.-made component parts. These tariff savings are available only where the imports were assembled in the foreign plant (1) from U.S.-manufactured or fabricated components (2) that had been exported "ready for assembly without further fabrication" and (3) that have not lost their physical identity and have not been advanced in value or improved in condition abroad except by being assembled and except "by operations incidental to the assembly process" such as cleaning, trimming, calibrating, or lubricating.

Examples of fabricated components that would qualify as being ready for assembly without losing their physical identity include circuit boards, machine parts, semiconductors, precut parts of wearing apparel, lug nuts, and automobile engines or tires. Sending bolts of fabric abroad to be cut into parts of shirts does not qualify as assembly, but sewing two sleeves to the body of a shirt does. It is not "assembly" when lumber, leather, or plastic is sent abroad to be formed into new and different articles that will become components of finished goods. Section 9802 applies only to assembly operations, which include any method of joining two or more solid articles, such as welding, screwing, gluing, or sewing. Combining chemicals, liquids, gases, or food ingredients is not considered assembly. In addition to automobiles and clothing, other representative products include telecommunications and electronic equipment, computers, televisions, sausage casings, mini-blinds, stuffed toys, and almost any product capable of assembly. In *Samsonite Corp. v. United States,* the operations of the plant were held to be a fabrication and not a mere assembly.

Samsonite Corp. v. United States

889 F.2d 1074 (1989) United States Court of Appeals (Fed. Cir.)

BACKGROUND AND FACTS

Samsonite Corporation assembles luggage in Mexico for import into the United States. Many component parts used in the assembly process are made in the United States. Samsonite had shipped steel strips from the United States to Mexico for use as luggage handles. When the strips left the United States, they were five inches long, straight, and bearing a coat of oil. Their value ranged from 95 cents to $1.26. In Mexico, the strips were bent by machine into a form resembling a square-sided letter C, cleaned, covered with a vinyl sheath, and riveted to plastic frame assemblies. The assemblies were then placed in, and fastened to, bags of vinyl to make soft luggage. On import into the United States, the Customs Service dutied the luggage, including the value of the steel strips at the rate of 20 percent *ad valorem.* The Court of International Trade upheld the government's contention that the steel strips had not been "exported in a condition ready for assembly" and that the process in Mexico amounted to a fabrication and more than a mere assembly. Samsonite appealed.

continues

continued

SENIOR CIRCUIT JUDGE FRIEDMAN

To obtain a deduction for American-fabricated articles assembled abroad, the components

a. must have been exported from the United States "in condition ready for assembly without further fabrication,"
b. not have lost their physical identity in the articles by change in form, shape, or otherwise, and
c. not have been advanced in value or improved in condition "except by being assembled" and except "by operations incidental to the assembly process such as cleaning, lubricating, and painting."

As the Court of International Trade correctly pointed out, since the "foregoing three conditions for a deduction are set forth in the conjunctive, ... each must be satisfied before a component can qualify for duty-free treatment." We agree with that court that the steel strips involved in this case did not meet those conditions.

The critical inquiry is whether the bending and shaping that the strips underwent constituted "fabrication" or mere assembly and operations incidental to the assembly process. We hold that what was done to the strips in Mexico was fabrication and not mere assembly.

When the steel strips were exported from the United States, they were just that: five-inch strips that could not serve as the frame of the luggage without undergoing a complete change in shape. Prior to assembling the luggage, the strips were bent by machine into a carefully and specially configured rectangular shape that was necessary before the original strip would serve its ultimate function as part of the frame of the luggage.

In short, what emerged after the bending operation was a different object from that which left the United States. The latter was a steel strip, the former was a metal frame for a piece of luggage. The transformation of the strip in this manner into a luggage frame was a fabrication. The strips therefore had not been exported from the United States "in condition ready for assembly without further fabrication."

Samsonite contends, however, that prior decisions of the Court of Customs and Patent Appeals require a contrary conclusion. It relies particularly on *General Instrument Corp. v. United States,* 499 F.2d 1318 (CCPA 1974). That case involved wire wound on spools that had been exported from the United States to Taiwan. There the wire was removed from the spools, formed into a horizontal coil by a winding machine, taped to prevent unraveling, dipped in cement, dried, precision shaped, removed from the spools, and wound around a core. The end product made from the wire was a component of a television set that was imported into the United States.

The Court of Customs and Patent Appeals held that: "The steps performed upon the wire after its exportation to Taiwan are not 'further fabrication' steps, but rather assembly steps within the meaning of [the statute]."

Samsonite argues that far more was done to the wire in *General Instrument* than was done to the steel strips in this case. It argues that if the processing the wire underwent in *General Instrument* was not "fabrication," a fortiori "the one simple-minded act of bending a straight frame into a C was neither a further fabrication nor a nonincidental operation."

The critical inquiry in determining whether fabrication rather than mere assembly took place here, is not the amount of processing that occurred in the two cases, but its nature. In *General Instrument,* the wire, when it left the United States and when it returned as part of a finished product, was a coil. The wire was taken directly from the supply spool on which it was wound and, after processing, was used in assembling the TV set components. The wire underwent no basic change in connection with its incorporation into the television set component.

In contrast, in the present case the steel strips had to undergo a significant change in shape before the actual assembly of luggage could begin. Until the steel strips had been made into C shapes they could not be used as a part of the luggage. Unlike the "assembly" that the court in *General Instrument* held the processing of the wire involved, here "further fabrication" of the steel strips was required in order to change them into frames for luggage, before the assembly of the luggage could take place.

Decision. The Court of Appeals upheld the decision of the lower court. The bending and processing of the steel strips in Mexico was fabrication and not a mere assembly and therefore did not qualify for duty-free treatment under Section 9802.

Comment. In *United States v. Haggar Apparel Co.,* 526 U.S. 380 (1999), the United States Supreme Court upheld regulations of the U.S. Customs Service that permapressing of men's pants was an additional step in manufacturing and not a minor operation incidental to assembly.

Case Questions

1. What was the court's holding with respect to the application of Section 9802 to Samsonite's steel strips?
2. Samsonite contended that the bending process in Mexico was less significant than the process upheld as mere assembly in the *General Instrument Corp.* case. Do you agree? Was the court correct in this regard, or is the purported difference one without substance?

Mexican Regulation of Maquiladoras. The *maquila* industry is governed by regulations and decrees of the Mexican government. These regulations are intended to promote Mexico's competitiveness in assembly and manufacturing and to promote exports by giving tariff and tax incentives to Mexican exporters. *Maquiladoras* are chief beneficiaries of the incentives. The incentives include the elimination or reduction of tariffs on imports of certain component parts or raw materials destined for re-export as finished goods. The duty reductions apply only to products in select industry sectors. In order to qualify for favorable tariff treatment, a Mexican company must meet complex regulatory and tax law requirements that require companies to rely on sophisticated legal and accounting advice.

Mexico's tariff incentives for exporting firms have changed several times in recent years. In large part, the changes are due to changes in NAFTA rules. In 2007, the Mexican Ministry of the Economy merged the *maquila* program with another government export program into the *Maquiladora Manufacturing Industry and Export Services Program,* or IMMEX The IMMEX law covers eligibility requirements for IMMEX companies and their certification, operation, taxation, inspection, and reporting requirements.

Issues Related to the Mexican Maquila Industry

Mexico has encouraged development in the *maquila* industry since 1965, offering incentives for investment and favorable tariff and tax treatment for *maquiladoras.* Since then, *maquiladoras* have contributed significantly to Mexico's job growth and to its economy generally. For most of that time, *maquiladoras* were used only for low-wage assembly operations, whereas most capital investment remained in true "manufacturing" plants in the United States. Today, many Mexican plants use state-of-the-art production equipment and techniques and employ many more higher-skilled workers than in the past. Many U.S. businesspeople claim that the quality of workmanship in Mexican plants is on par with that anywhere in the world. Some plants are quality certified by the International Standards Organization (ISO). The average hourly wage for direct labor, however, is still only about $2.00 an hour, although ahead of average wages elsewhere in the country.

The success of the *maquila* industry has caused a migration of workers from all over Mexico to the border region. This has led to many social problems that are typical of fast-growing migrant areas. These include overcrowded living conditions, pollution, substandard housing, poor health care, inadequate sanitation and public utilities, poor roads and infrastructure, and many other problems. The electrical power and telecommunications industries are encumbered by a history of government protection and monopoly, and electricity and other utilities are often unreliable and inadequate for industry.

One of the most severe problems in the border region is an epidemic of crime that has spread to both sides of the border, including violent crimes such as kidnapping for ransom, smuggling and drug-related crimes, organized crime, and offenses related to illegal immigration and border crossings. Many foreign companies have to provide personal protective services for their employees.

Other political and societal factors have also detracted from the business climate in Mexico. The government bureaucracy is often encumbered by red tape and corruption, and officials at some levels of government maintain an anti-business attitude.

Still other problems have arisen in the *maquila* workplace. Many accusations of labor abuses have been made by governments, nongovernmental organizations, labor activists, and the popular press. These include unsafe or unhealthy working conditions, excessive working hours, sexual harassment, and violations of the right to organize. Although Mexico has enacted sophisticated labor and employment laws related to wages, working hours, and other areas, these laws are not always adequately enforced. As jobs become harder to find, unskilled workers become more vulnerable to a few unscrupulous supervisors and plant managers who are able to exploit workers desperate for well-paying jobs. Most global brand-name firms that operate *maquiladoras* or that have purchasing and supply arrangements with local plants try to monitor and "police" labor violations, although it is not always an easy task.

No issue is more pressing in the border region than the harm the plants have caused to the environment. In the early 1990s, the governments of the United States and Mexico began negotiations on protecting the Rio Grande and on building municipal sewer systems, water treatment plants, and solid-waste disposal sites. Their greatest concern was how to deal with hazardous waste. The two governments devised methods of tracking hazardous waste and regulating disposal sites. Complicating the problem are the thousands of trucks that cross the border daily, causing severe air pollution and damage to roads and bridges. Both governments have spent hundreds of millions of dollars to deal with these social and environmental problems.

CONCLUSION

The *North American Free Trade Agreement* was approved by the legislatures of Canada, Mexico, and the United States only after heated debate. Proponents saw it as a means of expanding trade opportunities for North American products, spurring cross-border investment, increasing the number of high-paying jobs in export industries, and bringing greater economic and social stability to Mexico. Opponents argued that it would result in large-scale loss of U.S. and Canadian jobs to low-wage workers in Mexico. Today, the impact of NAFTA is still disputed. NAFTA supporters point to an increase in the volume of trade and investment between the three countries and to an increase in living standards and strengthening of the Mexican middle class. Critics point to an increasing U.S. trade deficit with Mexico, which did not exist in 1993. They argue that NAFTA has caused a loss of U.S. jobs in many industries, particularly manufacturing, and in virtually every U.S. state. These critics maintain that despite an increase in manufacturing jobs in Mexico, real wages have not increased. Moreover, they point out that many of the new Mexican jobs are in plants along the U.S.–Mexican border, with many people working and living in crowded, slum-like conditions, with inadequate housing, health care, and sanitation. Environmentalists argue that NAFTA and the growth of border factories have created a social and environmental disaster in the region. One thing is certain: arguments over the impact of NAFTA are colored by American attitudes over increased illegal Mexican immigration into the United States. Certainly, the immigration issue has become the hottest topic in U.S.–Mexican relations.

Chapter Summary

1. The economic provisions of the U.S. Constitution constituted an agreement among the states to have their economies managed as a single unit by the federal government. Under the Constitution's economic provisions, Congress had the exclusive power to manage trade between the states and with foreign nations. The federal court system was empowered to strike down any state law that would impede the free interstate movement of goods or people or discriminate against businesses based in other states. The Constitution gave the federal government the sole right to issue currency and determine monetary policy and concentrated all control over commercial policy toward other nations in the federal government.
2. A free trade area (FTA) is created when a group of countries agrees to eliminate or phase out customs duties and other barriers to trade among the member countries as to goods originating in the FTA countries.
3. In a customs union, there is free trade of all goods that come through any of the union's members, even if they entered a member state through importation from outside the customs union. Because of this, a customs union can only function if all of its members agree to a common tariff on imports from outside the union and a common institution to negotiate such tariffs on behalf of the group.
4. A "common market" is a customs union that has reached a further state of integration. In addition to assuring the free movement of goods within the customs union, a common market seeks to further facilitate free competition within the union and protect the right of all enterprises and persons within the area to do business, invest capital, and sell their services within the area without discrimination on the basis of national origin. To achieve free economic competition in a common market, the members of the market establish common rules relating to anti-competitive behavior and subsidization of industry. Further, a court with jurisdiction and power to enforce its rulings is necessary to ensure compliance with the market's norms.
5. The provisions of the *WTO Agreement* do not prevent formation of a customs union or FTA. The WTO treats such a grouping as an economic actor and requires that tariffs against those outside the grouping not be increased as a consequence of the group's formation.

6. The *North American Free Trade Agreement* between Canada, Mexico, and the United States went into force in 1994. It created the world's largest free trade area. Today, this market encompasses about 451 million people and a combined gross domestic product of more than $17 trillion.
7. By 2008, all tariffs on goods originating and traded in Canada, Mexico, and the United States were eliminated.
8. NAFTA tariff rates apply only to articles that originate in Canada, Mexico, or the United States. Only goods that qualify under NAFTA's rules of origin can obtain NAFTA tariff rates. Goods originate in a NAFTA country if they are wholly produced or obtained in Canada, Mexico, or the United States. This includes live animals born and raised, minerals mined, and crops grown in these countries. However, if the goods contain non-originating inputs (components or raw materials), they qualify as having originated in a NAFTA country if they meet the regional value content requirements or the tariff shift rules of Annex 401 of NAFTA.
9. NAFTA's national treatment principle is similar to that found in GATT. It states that once goods arrive from another NAFTA country, they must be treated without discrimination and no differently than domestically made goods. Reports of the United States Trade Representative show that Mexico and Canada still maintain many non-tariff barriers to U.S. goods and services.
10. The country-of-origin marking and labeling rules are set out in Annex 311 to NAFTA and are enacted in the national customs regulations of the United States, Canada, and Mexico.
11. Canada and Mexico are significant purchasers of U.S. agricultural products. NAFTA has boosted U.S. agricultural exports to Canada and Mexico since 1994. The elimination of Mexican tariffs in 2008 on products such as corn and beans has been viewed as a threat by many small Mexican farmers, who fear competition from large-scale American farms. This remains a sensitive political issue in both countries.
12. NAFTA's side agreements on the protection of labor and the environment are controversial. The *North American Agreement on Environmental Cooperation* does not set environmental or ecological standards, but it does call for the three countries to cooperate in protecting the environment. The *North American Agreement on Labor Cooperation* is intended to make labor policies more uniform by promoting Mexico's enforcement of its labor laws.
13. The Fair Trade Commission supervises the implementation of the agreement and attempts to resolve disputes that may arise among the three governments. If a settlement is not reached, the commission may convene an arbitral panel that can recommend a solution. Panels do not have the authority to tell a country to actually change its laws or policies.
14. The Mexican *maquiladora* industry consists of "production-sharing" factories that assemble U.S. components into finished products for return to the United States. Products include electronics, automobiles, and apparel. This industry allows manufacturers to take advantage of low-cost labor that is located close to the United States. The *maquila* industry is attempting to compete with even lower-cost labor from China, as Chinese imports to the United States grow at faster rates than imports from Mexico. Since 2007, the *maquila* industry has been governed by new Mexican "IMMEX" regulations.

Key Terms

free trade area (FTA) 375
customs union 375
common market 376
national treatment 379
export taxes 379
customs user fees 379
substantial transformation test 380
tariff shift rule 381
regional value content 381
certificate of origin (CO) 382
arbitral panel 388
binational panels 398
production sharing 398
maquiladoras 401

Questions and Case Problems

1. Does the United States have any free trade agreements under negotiation at the present time? If so, what is their status? Are there countries with which the United States should contemplate future free trade agreements?
2. Consider a study of doing business in Mexico. How do the economic, cultural, social, and political climates affect a business there? Describe Mexico's form of government. How are business relations conducted there? Are they more or less formal than in other Western countries? Describe how Mexico's policies toward trade and investment have changed over the years. Do you believe that Mexico provides a stable climate for trade and investment? What products or industries would seem to do well in the Mexican market?
3. NAFTA contains provisions regarding the fair treatment of labor and the protection of the environment. Evaluate their potential for success. What labor and environmental issues are addressed in NAFTA? What issues should be addressed? Explain.
4. Your company produces "Big Duster" tires. Your most popular styles are the ones with the raised white lettering on the outside of the tire. You would like to export tires to Mexico but cannot pass the Mexican labeling and marking requirements. Among the many other requirements, a required remolding of the tires in Spanish would be costly. You do not think the regulations are fair. Do the requirements violate NAFTA? What course of action should you take?
5. Your company distills Kentucky bourbon. A Canadian competitor is selling "Kentucky bourbon" in Ontario, but its bourbon is made in Canada. Canada's liquor control agency has looked the other way and ignored your requests to enjoin the sale. Does the sale violate NAFTA? GATT? Would this action be heard before the NAFTA Free Trade Commission or the WTO? What steps can be taken to force Canada to enjoin the sale? What remedies are available? If the Canadian products are exported to the United States, can they be stopped at the border?
6. How does the function of a NAFTA arbitral panel differ from that of a binational panel? What is the standard of review in binational panel decisions? Describe the role of an extraordinary challenge committee. Why does NAFTA recommend that panelists on binational panels and extraordinary challenge committees be judges or former judges whenever possible, but allow arbitral panelists to be specialists in international business or trade?
7. What is a rule of origin? Why is it important to the operation of a free trade area?
8. Discuss the social responsibility of a Canadian or U.S. manager working in Mexico. If a certain course of action is illegal in the manager's own country but lawful and accepted in Mexico, which standard should the manager follow? Describe the social responsibility of firms operating in Mexico in regard to environmental protection, worker health and safety, and corrupt practices.

Managerial Implications

Consider the following NAFTA management problem in a global business context.

DownPillow, Inc., a small U.S. manufacturer of down comforters and pillows, sells nationally through high-quality retailers. The company is known for its quality of materials and production. Its raw materials include cotton fabric, unfilled cotton shells, and down fills. These materials are not produced in the United States in sufficient quantities to meet the needs of the U.S. market. The HTS classification for unfilled comforter shells is 6307.90. The classification for finished down comforters is HTS 9404.90.

For many years, DownPillow purchased materials from Europe and paid in foreign currency. Gradually, costs rose because European suppliers faced higher labor and overhead costs. A declining U.S. dollar made goods more costly, but as costs rose, the company could not pass them on in price increases. When the U.S. market became more competitive in the early 1990s, DownPillow looked to China for cheaper materials. China is the world's leading producer of cotton textiles and down fill. Chinese textiles enter the United States under strict quota limits, enforced by U.S. Customs. Quota category 362 includes unfilled shells, comforters, quilts, bedspreads, and other top-of-the-bed products. DownPillow negotiated with a Chinese manufacturer for low-cost materials priced in dollars. The new products were introduced to U.S. customers in 1993 at competitive prices. The new lower-priced goods quickly became an important part of the company's line.

However, the political situation changed over time. The United States accused China of illegally transshipping textiles through third countries to get around the U.S. quota. In response, the United States reduced the quota on category 362. The annual quota began to close in early fall. Goods anticipated for shipment during the Christmas season sat in a customs-bonded warehouse at the port until released by U.S. Customs the following January. In the following year, the largest U.S. importers of comforters and bedspreads had bought their merchandise early, and the quota closed in March. DownPillow was barely able to obtain sufficient unfilled shells for its production needs. When it tried to switch its customers back to the higher-priced merchandise made from European materials, they balked. Many threatened to take their business elsewhere.

1. Management is desperate for a solution. It has learned that Canada will permit the entry of Chinese textiles. They also know that Canadian trade negotiators put a little-known rule of origin in NAFTA providing that a product that undergoes a change from category 6307.90 to category 9404.90 will become a product of North America. (Tariff shifting is not generally available for textile articles, but widely available for many other manufactured and processed goods.) They would like your opinion on answers to the following questions:
   a. May they bring the Chinese cotton shells into Canada and ship them to the United States despite the quota? What processes would have to take place in Canada to do this? If they did, what would the tariff rate be? Would they see any net tariff savings?
   b. Production in Canada would give ready access to the Canadian home-fashions market. Should the company explore the possibility of investment in a plant in Canada? What are the pros and cons of such a move? How would they be affected by NAFTA investment provisions?
   c. Canada is a good supplier of goose down. If DownPillow produces finished comforters in Canada, would it make a difference if it used down from Canada geese, as opposed to down plucked from geese in, say, Poland, and imported into Canada?
   d. Every state requires that comforters may only be sold if they are manufactured or imported by licensed bedding manufacturers. Bedding manufacturers are subject to state health codes. Does NAFTA prohibit the application of state health codes to Canadian and Mexican companies or to products made by them?
   e. The company also has had some interest from buyers in Mexico. Would any import duties apply on shipments of either its U.S.- or Canadian-made products to Mexico? What would the tariff rate be? What special textile labeling rules are applicable, and how would they affect the company's ability to market there?
   f. Management is concerned about meeting foreign health standards applicable to a natural product like down and feathers. Where would they go for information on foreign regulations?

2. Discuss the wisdom of DownPillow's decision to switch its source of supply to China. Describe the impact of customs and tariff law on a North American firm's strategy. Describe how this small company was affected by international political events out of its control. Do you think the company underestimated its customers and its market?

Ethical Considerations

Maquiladoras have been subject to much criticism. Critics contend that the industry is merely an attempt to attract foreign investment by not strictly adhering to environmental and labor standards. As a result, environmental problems especially in border areas have been exacerbated, and social tensions have increased. Wages, while improving, may still be inadequate to meet basic needs, thereby causing workers to live in squalid conditions. The absence of mobility promoted by the low skill nature of many jobs locks workers into permanent cycles of poverty and dependency on the *maquila* industry. This dependency and the absence of mobility may encourage worker exploitation in the form of excessive work hours, unhealthy and unsafe working conditions, and discriminatory hiring practices. Finally, critics note that, to the extent the health of the *maquila* industry depends on companies and economies of other countries, it does not promote long-term economic stability. Economic stability is also lacking as other low wage countries, such as China and countries in Southeast Asia, develop their own productive capabilities, thereby causing companies to depart from Mexico and leaving a large pool of unemployed and unskilled workers in their wake.

By contrast, supporters of the *maquiladora* strategy have contended that the factories are a means of integrating

Mexico's developing economy and growing labor force into the global economy. *Maquiladoras* are an important source of foreign exchange and constitute a significant portion of Mexico's exports. Given their number and size, *maquiladoras* are a successful method of domestic job creation, which serves to keep Mexican workers at home. Proponents also note that conditions have improved in most *maquiladoras* since NAFTA's entry into force and effect. Furthermore, the *maquila* industry has evolved from simple assembly activity based on cheap labor with low added value through the adoption of best practices in the productive processes and industrial organization. Examples of such practices include increases and improvements in capabilities, just-in-time, continuous improvement, environmental performance, and occupational safety and health.

These tensions also exist when analyzing the *maquila* industry from an ethical standpoint. Which impact is the most persuasive from an ethical point of view? For example, utilizing a teleological framework, a moral relativist might contend that the *maquila* industry is appropriate given Mexico's status as a developing economy and the level of skill of a significant portion of its workforce. However, a moral relativist could also argue that, although perhaps appropriate at the present time, the *maquila* industry is not a viable long-term strategy for economic prosperity.

A utilitarian point of view may reach similar conclusions. One may contend that the *maquila* industry is ethical given that it results in the greatest overall good for the community by providing economic growth for Mexico and jobs for Mexican workers. However, a utilitarian approach may also conclude that the *maquila* industry will not result in the greatest overall good for the greatest number in the long term. Furthermore, the tendency to focus on short-term profits and employment may justify many otherwise objectionable behaviors with respect to environmental protection and labor rights.

By contrast, deontological frameworks may provide clearer guidance. Divine command theory, which resolves dilemmas on the basis of tenets of faith within religious beliefs, may find the *maquila* industry objectionable to the extent that it encourages the exploitation or mistreatment of labor contrary to human dignity. *Maquiladoras* may also be subject to condemnation pursuant to the Categorical Imperative as no one would wish for the practices within the industry to become universal laws with respect to the treatment of laborers engaged in manufacturing. The industry is subject to further condemnation to the extent that it treats workers as a means to an end. Finally, the lack of fairness and equality in the *maquila* industry may subject it to criticism pursuant to contractarianism. Exploitation of labor, to the extent it occurs in the industry, may also be deemed to violate the duties and responsibilities placed on employers with respect to low-skilled workforces in developing economies.

What point of view best represents your thinking with respect to the *maquila* industry? Why?

CHAPTER 15

The European Union

Europe's history is long and tumultuous with alliances formed and dissolved over thousands of years. A significant trend in the post-World War II period has been the development of regional economic alliances to facilitate trade, as well as to maintain peace and security. These regional agreements have had significant impact on the conduct of business.

Historical precedents for European economic integration go back to before the Roman Empire. However, the devastation of Europe caused by World War II and efforts to rebuild were the major forces in bringing six European countries—Belgium, France, Italy, Luxembourg, the Netherlands, and West Germany (the western portion of modern Germany)—together to form the European Common Market or **European Economic Community**, now known as the European Union (EU). As of August 2013, the number of member states grew to 28 with the addition of Croatia. The EU is now the largest single market in the world with a population of more than 500 million people and a combined gross domestic product of more than $16 trillion. The primary focus of this chapter is to examine the structure and operation of the EU to the extent that it is relevant to business. It also examines the process of gradually greater economic integration within the EU and its impact on business.

HISTORY OF THE EUROPEAN UNION

The EU did not spring forth fully developed in its current form. Rather, it developed over a period of years and with successive modifications. Understanding the present issues requires an examination of the EU's history.

Founding Treaties

Winston Churchill, a former prime minister of Great Britain, stated in 1946 that postwar Europe needed a "... [s]overeign remedy ... to re-create the European family, or as much of it as we can, and provide it with a structure under which it can dwell in peace and safety and freedom. We must build a kind of United States of Europe." Jean Monnet, a French government official considered the founding father of the EU, said that "the states of Europe must form a federation." They hoped this type of partnership would prevent the development of conditions that might result in a third world war.

Although the EU is a single unit, it actually started as three "communities," each created and operating under a separate treaty. The best known was the European Community (EC), formerly known as the European Economic Community, established under the 1957 *Treaty of Rome.* This treaty, like the U.S. Constitution, created a set of market-wide institutions empowered to develop common policies, but it left the substance of the policies to the new institutions. The second community, the **European Coal and Steel Community (ECSC)** was established in 1952 under the *Treaty of Paris,* which specifically defined the outlines of an agreed common policy, covering combined price and output controls, investment subsidies, tariff protection, and competition rules with respect to coal and steel. The third community, the **European Atomic Energy Community (Euratom)**, established on the same day as the EC by a second, separate *Treaty of Rome,* focused primarily on creating a market for and distributing atomic energy throughout the European states. It also was responsible for selling excess nuclear energy outside member states. All three of these "communities" existed under the administration of a single institution, the **Commission of the European Communities** (the Commission).

The **European Union** is a concept added by the *Maastricht Agreement,* also known as the *Treaty on European Union.* The *Maastricht Agreement* did not abolish the Communities, but created the concept of a Union as an expression of the member states' underlying unity, as reflected in the Communities. Maastricht also added goals, to which the member states aspired, that might permit the eventual development of political integration. In practice, the level of political integration was very loose: Member states had very different positions on political, military, social, and labor questions and made little attempt to coordinate them. Legally, there were three communities. Thus, the somewhat confusing result was that, although the EU was a single set of institutions, each of which we will discuss in depth below, it acted as ECSC on steel and coal matters; it acted as Euratom on atomic energy matters; and when it acted on most other economic matters, it did so as the EC.

Because the general rule is that the EU has only the powers its member states confer on it in treaties, we will review some of the major treaties in more detail.

Treaty of Rome. The *Treaty of Rome* stated the original objectives of the EU (see Exhibit 15.1). The *Treaty of Rome* launched the process of establishing a customs union, gradually turning over international trade policy to the Commission. The *Treaty of Rome* also launched internal multinational regulation, as it contained "competition law" calculated to prevent the creation of market-wide private combinations in restraint of trade. The *Treaty of Rome* is still important in the area of competition law. Notwithstanding the earlier ECSC effort, the *Treaty of Rome* is commonly regarded as the true beginning of European economic integration.

The Single European Act. Despite the professed goals of the *Treaty of Rome,* progress on economic integration was quite slow. Approaching the thirtieth anniversary of the *Treaty of Rome,* the EU was still more a loose free trade area than a customs union. It posed significant barriers to imports from other member states, and its divergent approaches on trade policy with nonmember states made a customs union untenable. The 12 existing members thus enacted the *Single European Act* (SEA), effective in July 1987. The purpose of the SEA was to strengthen the institutions and enable them to act to further the goals of the *Treaty of Rome.*

The SEA signaled a dramatic move away from the *Treaty of Rome's* slow, consensus-based system. The members abandoned the requirement of unanimous consent to move forward and instead adopted the concept of **qualified majority voting**. This change meant that not all the member states had to agree on proposals that related to the internal market. This allowed the institutions to make decisions even if there was some objection.

Exhibit 15.1

Treaty of Rome

Article 2

The Community shall have as its task, by establishing a common market and progressively approximating the economic policies of Member States, to promote throughout the Community a harmonious development of economic activities, a continuous and balanced expansion, an increase in stability, an accelerated raising of the standard of living, and closer relations between the States belonging to it.

Article 3

For the purposes set out in Article 2, the activities of the Community shall include, as provided in this Treaty and in accordance with the timetable set out therein.

A. the elimination, as between Member States, of customs duties and of quantitative restrictions on the import and export of goods, and of the other measures having equivalent effect;
B. the establishment of a common customs tariff and of a common commercial policy toward third countries;
C. the abolition, as between Member States, of obstacles to freedom of movement for persons, services, and capital;
D. the adoption of a common policy in the sphere of agriculture;
E. the adoption of a common policy in the sphere of transport;
F. the institution of a system ensuring that competition in the common market is not distorted;
G. the application of procedures by which the economic policies of Member States can be coordinated and disequilibrium in their balances of payments remedied;
H. the approximation of the laws of Member States to the extent required for the proper functioning of the common market;
I. the creation of a European Social Fund in order to improve employment opportunities for workers and to contribute to the raising of their standard of living;
J. the establishment of a European Investment Bank to facilitate the economic expansion of the Community by opening up fresh resources;
K. the association of the overseas countries and territories in order to increase trade and to promote jointly economic and social development.

The Maastricht Treaty. After the passage of the SEA, the pace of change quickened. In 1991, EU leaders hammered out an agreement at Maastricht, Netherlands, that advanced economic integration and set the stage for a measure of political integration. The EU concept was established, along with EU "citizenship," which facilitated movement of labor. It set the stage for a single European currency, the euro, and a European Central Bank to control monetary policy. The agreement also set goals for common policy on internal environmental and other issues important to business. The *Maastricht Treaty* also increased the use of qualified majority voting.

Treaty of Lisbon. The period from 1991 through 2007 was marked by difficulties in furthering economic integration. Attempts to address institutional reform in the *Treaty of Nice* (2003) failed, and the rejection of an attempt to consolidate the EU's authority in the *Treaty Establishing a Constitution for Europe* by voters in France and the Netherlands in 2005 led to a period of reflection and inaction. The period of reflection ended in 2007, when a new effort was initiated to salvage some of the reforms set forth in the Constitution for Europe. These efforts resulted in the *Treaty of Lisbon,* which was signed in December 2007 and entered force in December 2009. The *Treaty of Lisbon* significantly modified the EU's existing institutions as well as its underlying structure. The treaty abolished the separation between the policy areas and introduced a single consolidated entity with a legal personality. The word "Community" was removed from the name of all existing institutions.

The *Treaty of Lisbon* redefined the relationship between EU institutions and the national governments of the member states. This relationship has been redefined in three separate principles. First, the *Treaty of Lisbon* distinguishes between exclusive competence, shared competence, and supporting competence. The EU has exclusive competence or power in areas such as the functioning of the customs union, common trade policy, competition law, and monetary policy. The member states share competency with the EU in such areas as the internal market, social policy, agriculture, environmental and consumer protection, transportation, energy, and public health. However, the member states' power is limited to those areas where the EU has not otherwise acted. The EU may support, coordinate, or supplement actions in fields left primarily to the member states, such as industry, tourism, culture, and education. The second principle is a greater role for national governments in EU affairs. National parliaments may now object to proposed EU legislation on the basis that it oversteps EU authority. The EU may be forced to reexamine or explain the proposed legislation depending on the number of national parliaments that file objections. Finally, for the first time, the *Treaty of Lisbon* formalizes a procedure by which member states may withdraw from the EU.

The *Treaty of Lisbon* also redefined the relationship between the EU and citizens of the member states. The treaty creates a new citizens' initiative that requires the consideration of proposals signed by one million citizens from any number of member states. The treaty also provides that the political, social, and economic rights set forth in the *Charter of Fundamental Rights* are legally binding on the member states.

The *Treaty of Lisbon* represents the most significant change to the EU since the beginning of European economic integration as represented by the *Treaty of Rome* (now known as the *Treaty on the Functioning of the European Union,* which for purposes of clarity we will continue to refer to as the *Treaty of Rome).* The structure of the EU is discussed in the next section.

MEMBERSHIP IN THE EUROPEAN UNION

The EU currently consists of 28 states. Table 15.1 lists the current EU member states alphabetically with the year each state applied for and acceded to membership. Membership in the EU has been highly desired by the vast majority of states as noted by the fact that only one state (Norway) has refused an invitation to join, and states are willing to wait for long periods of time while their applications are undergoing review. This long period of time begs the question–how does a state join the EU?

The Accession Process

Becoming a member of the EU is a long and complex process. The *Maastricht Treaty* provides that any European state may apply for membership if it respects democratic values. These values include stable institutions guaranteeing democracy and respect for the rule of law and human rights, a functioning market economy, and acceptance of EU laws and practices. A state wishing

Table 15.1 MEMBERSHIP IN THE EUROPEAN UNION AND ITS PREDECESSORS (2013)

STATE	DATE OF APPLICATION	ACCESSION DATE
Austria	July 1989	January 1995
Belgium	Founding Member	July 1952
Bulgaria	December 1995	January 2007
Croatia	February 2003	July 2013
Cyprus	July 1990	May 2004
Czech Republic	January 1996	May 2004
Denmark	May 1967	January 1973
Estonia	November 1995	May 2004
Finland	March 1992	January 1995
France	Founding Member	July 1952
Germany, West	Founding Member	July 1952
Greece	June 1975	January 1981
Hungary	March 1994	May 2004
Ireland	May 1967	January 1973
Italy	Founding Member	July 1952
Latvia	September 1995	May 2004
Lithuania	December 1995	May 2004
Luxembourg	Founding Member	July 1952
Malta	July 1990	May 2004
Netherlands	Founding Member	July 1952
Poland	April 1994	May 2004
Portugal	March 1977	January 1986
Romania	June 1995	January 2007
Slovakia	June 1995	May 2004
Slovenia	June 1996	May 2004
Spain	June 1977	January 1986
Sweden	July 1991	January 1995
United Kingdom	May 1967	January 1973

to join must first reach a stabilization and association agreement with the EU whereby the potential candidate state is offered free trade incentives in return for commitments to political and economic reform. A state may submit an application for membership once such an agreement is completed. At this juncture, an applicant becomes an official candidate. However, this status does not mean that formal membership negotiations have commenced.

Membership negotiations are conducted in chapters relating to specific EU legislation, legal acts, and court decisions otherwise known as the ***acquis communautaire*** (literally meaning that which has been agreed upon by the community). An accession treaty is only drafted once negotiations are concluded on all chapters and topics. Accession treaties granting new membership must be ratified by all existing members. A date is then set for the commencement of formal membership. Any existing member state may effectively veto a new membership application although such an occurrence would be rare at this stage. Of course, negotiations may take place over such a long period of time as to constitute an effective veto of membership. Such is the case with Turkey, which has been an applicant for membership since 1987 with no end in sight to membership negotiations. Table 15.2 lists the current candidates for EU membership and the status of each application.

The Advantages and Disadvantages of Further Expansion. Expansion of membership slowed considerably after rapid growth in the mid-1990s and from 2004 through 2007. This may be due to several factors, including a declining number of suitable expansion candidates and the financial crisis which has taken some of the luster off of membership (to be discussed later in this chapter). The most recent enlargements have focused on poorer, eastern European states that may pose a threat to western

Table 15.2 CANDIDATES FOR EU MEMBERSHIP AS OF AUGUST, 2013

STATE	DATE OF APPLICATION	STATUS
Albania	April 2009	Potential Candidate
Bosnia & Herzegovina	-	Potential Candidate
Iceland	July 2009	Official Candidate
Kosovo	-	Potential Candidate
Macedonia	March 2004	Official Candidate
Montenegro	December 2008	Official Candidate
Serbia	December 2009	Official Candidate
Turkey	April 1987	Official Candidate

European dominance of EU institutions and a drain on resources. Enlargement to Eastern Europe has resulted in increased development aid to these new and poorer member states. Expansion may also increase migration by Eastern Europeans and exacerbate the unemployment problem facing Western Europe. Expansion has also occurred in a somewhat undemocratic manner as there has never been an EU-wide referendum on any of the previous additions. Finally, possible future expansion has caused the EU to consider what it means to be European. As noted by German chancellor Angela Merkel in 2006, "[i]f we do not want to stop completely or even reverse integration, we have to say where the borders of Europe are." For example, should a state like Turkey be admitted given that the majority of its territory is located in Asia and its population is predominantly Muslim? If geography is an important factor, what should become of Iceland's application? If religion is a determinant, what should be done about a candidate such as Bosnia which is a part of the European continent but a predominantly Muslim country? These are questions which the EU will need to answer as it considers future expansion.

Conversely, there are several benefits of enlargement. Expansion provides greater security for the European continent and minimizes the likelihood of future armed conflict. Democratization, the rule of law, and respect for human rights are promoted through the enlargement process. Expansion to Eastern Europe provides Western European states with access to new markets for goods and services and cheaper labor. The EU must take action to retain its economic clout as regional trading blocs become more commonplace in the absence of progress on greater global integration at the World Trade Organization. The EU cannot afford to be left behind by economic events in the Pacific Rim and on the Indian subcontinent and greater regional integration on a worldwide scale.

STRUCTURE OF THE EUROPEAN UNION

Power in the EU is allocated by the member states to several institutions. The primary institutions are the European Council, the Council of Ministers of the European Union, the Commission of the European Union, the European Parliament, and the Court of Justice.

The European Council

A potential source of confusion arising from the *Treaty of Lisbon* is the **European Council** (the Council), which should not be confused with the Council of Ministers, to be discussed shortly. The Council became a full EU institution as a result of the *Treaty of Lisbon.* It is composed of the heads of state or government of the EU's member states along with the president of the European Commission. The Council has jurisdiction over a wide range of areas, including the composition of the Parliament and Commission and law enforcement, foreign policy, and constitutional matters. The Council is headed by a president. The president is elected by the Council to a term of two and one-half years and can be reappointed once. The president's work is largely administrative with responsibility for preparing the Council's work, hosting its meetings, reporting its work to the European Parliament, and working to secure consensus among member states. The president also acts as the EU's external representative on issues concerning common foreign policy and security.

The Council of Ministers of the European Union

The **Council of Ministers of the European Union** (the Council of Ministers) sits in Brussels, Belgium, the effective "capital" of the EU. It is composed of one representative from each member state. Each member state has several ministers, each specializing in a different area. A member state will designate a different minister to be its representative on the Council of Ministers, depending on the subject on the agenda at a given meeting. Different areas of specialization include international affairs, finance, agriculture, and transportation. The position of president of the Council of Ministers is elected by European leaders to chair quarterly summits and establish the agenda. The purpose of the Council of Ministers is to coordinate economic policies of member states and to make decisions on issues within its jurisdiction, which includes approving legislative directives to the member states and international agreements.

The Council of Ministers reaches decisions through a complex "qualified majority" voting system (unless unanimity or simple majority is otherwise required). A qualified majority is achieved if (1) a majority of member states (in some cases a two-thirds majority) approve a proposal; (2) member states with a population of at least 62 percent of the total EU population approve it; and (3) a minimum of 255 votes are cast in favor of the proposal. This formulation will change in November 2014 when proposed legislation must also garner the votes of 55 percent of member states representing 65 percent of the EU's population. The votes are presently divided as follows:

Votes for each member state	
Germany, France, Italy, United Kingdom	29
Spain, Poland	27
Romania	14
Netherlands	13
Belgium, Czech Republic, Greece, Hungary, Portugal	12
Austria, Bulgaria, Sweden	10
Croatia, Denmark, Ireland, Lithuania, Slovakia, Finland	7
Cyprus, Estonia, Latvia, Luxembourg, Slovenia	4
Malta	3
TOTAL	352

The *Treaty of Lisbon* also obligates the Council of Ministers to meet in public when it deliberates and votes on legislation.

The European Commission

The **European Commission** serves as the EU's executive body carrying out the decisions of the Council of Ministers. It also is the only body that can make legislative proposals for the Council of Ministers and European Parliament to consider. As a practical matter, however, the Commission proposes whatever the Parliament or the Council of Ministers requests that it propose. The Commission is headed by the College of Commissioners. It consists of one member appointed by each member state, each of whom is theoretically obligated to represent the interests of the EU as a whole rather than the interest of their home state. The Commission is headed by a president who is elected by the European Parliament.

The term *Commission* also refers to the bureaucracy that performs the Commission's day-to-day work: more than 25,000 civil servants who serve in the different **Directorates-General**, which are specialized areas of interest of the Commission. For example, *DG-IV* is the part of the Commission responsible for development of its competition law. Each commissioner has special responsibilities at a directorate. There is some overlap among directorates, and fierce turf battles often rage among the bureaucrats.

The European Parliament

The **European Parliament** (the Parliament) is the only EU institution whose members are elected by European citizens. Each member state elects a different number, based on population who are known as Members of the European Parliament or MEPs. However, no member state can have more than 96 nor less than 6 MEPs. The allocation of MEPs is set forth in the following table.

Austria	19
Belgium	22
Bulgaria	18
Croatia	12
Cyprus	6
Czech Republic	22
Denmark	13
Estonia	6
Finland	13
France	74
Germany	96
Greece	22
Hungary	22
Ireland	12

Italy	73
Latvia	9
Lithuania	12
Luxembourg	6
Malta	6
Netherlands	26
Poland	51
Portugal	22
Romania	33
Slovakia	13
Slovenia	8
Spain	54
Sweden	20
United Kingdom	73
TOTAL	766

The MEPs are elected to five-year terms. Each member state determines the electoral rules for its own candidates. The Parliament comprises members of various political factions that create alliances across national boundaries, including the Socialists, Christian Democrats, European Democrat Alliance, Greens, and other groups.

The power of the European Parliament has progressively grown over time. This expanding power is an attempt to address concerns that the EU relies too heavily on appointed officials and is undemocratic. As a result of the *Treaty of Lisbon,* the Parliament now has the same degree of lawmaking power as the Council of Ministers in some areas where previously it was merely consulted or not involved at all. These areas include immigration, law enforcement and judicial cooperation, and some aspects of trade policy and agriculture. The Parliament must also approve the EU's budget, which is set forth within a multiannual financial framework (unlike the United States). Parliamentary assent is required for many international agreements to which the EU may ascribe. Finally, the Parliament is responsible for the selection of the president of the European Commission.

The Court of Justice of the European Union

The **Court of Justice of the European Union (ECJ)** in Luxembourg functions as the final arbiter of EU law. For private parties, its main function is to hear appeals from the European trial court, the **General Court**. It also has original jurisdiction in cases brought by EU institutions to compel member states to comply with their treaty obligations or by member states against EU institutions alleged to have overstepped their powers under the treaties.

One judge is appointed by each of the member states for a renewable term of six years. The judges elect a president of the Court for a renewable term of three years. Unlike most national high courts, the Court may sit as a full court, in a Grand Chamber of 11 judges, or in smaller chambers. The Court only sits as a full court when the judges determine that a case is of unusual importance, when different small chambers are in conflict, or, in rare cases, to remove a commissioner. The Court of Justice sits in a Grand Chamber in important cases or when petitioned by a member state or an EU institution. The Court hears most cases in chambers of three or five judges, much like the Courts of Appeals in the U.S. federal court system.

The General Court (formerly known as the Court of First Instance) is the general trial court of the EU. It has original jurisdiction over lawsuits brought by private parties and member states (other than those assigned to the Court of Justice). Like the Court of Justice, the General Court is comprised of one judge from each member state, who serve renewable six-year terms. A party bringing a suit in the General Court will probably encounter a three-judge chamber. The General Court hears about three-quarters of its cases in this fashion. If it deems a case important enough, the General Court can sit as a Grand Chamber of 13 judges or as a full court.

The EU courts follow the civil law tradition because all but the British and Irish judges come from this tradition. For example, the court itself calls witnesses, demands the production of documents, and hires necessary experts. The court allows limited cross-examination by the parties and permits parties to present their own experts on factual disputes.

Adherence to the civil law tradition is not the only difference between EU and U.S. courts. EU courts often handle cases that are different from their U.S. counterparts. For example the ECJ may be asked by a national court to issue a preliminary ruling on a point of EU law. Resort to such an advisory opinion is largely absent in the U.S. judicial system. EU courts also decide cases brought against member state governments for failing to fulfill treaty obligations or apply EU law. Additional types of cases include annulment actions to set aside EU laws alleged to violate EU treaties or fundamental rights and direct actions brought by individuals, companies, or organizations challenging EU decisions or actions.

Another distinguishing feature is that decisions are issued without any dissenting opinions. This practice does not indicate total agreement among the judges; however, the public is not privy to their differences. This is in contrast to the U.S. judicial tradition, where the public, press, and legal scholars examine dissenting opinions to divine the philosophical differences among judges and predict future outcomes on different cases. The rationale for this EU practice is to protect the national judges from pressure within their home states.

National courts are obligated to follow EU law and the ECJ's decisions. An English court recognized this authority in a famous opinion that noted the difference between English and EU law, but nonetheless followed the controlling EU law. Lord Denning in *Bulmer v. Bollinger* [1974] stated:

> The (EC) Treaty is quite unlike any of the enactments to which we have become accustomed… . It lays down general principles. It expresses its aims and purposes. All in sentences of moderate length and commendable style. But it lacks precision. It uses words and phrases without defining what they mean. An English lawyer would look for an interpretation clause, but he would look in vain. There is none. All the way through the Treaty there are gaps and lacunae. These have to be filled in by the judges, or by the regulations or directives. It is the European way… . Seeing these differences, what are the English courts to do when they are faced with a problem of interpretation? They must follow the European pattern. No longer must they argue about the precise grammatical sense. They must divine the spirit of the Treaty and gain inspiration from it. If they find a gap, they must fill it as best they can… . These are the principles as I understand it, on which the European Court acts.

The Court of Justice must also interpret EU law and is the ultimate authority for these conflicts.

Distinctions among Institutions

Non-Europeans have some difficulty following developments in the EU because of a lack of clarity about the roles of its various institutions. The European Council and the Council of Ministers easily can be confused with the Council of Europe. The Council of Europe comprises all the EU members plus a number of other countries, including Switzerland. The Council of Europe works to support democracy and human rights and to address the issues facing Europe as a whole. The Council of Europe has a European Court of Human Rights that hears complaints about violations of the *European Convention on Human Rights* and the *Anti-Torture Convention.*

Similarly, one should not confuse the EU's Court of Justice, which sits in Luxembourg, with the International Court of Justice, a court of final jurisdiction annexed by statute to the *United Nations Charter,* or the European Court of Human Rights. As discussed earlier in this chapter, the Court of Justice, an EU institution, hears cases dealing with the interpretation of EU treaties and legislation and conflicts between EU and national law.

The EU also should not be confused with the European Free Trade Association (EFTA). EFTA was founded in 1960 for the purposes of promoting free trade and closer economic cooperation among Western European countries. EFTA membership consisted of several countries that are now EU members such as Austria, Denmark, Finland, Portugal, Sweden, and the United Kingdom. These states withdrew from EFTA to join the EU, leaving the current membership of Iceland, Liechtenstein, Norway, and Switzerland. Despite its small size, EFTA has pursued trade relations around the world and has concluded several free trade agreements, including one with the EU.

Harmonization: Directives and Regulations

One of the principal goals of the EU is to harmonize national laws and create a common legal environment for business. How does the EU accomplish this goal? The Council of Ministers, Commission, and Parliament have several avenues open to them to achieve this objective. Article 189 of the *Treaty of Rome* identifies the four principal means:

- An **EU regulation** shall have general application. It shall be binding in its entirety and directly applicable in all member states.
- An **EU directive** shall be binding as to the result to be achieved on each member state to which it is addressed but shall leave to the national authorities the choice of form and methods.
- A *decision* shall be binding in its entirety on the member state or individual to whom it is addressed. Decisions are commonly used with respect to proposed mergers and agricultural matters.
- Recommendations and opinions shall have no binding force.

Regulations take effect immediately in the states and circumvent the need to pass legislation on the national level. Many **EU regulations** exist in the agriculture and competition law areas. *EU directives*, in contrast to regulations, require that members bring their laws into harmony with the standard stated in the directive within a stated time period, most often three years. The EU has used this approach in the environmental, products liability, and employment arenas. Directives give member states more autonomy to implement legislative programs in ways that are most consistent with local conditions. The problem with local autonomy, however, is that the national legislation may not advance the purposes of the directive. If the Commission believes that has happened, the Commission may initiate action in the EU courts to force the member state to comply. The member state will, of course, try to show that its action adequately complied with the directive.

There are two concepts of primary importance in any discussion of EU law. The first concept is the direct effects doctrine. The direct effects doctrine provides that provisions within EU treaties are applicable to individual businesses and persons and thus these businesses and individuals are empowered to seek enforcement without the necessity of state intervention or participation. The doctrine had its origin in *Van Gend en Loos v. Nederlandse Administratie der Belastingen*, Case 26/62 [1963] in which a transportation company sought a refund of a tariff from Dutch customs authorities that the company claimed was contrary to the free movement of goods provision of the Treaty of Rome. In permitting the transportation company to proceed with its action to enforce the free movement provisions, the ECJ stated:

> community law … not only imposes obligations on individuals but is also intended to confer upon them rights which become part of their legal heritage. These rights arise not only where they are expressly granted by the treaty, but also by reason of obligations which the treaty imposes in a clearly defined way upon individuals as well as upon the member states and upon the institutions of the community.

The direct effects doctrine has thus empowered businesses and individuals to serve as enforcers of obligations imposed by EU treaties.

The second concept is the supremacy doctrine. In a manner similar to the relationship between U.S. federal and state law, EU law is superior to the laws of the member states in areas in which integration has been occurred. Where a conflict arises between EU law and the national law of a member state, the EU law takes precedence. This principle was first announced in *Costa v. ENEL*, Case 6/64 [1964], in which the ECJ stated:

> [t]he law stemming from the treaty, an independent source of law, could not, because of its special and original nature, be overridden by domestic legal provisions … without being deprived of its character as community law and without the legal basis of the community itself being called into question.

The supremacy doctrine has had the effect of overturning numerous national laws regardless of their ancient pedigree. For example, in 1987, the ECJ struck down the *Reinheitsgebot*, the German beer purity law, originally adopted in 1516, which mandated that only four ingredients (water, hops, barley, and yeast) could be contained in any beverage sold to the German public as "beer." The effect of this law was to exclude beer brewed using rice, maize, sorghum, or other raw cereals. The ECJ dismissed Germany's contention that sales of products labeled as "beer" containing other ingredients would deceive German consumers and would imperil public health. The ECJ struck the law down as an artificial and unwarranted barrier to trade. The decision evoked widespread outcry in Germany but nevertheless opened the German market to a wide variety of beverages that could now be labeled as beer. It also demonstrated the ECJ's commitment to the supremacy doctrine.

Another example of the supremacy doctrine in operation may be found in the following case. It is important to note the wide scope of the doctrine in this case, extending all the down to admissions fees to cultural sights and museums operated by local government authorities.

As a result of the supremacy doctrine, the EU has achieved considerable integration in a wide variety of areas. Four of these areas, the so-called **Four Freedoms**, are discussed in the next section. Other areas where significant integration has occurred or been attempted are discussed later in this chapter.

Commission of the European Communities v. Italian Republic

C-388/01 [2003] European Court of Justice

BACKGROUND AND FACTS

Decree No. 507 of the Italian Ministry of Cultural Assets and Natural Sites regulated tickets for admission to monuments, museums, galleries, archaeological digs, parks and gardens classified as "national monuments." Article 4(3) of the Decree provided for free admission to EU citizens under the age of 18 years or over the age of 65 years. However, the Decree was only applicable to national monuments and did not apply to public monuments operated by local government authorities. Examples of public monuments included tourist attractions located in Treviso, Padua, Florence, and Venice. Italian authorities tolerated reduced rates restricted to Italian nationals and persons residing within the territory of the local authority operating these public monuments. Favorable admission was denied to tourists who were nationals of other member states who fulfilled the same age requirements.

Italy defended this distinction on the basis that free admission to the sites could not be granted in disregard of economic considerations with respect to the management of local cultural sights and that the national government had no authority with respect to museums and other cultural sites operated by local authorities.

The Commission challenged the distinction between national and public monuments before the European Court of Justice. It claimed that Italy permitted discrimination in violation of its treaty obligations by allowing local governments to grant advantageous conditions for admission to Italian nationals and persons resident within the territory of those authorities running the cultural sites in question and by excluding from such advantages tourists who were nationals of other member states.

FINDINGS OF THE COURT

The Court has already held that national legislation on admission to the museums of one Member State which entails discrimination affecting only foreign tourists is, for nationals of other Member States, prohibited by Articles 7 and 59 of the EEC Treaty (which became Articles 6 and 59 of the EC Treaty, now, after amendment, Articles 12 EC and 49 EC) (Case C-45/93 *Commission v. Spain* [1994] ECR I-911).

It is also clear from the Court's case-law (see, Case C-3/88 *Commission v. Italy* [1989] ECR 4035, paragraph 8) that the principle of equal treatment, of which Article 49 EC embodies a specific instance, prohibits not only overt discrimination by reason of nationality but also all covert forms of discrimination which, by the application of other criteria of differentiation, lead in fact to the same result.

* * *

The Italian Republic none the less puts forward various reasons in the general interest in order to justify the advantageous rates at issue. First, in the light of the cost of managing cultural assets, free admission to the sites cannot be granted in disregard of economic considerations.

* * *

First of all, to the extent that the advantageous rates at issue provide for a distinction on the basis of nationality, it should be recalled that such advantages are compatible with Community law only if they can be covered by an express derogating provision ... namely public policy, public security or public health. Economic aims cannot constitute grounds of public policy within the meaning of Article 46 EC (see, Case C-484/93 Svensson and Gustavsson [1995] ECR I-3955, paragraph 15)... . [As] neither the necessity to preserve the cohesion of the tax system nor the economic considerations put forward by the Italian Government come within the exceptions allowed by Article 46 EC, the advantageous rates at issue, in so far as they are allowed only for Italian nationals, are incompatible with Community law.

* * *

As regards, the economic grounds put forward by the Italian Government, suffice it to note that they cannot be accepted, since aims of a purely economic nature cannot constitute overriding reasons in the general interest justifying a restriction of a fundamental freedom guaranteed by the Treaty (see, Case C-35/98 Verkooijen [2000] ECR I-4071, paragraph 48).

* * *

Finally, the Italian Government contends that the regulations which introduced the advantageous rates at issue are not within its competence. They concern museums or other exhibition spaces run by local authorities, whereas, in accordance with Article 47 of Presidential Decree No. 616 of 1977, "all services and activities relating to the existence, conservation, functioning, public enjoyment and development of museums, collections of artistic, historic or bibliographic interest ... belonging to the region or to other local authorities including non-territorial authorities subject to its control or, in any event, of local interest" come within the exclusive competence of the regions.

continues

continued

In that regard, suffice it to recall that a Member State cannot plead conditions existing within its own legal system in order to justify its failure to comply with obligations arising under Community law. While each Member State may be free to allocate areas of internal legal competence as it sees fit, the fact still remains that it alone is responsible towards the Community under Article 226 EC for compliance with its obligations (see, Case C-33/90 *Commission v. Italy* [1991] ECR I-5987, paragraph 24).

Costs

Article 69(2) of the Rules of Procedure provides that the unsuccessful party is to be ordered to pay the costs if they have been applied for in the successful party's pleadings. Since the Commission has applied for costs and the Italian Republic has been unsuccessful, the latter must be ordered to pay the costs.

On those grounds, THE COURT (Sixth Chamber), hereby:

1. Declares that, by allowing discriminatory, advantageous rates for admission to museums, monuments, galleries, archaeological digs, parks and gardens classified as public monuments, granted by local or decentralized State authorities only in favor of Italian nationals and persons resident within the territory of those authorities running the cultural sites in question, who are aged over 60 or 65 years, and by excluding from such advantages tourists who are nationals of other Member States and non-residents who fulfill the same objective age requirements, the Italian Republic has failed to fulfill its obligations under Articles 12 EC and 49 EC;
2. Orders the Italian Republic to pay the costs.

Decision and Comment. The Court prohibited local governments in Italy from maintaining different fees for Italian nationals and citizens of other EU member states with respect to admission to local museums and cultural attractions. The Court rejected Italy's contention that it did not possess authority to regulate the fees charged by local governments. Rather, the Court extended the non-discrimination principle from cultural attractions and museums operated by national governments to such sights operated by regional and local governments.

Case Questions

1. What was the ECJ's holding with respect to Italy's claims regarding the cost to local governments of maintaining cultural attractions and historic locations?
2. What was the basis for the ECJ's decision that the Italian national government was responsible for the conduct of local governments with respect to the fees charged for admission to museums and cultural attractions?

THE EUROPEAN UNION AND THE REGULATION OF BUSINESS: THE FOUR FREEDOMS

The Four Freedoms refer to a body of EU law originating with the Treaty of Rome in which the EU committed itself to achieving the free movement of goods, services, capital, and people in the common market. The Four Freedoms constitute the very essence of the EU and are at the heart of its substantive law. These freedoms constitute the most important economic factors and are central to the EU's goals of enhancing continental integration and prosperity. All factors of production are entitled to move freely between the member states. This guarantee creates a truly free market and permits efficient allocation of factors of production to areas where they are most needed and valued. The following sections briefly describe each of the Four Freedoms.

The Free Movement of Goods

The *Treaty of Rome* provides that the common market "shall cover all trade in goods" and prohibits between member states "customs duties on imports and exports and … all charges having equivalent effect." This article also mandates the adoption of a common external tariff with respect to goods entering the member states from nonmember states. Once a good has entered a member state from a nonmember state and the appropriate customs duty has been paid, it must then be permitted to circulate freely between member states. Exceptions exist for goods that pose risks to consumers or harm the public health or the environment. The free movement of goods prohibits not only customs duties on imports and exports but also charges having the equivalent effect of a customs duty. Charges having equivalent effects include any pecuniary charge, no matter how small or its designation, that are unilaterally imposed on domestic and foreign goods upon crossing a border within the EU. It does not matter if a charge does not benefit the charging state, does not discriminate, and does not attempt to protect a like competitive domestic product. Internal taxes imposed on products of other member states in excess of those imposed on like domestic products are also prohibited.

In addition to customs duties and taxes, free movement of goods also prohibits quantitative restrictions and non-tariff measures having an equivalent effect. This prohibition is applicable to discriminatory rules that expressly distinguish between national and imported goods as well as rules that have the effect of hindering the free movement of imported goods. The following case is an example of a measure that had the effect of hindering the free movement of goods.

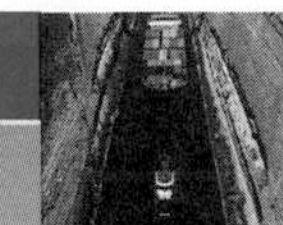

Commission of the European Communities v. Portuguese Republic

265/06 [2008] European Court of Justice

BACKGROUND AND FACTS

Article 2(1) of Portuguese Law No. 40/2003 provided that "the affixing of tinted film to the windows of passenger or goods vehicles shall be prohibited with the exception of lawful stickers and dark, non-reflective film to the goods compartment of goods vehicles."

Portugal acknowledged that its law constituted a restriction on the free movement of goods but contended that it was justified by the objectives of road safety and public safety. Portugal argued that the ban was intended to enable law enforcement authorities to make a rapid external inspection of the interior of motor vehicles in order to ensure that the vehicle's occupants were wearing seat belts and to identify potential criminals for the purpose of combating crime.

There was no Community legislation on tinted film designed to be affixed to the windows of motor vehicles at the time Portugal adopted its legislation. However, Community legislation existed in relation to safety glazing which was fitted from the outset to motor vehicles. This legislation included Council Directive 92/22/EEC of March 31, 1992 on safety glazing and glazing materials on motor vehicles and their trailers. This legislation provided that with respect to windshields, light transmittance could not be less than 75%. The light transmittance was required to be at least 70% in other areas within the driver's forward line of sight. Light transmittance could be less than 70% with respect to safety glazing located within the driver's rearward field of view if the vehicle was fitted with two exterior rear-view mirrors.

The Commission claimed that Portugal failed to fulfill its obligations under Articles 28 and 30 of the EC Treaty by affecting the marketing of almost all colored film, lawfully manufactured and marketed in other Member States intended to be affixed to the windows of motor vehicles. No potential customers, traders or individuals would purchase such film, since they knew that they could not affix it to the windows of motor vehicles. The Commission also claimed that the ban was excessive and disproportionate with respect to the objectives of combating crime and ensuring road safety. The Commission claimed a visual inspection was only one means among others in order to fight crime and prevent offenses relating to the obligation to wear seat belts, and at least some films, namely those with a sufficient degree of transparency, permitted the desired visual inspection of the interior of motor vehicles. Finally, the Commission noted that glazing of windows was permitted on motor vehicles before they were released into the stream of commerce as provided by Council Directive 92/22/EEC.

FINDINGS OF THE COURT

According to settled case-law, all rules enacted by Member States which are capable of hindering, directly or indirectly, actually or potentially, intra-Community trade are to be considered as measures having an effect equivalent to quantitative restrictions, prohibited by Article 28 EC. In this case, the Portuguese Republic acknowledges that the ban restricts the marketing of products in Portugal.

It must be held that potential customers, traders or individuals have practically no interest in buying [such products] in the knowledge that affixing such film to the windscreen and windows alongside passenger seats in motor vehicles is prohibited.

* * *

The contested provision therefore affects the marketing in Portugal of almost all tinted film legally manufactured and sold in other Member States or in States party to the EEA Agreement intended to be affixed to the windows of motor vehicles.

It follows that the ban in Article 2(1) of Law No. 40/2003 constitutes a measure having equivalent effect to quantitative restrictions within the meaning of Article 28 EC. That provision is incompatible with the obligations arising from those provisions, unless it may be objectively justified.

continues

continued

According to settled case-law, a measure having an effect equivalent to a quantitative restriction on imports may be justified only by one of the public-interest reasons laid down in Article 30 EC or by one of the overriding requirements referred to in the judgments of the Court (see, in particular, Case 120/78 *Rewe-Zentral* (*'Cassis de Dijon'*) [1979] ECR 649, paragraph 8), provided in each case that that measure is appropriate for securing the attainment of the objective pursued and does not go beyond what is necessary in order to attain it (Case C-14/02 *ATRAL* [2003] ECR I-4431, paragraph 64; Case C-432/03 *Commission* v *Portugal* [2005] ECR I-9665, paragraph 42; and Case C-254/05 *Commission v. Belgium*, paragraph 33).

In this case, the justifications put forward by the Portuguese Republic relate, first, to the fight against crime in the context of public safety and, second, to ensuring that the obligation to wear seat belts is complied with, which comes within the sphere of road safety. The fight against crime and ensuring road safety may constitute overriding reasons in the public interest capable of justifying a hindrance to the free movement of goods (see, with regard to road safety, Case C-54/05 *Commission v. Finland* [2007] ECR I-2473, paragraph 40).

However, it is for the Member States to show that their legislation is appropriate to ensure the attainment of such objectives and that it is in conformity with the principle of proportionality (see, to that effect, inter alia, Case C-297/05 *Commission v. Netherlands* [2007] ECR I-0000, paragraph 76).

In that regard, the Portuguese Republic has produced only one argument in support of the contested measure, namely, that it enables the passenger compartment of motor vehicles to be immediately inspected by means of simple observation from outside the vehicle.

Although the ban in Article 2(1) of Law No. 40/2003 does indeed appear to be likely to facilitate such inspection and, therefore, appropriate to attain the objectives of fighting crime and ensuring road safety, it does not follow that it is necessary to attain those objectives or that there are no other less restrictive means of doing so.

The visual inspection in question is only one means among others available to the competent authorities in order to fight crime and prevent offences relating to the obligation to wear seat belts.

The claim that the contested measure is necessary was further undermined when the Portuguese Republic admitted at the hearing that it allows the marketing on its territory of motor vehicles fitted from the outset with tinted windows within the limits laid down by Directive 92/22. Tinted windows, like the tinted film at issue, may prevent any external visual inspection of the interior of vehicles.

Therefore, unless it is accepted that, as regards motor vehicles fitted at the outset with tinted windows, the competent authorities have abandoned their campaign to fight crime and their efforts to enforce road safety, it is clear that they must use other methods to identify criminals and persons who may be breaking the rules concerning the wearing of seat belts.

Furthermore, the Portuguese Republic has not shown that the ban, in so far as it concerns all tinted film, is necessary to promote road safety and combat crime.

As stated by the Commission at the hearing, there is a wide range of tinted film, from transparent film to film which is almost opaque. That information, which was not challenged by the Portuguese Republic, means that at least some films, namely those with a sufficient degree of transparency, permit the desired visual inspection of the interior of motor vehicles.

It follows that that ban must be regarded as being excessive and, therefore, disproportionate with respect to the objectives pursued.

COSTS

Under Article 69(2) of the Rules of Procedure, the unsuccessful party is to be ordered to pay the costs if they have been applied for in the successful party's pleadings. Since the Commission has applied for costs and the Portuguese Republic has been unsuccessful, it must be ordered to pay the costs.

On those grounds, the Court (Third Chamber) hereby:

1. Declares that, by prohibiting in Article 2(1) of Decree-Law No 40/2003 of 11 March 2003 the affixing of tinted film to the windows of motor vehicles, the Portuguese Republic has failed to fulfill its obligations under Articles 28 EC and 30 EC; and
2. Orders the Portuguese Republic to pay the costs.

Decision and Comment. The court struck down Portugal's absolute prohibition upon the tinting of automobile windows after they have been released into the stream of commerce despite the absence of an EU law directly in contravention of the Portuguese law and the concerns regarding public safety and combatting crime.

Case Questions

1. What was the ECJ's holding with respect to Portugal's claims that the prohibition upon window tinting was in the interest of public safety and eradication of crime?
2. What was the basis for the ECJ's decision that Portugal's law constituted an obstacle to the free movement of goods?
3. How did the ECJ conclude that the prohibition on window tinting was an obstacle to the free movement of goods when the Portuguese law did not contravene a directly applicable EU law?

The Free Movement of Services

Services have long been recognized as an important part of EU economic activity. Services presently account for approximately 70 percent of all economic activity and employment in the EU. Free movement of services is thus of vital importance to the smooth operation of the internal market. Such free movement allows businesses to pursue continuous economic activities across national borders throughout the EU. Free movement also allows service providers in one member state to offer temporary services in other member states without having to be established already in these states.

The *Treaty of Rome* prohibits restrictions on the freedom to provide services within the EU with respect to nationals in one member state who provide services in another member state. Services are broadly defined to include any economic activity for remuneration not governed by treaty provisions relating to the free movement of goods, capital, and persons. This includes activities of an industrial or commercial character and activities of craftspeople and of the professions.

Prohibited restrictions on services include those which are directly discriminatory as well as those which are neutral on their face but have a negative impact on the free movement of services. Service providers in one member state offering their services across the border in another member state are entitled to the same treatment as domestic service providers in the same industry, trade, or profession. In the following case, the ECJ was requested to determine whether a licensing scheme for debt collectors imposed by the Italian government was inconsistent with the free movement of services.

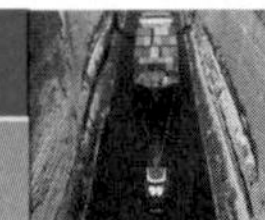

Commission of the European Communities v. Italian Republic

Case C-134/05 [2006] European Court of Justice

BACKGROUND AND FACTS

The EU sought a declaration that, because of the way in which long-standing Italian law permitted extrajudicial debt recovery by creditors against entities established in other member states, Italy had failed to fulfill its treaty obligations. The EU had not passed directly applicable legislation in the area of extrajudicial debt recovery. Italian law provided that, in order to recover debts extrajudicially, a creditor needed to obtain a license from the *Questore* (the local police authority). This license permitted action only in the Italian province where it was issued. Further, the Questore could place such conditions on the grant of a license as it thought appropriate. The license holder needed to display a list of all services provided and their cost on its business premises so that the Questore could confirm that prices for the services did not vary significantly. Further, license holders could not provide banking or credit services. Only banks and financial institutions listed with the ministry of the treasury could provide these services.

The Commission brought an action against Italy, as it considered these requirements to be in restraint of commerce among the member states. The Commission asked the Court of Justice to clarify the degree of discretion that member states retain vis-à-vis the European Commission in intermember state economic matters.

ADVOCATE GENERAL POIARES MADURO

By its application, the Commission once again asks the Court to clarify the margin of discretion available to the Member States in regulating the pursuit of an economic activity which has not yet been the subject of Community legislation. In that regard, it should be pointed out at the outset that, according to the case-law of the Court, "in the absence of harmonization of a profession, Member States remain, in principle, competent to define the exercise of that profession but must, when exercising their powers in this area, respect the basic freedoms guaranteed by the Treaty" … . It is true that the freedoms of movement, such as the rights to freedom of establishment and freedom to provide services, are not intended to liberalize national economies by precluding any legislation by the State which might affect economic and commercial freedom; if they were, they would sound the death knell for the powers of the Member States to legislate in economic matters. They do serve, however, to promote the decompartmentalisation of national markets by making it easier for operators to carry on their activity at a transnational level. To that end, they are intended to cover all transnational situations and to prohibit not only any direct or indirect discrimination on grounds of nationality introduced by the Member States, but also any national measure resulting in the treatment of transnational situations less favourably than purely national ones … . In other words, in accordance with the logic of the internal market, they serve to ensure that discrimination which obstructs the exercise of the freedom of movement will be challenged by legal action … . More specifically, the less favourable treatment of transnational situations which the principle of freedom of

continues

continued

movement prohibits may take different forms. It may, of course, be the effect of discrimination advantageous to its own nationals. It may also arise from a restriction on market access, be it that the national rules have the effect of protecting the positions acquired by economic operators established in the national market or that they make the pursuit of a transnational activity or trade between Member States more difficult.

It is in the light of this analytical framework that the relevance of the complaints raised by the Commission should be assessed. As the following analysis will make apparent, those complaints are well founded. This does not mean that a Member State cannot regulate the activity of extrajudicial debt recovery ... . However, the conditions which the Italian Republic has attached to the pursuit of that activity are far too restrictive of the freedom of establishment and the freedom to provide services.

A. THE REQUIREMENT OF A LICENCE AND THE ADDITIONAL CONDITIONS GOVERNING THE AWARD OF LICENCES

The Commission first calls into question the condition, which the Italian rules attach to pursuit of the activity of extrajudicial debt recovery, that prior administrative authorisation must be obtained from the local police authority... . [Insofar] as that requirement is also imposed on providers of services established in another Member State, without regard to whether they have complied with any obligations laid down by the rules of the country in which they are established... those rules infringe the freedom to provide services. This is particularly true given that the Italian rules give the Questore the power to impose requirements additional to those which they expressly lay down ... .

[I]t is common knowledge that, in keeping with the approach originally adopted with regard to the free movement of goods, the principle of the freedom to provide services has gradually come to be interpreted as prohibiting not only directly or indirectly discriminatory restrictions, but also obstacles applicable without distinction. In the light of the foregoing considerations, I therefore propose that the Court should uphold the complaint alleging that Article 49 EC has been infringed by virtue of the fact that the activity of extrajudicial debt recovery is made subject to the grant of a licence.

B. THE TERRITORIAL DELIMITATION OF THE LICENCE

The Commission takes the view that limiting the validity of the licence to the territory of the province in which the Questore that granted it has authority, unless an authorised representative is awarded a contract of agency to pursue the activity in a province for which the operator does not have a licence, constitutes an unjustified restriction on both the freedom to provide services and the freedom of establishment. Since Italy is divided into 103 provinces, that geographical delimitation of the scope of the licence indisputably constitutes a restriction on the exercise of those two fundamental freedoms. An operator who wishes to extend his business throughout much of Italy with a view to operating there on an occasional or stable and continuous basis must submit as many licence applications as there are provinces in the area which he intends to cover, and 103 applications if he intends to carry on his business throughout the Italian territory. Contrary to the Italian Government's submission, it is in this regard also irrelevant that the same requirement is imposed on operators established in Italy because, in any event, indistinctly applicable obstacles to the freedom of establishment are prohibited in the same way as those to the freedom to provide services.

It remains to be determined whether that restriction is appropriate and necessary on the legitimate public security grounds put forward by the defendant, namely to ward off the risk of infiltration by organised crime. In the defendant's view, it is, since the province is the most appropriate territorial level for assessing the impact on public order of the activities of an additional extrajudicial debt recovery operator and supervising existing operators. I am not persuaded by that defence. In my view, the limitation of the territorial scope of the licence is, first of all, an unjustified restriction on the freedom to provide services. If, as I suggested earlier, the general and absolute requirement of a licence infringes the principle of the freedom to provide services, then the same is particularly true of a system under which the number of applications for authorisation which a crossborder service provider must make increases with the size of the geographical area he wishes to cover in the host Member State. Moreover, the Court has already called into question the obligation on an architect to enrol on the professional register of each province in which he plans to provide his services, on the ground that such a delimitation of the territorial scope of registration "further complicates" the exercise of the freedom to provide services, which is already restricted by that obligation in itself.

I therefore propose that the Court should find that, by limiting the validity of the licence to the provincial jurisdiction of the police authority which granted it, and by requiring the operator to award a contract of agency

continues

continued

to an authorised representative in order to pursue his activity in a province for which he does not have a licence, the Italian Republic has failed to fulfil[l] its obligations under the principles of the freedom of establishment and the freedom to provide services.

C. MAKING PURSUIT OF THE ACTIVITY SUBJECT TO THE POSSESSION OF PREMISES BY THE OPERATOR

According to the Commission, the contested Italian rules show that there is an obligation to possess premises in which the debt recovery activity is to be carried out, which obligation applies to each province for which the operator has a licence. It argues that such a requirement infringes both the freedom of establishment and the freedom to provide services... . This obligation is therefore closely linked to limiting the validity of the authorisation to the territory of one province: the territorial limitation of the establishment makes it necessary to have multiple establishments. I have already set out the reasons why such a limitation of the geographical scope of the licence infringes the freedom of establishment... .

D. LIMITATION OF THE FREEDOM TO FIX SCALES OF CHARGES

The Commission also criticises the Italian Republic for having restricted the freedom of establishment and the freedom to provide services without justification by recommending... that the Questore control scales of charges by setting objective and uniform parameters, in order to ensure that the prices charged within a single province do not vary too greatly. I concur with the Commission's view that that recommendation must be regarded as a limitation of the freedom to fix scales of charges, in spite of the denial that that is the case by the Italian authorities, according to which that recommendation simply suggests that the Questore should provide operators with details of price lists based on objective factors (costs, the ratio of supply and demand in relation to services, etc.). However, the fact that those details are binding is apparent from the defendant's own admission that the development of excessive price competition could prompt the law enforcement authority to suspend or even revoke the licences of responsible operators.

Like the Commission, I consider that that limitation of the freedom to fix scales of charges is such as to hinder or make less attractive the exercise of the freedom of establishment and the freedom to provide services and therefore constitutes an obstacle to those two fundamental freedoms. Even if it is not discriminatory, it is such as to restrict access to the Italian market in activities concerned with extrajudicial debt recovery by operators wishing to establish themselves in Italy or provide their services in that State. As the Court made clear in CaixaBank France, price competition is often the best way of attracting customers and thus entering a market, in particular for operators who are not yet present in that market and are therefore unknown to customers. Accordingly, any national measure which has the effect of limiting it constitutes a restriction on the exercise of the right of establishment and the right to provide services... .

It is therefore appropriate to uphold the complaint alleging that Articles 43 EC and 49 EC have been infringed by the limitation of the freedom to fix scales of charges.

E. THE PROHIBITION ON THE PURSUIT OF DEBT RECOVERY ACTIVITIES CONCURRENTLY WITH THE PROVISION OF BANKING AND CREDIT SERVICES

Finally, the Commission alleges that the Italian Republic has infringed the freedom of establishment and the freedom to provide services, inasmuch as [Italian law] makes the activity of extrajudicial debt recovery incompatible with the banking and credit services... .]Insofar as that incompatibility has the effect of prohibiting banking operators from other Member States who are authorised, if they so wish, to pursue both lines of activity concurrently in their country of origin from pursuing debt recovery activities in Italy, it indisputably hinders their right to freedom of establishment and freedom to provide services.

I therefore propose that the Court should also uphold the complaint alleging that Articles 43 EC and 49 EC have been infringed by the incompatibility between the activity of debt recovery and banking and credit services.

Decision. The Advocate General proposed that the Court enter a judgment consistent with his opinion.

Case Questions

1. What was the recommendation to the ECJ with respect to the consistency of Italy's regulation of debt collectors with its obligation to ensure free movement of services?
2. What provisions of the Italian debt collection licensing scheme were deemed inconsistent with the free movement of services? How was each of these provisions inconsistent with free movement?
3. The opinion noted that the EU had not adopted rules with respect to the regulation of debt collectors. Nevertheless, the conclusion was that Italy's regulations were inconsistent with the free movement of services. Is this an example of the EU improperly interfering with an area of economic activity that should be left to national governments? Why or why not?

The Free Movement of Capital

The *Treaty of Rome* prohibits all restrictions on the movement of capital between member states. This includes a prohibition on restrictions on payments. Thus, capital may be freely transferred in any amount between member states. All such transfers are deemed domestic payments and can only be subjected to domestic transfer costs if any. Credit and debit card charging and withdrawals from automated teller machines within member states are also deemed domestic transactions. The EU has yet to achieve complete standardization on paper-based payment forms such as checks but is continuing its work on harmonization in this area.

Efforts to integrate the free flow of capital are best exemplified by two events. The first was the creation of the **European Central Bank.** Located in Frankfurt, Germany, and founded in 1998, the European Central Bank's mission is to "promote price stability" and "to define and implement the monetary policy of the euro zone, conduct foreign exchange operations, issue notes, and promote the smooth operation of payment systems." The European Central Bank is effectively in charge of monetary policy relating to the euro, the common currency within the majority of the EU member states.

There is considerable historical precedent for the euro, including common currencies that were utilized in the Roman Empire, the Holy Roman Empire, the Hanseatic League, the "Latin Monetary Unit" used during the reign of Napoleon III, and the Scandinavian Monetary Unit used from 1872 to 1914. One of the EU's founders, Jean Monnet, advocated creation of a single European currency in the late 1940s. At the time of the creation of European Coal and Steel Community, French economist Jacques Rueff stated, "Europe will become united through its money or not at all." However, despite these sentiments, early efforts at monetary union failed.

The euro resulted from the Delors Report drafted by a committee of appointed fiscal experts and released in April 1989. After years of legislative wrangling, the euro became fully effective in January 2002, when the national currencies of participating states were retired. They were replaced with 14.25 billion notes ($577 billion in circulation) and 50 billion coins with $15.4 billion in value.

Every state that wanted to utilize the euro was permitted to join the monetary union. However, a few states chose to retain their national currencies. Denmark opted out in 2001 and retained the kroner due to concerns about cuts to its generous health, pension, and education benefits. The United Kingdom opted out in 2003 because of high costs, slower economic growth in the EU, and national pride in the British pound. Sweden opted out in 2003 due to opposition to monetary centralization, faster economic growth, cultural differences, and high social spending. The states listed in Table 15.3 currently utilize the euro as their national currency and are part of the so-called **Eurozone.** The *Eurozone* encompasses more than 331 million people (66 percent of all people in the EU) and

Table 15.3 EUROZONE MEMBER STATES

STATE	DATE OF ADOPTION
Austria	January 1999
Belgium	January 1999
Cyprus	January 2008
Estonia	January 2011
Finland	January 1999
France	January 1999
Germany	January 1999
Greece	January 2001
Ireland	January 1999
Italy	January 1999
Luxembourg	January 1999
Malta	January 2008
Netherlands	January 1999
Portugal	January 1999
Slovakia	January 2009
Slovenia	January 2007
Spain	January 1999

has a gross domestic product of $12.4 trillion (more than 75 percent of the EU's gross domestic product). Other than Denmark and the United Kingdom, all other EU member states are required to eventually join the Eurozone.

The euro is revolutionary for many reasons. Monetary union has never been attempted on such a large scale—replacing so many successful currencies, serving millions of people and on a continent-wide basis. Several replaced currencies had long histories of successful use. For example, the Greek drachma was one of the world's oldest currencies, dating from the fifth century BC. The French franc was first minted in 1360, the Dutch guilder in the fourteenth century, and the Spanish peseta in 1497. The Italian lira was created in the sixteenth century and was used to pay Michelangelo and other Renaissance artists.

The euro was intended to create be a currency to challenge the U.S. dollar as the world's preferred reserve currency and standard unit of exchange in international transactions. The continued viability of the euro in light of the EU's ongoing financial crisis will be discussed later in this chapter. To its credit, the euro also eliminates the cost of currency conversion, specifically, $15 for every border crossing in Europe with an estimated annual cost of $10 billion. It also serves to integrate markets, makes comparison shopping easier, leads to price convergence throughout Europe, and eliminates exchange rate risk.

The Free Movement of People

The final freedom is the free movement of people. All EU residents have the right to travel, live, study, and work in another member state without being subject to nationality-based discrimination. Workers traveling within the EU are to be free from nationality-based discrimination with respect to employment, pay, and all other conditions of work. This freedom entails the rights to accept employment offers in other member states, travel to other member states to engage in such employment, and stay in another member state while performing such employment. This freedom of movement extends to close family members even if they are not citizens of an EU member state. Workers may remain in another member state after completing such employment if they choose to do so.

These rights are subject to limitations on the grounds of public policy, security, and health, and they do not apply to public employment. Additionally, EU citizens must not become an undue burden on their country of residence. Citizens of member states may reside in another member state for up to three months without being subject to any condition or formalities other than the requirement to hold a valid passport or identity card. After three months, such persons may be required to register with local government authorities. After five years, the right to residence is permanent without any preconditions.

Free movement of people has also resulted in the removal of border controls when traveling by land between 22 of the member states. Border controls remain in place in six states and, of course, for travelers entering from outside of the EU.

OTHER AREAS OF INTEGRATION: SOME EXAMPLES

It is important to note that the EU's efforts at harmonization and the removal of barriers to free movement of goods, services, capital, and people are comprehensive. These efforts cut across a wide range of industrial sectors, and they affect every business operating in the EU. Individuals residing in member states are also significantly affected by the EU's efforts at harmonization and removal of barriers—from the products they consume to the energy that they use and the environment in which they live. This next section summarizes developments in some of these areas with respect to industry and individuals.

The Common Agricultural Policy

The EU is committed to the establishment of a **common agricultural policy** (the **CAP**). First implemented in 1962, the CAP has been central to the EU's mission ever since. Its goals, which are set forth in Article 39 of the *Treaty of Rome,* are as follows:

1. to increase agricultural productivity
2. to ensure a fair standard of living for the agricultural community
3. to stabilize markets
4. to guarantee regular supplies
5. to ensure reasonable prices to consumers

The EU has implemented these objectives through the CAP, which ensures minimum prices to farmers, imposes import tariff barriers and quotas on agricultural products from nonmember states, and pays subsidies to farmers for cultivated land. The CAP effectively maintains European agricultural firms that otherwise would not be able to withstand competition from lower-cost producers from outside the EU and increases the cost of agricultural products. This does provide the EU with some ability to feed itself in the event of hostilities. However, there is a difference of view between those who benefit from these policies and those who pay for them as to how much protection the EU should provide.

The CAP has been divisive within the EU for many reasons. First, the CAP is extremely expensive. The CAP has traditionally been the largest single item of EU expenditure and accounted for more than 30 percent of the EU's total budget in 2013 (down from 48 percent in 2006). The CAP also involves considerable administrative expenses, which have been subject to allegations of mismanagement and fraud. It has been contended that the primary beneficiaries of the program are not small family farms but rather large producers and agribusinesses that have reaped considerable financial windfalls. Program costs and administrative expenses have been passed on the consumers in the form of artificially high food prices. The CAP is alleged to have contributed to overproduction of certain products (such as cereals, dairy, and alcohol). The production encouraged by the CAP has been criticized as damaging to the environment and contributing to unhealthy diets within the EU. The CAP has also contributed to inequities within the EU as member states with larger agricultural sectors, such as Portugal, Spain, and France (the largest recipient of CAP funds), receive large amounts of money at the expense of states with smaller agricultural sectors. Finally, the CAP has limited the ability of lesser-developed states to increase their earnings through agricultural exports to the EU. The EU has attempted to address some of these concerns in recent years, and additional revisions to the CAP will coincide with the new EU budget starting in 2014. It is expected that the revisions to the CAP will focus on decreasing direct payments and ensuring viable food production and sustainable use of natural resources and promoting balanced territorial development within the EU.

The EU's response to the concern about bovine spongiform encephalopathy (BSE)—more commonly known as mad cow disease—emanating from the United Kingdom illustrates some of the problems with the implementation of the single market in the agricultural context. In 1996, the Commission banned exports of beef and other meat products from the United Kingdom because of concerns about BSE. In 1998, the ban was lifted but not all countries felt comfortable about British meat exports. France continued to balk at compliance with the court decision in the *National Farmers' Union* case.

National Farmers' Union and Secrétariat

Général du gouvernement (France) C-241/01 [2002] European Court of Justice

BACKGROUND AND FACTS

Following the discovery of a probable link between a variant of Creutzfeldt–Jakob disease, a disease affecting human beings, and bovine spongiform encephalopathy (BSE), which was widespread in the United Kingdom in the mid-1990s, the Commission adopted *Decision 96/239/EC* of 27 March 1996, which contained emergency measures to protect against BSE. This decision prohibited the United Kingdom from exporting certain products, in particular live bovine animals, meat of bovine animals, and products obtained from bovine animals, from its territory to the other member states and third countries.

Article 14 The Commission shall carry out Community inspections on-the-spot in the United Kingdom to verify the application of the provisions of this decision, in particular in relation to the implementation of official controls.

Article 15 The United Kingdom shall send the Commission every month a report on the application of the protective measures taken against BSE, in accordance with national and Community provisions. By its third question, the national court seeks to ascertain whether a Member State is justified in invoking Article 30 EC in order to prohibit imports of agricultural products and live animals, inasmuch as *Directives 89/662 and 90/425* cannot be regarded as harmonising the measures needed in order to attain the specific objective of protecting the health and life of humans provided for by that article.

FINDINGS OF THE COURT

According to settled case-law, where Community directives provide for the harmonisation of the measures necessary to ensure the protection of animal and

continues

continued

human health and establish Community procedures to check that they are observed, recourse to Article 30 EC is no longer justified and the appropriate checks must be carried out and the measures of protection adopted within the framework outlined by the harmonizing directive.

* * *

The Court has also held that even where a directive does not lay down any Community procedure for monitoring compliance or any penalties in the event of breach of its provisions, a Member State may not unilaterally adopt, on its own authority, corrective or protective measures designed to obviate any breach by another Member State of rules of Community law … .

It should indeed be made clear that in the European Community, which is a community based on law, a Member State is bound to comply with the provisions of the Treaty and, in particular, to act within the framework of the procedures provided for by the Treaty and by the applicable legislation.

It is in the light of those various factors that it is necessary to determine whether the French Government was able, at the date of the implicit decisions at issue in the main proceedings, to invoke Article 30 EC in order to maintain the prohibition on imports of beef and veal from the United Kingdom.

Although Regulation No 999/2001 no doubt achieved full harmonisation of the rules relating to the prevention, control and eradication of certain transmissible spongiform encephalopathies, it should be noted, as has the Advocate General in points 91 to 94 of his Opinion, that *Decisions 98/256 and 98/692*, defining the DBES, laid down the rules necessary for the protection of public health upon the resumption of exports of beef and veal from the United Kingdom to the other Member States.

Those decisions, which are additional to the general legislation already in existence, specify the requirements of eligibility and traceability of animals liable to be used under the DBES, the requirements to be satisfied by slaughterhouses and the conditions specific to the cutting of meat, which are imposed as a supplement to the provisions in force relating to the withdrawal of specific offal.

Moreover, Article 14 of *Decision 98/256* as amended provides that Community inspections must be carried out by the Commission in the United Kingdom to verify the application of the provisions of that decision, while Article 15 thereof provides for the United Kingdom to send to the Commission every month a report on the application of the protective measures taken against BSE.

As regards the obligations of the Member States other than the United Kingdom, Article 17 of *Decision 98/256* as amended provides that they are to adopt the necessary measures to comply with that decision and are immediately to inform the Commission thereof.

Furthermore, as was stated in paragraph 38 of this judgment, Article 16 of *Decision 98/256* as amended specifies that that decision must be reviewed regularly in the light of new scientific information and that any amendments are to be made in accordance with the procedure laid down in Article 18 of *Directive 89/662.*

Examination of these various provisions show that, in addition to the harmonisation of the measures necessary to ensure the protection of human health. *Decision 98/256* as amended lays down procedures for monitoring compliance with it and specifies, by reference to *Directive 89/662,* the appropriate procedure for making the amendments which might be made essential by the development of scientific knowledge.

As regards the emergency measures liable to be taken by a Member State in the event of a serious hazard to human health, it is important to note that Decision 98/256 was adopted on the basis of *Directives 89/662 and 90/425,* and *Decision 98/692* on the basis of *Directive 89/662* alone.

Directive 89/662 describes, in Article 7, 8 and 9, the measures which may be adopted by a Member State of destination, in particular where its competent authorities establish that the goods imported do not meet the conditions laid down by Community legislation. Article 7 authorises the destruction or return of those goods and Article 9 authorises in particular the adoption, by that Member State, of interim protective measures on serious public-health or animal-health grounds.

It is in accordance with those provisions, which require the measures adopted to be notified without delay to the other Member States and to the Commission and close to collaboration between the Member States and the Commission, that a Member State must act when faced with a situation endangering the health of its population … .

It is moreover the application of the interim protective measures referred to in Article 9 of *Directive 89/662* which is envisaged by the 13th recital in the preamble to *Decision 98/692* in the event that it is discovered, after the dispatch of products which were believed to fulfil the conditions of the DBES, that those products came from an animal subsequently found to be ineligible under that scheme.

Examination of all these provisions shows that the existing legislation and, in particular, *Directive 89/662* and *Decisions 98/256 and 98/692* provide for the harmonisation necessary to ensure the protection of public health upon the resumption of exports of beef

continues

continued

and veal from the United Kingdom to the other Member States and lay down Community procedures to monitor compliance with them.

It is true that, in paragraph 134 of *Commission v. France,* cited above, the Court noted that there were difficulties in interpreting *Decision 98/256* as amended in respect of the Member States' obligations relating to the traceability of products. Suffice it to state, however, that, as paragraph 135 of that judgment shows, those difficulties of interpretation had disappeared by the date of the implicit decisions refusing to lift the ban at issue in the main proceedings.

As regards products subject to the *DBES* which have been cut, processed or rewrapped in another Member State and subsequently exported to France without the affixing of a distinct mark, suffice it to state that the main proceedings do not concern such products and that, in any event, the French Government has never prevented their importation.

It follows from all the foregoing that, since *Directive 89/662* and *Decision 98/256* as amended lay down the rules necessary for the protection of public health upon the resumption of exports of beef and veal from the United Kingdom to the other Member States, lay down a Community procedure to monitor compliance with that decision and a procedure for amending it in the light of new scientific information and provide the appropriate legal framework for the adoption of interim protective measures by a Member State of destination for the purpose of protecting public health, a Member State is not entitled to invoke Article 30 EC in order to prevent the resumption of imports to its territory of beef and veal from the United Kingdom which were carried out in accordance with *Decisions 98/256* as amended and *1999/514.*

Decision and Comment. The UK was allowed to ship beef and veal outside the country. France finally complied in the face of heavy fines.

Case Questions

1. What was the ECJ's holding with respect to continued French prohibitions on the importation of British beef and veal?
2. Does the decision give adequate regard to France's concerns about the safety of British meat products or does it sacrifice such concerns in the interest of eliminating a barrier to the free movement of goods? What are the reasons for your conclusion?

Consumer Protection

Consumer protection is an important aspect of EU legislation in all relevant policy areas. As the free movement of goods and services as well as the common currency have opened borders and use of the Internet and electronic commerce have expanded, the need for adequate consumer protection has increased. The EU has adopted numerous measures to safeguard consumer interests with respect to fair business practices, misleading and comparative advertising, labeling, and a host of products including toys, electrical appliances, cosmetics, pharmaceutical products, and machinery. In January 2004, the EU adopted stricter rules on the recall of dangerous products with specific concentration on toys, electrical appliances, and lighting equipment. The rules also set safety standards across the EU for numerous consumer products including sports equipment, childcare articles, gas appliances, textiles, and household furniture. In December 2007, the EU adopted rules strengthening the ban on misleading advertising and prohibiting coercive and harassing sales practices. Efforts to reach agreement on EU-wide rules relating to online business practices and consumer credit and other non-cash means of payment are being considered.

Energy and the Environment

EU energy policy is based on a number of concerns. There is a recognized need to develop alternative sources of energy in order to lessen dependence on foreign sources of energy, which is currently at 50 percent. The reduction of dependence on foreign sources of energy also requires increasing energy efficiency. The EU has undertaken numerous efforts to increase energy efficiency at the macroeconomic level as well as informing consumers of the energy usage of household items. Consumer products sold in the EU now carry energy efficiency ratings and consumption statistics. In July 2007, EU households were free to pick gas and electricity suppliers of their choice and were no longer required to bundle such services through one supplier.

EU environmental legislation is far too comprehensive and detailed for adequate discussion here. However, it bears to note that in December 2008, the EU approved a comprehensive set of emissions standards designed to reduce greenhouse gases by 20 percent by 2020. This plan also mandated raising the market share of renewable energy sources to 20 percent and cutting overall energy consumption by a corresponding 20 percent. Renewed efforts were also initiated with respect to the use of biofuels, electricity, and hydrogen with the goal of 10 percent of fuel for transport coming from these sources by 2020.

The Business Implications of the European Union

The main object of the EU is to make it easier to do business within Europe. The elimination of intra-EU tariffs means that, once a product enters the EU, an enterprise need not concern itself further with customs duties. Harmonization of laws and standardization of equipment means that companies can manufacture the same product for the entire European market, creating significant economies of scale and streamlining regulatory compliance costs. Companies can centralize or regionalize corporate offices and distribution centers rather than have a separate office for each country. Firms must still comply with separate national laws, particularly those that regulate health and advertising. However, because such laws must increasingly comply with EU directives, they are less of a hindrance to intermember state commerce. The EU seems relentless in its efforts to impose its economic will on the member states.

These commercial unification developments particularly benefit competitive European businesses that have a larger duty-free market. They harm marginal European businesses that owe their survival to trade barriers against competition from other member states. Economic theory suggests that ultimately, as more efficient and qualified firms vanquish corporate deadwood, the majority of Europeans will benefit. These developments also benefit competitive firms from non-EU countries. While non-EU concerns must still confront the hurdle of EU tariffs and quotas, once they surmount that barrier, the customs union gives them the same advantages as entities in member states. The dynamic of free internal trade was largely responsible for the economic success of the United States. Today, it appears to be having a similar effect within the EU.

In many areas, the EU is the principal government regulator. This is particularly true in competition law, where Directorate-General IV has long exercised ultimate authority. In 2007, Sun Microsystems succeeded in compelling Microsoft Corporation to modify its licensing practices by enlisting the assistance of the Commission. Thus, an American company was able to obtain relief from the practices of another American company that it could not obtain in the United States because both companies had substantial European operations. If a company is in Europe, it is under the jurisdiction of the EU, whose policies can be quite different from those of its home country.

The EU's treaty-making powers also have a direct effect on businesses from nonmember states. Article 133 of the *Treaty of Rome* gives the EU the exclusive power to conclude trade and tariff agreements with other nations, a necessary precondition to a customs union. Thus, if the EU decides that it needs to protect a particular European industry from nonmember state competition, nonmember state firms will be directly and adversely affected by EU action. In 2007, it was the EU, and not any single member state, that negotiated with China over possible tariffs on Chinese products, which it wished to impose in retaliation for the artificially low exchange rate of the yuan. In recent years, the EU negotiated with the United States and litigated against it in the WTO with respect to bananas, commercial aircraft, beef hormones, and information technology products. The businessperson from a nonmember state must recognize that in modern Europe, the commercial side of foreign policy is largely in the hands of the EU.

THE EUROPEAN ECONOMIC INTEGRATION MODEL AND THE FINANCIAL CRISIS

The financial crisis currently confronting the EU is complex, multifaceted and beyond detailed discussion in this book. The following section discusses some aspects of the financial crisis with a focus on the most severely impacted states, the EU's response and the future of the euro. Predictions regarding the outcome of the crisis are uncertain at best given its ever-changing nature. Undoubtedly, circumstances will change over time, and readers will need to update themselves as events warrant.

The Financial Crisis in Specific States

The financial crisis in the EU was the result of a convergence of many different factors, including the liberal extension of credit, high-risk lending practices, the global recession starting in 2008, and the collapse of real estate markets in some Eurozone states. There were other factors as well that undoubtedly contributed to the crisis, including unsustainable levels of sovereign debt in some Eurozone states, the inability or lack of willingness to address financial problems within these states, and an underestimation of the magnitude of the crisis which in turn delayed an effective coordinated response.

The EU itself is also to blame. As previously discussed, the EU created a continental currency without also creating a strong central financial authority. The European Central Bank is significantly limited in its powers with respect to the national budgets and financial affairs of the Eurozone members. The EU was and remains hampered in responding to the crisis due to the absence of full integration of European banking and fiscal management and the continuing responsibility for national budgetary policy at the member state level.

The causes, impacts and responses to the financial crisis vary widely within the Eurozone members. The following discussion will focus on Greece and Spain, two Eurozone members that have been severely impacted by the financial crisis. It must be remembered while reviewing this section that many of the issues that have received widespread attention in Greece and Spain are also present in other Eurozone states. For example, the bursting of the real estate bubble that helped fuel the crisis in Spain was also a significant factor in the crisis as it developed in Ireland. Excessive government debt, which has been a hallmark of the crisis in Greece, was a factor in the worsening of the crisis in Portugal.

It can be concluded from this discussion that there is no one cause of the financial issues currently plaguing the Eurozone and thus no one solution. The other conclusion is that no member of the Eurozone is immune—the crisis has proven contagious and has spread to other member states such as Cyprus, Ireland, Italy, Portugal, and Romania. Even those member states with the strongest economies, most importantly, Germany, have experienced the fallout of the crisis. For better or worse, the fates of the strongest and weakest economies within the Eurozone are inextricably linked to one another.

Greece. The Greek economy was characterized by rapid growth in the first half of 2000s. Its budgetary deficit was also one of the largest in the Eurozone. These deficits increased substantially as the Greek government attempted to prop up the economy after the impact of the global recession in 2008. The size of the country's debt required it to seek loans from the EU, the European Central Bank, and international financial institutions such as the International Monetary Fund. These loans and other bailouts are expected to total more than € 245 billion by 2016.

The financial bailout package the EU offered to Greece came with significant strings attached. The primary string was the imposition of austerity measures to reduce the budget deficit and return the country to a level of fiscal health close to that required by the criteria for admission to the Eurozone. These austerity measures had the side effect of contributing to the worsening of the recession. Greece's gross domestic product declined by almost 7 percent in 2011, and industrial output was more than 28 percent lower than it had been at the height of Greek prosperity in 2005. More than 100,000 businesses closed, and unemployment skyrocketed to more than 26 percent at the end of 2012. The unemployment rate among young adults was estimated at more than 50 percent during this period of time. As a result, massive street protests became commonplace throughout the country.

There was considerable discussion in 2012 of negotiating a structured default for Greece whereby it would be permitted to exit the Eurozone and reinstate its former national currency, the drachma, at a debased rate. This option did not gain traction primarily due to concerns about its impact upon the financial health of institutions holding Greek sovereign debt denominated in euros and the impact on the Greek economy. For example, a return to the drachma, even in a structured manner, would severely affect Greece's gross domestic product, create the potential for hyperinflation, and plunge an already reeling Greek political system and distressed citizenry into severe crisis. The approach taken to date consists of continued financial bailout packages, related domestic austerity measures and hope that the situation improves as the EU and world economies emerge from the recession.

Spain. The cause of the financial crisis in Spain differs from that in Greece. The Spanish crisis was not the initial product of excessive government debt but rather was fueled by the collapse of the residential real estate market (which had seen prices rise by 200 percent from the mid-1990s), a growing trade deficit, rising inflation, and the advent of the global recession. The collapse caused the Spanish government to spend billions of euros in bank bailouts which in turn substantially increased the fiscal deficit and debt. These increases were a primary factor in the downgrading of the country's credit rating.

Unlike Greece, the Spanish government did not wait for the imposition of austerity measures by potential financial rescuers. Rather, the government introduced voluntary austerity measures starting in 2011 designed to rebuild trust in financial markets and within the EU. However, in a manner similar to Greece, these austerity measures deepened the recession. Unemployment has been of particular concern in Spain. The unemployment rate was more than 24 percent by the end of 2012, and unemployment for those under the age of 25 years was 50 percent.

Unlike Greece and other states negatively impacted by the financial crisis, there has been less discussion of Spain exiting the Eurozone. This is due to the size of the Spanish economy which is larger than Greece, Ireland, and Portugal combined. If a Greek exit from the Eurozone would be ruinous, a Spanish exit would be catastrophic. As a result, Spain received an economic bailout for recapitalization of the financial sector primarily from European sources totaling up to € 100 billion in 2012. The Spanish government was negotiating a further bailout package with the International Monetary Fund at the time of preparation of this book. It remains to be seen if a combination of financial assistance, self-imposed and mandated austerity measures, and a recovering global economy will be sufficient to return Spain to some degree of economic normalcy.

The EU's Response to the Financial Crisis

The EU's response to the financial crisis has been as complex and multifaceted as the crisis itself. There are two responses in particular worthy of separate mention in addition to the responses discussed above with respect to Greece and Spain (and financial assistance packages to other adversely affected states). In September 2012, the Eurozone states launched the **European Stability Mechanism (ESM)**. The ESM is a permanent funding program for the rescue of states undergoing financial crisis. The ESM is designed to prevent financial contagion within the Eurozone by containing such crises within the borders of an affected state. The containment of such crises is to occur through guarantees of all or a portion of the debts of an affected state.

A second notable response to the crisis is the creation of the **European Fiscal Compact (EFC)**. The EFC became effective on January 1, 2013 after its ratification by 12 of the 17 Eurozone members. The EFC requires that ratifying states adopt laws within one year of ratification requiring their national budgets be in balance or in a surplus. The EFC defines the term *balanced budget* to mean a general budget deficit of less than 3 percent of gross domestic product. Structural deficits of no more than 1 percent of gross domestic product are also permissible. States not in compliance with these limitations will be required to correct the issue within designated timeframes. Ratifying states that are not in compliance at the time that the EFC entered force and effect will be provided with a state-specific "adjustment path" for eventually achieving compliance. States failing to implement the EFC within one year of ratification may be subject to a compliance action brought in the European Court of Justice at the request of another ratifying state. The EFC also provides for financial penalties for failure to adequately implement its provisions.

The Future of the Euro

The future of the euro in light of the financial crisis remains difficult to predict. Some commentators have suggested that one or more of the most significantly affected states voluntarily leave the Eurozone and return to their former national currencies. As previously mentioned with respect to Greece, this proposal would most likely prove disastrous for creditors, exiting states, and their citizens alike. The political and reputational damage to the EU, should such withdrawals occur, are equally serious and would be difficult, if not impossible, to calculate. Other commentators have discussed the possibility of withdrawal from the Eurozone by economically healthy states (primarily Germany) thereby preserving German fiscal strength, which could in turn be utilized to provide an economic boost to the EU through reintroduction of the deutsche mark. All of these options seem unlikely given the repeated commitments to the euro expressed by national leaders within the Eurozone member states and by representatives of the European Central Bank and enormous efforts and funds that have been committed to preserving the euro and the Eurozone.

It is much more likely that the efforts to forge closer economic ties among the peoples of Europe as expressed most forcefully in the euro will continue for the foreseeable future. Eurozone members will undoubtedly monitor the EFC to determine its effectiveness as well as proceed with establishment of the ESM to address future financial problems. It is unlikely that the current crisis will result in the creation of an EU treasury department empowered to make financial decisions at the regional, national, and continental levels. However, it can be safely predicted that greater integration of the banking and financial sectors and budgetary processes will emerge from this most recent and serious threat to the EU in its history.

CONCLUSION

The development of integrated trade areas reflects an increasing recognition of the accepted economic principle that free trade maximizes benefits to the whole by allowing each country to specialize in its areas of relative competitive advantage. The United States is a successful model of such an effort. Until recently, the EU was also demonstrating the advantages of economic integration. The current challenges facing the EU have severely tested its ability to maintain its current structure let alone move forward with its vision of greater integration and harmonization. In reaction to the EU and NAFTA, other countries have been stimulated to consider cooperative efforts to reduce trade barriers. In every context where free trade has been allowed to proceed, the economic fortunes of the populations have improved. The message is unmistakable: Free trade—or at least enhanced economic cooperation—is the most prosperous path forward.

Chapter Summary

1. The European Union (EU) started as a concept that represented three "communities," each created and operating under a separate treaty: the European Community, formerly known as the European Economic Community; the European Coal and Steel Community; and the European Atomic Energy Community. Today, the EU is a fully integrated single entity.
2. The EU consists of numerous institutions. These institutions include the Council of Ministers of the European Union, the European Council, the Commission, and the Parliament. Broadly speaking, these institutions are responsible for proposing and adopting legislation, enforcing such legislation and the EU treaties against encroachment, attempting to further harmonize national legal and regulatory regimes within the individual member states, and representing the EU to the rest of the world.
3. The Court of Justice and the General Court hold the judicial power of the European Union. The Court of Justice is comprised of one judge from each member state. The judges are appointed by the member states for a renewable term of six years. In cases involving private parties, it generally hears appeals of judgments from the General Court, which is the trial court of the EU.
4. Substantive law in the EU consists of many different types of legislation. Regulations have general application and are binding on the member states without further action. Directives are binding as to the result to be achieved but leave to each member state the means by which they are to be implemented. Decisions are binding on the parties to whom they are addressed. Recommendations are nonbinding statements of policy.
5. The hallmark of EU regulation is the free movement of goods, services, capital, and people, the so-called Four Freedoms. Measures by member states that place limitations on these freedoms or directly or indirectly discriminate on the basis of national origin are not tolerated and may be subject to nullification by the ECJ.

Key Terms

European Union 407
qualified majority voting 408
acquis communautaire 410
EU regulation 414
EU directive 414
Four Freedoms 415
common agricultural policy (CAP) 424

Questions and Case Problems

1. Rewe, a limited liability company with an office in Germany, imported goods from the EU countries. In 1976, Rewe applied to a German agency for permission to import Cassis de Dijon. The agency responded that spirits needed to contain 32 percent alcohol to be marketed in Germany. (The only exception to this rule was beer.) Cassis had only 15–20 percent spirit content, so it could not be imported. The German court referred the case to the ECJ to deal with conflicts between German law and Articles 30 and 37 of the *Treaty of Rome*. The German government argued that it was trying to protect public health and consumers. How did the court rule? Why? Did this settle the issue for the future? See *Rewe-Zentral [Cassis de Dijon]*, C-120/78 [1979].
2. Italy required chocolate products manufactured in other member states that contained vegetable fats other than cocoa butter to be sold in Italy as "chocolate substitutes." The Commission claimed that Italy had failed to fulfil its obligation under Article 30 of the EC treaty and *Council Directive 73/241/ EEC* of July 24, 1973, which permitted the use of vegetable fats other than cocoa butter in chocolate products. The Commission stated that chocolate containing vegetable fats other than cocoa butter up to a maximum of 5 percent of the total weight of the product is manufactured under the name "chocolate" in six member states (Denmark, Ireland, Portugal, Sweden, Finland, and the United Kingdom) and that it is accepted under that name in all member states with the exception of Spain and Italy. The Commission considered that it was not possible to claim that the addition of vegetable fats other than cocoa butter to a chocolate product that contains the minimum contents required under *Directive 73/241* substantially changed the nature of the product to the point where the use of the name "chocolate" would create confusion as regards its basic characteristics. However, the Italian government refused to change its interpretation of the Directive or the Italian law. What should be the ECJ's holding in this case? Based upon its decision, are the member states required to harmonize their product descriptions regardless of differences between their populations? Why or why not? See *Commission of the European Communities v. Italian Republic*, 14/00 [2003].
3. How does the EU's approach to GMOs differ from that of the United States? How does this affect international business? Find some current articles or cases that address the controversy. What role does the WTO play? How interrelated are other trade disputes?
4. May Germany require waste that is shipped to another member state to be disposed of according to Germany's environmental protection laws? See *Daimler Chrysler AG v. Land Baden—Wurttemberg*, C-324/99 [2001]. What impact does this ruling have on business? Does the result suggest a need for more EU standards? Why or why not?
5. How do a directive, a regulation, and a recommendation differ? Why would the EU choose one over the other? Give examples. What impact does this decision have on businesses?
6. The financial crisis in the Eurozone has led to considerable debate about the future of not only the euro but also the EU. What is your prediction regarding the future of the euro? What is your prediction regarding the future of the EU?

Managerial Implications

1. Your company has an office in Spain. You have hired a worker, Ms. Jimenez, for a float term and have renewed her contract twice. Shortly after renewing it for the second time, you discover that she will be giving birth within three months. You send her a notice stating that she is terminated effective in one month (which is two months before her due date). You believe that since she was only on a limited-term contract she cannot expect to be treated like a more permanent employee and given all maternity benefits. Are there any legal concerns here? What impact might this decision have on the advancement of women in employment? How will this affect your hiring practices?
2. Your company is expanding into Europe. You must pick a location for your office and have two locations to consider.
   a. How will you make this decision?
   b. Will whether the country has adopted the euro have an impact on your decision?
   c. Would you be discouraged from locating to a country that has had a poor record of implementing EU directives?

d. Would you consider locating an office in one of the countries that plans to join but has not done so yet?

3. Labco is a small manufacturing company that wants to do more exporting to the EU. They discover that the Commission is considering a directive that might limit their ability to do business in those countries.
   a. What can they do? The president of the company has asked you to research this matter and outline a plan of action.
   b. What difference does it make if Labco is a very large, publicly traded corporation?
   c. What are your options if the EU implements a directive or regulation that you believe discriminates against you as a foreign business?
4. Imagine that you are a student intern and will be spending this semester on assignment to the vice president of international sales at a toy firm. Up until now, the firm's primary markets have been in the United States and Canada. The toys are designed in the United States and manufactured by vendor firms in China. At a meeting with the vice president's design and marketing staff, he asks about opening new markets in Europe. He explains that in the United States, the design and sale of children's toys are highly regulated by the U.S. Consumer Products Safety Commission. Indeed, some other companies have had their toys removed from store shelves for noncompliance with federal regulations. He feels there must be some consumer safety regulations in effect in Europe that will act as a barrier to his firm's access to European markets. After all, if the regulations are very different from those in the United States, it may be costly to redesign the toys to comply with European standards. After the meeting, the vice president asks you to find answers to the following questions:
   a. Are there any standards or technical regulations in effect in Europe that govern the sale of toys? Where can he locate the regulations on the design, manufacture, and marketing of children's toys in Europe? Can you give a specific Web address so he can look at them himself?
   b. Do the toys have to meet different requirements in every European country, or is there a single standard that covers all of Europe?
   c. To which toys do the standards apply, and what toys, if any, are exempt?
   d. What are the design and manufacturing standards for toys covered by the regulations, and what is the standard for safety? Are there any specific provisions covering the toys' physical or mechanical properties?
   e. Do the toys have to be tested in advance for compliance with safety regulations?
   f. What are the toy labeling requirements? Is there a certain label or mark that will let consumers know that the toy has been tested for safety?

Ethical Considerations

Despite its relative success in building a common market for European goods, services, and capital, the EU faces many difficult challenges in the coming years. Concerns include the growing bureaucracy necessary to govern the EU, divergence on foreign policy with some states taking a more pro-U.S. approach to international affairs, and increasing cultural and social diversity. Many of the challenges confronting the EU are economic. The financial meltdown in some member states and its effect across the continent is only one of many challenges confronting the EU.

These concerns also raise the issue of the extent to which the interests of citizens of member states are best served by the present state of integration and possible closer integration in the future. Citizens of wealthier states have justifiable concerns about subsidizing poorer states and the fact that these wealthier states receive less money from the EU than they contribute. Smaller states worry that they will be overpowered in the EU's institutions by larger, more populous states. Less developed states may also be concerned about dominance of important areas such as media and technological innovation by more developed states such as France, Germany, Italy, and the United Kingdom. States with liberal social policies may be concerned that such policies will come under attack by states with more conservative social views. Conversely, more conservative states may be concerned that socially liberal policies will be imposed on them.

Citizens of all member states worry about the surrender of sovereignty to "Eurocrats" in Brussels and resultant loss of concern about local issues. In particular, the EU has been criticized in the past for a "democratic deficit." This deficit arises from the fact that the EU's institutions (other than the Parliament) are not directly elected by European citizens. Furthermore, the operations of these institutions are so complex as to be inaccessible to ordinary citizens. The *Treaty of Lisbon* was, in part, an effort to address these concerns primarily through the expansion of the role of the Parliament in the EU's governance structure.

Utilitarianism focuses on whether a given action adds to the overall utility of the community. Ethical conduct is that which is likely to produce the greatest overall good not just for the decider but for all persons who will be affected by the decision. Based on the above-referenced concerns, is the current state of integration in Europe consistent with principles of utilitarianism? Is greater integration, which may occur in the future, consistent with the greatest overall good of European citizens? Is the success of greater economic integration an adequate measure of the utilitarian nature of the EU? Who should determine the course of future integration in the EU—its citizens or the institutions? What local concerns and individual well being of European citizens are sacrificed as a result of the current state of integration? What local concerns and individual well being of European citizens will be sacrificed as a result of greater future integration? Are such individual and national sacrifices worth the price of greater European prosperity and global influence? Why or why not?

PART 4
Regulation of the International Marketplace

The issues addressed in Parts Two and Three of this text apply to any enterprise wishing to export its goods to another country, even if the enterprise does not have operations in that country. Part Two considered international commercial law, which creates a reliable framework to assure exporters and importers in different parts of the world that they will receive money for goods and services. International trade law, discussed in Part Three, involves the framework of barriers and openings to trade among nations. In Part Four, the focus turns to the legal complications that arise when a business actually moves a portion of its enterprise or employs an agent in another country.

Many business factors may prompt a business to take this step. First, most businesses—from Madagascar to Minnesota—find that they sell more goods if they employ a local sales representative. A business that wishes to promote sales abroad will hold a greater advantage if it retains the services of an individual abroad to promote sales. If such retention proves successful, the business may then wish to establish an office in that country. Indeed, the business might eventually generate greater profits from making its product abroad and selling it there—or even exporting it back into the United States.

When a business first establishes a presence abroad, it becomes subject to regulation by the foreign country being "penetrated" and, if it is a U.S. company, to a series of U.S. laws that apply to such "penetrators." As the presence in such a foreign "host country" progresses from a local office through a manufacturing plant, the level of host-country regulations becomes more intense. For instance, a U.S. company that builds a factory in a foreign nation may become subject to national and provincial norms, such as labor, environmental, and/or tax laws; technology transfer laws; laws governing the appropriate level of foreign ownership of businesses; and laws governing the repatriation of profits to the United States. In addition, the company may encounter possible nationalization by the foreign country, the U.S. *Foreign Corrupt Practices Act* or similar legislation in other nations, and a plethora of U.S. and foreign country antitrust laws.

Part Four treats that immense body of law in a general, thematic way—as the great diversity of local laws governing investment demands. In contrast to international commercial law—in which great consistency has developed over millions of commercial transactions—and to trade law—in which substantial harmonization has emerged through WTO—laws governing foreign investment are peculiarly reflective of local culture and attitudes. Like culture, these laws vary widely among the world's more than 200 nations. Further, these laws—like the attitudes they reflect—are constantly evolving. Many countries, including the United States, have fluctuated from the extreme of being aggressively hostile to foreign investment, to a friendlier attitude, and back to hostility yet again.

The position of a country at any given time on this spectrum depends on mercurial international and domestic political conditions. For instance, from the 1950s through the mid-1970s, many developing countries grew progressively more antagonistic toward foreign investment, reflecting emerging national self-esteem and wariness of former colonial masters. But when anti–foreign investment laws caused those economies to run out of capital resources in the late 1970s and early 1980s, many of the governments reversed course and passed more investment-friendly laws. In the twenty-first century, the pendulum has swung back in many nations to economic nationalism, as recessionary forces and a new populism have impaired Latin economies and revived suspicions of foreigners.

No one can possibly predict precisely what foreign investment laws will be in force tomorrow. However, one can identify different approaches that nations have taken in regulating foreign business penetration. A working knowledge of these approaches provides a framework that a business can employ to analyze different aspects of the legal environment in the country in which it is considering investment.

Part Four begins at the least intrusive—and therefore least regulated—foreign presence and moves through increasingly substantial and regulated forms of establishment. Chapter Sixteen reviews issues that arise once the enterprise retains an agent or a representative abroad. Such retention triggers the host country's requirements for *agency relationships,* as well as its laws relating to advertising and marketing. It also brings into play one of the principal concerns of U.S. business abroad, the U.S. *Foreign Corrupt Practices Act*.

Chapter Seventeen reviews licensing and other arrangements through which a U.S. enterprise is paid for permitting a foreign entity to use its intellectual property. Many host countries closely regulate these arrangements because they wish to capture the intellectual property for their own nationals.

Chapter Eighteen considers the political risk associated with committing capital resources in a foreign country: nationalization or expropriation of a firm's investment by the foreign sovereign. The chapter also addresses the legal peculiarities of operating in another country—subjecting the firm and its employees to the full array of the host country's corporate, currency, and tax laws.

Chapter Nineteen discusses labor laws, which mirror the broadly varying concepts of the proper relationship between employees and their places of work.

Chapter Twenty provides an in-depth treatment of international environmental law, one of the most dynamic legal disciplines in recent years.

Finally, Chapter Twenty-one addresses the pinnacle of foreign penetration—situations in which U.S. investors become so dominant in the relevant country that they become subject to its antitrust or competition laws.

Confronting foreign law is a bit like taking on Hydra, the many-headed monster of Greek mythology. In the following chapters, the student may find that every time he or she cuts off one of the law monster's heads, this monster—like Hydra—will replace it with two new ones.

CHAPTER **16**

Marketing: Representatives, Advertising, and Anti-Corruption

As shown in earlier chapters, an American business can sell its goods abroad by simply delivering them FOB a U.S. port to an ocean-bound vessel. While the products of the business must comply with local regulations, if the business sells its products in that fashion and does not otherwise have any contacts with the country to which its goods are bound, the enterprise itself will generally escape regulation by the foreign country. Why then, would a U.S. business place a representative abroad and enmesh itself in foreign regulation?

First, a business can expand its geographic market by expanding the geographic scope of its marketing. If a company advertises popcorn poppers only in Topeka, Kansas, it will sell popcorn poppers only to Zimbabwean buyers who happen by Topeka or who stumble on its Internet site. If, on the other hand, the company markets in Harare, Zimbabwe, the enterprise will encounter more prospective Zimbabwean buyers. Thus, the enterprise that believes Zimbabwe is a "hot" prospective market for poppers will retain the services of a sales representative in Zimbabwe.

Second, a local presence permits the Topeka enterprise to maintain the popcorn poppers sold abroad. Zimbabweans are more likely to buy a Topeka popper through the Internet if they know they can get it repaired in Harare rather than have to send it back to Topeka for maintenance. If the initial sales efforts bear some fruit, the Topeka enterprise may wish to establish a sales and service facility in Harare. Before embarking on these initiatives, the Topeka enterprise should review the Zimbabwe law affecting representatives of foreign enterprises.

This chapter addresses the major issues associated with marketing in a foreign jurisdiction. First, it sets forth the norms governing the relationship of a foreign enterprise with its local in-country representatives. Second, Chapter Sixteen explains the different types of rules that govern the advertising those representatives advance to promote sales. Finally, it treats the extensive regulation against unethical practices such as bribery to conclude sales directly or indirectly through local representatives.

REGULATION OF RELATIONSHIPS WITH REPRESENTATIVES

Relationships with representatives take two basic forms: the agency and the independent contractor. An **agency relationship** is a business arrangement in which one party, the **agent**, performs a variety of functions on behalf and at the direction of another party, the **principal**. Most employees of a corporation, for example, are agents of that corporation for one purpose or another.

Independent contractors, often called *independent agents* outside the United States, perform general tasks for the business, but retain substantial discretion and independence in carrying them out. Consultants to a corporation are often viewed as independent contractors. Under U.S. law, a primary importance of the distinction between agents and independent contractors is that third parties can generally sue the principal for acts of an agent, but not for those of an independent contractor. This distinction is important to principals because they wish to avoid paying for their representatives' injuries to third parties. However, the distinction does not change the deal between the agent and principal. The substantive terms of the agreement are those developed between the principal and the agent.

The United States places few restrictions on the substantive terms of the representative–principal relationship. Two sophisticated parties can agree on virtually any compensation they wish, from a few dollars to an ownership interest in the principal's enterprise. They can decide on the extent to which one will indemnify the other. They can expand or restrict the representative's scope of discretion as they mutually deem appropriate. Accordingly, U.S. businesses are accustomed to shaping representative–principal relationships without worrying about governmental intervention. The enterprise assumes it will make its own deal with the agent and further assumes that the government will not alter that arrangement.

Supersession of Agreement with Representative

In many countries, the assumption of governmental non-interference would be in error. Nations often enact laws calculated to protect local representatives, regardless of the deal that a particular representative has negotiated. In effect, a local law may state that—notwithstanding the written agreement between the principal and the representative—it will supersede the agreement's language to protect the representative. Stated another way, even if the representative agrees to a 1 percent commission with the U.S. principal, the principal might find that it is obligated under local law to pay the representative no less than 2 percent. Little surprises like this can greatly affect the profitability of a foreign venture.

The supersession problem is particularly acute when the foreign business terminates the agency arrangement. No matter what the contract provides, the foreign principal may need to make a large payment to the representative in order to terminate the arrangement, or may not have a right to terminate the agent at all. For example, a *Voyageur, Representant, et Placier* (VRP)—a type of commercial agent—is entitled to special protection under the French labor code, and every representative is assumed to be a VRP unless the written agreement specifies otherwise. Similarly, under *European Union (EU) Council Directive 86/653*, parties may agree to a fixed-term contract. But if the parties continue their relationship after the stated term of the contract, it becomes an **evergreen contract**—one that the parties may terminate only by a three-month written notice once the relationship has lasted for three years or more.

The *Puerto Rico Dealer's Act* provides an example of the Spanish–American civil law that strictly limits the termination of an agency. Regardless of whether the parties have reserved the right to terminate in the terms of their agreement, the *Dealer's Act* prohibits the principal from terminating the agreement or from refusing to renew without "**just cause.**" Just cause is often difficult to establish. The Act states that even non-performance or violation of the contract is not considered just cause unless the principal can prove that the breach affected it in a "substantial manner." Indeed, in the *Waterproofing Systems, Inc. v. Hydro-Stop, Inc.* case in 2006, a federal appellate court with jurisdiction over Puerto Rico found that even continual late payments and alleged fraud involving the distributor retaining the funds from a joint check might be insufficient to constitute "just cause" under the Act. The foreign investor is at a very significant disadvantage because the entity that determines whether "just cause" exists is a local court, which often favors the local representative.

To American eyes, this web of laws favoring local representatives is viewed as protectionism. However, host countries view such laws quite differently. They regard them as providing a level playing field for local small businesses against multinational giants. In the following case, Paraguay's Supreme Court of Justice stated the rationale for such laws quite capably.

Electra-Amambay S.R.L. v. Compañía Antártica Paulista Ind.

Brasileira de Bebidas E Conexos Order No. 827
(November 12, 2001) Paraguay Supreme Court of Justice

BACKGROUND AND FACTS

The Paraguayan government enacted a law that specifically protects Paraguayan representatives of foreign companies. Among other things, the law requires a foreign company to make an extraordinarily large payment to the Paraguayan representative if the representative is terminated for some reason other than "just cause." The Paraguayan statute narrowly defines "just cause." There is no similar law protecting Paraguayan distributors or other representatives of Paraguayan-based enterprises.

continues

continued

Compañía Antártica, a Brazilian firm, terminated Electra-Amambay, its Paraguayan representative. Electra-Amambay argued that the termination was not for good cause and sought its statutory penalty. Compañía Antártica countered by arguing that the Paraguayan statute was an unconstitutional discrimination based on national origin.

JUDGE CARLOS FERNANDEZ GADEA

Compañía Antártica advances the objection that [the] Articles ... of the Law No. 194/93, on which the [Electra-Amambay] bases its lawsuit, is unconstitutional.

The objection maintains that Articles 1, 4, 5, 6, 7, and 8 constitute an unjust and arbitrary discrimination against foreign manufacturers and companies ... . They establish obligations, assumptions, and sanctions only and exclusively against foreign manufacturers and firms, but not against persons domiciled within the country. [The objection is that] this inequality violates Articles 46 and 47, paragraph 2 of the National Constitution.

***

This Law, *194/93*, is of a special character, regulating the relationships between foreign manufacturers and firms and their representatives, agents, and distributors of their products domiciled in the country. And in the case of the termination of these relationships without a statement of just cause, it sets forth how the amount of damages should be calculated. It is customary that a foreign firm which contracts for the services of physical and legal persons domiciled in Paraguay lays down the ground rules of said relationship, establishing the rights and obligations of both parties. With the promulgation of this law, the parties are placed on an equal footing, establishing the damages that should be paid by the foreign firm in the case of a rupture of the contractual bond without just cause. The firm or persons who find themselves in the country, for the promotion, sale, or placement within the republic of products or services provided by the foreign firm necessarily had to incur expenses in investments so that the referred product would have success in the local market. However, it is necessary to underscore that if there exists just cause, the foreign firm or provider has suitable and appropriate means at its disposal to seek exoneration from liability for the damages.

***

[Compañía Antártica makes the further point] that Article 2 of the mentioned law ... in defining the different types of contractual relationships, abusively exceeds the intention, will and interest of the manufacturers who simply wish to export their products without creating any contractual relationship other than that of the simple purchase and sale of goods. [Moreover, it notes] Article 9 [of the law] presumes to rise to the level of "public order" [but] in this case, the social order is not implicated. The implicated interests involve a small minority of the population and not the general interest.

***

With respect to this point, I believe that it is not logical to think that the foreign manufacturers have an interest only in a simple purchase and sale transaction. The relationship between the parties can go much further than a single transaction. Such a relationship should be found to exist [before the statute applies]. As to Article 9 ... the law was clothed as a matter of "public order" when it was enacted as such by the public legislative power.

***

Finally, it is important to emphasize that this law does not reflect an exaggerated protectionism of the State, but rather legal security and equality, bearing in mind that one of the parties (the foreign company) is in better economic condition than its local representative and that the latter finds itself in a unequal state, whether for lack of technical training, economic resources or qualified personnel. It is because of this that the State intervenes in this relationship, setting forth precise rules with which the parties must comply, especially when the foreign enterprise unilaterally decides to terminate this relationship, without cause. It is in this situation, when the national representative is economically prejudiced, that [the law] compensates for this prejudice in some way by an award of damages ... . As has been said, there exist causes that are justifications exempt from the obligation to pay damages through which the foreign enterprise can exonerate itself from this responsibility. These causes are found itemized in the law.

Decision. The court rejected the objection as inadmissible and charged Compañía Antártica with all costs.

Case Questions

1. What is the "special character" of Law 194/93, and how is its purpose achieved?
2. How does the court justify not implicating the social order of Paraguay?
3. What are alternative methods for Paraguay to achieve the results it seeks under this law?

The European Union also aggressively protects its local agents. *European Union (EU) Council Directive 86/653* on agency requires each EU member state to pass consistent national laws on representatives. These include a few mandatory provisions that may seem odd to Americans:

- The directive provides for an **economic conditions alarm**: The principal must notify the agent if it expects that the agent's volume of business—and thus the agent's commission—will be "significantly lower" than what the agent "normally" expects.
- The directive also requires payment of a commission, not only when a transaction is concluded because of the agent's efforts but also whenever a transaction is made between the principal and a party that the agent previously acquired as a customer.
- A **commission override** is included: Whenever a principal makes a sale in a territory or a market sector reserved for the agent, the principal must pay the agent a commission, whether or not the agent actually participated in the sale, no matter what the agency agreement provides.

Under the directive, these commissions accrue when the customer "should have [executed its part of the transaction] if the principal has executed his part of the transaction." The principal must also pay the commission even if the deal is not consummated.

Tax and Labor Regulation and Principal Liability: The Dependent–Independent Distinction

The retention of a representative often leads to principal liability and triggers tax and labor law requirements. The burdensomeness of these regulations frequently increases upon a finding by the host country that the representative is a **dependent agent** rather than an **independent agent**.

For tax purposes, the principal is often viewed as having opened an office—sometimes referred to as a **permanent establishment**—once it hires a dependent agent within the host country. Upon such an establishment, the principal's transactions become subject to the host country's corporate tax laws.

Similarly, a dependent agent is an employee for purposes of the host country's labor laws. As in the United States, having an *employee* subjects a company to pension law, tax withholding, labor laws, and other legal consequences. In many countries, such a determination can also affect the control of the U.S. investor's foreign enterprise. For example, as Chapter Nineteen explains, in many countries employees may have rights under the national laws to representation on the company's board of directors.

Finally, if an agent is dependent, the principal will be vicariously liable to third parties for the agent's misdeeds. In the context of **product liability**—responsibility to consumers for defects in one's product—the agent–principal relationship is not a critical consideration. As long as the U.S. manufacturer's product enters the foreign market, the manufacturer is likely to be in the "chain of distribution" and subject to suit, whether it does business through a dependent or independent agent. But it makes a difference if the U.S. manufacturer did not participate in the agent's liability-creating act. If the entrepreneur's Nairobi dependent agent runs over a law student in the agent's delivery truck, the entrepreneur may be liable in Kenya to pay damages equal to a lifetime of lost income. If the agent is independent, the entrepreneur probably has no such liability.

In hiring a representative, a firm should therefore determine whether the arrangement is to be characterized as creating a dependent agency or an independent agency. Unfortunately, this distinction is not based on any single definitive test. Instead, courts review a variety of factors and determine whether, on balance, the parties have created a dependent agency. The more flexibility and discretion the representative has, the more likely the representative is to be considered independent. Representatives who personally organize, pursue, and set the schedule for the marketing program—that is, those who have great discretion in organizing their time and work—are more likely to be considered independent. If, on the other hand, the U.S. principal creates the marketing program in detail and the representatives simply carry it out, the representatives are likely to be dependent. Similarly, agents who have an obligation to follow the specific instructions of the principal are likely to be dependent. In contrast, agents who are given a task to perform, but have no obligation to follow the principal's instructions in carrying out that task, are more likely to be viewed as independent. The *EU Agency Directive*, for example, simply defines an independent agent as someone with "continuing authority to negotiate the sale or purchase of goods" on behalf of the principal. A compensation package that is based solely on commissions, rather than on periodic payments or a fixed salary with reimbursement of overhead expenses, is also indicative of independence. Independent agents typically rent their own office space and hire subagents to carry out the tasks. Finally, representatives who serve more than one principal are more likely to be considered

Exhibit 16.1

The Distinction Between Independent and Dependent Agents		
	Independent	**Dependent**
Scheduling	Details created by agent within principal's general requirements	Details provided by principal
Work Organization	Principal identifies strategic objectives; agent determines tactics and has continuing authority for achieving objectives	Principal is involved in working out details
Instructions	Principal does not instruct; change in direction causes change in compensation	Agent is always subject to change in instructions
Compensation	Commissions; float amount of money	Hourly pay or salary
Expenses	Included in compensation amount	Specific expense reimbursement
Number of Principals	Works for many clients	Works for one client

independent. Exhibit 16.1 lays out these considerations in graphic form.

Of course, the U.S. investor may not wish to give an agent the level of discretion required to be an independent agent. The U.S. investor may wish to have a greater level of quality control or a greater share of the entrepreneurial profits in the venture. These benefits of a dependent agent often outweigh the costs of greater regulation. But in weighing the business benefits of retaining a dependent agent, the U.S. investor should thoroughly understand the local legal costs and risks that it will incur.

Once the foreign direct investor has representatives in place, they will launch a marketing effort in the target nations. Where the foreign investor is selling to the consumer market, it will need to develop an advertising campaign with its local representative. We now turn to the laws governing that content.

REGULATION OF ADVERTISING ABROAD

If the Topeka enterprise described at the beginning of the chapter wishes to sell its popcorn poppers to the Zimbabwean public, hiring an agent in Zimbabwe may not be enough. The enterprise will need to determine how best to advertise its poppers to the Zimbabwean consumer. This will require development of marketing strategies attractive to the local culture. Obviously, the soccer-loving Zimbabweans will be unimpressed by endorsements from U.S. football players. Just as cultural differences affect what advertising is attractive to foreign consumers, they also affect what advertising is forbidden. Marketing abroad requires sensitivity to the limits that foreign law can place on marketing efforts.

The marketer may not place just anything on the television screens or in the newspapers. These local legal limitations do not always correspond with local interests. For instance, a television commercial that features an explicit sexual message might well spur sales both in Denmark and in Saudi Arabia; after all, a significant percentage of individuals in all cultures have an interest in racy things. In Denmark, the authorities would take no interest in such an advertisement. However, in Saudi Arabia, the "religionus police" might mete out corporal punishment to one's local representative. An ineffective advertising campaign may simply prove unprofitable, but an illegal advertising campaign may result in a prison term.

Truth in Advertising

One of the founding concepts of libertarian capitalism is ***caveat emptor*** ("let the buyer beware"). According to this precept, government should not intervene in commercial relations. Buyers should investigate the seller's claims or obtain contractual representations and warranties. If they fail to do so and the seller's claims turn out to be false, the buyer only has himself or herself to blame. Under classic capitalist theory, the "invisible hand" of the market will eventually ferret out consistently dishonest sellers and consistently careless buyers.

Ultimately, the Ninth Commandment of the Judeo-Christian Old Testament Scriptures—"thou shalt not bear false witness"—triumphs over *caveat emptor* in most cultures. Today almost every nation prohibits false advertising, at least formally. The European Union, for example, specifically excludes fraudulent advertising from its general protection of commercial speech. Even during the late nineteenth century—the high-water mark of libertarian capitalist thought—courts found ways to protect the unwary. Before the United Kingdom enacted consumer protection laws, English courts protected consumers by stretching ancient contract law principles to newspaper advertising. If a company promises that its product can specifically do something, they reasoned, the company is liable in contract if the product fails to live up to the promise.

As shown in the *Carbolic Smoke Ball* case, the distaste for deceptive advertising is shared to varying degrees throughout the world. But some cultures are less tolerant than others of **"puffing"**—vagueness and exaggeration—in advertising. The Teutonic penchant for accuracy, for example, prevented a German snack food marketer from making an unspecific claim that its potato chips contained "40 percent less fat." When a competitor sued, a German court interpreted the ambiguous statement to be a representation that the chips contained 40 percent less fat than *any* existing brand. Finding that the chips did not, the court enjoined the entire advertising program.

The exacting standards of the Japanese are similarly intolerant of exaggeration. In Japan, the Fair Trade

Carlill v. Carbolic Smoke Ball Co.

1 Q.B. 256 (1893) Queen's Bench

BACKGROUND AND FACTS

The defendant, who made and sold a medical preparation called the "Carbolic Smoke Ball," inserted the following advertisement in the *Pall Mall Gazette* on November 13, 1891:

> £100 reward will be paid by the Carbolic Smoke Ball Company to any person who contracts the increasing epidemic influenza, colds, or any disease caused by taking cold, after having used the ball three times daily for two weeks according to the printed directions supplied with each ball. £1000 is deposited with the Alliance Bank, Regent Street, showing our sincerity in the matter. During the last epidemic of influenza many thousand carbolic smoke balls were sold as preventives against this disease, and in no ascertained case was the disease contracted by those using the carbolic smoke ball.

The plaintiff was a woman who, relying on this advertisement, bought one of the balls at a drugstore and used it as directed, three times a day, from November 20, 1891, to January 17, 1892, when she developed influenza.

LORD JUSTICE LINDLEY

The first observation I will make is that we are not dealing with any inference of fact. We are dealing with an express promise to pay £100 in certain events. Read the advertisement how you will, and twist it about as you will, here is a distinct promise expressed in language which is perfectly unmistakable—"£100 reward will be paid by the Carbolic Smoke Ball Company to any person who contracts the influenza after having used the ball three times daily for two weeks according to the printed directions supplied with each ball."

We must first consider whether this was intended to be a promise at all, or whether it was a mere puff which meant nothing. Was it a mere puff? My answer to that question is No, and I base my answer upon this passage: "£1000 is deposited with the Alliance Bank, showing our sincerity in the matter." Now, for what was that money deposited or that statement made except to negate the suggestion that this was a mere puff and meant nothing at all... .

Then it is contended that it is not binding. In the first place, it is said that it is not made with anybody in particular. Now that point is common to the words of this advertisement and to the words of all other advertisements offering rewards. They are offers to anybody who performs the conditions named in the advertisement, and anybody who does perform the condition accepts the offer... .

[I]t is said that this advertisement is so vague that you cannot really construe it as a promise—that the vagueness of the language shows that a legal promise was not intended or contemplated. The language is vague and uncertain in some respects, and particularly in this, that the £100 is to be paid to any person who contracts the increasing epidemic after having used the balls three times daily for two weeks. It is said. When are they to be used? According to the language of the

continues

continued

advertisement no time is fixed, and, construing the offer most strongly against the person who has made it, one might infer that any time was meant ... . I do not think that business people or reasonable people would understand the words as meaning that if you took a smoke ball and used it three times daily for two weeks you were to be guaranteed against influenza for the rest of your life, and I think it would be pushing the language of the advertisement too far to construe it as meaning that ... . [I]t strikes me that there are two, and possibly three, reasonable constructions to be put on this advertisement, any one of which will answer the purpose of the plaintiff. Possibly it may be limited to persons catching the "increasing epidemic" or any colds or diseases caused by taking cold, during the prevalence of the increasing epidemic. That is one suggestion; but it does not commend itself to me. Another suggested meaning is that you are warranted free from catching this epidemic, or colds or other diseases caused by taking cold, whilst you are using this remedy after using it for two weeks. If that is the meaning, the plaintiff is right, for she used the remedy for two weeks and went on using it till she got the epidemic. Another meaning, and the one which I rather prefer, is that the reward is offered to any person who contracts the epidemic or other disease within a reasonable time after having used the smoke ball ... . What is a reasonable time? It has been suggested that there is no standard of reasonableness; that it depends upon the reasonable time for a germ to develop! I do not feel pressed by that. It strikes me that a reasonable time may be ascertained in a business sense and in a sense satisfactory to a lawyer ... . It strikes me, I confess, that the true construction of this advertisement is that £100 will be paid to anybody who uses this smoke ball three times daily for two weeks according to the printed directions, and who gets the influenza or cold or other diseases caused by taking cold within a reasonable time after so using it; and if that is the true construction, it is enough for the plaintiff.

Decision. Under British contract law, Queen's Bench found that the advertisement was a "definite and operative offer" that the plaintiff had accepted through her performance. It entered judgment of £100 on her behalf.

Case Questions

1. Give at least three examples of how the advertising or the subsequent acts that led to this suit suffered from vagueness problems.
2. What other factors could have influenced the court's determination that there was a promise and not mere puffery?

Committee prevented PepsiCo, Inc., from advertising its cola drink as "the choice of the next generation" as it did in the United States. Its rationale was that Pepsi was second to Coca-Cola in the Japanese market.

Other nations are far more flexible. In some countries, hucksters have been victimizing others for centuries. While investors are still able to do so, they may wish to take advantage of such greater latitude abroad. But the trend is clear: In most countries, the authorities are catching up to the philosophical descendants of the *Carbolic Smoke Ball* medical science entrepreneurs.

The sanctions for false advertising vary from place to place. The advertising laws in some of the relatively new Eastern European democracies indicate a remaining socialist distrust of capitalist advertising. The Czech Republic bans "hidden seduction" and insists that advertising be based on the "specific features of the goods." And Hungary formerly demanded that the advertiser have sufficient inventories of advertised goods on hand before beginning an advertising campaign. Of particular interest is the South Korean requirement of a public apology. Although to a Westerner such a sanction would be little more than a slap on the wrist, the ignominy of a public apology caused an advertiser to appeal the public apology sentence to the High Court of Seoul. The Seoul court found that the advertiser was guilty of deception, but it also found extenuating circumstances in the case. Therefore, it reversed the sentence of a public apology, finding it too harsh a penalty.

Content-Specific Regulations

Advertising can be unlawful even if its content is perfectly true. Advertising aimed at children, for example, is closely and diversely regulated. More than 40 countries prohibit or greatly limit such advertising, reasoning that children cannot intelligently assess the content of commercials. Many of these bans reflect idiosyncratic cultural values.

Language Laws. In some nations, **language laws** can complicate cross-border advertising. The municipal government of Jakarta, Indonesia, worried about cultural invasion by ethnic minorities, bans languages other than Indonesian from billboards and imprisons violators for up three months. The marketing difficulties created by this law become apparent when one considers that, for most of the 207 million people in the Indonesian islands, Bahasa Indonesia is a second language. And under *Law 24* of 2009, all international agreements must have a Bahasa Indonesia version.

France is famous—or infamous perhaps—for its policing of language in commercial advertising. In France, every word used in advertising is legally required to be French, even if the French population more commonly uses the English word. For example, although virtually all French businesspeople prefer to use the simple English term *cash flow,* the language law recently required them to reflect the concept in its seldom-used French incarnation of *marge brute d'autofinancement.* If similar laws prevailed in the United States, advertisers would have to refer to *paté* by its less appetizing English name, *ground goose liver.* In March 2006, the Versailles Court of Appeal ordered GE Healthcare to pay $689,920 to trade unions representing its employees because GE Healthcare failed to translate technical security directions for sophisticated devices into French. The court also ordered several other classes of documents translated into French and threatened to impose a daily fine of roughly $24,000 per day per document for failure to provide the translations by certain target dates. Despite this law and its occasional enforcement, recent studies suggest that French advertising agencies continue to include common English words—easily understood by their audience—in advertising copy without incident.

The Canadian province of Québec has also attempted to preserve the use of the French language and the unique cultural identity that Québecers derive from their French–Canadian heritage. In 1998, the Canadian Supreme Court held that the protection of the French language justified a limit on freedom of expression but that banning all commercial speech not in French went too far. Today in Québec, items such as menus and labels should feature French that is at least as prominent as any other language. On signs and posters, French must be "markedly prominent" in relation to other languages. As described below, the latest challenge to this Québec restriction was upheld by the Court of Appeal of Québec. The Canadian Supreme Court declined to grant a review of the case.

Québec (Procureur général) c. Entreprises W.F.H. ltée

2000 CarswellQue 826 Cour supérieure du Québec, 2000

BACKGROUND AND FACTS

The accused challenged the validity of Article 58 of the Charter of the French Language, which required the predominance of French on bilingual commercial signs. The accused had a wooden sign that read:

> ***La Lionne et le Morse***
> ***Antiquités***
> ***Hot Tubs & Saunas***
> ***Encadrement Gifts***
> ***Lyon and the Wallrus***
> ***Antiques***
> ***Hot Tubs & Saunas***
> ***Cadeaux***

Article 58 requires: "That public signs and commercial advertising must be in French. They can also be in both French and another language provided that the French is markedly predominant." A regulation related to this article explained that: "French is markedly predominant where the text in French has a much greater visual impact in comparison to the text written in another language ... . French is deemed to have a much great visual impact if ... space allotted to the text in French is at least twice as large as that devoted to the text in another language; characters used in the text written in French are at least twice as large as those used in the text written in another language; and other characteristics of the display did not reduce the visual impact of the text in French."

The accused did not disagree that Article 58 was violated but asserted that Article 58 was void under the Equality Clause of *The Canadian Charter of Rights and Freedoms.*

SUPERIOR COURT JUDGE BELLA VANCE

I do not think that Québec is comparable to the whole or even individual countries ... Québec, for its population of 6 million French surrounded on all sides by a population of 300 million people speaking English, the language of the dominant and most economically important people on the planet, cannot be compared to the States targeted by the report.

continues

continued

Québec has on its borders, unlike the Swiss, Germans, French, or Italians, an adjacent monolingual neighbor who does not speak its language. Furthermore, the French in Québec is not a regional or ancestral language that you want to keep just for cultural reasons, but for centuries a language of daily use for millions of people who for many, especially in the rural and semi-urban areas, is the only language they know.

***

Québec is in a unique linguistic situation, which prompted the Supreme Court of Canada's Confederation, to propose a unique legislative solution that does not exist elsewhere in the world.

***

The existence of the use of French has a rational connection with the concern of urgency and reality of the National Assembly to ensure that the face of Québec's language reflects the predominance of French. Does this requirement minimally impair the right to equality before the law and the right to equal benefit and protection under the law without discrimination? It is designed so as not to interfere with that right to the point that the reduction outweighs the objective legislation. Ensuring that non-Francophones could write job applications forms, purchase orders, invoices, and receipts in the language of their choice, creates, at most, a minimal impairment of equality rights. Although, as argued by appellant, the required use of French might create an additional burden for merchants and shopkeepers who are non-native speakers, there is nothing that undermines their ability to use another language.

***

The distinctions created by the laws do not involve discrimination.

Decision. The Court affirmed the lower court's ruling, upholding the French language law.

Case Questions

1. Do you think that geography is a valid reason to favor one language over another?
2. Is it appropriate to favor one language over another provided people who do not speak that language are given the opportunity to conduct normal life functions in a different language?
3. If French is so important and powerful to millions of people, why does it need legal protection?

Advertising Restrictions on "Sin" Products: Tobacco and Alcohol. Other advertising regulations target specific types of products deemed to be corrosive to society—"sin" products. As in all advertising, regulations reflect the customs of the countries that enact them. With ferocity mindful of its recent totalitarian heritage, Bulgaria has banned all tobacco advertising outside of tobacco shops and threatened violators with a $50,000 fine per violation. The antiauthoritarian British, on the other hand, do not forbid tobacco advertising. Instead, they insist on self-imposed and highly subjective industry guidelines. This approach led to the banning of an ad campaign featuring two overweight, balding, middle-aged men whom the industry watch group deemed "too appealing" to young people. Belgium permits cigarette ads, but only those that focus on the package or on part of its design. A directive by the European Union that would have effectively banned all advertising of tobacco products was annulled in 2000 by the European Court of Justice for being overreaching. (*Federal Republic of Germany v. European Parliament and Council of the European Union*, Case #C-376/98 [2000].)

Although the comprehensive European Union ban was annulled, states within the EU have addressed the advertising of tobacco in their own form. Additionally, Japan has instituted its own ban on advertising of tobacco products. Since 2004, Japan has banned outdoor advertising of tobacco and limited newspaper advertising to 12 ads each year, no more than three per month, for each tobacco manufacturer. The World Health Organization's **Framework Convention on Tobacco Control (FCTC)** has a total of 168 signatories and 168 parties. The FCTC institutes a comprehensive ban on tobacco advertising in those states that are signatories to the convention. The minimum requirement is that each party "prohibit all forms of tobacco advertising, promotion and sponsorship that promote a tobacco product by any means that are false misleading or deceptive or are likely to create an erroneous impression."

Alcohol is also considered "sinful" and its advertising is thus regulated, with interesting local peculiarities. Starting in 1993, France banned most liquor advertising—direct or indirect—including sponsorship of sports events. The only exception was French wine. Sweden bans all television alcohol advertising except for low alcohol beer, although stronger beers share a name with some of the low alcohol beers and arguably are advertised every time one of their namesake "light" beers is mentioned. Saudi Arabia, which enforces a strict interpretation of Islamic law, bans alcohol and alcohol advertising altogether. Even the definition of "sinful liquor" can be counterintuitive. In June 2010, Iranian President Mahmoud Ahmadinejad signed a law barring broadcast advertising by "Zionist" companies, which according to him include beverages sold by Coca-Cola and Nestlé.

Other Restrictions on Advertising. At the other end of the spectrum are laws that prohibit advertising of products too important to allow mere marketing to affect their distribution, such as prescription drugs or other medicines. Spain prohibits the advertisement of medicines that may be dispensed only with a prescription, are psychoactive or narcotic drugs, or are part of the National Health System. Similarly, the European Union prohibits the advertising of prescription drugs, through advertisements for over-the-counter drugs are permitted.

The central point in advertising abroad is that the U.S. enterprise must seek legal advice from local practitioners and fashion local advertising appropriately. Indeed, in many countries, the guiding norms are embodied not in laws but in industry codes observed by the local marketing organizations. The rules in this area are as diverse and arbitrary as human culture itself and as transitory as political opinion. Perhaps the primary general principle is that no useful general principles apply to all cultures.

Marketing Considerations: The Nestlé Infant Formula Case

An enterprise that seeks to market a product in a new nation must be alert to unanticipated risk associated with the product in the new environment. If such risk exists—even if a marketing campaign is technically lawful—the law, public scorn, or both will catch up with the entrepreneur eventually. The Nestlé infant formula case is an excellent illustration of this problem.

Infant formula manufacturers have long provided hospitals with free or low-cost formula as a marketing technique. The concept is that if the mother develops a brand loyalty when her child is a newborn, her loyalty is unlikely to change over time. Formula manufacturers, like all other merchants, have also promoted their products through mass media. Some have argued that these marketing techniques have the effect of discouraging mothers from breast-feeding, which is widely regarded to be superior to feeding infant formulas. This discouragement is said to be particularly influential in the Third World, where mothers are less educated and more impressionable.

Critics argue that in such developing countries, forsaking breast-feeding can have especially grim consequences. Outside hospitals, the water supply may not be sanitary and mothers may not understand formula usage instructions. Improper use can lead to malnutrition, diarrhea, and gastroenteritis.

Nestlé, S.A., a Swiss concern with more than 40 percent of the $3 billion baby formula market, became a lightning rod for criticism. Critics charged that Nestlé was luring uneducated Third World mothers away from breast-feeding through its marketing activities. These critics organized a series of boycotts against all Nestlé products throughout developed countries.

In response, Nestlé changed its promotional practices and, in 1976, phased out mass-media advertising. But still Nestlé did not escape criticism because it continued to provide free and low-cost formula. The World Health Organization promulgated an "International Code of Marketing of Breast Milk Substitutes," which many countries have implemented as law. Nestlé voluntarily agreed to follow the code in 1982, agreeing to supply formula only upon request by hospital administrators. However, Third World administrators continued to order formula and give it to virtually all mothers. Accordingly, in 1989, several groups in Britain, Ireland, and Sweden reactivated the boycott because of what they viewed as continued promotion. Finally, in January 1991, Nestlé committed to stop supplying free and low-cost formula completely.

In short, although Nestlé acted in conformance with the law, it still found itself in a vortex of controversy that adversely affected its profitability throughout the world. Marketing often involves understanding that corporations may be held to a higher standard than that mandated by law.

In many countries, a frequent marketing strategy had been to bribe government officials to gain their assistance. This was particularly true in the case of larger government purchases such as defense products, but it also was a means of avoiding government prosecution or evading legal requirements. Many local representatives were expert at this, asking for large sums in order to allow foreign direct investors to be able to disclaim actual knowledge of corruption. This type of marketing is now highly dangerous. The next section sets out the extensive regulatory network that has grown to prevent corrupt marketing methods.

THE FOREIGN CORRUPT PRACTICES ACT

In most nations, the government is far more immersed in the day-to-day functioning of commerce than is the government of the United States in its own commerce.

In emerging nations, favorable government action or inaction is often a prerequisite to concluding a transaction. Government officials have discretion over such government action or inaction, so they have greater influence over commercial transactions than their United States counterparts. Many of these foreign government officials are not above informing their discretion with a bribe. Indeed, in many countries, bribery of public officials has long been a way of life.

This is the case even though almost every nation in the world formally outlaws bribery of its own officials. For example, the Russian Federation has enacted a complex legal framework prohibiting official corruption. Since April 1992, *Presidential Decree 351* has, as a preventive measure, barred civil servants from participating in entrepreneurial activities, managing commercial activities, or accepting foreign business trips paid by commercial entities. Nonetheless, Russia has earned a reputation for official corruption that often inhibits foreign investment.

South Korea also has an impressive and strict antibribery legal framework. The Korean *Criminal Code* prohibits not only receipt or solicitation of a bribe but also "manifestation of a will to deliver" a bribe. In August 1996, two former South Korean presidents were convicted of criminal bribery after they accepted hundreds of millions of dollars from business enterprises. One was sentenced to death, while the other was sentenced to 22 years and six months in prison. Yet despite these enforcement efforts, South Korea was rocked by a series of official corruption scandals from 1998 through 2008 that battered its economy.

A foreign investor who makes a payoff to a foreign official therefore risks criminal prosecution by the official's country. But in many countries, this risk is not great. For instance, in the past, South Korean prosecutors had enforced bribery laws only against lower-level officials and had exercised their prosecutorial discretion to avoid actions against politically powerful high-level officials. Similar stories about other nations are rampant, particularly in emerging markets. In fact, for the foreign investor, there is often a much greater risk of official persecution if a corrupt payment is not made.

At least 38 countries in the world now also outlaw payment of bribes by their citizens to public officials in other countries. Because one of those countries is the United States, every American who retains an agent abroad should be familiar with the *Foreign Corrupt Practices Act (FCPA).*

Origins of the FCPA and Other Antibribery Laws

In the mid-1970s, the press in the United States uncovered a number of instances of U.S.-based corporations making payments to foreign leaders for official favors. For example, an aircraft manufacturer was widely alleged to have made payments to the Japanese prime minister and a Dutch prince in exchange for assistance in obtaining government contracts. At the same time, alleged payments to a number of members of the Italian government caused its president to resign.

Concerned that American industry might be widely engaged in anti-democratic behavior, the U.S. Securities and Exchange Commission (SEC) instituted a voluntary disclosure program to assess the frequency of the phenomenon. Firms were invited to tell of their payoffs abroad under a loose understanding that they would not be prosecuted. The volume of the response was remarkable. More than 400 U.S. companies revealed that they had bribed foreign public officials. The amounts paid aggregated into the hundreds of millions of dollars. Although corporations based in other countries allegedly engaged in the same practices, no nation had ever publicly confessed to such a massive pattern of corrupt behavior.

The U.S. public was in no mood to condone frank admissions of immorality. Scarcely a year before, the President of the United States had resigned because of the Watergate cover-up. No other nation had ever faced the embarrassment of revealing such an extensive pattern of corrupt activity. Public opinion at home and disdain abroad demanded prompt and decisive action. They got it. By December 1977, Congress had passed—and the president had signed—the world's first law outlawing citizens' bribes to officials of another nation.

For two decades, the United States was alone in forbidding its citizens from bribing foreign officials. Indeed, some nations permitted tax deductions for such payments. However, the tide finally turned. In February 1999, the *Convention on Combating Bribery of Foreign Public Officials in International Business Transactions (OECD Convention)* became effective. The *OECD Convention* obligated each member state of the Organization for Economic Cooperation and Development (OECD) to enact a law making the bribery of foreign public officials a criminal act. The *OECD Convention* mirrors the accounting provisions of the FCPA, which require that public companies' accounting systems detect and report corrupt payments. As of November 2012, 34 OECD member countries and six non-member countries had ratified the *OECD Convention*, including all major European countries and Latin American economic powers such as Argentina, Brazil, Chile, and Mexico. The *OECD Convention* is particularly significant because the nations that have ratified it are home to virtually all of the word's large international corporations.

The *OECD Convention's* restraints are limited to active corruption of foreign public officials and are not as stringent as the FCPA standards. In most aspects, the *OECD Convention* is consistent with the FCPA and was even amended in 1998 to harmonize its terms with those of the *OECD Convention*.

Other international legal efforts are also developing. In late 2003, the United Nations General Assembly adopted the *UN Convention against Corruption (UN Convention)*. The *UN Convention* was formulated through negotiations involving 125 countries, including many less-developed nations. The *UN Convention* entered into force in December 2005, and 161 countries had ratified or acceded to it as of February 2013. Although the *UN Convention* is unlikely to enhance existing enforcement mechanisms, it provides additional international focus on the problem of corruption as a serious obstacle to development.

Separately, the Council of Europe promulgated a *Criminal Law Convention on Corruption* that included a broader definition of corruption than does the *OECD Convention*, one that is closer to that in the FCPA. Like the FCPA, the *Criminal Law Convention on Corruption* covers active and passive bribery and transnational bribes. The *Criminal Law Convention on Corruption* entered into force in January 2002, and 43 states had ratified or acceded to it as of February 2013.

The European Union has enacted four treaties and protocols focused on criminalization of transnational bribery. Under the *First Pillar Provisions of Community Law*, the European Commission is trying to promote a comprehensive European Union-wide policy against corruption. Under this policy, all members should join in implementing existing anticorruption treaties, harmonize their legal standards and law enforcement techniques, and properly implement specialized audit rules. All members have banned tax deductions for bribes to foreign public officials. The European Council also adopted a decision, known as the *Framework Decision*, which requires members to criminalize private-sector corruption. To understand how these antibribery statutes work, this chapter now turns in depth to the FCPA, which is the law that applies to U.S. enterprises.

Structure of the FCPA

The Foreign Corrupt Practices Act (FCPA) seeks to punish bribery of foreign officials through civil and criminal penalties and to establish internal accounting mechanisms that will prevent such bribery. The law's so-called **antibribery** provisions authorize criminal punishment. The law's prevention function is accomplished through provisions that seek to detect illegal payments by examining the accounting and record-keeping systems of the enterprise.

The Antibribery Provisions. In essence, the FCPA's antibribery provisions prohibit U.S. firms from "corruptly" paying or offering to pay a "foreign official" for assistance in obtaining or retaining business. They also prohibit payments to a person, such as a foreign agent, when the payer had reason to know that a portion of the payment would go to a public official. In light of the increasing importance of multinational organizations, in March 2002, President George W. Bush signed an executive order designating European Union officials and officials of public international organizations as within the definition of "foreign official."

Violating antibribery provisions is a serious offense. In November 2002, the U.S. Sentencing Commission promulgated amendments making FCPA violations subject to the same sentencing guidelines as domestic bribery cases. Any individual convicted under these provisions can be imprisoned for up to five years and fined up to $100,000, even if that person acted with a reckless disregard of possible bribery but no actual knowledge. An individual may also face a $10,000 civil penalty. Furthermore, under the *Alternative Fines Act*, a statute which applies to all crimes that resulted in a gain to the criminal, the individual may be fined up to twice the amount of the benefit sought to be obtained by making the corrupt payment. Any corporation convicted of a criminal violation can be fined $2 million per violation and may be subject to the *Alternative Fines Act*. Willful criminal violations of the FCPA are subject to even stricter penalties. Individuals may be fined up to $5 million and imprisoned for up to 20 years, and corporations may be fined up to $25 million. Civil fines can range from $5,000 to $500,000, or the amount of the pecuniary gain from the violation, whichever is greater.

Unfortunately, the law does not clearly define what one has to do to commit these serious offenses. It contains three principal points of ambiguity: the *routine governmental action exception*, the *corruptness requirement*, and the *knowing requirement*.

Congress recognized that in many countries petty graft is so common that to forbid U.S. companies from engaging in it would be tantamount to forbidding them to do business there. Accordingly, Congress excluded from the coverage of the FCPA "any facilitating or expediting payment ... the purpose of which is to expedite or secure the performance of a routine governmental action." Such routine governmental actions must be *non-discretionary.* In other words, the government official must just be getting paid to do the routine tasks of his or her job: granting qualifications to do business, processing visas, providing police and mail service, or providing basic utilities or transportation services. But there is no *de minimis* exception. The SEC has alleged FCPA violation for providing, *inter alia*, flowers for the wife of the CEO of a company controlled by a foreign government.

The routine governmental action exception (sometimes called the **"grease payments" exception**) is limited. For instance, payments made to foreign customs officials to store shipments longer than otherwise permitted were deemed to fall outside of the exception. Few government actions do not involve some discretion, particularly in countries outside the United States. As discussed in other chapters, many national statutes tend to lay out broad, general outlines and allow government officials to fill in the blanks. In short, U.S. executives largely must guess whether the role of any given government official will ultimately be determined by some court to be "routine." If they guess wrong, they can go to prison. Under such circumstances, taking chances is not advisable. Today, businesses in the United States are generally considered more reluctant than those in other countries to make any payments to officials.

In environments where making gratuity payments to customs officials is routine, the U.S. investor must make a careful assessment of its potential FCPA liability vis-à-vis its ability to operate effectively without making such payments. Many U.S. companies have determined that the profits of operating in such countries are not worth the risk. This is one reason U.S. investment in Russia, for example, has greatly declined.

To violate the antibribery provisions, a payment must also be "corrupt." Although the word *corrupt* is used in a number of criminal statutes, the legal concept of corruption is not well defined. In the case of *Stichting ter Behartiging van de Belangen van Oudaan-deelhouders in Het Kapitaal van Saybolt International B. V. v. Schreiber*, the U.S. Court of Appeals for the Second Circuit, which is the highest federal court for the region that includes New York City, found that acting "corruptly" requires "an evil motive or purpose and an intent to induce an official to misuse his position." Someone who is simply negligent in making a payment is not generally considered corrupt. A businessperson who—through lack of sophistication—fails to realize that part of a payment to a local foreign agent is in fact going to a government official may not have the corrupt state of mind required to violate the antibribery provision. (However, as discussed in the next section, that businessperson might be in violation of the accounting provisions, which have no corruptness requirement.) **Corruptness** requires that the businessperson display a reckless or conscious disregard for the consequences of personal actions. Even if payers do not have actual knowledge that they are making a payment to a government official, they are corrupt if they act as if they do not care whether it is going to a government official.

The corruptness requirement even applies to victims of extortion. If a foreign official is extorting a payment from a U.S. investor—threatening to take action against the investor's business if the payment is not made—the investor is corrupt if it makes the payment. When a U.S. firm is faced with an extortion request in a country in which it already has substantial assets, therefore, the firm must refuse to make the payment and suffer the official's retribution against its assets. This situation, too, suggests that the investor should carefully review the business climate in the foreign country before entering it.

The ambiguities that accompany the corruptness concept are similar to those that surround the **knowing requirement.** Although Congress has made clear that "mere foolishness" is insufficient for liability, the standard is intended to cover "any instance where 'any reasonable person would have realized' the existence of the circumstances or result and the [person] has 'consciously chosen not to ask about what he had reason to believe he would discover.'" The danger is that a foreign agent will ask for a commission that will ultimately end up in the hands of a foreign official. If a firm discovers that its agent made a payment to a government official, U.S. prosecutors would review the circumstances surrounding the payment to the agent to determine whether the firm "knew" of the agent's bribe. Moral: Whenever an agent asks for an unusually large fee or commission, a U.S. investor has reason to be nervous.

The Accounting and Record-Keeping Requirements. The FCPA also requires public U.S. companies to "make and keep books, records, and accounts which, in reasonable detail, accurately and fairly reflect the transactions and dispositions of [their] assets." It further requires an investor to "devise and maintain a system of internal accounting controls sufficient to provide reasonable assurances" that all transactions are properly authorized and that access to assets is tracked. These requirements are commonly referred to as the **accounting and record-keeping provisions**. The SEC may bring an enforcement action against any company that knowingly violates the accounting and record-keeping provisions. The *Sarbanes–Oxley Act* of 2004 imposed further accounting and record-keeping requirements on companies.

The principal objection to the accounting provisions is that they fail to incorporate any concept of relative importance, known in financial circles as **materiality**. U.S. businesses are not normally expected to unearth every fact in their financial statements because doing so would be impractical and would drown the reader of the financial statements in a sea of detail. Accounting systems are generally geared to track *material* facts—facts of a financial magnitude that a prudent investor in the company should know. A $5,000 problem in a $5 billion company, for instance, would not normally be perceived as material.

By not including a concept of materiality, the accounting provisions of the FCPA require the U.S. company's accounting system to be able to identify bribery regardless of how small it may be. Although $5,000 might be a great deal of money to an individual, tracking every such problem represents a formidable task for a multibillion-dollar company. Nevertheless, as a technical matter, failing to track even a small problem is a possible violation of the FCPA.

The Department of Justice Review Process

Before entering a transaction that raises a possible FCPA issue, an investor can seek an interpretation of these somewhat ambiguous provisions from the U.S. Department of Justice (DOJ). But this process is quite flawed.

The inquiring firm first must submit all relevant details of the proposed transaction to the DOJ, including appropriate documentation. The DOJ will not respond to hypothetical fact situations. The firm must be willing to risk the confidentiality of the deal. All documents submitted to the DOJ are subject to the *Freedom of Information Act*, which permits any American, including a journalist, to request disclosure of documents in the government's possession. Even in a deal whose specifics receive confidential treatment, the DOJ will issue a release that describes the general nature of the transaction. Because of this, the procedure has the initial disadvantage of subjecting the transaction to the scrutiny of the public at large, including the U.S. firm's competitors, before the transaction closes. In a highly competitive world with near-instant communications, these competitors may be attracted to the opportunity and lure the U.S. firm's proposed business partners away with a more attractive deal.

Disclosure of the deal can have other adverse effects. The public officials involved may resent having their integrity publicly questioned, or such public disclosure might adversely affect the officials' standing in their own home country.

The DOJ will respond in 30 days unless it requires the submission of additional information. If it does require additional information, the DOJ will have an additional 30 days from the time of receipt of that information. At the end of this two-month period, the DOJ will either express an interest to pursue or not to pursue a prosecution under the FCPA, or will decline to state any position. This delay is burdensome to most business transactions. While the parties await a response, market conditions may change and make the deal less attractive or entirely unattractive for one of the parties.

Perhaps because of these problems, the DOJ review procedure is used quite infrequently. Although millions of foreign transactions have occurred since the procedure was instituted in 1980, only a few dozen requests have been made under it since 1993. In the overwhelming majority of cases, U.S. firms choose not to avail themselves of the procedure. Nonetheless, the following example will help illustrate the process.

FCPA Enforcement Actions

For more than two decades, the FCPA was seldom enforced, but this has markedly changed. Civil and criminal enforcement actions in connection with alleged payments to foreign officials have increased greatly in recent years. In the three years from 2004 through 2006, 22 DOJ enforcement actions and 19 SEC enforcement actions were initiated. From 2007 through 2009 those numbers exploded to 96 DOJ actions and 52 SEC actions; 2010 was a particularly busy year with 61 DOJ actions and 29 SEC actions. Enforcement efforts continued in 2011 and 2012 with

Foreign Corrupt Practices Act Review Opinion Procedure Release 12-02

October 18, 2012 United States Department of Justice

The Department of Justice (the "Department") has reviewed the *Foreign Corrupt Practices Act* ("FCPA") Opinion Procedure Request from 19 non-profit adoption agencies headquartered in the United States (the "Requestors") submitted on August 21, 2012 ...

The Requestors seek an opinion related to their proposal to host 18 government officials from a foreign country (the "Foreign Country") during visits to the United States. Of those officials, 13 are from the government ministry in the Foreign Country that oversees adoptions (the "Adoption Ministry"), and one is the presiding judge of the court in the Foreign Country that ultimately approves or disapproves adoption requests (the "Adoption Court") ... . The remaining officials are the director of the Foreign Country's agency that oversees orphanages, a minister in the Office of the Foreign Country's head of government, and two members of the Foreign Country's legislature.

The Requestors represent that the purpose of the trip is to allow government officials from the Foreign Country to learn more about the Requestors' work, which includes processing adoptions in the Foreign Country. During the trip, the government officials will interview the Requestors' staff members, inspect the Requestors' files, and meet with families who adopted children from the Foreign Country.

Based on the Department's review of the Request and additional information received from the Requestors, it is the Department's opinion that the Requestors' proposed funding of the trip to the United States by the government officials from the Foreign Country is a reasonable and bona fide expenditure that is directly related to the promotion, demonstration, or explanation of the Requestors' products or services. Therefore, the Requestors' proposed funding of the trip may go forward without enforcement action.

* * *

THE PROPOSED TRIP

The amount that the Requestors spend on hotels and meals will not exceed General Services Administration ("GSA") rates. The Requestors will pay for business class airfare for high-ranking officials, which, as proposed, is permitted by the Foreign Country's government. The Requestors will pay all expenses directly to the providers and will not give any money, including per diems, directly to the government officials. If some of the trips require staying over a weekend, the Requestors will pay for hotels and meals during those periods, subject to the same limitations above. The Requestors will share the costs of the trips ...

ANALYSIS

... The officials whom the Requestors will sponsor, as officers or employees of the Foreign Country's government, are "foreign officials" under the FCPA ... Additionally, the FCPA contains an affirmative defense covering "reasonable and bona fide expenditure[s], such as travel and lodging expenses, incurred by or on behalf of a foreign official ... directly related to ... the promotion, demonstration, or explanation of products or services ... ."

In other instances, with appropriate protections, the Department has recently issued favorable Opinion Releases with respect to sponsoring travel and related expenses for foreign officials. In FCPA Opinion Release 11-01, the Department issued an opinion in response to a request from an adoption service provider, declining to take enforcement action if the company proceeded with sponsoring expenses for a trip, including international airfare to the United States, by one official from each of two foreign agencies of a Central American government. In FCPA Opinion Releases 07-02 and 07-01, the Department issued opinions in response to requests from private companies in the United States, declining to take enforcement action if the companies proceeded with paying domestic expenses for trips by officials from Asian governments. In all three FCPA Opinion Releases, the requestors made representations and took corresponding measures to ensure that the proposed trips met the criteria of the affirmative defense covering reasonable and bona fide expenditures under 15 U.S.C. §78dd-2(c)(2)(A).

Based on their representations and proposed safeguards, the payments that the Requestors propose to make here fall within the same affirmative defense. First, the expenses described above are reasonable under the circumstances. This includes the provision of business class airfare for high-ranking officials, which, as proposed, is permitted by the Foreign Country. Second, the expenses are directly related to the promotion, demonstration, and explanation of the Requestors' services. The Requestors represent that the purpose of the trip is to demonstrate the Requestors' work to the government officials by allowing the government officials to interview the Requestors' staff members, to inspect the Requestors' files, and to meet with families who have adopted children from the

continues

continued

Foreign Country. The proposed itineraries are consistent with this purpose.

Based upon all of the facts and circumstances, as represented by the Requestors ... the proposed expenses reflect no corrupt intent and appear to be bona fide promotional expenses .... The expenses contemplated are reasonable under the circumstances and directly relate to "the promotion, demonstration, or explanation of [the Requestors'] products or services."

Accordingly, with respect to the trips that the Requestors propose paying for, based on the representations made in the Request ... the Department does not presently intend to take enforcement action.

This FCPA Opinion Release has no binding application to any party that did not join in the Request, and can be relied upon by the Requestors only to the extent that the disclosure of facts and circumstances in their Request is accurate and complete.

Case Questions

1. How important are the following two representations made by the Requestors to the DOJ's decision?

   (a) The Requestors will not give any money directly to the foreign officials, but will pay expenses directly to the providers.

   (b) The amount spent on hotels and meals will not exceed the GSA rate (which is the maximum *per diem* allowance that U.S. federal employees are entitled to receive as reimbursement for expenses incurred while on official trip within the continental United States).
2. Is this opinion sufficient to safeguard the identities of the parties involved in the proposed visit?
3. What role do DOJ's prior Opinion Releases play in this decision?

a total of 40 SEC actions and DOJ actions. As of the end of 2012, there were about 150 active FCPA investigations.

Record fines have been levied against companies under the FCPA in the last few years. Aside from the $1.6 billion in fines in the *Siemens* case to be discussed later, Kellogg Brown & Root LLC (KBR), a Houston-based global engineering firm, agreed to pay $402 million in criminal fines in 2009 for paying Nigerian officials at least $182 million in bribes to procure engineering, procurement, and construction contracts to build liquefied natural gas facilities in Bonny Island, Nigeria. On the same day, KBR's parent company, KBR Inc., and its former parent company, Halliburton Company, settled civil FCPA charges with the SEC agreeing to be jointly liable to pay $177 million in disgorgement. Similarly, BAE Systems plc settled an SEC enforcement action on June 29, 2010, for $400 million dollars, and just the day before, Technip S.A. settled for $338 million. Corporate fines (including penalties, disgorgement, and pre-judgment interest) totaled $508 million in 2011, and dropped to $259 million in 2012. This drop likely reflects the significant resources that have been diverted from corporate settlements to individual trials over the past few years. With some important cases in the pipeline, 2013 could see an increase in corporate fines under the FCPA.

Prosecution of individuals for FCPA violations has also increased dramatically. From 2005 to 2007, the DOJ charged 16 individuals with FCPA criminal offenses. This number more than quadrupled to 65 in the following three years from 2008 to 2010. The numbers have fallen in the past two years with a total of 12 individuals charged in 2011 and 2012. On November 2012, Assistant Attorney General Lanny Breuer stated that the DOJ has been really "vigorous about holding individuals accountable" over the past four years.

A closer look, however, reveals a more complex picture. Of the 77 individuals criminally charged with FCPA offenses by the DOJ since 2008, 46 were involved in just four cases. In particular, the "Africa Sting" case alone resulted in the arrests of 22 individuals in January 2010. A majority of DOJ's corporate enforcement actions so far have not resulted in any DOJ charges against the company employees. So although individual prosecution has become more prominent, the majority of these individual prosecutions result from a limited number of cases.

Territorial Jurisdiction over Non-U.S. Persons

The *OECD Convention* requires that transnational bribery laws apply to "any person." In order to implement this requirement, the FCPA was amended in 1998 by adding new language that provides for jurisdiction over non-U.S. persons who commit an FCPA violation "while in the territory of the United States." The DOJ and the SEC have interpreted this requirement broadly, but courts have not always agreed. For instance, the DOJ has claimed jurisdiction over a non-U.S. person for merely operating a "U.S.-based email address." The DOJ has also advanced the "correspondent account jurisdiction" theory to claim jurisdiction over non-U.S. persons that arrange for payments to foreign officials through wire transfers that pass through U.S. financial institutions.

The February 2013 decision of a New York District Court in *SEC v. Uriel Sharef et al.* is a rare dismissal of a government FCPA suit against a foreign national for lack of jurisdiction. The defendant, Herbert Steffen, was a German citizen who served formerly as the CEO of Siemen's Argentine subsidiary where some of the alleged bribes to U.S. and German authorities took place. The SEC sued Steffen, who had no direct ties to the United States, on grounds that his alleged misconduct was part of a scheme that involved filing misleading financial statements with the SEC. But Steffen had not authorized the bribe, directed the cover-up, or played any role in the falsified filings. The District Court found that the SEC failed to show that Steffen had "minimum contacts" in the United States and dismissed the suit for lack of personal jurisdiction. This decision underscores that there are indeed limits to the reach of U.S. administrative agencies.

Difficulty in Prosecuting Individuals for FCPA Violations

The DOJ has struggled to win convictions in court against individuals charged with FCPA violations. For example, a U.S. district judge in California vacated convictions of several employees of Lindsey Manufacturing, an electric-equipment maker, for allegedly paying bribes to officials at the Mexican state-owned utility Comisión Federal de Electricidad from 2002 to 2009 in order to procure supply contracts. The judge cited flagrant prosecutorial misconduct to justify his decision. The prosecutor withheld evidence from the defense and used false statements to obtain search warrants. Elsewhere, federal judges as well as juries have acquitted employees charged with bribing foreign officials. These cases show that prosecutors face serious evidentiary hurdles in proving FCPA violations beyond a reasonable doubt.

Foreign Enforcement Actions

A few other countries with FCPA-like laws have also intensified their efforts to step up enforcement. While the number of countries actively enforcing the *OECD Convention* rose steadily between 2006 and 2008, there was a backslide in 2009, when only four nations had active enforcement and 21 nations had little to no enforcement. In 2010, the numbers rose again, with Denmark, Italy, and the United Kingdom becoming more active. But one of the actions was the London police's involvement in DOJ's 2010 bi-continental raid, an action initiated by the Americans. In 2011, there was a further increase in enforcement of the *OECD Convention*, with 13 countries sanctioning individuals or entities. The United Kingdom, Germany, Hungary, Italy, and South Korea have been among the most aggressive enforcers outside the United States.

The most dramatic enforcement of an FCPA-like statute came in a case against Siemens, A.G., set forth later. The United States imposed massive fines on the company for violating statutes prohibiting bribery of foreign public officials. In May 2007, a German court also convicted two former employees of Siemens AG of bribing officials at an Italian utility to award them contracts for the sale of gas turbines. One received a two-year suspended prison sentence for bribery. The other received a nine-month suspended sentence for aiding the bribery. The court also ordered Siemens to pay €38 million ($51.4 million) of the profit from the contracts.

Despite these efforts, 20 of the 40 signers of the *OECD Convention* have had little to no enforcement action; 14 of those nations have not brought a case since 1999. The United States is by far the most aggressive enforcer.

Securities and Exchange Commission v. Siemens Aktiengesellschaft

SEC Litigation Release no. 20829 (December 15, 2008)

BACKGROUND AND FACTS

Siemens, a German company that subjected itself to U.S. jurisdiction through its very significant U.S. business, violated the FCPA by engaging in a widespread and systematic practice of paying bribes to foreign government officials to obtain business. Siemens created elaborate payment schemes to conceal the nature of its corrupt payments, and the company's inadequate internal controls allowed the conduct to flourish. The misconduct involved employees at all levels, including former senior management, and revealed a corporate culture long at odds with the FCPA.

During this period, Siemens made thousands of payments to third parties in ways that obscured the

continues

continued

purpose for, and the ultimate recipients of, the money. At least 4,283 of those payments, totalling approximately $1.4 billion, were used to bribe government officials in return for business to Siemens around the world. Among others, Siemens paid bribes on transactions to design and build metro transit lines in Venezuela; metro trains and signalling devices in China; power plants in Israel; high voltage transmission lines in China; mobile telephone networks in Bangladesh; telecommunications projects in Nigeria; national identity cards in Argentina; medical devices in Vietnam, China, and Russia; traffic control systems in Russia; refineries in Mexico; and mobile communications networks in Vietnam. Siemens also paid kickbacks to Iraqi ministries in connection with sales of power stations and equipment to Iraq under the United Nations Oil-for-Food Program. Siemens earned more than $1.1 billion in profits on these transactions.

An additional approximately 1,185 separate payments to third parties totaling approximately $391 million were not properly controlled and were used, at least in part, for illicit purposes, including commercial bribery and embezzlement.

From 1999 to 2003, Siemens' Managing Board or "Vorstand" was ineffective in implementing controls to address constraints imposed by Germany's 1999 adoption of the Organization for Economic Cooperation and Development (OECD) anti-bribery convention that outlawed foreign bribery. The Vorstand was also ineffective in meeting the U.S. regulatory and anti-bribery requirements that Siemens was subject to following its March 12, 2001, listing on the New York Stock Exchange. Despite knowledge of bribery at two of its largest groups—Communications and Power Generation—the company's conductat the top was inconsistent with an effective FCPA compliance program and created a corporate culture in which bribery was tolerated and even rewarded at the highest levels of the company.

Employees obtained large amounts of cash from cash desks, which were sometimes transported in suitcases across international borders for bribery. Authorizations for payments were placed on post-it notes and later removed to eradicate any permanent record. Siemens used numerous slush funds, off-book accounts maintained at unconsolidated entities, and a system of business consultants and intermediaries to facilitate the corrupt payments.

Siemens failed to implement adequate internal controls to detect and prevent violations of the FCPA. Elaborate payment mechanisms were used to conceal the fact that bribe payments were made around the globe to obtain business. False invoices and payment documentation were created to make payments to business consultants under false business-consultant agreements that identified services that were never intended to be rendered. Illicit payments were falsely recorded as expenses for management fees, consulting fees, supply contracts, room preparation fees, and commissions. Siemens inflated UN contracts, signed side agreements with Iraqi ministries that were not disclosed to the UN, and recorded the ASSF payments as legitimate commissions despite UN, U.S., and international sanctions against such payments.

In November 2006, Siemens' current management began to implement reforms to the company's internal controls. These reforms substantially reduced, but did not entirely eliminate, corrupt payments. All but $27.5 million of the corrupt payments occurred before November 15, 2006. The company conducted a massive internal investigation and implemented an amnesty program to its employees to gather information.

RESOLUTION

Siemens agreed to pay a total of $1.6 billion in disgorgement and fines, the largest amount a company has ever paid to resolve corruption-related charges. Siemens agreed to pay $350 million in disgorgement to the SEC. In related actions, Siemens will pay a $450 million criminal fine to the U.S. Department of Justice and a fine of €395 million (approximately $569 million) to the Office of the Prosecutor General in Munich, Germany. Siemens previously paid a fine of €201 million (approximately $285 million) to the Munich Prosecutor in October 2007. In addition, Siemens consented to the entry of a court order permanently enjoining it from future violations of Sections 30A, 13(b)(2)(A), and 13(b)(2)(B) of the *Exchange Act;* and ordering it to comply with certain undertakings regarding its FCPA compliance program, including an independent monitor for a period of four years.

Case Questions

1. How do the Siemens' penalties relate to the limits on fines imposed by the *Alternative Fines Act*, discussed earlier in this chapter?
2. Why was a German company subject to the U.S. FCPA? Do you think FCPA enforcement is effective if the foreign officials accepting the bribes are not held accountable?
3. Why did Siemens' internal efforts to stop corruption not result in more lenient treatment from the U.S. government?

International Refusal to Enforce Contracts Induced by Bribery

Civil and criminal penalties under the FCPA and foreign antibribery statutes are not the only possible legal sanctions for investors who use bribes to induce foreign public officials to award them contracts. In the past few years, international tribunals have refused to enforce contracts based on bribery, leaving the briber to forfeit its bribe payment and lose the benefit of its wrongdoing. In the 2006 English case *Marlwood Commercial Inc. v. Kozeny*, the Queen's Bench Commercial Court held that English courts will not enforce contracts involving bribery of foreign officials or sale of influence because they are illegal in England and contrary to English public policy. This rule applies even if the bribery is not a crime in the foreign country.

In the 2006 arbitration of *Inceysa Vallisolenta, S.L v. Republic of El Salvador*, the International Centre for Settlement of Investment Disputes (ICSID) tribunal similarly refused to enforce a contract entered into by the Salvadoran government with a contractor who acted fraudulently. The panel relied on the interpretation of the specific language of the *Bilateral Investment Treaty* at issue. However, in the 2007 arbitration of *World Duty Free Co. v. Republic of Kenya*, produced later in this section, the ICSID tribunal went a step further and established a general rule that bribe payments are unacceptable under transnational public policy.

The International Monetary Fund (IMF) has said that IMF officials will press for anticorruption reforms in countries seeking to borrow money. The World Bank has declared that if it finds evidence of corruption in any project it finances, it will cancel the project. The developing world has weighed in through the *UN Convention against Corruption*. Courts will give no refuge to a bribe-giver, no matter how sympathetic its circumstances or how insignificant the bribe is to the underlying dispute.

Bribe-givers could also face private lawsuits from their competitors. Catering giant Compass was investigated by the United Nations for allegedly bribing its officials in connection with a bid to provide food rations to its peacekeeping forces. Compass's two rivals—Es-Ko International and Supreme Foodservice AG—sued Compass in a New York court alleging various non-FCPA violations for contaminating the bidding process and cheating them out of contracts that could be worth hundreds of millions of dollars. Compass reportedly settled the case for $74 million.

The World Bank has also declared that it will stop financing a project in which it finds any evidence of corruption. For instance, on June 2012 the World Bank claimed that it had credible evidence pointing to a high-level "corruption conspiracy" among Bangladeshi government officials, executives of a Canadian engineering firm SNC-Lavalin, and others in connection with the Padma Bridge Project in Bangladesh. As a result, the World Bank cancelled its $1.2 billion credit in support of the project. The Canadian authorities had earlier charged two former executives of SNC-Lavalin under the *Corruption of Foreign Public Officials Act*—Canada's FCPA-like statute—for bribing Bangladeshi officials in connection with a bid to build the bridge.

World Duty Free Company Limited v. The Republic of Kenya

ICSID Award, Case No. ARB/00/7, October 4, 2006

TRIBUNAL MEMBERS H. E. JUDGE GILBERT GUILLAUME; HON. ANDREW ROGERS, QC; V. V. VEEDER, QC

... the Tribunal recalls that the Government of Kenya, on 27 April 1989, concluded an agreement with a company, called the "House of Perfume" for the construction, maintenance and operation of duty-free complexes at Nairobi and Mombasa Airports. This agreement was amended on 11 May 1990 to substitute "World Duty Free Ltd" for the "House of Perfume." As a follow-up to this agreement, a Lease was concluded on 25 August 1995 between the Kenya Airports Authority—acting on behalf of the Government of Kenya—and World Duty Free. All of these documents were signed by Mr. Nassir Ibrahim Ali, acting on behalf of the Companies.

World Duty Free contends that Kenya breached the 1989 Agreement in several respects, illegally expropriated its properties and destroyed its rights under the agreement. On this basis, it requests restitution or, in the alternative, compensation ... .

Kenya, for its part, submits that the 1989 Agreement was procured by paying a bribe to the then President of Kenya, Daniel arap Moi. It adds that the payment of such a bribe is criminal and that the resulting contract does not have the force of law. It is unenforceable and the claims

continues

continued

cannot be heard as a matter of public policy. Furthermore, as a matter of applicable law, the contract is voidable and has been validly avoided by Kenya. Consequently, the claims must be dismissed with prejudice ... .

[The tribunal finds that a bribe of $2 million had been paid by Mr. Ali to President Moi, and that the 1989 Agreement was in fact procured as a result of such a payment. The tribunal then addresses Kenya's argument that as a matter of international public policy, as well as Kenyan and English law, the 1989 Agreement "does not have force of law" and that World Duty Free's claims should therefore be dismissed.]

The Tribunal first notes that bribery or influence peddling, as well as both active and passive corruption, are sanctioned by criminal law in most, if not all, countries. This was the case in Kenya in particular in 1989, under the Kenyan *Prevention of Corruption Act* of 1956, and is still the case under the *Anti-Corruption and Economic Crimes Act* of 2003.

In order to render more effective this general condemnation, a number of international conventions were concluded during the last decade. [The tribunal here mentions conventions adopted by the Organisation of the American States, OECD, and the Council of Europe.]

The same trend can be observed in Africa: on 11 July 2003, in Maputo, Mozambique, the Heads of States and Governments of the African Union approved a *Convention on Preventing and Combating Corruption*, which has been signed by 39 African States (including Kenya) and has already been ratified by 11 of these 39 States. In this Convention, the Member States of the African Union declare themselves "concerned about the negative effects of corruption and impunity on the political, economic, social and cultural stability of African States and its devastating effects on the economic and social development of the African peoples." They "acknowledge that corruption undermines accountability and transparency in the management of public affairs as well as socio-economic development in the continent." Article 4 of the Convention lists the acts of corruption to which it applies and covers in particular "the solicitation or acceptance, directly or indirectly, by a public official or any other person, of any goods of monetary value or other benefit, such as a gift, favour, promise or advantage for himself or herself or for another person or entity, in exchange of any act or omission in the performance of his or her public functions." Under Article 5 of the Convention, legislative and other measures must be taken to establish such acts as offences.

These various Conventions only bind State parties and do so only from the date States become parties. They deal mainly—and sometimes exclusively—with criminal law. In concluding these Conventions, States have shown their common will to fight corruption, not only through national legislation, as they did before, but also through international cooperation. In doing so, States not only reached a new stage in the fight against corruption, but also solidly confirmed their prior condemnation of it.

In light of domestic laws and international conventions relating to corruption, and in light of the decisions taken in this matter by courts and arbitral tribunals, this Tribunal is convinced that bribery is contrary to the international public policy of most, if not all, States or, to use another formula, to transnational public policy. Thus, claims based on contracts of corruption or on contracts obtained by corruption cannot be upheld by this Arbitral Tribunal.

[The tribunal then examines English and Kenyan law—the laws chosen by the Parties in the agreements—and finds that no English or Kenyan statute or law render legal any part of claimant's conduct. The tribunal then addresses claimant's argument that the bribe was a transaction independent of, and therefore severable from, the 1989 Agreement.]

The Tribunal dismisses the Claimant's submissions that the bribe was an independent collateral transaction or at least severable from the Parties' Agreement of 27th April 1989. On the facts found in this case, the bribe was no separate agreement or otherwise severable from the Agreement. As to separateness, it is no answer for the Claimant to assert that the fact that the bribe was covert and kept confidential (with no mention of any such payment in the Agreement) is proof that it was a distinct transaction from the Agreement itself. Its secrecy was because it was a bribe; and as such, it therefore cannot be invoked by the Claimant to establish its separateness from the Agreement. This was one overall transaction and not two unrelated bargains. Moreover, the Claimant's submission proves too much: every bribe is intended to be secret by payer and payee; and accordingly the submission of a separate or collateral bribe based on such secrecy would save every illegal transaction tainted by bribery—if the Claimant was right. The Tribunal considers the Claimant's submission to be wrong both in principle and on the facts of the present case.

In conclusion ... the Claimant is not legally entitled to maintain any of its pleaded claims in these proceedings as a matter of *ordre public international* and public policy under the contract's applicable laws.

Case Questions

1. How does the tribunal support its conclusion that bribe payments are unacceptable under international public policy? What role does the *Convention on Preventing and Combating Corruption* that is approved by the African Union play in the tribunal's reasoning?
2. How important is it that Kenyan and English law also prohibit bribe payments?
3. What does the tribunal mean when it says that the bribe and the 1989 Agreement were "one overall transaction"?

Best Practices for the U.S. Businessperson

Achieving greater profits for one's company is not worth a prison sentence. With the United States' new aggressive enforcement of the FCPA, it is increasingly likely that if any corruption is detected, it will cause multilateral institutions to pull financing and may even void the ill-procured contract, leading to disastrous consequences for the investor. Therefore, the best course of action for the U.S. entrepreneur abroad is to be vigilant against foreign corruption. Here are a few ground rules:

1. Avoid making direct payments to government officials, other than payments associated with the most ministerial aspects of clearing customs. Payments should be avoided even if the foreign official threatens to terminate existing contracts with one's firm unless he or she is paid off. The simplest course may be to avoid doing business in nations in which such extortion is known and likely to occur. Such situations put a firm in a difficult position: If it accepts the extortion demand, it risks U.S. criminal conviction; if it refuses the demand, it faces a substantial business loss.
2. Foreign agents should be carefully selected and even more carefully paid. Preferably, companies should build an ample "due diligence" file containing the foreign agent's trade references and records of investigations into the person's character. Commissions and other payments should conform to customary rates in that nation.
3. Avoid "premium" transactions in nations with suspect reputations. Make appropriate inquiry with respect to the government officials whose discretion is involved in any given transaction.

CONCLUSION

A U.S. enterprise that uses an independent agent to expand into a foreign nation can avoid much of the foreign regulation that is inherent in establishing a full corporate presence or in cross-border licensing. However, in order to avoid such regulation, it will need to make sure that its agent is recognized as independent. The enterprise will benefit from becoming familiar with the statutory framework of rights that protect the agent—rights that exist regardless of the terms of its contract with the agent. Once it engages a local agent, the U.S. enterprise must make sure that its advertising and promotional efforts abroad comply with local regulations and laws and reflect the sensitivities of the local culture. Finally, the enterprise must be particularly careful that its "promotions" do not include payments that are indirectly intended to go to a local official as this violates national criminal laws and international agreements.

Chapter Summary

1. The United States places few restrictions on the terms of the agent–principal relationship. The principal and the agent each have discretion to agree on appropriate terms, including compensation, exclusivity, and termination of the relationship. However, many nations enact laws that supersede contractual arrangements. These laws protect local representatives against enforcement of certain contract terms, no matter what is written in a representative's agreement.
2. For tax purposes, if the principal works through an agent rather than an independent contractor, the principal is often viewed as having opened an office and is subject to taxation. This tends not to occur with independent contractors. In particular, if an investor has a dependent agent in a country, he or she will often be regarded as an employee. This classification may subject the principal to local law regarding pensions, tax withholding, and labor negotiations. Further, if an agent is found to be dependent, the principal will be vicariously liable to third parties for the agent's misdeeds, particularly in the context of product liability.
3. Virtually every country prohibits false advertising, but what is "false" differs according to how exacting the local culture is. What is false advertising in one culture may be acceptable "puffing" in another. In some nations, language laws require that every word

in advertising—including technical jargon—be in the local language.

4. Countries tend to impose particularly tight regulations on advertising of products that are considered to be (or lead to) "sin" in the local culture. For example, many countries regulate the advertising of alcoholic beverages or tobacco products. Many countries also restrict the advertising of medicines because such products are too important to allow mere marketing to affect their distribution.
5. Virtually all countries have laws against the bribery of public officials. However, in many of these countries, the local authorities do not enforce these laws. However, businesspeople must consider the risk of prosecution in their home country for bribing an official in another country. At least 38 countries, including the United States, have laws that forbid their citizens to bribe foreign public officials. The U.S. *Foreign Corrupt Practices Act* prohibits U.S. citizens from "corruptly" paying or offering to pay a "foreign official" for assistance in obtaining or retaining business. It also prohibits payments to a foreign agent when the payer had reason to know that a portion of the payment will go to a public official.
6. The U.S. *Foreign Corrupt Practices Act* does not prohibit a "facilitating or expediting payment… the purpose of which is to expedite or secure the performance of a routine governmental action." Routine governmental actions are those that are nondiscretionary. This facilitating payments exception has been narrowly interpreted. The FCPA does not contain a *de minimis* exception.
7. The FCPA also requires publicly held U.S. companies to "make and keep books, records, and accounts which, in reasonable detail, accurately and fairly reflect the transactions and dispositions of [their] assets" and requires an investor to "devise and maintain a system of internal accounting controls sufficient to provide reasonable assurances" that all transactions are properly authorized and that access to assets is tracked. These requirements mean that a company may be liable for failing to identify bribery even if the amount would not otherwise be material to the investor company.
8. Before jurisdiction could be established over a foreign entity, the FCPA requires that the foreign entity commit an FCPA violation "while in the territory of the United States." But the DOJ and the SEC have interpreted this requirement broadly. Courts have rarely dismissed an FCPA case against a foreign defendant for a lack of jurisdiction.
9. In recent years, the U.S. Department of Justice has greatly increased its civil and criminal enforcement of the FCPA. In the three years from 2004 through 2006, 22 DOJ enforcement actions and 19 SEC enforcement actions were initiated. From 2007 through 2009 those numbers exploded to 96 DOJ actions and 52 SEC actions; 2010 was an especially busy year with 29 SEC actions and 61 DOJ actions. Enforcement efforts continued in 2011 and 2012 with a total of 40 SEC actions and 36 DOJ actions. As of the end of 2012, there were about 150 active FCPA investigations. But the DOJ has struggled to win convictions in court against individuals charged with FCPA violations.
10. Other states, particularly in Western Europe, have been inconsistent in enforcement of their anti-bribery of foreign official's law.
11. In the past few years, international tribunals have refused to enforce contracts obtained through bribery, leaving the bribe-givers no way to recapture their investments.

Key Terms

agency relationship 436
agent 436
principal 436
independent contractor 436
evergreen contract 437
just cause 437
economic conditions alarm 439
commission override 439
dependent agent 439
independent agent 439
permanent establishment 439
product liability 439
caveat emptor 440
puffing 441
language laws 442
antibribery 447
"grease payments" exception 448
corruptness 448
knowing requirement 448
accounting and record-keeping provisions 449
materiality 449

Questions and Case Problems

1. Suppose that Roger Sobodka, a U.S. executive stationed in Paris, wishes to build a support office for his firm's technicians in the Parisian suburb of Asnieres. He enters into an agreement with Francois Demblans, a homebuilder, to do the work for $100,000. Under the agreement, M. Demblans may seek reimbursement of costs attributable to unforeseen circumstances. The agreement further specifies that construction of the office building will be complete in nine months, and that M. Demblans will modify his work upon Mr. Sobodka's reasonable instructions. Assuming that French agency law is consistent with that discussed in this chapter, is M. Demblans a dependent or an independent agent of Mr. Sobodka?
2. After conducting a market survey, Penton Intergalactic, Ltd., a manufacturer of plows, believes that there is pent-up demand for its product in the expanding agricultural economy of Paraguay. Penton retains Saul Ortiz, a Paraguayan who operates a substantial business selling agricultural implements. Penton's New York City advertising agency develops the ad campaign and strategy for introduction of the product, including a rather precise time schedule. Sr. Ortiz is to follow Penton's instructions as the project develops. Sr. Ortiz will use the same employees that he uses in his business operations, except that a few Penton employees will be on-site to assist him. He will receive a commission on each plow sold, plus reimbursement of marketing expenses identifiable as related to the Penton program. Assuming that Paraguayan agency law is consistent with that discussed in this chapter, is Sr. Ortiz a dependent or an independent agent?
3. Jordan Motors, Inc., opens a dealership in Frankfurt, West Germany, selling American cars. In its advertising campaign, Jordan claims that for the next two weeks only, it will beat the price on any comparable German car by 1,000 euros. Faced with this threat to its market share, Hartman Autos, A. G., slashes its prices to cost. Andrea Giebbels comes to Jordan's showroom with a written quote of Hartman's price for its bottom-of-the-line German car and demands that Jordan sell her 20 of its bottom-of-the-line American cars for a substantial loss. Jordan refuses. If Fraulein Giebbels brings an action, will she be able to enforce Jordan's offer? If Hartman sues, can it have Jordan's advertising campaign enjoined?
4. Borges Meat Marketing, Inc., a Nebraska corporation, wishes to establish a network of gourmet butcher shops in India. It has a well-developed introductory advertising campaign that it has employed in establishing similar butcher shops in the United States and does not wish to go to the expense of developing a new one. What should it do?
5. Joseph Supersonic Company, a U.S. jet fighter manufacturer, is eager to sell its aircraft to the state-owned airline of the Republic of Platano and wishes to retain a local representative to assist it. Maria de la Concepcion Casañas y Diaz is reputed to have the best government contracts in Platano; her clients have been successful in garnering contracts a high percentage of the time. Accordingly, she is more in demand than other local representatives, and her fee is the highest in the country. What are the implications of hiring Srta. Casañas y Diaz?
6. Using the facts in Question 5, assume that a reference check has uncovered rumors that Srta. Casañas y Diaz has had an intimate relationship with Platano's assistant secretary for government procurement, although they have no plans for a more permanent relationship. What are the FCPA implications now?
7. Assume that Joseph retained Srta. Casañas but failed to obtain the contract. To Joseph's chagrin, it subsequently learns that Srta. Casañas y Diaz used part of her fee to make a $10,000 payment to a government official. If Joseph has total assets of $5 billion, should it report the episode on its financial statement?

Managerial Implications

Your firm, Flyboy, Inc., is a successful U.S. manufacturer of aircraft. Flyboy would like to expand its market to Pamonia, a small, oil-rich kingdom that was once an Italian colony. The principal purchaser of aircraft in Pamonia is the government, although some private families have the resources to purchase the product. The same private families are, not coincidentally, also the nobility of the Pamonian kingdom. For a new entrant like Flyboy, breaking into the market without a local representative is not possible. You are also aware that local custom includes "grease payments" and lavish gifts to customers in Pamonia.

1. Prepare a five-page paper considering the pluses and minuses of entering the Pamonian market. Focus on the legal risks inherent in the proposed investment and how Flyboy might avoid them.
2. Describe the arrangements into which you would enter with your Pamonian agent.
3. Evaluate the possibility of using an Italian firm as your distributor in Pamonia. What would be the FCPA implications if Flyboy simply delivered the aircraft FOB Pamonia and had no involvement in marketing? What implications would this have for Flyboy's profit margin?

Ethical Considerations

1. Agent protection laws ostensibly protect small, local entities from powerful foreign companies. It is true that because it is easy for a big company to communicate with and transport people to faraway lands, it can easily displace its local agent after it launches the business. In light of the much greater power of a multinational corporation against even a wealthy local, there may be justification for these laws. Yet, local representatives tend to become extremely wealthy for not doing very much work. Cynics suggest that the political influence of these local elites has more to do with agent protection laws than with any real desire to help "little guys." Furthermore, where such laws are enforced, local consumers typically have to pay more for the same product. Who is right, the countries that enact agent protection laws or the countries that do not?
2. In the summer of 2007, the media revealed that the British defense firm BAE had paid more than $2 billion in bribes over 20 years to Prince Bandar, a powerful member of the Saudi royal family. The Prince had delivered a contract under which Saudi Arabia purchased hundreds of British warplanes, spare parts, and training for Saudi pilots. When the British Fraud Office began investigating the transaction, Prime Minister Tony Blair terminated it for "national security" reasons, but the truth came out through the media. Prime Minister Blair ultimately defended the transaction on a national security basis and pointed to the many jobs it provided to the U.K. economy. The contracts continue today, and arms sales to the Middle East typically entail 10–15 percent commissions to "agents" widely reported to channel them to heads of state, generals, and their friends. What is your view as to the prime minister's position?

CHAPTER 17

Protection and Licensing of Intellectual Property

INTRODUCTION

Intellectual property rights (IPRs) are increasingly becoming an extremely important asset of any large corporation, whether in the United States or in other countries. In today's global economy, IPRs are critical to a company's ability to compete effectively, and they are often a key reason behind a company's dominance in the marketplace. It is no surprise then, that IPRs are central to various intercorporate transactions including mergers and acquisitions, licensing, and cross-licensing. In fact, because large corporations have universally recognized the need to build strong IPR portfolios, cross-licensing agreements are proliferating and are becoming a routine part of business operations.

Innovation and intellectual property have been recognized as a central driver for growth as well as stock market value. As market capitalization and the global economy have moved from a manufacturing-based to a knowledge-based economy, the type of assets on companies' balance sheets has significantly shifted from tangible assets to intangible assets (which include IPRs). For instance, Research in Motion's BlackBerry patents have been estimated to contribute more than 20 percent to its share value, although the value may be declining due to increased competition from Apple, Samsung, and others.

As a result, companies are racing to build substantial intellectual property portfolios to maintain a strong position in the marketplace and to improve their bottom line and share value. In 2011, a consortium including Microsoft, Apple, Ericsson, Research in Motion, and others paid $4.5 billion for 6,000 patents owned by bankrupt Nortel Networks. Google purchased Motorola Mobility for $12.5 billion and acquired Motorola's 17,000 patents in that transaction.

IPRs give their owners a monopoly within the four corners of the IPRs: the literal meaning stated in the granted IPR. If a company owns an IPR, it can bring lawsuits to prevent others from competing with products with features that fall within the literal bounds of the legal description of the IPR. The international marketplace is thus increasingly driven by IPR litigation. Companies secure intellectual property rights to ensure freedom to operate in their IP space, to preempt litigation, and to strengthen their bargaining position against competitors. For instance, in a crowded technology space, a company can defend itself in litigation by countersuing and asserting its own patents against a competitor. In addition, armed with a strong intellectual property portfolio, companies are in a better position to negotiate favorable terms in a licensing or cross-licensing agreement to obtain use of another company's IPR.

Emerging countries are quickly catching up on IPR-driven growth strategies. China was the world's second largest research-and-development spender in 2009. Further, a Chinese telecommunications company, ZTE Corporation, was the biggest filer of international patent applications in 2011. Another Chinese company, Huawei Technologies, ranked third.

While this global race to build IPR portfolios has promoted innovation and growth, in certain crowded fields, it has also resulted in global IP wars, such as the multinational Apple/Samsung litigation. This wealth of litigation sometimes paradoxically results in the inefficient underuse of IP resources, a situation in which too many patent owners are excluding each other, and as a result, no one can effectively use the invention. Licensing or cross-licensing arrangements solve or lessen these inefficiencies and should be considered and used early in any potential transaction or dispute.

This chapter analyzes how IPRs affect companies' behavior, strategies, and interrelations, including litigation and licensing arrangements between private parties. In addition, the chapter will examine the various IPR protection and enforcement laws and treaties and how governments attempt to promote innovation, development, and trade through these laws and treaties. Finally, the chapter will discuss practical limitations on the protection and enforcement of IPRs, including historical attitudes towards IPRs, social considerations, and ethical issues.

LITIGATION

If a company can gain a monopoly by defining its IPR broadly, there is a great incentive to broad patents. And the government authorities with the power of granting patents are extremely busy and do not have the resources of those seeking the patents. For example, in late 2012, Apple obtained a U.S. design patent on a computer in the shape of a triangle with rounded corners. That may mean that no other computer manufacturer can make a computer of a similar shape unless Apple consents. Whatever one might say about the policy merits of granting a company a monopoly on such a common shape, if successful, the patent holder would be able to exclude competitors from entering the computer tablet market, irrespective of whether the contents and quality of the tablet are entirely different. If the courts uphold this patent, Apple would dominate the tablet market. The same incentive exists for all companies, in virtually all fields: Companies can foreclose competition, irrespective of quality or price, simply by "owning" some attribute essential to the product. Thus, it is not surprising that virtually every technological field is now crowded with similarly broadly worded patents.

In the current IPR-crowded environment, litigation has become unavoidable, particularly in profitable industries dominated by one or more market leaders. A company with a strong IPR portfolio can refuse to license its IPR and can threaten or pursue litigation, which can result in significant litigation expenses and potential market hold-up. This situation is highlighted, for instance, in the ongoing smartphone wars that are pitting the smartphone tech giants against each other in multinational disputes. Apple is spending millions of dollars in litigation expenses in several countries and continents, against multiple mobile-device manufacturers including Samsung, Motorola Mobility, and HTC.

One of the issues being litigated involves Apple's patent covering the "bounce-back effect" in iOS, Apple's operating system for iPhones and iPads. Apple claims that Google's operating system Android and Android-equipped mobile devices infringe Apple's "bounce-back" patent. Apple's offensive litigation strategy, however, has prompted its rivals to retaliate in kind. For every allegation of patent infringement, Apple has to face allegations that Apple's patent is invalid and counterclaims for infringement of the competitor's own patents.

In litigation, an IPR owner plaintiff typically asserts infringement of one or more IPRs by products sold or manufactured by the accused infringer. The accused infringer can assert defenses of non-infringement, invalidity, and/or unenforceability. In addition, the accused infringer can counterclaim and assert the accused infringer's own IPRs against the plaintiff. In the United States, federal district courts have exclusive jurisdiction over patent cases. And because, like all trials, patent trials involve resolution of issues of fact, juries often decide these cases. All appeals in patent cases are heard by the Court of Appeals for the Federal Circuit, which sits in Washington, DC. An unsatisfied patent litigant can further appeal decisions from the Federal Circuit to the Supreme Court of the United States, but such appeals are discretionary and the Supreme Court hears very few patent cases.

Apple, Inc. v. Samsung Electronics Co., Ltd.

—— F. Supp. 2d —— (2013) WL 772525 (N.D. Cal.)

BACKGROUND

In August 2012, a jury awarded Apple more than $1 billion in damages for infringement against Samsung. Samsung filed a motion with the court for reduction of the jury award and for a new trial, and Apple filed a motion for supplemental damages.

JUDGE LUCY H. KOH

Apple's motion for an increase in the jury's damages award is DENIED. The Court declines to determine the amount of prejudgment interest or supplemental damages until after the appeals in this case are resolved.

continues

continued

Because the Court has identified an impermissible legal theory on which the jury based its award, and cannot reasonably calculate the amount of excess while effectuating the intent of the jury, the Court hereby ORDERS a new trial on damages for the following products: Galaxy Prevail, Gem, Indulge, Infuse 4G, Galaxy SII AT&T, Captivate, Continuum, Droid Charge, Epic 4G, Exhibit 4G, Galaxy Tab, Nexus S 4G, Replenish, and Transform. This amounts to $450,514,650 being stricken from the jury's award. The parties are encouraged to seek appellate review of this Order before any new trial.

The jury's award stands for the Galaxy Ace, Galaxy S (i9000), Galaxy S II i9100, Galaxy Tab 10.1 WiFi, Galaxy Tab 10.1 4G LTE, Intercept, Fascinate, Galaxy S 4G, Galaxy S II Showcase, Mesmerize, Vibrant, Galaxy S II Skyrocket, Galaxy S II Epic 4G Touch, and Galaxy S II T-Mobile. The total award for these 14 products is $598,908,892.

It is so ordered.

Case Questions

1. Should patent cases be decided by lay judges and juries?
2. Are litigation damages too high in patent cases?
3. How can the legislature improve the patent system and reduce the inefficiencies of litigation?

Certain courts have imposed mandatory licensing for patented technologies that are essential to the implementation of a standard. For example, in 2011, the Hague District Court in the Netherlands denied Samsung's request for an injunction against Apple in connection with patents essential to comply with the 3G telecommunications standard. Samsung was required to give a license to Apple on **fair, reasonable, and nondiscriminatory** (**FRAND**) terms before seeking injunctive relief. FRAND licensing can significantly reduce the risk of patent hold-up and the perceived advantages of litigation, e.g., keeping competitors out of the marketplace. Unfortunately, FRAND licensing applies only in limited circumstances and has not curbed litigation in a meaningful way. Because companies are learning that litigation is costly and risky, however, the free market may itself correct the inefficiencies of litigation by deterring parties from litigating and pushing them to enter in licensing and/or cross-licensing arrangements.

REASONS FOR INTELLECTUAL PROPERTY TRANSFER ARRANGEMENTS

The most rapidly growing method of doing business abroad is to transfer intellectual property rights (IPRs) to a foreign business in exchange for a fee or other form of remuneration. Intellectual property rights are rights to technological know-how or artistic work. Like the simple engagement of a representative discussed in the preceding chapter, IPR transfers need not involve any capital investment abroad. They usually involve manufacturing or merchandising a product or service in the foreign country. By engaging a foreign party to do this manufacturing or merchandising, the U.S. investor can avoid the substantial risks and legal entanglements of capital investments abroad, discussed in chapters to follow.

Owners of IPRs transfer them for a variety of reasons. The U.S. firm might grant a license for a fee—such a license fee is called a **royalty**—to a foreign company. A **license** is a limited permission to use the U.S. firm's trademarks, copyrights, or know-how in making products for sale in the vicinity of the foreign company's country. Alternatively, the U.S. company might provide the IPR and physical components to a foreign manufacturing plant that will fabricate the product for re-export back to the U.S. concern.

In many cases, the foreign product is itself a component of the U.S. company's ultimate product. Upon receipt, the U.S. company will integrate it into the ultimate product in the United States. In addition, a U.S. firm can use a transfer of technology as its contribution to a joint venture abroad in exchange for a share of the joint venture. The joint venture would use the technology to manufacture and, perhaps, market the product.

A U.S. company typically enters into one of these arrangements because it provides marketing or other opportunities that the firm otherwise could not exploit efficiently. The firm may already be producing at the full extent of its domestic manufacturing capacity and may not have the resources to expand significantly. Licensing or teaming with a foreign company with adequate capital and perhaps other attractive assets—for instance, a ready marketing network in desired export markets—is a way to expand the company's market without raising substantial additional capital.

Another U.S. firm may have ample funds and a good product, but an inadequate research and development (R&D) capability. If it needs to improve its technology quickly before it is nudged out of market share by competing technologies, such a company may wish to team with a foreign company that has strong R&D infrastructure in order to expand to new geographic markets in the short term, while developing enhanced products for the future.

Still another company may possess a **utility patent** (one that has a broad range of potential applications), but lack the breadth of management capabilities, developmental resources, or marketing skills to exploit all its applications simultaneously. After such a company reserves for itself the patent applications that seem most consistent with its skills and orientation, the company might license the basic technology to other firms, each of which is authorized to develop a specified product or geographic market.

If labor is substantially cheaper in a foreign country, it may entice an IPR owner to shift production offshore. The U.S. company, however, may not know its way around the foreign country or may fear the risk of nationalization. In such a situation, the U.S. firm might prefer contracting with a local firm for its production requirements, rather than setting up its own factory abroad.

Companies also enter into licensing or cross-licensing arrangements to expand their business operations and gain access to new product lines. For instance, in 2013 Syngenta and DuPont recently entered into a technology licensing agreement that will expand each of the companies' crop protection product portfolios. Under the agreement, Syngenta obtained a license from DuPont to develop products containing DuPont's fungicide oxathiapiprolin. In exchange, DuPont received exclusive access to Syngenta's Solatenol product for mixture with DuPont's picoxystrobin fungicide on soybean and other crops in Brazil. Companies may also enter into licensing or cross-licensing arrangements to share initial costs, which can present barriers to entry into a new market, and maintenance costs. For instance, Nokia Siemens Networks agreed with Ericsson and Huawei in 2013 to enter into cross-licensing agreements for multi-vendor network management and to jointly utilize the Operations Support Systems (OSS) that they use to manage networks.

In short, there are many reasons for an IPR owner to transfer its intellectual property. Regardless of the motivation for a transfer, the risk is the same—losing control of the IPRs and helping to establish a competitor. For example, a small U.S. chemical manufacturer may provide its basic patent to a large French manufacturer through a joint venture in the hope of exploiting the European market and obtaining added R&D capacity. But in doing so, it may give the powerful foreign firm an opportunity to "research around" the patent and develop non-infringing alternatives, or other products whose infringement cannot be proved. With such products, the French firm may come to dominate the European market, as well as pose a threat in the U.S. firm's own home market.

IPR transfers are becoming so common that numerous firms are emerging to facilitate transactions between IPR owners and potential purchasers. These include (1) IPR clearinghouses, which provide IPR strategy advice, valuation, infringement analysis; (2) IPR brokers which handle IPR auctions and brokerages; (3) IPR aggregation funds for open source software; and (4) firms that identify and acquire patents for the purpose of preventing violations and litigation costs.

INTELLECTUAL PROPERTY RIGHTS: TRANSFER ARRANGEMENTS

The heart of any IPR transfer is a grant of license that permits the other party to use the relevant right. The conditions of that use and the compensation to the licensor form the balance of the agreement.

Right to Use and Conditions of Use

The licensor often agrees to provide services to facilitate the anticipated activities, such as assistance in setting up an assembly line or other training and technical support. The licensor generally seeks to restrict the licensee's use of the transferred IPR. One common type of restriction is **geographical limitations**. For example, a licensor of a "name brand" doll may limit the licensee's sale of that doll within a specific nation. **Field of use limitations** restrict the applications for which the licensee may employ the IPR. For example, the licensor of a laser technology might permit one licensee to use the technology only in connection with medical applications, while retaining for itself the right to use the technology for communications applications and other uses. Other potential restrictions include **output or customer restrictions**, especially if the licensor plans to use the licensee as a source of products for the licensor's own distribution requirements.

When the licensor's economic return depends on the licensee's marketing success, the licensor may seek to impose various obligations on the exploitation of the licensed IPR. The licensee usually will be expected to pledge to use its "best efforts" to develop a market for the products manufactured with the IPR. Many licensors go farther, demanding that the licensee comply with specific marketing quotas under pain of losing its license.

Competitive Circumstances

When exploitation of the licensed IPR requires significant financial or other resources of the licensee, it will often demand **exclusive rights** in the IPR within some geographic area in order to enhance its chances of earning an adequate return on its investment. The licensor, on the other hand, may not want to "put all of its eggs in one basket." A licensee may fail for many reasons, such as lack of commitment, inability to secure financing, or marketing inadequacies. Meanwhile, competing technologies may come into the market, the licensor's patents may expire, or other events may intrude to reduce the long-term prospects for the venture. Licensors who are concerned about such risks sometimes grant rights to two or more licensees who are willing to compete to develop the target market.

Licensees faced with this situation will probably attempt to negotiate some compensating advantage, such as a reduced royalty obligation. Setting the royalty level for a particular IPR can be a difficult proposition, especially when the degree of market demand for the IPR may not yet be clear. Setting the royalty level too high may boost the total price for the end products to a level that is not competitive with substitute products available in the market. Demand may be high in Dijon for a hamburger sold using McDonald's trademarked materials and quality control practices, justifying a higher price, but at some point, consumers will be happier with a Brand X hamburger produced by someone who does not pay royalties. This will cause sales and royalties to decline, hurting licensor and licensee alike. The trick is to identify a royalty level that allows both licensor and licensee to optimize their respective returns.

Confidentiality and Improvements

Another key license provision is the clause that sets forth the licensee's obligation to keep the licensed technology confidential so that third parties cannot exploit the technology. Such provisions are critical when the IPR being licensed is a technology that is protected primarily by trade secret procedures rather than patent law. The licensee often will try to limit the length of time during which it must maintain confidentiality, while the licensor will try to preserve confidentiality for the anticipated useful life of the trade secret. The parties may also bargain over the specific means by which the licensee will be expected to safeguard the confidential technology. For instance, the licensor may demand that the licensee's employees enter into confidentiality and non-exploitation agreements that the licensor can enforce in the event of a breach. The licensor might also demand that only employees who "need to know" the technology be informed of it.

The parties will also usually negotiate over ownership and use rights if the licensee develops improvements in the licensed technology or creates new inventions based on that technology. Reasoning that the licensee would not have had the opportunity to develop these useful technologies without the know-how supplied by the licensor, the licensor may seek a **grant back** to itself of ownership in or at least the right to use—often without compensation—such new technology.

Licensors and licensees also haggle about termination issues. These principally focus on the length of time during which the licensee may exploit the licensed IPR; what events may cause the license to terminate early; and what, if any, rights the licensee will have in the IPR after termination. Thus, the licensor will try to be sure that the licensee agrees not to use the IPR in competition with the licensor or to disclose it to a potential competitor. The licensee, on the other hand, will try to keep royalties low and minimize or abbreviate the duration of noncompetition or nondisclosure provisions.

Many of the conflicts discussed here are often at issue during negotiations of IPR transfer agreements, whether domestic or international. The principal difference in the international scenario is that the host government often creates circumstances that favor the local licensee.

INTERNATIONAL PROTECTION FOR PATENTS, TRADEMARKS, AND OTHER INTELLECTUAL PROPERTY

Host countries regulate transfers of IPRs through a variety of direct and indirect means. Governments will be more or less protective of intellectual property, depending on its economic interests. Nations that generate intellectual property tend to favor strong protection, and those that do not create such property tend to oppose it. This conflict has been played out in international treaty negotiations where these nations work out common interests.

Whatever differences there are in the scope of protection, there is general agreement that some protection is necessary. If not, inventors will not take their innovations to non-protecting states and their commercial development will be disadvantaged.

During the last century, nations struggled to establish a consistent international legal system of intellectual property, with only limited success. The benefits of open trade in IPRs were often outweighed by a desire not to permit foreigners to profit through the sale of mere ideas. Progress was slow when intellectual property was a less important engine of wealth than industrial organization. The digital and telecommunications revolution made intellectual property an increasingly significant source of product value. Not surprisingly, the creators of this new value have moved rapidly to protect it through a comprehensive series of treaties. Nations that formerly opposed such treaties have conceded many issues, recognizing the hopelessness of competing without access to the new technology. These treaties streamline and standardize procedures, expand the geographic scope of protection, and create a much stronger international IPR enforcement network.

Paris Convention

The first international property treaty was the International *Convention for the Protection of Industrial Property*, better known as the *Paris Convention*. The Paris Convention, originally prepared in 1883 and since revised many times, guarantees that in each signatory country, foreign trademark and patent applications from other signatory countries will receive the same treatment and priority as those from domestic applicants. "Nationals of each of the [signatory] countries … shall, as regards the protection of industrial property, enjoy in all the other countries … the advantages that their respective laws now grant, or may hereafter grant, to nationals … ." In other words, no signatory country can give intellectual property protection to its own citizens unless it provides the same protection to the citizens of the other signatories. By implementing this principle of "national treatment"—an animating principle of all intellectual property treaties—the *Paris Convention* targeted discrimination against foreigners in obtaining patents.

The *Paris Convention* also gives a patent holder in any signatory country a **right of priority**. The convention provides that the date of an applicant's foreign application is deemed to be the same as the date of the applicant's original application on the same invention, so long as the foreign application was filed before the first anniversary of the original application. Because in most countries the first to file is the patent holder, this principle prevented a "race to the patent office" in other countries after the original filing.

There were two main problems with the *Paris Convention* scheme. First, the convention does not require any minimum substantive standard of patent protection. Thus, if a nation has no pharmaceutical R&D capability, it can decide that it is "immoral" to permit pharmaceutical patents and deny patent protection to pharmaceuticals. Although as a practical matter such a law is aimed at foreigners—because no locals have pharmaceutical patents—it is in compliance with the *Paris Convention*.

Another drawback of the convention is its lack of an enforcement mechanism. Disputes under the treaty are to be resolved by the International Court of Justice, but most signatory countries either do not recognize the court's jurisdiction or ignore rulings with which it does not agree. Consequently, there is no real procedure for enforcing verdicts other than voluntary compliance. In the 1990s, the developed nations determined to resolve these two defects of the *Paris Convention*. The result was the *TRIPS Agreement*, discussed later.

Patents

In 1970, the *Patent Cooperation Treaty* (PCT) supplemented the *Paris Convention* by establishing a centralized utility patent application process. The PCT has been signed by 142 states. A PCT application is filed on a standard form with the World Intellectual

Property Organization (WIPO). The WIPO, a United Nations agency headquartered in Geneva, Switzerland, processes the common application and forwards it to the countries designated by the applicant. If at least one of the applicants named in the PCT application is a national or resident of a PCT signatory, the PCT gives the application a **priority claim** on that invention in all signatory states. With a priority claim, the applicant business has up to 30 months after filing to begin the administrative processing (prosecution) of the application in the countries in which it wishes to obtain protection. This allows the applicant to lock in an application date while giving it time to raise capital on the basis of the patent filing. If capital cannot be raised—which suggests that there is inadequate commercial interest—the applicant can walk away without having spent needless sums in worldwide patent prosecution.

Europe has a consolidated multinational patent application. Since 1978, a patentee can obtain protection in all EU countries by filing a single application under the *European Patent Convention*. The convention is now in force in 38 countries. This system was enhanced in December 1989 when the member states signed the *Agreement Relating to Community Patents*, which created a unitary system for the application and grant of European patents and a uniform system for the resolution of litigation concerning patent infringement. Under this system, all persons seeking a European patent complete the same PCT application form and file it with the European Patent Office (EPO), located in Munich, Germany. The EPO's Revocation Division and Patent Administration Division grant and revoke patents for the entire EU. The grant of a European patent by the EPO must be "validated" in a member state and enforcement occurs in the member state's courts rather than a common European court system.

Infringement actions are brought in Community Patent Courts of First Instance and Second Instance, with all appeals to a single Common Patent Appeal Court for the entire EU. As a further bit of streamlining, the EPO filing is coordinated with the PCT process. An applicant can complete the PCT standard filing and designate the EPO as a "country" of origin to obtain both EPO and PCT protection.

The PCT system applies only to **utility patents**, that is, patents protecting a novel and useful process, machine, manufacture, or composition of matter. There is a separate but similar treaty system for **design patents**, patents protecting the ornamental features of an article of manufacture.

The Hague System for the International Registration of Industrial Designs first entered into force in 1925. It has been amended and supplemented several times, most recently by the *Geneva Act of the Hague Agreement Concerning the International Registration of Industrial Designs* (better known as the *Geneva Act*), which establishes a single standard application and single design patent filing process. The *Geneva Act* entered into force in December 2003. To date, the act has been ratified or acceded to by only 45 members. The United States has signed the act but has not yet ratified it. On December 19, 2012, President Obama signed into law the *Patent Law Treaties Implementation Act* of 2012 (PLTIA). The PLTIA harmonizes U.S. law for design patents with the *Geneva Act*. For example, the PLTIA extends the term of all U.S. design patents to 15 years from the date of grant (instead of the current 14-year term). The United States also reformed its utility patent system in 2011, in part to harmonize it with the rest of the world. For example, section 3(p) of the *Leahy-Smith America Invents Act* states that "[i]t is the sense of the Congress that converting the United States patent system from 'first to invent' to a system of 'first inventor to file' will improve the United States patent system and promote harmonization of the United States patent system with the patent systems commonly used in nearly all other countries throughout the world … ."

One area that has generated significant controversy is the scope of patentable subject matter. Governments and organizations in some emerging countries have argued that corporations from more developed nations engage in **biopiracy**, meaning they extract native or indigenous plants and animals for research (with the help of local knowledge), alter the plant or animal (such as through genetic engineering), and then obtain patents related to this research without providing the host country with compensation or affordable access to the inventions. Biotechnology corporations argue that they are performing research and pursuing innovation that would not occur without the ability to protect inventions that arise from this research. For example, a company might patent a particular strain of rice that has been genetically altered to withstand pests and provide greater yields. Even if the unaltered strain came from a particular country, the company would argue it provided significant resources to develop the new strain and should not have to give away this invention for free. As discussed in the following case, the scope of patentable subject matter continues to be a subject of dispute.

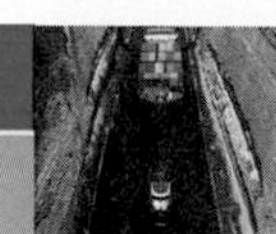

Diamond v. Chakrabarty

447 U.S. 303 (1980) United States Supreme Court

BACKGROUND AND FACTS

After genetically engineering a bacterium capable of breaking down crude oil, Ananda Chakrabarty sought to patent his creation under Title 35 U.S. Code Section 101, which states that "[w]hoever invents or discovers any new and useful process, machine, manufacture, or composition of matter, or any new and useful improvement thereof, may obtain a patent ... ." The U.S. Patent Office (PTO) rejected a claim to the bacterium itself on the grounds that living things are not patentable under Section 101. The Court of Customs and Patent Appeals reversed the PTO's decision and the U.S. Supreme Court agreed to hear Diamond's appeal. The Court was faced with the question of whether the creation of a live, human-made organism was patentable under Title 35 U.S.C. Section 101.

CHIEF JUSTICE BURGER

In 1972, respondent Chakrabarty, a microbiologist, filed a patent application, assigned to the General Electric Co. The application asserted 36 claims related to Chakrabarty's invention of "a bacterium from the genus Pseudomonas containing therein at least two stable energy-generating plasmids, each of said plasmids providing a separate hydrocarbon degradative pathway." This human-made, genetically engineered bacterium is capable of breaking down multiple components of crude oil. Because of this property, which is possessed by no naturally occurring bacteria, Chakrabarty's invention is believed to have significant value for the treatment of oil spills ... . The patent examiner allowed [some] claims ..., but rejected claims for the bacteria. His decision rested on two grounds: (1) that microorganisms are "products of nature," and (2) that as living things they are not patentable subject matter under 35 U.S.C. § 101 ... . The Constitution grants Congress broad power to legislate to "promote the Progress of Science and useful Arts, by securing for limited Times to Authors and Inventors the exclusive Right to their respective Writings and Discoveries." Art. I, § 8, cl. 8. The patent laws promote this progress by offering inventors exclusive rights for a limited period as an incentive for their inventiveness and research efforts ... . The authority of Congress is exercised in the hope that "[t]he productive effort thereby fostered will have a positive effect on society through the introduction of new products and processes of manufacture into the economy, and the emanations by way of increased employment and better lives for our citizens."

The question before us in this case is a narrow one of statutory interpretation requiring us to construe 35 U.S.C. § 101, which provides: "Whoever invents or discovers any new and useful process, machine, manufacture, or composition of matter, or any new and useful improvement thereof, may obtain a patent thereof, subject to the conditions and requirements of this title." Specifically, we must determine whether respondent's microorganism constitutes a "manufacture" or "composition of matter" within the meaning of the statute.

In cases of statutory construction we begin, of course, with the language of the statute. And "unless otherwise defined, words will be interpreted as taking their ordinary, contemporary common meaning." We have also cautioned that courts "should not read into the patent laws limitations and conditions which the legislature has not expressed."

Guided by these canons of construction, this Court has read the term "manufacture" in § 101 in accordance with its dictionary definition to mean "the production of articles for use from raw or prepared materials by giving to these materials new forms, qualities, properties, or combinations, whether by hand-labor or by machinery." Similarly, "composition of matter" has been construed consistent with its common usage to include "all compositions of two or more substances and ... all composite articles, whether they be the results of chemical union, or of mechanical mixture, or whether they be gases, fluids, powders or solids." In choosing such expansive terms as "manufacture" and "composition of matter," modified by the comprehensive "any," Congress plainly contemplated that the patent laws would be given wide scope.

The relevant legislative history also supports a broad construction. The *Patent Act* of 1793, authored by Thomas Jefferson, defined statutory subject matter as "any new and useful art, machine, manufacture, or composition of matter, or any new or useful improvement [thereof]." Act of Feb. 21, 1793, § 1. The Act embodied Jefferson's philosophy that "ingenuity should receive a liberal encouragement." Subsequent patent statutes in 1836, 1870, and 1874 employed this same broad language. In 1952, when the patent laws were re-codified, Congress replaced the word "art" with "process," but otherwise left Jefferson's language intact. The Committee Reports accompanying the 1952 Act inform us that Congress intended statutory subject matter to "include anything under the sun that is made by man."

continues

continued

This is not to suggest that § 101 has no limits or that it embraces every discovery. The laws of nature, physical phenomena, and abstract ideas have been held not patentable. Thus, a new mineral discovered in the earth or a new plant found in the wild is not patentable subject matter. Likewise, Einstein could not patent his celebrated law that $E=mc^2$; nor could Newton have patented the law of gravity. Such discoveries are "manifestations of … nature, free to all men and reserved exclusively to none."

Judged in this light, respondent's micro-organism plainly qualifies as patentable subject matter. His claim is not to a hitherto unknown natural phenomenon, but to a non-naturally occurring manufacture or composition of matter-a product of human ingenuity "having a distinctive name, character [and] use … . " Here … , the patentee has produced a new bacterium with markedly different characteristics from any found in nature and one having the potential for significant utility. His discovery is not nature's handiwork, but his own; accordingly it is patentable subject matter under § 101.

Two contrary arguments are advanced, neither of which we find persuasive. The petitioner's first argument rests on the enactment of the 1930 *Plant Patent Act*, which afforded patent protection to certain asexually reproduced plants, and the 1970 *Plant Variety Protection Act*, which authorized protection for certain sexually reproduced plants but excluded bacteria from its protection. In the petitioner's view, the passage of these Acts evidences congressional understanding that the terms "manufacture" or "composition of matter" do not include living things; if they did, the petitioner argues, neither Act would have been necessary … . We reject this argument. Prior to 1930, two factors were thought to remove plants from patent protection. The first was the belief that plants, even those artificially bred, were products of nature for purposes of the patent law. The second obstacle to patent protection for plants was the fact that plants were thought not amenable to the "written description" requirement of the patent law. Because new plants may differ from old only in color or perfume, differentiation by written description was often impossible.

In enacting the *Plant Patent Act*, Congress addressed both of these concerns. It explained at length its belief that the work of the plant breeder "in aid of nature" was patentable invention. And it relaxed the written description requirement in favor of "a description … as complete as is reasonably possible." No Committee or Member of Congress, however, expressed the broader view, now urged by the petitioner, that the terms "manufacture" or "composition of matter" exclude living things … . Congress [] recognized that the relevant distinction was not between living and inanimate things, but between products of nature, whether living or not, and human-made inventions. Here, respondent's microorganism is the result of human ingenuity and research. Hence, the passage of the *Plant Patent Act* affords the Government no support.

Nor does the passage of the 1970 *Plant Variety Protection Act* support the Government's position. As the Government acknowledges, sexually reproduced plants were not included under the 1930 Act because new varieties could not be reproduced true-to-type through seedlings. By 1970, however, it was generally recognized that true-to-type reproduction was possible and that plant patent protection was therefore appropriate … .

To buttress his argument, the petitioner, with the support of amicus, points to grave risks that may be generated by research endeavors such as respondent's. The briefs present a gruesome parade of horribles. Scientists, among them Nobel laureates, are quoted suggesting that genetic research may pose a serious threat to the human race, or, at the very least, that the dangers are far too substantial to permit such research to proceed apace at this time. We are told that genetic research and related technological developments may spread pollution and disease, that it may result in a loss of genetic diversity, and that its practice may tend to depreciate the value of human life … . We disagree. The grant or denial of patents on microorganisms is not likely to put an end to genetic research or to its attendant risks. The large amount of research that has already occurred when no researcher had sure knowledge that patent protection would be available suggests that legislative or judicial fiat as to patentability will not deter the scientific mind from probing into the unknown any more than Canute could command the tides … .

Decision. Accordingly, the judgment of the Court of Customs and Patent Appeals was affirmed, allowing the patenting of living organisms in the United States.

Case Questions

1. The foregoing decision was decided by the Supreme Court by only a 5 to 4 vote. Do less-developed nations agree with the majority or the minority? Why?
2. Has the development of artificial life forms been encouraged by the Supreme Court's decision? Is this a good thing? What would have happened to the *Horizon* oil spill in the Gulf of Mexico without crude oil-ingesting organisms?
3. Do industrialized nations like the United States tend to expand the scope of IPRs? Why?

Trademarks

As previously noted, registered trademarks are assured national treatment by the *Paris Convention*. The *Paris Convention* also confers a right of priority to a trademark holder if the foreign registrations are made within six months after the original registration. In contrast, trademark prosecution is usually based on the law of the country where registration is sought.

Europe has a centralized multinational trademark registration system. Since 1996, the *Community Trademark Regulation*, administered by the Office for Harmonization in the Internal Market (OHIM), has allowed a single trademark registration enforceable throughout the EU. The *Trademark Regulation* also provides a unified enforcement authority, the Office for Harmonization in the Internal Market. Infringement in any member state can be prosecuted through this office.

The system established in the 1989 protocol to the *Madrid Agreement Concerning the International Registration of Marks* of 1891 (*Madrid Protocol*), like the PCT, provides a centralized filing system on a standard form and a designation of the countries in which trademark registration is sought. The WIPO also administers the prosecution and notifies designated countries. Although 89 countries have joined the Protocol (including the United States), the European Union and many other nations have not.

Domain Names

Trademark law also protects Internet domain names. After much international negotiation, in August 1999, the Internet Corporation for Assigned Names and Numbers (ICANN) adopted the *Uniform Domain Name Dispute Resolution Policy* (UDRP). The UDRP set forth general "first to file" rules for domain names, but excepted bad-faith filings. This "first to file rule" led to the practice of **cybersquatting**, which is the registering of a domain name with the intent to profit from the goodwill of a trademark belonging to another. Typically, the cybersquatter offers to sell the domain to the company who owns the trademark at an inflated price. Over time, the desire to stop cybersquatting led to an expansion of what "bad faith" means in the UDRP context. At common law, **bad faith** means intentional wrongful behavior, but in the UDRP, it now includes some negligence without a finding of intent. For example, a negligent failure to conduct prior checks for third-party rights has been held to constitute bad faith. The UDRP also created an innovative dispute resolution process that submits complaints and replies electronically over the Internet to a WIPO Arbitration and Mediation Center.

In January 2000, the first case was decided under the UDRP. The WIPO panel determined that the defendant cybersquatter had registered the domain name "worldwrestlingfederation.com" in bad faith and ordered him to cease using it. The new process meted out swift justice: It took only six weeks from submission of the initial complaint to the ultimate decision. In the years since, the UDRP process has continued to provide a refreshingly quick and uncomplicated way of resolving Internet IPR disputes. More than 18,000 complaints have already been filed under the UDRP, concerning more than 30,000 domain names. Ninety-seven percent of these cases have been resolved.

Individual countries can also pass legislation to curb cybersquatting. The United States was the first nation to pass such legislation. In 1999, the United States enacted the *Anticybersquatting Consumer Protection Act*, which prohibits registering, trafficking in, or using a domain name with bad faith intent to profit from the goodwill of a trademark owner. Other countries have followed, including Japan, which passed legislation in 2001 expanding their unfair competition prevention laws to include domain name protection.

WIPO Arbitration and Mediation Center

Mobile Communication Service Inc. v. WebReg, RN Administrative Panel Decision (February 24, 2006), Case No. D2005-1304

BACKGROUND AND FACTS

The complainant was Mobile Communication Service, Inc., which did business under the name Mobilcom. The domain name in question was "mobilcom.com," which had been registered by respondent WebReg, RN. Mobilcom contended that the domain name consisted entirely of its trademark, that WebReg lacked any rights or legitimate interests in that name, that there was no evidence that WebReg was making a legitimate non-commercial or fair use of the domain name, and that the domain name was registered and being used in bad faith. Mobilcom noted that WebReg had offered to sell the domain name for $35,000, which they argued was consistent with WebReg's pattern of registering domain names that incorporate the marks of third parties and offering them for sale.

continues

continued

DISCUSSION AND FINDINGS

The burden for Complainant under paragraph 4(a) of [UDRP] is to prove:

(i) that the Domain Name registered by Respondent is identical or confusingly similar to a trademark or service mark in which Complainant has rights; and

(ii) that Respondent has no rights or legitimate interests in respect of the Domain Name; and

(iii) that the Domain Name has been registered and is being used in bad faith.

A. Identical or confusingly similar Complainant alleges that it owns a Pennsylvania trademark registration. State trademark registrations, though, are entitled to minimal weight because they are not examined and thus do not represent persuasive evidence of ownership of a valid, distinctive trademark … . Thus, to prevail under the first factor, Complainant will need to establish common law trademark rights in the MOBILCOM name … . Turning to the evidence in this case, the Panel finds that Complain ant has alleged sufficient facts to establish common law trademark rights … .

B. Rights or legitimate interests The website to which the Domain Name resolves is entitled "Tech Buyer.com" and contains links to other sites that offer technology and Internet-related services that appear to compete with those offered by Complainant. This type of use is neither a bona fide offering of goods or services pursuant to paragraph 4(c)(i) of the Policy nor a legitimate non-commercial or fair use pursuant to paragraph 4(c)(iii) … . The Panel thus finds that Complainant has satisfied the requirements of paragraph 4(a)(ii) of the Policy.

C. Registered and used in bad faith As noted above, Internet users who access the website associated with the Domain Name are directed to a website that offers certain services that compete with those offered by Complainant. Using a domain name "to redirect Internet users to websites that host links to external websites, including websites of Complainant's competitors," is evidence of bad faith … .

In addition, Respondent offered the Domain Name for sale for $35,000, a sum that is far in excess of the cost of registering a domain name. In the absence of a legitimate interest by Respondent, the offer to sell the Domain Name for a price in excess of registration costs supports an inference that Respondent registered the Domain Name in bad faith, with the primary purpose of selling it in violation of paragraph 4(b)(i) of the Policy … .

Finally, Complainant asserts that Respondent is guilty of a pattern of registering domain names to prevent the owners of trademarks from reflecting their marks in the corresponding domain names. [The Panel then summarized seven other UDRP complaints in which WebReg had been found to be in violation of the bad faith standard.] Based on a review of these decisions, it appears that Respondent's business practice includes the registration of domain names containing fanciful trademarks … trademarks created by the joinder of common or dictionary words … and [those] that have expired … followed by efforts to resell those names. Although this Panel has held (including in a number of cases in which Respondent's counsel represented the respondent) that it is not bad faith to resell domain names that incorporate common dictionary terms if the respondent was unaware of complainant's trademark rights at the time of registration … respondents cannot rely on this precedent to shield their conduct by closing their eyes to whether domain names they are registering are identical or confusingly similar to trademarks. In other words, where a respondent has registered a domain name consisting of a dictionary term because the respondent has a good faith belief that the domain name's value derives from its generic qualities, that may constitute a legitimate interest and the offer to sell such a domain name is not necessarily a sign of bad faith. Where, in contrast, a respondent registers large swaths of domain names for resale, often through automated programs that snap up domain names as they become available, with no attention whatsoever to whether they may be identical to trademarks, such practices may well support a finding that respondent is engaged in a pattern of conduct that deprives trademark owners of the ability to register domain names reflecting their marks.

On the record of this case, the Panel believes it a fair inference that Respondent's conduct falls into the latter category … . [E]ven a cursory search on search engines like Yahoo! and Google would have shown that MOBILCOM is a trademark. The Panel thus concludes that Respondent has registered this Domain Name to prevent Complainant from reflecting its mark in the corresponding .com Domain Name, and that Respondent is engaged in a pattern of such conduct.

Complainant has therefore satisfied the requirements of paragraph 4(a)(iii) of the Policy.

Decision. For all the foregoing reasons, in accordance with paragraphs 4(i) of the Policy and 15 of the [UDRP], the Panel orders that the Domain Name <mobilcom.com> be transferred to Complainant.

Case Questions

1. Would the complainant have won the case if it could not show that it had an interest in the name Mobilcom? Must all of the elements be shown to get relief?
2. Is it acceptable to have a business selling domain names? How must such a business show that it creates domain names?
3. How could it be shown that the company creating domain names was aware of another firm's use of a dictionary word as a trademark?

Copyrights

The *Berne Convention for the Protection of Literary and Artistic Works*, better known as the *Berne Convention*, deals with the granting of **copyrights** among signatory nations. Like the *Paris Convention*, the *Berne Convention* is based on a national treatment scheme: Each signatory nation must afford foreigners the same treatment as its own citizens. Unlike the *Paris Convention*, the *Berne Convention* requires all 164 signatory nations to enact certain minimum substantive laws. These include prohibitions against copying literary and artistic works and granting authors exclusive rights to adaptations and broadcasts of works. In contrast to the fragmented patent and trademark system, there is no filing requirement. All an author needs to do is affix the symbol (©) and the year of authorship to provide copyright protection throughout the world. The *Berne Convention* signatories agree to grant national treatment to copyright holders from other signatories automatically from the moment of creation rather than the time of filing.

The computer revolution and the growth of the Internet have brought software copyright issues to the forefront. First, there was a significant dispute as to whether computer programs were copyrightable subject matter. This was resolved in late December 1996, when WIPO approved the *Draft Treaty on Certain Questions Concerning the Protection of Literary and Artistic Works*, providing that: "Computer programs are protected as literary works within the meaning of Article 2 of the *Berne Convention*. Such protection applies to the expression of a computer program in any form." This treaty, also known as the *WIPO Copyright Treaty* or the *Protocol to the Berne Convention*, entered into force in 2002, and 88 countries are signatories. It expands the scope of broadcasts that an author must permit to include "any communication to the public of their works, by wire or wireless means, including the making available to the public of their works in such a way that members of the public may access these works from a place and a time individually chosen by them." Naturally, this is carefully crafted to include access through the Internet. Together with the *Performances and Phonograms Treaty*, passed at the same time, the *Protocol to the Berne Convention* sought to tighten international law by requiring signatory nations to provide adequate legal protection against the circumvention of technological security measures, effective remedies against the knowing removal of electronic rights-management information and the related acts of distribution, and necessary measures to permit effective action against any act of infringement of rights covered by the treaties.

The United States wanted this protection to go even further. It sought to cover even temporary reproduction of copyrighted material unless the nation enacted certain minimum standards of protection. Because the Internet works by sending packets of data into a computer's temporary memory, this would have created significant issues as to Internet "browsing." The dispute was resolved through an Agreed Interpretation of a Treaty provision, and that interpretation has been implemented in different contexts.

All of these provisions had dubious significance in the context of the *Berne Convention*. Like the *Paris Convention*, it has been difficult to enforce the *Berne Convention* effectively. This enforcement problem was one of the principal forces that drove negotiations on the *TRIPS Agreement*.

Because of their substantial film and music industries, developed countries, particularly the United States, have strong incentives to protect copyrighted works. In 1998, the United States passed the *Copyright Term Extension Act* (CTEA) that extended copyright terms in the United States. The law, also known as the Sonny Bono Copyright Term Extension Act or as the Mickey Mouse Protection Act, effectively delayed the date at which copyrighted works would enter the public domain until at least 2019. Emerging economies, on the other hand, do not have strong incentives to pass legislation protecting and enforcing IPRs and have historical or societal conditions that have hindered such legislation. For instance, with the advent of the communist regime in China in 1949, all existing statutes, including copyright law, were repudiated. In addition, intellectuals lost all political power under Mao Zedong. China started legislating IPRs again after it officially reestablished diplomatic relations with the United States in 1979. The two countries entered bilateral agreements covering copyright law. In 1990, China enacted its first comprehensive copyright laws, and after China entered into the World Trade Organization in 2001, it completely overhauled its intellectual property system, amending the patent, copyright, and trademark laws, to comply with the *TRIPS Agreement*.

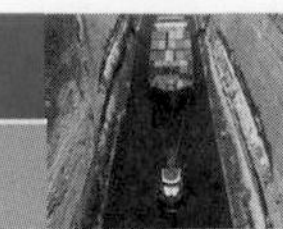

TVBO Production Limited v. Australia Sky Net Pty Limited

FCA 1132 (2009) Federal Court of Australia

BACKGROUND AND FACTS

Television Broadcasts Limited (TVB), based in Hong Kong, owned a Chinese language miniseries called *Twin of Brothers.* Its subsidiary, TVBO, owned the copyright in each episode in all countries except Hong Kong. TVB and affiliated companies filed a complaint against four respondents in the Federal Court of Australia. The first respondent, Australia Sky Net, was a pay television service in Australia. The fourth respondent, Chinese Satellite Communications, was a media company based in Taiwan. TVB's complaint alleged that the four respondents worked together to intercept and rebroadcast TVB's *Twin of Brothers* miniseries to Australia in violation of Australia's *Copyright Act* of 1968 and *Copyright (International Protection) Regulations* of 1969. The fourth respondent refused to appear in the lawsuit.

JUSTICE FOSTER

Section 184 of the Act provides that the Regulations made under the Act may make provision applying any of the provisions of the Act…, in relation to a country (other than Australia) so specified, in a number of different ways set out in that section. Regulation 4(1) of the *Copyright (International Protection) Regulations* 1969 provides that a provision of the Act that applies in relation to (amongst other things) cinematograph film made or first published in Australia applies in relation to such film made or first published in a *Berne Convention* country or in a WTO country: (a) In the same way as the provision applies, under the Act, in relation to an Australian work or subject-matter; and (b) As if the foreign work or subject matter were made or first published in Australia.

China is a *Berne Convention* country and a WTO country within the meaning of that Regulation… . copyright under the Act will subsist in any cinematograph film made in Hong Kong and protection will be afforded to such film under the Act. The evidence demonstrates that the *Twin of Brothers* series was made in Hong Kong in the period from July 2003 to August 2004. Copyright therefore subsists in each episode of the *Twin of Brothers* series… . The applicants [] tendered two VCD box sets of the title *Twin of Brothers,* one for sale in Hong Kong and one for sale in Macau. The box set for sale in Hong Kong bore the following statement on its packaging: © Television Broadcasts Limited & TVBO Production Limited (Release in 2004). That tender was made for the purpose of placing the applicants in a position to rely upon the presumptions contained in §131 of the Act, should it become necessary to do so. Section 131(1) provides that a person shall be presumed to be the maker of the film where the name of a person appears on copies of a cinematograph film made available to the public in such a way as to imply that the person was the maker of that film. Subsections 131(2) and 131(3) provide that where articles or things embodying the film have been supplied commercially and, at the time of supply, the article or their container bore a label with a "©" and the year and name of a person, then it is presumed that the film was made in that year and that the person so named is the owner of the copyright in that film… . [I]n the present case, the applicants are entitled to rely upon the presumptions raised by §131 of the Act with the consequence that, unless the contrary is established, the Court will presume that TVB and TVBO are the owners of copyright in the cinematograph films which comprise the series *Twin of Brothers* and that those films were made in 2004.

The applicants tendered certain paragraphs of an affidavit sworn by the third respondent in certain proceedings in the Supreme Court of New South Wales in order to prove several facts and matters relevant to an understanding of the way in which subscribers to the first respondent's [Australia Sky Net] subscription service are able to view television signals in Australia. In that affidavit, the third respondent swore that: (a) The fourth respondent [Chinese Satellite Communications] retransmits 16 free-to-air programs available in Taipei (the Taipei channels) from Taiwan to the east coast of Australia using the Measat-2 satellite; (b) Each of the Taipei channels is transmitted within and/or received in Taiwan using different signals of different frequencies; (c) In retransmitting the Taipei channels, the fourth respondent encrypts 14 of the 16 signals and then uplinks all of the Taipei channels' signals from the transmitters to the Measat-2 satellite. The remaining two of the 16 signals are uplinked and transmitted without encryption; (d) The satellite transponder downlinks the signals into Australia; (e) Subscribers to the first respondent's pay television service are able to view the scrambled 14 Taipei channels using [certain] equipment provided by the first respondent to those subscribers… ; (g) The fourth respondent is responsible for activating and deactivating the smart cards which allow the signals to be de-encrypted.

continues

continued

The retransmission of the Taipei channels is only made possible by the fourth respondent leasing capacity on the Measat-2 satellite. Having leased such capacity, the fourth respondent then sends its signal containing the Taipei channels from its base station in Taiwan to the Measat-2 satellite. The signal is then downlinked by the satellite to the east coast of Australia. This enables subscribers of the first respondent's service located in New South Wales, Victoria and Queensland to view the channels ... .

The evidence establishes that, on 28 January 2007, the fourth respondent transmitted Episode 5 of *Twin of Brothers* to subscribers of the first respondent's pay television service in Australia. The transmission was made on Channel 8 of the first respondent's pay television service and was available only to subscribers of that service. It was encrypted. The applicants submitted that this transmission probably occurred in the following way: Episode 5 of *Twin of Brothers* was originally broadcast by the Fujian Media Group on its channel SETV. That organisation is based in China. That broadcast occurred with the permission and licence of TVBO. That broadcast was received by the fourth respondent and intercepted by it. It was then retransmitted to Australia without the permission of the appropriate entities. It is clear that the retransmission by the fourth respondent of Episode 5 of *Twin of Brothers* on this occasion was not licensed by or on behalf of TVBO.

I accept these submissions and make findings accordingly ... . Having regard to the means deployed by the fourth respondent to transmit to Australia Episode 5 of *Twin of Brothers,* it seems to me that it communicated by electronic transmission that episode to the public in Australia. It caused the requisite signals to be transmitted from its base station in Taiwan to subscribers of the first respondent's pay television service within Australia. It determined the content of the communication ... . The fourth respondent's transmission emanated from Taiwan, but this circumstance does not absolve it from liability. The transmission was received by pay TV subscribers within Australia. The fourth respondent did not have a licence to transmit that episode to the first respondent's subscribers within Australia. I find that, unless restrained, the fourth respondent will, in all probability, repeat this conduct. For these reasons, I consider that the fourth respondent infringed TVBO's copyright in Episode 5 of *Twin of Brothers* ... .

Decision. The Court found the defendants guilty of copyright infringement and granted TVBO its requested relief.

Case Questions

1. How difficult would it have been for plaintiffs like TVBO to find out who was stealing and rebroadcasting its signal?
2. How would an Australian court enforce its jurisdiction over a foreign copyright infringer?
3. If it were difficult to trace this type of piracy, would it be worthwhile for the pirate to continue? How would a court system discourage this type of piracy?

TRIPS

As intellectual property became increasingly valuable, the developed world—which created virtually all such property—increased pressure to cure the defects of the *Paris* and *Berne Convention* systems. These efforts bore fruit in the GATT *Agreement on Trade-Related Aspects of Intellectual Property Rights* (TRIPS), which became effective in most nations on January 1, 2000. TRIPS requires its signatories to enact minimum substantive standards of protection and create a viable enforcement mechanism. In effect, TRIPS has caused developing countries to adopt intellectual property laws that approximate those of Europe and North America and has created a system to enforce them.

TRIPS requires every member of the World Trade Organization (WTO) to abide by the *Paris* and *Berne Conventions*—including the recent protocols to those treaties—and apply the treaties' national treatment requirements so that all foreign IPR owners receive the same protection as local nationals. It establishes 50-year copyright protection pursuant to the *Berne Convention*. All WTO members must recognize the patent holders' right to assign or license their patents and the term of patent protection must be at least 20 years.

Patent protection is also now available for "any new inventions, whether products or processes, in all fields of technology, provided that they are new, involve an inventive step (**nonobvious**) and are capable of industrial application (**useful**)." TRIPS even established minimum standards for trade secret protection after the model of uniform trade secret statutes in the United States.

TRIPS seeks to remedy some of the acknowledged problems of the *Paris* and *Berne Conventions*. First, unlike the *Paris Convention*, TRIPS sets minimum standards of intellectual property protection. A nation can no longer comply with international intellectual property law if its law provides no effective protection. Second, TRIPS requires signatory countries to ensure that enforcement procedures as specified in this Part are available under their laws so as to permit effective action against any act of infringement of intellectual property rights covered by this Agreement, including expeditious remedies to prevent infringements and remedies which constitute a deterrent to further infringements.

If one nation believes that another is out of compliance, it can initiate a dispute proceeding before a WTO panel.

Because most industrialized countries had effective patent, copyright, and trademark systems in place before TRIPS, these countries became compliant with minor adjustments. However, TRIPS required many emerging nations to enact a new statutory scheme, including an adequate domestic enforcement mechanism. TRIPS was the first WTO agreement to impose "positive" obligations on WTO signatories to adopt new laws; previously, WTO agreements had relied on negative prohibitions. Although much stronger than previous WTO agreements, TRIPS has a number of drawbacks. The developed nations accepted an "escape clause" to the minimum substantive standards in Article 8 of TRIPS. Signatory nations may exclude from patentability inventions, the prevention within their territory of the commercial exploitation of which is necessary to protect *ordre public* or morality, including to protect human, animal, or plant life or health or to avoid serious prejudice to the environment.

Although any actions taken under Article 8 must be "consistent with the provisions" of the TRIPS, Brazil may again refuse to grant pharmaceutical patents if it determines they are at odds with its concept of the *ordre public* (public order).

Developed nations counter that the exception was intended to be narrow, permitting patent infringement only for (1) noncommercial purposes, (2) research, (3) experimentation for testing or improvement, and (4) educational purposes. Litigation on the issue seems likely because many emerging countries are not inclined to pay large royalties on certain types of intellectual property, particularly in the area of medicines.

Complaints that a signatory nation is not complying with its obligations under TRIPS are adjudicated through a WTO dispute settlement mechanism. The majority of the complaints filed have been between developed countries. As of this writing, no country had been awarded the power to retaliate in response to the failure of another nation to fulfill its obligations under TRIPS.

Emerging nations fear that high-tech exports protected by intellectual property rights will slow development of their own industries and transfer local wealth abroad. Because local licensees form the local political constituency in emerging nations, these fears easily translate into massive domestic political pressure, leading signatory governments to reinterpret their treaty commitments. To the extent these nations seek to comply at all, they do so in the least restrictive way possible.

The Philippines, for example, created a TRIPS-compliant system for patenting and trademarking foreign drugs, but the legislature then took away most of the system's economic value by requiring branded drug manufacturers to produce generic versions of their drugs. Another example of an attempt at reinterpretation is Canada's assault on Article 33, which provides a 20-year term for patents. In the Canada 17-20 case, Canada defended its term of 17 years from grant for certain patents as sufficiently "consistent" with the term of 20 years from filing.

As discussed earlier, the TRIPS Agreement (Article 64) provides a mandatory mechanism for resolving disputes between WTO countries—the WTO dispute settlement process. For example, the United States filed a WTO dispute settlement case against China to resolve or curb piracy issues in China. Such an action was not available when China was outside the WTO. China's WTO membership gave the United States a new process that includes consultations, negotiations, dispute settlement, and arbitration. Because of China's WTO membership, however, the United States can no longer impose unilateral sanctions against China concerning the lack of intellectual property protection, as it threatened to do more than a decade ago. Indeed, the WTO process prohibits a member state from taking retaliatory measures before it exhausts all of the actions permissible under the rules.

Therefore, in 2007, under the pressure from lobby groups representing companies such as Microsoft and Walt Disney, the United States initiated WTO dispute settlement proceedings over the deficiencies in China's legal regime for protecting and enforcing copyrights and trademarks in a proceeding called "China—Measures Affecting the Protection and Enforcement of Intellectual Property Rights." The European Community, Japan, Canada, and Mexico joined in the consultations. The United States brought three main claims before the WTO panel: (1) China's criminal laws maintain safe harbors that allow commercial-scale counterfeiting and piracy without the possibility of criminal prosecution or conviction for those acts; (2) China has failed to give Chinese Customs officers the required authority for disposing of counterfeit and pirated imports; and (3) China denies automatic and immediate copyright protection to certain works, including those that have not yet cleared China's content review process. In 2009, the Dispute Settlement Body of the WTO issued a report on the dispute between China and the United States, siding with China on the first claim and with the United States on the other two claims. In 2010, China implemented the recommendations of the report and amended its copyright laws and its regulations on customs protection of IPRs.

THE DOHA DECLARATION ON TRIPS AND PUBLIC HEALTH

The effect of TRIPS on the pharmaceutical industry has been extensively debated. Increased protection of drug patents has serious implications for the availability of generic versions of drugs, an area of international concern in light of the exponential increase of HIV/AIDS in emerging nations. Worldwide debate focused on the connection between the cost of pharmaceuticals and the worsening public health of citizens of emerging countries. Emerging nations were concerned that TRIPS was being narrowly interpreted in a way that unduly limited the supply of generic drugs. Responding to these concerns, in November 2001 ministers of WTO member countries agreed to approve what is known as the Doha Declaration on the TRIPS Agreement and Public Health (Doha Declaration). The final text of the Doha Declaration recognizes the "gravity of the public health problems afflicting many developing and least-developed countries especially those resulting from HIV/AIDS, tuberculosis, malaria and other epidemics" and the "need for TRIPS to be a wider national and international action to address these problems." The WTO ministers stressed the importance of the implementation and interpretation of TRIPS in a manner that supports public health through improving access to existing medicines and formulating new medicines.

Developed countries were required to comply immediately with the requirements. Countries classified as "developing," such as India, were given ten years from the effective date of TRIPS, or until 2005, to become compliant. The least-developed countries, including many African states, are exempt from providing patent and trade secrets protection for pharmaceuticals until 2016. These least-developed countries were also permitted to retain their right to apply for additional extensions.

One key issue that was not resolved at the time of the Doha Ministerial Conference involved the interpretation of Section 31 of TRIPS, which permitted governments to issue compulsory licenses to allow companies to make patented products or use a patented process under license without the consent of the patent owners, but only under certain conditions intended to protect the legitimate interests of the patent holder. Article 31 (f) of TRIPS states that products made under compulsory licensing must be "predominantly for the supply of the domestic market." While this section directly applies to countries that have the resources or host companies that have the capability to manufacture these pharmaceuticals, it indirectly affects less-developed countries not equipped to manufacture pharmaceuticals by effectively limiting their ability to import cheaper generic drugs from countries that produce pharmaceuticals under the compulsory licensing provisions of TRIPS.

The Doha Declaration assigned to the TRIPS Council the task of determining whether to provide additional flexibility so that countries unable to produce pharmaceuticals domestically could import patented drugs made under compulsory licensing. In August 2003, the TRIPS Council decided to allow any WTO member country to export pharmaceuticals made under compulsory licenses. The TRIPS Council decision took the form of an "interim waiver" of Section 31(f) that allowed countries producing generic copies of patented products under compulsory licenses to export the products to eligible importing countries. The waiver is intended to last until the relevant portion of TRIPS is amended. A decision to permanently amend TRIPS to incorporate this waiver was reached in December 2005, and this decision will become part of the agreement when two-thirds of the member states agree to it.

All WTO member countries are permitted to import pharmaceuticals under the TRIPS Council's decision. However, 33 developed countries have voluntarily announced that they will not avail themselves of this provision to import pharmaceuticals. Eleven other countries have announced that they will import pharmaceuticals under this provision only in a national emergency.

The War of Geographical Indications

Notwithstanding these attempts to standardize the law, a "mark" in one nation may still be a generic name in another. Until the recent attempts to standardize practice take effect, the determination of whether an item is generic requires an analysis of the conditions in the country where a mark is sought. This is particularly well illustrated in the context of **geographical indications**, where a product, particularly a wine or liquor, is marketed by reference to a geographic region. For example, there has long been a dispute as to whether it is appropriate to label a sparkling wine made in the style developed in Champagne, France, as "champagne." The following New Zealand case illustrates this "geographic indications" dispute, while underscoring just how narrowly national the focus in trademark law can be.

New Zealand—Comite Interprofessionel du Vin de Champagne v. Wineworths Group, Ltd.

2 N.Z.L.R 432 (1991) High Court of Wellington

BACKGROUND AND FACTS

An Australian company sought to sell sparkling wine in New Zealand. The wine was made in Australia from grapes grown in Australia, but was packaged in bottles that included the word "champagne" on the label. The Comite Interprofessionel du Vin de Champagne (CIVC), a group of champagne producers from the French department of Champagne, sought an injunction to prevent the Australians from "passing off" Australian sparkling wine as wine actually produced in the region of Champagne.

JUDGE JEFFRIES

These proceedings are brought by the plaintiffs to protect their claimed property right in the word "Champagne." As an editorial policy in this judgment I am using the word champagne with a capital when it refers to the district and the wine from the district. The plaintiffs seek in effect to prevent the defendant from importing into New Zealand sparkling wine from Australia labeled champagne... .

Champagne... is relatively new, having its origin in time at the end of the seventeenth century but its final development was a nineteenth century phenomenon. Dom Perignon of the Benedictine Abbey of Hautvillers near Epernay in the Champagne district is credited with its beginning... . The two features of Champagne of prime importance for its uniqueness are the soil and climate in which the grapes are grown, and the method of manufacture by skilled personnel... . For the production of grapes for Champagne there are strict geographical limitations imposed by law... . By [French] law the wine allowed to carry the appellation Champagne must be produced exclusively within precise zones... . The essence of the methode champenoise is that the process of second fermentation takes place in the bottle in which it is sold... .

This proceeding is about New Zealand law and the understanding of its people so it is appropriate to say something of the wine industry and wine drinking by New Zealanders. Viticulture commenced with the first settlers 150 years ago and never abated, but New Zealanders did not early develop a widespread interest in and use of wines either locally made or imported. This was in contrast to Australia where indigenous wine manufacture and drinking became a more integral part of the lifestyle of that country... . New Zealanders' attitude toward wine underwent a marked change commencing from about thirty years ago... . The population became markedly more knowledgeable on wines and the demand for information was met principally by newspaper columns and books on wine.

Champagne has been exported to New Zealand from about the middle of the last century in small quantities until 1979, and increasingly in the 1980s. It is certain there were quite small volume exports of Australian champagne from 1977 onwards... . New Zealand has, apart from the foregoing, no history of material consumption, or manufacture, of sparkling wine prior to 1980... . In about 1981 Montana Wines, Ltd., which is New Zealand's largest maker, launched a sparkling wine produced by methode champenoise and labeled it "Lindauer New Zealand Champagne." Proceedings were issued in 1982 against Montana and after four years were settled by a consent order of the Court issuing an injunction generally restraining the use of the word champagne on that defendant's products.

continues

continued

[In Australia,] [s]parkling wine calling itself champagne made from grapes grown in Australia by the methode champenoise, and by other methods, has been entirely accepted and without direct challenge from the CIVC. The plaintiffs recognize, and although reluctantly accept, for Australia, like Canada and the United States of America, there is no legal protection available to them over the use of the appellation champagne.

The sparkling wine market in New Zealand changed dramatically with the introduction here from Australia in 1986 of Yalumba Angas Brut Champagne. The wine was of good quality and reasonably priced. It was a stunning success and other wine importers began a serious search in Australia for competitors ... .

It is appropriate here to emphasize the plaintiffs' view of what makes the product and therefore the name of Champagne so special. The product is a quality one and by virtue of the cost of manufacture it is necessarily expensive, which is part of its exclusivity. From the quality product the reputation has developed, which reflects the specialness of the wine itself arising from factors outlined above. Whilst it has developed a reputation as a quality sparkling wine, the consumption of it has also become widely associated with certain types of human activity that are mobilized around celebration and joy. Champagne is appropriate as a wine with which to celebrate (a characteristic is that it palpably agitates in the glass) and that is reinforced by exotic origin (for all but the French) and its cost. The plaintiffs say the excellent wine, whose quality is secured by the law of France, is rolled up with its deserved reputation and the name is a valuable right to them as owners ... .

It is appropriate here to deal with a phenomenon which is occurring in Australia ... whereby [s]parkling wines at the lower end of the price range not made from the classic Champagne grape varieties and using the transfer method are continued to be called champagne but those at the upper end of the price range made by methode champenoise are tending not to be called champagne, but given a brand name with the label showing it was produced by methode champenoise. That trend clearly suggests that the word champagne has been so devalued in the market in Australia that the public now needs a word, or words, that will convey the excitement and quality surrounding the word champagne say in New Zealand or the United Kingdom.

What the defendant [says] is that the word champagne has in New Zealand lost its distinctive significance so as to be properly defined now as a generic term having generic use within the wine market ... .

The task of the Court is to decide how the adult population of New Zealand as a group perceives the word. One has only to frame the task in that way to demonstrate its immense difficulty.

The Court holds [market research] studies supporting the contention that there is significant evidence that champagne is not a generic word by usage in New Zealand ... . From the evidence of the wine experts emerged two other observations worth making. If Australian wine interests were able to export sparkling wines to New Zealand it would have overall a deleterious effect by setting back the desirable goal of attainment of the maximum accuracy and fair labeling on wine bottles ... . The countries who are members of the Common Market strictly adhere to France's proprietary right in the word Champagne ... . There was a conscious attempt to supply [restaurant wine] lists encompassing a wide range of restaurants from the select and expensive ones downwards ... the great majority make the distinction between sparkling wines and Champagne. [T]he Court's decision is that the word champagne in New Zealand is not generically used to describe any white sparkling wine.

The word *champagne* does, in my view, have a special impact or impression on ordinary, average New Zealanders for whom wine drinking generally plays no significant part in their lives. This nonexpert, phlegmatic, even uninterested representative New Zealander does have a definite response to the word *champagne* over and above noting it to be a white sparkling wine, or one with bubbles in it. That response if pushed to articulation might be, a wine for celebration, expensive, of French origin, special method of manufacture, name of district in France, consumed by a certain social class, a wine ships are launched with or crowds are sprayed with after a major sporting event is won ... .

The question for the Court is whether importation into New Zealand, as aforesaid by the defendant advertising and selling Seaview Champagne, is deceptive in the way complained of by the plaintiffs. The Court's decision is that it is deceptive. To begin with the finding of the Court is that the word *champagne* is distinctive and that in New Zealand it has not passed into generic territory. Having found it is not generic then to use it in the market previously described is deceptive ... . By using the word *champagne* on the label the defendant is deceptively encroaching on the reputation and goodwill of the plaintiffs.

continues

continued

Decision. The court enjoined the Australian defendants from using the word *champagne* in New Zealand.

Case Questions

1. The result in this case means that "champagne" is an enforceable IPR in New Zealand and the United Kingdom, but not in Australia, Canada, or the United States. Do you think that the court's approach was objective or subjective? What does this suggest about trademark law?
2. The court reached its decision by reviewing evidence about association between the word *champagne* and the product from France. Such surveys were organized and conducted by experts for each of the parties. Were these surveys subjective or objective? Whose job is it to determine which surveys are more reliable?
3. The Coca-Cola Company hires personnel worldwide to assure that when consumers order a "coke," they are either served Coca-Cola products or are advised that none are available. Why?

For a time, these worldwide liquor name wars resulted in an armistice of sorts between the United States and the EU. In a bilateral agreement concluded in 1994, the United States agreed to prevent its companies from labeling U.S.-made liquor as *Scotch whiskey, Irish whiskey, cognac, Armagnac, Calvados,* or *brandy de Jerez.* In exchange, Europeans may not label European-made products as *bourbon* or *Tennessee whiskey.* The debate over trademarks for "geographic indications," however, grew heated. In October 2003, the WTO agreed to establish a panel to examine *EC Council Regulation 2081/92,* which creates restrictive rules to protect trademarks and geographical indications for geographical products and foodstuffs. *Regulation 2081/92* does not allow a nation to register its geographical indications in the EU's Register of Protected Designations of Origin and Protected Geographical Designations (EU's Geographical Designations Register) unless the nations provide the same enhanced protection as the EU. The United States and Australia each complained separately about the regulation, and in 2003 a single panel was established by the WTO to adjudicate these allegations.

The United States and Australia argued that by not permitting the names of agricultural products from non-EU member countries to be registered without reciprocity in the EU's Geographical Designations Register, the EU violated its national treatment and most favored nation obligations under the GATT and TRIPS. In addition, the terms of the regulation mean that the EU did not grant the advantages that EU products receive to products of non-EU member countries. For example, *EC Council Regulation 2081/92* granted certain monitoring and enforcement benefits to geographical indications of EU members but does not grant the same benefits to non-EU member countries.

In a report formally issued in early 2005, the WTO panel agreed with some of the arguments the United States and Australia made. The panel held that the EC's regulatory system failed to provide national treatment to non-EC nations, but only to the extent that it required non-EC nations to (1) adopt a system of GI protection equivalent to the EC's system and offer reciprocal protection to EC GIs and (2) have applications and objections from citizens of non-EC members examined and transmitted by the governments of those members and required those governments to operate systems of product inspection equivalent to EC nations. In April 2006, the EC implemented new regulations, which it claimed brought the EC into full compliance with its obligations under TRIPS. The United States and Australia continue to maintain that further reforms are required to fully address the WTO panel requirements. The geographical indications war rages on.

Geographical Indications under the Doha Development Agenda

The battle of geographical indications is not limited to the developed worlds of North America, Australia, and Europe and is not limited to wines and liquors. The Development Agenda of the Doha Ministerial Conference included two issues relating to geographical indications: (1) creating a multi-register for wines and spirits and (2) extending the higher or enhanced level of protection accorded to wines and spirits under TRIPS to other products.

The negotiations for the creation of a multi-register for geographical indications for wines and spirits are required under TRIPS and the Doha Declaration.

There are two main arguments in the negotiations. On one hand, countries led by the United States, Argentina, Australia, and Japan propose a voluntary system where notified geographical indications would be registered in a database. Under this proposal, governments choosing to participate would have to consult the database when making decisions on protection in their countries. Countries that do not wish to participate would simply be "encouraged" but not "obliged" to consult the database. In contrast, the so called "EU proposal" suggests that the registration would establish a "presumption" that the geographical indication is to be protected in all countries. The presumption of protection can be challenged on certain grounds, but once a name or term has been registered, a nation can no longer refuse protection to the registered name or term unless the name or term is challenged within 18 months from registration.

A number of countries, including EU member-states, China, Thailand, Pakistan, and Nigeria, have requested extending the enhanced protection given to wines and spirits by TRIPS to other products. They argue that a key component of the value of certain agricultural products (such as basmati rice and Parma ham) is the well-established link to the regions where these goods are produced. As in the case of wines and spirits, the demand for these products provides opportunities for producers from those regions. To protect these producers from usurpation, the extension advocates argue that safeguards similar to those of wines and spirits need to be in place.

The opponents of the extension—including the United States, Japan, Canada, Australia, and New Zealand—argue that the existing level of protection under Article 22 of TRIPS is adequate and that providing the enhanced protection would be expensive to enforce. The opponents of enhanced protection also argue that the usurpation claim is flawed, especially since the world has seen a great number of immigrants taking the methods of producing or making these products with them to their new home countries. In July 2006, the general council of the WTO suspended the Doha Round of negotiations, citing a failure of the parties involved to draw any closer to consensus on the issues before it, including extending the broader protection of Article 23 to all geographical indications. There has been little progress since then.

Continuing TRIPS Turmoil on Biodiversity

As we have seen, the patenting of living organisms was controversial even in the United States. Beginning in 1999, the TRIPS Council commenced its review of Article 27.3 of TRIPS, which relates to biotechnological inventions. Article 27.3 of TRIPS permits countries to exclude plants, animals, and biological processes from patent protection. (Microorganisms and nonbiological and microbiological processes are eligible for patents.) However, Article 27.3(b) requires member countries to provide for the protection of plant varieties either by patents, through a system created specifically for that purpose *(sui generis),* or by a combination of both.

The TRIPS Council's discussions include a variety of controversial topics. First, the council addressed the modification of existing TRIPS provisions on the patentability or nonpatentability of plant and animal inventions. Second, the council addressed the interpretation of effective protection for new plant varieties, including a discussion on the effects of other laws such as the International Union for the Protection of New Variety of Plants. Third, it focused on the handling of certain moral and ethical issues such as the extent to which invented life forms should be eligible for patent protection. Finally, the council considered the issue of traditional knowledge and genetic material, and the rights of communities or countries where this knowledge or genetic material originates.

A key topic under consideration by the TRIPS Council is whether TRIPS conflicts with the *UN Convention on Biological Diversity* (CBD). Those who argue that a conflict exists claim that while the CBD appears to grant sovereignty in biological resources to the countries that possess them, TRIPS permits these resources to be patented. Consequently, there is currently a dispute as to whether rights and benefits given to the resource holders under the CBD are taken away by TRIPS.

In November 2001, the Doha Declaration linked the issues of biotechnology, biodiversity, and traditional knowledge and declared that further work by the TRIPS Council on these reviews should be guided by the TRIPS objectives and principles and must take development into account.

Since the Doha Ministerial Conference, a number of proposals have been submitted for dealing with these complex subjects on biodiversity. On October 17, 2002, the EU submitted a paper that included a proposal to examine the requirement that patent applicants disclose the origin of genetic material. Switzerland submitted a proposal on May 28, 2003, suggesting an amendment to WIPO's *Patent Cooperation Treaty*, which in essence would require domestic law to ask patent applicants to disclose the origins of genetic resources and traditional knowledge. Under this proposal, a failure to disclose required information could delay the grant of patent protection or affect its validity.

Similar proposals have been submitted by nations that are home to biological resources. A paper submitted by Brazil, Cuba, Ecuador, India, Peru, and Venezuela in June 2003 developed earlier proposals on disclosure of the origins of biological resources. This led to the six nations advancing, in May 2006, a proposal to add a new Article 29bis to the TRIPS agreement. Under this amendment, it would become mandatory to disclose in patent application forms the source of biological resources and associated traditional knowledge to show that authorization has been given for this use and to show that the applicant has entered into a benefit-sharing arrangement with the source of the biological resources. Many EU nations support this suggestion.

Several other developed countries—particularly the United States, the residence of most owners of pharmaceutical IPRs—have opposed these provisions. These countries argue that further legislation on these subjects is not necessary because these issues can be adequately addressed in contractual agreements between the researching entities and the communities that own these genetic materials and traditional knowledge. Private pharmaceutical entrepreneurs are less circumspect: They characterize the proposal as little more than an attempt by Third World elites to profit without making real contributions. Indeed, emerging nations loudly complain about the potential that biopiracy will develop as pharmaceutical firms take evasive action. The outcome of this conflict remains to be seen.

NONENFORCEMENT OF IPR LAWS

As seen throughout this book, the varying attitudes of nations are generally reflected in their laws. However, in the IPR context, TRIPS now mandates what each country's laws must say. Attitudes in this context are now more accurately reflected in how the words of these laws are actually enforced.

It is one thing to enact laws as TRIPS requires and quite another to enforce them. Industrialized emerging countries often have panoply of laws designed to protect domestic and foreign IPRs but fail to enforce the laws or do not have adequate procedures to enable foreign parties to enforce them. After NAFTA, for example, Mexico adopted most internationally accepted standards with respect to IPRs. Yet to this day, Mexico City streets are littered with pirated music CDs and videos because Mexico has not devoted many of its scarce resources to enforcing those laws.

Still other nations enforce their laws in a discriminatory fashion so that foreign parties do not have confidence that their rights will be vindicated against clear infringement. Indeed, some nations tacitly encourage piracy of such IPRs by their citizens. In South Korea, the government once published details of pharmaceutical and pesticide formulations to facilitate their copying by locals.

After a great deal of prodding from developed nations, the Chinese government enacted modern copyright infringement legislation and even created special IPR tribunals. But in the meantime, China allowed construction of 26 compact disc plants with the capacity to manufacture more than 50 million CDs per year, despite the fact that China had a relatively small number of consumers who can purchase CDs and that virtually no Western companies had licensed the reproduction of their products in China. A particularly flagrant violation occurred in 1994, when a relative of the Chinese premier opened a huge laser disk and compact disc factory with the capacity to manufacture 5.5 million CDs and 1.5 million laser disks per year. Despite open violations of the ostensible IPR protection laws, Chinese authorities refused to permit even an inspection of the facility by Westerners.

This piracy is very big business. The FBI has estimated that U.S. businesses lose over $250 billion per year to **counterfeit goods**. In recent years, the U.S. government and leaders of its domestic high-tech and entertainment industries have focused a great deal of attention on the interrelation between the quality of foreign intellectual property protection and the vitality of U.S. trade in foreign countries and, indeed, the U.S. domestic market. In 1979, international firms from developed nations joined to form the International Anti-Counterfeiting Coalition, a trade group that pressures governments to enforce IPR laws, and the group has grown exponentially in recent years. At the urging of these industry groups, the U.S. government has become active in promoting the adoption and effective enforcement of intellectual property laws by its various trading partners. As noted previously, the TRIPS Agreement requires WTO countries to ensure that IPR laws are enforced and to call for the seizure of goods infringing on IPR rights. A failure to enforce such laws now can give rise to a WTO trade proceeding. Taiwan, once an internationally notorious haven of piracy, largely eliminated piracy after the United States was on the verge of enacting retaliatory tariffs on Taiwanese products. When the United States threatened to block hundreds of millions of Brazilian products from entering the United States, the government of Brazil agreed to a strict timetable for implementing patent and copyright reforms. U.S. movie industry officials, in partnership with the U.S. government, have used the threat of Super 301 trade proceedings, discussed below, against Italian products to prod Italian officials into more diligent enforcement of its copyright laws.

In April 2007, the United States filed two complaints with the World Trade Organization against the People's Republic of China for its "unfair trade practices," centering on "deficiencies in China's legal regime for protecting and enforcing copyrights and trademarks." In other words, after years of attempting to persuade the Chinese to police their rampant piracy and counterfeiting of U.S. entertainment products, it decided to initiate hostilities. The United States argued that Chinese laws actually impeded the legitimate distribution of such products, which further increased the demand for pirated products.

In addition to the TRIPS Agreement and the WTO dispute settlement proceedings, countries can combat IPR violations and copyright piracy through other means. Under Section 301 of the *Trade Act* of 1974, each year, the Office of the United States Trade Representative (USTR) issues the Special 301 Report, which is an annual review of the global state of intellectual property rights. For instance, the 2013 Special 301 Report maintains China on the Priority Watch List and states that China will continue to be subject to Section 306 monitoring. In particular, the 2013 Special 301 Report recognizes that China has increased its IPR enforcement efforts but also notes that issues of widespread piracy and "the apparent growth of trade secret theft" remain. In addition, the United States can use the Joint Commission on Commerce and Trade (JCCT) to get results on IPR protection and enforcement. As a result of past JCCT commitments, China introduced rules that require computers to be preinstalled with licensed operating system software, agreed to step up work to combat counterfeit goods at trade fairs and consumer markets, and joined the WIPO Internet Treaties, which are critical to ensuring IP protection in the digital age.

The Proposed Anti-Counterfeiting Trade Agreement

In 2006, Japan and the United States began confidential discussions related to a new plurilateral treaty to help in the fight against counterfeiting and piracy. The aim was to bring together countries that are interested in fighting counterfeiting and piracy and to negotiate an agreement that enhances international cooperation and contains international standards for enforcing intellectual property rights. Preliminary talks about such an anti-counterfeiting trade agreement took place throughout 2006 and 2007 among an initial group of interested parties (Canada, the European Union, Japan, Switzerland, and the United States). Negotiations started in June 2008 with the participation of a broader group of participants (Australia, Canada, the European Union and its 27 member-states, Japan, Mexico, Morocco, New Zealand, Republic of Korea, Singapore, Switzerland, and the United States).

The *Anti-Counterfeiting Trade Agreement* (ACTA) would establish a new international legal framework that countries can join on a voluntary basis and would create its own governing body outside existing international institutions such as the WTO and WIPO. Negotiating countries have described it as a response "to the increase in global trade of counterfeit goods and pirated copyright protected works." As negotiations have progressed, partial drafts of the agreement have become public. The U.S. government published a partial draft for public release in April 2010. The scope of ACTA is broad and would call for cooperation among member-states and civil and criminal enforcement of intellectual property laws that protect patent, industrial design, trademark, and copyright or related rights. As one example, member-states would enforce laws and cooperate to prevent cross-border distribution of pirated movies and music over the Internet. At the time of this writing, negotiations related to ACTA are ongoing.

THE MECHANICS OF IPR TRANSFER REGULATIONS

Three basic types of regulatory schemes provide the format for IPR transfer agreements. They range from preapproval to notification-registration to no regulation. The third scheme is obviously the most beneficial to the U.S. entrepreneur. But because the absence of law would be uninteresting to legal scholars, this section focuses on the preapproval and registration-notification systems in selected countries.

Prior-Approval Schemes

Requiring substantive **prior approval** from a government agency is a more intrusive type of regulatory scheme. It is indicative of a relatively protectionist government policy. The degree to which such a scheme intrudes on private enterprise depends largely on the attitude and mandate of the relevant regulatory agencies.

Some prior-approval schemes delegate specific types of authority to government entities and contain relatively objective standards. In others, the laws are written in general terms and vest broad interpretive powers in the bureaucracy. Some nations call for the exercise of this discretion by giving government officials a broad range of reasons for disapproving a transfer of technology. The Royalties Committee in Colombia could refuse to register a technology transfer agreement if the proposed license continued confidentiality obligations after its term or if the term extended for more than three to five years.

Other countries have taken an approach that depends even more on discretion: All transfer-of-technology agreements are prohibited unless a specific reason can be found for them to be permitted. The Japanese *gensoku kinshi* (prohibited in principle) system was a good example. In this system, transactions were presumed to be prohibited, but there were some exemptions. These exemptions were not based on law, but instead reflected an evolving bureaucratic tradition that decided what transactions should be exempt. Therefore, a foreign investor could only obtain key "legal" insights from someone familiar with the personalities who administered the process.

These discretionary systems make it easy for a government to reject requests for technology transfers by mere delay. In its heyday, the Japanese approval mechanism held up for more than four years a request for a technology transfer by Texas Instruments, Inc., to a proposed Texas Instruments subsidiary in Japan. While Texas Instruments was stalemated, Japanese competitors were able to develop technologies that would help them combat the Americans once they arrived. Many other foreign companies that were not as dogged as Texas Instruments were simply driven away by delay.

Delay is also used to deter technology transfers that require a patent. For instance, in some Latin American countries, the patent process sometimes took eight years from start to finish. During that entire period, there was an embargo on all fees payable to the owner of the patent.

Notification-Registration Schemes

A **notification-registration** system is more open to technological transfer. The Japanese *gensoku kinshi* (prohibited in principle) system transformed over time into the *gensoku jiyu* (free in principle) system. Similar instances may be found in South Korea, Venezuela, and Mexico, where prior-approval schemes have been replaced by a simple registration procedure. Countries with a general system of notification often make exceptions for areas of heightened concern, such as technology agreements between foreign companies and their controlled subsidiaries. Because of the patent inequality in bargaining position in such situations, many countries with a notification-registration system will still require specific approval of technology transfer agreements between such companies.

A danger in notification-registration countries is that some provisions of a registered contract might not be enforceable under a country's laws. License royalties in a given contract might be retroactively ruled excessive and recharacterized as taxable income to the foreign company. For instance, in some Chinese special economic zones, the foreign investor must compensate the local licensee for losses it incurs on sales of products manufactured by the transferred technology.

A significant danger in any approval-notification system is the risk that the government bureaucracy can make an unauthorized disclosure of the foreign party's intellectual property. Some commentators have suggested that, notwithstanding its advanced IPR protection laws, Mexico is not acquiring the most modern industrial technology because foreign investors do not wish to risk piracy of their IPRs. In Japan, foreign investors cast a wary eye on the Japanese government's continuing requirements for specificity in describing transferred technology under its notification system. Although Japanese authorities respond that they need such information for statistical purposes and that any disclosure by a government official could lead to criminal sanctions, foreign investors remain concerned about possible leaks from government ministries to Japanese firms.

A relevant provision of U.S. trade law is Section 337 of the *Tariff Act*, which took its current form in 1974.

Among other things, Section 337 prohibits the importation of articles that infringe a U.S. patent, trademark, or copyright. For example, if someone tries to import fake Rolex watches into the United States from a country that does not enforce its IPR laws, the Rolex trademark holder may seek to exclude the fakes through Section 337. The International Trade Commission (ITC), an independent, quasi-judicial federal agency, carries out investigations under this provision upon the filing of a complaint by the trademark holder or by the ITC on its own initiative. Under Section 337, the complainant must establish that its trademark is being infringed and that it has a "domestic industry" that uses the trademark (for example, a business that distributes and sells genuine Rolex watches in the United States). If the ITC determines that an article is being imported in violation of Section 337, it can issue a limited-exclusion order (excluding some of the items in question) or a general-exclusion order (excluding all of the items in question). Under Section 337, the president can reject or modify an exclusion order issued by the ITC before it becomes final. Once an exclusion order is final, U.S. Customs will attempt to stop the article from entering the United States and may seize inventories of the fakes already in the United States.

The ITC can also exclude a product that has one or more components that infringe a U.S. patent. For example, many cell phones imported into the United States contain semiconductor chips manufactured overseas. An owner of a U.S. patent may allege that the internal operations of one or more of these chips infringe its patent. The patent holder may ask the ITC to institute an investigation into the alleged infringement. If the ITC determines that the accused chips infringe the patent in question, it could issue an order excluding some or all of the cell phones, even though the cell phone companies may have little knowledge about how the chip is made or how it functions internally.

Resolutions of intellectual property disputes at the ITC are often much faster than in federal courts, and the ITC has broad power to order discovery overseas (for example, by ordering inspection of foreign plants, production of documents located abroad, or depositions of foreign employees). While a foreign respondent (i.e., the accused party) might refuse to comply, the ITC can consider such noncompliance when it determines whether it will issue an exclusion order. As can be seen, Section 337 is a powerful tool for preventing importation of goods that infringe a U.S. trademark, patent, or copyright. Certain foreign governments have raised concerns that Section 337 may be used in a discriminatory fashion to protect particular industries or companies in the United States or favor certain foreign companies over others. After TRIPS was accepted by other nations effective in 1995, Congress amended Section 337 in the *Uruguay Round Agreement Act* to respond to concerns about allegedly discriminating aspects of Section 337.

THE GRAY MARKET

As noted earlier, a prospective U.S. licensor fears that the IPR that it licenses abroad may come back into its home market to compete with the licensor's goods. After a license's anti-competition restrictions expire, the licensee might take the product it makes with the IPR and invade the U.S. market. But even before that occurs, a licensor must contemplate the danger that a completely unrelated party with whom the licensor has no anti-competition agreement will purchase the licensed product and import it back into the United States. This importation of merchandise produced and sold abroad and then imported back into the United States for sale in competition with the U.S. trademark owner is referred to as the **gray market** or **parallel trade**. The products imported back are **gray market goods** or **parallel imports**.

The Nature of the Problem

The gray market principally threatens the U.S. licensor if the product is sold at a lower price abroad than in the United States. This can happen for a variety of reasons. The U.S. licensor might have established such a reputation for quality in the U.S. market that it can command a substantial premium for its product there. But until its product builds a similar reputation abroad, the licensor will not be able to charge a similar premium. In the meantime, the gray marketer could purchase the goods abroad more cheaply, transport them back to the United States, and place them in direct competition with the U.S. licensor.

The gray market is also stimulated by international currency fluctuations. Relative currency values vary minute by minute during each business day. Retailers and wholesalers of goods are much slower to react, however. If the Canadian dollar goes down in value relative to the U.S. dollar, a nimble arbitrageur can purchase the U.S. product in Canada at a price that is a bargain in U.S. dollars.

Holders of trademarks oppose the gray marketers. They note that some products sold abroad under their trademarks are actually different from the domestic products. For instance, soft drinks sold in the Far East are sweetened more than their U.S. counterparts. U.S. licensors argue that sale of the foreign product in the United States could have a detrimental impact on the reputation of their domestic product.

U.S. licensors also argue that gray marketers receive a "free ride" on their U.S. marketing efforts. They point out that they make a substantial investment in time, effort, and capital to develop the sort of reputation that commands a premium in the U.S. market. Consequently, they argue, the gray marketer who comes in without making any payment to the U.S. trademark holder is stealing some of the return on the holder's investment.

Consumers, on the other hand, are generally delighted by the gray market. It often enables them to obtain goods of the same or comparable quality as well-known brands at a lower price. U.S. consumer advocates and merchandise retailers favor the gray market.

Resolution of the Dispute

In this hotly debated area, courts have gone in a variety of directions. National legislatures, including the U.S. Congress, are often called upon to provide assistance to one side or the other in the struggle.

Under one view, the trademark holder has no right to control goods after it sells them in commerce. After such a sale, the trademark holder has exhausted its control, and once its control is exhausted, the trademark holder cannot complain of competition by others. The exhaustion doctrine, if pursued to its logical end, would create a wide-open gray market.

Courts seem to have accepted the proposition that if a gray market product is so different as to call into question the quality of the domestic product, the licensor should be granted relief, especially if the seller of the domestic product has independently developed goodwill in its home country. Justice Oliver Wendell Holmes wrote one of the opinions that formed the foundation for analysis in this area.

A. Bourjois & Co. v. Katzel

360 U.S. 689 (1923) United States Supreme Court

BACKGROUND AND FACTS

A French cosmetic company with a business in the United States sold that business to a U.S. company, A. Bourjois & Co., along with its trademark for face powder. A. Bourjois reregistered the trademark and continued with the face powder business, using the same box and trademark for the product. Katzel bought a quantity of the same powder in France and sold it in the United States in boxes closely resembling the A. Bourjois boxes, but with its own labels. The plaintiff, A. Bourjois, sued for copyright infringement. It sought a preliminary injunction restraining the defendant from infringing its copyrights.

JUSTICE HOLMES

In 1913 A. Bourjois & Cie., E. Wertheimer & Cie., Successeurs, doing business in France and also in the United States, sold the plaintiff for a large sum their business in the United States, with their good will and their trade marks registered in the Patent Office. The latter related particularly to face powder, and included the above words. The plaintiff since its purchase has registered them again and goes on with the business that it bought, using substantially the same form of box and label as its predecessors and importing its face powder from France. It uses care in selecting colors suitable for the American market, in packing and in keeping up the standard, and has spent much money in advertising, so that the business has grown very great and the labels have come to be understood by the public here as meaning goods coming from the plaintiff. The boxes have upon their backs: "Trade Marks Reg. U.S. Pat. Off. Made in France—Packed in the U.S.A. by A. Bourjois & Co., Inc., of New York, Succ'rs. in the U.S. of A. Bourjois & Cie., and E. Wertheimer & Cie."

The defendant, finding that the rate of exchange enabled her to do so at a profit, bought a large quantity of the same powder in France and is selling it here in the French boxes which closely resemble those used by the plaintiff except that they have not the last quoted statement on the backs, and that the label reads, "Poudre de Riz de Java," whereas the plaintiff has found it advisable to strike out the suggestion of rice powder and has "Poudre Java" instead. There is no question that the defendant infringes the plaintiff's rights unless the fact that her boxes and powder are the genuine product of the French concern gives her a right to sell them in the present form.

After the sale the French manufacturers could not have come to the United States and have used their

continues

continued

old marks in competition with the plaintiff… . If for the purpose of evading the effect of the transfer, it has arranged with the defendant that she should sell with the old label, we suppose that no one would doubt that the contrivance must fail. There is no such conspiracy here, but, apart from the opening of a door to one, the vendors could not convey their goods free from the restriction to which the vendors were subject… . It deals with a delicate matter that may be of great value but that easily is destroyed, and therefore should be protected with corresponding care. It is said that the trademark here is that of the French house and truly indicates the origin of the goods. But that is not accurate. It is the trademark of the plaintiff only in the United States and indicates in law, and, it is found, by public understanding, that the goods come from the plaintiff although not made by it. It was sold and could only be sold with the good will of the business that the plaintiff bought. It takes the reputation of the plaintiff upon the character of the goods.

Decision. The U.S. Supreme Court reversed the decision of the U.S. Court of Appeals not to grant the plaintiff, A. Bourjois, a preliminary injunction.

Case Questions

1. Certain German automobiles that are regarded as non-luxury in Germany have upgraded options before shipment to the United States, where they are marketed by U.S. licensees as luxury cars. How would this business model be adversely affected if not for the *Bourjois* decision?
2. How does the protection afforded by *Bourjois* hurt U.S. consumers?
3. If the *Bourjois* protection were not afforded, what would this mean for U.S. licensees of products from outside the United States?

In situations with relatively little possibility of confusion, in which the quality of the gray market product is indistinguishable from the domestic product, U.S. courts have not been solicitous of the rights of licensors. In such cases, courts prize the benefits of price competition over concerns about a free ride for the gray marketer. More recent Supreme Court cases confirm this trend, favoring gray market forces where there is little chance of confusion. In *K Mart Corp. v. Cartier, Inc.*, 486 U.S. 281 (1988), the U.S. Supreme Court allowed the entry of gray market imports as long as the foreign manufacturer and the domestic trademark owner were subject to common control.

The European Court of Justice has charted a different course. In the cases of *Sebago Inc. v. GB Unie, SA*, [1999] E.T.M.R. 681 and *Silhouette International Schmied GmbH & Co. KG v. Hartlauer Handelsge-sellschaft mbH*, [1999] E.C.R. 1-4799, the ECJ interpreted the EU's Trademark Directive to permit reimport from one Union country to another, but to forbid reimport from other countries into the European Union. This "regional trademark exhaustion" principle was calculated to protect free access to markets within the Union while protecting the integrity of the common market from nonmembers. Other nations, led by Australia, have charted yet another course. Australia advocates the principle of "international exhaustion," meaning free reimport whether or not there is a danger of confusion. The Australians argue that rights to trade are part of the property purchased. Therefore, the purchaser should be free to trade its property regardless of where it finds the buyer.

The parallel import issue was purposefully left open in the TRIPS agreement. The divisions among nations are too wide to permit comprehensive agreement in the foreseeable future. Until the future day when agreement is reached, the exporter must simply inform itself of the law in the area to which it is sending product.

FRANCHISING: LICENSING OUTSIDE THE TECHNOLOGICAL CONTEXT

Franchising seldom involves technological complexity. It is an arrangement in which the licensor permits the licensee to sell certain goods under the licensor's trademark or service mark under a franchising agreement. To prevent devaluation of its trademark, the licensor will typically condition its use on the licensee's observance of certain quality standards. A Muscovite who wishes to open a McDonald's restaurant will contract with McDonald's Corporation for a franchise. A condition of the franchise might be that the franchisee must follow specified processes in cooking hamburgers.

Several observations may be made about franchises:

1. Although franchising seldom involves significant patent law or other technological issues, many of the considerations noted in other licensing contexts apply with equal force. Often, the franchiser will only keep renewing a franchise if the franchisee meets defined marketing quotas. The franchisee will attempt to obtain exclusive rights within some geographic area, while the franchiser will resist granting such rights or will try to narrow the geographic area. Franchisers must make the same balancing considerations as other licensors in arriving at an appropriate royalty level and duration for the franchise.
2. While patent law protection is generally not a significant issue in franchising, trademark protection is a big issue. Often the most valuable asset that the franchisee purchases is the right to use the franchiser's good name and trademarks on other wise local products. If trademark protection or enforcement is lax in the local jurisdiction, the value of the franchise accordingly declines.
3. Competition laws have greatly affected a number of franchising issues. For instance, the European Commission has invalidated franchisers' quality assurance provisions when they were deemed unduly restrictive of the franchisee's ability to compete. Franchisers must also be concerned about the application of competition laws to **tied-purchase clauses** in franchise contracts. These clauses require the franchisee to buy certain goods from the franchiser. Such provisions are sometimes difficult to justify on quay control grounds. Courts will also deny geographic exclusivity if it unduly restricts competition within the host country.
4. Because franchisees typically sell to the local domestic market and generate few exports, franchisers face special difficulties repatriating profits from soft currency countries. This problem is often solved by creating hard currency sections within franchise stores where you can buy the same products for hard currency at relatively favorable exchange rates. Even if hard currency transactions are a small part of the total sales, as long as they are equal to the franchisee's payments due to the franchiser, they can largely relieve the problem.

   Another approach has been to make **countertrade** payments to the franchiser with goods instead of hard currency. PepsiCo, Inc., is partially paid for its cola products by its Russian co-venturers with mushrooms for the pizzas of PepsiCo's Pizza Hut subsidiary. The potential for countertrade is limited in most soft currency countries because goods from such nations are often not competitive with those from hard currency countries.
5. A few nations have a number of laws that are specifically directed at the franchising phenomenon. The franchiser must be alert for **franchise tax** laws, which can impose taxes based on the franchiser's worldwide operations even if its local operations fizzle. A business may sometimes avoid such taxes by structuring the franchise agreement in accordance with local preferences.
6. System franchisers—those with a prepackaged program of instruction and initiation for prospective franchisees—should be careful to avoid the entanglements of **language politics**. This term describes the situation, found in regions of a few countries, where laws require that companies conduct business in a certain language. A prominent example is in the province of Quebec in Canada, where the law requires that business be done in French. A U.S. franchiser that brings its standard English-language package into such an area may be subject to significant civil penalties.

Finally, some nations impose stringent disclosure requirements on who may be a franchiser and what must be disclosed to prospective franchisees. These restrictions include registration requirements and highly detailed disclosure requirements under which a franchiser must reveal information about its business that it may not wish to make known.

ANTITRUST CONSIDERATIONS

IPRs can sometimes allow a company to monopolize a market. Thus, there is a tension between antitrust laws and intellectual property laws, because antitrust laws seek to foster competition in the marketplace and to eliminate monopolies while intellectual property laws can provide inventors with a legal monopoly. In the 1970s, the United States Federal Trade Commission (FTC) and the Department of Justice (DOJ) subjected IPRs to stringent scrutiny and prohibited certain IPR arrangements including: mandatory package licensing (also known as patent pools), tying of unpatented supplies, compulsory payment of royalties in amounts not reasonably related to sales of the patented product, and mandatory grant-backs. In the 1990s, however, the FTC and DOJ abandoned most of these rules and indicated that intellectual property should be treated no differently than other forms of property, patents do not necessarily confer market power, and licensing is generally procompetitive. The Federal Circuit has supported this exclusion of antitrust principles from the world of intellectual property. It is this exemption that has, in the first two decades of the twenty-first century, fueled the explosion of IPR accumulation by major companies.

In re Independent Service Organizations Antitrust Litigation CSU et al. v. Xerox Corporation

203 F.3d 1322 (Fed. Cir. 2000)

BACKGROUND

CSU sued Xerox, claiming that the copier manufacturer's refusal to sell patented parts and copyrighted manuals and to license copyrighted software violated antitrust laws. The district court granted summary judgment in favor of the copier manufacturer, and CSU appealed. The Court of Appeals for the Federal Circuit held that the copier manufacturer's refusal to sell or license its patented parts did not violate antitrust laws.

CHIEF JUDGE HALDANE ROBERT MAYER

Intellectual property rights do not confer a privilege to violate the antitrust laws. But it is also correct that the antitrust laws do not negate the patentee's right to exclude others from patent property. The commercial advantage gained by new technology and its statutory protection by patent does not convert the possessor thereof into a prohibited monopolist. The patent right must be 'coupled with violations of § 2,' and the elements of violation of 15 U.S.C. § 2 must be met. Determination of whether the patentee meets the *Sherman Act* elements of monopolization or attempt to monopolize is governed by the rules of application of the antitrust laws to market participants, with due consideration to the exclusivity that inheres in the patent grant.

The patentee's right to exclude, however, is not without limit. As we recently observed, a patent owner who brings suit to enforce the statutory right to exclude others from making, using, or selling the claimed invention is exempt from the antitrust laws, even though such a suit may have an anticompetitive effect, unless the infringement defendant proves one of two conditions. First, he may prove that the asserted patent was obtained through knowing and willful fraud. Or he may demonstrate that the infringement suit was a mere sham to cover what is actually no more than an attempt to interfere directly with the business relationships of a competitor.

Case Questions

1. Is there a conflict between antitrust laws and IPR laws? If so, how can such a conflict be resolved by the legislature or the courts?
2. Should the courts or the legislatures impose a duty to license to prevent a company to monopolize a market?

CONCLUSION

In a world dominated by technological and design innovation, intellectual property rights have become vital to many companies' very existence. Companies are investing in research and development and in flooding overburdened and under-sophisticated governmental authorities with IPR requests in order to obtain IPRs to dominate the markets in which they compete. And litigation of conflicting IPRs has become a normal cost of doing business. It is not clear whether the existing and sometimes outdated IPR governmental and legal framework is adapted to this new reality. Should governments step in and correct the inefficiencies of litigation, or should companies and the free market correct these inefficiencies themselves? Licensing and cross-licensing provide alternative tools for companies to resolve disputes. They are also less costly and less risky.

Licensing can also allow a firm with intellectual property to increase the IPR's returns by permitting someone else to exploit it in another market. In the international context, this capability is particularly useful. For example, a U.S. concern with little or no experience in Nepal can contract with someone with such experience to exploit the Nepalese market. In the normal course, licensor and licensee will negotiate over matters such as conditions and extent of use, compensation, and confidentiality. However, negotiations between licensor and licensee are complicated in the international context. Many countries seek to assist local licensees in their efforts to acquire advanced technology. Local legislation may supersede contractual provisions in order to permit host-country nationals to possess the intellectual property more rapidly, while lax enforcement of such legislation can also ease this process. Under some approval systems, nothing is likely to happen without cooperation of a local licensee.

The TRIPS agreement should greatly standardize and improve the situation. After it is fully implemented, TRIPS should provide minimum standards of intellectual property protection and a reliable worldwide system of enforcement. It will take a while for the parties to work through continuing disagreements on TRIPS implementation.

If all these complications are not bad enough, the U.S. firm that sends goods abroad may find them exported back to its local market. The trend among developed countries has been to permit such increased competition.

Though the logic of efficiency and accelerating technical advances that underlie licensing make it a rapidly expanding—and highly profitable—form of doing business abroad, it is still an endeavor that must be pursued cautiously.

Chapter Summary

1. Intellectual property rights (IPRs) are extremely valuable assets in today's global economy. Companies universally recognize the necessity of investing in research and development to build strong IPRs. Litigation of IPRs in courts is becoming a normal part of competition between companies. They compete in open markets for customers and in courts to obtain the right to exclude each other in the marketplace. Licensing and cross-licensing lessen the risk and cost of litigation and should be pursued aggressively.
2. IPRs are licensed for many business reasons, such as the receipt of royalties or for use in contract manufacturing. IPR licensing agreements are drafted to protect the IPR owner by restricting the licensee's use of the IPR. Common restrictions include geographical limitations, field of use limitations, and output or customer restrictions. The parties will also negotiate on exclusivity of license, royalty levels, confidentiality, rights to IPR improvements, and termination provisions.
3. The first international property treaty was the *International Convention for the Protection of Industrial Property,* known as the *Paris Convention*. It guarantees that in each signatory country, foreign trademark and patent applications from other signatory countries receive the same treatment and priority as those from domestic applicants. The *Paris Convention* has major drawbacks. First, it does not require any minimum substantive standard of patent protection. Second, it lacks an enforcement mechanism. *The Patent Cooperation Treaty* (PCT) supplemented the *Paris Convention* by establishing a centralized utility patent application process.
4. The *European Patent Convention* and the *Agreement Relating to Community Patents* created a unitary system for the application and grant of European patents and a uniform system for the resolution of litigation concerning patent infringement.
5. The international treaty system for design patents is the Hague System for the International Registration of Industrial Designs. This system was significantly enhanced by the *Geneva Act*, which established a single standard application and single design patent filing process in 2003.
6. The *Madrid Protocol* provides a centralized filing system on a standard form and a designation of the countries in which trademark registration is sought. The WIPO administers trademark prosecution and notifies designated countries. Many important economic powers have not ratified the *Madrid Protocol.*
7. The *Internet Corporation for Assigned Names and Numbers* (ICANN), which regulates the Internet, has adopted the *Uniform Domain Name Dispute Resolution Policy* (UDRP). Under the UDRP, the "first to file" has the right to a domain name, unless the filing is made in "bad

faith." "Bad faith" under the UDRP is much easier to show than it generally is at law. In the URDP context, it now includes some negligence without a finding of intent.

8. Under the *Berne Convention*, each signatory nation must afford foreigners the same copyright protection as its own citizens. The *Berne Convention* requires all 164 signatory nations to enact certain minimum substantive laws. These laws, known as *minima,* include prohibitions against copying literary and artistic works and grant authors exclusive rights to adaptations and broadcasts of works. There is no filing requirement.
9. The *Draft Treaty on Certain Questions Concerning the Protection of Literary and Artistic Works* provides that computer programs are protected as literary works under the *Berne Convention.*
10. The GATT *Agreement on Trade-Related Aspects of Intellectual Property Rights* (TRIPS), effective since 2000, obligates its signatories to enact minimum substantive standards of protection for intellectual property rights and to create a viable enforcement mechanism. If one nation believes that another is out of compliance, it can initiate a dispute proceeding before a WTO panel. TRIPS has caused the enactment of IPR protection laws in many countries where the prevailing culture and political elites do not support protection. Thus, many countries with extensive IPR protection laws on the books do little to enforce those laws. Under TRIPS, this has resulted in international proceedings regarding nonenforcement of IPR laws.
11. The terms *gray market* and *parallel trade* refer to the importation of merchandise produced and sold abroad and then imported back into the country of origin for sale in competition with the IPR owner.

Key Terms

intellectual property rights (IPRs) 460
fair, reasonable, and nondiscriminatory (FRAND) 462
royalty 462
license 462
utility patent 463
field of use limitations 463
geographical limitations 463
output or customer restrictions 464
exclusive rights 464
grant back 464
right of priority 465
priority claim 466
design patent 466
biopiracy 466
bad faith 469
cybersquatting 469
copyright 471
nonobvious patent 473
useful patent 473
geographical indications 476
counterfeit goods 480
prior approval 482
notification-registration 482
gray market 483
parallel trade 483
gray market goods 483
parallel imports 483
franchising 485
tied-purchase clause 486
countertrade 486
franchise tax 486
language politics 486

Questions and Case Problems

1. Hirt Systems Company is a U.S. company that has a strong market in the United States for securing computer terminals. It envelops such terminals with lead to prevent them from emitting microwaves that can be picked up by "spy receivers." The key to Hirt's success is its design know-how. Because the application is labor intensive, models produced abroad are significantly cheaper. Hirt has been affected by these lower-priced models, although it has held its own because its design is superior. As part of its expansion program, Hirt is considering constructing a new assembly plant. Compare the relative benefits and risks of building it as a Hirt-owned concern in a developing country under the direction of Hirt's U.S. management with building the plant in the United States.
2. Assuming the facts from Question 1, what would be the advantages and disadvantages of a joint venture with a major foreign company abroad compared to the alternatives discussed in Question 1?

3. David Wise, a U.S. inventor, has developed and patented a revolutionary new running shoe that increases one's speed significantly. His invention has achieved considerable success in the Midwestern region of the United States. Two European companies have offered him joint venture packages to take his invention to the track-happy Europeans. Barthelemy Plus Grande, S.A. is a French sportswear giant with a marketing and distribution system that includes every major city in Western Europe and massive capital resources. Pék Társaság, a recently privatized Hungarian firm, offers substantially lower labor costs. Which should Mr. Wise choose as a joint venture partner? Why?
4. Mr. Wise's marketing experts advise him that the Japanese market is hungry for his shoes. Focusing on technology transfer issues, discuss whether he should seek a Japanese joint venture partner or enter through a wholly owned subsidiary.
5. Analyze the same issues raised in Question 4, but assume Mr. Wise is considering entry into a "prior-approval" country.
6. Laffite Enterprises, Inc., a U.S. firm, has purchased the right to use the trademark of Wellington Imperial, Ltd., in the United States for a high-quality line of Napoleonic War reproductions. Wellington has a cheap line of Napoleonic trinkets that it sells in France. Degas Magazines, S.A., a French firm, begins to import the low-priced Wellington line into the United States. If Laffite brings an action against Degas, how would a U.S. court address the policy considerations presented?
7. Geyer Schokolade, A.G. makes the bonbon of choice for the German yuppie. Its product's cachet permits Geyer to charge a hefty premium at home. Geyer expands into the U.S. market, where no one has heard of its bonbons, and charges a more reasonable price to garner market share. Henry Joseph, a U.S. entrepreneur, reimports the bonbons into Germany and offers them at a substantial savings below Geyer's price. What will be the result of Geyer's attempt to stop Mr. Joseph at the EEC Court of Justice?

Managerial Implications

1. You work for Wilbur Intergalactic, Ltd., a leading North Carolina processor and purveyor of North Carolina-style pork barbecue. Certain areas of North Carolina around Wilson, N.C., are known for producing superior pork barbecue because of the peculiar nature of the soil in which the pigs wallow and because of the method for preparing barbecue developed in that area. Soon, Wilbur Ltd. and other purveyors begin to promote their barbecue pro ducts as "Wilson-Style Barbecue." In 1999, the North Carolina legislature designates Wilson County as a special barbecue area and prohibits anyone from using the designation "Wilson-Style Barbecue" for barbecue not made from Wilson-bred hogs, in Wilson, pursuant to the Wilson method. Soon thereafter, the Professional Committee of Wilson Barbecue secures the U.S. trademark "Wilson-Style Barbecue" for Limited Wilbur and its other members.

   In 2001, Limited Wilbur management learns that at France's Euro Wally World, a French firm has been selling pork barbecue with the words "Method Wilson" on the label. The barbecue is made from local French hogs, but pursuant to the Wilson method of barbecuing. The committee has not secured trademark protection in France.

   a. Explain how a French court would analyze the issue of whether the French barbecuers are infringing on Limited Wilbur's property rights. In this analysis, discuss whether "Wilson-Style Barbecue" is too generic to receive protection and what Limited Wilbur's rights are under the various intellectual property treaties.
   b. Develop a plan for expanding Limited Wilbur's product marketing to France, giving consideration to steps that it should take to preserve its "Wilson-Style Barbecue" trade name.
2. Undertake a study of the trade war between China and the United States over intellectual property rights. After years of trying to get China to protect American IPRs, an agreement was reached between the two countries in 1992. Reports of copyright and trademark violations continued, and in June 1994, an investigation was initiated under Special 301. China was identified as a priority country in July 1994 (59 FR 35558). A determination was made to take action against China on February 7, 1995 (60 FR 7230). The nation's press

covered the story daily, describing how it would cost U.S. consumers billions of dollars per year. China embarked on its own public relations campaign, with U.S. television showing bulldozers crushing thousands of bootlegged and counterfeit CDs on a street in China. A month later, on March 7, 1995, the USTR announced that China had agreed to take the needed action to protect IPRs of U.S. film, recording, and software companies. As shown in this chapter, the United States continues to take the view that China is engaged in massive IPR piracy. In April 2007, the United States initiated two WTO proceedings.

a. What is the annual cost of Chinese IPR violations to U.S. companies? How have IPR violations affected the decision of American companies to do business there? What has been the response of private firms to these violations, and how have they tried to control them?
b. What positive actions has China taken to correct the problem? What new laws have been passed for the protection of IPRs, and how are they enforced?
c. Consider specifically the problems of U.S. software companies in China. Can you find any information about Microsoft's position on doing business in China? What has been their strategy for tapping into the potentially huge Chinese market, while ensuring that their copyrights on software remain protected? If the Chinese government views IPR violations as a legitimate way to make a profit, would bringing the government in as a joint venture partner be one way to get the Chinese to see the need for IPR protection?

3. L'anza Research, Inc., manufactures high-quality hair care products in California. Copyrighted labels are attached to all products and packaging. In the United States, L'anza sells exclusively to authorized distributors who resell within limited geographic areas and only to authorized retailers such as hair salons. Exports to foreign distributors are sold at a 40 percent discount. L'anza sold three shipments containing several tons of merchandise to its distributor in the United Kingdom, Quality King, who resold them to a buyer in Malta. L'anza later discovered that the products had been resold to a U.S. buyer for less than the wholesale price and were being sold at discounted prices by unauthorized retailers in California. L'anza complained that because it held the right to the copyrighted language and design of the labels, the unauthorized resale violated U.S. copyright laws. The lower courts agreed. The U.S. Supreme Court reversed, unanimously holding that under the "first sale" doctrine, once a copyright owner places an authentic, copyrighted item in the stream of commerce, it has no further right to control its distribution or reimportation. Thus any lawful purchaser of the products may dispose of them as they please without further obligation. This decision does not apply to counterfeited, pirated, or illegally copied goods shipped into the United States in violation of the copyright or trademark laws. What should L'anza have done to protect itself? Why is a foreign distributorship agreement important? What specific areas of concern should it address? See *Quality King Distributors v. L'anza Research Intl. Inc.*, 523 U.S. 135(1998).

Ethical Considerations

The number of people living with HIV has grown by a factor of 4.5 times since 1990 when approximately 7.5 million people were HIV-positive. According to the World Health Organization (WHO), there were approximately 33 million people living with HIV worldwide in 2008, including 30.8 million adults and 2.2 million children. An additional 2.7 million people are newly infected with HIV every year, which represents a daily new infection rate of 7,397 persons. Two million people die every year as a result of AIDS, which represents a daily death rate of 5,479 persons. Most new infections and deaths are due to inadequate access to HIV prevention and treatment services. As a result, the WHO has concluded that the HIV pandemic remains the most serious of infectious disease challenges to public health.

The HIV epidemic outside of sub-Saharan Africa, while serious, remains primarily concentrated among at-risk populations, such as men who have sexual relations with other men, drug users, and sex workers and their partners. However, the epidemic in sub-Saharan Africa is generalized throughout all strata of the population. More than 22.5 million people in sub-Saharan Africa, 5 percent of the entire adult population in the region, are infected with HIV, an increase of more than 4.5 million since 2001. Nine states in the region have adult infection rates in excess of 10 percent.

These states are Botswana (25.2 percent), Lesotho (23.5 percent), Malawi (12.7 percent), Mozambique (12.5 percent), Namibia (15.3 percent), South Africa (16.2 percent), Swaziland (25.9 percent), Zambia (15.6 percent), and Zimbabwe (18.1 percent). By comparison, the highest infection rate in the Western Hemisphere is Haiti at 2.2 percent of the adult population.

Despite declines in the rate of new infections, the death toll as a result of AIDS increased from 1.4 million in 2001 to 1.6 million in 2007. Seventy-six percent of all deaths due to AIDS worldwide occur in sub-Saharan Africa, and more than 25 million people living in the region have perished to date in the pandemic. These deaths have resulted in 11.4 million orphans.

Treatment of people infected with HIV has benefited in recent years with the development of antiretroviral drugs (ARV). ARVs are medications used to treat infections by retroviruses such as HIV. When several such drugs, typically three or four, are taken in combination, the approach is known as highly active antiretroviral therapy (HAART). HAART first became available in the developed world in 1996 and resulted in an 84 percent drop in the HIV/ AIDS death rate. At a cost of $15,000 per person per year, ARVs were too expensive for the majority of HIV patients in the developing world. Five years after HAART was introduced, fewer than 8,000 people in sub-Saharan Africa were receiving ARVs. Widespread introduction in the developing world could only occur if the price of ARVs was reduced.

In early 2000, an Indian pharmaceutical company began to produce generic ARVs that were identical to the brand name drugs produced by companies in the developed world but significantly cheaper. This sparked a price war between branded and generic drug manufacturers, which resulted in the lowering of prices for ARVs. By June 2001, ARVs were available in generic form from Indian manufacturers for as little as $295. By 2008, the price had fallen to $88 per person per year.

In addition to lowering prices, branded manufacturers of ARVs responded by filing lawsuits against generic manufacturers. The first such lawsuit to proceed to trial, the so-called "AIDS Medicine Trial," opened in Johannesburg, South Africa, in March 2001. The Pharmaceutical Manufacturers' Association of South Africa and 39 global drug companies filed this action in 1998 challenging a 1997 South African law that permitted the national health minister to ignore patent rights to obtain essential medicines, including ARVs, at cheaper prices through the purchase of generic alternatives or purchasing name brand drugs in states where they are cheaper.

The pharmaceutical companies abandoned their lawsuit on April 19, 2001, after a wave of bad publicity, including condemnation by the European Parliament and a petition signed by 300,000 people in 130 states denouncing the lawsuit. Later in the month, Merck announced that it would sell two ARVs (Crixivan and Sustiva) in the developing world at a 90 percent discount. The price of Crixivan was subsequently reduced from $6,016 per patient per year to $600, and Sustiva's price was reduced from $4,730 per patient per year to $500. In addition, GlaxoSmithKline granted a voluntary license to a South African generics manufacturer to share the rights to three of its ARVs (AZT, 3TC, and Com-bivir) without charge.

Despite this progress, continuing success of HIV/ AIDS prevention and treatment programs remains uncertain. In April 2007, United Nations Program on HIV/AIDS estimated that spending would need to increase from $8 billion to $20 billion to make access to ARVs universal. Considering that less than $14 billion was invested in HIV/AIDS programs in 2008, a funding shortfall appears inevitable, especially given economic recession and deepening budget crisis confronting many states. Another financial barrier to universal treatment is that infected individuals who begin taking ARVs must remain on them for the rest of their lives. This places enormous pressures on governments and international organizations to ensure consistent funding for access to ARVs for a period of time that will most likely span several decades. This also places pressure on pharmaceutical manufacturers who may be confronted by the specter of ARV-immune strains of HIV due to incomplete or discontinued treatment.

In June 2008, the WHO reported that it had reached its goal set forth in 2002 to guarantee ARV access to three million people infected with HIV in the developing world. More than 2.2 million of these people are located in sub-Saharan Africa. However, only one in ten of the 2.1 million infected children under the age of 15 are receiving ARVs and for every two people who start drug treatment, another five people are infected worldwide. In November 2009, the International AIDS Vaccine Initiative concluded that the HIV pandemic would remain out of control by its 50th anniversary in 2031 unless funding was increased to $35 billion per year. The initiative predicted that the developed world and rapidly developing states such as Brazil, China, India, Mexico, and Russia would be able to finance efforts to combat their domestic epidemics. However, the vast majority of states in the developing world would remain heavily dependent on the developed world, international organizations, private donors, and pharmaceutical companies to assist in combating the pandemic in the foreseeable future.

1. Applying teleological frameworks for ethical thinking, what is your analysis of the pharmaceutical industry's behavior prior to and after 2001?
2. Based on teleological frameworks, what is the appropriate course of action for the industry to take in the future with respect to the ongoing HIV/AIDS crisis?
3. Applying deontological frameworks for ethical thinking, what is your analysis of the pharmaceutical industry's behavior prior to and after 2001?
4. Based on deontological frameworks, what is the appropriate course of action for the industry to take in the future with respect to the ongoing HIV/AIDS crisis?

CHAPTER 18

The Legal Environment of Foreign Direct Investment

Foreign direct investment (FDI) signifies a class of investments in a foreign host country that involves the investing business carrying on some significant portion of its physical operations in the host country itself. In Chapter One, the term *foreign direct investment* was defined as the ownership and active control of the productive assets of ongoing business concerns by an investor in a foreign country. Foreign direct investment can take many different forms: from opening a branch that operates in the host country but that is still a part of the investing business organized in the home country, to starting or acquiring a foreign subsidiary, to operating through a joint venture with a foreign business entity. The distinguishing feature of foreign direct investment, however, is that the investing business carries on operations directly in the host country. Foreign direct investment is thus a market-entry method that involves significantly greater penetration into the foreign host country than is involved in trade through an agent or representative in the home country (discussed in Chapter Sixteen), or in intellectual property licensing (discussed in Chapter Seventeen), or in foreign indirect investment, such as passive debt investments or portfolio investments or in foreign companies that do not represent a controlling interest.

This greater market penetration presents enhanced opportunities for long-term investment and for earning profit, both because of the ability to take on a more active role in the host country and to take advantage of inducements to foreign direct investment offered by many countries. But these opportunities are accompanied by a host of unique legal obligations and risks. The unique risks of operating directly in a foreign host country make it important for the investing firm to assess its ability to manage and handle them. This chapter discusses the legal risks and the potential rewards associated with foreign direct investment.

This chapter begins with a description of the different forms of FDI and how to choose among them. It then explains two distinctive risks of FDI, currency and political risk, and how they are controlled in international transactions. The chapter develops political risk further, explaining the historical, cultural, and economic bases and theories that underlie nationalization and expropriation. The nationalization/expropriation discussion ends with a section on the remedies available to foreign direct investors. Finally, the chapter outlines the principal U.S. tax law issues that drive FDI and the taxation risks associated with FDI.

CHOOSING FOREIGN DIRECT INVESTMENT

The legal environment for foreign direct investment varies depending not only upon the identity of the host country but also upon the form the investment takes. Therefore, the firm must make two key decisions before a full assessment of its ability to grow in the relevant legal environment can proceed. First, the firm must determine whether there are desirable investment opportunities in the foreign host country. Second, the firm must establish its rationale for determining what form or method of investment will best suit its needs.

Reasons for Foreign Direct Investment

There are many different reasons that U.S. investors find direct investments in foreign countries desirable. The particular motivations of any given U.S. investor can inform the choice of where and when to invest, as well as the structure the investment will take.

One of the chief motivations for foreign direct investment is to bring a business in more direct contact with the resources that the foreign host country's economy has to offer. This sometimes is the natural resources of a foreign country, such as timber, petroleum, or iron ore. Direct investment in a foreign country can also give access to that country's workforce, which may give the investor advantages, such as specific training or capacity (e.g., Swiss watchmakers), lower wages, or lower regulatory hurdles than in the home country (e.g., Vietnamese low-tech industry). Foreign direct investment can improve sales by creating closer ties to and relationships with customers in the host country. If a business's suppliers are located in a foreign country, a direct investment in that country may place production closer to those suppliers, increasing the efficiency of production. And the acquisition of a valuable target company that operates in a foreign country will naturally lead to foreign direct investment. Similarly, manufacturing or marketing joint ventures present attractive opportunities that require foreign direct investment. Foreign direct investment can also allow the investor to avoid trade barriers in certain circumstances. Direct investment may also be necessary to acquire the right to use intellectual property. Investing in many different countries can have a diversification benefit—a booming economy in host country can make up for poor performance in the economy of the investor's home country.

Methods of Foreign Direct Investment

Just as there are many possible motives for making an investment in a foreign country, there are many forms that such an investment can take. This section outlines the classic methods of foreign direct investment and explores the different legal consequences that attach to each. The discussion begins with a review of the forms that grant the U.S. investor the most direct control over the enterprise created by the investment, and proceeds to an exploration of the rationale for choosing among these forms.

Opening a Foreign Branch or Forming a New Foreign Subsidiary. An enterprise that wishes to establish an entity abroad under its control may create a subsidiary (a separate corporate entity organized under the laws of the foreign host country) or a branch (a division of the home country corporation that is not a separate legal person). Neither step is to be taken lightly. Whether the company establishes a subsidiary or a branch, it may waive rights of protection under the bilateral investment protection agreements of the United States. In many cases, the company also subjects itself completely to the foreign nation's corporate tax laws.

Certain differences distinguish the subsidiary from the branch approach. If a company chooses to establish a branch abroad, it faces greater potential vicarious liability. In essence, the mother company is directly accountable for any liabilities of a branch, but not those of a subsidiary, which is a separate corporation. Thus, if the foreign activity involves potential product liability or environmental liability, a subsidiary corporation is indicated. On the other hand, the establishment of a branch rather than a subsidiary may have significant consequences under local tax law and U.S. tax law. Because tax laws often distinguish between different forms of an enterprise, such laws will often dictate the choice of entity: a U.S. branch, a U.S. partnership, a foreign corporation, or a foreign partnership. In many cases, for instance, because taxes are generally deferred until dividends are declared, remittances from branches may be taxed at higher rates than dividends from a foreign subsidiary.

Acquiring a Foreign Firm. Instead of creating a new business through opening a foreign branch or starting a foreign subsidiary, an investor can acquire an existing business in the foreign host country. The phenomenon of transnational takeovers—mergers between companies in developed economies—has become more common. European and Japanese investors have taken over U.S. concerns, and U.S. investors have taken over European companies. In Europe, many national firms have responded to the continent-wide competitive environment by merging across borders to form multinational concerns that can serve clients throughout the European Community.

Acquisitions can be structured in many ways. The investor may acquire the business through a purchase of substantially all of the assets of the existing business or through a purchase of the assets or equity of the existing business. This choice is typically driven either by the different tax consequences that attach to each form of acquisition or by the desire to avoid certain liabilities that the existing business holds. While an asset purchase may be more complicated than the other forms, it generally allows liabilities to be left behind with the sellers of the business. In addition, the purchaser of assets can select only those parts of the target that complement the purchaser's existing business and leave other assets behind. On the other hand, an equity acquisition will allow the transfer of the valuable contracts of the acquired entity without the purchaser needing to seek the consent of contract counterparties, allowing a very smooth transition. Also, a correctly structured equity acquisition will effectively transfer valuable tax attributes, such as net operating losses to the acquirer. Purchasing the equity of the foreign business will cause the U.S. investor to hold the business as a foreign subsidiary. An asset purchase may be accomplished either directly by the

U.S. investor, in which case the business will be held as a foreign branch, or by a foreign subsidiary created especially for the acquisition.

As can be seen, the choice between an asset and stock acquisition will depend on the individual circumstances of the purchaser and the foreign target. Different approaches are right for different situations.

Joint Ventures. For the U.S. investor that wishes to exercise a measure of control over its minority investment, joint ventures are often the vehicle of choice. A foreign investor may enter into a joint venture by creating a new entity together with a host country national or by acquiring a portion of an existing local entity. The four basic forms of a joint venture are (1) a foreign corporation, (2) a foreign partnership, (3) a U.S. corporation with a foreign branch, and (4) a U.S. partnership with a foreign branch. The precise shape of the joint venture depends largely on the participants' relative treatment under the tax laws and treaties of the host country and the United States.

Majority versus Minority Ownership. The forms of foreign direct investment just discussed, with the possible exception of the joint venture, all involve the U.S. investor taking on a majority or controlling interest in the foreign business. There are a number of business reasons an enterprise would prefer to establish an entity it can control through majority ownership rather than an entity in which it owns a minority interest. For instance, a firm that greatly fears disclosure of its software know-how would be reluctant to enter into any venture that it did not fully control, whether the potential co-venturer was Mongolian or Virginian. The international dimension adds an additional layer of complexity.

Control, however, does not require voting equity. It can be achieved indirectly by entering into key contracts with the venture. For example, if the joint venture is to assemble components manufactured in the United States under terms that give the U.S. investor substantial discretion over whether to continue supplying the components, the U.S. investor retains significant control over the venture no matter who formally owns the venture. Other control mechanisms include supply contracts, marketing agreements, management contracts, and veto powers in the joint venture agreements.

Minority investments can also include so called passive investments. A **passive investment** can involve either a passive debt investment—making a loan to a foreign business—or a passive equity investment—purchasing an equity interest in the foreign business as a portfolio investment that does not allow for control of the business. Passive investments tend to be the least regulated type of foreign investment because, unlike active minority ownership investments, they do not raise the specter of "outsider" influence that often leads foreign governments to exercise greater governmental regulation. But this type of investor is very different from a faceless purchaser of equity on a foreign stock exchange. The "passive" investor can, nonetheless, exercise significant control through covenants in debt or preferred equity investments that effectively set the direction of the enterprise through mandatory milestones, production triggers, and the like that compel the majority owners to manage their enterprise in the manner the foreign investor prefers.

Possible Restrictions on Majority Ownership. Virtually every country prohibits entities in sensitive sectors from being controlled by foreigners. Governments that feel more insecure about foreign domination tend to exclude foreign-owned investments from even more sectors of their economies. Until NAFTA and the privatizations of the 1990s, Mexico generally prohibited 100 percent foreign investment, permitting it only in 34 designated industrial activities. These laws have been modified as Mexico's private sector success—in the recent past, the world's richest man was Carlos Slim, a Mexican—made it less concerned about foreign economic domination and more interested in attracting foreign capital.

Other countries are more restrictive, permitting foreign control only in sectors in which they have the greatest interest in development. India and China, for example, have until recent years generally permitted full foreign ownership only in firms that manufacture exclusively for export. Such firms were tolerated because they earned needed foreign exchange for the host country. India and China also permitted high levels of foreign majority ownership in high-technology firms. In that instance, the desire for modernization and training of locals in key industries outweighed distrust of foreign control.

Finally, a few nations such as North Korea have been so xenophobic that they have not permitted foreign majority ownership at all. But such rules dry up development capital. India's enactment of a general 40 percent limitation on foreign ownership, for example, led to a 55 percent drop in foreign investment between 1975 and 1987. Similarly, Mexico's enactment of a 49 percent foreign investment limit—since modified in most industries outside petroleum—led to an abrupt reduction of foreign investment from more than 10 percent of all private investment to about 3 percent. And Cuba's continuing intolerance of foreign majority ownership largely accounts for its slide from being one of Latin America's most developed nations in 1959 to being one of its most economically backward in 2013.

The unavailability of capital to isolationist nations has pushed nearly all countries to accept foreign majority ownership in the early twenty-first century. Nominally communist nations such as Vietnam now permit foreigners to own and control investments there. Occasionally nationalist governments toy with restricting foreign investment, but such efforts generally prove short-lived or limited in practice, as in Venezuela and Bolivia.

Special Restrictions on Investments in Key Industries. Many nations strictly limit foreign investment in some strategic sectors of their economies. Even in the United States, foreign nationals may not hold more than a 25 percent voting interest in an airline or a company that owns an earth station or microwave license. These restrictions led Australian Rupert Murdoch to become a U.S. citizen before completing his acquisition of the Fox television network. Foreigners are also prevented from controlling U.S. defense contractors that own technologies deemed important to national security. Analogous concerns prevented Dubai Port World from acquiring control over certain U.S. port operations a few years ago. Certain nations either forbid 100 percent foreign ownership of software manufacturers or impose taxes that make such ownership extremely unattractive.

Countries that are more concerned about overseas domination exclude foreigners from a larger number of sectors. Some nations have historically required prior approval of any investments in defense or national security, electricity, gas, telecommunications, public utilities, radio and television stations, insurance companies, or financial entities.

The administrative difficulties and expense involved in such a process discourage foreign investment. Because almost all nations covet foreign investment, there has been an increasing trend to simplify and streamline these processes. For example, in India, if the foreign investor limits its equity stake to 51 percent or less in 34 formerly closed industries, only the Reserve Bank of India needs to approve the transaction. Many countries now have a unified national entity that approves projects. Examples include Egypt's semiautonomous Investment Authority and Kenya's Foreign Investment Agency.

Conversely, many countries give preferences and incentives to certain types of foreign investments. For instance, India grants export-oriented businesses special relief from duties and assists these businesses in obtaining import licenses. China tries to compensate for its poor infrastructure by giving high-technology firms priority access to its public utilities.

The Legal Consequences of Foreign Direct Investment

A U.S. investor that engages in foreign direct investment, an investment in assets or a company domiciled in a foreign nation, subjects its investment to the laws of the foreign host country. Whatever form the investment takes, if a U.S. investor makes an **active investment** in a host country, it ultimately will result in the investor having an ownership interest in the foreign business as either a foreign branch or subsidiary. If the business is held through a foreign subsidiary, the assets of the business will be legally owned by a business entity organized under the laws of the foreign host country. The investor becomes, quite literally, a corporate citizen of the foreign country. Even if the business is held as a branch, the physical assets of the business will be located in the host country. This can make the assets a tempting target for expropriation or nationalization. And because international tax norms typically grant the country in which income is earned the first crack at taxing the income, the host country will have the primary power to tax income earned by the foreign business.

Because many nations, especially developing countries, are concerned about a resurgence of foreign domination of their economies, foreign investment is regulated under a wide assortment of domestic corporate laws. Particularly prevalent in strategic sectors, these laws often reflect the same concerns about foreign economic domination that had previously led to outright nationalization.

Not coincidentally, nations with greater apprehensions about foreign economic domination tend to have more restrictive laws. The massive U.S. economy, having relatively little to fear from outsiders, has few obstacles to foreign investors. On the other hand, developing countries, which can be easily overwhelmed by sophisticated foreign capitalists, are more wary. Suspicions about foreign penetration continue to concern these nations even as they try to transition to free-enterprise legal systems.

COUNTRY AND REGIONAL RISKS IN FOREIGN DIRECT INVESTMENT

Engaging in foreign direct investment subjects investors to risks unique to the countries and regions in which investments are made. Chief among these risks are currency risk—the risk that profits in the foreign host country's currency will not translate into equivalent profits in the investor's home country—and **political risk**—the risk that profits will be affected by changes in the host country's political structure or instability. This section discusses these two types of risk and what an investor can do to mitigate each.

Currency Risk

One of the most distinctive aspects of doing business outside one's own country is **currency risk.** If the investment is in an enterprise that will be earning foreign currency, the business must consider the two forms of currency risk: fluctuation risk and inconvertibility risk.

Fluctuation risk is the possibility that the currency of the country in which the U.S. investor has put its money will devalue against the U.S. dollar. For example, in 2000, the Argentine currency abruptly devalued more than 50 percent against the U.S. dollar. The pesos earned in Argentina could no longer repay the U.S. dollar loans that foreign investors had taken out for their Argentine investments. When a foreign currency devalues against the dollar, the value of the investment's revenues declines. Thus, a sudden variation in the exchange rate can ruin an operationally successful business investment.

Inconvertibility risk is the risk that the government of a country with soft currency will hinder the foreign entrepreneur from trading the foreign currency back into U.S. dollars. A **soft currency** is one that is not freely exchangeable for currencies of other nations. Generally, this is because international currency arbitrageurs view the currency's fluctuation risk as too great to maintain markets in it.

In a soft-currency nation, hard currency is in short supply. At the time of the initial investment, the U.S. investor must often hand over its dollars to the local central bank, which will exchange them for the local currency. To obtain dollars back for the local soft currency, the U.S. investor must fill out an application and await a response. The government then decides who gets to exchange the local soft currency for its supply of hard currency. Through a wide variety of diverse and imaginative ceilings, prohibitions, and controls, such governments can limit access to hard currency for foreigners seeking to take profits out of the local economy. An effective unofficial technique is for the government to sit on the investor's application indefinitely.

Because inconvertibility controls can effectively destroy profit, investors need to understand how to limit this risk. A number of options are available.

Currency Swaps. The foreign entrepreneur's principal concern is how to limit the risk posed by the fact that the investment will be earning profits in a currency different from its own. A broad assortment of financial contracts, generically known as **currency swaps,** may be purchased from financial intermediaries to hedge against fluctuation risk. For example, a party who will need dollars in the future can enter into an agreement to deliver a certain number of Argentine pesos in the future for a stated number of U.S. dollars to a currency arbitrageur or other financial intermediary. The currency swap transfers the risk of fluctuation to the intermediary, leaving the investor with only the risk of the business itself.

The intermediary will then seek to "hedge" its risk by a matching transaction with another, unrelated party in which the intermediary agrees to deliver the Argentine pesos it receives in the first transaction for the U.S. dollars the intermediary has agreed to deliver in the first transaction. Done properly, the intermediary matches business parties' needs and takes a spread. To facilitate these transactions, the International Swap Dealers Association has developed a standard form agreement so that all legal terms in these deals are consistent and the intermediary bears no legal risk from gaps in documentation. This is now a highly efficient international currency market that an entrepreneur may easily access through its investment banker.

Arrangements with the Soft-Currency Country. The most direct way of ensuring access to hard currency is to obtain that access from the government of the soft-currency country. The essential problem in soft-currency countries is the great demand for a limited amount of hard currency. The queue for hard currency is long. When the investor finally gets to the front of the queue, it receives only its ration of foreign currency.

If the investor proposes bringing a desired industry to the soft-currency nation—a high-technology plant or a hard-currency earner—it can negotiate with the government in advance for preferential access to hard currency. The resulting **currency exchange rights** can help solve the inconvertibility problem for the foreign investor.

If preferential currency exchange rights are not available, the U.S. investor may seek **import substitution rights** from the government. These rights are available when the new venture will manufacture a product in the soft-currency country that the nation had previously imported. However, an investor must still reach this agreement before actually committing capital to the soft-currency nation.

Payment and Price Adjustment Approaches. In most situations, the government will not be willing or legally able to provide the foreign investor with either currency exchange or import substitution rights. The investor must therefore create legal structures to maximize the foreign venture's U.S. dollar resources. One way to protect against currency risk is through the structure of payments back to the foreign investor.

First, whenever possible, the foreign investor should negotiate to receive lump-sum, hard-currency payments as early as possible rather than in a series of future installments. This up-front payment avoids the uncertainty of whether the foreign customer will receive hard-currency allocations in future years.

The obvious drawback of this approach is that most foreign customers and foreign investments cannot yield immediate cash. Many foreign ventures are start-up operations and rely on future earnings to pay a return. Further, the approach does not work at all for a U.S. firm that plans to generate revenue by selling its products abroad for foreign currency.

A second approach is to build currency adjustment mechanisms into contractual payment terms through **profit margin preservation** provisions or **unitary index adjustment** factors. Under the profit margin preservation approach, the price or payment to the foreign investor will be adjusted periodically to maintain the same profit margin. This can disclose the foreign company's cost structure, information that is highly confidential, because it permits competitors to price effectively against the firm.

This serious problem does not exist if the parties provide for formulaic adjustment of payment terms based on an accepted unitary index. This index can be a commonly accepted measure of relative currency value or national inflation. Unfortunately, indexes are frequently independent of the facts of the transaction or notoriously unreliable. Moreover, neither the profit margin preservation nor the unitary index adjustment approaches address the issue of repatriation. In other words, if your cost structure is stated in Polish zlotys or adjusted to an acceptable index, you may be technically protected against 300 percent devaluation against the dollar, but still have no way of exchanging your zlotys for dollars.

Structuring of Hard-Currency Obligations and Revenues. Another series of methodologies for ameliorating currency risk involves structuring transactions so as to conserve U.S. dollar resources. An investor can achieve this type of risk reduction by avoiding obligations denominated in currencies outside of the investment site and by conserving hard currency earned by the venture.

Few investments are funded entirely through contributions of equity from the entrepreneur. In most cases, the entrepreneur borrows a significant portion of the capital necessary to launch the venture. An important rule for avoiding currency risk in a venture that will be generating local currency revenues is to borrow that in local currency. This minimizes exposure to the vagaries of the international currency markets or the whims of local authorities.

The Argentine devaluation of the early 2000s again illustrates this point. In view of Argentina's decade-long commitment to maintaining fiscal stability, many North American entrepreneurs came to regard the peso as relatively stable. They invested in Argentine power plants and other infrastructure projects, borrowing money through lower-interest U.S. dollar loans. When the peso crashed, the peso earnings of the Argentine power plants were worth 50 percent less. Many ventures could no longer make their debt payments and went into bankruptcy.

By contrast, those investors who had borrowed in pesos did not face this financial problem: Within Argentina, the peso was still the unit of exchange. Indeed, because devaluation was accompanied by inflation, those with fixed-interest-rate peso debt had to devote less of their cash flow to debt service.

The same rule applies with respect to contracts between the venture and **trade creditors**, the entities that sell supplies or services to the venture. To the greatest extent possible, the venture should buy locally in local currency, conserving hard-currency resources for repatriation.

If the investor anticipates that the foreign venture will earn significant hard currency, it should prevent the hard currency from reentering the soft-currency country. It can instruct hard-currency customers to pay the U.S. investor directly instead of through the venture. Similarly, the U.S. investor can "call" a percentage of the foreign venture's production: The investor conducts a hard-currency sale, obtains the payment, takes its agreed-upon share, and transfers the residue to the venture.

Countertrade. **Countertrade**, another popular way of dealing with the inability to convert currency—known as **currency inconvertibility**—is a reciprocal arrangement between buyer and seller for the sale of goods or services intended to minimize the outflow of foreign exchange from the buyer's country. In countertrade, local currency earnings are used to purchase local products, which are then exported to a hard-currency country. The proceeds are then converted into dollars and returned to the foreign investor.

Counterpurchase. A common type of countertrade is the **counterpurchase agreement**. Counterpurchase involves the sale of goods to a buyer, often a foreign government, which requires as a condition of the sale that the seller buy other goods produced in that country. These deals are usually structured as two separate contracts where each party is paid in currency when its products are delivered to the other party. Usually, the seller will be given a selection of items for export. The goal of a counterpurchase arrangement is for export transactions to offset the "cost" of import transactions.

Barter. **Barter** is the direct exchange of goods for goods (or services). Barter transactions can involve a wide range of items, from pharmaceuticals and aircraft to agricultural commodities, oil, natural resources, and even consumer goods. In 1972, Pepsi famously agreed to trade products and build bottling plants for Pepsi-Cola in Russia in return for Stolichnaya vodka and other Russian-made products. Barter specialists have developed creative schemes for minimizing risks for exporters.

Buy-Back. In a **buy-back agreement**, the provider of the equipment or technology used in manufacturing will receive, as its payment, a portion of the goods manufactured by the supplier's equipment or the factory in which the equipment is installed. Lack of control over the manufacturing process or the making of a market for the ultimate product are obvious concerns.

Informal Consortia or Parallel Exchanges. In some soft-currency countries, foreign investors form consortia to trade local soft currency, in effect forming a private **parallel exchange**. In this arrangement, the investors—all committed to the local incontrovertibility risk—spread that risk over a larger group, with the hoping of reducing the vagaries of local bureaucracy.

Inconvertibility Insurance. A final alternative for the U.S. investor is an **inconvertibility** or **nontransfer insurance policy.** Investors can purchase such policies to insure against **hard blockages**, which occur when the foreign government passes a law that prevents conversion or transfer. For a somewhat higher fee, a businessperson may purchase a policy that also protects against **soft blockages** or delays in processing conversion requests by the local authorities. Inconvertibility insurance is a type of political risk insurance.

Political Risk and Government Stability

A company's ability to turn a profit rests in part on its ability to earn a return on capital, reap the rewards of its effort, and form stable and predictable contracts and relationships with other parties. None of this can occur without a stable political environment that supports a market economy and provides basic protections for personal property and enforcement of contracts. Stable governments are thus often a precondition to being able to earn a reasonable profit from a foreign investment.

But government stability is never completely assured, especially in developing countries. Regime changes can dramatically change the prospects of one's investments. Civil war or terrorism can place physical infrastructure and personnel located in a foreign country at risk. In Iran in 1979 and the early 1980s, a combination of a regime change from Shah Pahlavi to Ayatollah Khomeini, a full-scale war with Iraq, and unrest among ethnic minorities that led to shifts in both the price and sources of oil caused an energy crisis in the United States. Expropriation and nationalization, as discussed later in this chapter, can result in the taking of an investor's entire business for inadequate, or even no, compensation. Even in a developed country, decisions about fiscal and monetary policy can have an impact on the macroeconomy and the presence of demand for one's products, and tax laws can be changed in a manner that cuts into profits. Government threats of debt default in the Eurozone have dramatically affected the prospects of companies with heavy exposure to European markets.

Managing Political Risk. As with any risk that affects a business's profitability, investors need to consider the tools at their disposal to mitigate and manage the risk of loss through political changes or instability. As with any business risk, one can try to manage political risk by learning about it and seeking to avoid it. But the primary legal apparatus for handling such risk is through **political risk insurance**. There are two primary means of managing political risk: political risk analysis and political risk insurance. **Political risk analysis** is another form of proactive management: the enterprise retains a firm or its own personnel to analyze a host country's risk of nationalization/expropriation as it would study any other business problem. Legal political risk insurance contracts allow investors to recuperate losses suffered when political risks are borne out.

Political Risk Insurance. Entrepreneurs normally assume the risk that their business will fail because their product is unable to find an adequate market, though they will try to avoid the risks of events beyond their control such as fire, earthquake, or employee dishonesty. To cover those risks, they normally contract with an insurance company, which assumes this risk for a fee. The fee, or *premium* is based on an actuarial assessment of the probability of loss among all of the company's insureds. Insurance against political risk arose from this practice. Entrepreneurs who are unwilling to hazard the risk of a foreign government taking will pay a premium to a public or private insurance company.

Obviously, the cost of this insurance is a disincentive to investment abroad. In order for the U.S. or European investor to justify foreign investment, the anticipated increased marginal returns on the emerging market venture—relative to a comparable U.S. or European investment—must be greater than the cost of the insurance. Otherwise, the emerging market investment becomes financially unjustifiable.

Political Risk Insurance from Government Agencies. A number of capital-exporting nations have established government corporations that provide political risk insurance, such as the United States' Overseas Private Investment Corporation (OPIC). Agencies like OPIC aim to promote exports by insuring domestic firms that do business abroad against expropriation (including creeping expropriation), nationalization, revolution, insurrections, and currency inconvertibility. They provide insurance at rates that do not include a significant profit for the insurer. But the availability of insurance is sometimes subject to politically motivated conditions that exclude many projects. For example, when India tested nuclear weapons in May 1998, OPIC funding for projects based in India became unavailable.

OPIC investments must also not adversely affect the U.S. balance of payments or U.S. employment. The host country must not impose performance regulations that are likely to reduce "positive trade benefits likely to accrue to the United States" so that a joint venture that makes nothing but components for export back to the United States may not qualify. OPIC also gives preference to investments in countries with relatively low per capita annual income. This condition targets the insurance coverage to the poorest countries, which coincidentally have the least viable commercial infrastructure.

Finally, OPIC can operate only in a country with which the United States has concluded a bilateral investment agreement. Because bilateral investment agreements require the host country to agree to waive its sovereign rights views on takings in disputes with the United States, many nations have either not entered into them or canceled them as political views change.

Other developed nations have similar public **export credit agencies** that promote investment from their own countries. These include Japan's Bank for International Cooperation, Germany's Hermes Kreditversicherung-AG, France's Compagnie francaise d'Assurance pour le commerce extérieur, and the Export Development Corporation of Canada. The conditions and limitations of these political risk programs are quite similar to those of OPIC. In some projects, a number of these export credit agencies will pool their efforts.

A similar but internationally based investment insurance company is the Multilateral Investment Guarantee Agency (MIGA). An independent affiliate of the World Bank, MIGA issues insurance guarantees to protect foreign investors from losses relating to currency transfer restrictions, expropriation, war, civil disturbance, and breach of contract. MIGA guarantees are granted for a 15-year term. Both the investor's home country and the country in which it is investing must be parties to the *MIGA Convention.*

Private Political Risk Insurance. Trends toward the modern–traditional expropriation theory, discussed later in this chapter, and international investment treaties and codes lowered the perceived risk of political risk insurance. The result was an increase in the availability of such insurance from private insurers. And as the trend to modern–traditional theory has at least partially reversed, the availability of private insurance has once more began to ebb.

Two principal markets provide **private political risk insurance**. Lloyd's of London and other **insurance syndicates**—pools of money provided by investors to insure specific projects—provide such insurance on a case-by-case basis. In this market, the U.S. investor engages a broker for a specific transaction. In turn, the broker negotiates terms with heads of syndicates specializing in political risk insurance. The syndicate heads then obtain commitments from other syndicates in order to spread the risk exposure.

Alternatively, the investor can approach a lead underwriter of a group operating under a **reinsurance treaty**. The reinsurance treaty is an agreement among insurance companies that spreads the risk among its members. Under its terms, the lead underwriter can commit the resources of the entire group after negotiating the transaction with the U.S. investor.

If available at a competitive price, private insurance has advantages. First, private insurers have no political agendas and hence no political prerequisites. In addition, the private insurance approval process can be faster than that of public agencies. But private insurance has disadvantages. Coverage can be expensive, and many private syndicates will not enter politically volatile areas without a public agency as a partner. Finally, the term of private insurance policies is generally limited to five to seven years. This is too short for an adequate return from larger capital-intensive construction projects.

ATTITUDES TOWARD FDI IN DEVELOPING COUNTRIES AND THE TAKING OF INVESTOR'S PROPERTY

A business that operates in a foreign host country subjects its property there to the power of that sovereign government. One of the greatest threats facing an investor is the threat that the investor's property may be taken by the host government through *expropriation* or *nationalization*. These threats are often considered types of political risk because a government's decision to seize or nationalize private property is usually based on a certain political, economic, or social ideology. There is a long history of the threat of expropriation or nationalization of private property in some countries. Although this is a threat most commonly associated with developing countries, it has occurred in developed countries as well. A typical example might be a leftist government in Latin America that views multinational corporations not as investors that bring technology, create jobs, and pay taxes, but as powerful representatives of capitalist governments in the Northern Hemisphere, bent on exploiting natural resources, channeling profits out of the country, and favoring their local capitalism-inclined adversaries. Governments in developing countries with this hostile attitude toward multinational corporations want the benefits of their investment but then seek to control the company for the benefit of the government, its functionaries, and ultimately, they believe, the general public. In some cases, this has led to the expropriation or nationalization of the investor's property.

We begin this topic by explaining the theoretical basis for such "takings," a term that we will use often in this chapter. We explore the reasons a government might take property and the legal theories that have developed around these takings. We will also look at privatization—the opposite of a taking—in which government-owned firms or industries are sold or turned over to private investors.

Nationalization is quite au courant, but Western legal scholars have been debating the propriety of the takings of foreign property for hundreds of years. This anti-nationalization dialectic comprises two major theories: the traditional theory and the modern–traditional theory. These theories dominate thinking on expropriation and nationalization in developed countries.

The **traditional theory** prohibits all takings of foreign property. Grotius' fundamental principle was that foreign investors—unlike local merchants—should be exempt from the sovereign's condemnation rights: "The right of subjects then differs from the right of foreigners in this, that over those who are in no way subject, the power of eminent domain has no control." This made some sense in the context of the pre-twentieth-century international system, in which citizens of the advanced mercantile or industrial countries were considered to be wholly immune from the judicial power of the less-developed host state. Thus, in the nineteenth century, Britain dispatched gunboats to Venezuela to compel restitution for expropriated property of British subjects.

Exhibit 18.1

Diplomatic Note from the Secretary of State of the United States of America to the Minister of Foreign Affairs of Mexico
July 21, 1938
United States Department of State

BACKGROUND AND FACTS

Agrarian expropriations began in Mexico in 1915. As of August 30, 1927, 1,621 moderate-sized properties of American citizens had been taken. Subsequent to 1927, additional properties, chiefly farms of a moderate size, with a value claimed by their owners of $10,132,388, were expropriated by the Mexican government. The claims were referred to a General Claims Commission established by agreement between the two governments. However, as of 1938, when Secretary Hull sent his letter, not a single claim had been adjusted and none had been paid.

SECRETARY OF STATE CORDELL HULL

The taking of property without compensation is not expropriation. It is confiscation. It is no less confiscation because there may be an expressed intent to pay at some time in the future. If it were permissible for a government to take the private property of the citizens of other countries and pay for it as and when, in the judgment of that government, its economic circumstances and its local legislation may perhaps permit, the safeguards which the constitutions of most countries and established international law have sought to provide would be illusory. Governments would be free to take property far beyond their ability or willingness to pay, and the owners thereof would be without recourse. We cannot question the right of a foreign government to treat its own nationals in this fashion if it so desires. This is a matter of domestic concern. But we cannot admit that foreign government may take the property of American nationals in disregard of the rule of compensation under international law. Nor can we admit that any government unilaterally and through its municipal legislation can, as in this instant case, nullify this universally accepted principle of international law, based as it is on reason, equity and justice… .

The whole structure of friendly intercourse, of international trade and commerce, and many other vital and mutually desirable relations between nations indispensable to their progress rest upon the single and hitherto solid foundation of respect on the part of governments and of peoples for each other's rights under international justice. The right of prompt and just compensation for expropriated property is a part of this structure. It is a principle to which the government of the United States and most governments of the world have emphatically subscribed and which they have practiced and which must be maintained. It is not a principle which freezes the status quo and denies changes in property rights but a principle that permits any country to expropriate private property within its borders in furtherance of public purposes. It enables orderly change without violating the legitimately acquired interests of the citizens of other countries.

Modern–traditional theory permits takings but imposes certain requirements on the nation exercising its takings power. This theory recognizes the sovereign's right to nationalize foreign-owned property, that is, to exercise *eminent domain* over the property of foreigners just as it can over nationals. But modern–traditional theory places conditions on the proper exercise of that right. The exercise of the right must be (1) for a public purpose; (2) nondiscriminatory (not directed against a specific foreign person); and (3) accompanied by prompt, adequate, and effective compensation. Secretary of State Cordell Hull eloquently advanced this modern–traditional theory in his response to the expropriations of the Mexican Revolution in the early twentieth century (see Exhibit 18.1). In the 1970s and 1980s, arbitrations arising out of the expropriation of foreign petroleum holdings by the Iran–United States Claims Tribunal in The Hague confirmed that modern–traditional theory remains the accepted, if not universal, international standard.

Sovereign Rights versus Investor Rights in Developing Countries

In contrast to the modern–traditional theory of takings that has come to dominate developed countries, developing countries have seen a greater willingness to relax the requirements typically associated with a taking, especially the requirement of adequate compensation. Instead, takings in these countries have often been viewed as an area where the rights of individual investors must be balanced against the rights and needs of the sovereign government.

In the nineteenth century, the first intellectual counterpoint to the traditional theory came from Latin America, the most developed of the capital importing regions. The so-called **Calvo Doctrine**—named after the Argentine scholar who first articulated it—placed the sovereign ahead of the foreign investor within the sovereign's territory. It challenged any intervention by foreign states in investment disputes as a violation of the sovereign's jurisdiction. Calvo proponents argued that nationalization is a legitimate exercise of the sovereign's preeminent right to restructure the economy. As such, it was not subject to the law of any other jurisdiction, including international law.

The Calvo Doctrine maintained that a sovereign nation should be free to determine compensation for a taking. The recourse available to the foreign investor should be no greater than that of the domestic investor: appeal to the courts or political branches of the host nation. No foreign nation or foreign arbitral panel may interfere on behalf of an investor that happens to be of foreign origin. This meant that it was within the sovereign power of each state to allow nationalizations without observing the three modern–traditional preconditions.

Calvo's emphasis on state primacy corresponded neatly with the concept of state property inaugurated by the Bolshevik Revolution. To communists, the theory that the sovereign state had a right to restructure its own economy was consistent with the expropriations that followed the revolution. Other communist states followed the Soviet example, justifying it along Calvo lines.

Finally, when Europe's former Asian and African colonies became independent in the years following World War II, they came to view nationalization as integral to economic independence: Foreigners directing the economy effectively controlled the country, despite their lack of political control. These new states could not afford to pay full compensation for nationalizations. Hence, the sovereign state countertheories came into vogue.

In short, during the twentieth century, much of the world adopted theories asserting the state's right to take foreigners' property for less than full compensation. Whatever the intellectual rationale, the outcome for the foreign investor was the same: minimal compensation for the loss of its property.

In the 1980s and 1990s, sovereign rights theories declined. When Latin American governments and their nationalized enterprises defaulted on foreign loans, their access to capital dried up, exacerbating their economic difficulties. These difficulties led to the election of governments supportive of private enterprise. To attract new capital investment, the governments were compelled to assure prospective foreign investors, through legislation and treaties, those future investments would be treated under the modern–traditional theory. When the Eastern European communist bloc collapsed in the 1989–1991 period, the new democracies also followed the same modern–traditional approach to attract foreign investment. By the 1990s, most former colonies also accepted the modern–traditional theory through bilateral treaties in order to attract foreign capital. The sovereign rights theories seemed dead.

The sovereign rights theory made a comeback in the first decade of the twenty-first century. A clear trend seems to have emerged in the Latin American nations of Argentina, Bolivia, Venezuela, Nicaragua, and Ecuador. In 2007, Bolivia became the first country to denunciate and, hence, officially withdraw from the *ICSID Convention*, discussed later. Bolivia was joined by Ecuador in 2009 and Venezuela in 2012. Nicaragua has also announced plans to denunciate the *ICSID Convention*. These nations suggest that because ICSID is a branch of the World Bank, ICSID rulings are subject to conflicts of interest between the World Bank as stakeholder and as arbitrator. They argue that ICSID proceedings are partial, shrouded in secrecy, and inconsistent.

Some Latin American governments are also assertively re-imposing state control. Venezuela has steadily reduced the role of private capital in the oil industry through a series of "offer you can't refuse" buyouts. On May 1, 2006, Bolivia nationalized the energy industry. Bolivia has continued nationalizations in other industries, including the mining industry, while refusing to pay any compensation. Ecuador has reasserted state control over the oil industry. In Argentina, selective renationalization of previously privatized enterprises is proceeding, banks have been forced to make loans at below-market rates, and the country's largest oil producer was nationalized in May 2012.

Other countries are using the reassessment of taxes as a means of nationalizing businesses or at least taking a larger share of profits in extractive businesses. In 2006, Yukos, a Russian oil company declared bankruptcy after its assets were frozen and the Russian government claimed more than $30 billion in back taxes. Many of the company's assets were then purchased at auctions by oil companies owned by the Russian government, with little if any competitive bidding. Brazil has sought more than $12 billion in back taxes against the mining company Vale. Mongolia, Algeria, and China have all recently imposed windfall taxes on natural resources such as gold, copper, and oil in order to share in the increased revenue generated by rising global commodity prices.

There are some signs, however, that this trend toward increased nationalizations may be waning. Mexican President Enrique Peña Nieto, who took office in December 2012, has pledged to allow private investment in Pemex—Mexico's largest oil company, which has been state run since it was nationalized in 1938. Bolivia and Ecuador have seen increased use of joint service contracts with private entities, which allow the governments to take advantage of the knowledge and expertise of the private sector while still retaining ultimate control of the businesses. Currently, however, nationalization risk is at its highest point in decades.

Threats to an Investor's Private Property

Sovereign rights proponents like Professor Calvo rejected the modern-traditional theory's prerequisites for takings: public purpose and nondiscrimination. The right to take foreign property was an attribute of sovereignty. It could not be conditioned on whether an international tribunal characterized the taking as discriminatory or as furthering a private purpose.

While sovereign rights states believe that they can take foreign property for any purpose, under their theory, the level of compensation that the foreigner deserves does hinge on the purpose of the taking. An *expropriation* merits full compensation; nationalization merits less compensation. The classic **expropriation** is a taking of an isolated item of property. By contrast, **nationalization** is the taking of an entire industry or a natural resource as part of a plan torestructure the nation's economic system. In nationalization, the values underlying sovereign rights theories are most strongly implicated. Full compensation is not required by those theories.

In recent years, the Islamic Republic of Iran has not been precluded by treaty from espousing sovereign rights theories. The *INA Corp.* arbitration demonstrated that some jurists still accept sovereign rights concepts. The approach suggested by the panel in the *INA* case—that less than full compensation could be paid in the event of any large-scale nationalization—remains a very small minority view. See the case *INA Corp. v. Islamic Republic of Iran,* below.

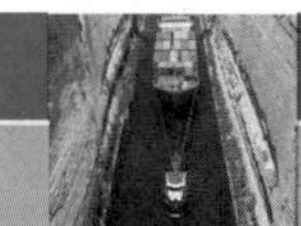

INA Corp. v. Islamic Republic of Iran

8 Iran-U.S. Cl. Trib. Rep. 373 (1985) Iran-United States Claims Tribunal

BACKGROUND AND FACTS

On May 3, 1978, a subsidiary of INA Corporation (INA), INA International Insurance Company, Ltd. (INA International), acquired 20 percent of the shares of Bimek Shargh (Shargh), an Iranian insurance company. The proposed investment by INA International was approved by Central Insurance of Iran (CII), the government body responsible for the regulation of insurance activities in Iran, by a letter to Shargh management dated December 27, 1977. INA International paid 20 million rials for the shares of Shargh. On June 25, 1979, Iran's government enacted the *Law of Nationalization of Insurance and Credit Enterprises.* Article 1 provided as follows:

> To protect the rights of the insured, to expand the insurance industry and the entire State and to place it at the service of the people, from the date of this law, all Insurance enterprises in Iran are proclaimed nationalized with acceptance of the principle of legitimate ownership.

INA sued for what it alleged to be the going value of its Shargh shares, together with interest and legal costs.

JUDGE LAGERGREN

The essence of the dispute between the Parties lies not in the fact of nationalization having taken place, which is agreed, but in the determination of the level of compensation, if any, which should be paid to the shareholders of Shargh as a consequence. No compensation has been paid to date, INA argues for compensation that is prompt, adequate and effective, on the basis both of general principles of international law and the *Treaty of Amity, Economic Relations, and Consular Rights* of 15 August 1955. INA asks the Tribunal to accept the amount of its initial investment in Shargh as the best available indicator of the value of the company as a going concern at the time of nationalization just over one year later.

The respondent government concedes that, in principle, the working of Article I of the nationalization law does, in appropriate cases, envisage the payment of compensation to private shareholders of nationalized insurance companies, but that this must be based on the "net book value" of the company.

It has long been acknowledged that expropriations for a public purpose and subject to conditions provided for by

continues

continued

law—notably that category which can be characterized as "nationalizations"—are not *per se* unlawful. A lawful nationalization will, however, impose on the government concerned the obligation to pay compensation.

This case presents, in addition, a classic example of a formal and systematic nationalization by decree of an entire category of commercial enterprises considered of fundamental importance to the nation's economy… .

In the event of such large-scale nationalizations of a lawful character, international law has undergone a gradual reappraisal, the effect of which may be to undermine the doctrinal value of any "full" or "adequate" (when used as identical to "full") compensation standard as proposed in the case.

However, the Tribunal is of the opinion that in a case such as the present, involving an investment of a rather small amount shortly before the nationalization, international law admits compensation in an amount equal to the fair market value of the investment.

Decision. The Iran-United States Claims Tribunal awarded INA Corporation the amount it sought plus simple interest at 8.5 percent per annum from the date of nationalization.

Case Questions

1. What, according to Judge Lagergren, is the general rule relating to compensation of nationalizations?
2. Judge Lagergren notes that the Iranians had conducted a nationalization. Does he apply the rule for compensation of nationalizations? Did he craft an exception to that rule?
3. If Venezuela nationalizes the petroleum industry, what measure of damages would Judge Lagergren apply? Does net book value reward the foreign investor for the appreciation in value of assets due to his entrepreneurial efforts?

Most international tribunals adhere to the modern–traditional theory. But no less an authority than the *Restatement (Third) of Foreign Relations Law*—which ostensibly reflects the consensus view—states that less than full compensation may be acceptable in "exceptional circumstances" such as agricultural land reform. Modern–traditional theory continues to be under attack.

Level of Compensation for Nationalizations. Sovereign rights advocates uniformly reject the modern–traditional formula of "prompt, adequate, and effective compensation" in instances of nationalization. First, they often disavow the obligation to provide compensation at fair market value. For instance, with respect to the taking of lands or natural resources, they argue that the state already owns the resource, denying the value of the foreigner's land title, so it need pay only for the foreign owners' improvements.

Beneath the surface of these arguments is the reality that the taking government usually cannot afford its fair market value. Thus, a number of sovereign rights states have favored measures of compensation that bear only an attenuated relationship to fair value. One such measure is **net book value** of the nationalized asset. This value reflects the tax-related depreciated cost of assets (calculated using accounting conventions) without regard to whether there has in fact been true depreciation in value. Many assets, for example, actually appreciate over time because of appreciation in the value of what they produce or because the business of which they are a part has a "going concern value" over and above the value of the asset in isolation.

These issues are dramatically illustrated in the recent disputes between international oil companies and the Venezuelan government. Venezuela effectively seized petroleum-producing assets of ExxonMobil and ConocoPhillips. These companies sought compensation in cash for the market value of the projects. But Venezuela insisted on paying book value in crude or reserves. Exxon's stake purportedly had a book value of $750 million and a market value above $2 billion. Conoco's assets had an estimated book value of $4.5 billion and a market value of about $7 billion. Clearly, determination of the measure of compensation has significant financial repercussions.

Promptness of compensation is also a concern. Sovereign rights states generally insist on the right to schedule payment of the compensation over time. These installments sometimes are paid through devices such as the issuance of national bonds payable in the local currency. In such instances, the victim of nationalization must bear the devaluation risk associated with the local currency in addition to its less than market value compensation. Not only is the value of such currencies subject to erosion—particularly when the government does not respect private property rights—but there is also a substantial risk that the local country will not be able to repay its bonds. Because of these risks, such bonds might be transferable to others only at a massive discount, if at all.

Creeping Expropriation. Short of outright expropriation, a foreign nation may impose regulations that limit the exercise of ownership rights—so-called creeping expropriation. **Creeping expropriation** is the effect of laws and regulations that subject the investor to discriminatory taxes, legislative controls over management of the firm, price controls, forced employment of nationals, license cancellation, and restrictions on currency convertibility. Creeping expropriation requires a careful fact-based determination to ascertain whether the sovereign has gone beyond its right to regulate industry. This ambiguity makes creeping expropriation even more difficult for the foreign investor.

For instance, in 2010, the joint oil exploration venture between British Petroleum (BP) and Russian TNK (TNK) came under severe regulatory pressure in Russia after the venture developed differences with national state-owned giant Gazprom over issues of pipeline access and development strategy. Russia also revoked other foreign oil permits, ostensibly on the basis of environmental concerns. Such problems or "regulatory expropriation" are really a subtle form of political risk. The prudent business manager should weigh whether to insure against such occurrences.

Privatization

Privatization is the opposite of nationalization: The national sovereign transfers a government-owned asset to private parties. **Privatization** can be accomplished by the outright sale of assets or ownership interests in a state-owned enterprise being sold to private investors, by granting concessions that allow private entities to operate and derive a profit from state-owned infrastructure, through the widespread issuance of vouchers representing a right to profits to all citizens, or simply by allowing new private businesses to form in a sector formerly reserved to the government.

Privatization has a long history. During the Middle Ages in the Western World, the sovereign owned most of the property. Not until the rise of the merchant classes did private property become important. At that time and context, Grotius, a son of merchant burghers, shaped the limitations on the powers of a sovereign to "nationalize" the property of a foreign merchant. Sovereigns began to realize that if they transferred undeveloped property, from which the sovereign earned nothing, to private entrepreneurs who developed the property, the sovereign could get revenues by taxing the entrepreneurs. One of the first sovereigns to do so extensively was the United States of America. For example, to encourage the building of canals, entrepreneurs were given concessions to build and collect tolls from canals they built. The *Homestead Acts* transferred government land to those who agreed to create farms. A similar privatization trend was taking place throughout the world, particularly in Europe's colonial possessions.

This trend was reversed by Karl Marx's indictment of capitalist excesses. Marxist views were fully or partially accepted in Russia and other communist countries, newly independent African and Asian nations, and newly elected labor or other leftist governments in Western Europe and Latin America. As discussed earlier, these governments nationalized or expropriated all or large parts of the private sector, especially those parts of the private sector owned by foreigners.

But government's ability to extract value from property had not improved in the intervening centuries. Privatization in the modern era began following the end of World War II. In the 1950s, Winston Churchill privatized Britain's steel industry.

The privatization movement picked up steam in the mid-1970s. In 1979, the conservative government of Margaret Thatcher sold its stake in British Petroleum. Britain went on to sell British Aerospace, National Freight Company, Britoil, British Ports, Jaguar Cars, British Telecom, and British Airways in the 1980s. Japan privatized its tobacco and salt industries in 1984 and the telephone and railway industries in 1986. The United States saw privatization through the sale of Conrail to the public in 1987 and the subsequent privatizations of the U.S. Investigations Service, U.S. Enrichment Corporation, and Elk Hills Naval Petroleum Reserve. Even mainland China and Vietnam, the last major bastions of communism, developed business forms that transferred control of assets to private entrepreneurs, especially foreign investors.

Many formerly socialist countries went through privatization of government-held businesses when the USSR dissolved in the early 1990s. The World Bank and many other governmental organizations helped guide these transitioning countries through the process of privatization. During that decade, hundreds of thousands of small-scale operations and approximately 60,000 medium- or large-scale service providers were sold to private investors. East–Central Europe, the Balkan states, and Russia privatized most aggressively. For example, the private-sector share of the economy in Russia went from around

5 percent in 1991 to around 70 percent by the end of the decade. Other countries, such as Belarus, privatized much more slowly, seeing the private-sector share of the economy increase only to around 20 percent by the year 2000.

The 1980s and 1990s also saw sweeping and rapid privatization in many Latin American countries, a trend that has reversed itself in a few Latin nations, as discussed earlier. Between 1975 and 1989, the Pinochet government in Chile, advised by free market economist Milton Friedman, sold publicly held interests in more than 160 corporations to private parties. Bolivia re-elected Victor Paz Estenssoro as president once again in 1985. In order to curb the hyperinflation occurring at the time, Estenssoro implemented the so-called New Economic Policy, which included the privatization of many government-controlled businesses. In Argentina, similar bouts of hyperinflation in 1989 and 1990 prompted a rapid privatization of the country's holdings in Aerolineas Argentinas, Entel (a telecommunications company), petrochemical companies, and televisions stations, among other companies. Altogether, more than 120 companies were privatized through direct sales, concessions, or franchises. Many other Latin American countries, such as Colombia, Guatemala, Panama, Paraguay, and Uruguay, also went through a wave of privatizations in the early 1990s.

The Privatization Process. Privatization takes many forms. At the outset of the process, the industry to be privatized is a functioning unit of the national government. Whether it is a steel manufacturer or an individual power plant, its purpose is to further national interests. All revenues go into the state, and all expenses are covered by the state. Government employees staff the enterprise. This is why the privatizing government needs to prepare the asset for sale before privatizing it.

The privatization process typically begins with a functioning unit of the government, such as the national telecommunications ministry or the national steel manufacturing ministry. The assets that are necessary for the unit to function are transferred to a new corporate entity. To clear title to property, governments frequently create a legal network whereby the victim of expropriation must either assert its claim within a specified period or waive it.

In countries where there has been no functioning capitalist system, the legal infrastructure for private investment must be created. The recognition of private property rights is essential to privatization. A functioning system of private property requires establishment of laws governing the acquisition and transfer of title, filing registries for real property mortgages, systems for acquiring and recording chattel mortgages, and other unglamorous mechanisms. International investors also require a functioning commercial code. They require an understandable regulatory regime governing the newly privatized enterprise. All of this legal infrastructure must be laid out before significant privatization can occur.

Nicaragua: A Privatization Example. From 1979 through 1990, Nicaragua was ruled by a populist left-wing party known as the Sandanista National Liberation Front. The Sandanistas nationalized many of the businesses and properties that had been owned by the Somoza family—who ruled Nicaragua as dictators from 1936 through 1979—and its allies. When the Sandanista party lost to the National Opposition Union, a political union of several anti-Sandanista parties from across the political spectrum, in elections held in 1990, major free-market reforms were adopted by the new governing coalition.

These reforms included efforts to privatize many state-controlled entities. *Decree-Law No. 7-80* established the General National Public Sector Corporations Board (CORNAP). CORNAP was granted control over 22 separate state-owned corporations and business entities across the agriculture, forestry, fishing, mining, foreign trade, transport, construction and other sectors. CORNAP had a mandate to "authorize legal, non-judicial or legislative acts of privatization of the Corporations, their enterprises and assets."

Additionally, *Decree-Laws No. 11-90* and *23-91* set up procedures for submitting claims that the Sandanista regime had expropriated certain property and authorizing restitution or indemnification as a remedy for such confiscations. Under the *Coordination Agreements* signed the following year, workers in state-owned enterprises were granted an option to receive a 25 percent participation in the profits in any privatization, mitigating one of the largest political concerns with the privatization experiences in other Latin American countries—job losses following privatizations.

Substantial clean-up was required prior to privatization. Claims for restitution had to be resolved. Corporate formalities had rarely been observed. These business entities had a variety of different structures, and some were held jointly with private entities. Most of them had large amounts of debt—to the tune of at least $400 million combined. Many of the entities, especially in the agriculture sector, did not have well-defined property rights with established boundaries to their real estate under existing laws. CORNAP developed separate procedures to deal with (1) entities that presented desirable and potentially profitable investments to private investors, (2) entities whose assets consisted primarily of valuable real estate, and (3) entities in crisis that needed accelerated privatization or closure.

CORNAP worked together with international institutions such as the United Nations Development Programme, the Inter-American Development Bank, and the U.S. Agency for International Development to help coordinate its privatization efforts. Assets and liabilities of each entity to be privatized were typically valued by independent financial consultants, and a competitive bidding process was used to determine the ultimate price. Private property rights were legally formalized in the assets to be transferred prior to physical transfer of the enterprise. Most properties privatized by means other than restitution were transferred by direct sale often paid for at least in part by an assumption of the companies' debts.

Overall, entities responsible for generating approximately 28 percent of Nicaragua's total 1988 GDP were privatized through CORNAP in the early 1990s. A second wave of privatization in the late 1990s and early 2000s, under pressure from the IMF and World Bank, replaced public utilities with private markets in the provision of utilities such as electricity, water, sewage, and telephone services. By 2006, however, the anti-Sandanista coalition fractured, and the Sandanistas returned to power in a three-way race. Nicaragua joined the Bolivarian Alliance for the People of Our America, along with other socialist-aligned countries such as Venezuela and Cuba. In February 2012, the group declared its support for nationalizations and a desire to "strengthen the role of the State as a central player in the economy." Although it remains to be seen how far the current regime goes in pushing for renationalization, Nicaragua illustrates the fragility of privatization. Any foreign investor purchasing an asset in a privatization should consider the risk of renationalization. Nations that have once nationalized have a high recidivism rate.

RESOLVING INVESTMENT DISPUTES

Investors seeking relief from what they believe to be unlawful expropriation or nationalizations of their property by a foreign host country have three basic options. First, a large number of host countries have consented or will consent to the arbitration of disputes either by contract or treaty. Second, U.S. investors can seek relief from the courts of the host country or from the U.S. court system. This section will discuss each of these possible avenues for relief.

The Use of Arbitration in Settling Investment Disputes

An aggrieved investor can explore the possibility of dispute resolution in an international tribunal, a subject addressed in Chapter Three. Unless the host nation has generally consented to international arbitration for foreign investment disputes in bilateral investment treaty, the host nation cannot be compelled to arbitrate. The time to seek the host state's consent to arbitration is before the investment is made, when the investor has negotiating leverage. A carefully drawn arbitration clause in a contract with a government agency can provide a strong argument that an expropriation will be adjudicated according to the prevailing principles of international law, which require full compensation.

When contracting with a government agency, the entrepreneur should not blindly rely on the arbitration provision in the contract (the *clause compromissoire*) because the government official agreeing to the provision might have no power to do so. National legislation may supersede the contractual provisions that the arbitrator is called on to interpret. For example, *Andean Pact Decision 24* once excluded foreign investment contracts and foreign transfer of technology contracts from the jurisdiction of any foreign court or arbitrator. Similarly, Article 100 of the Argentine Constitution prohibits the state from submitting to arbitration on issues arising out of remittance of capital or profits abroad. Under national legislation, relatively straightforward matters such as the payment of damages to an entrepreneur upon the state's breach of an agreement not to take property are generally deemed to be within an arbitrator's power.

The entrepreneur should also be on the alert for special procedural requirements imposed by national laws. Perhaps the most common of these in the arbitration context is the requirement of a document (the *compromise*), signed by the parties to the *clause compromissoire,* which submits the specific dispute at issue to arbitration. The theory of the compromise is that the parties will begin to come together through the process of framing the dispute for the arbitrator.

Obviously, a recalcitrant party can instead make this process the source of unnecessary delay.

These national procedural requirements are as diverse as nations themselves. In the following case, a foreign investor neglected to structure its contract with a government entity so as to ensure that its choice of an international arbitral tribunal would be honored under local law. The result was very bad for the foreign investor.

Convention on the Settlement of Investment Disputes Between States and Nationals of Other States. Many countries have agreed to arbitration in cases of investment disputes in foreign investment codes. Another source of consent to arbitration is by treaty. The United States has negotiated bilateral investment treaties with a large number of its trading partners under which the host countries consent to arbitration in case of dispute with U.S. investors. The arbitration

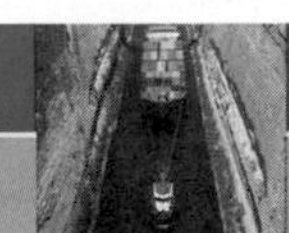

National Thermal Power Corp. v. The Singer Co.

1993 Y.B. Com. Arb. 403 (1992) The Supreme Court of India

BACKGROUND AND FACTS

The National Thermal Power Corporation of India (NTPC) entered into a contract with The Singer Company (Singer), a British concern, to supply equipment and erect certain projects in India. A dispute arose and Singer sought arbitration under International Chamber of Commerce (ICC) rules in London, as provided in the contract. Singer won the arbitration and was granted an award by the ICC tribunal. Singer then sought to enforce the award in India under the *Indian Foreign Awards Act,* which limits the role of Indian courts to recognition and enforcement of the foreign arbitral award. NTPC argued against enforcement, claiming that because the contract was governed by Indian law, it was not a "foreign award" under the Act. Therefore, despite the contract's clear submission to ICC arbitration, the whole case should be retried in India under the *Indian Arbitration Act.* The Delhi High Court dismissed NTPC's application, and NTPC appealed to the Supreme Court of India.

JUSTICE THOMMEN

The General Terms and Conditions of Contract ... are expressly incorporated in the agreements and they state: "the laws applicable to this Contract shall be the laws in force in India. The Courts of Delhi shall have exclusive jurisdiction in all matters arising under the contract." [Another clause] of the agreement deals with arbitration in respect of a foreign contractor. The latter provision says:

> In the event of foreign Contractor, the arbitration shall be conducted by three arbitrators ... all Rules of Conciliation and Arbitration of the International Chamber of Commerce shall apply to such arbitrations. The arbitration shall be conducted at such places as the arbitrators may determine.

The fundamental question is whether the arbitration agreement contained in the contract is governed by the law of India so as to save it from the ambit of the *Foreign Awards Act* and attract provisions of the *Arbitration Act* ... .

[Counsel for Singer contends] that while the main contract is governed by Indian law, as expressly stated by the parties, arbitration being a collateral contract and procedural in nature, it is not necessarily bound by the proper law of the contract ... London having been chosen in accordance with the ICC Rules to be the seat of arbitration, English law is the proper law of arbitration, and all proceedings connected with it are governed by that law ... .

The proper law of the contract in the present case being expressly stipulated to be the laws in force in India and the exclusive jurisdiction of the courts in Delhi in all matters arising under the contract having been specifically accepted, ... the proper law governing the arbitration agreement is indeed the law in force in India, and the competent courts of this country must necessarily have jurisdiction over all matters concerning arbitration. Neither the rules of procedure for the conduct of arbitration contractually chosen by the parties (the ICC Rules) nor the mandatory requirements of the procedure followed in the courts of the country in which the arbitration is held can in any manner supersede the overriding jurisdiction and control of the Indian law and the Indian courts ... .

A "foreign award," as defined under the Foreign Awards Act means an award made ... on differences arising between persons out of legal relationships ... which are considered to be commercial under the law in force in India. To qualify as a foreign award under the Act, the award should have been made in pursuance of an agreement in writing for arbitration to be governed by the New York Convention or the Recognition and Enforcement of Foreign Arbitration Awards ... and not to be governed by the law of India ... . An award is "foreign" not merely because it is made in the territory

continues

continued

of a foreign State, but because it is made in such a territory on an arbitration agreement not governed by the law of India. An award made on an arbitration agreement governed by the law of India, though rendered outside India, is ... not treated in India as a "foreign award." ... .

Such an award necessarily falls under the Arbitration Act and is amenable to the jurisdiction of the Indian Courts and controlled by the Indian system of law just as in the case of any other domestic award ... .

Decision. The Supreme Court of India set aside the judgment of the Delhi High Court and ordered a retrial of the entire case in India, effectively finding that if Indian law governs a contract, an international arbitration provision is void.

Case Questions

1. Does this decision mean that foreign investors doing business in India cannot choose international arbitration?
2. What would the result have been if the parties had chosen to have the contract governed by the laws of England and Wales instead of the laws of India?
3. Does this result suggest that arbitration leads to faster results than courtroom litigation?

agreement can provide for *ad hoc* arbitration, as under the United Nations' UNCITRAL Rules, or may refer to an arbitral institution. Perhaps the most significant arbitration agreement involving a government is the *Convention on the Settlement of Investment Disputes Between States and Nationals of Other States,* to which the United States is a party. The Convention provides a forum and a set of rules for the arbitration of disputes between U.S. citizens and signatory countries. Both the citizen and the host country agree that the Convention governs and that all disputes will be resolved by the **International Centre for the Settlement of Investment Disputes (ICSID).** As of January 2013, 159 countries were signatories to the Convention. Three Latin American countries—Bolivia, Ecuador, and Venezuela—are former members who have recently withdrawn from the Convention.

The growth of cross-border trade and investment also led to a proliferation of bilateral investment treaties (BITs) from the 1980s through the first years of the twenty-first century. Each BIT is a treaty between two trading nations in which each agrees to provide the other's citizens specific investment protections. Typically, BITs offer foreign investors a set of substantive rights, such as national treatment, most-favored-nation treatment, fair and equitable treatment, and guarantees of compensation for expropriation. They also provide foreign investors with direct access to international arbitration to address violations of those substantive rights. At the end of the 1980s, there were approximately 385 BITs. Most BITs designate ICSID as a forum for arbitration. The principal focus of this network of treaty-enforced international adjudication is to protect investors against state action.

In light of the resurgence of sovereign rights theory in Latin America, it is not surprising that this adjudication system focuses on that area. A majority of the pending cases before ICSID are currently against Latin American countries. While developments there demand closer scrutiny, concerns are not limited to Latin America. For instance, although Russia signed the ICSID convention, it has never ratified the convention and generally remains out of the ambit of international arbitration.

ICSID Cases. An important issue in ICSID cases is how damages are to be measured because this plays a crucial role in whether or not arbitration can provide an effective remedy for investors whose property has been expropriated by a host country. The following case provides some insight into how ICSID approaches creeping expropriation and how it determines the amount of damages to be awarded in a context where the host nation is forced into arbitration by a BIT.

Resolving Investment Disputes Before Courts

If the host country has not consented to international arbitration, the foreign investor must seek relief from the courts in the host country or in the United States. Indeed, because international arbitration has become quite expensive and slow, the investor may actually wish to consider alternatives to arbitration. Seeking relief in the courts of the country where the property was expropriated is seldom a good idea. As German or Japanese investors in the United States will testify, the foreigner is at a disadvantage even in judicial systems independent of the executive branch. This disadvantage becomes grave in countries with significant

ADC Affiliate et al. v. The Republic of Hungary, International Center for Settlement of Investment Disputes

Case No. ARB/03/16 (March 15, 2006)

BACKGROUND AND FACTS

The claimants were foreign entities that had invested in the 1999 expansion of an airport near Budapest, Hungary. The airport was owned by the Government of Hungary. In 2002, the government enacted a decree that resulted in the privatization of the airport and caused the effective termination of the claimants' long term leases from which they sought to recover their investment. Arbitration against Hungary ensued. The ICSID panel ruled that this was a violation of the agreement with the investors which took the investors' property, an unlawful expropriation. After the expropriation, the airport boomed; thus, had the expropriation not occurred, the investors would have greatly profited. The ICSID panel focused on the measure of damages owed under the circumstances.

HON. CHARLES BROWER

1. The Applicable Standard for Damages Assessment

The applicable standard for assessing damages has given rise to considerable debate between the Parties.

The principal issue is whether the BIT standard is to be applied or the standard of customary international law. The Claimants argue that the Respondent's deprivation of its investments was a breach of the BIT and as an internationally wrongful act is subject to the customary international law standard as set out in Chorzów Factory (Claim for Indemnity) (Merits), *Germany v. Poland,* P.C.I.J. Series A., No. 17 (1928). The Respondent contends that the BIT standard is a lex specialis which comes in lieu of the customary international law standard.

There is general authority for the view that a BIT can be considered as a lex specialis whose provisions will prevail over rules of customary international law (*see, e.g., Phillips Petroleum Co. Iran v. Iran,* 21 Iran-U.S. Cl. Trib. Rep. at 121). But in the present case the BIT does not stipulate any rules relating to damages payable in the case of an unlawful expropriation. The BIT only stipulates the standard of compensation that is payable in the case of a lawful expropriation, and these cannot be used to determine the issue of damages payable in the case of an unlawful expropriation since this would be to conflate compensation for a lawful expropriation with damages for an unlawful expropriation. This would have been possible if the BIT expressly provided for such a position, but this does not exist in the present case... .

Since the BIT does not contain any lex specialis rules that govern the issue of the standard for assessing damages in the case of an unlawful expropriation, the Tribunal is required to apply the default standard contained in customary international law in the present case.

The customary international law standard for the assessment of damages resulting from an unlawful act is set out in ... the Chorzów Factory case ... which reads: "reparation must, as far as possible, wipe out all the consequences of the illegal act and re-establish the situation which would, in all probability, have existed if that act had not been committed."

In the same case ... the PCIJ also pointed out that "reparation therefore is the indispensable complement of a failure to apply a convention."

Moreover, the PCIJ considered that the principles to determine the amount of compensation for an act contrary to international law are: "Restitution in kind, or, if this is not possible, payment of a sum corresponding to the value which a restitution in kind would bear; the award, if need be, of damages for loss sustained which would not be covered by restitution in kind or payment in place of it... ."

This statement of the customary international law standard has subsequently been affirmed and applied in a number of international arbitrations relating to the expropriation of foreign owned property... .

The present case is almost unique among decided cases concerning the expropriation by States of foreign-owned property, since the value of the investment after the date of expropriation (1 January 2002) has risen very considerably while other arbitrations that apply the Chorzów Factory standard all invariably involve scenarios where there has been a decline in the value of the investment after regulatory interference. It is for this reason that application of the restitution standard by various arbitration tribunals has led to use of the date of the expropriation as the date for the valuation of damages.

However, in the present, sui generis, type of case the application of the Chorzów Factory standard requires that the date of valuation should be the date of the Award and not the date of expropriation, since this is what is necessary to put the Claimants in the same position as if the expropriation had not been committed... .

2. Discounted Cash Flow (DCF) *Method v. Balancing Payment Method*

The next focus of the legal debate between the Parties is the appropriate method to compute the fair

continues

continued

market value of the expropriated investments of the Claimants. The Claimants submit, based on their expert reports, i.e., the LECG reports, that the DCF method is appropriate in the present case. The Respondent contends that, based on the NERA Report and the later Hunt Report, a Balancing Payment method is to be followed.

Like many other tribunals in cases such as the present one, the Tribunal prefers to apply the DCF method, although it is mindful of the Respondent's admonishment that: "international tribunals have exercised great caution in using the [DCF] method due to its inherently speculative nature." (Counter-Memorial at para. 590).

The Respondent's Balancing Payment method "is the sum required to provide the Claimants with an IRR return of 17.5 percent at the date of termination, after accounting for the payments already made." (Counter-Memorial at para. 739). In the Tribunal's view, the Balancing Payment method does not take into account, at least not sufficiently, the remaining term of the investments… . The Respondent's argument that the Balancing Payment method shall be used instead of the DCF method is therefore rejected… .

Case Questions

1. The measure of damages was quite high because the case was deemed an unlawful expropriation. Why was it unlawful? Would damages have been lower if it had been lawful?
2. The panel found damages as of the date of the Award rather than the date of the taking. Why? How can one tell whether to apply the Chorzow date of valuation rule or the rule in this case?
3. The panel chose the DCF method. Why was that necessary under the circumstances of this case?

political risk, which tend to have judiciaries that are only nominally independent. To have as a judge the ally of one's adversary is an unhappy litigation situation. Finally, if a country happens to ascribe to sovereign right principles, recourse to its judiciary would be rather fruitless. Nevertheless, under traditional international law principles, an injured investor may need to exhaust local remedies before invoking diplomatic or international adjudication.

A more promising option is for the investor to sue the host state in the United States. After all, most governments have assets in the United States that are subject to attachment by U.S. courts. For example, if a Boeing 747 owned by a state-owned airline was sitting on the tarmac at Chicago's O'Hare Airport, it could be attached to satisfy most types of judgments. But there are obstacles to this course of action, principally under the *Foreign Sovereign Immunities Act* and the *Act of State Doctrine.*

Foreign Sovereign Immunities Act and Investment Disputes. In 1976, Congress enacted the *Foreign Sovereign Immunities Act* (FSIA). Under FSIA, foreign states are generally immune from the jurisdiction of U.S. courts, save for seven exceptions: (1) the foreign state waives immunity; (2) the state's action constitutes "commercial activity" carried on by the state; (3) rights in property are taken in violation of international law; (4) rights in property are acquired through inheritance or gifts in the United States; (5) the suit involves noncommercial torts within the United States; (6) the suit involves maritime liens based on the foreign state's "commercial activity"; or (7) the suit involves certain types of counterclaims and the foreign state instituted the lawsuit against a U.S. citizen. In addition, in light of the rising terrorist threat, Congress amended FSIA to allow a U.S. citizen to sue a foreign state in a U.S. court for damages resulting from a state-sponsored act of terrorism. The U.S. Supreme Court has held that these are the only exceptions to FSIA's grant of immunity and has interpreted these exceptions narrowly.

The Commercial Activities Exception. The most significant of FSIA exceptions is the **commercial activity exception**. This exception is principally aimed at situations in which the state enters into a commercial contract and is acting as a private commercial party: "a foreign state shall not be immune from the jurisdiction of the United States or the states in any case … in which the action is based … upon an act outside the territory of the United States in connection with the commercial activity of the foreign state elsewhere and it causes a direct effect on the United States." One of the most comprehensive analyses by the Supreme Court on what constitutes "commercial activity" under the FSIA is found in the *Saudi Arabia v. Nelson* case (see below). Writing for a slim majority of the Court, Justice Souter was careful to contrast the actions charged against Saudi Arabia with the *Republic of Argentina v. Weltover, Inc.* case, where Argentina had clothed its actions in official enactments.

Saudi Arabia v. Nelson

507 U.S. 349 (1993) United States Supreme Court

BACKGROUND AND FACTS

The Nelsons, a married couple, filed an action for damages against the Kingdom of Saudi Arabia, a Saudi hospital, and the hospital's purchasing agent in the United States. The purchasing agent had, at the direction of the Saudi government, recruited the husband through advertising in the United States to work at a hospital in Saudi Arabia. The plaintiffs alleged that, once in Saudi Arabia, the Saudis had unlawfully detained and tortured the husband. The Court of Appeals found subject matter jurisdiction. It concluded that the husband's recruitment and hiring were "commercial activities" that Saudi Arabia and the hospital carried on in the United States and that the Nelsons' action was "based upon" these activities within the meaning of the statute.

JUSTICE SOUTER

The *Foreign Sovereign Immunities Act* of 1976 entitles foreign states to immunity from the jurisdiction of courts in the United States ... subject to certain enumerated exceptions. One is that a foreign state shall not be immune in any case "in which the action is based upon a commercial activity carried on in the United States by the foreign state ... " The Act defines such activity as "commercial activity carried on by such state and having substantial contact with the United States ... ."

We begin our analysis by identifying the particular conduct on which the Nelsons' action is "based" for purposes of the Act ... . In denoting conduct that forms the "basis," or "foundation," for a claim ... the phrase is read most naturally to mean those elements of a claim that, if proven, would entitle a plaintiff to relief under his theory of the case ... . Earlier ... we noted that [the commercial activity exception] contains two clauses following the one at issue here. The second allows for jurisdiction where a suit "is based ... upon an act performed in the United States in connection with a commercial activity of the foreign state elsewhere," and the third speaks in like terms, allowing for jurisdiction where an action "is based ... upon an act outside the territory of the United States in connection with a commercial activity of the foreign state elsewhere and that act causes a direct effect in the United States ... ." Congress manifestly understood there to be a difference between a suit "based upon" commercial activity and one "based upon" acts performed "in connection with" such activity ... .

In this case, the Nelsons have alleged that petitioners recruited Scott Nelson for work at the hospital, signed an employment contract with him, and subsequently employed him. While these activities led to the conduct that eventually injured the Nelsons, they are not the basis for the Nelsons' suit. Even taking each of the Nelsons' allegations about Scott Nelson's recruitment and employment as true, those facts alone entitle the Nelsons to nothing under their theory of the case. The Nelsons have not, after all, alleged breach of contract ... but personal injuries caused by petitioners' intentional wrongs and by petitioners' negligent failure to warn Scott Nelson that they might commit those wrongs. Those torts, and not the arguably commercial activities that preceded their commission, form the basis for the Nelsons' suit. Petitioners' tortious conduct itself fails to qualify as "commercial activity" within the meaning of the Act ... . [T]he Act defines "commercial activity" as "either a regular course of commercial conduct or a particular commercial transaction or act," and provides that "[t]he commercial character of an activity shall be determined by reference to the nature of the course of conduct or particular transaction or act, rather than by reference to its purpose ... ." If this is a definition, it is one distinguished only by its diffidence; as we observed in our most recent case on the subject, it "leaves the critical term 'commercial' largely undefined." *Republic of Argentina v. Weltover, Inc ...* . We do not, however, have the option to throw up our hands. The term has to be given some interpretation, and congressional diffidence necessarily results in judicial responsibility to determine what a "commercial activity" is for purposes of the Act.

We took up the task just last Term in *Weltover...* which involved Argentina's unilateral refinancing of bonds it had issued under a plan to stabilize its currency. Bondholders sued Argentina in federal court, asserting jurisdiction under the third clause of [the exception]. In the course of holding the refinancing to be a commercial activity for purposes of the Act, we observed that the statute "largely codifies the so-called 'restrictive' theory of foreign sovereign immunity first endorsed by the State Department in 1952." We accordingly held that the meaning of "commercial" for purposes of the Act must be the meaning Congress understood the restrictive theory to require at the time it passed the statute.

Under the restrictive, as opposed to the "absolute," theory of foreign sovereign immunity, a state is

continues

continued

immune from the jurisdiction of foreign courts as to its sovereign or public acts (jure imperii), but not as to those that are private or commercial in character (jure gestionis) ... . We explained in *Weltover*... that a state engages in commercial activity under the restrictive theory where it exercises "only those powers that can also be exercised by private citizens" as distinct from those "powers peculiar to sovereigns." Put differently, a foreign state engages in commercial activity for purposes of the restrictive theory only where it acts "in the manner of a private player within" the market ... . We emphasized in *Weltover* that whether a state acts "in the manner of" a private party is a question of behavior, not motivation.

We did not ignore the difficulty of distinguishing "purpose" (i.e., the reason why the foreign state engages in the activity) from "nature" (i.e., the outward form of the conduct that the foreign state performs or agrees to perform), but recognized that the Act "unmistakably commands" us to observe the distinction. Because Argentina had merely dealt in the bond market in the manner of a private player, we held, its refinancing of the bonds qualified as a commercial activity for purposes of the Act, despite the apparent governmental motivation.

Unlike Argentina's activities that we considered in *Weltover,* the intentional conduct alleged here (the Saudi Government's wrongful arrest, imprisonment, and torture of Nelson) could not qualify as commercial under the restrictive theory. The conduct boils down to abuse of the power of its police by the Saudi Government, and however monstrous such abuse undoubtedly may be, a foreign state's exercise of the power of its police has long been understood for purposes of the restrictive theory as peculiarly sovereign in nature ... .

The Nelsons ... urge us to give significance to their assertion that the Saudi Government subjected Nelson to the abuse alleged as retaliation for his persistence in reporting hospital safety violations, and argue that the character of the mistreatment was consequently commercial ... . But this argument does not alter the fact that the powers allegedly abused were those of police and penal officers. In any event, the argument is off the point, for it goes to purpose, the very fact the Act renders irrelevant to the question of an activity's commercial character. Whatever may have been the Saudi Government's motivation for its allegedly abusive treatment of Nelson, it remains the case that the Nelsons' action is based upon a sovereign activity immune from the subject-matter jurisdiction of United States courts under the Act.

Decision. The Supreme Court reversed the judgment of the Court of Appeals, dismissing the case. This meant that the Nelsons could not bring suit in an American court over the alleged actions in Saudi Arabia.

Case Questions

1. Would the Nelsons have had a claim in U.S. courts if the employment contract Mr. Nelson had signed in the United States had expressly agreed not to detain him in the absence of criminal activity? Would such a clause have made his action one for breach of contract? Would that have made a difference?
2. If his Saudi employer had failed to pay him the amounts he had contracted to pay, would Mr. Nelson been barred from suing in the United States by the FSIA? Would a U.S. court have had jurisdiction to hear such a suit?
3. What would have been the result in the case if Congress had adopted the "absolute" theory of foreign sovereign immunity?

The Act of State Doctrine and Investment Disputes. If a court decides that, under the FSIA, it can hear the U.S. investor's case against the sovereign state, the investor must still persuade the court to exercise this jurisdictional power despite the *Act of State Doctrine.* The doctrine was historically referred to as a principle under which—for reasons of **comity** (good relations) among nations—a U.S. court will refuse to inquire into the validity of any act of a foreign government. In the more recent case *Kirkpatrick* case that follows, the U.S. Supreme Court has narrowed the impact of the doctrine by abandoning the comity rationale. The *Act of State Doctrine* is also inapplicable if the foreign state has entered into an investment treaty that effectively waives the policy as regards U.S. investors.

In *Kirkpatrick,* Justice Scalia noted that "some Justices have suggested" a possible exception to the *Act of State Doctrine* for commercial activity. He was alluding to the plurality opinion of Justice Byron White in *Alfred Dunhill of London, Inc. v. Cuba,* 425 U.S. 682 (1976). Other lower courts have split on the question of whether such an exception exists. Until a majority of the Supreme Court revisits the issue, the matter will remain open.

The State Sponsor of Terrorism Exception. In the wake of the terrorist attacks on September 11, 2001, the "state-sponsored terrorism" exception to the FSIA has received increased attention. This exception requires a plaintiff to satisfy a number of prerequisites. First, the

W.S. Kirkpatrick v. Environmental Tectronics Corp.

493 U.S. 400 (1990) United States Supreme Court

BACKGROUND AND FACTS

The government of Nigeria awarded a military contract to W. S. Kirkpatrick & Co. The losing bidder, Environmental Tectronics Corporation (ETC), investigated the circumstances under which the contract had been awarded and learned that the winner had bribed key government officials who were responsible for making the award. Ultimately, the U.S. Department of Justice conducted an investigation that confirmed ETC's findings, and high Kirkpatrick officials pled guilty to violations of the *Foreign Corrupt Practices Act.* Thereafter, ETC brought a civil lawsuit against Kirkpatrick in the United States under the *Racketeer Influenced Corrupt Organizations Act* and U.S. antitrust laws. Kirkpatrick moved to dismiss the lawsuit on the basis that the *Act of State Doctrine* prohibited the federal court from considering the matter. The district court granted Kirkpatrick's motion, but the Court of Appeals reversed the district court.

JUSTICE SCALIA

This Court's description of the jurisprudential foundation for the act of state doctrine has undergone some evolution over the years. We once viewed the doctrine as an expression of international law, resting upon "the highest considerations of international comity and expediency." We have more recently described it, however, as a consequence of domestic separation of powers, reflecting "the strong sense of the Judicial Branch that its engagement in the task of passing on the validity of foreign acts of state may hinder" the conduct of foreign affairs … .

We find [that] the factual predicate for application of the act of state doctrine does not exist. Nothing in the present suit requires the Court to declare invalid, and thus ineffective as "a rule of decision for the courts of this country," the official act of a foreign sovereign.

In every case in which we have held the act of state doctrine applicable, the relief sought or the defense interposed would have required a court in the United States to declare invalid the official act of a foreign sovereign performed within its own territory. In the present case, by contrast, neither the claim nor any asserted defense requires a determination that Nigeria's contract with Kirkpatrick International was, or was not effective. Petitioners point out, however, that the facts necessary to establish respondent's claim will also establish that the contract was unlawful. Specifically, they note that in order to prevail, respondent must prove that petitioner Kirkpatrick made, and Nigerian officials received, payments that violate Nigerian law, which would, they assert, support a finding that the contract is invalid under Nigerian law. Assuming that to be true, it still does not suffice. The *Act of State Doctrine* is not some vague doctrine of abstention but a "principle of decision binding on federal and state courts alike." "The act within its own boundaries of one sovereign State … becomes … a rule of decision for the courts of this country." Act of state issues only arise when a court must decide—that is, when the outcome of the case turns upon—the effect of official action by a foreign sovereign. When that question is not in the case, neither is the act of state doctrine. That is the situation here. Regardless of what the court's factual findings may suggest as to the legality of the Nigerian contract, its legality is simply not a question to be decided in the present suit, and there is thus no occasion to apply the rule of decision that the act of state doctrine requires.

But what is appropriate in order to avoid unquestioning judicial acceptance of the acts of foreign sovereigns is not similarly appropriate for the quite opposite purpose of expanding judicial incapacities where such acts are not directly (or even indirectly) involved. It is one thing to suggest, as we have, that the policies underlying the act of state doctrine should be considered in deciding whether, despite the doctrine's technical availability, it should nonetheless not be invoked; it is something quite different to suggest that those underlying policies are a doctrine unto themselves, justifying expansion of the act of state doctrine (or, as the United States puts it, unspecific "related principles of abstention") into new and uncharted fields.

The short of the matter is this: Courts in the United States have the power, and ordinarily the obligation, to decide cases and controversies properly presented to them. The act of state doctrine does not establish an exception for cases and controversies that may embarrass foreign governments, but merely requires that, in the process of deciding, the acts of foreign sovereigns taken within their own jurisdictions shall be deemed valid. That doctrine has no application to the present case because the validity of no foreign sovereign act is at issue.

Decision. The U.S. Supreme Court affirmed the decision of the Court of Appeals, permitting ETC to proceed with its lawsuit against Kirkpatrick.

Case Questions

1. In light of *Kirkpatrick,* should *Act of State Doctrine* ever be relevant in foreign corruption cases?
2. What is the policy favoring the *Act of State Doctrine*? What policy does Justice Scalia note against it?
3. How would the *Act of State Doctrine* affect an attempt to challenge a Venezuelan government official edict that breaches a commercial agreement to comply with the modern–traditional doctrine?

plaintiff must seek money damages, not injunctive relief, for personal injury or death resulting from "an act of torture, extrajudicial killing, aircraft sabotage, hostage taking, or the provision of material support … for such an act." Second, the plaintiff must be a U.S. national when the act of terrorism occurs. Third, the defendant sovereign nation must be designated a "state sponsor of terrorism" by the State Department at the time the act occurs. Finally, if the terrorism occurred in the defendant state's territory, the plaintiff must have first tried to seek an international arbitration.

In *Cicippio-Pueblo v. Islamic Republic of Iran,* the District of Columbia Court of Appeals ruled in 2004 that while the "state-sponsored terrorism" exception to the FSIA waives the immunity of a foreign state, this exception did not provide a cause of action against the foreign state itself. Instead, the court held that the exception only allows a private right of action for U.S. citizens against officials, employees, and agents of a foreign state in their individual capacity, not their official capacity. Victims can still bring suit, but they must do so under other statutes or the common law.

For a U.S. entrepreneur, the act becomes relevant if it is considering doing business, directly or indirectly, with a nation that is on the State Department's list of "state sponsors of terrorism." For example, there are more than 6,000 claims against Cuba alone. If any of the claimants can show that the entrepreneur owes an account payable to such a "state sponsor of terrorism," it might find itself to be the recipient of an order of attachment, seizing funds ostensibly owed to the terrorist sponsor. Doing business in such nations has become risky.

TAXATION OF MULTINATIONAL FIRMS

Tax issues are as varied as the local tax laws, the tax treaties between the target market and the investor's home country, and the circumstances of the individual venture. Even if nations have entered into tax treaties, methods of calculating income, deductions, and depreciation differ significantly. Further complications occur when these different systems are applied to multinational transactions. A general international business law textbook could not possibly address the tax systems of all nations in the world. Even U.S. federal tax law—as embodied in the *Internal Revenue Code*—is the subject of multiple courses in most American law schools. The U.S. investor should be aware, however, of the main provisions of the U.S. tax law that affect international transactions. This section provides a brief introduction into the highlights of these provisions.

The Government Dilemma in Taxing Multinational Firms: Economic and Enforcement Problems

International transactions present a dilemma for tax authorities. In order to ensure that revenue is collected in a manner that is both fair and economically efficient, tax policymakers typically try to tax each item of income once and only once and at equal rates. This ensures that economic decisions are minimally distorted by the presence of taxation and that persons or businesses that are in similar situations are taxed similarly. The international tax system, however, is of necessity a complex puzzle composed of many overlapping pieces. Each nation needs to ensure that it can raise sufficient revenue and that it otherwise looks after the interests of its citizens, such as by promoting international competitiveness of its businesses.

Nations are also seeking to advance different policy objectives: Less developed nations wish to encourage foreign investments that promote technological advancement, while more developed nations are indifferent to such goals. And while each of these overlapping tax systems is tied to the geographic boundaries of the nation, the income earned by international transactions may not have such a definite source. Thus, even a benevolent, omniscient, and perfectly rational planner would have a difficult challenge in developing an international taxation system that functioned smoothly. These problems are exacerbated by the fact that in practice, governments must deal with many competing interests and do not have complete knowledge of what transactions are occurring. Nor do tax authorities always have the power to reach potential taxpayers' assets in the international context. These enforcement issues complicate the ability to enforce the tax systems that are, in fact, in place and frequently lead tax authorities to rely on withholding by payers rather than collection from payees.

Territorial and Extraterritorial Income

One of the most pressing problems in international taxation is to identify the geographic source of each item of income. The U.S. Internal Revenue Service

(IRS) has developed a complex set of rules to determine whether any given item of income has a domestic source or a foreign source. Other countries have similar sourcing rules, although they do not perfectly agree with one another. Sourcing is an important threshold issue in international taxation because, as a general rule, the country from which the income is sourced gets the first crack at taxing the income under tax treaties. Moreover, countries that rely on a territorial tax system do not tax foreign source income, and countries (such as the United States) that tax worldwide income typically give a tax credit for foreign taxes paid on foreign source income. And even countries with worldwide income taxes would not typically attempt to tax foreign persons on their foreign source income.

The manner in which the source of an item of income is taxed depends on what type of income the item represents. For example, wage income from the performance of services is typically sourced to the country in which that service was performed. In the United States, interest is typically sourced to the residence of the payer, and dividend income is typically sourced to the country in which the company paying the dividend is organized. Rents and royalties are typically sourced to the country in which the properties at issue are located or used. U.S. source rules for income earned on the sale of tangible property are quite complex and can depend on the location where title is passed under the sales contract, the location of assets used in the production of the property, and the residence of the seller, among other factors. All of these source rules have a rich set of exceptions.

Systems for Taxing Multinational Firms

As alluded to earlier, different countries have different scopes for which they tax domestic persons. The United States uses, at least in the first instance, a *worldwide* system of income taxation for U.S. persons, although this scope is significantly altered by the *deferral principle* and rules related to *controlled foreign corporations.* This section discusses first the U.S. system of international tax and then briefly discusses alternatives used by other nations.

United States: Worldwide "Tax Credit" System. As a default rule, all income earned anywhere in the world, regardless of source, by U.S. persons is taxable by the U.S. government. This is why the U.S. system is referred to as a worldwide system of income taxation. There are two very important limitations on this default rule that make the U.S. international tax system work quite differently in practice than this simple principle might suggest.

Foreign Tax Credit. The first of these limitations is the Foreign Tax Credit. To reduce the incidence of **double taxation**—where the same item of income is taxed by two different tax authorities—the United States offers a dollar-for-dollar tax credit for foreign income taxes paid on foreign source income. For example, if a U.S. investor receives a $100 dividend from a foreign corporation and faces $35 in U.S. tax, but has already paid $30 in tax to the foreign country in which the corporation is organized, then the Foreign Tax Credit would allow the U.S. investor to pay only $5 in U.S. income tax on the dividend. This prevents the investor from paying an effective 65 percent rate by being taxed by both foreign and U.S. tax authorities. The Foreign Tax Credit reflects the general principle of international taxation that the source country has the first chance to tax an item of income and the residence country only has a secondary authority to tax. This principle is also supported by various tax treaties, which typically have many mechanisms for reducing the incidence of double taxation. The Foreign Tax Credit is subject to very complex limitations that can often drive tax-planning decisions in practice.

One recurring tax issue is the U.S. investor's ability to credit taxes it has paid to a foreign country against taxes payable to the United States. Put simply, with respect to income from foreign sources, a U.S. enterprise receives a credit for certain foreign taxes against its U.S. taxes. Thus, an investor needs to consider the tax rates applicable to a particular form of organization and whether the foreign impositions are creditable taxes for U.S. purposes. The following case illustrates the importance of this issue to an enterprise's investment decision.

The Deferral Principle. The second limitation on the worldwide taxation principle is the deferral principle. Under U.S. tax law, a U.S. person is a legally separate person from any foreign corporation it may own. Thus, while the U.S. person will be subject to tax currently on any income it owns, it will not be taxed immediately on any income earned by the foreign corporation it owns. Instead, tax on this income will be deferred until it is **repatriated**—paid out to the U.S. person, typically in the form of a dividend. Because it is a relatively simple matter to create a corporation organized under the laws

Bank of America Nat'l Trust & Savings Assn. v. United States

459 F.2d 513 (1972) United States Court of Claims

BACKGROUND AND FACTS

Plaintiff Bank of America conducted a general banking business in the Kingdom of Thailand, the Republic of the Philippines, and the Republic of Argentina. With respect to this business, Bank of America paid the three jurisdictions various types of taxes. Bank of America demanded a credit for most of these assessments either on its federal income tax returns or by refund claim.

The Internal Revenue Service disallowed a number of the credits claimed, and Bank of America appealed to a trial commissioner. The trial commissioner held for the Bank of America with respect to the Thailand Business Tax, Type 1 and Type 2; the Philippine Tax of Banks; and the City of Buenos Aires Tax on Profit-Making Activities. Bank of America appealed the matter to the Court of Claims.

JUDGE DAVIS

For a domestic corporation, § 901 (a) and (b)(1) of the *Internal Revenue Code*... allows a credit against federal income taxes of "the amount of any income, profits, and excess profits taxes paid or accrued during the taxable year to any foreign country or to any possession of the United States." It is now settled that the question of whether a foreign tax is an "income tax" within § 901 (b) (I) must be decided under criteria established by our revenue laws and court decisions, and that the foreign tax must be the substantial equivalent of an income tax as the term is understood in the United States... .

[T]he Thailand Business Tax... states that... persons engaged in business have the duty to pay business tax on the "gross takings" for each tax month at [rates ranging from 2.5 percent to 10.5 percent]. "[G]ross takings" from the business of banking [are] (a) interest, discounts, fees, or service charges, and (b) profit, before the deduction of any expense, from the exchange, purchase, or sale of currency, issuance, purchase, or sale of notes or foreign remittances.

The City of Buenos Aires Tax on Profit-Making Activities... imposes a tax on the gross receipts of banks, insurance, savings and loan, and security and investment companies, and... provides that, in the case of banks... "the taxable amount shall be composed of interest, discounts, profits from non-exempt taxable securities, and other revenue, resulting from profits and remuneration for service received in the course of the last business year."

The Philippines Tax on Banks provides... that there shall be collected a tax of 5 percent on the gross receipts derived by all banks doing business in the Philippines from interest, discounts, dividends, commission, profits from exchange, royalties, rentals of property, real and personal, and all other items treated as gross ... For none of the three taxes was the taxpayer permitted to deduct from gross income the costs or expenses of its banking business or of producing its net income ... The problem, then, is whether such imposts on gross banking income... are "income taxes" under the foreign tax credit—"income taxes" as we use that term in the federal system under our own revenue laws.

There is consensus on certain basic principles, in addition to the rule that the United States notion of income taxes furnishes the controlling guide. All are agreed that an income tax is a direct tax on gain or profits, and that gain is a necessary ingredient of income... . Income, including gross income, must be distinguished from gross receipts which can cover returns of capital... . Only an "income tax," not a tax which is truly on gross receipts, is creditable.

[W]e cannot accept the position that all foreign gross income taxes, no matter whether or not they tax or seek to tax profit or net gain, are covered by that provision... for almost sixty years the concept that the income tax seeks out net gain has been inherent in our system of taxation. That is the "well-understood meaning to be derived from an examination of the [United States] statutes which provide for the laying and collection of income taxes"—the basic test... for determining whether a foreign tax is an "income tax" under the foreign tax credit... Where the gross income levy may not, and is not intended to, reach profit (net gain), allowance of the credit would serve only haphazardly to avoid double taxation of net income, since only the United States tax—underthe concept followed since 1913—would necessarily fall upon such net gain. There would not then be any significant measure of commensurability between the two imposts (except by chance).

We do not, however, consider it all-decisive whether the foreign income tax is labeled a gross income or a net income tax, or whether it specifically allows the deduction or exclusion of the costs or expenses of realizing the profit. The important thing is whether the other country is attempting to reach some net gain, not the form in which it shapes the income tax or the name it gives. In certain situations a levy can in reality be directed at net gain even though it is imposed squarely on gross income.

Our review of the [law] persuades us that the term "income tax" in 901(b)(1) covers all foreign income taxes designed to fall on some net gain or profit, and

continues

continued

includes a gross income tax if, but only if, that impost is almost sure, or very likely, to reach some net gain because costs or expenses will not be so high as to offset the net profit... .

Do the three foreign taxes we are now discussing... meet this test? Each of the taxes is levied on gross income from the banking business and allows no deductions for the costs or expenses of producing the income. Any taxpayer could be liable whether or not it operated at a profit during the year.

The only question is whether it is very unlikely or highly improbable that taxpayers subject to the impost would make no profit or would suffer a loss. Obviously, plaintiff and the other institutions subject to the taxes had substantial costs in their banking business, salaries and rent being the major items. The covered banks must also have had bad debts and defaults, and these would have to be taken into account in calculating annual net gain... .

Nor can one say on this record that the three governments felt that net gain would always (or nearly so) be reached by these special banking levies, or that they designed these particular taxes to nip such net profit. Each of the three jurisdictions had a general net income tax (comparable to ours, and admittedly creditable) that the Bank of America and other banks had to pay. That was the impost intended to reach net gain. We cannot say, therefore, that there was only a minimal risk that the combination of a bank's expenses plus its debt experience (and other losses) would outbalance its net gain or profits in any particular year—or that the foreign countries so considered.

Decision. The United States Court of Claims dismissed the petition for a tax credit.

Case Questions

1. Do U.S. courts accept foreign nations' designation of a tax as being on "gross" or "net" receipts? Is this second-guessing a foreign judgment? Does the *Act of State Doctrine* apply?
2. Was the foreign law at issue structured like U.S. tax law? Did the court try to recharacterize the foreign tax law so that it could be analyzed in terms of U.S. tax categories?
3. How complicated would tax compliance be for a bank operating in many nations? Why?

of another country, the deferral principle is a powerful limitation on the default rule of worldwide tax.

The deferral principle so favors taxpayers that U.S. tax authorities have carved out a large class of exceptions to the principle. Under the controlled foreign corporation rules of Subpart F of the Internal Revenue Code, certain income that is earned by foreign corporations controlled by U.S. shareholders is taxed currently to those shareholders even though it is earned by a separate legal person. Without these rules, the deferral principle could be used to avoid tax on many items indefinitely.

For the purposes of Subpart F, a U.S. shareholder is defined as any U.S. person who owns 10 percent or more of a foreign corporation. A foreign corporation is a controlled foreign corporation if U.S. shareholder own more than 50 percent of the corporation. The U.S. shareholders are then taxed currently on any Subpart F income of the controlled foreign corporation. The definition of Subpart F income is complex but typically includes passive income such as dividends, interest, rents and royalties, income earned from selling goods that are neither made nor used in the controlled foreign corporation's country of origin to a related parties, and income earned by selling services to a related party. Income previously taxed under the controlled foreign corporation rules is not taxed a second time when it is repatriated.

Other Systems: Territorial and Formulary Apportionment Systems. There are two primary alternatives to the worldwide system of income taxation used by the United States. Some countries use a so-called territorial system where only domestic source income is subject to taxation. Another alternative is a system that works based on a formulary apportionment. In a formulary apportionment system, rather than trying to identify the source of each item of income, all income earned by a given person is put into a single category. This income is then apportioned between the various nations that have some claim to tax the person on the basis of a predetermined formula that relies on factors such as proportion of sales, assets, or payroll located in a jurisdiction. This is similar to the methods typically used to determine to which states a U.S. taxpayer owes income tax. A formulary apportionment system has not been adopted in the international setting, primarily because of the difficulty of coordinating across different countries and concerns about increased compliance costs.

Other Issues in International Taxation

The preceding discussion gave an overview of some of the basic foundations of the U.S. taxation of international transactions. The remainder of this section discusses a few prominent international taxation issues.

Transfer Pricing. Because the amount of tax to which an item of income is subject depends upon the source of that income, there can be a large incentive to shift income from high-tax jurisdictions to low-tax jurisdictions. Furthermore, a very large proportion of international trade occurs between related parties. Related parties are free to fix prices that they pay to one another on any basis they choose because market forces do not discipline the prices. This fact, combined with the incentive to shift income between countries, creates another fundamental problem for international taxation: **transfer pricing.**

The problem of transfer pricing can be illustrated by a simple example. Suppose that Company X sells widgets to U.S. customers for $12 and that these widgets are manufactured by related Company Y in a low-tax jurisdiction. Suppose further that it costs Y $2 to make each widget and that if X and Y were unrelated, then the market price that X would pay to Y would be $7 per widget. X is subject to a 50 percent tax while Y is only subject to a 10 percent tax. If X and Y were unrelated, Y would pay 10 percent × ($7 – $2) = $.50 per widget in tax and X would pay 50 percent × ($12 – $7) = $2.50, for a combined total of $3 per widget. However, because X and Y are related, they can fix the price at, say, $11 instead. In these circumstances, Y pays 10 percent × ($11 – $2) = $.90 and X pays 50 percent × ($12 – $1) = $.50. X and Y have reduced their joint tax liability from $3 to $1.40 per widget simply by changing an essentially meaningless number.

In order to mitigate this transfer problem, countries, including the United States, require that transactions between related parties be priced for tax purposes as if the transaction had been arm's-length between unrelated parties. The IRS has authority to reexamine any transfer pricing and adjust it to reflect this arm's-length standard. Of course, there is no perfect way for determining what price would be paid in an arm's-length transaction, so imperfect comparisons and estimation techniques must be used. Transfer pricing is thus a very large source of compliance costs and confusion for both tax authorities and taxpayers who have a large number of international affiliates.

In the *Compaq* case, discussed below, the U.S. Tax Court delineated the limits of the discretion of the IRS in this area, decisively underscoring the preeminence of market-based transactions over cost-plus methodologies in transfer-pricing cases.

Compaq Computer Corp. Subsidiaries v. Commissioner of Internal Revenue

113 T. C. 214 United States Tax Court

BACKGROUND AND FACTS

Petitioner Compaq Computer Corporation manufactures personal computers (PCs). Printed circuit assemblies (PCAs) are the electronic circuitry inside a PC's central processing unit that allows the PC to operate. Compaq set up a PCA manufacturing subsidiary in Singapore. The petitioner purchased PCAs from its Singapore subsidiary at actual market prices based on purchases of similar PCAs from unrelated subcontractors that were primarily located in the United States, with a "turnkey equivalent" adjustment based not on actual transactions, but on industry practice. The IRS took the position that such pricing resulted in too much profit being left in low-tax Singapore. The IRS argued that a "cost-plus" approach should have been used and declared a deficiency in Compaq's consolidated returns. Compaq appealed to the Tax Court.

COHEN, CHIEF JUDGE

The issue addressed in this opinion is whether income relating to printed circuit assemblies (PCA's) should be reallocated ... to petitioner from its Singapore subsidiary for its 1991 and 1992 fiscal years ... .

Compaq U.S. bought 3.6 million PCA's worth $597 million on a turnkey equivalent basis from unrelated subcontractors. The PCA's were nearly identical to PCA's sold by Compaq Asia to Compaq U.S.. After adjustment for differences in physical property and circumstances of the sales, the prices that Compaq U.S. paid to the unrelated subcontractors for PCA's were comparable to the prices that Compaq U.S. paid to Compaq Asia for PCA's.

The issue that we are considering here is whether the transfer prices for PCA's that were charged between Compaq U.S. and Compaq Asia meet the arm's-length

continues

continued

standard ... . Petitioner asserts that [the IRS] notice determinations are unacceptable and that comparable transactions between unrelated parties prove that the transfer prices satisfy the arm's-length standard ... . [The IRS] asserts that petitioner has not presented comparable uncontrolled prices to prove that its transfer pricing system should be upheld ... . [The IRS's] primary argument is that petitioner''s turnkey equivalent analysis is not based on actual transactions ... .

Section 482 gives [the IRS] broad authority to allocate gross income, deductions, credits, or allowances between two related corporations if the allocations are necessary either to prevent evasion of taxes or to reflect clearly the income of the corporations ... .

The purpose of section 482 is to prevent the artificial shifting of the net incomes of controlled taxpayers by placing controlled taxpayers on parity with uncontrolled, unrelated taxpayers.

* * *

[T]he regulations attempt to identify the "true taxable income" of each entity based on the taxable income which would have resulted had the entities been uncontrolled parties dealing at arm's length.

* * *

When [the IRS] has determined deficiencies based on section 482, the taxpayer bears the burden of showing that the allocations are arbitrary, capricious, or unreasonable ... . "Whether respondent has exceeded its discretion is a question of fact."

* * *

In reviewing the reasonableness of respondent's determination' the Court focuses on the reasonableness of the result, not on the details of the methodology used.

[The IRS] used unrealistic material, labor, and overhead markups in applying its formulas. If markups in the range of industry markups are used, the results of [IRS] analysis bear no recognizable relation to [the IRS] notice amounts. [Compaq's] analysis establishes an arm's-length price for PCA purchases by Compaq U.S. from Compaq Asia that is approximately $232 million greater than [the IRS] determination in the notice. Due to the significant difference in these arm's-length prices and [the IRS] determination in the notice of deficiency, we conclude that [the IRS] allocations lead to an unreasonable result and are thus arbitrary, capricious, and unreasonable.

In addition to proving that the deficiencies set forth in the notice are arbitrary, capricious, or unreasonable, petitioner must also prove that the prices charged by Compaq Asia were consistent with arm's-length pricing ... . The regulations set forth three pricing methods to determine whether there is an appropriate arm's-length price. First, if comparable uncontrolled sales exist, the regulations mandate that the CUP method be used. If there are no comparable uncontrolled sales, the resale price method must be utilized if the standards for its application are met. If the standards for the resale price method are not satisfied, either that method or the cost-plus method may be used, depending upon which method is more feasible and is more likely to result in an accurate estimate of an arm's-length price. Where none of the three methods can be reasonably applied, some other appropriate method may be used.

Under the CUP method, the arm's-length price of a controlled sale is equal to the price paid in comparable uncontrolled sales including necessary adjustments. "Uncontrolled sales" are sales in which the seller and the buyer are not members of the same controlled group ... . Uncontrolled sales are considered "comparable" to controlled sales if the physical property and circumstances involved in the uncontrolled sales are identical to the physical property and circumstances involved in the controlled sales or if such properties and circumstances are so nearly identical that differences either have no effect on price or such differences can be reflected by a reasonable number of adjustments to the price of the uncontrolled sales. Adjustments can be made only where such differences have a definite and reasonably ascertainable effect on price. Some of the differences listed in the regulations as possibly affecting price are differences in quality, terms of sale, intangible property associated with the sale, level of the market, and geographic market in which the sales take place. Whether differences render sales noncomparable depends upon the particular circumstances and property involved ... .

Petitioner has presented substantial evidence of uncontrolled transactions with unrelated subcontractors. Petitioner's CUP analysis is predicated on Compaq U.S. purchases of 3.6 million PCA's from unrelated subcontractors between 1990 and 1993. The aggregate purchase price of these PCA's totaled $597 million on a turnkey equivalent basis and was 93.1 percent of the Compaq U.S. standard cost. In addition, the purchases occurred in the regular course of business and were substantial in both frequency and amount ... . Although these transactions were not identical to the controlled transactions involving Compaq Asia, we conclude that they are sufficiently similar to provide a reliable measure of an arm's-length result. Thus, the purchases from unrelated subcontractors identified by petitioner qualify as comparable uncontrolled sales for purposes of application of the CUP method.

Compaq U.S. purchases of PCA's from unrelated subcontractors, however, differ in some respects from the PCA purchases from Compaq Asia. Accordingly, within the context of [tax regulations] and the particular facts in this case, the specific differences between the

continued

Compaq U.S. purchase of PCA's from Compaq Asia and unrelated subcontractors must be examined to determine "Whether and to what extent differences in the various properties and circumstances affect price … . The record demonstrates that the only differences in PCA's within each product category were the particular components used on each individual PCA and the time required to process PCA's on the manufacturing line. We are persuaded that these differences can be corrected with adjustments to Compaq U.S. standard costs" … .

Based on the uncontrolled purchases of 3.6 million PCA's, the turnkey equivalent price of PCA's purchased from unrelated subcontractors was 93.1 percent of the Compaq U.S. standard costs weighted to the Compaq Asia production amount. Compaq Asia turnkey prices were 93.9 percent of the Compaq U.S. standard cost. Thus, the relationship between Compaq Asia prices and unrelated subcontractors prices is definite, and a reasonably accurate adjustment can be made using these ratios … .

Ultimately, [the IRS] argues that, because the CUP method cannot be applied, a profits-based fourth method is the appropriate method of determining arm's-length prices in this case. The Court was faced with the same "prices v. profit" argument [in a prior case]. This Court held:

The fact that B&L Ireland could, through its possession of superior production technology, undercut the market and sell at a lower price is irrelevant. Petitioners have shown that the $7.50 they paid for lenses was a "market price" and have thus "earned the right to be free from section 482 reallocations."

* * *

The same is true in the present case. The CUP method establishes arm's-length prices for PCA's that were sold by Compaq Asia, and a large profit margin does not prevent use of the CUP method.

Decision. The Tax Court found that petitioner satisfied its burden of proving that the prices in the intercompany transactions were consistent with arm's-length prices and ordered the IRS to reduce its deficiency notices accordingly.

Case Questions

1. What standard does a taxpayer have to meet in order to overcome the IRS determination that the transfer prices were not arm's-length? Does this give the IRS the great benefit of the doubt?
2. Why was the IRS unable to show that its ruling against Compaq was not "arbitrary and capricious"?
3. What does this tell the U.S. investor about playing games with inter-affiliate transfer pricing to avoid taxes?

Illegal Schemes to Avoid Taxation: Invoice Faking. The last decade has seen a rapid rise in *invoice faking*, an international tax fraud scheme. In an invoice-faking scheme, transfer prices are manipulated to systematically overstate or understate quantities and prices of goods that are being shipped internationally. Rather than accurately recording the amount of money changing hands between parties, the invoices show a greater amount of cash flowing into low-tax jurisdictions than is actually the case. This invoice faking allows paper profits to be shifted into the low-tax jurisdiction, lowering the overall tax paid on the transaction.

For example, imagine that Company A in a high-tax jurisdiction sells 10,000 widgets at $10 per widget to Company B in a low-tax jurisdiction. A faces a 50 percent tax while B faces a 10 percent tax. Instead of accurately reflecting the $10 per widget paid, however, A and B submit invoices to the tax authorities showing a $20 purchase price. A and B's economic situation is the same, but together they have just saved 40 percent × 10,000 × $10 = $40,000 in net taxes. While it is true that B is paying higher taxes than they otherwise would have, A can easily share some of its tax savings with B so that both parties come out ahead.

Tax fraud due to fake invoicing is a serious enforcement problem for many developing countries. Global Financial Integrity, a Washington, DC-based research nonprofit, estimates that developing countries lost approximately $100 billion in tax revenue between 2002 and 2006 to fake invoicing schemes. In some countries, such as Zimbabwe, the losses represented more than 30 percent of total government revenues. This significantly exacerbates the already-existent problem of chronically underfunded governments in the developing world, which prevents further economic development and dims the prospects for future prosperity in some of the hardest hit countries.

Taxation of E-Commerce. Products and services sold over the Internet to a foreign nation are subject to that nation's taxation. An e-company marketing abroad has to consider the foreign tax liability incurred in such transactions.

In particular, all European Union purchases are subject to a **value-added tax (VAT)**. The VAT is similar to, but much higher than, U.S. states' sales taxes on retail goods. Each EU member-state has its own VAT rate, ranging from 15 percent to 25 percent. Application of land-based law to Internet transactions has bizarre consequences. For example, a U.S. customer who buys a European vendor's product over the Internet owes no VAT at the time of purchase. If he or she later visits Europe, he or she would owe the VAT upon arrival. If the customer pays it (a big "if"), he or she will be eligible for reimbursement of the VAT upon leaving European territory. Obviously, authorities are not enforcing VAT against U.S. consumers. The provision was enacted to impose a tax obligation on U.S.-based merchants selling to European consumers. All such suppliers that make more than 100,000 € in sales to an EU nation must file returns and pay VAT on all sales.

More controversially, the EU treats sales on the Internet, including downloadable music or software, as services for tax purposes. Because EU member-states tax services at even higher VAT rates than goods and because most music and software downloads originate in the United States, many viewed this treatment as a political decision aimed at American business. A confrontation between the United States and Europe immediately followed, which resulted in an apolitical resolution.

Under VAT rules, services—unlike goods—are taxed at the place where they are provided. Therefore, there was no way for the EU to enforce the law without U.S. government cooperation. That cooperation has not been forthcoming. More debates like this are likely to unfold before nations' e-commerce tax systems are coordinated in a manner similar as those for income taxation.

Mechanisms to Reduce Global Tax Liabilities. Despite the complexity of the rules governing international taxation, and sometimes even because of such complexity, there are many ways by which multinational corporations can structure their transactions in order to legally pay less tax. This section discusses some of the more high-profile examples of legal tax planning. While these techniques are often legal, they can deprive governments of revenue, distort taxpayer decision-making and result in distribution of the tax burden in a manner inconsistent with government policy.

Governments are not powerless against such tax-planning techniques. In the United States, for example, the IRS can rely on judicial doctrines such as the economic substance doctrine, which permits transactions to be recharacterized or ignored if they serve no legitimate business purpose beyond the reduction of tax liability. In 2010, this doctrine was codified in the *Internal Revenue Code*, along with penalties up to 40 percent of any underpayment when the doctrine is violated by abusive tax-planning maneuvers. But these techniques are legal and illustrative of why tax lawyers are so important in significant international transactions.

What Is a "Tax Haven"? A **tax haven** is a country where the effective tax rate on a relevant item of income is very low or zero. Because the effective tax rate may vary between different types of income, some countries are tax havens only with respect to certain types of income. Some tax havens have been created by historical accident. For example, a large proportion of foreign direct investment in India is funneled through Mauritius entities because the Mauritius–India bilateral tax treaty contains some especially favorable provisions for investors. In other instances, small countries deliberately make themselves tax havens so as to attract the accompanying corporation creation and banking business. The Cayman Islands is a prototypical example of this kind of tax haven for hire arrangement.

Tax havens may even appear in high-tax jurisdictions. The classic example of this phenomenon is the Netherlands. Despite having a top marginal rate of 52 percent on individuals and 25.5 percent on corporations, the Netherlands is often seen as an attractive location for tax planning for at least two reasons. First, the Netherlands exempts dividends and capital gains from foreign subsidiaries from its corporate income tax. Second, the Netherlands has a large number of income tax treaties with other countries that reduce or eliminate the rate of withholding taxes required on dividends, interest, and royalties. These provisions allow the Netherlands to frequently serve as an effective conduit in tax-planning transactions, such as the Dutch Sandwich discussed next.

The "Double Irish" or "Dutch Sandwich." The *Double Irish* and the *Dutch Sandwich* are related tax-planning techniques that U.S. multinationals use if they have significant income from non-U.S. intellectual property rights. In the simplest form of the Double Irish, the taxpayer forms two Irish corporations. The first Irish corporation locates its management functions in a tax haven such as the Cayman Islands. Under Irish tax laws, a corporation is resident in the country where its management is located, while under U.S. tax laws, a corporation is resident in the country in which it is organized. Therefore, this first Irish corporation is an Irish person for U.S.-tax purposes and a Cayman Islands person for Irish-tax purposes. This corporation holds the non-U.S. intellectual property rights and enters into a cost sharing agreement with the U.S. parent company, as allowed under U.S. transfer pricing regulations. The second Irish corporation, formed as a subsidiary to the first, is an Irish person for both U.S. and Irish tax purposes. The first Irish corporation then licenses the rights to the second Irish corporation. The second corporation receives income from the use of the intellectual property rights outside of the United States but pays most of this income to the first Irish corporation in the form of a royalty. The second Irish company is thus taxed at the low 12.5 percent Irish tax rate on just a small fraction of the revenues earned. The rest of the income is left untaxed in the Cayman Islands. Because the second Irish company is a subsidiary of the first, an election under U.S. tax laws allows for the transaction between them to be disregarded, so the companies will not earn Subpart F income under the controlled foreign corporation rules, and the parent will not have to pay current U.S. tax.

In a variant on the Double Irish, a Netherlands entity is interposed between the two Irish corporations. Because Ireland exempts certain payments to the Netherlands from withholding taxes, this transfer can be used to avoid paying Irish tax on even the small amount of profits that are taxed in the pure Double Irish. Because of the generous provisions of Dutch tax law discussed earlier, the Netherlands does not collect any tax on this series of transactions either. This arrangement results in almost no taxes being paid on the income earned through the use of non-U.S. intellectual property rights. To the uninitiated, this may seem like an evasion of the tax laws, but the legality of this planning device has been approved by the IRS. In international tax law, form can be very important.

Multilateral Cooperation and Enforcement. Efforts to improve communication and cooperation among the tax authorities of different countries have grown in recent years as an increasingly global marketplace has required tax authorities to either work together or see their tax bases systematically dwindled by intelligent tax lawyers. In 2002, the OECD released a model *Tax Information Exchange Agreement* (TIEA). Bilateral information sharing agreements based on this model have been entered into between many countries. The United States alone has entered into at least 30 such agreements. In addition, in 2004 the tax authorities of the United States, the United Kingdom, Australia, and Canada created the *Joint International Tax Shelter Information Center* (JITSIC) as a tool for the multilateral exchange of information related to international tax shelters.

Although the OECD model agreement only covers exchange of information upon request of one of the parties to the agreement, many TIEAs also have provisions for the routine or automatic exchange of information that may be relevant to the application of tax laws of the other party. The routine exchange of information related to transfer pricing is becoming more common. Requests can typically made for any information that might be "foreseeably relevant" to the application of the requesting party's tax laws. TIEAs typically require that tax authorities not only divulge information in their possession when it is requested but also tax affirmative steps to gain access to such information, even if it is not relevant for the application of their own domestic tax laws. Protections of taxpayer confidentiality are routinely included. TIEAs also often authorize tax authorities to conduct extraterritorial investigations with the consent of the potential taxpayers concerned.

JITSIC's primary function is to help participating countries identify abusive tax avoidance transactions. Such information is exchanged on an ongoing basis to fight tax evasion in real time. Japan joined JITSIC in 2007, and China and South Korea have been granted observer status. JITSIC's original mission has also been expanded to include heightened scrutiny of offshore arrangements and high net-worth individual taxpayers.

Increased information sharing and cooperation among tax authorities has been quite successful. The IRS has used JITSIC information to successfully identify and crack down on so-called "foreign tax credit generator" transactions among other tax shelters. Tax practitioners are increasingly seeing the effects of better information sharing and joint audits. Such trends are likely to continue and deepen, mitigating some of the enforcement problems that have plagued the taxation of international transactions.

CONCLUSION

Foreign direct investment can open up many desirable financial opportunities across the globe for an investor. It can allow for greater access to the customers, natural resources, suppliers, and workforce located in a foreign country. It can help to avoid certain barriers to trade. However, there are particular nationalization and expropriation risks associated with direct investment in a foreign host country, and the investor needs to understand these risks and how to ameliorate them and remedy them if they occur. Finally, before committing capital abroad, the investor needs to understand how its profits will be taxed by the jurisdictions with a stake in the transactions.

This chapter provided a brief overview of the highlights of this legal landscape. It began by discussing the various choices that must be made before making an investment. Why invest in a particular country or enterprise? How should that investment be structured as a matter of the corporate law of the host country? These are important decisions that need to be carefully considered to maximize the return on the investment.

This chapter then discussed two of the most important risks that are unique to foreign direct investment. Currency risk is the risk that profits earned in the host country's currency will not translate into profits in the investor's home country currency—either due to exchange rate fluctuation or legal impediments to convert a soft currency. A host of techniques for mitigating this risk were presented. Political risk is the risk that policy changes or political instability in the host country will prevent the realization of a profit. Getting information first through political risk analysis services and obtaining political risk insurance offer the best protection against political risk.

The next section of this chapter discussed one of the most important forms of political risk: the risk that one's investment will be expropriated or nationalized by the host country. While takings by developed countries typically must be accompanied by adequate and prompt compensation, these protections do not always exist in the developing world. Particular in Latin America, the pendulum has swung back and forth several times on the prevailing attitudes of developing country governments to the property rights of investors.

If an investment is expropriated or nationalized unlawfully, it is important to understand what remedies might be available. The next section of this chapter discussed the means for obtaining relief from foreign governments unlawful takings. ICSID provides a unified framework for the arbitration of such disputes. While a large number of countries participate in ICSID arbitrations, a few Latin American countries have recently withdrawn from the convention that created the organization. As an alternative to arbitration, actions can potentially be brought in the local courts of the host country or in U.S. courts. Both of these options suffer from several impediments, however.

This chapter ended with an overview of the U.S. taxation of international transactions. While such a topic is very large and complex, the basics were discussed. The United States has, in the first instance, a worldwide system of international taxation where U.S. persons are taxed on both their foreign and domestic income. The foreign tax credit and the deferral principle represent to important limitations on the worldwide reach of U.S. tax law. The controlled foreign corporation rules, however, carve back some of the income that would be deferred under the deferral principle. Transfer pricing, invoice faking, tax-planning techniques, and multilateral cooperation and information sharing were also discussed.

Chapter Summary

1. Many host nations, particularly in the developing world, regulate foreign direct investment in order to prevent foreign economic domination. Passive debt investments are the least regulated; active majority equity investments are most closely regulated.
2. Because passive equity investments provide capital without allowing foreign control of management, nations generally facilitate entry by foreigners into equity capital markets. Most developed nations have sought to attract foreign passive equity investment.
3. Most nations limit the types of businesses over which a foreign investor can exercise control. These range from limits on investment in sectors affecting national security—such as those found in the United States—to sweeping limits on majority ownership in all businesses, or on all but those directed at the export

market. This type of limit is common in China and many developing countries.

4. Because active foreign investors greatly value the ability to control their enterprises abroad, limits on control tend to reduce the amount of investment into a country. Nations that have imposed such controls have experienced dramatic drops in capital investment in affected industries. Thus, the trend over time has been for nations to remove control limitations as they become more developed and capital needs increase.
5. A foreign investor may operate in another country through a subsidiary/partnership organized in that country or through a branch of its entity. Generally, the foreign branch gives certain tax advantages to the foreign investor, but can subject its entire business to the jurisdiction of the host country regulators and legal liability.
6. Nations generally enter into tax treaties to prevent double taxation of international investors. This is most often achieved by limiting taxation to the "water's edge" and providing credit for analogous taxes on the same activity. There are also tax laws that prevent evasion of tax through artificial transactions such as transfer pricing. Nonetheless, there are a variety of corporate structures that can legitimately reduce the overall tax burden to the enterprise.
7. There are two forms of currency risk: fluctuation risk and inconvertibility risk. Fluctuation risk is the possibility that the value of the currency in the country where one has invested will go down relative to the currency of the foreign investor's home country. Inconvertibility risk is the possibility that the foreign investor will not be able to convert local currency earned by its investor into a hard currency.
8. In modern international business, currency swaps are the principal method for controlling currency fluctuation risk. A financial intermediary agrees to pay the business party if currency rates go over a certain level and the business party agrees to pay the intermediary if it does not, effectively negating fluctuation risk for the operating company. To facilitate these transactions, the International Swap Dealers Association has developed a standard form agreement so that all legal terms in these deals are consistent and parties can easily redistribute the risk inherent in swaps.
9. Inconvertibility risk can be reduced by negotiating with the local government for currency exchange rights that provide preferred access to hard currency reserves or import substitution rights, which are available when the new venture will manufacture a product in the soft-currency country. Foreign investors can also ameliorate inconvertibility risk by structuring transactions correctly. Structuring techniques include requiring lump-sum, hard-currency payments as early as possible; negotiating with local partners for profit margin preservation provisions; or applying unitary index adjustment factors. It is also important, in investments that will be generating local currency revenues, to borrow to the greatest extent possible in local currency and purchase services and supplies from parties who can be paid in the local currency.
10. Countertrade is a way of controlling inconvertibility risk by trading goods. The principal forms are counterpurchase, barter, offsets, and buy-back. In light of the rise of currency swaps and parallel exchanges, the importance of countertrade has declined. A final method for containing inconvertibility risk is to buy insurance against it.

Key Terms

foreign direct investment 494
passive investment 496
active investment 497
currency risk 498
currency swaps 498
political risk 498
fluctuation risk 498
inconvertibility risk 498
soft currency 498
currency exchange rights 499
import substitution rights 499
profit margin preservation 499
unitary index adjustment 499
trade creditors 499
countertrade 500
currency inconvertibility 500
counterpurchase agreement 500
barter 500
buy-back agreement 500
informal consortia or parallel exchanges 500
inconvertibility insurance 500
non-transfer insurance 500
hard blockages 500

soft blockages 500
political risk analysis 501
political risk insurance 501
export credit agencies 501
private political risk insurance 502
insurance syndicates 502
reinsurance treaty 502
traditional theory 502
modern–traditional theory 503
nationalization 505
expropriation 505
net book value 506
creeping expropriation 507
privatization 507
commercial activities exception 513
act of state 515
comity 515
double taxation 518
repatriated 518
transfer pricing 521
value-added tax (VAT) 523
tax haven 524
eminent domain 530
condemnation 530

Questions and Case Problems

1. Keefe Energy, Inc., a U.S. firm, enters into a joint venture with Energia Guerra, S.A., a Mexican firm, to build and operate a coal-fired electric-power-generating plant with an estimated useful life of 35 years. The building and land will be owned by G/K, S.A., a company 80 percent owned by Guerra and 20 percent owned by Keefe. G/K will enter into an agreement with Keefe under which Keefe is to build and operate the plant and receive 95 percent of the projected profit from the plant for the first 20 years of its operation. Is Keefe making a minority investment? What sort of scrutiny is the joint venture likely to receive from government officials?
2. Assume the same facts as in Question 1, except that the joint venture is to build and operate a computer microcircuit manufacturing plant. What different considerations come into play in government review? What is the likely outcome?
3. What financing alternatives would be available to a U.S. firm that was interested in investing in a proposed manufacturing plant in a small country that recently left the communist bloc and did not wish to invest many of its own resources?
4. If a U.S. company establishes a 100 percent subsidiary in another country, what three general aspects of U.S. income tax law should the company be sure it has addressed?
5. What are the implications for an American who purchases shares in a German company on the basis of inside information?
6. Pursuant to Bulgaria's new joint venture program, Zasada, Inc., a U.S. firm, constructs a football helmet manufacturing facility in Sofia to produce helmets for export to the United States. Four years later, a change in the Russian Parliament leads to domestic policy reversals. Russia annexes Bulgaria as a member of its federation and takes possession of all Bulgarian factories that employ more than 25 people, including Zasada's helmet facility. Was this a nationalization or an expropriation? How would the *INA Corp.* tribunal assess the appropriate compensation to Zasada? How would a traditional theory court measure that compensation? How would a modern–traditional theory court measure that compensation? What do these decisions suggest about the development of compensation theory?
7. Economic development in the Republic of Costa Azul is perceived to be hindered by the ownership of all farm land by a few families and a few firms, some of which are U.S.-owned. A new government is democratically elected on a platform of land redistribution. The government has no currency to buy such land and lacks the credit necessary to borrow significant sums. If Costa Azul cannot afford to pay "prompt and just" compensation for foreign private property, should it refrain from initiating social change? Does it make a difference if Costa Azul refrains from taking the land and instead increases property taxes on lots greater than 25 hectares by a factor of 100?
8. How should the FSIA apply if a government purchases private property as an embassy and violates local ordinances in its operation? What if a government-owned airline sells a tour package to a private citizen, and then detains her and refuses her entry into the country as an undesirable? What if the government retains a consulting firm to develop a national agricultural development plan and then refuses to pay the firm because the nation changes its agricultural policy? Was the "confiscation" of all cigar manufacturers by the Cuban government in the early 1960s an expropriation or a nationalization?
9. Was this confiscation commercial activity in which a private businessperson could engage? Was the Cuban

government's assertion of rights to post-intervention sums paid for cigars a commercial act? Is the analysis any different with respect to pre-intervention shipments?

10. Maria Hartman, a U.S. investor, owns a toy assembly plant in the Kingdom of Fromage Vert. At a tennis match between a leading U.S. player and a star Fromagian, Maria irritates the king by cheering for the American. The next day, the king issues an edict taking Ms. Hartman's plant for the kingdom. Ms. Hartman sues Fromage Vert in U.S. District Court for the Southern District of New York, where the kingdom's airline owns an office. Would the U.S. court have jurisdiction in the absence of a treaty? Do you think the Fromagian taking of the toy assembly plant was a commercial activity? Was it an "act of state"?
11. Is privatization a recent phenomenon? Why has it become more prominent in recent years? What triggered the move to more privatization in Latin American countries? What triggered increased privatization in former communist nations?
12. Briefly describe the partial sale model of privatization. What is the predominant characteristic of the partial sale? How can a minority private investor try to protect itself from abuse by the majority government owner?
13. Briefly describe the trade sale model of privatization. What is the distinguishing feature of the trade sale? How is privatization achieved through management contracts?
14. List three reasons why giving employees equity shares in the new private entity makes sense. Give a reason that is principally applicable in Eastern Europe. What are two disadvantages associated with transferring shares to employees? What are two types of consideration that employees can be asked to give in exchange for their shares?
15. Briefly describe the concession model of privatization. How long should the term of the concession be?
16. Name four types of adjustments to regulations that are often addressed in the context of privatizations. Explain how they may be addressed.
17. Ernesto Ortiz, famed American corporate raider, initiates a hostile takeover of Bundesbank Freidumia (BF), the largest commercial bank in Freidumia. In purchasing 70 percent of BF's shares, Ortiz pays a substantial premium for control. After he concludes the transaction, Freidumia outlaws any foreigner or person under foreign control from voting shares in a commercial bank corporation, thereby wresting control from Mr. Ortiz. Has a nationali zation taken place? An expropriation?

Managerial Implications

1. You work for Luree Intergalactic, Inc., a Montana Alpine ski manufacturer. Because of Latvia's attractive relative labor costs, Luree joins forces with Aivars, AG, a Latvian firm, to build a new factory in Riga to serve the European market. Together, Luree and Aivars establish Udris, Ltd., a Latvian joint-stock company that will own the factory and sell products from it. Udris will be free to sells its skis to anyone, but expects to sell most of its initial output to Luree and Aivars. Under an agreement between Luree and Aivars, Luree will purchase skis from Udris for resale in Europe east of Ukraine, and in North and South America, New Zealand, and Japan; Aivars will market the remaining portion of Udris's production to the rest of the world,
   a Because Luree has greater financial resources than does Aivars, its capital contribution will entitle it to 90 percent ownership of Udris. Aivars also recognizes that it has received the less attractive ski markets. It expects to derive most of its income from a special contract with Udris to test new ski models on mogul runs. Prepare a memorandum that anticipates what principal corporate law concerns will need to be addressed in this arrangement.
   b Aivars suggests that, as compensation for being Udris's first customers, Luree and Aivars receive a discount off the price that Udris charges other purchasers. Analyze the transfer-pricing issues raised by this proposal.
2. Your firm, Lloyd Aviation Company, is a leading U.S. manufacturer of helicopters. While on a trip to Moscow, you met Gennady Tupolev, the head of the former Soviet Air Force division that once manufactured military helicopters. The Russian government has no funds to finance further operations for the Tupolev Division and he needs to privatize its operations. The Russian government is reluctant to cede control over an industry that is so central to its national security. However, its conversion to com-

mercial production will require thorough control by Lloyd. The division has a strong research and development department. Many of the division's lower-level employees will need to be laid off if it is to be a commercially viable operation.

a Prepare a memorandum to Lloyd's board of directors outlining your plan for privatizing the Tupolev Division.

b What regulatory arrangements should Lloyd make with the Russian government?

Ethical Considerations

As noted in this chapter, the taking of private property is a controversial issue in international business law. Recent examples include Thailand and Venezuela. In January 2007, the Thai government approved a new investment law barring foreign ownership of more than 50 percent in telecommunications companies and other sectors vital to national security. Companies violating the law were required to find a Thai partner and sell off their interests to get under the cap or surrender voting rights by 2009. Also in January 2007, Venezuelan president Hugo Chavez announced plans to nationalize all businesses in telecommunications and electricity and control four multibillion-dollar oil projects in the Orinoco River Basin. Impacted investors included Verizon Communications, ExxonMobil, Chevron, BP, and ConocoPhillips. This nationalization decree was expanded in May 2008 to include steel, cement, sugar plantations, dairy products, and cattle.

The taking of private property is also a controversial topic in the United States. **Eminent domain** (also referred to as **condemnation**) is the government's power to take private property for public purposes. In the United States, eminent domain implicates constitutional considerations. Specifically, the Fifth Amendment to the U.S. Constitution prohibits the taking of private property by the federal government without just compensation. The Fourteenth Amendment prohibits states from taking private property without due process. Private property rights are also protected in state constitutions.

In the United States, in addition to just compensation, the taking of private property must be accompanied by a public purpose. However, courts generally will only require that government statements of public purpose be minimally rational and will not give them close scrutiny. Examples of public use include slum clearance, environmental protection, historic preservation, public safety, shortages of residential property, economic revitalization, job creation, and increases in tax revenues associated with commercial development. The last two examples were relied upon by the U.S. Supreme Court in its controversial 2005 decision in *Kelo v. City of New London,* in which the Court upheld the condemnation of a 90-acre residential neighborhood in New London, Connecticut, for transformation into commercial development, including office buildings, upscale housing, a marina, and enhancement of a research facility operated by Pfizer, Inc. Property owners can only defeat such initiatives if the state constitution or state law prohibits condemnation under such circumstances.

Despite legal concerns arising from these takings, are such takings nevertheless defensible from an ethical standpoint? For example, are these takings defensible on at least an individual basis utilizing moral relativism, which focuses on determining right behavior based on the time and place of circumstances? Should courts and arbitral bodies second-guess determinations by national and state sovereigns that the taking of private property is appropriate at a given time and under the circumstances? If they so frustrate the will of democratically elected bodies, what is the moral basis for doing so? Are takings of private property consistent with *utilitarianism?* In the international arena, private property takings are often portrayed as decentralizing economic concentration or preventing exploitation by large businesses for the benefit of the general public? Is this true? Or is the expropriation being effected to place a large, money-making asset in the hands of the people who run the government? A similar argument may be advanced with respect to takings in the United States, specifically, that deprivation of individual property rights serves the best interests of the public at-large through economic development, environmental protection, historic preservation, job creation, and enhancement of tax revenues. However, under both circumstances, individual well being is sacrificed for the perceived benefit of the community. Does this undermine the defense of takings through utilitarianism?

Utilizing a *deontological framework,* do takings violate fundamental rights to private property recognized by the natural school of law and enshrined in national and international instruments such as the U.S. Declaration of Independence, the U.S. Constitution, and the Universal Declaration of Human Rights? Are such takings indefensible pursuant to the *categorical imperative* as no one would wish for the disregard of private property rights to become a universal standard of conduct? Do such takings treat private property as a means to achieve a perceived benefit to the community without sufficient regard for those individuals who are negatively impacted? Finally, are such takings fair and equitable pursuant to *contractarianism,* especially to the extent that they disproportionately impact the poor and politically disenfranchised groups? On the other hand, are the inequalities resulting from such takings defensible if they generate benefits for society as a whole?

CHAPTER 19

Labor and Employment Discrimination Law

Some say that corporations are lifeless entities with one principal objective: to maximize profit for their stockholders. While many corporate leaders find it good business to be thoughtful of those who work for the firm, others often subordinate the interests of their workers to those of their stockholders unless government intervenes. Accordingly, virtually all societies have enacted laws that protect workers from abusive or discriminatory practices.

This regulation varies widely from place to place. For example, the paternalistic protective framework that safeguards and enfranchises German workers is extremely different from the United States' emphasis on individual achievement by workers and on control by managers. This chapter examines different approaches in this important area and their effect on international business transactions.

DIFFERENT APPROACHES TO LABOR LAW

Any foreign direct investment, whether controlled by investors from the United States or from some other country, relies on employees and is thus influenced by the host country's labor laws. Because these laws are often different from those encountered in the investor's home country, investors must review the laws and the attitudes they reflect. Although a more detailed study would reveal countless differences between U.S. and foreign labor laws, a review of three principal areas gives a general sense of the distinctions.

1. Many nations' laws require employee consultation or participation in management decisions that Americans view as being the owner's prerogative.
2. Many countries place legal constraints on employee dismissal that are completely unfamiliar to the U.S. investor.
3. When a U.S. investor acquires a foreign business, by operation of law, it may also be acquiring the foreign industry's labor arrangements.

Employee Participation in Strategic Decisions

A running controversy in managerial theory involves the level of discretion owners and management should have in making strategic decisions and whether labor should participate in such decisions. A nation's laws on these issues have historically been shaped by its sociopolitical traditions. For example, in the Scandinavian countries, workers participate in management decisions solely through labor unions. France, Greece, Portugal, and Spain utilize both trade unions and a body elected by all employees to participate in management's decision making. Ireland and the United Kingdom do not permit trade unions this type of access. One of the interesting phenomena of modern labor law is that these approaches seem to be merging as the world's economies merge.

The U.S. Approach. Notwithstanding legislative initiatives such as the *Worker Adjustment, Retraining, and Notification Act*—which at times requires a company to give 60 days' notice of plans to close a plant with more than 100 employees—U.S. companies allow owners greater flexibility. Traditionally, U.S. management, completely by itself and in secret, makes strategic decisions such as whether to close a plant or reduce manpower levels. In the United States, management decides and labor carries out those decisions at an agreed hourly rate.

U.S. law mirrors this perspective. The U.S. Supreme Court has squarely held that an employer need not bargain with its employees over whether to shut down part of its business. The Court viewed this prerogative as akin to the closing of a business, where "an employer has the absolute right to terminate his entire business for any reason he pleases."

The German Approach. Europeans have traditionally viewed the role of workers quite differently. The law in many Continental countries grants workers a right of consultation about, or notice before, the implementation of decisions resulting in workforce reductions. German law illustrates these worker rights of participation. Each place of business with more than five employees must have a ***Betriebsrat*** (works council) to represent that plant's interest. In contrast to their U.S. counterparts, these works councils are independent from trade unions. They represent the interests of plant employees as distinct from those of the employer or trade unions.

Under the *German Works Constitution Act*, the employer must fully inform the works council in "due time" of any plant changes that might result in "substantial disadvantages for employees" and consult with it on such proposals. In the course of that consultation, the employer solicits the works council's approval of the employer's method of selecting persons to be terminated as a result of the plant change. If the employer and the works council cannot resolve a dispute by this method, they then appear before an arbitration committee. In addition, the employer notifies the regional office of the Federal Employment Institute. If this office believes the plant change would strain local resources, it can delay the change until two months after notice is given. As these examples illustrate, U.S. companies can be confronted with radically different labor situations once they go abroad.

A number of countries also require substantial employee representation on the corporate board of directors. This is often accomplished by mandating a two-tiered board: a large supervisory board (in Germany, the ***Aufsichtsrat***) and a management board (in Germany, the ***Vorstand***). The *Aufsichtsrat* is responsible for representing shareholder interests, while the *Vorstand* manages the firm from day to day.

In Germany, the Netherlands, Austria, and Luxembourg, employees have direct representation in the *Aufsichtsrat*. Indeed, in Germany, companies that employ more than 2,000 workers must establish *Aufsichtsrat* representation that is 50 percent labor and 50 percent shareholders. In companies with more than 500 workers, one-third of the *Aufsichtsrat* must be composed of workers. This focus on worker participation in corporate decisions has proved attractive to the former communist nations, which for half of the twentieth century emphasized the rights of workers. Laws in the Czech Republic and Poland, among others, have followed the German law model of worker boards.

The implications for U.S. investors are important. All significant strategic decisions in these countries require supervisory board approval. Thus, the *Vorstand* must present persuasive reasons for a strategic plan that involves workforce reductions. In short, the flexibility of management is not as great in German-model countries as in the United States.

The Japanese Approach. In Japan, management–labor strife is rare because of traditional and structural factors that blur distinctions between management and workers. Union leadership is a stepping-stone to management. Nearly 15 percent of union officials rise to serve as executives of the company. Consequently, union leaders have little incentive to take strident labor positions against those responsible for their advancement. Under Japanese tradition, the income differentiation between management and labor is not nearly as great as in the West. Japanese culture prizes consensus and encourages cooperation over confrontation. There is less of a perceived need for labor–management confrontation, and labor laws are generally inoffensive.

The Chinese Approach. Unions in China differ greatly from their counterparts in works council countries. Establishing a union in China is theoretically easy. To establish a union, 25 workers simply join, and the employer is typically required to accept the request for the union. Therefore, employers, often to preempt organization of workers, will set up a "company union." Company unions are typically prohibited in developed countries because they tend to prevent workers from organizing independently and choosing their own advocates. If employees are able to administer their own union, all negotiations with the employer are conducted under the watch of the local or national union.

Traditionally, the Chinese union's function has not been to advocate for the interests of the workers but to avoid labor unrest. In addition, while many unions exist in China, all unions must maintain an affiliation with the All-China Federation of Trade Unions (ACFTU). The national labor organization largely shapes the local work council's efforts. Unions in China may best be described as intermediaries between workers and management that do most of their work by negotiating behind closed doors.

While the ACFTU is nominally independent, China is neither a democracy nor a nation with truly independent legal institutions. Thus, government officials selectively influence ACFTU. In 2006, the ACFTU negotiated collective agreements covering more than 110 million workers in a fashion consistent with promotion of Chinese commercial interests. The collective bargaining was not adversarial to management. Rather, the union sought to maintain both the profitability of the company and to prevent worker strife. Union officials, who often are members of management and who are paid by the company, not the workers, have broader considerations than just the interests of the workers. Unions must spread their efforts between advocating for workers, maintaining a positive economic environment for employers, and preventing industrial instability that could threaten broader economic policy. Since 2008, the government has revisited its policy somewhat, and the ACFTU is advocating a bit more for the rights of workers than it did in previous years. That said, the government continues to imprison workers who campaign for independent trade unions.

Workers in China do not have the right to independently organize and strike. Yet in the summer of 2010, workers in Guandong Province pressured their factory owners for better wages and working conditions by having work stoppages. The workers were relentless, and this was a pivotal point in labor disputes for China because the government sided with the employees and allowed the strikes to proceed. Ultimately, the strikes continued without an intervention by the ACFTU, and the workers were victorious in securing a 24 to 34 percent wage increase. These 2010 strikes, coupled with a tragic series of worker suicides at the Foxconn electronics manufacturing factories (Apple's number one foreign supplier), pressed the government to alter labor policies. The government has intervened in many areas to meet growing expectations, mainly regarding wages and working conditions, of its workers and the international community.

As a matter of changing social policy, the government is now encouraging workers to engage in collective bargaining. The government is adopting this approach in the hope that it will address the growing income inequality gap by pressuring companies to use their profits to pay workers higher wages. However, even with a surge in collective bargaining in recent years, the results have been only the establishment of minimum labor standards and have accomplished little to improve employee wages or benefits. As foreign investment becomes more mainstream in China, the workers' union will surely continue to undergo development.

Impediments to Dismissal

Prevailing national norms also create different legal frameworks on the issue of *impediments to employee dismissal.* National attitudes toward the proper relationship between manager and employee heavily color the content of national law.

Underlying Philosophical Foundations. People in the United States, perhaps the most capitalist of nations, do not commonly believe that anyone is entitled to a job. Once an individual ceases to be productive, his/her future employment is in jeopardy. Legally required severance pay is low and is viewed as a humane cushion to help the discharged worker until he or she can find new employment.

Europeans, on the other hand, tend to feel that employees acquire a property interest in their jobs over time. The more senior an employee is, the greater his or her property interest. Accordingly, severance pay is legally required as compensation for the taking of this substantial property, and it increases as the employee becomes more senior. For the most senior employees, severance pay can be so high as to strongly discourage involuntary dismissal. This system is often criticized as creating a very senior workforce with little incentive to perform.

The traditional Japanese view is that one's job is a central part of his or her place in society and that a job largely defines the person. An individual is expected to hold a job for the same company for a lifetime. In Japan, the focus is not on the conditions of dismissal but on the propriety of dismissal in the first place.

China's government has always played a central role in the workplace. Prior to the 1980s, China's labor market was referred to as the "Iron Rice Bowl" because all jobs were allocated to citizens through an administrative bureau. Employees could not choose their employer. Likewise, the employer was expected to provide job security and guaranteed benefits for life. However, as China experienced the largest labor movement in history, the country underwent a liberalization of the labor market in the 1990s, which ushered in a period of "at-will" employment that proved to be central to many of the unsafe and horrendous work conditions found in China. When the *Labor Contract Law* was introduced in 2008, it abolished at-will employment and required employers to provide employees with written contracts. This change means employers may no longer terminate employees for no reason. Only during the probationary period may the employer terminate the employee unilaterally. Moreover, under the *Labor Contract Law*, an employer cannot terminate an employee for incompetence alone. If an employee is incompetent, the employer must re-assign the employee or provide further training before terminating the contract. The employer is restricted to unilaterally terminating an employee only if he or she seriously breaches the employer's rules and regulations. The job-for-life concept continues in Chinese society, but on different terms and conditions. As China struggles to balance its position in the industrial world and its internal traditions, the country will surely re-examine its approach.

Other nations tend to fall within one of these models or between them.

Legal Frameworks Reflecting Philosophy. In the United States, employers historically have been able to terminate employees with little notice. Unless a collective bargaining agreement was in place, U.S. management had few limits on its employee termination options. This picture has changed somewhat as U.S. businesses have been influenced by European and Japanese practices. Relatively recent federal legislation now gives employees unpaid leave to care for family members, guarantees workers their jobs back after such leave, and requires a warning of plant closings. More and more U.S. managers now take a page from Japanese companies and seek ways of providing greater assurance of employment. Nonetheless, U.S. law gives entrepreneurs great flexibility to do as they wish with their employees. U.S. businesses face a very different legal world beyond these shores.

In the United Kingdom, the law mandates that an employer consult with the appropriate trade union before making a dismissal. If the workforce is to be reduced by ten or more employees, a consultation must take place sixty days prior to termination. Under German law, the works council must approve any dismissal. If it does not, the employer may appeal to a labor court. Indeed, the *Betriebsrat* can affirmatively call for the dismissal of employees even without a request from the employer.

In China, if a company determines a reduction in workforce is eminent that will involve at least 20 employees or 10 percent of the employer's workforce, then one of the following conditions must be satisfied:

1. The employer is under restructuring according to a bankruptcy claim.
2. The employer is experiencing difficulties in production and operations.
3. There is going to be a change to production, a technology makeover, or an adjustment to mode of operation that still requires cutbacks after employment contracts have been amended.
4. A material change in the objective economic circumstances occurred, making performance and fulfillment of the contract impossible.

In addition, the employer must provide a written explanation to either the labor union, or if there is not a labor union, to all the employees at least 30 days prior to the implementation of the excess employee issues. The reporting does not stop at the factory level. Once the opinion of the employees is expressed either through the union or individually, the employer must report the redundancy scheme to the local labor authorities. If mass layoffs are involved, there are typically supplemental reporting requirements to higher government levels that must include supporting documentation and a proscribed reporting format.

Japan is perhaps the most interesting case. There, the written law seems to permit relatively free dismissal of employees. However, tradition—embodied in decisional law—protects the employee (see *Kochi Hoso*). A similar attitude was reflected in Japan's approach to plant closings. Japanese companies in financial stress seldom closed factories. Instead, plants were taken over by friendly affiliates in good financial condition, or workers were turned over to local successful firms. Again, the discretion implicit in Japanese labor law was interpreted to enforce these cultural traditions. U.S. companies, such as Procter & Gamble and Chase Manhattan Bank, have faced court proceedings from local unions challenging facility shutdowns in Japan as "unfair labor practices." This has occurred even when the U.S. firms offered the dismissed employees new jobs in different locations.

Just as U.S. employment practices are being influenced by those of Europe and Japan, the Japanese are being influenced by Westerners. During the long recession of the 1990s and early twenty-first century, giants such as Nippon Telephone & Telegraph, NKK Corporation, and Nissan Corporation all successfully implemented reductions in their workforces. These companies did not actually lay off employees, but effected the reductions through normal attrition, intracompany transfers, and transfers to subsidiaries. Because many employees rejected unattractive transfers and many of the subsidiaries went out of business, this shift proved to be significant. At the same time, surveys of Japanese executives indicated a broad consensus that the days of lifetime employment and strict seniority advancement systems were numbered. The differences between nations regarding the permanence of employment are still quite significant. However, they are becoming less profound over time.

Assumption of Employment Arrangements

To a far greater extent than in the United States, many nations—particularly in Europe—compel corporate acquirers to adhere to existing employment arrangements.

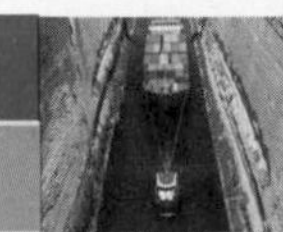

Kochi Hoso (Broadcasting Co.)

Supreme Court of Japan Rokeisoku No. 937 (1977)

BACKGROUND AND FACTS

Like all Japanese firms with more than ten employees, Kochi Hoso, a radio broadcasting company, was required to maintain rules of employment that specified the conditions under which an employee could be discharged. Kochi Hoso clearly specified that tardiness for a broadcast was cause for dismissal. No contractual provision excused such tardiness. The plaintiff, a radio announcer, had failed twice to arrive at the studio in time for a news broadcast. After the second offense, Kochi Hoso discharged the plaintiff, pointing to the unambiguous rules. Plaintiff sought reinstatement, arguing that although the discharge was within the rules, it was unreasonable or contrary to public policy. The Supreme Court found no reasonable cause for termination.

PER CURIAM

Even when an employee's conduct constitutes a cause for a discharge, an employer may not always discharge the employee. It should be noted that when the said discharge is found to be significantly unreasonable under the specific situation so that it could hardly be approved as being appropriate in the light of the socially accepted view, such a discharge should be considered to be an abusive exercise of an employer's power to discharge employees and, thus, to be invalid.

Decision. The Supreme Court of Japan ordered that the radio announcer be reinstated in his job.

Case Questions

1. If a firm were establishing an office in Japan, how would it determine the "socially accepted" view on the discharge of employees for tardiness? Would it look in the relevant statutes?
2. Traditionally, Japanese work for an employer their entire careers. How does that influence the "socially accepted" view reflected in this opinion? Is employment law affected by social norms in the United States?
3. In a country that views employment as strictly a contractual relationship, how would this case have come out?

In other words, when acquiring a manufacturing plant, one may be acquiring the collective bargaining agreement that the seller had negotiated with the trade union prior to the purchase of the company. A U.S. investor must assess this inheritable liability before acquiring a foreign company. Knowing each country's domestic laws in advance of a merger or purchase assists in overseeing the seller's duties with regard to the existing employees. For example, in the U.K., the *Transfer of Understanding Protection of Employment Regulations 2006* (TUPES) imposes distinct duties on the employer to inform and consult with the appropriate representatives or employees regarding the proposed transfer of a company to a buyer. Failure to perform these duties in a timely manner, or if not carried out at all, can result in an employment complaint, which may be remedied by as much as 13 weeks' pay to existing company employees for which both the seller and new owner are liable. The risks of overlooking employment measures in connection with acquisitions can create unnecessary and substantial costs.

EMPLOYMENT DISCRIMINATION OUTSIDE THE UNITED STATES

The United States almost certainly has the world's most comprehensive set of laws against discrimination of all sorts in employment. Because most countries outside of the Americas were created as the geographic homes of homogeneous ethnic groups, they have perceived relatively little need to develop antidiscriminatory schemes. Germany is the nation-state created by the ethnic Germans who lived in that area, and the Japanese islands are those where ethnic Japanese live. In many countries, the overwhelming ethnic majority has not felt a need to protect against ethnic discrimination. Indeed, at the opposite extreme, the Baltic countries, formerly part of the Soviet Union, have passed laws mandating discrimination against the ethnic Russian minority.

The Common Market's goal of allowing people of all member nations to work in other member states has given rise to laws against ethnic discrimination in those economies. As Europe's declining populations require increasing numbers of immigrant workers from Africa and the Middle East, these issues are likely to expand.

The issue of discrimination against women has brought a new legal complexity to employment issues. However, all of these schemes are in formative stages. The principal employment discrimination issue for U.S. companies remains whether the comprehensive U.S. laws apply to their overseas operations.

The Extraterritorial Application of U.S. Employment Discrimination Law

There has been significant disagreement in Congress and the legal community concerning the extent to which U.S. discrimination laws apply abroad and how such can be enforced if they are applicable. This concept is known as extraterritoriality. For instance, how can a U.S. company operate in Islamic countries that legally require discrimination against Christians and Jews if it has to treat everyone equally? In 1991, the U.S. Supreme Court first gave some direction in this area.

Soon after the Supreme Court limited extraterritoriality of U.S. labor law by reading existing law narrowly in the *Aramco* case, Congress sought to overrule the *Aramco* case by partially extending U.S. employment law overseas. Congress expressly extended Title VII to firms operating outside the United States under the "control" of a U.S. entity. Congress also expanded Title VII's definition of "employee" to include U.S. citizens employed abroad. In addition, as the *Aramco* court predicted, Congress made an exception for situations where compliance with Title VII would violate the law of the country where the firm is located.

Congress's action did not prove to be the last word. Since *Aramco,* courts have interpreted Title VII, the *Age Discrimination in Employment Act* (ADEA), and the *Americans with Disabilities Act* (ADA) to prohibit U.S. employers and foreign companies controlled by a U.S. employer from discriminating in employment of U.S. citizens in other countries.

In *Watson v. CSA, Ltd.,* 376 F. Supp. 2d 588 (D. Md. 2005), the United States District Court for the District of Maryland found that American companies operating in a U.S. military base in Kuwait were potentially liable under Title VII. Watson was an African American employed by a foreign subcontractor headquartered in the Cayman Islands to work in a U.S. base in Kuwait. He filed a Title VII suit against his employer and the unincorporated American joint venture, of which the subcontractor was a wholly owned subsidiary. Focusing on the interrelation of operations, common management, centralized control of labor relations, and the common ownership or financial control of the employer and the joint venture, the *Watson* court found that the foreign subcontractor was controlled by the American joint venture and denied defendants' motion to dismiss.

Similarly, in *Rajoppe v. GMAC Corp. Holding Corp.,* No. 05-2097, 2007 WL 846671 (E.D. Pa. Mar. 19, 2007), the United States District Court for the Eastern District of Pennsylvania found an American corporation potentially liable under Title VII in connection with its employment of an American citizen in Japan. Rajoppe, an American citizen employed by GMAC Commercial Mortgage Japan, a foreign subsidiary of defendant GMAC Commercial Holding Corp., filed a Title VII suit alleging that he was terminated because of his race. Focusing on the same four factors that the *Watson* court had relied on to determine whether related entities constitute an "integrated enterprise," the *Rajoppe* court found that Rajoppe had raised genuine issues of material fact regarding whether the Japanese subsidiary was "controlled" by the defendant and denied GMAC's motion to dismiss for lack of subject matter jurisdiction.

However, courts have found that the same laws do not give rights to foreigners seeking work from U.S. entities outside the United States.

Equal Employment Opportunity Commission v. Arabian American Oil Co.

499 U.S. 244 (1991) United States Supreme Court

BACKGROUND AND FACTS

The respondents are two Delaware corporations: Arabian American Oil Company (Aramco) and its subsidiary, Aramco Service Company (ASC). Aramco's principal place of business is Dhahran, Saudi Arabia, and it is licensed to do business in Texas.

In 1979, Boureslan was hired by ASC as a cost engineer in Houston. A year later, he was transferred, at his

continues

continued

request, to work for Aramco in Saudi Arabia. Boureslan remained with Aramco in Saudi Arabia until he was discharged in 1984. He instituted this suit in the United States District Court for the Southern District of Texas against Aramco and ASC. He sought relief under Title VII of the *Civil Rights Act* on the ground that he was harassed and ultimately discharged by respondents on account of his race, religion, and national origin.

CHIEF JUSTICE REHNQUIST

Both parties concede, as they must, that Congress has the authority to enforce its laws beyond the territorial boundaries of the United States. Whether Congress has in fact exercised that authority in this case is a matter of statutory construction. It is our task to determine whether Congress intended the protections of Title VII to apply to United States citizens employed by American employers outside of the United States.

It is a long-standing principle of American law "that legislation of Congress, unless a contrary intent appears, is meant to apply only within the territorial jurisdiction of the United States." It serves to protect against unintended clashes between our laws and those of other nations which could result in international discord.

Title VII prohibits various discriminatory employment practices based on an individual's race, color, religion, sex, or national origin. An employer is subject to Title VII if it is "engaged in an industry affecting commerce." "Commerce," in turn, is defined as "trade, traffic, commerce, transportation, transmission, or communication among the several States; or between a State and any place outside thereof... ."

Petitioners ... assert that since Title VII defines "States" to include States, the District of Columbia, and specified territories, the clause "between a State and any place outside thereof" must be referring to areas beyond the territorial limit of the United States. The language relied upon by petitioners—and it is they who must make the affirmative showing—is ambiguous, and does not speak directly to the question presented here. The intent of Congress as to the extraterritorial application of this statute must be deduced by inference from boilerplate language which can be found in any number of congressional acts, none of which have ever been held to apply overseas.

If we were to permit possible, or even plausible, interpretations of language such as that involved here to override the presumption against extraterritorial application, there would be little left of the presumption.

Petitioners argue that Title VII's "alien exemption provision ... clearly manifests an intention" by Congress to protect U.S. citizens with respect to their employment outside of the United States. The alien exemption provision says that "the statute" shall not apply to an employer with respect to the employment of aliens outside any State. Petitioners contend that from this language a negative inference should be drawn that Congress intended Title VII to cover United States citizens.

If petitioners are correct that the alien-exemption clause means that the statute applies to employers overseas, we see no way of distinguishing in its application between United States employers and foreign employers. Thus, a French employer of a United States citizen in France would be subject to Title VII—a result at which even petitioners balk. The EEOC assures us that in its view the term "employer" means only "American employer," but there is no such distinction in this statute.

It is also reasonable to conclude that had Congress intended Title VII to apply overseas, it would have addressed the subject of conflicts with foreign laws and procedures. In amending the Age Discrimination in Employment Act of 1967 to apply abroad, Congress specifically addressed potential conflicts with foreign law by providing that it is not unlawful for an employer to take any action prohibited by the ADEA "where such practices involve an employee in a workplace in a foreign country, and compliance with the ADEA would cause such employer ... to violate the laws of the country in which such workplace is located." Title VII, by contrast, fails to address conflicts with the laws of other nations.

Decision. Petitioners failed to present sufficient affirmative evidence that Congress intended Title VII to apply abroad. Accordingly, the judgment of the Court of Appeals was affirmed.

Case Questions

1. Is it the presumption that a federal law will or will not have extraterritorial application if not otherwise stated?
2. What type of a legal analysis did the court apply—literal construction or contextual construction?
3. In light of immediate, subsequent action by Congress, did it appear that the statute had accurately reflected (and the court had iterated) Congress's intent?

The Fourth Circuit Court of Appeals followed the Supreme Court's lead and expanded it. In the *Reyes-Gaona* case that follows, the appellate court held that the Act does not apply just because the workplace is in the United States regardless of other circumstances.

Reyes-Gaona v. North Carolina Growers Ass'n, Inc.

250 F.3d 861 (2001) United States Court of Appeals (4th Cir.)

BACKGROUND AND FACTS

Plaintiff Luis Reyes-Gaona was a Mexican national over the age of 40. Defendant North Carolina Growers Association (NCGA) was an American corporation that assisted agricultural businesses in North Carolina in securing farm labor through a legal federal program. Defendant Del-Al was an agent of NCGA that recruited workers for NCGA and its members. Reyes-Gaona went to a Del-Al office in Mexico and asked to be placed on a list of workers seeking employment in North Carolina. Del-Al told Reyes-Gaona that NCGA would not accept a worker over 40 years old unless that person had worked for NCGA before. With the support of the United States Equal Employment Opportunity Commission, Reyes-Gaona filed suit against NCGA and Del-Al, alleging age discrimination in violation of the Age Discrimination in Employment Act.

WILKINSON, CHIEF JUDGE

This case requires us to decide whether the Age Discrimination in Employment Act (ADEA) covers foreign nationals who apply in foreign countries for jobs in the United States. We hold that the Act does not cover such persons... .

Plaintiff is a foreign national who applied in a foreign country for work in the United States. Accordingly, we begin, as we must, by acknowledging the "longstanding principle of American law 'that legislation of Congress, unless a contrary intent appears, is meant to apply only within the territorial jurisdiction of the United States.'" ... This interpretive canon is an especially important one as it "serves to protect against unintended clashes between our laws and those of other nations which could result in international discord." ... Thus, the presumption against extraterritorial application of a federal statute can be overcome only if there is an "affirmative intention of the Congress clearly expressed." ... Since this determination is necessarily "a matter of statutory construction," we begin with the text of the ADEA itself.

The ADEA makes it unlawful "for an employer" to "fail or refuse to hire" or "otherwise discriminate against any individual with respect to his compensation, terms, conditions, or privileges of employment, because of such individual's age." The term "employer" means any company "engaged in an industry affecting commerce who has twenty or more employees" and includes the agents of such companies ... . The term "employee" means "an individual employed by any employer," and "includes any individual who is a citizen of the United States employed by an employer in a workplace in a foreign country." ... Prior to 1984, the ADEA did not contain the language regarding U.S. citizens employed in foreign workplaces. To the contrary, [the ADEA] adopted language from the Fair Labor Standards Act (FLSA) excluding from coverage any individual " whose services during the workweek are performed in a workplace within a foreign country ... ."

Based on the exclusionary language adopted from the FLSA, many courts held that, before 1984, the ADEA had a purely domestic focus and did not cover American citizens working for American companies in foreign countries ... . The presumption against the extra-territorial application of American laws required this result because absent a clear statement from Congress, the scope of American law is limited to "the territorial jurisdiction of the United States." ... Thus the presumption prevented the ADEA from regulating events taking place in foreign countries even when they involved citizens of the United States. And the Act certainly could not have reached the even more attenuated situation of a foreign national applying in a foreign country for work in the United States.

In 1984, Congress partially closed this gap. Congress [amended] the ADEA to give it limited extraterritorial application. The definition of "employee" was amended to include "any individual who is a citizen of the United States employed by an employer in a workplace in a foreign country." ... This new statutory language explicitly expanded the ADEA to prohibit U.S. companies from discriminating against U.S. citizens employed in foreign countries. Congress also included an accompanying provision outlawing such discrimination by subsidiaries of U.S. corporations ... . The language was "carefully worded to apply only to citizens of the United States" who worked for a U.S. company or its subsidiary because Congress recognized that the "well-

continues

continued

established principle of sovereignty" prohibited the United States from imposing "its labor standards on another country." ... These amendments demonstrated that "when it desires to do so, Congress knows how to" expand "the jurisdictional reach of a statute." ... Notably missing from the 1984 amendments, however, is any provision regulating the conduct at issue here. Congress explicitly gave the ADEA extra-territorial application with respect to certain U.S. citizens while simultaneously declining to extend coverage to foreign nationals like Reyes-Gaona. Nothing in the amendments regulates age discrimination by U.S. corporations against foreign nationals in foreign countries. And the doctrine of ***expressio unis est exclusio alterius*** instructs that where a law expressly describes a particular situation to which it shall apply, what was omitted or excluded was intended to be omitted or excluded... . Thus, a faithful reading of the plain text of the statute, especially in light of the 1984 amendments, compels the conclusion that Reyes-Gaona's claim is not sustainable under the ADEA.

Reyes-Gaona and the EEOC disagree. They claim that this case does not require extra-territorial application of the ADEA because the job Reyes-Gaona applied for was in the United States. The crux of their argument is that when determining whether a suit requires extraterritorial application of the ADEA, courts always look to the place of employment rather than the place where the decision was made. Because Reyes-Gaona applied for a job in the United States, they argue, the presumption against extra-territoriality is not implicated by this suit. In support they note that the ADEA itself contains the term "workplace." For example, "employee" is defined to include U.S. citizens employed "in a workplace in a foreign country." ... And the Act excepts from its reach employees "in a workplace in a foreign country" where compliance would conflict with the laws of the country "in which such workplace is located."

We are not persuaded. All of these statutory references come from the 1984 amendments to the ADEA which, as previously explained, do not cover Reyes-Gaona. Nothing in the ADEA provides that it shall apply anytime the workplace is in the United States regardless of the nationality of the applicant or the country in which the application was submitted. And the fact that the 1984 amendments refer to workplace does not mean that the Act focuses on work situs to the exclusion of the situs of the application or the nationality of the applicant... .

The simple submission of a resume abroad does not confer the right to file an ADEA action. Indeed, such a broad reading of the Act could have staggering consequences for American companies. Expanding the ADEA to cover millions of foreign nationals who file an overseas application for U.S. employment could exponentially increase the number of suits filed and result in substantial litigation costs. If such a step is to be taken, it must be taken via a clear and unambiguous statement from Congress rather than by judicial fiat.

The Supreme Court has instructed the lower courts to take seriously the presumption against extra-territorial application of U.S. laws. In keeping with these instructions, many lower courts, including this one, held that the ADEA had no extra-territorial application prior to 1984. Congress responded by amending the Act to provide for limited extra-territorial reach. Since these amendments do not reach the case at bar, there remains nothing in the text of the ADEA to rebut the presumption against extending it to cover Reyes-Gaona. And the limited nature of the 1984 amendments indicates that foreign nationals in foreign countries are not covered by the ADEA, regardless of whether they are seeking employment in the United States or elsewhere.

Decision. The Fourth Circuit Court of Appeals affirmed the district court's dismissal of Mr. Reyes-Gaona's suit.

Case Questions

1. Why did the EEOC file a complaint against NCGA for a position Reyes-Gaona was applying for in Mexico?
2. Could American firms avoid the ADEA by conducting the hiring process in Mexico?
3. What was the court's reasoning to deny the EEOC complaint? How did legal presumptions factor into its decision?

In 2005, the U.S. Court of Appeals for the District of Columbia provided additional guidance on the limits of extraterritorial application of U.S. antidiscrimination laws in *Shekoyan v. Sibley International Corp.*, 217 F. Supp. 2d 59 (D.D.C.), *aff'd*, 409 F.3d 414 (D.C. Cir. 2005). In *Shekoyan*, the court excluded a permanent U.S. resident alien who worked abroad for a U.S. government contractor from the extraterritorial protection of Title VII and the ADEA. The *Shekoyan* court held that although the employee was a U.S. resident and his employment and training occurred in the United States, he was an alien and therefore was not protected by U.S. antidiscrimination laws when his job was solely located abroad.

Neither Title VII nor ADEA apply to non-citizens employed outside the United States, but both statutes apply to non-citizens legally employed within the United States. Thus, with the rise of Internet communications, some firms have sought to avoid legal burdens associated with U.S. employees by placing employees outside its boundaries. American courts have pushed back: Whether an individual is employed within the United States is a factual determination courts make. In *Gomez v. Honeywell Int'l, Inc.*, 510 F. Supp. 2d 417 (W.D. Tex. 2007), the United States District Court for the Western District of Texas determined that a non-U.S. citizen over the age of 40, employed by Honeywell International, Inc., as an operations manager in Mexico, performed work in the United States when she reported to a supervisor in the United States and traveled to the United States on a regular basis. The *Gomez* court rejected the primary-work-station test in favor of the more comprehensive center-of-gravity test in determining whether Ms. Gomez worked within the United States for purposes of her ADEA and Title VII claims. The court considered several factors, including the site of the creation of the employment relationship, the intent of the parties regarding the location of the employment, the locations of the reporting relationships, the actual locations where the employee performed her duties, and the location of the employee's domicile. In short, courts will not allow firms to avoid the law by using employees who are functionally within the United States, even if they are physically across the border.

Apart from non-citizens employed outside of the United States, there are other instances in which courts have declined to apply U.S. employment law abroad. In its opinion in *Ofori-Tenkorang v. American International Group, Inc.*, 460 F.3d 296 (2d Cir. 2006), the United States Court of Appeals for the Second Circuit held that the provisions against racial discrimination found at 42 U.S.C. § 1981 did not apply outside of the United States. In addition, a number of other American laws by their terms have no extraterritorial application. These include the *National Labor Relations Act, the Employee Retirement Income Security Act of 1974 (ERISA), the Occupational Safety and Health Act, the Worker Adjustment and Retraining Notification Act, the Fair Labor Standards Act, the Equal Pay Act, the Family and Medical Leave Act, the Sarbanes–Oxley Act of 2002 (SOX)*, and state equal employment opportunity laws.

That SOX has no extraterritorial application seemed well established in case law until *O'Mahony v. Accenture Ltd.*, 537 F. Supp. 2d 506 (S.D.N.Y. 2008). The case was filed in the United States District Court for the Southern District of New York by an Irish national who was a partner and employee of Accenture LLP, a U.S. subsidiary of Accenture Ltd., a Bermuda company listed on the New York Stock Exchange. The plaintiff sought relief under SOX's whistleblower provision, alleging that her employer retaliated against her because of her objection to the company's fraudulent scheme to evade paying French social security contributions. Contrary to earlier decisions the administrative law judges of the Department of Labor had reached, the court found that it had subject matter jurisdiction over the dispute and denied the defendant's motion to dismiss. The *O'Mahony* court did not directly address whether SOX conferred extraterritorial jurisdiction on the court. Instead, the court primarily considered the plaintiff had worked for several years in the United States, that Accenture LLP was a subsidiary of a SOX-regulated company, and that the decisions to perpetrate fraud and retaliate against plaintiff were taken in the United States. The decision in *O'Mahony* leaves open the possibility that courts in the future might find extraterritorial application of SOX, extending protection even in circumstances where Title VII, ADA, or ADEA would not reach.

Defenses to U.S. Employment Law When Applied Extraterritorially

There are three principal defenses to U.S. challenges of employment decisions abroad: (1) the decision is made by "a foreign person not controlled by an American employer"; (2) the U.S. equal employment opportunity law (EEO law) conflicts with a host country's laws, so that the employer faces "foreign compulsion" because complying with U.S. law would violate the host country's laws; and (3) the performance of the job requires a trait, such as a specific religion or gender, allowing the employer the "bona fide occupational qualification" defense. We will review each of these in turn.

Control by a Foreign Person. When Congress passed the ADEA amendments, it was generally possible to define clearly the nationality of a corporation's controlling person. However, because now the stock of an international company may be simultaneously offered on many international exchanges—allowing people of all nationalities to purchase stock anonymously—it becomes virtually impossible to identify the nationality of owners in industrialized countries. However, courts have prevented the EEOC and U.S. citizens from bringing suit against "foreign" firms with very substantial U.S. operations.

The Foreign Compulsion Defense. Congress also intended to provide a **foreign compulsion defense,** permitting U.S. firms flexibility when the enforcement of U.S. employment laws overseas would result in a violation of foreign law. This defense does not apply to foreign employers who are charged with employment discrimination in the United States. As in all legal situations, interesting questions arise in difficult cases. In the *Mahoney v. RGE/RL, Inc.* case which follows, the U.S. Court of Appeals for the District of Columbia found that where U.S. law would cause a U.S. firm to violate a foreign collective bargaining agreement—not a law, strictly speaking—the foreign compulsion defense nonetheless applied.

The EEOC has taken a different position. Because the firm voluntarily entered into the discriminatory labor agreement, the EEOC maintains that foreign compulsion defense does not apply. In situations where there is genuine conflict with foreign law, the EEOC provides for possibility of intervention by the U.S. Department of State.

The Bona Fide Occupational Qualification Defense. The **bona fide occupational qualification (BFOQ) defense,** both in Title VII and the ADEA, provides that an employer may engage in discrimination if it is "reasonably necessary to the normal operation of the particular business or enterprise." This is not much of a "safe harbor" for U.S. employers. What is "reasonably necessary" for one person may not be for another. For example, when an American hospital refused to send Jewish anesthesiologists to Saudi Arabia, a court held that the BFOQ defense did not defeat a suit by a group of Jewish doctors. The court found that the employer had not made appropriate efforts to determine the Saudi Arabian policy regarding the entry of Jewish doctors into the country and that the Saudi government had never directed the employer that American Jews could not participate in the program. Another court found the BFOQ defense did not justify a refusal to promote a woman to a senior position at a U.S. company's Latin American office. The court found inadequate the company's reasoning that she would have to deal with men in Latin America, where, they argued, businesspeople believe that women belong in the home. The BFOQ defense might be useful to the litigator trying to defend a company's action after the fact, but it seems too uncertain to be a useful tool for business planning.

Mahoney v. RFE/RL, Inc.

47 F. 3d 447 (1995) United States Court of Appeals for the District of Columbia Circuit

BACKGROUND AND FACTS

RFE/RL, Inc., is a Delaware non-profit corporation that is funded but not controlled by the federal government. It is best known for its broadcast services, Radio Free Europe and Radio Liberty. RFE/RL's principal place of business is Munich, Germany. In 1982, the company entered into a collective bargaining agreement with unions representing its employees in Munich. One of the provisions of the labor contract, modeled after a nationwide agreement with the German broadcast industry, required employees to retire at age 65.

After Congress amended the Age Discrimination in Employment Act (ADEA) to cover American citizens working for American corporations overseas, RFE/RL thought its American employees in Munich would no longer have to retire at the age of 65, as the collective bargaining agreement provided, and could continue to work if they chose. In order to implement this understanding, the company applied to the Works Council for limited exemptions from its contractual obligation. Rejecting RFE/RL's requests, the Works Council determined that allowing only those employees who were American citizens to work past the age of 65 would violate not only the mandatory retirement provision but also the collective bargaining agreement's provision forbidding discrimination based on nationality. RFE/RL appealed the Works Council's decisions with respect to the plaintiffs to the Munich Labor Court and lost. The Labor Court agreed with the Works Council that RFE/RL must uniformly enforce the mandatory retirement provisions because exemptions would unfairly discriminate against German workers. The Labor Court also held that the company's retaining employees over the age of 65 despite the collective bargaining agreement would be illegal. The company terminated plaintiff De Lon in 1987 and plaintiff Mahoney in 1988. Both plaintiffs were working for the company in Munich, both were U.S. citizens, and both were discharged pursuant to

continues

continued

the labor contract because they had reached the age of 65.

CIRCUIT JUDGE RANDOLPH

If an American corporation operating in a foreign country would have to "violate the laws" of that country in order to comply with the Age Discrimination in Employment Act, the company need not comply with the Act. The question here is whether this "foreign laws" exception ... applies when the overseas company, in order to comply with the Act, would have to breach a collective bargaining agreement that foreign unions ... .

The parties agree that RFE/RL thereby violated the ADEA unless the "foreign laws" exception applied. The Act prohibits employers from discriminating against employees on the basis of age. "Employee" includes "any individual who is a citizen of the United States employed by an employer in a workplace in a foreign country;" and it is common ground that the Act covers RFE/RL.

The "foreign laws" exception to the Act states: It shall not be unlawful for an employer, employment agency, or labor organization (1) to take any action otherwise prohibited under subsections (a), (b), (c), or (e) of this section where ... such practices involve an employee in a workplace in a foreign country, and compliance with such subsections would cause such employer, or a corporation controlled by such employer, to violate the laws of the country in which such workplace is located. The district court held [the provision] inapplicable because the mandatory retirement provision is part of a contract between an employer and unions—both private entities—and has not in any way been mandated by the German government. Second, the provision does not have general application, as laws normally do, but binds only the parties to the contract ... .

If RFE/RL had not complied with the collective bargaining agreement in this case, if it had retained plaintiffs despite the mandatory retirement provision, the company would have violated the German laws standing behind such contracts, as well as the decisions of the Munich Labor Court. In the words of [the foreign compulsion defense], RFE/RL's "compliance with [the Act] would cause such employer ... to violate the laws of the country in which such workplace is located." Domestic employers of course would never face a comparable situation; the Supremacy Clause of the Constitution would force any applicable state laws to give way, and provisions in collective bargaining agreements contrary to the Act would be superseded. Congressional legislation cannot, however, set aside the laws of foreign countries. When an overseas employer's obligations under foreign law collide with its obligations under the Age Discrimination in Employment Act, [the foreign compulsion defense] quite sensibly solves the dilemma by relieving the employer of liability under the Act ... .

We recognize that RFE/RL's collective bargaining agreement is legally enforceable, which necessarily means that breaching the agreement in order to comply with the Act would ... "cause" RFE/RL "to violate the laws of" Germany. Plaintiffs complain that RFE/RL could have bargained harder for a change in the labor contract. But application of [the foreign compulsion defense] does not depend on such considerations. The collective bargaining agreement here was valid and enforceable at the time of plaintiffs' terminations, and RFE/RL had a legal duty to comply with it. There is not, nor could there be, any suggestion that RFE/RL agreed to the mandatory retirement provision in order to evade the Age Discrimination in Employment Act. Such provisions are, the evidence showed, common throughout the Federal Republic of Germany, and RFE/RL entered into this particular agreement before Congress extended the Act beyond our borders.

Decision. The Court of Appeals reversed the District Court's opinion and remanded the case to the District Court with instructions to dismiss the matter.

Case Questions

1. Does the court's decision mean that any collective bargaining agreement falls within the "foreign laws" exception? What if refusal to recognize CBA had been acceptable under German law?
2. Recalling the Denty court's comments about attempts to avoid the ADEA, why could it not be said that RFE/RL agreed to the CBA provision in order to circumvent the ADEA? When was the CBA entered into?
3. What does this decision reflect about courts' tendencies when faced with a potential conflict of laws?

Antidiscrimination Laws Outside the United States

The history of the United States is peppered with successive waves of immigration by various ethnic groups, each seeking civic or economic freedom. Even the framers of the Constitution, who were virtually all of British ancestry, were products of four different migrations from different parts of Britain and came from distinctly different religious traditions. Not surprisingly, the United States has a highly developed legal system proscribing discrimination based on religion or national origin. As we have seen in the preceding section, this body of law has in turn given rise to related legal principles prohibiting discrimination based on other criteria that have become socially unacceptable bases for differentiation, such as race, age, and gender.

The multi-ethnic makeup of the United States has been relatively unusual. As F. Scott Fitzgerald elegantly noted, "France was a land, England was a people, but America having about it that quality of the idea, was harder to utter… . It was a willingness of the heart." Most Europeans and Asians live in geographic regions inhabited by their ethnic brethren. The same has been true to a lesser extent in Africa, where traditional ethnic groups remain dominant in regions of multi-tribal nations created by European colonists. Even today, the competing desires of ethnic groups to dominate a geographically contiguous zone are a primary cause of civil strife in these continents. "Ethnic cleansing" in Bosnia and post-1999 "counter-cleansing" in Kosovo were efforts to create geographic regions where only one ethnic group resides. Although Latin Americans do not have the same tie to the land as do the peoples of the Eastern Hemisphere, the dominance of the Spanish culture in Hispanic America and of the Portuguese culture in Brazil have prevented legal developments similar to those in the United States. As the result of these social conditions, these countries have few antidiscrimination laws.

The revolution in transport and communications is ending ethnic homogeneity in the Old World. Ethnic North Africans work in Paris, ethnic Pakistanis work in London, and ethnic Turks work in Frankfurt. Women are not as willing to accept discrimination in the workplace. Moreover, as the population of Europe ages and declines, more and more companies are grappling with issues of an older workforce. In 2000, the European Union adopted *Council Directive 2000/78/EC*, which prohibits employment discrimination on the bases of religion or belief, disability, age, or sexual orientation (see the Czech Republic case). The same year, the European Union adopted *Council Directive 2000/43/EC*, which prohibits discrimination on the bases of race or ethnic origin. As member states have enacted legislation or regulations to incorporate these directives' general framework, more U.S. employers are likely to see more claims brought by their European-based employees.

European Commission Proceedings against Czech Republic on the Race Equality Directive and the Employment Equality Directive

2006/2262 and 2006/2434

BACKGROUND AND FACTS

While member states are responsible for implementing EU law, the European Commission ensures that EU law is properly applied. When a member state does not comply with EU law, the Commission can bring an action for non-compliance to end the infringement, and, if necessary, may refer the case to the European Court of Justice. The Commission launches a formal infringement proceeding by submitting a "reasoned opinion" to a member state detailing the Commission's position on the infringement. The Commission then allows the member state an opportunity to voluntarily comply with the requirements of EU law.

The Commission began an infringement proceeding against the Czech Republic for non-compliance with the Race Equality Directive in June 2007 and a proceeding for non-compliance with the Employment Equality Directive in January 2008. Following are excerpts from the two Reasoned Opinions issued by the European Commission after the Czech Republic had replied to the Commission's letters of formal notice concerning the two directives. Both cases were eventually closed in May 2010 after the Czech Republic adopted a comprehensive Anti-discrimination Act in compliance with EU requirements.

REASONED OPINION ON COUNCIL DIRECTIVE 2000/78/EC

The letter of formal notice raised four issues: the lack of definitions of the different types of discrimination and the lack of reference to the ground of disability; the conditions of recruitment of customs administration officials; the lack of transposition concerning part of the material scope of the Directive; and the justification of differences of treatment on the grounds of age.

In light of the reply to the letter of formal notice, the following issues remain problematic.

continues

continued

[I]n the Czech legal order, where specific legislative instruments concerning a professional activity or a group of workers do prohibit discrimination on the grounds of religion or belief, age or sexual orientation, those legal instruments often do not include a definition of direct and indirect discrimination, harassment and instruction to discriminate ... .

[S]everal legal instruments do not include disability as a ground [on] which discrimination is forbidden, but prohibit discrimination concerning the "state of health" of a person ... .

[T]he legal rules concerning the conditions for recruiting customs administration officials include among the health criteria required for the job, characteristics such as the absence of "sexual preference defect," "defects of psychology and behaviour (sexual development and orientation)" and "sexual identity defect." [These] rules allow for a general and unjustified exception to the principle of equal treatment on the grounds of sexual orientation in access to employment which goes beyond the requirements of the Directive ... .

[For these reasons, the Commission declared that the Czech Republic failed to meet its obligations under Articles 2, 3(1), and 4(1) of the *Council Directive 2000/78/EC* establishing a general framework for equal treatment in employment and occupation. The Commission summarized Czech Republic's failures as:]

(1) not providing for a definition of the different types of discrimination (direct and indirect discrimination, harassment and instruction to discriminate) mentioned in Article 2 of the Directive in all the legal instruments that prohibit discrimination on the grounds of religion or belief, disability, age or sexual orientation as regards employment and occupation,
(2) not providing for a definition of the different providing certain conditions for recruiting customs administration officials which allow for a general and unjustified exception to the principle of equal treatment on the grounds of sexual orientation in access to employment,
(3) not providing for a definition of the different not providing for the prohibition of discrimination on the grounds of religion or belief, disability, age or sexual orientation concerning several fields covered by Article 3(1) of the Directive.

REASONED OPINION ON COUNCIL DIRECTIVE 2000/43/EC

The letter of formal notice raised five issues: the lack of definitions of the different types of discrimination, the lack of transposition concerning part of the material scope of the Directive, the rule on the burden of proof, the protection against victimi[z]ation and the lack of an Equality Body.

With the exception of the Labour Code, in the Czech legal order, where specific legislative instruments prohibit racial or ethnic discrimination, the laws in force do not include a definition of the different types of discrimination: direct, indirect, harassment and instruction to discriminate. This situation cannot adequately ensure the level of protection required by the Directive, especially in view of the legal certainty that the transposition of a Directive should involve ... .

In the Czech Republic, no legislative anti-discrimination rules cover, or cover sufficiently, several fields mentioned in Article 3 (1) of the Directive, such as the following: [p]rofessions and activities not covered by the Labour Code, such as access to employment and occupation regarding labour relations of judges, state attorneys, members of parliament, members of local government, and the labour relations of prisoners and volunteers; [s]elf-employment ...... ; [v]ocational training ... ; [m]embership of an involvement in an organi[s]ation of workers or employees ... ; [s]ocial protection, including social security and healthcare; [s]ocial advantages; [a]ccess to [g]oods and [s]ervices, including [h]ousing.

Article 8 (1) of the Directive provides as follows: "when persons who consider themselves wronged because the principle of equal treatment has not been applied to them establish, before a court or other competent authority, facts from which it may be presumed that there has been direct or indirect discrimination, it shall be for the respondent to prove that there has been no breach of the principle of equal treatment."

[I]n the Czech legislation the rule on the burden of proof is not applicable to housing and, concerning access to goods, it is only applicable regarding sales of goods in shops—excluding other types of sales of goods available to the public, like sales through internet, for example.

[I]n the legislation of the Czech Republic there is a lack of general legislative protection against victimi[z]ation outside the employment field. [Also], in the employment field, protection against victimi[z]ation only covers employees, excluding other people, such as clients who help a worker to present a discrimination complaint ... .

In the Czech Republic, no body was created or designated to ensure the promotion of equal treatment of all persons without discrimination on the grounds of racial and ethnic origin ... .

continues

continued

[For these reasons, the Commission declared that the Czech Republic failed to meet its obligations under Articles 2, 3(1), 8(1), 9 and 13 of the *Council Directive 2000/43/EC* implementing the principle of equal treatment between persons irrespective of racial or ethnic origin. The Commission summarized Czech Republic's failures as:]

(1) not providing for a definition of the different types of discrimination mentioned in Article 2 of the Directive in all the legal instruments that prohibit racial or ethnic discrimination,
(2) not providing for the prohibition of discrimination on the grounds of racial or ethnic ori gin concerning several fields of social life covered by Article 3(1) of the Directive, ...
(3) restricting ... the application of the obligation to shift the burden of proof to "the sale of goods in shops" and by not including other types of sales, as well as by excluding housing , when not regarded as a service, from the application of the same obligation,
(4) not providing for a complete protection against any adverse treatment or adverse consequence as a reaction to a complaint or to proceedings aimed at enforcing compliance with the principle of equal treatment,
(5) not designating a body or bodies for the promotion of equal treatment of all persons without discrimination on the grounds of racial or ethnic origin which have all the three competences required and comprise all fields covered by the Directive.

Case Questions

1. The Czech Republic is about 95 percent ethnic Czech. Knowing this, do you think that there was much racial or ethnic discrimination? Do you think that might have been why no written laws forbade it? What was accomplished by having such laws passed in accordance with the Directive?
2. What does this case reflect about EU recognition of gay and lesbian rights?
3. Do you think that official government offices to promote discrimination are helpful? In what way?

Globalization of trade and finance has had ramifications in the area of employment as well. For the past fifteen years, most of the trade agreements that the United States has signed have included labor standards, even though these are typically aspirational and without any true monitoring or enforcement mechanism. Financing entities, including the World Bank's International Finance Corporation, are incorporating labor standards as a condition of their loans. **Friendship, Commerce, and Navigation treaties** between the United States and other nations, which allow a foreign employer to choose its own executives and experts to run its operations in the other signatory nations, have come under greater scrutiny as to which levels and positions the foreign executives can occupy.

The strength of the World Trade Organization and other international institutions will become more influential as China and other emerging nations start entering trade agreements. Since 2011, China has entered into eight free trade agreements or regional trade agreements. These agreements have included labor and environmental laws. These provisions impose legally binding obligations that incorporate sustainable legal developments to eliminate employment discrimination. China did not become a full member of the WTO until November 2001. Therefore, these agreements help assess China's reforms and attitude toward labor principles.

Nations like Japan and China are reforming their equal employment opportunity laws to provide greater protections against discrimination in employment.

Laws Favoring Discrimination Based on National Origin or Religion. Despite these movements, some nations still permit discrimination based on their historical and cultural backgrounds. In many countries, the law actually requires discrimination based on religion or national origin. When a country is synonymous with an ethnic group, that ethnic group sometimes justifies preservation of ethnic identity by methodically excluding those outside it. Estonia has created citizenship laws, the plain intent of which is to deny citizenship to ethnic Russians who arrived during the 70 years of Soviet rule. Because Estonia confers employment and other benefits on the basis of citizenship, its citizenship law is a device for favoring ethnic Estonians over ethnic Russians in employment opportunities. Dominant ethnic groups in small, wealthy nations threatened by large numbers of industrious ethnic outsiders often enact laws to prevent those outsiders from holding certain types of jobs. For example, ethnic Kuwaitis and Jordanians have excluded Palestinian co-religionists from key jobs and properties. Likewise, when a nation does not distinguish between religion and the state, the law often calls for discrimination against infidels. Pro-discrimination laws are most frequently found in Middle Eastern Islamic countries such as Pakistan, Iran, and Saudi Arabia. One may also encounter such pro-discrimination statutes in countries where atheism is the state "religion," such as Cuba and North Korea.

China presents one of the most serious form of institutional discrimination through the ***Hukou.*** Hukou is the registration of households. Instituted in 1958, the system categorizes citizens according to their place of residence, essentially dividing the population into agriculture and urban. It is a mechanism for determining social entitlements. It is the core of living and working conditions in China. The rural migrant worker is prevented from sharing in the newfound prosperity of the industrial change sweeping through China. Only the lowest-paying jobs and often the most dangerous jobs are available to migrant workers. Their living conditions are squalid because most have to live in the factory dormitories. Furthermore, rural migrant workers cannot access local social benefits such as bus passes, welfare, and government services and cannot enroll their children in local schools. This system is such a part of China's culture that, even with modifications and changes to many employment laws, the structure remains intact. It is so entrenched in the way of life that cities have quotas on how many migrant workers are permitted to work in a city limit. Apart from job restrictions and prohibitions, cities will enforce these discriminatory practices by issuing fines on employers that hire outside workers. These fines fall under the various guises of registration fees, work management fees, administrative fees, and so on. Although recent reform efforts aim to restructure the discriminatory burdens cities have attached to migrant workers, the systemic discrimination remains untouched.

There are no such pro-discrimination laws in the United States. Nonetheless, the U.S. investor must take such laws into account in staffing foreign operations. Because they are rooted in deep cultural or political fear of outside influence, violations of their terms generally lead to adverse action by the local government.

Non-U.S. Laws Prohibiting Discrimination Based on National Origin or Religion. The U.S. investor must understand foreign laws prohibiting ethnic discrimination. They are both similar to and different from their U.S. counterparts. Articles 7, 48, 52, and 59 of the *European Union Treaty* forbid different types of discrimination within the Union based on nationality. The motivating principle behind these provisions is that nationals from each member state should be free to pursue their economic interests anywhere within the unified European economy without fear of differential treatment. The *Jany* case that follows demonstrates the Community's commitment to protect even the oldest of professions.

In the past, EU antidiscrimination law has not prohibited discrimination against ethnic individuals who are not member state nationals. But this is changing. The EU's Group on Treaty Amendment and Community Competence has, in recent years, noted that measures prohibiting racism and xenophobia should become part of the EU's discussion on EU treaty amendments. Among the measures discussed have been granting legal status to resident non-EU citizens and granting third-country nationals EU-citizen status upon completion of a five-year lawful residency requirement in one of the member states.

Malgorzata Jany & Others v. Staatssecretaris van Justitie

2001 E.C.R. I-8615 Court of Justice of the European Communities

BACKGROUND AND FACTS

Ms. Jany and Ms. Szepietowska, Polish nationals, and Ms. Padevetova, Ms. Zacalova, Ms. Hrubcinova, and Ms. Uberlackerova, Czech nationals, had established their residence in the Netherlands at various dates between May 1993 and October 1996, working as window prostitutes in Amsterdam. The Netherlands Secretary of State for Justice (Secretary of State) rejected their application for residence permits on the ground that prostitution is a prohibited activity or at least not a socially acceptable form of work and cannot be regarded as being either a regular job or a profession. In July 1997, the District Court of The Hague ruled that the appeals brought against the Secretary of State's decisions were well founded, and it set those decisions aside for failure to provide reasons. In a subsequent decision in 1998, the Secretary of State, ruling afresh on the applicants' objections, declared all of them to be unfounded. The six applicants then sought the annulment of the new decision taken by the Secretary of State to the Court of Justice of the European Communities.

Poland and the Czech Republic each had signed an agreement with the European Communities to transition their accessions into the Communities (*Association Agreement between the Communities and Poland*

continues

continued

signed in 1991, and *Association Agreement between the Communities and the Czech Republic* signed in 1993). The Court based its judgment primarily on its interpretation of the agreements between the Communities and Poland and the Czech Republic.

G. C. RODRIGUEZ IGLESIAS, PRESIDENT; P. JANN, F. MACKEN AND N. COLNERIC, PRESIDENTS OF CHAMBERS; C. GULMANN, D. A. O. EDWARD, A. LA PERGOLA (RAPPORTEUR), L. SEVON, M. WATHELET, V. SKOURIS, AND C. W. A. TIMMERMANS, JUDGES

Can Polish and Czech nationals rely directly on the Agreements in the sense that they are entitled, vis-à-vis a Member State, to claim that they derive a right of entry and residence from the right laid down in Article 44 of the Agreement with Poland and Article 45 of the Agreement with the Czech Republic in order to take up and pursue economic activities as self-employed persons and to set up and manage undertakings, irrespective of the policy which the Member State in question pursues in this regard?

[Does the Agreement] allow prostitution to be excluded from the notion of "economic activities as self-employed persons" on the ground that prostitution does not come within the description [or opening words of the Agreements] for reasons of a moral nature, on the ground that prostitution is prohibited in (a majority of) the associate countries, and on the ground that it gives rise to problems concerning the freedom of action of prostitutes and their independence which are difficult to monitor?

[The Agreements] must be construed as establishing, within the respective scopes of application of those two Agreements, a precise and unconditional principle which is sufficiently operational to be applied by a national court and which is therefore capable of governing the legal position of individuals. The direct effect which those provisions must therefore be recognized as having means that Polish and Czech nationals relying on those provisions have the right to invoke them before the courts of the host Member State, notwithstanding the fact that the authorities of that State remain competent to apply to those nationals their own national laws and regulations regarding entry, stay and establishment. The right of establishment [defined in the Agreements] means that rights of entry and residence, as corollaries of the right of establishment, are conferred on Polish and Czech nationals wishing to pursue activities of an industrial or commercial character, activities of craftsmen or activities of the professions in a Member State. However, it follows from [the Agreements] those rights of entry and residence are not absolute privileges, inasmuch as their exercise may, in some circumstances, be limited by the rules of the host Member State governing the entry, stay and establishment of Polish and Czech nationals.

Although Community law does not impose on Member States a uniform scale of values as regards the assessment of conduct which may be considered to be contrary to public policy, conduct may not be considered to be of a sufficiently serious nature to justify restrictions on entry to, or residence within, the territory of a Member State of a national of another Member State where the former Member State does not adopt, with respect to the same conduct on the part of its own nationals, repressive measures or other genuine and effective measures intended to combat such conduct.

Consequently, conduct which a Member State accepts on the part of its own nationals cannot be regarded as constituting a genuine threat to public order within the context of the Association Agreement between the Communities and Poland and that between the Communities and the Czech Republic. Applicability of the public policy derogation ... in the case of Polish and Czech nationals wishing to pursue the activity of prostitution within the territory of the host Member State, to the condition that that State has adopted effective measures to monitor and repress activities of that kind when they are also pursued by its own nationals.

That condition is not met in the present case. [W]indow prostitution and street prostitution are permitted in the Netherlands and are regulated there at the communal level.

Decision. On those grounds, the court ruled [T]hat Polish and Czech nationals relying on those provisions have the right to invoke them before the courts of the host Member State, notwithstanding the fact that the authorities of that State remain competent to apply to those nationals their own national laws and regulations regarding entry, stay and establishment... .

The right of establishment ... means that rights of entry and residence, as corollaries of the right of establishment, are conferred on Polish and Czech nationals wishing to pursue activities of an industrial or commercial character, activities of craftsmen or activities of the professions in a Member State. However, it follows from [the Agreements] that those rights of entry and residence are not absolute privileges, inasmuch as their exercise may, in some circumstances, be limited by the rules of the host Member State governing the entry, stay and establishment of Polish and Czech nationals.

continues

continued

[The Agreements] must be construed to the effect that prostitution is an economic activity pursued by a self-employed person as referred to in those provisions, where it is established that it is being carried on by the person providing the service.

Case Questions

1. What would have been the result of the case if prostitution in the Netherlands were illegal for Dutch women? Is this a case about privacy rights or ethnic discrimination?
2. What would have been the result in the case if the plaintiffs had been Russian nationals rather than nationals of Poland and the Czech Republic?
3. Would Czech and Polish nationals be equally free to practice other professions, such as law? What legitimate barriers might there to be their entry into those professions?

Discrimination Based on Gender. The movement to abolish discrimination based on gender is relatively new. Until the twentieth century, few nations even granted women the right of suffrage. The great majority of nations imposed many restrictions on work outside the home.

During the twentieth century, women's legal status changed radically. Gender discrimination laws were largely replaced with antidiscrimination provisions. Legal restrictions on women's roles in the workplace are now principally limited to a few Islamic nations. Due to the global economic crisis, in 2011 the International Labor Organization (ILO) reported that there were 29 million fewer people in the worldwide labor force with woman comprising 49 percent of the workers. The highest rates are in North America (75 percent) and the lowest are in the Middle East (26 percent).

Notwithstanding these legal advances, some level of gender discrimination remains almost universal in the twenty-first century. According to the International Trade Union Confederation, women on average earn 18 percent less than their male counterparts worldwide. In Japan, women earn only 63 percent of what men earn. In the United States, the figure is now 77 percent. Pay rates in Northern European nations are among the most equal. In Sweden and Denmark, the figures are 87 and 88 percent, respectively. In other countries, however, women's pay is dramatically less equal. Chile's booming economy has done little to improve the pay ratio of 54 cents for women to every dollar men make. Discriminatory access to educational opportunity is not the explanation.

In Latin America, on the average, a woman needs 15 years of education to make the same amount of money as a man with 11 years of education. Similarly, a 2003 study of gender discrimination in the Ukraine found widespread discrimination against women in all employment sectors, despite broad legal guarantees of equal protection. The discrimination included job announcements that specified male applicants only and job announcements requiring an attractive appearance for female applicants. In addition, the study found discrimination against unmarried women and women with small children. In 2011, the United Nations organization noted that the Ukraine continues to lag behind the European standards on gender equality.

Gender discrimination is widespread in China, despite various improvements made in China's *2008 Labor Law*. Job advertisements and the interview process specifically address marital status, height, attractiveness, and age as requirements for women applicants. In fact, the concept of discrimination is not widely known in all parts of China, including among judges. It is not entirely surprising that no Chinese woman seems to have filed a lawsuit based on gender discrimination in hiring.

Sexual harassment is also said to be quite prevalent in Chinese employment situations. In a national survey of 8,000 people, conducted by two major media organizations, 79 percent of women said they experienced sexual harassment in the work place.

Women are often required to retire at the age of 55, while men do not retire until 60 or older. This early retirement age is significant because typically women in China do not begin their professional lives until later as they are required to defer their attainment of advanced degrees and professional commitments to raise children or tend to other domestic obligations.

Lawmakers have particularly focused on the issue of maternity leave. Presently, the EU law provides for a minimum of 14 weeks' maternity leave and an allowance of at least 75 or 80 percent of net salary. It further stipulates that pregnant workers cannot be fired. Most recently, the European Parliament has proposed extending the leave to 20 weeks with 100 percent pay. In Hong Kong, a new law provides for ten weeks' maternity leave at two-thirds of the woman's latest salary. India requires six weeks' leave at full pay.

The Ukraine allows ten weeks' pre-birth and eight weeks' post-birth salaried maternity leave, as well as additional unpaid leave until the child reaches age three. The up-to-age-three leave allows the mother to collect benefits from the state.

China recently addressed the issue of maternity leave. The Special Protection Provisions in China's *2008 Labor Law*, Chapter VII, Article 61-63, mandates a reduced workload and a system of rest breaks for women who are pregnant and who are still breast feeding their children up to one year after birth. All women are entitled to a minimum of 98 days paid leave or 128 days paid leave, if they are older than 24 at the time of the birth. China has also established a maternity insurance fund that compensates a woman for any lost wages during maternity leave. The employer funds this program by contributing approximately 1 percent of payroll expenses. Unlike many Western countries, men are not covered under the maternity leave provisions.

There has also been change in the area of equal pay for equal work. While Chinese practice remains generally hostile to women, the laws on the Chinese books have improved markedly. Most notable is the *Equal Promotion Law*, which became effective in 2008. This law advances the concept that employees shall have the right to equal employment; shall have the right to select their job in accordance with the law; and, in seeking employment, will not be subject to discrimination based on factors such as ethnicity, race, gender, or religion.

China's amendment of the 2008 *Labor Contract Law* in early August 2012 will have an especially important impact on foreign direct investors. This amendment provides that workers hired through "labor dispatches," or contracting agents, receive the same treatment as direct recruits. Casual laborers have become the main source of labor in some regions. Under the old law, factory owners did not need to pay for these workers' social and medical insurance. But the new amendment explicitly stipulates that labor dispatches should not become the main labor channel and all temporary laborers should receive payments, including all welfare and benefits, equal to their permanent counterparts. This will have a direct impact onfirms in which there is a foreign investment, **foreign-invested enterprises (FIE)**. By law, FIEs have to hire employees through labor agencies. Previously this allowed the FIE to pay a lower wage rates. With the 2012 amendment, all companies will be required to pay employees equally.

The EU proscribes to this standard as well. Article 119 of the EU treaty and *Community Directive 2006/54/EC* requires equal pay for equal work and equality in access to employment. As illustrated in the following case involving Kathleen Hill and Ann Stapleton, compliance with these principles is determined through a practical *effect-oriented test.*

Kathleen Hill & Ann Stapleton Revenue Comm'rs & Dpt. of Finance

1998 E.C.R. I-3739 Court of Justice of the European Communities

BACKGROUND AND FACTS

Under job-sharing, established in 1984 by an Irish Government Circular, two civil servants may decide to equally share one full-time job so that the benefits are shared equally by both persons concerned and the costs of the post to the administration remain the same. The two civil servants retain the right to return to full-time employment at the end of the period for which they had opted to job-share, provided that suitable vacancies exist. Each year's job-sharing service counts as six months' full-time service, so an officer who has served for two years in a job-sharing capacity is placed on the second point of the full-time scale (equivalent to one year's full-time service).

A dispute arose between Ms. Hill and Ms. Stapleton, who had previously worked in a job-sharing capacity, and the Revenue Commissioners and Department of Finance of Ireland concerning the latter's decision to place them, on their return to full-time employment, on a point of the full-time pay scale lower than that of the job-sharing pay scale that they had previously occupied. Ms. Hill and Ms. Stapleton challenged their classification before an Equality Officer, who found in their favor on the ground that their employer was precluded from applying a provision to the effect that only paid service should be taken into account for progression on the incremental scale. The Labor Court, faced with appeal from the Revenue Commissioners and Department of Finance, referred these questions to the Court of Justice of the European Communities.

(a) [I]s the principle of equal pay [for men and women], as defined in *[European Council] Directive 75/117/EEC*, contravened if employees, who convert from job-sharing to full-time work, regress on the incremental scale, and hence on their salary scale,

continues

continued

due to the application by the employer of the criterion of service calculated by time worked in a job?

(c) If so, can a practice of incremental progression by reference to actual time worked be objectively justified by reference to factors other than the acquisition of a particular level of skill and experience over time?

H. RAGNEMALM, PRESIDENT OF THE CHAMBER; R. SCHINTGEN, G. F. MANCINI, J. L. MURRAY (RAPPORTEUR), AND G. HIRSCH, JUDGES

[T]he national tribunal is in substance asking whether there is discrimination in a case where workers who convert from job-sharing to full-time work regress on the incremental scale, and hence on their salary scale, due to the application by the employer of the criterion of service calculated by the length of time actually worked in a post. If application of that criterion gives rise to indirect discrimination, the national tribunal asks whether this can be justified.

It is apparent from the case-file that the national system in question places workers who convert from job-sharing to full-time work at a disadvantage compared with those who have worked on a full-time basis for the same number of years in so far as, when converting to full-time work, a job-sharing worker is placed, on the full-time pay scale, at a level below that which he or she previously occupied on the pay scale applicable to job-sharing staff and, consequently, at a level lower than that of a full-time worker employed for the same period of time.

It must be recalled at the outset that Article 119 of the Treaty sets out the principle that men and women should receive equal pay for equal work.

[D]iscrimination can arise only through the application of different rules to comparable situations or the application of the same rule to different situations.

[I]t has not been established that the unfavorable treatment applied to Ms Hill and Ms Stapleton constitutes direct discrimination on grounds of sex. It is thus necessary to examine whether that treatment may amount to indirect discrimination.

According to settled case-law, Article 4(1) of the Directive precludes the application of a national measure which, although formulated in neutral terms, works to the disadvantage of far more women than men, unless that measure is based on objective factors unrelated to any discrimination on grounds of sex.

It is apparent from the case-file that 99.2% of clerical assistants who job-share are women, as are 98% of all civil servants employed under job-sharing contracts. In those circumstances, a provision which, without objective justification, adversely affects the legal position of those workers coming within the category of job-sharers has discriminatory effects based on sex.

[D]uring the entire period for which they job-shared, Ms. Hill and Ms. Stapleton progressed by one incremental point each year and were paid at the rate of 50% of the salary for clerical assistants, according to the point each had reached on the scale.

[W]hen workers convert from job-sharing, under which they will have worked for 50% of full time, receiving 50% of the salary corresponding to that point on the pay scale for full-time work, they should expect both their hours of work and the level of their pay to increase by 50%, in the same way as workers converting from full-time work to job-sharing would expect those factors to be reduced by 50%, unless a difference in treatment can be justified.

However, there is no such progression in this case. When job-sharing workers convert to full-time work, their situation is automatically reviewed in such a way that they are placed, on the full-time pay scale, at a level lower than that which they occupied on the pay scale applicable to job-sharing.

The regression to which workers are subject when entering or returning to full-time work directly affects their pay. They are in fact paid less than double what they would have earned had they been job-sharing. Consequently, their hourly rate of pay is reduced. Reference to the criterion of hours worked during the period of job-sharing employment, as provided for under the scheme applicable here, fails to take account either of the fact that job-sharing ... is in a unique category as it does not involve a break in service, or of the fact ... that a job-sharer can acquire the same experience as a full-time worker. Furthermore, a disparity is retroactively introduced into the overall pay of employees performing the same functions so far as concerns both the quality and the quantity of the work performed. The result of this disparity is that employees working full time but who previously job shared are treated differently from those who have always worked on a full-time basis.

Within the category of full-time workers, therefore, there is unequal treatment, as regards pay, of employees who previously job-shared, and who regress in relation to the position which they already occupied on the pay scale.

In such a case, provisions of the kind at issue in the main proceedings result in discrimination of female workers vis-à-vis male workers and must in principle be treated as contrary to Article 119 of the Treaty and therefore contrary to the Directive. It would be otherwise only if the difference of treatment found to exist between the two categories of worker were justified by

continues

continued

objective factors unrelated to any discrimination based on sex … .

Community policy in this area is to encourage and, if possible, adapt working conditions to family responsibilities. Protection of women within family life and in the course of their professional activities is, in the same way as for men, a principle which is widely regarded in the legal systems of the Member States as being the natural corollary of the equality between men and women, and which is recognised by Community law.

The onus is therefore on the Revenue Commissioners and the Department of Finance to establish before the Labour Court that the reference to the criterion of service, defined as the length of time actually worked, in the assessment of the incremental credit to be granted to workers who convert from job-sharing to full-time work is justified by objective factors unrelated to any discrimination on grounds of sex. If such evidence is adduced by those authorities, the mere fact that the national legislation affects far more women than men cannot be regarded as constituting a breach of Article 119 of the Treaty and, consequently, a breach of the Directive.

Article 119 of the Treaty and the Directive are to be interpreted as precluding legislation which provides that, where a much higher percentage of female workers than male workers are engaged in job-sharing, job-sharers who convert to full-time employment are given a point on the pay scale applicable to full-time staff which is lower than that which those workers previously occupied on the pay scale applicable to job-sharing staff due to the fact that the employer has applied the criterion of service calculated by the actual length of time worked in a post, unless such legislation can be justified by objective criteria unrelated to any discrimination on grounds of sex.

Decision. The court ruled that Article 119 of the EC Treaty and Council Directive preclude legislation that provides that, where a much higher percentage of female workers than male workers are engaged in an employment category, rules that disadvantage that category are presumed invalid unless the employer can show an objective, non-sex related economic basis for the distinction. It thus remanded the case to the national courts for proceedings to determine if such a basis existed.

Case Questions

1. What would have been the result of this case if more men had availed themselves of a job-sharing option?
2. If, in the future, more men take care of the children and the percentage of women job-sharers drops, could the employer change its rules back to what they were before this case in order to reduce its expenses?
3. What effect will this ruling have on Irish taxpayers? Would this decision prevent the government agencies from eliminating the job-sharing program to save expenses?

Gender discrimination cases have found only mixed success in Japan. In July 1990, a Tokyo district court ruled for the first time that female employees had been improperly denied promotions due to gender discrimination. Although the court awarded 18 women $640,000, consistent with Japan's respect for the integrity of the workplace, the court declined to direct promotions because such action would interfere with personnel decisions. However, in November 2003, the Tokyo District Court found that different, lower pay for women was acceptable. As illustrated in the *Sumitomo* case, gender discrimination in employment was tolerated until very recently in Japan. Notwithstanding occasional setbacks, movement on gender discrimination issues seems consistent throughout the world.

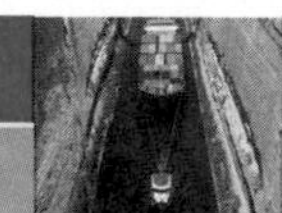

Sumitomo Electric Industries Ltd.

Osaka District Court of Japan (July 2000)

BACKGROUND AND FACTS

The plaintiffs, female employees of Sumitomo Electric Industries Ltd., sued their employer in 1995 in the fifth Civil Section of the Osaka District Court, alleging gender discrimination. During the mid-1960s, the company had hired female employees in the clerical position without an opportunity for them to transfer to specialist jobs. The male employees with the same education degrees were placed on a management track. The hiring practice, which the plaintiffs were

continues

continued

challenging, resulted in a wage and positional gap between the male and female workers with similar educational background and years in service.

JUDGE MATSUMOTO

Companies have a broad freedom in deciding who they hire, and under what conditions they hire. Yet such freedom in hiring is restricted by limitations provided for by law ... and even when there are none, by the principles of basic human rights, public welfare, public order and good morals ... .

[The company practice of hiring and promotion] is nothing but discrimination against women, and is against the objectives of Article 14 of the Constitution prohibiting discrimination based on sex.

However, Article 14 of the Constitution is not applied directly between private individuals, and although the *Labor Standards Act* stipulates the principle of equal wages for men and women (Article 4), it does not include a provision prohibiting discrimination between men and women in hiring. It goes without saying that the objectives of Article 14 of the Constitution should be respected even between private individuals ... . On the other hand, as companies have been recognized the freedom in hiring based on the freedom of economic activity (Article 22) and the protection of the right to property (Article 29) under the Constitution, harmonization must be sought between the various rights in deciding whether measures amount to unreasonable discrimination ... .

Around the mid-1960s, the ideas of division of roles, in which men supported the families economically while women married and stayed at home to concentrate in household work and raising children, were still strong ... . [I]t was not unusual for many companies in this country to try to raise the capacity and labor productivity for men through in-house training and other measures, on the assumption that they will work long-term until retirement, while not bearing the cost of providing opportunities for training for women, who had the high possibility of retiring after a few years ... .

The above ideas on role divisions for men and women are currently being overcome, and are no longer general ... . Therefore, the status of female clerical workers and gender-separate hiring methods, which had been adopted by the respondent company, has no room for acceptance now. But looking from the [vantage] point [of] mid-1960s, when the plaintiffs were hired, the respondent company's measure ... of categorizing high-school women in only routine assistant work ... cannot be considered as being in violation of public order and good morals ... .

Decision. The District Court dismissed the gender discrimination claims.

Case Questions

1. How is this employment law determination similar to that in the *Kochi Hoso* case earlier in this chapter? Was the judge overruling written law with his view of a "socially accepted" view?
2. Do "socially accepted" views change over time? What would you expect the result to have been next time a similar suit was brought in this court?
3. Is it appropriate for different cultures to have different laws relating to gender employment regulation?

Following an international public outcry after the decision, the Osaka Appeals Court issued a settlement recommendation in 2003, accepted by the parties, which essentially overturned the decision of the District Court. Under the terms of the settlement, the company will revise its hiring and promotion policies pursuant to the objectives of the amended *Equal Employment Opportunity Law* that prohibits gender discrimination in employment. The plaintiffs were promoted to either manager or assistant manager positions based on their experiences.

FOREIGN LAWS PERMITTING DIFFICULT WORK CONDITIONS

One of the principal reasons for locating a plant abroad is relative cost advantage. Particularly in low-skill manufacturing, a company's dollars, marks, or yen go farther paying salaries in an economy with a weak currency and a low cost of living. Many developing countries lack burdensome work rules that add costs.

Other nations boast smooth labor–management relations that avoid expensive disputes. In some cases, cost savings are attributable to work conditions that, while lawful in the host country, are not legal in industrialized Western nations. In fact, these labor practices may not even be legal under local law. U.S. companies seldom directly engage in illegal employment practices. Instead, they often place orders for a product or a component with a foreign buying agent that submits a low bid. These agents procure foreign suppliers to assemble the products or components in accordance with the U.S. company's specifications. These suppliers in turn subcontract parts of the product to smaller shops. Typically, the worst abuses occur in low-cost small shops that are several steps removed from the U.S. purchaser.

A U.S. firm, even if operating legally within the host country, must concern itself with whether those practices violate nonbinding standards issued by the ILO and other international standards. If a business is unaware of dubious labor practices but uses foreign buying agents, it should conduct due diligence to satisfy itself that such practices are not in use. As will be seen, a failure to do so can have adverse consequences in the U.S. firm's target markets.

Unsafe Labor Conditions

In developed countries, government agencies similar to the U.S. Occupational Safety and Health Administration regulate conditions in the workplace. In many emerging nations, there is no such legal framework, and working conditions can be quite hazardous. One of the more common and dangerous of these practices is the blocking and locking of all exits in manufacturing facilities as a low-cost measure to prevent pilfering. This practice has caused thousands of workers to be trapped and burned alive when fire broke out in such buildings. For example, a fire in a locked toy factory near Bangkok killed more than 240 workers and injured hundreds of others. In a separate incident, a fire in a locked facility killed 80 young women in Dongguan, China. The lack of ventilation in such factories also increases the incidence of tuberculosis and sinusitis among workers.

A second common safety issue is the use of antiquated and poorly maintained equipment, which causes the rate of work injuries to balloon. Indeed, in many emerging nations where such equipment predominates, work-related injuries are rising precipitously.

Harsh work rules, which are legal in many developing nations, are a third major concern. For instance, in order to maximize output per worker and thereby reduce cost per unit, some manufacturers permit assembly-line workers to use the restroom only three times in a 12-hour day. This practice not only subjects workers to great physical discomfort but it also increases the incidence of urinary tract infections. Harsh work rules also involve very long work hours. In China's Guandong Province, some factory employees must endure 130-hour work weeks—with dormitory rent deducted from their wages.

Prison Labor

Prison labor exists to some extent in virtually all countries. State prisoners manufacture most of the license plates in the United States. However, in a few nations—including China—it is legal for prisoners to work in traditionally commercial forms of manufacturing. If developed nations have difficulty competing with low-cost labor in underdeveloped countries, they have even less chance of competing with free, involuntary labor from such nations. The use of such labor is unacceptable to Western governments.

Because China has close relations between government and business, the practice of prison labor became particularly prevalent in the late 1980s. In 1992, the United States stepped up the pressure on China to exclude prison-labor products from exports to the United States. The result was a diplomatic Memorandum of Understanding. But the United States continued to receive reliable reports of prison labor.

The United States threatened trade sanctions to enforce the Memorandum before concluding a new agreement with China in 1994. Under the 1994 agreement, the United States is allowed to inspect "labor reform camps." However, the United States has complained that it has received only modest cooperation in implementing the agreements.

As in other areas, the Chinese government is far more willing to enact progressive laws and enter into diplomatic pacts than to enforce them. As of the end of 2012, human rights sources estimated that there were 5.5 million prison laborers turning out products, from toys to Christmas lights. In early 2013, with mounting dissatisfaction among its own citizens and with new leaders in Beijing, China appears to be turning its attention to this subject with potential for real change. Yet, whether China will seize this moment to conduct real reform, close the camps, or stop the institution of "re-education" through labor is unclear. One concern is that Beijing may merely retool the policy on labor camps. That is, officials will create new legal measures that appear improved but that change little, except to make it more difficult for monitors to claim or prove violations.

Child Labor

Because wages for children tend to be quite low, child labor is common—if illegal—in "low-cost" nations. For instance, although work during school hours is illegal for anyone under 14 years of age in Sri Lanka, Zambia, and Mexico, 500,000 children under 14 work in Sri Lanka, 700,000 work in Zambia, and millions work in Mexico. Children are the labor foundation of Bangladesh's garment industry and India's oriental carpet industry. In 2008, the ILO reported that 306 million children between the ages of 5 and 17—out of 1.6 billion worldwide—were engaged in some form of child labor.

Most working children are ages 11 to 14 years old, but as many as 60 million are between the ages of 5 and 11. Although the exact numbers are not known, available statistics indicate that approximately 96 percent of child workers reside in developing countries in Africa, Asia, and Latin America; there are also pockets of child labor in many industrialized countries. In spite of a reported decline in child labor during the period from 1995 to 2000, child labor remains a major concern. Working under circumstances that jeopardize their health and even their lives, most child laborers are malnourished and work long hours in hazardous occupations. Frequently, they do not attend school. Children working in Indian carpet shops, for example, have a high incidence of tuberculosis, worm infestation, skin disease, and enlarged lymph glands.

Consequences of Participation in Illegal or Harsh Work Conditions

Participating in illegal or harsh work conditions raises much more than an ethical dilemma for foreign direct investors. The U.S. investor might have to see the workers on the other end of a summons in the United States. Since the U.S. Supreme Court's decision in *Sosa v. Alvarez-Machain,* 542 U.S. 692 (2004), U.S. employers in foreign countries had begun to face lawsuits filed by their foreign employees. In *Sosa,* Justice Souter interpreted the ***Alien Tort Statute (ATS)*** to permit non-U.S. citizens to bring private causes of action in U.S. courts based on torts (such as piracy) that violate norms of international law that are as widely accepted and definite as those recognized by Congress when the ATS was passed in 1789. In April 2013, however, the Supreme Court appeared to limit very significantly this type of lawsuit, as described in the following case.

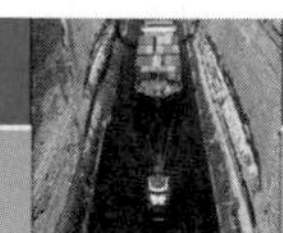

Kiobel v. Royal Dutch Petroleum Co.,

United States Supreme Court (April 16, 2013)

BACKGROUND AND FACTS

The Kiobel suit was filed in 2002 by Nigerian citizens from the Ogoni region of Nigeria against Dutch and British holding companies that were operating in the region through their Nigerian subsidiary. The petitioners alleged that the respondents aided and abetted human rights abuses committed by the Nigerian government, including torture, crimes against humanity, and arbitrary arrest and detention. The District Court granted in part and denied in part the respondents' motion to dismiss the petitioners' claims and certified an order on its own initiative for interlocutory appeal to the Second Circuit Court of Appeals. A divided Second Circuit panel held as an issue of subject matter jurisdiction that no corporate liability exists under the ATS. After the Second Circuit's decision in *Kiobel,* the Seventh Circuit, Ninth Circuit, and DC Circuit each issued decisions in separate ATS cases, finding that corporations were proper defendants under the ATS. The Supreme Court granted certiorari to consider the issue of corporate liability. Following oral argument, the Court directed the parties to submit supplemental briefs on the question of "[w]hether and under what circumstances the [ATS] allows courts to recognize a cause of action for violations of the law of nations occurring within the territory of a sovereign other than the United States."

CHIEF JUSTICE JOHN ROBERTS

Passed as part of the *Judiciary Act* of 1789, the ATS was invoked twice in the late 18th century, but then only once more over the next 167 years... The statute provides district courts with jurisdiction to hear certain claims, but does not expressly provide any causes of action. We held in *Sosa v. Alvarez-Machain*, however, that the First Congress did not intend the provision to be "stillborn." The grant of jurisdiction is instead "best read as having been enacted on the understanding that the common law would provide a cause of action for [a] modest number of international law violations." We thus held that federal courts may "recognize private claims [for such violations] under federal common law." The Court in Sosa rejected the plaintiff's claim in that case for "arbitrary arrest and detention," on the ground that it failed to state a violation of the law of nations with the requisite "definite content and acceptance among civilized nations."

The question here is not whether petitioners have stated a proper claim under the ATS, but whether a claim may reach conduct occurring in the territory of a

continues

continued

foreign sovereign. Respondents contend that claims under the ATS do not, relying primarily on a canon of statutory interpretation known as the presumption against extraterritorial application. That canon provides that "[w]hen a statute gives no clear indication of an extraterritorial application, it has none," ... and reflects the "presumption that United States law governs domestically but does not rule the world, ..."

We typically apply the presumption to discern whether an Act of Congress regulating conduct applies abroad. See, e.g., *Aramco,* ("These cases present the issue whether Title VII applies extraterritorially to regulate the employment practices of United States employers who employ United States citizens abroad"); ... The ATS, on the other hand, is "strictly jurisdictional." It does not directly regulate conduct or afford relief. It instead allows federal courts to recognize certain causes of action based on sufficiently definite norms of international law. But we think the principles underlying the canon of interpretation similarly constrain courts considering causes of action that may be brought under the ATS.

Indeed, the danger of unwarranted judicial interference in the conduct of foreign policy is magnified in the context of the ATS, because the question is not what Congress has done but instead what courts may do. This Court in *Sosa* repeatedly stressed the need for judicial caution in considering which claims could be brought under the ATS, in light of foreign policy concerns. As the Court explained, "the potential [foreign policy] implications ... of recognizing ... causes [under the ATS] should make courts particularly wary of impinging on the discretion of the Legislative and Executive Branches in managing foreign affairs." ... These concerns, which are implicated in any case arising under the ATS, are all the more pressing when the question is whether a cause of action under the ATS reaches conduct within the territory of another sovereign ... .

Petitioners contend that even if the presumption applies, the text, history, and purposes of the ATS rebut it for causes of action brought under that statute... . But to rebut the presumption, the ATS would need to evince a "clear indication of extraterritoriality." It does not.

To begin, nothing in the text of the statute suggests that Congress intended causes of action recognized under it to have extraterritorial reach. The ATS covers actions by aliens for violations of the law of nations, but that does not imply extraterritorial reach—such violations affecting aliens can occur either within or outside the United States ... .

Petitioners make much of the fact that the ATS provides jurisdiction over civil actions for "torts" in violation of th elaw of nations... . For support, they cite the common-law doctrine that allowed courts to assume jurisdiction over such "transitory torts," including actions for personal injury, arising abroad ... .

Under the transitory torts doctrine, however, "the only justification for allowing a party to recover when the cause of action arose in another civilized jurisdiction is a well-founded belief that it was a cause of action in that place."... The question under *Sosa* is not whether a federal court has jurisdiction to entertain a cause of action provided by foreign or even international law. The question is instead whether the court has authority to recognize a cause of action under U.S. law to enforce a norm of international law. The reference to "tort" does not demonstrate that the First Congress "necessarily meant" for those causes of action to reach conduct in the territory of a foreign sovereign. In the end, nothing in the text of the ATS evinces the requisite clear indication of extraterritoriality.

Nor does the historical background against which the ATS was enacted overcome the presumption against application to conduct in the territory of another sovereign ... . We explained in *Sosa* that when Congress passed the ATS, "three principal offenses against the law of nations" had been identified by Blackstone: violation of safe conducts, infringement of the rights of ambassadors, and piracy. The first two offenses have no necessary extraterritorial application ... .

Two notorious episodes involving violations of the law of nations occurred in the United States shortly before passage of the ATS. Each concerned the rights of ambassadors, and each involved conduct within the Union. In 1784, a French adventurer verbally and physically assaulted Francis Barbe Marbois—the Secretary of the French Legion—in Philadelphia. The assault led the French Minister Plenipotentiary to lodge a formal protest with the Continental Congress and threaten to leave the country unless an adequate remedy were provided ... . And in 1787, a New York constable entered the Dutch Ambassador's house and arrested one of his domestic servants ... . At the request of Secretary of Foreign Affairs John Jay, the Mayor of New York City arrested the constable in turn, but cautioned that because "neither Congress nor our [State] Legislature have yet passed any act respecting a breach of the privileges of Ambassadors," the extent of any available relief would depend on the common law ... .

These prominent contemporary examples—immediately before and after passage of the ATS—provide no support for the proposition that Congress expected causes of action to be brought under the statute for violations of the law of nations occurring abroad.

The third example of a violation of the law of nations familiar to the Congress that enacted the ATS was piracy. Piracy typically occurs on the high seas, beyond the territorial jurisdiction of the United States or any

continues

continued

other country... . This Court has generally treated the high seas the same as foreign soil for purposes of the presumption against extraterritorial application... . Petitioners contend that because Congress surely intended the ATS to provide jurisdiction for actions against pirates, it necessarily anticipated the statute would apply to conduct occurring abroad.

Applying U.S. law to pirates, however, does not typically impose the sovereign will of the United States onto conduct occurring within the territorial jurisdiction of another sovereign, and therefore carries less direct foreign policy consequences. Pirates were fair game wherever found, by any nation, because they generally did not operate within any jurisdiction... . We do not think that the existence of a cause of action against them is a sufficient basis for concluding that other causes of action under the ATS reach conduct that does occur within the territory of another sovereign; pirates may well be a category unto themselves...

Finally, there is no indication that the ATS was passed to make the United States a uniquely hospitable forum for the enforcement of international norms. As Justice Story put it, "No nation has ever yet pretended to be the custosmorum of the whole world ... " It is implausible to suppose that the First Congress wanted their fledgling Republic—struggling to receive international recognition—to be the first. Indeed, the parties offer no evidence that any nation, meek or mighty, presumed to do such a thing.

* * *

We therefore conclude that the presumption against extraterritoriality applies to claims under the ATS, and that nothing in the statute rebuts that presumption. "[T]here is no clear indication of extraterritoriality here,"...

On these facts, all the relevant conduct took place outside the United States. And even where the claims touch and concern the territory of the United States, they must do so with sufficient force to displace the presumption against extraterritorial application... . Corporations are often present in many countries, and it would reach too far to say that mere corporate presence suffices. If Congress were to determine otherwise, a statute more specific than the ATS would be required.

Decision. The U.S. Supreme Court dismissed the case for failure to state a cause of action.

Case Questions

1. *Kiobel* limits the availability of ATS claims premised on overseas conduct, but the decision "leaves for another day the determination of just when the presumption against extraterritoriality might be 'overcome.'" Should multinational companies expect plaintiffs to continue asserting ATS claims premised on at least some U.S.-based conduct in connection with the underlying tort?
2. Do you think plaintiffs will try their chances with ATS claims against corporate defendants that have a more substantial connection to the United States than "mere presence" through an investment office, securities exchange listing, or the like?
3. *Kiobel* did not rule on the availability of aiding and abetting liability under the ATS. Do you think that ATS claims premised on indirect acts of "help[ing] others" to commit human rights abuses are likely to be recognized?

The lower courts will, on a case by case basis, rule on whether claims "touch and concern" the United States of America with "sufficient force" to "displace" the Court's presumption against extraterritoriality. Courts will probably continue to avoid foreign policy friction, something all justices wanted, and to apply "principles such as exhaustion, *forum non conveniens* ... comity," and deference to the Executive Branch to limit many of such claims. *Kiobel* will be a barrier to lawsuits against U.S. companies based on actions abroad. But if there is a U.S. nexus for the labor practice, a plaintiff can surmount the barrier.

Despite the significant limitations Kiobel imposes on ATS claims, the decision does not foreclose other avenues for human rights-related litigation that plaintiffs have pursued in recent years. In particular, plaintiffs can be expected to continue bringing common law tort claims in U.S. state courts, which already are the most common form of human rights-related action; claims under securities and racketeering-related laws; and lawsuits in non-U.S. courts. Nor does Kiobel limit the wide array of out-of-court tactics used by plaintiffs to severely tarnish a company's reputation and brand. As a result, multinational companies must remain vigilant in their efforts to root out human rights abuses throughout their operations.

There are other obstacles to litigation in the U.S. over extraterritorial acts. Courts have dismissed ATS claims under ***forum non conveniens*** grounds—that the U.S. court was not a convenient forum to hear the claim. In *Aldana v. Del Monte Fresh Produce N.A., Inc.*, 578 F.3d 1283 (11th Cir. 2009), the United States

Court of Appeals for the Eleventh Circuit affirmed the district court's dismissal of action under *forum non conveniens* grounds. Guatemalan labor unionists sued the owner of a Guatemalan banana plantation and a Delaware company with its principal place of business in Florida under the ATS and the *Torture Victim Protection Act*, claiming that the defendants participated in torture and other human rights violations in connection with a protracted labor dispute in Guatemala in 1999. The private interests that the Eleventh Circuit considered in affirming the district court's *forum non conveniens* dismissal included the relative ease of access to sources of proof, the ability to compel unwilling witnesses who are in Guatemala to appear, and other practical and logistical issues.

U.S. companies must carefully consider the working conditions that their operations in foreign countries support. As litigation under the ATS increases, more and more companies will consider taking a closer look at the foreign-based operations for any exposure to these types of lawsuits.

U.S. companies whose foreign operations use such practices may also face consumer boycotts in their markets. Labor organizations and other increasingly active opponents of dubious labor practices are identifying and targeting companies involved—directly or indirectly—in such practices. The threat of such protests has proved a potent incentive for investors to avoid them.

The developed nations are attempting to stop these labor practices through international trade treaties. Under these proposals, non-enforcement of employment standards would be a violation of international trade agreements, as are dumping or subsidies discussed in Chapte Ten. The United States has proposed amendments to the WTO trade rules that tie labor standards to international trade. These amendments were stalled, and the delegates decided that labor issues should instead be discussed in the context of the ILO, where discussion has not been particularly effective. In its effort, the United States has focused on providing a tool for enforcing ILO conventions on unsafe working conditions, minimum age for child labor, and forced labor, without addressing any issues on minimum wages. Developing nations cried foul, asserting that such standards would be misused by the developed world to bar their products from developed markets. Although this matter remains under intense negotiation, some nations have agreed to combat practices like child labor in order to secure trade deals with the United States.

The U.S. Congress has reacted to the stalled effort to tie labor standards to international trade by entertaining a unilateral expansion of its own trade laws. Under a proposed revision of Section 301 of the Trade Act of 1974—discussed in Chapter Eleven—the harsh Section 301 sanctions and retaliatory measures would be available if a U.S. firm could prove that an importer is violating an established set of labor standards. However, because such a measure is not addressed in the global trade rules, the passage of such a law might be viewed as a violation of the international trade agreement.

In October 1997, Congress passed the *Sanders Amendment*, which bans the import of any product made by forced child labor. In addition, Congress established the Child Labor Command Center, located at U.S. Customs headquarters, which acts as a clearinghouse for information and provides 24-hour "hotline" telephone service to a wide variety of audiences in order to provide a venue for allegations about prohibited importations. The initiative increases foreign staffing by assigning three additional special agents to areas where forced child labor is the most common. In addition, Customs is to engage in outreach programs with trade, government, and nongovernmental organizations to achieve successful enforcement of the Sanders Amendment.

Multinational corporations (MNCs) are showing they, too, can play a role. Many MNCs have developed international codes of conduct that can assist in improving labor standards and working conditions in their affiliates and subcontractors in host developing countries.

Some U.S. firms—of which Levi Strauss & Co., Nike, Intel, and Apple are particularly prominent—have instituted global "sourcing guidelines" or "codes of conduct" to determine with whom they will do business. Levi Strauss requires a certification from suppliers that they are in compliance with the guidelines. If Levi Strauss has reason to believe that a supplier or its subcontractors have violated one of these guidelines, it will investigate the matter. If it finds a violation, it will terminate its contract with the supplier. As a result of this program, Levi Strauss stopped manufacturing jeans in China in 1993. By April 1998, China had made sufficient concessions to human rights to permit Levi Strauss to return.

In 2005, Apple took similar steps to bring its suppliers in line with working conditions that were safe, were environmentally responsible, and promoted employee respect. The company conducted more than 312 audits over the next three years and trained more than a million workers about their rights and methods for injury and disease prevention. Apple has been sharply criticized for not doing more. However, the general goal of these MNCs, including Apple, is a commitment to establishing core labor standards. Such "sourcing guidelines" or "code of conduct" approaches, if adopted by more firms, would go a long way toward eradicating questionable working conditions.

CONCLUSION

Labor law poses particular difficulties for the U.S. investor due to markedly different attitudes toward employer–employee relations in other nations. Especially surprising are laws that require employee input into strategic decisions, prescribe employee representation on boards of directors, and place impediments on dismissals. The investor must also familiarize itself with different countries' approaches to employment discrimination and coordinate such approaches with U.S. requirements for such operations. Finally, the U.S. investor abroad should avoid companies that permit types of harsh work conditions that are illegal in the West. Such practices may come back to haunt the investor in his or her home jurisdiction through personal injury lawsuits and consumer boycotts.

Chapter Summary

1. Nations approach worker participation in corporate decision making differently. U.S. law gives great discretion to the owner of the enterprise, with no input from workers. Most European nations formally require worker input on corporate decisions and representation on boards of directors. In Japan's more collective system, there is not as much distinction between management and labor, because union officials are often promoted into management ranks.
2. Different countries have varying legal approaches to employee dismissal. In the United States, in the absence of a collective bargaining agreement or an employment agreement, company owners have near-total discretion to terminate employees. In Europe, dismissal of employees typically requires consultation with a works council or some employee group. In Japan, it can be very difficult to terminate an employee at all. However, as business has globalized, the approaches have tended to merge toward one another.
3. Employment discrimination law in many countries is less developed than that in the United States. Indeed, the greatest employment discrimination problem U.S. firms operating in some foreign countries face is that many countries, by custom, require employment discrimination. Thus, U.S. firms must determine when U.S. law might make illegal their compliance with foreign discriminatory norms.
4. Congress has provided that Title VII of the *Civil Rights Act* does not apply where it would violate the law of the country where the firm is located. However, courts have since interpreted both the *Age Discrimination in Employment Act* and the *Americans with Disabilities Act* to prohibit U.S. employers and foreign companies controlled by a U.S. employer from discriminating in employment of U.S. citizens in other countries. Courts have found that the same laws do not give rights to foreigners seeking work from U.S. entities. In other cases, discrimination laws have been found inapplicable to U.S. residents hired to work exclusively abroad. The law is unsettled in this area.
5. Courts have found and Congress has now provided that quite a number of other U.S. antidiscrimination laws do not apply outside the United States. These laws include the *National Labor Relations Act, the Occupational Safety and Health Act, the Fair Labor Standards Act, the Equal Pay Act, the Family and Medical Leave Act*, and other federal and state laws.
6. The three principal defenses to U.S. challenges of employment decisions are that (a) the decision is made by "a foreign person not controlled by an American employer;" (b) the U.S. law conflicts with a host country's laws, and therefore the employer faces "foreign compulsion" because to comply with U.S. law would violate the host country's laws; and (c) the performance of the job requires a trait such as a specific religion or gender, allowing the employer the "bona fide occupational qualification" defense.
7. The European Union now has a significant body of law prohibiting discrimination based on age, gender, and (as to nationals of other member states) national origin or ethnicity. Despite some study groups on th

question, there is not yet Community-wide protection for immigrants from other nations.

8. Unsafe working conditions, harsh work rules, forced/prison labor, and child labor are commonplace in less-developed countries. Because these practices create cost advantages and usually occur several levels away from the purchasers of these products in developed countries, they have not historically been a cause for private enterprise concern. Most advances in this area have resulted from government-to-government pressure.
9. In the *Kiobel* case, the United States Supreme Court held that a party could bring a suit under the *Alien Tort Statute* for violations of norms of of international law that do not "touch and concern" the United States. This means that foreign parties wronged by an American firm's use of proscribed practices in child labor, unduly harsh work rules, and the like can only win a judgment in a U.S. court if they can prove the existence and violation of an applicable international norm and that the violation touched and concerned the United States. This showing can be quite difficult to make, but it creates a significant issue for any international enterprise with significant operations in the United States. For example, if a U.S. firm knowingly participates in maintaining a work environment that violates international norms in a clothing plant dedicated for export to theUnited States, it may satisfy the test. *Kiobel* and its principles must now be developed by the lower courts.
10. Faced with the prospect of adverse publicity, potential liability, and dubious ethics, international companies are increasingly investigating their supply chains to ensure that their products or product components are not being manufactured through the use of ethically questionable practices.

Key Terms

Betriebsrat 533
Aufsichtsrat 533
Vorstand 533
expressio unis est exclusio alterius 540
foreign compulsion defense 542
bona fide occupational qualification (BFOQ) defense 542
Friendship, Commerce, and Navigation treaties 546
Hukou 547
foreign-invested enterprise (FIE) 550
Alien Tort Statute 555
forum non conveniens 557

Questions and Case Problems

1. Would a U.S. court override an employer's contractual rights (as the Supreme Court of Japan did) because of a countervailing "socially accepted view"? What if the employment contract was between a drug lord and his "trigger man"? Do you think that the relative homogeneity of a national culture affects the breadth of issues on which there is a "socially accepted view"?
2. Susan Currie is a U.S. manufacturer of tear gas, which she sells to various governments for crowd control. To reduce transportation costs to the interested governments, Ms. Currie is considering building a new plant in Germany. The plant will employ 2,500 people. What foreign labor law considerations should she take into account?

Managerial Implications

Your firm is Crystallina, a U.S. mineral water producer and distributor. A strong market for mineral water is South Moravia, a nation dominated by a fundamentalist state religion that prohibits drinking any alcohol or carbonated beverages. Market studies indicate that if Crystallina established offices in South Moravia, it would reap rich profits. However, if employees of a company like Crystallina violate South Moravian religious law, the company is liable for severe fines.

1. South Moravian religious law prohibits women from engaging in gainful employment. Accordingly, if Crystallina establishes an office there, it will not be able to offer any of

its women executives an opportunity to work there. What U.S. legal issues are raised for Crystallina? Should Crystallina establish an office in South Moravia?

2. Now assume that South Moravian religious law permits women to work, but strictly prohibits homosexual behavior of any kind. Accordingly, if Crystallina establishes an office there, it will not be able to offer any of its gay executives an opportunity to work there. Does this raise any U.S. legal issues for Crystallina? Should Crystallina establish an office in South Moravia?
3. Now assume that South Moravian religious law permits women to work and has no particular concern about private homosexual behavior, but it strictly prohibits Christian worship of any kind. Because Roman Catholics recognize a duty to worship on Sundays and holy days, if Crystallina establishes an office in South Moravia, it will not be able to offer any of its Catholic executives an opportunity to work there. What U.S. legal issues are raised for Crystallina? Should Crystallina establish an office in South Moravia?

Ethical Considerations

The *World Economic Forum's Global Gender Gap Index* examines the gap between men and women in four fundamental categories: economic participation and opportunity, educational attainment, political empowerment, and health. Economic participation and opportunity is captured through the difference in labor force participation rates, wage equality, the ratio of women to men among legislators, senior officials and managers, and the ratio of women to men among technical and professional workers. A high ranking indicates a smaller gap between men and women in economic participation and opportunity for women. Educational attainment is captured through ratios of women to men in primary-, secondary-, and tertiary-level education differences in literacy rates. A high ranking indicates a smaller gap between men and women in educational attainment. The political empowerment gap is captured through the ratios of women to men in minister-level, parliamentary, and executive positions in the past 50 years. A high ranking indicates a smaller gap between men and women in political empowerment. The health gap is measured through a comparison of life expectancies for men and women as reported by the World Health Organization and the sex ratio at birth. A high ranking indicates a smaller gap between men and women with respect to life expectancy and sex ratio at birth.

The following chart summarizes the top 20 and bottom 20 countries and the United States as ranked in the most recent *Global Gender Gap Index* (utilizing data from 2007).

Rank	State	Economics	Education	Politics	Health
1	Sweden	6	27	1	73
2	Norway	10	17	3	51
3	Finland	22	21	2	1
4	Iceland	23	67	4	95
5	New Zealand	8	19	9	67
6	Philippines	2	1	14	1
7	Germany	29	35	6	56
8	Denmark	18	1	13	96
9	Ireland	48	1	8	80
10	Spain	84	39	5	74
11	United Kingdom	32	1	12	67
12	Netherlands	49	44	11	70
13	Latvia	17	70	19	1
14	Lithuania	7	29	38	37
15	Sri Lanka	94	56	7	1
16	Croatia	40	61	18	37
17	Australia	12	1	35	71
18	Canada	13	26	36	51
19	Belgium	46	1	20	50
20	South Africa	85	52	10	65
31	United States	14	76	69	36
109	Qatar	115	45	124	123
110	Angola	87	119	92	1
111	Mauritania	108	114	74	1
112	Mali	33	126	75	98
113	Ethiopia	86	121	68	100
114	India	122	116	21	126
115	Bahrain	124	59	121	110
116	Cameroon	107	115	97	100
117	Burkina Faso	67	124	94	92
118	Iran	123	90	122	58
119	Oman	125	83	119	89
120	Egypt	120	101	123	83
121	Turkey	118	110	108	87
122	Morocco	121	113	103	84
123	Benin	102	125	81	65
124	Saudi Arabia	127	87	128	60
125	Nepal	114	122	83	117
126	Pakistan	126	123	43	121
127	Chad	58	128	102	60
128	Yemen	128	127	127	1

Do any of the results of the *Global Gender Gap Index* surprise you? Is there a correlation between the level of economic development in these states and the gender gap? Given these results, are differences in the treatment of women defensible on the basis of cultural relativism, which teaches that different societies have different moral codes and there is no objective standard that can be used to judge one moral code better than another? Why or why not?

CHAPTER 20

Environmental Law

Laws protecting the environment were once only briefly mentioned in a book about laws affecting foreign investments. However, in recent years, there has been extraordinary activity in international environmental law. There have been large-scale international environmental disasters, and concern over climate change has greatly intensified. "Green" political parties have formed around environmental issues. In some important nations, these parties have become part of governing coalitions. Consequently, nations have been furiously enacting legislation, investing in the development of alternative energy, and entering into treaties concerning the environment. Although this area of international law is not as well developed as other, centuries-old legal canons, its impact on commercial activity has become noteworthy.

CONSIDERATION OF VARYING ENVIRONMENTAL REQUIREMENTS

Virtually all human activity alters the environment in some way. The central problem of environmental law is determining which activities alter the environment to an unacceptable degree. Those determinations vary depending on the circumstances of the person making them. Cutting down huge forests is as acceptable to Brazilian pioneers as it was to the North American pioneers—such as Abraham Lincoln—who turned the virgin forests of Illinois and Indiana into the heart of the grain belt. In the twenty-first century, most North Americans find Brazilian tree cutting unacceptable, even though none have proposed a reforestation of Peoria.

All things being equal, most people favor a clean and aesthetic environment. But all things are not equal. Poorer nations tend to oppose extensive, international environmental regulation because it impairs their ability to profit from less-sophisticated production procedures. Wealthy countries tend to favor environmental protection, not only because they can afford to but also because they profit from it. Citizens of wealthy nations design and manufacture the sophisticated equipment that makes production pollution-free. Wealthy nations sometimes use environmental and health issues as a pretext for keeping price-competitive foreign competition at bay.

Understanding the reasons for differences in environmental views among nations is critical to understanding the dynamics of traditional and emerging legal remedies.

Differences in Regulatory Schemes

Differences in nations' circumstances and views lead to differences in their environmental laws. First, the cost-benefit analysis for any environmental modification often varies from country to country. A country with an opportunity to profit from a sulphur-belching power plant is more likely to think that the plant's modification of the environment is acceptable than a neighbor nation, which does not profit from the plant but suffers from its acid rain. Second, countries that are happy with the economic status quo are more inclined to favor environmental measures. Wealthy nations tend to have more laws to reduce pollution from industrial processes than countries plagued with malnutrition. Third, some nations lack the technological infrastructure to produce goods without pollution. In a strict economic sense, enacting a regulatory scheme that mandates buying such infrastructure greatly benefits wealthier nations, which manufacture and sell such equipment, and hampers less-developed nations that must spend scarce resources to purchase it. Finally, some governments permit officials to profit from environmental modifications. Thus, a nation may be lax in regulating hazardous waste disposal if the families of government officials greatly profit from the activity.

Obviously, many of these factors tend to place the wealthier, more-developed democracies on the side of international environmental regulation and the less-developed nations in opposition to such regulation. This dichotomy between the rich "North" and the poor "South" forms the principal dividing line in virtually all issues relating to international environmental law.

For foreign investors, these differences mean they may prefer to locate their facilities in countries with fewer environmental restrictions. A steel factory will cost millions less to build in South Korea than in the

United States, where sophisticated antipollution equipment is required. A hazardous waste dump is easier to locate in Ghana than in Germany because Germany has a more comprehensive legal framework protecting groundwater from such waste.

These incentives have not been lost on countries pursuing conservation. First, because nature does not recognize political boundaries, European nations' compliance with climate change treaties will not reverse the upward trend in temperatures if China and India vastly increase their productive capacity. Canada's laws against acid rain are not fully effective if its populous southern neighbor does not enact similar laws. Second, the environmental regulations of the conservation-minded nations will make their products more expensive, placing them at a competitive disadvantage vis-à-vis countries less concerned about the environment. To level the playing field, conservationists have sought legal relief through international dispute resolution, import bans, and multilateral treaties.

Foreign investors must consider the risk that the host country's less-restrictive environmental laws will be changed through international action. This risk can be substantial. Installing antipollution devices after a plant is built, for example, can be vastly more expensive than including them during construction. In many circumstances, the better choice for the risk-averse investor is to build on the assumption that local environmental laws will evolve to the standards of developed nations.

Environmental Law as an Anticompetitive Tool

"Environmentally responsible" nations are not without sin. Such nations often enact strict local environmental laws not so much to save the environment as to prevent foreign competition.

The European Union (EU) has been accused of doing this to protect its meat and dairy industries, which have been battered by foreign competition. In 1993, the EU traced an outbreak of hoof and mouth disease in Italian livestock to Croatia. Rather than banning Italian meat or Croatian meat, the Union banned meat from the entire former Eastern bloc. Needless to say, banning meat from half a continent on the basis of a disease outbreak in a region of one small nation—especially while not banning meat from the only country where the disease had actually occurred—struck many producers as unfair. However, Eastern bloc meat was cheaper. Similarly, members of the EU banned U.S. beef because many U.S. producers enhanced their livestock through bovine growth hormones. proof that the hormones had any adverse effect on the meat has not yet been shown. However, U.S. meat was demonstrably less expensive and more popular among European consumers.

Another, more recent example, where the United States suffered as a result of strict local environmental or health regulations involved the swine flu. A new variety of flu was detected in Mexico in the spring of 2009. Whether this flu originated in Mexico or the southwestern United States is unclear. On June 11, 2009, the World Health Organization (WHO) declared the A(H1N1) strain of swine flu the first worldwide pandemic in 41 years. In late June 2009, federal agriculture officials said they believed the pandemic emerged in pigs in Asia and then traveled to North America in a human. As the number of cases rose, the lethality of the strain fell far below original estimates.

The U.S. Department of Agriculture claimed that by calling the pandemic H1N1 influenza in humans "swine flu," the media caused undue and undeserved harm to the agriculture industry, especially pork producers. Despite statements from the World Organization for Animal Health (OIE), the United Nations' Food and Agriculture Organization, and the World Health Organization that pandemic H1N1 influenza is not transmitted by eating meat, a number of the United States' trading partners banned live pigs and pork or pork products after the initial outbreak of H1N1 in humans. By April 2009, Ukraine, St. Lucia, Indonesia, the United Arab Emirates, Thailand, Honduras, and Croatia had banned U.S. pork imports. Russia, China, and Kazakhstan also banned U.S. pork from certain states. U.S. exports of pork dropped 20 percent in the first half of 2009.

The United States has also been accused of using environmentally disguised trade barriers. The EU has complained of a variety of U.S. taxes and fines that they assert are disproportionately directed at European auto imports. In the mid-1990s, the United States enacted Corporate Average Fuel Efficiency (CAFE) standards and "gas-guzzler" surtaxes. These measures were ostensibly enacted to encourage fuel conservation and reduce air pollution. At the same time, the United States enacted a luxury tax on certain high-priced vehicles. The taxes nominally apply to domestic cars as well as European autos. Interestingly, European automakers pay about 90 percent of the combined gas-guzzler taxes, luxury taxes, and CAFE fines, although they hold only about 4 percent of the U.S. automobile market.

An amusing example of alleged "environmental" anticompetitive behavior occurred in the French resort town of Grenoble. The city's leaders banned Bermuda shorts in public pools and encouraged bathers to wear bikinis and other skimpy traditional French bathing suits. They argued that the added material in the Bermuda shorts polluted their pools. Interestingly, all Bermuda shorts were foreign made.

TRADITIONAL INTERNATIONAL REMEDIES

The Polluter Pays: Responsibility for Pollution

In the absence of an agreement, the only way a country may address its neighbor's environmental pollution is through the dispute resolution mechanisms available under international law. Binding adjudication has not been common because, in the absence of treaties such as those recently implemented with Europe, the alleged polluter would not consent to jurisdiction in such cases. An instance in which the alleged polluter did consent to arbitration involved a Uruguayan pulp mill on the River Uruguay, which forms the border between Uruguay and Argentina. In this case, the International Court of Justice (ICJ) concluded that Argentina had failed to establish environmental infractions under the relevant bilateral agreement.

Pending ICJ Matters

Since the institution of the *Pulp Mills* case in 2006, there have been several other cases brought before the ICJ cases involving environmental infractions.

In April 2008, Ecuador instituted proceedings against Colombia involving its aerial herbicide spraying along the Ecuadorian–Colombian border. For

Pulp Mills on the River Uruguay (Argentina v. Uruguay)

Apr. 20, 2010 International Court of Justice

BACKGROUND AND FACTS

On May 4, 2006, Argentina brought a complaint before the ICJ against Uruguay. Argentina alleged that Uruguay had breached obligations to provide notice to and consult with the Administrative Commission for the River Uruguay (CARU) before authorizing the construction of paper mills on the banks of the river. CARU is the body charged with regulating and coordinating bilateral issues affecting the river, including pollution prevention, and has an equal number of experts from Uruguay and Argentina. The reporting obligations and the duties of CARU are embodied in the *Statute of the River Uruguay*, a 1975 treaty between the two parties that has the goals of utilizing, conserving, and preventing pollution of the River Uruguay.

As a basis for the ICJ's jurisdiction, Argentina cited Article 60 of the 1975 treaty, which allows submission to the ICJ if the parties fail to settle the dispute through negotiations. Discussions between the presidents of the two countries and among members of a technical group had failed to resolve the issue in 2006.

Argentina alleged that the paper mills would release toxic air and liquid, resulting in damage to the ecosystem of the River Uruguay and risks to the health of more than 300,000 Argentine residents. Further, Argentina claimed that the mills would cause significant injury to the local Argentine economy, particularly to fisheries and tourism, because the mills were proposed to be located 25 kilometres from the Argentine tourist resort of Gualeguaychú.

Uruguay contended that, based on its environmental impact assessments, the proposed mills would not meet the threshold level of emissions to trigger notification requirements under the 1975 statute. The plan would consist of two brand-new eucalyptus pulp mills that would produce air-dried pulp for use in paper products. Uruguay conceded that the production process would rely on "elemental" chlorine-free technology, which, unlike totally chlorine-free technology, results in the emission of some dioxins, but argued this emission was of immaterial quantities.

In an intermediate decision in March 2007, the ICJ declined to exercise its power under Article 41 of the *Statute of the Court* to enter "provisional" measures pending resolution of the case, such as preventing operation of the pulp mills. The standard for exercising provisional measures is that there be an urgent necessity to prevent irreparable prejudice to the party seeking relief before the court rendered its final decision and the court found that standard had not been satisfied.

On April 20, 2010, the ICJ issued a judgment holding that Uruguay had violated its procedural obligations

continues

continued

under the 1975 statute by beginning construction on the mill before concluding negotiations with Argentina. With respect to Argentina's allegations of substantive treaty violations, however, the ICJ held that Uruguay had not breached its environmental duties. It rejected, among other claims, Argentina's contention that Uruguay had failed to "prevent pollution and preserve the aquatic environment." Judges Al-Khasawneh and Simma stated in dissent that the ICJ, in failing to appoint its own experts, had produced a methodologically flawed decision. They described the case as a "missed opportunity to cope with scientific uncertainty in a state-of-the-art manner" that would "increase doubts in the international legal community whether [the ICJ], as an institution, is well-placed to tackle complex scientific questions."

TOMKA, VICE PRESIDENT; JUDGES KOROMA, ABRAHAM, KEITH, SEPÚLVEDA-AMOR, BENNOUNA, SKOTNIKOV, CANÇADO TRINDADE, YUSUF, GREENWOOD; JUDGE AD HOC TORRESS BERNÁRDEZ

Having concluded that Uruguay breached its procedural obligations under the 1975 Statute ..., it is for the Court to draw the conclusions following from these internationally wrongful acts giving rise to Uruguay's international responsibility and to determine what that responsibility entails.

Argentina first requests the Court to find that Uruguay has violated the procedural obligations incumbent on it under the 1975 Statute and has thereby engaged its international responsibility. Argentina further requests the Court to order that Uruguay immediately cease these internationally wrongful acts.

The Court considers that its finding of wrongful conduct by Uruguay in respect of its procedural obligations per se constitutes a measure of satisfaction for Argentina. As Uruguay's breaches of the procedural obligations occurred in the past and have come to an end, there is no cause to order their cessation.

Argentina nevertheless argues that a finding of wrongfulness would be insufficient as reparation, even if the Court were to find that Uruguay has not breached any substantive obligation under the 1975 Statute but only some of its procedural obligations. Argentina maintains that the procedural obligations and substantive obligations laid down in the 1975 Statute are closely related and cannot be severed from one another for purposes of reparation, since undesirable effects of breaches of the former persist even after the breaches have ceased. Accordingly, Argentina contends that Uruguay is under an obligation to "re-establish on the ground and in legal terms the situation that existed before [the] internationally wrongful acts were committed." To this end, the Orion (Botnia) mill should be dismantled. According to Argentina, restitution in inte-grum is the primary form of reparation for internationally wrongful acts. Relying on Article 35 of the International Law Commission's *Articles on the Responsibility of States for Internationally Wrongful Acts*, Argentina maintains that restitution takes precedence over all other forms of reparation except where it is "materially impossible" or involves "a burden out of all proportion to the benefit of deriving from restitution instead of compensation." It asserts that the dismantling of the mill is not materially impossible and would not create for the Respondent State a burden out of all proportion ... .

Taking the view that the procedural obligations are distinct from the substantive obligations laid down in the 1975 statute ..., Uruguay maintains that restitution would not be an appropriate form of reparation if Uruguay is found responsible only for breaches of procedural regulations. Uruguay argues that the dismantling of the Orion (Botnia) mill would at any rate involve a "striking disproportion between the gravity of the consequences of the wrongful act of which it is accused and those of the remedy claimed". [...]

Like other forms of reparation, restitution must be appropriate to the injury suffered, taking into account the nature of the wrongful act having caused it. [...]

Decision. The ICJ found that Argentina's failure to consent to the project would not have "entail[ed] any ensuing prohibition" on Uruguay's decision to proceed with construction, and that Uruguay had not engaged in any substantive violations of its statutory duties. The ICJ denied Argentina's claim for reparations. It concluded that the parties would have an ongoing duty to cooperate in monitoring the environmental impact of the pulp mill.

Case Questions

1. The court found that Uruguay violated its procedural duties to provide notice and seek agreement with Argentina before launching on the project, and then it argued that it was disproportionate to dismantle the pulp mills as a remedy for its violation. Did Uruguay then benefit from proceeding with construction without seeking consent? How might Argentina have prevented this from happening?
2. Was Argentina able to show that Uruguay's new mills were polluting in violation of the treaty? What would have happened if Argentina had been able to prove that?
3. The court imposed a duty to cooperate in monitoring ongoing pollution. Did such a duty not already exist? What do you think will happen as a result of this future monitoring?

more than a decade, Colombia had been spraying the border with herbicides as part of the "Plan Colombia" initiative to mitigate the cocaine and heroin production in that area. Ecuador's complaint alleges that Colombia's herbicides had negatively affected Ecuadorian people, property, and environment, resulting in numerous reports of serious health problems, destruction of food crops, and irrevocable damage to surrounding wilderness areas, such as the contamination of surface water. Ecuador argues that Colombia's spraying is a breach of national sovereignty and demands compensation for its many losses. Most recently in 2011, the ICJ extended the time limit allotted to Colombia to file its rejoinder in this case.

On May 31, 2010, Australia brought a complaint against Japan for its continued pursuit of whaling under the Second Phase of its Japanese Whale Research Programme under Special Permit in the Antarctic (JARPA II). Australia alleges that Japan, which is making its first appearance before the ICJ in this matter, is in breach of its obligations under the *International Convention for the Regulation of Whaling* (ICRW) of 1946, as well as other responsibilities for the preservation of marine mammals and marine environment. Specifically, Australia argues that Japan is violating the zero catch limits in relation to the killing of whales for commercial purposes and is not acting in good faith by refraining from undertaking commercial whaling of humpback and fin whales in the Southern Ocean Sanctuary. Additionally, Australia alleges that Japan is in further violation of international environmental convention in its failure to ensure that activities under its jurisdiction and control do not cause damage to the environment of other states or areas beyond the limits of national jurisdiction. Australia asks that the Court require that Japan cease implementation of JARPA II; that it revoke any authorizations, permits, or licenses; and that it provide assurances that it will guarantee that any further action under JARPA II or similar programs be brought into conformity with international law.

In November 2011, Costa Rica filed a complaint against Nicaragua alleging that Nicaragua's Army felled trees and dredged the San Juan River from August through November 2010 to build a canal, resulting in the incursion into and occupation of Costa Rican territory; the infliction of serious damage to its protected rainforests and wetlands; intended damage to the Colorado River, wetlands, and protected ecosystems; and the dredging and canalization activities being carried out by Nicaragua on the San Juan River. In turn, Nicaragua argues that the activities undertaken were on Nicaraguan territory. In 2011, the ICJ ordered provisional measures by mandating that neither party maintain government personnel in the disputed territory, permitting Costa Rica to send civilian personnel to the disputed territory to protect the environment from potential irreparable harm, prohibiting both parties from engaging in activity that may further aggravate the dispute before the Court renders its final decision, and requiring both parties to inform the Court of their compliance.

All of these matters are still pending resolution and, if they do result in binding arbitration, may significantly boost the power of international tribunals to enforce international and regional environmental conventions. They will also help shape the extent that nations are responsible to their neighbors for environmental damage done to border areas. International environmental law could be on the brink of a breakthrough.

Regulation of Products That Violate Environmental Objectives

Because international binding arbitration of environmental disputes such as in the *Pulp Mills* case is rare and, as demonstrated in the preceding pending actions, often requires a period of years before resolution, a more frequent method for counterattack is for the conservation-minded nation to enact domestic legislation outlawing importation of the offending product. These regulations are imposed against a product for two reasons: because the product itself violates environmental norms in the regulating country, or because it is manufactured through a process that is environmentally objectionable.

This type of domestic counterattack is somewhat restricted by the General Agreement on Tariffs and Trade (GATT), but GATT restrictions do not prevent nations from excluding products that are environmentally offensive by their very nature. Thus, if meat or a bathing suit poses a health or other environmental threat under local standards, and local standards are applied in a nondiscriminatory way, GATT presents no difficulty. In the following case, the French government was allowed to keep out Canadian asbestos products on the grounds that a ban was necessary to protect human health.

As the following *EC-Asbestos* case demonstrates, states have a great deal of flexibility in excluding products that are contrary to local environmental standards. In fact, the flexibility is so great that nations at times misuse facially neutral standards—such as "no baggy swimsuits or Bermuda shorts"—to give preference to local products. But if nothing is wrong with the product itself, a country will have more difficulty excluding the product on an environmental basis.

European Communities—Measures Affecting Asbestos and Asbestos-Containing Products

5/AB/R40 (Feb. 16, 2001) WTO Appellate Body

BACKGROUND AND FACTS

Chrysotile asbestos poses significant risks to human health. It is generally recognized to cause lung cancer and other respiratory diseases. Nonetheless, because it has such favorable qualities as resistance to high temperatures, it has been used widely in many industries.

This case involved a ban on asbestos products instituted by the French government, which had previously been a large importer of chrysotile asbestos. The ban entered into force on January 1, 1997. Canada, as the second-largest asbestos producer in the world, challenged the prohibition in the WTO. It claimed that the French ban violated several articles of the GATT in addition to the Agreement on Technical Barriers to Trade (TBT Agreement), which ensures that domestic product standards and regulations do not create unnecessary trade barriers. The EC contended that the ban was necessary to protect both workers subject to prolonged asbestos exposure and members of the general population who could be subject to occasional exposure, and that it was therefore permissible under GATT Article XX(b). Article XX(b) allows domestic measures that affect foreign products if those measures are "necessary to protect human, animal or plant life or health."

The WTO Panel concluded that the banned asbestos products and the domestic products used to replace them were "like products." The French ban was accordingly determined to be discriminatory under GATT Article III. The Panel concluded, however, that the ban was justified under Article XX(b). The Panel also found that the TBT Agreement did not apply. Canada appealed the Panel's decision.

In reading the following excerpt from the Appellate Body report, note that both the Panel and the Appellate Body confirmed France's ability to implement measures to exclude a harmful product, albeit on different grounds.

MESSRS. FELICIANO, BACCHUS, EHLERMANN

[I]t is undisputed that WTO Members have the right to determine the level of protection of health that they consider appropriate in a given situation. France has determined, and the Panel accepted, that the chosen level of health protection by France is a "halt" to the spread of asbestos-related health risks. By prohibiting all forms of amphibole asbestos, and by severely restricting the use of chrysotile asbestos, the measure at issue is clearly designed and apt to achieve that level of health protection. Our conclusion is not altered by the fact that PCG fibres might pose a risk to health. The scientific evidence before the Panel indicated that the risk posed by the PCG fibres is, in any case, less than the risk posed by chrysotile asbestos fibres, although that evidence did not indicate that the risk posed by PCG fibres is non-existent. Accordingly, it seems to us perfectly legitimate for a Member to seek to halt the spread of a highly risky product while allowing the use of a less risky product in its place... .

... Canada asserts that the Panel erred in finding that "controlled use" is not a reasonably available alternative to the Decree ... . The remaining question, then, is whether there is an alternative measure that would achieve the same end and that is less restrictive of trade than a prohibition. Canada asserts that "controlled use" represents a "reasonably available" measure that would serve the same end. The issue is, thus, whether France could reasonably be expected to employ "controlled use" practices to achieve its chosen level of health protection—a halt in the spread of asbestos-related health risks.l

In our view, France could not reasonably be expected to employ *any* alternative measure if that measure would involve a continuation of the very risk that the Decree seeks to "halt." Such an alternative measure would, in effect, prevent France from achieving its chosen level of health protection. On the basis of the scientific evidence before it, the Panel found that, in general, the efficacy of "controlled use" remains to be demonstrated. Moreover, even in cases where "controlled use" practices are applied "with greater certainty," the scientific evidence suggests that the level of exposure can, in some circumstances, still be high enough for there to be a "significant residual risk of

continues

continued

developing asbestos-related diseases." The Panel found too that the efficacy of "controlled use" is particularly doubtful for the building industry and for DIY enthusiasts, which are the most important users of cement-based products containing chrysotile asbestos. Given these factual findings by the Panel, we believe that "controlled use" would not allow France to achieve its chosen level of health protection by halting the spread of asbestos-related health risks. "Controlled use" would, thus, not be an alternative measure that would achieve the end sought by France.

Decision. The Appellate Body concluded that there was no "reasonably available alternative" to France's chosen method of preventing asbestos-caused harm. It upheld the Panel's finding that France had acted consistently with international trade law.

Case Questions

1. Was there any question that France's ban would have a discriminatory impact on Canadian asbestos products?
2. If France's ban had been based on grounds other than protecting the health of French residents, would it have been upheld? Do nations have greater discretion to discriminate against foreign products if they base the discrimination on health concerns?
3. How would the Appellate Body have been perceived if it compelled France to accept products that its democratically elected government deemed unhealthy? Do you think that this judicial rule might be partially based on the tribunal's desire to preserve its legitimacy?

Regulation of Products with Environmentally Objectionable Production Processes

The *EC-Asbestos* case is an example of a trade restriction based on a threat to the environment inherent in a product itself—asbestos contamination posing a threat to human health. However, the environment is more frequently injured by the process used to make a particular product. Nothing about finished steel is environmentally harmful. But if the plant that manufactures the steel has no pollution-control devices, the plant will destroy the ecosystems in bodies of water surrounding it, darken the atmosphere, and contribute to acid rain. In *EC-Asbestos,* Articles III and XX of GATT were interpreted to allow highly discriminatory restrictions if a foreign product threatened the environment or human health. Ironically, the GATT has also been interpreted to *forbid* discriminatory restrictions if they target an environmentally offensive process used to create the product, unless the proscribing party is flexible in the application of standards, as shown in the following case.

United States—Import Prohibition of Certain Shrimp and Shrimp Products Recourse to Article 21.5 of the DSU by Malaysia

WT/DS58/AB/RW (Oct. 21, 2001) WTO Appellate Body

BACKGROUND AND FACTS

To protect endangered sea turtle populations from further decline by reducing their incidental mortality in commercial shrimp trawling, U.S. commercial shrimp trawlers are required to use Turtle Excluder Devices (TEDs) approved in accordance with standards established by the U.S. National Marine Fisheries Service. In 1989, the U.S. Congress enacted Section 609 of *Public Law 101-162*, under which the Department of State was to certify whether nations that export shrimp to the United States had adopted programs to reduce the incidental capture of sea turtles in their shrimp fisheries that were comparable to the program in effect in the United States. If the State Department did not certify a nation, that nation would be banned from exporting shrimp to the United States. In practice, the State Department effectively required that other countries adopt a TED requirement. In 1998, the WTO Appellate Body found the U.S. measure to be a forbidden prohibition on imports that was not justified under Article XX(b)'s exception for measures taken to protect animal life "not applied in a manner which would constitute a means of arbitrary or unjustifiable discrimination between countries." In essence, the Appellate Body found that the United States' de facto insistence on a U.S. excluder device was "unjustifiable discrimination" and therefore recommended that the United States bring Section 609 into conformity with the GATT.

continues

continued

Congress did nothing to the law, but the State Department revised the guidelines it used in enforcing the law. Where the government of a harvesting country requested certification based on its having adopted a program based on TEDs, the Department of State was to issue it so long as the program included a requirement that commercial shrimp trawlers use TEDs "comparable in effectiveness" to those used in the United States. The program also had to include a credible enforcement effort that included monitoring for compliance.

In May 1998, the State Department certified that 16 nations had indeed adopted such programs. It also certified that the fishing environments in 23 other countries did not pose a threat of the incidental taking of sea turtles protected under Section 609. Under Section 609, shrimp imports from any nation not certified were prohibited effective May 1, 1998.

Malaysia was not certified and challenged the revised procedure. The WTO panel ruled that, as enforced under the revised State Department guidelines, Section 609 no longer constituted an "unjustified discrimination." Malaysia appealed to the WTO Appellate Body.

CHAIRMAN BACCHUS AND MESSRS. GANESAN AND LACARTE-MURÓ

In 2000, Malaysia informed the [WTO Dispute Settlement Body] DSB that it was not satisfied that the United States had complied with the recommendations and rulings of the DSB, and announced that it wished to seek recourse to a panel ... .

[In this appeal, the] issue was whether the Panel had erred in finding that the measure at issue was now applied in a manner that no longer constituted a means of "arbitrary or unjustifiable discrimination between countries where the same conditions prevail" and was, therefore, within the scope of measures permitted under Article XX of the GATT 1994. To answer this question, the Appellate Body analyzed (1) the nature and extent of the duty of the United States to pursue international cooperation in the protection and conservation of sea turtles and (2) the flexibility of the Revised Guidelines. Regarding the issue of international cooperation, the Panel reached the conclusion that the United States had an obligation to make serious good faith efforts to reach an agreement before resorting to the type of unilateral measure currently in place.

> ... whereas subject to the requirement that such measures are not applied in a manner which would constitute a means of arbitrary or unjustifiable discrimination between countries where the same conditions prevail, or a disguised restriction on international trade, nothing in this Agreement shall be construed to prevent the adoption or enforcement by any contracting party of measures: ...

The Appellate Body also mentioned its conclusion in the *United States—Shrimp* case that the United States had to provide all exporting countries "similar opportunities to negotiate" an international agreement to avoid "arbitrary or unjustifiable discrimination." ... With respect to that measure, the United States could conceivably respect that obligation, and the conclusion of an international agreement might nevertheless not be possible despite the serious, good faith efforts of the United States. Requiring that a multilateral agreement be concluded by the United States in order to avoid "arbitrary or unjustifiable discrimination" in applying its measure would mean that any country party to the negotiations with the United States, whether a WTO Member or not, would have, in effect, a veto over whether the United States could fulfill its WTO obligations. Such a requirement would not be reasonable. The Appellate Body concluded that the United States could not be held to have engaged in "arbitrary or unjustifiable discrimination" under Article XX solely because one international negotiation resulted in an agreement while another did not. The Appellate Body upholds the Panel's finding ... .

Afterwards, the Appellate Body turned to the analysis of the next issue, the flexibility of the Revised Guidelines. Malaysia claimed that the United States unilaterally imposed its domestic standards on exporters. Moreover, Malaysia disagreed with the Panel that a measure could meet the requirements of the chapeau of Article XX if it would be flexible enough, both in design and application, to permit certification of an exporting country with a sea turtle protection and conservation programme comparable to that of the United States. The Appellate Body stated that "conditioning access to a Member's domestic market on whether exporting Members comply with, or adopt, a policy or policies unilaterally prescribed by the importing Member may, to some degree, be a common aspect of measures falling within the scope of one or another of the exceptions (a) to (j) of Article XX." However, a separate question arises, when examining under the chapeau of Article XX, a measure that provides for access to the market of one WTO Member for a product of other WTO Members conditionally.

In *United States—Shrimp,* the Appellate Body concluded that the measure at issue there did not meet the requirements of the chapeau of Article XX relating to "arbitrary or unjustifiable discrimination" because, through the application of the measure, the exporting members were faced with "a single, rigid and unbending requirement to adopt essentially the same policies and enforcement practices as those applied to, and enforced on, domestic shrimp trawlers in the United States." In this dispute, on the other hand, the

continued

Panel found that the new measure is more flexible than the original measure and had been applied more flexibly than was the original measure. The new measure, in design and application, did not condition access to the United States market on the adoption by an exporting Member of a regulatory programme aimed at the protection and the conservation of sea turtles that was essentially the same as that of the United States.

The Appellate Body noted that the Revised Guidelines contained provisions that permitted the United States authorities to take into account the specific conditions of Malaysian shrimp production, and of the Malaysian sea turtle conservation programme, should Malaysia decide to apply for certification. It concluded that the provisions of the Revised Guidelines, on their face, permitted a degree of flexibility that would enable the United States to consider the particular conditions prevailing in Malaysia if, and when, Malaysia applied for certification.

Decision. The Appellate Body upheld the finding of the Panel and therefore made no recommendations to the DSB with respect to Section 609.

Case Questions

1. The United States had to change its original regulation regarding the preservation of turtles. How does this compare to the treatment given to France's law on asbestos? Do nations have more discretion in discriminating to protect human health within their borders than animal species around the world?
2. What changes in the new regulations made them acceptable "discrimination"?
3. Can a large market such as the United States change environmental policy throughout the world using measures like this? Why? Is it antidemocratic to have the United States impose its policies on other nations through its bargaining power?

As the *Shrimp* case shows, the WTO Appellate Body is quite tolerant of a nation that attempts to force foreign producers to comply with the same environmentally conscious procedures as are required within the nation, so long as the importing nation is flexible in accepting other nations' approaches to achieving the same environmental objective. But when a nation attempts to create different standards for foreign parties, the WTO can be very demanding. For example, in the famous *Reformulated and Conventional Gasoline* case, the WTO found that an anti-air pollution regulation that placed fuel standards on automobiles violated GATT because it allowed domestic car manufacturers to comply with a "baseline" of their own performance, while forcing foreign manufacturers to judge performance off industry averages, which may be well below their own. Anti-pollution laws must not distinguish solely on the basis of national origin.

Litigation Against Polluters in an Affected Country. If the polluting foreign investor is subject to the jurisdiction of the conservationist nation's courts, it might be hauled into court there. This scenario is quite possible where the pollution directly affects the territory of the conservationist nation.

An interesting classic example involves international emissions from a nuclear plant. The Supreme Court of Austria held that Austrian landowners could sue the former Czechoslovakia in Austrian courts for the environmental effects of such emissions. Note especially the court's reliance on the absence of a valid claim under Czech law.

Judgment of February 23, 1988

39 Österreichische Zeitschrift für Öffentliches Recht und Völkerrecht 360 Supreme Court of Austria

BACKGROUND AND FACTS

The plaintiff, an owner of real estate in Austria near the former Czechoslovakia, brought action in Austrian courts seeking to prevent the construction of a nuclear power plant 115 kilometers away in Czechoslovakia. The plaintiff alleged that the plant had not been properly licensed and that the effects of radionuclides generated during the plant's normal operation, as well as those that would be released in a nuclear accident, threatened his real estate. The plaintiff alleged that the plant could not operate without emitting radioactive-contaminated water vapor and excessive warmth.

continues

continued

The Court of First Instance denied the plaintiff's claim, holding that it lacked ***jurisdiction ratione loci****—geographic jurisdiction over the matter. On appeal, the Court of Second Instance affirmed the lower court decision. The Oberste Gerichtshof (Supreme Court) of Austria, however, disagreed with the courts below it.*

PER CURIAM

The Court of First Instance—affirmed by the Court of Second Instance—has disavowed its [own] *jurisdiction ratione loci* ... but the Supreme Court is of the opinion that [the statute governing venue of claims related to real estate] also provides *jurisdiction ratione loci* for Austrian courts over claims ... of real estate owners affected by emissions [of a foreign state]. No treaty rules exist in the case in question with respect to Czechoslovakia.

It is unreasonable to require the claimant to pursue legal proceedings in Czechoslovakia, which obviously are not possible because there the problem under consideration is treated as a public law problem and acts ***jure imperii*** [official acts] cannot give rise to civil law obligations. This view is not consistent with Austrian law [under which] foreign states can be sued for acts ***jure gestionis*** [commercial activity] before courts [of another state]; and the question whether acts of the state are acts jure imperii or jure gestionis is not to be determined by the national law in question but according to general international law. Under such international law, the construction and the operation of a ... plant for the generation of electricity are not within the scope of jure imperii, but are jure gestionis and therefore not excluded from the national [Austrian] jurisdiction ... .

It cannot be said that legal proceedings in Austria would only lead to a judgment which is not enforceable and therefore would only have academic, and not protective, importance; although in the absence of a treaty on execution of judgments with the state in question, an execution of the judgment would presumably not be possible in Czechoslovakia, the pecuniary penalties imposed to enforce the claim ... could probably be enforced in Austria and a violation by the defendant of the restraining order of a court could be a legal ground for possible claims of damages by the plaintiff.

As all conditions for Austrian jurisdiction exist but the *jurisdiction ratione loci* has been rejected by the court which would have been competent according to [Austrian law], the Supreme Court ... is competent to designate a Court of First Instance as the court having *jurisdiction ratione loci* in this case.

Decision. The Supreme Court of Austria reversed the finding of the Court of Second Instance that Austrian courts lacked jurisdiction over the plaintiff's claim. It remanded the matter to the trial court where the plaintiff's real estate was situated for further litigation.

Case Questions

1. What is the major difference between this case and the *Pulp Mills* case?
2. How did the Austrian court justify taking jurisdiction over a matter more than 100 kilometers inside the territory of another country?
3. If an Austrian court issues a judgment and the Czech party refuses to comply, how do you think that the plaintiff will seek to enforce the judgment?

Litigation Against Polluters in Polluter's Home. Another traditional approach to obtaining relief against a polluter is to sue it in its home jurisdiction. In many countries, this approach is not practical. The local judges would be disinclined to rule against a significant local enterprise. Even in a neutral forum, such a suit can still run into significant difficulties.

In the United States, the *Alien Tort Claims Act* (ATCA), discussed in Chapter Nineteen, had been interpreted to provide non-U.S. citizens with the ability to sue U.S. companies that cause environmental damage abroad. As noted in Chapter Nineteen, however, in the *Kiobel v. Royal Dutch Petroleum Co.* case which the U.S. Supreme Court handed down in April 2013, such suits were limited to those with claims that "touch and concern" the United States with "sufficient force" to "displace" the presumption against extraterritoriality. Over the next few years the federal courts will develop the meaning of *Kiobel* in environmental cases as plaintiffs try to show that their complaints "touch and concern" the United States.

An approach centered on the jurisdiction of U.S. courts may be effective against U.S. companies, but it seems ultimately doomed to be ineffective because it cannot provide relief if none of the acts relating to environmentally suspect behavior occurred in the United States or sufficiently "touch and concern" the United States. A U.S. investor could, for example, ensure that all discussion relating to a specific polluting project take place in the country with the most forgiving environmental laws. For an approach to be effective in furthering conservation, therefore, it needs to be multinational in scope.

Inadequacies of the Traditional International Pollution-Control System

Existing international remedies can be effective in specific instances, but they are unlikely to be effective in transforming the international environmental legal system. International arbitration can proceed only if both parties have consented. Such consent is infrequent in the environmental context, because a nation usually does not voluntarily subject itself to a proceeding about pollution generated on its own territory.

As we have seen, trade sanctions must be couched in product defects. However, most environmental damage is caused by manufacturing processes and, as illustrated in the *Import Prohibition of Certain Shrimp and Shrimp Products* decision, such processes are largely exempt from regulation under GATT. Litigation in the affected conservationist nation can be effective against investors, but the affected nation must be sufficiently close to suffer a direct physical adverse effect. Litigation in the polluter's home country can be circumvented by having all actions and decisions occur in the less conscientious nation. Accordingly, new approaches are being pursued to address the problem of global pollution.

EMERGING PROBLEMS AND SOLUTIONS

In light of the perceived shortcomings of traditional legal methodologies for addressing environmental controversies, environmentalists have been developing regional and global solutions. This section surveys a representative group of the more important of these approaches.

Regional Approaches

The most common regional approach to environmental protection is in national environmental regulations of exports. Even if GATT constrains a nation from excluding imports created in environmentally suspect ways, the nation can regulate its exports. The U.S. law relating to the export of environmentally hazardous materials is an excellent case in point.

National Constraints on Exports. The cornerstone of U.S. environmental regulation of the export of hazardous materials is the principle of **prior informed consent (PIC)**. The export of pesticides, for example, is regulated by the U.S. Environmental Protection Agency (EPA) under the *Federal Insecticide, Fungicide, and Rodenticide Act* (FIFRA). FIFRA requires that before a U.S. seller can export pesticides that are not registered for use in the United States, it must obtain the PIC of the purchaser and give notice to the appropriate official in the receiving country. The restrictions of the *Resource Conservation and Recovery Act* (RCRA) are even more demanding on the export of hazardous waste. RCRA requires the exporter to provide notice to the EPA of any forthcoming shipment. Then, the government of the receiving country must expressly accept the shipment and provide written notice to the EPA of that consent. Special manifest requirements apply to the shipment, and the exporter has annual reporting obligations to the EPA.

U.S. legislation also seeks to ensure that the foreign government's consent is thoroughly informed. The *Toxic Substances Control Act* (TSCA) imposes reporting and record-keeping requirements on all chemical substances. In international transactions, TSCA requires exporters to notify the EPA of the export of any chemical or article containing a chemical that is or has been subject to testing under the statute. The EPA must then notify the foreign government of the EPA action with respect to the chemical.

The United States has many laws regulating pesticide use within its borders, but no law exists that forbids manufacturers from exporting banned pesticides to countries with less stringent or poorly enforced laws. This creates the so-called **Circle of Poison**. U.S.-banned pesticides are exported to developing nations and are used on crops, which are then exported back to the United States. These pesticides then reenter the United States as residues on food products.

Because it dramatized the inherent inadequacy of domestic legislation, the Circle of Poison problem motivated the developed world to seek global solutions to the international distribution of toxins. As discussed later, nations are now turning to international treaties.

In certain substantive areas, national legislation—even in a nation as large as the United States—has virtually no effect. For most environmental issues, global and regional problems require multinational solutions.

North American Environmental Treaties. In North America, progress toward common environmental standards has been made through bilateral treaties and the North American Free Trade Agreement (NAFTA). NAFTA's Environmental Side Agreements established the North American **Commission for Environmental Cooperation** (CEC), headquartered in Montreal. Although the North American Free Trade Commission normally considers all trade disputes, including disputes with environmental implications, the CEC determines whether any party to NAFTA has shown a "persistent pattern of failure" to "effectively enforce its environmental law." The CEC indicates these findings in *Factual Records*. In 2007, the CEC released a *Factual Record* on allegations that Canada was failing in its enforcement of pollution provisions of the *Fisheries Act* and provisions of the *Pulp Paper Effluent Regulations* (PPER). A finding of a pattern of failure can result in a broad range of sanctions, including suspension of NAFTA benefits. Thus, nongovernmental organizations now have an international forum to challenge the anticonservation activities of the three signatory governments (Canada, Mexico, and the United States). The following case discusses the requirements in one such challenge.

Under NAFTA, the United States, Canada, and Mexico also agreed to finance jointly a variety of border wastewater and water pollution projects. Further, NAFTA creates permanent committees for Standards-Related Measures and for Sanitary and Phytosanitary Measures to harmonize the environmental laws of the three nations. The objectives of these efforts, together with the CEC, are to convert such regulation into acceptable standards in NAFTA countries and ultimately to remove such standards as an impediment to trade.

Skeena River Fishery: Canada

Determination of Submission SEM 09-005 (Oct. 15, 2009) Secretariat of the North American Commission for Environmental Cooperation

BACKGROUND AND FACTS

The Submitter, North Coast Steelhead Alliance (NCSA), filed a submission on enforcement matters pursuant to Articles 14 and 15 of the North American Agreement on Environmental Cooperation (NAAEC or Agreement) with the Secretariat of the North American Commission for Environmental Cooperation. NCSA alleged that the Canadian Department of Fisheries and Oceans (DFO) was failing to effectively enforce its environmental laws in relation to commercial fishing licenses for salmon in the Skeena River, on the north coast of British Columbia. DEO was accused of allowing commercial salmon fishers to ignore license conditions aimed at protecting steelhead trout caught as "by-catch." The license conditions at issue included:

- having operating revival tanks on board while fishing;
- sorting, reviving and releasing non-target species with the least possible harm;
- not taking steelhead prohibited at any time;
- the taking and possession of chum, coho, and Chinook salmon only at certain specified times.

NCSA asserted in its submission that "effective enforcement of the commercial gill-net licenses and seine-net licenses is necessary to protect the health and biodiversity of the species these environmental laws are intended to protect" and concluded that "reduced fish stocks are a result of non-enforcement of license conditions." It asserted further that non-enforcement harms "the entire ecosystem, including people, other species of fish and their habitat."

MARION, LEGAL OFFICER, SUBMISSIONS ON ENFORCEMENT MATTERS UNIT ANALYSIS

NAAEC Article 14 authorizes the Secretariat to "consider a submission from any non-governmental organization or person asserting that a Party is failing to effectively enforce its environmental law ... ."

A. Opening Paragraph of Article 14(1) The Secretariat will now treat each component of NAAEC Article 14(1) in turn. Article 45(1) defines "nongovernmental organization." The Submitter, the North Coast Steelhead Alliance, represents itself as a nonprofit organization ... . The Submitter also represents itself as a non-governmental organization. The Submitter thus appears to meet the definition of "non-governmental" set out in Article 45(1) of NAAEC: its organization is a non-profit and a non-governmental organization and it does not appear to be affiliated with, nor is it under the direction of, any government.

[T]he Secretariat now considers whether the assertions relate to an "ongoing" alleged failure to effectively enforce environmental law. The Secretariat notes that the asserted failures to effectively enforce are best documented with regard to commercial gill-net and seine-net licenses issued in 2006, but these assertions

continues

continued

of failures to effectively enforce the laws at issue also appear to extend from at least 2005 to the time of the Submission. The Submitter also provides 2000–2007 commercial harvest data and the Party's own compliance and enforcement ("C&E") summaries for the latter years, as well as C&E sections of DFO's 2007 and 2008 post-season reviews.

It appears from the latter information, and from other information provided in the Appendices to the Submission, that the Party increased enforcement efforts in 2007 and 2008 as compared to 2006: it raised patrol hours and issued warnings and laid charges for violations of license conditions... . However, it is not entirely clear from the data provided how this evidence of increased enforcement efforts directly concerns the area in which the Submitter asserts that the laws at issue are not being effectively enforced. It also appears that the assertions alleging violations of license conditions with regard to vessels having operating revival boxes on board, and non-target fish being released with the least harm, cover a period prior to 2006 as well, and such assertions also appear to concern an ongoing situation in 2008, despite the increased enforcement efforts. Moreover, assertions of harmful effects of enforcement efforts which disproportionately target aboriginal and recreational fishers, rather than commercial fishers, concern an ongoing situation at the time of the Submission. For these reasons, the Secretariat considers that the assertions in the Submission meet the temporal requirement in the opening paragraph of Article 14(1)... .

The Secretariat now examines whether, first, the laws at issue in the Submission constitute "environmental law" and, secondly, whether the assertions allege a failure to "effectively enforce" such environmental law.

The environmental laws at issue

> "[E]nvironmental law" means any statute or regulation of a Party, or provision thereof, the primary purpose of which is the protection of the environment, or the prevention of a danger to human life or health, through ... (iii) the protection of wild flora or fauna, including endangered species, their habitat, and specially protected natural areas in the Party's territory, but does not include any statute or regulation, or provision thereof, directly related to worker safety or health.

Section 22(1) FGR provides for the authority of the Minister to set conditions on fishing licenses for the purpose of the conservation and protection of fish ... .

Section 22(2) FGR provides for the authority of the Minister to amend a license for the purposes of conservation and protection of fish ... .

[The Secretariat found that the laws at issue were "environmental laws" for the purpose of the NAAEC.]

Assertions on the failure to effectively enforce

The Secretariat now analyzes whether the assertions in Submission SEM-09-005 concern alleged failures of the "effective enforcement" of environmental laws, in accordance with the opening paragraph of NAAEC Article 14(1). The Secretariat has consistently interpreted Article 14(1) to exclude any assertions alleging a deficiency in the law itself. The Secretariat considers that the Submission as a whole does assert failures of effective enforcement of the Party's environmental laws, rather than deficiencies in the laws themselves.

The Secretariat finds the Submission meets the criterion of NAAEC Article 14(1) ... .;

> *(d) the Submission: "appears to be aimed at promoting enforcement rather than at harassing industry ... ."*

The Secretariat, on the basis of the information currently before it, considers that the Submission satisfies the requirements of Article 14(1)(d), as the Submission appears to be aimed at promoting enforcement of the laws at issue rather than at harassing industry. In making this determination, the Secretariat notes that the Submission is in part concerned with what the Submitter alleges is a disproportionate enforcement effort targeting recreational fishers. However, the Submitter also analyzes comparative data on enforcement efforts by DFO officials concerning commercial, recreational and aboriginal fishing licenses alike for 2006, 2007 and 2008 ... . It is not evident from the information before the Secretariat that the Submitter is in a competitive relationship with commercial licensees mentioned in the Submission, or that the Submitter is a competitor who could stand to benefit economically from the Submission.

> *(f) the Submission: "... is filed by a person or organization residing or established in the territory of a Party."*

Finally, the Secretariat considers whether the Submission was filed by a person or organization residing in or established in the territory of a Party. The Submitter reports its address as being in Hazelton, British Columbia, Canada.

B. Article 14(2) Factors ... Having determined in the preceding section that the Submission indeed meets the requirements of NAAEC Article 14(1), the Secretariat will now review the Submission under NAAEC Article 14(2), in order to determine whether the Secretariat should request a response to the Submission from the Party ... .

continued

NAAEC Article 14(2) provides that:

In deciding whether to request a response, the Secretariat shall be guided by whether:

(a) the Submission alleges harm to the person or organization making the Submission;
(b) the Submission, alone or in combination with other Submissions, raises matters whose further study in this process would advance the goals of this Agreement;
(c) private remedies available under the Party's law have been pursued; and
(d) the Submission is drawn exclusively from mass media reports.

(a) "the Submission alleges harm to the person or organization making the Submission"

First, the Secretariat examines whether the Submission alleges harm to the person or organization making the Submission under Article 14(2)(a). Following Guideline 7.4(a) and (b), the Secretariat further considers whether the alleged harm, according to the Submitter, is due to the asserted failure to effectively enforce the law, and whether the alleged harm relates to the protection of the environment. The Submitter states that it is "a non-governmental environmental organization whose members include individuals and other organizations that have a shared interest in the conservation and protection of Skeena salmonids, especially Skeena steelhead." The Submitter claims that its members make use of these fisheries, and it alleges that any "reduced viability of fish stocks harms (Article 14.2(a)) the entire ecosystem, including people, other species of fish and their habitat." The Submitter also asserts that Canada is failing to effectively enforce the *Fisheries Act "by* allowing marine commercial salmon fishers on the North Coast of British Columbia, Canada, to ignore licence conditions aimed at protecting and conserving certain kinds of fish, mainly steelhead trout, that are caught as 'by-catch.'" The Secretariat concludes that the Submission alleges harm to the organization making the Submission in accordance with Article 14(2) (a), and that this allegation relates to the protection of the environment.

(b) "the Submission, alone or in combination with other Submissions, raises matters whose further study in this process would advance the goals of this Agreement"

The Secretariat considered Article 14(2)(b) and whether the Submission raises matters whose further study in this process would advance the goals of the Agreement. In this connection, the Submission includes detailed information on fish preservation and conservation best practises, as well as information on fisheries law-enforcement practises. Further study of the matters raised in the Submission could thus advance NAAEC objectives found in Article 1 (a), (f), (g), and (h).

(c) "private remedies available under the Party's law have been pursued"

In accordance with Article 14(2)(c), the Secretariat has examined whether private remedies available under the Party's law have been pursued. The Secretariat was also guided in this connection by Guideline 7.5(b)88. The Submitter claims that "there are no realistic alternative private remedies available (Article 14(2)(c))." According to the Submission, "[t]he Submitter either does not have status for civil remedies or would find them impractical to pursue." Moreover, the Submitter states, "[w]hile Canadian citizens do have the right to commence private prosecutions of offences under the *Fisheries Act* and its regulations where the government refuses to enforce the law, such proceedings are usually stayed by the Attorney General and ... do not address the systemic problem of persistent non-enforcement by the Canadian government." The Submitter alleges that "[p]rivate prosecutions are ... not a viable option for effective enforcement where there are numerous ongoing violations of federal law."

In light of the foregoing, the Secretariat finds that the Submitter apparently does have access to private remedies under the Party's law, although the Submitter may not, by its own admission, be in a financial position to pursue them. It does appear that the Submitter has not pursued private remedies in the sense of going to the courts with its assertions. But the Submitter has engaged in other "actions," including participating in discussions on the government's integrated fishery-management plans, undertaking efforts to obtain government information through access-to-information legislation, and communicating about the matters at issue with the Party... . In accordance with Guideline 7.5(a) the Secretariat considers that it does not appear there would be duplication or interference if a Factual Record were prepared, and in accordance with Guideline 7.5(b), the Submitter appears to have taken reasonable actions to pursue private remedies, and as noted above it alleges that it faces barriers to the pursuit of such remedies. In light of the foregoing, the Secretariat finds that the Submission meets the requirements of Article 14(2)(c).

(d) "the Submission is drawn exclusively from mass media reports"

With respect to Article 14(2)(d) and guided by Guideline 7.6, the Secretariat examines whether the [sic] Submission is based exclusively on mass media reports. In reviewing the Submission along with its Appendices, the Submitter notes that the Submission is

continued

based primarily on information obtained from the federal and provincial governments, industry, and research resources, as well as the Submitter's direct involvement with the Skeena River Fishery and the North Coast Fishery of British Columbia.

The Secretariat considers that the Submission is not based solely on mass media reports..

Decision. The Secretariat concluded that the Submission met the requirements of Articles 14(1)-(2) and, accordingly, warranted a response from the Government of Canada. The Secretariat noted that Canada might wish to address "(1) enforcement efforts relating to the area concerned in the Submission, and the effectiveness of such efforts in conserving and protecting fish in accordance with the laws at issue; and (2) information concerning allocation of enforcement resources, and the Submitter's assertions of disproportionate targeting of non-commercial fishers, allegedly causing negative impacts on the conservation and protection of fish."

Case Questions

1. How is this approach different from that taken by Austrian plaintiffs against Czechs in the *Judgment* case? Does the international treaty make transnational environmental protection easier?
2. Do the complainants in *Skeena River Fishery* have to prove financial damage as a result of Canada's alleged non-enforcement? Do the plaintiffs in the Austrian *Judgment* case have to prove such damages?
3. How will the Canadian government's spending priorities factor into this decision? Should the Secretariat be able to order Canada to spend money on fisheries enforcement rather than unemployment insurance? Can the Secretariat do that?

In addition to resolving enforcement disputes, the CEC has conducted studies of proposed developments in border areas. For example, in 2007, the CEC hosted symposia focused on environmental technology, including a symposium featuring experts on green building and architecture. Research presented at the symposium evaluated how governments can encourage green and carbon-neutral building through zoning regulations, tax incentives, and government-supported research and development. The CEC has supported similar small "eco-projects."

The work of the CEC has been more that of a development agency than of an environmental cop. At its annual meeting in 2008, the CEC Council discussed conserving biodiversity, managing freshwater, reducing risks from toxic substances, and accelerating market-based environmental progress. Other topics included the elimination of environmental threats from non-compliant imports and the greening of the North American auto sector. The emphasis is on voluntary action, even though most effective compliance is achieved through involuntary means.

At its 2010 meeting, the CEC presented the proposed Strategic Plan for 2010–2015. As this plan's top priority, the CEC decided to focus on improving environmental health of children and other vulnerable communities. Following council resolutions 00-10 and 02-06, which recognize the particular vulnerabilities of children to environmental risks, resolution 10-02 set forth on the CEC's agenda a commitment to develop the capacity of health professionals to address the relationship between health and environment, particularly for children and other communities at risk. The CEC also committed to strengthen strategic linkages with health organizations, including the trilateral network of Pediatric Environmental Health Specialty Units (PEHSUs). This resolution supported the establishment of a PEHSU in the Lake Chapala district of Jalisco, expecting it to undertake community-based research projects addressing water pollution.

The CEC's Strategic Plan also drew attention to the importance of increasing the resilience of North America's shared ecosystems, and enhancing enforcement and management of chemicals of concern. Furthermore, the CEC committed to collaborate in improving the data gathering, methodologies, and inventories of **greenhouse gas emissions**, which are concentrated gasses in the Earth's atmosphere derived from the burning of fossil fuels. The CEC also took steps to boost the economy by committing to work with the private sector to improve environmental performance of small- and medium-sized enterprises in the areas of green building design, movement of e-wastes, etc.

At its annual meeting in July 2012, the CEC took action to modernize the implementation of the **Submissions on Enforcement Matters (SEM)** process. Improvements sought to increase timeliness, transparency, and accessibility of these submissions. A significant change in the process established target deadlines for key steps in the process in order to reduce processing time by half. Also, the modernization included a call for parties to follow up on concluded submissions with new developments and actions taken regarding matters raised. These revised guidelines were adopted through council resolution 12-06.

While NAFTA mechanisms have historically not permitted the CEC to impose environmentally progressive policies on less-developed Mexico, the United States and Canada have placed increasing attention and focus on Mexico. For example, the CEC instructed the Secretariat to prepare a *Factual Record* regarding assertions that Mexico was failing to effectively enforce environmental legislation that prohibited the dumping of hazardous waste and crimes against the environment. This resulted in effectively shutting down and dismantling the offending facility, which was operated by BASF Mexicana, S.A. de C.V., and an international chemical industrial company. In a separate instance, following a 2005 submission by a human rights organization based in Mexico, the CEC instructed the Secretariat to prepare a *Factual Record* on Mexico's alleged failure to effectively enforce its environmental laws regulating vehicle inspection programs and controlling polluting emissions.

European Union Environmental Initiatives. In 1985, the *Single European Act* made the environment an official responsibility of the EU, amending Section 13 of the *Treaty of Rome* with a new Title VII on the environment. In 1987, the European Council enacted a comprehensive environmental action program. In all, the Council of Ministers of the European Communities has adopted more than 200 different directives on environmental protection that the member states are obliged to implement through national legislation. Further, the European Commission has pursued hundreds of infringement procedures against member nations to compel implementation of these directives. Because of this aggressive approach, EU members generally are more thorough than the United States in environmental protection schemes.

A specific example of this aggressive approach is the EU's ban on **genetically modified organisms (GMOs)**, which are organisms that have been genetically altered. In the EU, all GMOs, along with irradiated food, are considered "new food" and subject to extensive, case-by-case, science-based food evaluation by the European Food Safety Authority (EFSA). As of August 2012, the EU had approved only 48 GMOs based on the evaluations submitted by the EFSA. Most of the GMOs were for animal feed imports or for feed and food processing. There is an additional layer of protection, which allows EU member states to temporarily restrict or prohibit the use and/or sale of a GMO within their territory if they have justifiable reasons to consider that the approved GMO constitutes a risk to human health or the environment. The EC is obliged to investigate these cases and either overturn the original registrations or request the country to withdraw its temporary restriction. By 2012, seven countries had submitted safeguard clauses, and the EC investigated and rejected those from six countries. The United Kingdom, the seventh restricting country, withdrew its submission.

The European Commission has also issued a number of "green papers" in its attempt to advance Union-wide environmental standards. First, it proposed a uniform system of civil liability for damage to the environment. The proposal would standardize the principles under which firms have to pay to repair environmental damage. It specifies situations under which strict liability concepts apply and compensation mechanisms for cases in which the responsible party cannot be identified. The Commission further intensified its approach through a directive, formally adopted in 2008, requiring member states to provide criminal sanctions for the most serious environmental offenses when committed intentionally or with gross negligence. This directive was created based on the belief that criminal sanctions are the most effective measure to deter noncompliance with European environmental legislation.

In 2003, the European Parliament issued a directive that established an emissions-trading scheme for the energy sector and large industrial installations. The scheme ensures that the greenhouse gas emissions from the energy and industry sectors covered are cut at least to meet emission commitments under the ***Kyoto Protocol***. The Commission made an initial assessment of National Allocation Plans (NAPs) in November 2006 in which it established emission caps from 2008 to 2012 for each member state. The Commission has also introduced legislation on the Registration Evaluation Authorization and Restriction of Chemicals (REACH), which entered into force in 2007. The REACH legislation creates the European Chemicals Agency, which is responsible for implementing requirements and publishing guidance documents to protect human health and the environment from the EU's chemical industry while keeping the industry competitive. On environmental issues, the Commission is increasingly in the position of clearinghouse and arbiter for policy differences within the EU.

In 2003, the European Parliament issued a directive to ensure that, on environmental matters, the public has full access to whatever information it needs to petition the Commission on these policy matters. The legislation creates an inherent public right to such information and a presumption that disclosure of information is the general rule. By creating this unusual right to information, the directive seeks to achieve greater awareness of environmental matters, a free exchange of views, and more effective participation by the public in environmental decision making in all the nations of the EU. The Commission will be pressed to continue in its efforts.

Regional Marine Treaties. Nations sharing bodies of water have cooperated significantly on environmental issues. Marine environmental protection was pioneered in 1972 by the *London Convention for the Prevention of Marine Pollution by Dumping from Ships and Aircraft*, which prohibited the dumping of specified hazardous wastes from ships at sea and required permits for the dumping of others. The *Helsinki Convention on the Protection of the Marine Environment of the Baltic Sea Area* improved on the London Convention by providing for an effective international inspection and enforcement network. *The Barcelona Convention for the Protection of the Mediterranean Sea from Pollution* took matters further by enlarging the *London Convention*'s list of prohibited substances. In November 2003, the environment ministers of the Mediterranean countries signed a declaration "to speed up the eradication of the at-risk single hull vessels which travel to and across the Mediterranean." Similar convention arrangements have been concluded for the Red Sea and the Gulf of Aden, the Caribbean, the Southeast Pacific, and the South Pacific. In 2007, 25 shipping states within the UN's International Maritime Organization (IMO) enacted legislation that bans the use of tributyltin (TBT). TBT is a compound, found in many anti-fouling paints on ships, which kills algae and barnacles and is toxic to many other marine organisms. The depopulation of commercial oysters in the 1970s near France and the United Kingdom is linked to TBT contamination. The ban was considered a victory for the IMO.

Developments in South Asia and the South Pacific. Countries in South Asia and the South Pacific are not renowned for vigilant enforcement of environmental policy. Nations in this region have emphasized industrial development rather than reduction of environmentally adverse by-products of that development. Indeed, as discussed later, China and India lead the emerging world's resistance to global attempts to outlaw technologies believed to deplete the ozone layer and cause climate change. Other nations in the region have made efforts at regional environmental cooperation.

A number of countries in the region have entered into the *ASEAN Agreement on the Conservation of Nature and Natural Resources*, under which each of the parties recognize "the responsibility of ensuring that activities under their jurisdiction or control do not cause damage to the environment or the natural resources under the jurisdiction" of other nations. In addition, a number of regional environmental programs have been established to coordinate policy. These include the South Asia Cooperative Environment Program (Afghanistan, Bangladesh, India, Iran, Maldives, Nepal, Pakistan, and Sri Lanka), ASEAN (Singapore, Thailand, and Brunei), and the South Pacific Regional Environment Program (comprising 21 South Pacific island nations).

Following the 2004 tsunami, several environmental issues emerged in the South Asia and South Pacific region. The tsunami was caused by an Indian Ocean earthquake measuring approximately 9.0 on the Richter scale and caused the deaths of 200,000 people. The disaster affected 12 countries, reduced 400,000 homes to rubble, and caused around $10 billion in damage. Among the many structures destroyed was the infrastructure for solid and liquid waste and industrial chemicals. Drinking water and soil were contaminated. The **United Nations Environment Programme (UNEP)** established an Asian Tsunami Disaster Task Force at the request of the affected countries. The Task Force assessed damage, mobilized recovery assistance, and worked to ensure that the environment was part of national recovery agendas.

Some of the nations most devastated by the tsunami had experienced warning signs such as rising sea levels. Losses of life and property were particularly high in areas with major erosion problems and in areas where mangrove forests had been logged and cleared for agricultural use or for fish farming. The UNEP has instituted rehabilitation and protection of natural ecosystems, including mangrove forests and coral reefs, as part of its effort to mitigate major destruction in future natural disasters.

Developments in Eastern Europe and Central Asia. During Eastern Europe's communist years, it was the most environmentally devastated region in Europe. The corruption and poverty of the communist system did not leave funds to protect the environment. In the first years after the fall of the Berlin Wall, Eastern Europe was preoccupied with economic recovery and did not expend significant resources on environmental compliance and monitoring. Now, finally, Eastern Europe has joined the "green" movement.

In 2003, the Czech Republic, Hungary, Montenegro, Poland, Romania, Serbia, Slovakia, and the Ukraine adopted the *Convention on Environment Protection and Sustainable Development of the Carpathians.* The *Carpathian Convention* creates treaty obligations among the signatories to protect, maintain, and sustainably manage the natural resources of that mountain region. The treaty specifically adopts (1) the precaution and prevention principles, (2) the "polluter pays" principle, and (3) public participation and stakeholder involvement in development initiatives in each country, ending the "race to the bottom" among these emerging European economic participants. By creating a multinational approach to the problem, the Carpathian nations seek to restore their collective environment. At the Pan-European Ministers' Conference, the environment ministers of the region's countries expressed their support of the Carpathian effort, noting their intent to contribute to improving environmental conditions by strengthening the efforts of these countries in environmental protection and by facilitating partnership and cooperation between these countries and other European countries.

At the Kyiv Conference in 2003, 22 European countries, including 11 nations formerly in the Eastern bloc, signed the *Protocol on Civil Liability and Damage Caused by the Transboundary Effects of Industrial Accidents.* The protocol arose from the accident at a dam at BaiaMare (Romania) in January 2000, which sent 100,000 tons of wastewater infused with highly toxic pollutants, including cyanide, into rivers in Hungary, Yugoslavia, and Romania. This protocol gives affected individuals a legal claim for compensation and fills in the major gap in remedies reflected in the *Judgment of February 23, 1988.* A wronged party in one signatory nation can now make the polluter pay in another nation. Memories are long, however. The Czech Republic, target of the *Judgment of February 23, 1988,* did not sign the protocol.

Middle East and Africa. The Middle East and Africa face a number of environmental challenges. In particular, several countries in this region face water scarcity, land and coastal degradation, and desertification. The Middle East and Africa have large natural resource endowments but are also plagued by civil unrest, both of which can contribute to environmental degradation. In recent years, countries in this region have begun to develop and coordinate policies to maintain and improve the environment.

For example, in February 2006, several North African national and local governments convened in Rabat, Morocco, to establish a regional network for environmental issues. The nations formed the Network for Environmental Compliance and Enforcement in the Maghreb (NECEMA). Morocco and Tunisia were co-chairs of the network. At the conference and in the following months, NECEMA participants discussed countries' environmental compliance and enforcement programs, analyzed examples of international experience, and developed a set of best practices for country assessment.

In 2007, representatives of 42 African countries gathered in Kigali, Rwanda, at the African Regional Conference to address desertification and climate change in Africa. This gathering was convened in preparation for a conference of the parties to the *United Nations Convention to Combat Desertification* (CCD). The CCD entered into force in 1996 and has 191 parties.

Several countries in attendance at the African Regional Conference had launched Green Belt initiatives in the late 1980s and throughout the 1990s. The Green Belt movement focused on tree planting to conserve the environment and stem the effects of **deforestation** (the clearing of forested land for non-forest use) and **desertification** (when a dry region becomes increasingly arid, losing water and vegetation). In 2004, Kenyan national Wangari Maathai received the Nobel Peace Prize in recognition of her efforts to promote ecologically viable development and her activities with the Green Belt movement.

Initiatives by Multilateral Agencies. Multilateral agencies have advanced the effort by applying uniform environmental standards to projects that they finance. The World Bank, for example, has published a 460-page volume of environmental guidelines for its personnel to use in evaluating the adequacy and effectiveness of pollution control measures for industrial projects. If a country wishes to obtain financing for its projects from the World Bank or its private project finance affiliate, the International Finance Corporation (IFC), the characteristics of the project must fall within accepted world environmental standards. In light of the importance of these financing sources in the Third World, the impact of these guidelines on both public and private projects has been very substantial.

Global Solutions

The United Nations began its work in the environmental arena in 1972 when it adopted the *Stockholm Declaration on the Human Environment* and founded the UNEP. UNEP has now been the catalyst for the formulation and adoption of almost 30 binding multilateral instruments and 10 sets of non-binding environmental guidelines and principles.

The World Trade Organization. As demonstrated in the *Reformulated Gasoline* and *Shrimp* cases, GATT affirmatively prevents a conservationist nation from imposing its environmental policies on others through trade law. Environmentalists are working hard to reverse this.

As with other international environmental initiatives, most developed nations favor the creation of a permanent trade and environment committee to advance and implement pro-environment proposals, while less-developed countries resist the concept strongly. Most proposals likely to come out of an environmental committee would, in their view, adversely affect their exports into the developed world. Some structure seems inevitable, but years of discussion have created little more than commissions to study the possibility further.

One proposal is to impose an additional *ad valorem* tax on all imports. This would promote environment-friendly development in poorer nations. This proposal addresses developing nations' inability to pay for the technology necessary to implement a cleaner environment. However, poor countries are not enthusiastic about the proposal. First, imposing a tax on their exports would make them less competitive with domestic products in developed countries. Second, the funds would ultimately find their way back to the richer countries that manufacture the antipollution infrastructure.

During debate on the Convention on Biological Biodiversity, the less-developed countries offered their own suggestion: that the richer nations simply make "green" technology available for no charge. This triggered strong opposition from the United States, the home of most inventors and manufacturers of that equipment. The less-developed world also was willing to ensure that species important to biomedical research would be kept alive. However, in return, the owners of intellectual property would have to share that information for free. Not surprisingly, the United States, the home country of most firms with important biomedical intellectual property, did not support that portion of the convention either. The crafting of provisions that left some of the more difficult questions open for another day allowed the United States to join in the convention.

Another set of proposals focuses on establishing uniform WTO-accepted standards for labeling and packaging. The objective is to establish standards that protect the environment but prevent nations from using such standards as a trade barrier. During the Ministerial Conferences in Doha (2001) and Cancún (2003), the ministers instructed the Committee on Trade and Environment to give attention to the impact of eco-labeling on trade and to examine whether existing WTO rules stand in the way of eco-labeling policies. Environmentalists were quite active among the groups that rioted at the 1999 WTO ministerial meetings in Seattle, Washington. The protests had relatively little impact on the trade-oriented group, but they did reflect long-term pressure from "green" constituencies that the WTO is taking into account. The continuing North–South conflict on these questions has prevented significant progress to date in that forum. More heartening news has come from other global gatherings.

Finally, at the Ministerial Conference in Cancún, the ministers agreed to launch negotiations on how WTO rules are to apply to WTO members that are parties to environmental agreements. Today, about 30 out of approximately 200 multilateral environmental agreements contain trade provisions. According to the ministers, the objective of the new negotiations will be a clarification of the relationship between trade measures taken under the environmental agreements and WTO rules. The ministers also agreed to negotiations on the reductions or elimination of tariff and non-tariff barriers to environmental goods and services.

The International Court of Justice. Another forum for addressing environmental disputes may be the ICJ. The ICJ, seated in The Hague, Netherlands, is the principal judicial organ of the United Nations and is charged with resolving disputes between sovereign states. Despite the fact that the ICJ set up a standing Chamber for Environmental Matters in 1993, the Argentina–Uruguay dispute, filed in 2006 and described earlier, is the first environmental matter to come before the ICJ.

The ICJ's failure to act at the preliminary stage for "lack of a risk of prejudice" cannot give other parties much incentive to use the ICJ in future disputes. It may well have been appropriate to decline Argentina's request for a temporary injunction based on lack of likelihood of success on the merits. Requests to stop construction are frequently denied on such grounds in domestic litigation. As the final judgment shows, there can be little doubt that once the paper mills were built, it would have prejudiced Uruguay enormously to disassemble them or make material structural modifications to them.

Whether the ICJ is equipped to decide questions of scientific uncertainty is an important question whose answer has the potential to undermine international willingness to submit to its jurisdiction.

Global Ban on Toxic Substances. As noted earlier, domestic legislation such as TSCA has banned certain toxic substances domestically and somewhat limited their circulation abroad. But so long as developing nations permit the use of these substances, their adverse effect is felt throughout the world. Beginning in 1998, nations began to discuss global solutions to the issue of proliferation of toxins.

These negotiations did not go smoothly. The environmental effects of toxins in the developed world are alarming. Because toxins drain into the world's waters, effects are often contracted through the eating of fish. American researchers have documented learning and behavioral problems in children exposed prenatally to coolants such as PCBs through mothers who ate Great Lakes fish. In Japan, high dioxin levels have been found in whale and dolphin meat. Research has detected toxins in animals thousands of miles from where the pollutant is used. However, toxins are often effective in controlling pests. Their use permits crops to grow more abundantly in areas where food is otherwise scarce. In light of its recurring history of famine, it is understandable that Ethiopia has 250 sites contaminated by dangerous pesticides, including 1,500 tons of aldrin, chlordane, and DDT.

In 2000, negotiators from 122 countries signed the first global ban on the use of specified chemical compounds. The banned substances were the acknowledged "dirty dozen" of chemical contamination, linked to birth defects and genetic abnormalities: PCBs, DDT, dioxins, and furans. The industrialized nations agreed to pay poor countries $150 million annually to help them find alternatives and permitted the limited use of DDT for public health reasons, such as malaria control.

The Basel Convention. One of the best examples of multinational cooperation in environmental matters is the *Basel Convention on Transboundary Movements of Hazardous Wastes and Their Disposal*, which was adopted by 170 nations under the auspices of UNEP. The Basel system is not as stringent as the U.S. law on movement of hazardous waste discussed previously, but is broader in scope.

As the volume of waste ballooned in the 1980s, a substantial trade developed in the transport of wastes from the United States and Western European countries to developing nations. Because there were strict environmental restrictions on disposal in the developed countries, and few or no restrictions in developing nations, waste generators could dispose of hazardous waste at a much lower cost by sending it on a barge to a less-developed country. For example, Guinea Bissau entered into contracts valued at more than $600 million over five years—about the size of its entire gross national product—to receive U.S. and European garbage. The downside of this system, of course, is that unremediated hazardous wastes enter the world's ecosystem in Bissau, Guinea Bissau, just as surely as if dumped in Champaign, Illinois. The emerging countries, which were realizing substantial revenues, were reluctant to change the arrangement.

The Basel Convention regulates the transport of wastes that display certain **hazardous characteristics**, such as flammability or toxicity. Transport is prohibited unless the disposer notifies the governments of the receiving and notifies transit nations of the nature and amount of wastes in a shipment. These governments must then authorize the shipment. The receiving nation must also confirm that arrangements are in place for the "environmentally sound management of the wastes in question." During shipment, the refuse must be clearly marked with the contents of the shipment. Upon completion of disposal, the exporter must notify the receiving nation. If completion does not happen, the exporting nation must accept a return of the wastes. And to prevent the development of "waste outlaw" nations, all signatories are prohibited from permitting the transport of wastes to nonsignatories.

The Basel Convention is hampered by a lack of consensus on a number of critical definitions. There is no widely accepted definition of what is "hazardous." Nor is there universal agreement on what management is sufficient for **remediation of wastes** (i.e., rendering them harmless to the environment). The difficulties in these areas are exacerbated by the substantial incentive that officials in receiving nations have to allow unrestricted transport of refuse. This can make them less demanding than officials in developed nations. If the governing elites in the receiving countries—many of which are not democratic—are unenthusiastic about enforcement, the Basel Convention does not work well. UNEP and others continue to work on these difficult definitional and enforcement issues.

The Convention on International Trade in Endangered Species. The *Convention on International Trade in Endangered Species of Wild Fauna and Flora* (CITES), which was enacted about two decades ago and is now in force in 177 nations, is an example of how well a treaty can work when it has broad political support. CITES created a system for identifying and listing endangered and threatened species. It forbids the import or export of such species unless a "scientific authority" finds that the import or export will not aggravate the species' situation. It currently governs trade in more than 30,000 protected plant and animal species.

Noncompliant nations—whether parties or non-parties to the convention—face potentially severe multilateral trade sanctions for violations. For example, CITES has identified certain species of Caspian Sea sturgeon as endangered. Unless leading exporters such as Russia and Iran demonstrate that the caviar trade is not detrimental to sturgeon, their caviar exports to all markets would be banned under CITES. Because of the broad support for CITES in both developed and most less-developed nations, the treaty is generally judged to be effective. The former outlaw nations have been brought to heel by overwhelming political pressure.

The Montreal Protocol. UNEP has sponsored a particularly comprehensive example of a global solution to a global environmental problem in the *Montreal Protocol on Substances That Deplete the Ozone Layer*. The *Montreal Protocol* called for a gradual reduction of substances feared to damage the ozone layer by imposing a freeze on consumption; a 10 percent limit on increases in production beginning in 1990; a 20 percent reduction in both consumption and production by 1993; and a further 30 percent reduction in production by 1998. The protocol used the same sanction as used in CITES against violators: all signatories to the protocol pledge to impose trade sanctions against violators.

The *Montreal Protocol* assuaged the concerns of the less-developed countries by permitting them greater flexibility in compliance than the more-developed countries. In other words, the developed countries were required to reduce their chlorofluorocarbon (CFC) levels before the emerging countries. For a period, factories in the emerging countries had to meet less-demanding standards than those in other nations. The idea was that, over time, the production levels of CFCs in the developed world would move toward parity with those in the less-developed world, and eventually, all would decline.

This inequality in treatment created a significant political issue in the United States. As manufacturers and workers discovered the difficulties of competing with foreign-based firms that could use less-expensive, dirtier equipment and processes, they objected loudly to the disparity in treatment. In fact, many U.S. corporations in affected industries have moved manufacturing facilities to such lower-cost nations, a trend that still continues. This has triggered adverse reactions from organized labor and increasing political backlash from politicians whom labor supports. The future of the Montreal Protocol may rest with how industrialized nations cope with this transitional period of inequality.

The Climate Control Convention. Difficult as resolving the issues of the ozone layer has proved to be, agreement is even more difficult in the context of **climate change** (significant and lasting change in weather patterns), addressed in the *UN Framework Convention on Climate Change* (UNFCCC). CFCs and halons make life somewhat easier—they facilitate the functioning of certain appliances and machines—but are not critical to industrial development. However, if the earth really is experiencing climate change, resolution of such a problem requires a substantial reduction in thermal energy use. Fossil fuels are the main source of thermal energy in the United States. They are used both in the internal combustion engines of automobiles and lawn mowers and in electric power generation. Most electric power used in the United States is generated from the burning of fossil fuels.

Because energy use is central to economic growth, the less-developed countries are not likely to agree quickly to any limitations that could restrict their economic development. And the less-developed world is not alone in its opposition. The United States, Canada, and the United Kingdom all rely heavily on fossil fuels for their energy needs and have all—through both liberal and conservative administrations—opposed proposed quantitative or temporal goals for carbon dioxide emissions. Arrayed against this alliance are the "green-influenced" governments of continental Europe and Japan, which rely on carbon dioxide-free nuclear power. The latter nations are impatient to push for hard restrictions, especially on the United States.

To complicate matters further, climate change would not affect all nations in the same way. A rise in the ocean levels from arctic ice melt may flood much of Southeast Asia while causing drought in some currently fertile areas. However, a warmer, moister climate would provide longer, frost-free growing seasons. According to a UNEP study, a temperature increase of 1.5 degrees Celsius in the central European section of the former Soviet Union would result in a 30 percent increase in its wheat yield.

Finally, some scientists continue to disagree about whether the thickening blanket of greenhouse gases is, in fact, increasing world temperatures. Various theories as to the circulation of air in the atmosphere and the cooling effect of other synthetic airborne materials—such as sulfate particles that impede sunlight's penetration of the atmosphere—support the arguments of those nations that oppose a climate change treaty.

At the 1992 United Nations Rio Conference on Environment and Development, the world community took its first tentative step toward a multilateral resolution of this problem with the Framework Convention on Climate Change. The convention did not resolve any of the foregoing disputes or require any measures from its parties. Rather, it established a framework for later discussions leading to more specific treaties on the issue. The convention identified two areas to address in the future: harmonization of national regulation and disguised discrimination against imports. In 1997, the *Kyoto Protocol* to the convention went a step further, setting quantitative targets for the reduction of greenhouse gases to 5 percent below 1990 levels. The EU agreed to reduce emissions by 8 percent, the United States by 7 percent, and Japan by 6 percent.

Then, from 1998 through 2000, officials from all corners of the globe fought over how to measure such reductions. The United States and Canada argued that they should be allowed to purchase **pollution credits** from countries with low emissions rather than meeting the goals immediately. They also argued that they should be allowed to deduct from their emission totals **carbon sinks**—areas such as forests and farmlands that absorb carbon compounds. In late 2000, the EU rejected these arguments, accusing the North Americans of evading their Kyoto commitments. There matters stood as the George W. Bush administration took power in the United States. The Bush administration quickly took the position that the carbon dioxide commitments were not enforceable against the United States in the absence of a pollution credit scheme.

There was little tangible progress over the next decade. In late 2003, nations again met to confer on the UNFCCC. While the ministers passed a resolution "that climate change remains the most important global challenge to humanity and that its adverse effects are already a reality in all parts of the world," there was no further agreement on enforcement apparatus. Instead, two funds were developed to support developing countries' efforts in the area, the Special Climate Change Fund and the Least Developed Countries Fund. These funds support technology transfer, adaptation projects, and other activities. Several countries renewed an earlier pledge to contribute US$410 million annually to developing countries. Obviously, in light of the magnitude of the problem, this is not very much money.

The *Kyoto Protocol*, which nearly 200 countries have now ratified, went into force in February 2005. However the *Kyoto Protocol's* effectiveness has been contested because the United States never ratified it and because pollution reduction targets were not assigned to developing countries, including the world's largest greenhouse gas emitter, China. Allegedly, the United States never ratified the protocol because of the 1997 *Byrd–Hagel Resolution*, which stated that the U.S. Senate would not consider an international climate treaty that created a distinction between responsibilities of developed and developing countries. In addition to the lack of support from the United States, countries have struggled to meet their *Kyoto Protocol* goals. Canada's domestic regulatory policies, for example, placed it out of line with its Kyoto obligations, causing it to announce that it would not attempt to meet its target in the first commitment period. The EU has instituted a regional Emissions Trading System (ETS) to assist member states in meeting their Kyoto targets; however, progress reports issued by the European Climate Change Programme indicate that existing measures will not be sufficient to allow the EU to fulfill its international commitments.

At the thirteenth meeting of the UNFCCC in Bali in 2007, the parties developed a two-year action plan to achieve an agreement in Copenhagen in 2009. President Barack Obama's inauguration in 2008 brought with it hopes of international progress with renewed U.S. leadership. But the disorganization at Copenhagen in 2009—resulting partly from the unwieldy attendance of representatives from 190 countries—produced the *Copenhagen Accord*, a weak agreement with uncertain legal status. The parties expressed their will to "urgently combat climate change in accordance with the principle of common but differentiated responsibilities and respective capabilities," affirming prior consensus that global temperature increases should be kept to under 2 degrees Celsius. But the agreement did not include a plan for reaching this goal.

In 2010 in Cancun, countries of the *Kyoto Protocol* made their emission reduction pledges official. In addition, the parties committed developed countries to $30 billion "fast-start financing" in 2010–2012 for developing countries' efforts in adaptation and mitigation. These funds, however, turned out to be poorly tracked by the developed nations. Furthermore, the agreements created the Green Climate Fund to distribute $100 billion per year by 2020 to developing countries for assistance with climate change mitigation and adaptation. Although this represented very ambitious plans to help developing nations deal with climate change, it has so far been vague as to what aid will be provided until 2020. Unlike in Copenhagen, the Cancun Agreements established clear goals and a schedule for keeping the global temperature increase below 2 degrees Celsius.

The *Durban Platform for Enhanced Action*, which determined that a second compliance period would be entered in 2013, was drafted and accepted in 2011. At this point, all industrialized countries and 48 developing countries affirmed their reduction pledges until 2020. Furthermore, the Climate Green Fund, established in Cancun, was officially launched in Durban along with the creation of a Standing Committee to advise the parties on exercising its functions. In Durban, the parties further agreed to work toward a new, legally binding instrument that, unlike the Kyoto agreement of 1997, would require actions of all parties.

The eighteenth meeting of the UNFCCC in Doha, Qatar, in 2012 brought about the adoption of the Doha Amendment to the *Kyoto Protocol* and concluded work under the Bali action plan. This amendment has not yet entered into force. The United States occupies a dual position as one of the world's most powerful actors in international negotiations and one of its largest per capita polluters. U.S. domestic action is therefore necessary to reaching an international agreement.

The House passed a climate bill in June 2009, but subsequent attempts to construct and pass a bill in the Senate have failed, due both to international and national concerns. This bill, "*The American Clean Energy and Security Act of 2009*," proposed a nationwide **cap-and-trade regime**—one in which all energy producers have a "cap" on the gases that they can produce, but can trade with others to get more "cap" room"—aiming for a 17 percent reduction in greenhouse gas emissions. However, this bill presented several vulnerabilities. It presents the potential for legal challenges from the WTO due to its grant of free emissions allowances, which may represent illegal subsidies under the WTO, to energy and trade intensive industries; its failure to qualify as a border tax adjustment because it represents a regulatory regime, and not a "tax" under the GATT; and the unlikelihood that the WTO will grant the bill an exception given the growing political pressure surrounding the global trading system. The bill also faces domestic political pressure due to concerns about maintaining U.S. industrial competitiveness and preventing job losses through border measures against high-carbon imports from developing countries.

In 2012 the American public's belief that global warming is a real phenomenon hit its highest acceptance level (70 percent). Although the Obama administration has repeatedly stated it would prefer congressional legislation to address climate change, the divided Congress has so far proven unwilling to take climate action. In 2007, the Supreme Court ruling in *Massachusetts v. EPA* determined that the EPA has the authority, but not necessarily the obligation, to regulate greenhouse gas emissions. It is therefore likely that the Obama administration will continue to assume authority under the EPA's *Clean Air Act*.

Countries that are particularly vulnerable to rising sea levels and changing weather patterns are looking for other ways to compel action on the part of larger polluting nations. Environmental disputes among nations traditionally took place between countries sharing a border, as in the *Pulp Mills* case. Yet global environmental challenges like climate change raise the possibility for conflict between countries that are geographically disparate. The probable distribution of the negative effects of climate change, moreover, increase the likelihood of disagreement between the priorities of high-emitting wealthy nations in the global North and those of low-emitting poor nations in the South. The Alliance of Small Island States, a coalition of low-lying coastal countries that are particularly vulnerable to rising sea levels, has repeatedly called for the developed countries to take on greater responsibility for emissions abatement and provide more support for mitigation in developing countries. The Federated States of Micronesia, a small island nation in the Pacific, recently filed a plea with the Ministry of the Environment in the Czech Republic protesting the country's plans to prolong the life of a coal-fired power plant. The Republic of Tuvalu has also announced its intention to sue Australia and the United States in the ICJ for their continued high rate of greenhouse gas emissions.

Alternative Energy Movement. The disconnect between the world's growing thirst for energy and its desire to avoid pollution and climate change has triggered a boom in alternative energy sources. This section addresses some of these developments.

Biofuels. Spurred by soaring fossil fuel prices more than environmental concerns, many nations have intensified their focus on **biofuels** as a source of energy. These technologies are not new: Both the

United States and Europe first developed biofuel industries in the early twentieth century. However, until recent technological developments and spikes in energy prices, these fuels were prohibitively expensive relative to traditional fuels.

The fuels are made from plant matter such as corn or sugar cane stalks and when combined with petroleum in liquid, gaseous, or solid form, they can produce electricity and heat. **Ethanol** (ethyl alcohol) is one of the more popular biofuels and is mixed with petroleum at varying ratios.

Several countries have adopted incentive programs for biofuel production. The U.S. Department of Energy has established a Renewable Energy Biomass Program to encourage the development and improvement of technology for biofuel. Producers currently enjoy an excise tax exemption and an earned income tax credit. The government increased regulation of producers in the *Energy Policy Act* of 2005 (EPACT). The Act established minimum requirements for ethanol and biodiesel fuel usage in automotive fuels through 2012.

Brazil is a pioneer in the field of biofuel. Its ethanol fuel program, which uses sugar cane, has been in use for more than 30 years. More recently, the Brazilian Parliament passed *Law 10438* to create the Program of Incentives for Alternative Energy Sources (PROINFA) in 2002. The Brazilian government requires that all gasoline contain a minimum of 20 percent ethanol, and on average, fuel for transportation includes more than 40 percent ethanol. Brazil has steadily increased its exports of ethanol to other markets, including Japan and other Asian countries. The U.S. EPA has approved more than 100 Brazilian sugarcane mills as ethanol exporters to the United States. In 2011, Brazil exported more than 1.8 billion liters of ethanol, and the Brazilian government expects that to increase to 6.8 billion liters by 2020. Brazil was actually forced to *import* more than 570 million liters of the biofuel to keep up with the growing foreign demand—and to avoid a shortage of the product in its domestic market.

However, national protectionism can still overshadow environmental concerns. Ethanol produced with sugar cane in Brazil is far less expensive to produce than corn-based ethanol. In reaction, the United States has thrown up trade barriers to protect its corn-based ethanol industry, needlessly making all biofuels in the United States more expensive and retarding the development of a renewable alternative to petroleum. Environmentalism has not yet overcome baser economic concerns.

The European Union is also encouraging the development of alternative energy. The EU has set a target: Fuels should contain 5.75 percent biofuels by 2010. To meet this target, member states are offering tax rebates to producers. For example, France offered a rebate for production of 80,000 tons of biodiesel and 320,000 tons of ethanol by the end of 2007. France, like other European countries, typically produces ethanol from sugar beets or cereals and produces biodiesel from rapeseed. Germany is Europe's leading biodiesel producer, accounting for 80 percent of production, while Spain is the leading ethanol producer.

Like the United States, the EU has high biofuel production costs relative to fossil fuels. This overall higher cost for biofuel has impeded market-based expansion in the United States and the EU. Brazil's lower cost of production has allowed biofuel to penetrate the market more easily.

Despite their initial popularity, biofuels have begun to fall out of favor. The United Kingdom recently reduced the EU goal of 5.75 percent to 3.25 percent in 2010 and abandoned its 20 percent tax incentive. Biofuels tend to be about 50 percent more expensive than petroleum that would provide an equivalent amount of energy. They also have the potential to distort food prices as fuel crops compete with food crops for a limited supply of arable land. Finally, as a recent EU study of palm oil production on Malaysia and Indonesia shows, deforestation for the purpose of growing fuel crops threatens biodiversity. The loss of trees that absorb carbon dioxide also potentially negates the benefit of reducing greenhouse gas emissions originally thought to accompany the replacement of fossil fuels with biofuels.

Wind and Solar. Notwithstanding high initial costs, wind and solar energy projects are becoming more prominent in several countries. In 2000, the German government implemented the *Renewable Energy Sources Act*, which requires utilities to purchase renewable energy and guarantees prices for renewable energy generators. Germany also produces a large percentage of the world's solar power. In April 2010, the U.S. Department of the Interior approved the first offshore wind farm in the United States, overcoming environmental objections about threats to marine species and concerns that offshore turbines might interfere with air traffic control. There are many other U.S. offshore wind projects in development encouraged by a federal tax grant program that provides public funding for 30 percent of project capital costs. In the United Kingdom, investments of more than £100 billion in offshore wind projects are expected over the next decade.

General Prospects for Global Environmental Solutions. In a world where emerging public opinion strongly favors environmental protection, one should not underestimate the potential for global solutions. A relatively short time ago, for example, the differences between whaling nations and environmentalists in nonwhaling nations were thought to be irreconcilable. The force of public opinion in the whalers' own countries led to an agreement to permit international regulation. Today, commercial hunting of whales is regulated by the International Whaling Commission, which meets periodically to determine how much, if any, whaling is to be allowed. From 1986 through 1992, the commission effectively banned whaling. This allowed whale stocks to replenish. The threatened mammal has come back from the edge of extinction to the point where limited hunting has begun again.

For "First World" investors, agreements like the *Montreal Protocol* mean that their "Third World" manufacturing plants will need to comply with international standards at some point in the future. Further, because the protocol also prohibits trade in CFCs between parties to the protocol and nonparties, foreign investors that manufacture products in the less-developed world for export to the developed world must expect that those export markets are likely to be closed to them if their plants are located in a country that is not a party to the agreement. The bottom line for foreign investors is that differences in environmental regulations are becoming increasingly difficult to exploit.

Environmental challenges are increasingly shared across national borders. International environmental law is accordingly becoming more central to the activities of national governments and corporations alike. In a striking confirmation of the "globalization of 'environmental policy'" and Europe's recognized "right to an acceptable environment and public responsibility for its preservation," the European Court of Justice (ECJ) held in 2005 that the European Commission had the ability to create a harmonized body of criminal law to protect the environment. The Commission may now promulgate criminal laws that all member states must adopt. Describing the use of criminal codes as "a last resort" used to defend against "threats to the values which sustain coexistence," the ECJ concluded that in certain cases the European Community must be able to "avail itself of criminal penalties as the only 'effective, proportionate, and dissuasive' response." It is arresting to consider this pronouncement alongside decisions by U.S. federal courts in Alien Tort Statute cases, discussed earlier, concluding that there is not yet a generally recognized right to a clean environment.

CONCLUSION

Environmental law is an area of rapidly increasing regulation as conservationism becomes an accepted goal of groups across the political spectrum. As this trend is internationalized through bilateral and multilateral treaties, the investor who seeks to avoid environmental protection laws runs the risk of being trapped abroad with an unusable investment.

Chapter Summary

1. Nations may enact domestic legislation outlawing import of a product because the product itself violates environmental norms in the regulating country or because it is manufactured through a process that is environmentally objectionable.
2. According to WTO rules, a nation may require foreign producers to comply with the same environmental standards that are required by domestic firms, but it may not subject foreign firms to more rigorous standards.
3. Victims of environmental misdeeds abroad can sometimes sue the foreign investor polluter in its home country, but such a ruling often depends on the demonstration that activities that contributed significantly to the pollution had occurred in the home country.
4. NAFTA established the North American Commission for Environmental Cooperation to determine whether any party to NAFTA has shown a "persistent pattern of failure" to "effectively enforce its environmental law." The Commission has declared it has no right to investigate actions by legislatures of NAFTA countries even if those actions effectively nullify other laws.
5. The Council of Ministers of the European Communities has adopted more than 200 different directives on environmental protection that the member states must implement through national legislation. The European Commission has pursued hundreds of infringement procedures against member nations to compel implementation of these directives. EU countries now

have the most rigorous environmental laws in the world.

6. The *London Convention for the Prevention of Marine Pollution by Dumping from Ships and Aircraft* prohibits the dumping of specified hazardous wastes from ships at sea and requires permits for the dumping of others.
7. If a country wishes to obtain financing for its projects from the World Bank or its private finance affiliate, the International Finance Corporation, the characteristics of the project must fall within accepted world environmental standards articulated in the World Bank's publications.
8. The *Basel Convention* regulates the transport of wastes that display certain hazardous characteristics. Transport is prohibited unless the disposer notifies the governments of the receiving and transit nations of the nature and amount of wastes in a shipment and confirms that arrangements are in place for environmentally sound management of the wastes.
9. The *Convention on International Trade in Endangered Species of Wild Fauna and Flora*, ratified by 172 nations, created a system for identifying and listing endangered and threatened species. It forbids the import or export of more than 30,000 protected plant and animal species unless a scientific authority finds that the import or export will not aggravate the species' situation.
10. The *Montreal Protocol* has gradually reduced substances feared to damage the ozone layer by imposing first a freeze on consumption, and then staged reductions in consumption and production. All signatories to the protocol are pledged to impose trade sanctions against violators.
11. The *Framework Convention on Climate Change* did not resolve any of the disputes as to numerical deadlines for reduction of carbon dioxide emissions. Rather, it established a framework for later discussions leading to more specific treaties on the issue. The *Kyoto Protocol* set quantitative targets for the reduction of greenhouse gases, but it was not approved by the United States and places no constraints on China or India. The 2009 *Copenhagen Accord* reiterated the international consensus that temperature rises should be kept to less than 2 degrees Celsius, but it did not lay out a plan for reaching that goal.

Key Terms

Questions and Case Problems

1. In the *Judgment of February 23, 1988*, what would the Austrian Supreme Court have done if a private cause of action had been available in Czechoslovakia? How do you think the court would handle complaints about a nuclear accident such as Chernobyl?
2. How would an Austrian judgment for money damages against the Czechoslovak government be enforced? What type of injunctive relief would be possible?
3. If a U.S. company is presented with the opportunity to build a plant in a former communist country with less stringent laws on carbon dioxide emissions, what factors should it take into consideration before proceeding with the project? To what extent should it consider the long-term investment interest of the company's shareholders? Are any other issues relevant to management's consideration? Would the company's president, who bypassed this low-risk opportunity to realize profit for the shareholders because of personal political views, have fulfilled management's fiduciary obligations to the shareholders?

4. Assume that a democratically elected government, after a favorable vote in a popular referendum, launches a program to clear 150,000 acres of tropical rain forest in order to promote economic development. To carry out the will of the people, the government issues a request for proposals to international engineering firms for a contract to help clear the acreage. A number of international firms have indicated that they will bid on the project. Prepare a memo to your U.S. firm expressing your views on whether the firm should submit a bid.
5. Despite the *Montreal Protocol*, the nation of Livy continues to produce CFC-emitting refrigerators and to export them to nations throughout the world. A number of governments object to Livy's practices and ban its exports pursuant to the protocol. Livy brings an action under GATT, alleging that under the principles stated in the *Shrimp* case, this is an attempt to impose conservationist policies on Livy. How should the GATT panel rule?
6. The Kingdom of Carolinium has a strong commitment to the preservation of wild horse herds. The neighboring Republic of Giles Run is a major dog food manufacturer and regularly uses wild horse meat in its products. These products are exported to and marketed in Carolinium. In accordance with its principles, Carolinium enacted the *Horse Conservation and Health Act* (HCHA), banning the use of all horse meat in any animal or human food products. Carolinium justified the HCHA on conservationist and health grounds. The evidence for any health hazard from horse meat is limited to a few scattered cases of botulism. The Carolinium ban effectively terminated all dog food exports from Giles Run. In response, Giles Run called for the creation of a GATT panel to consider the HCHA violation of GATT. How should the GATT panel rule?

Managerial Implications

Your employer, Ortiz-Hartman Steel Limited, is a specialty U.S. steel manufacturer. Over the past several years, Ortiz-Hartman has been underpriced in its specialty steel submarket by a manufacturer from the Bishopric of Saul, a nation that has virtually no environmental laws. Steel plants in Saul spew pollutants into the air and the rivers. Some of the pollutants damage the property and health of Saul subjects, but no cause of action in Saul affords them relief. Other pollutants damage the environment in neighboring countries. Faced with crippling competition, some members of Ortiz-Hartman management recommend that Ortiz-Hartman build a plant in Saul and take advantage of the more forgiving pollution laws.

1. Your employer asks you to prepare a memorandum summarizing the potential liability to Ortiz-Hartman associated with building a plant in Saul under current law. In your assessment, address all possible sources of liability, even those that you consider to be unlikely. Explain the detailed reasoning for your assessments.
2. Prepare a memorandum summarizing long-term risk in light of emerging international environmental legal standards.

Ethical Considerations

In March 1964, the Ecuadorian government invited Texaco, Inc. (Texaco) and Gulf Oil Corporation (Gulf) to conduct exploratory activities in the Oriente, an area that includes the eastern lowlands and slopes of the Andes and a portion of the Amazon River basin. Texaco and Gulf formed a consortium (Consortium) with equal ownership rights through their Ecuadorian subsidiaries to conduct this exploration. The Consortium discovered oil in commercial quantities in 1967 and began export operations in 1972 after completion of a pipeline to Ecuador's Pacific coast. Texaco served as the operator on behalf of the Consortium throughout this period of time.

The Consortium underwent significant changes in the 1970s. The state-owned oil company—Compania Estatal Petrolera Ecuatoriana (CEPE; later reorganized as Petroecuador)—assumed a stake in the Consortium in June 1974 and purchased Gulf's stake in December 1976. From 1977 to 1990, the Consortium operated with Texaco and CEPE/ Petroecuador as the only participants and Texaco as the operator. On July 1, 1990, Petroamazonas, a subsidiary of Petroecuador, replaced Texaco as the operator. The concession agreement expired on June 6, 1992. Ecuador elected not to renew the agreement and assumed complete control of the concession area. At the time of the termination of Texaco's interest, the Consortium had operations on more than one million acres; had 339 wells, 18 production stations, and 1500 kilometers of pipelines; and had extracted more than 1.4 billion barrels of oil.

The Consortium's operations exacted a heavy toll on the environment. Oil production and pipeline operations were alleged to have resulted in the discharge of 26 million gallons of crude oil and toxic wastewater into the surrounding environment. Approximately 2.5 million acres were impacted by oil-related discharges into wetlands, streams, and rivers and leeching into soil and groundwater. The Consortium dug and operated hundreds of unlined pits, which were used to store toxic chemicals utilized in drilling operations as well as other runoff. Additional sources of environmental contamination included the burning of crude oil, the flaring of approximately 235 billion cubic feet of natural gas, and spraying of roads with crude oil for maintenance and dust control.

Ecuador threatened to sue Texaco for environmental injuries. As a result, in May 1995, Texaco, Ecuador, and Petroecuador entered into a contract (Remediation Agreement) wherein Texaco agreed to perform work on designated sites in return for a release of claims from Ecuador and Petroecuador. The Remediation Agreement released Texaco and all related companies from claims arising from environmental degradation associated with the Consortium's activities other than those arising from remediation Texaco was obligated to perform. Texaco began remediation in 1995 and completed this work in 1998. Texaco spent $40 million in this effort, which included closing and remediating 161 waste pits and 7 overflow areas, plugging and abandoning 18 wells, and cleaning soil at 36 sites. Texaco also installed three produced water treatment and reinjection systems, provided Petroecuador with equipment for ten additional systems, designed three oil containment systems, and conducted extensive replanting of native vegetation at the remediated sites. Texaco also made two payments of $1 million each for socioeconomic projects and made payments totaling $4.6 million to affected municipalities in the region. In September 1998, the Ecuadorian government and Petroecuador signed a document (Final Act) in which they recognized that Texaco had fulfilled its obligations pursuant to the 1995 agreement and released it from current and future liability.

In November 1993, 74 Ecuadorians filed a class action lawsuit against Texaco in the U.S. District Court for the Southern District of New York. The plaintiffs purported to represent more than 30,000 persons residing in the Oriente who had suffered damages from hydrocarbon contamination as a result of the Consortium's operations. The claims were ultimately dismissed on Texaco's motion on the basis of *forum non conveniens*, which dismissal was upheld on appeal.

In May 2003, 46 Ecuadorian residents filed a lawsuit against Chevron Corporation (Chevron) in the Superior Court of Justice of Nueva Loja in the Sucum-bios Province. The Plaintiffs based their lawsuit on provisions of the Ecuadorian Constitution guaranteeing citizens the right to live in a healthy environment and the Environmental Management Law of 1999 that recognized a "popular action" to obtain damages for environmental injuries. The amount of damages was not initially specified but was later calculated at $27.3 billion.

Chevron asserted numerous defenses. Chevron initially contended that there was no valid claim against it or Texaco as the Environmental Management Law could not be applied retroactively pursuant to Ecuador's Constitution, Civil Code, and applicable case law. Furthermore, it asserted that the claims were barred by the Remediation Agreement and Final Act. Additionally, Chevron claimed that the Plaintiffs sued the wrong entity by failing to assert claims against Texaco. Specifically, Chevron contended that it did not acquire Texaco in 2001 and thus were not responsible for its liabilities, including responsibility for environmental injury in Ecuador. Rather, Texaco was merged with a wholly owned subsidiary of Chevron called Keepep, Inc. Chevron also alleged that the Superior Court lacked personal jurisdiction as Chevron had never operated in Ecuador, that the Plaintiffs' claims were barred by Ecuador's four-year statute of limitations, and that the Plaintiffs lacked standing as they failed to plead individualized personal injury or property damage.

The Superior Court deferred ruling on these defenses and commenced trial in October 2003. The conduct of the trial stirred considerable controversy and provided Chevron with additional defenses. These controversies include procedural anomalies relating to evidence collection, the testing of soil and water samples, the use of expert witnesses, and the methods utilized to calculate damages. Chevron also claimed that the Superior Court was influenced by political pressure exerted primarily by Ecuadorian President Rafael Correa and that the trial judge lacked integrity.

Although Texaco and Chevron's defense of the U.S. and Ecuadorian litigations is within the procedural rules in both jurisdictions, is it the appropriate moral response to environmental contamination in Ecuador? Is Chevron's conduct consistent with *teleological frameworks* for ethical thinking? Did Chevron's response to the litigation promote its self-interest to the greatest degree possible as set forth in *ethical egoism?* What might become of environmental protection in the developing world if Chevron successfully defends the litigation? Was Texaco's behavior ethical based on the time and place of its occurrence? Did Texaco's conduct and Chevron's litigation strategy produce the greatest overall good for affected persons as set forth in *utilitarianism?* Does the potential outcome of the Ecuadorian litigation demonstrate the difficulties inherent in utilitarianism with respect to measuring outcomes and predicting the success, failure, or utility of certain behaviors?

Is Chevron's conduct consistent with *deontological frameworks* for ethical thinking? Is Chevron setting an example by which other multinational corporations may conduct their operations in the developing world? Did Texaco's conduct treat Ecuadorians as means to the end of exploiting oil and gas resources? Is Chevron's decision to vigorously defend the Ecuadorian litigation and resist settlement the fairest and most equitable resolution as anticipated by contractarianism?

CHAPTER 21

Regulating the Competitive Environment

An enterprise with great market power must be concerned with the limits that competition or "antitrust" laws place on extensions of that power. Such extensions include not only the introduction of products, but also franchise and licensing arrangements. Unlike other bodies of law reviewed in Part Four of this book, the general substance of competition laws is markedly similar from nation to nation. The way in which that law is implemented, however, differs significantly from place to place.

HISTORICAL DEVELOPMENT OF INTERNATIONAL COMPETITION LAW

Antitrust law has been important in the United States since the end of the nineteenth century. At that time, Congress passed the *Sherman Antitrust Act* and the *Clayton Act* to permit government "trust-busters" to break up a number of "trusts" and cartels that used their size to crush the competition. After competition was wiped out, the "trusts" were free to hike prices to consumers' detriment. These laws, which had strong populist support and developed independently in American courts, are the foundation of an economic system that relies on maximizing competition to permit free-market forces to operate.

After the Second World War, the European equivalent of antitrust law—**competition law**—developed rapidly. Under Articles 101 and 102 of the *Treaty on the Functioning of the European Union* (TFEU) (formerly Articles 81 and 82 of the *Treaty of Rome*), the members of the European Union (EU) pledged to regulate anticompetitive actions and outlaw the abuse of dominant market power, both within the individual member states and in the Union as a whole. These articles, now implemented by the Commission of the European Communities, form the bedrock on which the EU's highly sophisticated competition law is based. In recent years, the Commission's Directorate-General COMP (DG-COMP) has prepared numerous regulations for adoption by the European Council of Ministers and issued a host of decisions and exemptions. The DG-COMP is the EU's combination of the Federal Trade Commission and the U.S. Department of Justice, which together regulate antitrust matters in the United States.

Competition law has also become an important focus for the European Court of Justice (ECJ), which hears appeals of Commission decisions and referrals from the courts of the EU member states on competition law issues. The European approach puts less confidence in market forces and is more fearful of unrestrained competition. The Europeans are more willing to rely on direct government action and less willing to count on litigation, although individual countries within Europe are beginning to emerge as more "litigation friendly."

Effective August 1, 2008, China implemented the *Anti-Monopoly Law* of the People's Republic of China. (AML). The new law, based in great part on European competition law, targets anticompetitive monopoly agreements, abuse of dominant market positions, and concentrations viewed as likely to eliminate or restrict competition. Like the U.S. and EU regimes, the AML covers certain extraterritorial transactions that have a domestic impact in China. Also like competition laws in many other countries, China's AML lays out a basic regulatory framework but leaves the details of implementation open-ended.

More than one hundred other nations around the world now have enacted competition policy-based national merger notification and review regimes. From South Korea to Brazil to the Czech Republic, many nations are concerned with private domination of sectors of the national economy.

Even as competition laws multiply, their content becomes more diverse. Some nations follow the U.S. model, some follow the EU model, some combine those approaches, and some opt for new ideas. The U.S. Attorney General's International Competition Policy Advisory Committee initially sought to promote substantive convergence among competition law schemes and procedural "best practices," but concluded that "… agreement on specific substantive rules is unlikely in the foreseeable future" and that "[c]omplete harmonization will be achieved only in the long run, if ever." Antitrust scholars agree that harmonization in the near future is highly unlikely, although the discord generated from divergent results on the two sides of the Atlantic in the same or similar cases will likely maintain pressure for harmonization. Indeed, many countries have entered into bilateral agreements, or **memoranda of understanding** that provide for coordination on cases, sharing of information, and dialogue concerning competition policy issues. In addition, multilateral organizations such as the International Competition Network (ICN) and the Organisation for Economic Cooperation and Development (OECD) strive to promote convergence in competition policies through exchange of information and best practices.

Still, businesses today face conflicting trends in competition law. To understand how these trends affect businesses, this chapter begins with a review of the basic structure of antitrust/competition law.

In the following section, we address the competition law approaches of the major commercial powers in the world—the United States, European Union, Japan, and China. Because this group constitutes well over 60 percent of the world's gross domestic product, their approaches drive the development of the lawworldwide.

BASIC REGULATORY FRAMEWORK

The form of antitrust laws differs somewhat from nation to nation. The German competition legislation—the *Gesetzgegen Wettbewerbsbeschrankungen*—is highly detailed and addresses many issues in advance. This limits the discretion of the administering agency and the courts to define and develop the law. In stark contrast, but consistent with its reliance on government policy implementation, the *Korean Monopoly Regulation and Fair Trade Act* is drafted in more general terms. Administrative regulations contain the specifics of what is prohibited and how it is prohibited. *The Japanese Antimonopoly Law* facially resembles the U.S. law from which it is largely drawn, but it is administered by the Japanese Fair Trade Commission and works more like EU law. Consistent with the United States' litigious tradition, antitrust laws in the United States are stated in general terms. The details are worked out in court.

Despite these differences in form and enforcement, the substance of competition law is remarkably similar in its focus on three types of activity. First, competition laws tend to prohibit agreements between competitors that restrict competition, such as cartel or price-fixing agreements. From this general principle flows a whole range of specific prohibitions against anticompetitive clauses in licensing, franchising, and other types of agreements. Second, competition laws prohibit the abuse of a dominant market position. From this general principle come a variety of concepts such as bans against predatory pricing and refusals to deal in certain circumstances. Third, competition laws oversee mergers and acquisitions to ensure that competition is not lessened and consumers are not harmed by a new consolidated firm's gain in market power or entry into anticompetitive combinations.

Prohibitions Against Agreements to Restrict Competition

Legislatures and competition authorities across the globe increasingly are enacting laws and regulations to prevent anticompetitive agreements such as price-fixing, bid-rigging, and market allocation. Many of these laws follow the U.S. approach reflected in Section 1 of the *Sherman Act* and the EU in Article 101 of the TFEU, both of which prohibit concerted anticompetitive conduct. The *Sherman Act* does so in broad, unspecific language. Article 101(1) of the TFEU flatly prohibits "all agreements between undertakings [firms], decisions by associations of undertakings and concerted practices which may affect trade between the Member States and which have as their object or effect the prevention, restriction, or distortion of competition within the Common Market." Article 101(2) automatically voids all agreements that violate Article 101(1), and Article 101(3) authorizes the European Commission to grant exemptions from this prohibition.

Prohibitions against agreements that restrict competition are ordinarily the most relevant to international transactions. For example, a principal objective of every licensor is to prevent its licensee from competing with it. Left to its own devices, the licensor would seek pledges of eternal noncompetition throughout the Milky Way. The licensor must, however, moderate its demands so they are consistent with local competition law.

This principle is implemented differently under different systems. Some nations require governmental review of virtually all such **vertical arrangements** between firms and their distributors, customers, or suppliers. For example, Chile generally prohibits the establishment of exclusive distribution systems that restrict trade. Because exclusive distribution agreements always restrict trade, this prohibition means that all such arrangements must be reviewed with officials from the Fiscalía Nacional Económica, the Chilean competition law enforcer, to obtain discretionary preclearance.

The U.S. View. The United States characteristically looks at such arrangements in the context of determining whether they enhance or inhibit the workings of a competitive marketplace. The regulators and courts will allow vertical restraints if a reasonable case can be made that they foster better service and, hence, enhance interbrand competition; encourage innovation; or do not foreclose a substantial part of the market to others. For instance, U.S. policy tends to accept a patent holder's restrictions, and the enhanced profit that follows, in the hope of giving greater encouragement to innovation.

The EU View. In the EU, the Commission is more likely to intervene to prevent vertical restraints. In the area of patent licensing, DG-COMP is forgiving of some anticompetitive restrictions but not as forgiving as U.S. authorities would be, particularly with respect to products that include both patented and unpatented components. For example, in the realm of patents, in contrast to U.S. authorities, the Europeans increasingly view the monopoly inherent in a patent as a danger to competition that should be minimized as much as possible.

The European Commission is more flexible with respect to know-how transfer agreements than to patent licenses. **Know-how** is a firm's intellectual property that is protected through secrecy and confidentiality agreements rather than through patents or copyright laws. The rationale is that because the owner of know-how does not have any legally cognizable right to its knowledge, it can rely only on secrecy. The only way to protect secrecy is through restrictive provisions that prohibit the licensee from competing against the licensor or from disclosing the know-how to any third party. If the Commission could not give the potential licensor of know-how confidence that its know-how would be kept secret, the licensor would be left with little incentive to enter into any agreement. The result would be anticompetitive because no one but the licensor would have the know-how.

The EU authorities also show flexibility in reviewing franchise agreements. Franchise agreements involve peculiar considerations because the franchiser must have substantial control over the franchisee. Like other licensors, the franchiser must protect its know-how. In addition, the franchiser must ensure that the franchisee is producing and marketing the product in a manner consistent with the franchiser's good name. Uniformity is important to most franchise businesses. One franchisee's poor performance can have adverse effects on the franchiser's operations internationally. In addition, the franchiser may want to prevent the franchisee from charging prices that are inconsistent with the pricing practices of other franchisees. The European Court of Justice has considered these unusual attributes of the franchiser–franchisee relationship and, in general, has given franchisers and franchisees great flexibility in structuring their relationships.

The Japanese View. Japan's consensus-oriented tradition has historically encouraged collaboration rather than competition among its major corporations. Consistent with this tradition, Japan permitted development of tightly wound ***keiretsu*** networks of suppliers and distributors. Although these networks competed against one another in Japan, their control over the means of distribution, exercised through highly restrictive distribution agreements, effectively prevented foreign firms from entering the Japanese market. In fact, when they could enter the market at all, foreign companies were compelled to enter into a single, exclusive distributorship agreement for all of Japan. Obviously, the single distributor was able to exact quite favorable terms, and the Japanese consumer was confronted with relatively high prices. In 1990, the Japan Fair Trade Commission (JFTC) ruled that companies with at least a 25 percent share of the Japanese market were prohibited from signing exclusive import distribution contracts. Enforcement of these restrictions has not been aggressive, however.

The Chinese View. China's *Antimonopoly Law* (AML) prohibits agreements, decisions, or concerted actions that eliminate or restrict competition. The National Development and Reform Commission (NDRC) and the State Administration for Industry and Commerce (SAIC) handle price- and non-price-related violations of the AML, respectively. These two agencies monitor for agreements that (1) fix or change the price of products or the price for resale, (2) limit the output or sales of products, (3) allocate sales markets or raw material purchasing markets, (4) limit the purchase of new technology or new facilities or the development of new products or new technology, (5) jointly boycott transactions, or (6) engage in other monopolistic agreements identified by the antimonopoly authorities.

While China's law and enforcement in this area is still relatively new, two recent cases illustrate the authorities' approach to agreements among competitors. NDRC investigated China Telecom and China Unicom in late 2011 for allegedly restricting broadband access through their pricing policies. NDRC suspended the investigation after the companies agreed to adjust their pricing systems and improve Internet interconnection and the broadband network in China. In 2012, SAIC imposed a fine and confiscated the illegal income of 11 used car dealerships that had entered into anticompetitive agreements to allocate markets and coordinate fees. China is moving decisively to keep its large markets competitive.

Abuse of Dominant Market Position

Section 2 of the *Sherman Act*, Article 102 of the TFEU, and their counterparts in other national competition statutes address the problem of monopolies and the abuse of monopoly power. To be in violation of such **monopoly** provisions, a company must have a **dominant market position**, which is defined differently in different countries and in different industries. In addition, the dominant party must be found to have abused this position.

In smaller countries where, by definition, fewer entities can survive in the relevant markets, market domination tends to be more widely tolerated. Thus, in Canada, where industry is considerably more concentrated than in the United States, optimal levels of industrial concentration are likely to be relatively higher than in the United States. Moreover, cultural and historical factors are also of considerable importance. For instance, in Germany and France, refusals to deal (***refus de vente***) are closely proscribed, even if the refuser has a relatively low level of market dominance.

The U.S. View. U.S. antitrust law prohibits a single firm from acting in a way that unreasonably restrains competition by creating or maintaining monopoly power, or attempting to do so. As noted, two elements are required: The firm must possess monopoly power in the relevant market, and it must have gained that position through improper conduct. Under U.S. law, a firm has monopoly power when it has the long-term ability to raise prices or exclude competitors. U.S. courts consider the product in question and available alternatives if prices are raised, and typically do not find monopoly power if the firm has less than 50 percent of market share or if the leading position is not sustainable over time. Improper conduct includes exclusionary or predatory acts such as exclusive supply or purchase agreements, tying, predatory pricing, or refusals to deal. A legitimate business justification for its actions, however, will save a firm with dominant market power from liability. As the Supreme Court noted in 1966 in *United States v. Grinnell Corp.*, 384 U.S. 563, 571 (1966), dominant market power is lawful if it resulted from "growth or development as a consequence of a superior product, business acumen, or historic accident."

The EU View. In the following case involving Microsoft, the European Commission took a decidedly different approach than the United States when addressing abuse of a dominant market position. Its more aggressive position was generally upheld by the European Court of First Instance in the following 2007 decision.

Microsoft Corp. v. Commission of the European Communities

Case T-201/04, 5 C.M.LR. 11 (2007); Available at 2007 WL 2693858
European Court of Justice Court of First Instance—Grand Chamber BB

BACKGROUND AND FACTS

Microsoft Corp., a U.S. company, designs, develops, and markets software products, including operating systems for client personal computers (client PCs), operating systems for work group servers, and streaming media players. Sun Microsystems, Inc., another U.S. company, lodged a complaint with the European Commission alleging that Microsoft had refused to give Sun the information necessary to allow Sun's work group server operating systems to interoperate with the Windows client PC operating system. In 2000, the Commission launched an investigation of Microsoft's Windows 2000 generation of client PC and work group server operating systems and Microsoft's integration of its Windows Media Player into the PC operating system. In March 2004, the Commission entered a decision finding Microsoft guilty of two abuses of dominant market position, violating Articles 82 and 54. The Commission ordered Microsoft to (1) make its operating system more accessible to competitors, (2) offer client PC systems that did not bundle the Windows Media Player, and (3) set up and pay for an independent monitoring trustee to ensure Microsoft did not violate the order.

continues

continued

Microsoft was ruled to have had a dominant position in the client PC operating systems market and in the work group server operating systems market. In the PC operating system market, this was because the Commission found that Microsoft's market share was consistently over 90 percent, there were significant barriers to market entry because users like platforms on which they can use a large number of applications, and software designers write applications for the most popular client PC operating systems. In the work group server operating systems market, this was because Microsoft's market share was at least 60 percent, no other competitor in the work group market had a share greater than 25 percent, and there were close commercial and technological links between the PC and work group markets.

The Commission found that, in light of Microsoft's dominant position, it was abusive for Microsoft to (1) refuse to share interoperability information and (2) make the availability of the Windows client PC operating system conditional on the simultaneous acquisition of the Windows Media Player software. The Commission thus imposed a fine and a number of remedies on Microsoft. Microsoft appealed the decision to the Court of First Instance. Because of its importance, the matter was ultimately referred to the Grand Chamber of that Court.

PRESIDENT VESTERDORF AND JUDGES JAEGER, PIRRUNG, GARCÍA-VALDECASAS, TIILI, AZIZI, COOKE, MEIJ, FORWOOD, MARTINS RIBEIRO, WISZNIEWSKA-BIALECKA, VADAPALAS AND I. LABUCKA THE CRITERIA ON WHICH AN UNDERTAKING IN A DOMINANT POSITION MAY BE COMPELLED TO GRANT A LICENCE, AS DEFINED BY THE COMMUNITY JUDICATURE, ARE NOT SATISFIED IN THE PRESENT CASE

It follows from [the facts presented to the Court] that ... Windows work group networks rely on an 'architecture' of both client/server and server/server interconnections and interactions and that that 'architecture'—which the Commission characterises as 'Windows domain architecture'—ensures 'transparent access' to the main services provided by work group servers. Those various factors also show that ... those interconnections and interactions are closely interlinked. In other words, the proper functioning of the Windows work group networks relies both on client/server communication protocols—which, by their nature, are implemented both in Windows client PC operating systems and in Windows work group server operating systems—and on server/ server communication protocols. [F]or numerous tasks, server/server communication protocols appear, in fact, as 'extensions' of the client/server communication protocols. In certain cases, a server acts as a client PC vis-à-vis another server ... . The Court therefore finds that the Commission is quite correct to conclude that 'the common ability to be part of [the Windows domain architecture] is a feature of compatibility between Windows client PCs and Windows work group servers ... .'

The first abusive conduct in which Microsoft is found to have engaged is its refusal to supply the interoperability information to its competitors and to allow its use for the purpose of developing and distributing work group server operating system products ... .

By way of remedy for that refusal, the Commission ordered Microsoft, ... to do the following:

> ... make the interoperability information available to any undertaking having an interest in developing and distributing work group server operating system products and ... on reasonable and non-discriminatory terms, allow the use of the interoperability information ... for the purpose of developing and distributing work group server operating system products[.] Microsoft's argument is that its refusal to supply interoperability information cannot constitute an abuse of a dominant position within the meaning of Article 82 EC because, first, the information is protected by intellectual property rights (or constitutes trade secrets) and, second, the criteria established in the case-law which determine when an undertaking in a dominant position can be required to grant a licence to a third party are not satisfied in this case. [T]he Commission contends that there is no need to decide whether Microsoft's conduct constitutes a refusal to license intellectual property rights to a third party, or whether trade secrets merit the same degree of protection as intellectual property rights, since the strict criteria against which such a refusal may be found to constitute an abuse of a dominant position within the meaning of Article 82 EC are in any event satisfied in the present case ... . While Microsoft and the Commission are thus agreed that the refusal at issue may be assessed under Article 82 EC on the assumption that it constitutes a refusal to license intellectual property rights, they disagree as to the criteria established in the case-law that are applicable in such a situation... . The Commission ... maintains that, in order to determine whether such a refusal is abusive, it must take into consideration all the particular circumstances surrounding that

continues

continued

> refusal ... . Thus it explains ... that '[t]he case-law of the European Courts ... suggests that the Commission must analyse the entirety of the circumstances surrounding a specific instance of a refusal to supply and must take its decision [on the basis of] the results of such a comprehensive examination ... .' At the hearing, the Commission, ... confirmed that it had considered in the contested decision that Microsoft's conduct presented three characteristics which allowed it to be characterised as abusive. The first consists in the fact that the information which Microsoft refuses to disclose to its competitors relates to interoperability in the software industry, a matter to which the Community legislature attaches particular importance. The second characteristic lies in the fact that Microsoft uses its extraordinary power on the client PC operating systems market to eliminate competition on the adjacent work group server operating systems market. The third characteristic is that the conduct in question involves disruption of previous levels of supply ... .

In response to those various arguments, the Court observes that ... although undertakings are, as a rule, free to choose their business partners, in certain circumstances a refusal to supply on the part of a dominant undertaking may constitute an abuse of a dominant position within the meaning of Article 82 EC unless it is objectively justified. The Court of Justice thus considered that a company in a dominant position on the market in raw materials which, with the aim of reserving such raw materials for the purpose of manufacturing its own derivatives, refused to supply a customer which was itself a manufacturer of those derivatives, and was therefore likely to eliminate all competition on the part of that customer, abused its dominant position within the meaning of Article 82 EC.

In [another case], the Court of Justice was asked whether the refusal by a car manufacturer which was the proprietor of a design right covering car body panels to license third parties to supply products incorporating the protected design must be considered to be an abuse of a dominant position within the meaning of Article 82 EC. In its judgment, the Court of Justice emphasised that the right of a proprietor of a protected design to prevent third parties from manufacturing and selling or importing, without his consent, products incorporating the design constitutes the very subject-matter of his exclusive right. The Court of Justice concluded ... that 'an obligation imposed upon the proprietor of a protected design to grant to third parties, even in return for a reasonable royalty, a licence for the supply of products incorporating the design would lead to the proprietor thereof being deprived of the substance of his exclusive right, and that a refusal to grant such a licence cannot in itself constitute an abuse of a dominant position'. The Court of Justice added, however, that 'the exercise of an exclusive right by the proprietor of a registered design in respect of car body panels [might] be prohibited by Article [82 EC] if it involve [d], on the part of an undertaking holding a dominant position, certain abusive conduct such as the arbitrary refusal to supply spare parts to independent repairers, the fixing of prices for spare parts at an unfair level or a decision no longer to produce spare parts for a particular model even though many cars of that model [were] still in circulation, provided that such conduct [was] liable to affect trade between Member States ... .

It follows ... that the refusal by an undertaking holding a dominant position to license a third party to use a product covered by an intellectual property right cannot in itself constitute an abuse of a dominant position within the meaning of Article 82 EC. It is only in exceptional circumstances that the exercise of the exclusive right by the owner of the intellectual property right may give rise to such an abuse.

It also follows from that case-law that the following circumstances, in particular, must be considered to be exceptional:

- in the first place, the refusal relates to a product or service indispensable to the exercise of a particular activity on a neighbouring market;
- in the second place, the refusal is of such a kind as to exclude any effective competition on that neighbouring market;
- in the third place, the refusal prevents the appearance of a new product for which there is potential consumer demand.

Once it is established that such circumstances are present, the refusal by the holder of a dominant position to grant a licence may infringe Article 82 EC unless the refusal is objectively justified ... .

[T]he Court considers that it is appropriate, first of all, to decide whether the [exceptional] circumstances ... are also present in this case.

The Court observed ... that ... in order to be able to compete viably with Windows work group server operating systems, competitors' operating systems must be able to interoperate with the Windows domain architecture on an equal footing with those Windows systems... . The Court has held that interoperability ... had two indissociable components, client/ server interoperability and server/server interoperability and

continues

continued

that it implied ... that a server running a non-Microsoft work group server operating system could act as domain controller within a Windows domain using Active Directory and, consequently, would be able to participate in the multimaster replication mechanism with the other domain controllers ... . [T]he Commission's analysis of that question in the contested decision is based on complex economic assessments and that, accordingly, it is subject to only limited review by the Court ... .

It follows from all of the foregoing considerations that Microsoft has not established that the Commission made a manifest error when it considered that non-Microsoft work group server operating systems must be capable of interoperating with the Windows domain architecture on an equal footing with Windows work group server operating systems if they were to be marketed viably on the market. The Court also concludes from those considerations that the absence of such interoperability with the Windows domain architecture has the effect of reinforcing Microsoft's competitive position on the work group server operating systems market, particularly because it induces consumers to use its work group server operating system in preference to its competitors', although its competitors' operating systems offer features to which consumers attach great importance.

THE BUNDLING OF WINDOWS MEDIA PLAYER WITH THE WINDOWS CLIENT PC OPERATING SYSTEM

Article 6 of the contested decision orders Microsoft, inter alia, to offer, within 90 days of notification of the decision, a full-functioning version of its Windows client PC operating system which does not incorporate Windows Media Player, although Microsoft is to retain the right to offer a bundle of the Windows client PC operating system and Windows Media Player ... .

[T]he Commission clearly demonstrated ... that ... Microsoft offered OEMs, for pre-installation on client PCs, only the version of Windows bundled with Windows Media Player had the inevitable consequence of affecting relations on the market between Microsoft, OEMs and suppliers of third-party media players by appreciably altering the balance of competition in favour of Microsoft and to the detriment of the other operators. [N]o third-party media player could achieve such a level of market penetration without having the advantage in terms of distribution that Windows Media Player enjoys as a result of Microsoft's use of its Windows client PC operating system .... The Court considers that the Commission was correct to find ... that it was on the basis of the percentages of installation and use of media players that content providers and software developers chose the technology for which they would develop their own products .... The Commission correctly stated, first, that those operators tended primarily to use Windows Media Player as that allowed them to reach the very large majority of client PC users in the world and, second, that the transmission of content and applications compatible with a given media player was in itself a significant competitive factor, since it increased the popularity of that media player, and, in turn, favoured the use of the underlying media technology, including codecs, formats ... .

Microsoft has not demonstrated the existence of any objective justification for the abusive bundling of Windows Media Player with the Windows client PC operating system ....

Decision. The Court of First Instance annulled the portion of the Commission Decision that ordered Microsoft to submit a proposal for the establishment of a mechanism that was to include a monitoring trustee empowered to have access, independently of the Commission, to Microsoft's assistance, information, documents, premises, and employees and to the source code of the relevant Microsoft products. It also annulled the requirement that Microsoft pay for the monitoring trustee. The Court upheld all other aspects of the Commission's decision.

Case Questions

1. Would Microsoft have been ordered to provide the interconnection instructions if it had controlled only a 40 percent market share in operating systems?
2. If Apple were to obtain a larger market share in the future, would there be a basis for relieving Microsoft from this judgment?
3. This order prohibits Microsoft from giving a program away when the computer is purchased. Why?

The Japanese View. In pursuing anticompetitive activity, JFTC guidelines provide that Japanese authorities will prioritize cases where the entity has a majority market share, and its actions have a "serious impact" on consumers' lives. Other factors are market size, scope of business activities, and characteristics of the product. Among other abuses of a dominant market position, the Japanese *Antimonopoly Act* prohibits "abuse of superior bargaining position," in which large buyers can impose unreasonable terms in dealings with small- and medium-sized suppliers. The JFTC has stated that preventing such conduct is of particular importance.

The Chinese View. Chinese law also prohibits abuse of dominant market positions, which the AML defines as "the ability to control the price, quantity, or other trading conditions of products in relevant market, or to hinder or affect other undertakings to enter the relevant market." The National Development and Reform Commission (NDRC) oversees abuses relating to pricing, and the State Administration for Industry and Commerce (SAIC) oversees non-price-related violations. The full impact of this new authority in China is not yet clear.

Mergers and Acquisitions

The foregoing commentary describes traditional enforcement mechanisms that are familiar to U.S. businesspeople. In these mechanisms, the parties act and the authorities react. But each of the major jurisdictions that we have discussed have exceptions to this general rule for mergers and acquisitions that hit certain criteria for potential damage to free competition. The best examples are the United States Hart–Scott–Rodino review and the EU's preapproval procedure.

The U.S. View. As is true in many countries, U.S. merger law allows authorities prospectively to prohibit mergers before potentially harmful effects occur. U.S. authorities may also investigate completed mergers if they appear to have harmed consumers. Section 7 of the *Clayton Act* prohibits mergers and acquisitions when the effect "may be substantially to lessen competition, or to tend to create a monopoly." *Horizontal mergers* between direct competitors are considered to pose the greatest threat to competition, because they are seen as most likely to create or enhance market power or facilitate dominance in the market. If a proposed merger presents competitive concerns, firms often are able to work with the U.S. Federal Trade Commission (FTC) or U.S. Department of Justice (DOJ) to resolve such concerns through a **consent agreement**, which maintains the beneficial aspects of the deal while removing the anticompetitive elements.

The United States does not have a preapproval system. The closest mechanism to **preapproval** is the review process created by the *Hart–Scott–Rodino Act*, under which mergers, joint venture agreements, and similar transactions of a certain size must be brought before the Department of Justice before they are concluded. Even if the DOJ gives the parties permission to conclude the transaction, the DOJ may later bring litigation relating to it. Indeed, parties entering into a combination that is facing particular scrutiny may sometimes enter into a pre-litigation settlement agreement with the FTC in order to secure more comfort than a bare Hart-Scott Rodino decision not to seek an injunction. Nor does the *Hart–Scott–Rodino Act* prevent any private party from bringing such a suit. In fact, in *California v. American Stores Co.*, 495 U.S. 271 (1990), the U.S. Supreme Court held that private parties and state authorities may sue in federal court for divestiture of a merger even after it has been approved by the DOJ or the FTC. Overall, antitrust policy in the United States has developed in the courts.

The EU View. In 1990, the Council of the European Communities' *Regulation 4064/89*—the *EC Merger Regulation*—became effective. In 2004, the European Council made substantial amendments to the *Merger Regulation* when it formally adopted *Regulation 139/2004*, which affects both procedural review and the substantive test for merger prohibition. Under the *Merger Regulation*, parties to all mergers, acquisitions, joint ventures, and other business combinations having a *Community dimension* must provide pre-transaction notification to the Commission.

The *EC Merger Regulation* had historically been administered by the Commission's Merger Task Force in rapid-fire fashion. Reorganization of DG-COMP in recent years has allowed for more sector-specific review of mergers. Under the Regulation, deals "notified" to the Commission automatically begin a five-week Phase 1 merger inquiry. During the five-week period, the Task Force intensively studies the competitive effects of the proposed transaction. It also entertains the views of third parties if they can demonstrate a sufficient interest in the proposed merger. The Task Force then renders a Phase 1 decision in which it determines whether the merger "raises serious doubts as to its compatibility with the common market." It will extend the ruling if the parties offer proposed undertakings in the hope of settlement. If no serious doubts result, the merger is cleared. If serious doubts arise, the merger review enters Phase II, a four-and-one-half-month review that can be extended. Phase II includes a meeting with the parties involved, possibly another meeting that includes third parties, a Statement of Objections describing the Commission's concerns, a reply by the parties involved, a formal hearing, and proposed undertakings to settle the case.

In Phase I, the Commission's Merger Task Force begins with an analysis of the materials submitted by the parties seeking approval. It also has broad investigative powers under the *Merger Regulation*, including the ability to request information, examine business records, ask "for oral explanations on the spot," and conduct on-site investigations. The Commission has broad powers to levy fines for noncompliance or failure to cooperate during the investigative process.

In any inquiry, the Commission first attempts to determine Community dimension in cases of any dispute on the issue. Such a dimension exists when either

1. The aggregate worldwide sales of all the firms being combined exceed 5 billion euros, and
2. The aggregate sales of each of two or more of the firms within the Union exceeds 250 million euros;

or

1. The aggregate worldwide sales of all the firms being combined exceeds 2.5 billion euros
2. In at least three member states, the aggregate sales of the firms exceeds 100 million euros
3. In each of those three member states the aggregate sales of at least two of the firms exceeds 25 million euros, and
4. The aggregate sales within the EU of each of at least two of the firms exceeds 100 million euros. (The value of the euro varies widely against the U.S. dollar; for example, in January 2013, 1 euro was worth roughly 1.3 dollars.)

Even if either of these tests is satisfied, a concentration does not have a Community dimension if more than two-thirds of the aggregate Community-wide sales are in only one member state. If the proposed concentration has a Community dimension, then only the Commission is to examine the transaction; member states cannot interfere with or contradict the Commission's findings.

Once the Task Force determines that the transaction has a Community dimension, it then determines whether the concentration is compatible with the common market. Under the test prior to the adoption of *Regulation 139/2004*, a concentration that created or strengthened a dominant position so as to "significantly impede" effective competition within the Union was "incompatible" with the common market. Following *Regulation 139/2004*, the Task Force asks whether a merger "would significantly impede effective competition, in particular as a result of the creation or strengthening of a dominant position." While the two tests appear similar on the surface, under the new test, dominance is not the sole impediment to "effective competition." In great part, the EC intended the modification to prohibit unilateral effects on the relevant market, such as where major competitors merge to form a large firm, even when the resulting entity is still not the dominant firm. Thus, those cases where the merged entity would not be the leader within the defined market, but nevertheless would maintain a substantial market share, are still "caught." Dominance remains the staple of the test, however, and ensures continuity with previous case law. The other major change in the 2004 modification is that it moves closer to an effects-based test by explicitly providing in Recital 29 to the Regulation that "[i]t is possible that the efficiencies brought about by the concentration counteract the effects on competition, and in particular the potential harm to consumers, that it might otherwise have and that, as a consequence, the concentration would not significantly impede effective competition."

The criteria employed in assessing compatibility with the common market include market share (compatibility is presumed if joint market share in the common market does not exceed 25 percent), legal or practical barriers to entry, supply and demand trends in relevant markets, competition from firms outside the Union, and the structure of the markets.

In essence, the Commission undertakes a two-step analysis to determine whether an *undertaking* in a merger creates or strengthens a dominant position. First, it defines the *relevant markets* affected by the merger in terms of both product line and geography. Second, the Commission determines the effect of the merger on the market so defined by the new test as noted.

If a proposed transaction does not have a Community dimension, it is jointly regulated by the Commission and member state enforcement authorities. The boundary between regulation under the *Merger Regulation* and "normal" DG-COMP review under Articles 101 and 102 is hazy. If a proposed joint venture is *concentrative*—if it will "independently and permanently perform all of the functions of an autonomous economic entity," without "coordination of the competitive behavior of the parties among themselves or between them and the joint venture"—it is deemed to be subject to review under the *Merger Regulation*. If, on the other hand, it is merely *cooperative*, regular review is appropriate.

A trio of cases decided in 2002 by the **European Court of First Instance (CFI)** in Luxembourg, beginning with *Airtours* below, ushered in a more hospitable climate for mergers within the European Community. In often scathing language, the CFI vetoed the Merger Task Force's decisions blocking the unions. Altogether, the three cases suggest that, by 2003, EC regulatory power over mergers had been curtailed and that any Merger Task Force rejection of a proposed merger will be held to a more stringent standard of proof. Thus, any companies undergoing a merger review should expect a more thorough and intense review.

Airtours v. Commission

Case T-342/99 2002 E.C.R. II-2585 European Court of First Instance

BACKGROUND AND FACTS

A U.K.-based travel company, Airtours (now MyTravel), sought to purchase a travel agency known as First Choice. It announced its planned merger to EC authorities in early 1999. Later that year, the Merger Task Force blocked the proposed merger, asserting that such a proposed combination of travel powerhouses would necessarily create a "collective dominant" position in the U.K. market for so-called short-haul travel vacations. The Merger Task Force asserted that this would lead to higher prices for consumers as well as the elimination of smaller, less visible agencies. Airtours appealed to the Court of First Instance.

PRESIDENT JUDGE LINDH

The prospective analysis which the Commission has to carry out in its review of concentrations involving collective dominance calls for close examination in particular of the circumstances which, in each individual case, are relevant for assessing the effects of the concentration on competition in the reference market… . [W]here the Commission takes the view that a merger should be prohibited because it will create a situation of collective dominance, it is incumbent upon it to produce convincing evidence thereof. The evidence must concern, in particular, factors playing a significant role in the assessment of whether a situation of collective dominance exists, such as, for example, the lack of effective competition between the operators alleged to be members of the dominant oligopoly and the weakness of any competitive pressure that might be exerted by other operators… .

Finally, contrary to the Commission's contention… the fact that to some extent (30 to 40% of the shares) the same institutional investors are found in Airtours, First Choice and Thomson cannot be regarded as evidence that there is already a tendency to collective dominance in the industry. It is sufficient to point out in that regard that… there is no suggestion in the Decision that the group of institutional shareholders forms a united body controlling those quoted companies or providing a mechanism for exchange of information between the three undertakings. Furthermore, the Commission cannot contend that those shareholders are a further force for cautious capacity management, unless it has examined to what extent they are involved in the management of the companies concerned. Finally, even assuming that it were proved they are capable of exercising some influence on the management of the undertakings, since the concerns of the common institutional investors with respect to growth (and thus capacity) merely reflect a characteristic inherent in the relevant market, the Commission would still have to establish that the fact that institutional investors hold shares in three of the four leading tour operators amounts to evidence that there is already a tendency to collective dominance… .

It is apparent from the foregoing that, since it did not deny that the market was competitive, the Commission was not entitled to treat the cautious capacity planning characteristic of the market in normal circumstances as evidence substantiating its proposition that there was already a tendency to collective dominance in the industry… .

In the light of all of the foregoing, the Court concludes that the Decision, far from basing its prospective analysis on cogent evidence, is vitiated by a series of errors of assessment as to factors fundamental to any assessment of whether a collective dominant position might be created. It follows that the Commission prohibited the transaction without having proved to the requisite legal standard that the concentration would give rise to a collective dominant position of the three major tour operators, of such a kind as significantly to impede effective competition in the relevant market.

Decision. The CFI annulled the Merger Task Force's decision prohibiting the merger. This was the first time that the CFI had overruled such a merger ban by the EC.

Case Questions

1. Does the order prevent Airtours from entering into mergers in the future with companies that have a smaller share of the U.K. market?
2. If Airtours proposed a merger with another firm with a very large share of the German market but no share of the U.K. market, how would the merger be treated, based on this opinion?
3. What "product" is Airtours selling? Would this decision prevent a merger with a party in the travel business that sold a different "product"?

In *Airtours*, the CFI frequently criticizes the Merger Task Force for not meeting the requisite standard of proof, affording the EC none of the deference normally accorded an administrative agency's decision. Indeed, the CFI stated that the Task Force did "not give the slightest indication that there is no competition between the main tour operators." Such harsh criticism was particularly damning when one considers that under the *Merger Regulation*'s scheme, businesses do not take the risk of going forward without the agency's approval.

The *Airtours* CFI did agree that the so-called collective dominance test was the proper analytic framework for analyzing mergers, but it redefined the test to make it more difficult to stop mergers. Specifically, it stated that mergers must have "the direct and immediate effect of creating or strengthening a position of [collective dominance], which is significantly and lastingly to impede competition in the relevant market." The CFI emphasized that if no competitive effects were immediately created, then the merger must be allowed.

Airtours was only the first part of a run of bad news for the Merger Task Force. In the following case, *Schneider Elec. SA v. Commission*, the CFI annulled an EC decision because it had not followed its own procedural rules. This decision served notice that the CFI would now require strict compliance with procedural safeguards in the preapproval process.

In addition to noting this procedural error, the CFI specifically criticized the finding that the merged entity's dominance in France would necessarily imply dominance in other countries. Indeed, the court suggested that the Merger Task Force had exaggerated the merged entity's probable strength.

Schneider Elec. SA v. Commission

Case T-77/02, 2002 E.C.R. II-04201 European Court of First Instance

BACKGROUND AND FACTS

Schneider Electric SA (Schneider), a company incorporated under French law, is the parent company of a group engaged in the manufacture and sale of products and systems in the electrical distribution, industrial control, and automation sectors. Incorporated under French law, Legrand SA is a company that specializes in the manufacture and sale of electrical equipment for low-voltage installations. Schneider launched its bid to acquire Legrand in a $6.43 billion purchase offer in January 2001. In accordance with the requirements in the Merger Regulation, Legrand notified the Commission of Schneider's proposal to make a public exchange offer for all shares of Legrand held by the public. Due to French merger rules, Schneider proceeded with its purchase of Legrand before the Merger Task Force ruled on the propriety of the merger. In August 2001 the Commission decided that the transaction would create an anticompetitive dominant position in a number of key markets. The CFI then considered the Schneider case under new fast-track provisions designed to hasten judicial review of such merger decisions.

PRESIDENT JUDGE VESTERDORF

The Court considers ... the claim that Schneider's rights of defence have been infringed in that the Commission included in the Decision a specific objection which was not clearly expressed in the statement of objections ... .

According to well-established case-law, the Decision need not necessarily replicate the statement of objections. Thus, it is permissible to supplement the statement of objections in the light of the parties' response, whose arguments show that they have actually been able to exercise their rights of defence. The Commission may also, in the light of the administrative procedure, revise or supplement its arguments of fact or law in support of its objections ... .

Nonetheless, the statement of objections must contain an account of the objections cast in sufficiently clear terms to achieve the objective ascribed to it by the Community regulations, namely to provide all the information the undertakings need to defend themselves properly before the Commission adopts a final decision ... .

In addition, in the procedures for reviewing concentrations, the statement of objections is not solely intended to spell out the complaints and give the undertaking to which it is addressed the opportunity to submit comments in response. It is also intended to give the notifying parties the chance to suggest corrective measures and, in particular, proposals for divestiture and sufficient time, given the requirement for speed which characterises the general scheme of *Regulation No 4064/89*, to ascertain the extent to which divestiture is necessary with a view to rendering the transaction compatible with the common market in good time ... .

continues

continued

The Commission was consequently required to explain all the more clearly the competition problems raised by the proposed merger, in order to allow the notifying parties to put forward, properly and in good time, proposals for divestiture capable, if need be, of rendering the concentration compatible with the common market.

It is not apparent on reading the statement of objections that it dealt with sufficient clarity or precision with the strengthening of Schneider's position vis-à-vis French distributors of low-voltage electrical equipment as a result not only of the addition of Legrand's sales on the markets for switchboard components and panel-board components but also of Legrand's leading position in the segments for ultraterminal electrical equipment. The Court observes in particular that the general conclusion in the statement of objections lists the various national sectoral markets affected by the concentration, without demonstrating that the position of one of the notifying parties on a given product market would in any way buttress the position of the other party on another sectoral market.... .

Competitive overlap is conceivable only within a single national sectoral market and is thus different in nature from the mutual support provided at distribution level where two undertakings hold leading positions in one country in two distinct but complementary sectoral markets.

It follows that the statement of objections did not permit Schneider to assess the full extent of the competition problems to which the Commission claimed the concentration would give rise at distributor level on the French market for low-voltage electrical equipment.

Decision. The CFI annulled the Merger Task Force's prohibition on the merger because of the Task Force's defective procedural handling of the case.

Case Questions

1. Schneider and Legrande did not sell the same product. Why was their concentration a threat to competition?
2. Why would a combination of parties with "complementary" products create a threat to competition? How would this disadvantage competitors with only one of the complementary products?
3. What implications does this have for a maker of a personal computer operating system acquiring a company that sells software applications?

The ultimate blow for the Task Force was the *Tetra Laval* case decided in the autumn of 2002. There, the CFI rejected the Task Force's factual analysis of the likely negative horizontal and vertical impacts of the merger at issue. Further, in the CFI's first comment on the leveraging analysis adopted by the Merger Task Force, it redefined the **leveraging theory** of concentration, making it virtually useless. "Leveraging" refers to a company's ability to leverage dominance in one market to become dominant in another market, as developed in the *Tetra-Laval* case below.

The CFI noted that the leveraging theory, while still viable, was speculative in its actual impact. Notably, the CFI elsewhere criticized the Merger Task Force for failing to presume that the merged firm would at least attempt to behave in a legal fashion (because the prospect of being branded a criminal would be a strong deterrent on the merged entity's leadership). The CFI reasoned that although a conglomerate may have the ability to leverage its dominance, this is not tantamount to having a realistic incentive for doing so. In considering a leveraging theory, the Commission was to consider the extent to which the incentive to act illegally would be reduced due to the illegality of the conduct in question, the likelihood of its detection, the action taken by the competent authorities, and the financial penalties that could result. Today, leveraging as a concept remains a viable force in merger review, but the CFI signaled that the Merger Task Force will have to come up with more tangible proof regarding such leveraged effects. Specifically, "the proof of anticompetitive conglomerate effects of such a merger calls for a precise examination, supported by convincing evidence, of the circumstances which allegedly produce those effects."

In 2005, the European Court of Justice upheld the CFI's major findings in *Tetra Laval.* On appeal, the Commission argued that the CFI had exceeded its authority in reviewing the merger decision by looking beyond purely legal grounds for reversal toward the Commission's economic and fact assessments. The Commission believed the CFI failed to give appropriate discretion to the Commission by requiring convincing evidence of conglomerate effects. The ECJ, while recognizing that the Commission does have a degree of discretion in making economic assessments, upheld the CFI's review of that assessment and stated that "[n]ot only the Community Courts ... establish whether the evidence

Tetra Laval BV v. Commission

Case T-5/02 2002 E.C.R. II-4381 and Case T-80/02 2002 E.C.R.;
II -4519 European Court of First Instance

BACKGROUND AND FACTS

Tetra Laval, a Swedish company that is the world's largest carton-packaging manufacturer, decided to expand into the field of plastic bottle plugs. It sought to buy the French company Sidel, which makes the equipment that blows plastic plugs into milk and soft drink bottles, commonly known as PET technology. The proposed deal was valued at 1.7 billion euros. Tetra purchased Sidel prior to EC approval. The EC Merger Task Force later prohibited the merger on the grounds that the union would be able to "leverage" its dominance in carton packaging to also become dominant in the PET packaging equipment market, thus reducing competition horizontally and vertically. This so-called "leveraging" theory had been used earlier by the Merger Task Force to reject the highly controversial GE/Honeywell merger, despite the fact that the United States does not utilize the concept in antitrust review.

PRESIDENT JUDGE VESTERDORFF

Whilst it is true that the modified merger would enable Sidel, through Tetra's presence in the market for plastic bottle capping systems, to offer almost totally integrated PET lines, it is obvious that the vertical effects of Sidel's entry into that market through the merged entity, and Sidel's concomitant disappearance as a potential customer of the other operators active on that market, would be minimal in the light of the relatively weak position held by Tetra on that market. In addition, the global capacity of the merged entity, compared with Sidel's current capacity, to offer such integrated PET lines would not be strengthened by the modified merger, because Tetra would divest itself of its PET preforms activities. The Sidel annual report shows that sales of those lines accounted for only around 20% of Sidel's SBM machine sales in 2001, despite the alleged exponential growth of 30% between 1999 and 2000 to which the Commission refers in its defence.

As for the alleged effects on the EBM machines market, the contested decision expressly acknowledges that, in the light of Tetra's reply of 1 October 2001 to the supplemental statement of objections, the position of other players allayed concerns about dominance in a potential market for machines producing aseptic HDPE bottles with handles ... It is thus clear that the modified merger would not have significant negative effects on the position of converters active in the HDPE market. That market would, post-merger, remain a highly competitive market.

Consequently, it has not been shown that the modified merger would result in sizeable or, at the very least, significant vertical effects on the relevant market for PET packaging equipment. In those circumstances, the Court finds that the Commission made a manifest error of assessment in so far as it relied on the vertical effects of the modified merger to support its finding that a dominant position on those PET markets would be created for the merged entity through leveraging ... .

It follows from the foregoing that the Commission committed manifest errors of assessment in relying on the horizontal and vertical effects of the modified merger to support its analysis of the creation of a dominant position on the relevant PET markets.

Decision. The CFI rejected the Merger Task Force's decision because the Force's decision lacked sufficient evidence.

Case Questions

1. What evidence would have supported the Merger Task Force's decision and led to a different result?
2. Is "leveraging" now wrong in the absence of an anticompetitive effect in the EU? How could the vertical restrictions have posed more of a competitive threat?
3. What effect does a reputation for being an overly aggressive regulator have on the regulator's ability to defend its position when appealed? Are competition law cases sometimes decided on factors other than a pure application of law to facts?

relied on is factually accurate, reliable, and consistent but also whether that evidence contains all the information which must be taken into account in order to assess a complex situation and whether it is capable of substantiating the conclusions drawn from it. Such a review is all the more necessary in the case of a prospective analysis required when examining a planned merger with conglomerate effect." In addition, the ECJ held that it was appropriate for the CFI to require a more thorough consideration by the Commission of the firm's behavioral commitments, which may prevent the emergence of a dominant position.

In line with the CFI's and the ECJ's decisions in *Tetra Laval*, the Commission's analysis of conglomerate effects took another harsh blow from the CFI's merger decision issued in 2005, involving General Electric and Honeywell. In 2000, General Electric and Honeywell had announced their intention to merge. The U.S. Department of Justice indicated that it would allow the merger, but in 2001, the Commission decided to block the merger. While the Commission's decision to block the merger was eventually upheld due to significant horizontal effects, the Commission's conglomerate effects analysis was dismantled. The CFI reaffirmed that in order to substantiate a merger prohibition based on conglomerate or vertical effects likely to harm competition, the Commission must have convincing evidence of the chain of events leading to that harm.

Together, the 2005 decisions in *Tetra Laval* and *GE/Honeywell [General Electric Co. v. Commission of the European Communities,* (2005) ECRII-5575 (CFI); *Honeywell International Inc. v. Commission of the European Communities,* (2005) ECR II-5527 (CFI)] suggest that using a conglomerate effects analysis to prohibit a merger will be viewed with great suspicion unless there is a detailed showing of a high probability of anticompetitive effects. Further, these opinions also indicate that the European analysis, as noted, has shifted in the direction of the analysis undertaken in the United States. Nonetheless, divergent merger decisions on either side of the Atlantic, as General Electric and Honeywell can attest to, pose a serious risk for companies considering a merger.

This string of decisions resulted in suggestions that the EU should abandon the current model of endowing the investigatory EC Merger Task Force with enforcement powers in favor of the U.S. antitrust regulatory model, which requires a court judgment to block a merger. As a result of such pressures, the EC adopted a set of fundamental reforms regarding mergers. The reform package includes a more flexible time frame regarding merger investigations, guidelines regarding horizontal mergers, guidance regarding key concepts such as how to analyze anticompetitive behavior, and greater fact-finding powers for the Merger Task Force. The investigatory watchdog powers are split among the antitrust units of the EC's general competition directorate. The number of mergers notified to the Commission under the new regime reached a record level of 402 in 2007 before dropping off in the deep recession of 2008 through 2010. When considering the new regime, the EC explored the merits of both the dominance test and the substantial lessening of competition (SLC) test for assessing anticompetitive effects, but settled on the significant impediment to effective competition (SIEC) test.

The Japanese View. In 2009, Japan revised its *Antimonopoly Act* (AMA) to require **prior notification** of business combinations that exceed a certain threshold, replacing Japan's after-the-fact reporting system. Japan also recently abolished its confidential prior consultation system, whereby an informal decision by the JFTC could be obtained before the formal merger filing procedure and later adopted as the official decision. In addition to allowing for greater efficiency and transparency in the review process, these revisions bring the Japanese system more in line with international practices. Like many of its foreign counterparts, the JFTC has published guidelines to illustrate when a merger may act "substantially to restrain competition" and thus violate the AMA. If a potential harm to competition is present, the JFTC may prohibit the merger or allow it to proceed with remedial conditions.

The Chinese View. A large part of antitrust enforcement in China is focused on merger and acquisition control. The Anti-monopoly Bureau of China's Ministry of Commerce (MOFCOM) is in charge of such regulation, investigation, and enforcement. A qualifying merger or acquisition (**concentration of undertakings**) must be referred to MOFCOM and, upon review, may be prohibited, approved, or approved subject to conditions. MOFCOM has acknowledged that it is late to the game of competition regulation, and it is formulating regulations to address the proposal, negotiation, evaluation, determination, and implementation phases of the merger and acquisition review process. For an undertaking to qualify for review by MOFCOM, a transfer of control must occur through a merger, the acquisition of control over another undertaking, or "the ability to exercise decisive influence" over another undertaking. The criteria for control is thus quite broad and unspecific. Also, the threshold must be met of (1) total worldwide sales of at least RMB10 billion, *or* (2) total sales in China of at least RMB2 billion, *or* (3) total sales in China by at least two of the involved enterprises of at least RMB400 million. (In January 2013, 6.2 RMBs were worth 1 U.S. dollar.) In 2012, MOFCOM settled 154 cases, of which 142 were unconditionally approved, 6 were withdrawn, and 6 were conditionally approved. Over the first four years of the law, more than 450 undertakings have been unconditionally approved, and just one has been rejected.

OTHER ATTRIBUTES OF U.S. AND NON-U.S. COMPETITION LAW

Foreign competition law is similar to U.S. antitrust law in substance, but it is enforced quite differently. The most obvious distinction—and the primary reason for the absence of much competition law litigation outside the United States—is in the sanctions for violating the law.

Private Causes of Action for Damages

Although the Department of Justice has brought marquee cases such as *United States v. Microsoft,* 87 F. Supp.2d 30 (D.D.C. 2000), U.S. law is enforced principally by "private attorneys general," meaning private parties ostensibly injured by the antitrust violation. Such plaintiffs are encouraged by the United States' recognition of a private cause of action for violations of antitrust rules and the award of treble damages to successful litigants. With this large pot of gold at the end of the litigation rainbow, and relatively little downside exposure (U.S. litigants need not pay the other side's lawyer's fees if they lose), plaintiffs are encouraged to take their shot. Similarly, risk-averse defendants are encouraged to settle out of court before trial.

In Europe, EU competition laws may be enforced only in national courts. A private party may not go to the pan-European forums of the EU. Article 101(2) declares void any agreement that violates the terms of Article 101(1) but does not explicitly take the further step of granting a private cause of action for damages. Thus, a private party must generally play in the alleged violator's "home court" where the judiciary might be inclined to favor local interests. There is no equivalent to the U.S. federal court system; indeed, in the United States the antitrust plaintiff may choose any forum in the nation that is reasonably convenient, and its choice is generally respected.

There has been a push from the EU's Competition Commissioner to enhance private enforcement of competition laws within the European national courts. The Commission adopted the Green Paper on damages actions for breach of the EU antitrust rules in 2005 in order to assess how private causes of action can be pursued more successfully in Europe. In 2008, the Commission released a White Paper proposing specific measures designed to overcome obstacles to effective private enforcement of the EU antitrust rules. The White Paper addresses topics such as standing, fault requirements, passing-on defenses, statute of limitation requirements, and collective redress mechanisms. To date, however, these actions have not triggered a change in traditional European reluctance to encourage litigation.

The American penchant for litigation is also rejected by other major commercial powers. Japanese law provides for private individuals to bring claims under the antitrust law, and plaintiffs can also recover damages based on the general tort provision of the Civil Code. However, apart from bid-rigging activity, private antitrust actions have had little effect on the Japanese competition environment. In China, the *Antimonopoly Law* similarly provides for private enforcement, but relatively few actions have been brought to date. According to China's Supreme People's Court, difficulties in evidence collection and a challenging burden of proof has deterred private claimants. Moreover, in countries outside the United States, if the plaintiff loses, it must pay the defendant's attorneys' fees, which are substantial. In addition, outside the United States, treble-damage awards are generally unavailable. Thus, plaintiffs have much greater risk, less probability of success, and less reward if they succeed. The result is drastically less litigation.

Potential Criminal Liability

In addition, U.S. antitrust law also poses the possibility of criminal liability, which is not possible under the European model. This is not an idle threat: At the end of 2007, the DOJ reported that it had 50 pending grand jury investigations involving alleged international cartels. In the five-year span from 2005 through 2009, the DOJ collected approximately $3.4 billion in fines and filed 232 criminal cases based on violations of the U.S. antitrust laws. In 2007, the department imposed fines on three firms of $300 million while another firm was fined $500 million—the largest criminal fine ever imposed in the United States at that time. The contrast with Europe's efforts in this respect could not be more profound.

U.S. antitrust lawyers might be somewhat bemused by the punishment meted out in South Korea. When the three largest Korean manufacturers of color televisions were conclusively found to have engaged in a price-fixing scheme, they were ordered to end the scheme and to offer a public apology to the Korean people. The manufacturers appealed!

Article 101(3) and the Rule of Reason

The analytical framework established by U.S. antitrust law distinguishes between actions that are ***per se*** wrong and actions to which the **rule of reason** applies. *Per se* violations are those that no amount of explanation can make legal, whereas actions subject to the rule of reason can be legal if, upon analysis, they are found not to be anticompetitive. In 2007, the Supreme Court of the United States further entrenched the rule of reason analysis in a 5–4 decision in *Leegin Creative Leather Products, Inc. v. PSKS, Inc.,* 551 U.S. 877, (2007). In *Leegin*, the Court overruled a 96-year-old precedent by holding that vertical agreements between manufacturers and distributors to fix minimum resale prices are now to be judged by the rule of reason rather than a *per se* rule.

A dispute surrounds the issue of whether the rule of reason is an appropriate mode of analysis under EU competition laws. The language of Article 101(2) does not lend itself to the suggestion that some literally restrictive agreements may nonetheless be valid because of overarching pro-competitive effects. Nonetheless, the Commission flirted with that interpretation of the language and included elements of the analysis in some of its decisions.

Previously under Article 101(3), the Commission could exempt agreements that violated the terms of Article 101(1) in advance by issuing a comfort letter, an individual exemption, or a negative clearance. An **individual exemption** allowed performance of an agreement that would otherwise violate Article 101 because it had favorable economic effects overall. For example, an individual exemption might have been granted if the proposed agreement improved the production of goods or promoted technological economic progress, imposed only restrictions indispensable to such product improvement, and did not eliminate competition as to a substantial part of the products in question. This concept of weighing public benefit against public loss from anticompetitive activity has been adopted in the antitrust laws of each of the formerly Communist nations of central and eastern Europe.

A **negative clearance**, on the other hand, was a confirmation that the proposed agreement did not fall within Article 101(1) at all. It required the Commission's analysis of whether, in fact, the proposed agreement would impair competition. The disadvantage of the negative clearance was that if the facts as to competition turned out to be different from those represented on the application, the parties could nonetheless be fined.

The Commission would, on occasion, also issue **comfort letters** that told companies that their anticipated transaction, if implemented as represented, was not likely to infringe competition rules.

The Commission's actions in these processes functioned much like the rule of reason analysis. Employing a similar analysis, the Commission today grants **block exemptions** to entire classes of contracts. Under the terms of the block exemption, the Commission identifies the type of agreement eligible for exemptions and the types of anticompetitive provisions permitted in such agreements. In considering each provision to be included in a block-exemption contract, the Commission weighs the EU's interest in promoting productive cooperation between parties against the costs of somewhat reduced competition. At present, there are ten block exemptions in place for transactions including vertical agreements, specialization agreements, and research and development agreements.

As the following discussion will make clear, while the block exemption remains a possibility, the issuance of other preapproval exemptions and comfort letters has been almost entirely discontinued under the new EC competition law regime.

Preapproval Procedures versus Litigation

The preceding examination of non-U.S. antitrust laws and European counterparts reveals another difference between the U.S. system and various foreign systems. In their exemption system and the EU *Merger Regulation*, Europeans traditionally structured their system to provide for a resolution of competition law issues prior to the transaction taking place, typically through administrative action. The parties to the request could generally rely on the European Commission's negative clearance. Other non-U.S. systems have similar preapproval procedures on which parties can rely. They significantly reduce the amount of private litigation brought to enforce competition law outside the United States.

If the European Commission had to clear every potentially anticompetitive action in Europe, it would need more people than are in DG-COMP. It ameliorated this problem through its ***de minimis* exceptions** and by granting block exemptions. The *de minimis* exception provides that Article 101(1) is not violated if (1) the aggregate market share of the parties to the agreement is less than 15 percent of any relevant markets affected where the parties are not competitors, or (2) the aggregate market share of the parties to the agreement is less than 10 percent of any relevant markets affected where the parties are competitors or where it is difficult to ascertain whether the parties are competitors. And, as noted previously, the EU *Merger Regulation* has a much higher Community dimension threshold. Thus, with the *de minimis* exception, the majority of agreements within the EU are not considered to be anticompetitive. The Commission issues block exemptions applicable to particular industries or types of agreements. The broad number of subject areas permits companies to proceed with confidence in not violating Article 101(1) as long as they follow the highly specific instructions of the Commission when forming their agreements. Parties whose agreements fall into these categories and precisely follow the wording approved by the Commission do not need to seek approval from the Commission in order to have their transaction considered exempt. Instead, firms bear the risk of correctly ascertaining whether a block exemption applies to their agreements.

The great benefit of the preapproval approach traditionally pursued by the EU and many other governments is that the parties can consummate the transaction without risk of subsequent nullification and fines. However, the preapproval approach has costs of its own. First, even with block exemptions, *de minimis* rules, and comfort letters to reduce the flow of work, the Commission became overwhelmed. Over time, an enormous backlog developed at the Commission. Disposition of pending requests became notoriously slow. In contexts where the passage of time would kill the commercial objective of the transaction, firms would go forward and take their chances on a rule of reason analysis. Additionally, the block exemption approach effectively prohibits virtually everything, and then exempts large areas. Businesses are burdened by the need to write agreements that fit the rigid categories of the exemptions. Such an approach greatly hinders innovation in fashioning contractual arrangements and restricts the flexibility of entrepreneurs. This is a substantial cost. One of the engines of capitalism is the ability of parties to invent mutually beneficial arrangements that permit them to serve customers better. All efforts to address these problems in the Commission's preapproval system have been widely judged insufficient.

In 2000, the Commission effectively proposed an end to its preapproval system. In 2004, that proposal became an operating reality. *Regulation 1/2003*, adopted by the EU Council of Ministers in 2002, became effective in 2004. Under the new regulation, the Commission eliminated the requirement that transactions be notified to the Commission in advance. Instead, parties, as in the United States, decide for themselves, based on Commission law and precedent, whether an arrangement violates competition law or is subject to an exemption. Unless an agreement falls within a block exemption, companies will now face more uncertainty. DG-COMP now must use its scarce resources to police serious infringements, especially in the area of cartel enforcement. In that enforcement, DG-COMP now has broader investigative powers, which include the ability to conduct unannounced "dawn raids," apply stiffer penalties for violations, and take oral statements from staff of the companies under investigation. National competition enforcement authorities now play an integral part in antitrust enforcement.

Under the revised regime, national courts and **national competition authorities (NCAs)** have increased responsibility for enforcement of Articles 101 and 102. When a transaction affects trade between member states, the national authorities must apply Articles 101 and 102, even if national law is also applied. To facilitate the new regime, a network of competition authorities has been established so that the Commission and NCAs can collaborate in enforcement activities. The Commission has abandoned the prior preapproval model in favor of an after-the-fact, decentralized enforcement regime, whereby companies decide in advance whether they are violating Article 101(1) and, if so, whether they are potentially exempted from coverage by Article 101(3).

Another area in which the United States differs from EU countries is the extent to which statutes are given extraterritorial application. This difference has engendered such international hostility that it deserves separate treatment.

EXTRATERRITORIAL EFFECT OF COMPETITION LAWS

In an increasingly interdependent world, no country or continent operates in isolation. Anticompetitive behavior in Costa Rica may well have an adverse effect on the price of bananas in the United States. The basic question is whether U.S. law can or should do anything to prevent Costa Rican monopolistic action. Although the trend is now changing somewhat, Europeans have historically been reluctant to apply their competition law outside the Common Market. Conversely, Americans have tended to apply their antitrust law to every corner of the globe.

The U.S. Effects Test

The United States started with a limited concept of extraterritorial jurisdiction but has since developed it in a way that accords U.S. antitrust law a substantial extraterritorial effect. The issue was first examined in *American Banana Co. v. United Fruit Co.*, 213 U.S. 347 (1909), by the great Justice Oliver Wendell Holmes.

In *American Banana*, the plaintiff, a U.S. corporation, alleged that a rival U.S. corporation had caused the Costa Rican government to seize the plaintiff's banana plantation and prevent the completion of the plaintiff's railway. The plaintiff argued that these acts prevented it from competing in the production and sale of bananas for export to the United States and therefore violated the *Sherman Antitrust Act*. Justice Holmes dismissed the complaint, interpreting the *Sherman Act* "as intended to be confined in its operation and effect to the territorial limits over which the lawmaker has general and legitimate powers." Because the United States could not control what happened in Costa Rica, Justice Holmes reasoned that Congress did not intend to regulate what happened there.

Justice Holmes's elegant prose was not long the law in the United States. Court decisions after *American Banana* tended to acknowledge it and its reasoning, but applied the ruling in odd ways. In time, ignoring the importance of the decision rendered it a virtual nullity and opened the way for a new interpretation of the intent of Congress in the *Sherman Act*. This set the stage for the creation of the so-called U.S. **effects doctrine**, which was developed in the landmark case of *United States v. Aluminum Co. of America* (more commonly known as the *Alcoa* case).

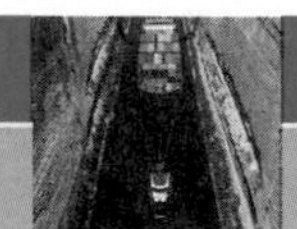

United States v. Aluminum Co. of America

148 F.2d 416 (1948) United States Court of Appeals (2d Cir.)

BACKGROUND AND FACTS

In 1931, a group of aluminum producers—one French, two German, one Swiss, one British, and one Canadian—formed a Swiss corporation named "Alliance." Each of the producers was a shareholder of Alliance.

In 1936, the shareholders instituted a system of royalties centered on Alliance. Each shareholder was to have a fixed production quota for every share it held, but when its production exceeded the sum of its quotas, it was to pay a royalty, graduated in proportion to the excess, to Alliance. Alliance then distributed the royalties as dividends to the shareholders in proportion to their shares. The effect was to create a cartel that controlled aluminum supplies and therefore kept prices high. Imports into the United States were included in the quotas.

The cartel ended in 1939 when the German shareholders became enemies of the French, British, and Canadian shareholders.

JUDGE LEARNED HAND

Did the agreement ... of 1936 violate Section 1 of the *[Sherman] Act*? [W]e are concerned only with whether Congress chose to attach liability to the conduct outside the United States of persons not in allegiance to it. That being so, the only question open is whether Congress intended to impose the liability, and whether our own Constitution permitted it to do so: as a court of the United States, we cannot look beyond our own law. Nevertheless, it is quite true that we are not to read general words, such as those in this act without regard to the limitations customarily observed by nations upon the exercise of their powers; limitations which generally correspond to those fixed by the "Conflict of Laws." ... We should not impute to Congress an intent to punish all whom its courts can catch, for conduct which has no consequences within the United States. On the other hand, it is settled law ... that any state may impose liabilities, even upon persons not within its allegiance, for conduct outside its borders that has consequences within its borders which the state reprehends; and these liabilities other states will ordinarily recognize. It may be argued that this act extends further. Two situations are possible. There may be agreements made beyond our borders not intended to affect imports, which do affect them, or which affect exports. Almost any limitation of the supply of goods in Europe, for example, or in South America, may have repercussions in the United States if there is trade

continues

continued

between the two. Yet when one considers the international complications likely to arise from an effort in this country to treat such agreements as unlawful, it is safe to assume that Congress certainly did not intend to act to cover them. Such agreements may on the other hand intend to include imports into the United States, and yet it may appear that they have had no effect upon them. That situation might be thought to fall within the doctrine that intent may be a substitute for performance in the case of a contract made within the United States; or it might be thought to fall within the doctrine that a statute should not be interpreted to cover acts abroad which have no consequence here. We shall not choose between these alternatives; but for argument we shall assume that the act does not cover agreements, even though intended to affect imports or exports, unless its performance is shown actually to have had some effect upon them. [The agreement] would clearly have been unlawful, had [it] been made within the United States; and it follows from what we have just said that [it was] unlawful, though made abroad, if [it was] intended to affect imports and did affect them ... . [T]he change made in 1936 was deliberate and was expressly made to accomplish [a restraint on exportation of aluminum to the United States for sale in competition with Alcoa] ... . The first of the conditions which we mentioned was therefore satisfied; the intent was to set up a quota system for imports.

[A] depressant upon production which applies generally may be assumed ... to distribute its effect evenly upon all markets. Again, when the [shareholders of Alliance] took the trouble specifically to make the depressant apply to a given market, there is reason to suppose that they expected that it would have some effect, which it could have only by lessening what would otherwise have been imported... .

There remains only the question whether this assumed restriction had any influence upon prices... . [A]n agreement to withdraw any substantial part of the supply from a market would, if carried out, have some effect upon prices, and was as unlawful as an agreement expressly to fix prices. The underlying doctrine was that all factors which contribute to determine prices, must be kept free to operate unhampered by agreements. For these reasons we think that the agreement of 1936 violated Section 1 of the *[Sherman Antitrust] Act.*

Decision. The U.S. Court of Appeals for the Second Circuit reversed the District Court's decision and remanded the case to it for further proceedings consistent with its opinion.

Case Questions

1. What are some of the complications that occur when U.S. courts order a foreign manufacturer to pay billions in damages for an agreement that would be acceptable under that country's competition laws?
2. Does Judge Hand see any limits placed by the U.S. Constitution on antitrust law?
3. Judge Hand's test requires that a "substantial" number of imports be affected by the anticompetitive conduct. To what measure was he referring by using that word? Would this be objectionable if only 1 percent of the U.S. market was affected?

Although careful to require consequences in the United States, Judge Hand in *Alcoa* pushed the reach of U.S. antitrust law further toward extraterritoriality than Justice Holmes. In subsequent cases, this trend intensified. U.S. courts interpreted the *Sherman Act* to require an ever-decreasing "effect" on the United States before it was applicable. Other courts soon turned to the question of whether actions by Americans affecting foreign markets could somehow satisfy the effects test.

Perhaps the crowning touch in this expansion came in *Joseph Muller Corp., Zurich v. Societe Anonyme De Gerance Et D'Armament,* 508 F.2d 814 (2d Cir. 1974), when a Swiss corporation sued a French corporation in the United States claiming a violation of U.S. antitrust laws, even though no U.S. companies or consumers were directly affected by any of the acts in question. In fact, a Franco–Swiss treaty required that any suits between French and Swiss citizens were to be brought in the defendant's country. Nevertheless, the U.S. trial court found the requisite effects for jurisdiction over the dispute. U.S. courts, in applying the effects test of *Alcoa,* effectively displaced foreign treaties and laws on the basis of minimal U.S. connections.

By the 1970s, some federal courts of appeal had grown disenchanted with the Alcoa test because of its failure to take into account the legitimate interests of foreign nations. These courts developed a **jurisdictional rule of reason** that took into account (1) whether the action had some effect on U.S. commerce, (2) whether the restraint was of a type and magnitude to be considered a violation of the U.S. antitrust laws, and (3) the comity (goodwill) interests of the foreign nation against the interests of the

United States in antitrust enforcement. Courts did not universally accept this approach and U.S. court intervention continued to spark international friction. Thus, in 1982, the U.S. Congress finally clarified the intent of the *Sherman Act* by adopting a strict version of the "effects" test in the *Foreign Trade Antitrust Improvements Act*. That statute provides that U.S. antitrust law does not apply to conduct unless such conduct has a "direct, substantial, and reasonably foreseeable effect on U.S. commerce or on the business of a person engaged in exporting goods from the United States to foreign nations."

The *Foreign Trade Antitrust Improvements Act* did not end disagreement. As the following case makes clear, five of the members of the U.S. Supreme Court had a rather sweeping view of the scope of the *Sherman Act*'s applicability. This case remains the law of the United States.

Hartford Fire Insurance Co. v. California

509 U.S. 764 (1993) United States Supreme Court

BACKGROUND AND FACTS

Nineteen states and numerous private parties brought antitrust suits against U.S. insurers, U.S. and foreign reinsurers based in London, and insurance brokers. The insurers, reinsurers, and brokers were alleged to have agreed to boycott commercial general liability (CGL) insurers that refused to change the terms of their standard domestic CGL insurance policies to conform to the policies the defendant insurers wanted to sell. The plaintiff states asserted that as a practical matter, the policies that the defendant insurers wanted to sell would (1) make occurrence CGL coverage unavailable for many risks; (2) make pollution liability coverage almost entirely unavailable for the vast majority of casualty insurance purchasers; and (3) limit coverage of seepage, pollution, and property contamination risks.

The U.S. District Court for the Northern District of California dismissed the suits because it refused to exercise *Sherman Act* jurisdiction over foreign reinsurers under principles of international comity. The Court of Appeals for the Ninth Circuit reversed this decision of the District Court.

JUSTICE SOUTER

[W]e take up the question ... whether certain claims against the London reinsurers should have been dismissed as improper applications of the *Sherman Act* to foreign conduct ... .

At the outset, we note that the District Court undoubtedly had jurisdiction of these *Sherman Act* claims ... . it is well established by now that the *Sherman Act* applies to foreign conduct that was meant to produce and did in fact produce some substantial effect in the United States ... . Such is the conduct alleged here: that the London reinsurers engaged in unlawful conspiracies to affect the market for insurance in the United States and that their conduct in fact produced substantial effect ... . According to the London reinsurers, the District Court should have declined to exercise such jurisdiction under the principle of international comity. The Court of Appeals agreed that courts should look to that principle in deciding whether to exercise jurisdiction under the *Sherman Act* ... . But other factors, in the court's view, including the London reinsurers' express purpose to affect United States commerce and the substantial nature of the effect produced, outweighed the supposed conflict and required the exercise of jurisdiction in this case ... .

When it enacted the *Foreign Trade Antitrust Improvements Act of 1982* ... Congress expressed no view on the question whether a court with *Sherman Act* jurisdiction should ever decline to exercise such jurisdiction on grounds of international comity ... .

We need not decide that question here, however, for even assuming that in a proper case a court may decline to exercise *Sherman Act* jurisdiction over foreign conduct (or, as Justice Scalia would put it, may conclude by the employment of comity analysis in the first instance that there is no jurisdiction), international comity would not counsel against exercising jurisdiction in the circumstances alleged here.

The only substantial question in this case is whether "there is in fact a true conflict between domestic and foreign law." ... The London reinsurers contend that applying the Act to their conduct would conflict significantly with British law, and the British Government, appearing before us as *amicus curiae,* concurs ... . They assert that Parliament has established a comprehensive regulatory regime over the London reinsurance market and that the conduct alleged here was perfectly consistent with British law and policy. But this is not to state a conflict. "[T]he fact that conduct is lawful in the state in which it took place will not, of itself, bar application of the United

continues

continued

States antitrust laws," even where the foreign state has a strong policy to permit or encourage such conduct ... . No conflict exists, for these purposes, "where a person subject to regulation by two states can comply with the laws of both." ... Since the London reinsurers do not argue that British law requires them to act in some fashion prohibited by the law of the United States ... or claim that their compliance with the laws of both countries is otherwise impossible, we see no conflict with British law ... . We have no need in this case to address other considerations that might inform a decision to refrain from the exercise of jurisdiction on grounds of international comity.

JUSTICE SCALIA, DISSENTING

I dissent from the Court's ruling concerning the extraterritorial application of the Sherman Act ... .

[V]arious British corporations and other British subjects argue that certain of the claims against them constitute an inappropriate extraterritorial application of the *Sherman Act*. It is important to distinguish two distinct questions raised by this petition: whether the District Court had jurisdiction, and whether the *Sherman Act* reaches the extraterritorial conduct alleged here.

On the first question, I believe that the District Court had subject-matter jurisdiction over the *Sherman Act* claims against all the defendants ... . The respondents asserted nonfrivolous claims under the *Sherman Act*, and [the U.S. judicial code] vests district courts with subject-matter jurisdiction over cases "arising under" federal statutes ... .

The second question—the extraterritorial reach of the *Sherman Act*—has nothing to do with the jurisdiction of the courts. It is a question of substantive law turning on whether, in enacting the *Sherman Act*, Congress asserted regulatory power over the challenged conduct ... . If a plaintiff fails to prevail on this issue, the court ... decides the claim, ruling on the merits that the plaintiff has failed to state a cause of action under the relevant statute ... .

There is, however, a type of "jurisdiction" relevant to determining the extraterritorial reach of a statute; it is known as "legislative jurisdiction," ... or "jurisdiction to prescribe." ... This refers to "the authority of a state to make its law applicable to persons or activities," and is quite a separate matter from "jurisdiction to adjudicate." ... There is no doubt, of course, that Congress possesses legislative jurisdiction over the acts alleged in this complaint: Congress has broad power under [the Constitution] "[t]o regulate Commerce with foreign Nations," and this Court has repeatedly upheld its power to make laws applicable to persons or activities beyond our territorial boundaries where United States interests are affected... . But the question in this case is whether, and to what extent, Congress has exercised that undoubted legislative jurisdiction in enacting the *Sherman Act*.

We have, however, found the presumption to be overcome with respect to our antitrust laws; it is now well established that the *Sherman Act* applies extraterritorially. See ... *United States v. Aluminum Co. of America* ... .

But if the presumption against extraterritoriality has been overcome or is otherwise inapplicable, a second canon of statutory construction becomes relevant: "[A]n act of Congress ought never to be construed to violate the law of nations if any other possible construction remains." ... Though it clearly has constitutional authority to do so, Congress is generally presumed not to have exceeded those customary international-law limits on jurisdiction to prescribe.

Consistent with that presumption, this and other courts have frequently recognized that, even where the presumption against extraterritoriality does not apply, statutes should not be interpreted to regulate foreign persons or conduct if that regulation would conflict with principles of international law... . "The controlling considerations" in this choice-of-law analysis were "the interacting interests of the United States and of foreign countries." ...

The solution ... adopted [by the Court in a maritime personal injury case] was to construe the statute "to apply only to areas and transactions in which American law would be considered operative under prevalent doctrines of international law." ...

The "comity" [authorities] refer to is not the comity of courts, whereby judges decline to exercise jurisdiction over matters more appropriately adjudged elsewhere, but rather what might be termed "prescriptive comity": the respect sovereign nations afford each other by limiting the reach of their laws. That comity is exercised by legislatures when they enact laws, and courts assume it has been exercised when they come to interpreting the scope of laws their legislatures have enacted ... .

Under the *Restatement [of Foreign Relations Law]*, a nation having some "basis" for jurisdiction to prescribe law should nonetheless refrain from exercising that jurisdiction "with respect to a person or activity having connections with another state when the exercise of such jurisdiction is unreasonable." ... The 'reasonableness' inquiry turns on a number of factors including, but not limited to: "the extent to which the activity takes place within the territory [of the regulating state], ... the connections, such as nationality, residence, or economic activity, between the regulating state and the

continues

continued

person principally responsible for the activity to be regulated, ... the character of the activity to be regulated, the importance of regulation to the regulating state, the extent to which other states regulate such activities, and the degree to which the desirability of such regulation is generally accepted, ... the extent to which another state may have an interest in regulating the activity, ... [and] the likelihood of conflict with regulation by another state." ...

Rarely would these factors point more clearly against application of United States law. The activity relevant to the counts at issue here took place primarily in the United Kingdom, and the defendants in these counts are British corporations and British subjects having their principal place of business or residence outside the United States. Great Britain has established a comprehensive regulatory scheme governing the London reinsurance markets, and clearly has a heavy "interest in regulating the activity." ... Finally, section 2 (b) of the *McCarran–Ferguson Act* allows state regulatory statutes to override the *Sherman Act* in the insurance field, subject only to [a] narrow "boycott" exception ... suggesting that "the importance of regulation to the [United States]" ... is slight. Considering these factors, I think it unimaginable that an assertion of legislative jurisdiction by the United States would be considered reasonable, and therefore it is inappropriate to assume, in the absence of statutory indication to the contrary, that Congress has made such an assertion ... .

If one erroneously chooses, as the Court does, to make adjudicative jurisdiction (or, more precisely, abstention) the vehicle for taking account of the needs of prescriptive comity, the Court still gets it wrong. It concludes that no "true conflict" counseling nonapplication of United States law (or rather, as it thinks, United States judicial jurisdiction) exists unless compliance with United States law would constitute a violation of another country's law ... . That breathtakingly broad proposition ... will bring the *Sherman Act* and other laws into sharp and unnecessary conflict with the legitimate interests of other countries—particularly our closest trading partners. [T]here is clearly a conflict in this case.

Decision. The Supreme Court affirmed that part of the judgment of the Court of Appeals that reversed the District Court's refusal to exercise jurisdiction over foreign reinsurers.

Case Questions

1. Do you think Justice Scalia would have spoken out the same way if, like the majority, he had read English and U.S. law not to be in conflict?
2. In determining whether the *Sherman Act* applies to a business outside the United States, if Congress's intent is not clear, to whom should courts give the benefit of the doubt?
3. What would happen if a U.S. judge decided that English insurance law created an unlawful monopoly under U.S. law?

As the operations and investments of U.S. and foreign businesses have become increasingly enmeshed, the DOJ and the Federal Trade Commission have been obliged to develop enforcement guidelines so that businesspeople would have a better sense of when they might expect prosecution. In 1995, they revised these Antitrust Enforcement Guidelines for International Operations, expressing a great "interest in international cooperation," and set forth 14 examples. Despite these protestations, the agencies showed that they intend to be aggressive. The 1995 guidelines cite the *Hartford Fire* holding to support the U.S. government view that interest balancing is a discretionary matter of comity

The FTAIA has qualified the application of the *Sherman Act* when the subject of the claim is transactions concluded in foreign nations. In 2004, the U.S. Supreme Court, in *F. Hoffman-La Roche Ltd. v. Empagran S.A.*, 542 U.S. 155, 164 (2004), clarified, in a class action suit by vitamin purchasers, that "[where] [t]he price-fixing conduct significantly and adversely affects both customers outside the United States and customers within the United States, but the adverse foreign effect is independent of any adverse domestic effect ..." the *Sherman Act* does not apply to the foreign purchases. Nonetheless, *Animal Science*, a recent Third Circuit decision made it easier for plaintiffs to have their claims heard before a U.S. court, even if U.S. antitrust laws ultimately are found not to apply. Whether other circuits, or the Supreme Court, will adopt this approach is an open question.

The European "Implementation" Test

Most nations take a more restrained approach to extraterritorial antitrust jurisdiction than the United States. Under the **territorial theory** of jurisdiction, which is widely accepted throughout the world, a nation may clearly assert jurisdiction over a merger involving a firm based in its territory. Thus, the People's Republic of Mozambique would be within its internationally recognized rights in asserting jurisdiction over a merger between a Mozambican company and a Canadian firm.

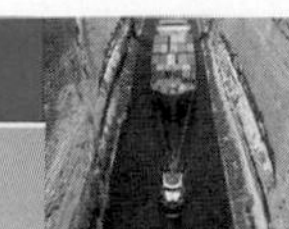

Animal Science Products, Inc. v. China Minmetals Corp., et al.

654 F.3d 462 (2011) United States Court of Appeals (3d Cir.)

BACKGROUND AND FACTS

The plaintiffs are domestic purchasers of "magnesite." The plaintiffs allege, on behalf of a putative class, that the defendants—Chinese producers and exporters of magnesite—engaged in a conspiracy since at least April 2000 to fix the price of magnesite that is exported to and sold in the United States. The plaintiffs allege that this conspiracy has affected hundreds of millions of dollars of United States commerce. Based on these allegations, the plaintiffs assert federal claims pursuant to the *Clayton Act*, 15 U.S.C. §§4, 16, predicated on the defendants' alleged violation of Section 1 of the *Sherman Act*, 15 U.S.C. §1.

In a remarkably comprehensive opinion dated April 1, 2010, the District Court engaged in extensive fact-finding and held that the FTAIA deprived it of subject matter jurisdiction... . The District Court thoroughly discussed the FTAIA's two exceptions but ultimately determined that the plaintiffs failed to demonstrate that either exception was applicable to this case. The District Court thus granted the defendants' motion and dismissed the plaintiffs' First Amended Complaint.

JUDGE POLLAK

This appeal involves interpreting the FTAIA, a statute that this Court has described as being "inelegantly phrased" and using "rather convoluted language." *Turicentro, S.A. v. Am. Airlines Inc.*, 303 F.3d 293, 300 (3d Cir. 2002) (quotation marks omitted)... . [T]he FTAIA first limits the reach of the U.S. antitrust laws by articulating a general rule that the *Sherman Act* "shall not apply to conduct involving trade or commerce ... with foreign nations." The FTAIA then creates two distinct exceptions that restore the authority of the *Sherman Act*. First, the FTAIA provides that it does not apply (and thus that the *Sherman Act* does apply) if the defendants were involved in "import trade or import commerce" (the "import trade or commerce" exception). Second, the FTAIA's bar is inapplicable if the defendants' "conduct has a direct, substantial, and reasonably foreseeable effect" on domestic commerce, import commerce, or certain export commerce and that conduct "gives rise" to a *Sherman Act* claim (the "effects" exception)... .

As noted above, the District Court construed the FTAIA as imposing a jurisdictional restriction, and, after engaging in fact-finding, determined that neither of the FTAIA's two exceptions applied ... .

... [W]e must determine whether, in enacting the FTAIA, Congress legislated pursuant to its Commerce Clause authority to articulate substantive elements that a plaintiff must satisfy to assert a meritorious claim for antitrust relief or whether Congress acted pursuant to its Article III powers to define the jurisdiction of the federal courts ... .

... The FTAIA neither speaks in jurisdictional terms nor refers in any way to the jurisdiction of the district courts ... . Indeed, the statutory text is wholly silent in regard to the jurisdiction of the federal courts.[2] The FTAIA reads only that the *Sherman Act* "shall not apply" if certain conditions are met. Assessed through the lens of Arbaugh's "clearly states" test, the FTAIA's language must be interpreted as imposing a substantive merits limitation rather than a jurisdictional bar. Or, in the terminology set forth above, in enacting the FTAIA, Congress exercised its Commerce Clause authority to delineate the elements of a successful antitrust claim rather than its Article III authority to limit the jurisdiction of the federal courts. We therefore overrule our earlier precedent that construed the FTAIA as imposing a jurisdictional limitation on the application of the *Sherman Act* ... .

[Next, Judge Pollack turned to the substantive elements of the claim.]

In light of the tremendous effort put forth by the District Court on the FTAIA issue, ... and for the sake of efficiency, we offer two brief instructions if the District Court addresses the FTAIA question again on remand.

First, the District Court correctly discerned that the import trade or commerce exception "must be given a relatively strict construction." *Carpet Group* [*Int'l v. Oriental Rug Importers Ass'n*, 227 F.3d 62, 72 (3d Cir. 2000)]. The District Court erred, however, in holding that this "strict construction" requires that the defendants function as the physical importers of goods ... . Rather, the relevant inquiry is whether the defendants' alleged anticompetitive behavior "was directed at an import market." *Turicentro*, 303 F.3d at 303 .... Or, to phrase it slightly differently, the import trade or commerce exception requires that the defendants' conduct target import goods or services.

We held that this requirement was not satisfied in *Turicentro*. *Turicentro* involved a group of foreign travel agents who sued various U.S. airline companies, alleging that they conspired to fix commission rates

continues

continued

paid to foreign travel agents. Based on these facts, we reasoned that:

> The alleged conspiracy in this case was directed at commission rates paid to foreign travel agents based outside the United States. That some of the services plaintiffs offered were purchased by United States customers is not dispositive under this inquiry. Defendants were allegedly involved only in unlawfully setting extra-territorial commission rates. Their actions did not directly increase or reduce imports into the United States.

Turicentro, 303 F.3d at 303. The conspiracy in Turicentro thus targeted a foreign market: fixing commission rates paid to foreign travel agents. Any subsequent "importing" of these rates into the United States occurred as a result of the plaintiffs' own activities, as it was the plaintiff travel agents (and not the defendant airline companies) who sold services with allegedly fixed rates to U.S. customers.

By contrast, we held that the import trade or commerce exception did apply in *Carpet Group*, deeming it sufficient that the plaintiffs "charge [d] that defendants engaged in a course of activity designed to ensure that only United States importers, and not United States retailers, could bring oriental rugs manufactured abroad into the stream of American commerce." *Carpet Group*, 227 F.3d at 72. In that case, the defendants' conduct targeted the U.S. import market in various ways:

> [The] defendants took steps to: (1) prevent foreign manufacturers from selling to United States retailers, (2) prevent at least one American retailer from purchasing rugs directly from foreign manufacturers, (3) prevent foreign governments and trade associations from sponsoring trade fairs at which retailers could purchase directly from foreign manufacturers, and (4) prevent an American rug retailers' trade association from sponsoring the trade fairs.
>
> Id. at 73.

On remand, therefore, if the District Court addresses the applicability of the import trade or commerce exception, the District Court should assess whether the plaintiffs adequately allege that the defendants' conduct is directed at a U.S. import market and not solely whether the defendants physically imported goods into the United States.

Second, the FTAIA's effects exception does not contain a "subjective intent" requirement. The plaintiffs noted that certain language utilized by the District Court appeared to require that the plaintiffs demonstrate that the defendants subjectively intended to impact U.S. commerce ... . [W]e clarify that the FTAIA's "reasonably foreseeable" language imposes an objective standard: the requisite "direct" and "substantial" effect must have been "foreseeable" to an objectively reasonable person. The text of the statute—"reasonably foreseeable"—makes plain that an objective standard applies.[3] Accordingly, if the District Court assesses the FTAIA's effects exception on remand, the relevant inquiry is whether the alleged domestic effect would have been evident to a reasonable person making practical business judgments.

Decision. The U.S. Court of Appeals for the Third Circuit vacated the District Court's decision and remanded the case to it for further proceedings consistent with its opinion.

Case Questions

1. Contrast the application of the import trade or commerce exception in *Carpet Group* with the application in *Animal Science*. Why did it not apply in *Carpet Group*? Why did it apply in *Animal Science*?
2. Under the effects test as interpreted in *Animal Science*, could an effect be "reasonably foreseeable" even if the defendant does not foresee the effect? In a trial, how would you prove that an effect was "reasonably foreseeable"?

A more controversial situation arises when a subsidiary of a foreign-based company seeks to engage in a transaction within the host country's jurisdiction. Although this situation does not involve questions as to jurisdiction over the subsidiary under the territorial theory, if the host country cannot also obtain authority over the foreign parent, that parent could evade the host country's competition laws merely by conducting all of its activities in the host country through a controlled subsidiary. Faced with this difficulty, the European Court of Justice devised the **single economic unit** concept, under which the court imputes the behavior of a controlled subsidiary to the parent. This concept also permits the court to consider the parent's level of market dominance in determining whether the subsidiary's actions are monopolistic. The court expanded this concept in the *Philip Morris* judgment (*BAT Reynolds v. Commission,* 1987 E.C.R. 4487), to find jurisdiction not only when actual voting control is acquired but also when the foreign acquirer would achieve "material influence" over an erstwhile European competitor.

The farthest reach of the accepted territorial jurisdiction doctrine is the principle of **objective territoriality**. Under this principle, a state may exercise jurisdiction over conduct commenced outside its territory when the act or effect of the act is physically completed inside its territory. However, many nations have vigorously resisted the extension of this effects test beyond physical effects in the host country to mere consequences that result in a nation, such as the effects from anticompetitive conduct.

The more restricted European effects test has meant that companies can conspire to limit competition in exports to a nation without that nation being able to claim jurisdiction over the conspiracy. For example, in Germany, each *exportkartell* unifies the marketing power of German corporations in a single industry for potent export activity outside the Common Market.

As Europeans have begun to develop their own massive multinational market, they have become more flexible in defining what constitutes a "physical completion" of an act within a territory. In the *A. Ahlstrom Osakeyhtio v. Comm'n* case, commonly referred to as the *Wood Pulp* case, the European Court of Justice found that the European Commission could assert jurisdiction over foreign companies that have no presence in the Union but that export to the Union through independent distributors. The court justified jurisdiction on the basis that the firms had engaged in price-fixing activity that was "implemented" within the Union.

The court in the *Wood Pulp* decision expressly declined to adopt the U.S. effects test, setting forth a new "implementation within the Community" test. The EU *Merger Regulation* literally applies to companies outside the EU. Its definition of Community dimension measures aggregate worldwide sales of the merged entities, not whether the assets are located inside the EU. If two large U.S. firms with significant sales to European distributors merge in the United States, must they comply with the regulation? Although it would be a logical extension of *Wood Pulp*, featured below, such an exercise of jurisdiction would convert the implementation test into a thinly veiled European effects test.

A. Ahlstrom Osakeyhtio v. Comm'n

1987–88 Tfr. Binder Common Mkt. Rep. (CCH) 14,491 (1988)
Court of Justice of the European Communities

BACKGROUND AND FACTS

Wood pulp is the principal raw material used in production of paper and paperboard. In 1988, the EU member states produced only a small fraction of their requirements for wood pulp. Virtually all of the product purchased in the Union originated from producers in countries that were then not members of the Union: Finland, Sweden, Canada, and the United States.

Many of these wood pulp producers had no presence in the Union. They sold their products to independent distributors and users located in the Union.

In each of these countries, the wood pulp producers organized into associations for export. In the United States, this group was the Pulp, Paper, and Paper Board Export Association of the United States (known as KEA), formed under the *Webb–Pomerene Act*, which exempts associations of U.S. exporters from U.S. antitrust laws. Each of these associations engaged in discussions on pricing policy regarding exports to the Union.

The European Commission brought an action against the members of the associations under the TFEU, found them guilty of anticompetitive activity under Article 81 of the Treaty, and imposed fines on them. The associations appealed to the Court of Justice, asserting that the Commission lacked jurisdiction over them.

PRESIDENT LORD MACKENZIE STUART

All the applicants that made submissions regarding jurisdiction maintain first of all that by applying the competition rules of the Treaty to them the Commission has misconstrued the territorial scope of Article 81. They note that ... the Court of Justice did not adopt the "effects doctrine" but emphasized that the case involved conduct restricting competition within the Common Market because of the activities of subsidiaries that could be imputed to the parent companies. The applicants add that even if there is a basis in [Union] law for applying Article 81 to them, the action of applying the rule interpreted in that way would be contrary to public international law, which precludes any claim by the [Union] to regulate conduct restricting competition adopted outside the territory of the [Union] merely by reason of the economic repercussions which that conduct produces within the [Union].

continues

continued

The applicants which are members of the KEA further submit that the application of [Union] competition rules to them is contrary to public international law insofar as it is in breach of the principle of noninterference. They maintain that in this case the application of Article 81 harmed the interest of the United States in promoting exports by United States undertakings as recognized in the Webb–Pomerene Act of 1918, under which export associations, like the KEA, are exempt from United States antitrust laws.

Insofar as the submission concerning the infringement of Article 81 of the Treaty itself is concerned, it should be recalled that under that provision all agreements between undertakings and concerted practices which may affect trade between Member States and which have as their object or effect the restriction of competition within the Common Market are prohibited.

It should be noted that the main sources of supply of wood pulp are outside the [Union]—in Canada, the United States, Sweden, and Finland—and that the market therefore has global dimensions. Where wood pulp producers established in those countries sell directly to purchasers established in the [Union] and engage in price competition in order to win orders from those customers, that constitutes competition within the Common Market.

It follows that where those producers concert on the prices to be charged to their customers in the [Union] and put that concentration into effect by selling at prices that are actually coordinated, they are taking part in concentration that has the object and effect of restricting competition with the Common Market within the meaning of Article 81 of the Treaty.

Accordingly, it must be concluded that by applying the competition rules in the Treaty in the circumstances of this case to undertakings whose registered offices are situated outside the [Union], the Commission has not made an incorrect assessment of the territorial scope of Article 81. The applicants have submitted that the decision is incompatible with public international law on the grounds that the application of the competition rules in this case was founded exclusively on the economic repercussions within the Common Market of conduct restricting competition which was adopted outside the [Union].

It should be observed that an infringement of Article 81, such as the conclusion of an agreement that has had the effect of restricting competition within the Common Market, consists of conduct made up of two elements: the formation of the agreement, decision, or concerted practice and the implementation thereof. If the applicability of prohibitions laid down under the competition law were made to depend on the place where the agreement, decision, or concerted practice was formed, the result would obviously be to give undertakings an easy means of evading those prohibitions. The decisive factor therefore is the place where it is implemented.

The producers in this case implemented their pricing agreement within the Common Market. It is immaterial in that respect whether or not they had recourse to subsidiaries, agents, sub-agents, or branches within the [Union] in order to make their contacts with purchasers within the [Union].

Accordingly, the [Union's] jurisdiction to apply its competition rules to such conduct is covered by the territoriality principle as universally recognized in public international law.

As regards the argument based on the infringement of the principle of non-interference, it should be pointed out that the applicants who are members of KEA have referred to a rule and the effect of those rules is that a person finds himself subject to contradictory orders as to the conduct he must adopt, each State is obliged to exercise its jurisdiction with moderation.

There is not, in this case, any contradiction between the conduct required by the United States and that required by the [Union] since the *Webb–Pomerene Act* merely exempts the conclusion of export cartels from the application of United States antitrust laws but does not require such cartels to be concluded.

Decision. The Court of Justice affirmed the Commission's imposition of fines on the foreign companies that had coordinated their pricing policies.

Case Questions

1. If the exporters were outside the United States and were exporting products to the United States, would a U.S. court have jurisdiction under the FTAA?
2. Is the holding in this case the same as or different from that of the majority in *Hartford?* Does it matter that the European Commission was declaring illegal activity of something that is legal from the U.S. perspective?
3. What effect does this have on the *Webb–Pomerene Act*?

Blocking Legislation

A necessary consequence of the U.S. effects doctrine is that the U.S. litigation system and pro-competition policies are carried into many foreign nations. The United States is by far the world's largest market. In addition, as noted earlier, both the U.S. system of litigation and the U.S. pro-competition policies are inconsistent with the systems and policies in other nations. The clash triggered a rash of dueling legislation. In an antitrust action brought by the Justice Department against the uranium production industry, an American producer alleged that uranium producers outside the United States had formed a cartel to raise the price of uranium. As the producer sought discovery against foreign producers to document its charges, foreign nations cried foul. They asserted that the uranium litigation was an attempt by the United States to enforce its economic policies abroad.

In short order, Canada, Australia, France, the Netherlands, New Zealand, Switzerland, Germany, and the United Kingdom enacted **blocking legislation**—statutes containing provisions that block the discovery of documents located in their countries and bar the enforcement of foreign judgments there. In addition, some contain **clawback provisions** under which the foreign companies can sue in their own country to recover against local U.S. assets all or part of the amount of an antitrust judgment rendered in the United States.

These blocking laws are tantamount to international legal warfare. However, blocking legislation is still a useful tool in other contexts. For example, many nations reacted against the *Cuban Democracy Act of 1992*, a U.S. law that prohibits foreign subsidiaries of U.S. corporations from doing business in Cuba, by forbidding those subsidiaries from obeying the act. Blocking legislation again appeared when the Clinton administration set forth its somewhat more aggressive international antitrust stance.

CONCLUSION

One of the prices of business success is regulation by antitrust laws. In recent years, antitrust/competition law, which had its roots in the United States, has spread around the world. This has created a new area for American entrepreneurs to be careful of when engaging in business activities.

Chapter Summary

1. Competition law, referred to in the United States as antitrust law, prohibits agreements between competitors that restrict competition. It also prohibits a firm from abusing a dominant market position through predatory pricing and refusals to deal.
2. Some nations require governmental review of virtually all vertical arrangements between firms and their distributors, customers, or suppliers. In the United States, regulators allow vertical restraints if a reasonable case can be made that they foster better service and hence foster interbrand competition, encourage innovation, or do not foreclose a substantial part of the market to others. In the EU, the Commission is more likely to intervene to prevent vertical restraints.
3. The European Commission is more flexible with respect to know-how transfer agreements than patent licenses. The rationale is that because the owner of know-how does not have any legally cognizable right to its knowledge, it can rely only on secrecy.
4. Competition authorities also show flexibility in reviewing franchise agreements because the franchiser must protect its know-how and the franchiser must ensure that the franchisee is producing and marketing the product in a manner consistent with the franchiser's good name. Poor performance by one franchisee can have adverse effects on the franchiser's reputation and operations internationally.
5. To be in violation of abuse of monopoly power provisions, a company must have abused its dominant market position, which is defined differently in different countries and in different industries.
6. In 1990, the Council of the European Communities' *Regulation 4064/89*—the *EC Merger Regulation*—became effective. Under the merger regulation, parties to all mergers, acquisitions, joint ventures, and other business combinations that have a "Community dimension" must provide pre-transaction notification to the commission. In 2004, the European Council put into effect substantial amendments to the merger regulation that strengthened EU competition laws.

7. In the United States, private parties harmed by anticompetitive activity may bring damage actions in federal court against a firm violating U.S. antitrust laws. In Europe, EU competition laws may be enforced only in national courts; a private party may not go to the pan-European forums of the EU. There has been a recent push from the EU's Competition Commissioner to enhance private enforcement of competition laws within the European national courts.
8. *Per se* competition law violations are those that no amount of explanation can make legal, while actions subject to the rule of reason can be legal if, upon analysis, they are found not to be anticompetitive. In 2007, the Supreme Court of the United States overruled a 96-year-old precedent by holding that vertical agreements between manufacturers and distributors to fix minimum resale prices are to now be judged by the rule of reason rather than a *per se* rule. A dispute surrounds the issue of whether the rule of reason is an appropriate mode of analysis under EU competition laws.
9. Under the U.S. Supreme Court case of *F. Hoffman-La Roche Ltd. v. Empagran S.A.*, where "[t]he price-fixing conduct significantly and adversely affects both customers outside the United States and customers within the United States, but the adverse foreign effect is independent of any adverse domestic effect ..." the *Sherman Act* does not apply to the foreign purchases. Europe and most other nations have a more restricted view of anticompetitive conduct jurisdictions. Under the principle of objective territoriality, a nation may exercise jurisdiction over conduct commenced outside its territory when the act or effect of the act is physically completed inside its territory.
10. Other countries with important markets and robust international trade, such as Japan and China, continue to build their competition policies and practices. Increasing attention to the competitive effects of business combinations, together with growing international cooperation in regulatory development and enforcement, means that businesses should remain aware of the competition laws in all jurisdictions where they do business or have an effect.

Key Terms

antitrust law 593
competition law 593
memoranda of understanding 594
vertical arrangement 594
know-how 595
keiretsu 595
monopoly 596
dominant market position 596
refus de vente 596
consent agreement 600
preapproval 600
leveraging theory 604
prior notification 606
concentration of undertakings 606
per se 608
rule of reason 608
individual exemption 608
negative clearance 608
comfort letter 608
block exemptions 608
de minimis exception 608
national competition authorities (NCAs) 609
effects doctrine 610
jurisdictional rule of reason 611
territorial theory 614
single economic unit 616
objective territoriality 617
blocking legislation 619
clawback provisions 619

Questions and Case Problems

1. The Slobovian Confederation's five producers control 95 percent of the world's supply of "goom," the key ingredient in the production of goomey bears. To maximize the Slobovian standard of living, the government passed a law creating a cartel among the five producers and forbidding access to Slobovian goom by any other entity. The price of goomey bears skyrocketed in the United States. Giggles Consolidated, a U.S. candy manufacturer, attempted to purchase a goom mine in Slobovia but was rejected by the cartel. As a result, Giggles brought an antitrust action against the cartel members in federal district court. Does U.S. law apply? If the U.S. court finds for Giggles, how can U.S. courts enforce such a judgment?
2. In the case in Question 1, if a U.S. court sought to enforce U.S. laws on Slobovia's leading export, how

would U.S.–Slobovian relations be affected? What if a key U.S. naval base was located in Slobovia? How well equipped are courts to conduct such relations?

3. In *Alcoa*, Judge Hand points out that even agreements to restrict trade only in Europe and South America would have anticompetitive repercussions in the United States. What additional element did he require before giving U.S. antitrust law extraterritorial effect?
4. If Judge Hand had written his decision in December 1941, at the beginning of World War II rather than in 1945, at its successful end, would he have handed down a judgment against the national aluminum company of a principal ally of the United States? Should a decision affecting the nation's relations with an ally reflect such considerations? Do you think the U.S. role in that war affected judges' perceptions of the relative importance of U.S. law?
5. Why would a British company bring a competition lawsuit under U.S. antitrust laws rather than EU competition law? What advantages does a company have in alleging an antitrust conspiracy? Describe the differences between U.S. law and EU law in the areas of pretrial discovery, attorneys' fees, and potential damage awards.
6. English courts have no authority to interpret treaties, whereas U.S. courts do. What arguments suggest that the English approach is preferable? What arguments indicate that the U.S. approach is better?
7. U.S. antitrust law reflects U.S. economic policy. If U.S. antitrust law resolves an economic dispute among British companies, has U.S. economic policy been extended to Britain? What are the implications of the United Kingdom's requirement that British companies comply with U.K. policy in resolving such disputes?

Index

See also Tables on pages xv–xxiv for listings of specific statutes, treaties, and cases.

A

B

D

J

K

L

M

N

O

U

V

W

Y

Z

List of Frequently Used Acronyms

ACTA	Anti-Counterfeiting Trade Agreement
ADA	Americans with Disabilities Act
ADEA	Age Discrimination in Employment Act
ADR	Alternative Dispute Resolution
AGOA	African Growth and Opportunity Act
AGP	Agreement on Government Procurement (WTO)
AID	Agency for International Development
ASEAN	Association of Southeast Asian Nations
ATS	Alien Tort Statute
BFOQ	Bona Fide Occupational Qualification
BIS	Bureau of Industry and Security (U.S. DOC)
BOP	Balance of Payments
BOT	Balance of Trade
CAFE	Corporate Average Fuel Efficiency
CAFTA-DR	Central American Free Trade Agreement
CAN	Andean Community of Nations
CAP	Common Agricultural Policy of the European Union
CARICOM	Caribbean Common Market
CBD	Convention on Biological Diversity
CBP	Bureau of Customs and Border Protection (U.S. DHS)
CCL	Commerce Control List
CE	Conformité Européene marking
CEC	Commission for Environmental Cooperation
CET	Common External Tariff (or CXT)
CFI	European Court of the First Instance
CIF	Cost, Insurance, Freight
CISG	Convention on Contracts for the International Sale of Goods
CIT	Court of International Trade
CITES	Convention on International Trade in Endangered Species of Wild Fauna and Flora
CO	Certificate of Origin
COD	Cash-on-Delivery
COGSA	Carriage of Goods by Sea Act
COOL	Country-of-Origin Label
CROSS	Customs Rulings Online Search System
CTEA	Copyright Term Extension Act
C-TPAT	Customs-Trade Partnership Against Terrorism
CVD	Countervailing Duty
DG-COMP	European Commission Directorate General for Competition
DOJ	Department of Justice
DSB	Dispute Settlement Body (WTO)
DSU	Dispute Settlement Understanding (WTO)
EAR	Export Administration Regulations
EC	European Community
ECCN	Export Control Classification Number
ECJ	European Court of Justice
EDI	Electronic Data Interchange
EEC	European Economic Community
EEI	Electronic Export Information
EFC	European Fiscal Compact
EFTA	European Free Trade Association
EPA	Environmental Protection Agency
EPACT	European Policy Act
EPI	Electonic Payment Services
EPO	European Patent Office
ERISA	Employee Retirement Income Security Act
ESM	European Stability Mechanism
ETC	Export Trading Company
EU	European Union
EXIMBANK	Export-Import Bank of the U.S.
FCN	Friendship, Commerce, and Navigation
FCPA	Foreign Corrupt Practices Act
FDI	Foreign Direct Investment
FIE	Foreign Invested Enterprise
FRAND	Fair, Reasonable, and Nondiscriminatory
FSIA	Foreign Sovereign Immunities Act
FTA	Free Trade Agreement or Area
FTC	Federal Trade Commission
FTZ	Foreign Trade Zone
GAFTA	Greater Arab Free Trade Area
GATS	General Agreement on Trade in Services
GATT	General Agreement on Tariffs and Trade
GDP	Gross Domestic Product
GMOs	Genetically Modified Organisms
GRI	General Rules of Interpretation
GSP	Generalized System of Preferences